# Management

*Comprehension,*
*Analysis, and*
*Application*

# Management

*Comprehension, Analysis, and Application*

**Robert D. Gatewood**
*University of Georgia*

**Robert R. Taylor**
*University of Memphis*

**O.C. Ferrell**
*University of Memphis*

AUSTEN
PRESS

*IRWIN*

Chicago • Bogotá • Boston • Buenos Aires • Caracas
London • Madrid • Mexico City • Sydney • Toronto

Publisher: William Schoof
Acquisitions Editor: John Weimeister
Production Manager: Bob Lange
Marketing Manager: Kurt Messersmith

Design and project management provided by Elm Street Publishing Services, Inc.

Compositor: Elm Street Publishing Services, Inc.
Typeface: 10/12 New Caledonia
Printer: Von Hoffmann Press, Inc.

LIBRARY OF CONGRESS CATALOGING-IN-PUBLICATION DATA
Gatewood, Robert D.
    Management: comprehension, analysis, and application/Robert D.
  Gatewood, Robert Taylor, O.C. Ferrell.
          p.        cm.
    Includes bibliographical references and index.
    ISBN 0-256-13784-6
    ISBN 0-256-17591-8 (Annotated Instructor's Edition)
    1. Management.    2. Industrial management.    I. Taylor, Robert
  (Robert Roy), 1948–    .    II. Ferrell, O.C.    III. Title.
  HD31.G367    1994
  658—dc20                                      94-31969

Printed in the United States of America
1 2 3 4 5 6 7 8 9 0 V H 9 8 7 6 5 4

Address editorial correspondence:
Austen Press
18141 Dixie Highway
Suite 105
Homewood, IL 60430

Address orders:
Richard D. Irwin, Inc.
1333 Burr Ridge Parkway
Burr Ridge, IL 60521

Austen Press
Richard D. Irwin, Inc.

We dedicate this book to our wives and families. Chris Riordan provided both emotional and logistical support to Bob Gatewood, meaning she patted him on the head when he missed deadlines (which is why he's kind of bald) and helped him prepare chapters to get caught up. Pat Taylor provided both technical and emotional support throughout to Bob. Pat's unyielding tolerance and interest gave Bob the strength to carry on. Linda Ferrell was involved in many aspects of the project including assisting with chapter content and writing the "Business Dilemma" boxes.

**Bob Gatewood**
**Bob Taylor**
**O.C. Ferrell**

# Preface

Management: Comprehension, Analysis, and Application is intended to assist students in acquiring knowledge and developing the cognitive processes necessary to make decisions in the practice of management. Our purpose was to craft a text and ancillary package that helps students learn the traditional foundations of management while developing decision skills to apply this knowledge in a real-world setting. Each chapter asks students to apply concepts to decision situations they could face in the daily practice of management and to address and successfully deal with challenges they may encounter in the first years of their careers.

This text also addresses the challenges faced by business schools in the 1990s, particularly the problems of declining enrollments and increasing competitive pressures from other disciplines and academic institutions. By bringing to life the concepts and processes of the demanding and exciting discipline of management, this book demonstrates that the study of management, and ultimately a career in one of the many subdisciplines or application areas of the field, can provide exciting challenges for interested students.

## THE DEVELOPMENT OF THIS TEXT

Management: Comprehension, Analysis, and Application differs from existing principles of management texts because it provides both knowledge and pedagogy in an integrated framework that is essential to helping students learn how to analyze, synthesize, and determine actions based on contemporary management thought. The American Assembly of Collegiate Schools of Business (AACSB) is currently promoting curricular innovation linked to each institution's mission. Many colleges of business are attempting to correlate this innovation with the reality of what students will encounter in the first few years of their careers. Criticisms from business leaders about business education indicate a need to improve students' abilities to communicate and to develop critical thinking and cognitive skills that will help them become problem solvers and decision makers. Consequently, many colleges are moving away from memorization of concepts and toward a focus on thinking, communicating, and making choices.

This movement has led many management faculties to critically review and redesign curricula. Traditional management knowledge will be taught in such a way as to enhance cognitive development and decision skills required in today's complex organizational environment. For students to be successful in a managerial career, they must understand how to evaluate situations characterized by an over-abundance of information and technology. As we move toward the twenty-first century, organizational productivity will be based on managing information, technology, and people to achieve organizational goals. *Management: Comprehension, Analysis, and Application* has been designed from the ground up to meet these challenges of business education and the realities of the practice of management in the future.

The development of this text began with an extensive survey of professors to determine the concepts, models, and techniques of management widely accepted as a basic requirement for the principles of management course. Benjamin Bloom's cognitive objectives, which identify the various levels of intellectual performance (knowledge, comprehension, application, analysis, synthesis, and evaluation), were used extensively in developing chapters. Each chapter asks the student to apply knowledge and concepts to organizational problems that they might face in daily practice. Key chapter features such as the "Business Dilemma" box challenge students to relate learned concepts to interesting applied problems. End-of-chapter exercises require students to appraise their own managerial skills and to utilize them in making choices in specific circumstances. In completing these two features of the text, students are asked to generalize, or compare and contrast a multitude of interesting concepts with everyday practices they can observe in local organizations. These exercises bring to life the practices and processes of management.

## Contemporary Topics

The recent concern with global management, business ethics and social responsibility, total quality management, and cultural diversity has been the key positioning statement of many textbooks. Attempts to meet AACSB requirements in these areas have led to principles texts with a main focus on one or more of these topics. The authors of this textbook, recognizing the importance of these four major imperatives to any organization moving into the twenty-first century, have included boxes entitled "Dynamics of Diversity," "Ethics Encounter," "Going Global," and "Quest for Quality," as well as individual chapters on each of these topics. In addition, chapter content integrates issues related to these topics throughout the text. We feel that it is not enough that students simply learn about these important topics; it is critical that they practice key concepts to reinforce understanding and to apply and expand on the concepts learned in the chapter.

This text was designed to attract students to the field of management. Assisted by a multitude of teaching aids, the instructor can make management an area worth exploring for a career. The "Careers Corner" box in each chapter demonstrates to the student the broad range of opportunities available for a lifelong involvement in management.

## OVERVIEW OF THE TEXT

*Management: Comprehension, Analysis, and Application* is divided into five parts. Part One explores the foundations of management, including the essence of management, the development of management thought and theory, and the organizational environment in which management occurs. Mark Butler of San Diego University really likes the "Business Dilemma" box on page 15 in Chapter One

part ■ one

because "these types of inserts give students a chance to 'experience' what is being illustrated in the text." Mel Schnake, Valdosta State College, says Table 2.2 on page 42 "is catchy—students will react well to it. It spices up an area of management that students often find somewhat dry."

Part Two highlights today's changing world of management, featuring individual chapters on ethics and social responsibility, global business, work-force diversity, total quality management, and small business and entrepreneurship. Robert Insley of the University of North Texas applauds the authors for placing the global chapter near the beginning of the book, not at the end as in most management texts. He also likes the cases because "they give students the opportunity to grapple with these tough issues! Cases are excellent in-class and outside-of-class, hands-on activities for both groups and individuals." Of the total-quality-management chapter, Allen Jedlicka of the University of Northern Iowa says, "The material is covered better than in my present textbook, and having this material could eliminate the additional readings I give on the subject."

**part ▪ two**

Part Three focuses on planning and organizing—developing and implementing plans, strategic management, decision making, designing jobs and departments, and structuring the overall organization. Robert Insley says a strength of the planning chapter is "the way the opening vignette, 'Careers Corner' box, and 'Strengthen Your Skills' exercise capture the students' attention by making them active participants mentally and physically." Marvin Karlins, University of Southern Florida, says the chapter on decision making is "one of the best presentations of decision making I have seen in an introductory management text, particularly because it is well conceptualized, logical, and the flow is sensible and easy to understand." Of the organizing chapter, Dennis Gibson of Troy State University says the "exhibits do a very good job of providing meaning to the text."

**part ▪ three**

Part Four covers directing and staffing, with chapters on human resource management, work teams, motivation, leadership, communication, and organizational change and development. Regarding the human resource management chapter, Richard Paulson, Mankato State University, says the "Levi Strauss case is interesting and useful. In addition to principles of human resources, the case illustrates principles from leadership, communications, and other areas." Meg Birdseye of Augusta College says she likes "the introduction of the motivation chapter, especially the tie-in to the various schools of management." Karen Froelich, North Dakota State University, says the organizational change and development chapter is "well organized and more realistic and successfully applied than most." She says she often skips this chapter, but "would include it if using this text."

**part ▪ four**

Finally, Part Five addresses issues related to operations and productivity, management information systems, and management control systems. Of the operations and productivity chapter, Stephen Winter of Orange County Community College says the "authors have taken a typically 'boring' chapter and crafted a very readable and interesting one. The content, presentation, and up-to-date information are superior to that of my current text." Ken Dunegan, Cleveland State University, says of the managing information chapter that he is "glad to see discussion of Internet and e-mail."

**part ▪ five**

## The Chapters

Chapter One, "The Essence of Management," presents the basic functions of management that are common in all organizations. It provides a detailed discussion of the various roles that managers must play within their organizations and the

**chapter ▪ one**

skills they must possess. It also explains why management activities appear to be different in different organizations and discusses what a student can reasonably learn about management in an introductory course.

Chapter Two, "The Development of Management Thought," is filled with interesting details about the history of management, which bring the discipline to life and put it into historical perspective. From the development of the Protestant work ethic through Taylorism and the Hawthorne studies and up to the introduction of Theory Z and Deming's TQM, this chapter lays the groundwork for the models, theories, and practices that comprise the remainder of the book. Students will complete this chapter both understanding how management came to be so important and excited about the intellectual challenge that follows.

Chapter Three, "Environmental Factors of Management," examines why managers' actions must be based on what they know about the organization itself as well as important factors external to the organization. An explanation of these factors and their significance is the basis of the chapter, which also describes methods that managers can use to try to manage the environment. The stakeholder approach to management is interwoven into this presentation.

Chapter Four, "Management Ethics and Social Responsibility," focuses on the emergence of business ethics and social responsibility as major concerns in the changing world of management. This chapter defines business ethics and social responsibility within the context of the field of management, introduces a number of management ethics issues, and provides a framework for understanding how ethical choices are made. While the focus is descriptive, specific guidelines for normative ethical decision making are provided. Students are informed about the role and importance of ethical decisions in management and how companies are developing programs to influence the ethical conduct of employees. Additionally, the history of social responsibility is presented and major social responsibility issues in management are identified.

Chapter Five, "Managing in a Borderless World," analyzes the factors that influence management around the globe. It covers the different levels of organizational involvement in international trade, as well as how global business affects management. Additionally, the chapter takes a unique look at various trade agreements and alliances that have developed worldwide and how they influence business activities.

Chapter Six, "The Dynamics of Diversity," focuses on the increasing importance of cultural diversity in the work force. It defines cultural diversity and surveys several important cultural groups among working Americans. The benefits and problems associated with a culturally diverse work force are analyzed, and ways organizations can manage their diverse human resources more effectively are evaluated. The chapter then explores how organizations have tried to address the issue of diversity through assimilation, affirmative action, and the development of a multicultural organization.

Chapter Seven, "Managing for Total Quality," focuses on the fact that product quality is the primary area of emphasis in America's most successful businesses today. It surveys the development of the quality movement through a discussion of the quality gurus W. Edwards Deming, Joseph Juran, and Philip Crosby. More importantly, this chapter teaches students the tools, techniques, and processes managers need to successfully implement a total quality management program. It ingrains in the reader the perception that quality management is not just another fad, but rather is the primary process through which American industry will successfully compete into the twenty-first century.

Chapter Eight, "Entrepreneurship and Small Business," presents entrepreneurship and small business from a management perspective. It discusses the importance of small business in the U.S. economy and evaluates the reasons certain industries attract small business. The chapter analyzes why small businesses succeed and fail and describes in detail how to start one. Finally, it discusses entrepreneurship from the perspective of large businesses—especially why large businesses are trying to "think small."

chapter ■ eight

Chapter Nine, "Developing Organizational Plans," describes the steps in planning within organizations and how these steps are interrelated. It emphasizes that planning is not only the process of specifying future actions; planning is also the implementation of plans. The chapter also discusses the three levels of organizational planning (strategic, tactical, and operational), as well as how these must be interrelated.

chapter ■ nine

Chapter Ten, "Strategic Management," simplifies the complex process of developing strategic plans and strategic management. Through numerous real-world examples, exercises, and a section focusing on personal career strategy, strategy development is made understandable. After reading this chapter, students appreciate that strategy development is important at all levels of the organization, and they learn how to use the tools developed for this type of planning.

chapter ■ ten

Chapter Eleven, "Making Decisions," provides an excellent overview of the many factors that influence the decision-making process—from emotions and stress to risk propensity, self confidence, and escalation of commitment. It contains a unique discussion of the impact intuition plays in decision making and also compares and contrasts the advantages and disadvantages of individual versus group decision making. The student will leave this chapter knowing how to utilize the tools and techniques necessary to make managerial decisions.

chapter ■ eleven

Chapter Twelve, "Organizing: Designing Jobs and Departments," defines organization and explains why it is necessary. Details on how managers form jobs and departments and the different bases for this formation are included. The chapter also discusses the central principles of organizations, including departmentalization, authority, and chain of command, as well as how these are put into practice within organizations.

chapter ■ twelve

Chapter Thirteen, "Organizing: Designing the Overall Organization," explains organizational structure and describes four types of formal structures—functional, multidivisional, matrix, and networks/outsourcing. The chapter describes characteristics that define the latent structure of an organization, as well as the contingency factors that influence the type of formal structure that is best for an organization. Different types of coordinating mechanisms that can be used to support an organization's structure are summarized, as are the five organizational archetypes: simple structure, machine bureaucracy, professional bureaucracy, divisionalized form, and adhocracy.

chapter ■ thirteen

Chapter Fourteen, "Managing Human Resources," focuses on the importance of human resource management to an organization in reaching its goals and explains how human resource management must be tied to the firm's strategic plans. It discusses how and why human resource management programs must be interrelated in order to contribute to the achievement of the organization's goals, and it highlights the features of those programs that are critical for their effectiveness.

chapter ■ fourteen

Chapter Fifteen, "Building Successful Groups and Teams in Organizations," introduces the notion that groups and teams are not necessarily the same. By learning how to control the key factors and processes that influence group functioning, such as roles, norms, group size, cohesiveness, and trust, students will learn how

chapter ■ fifteen

and when to turn a group into a highly effective team, even one that can direct and lead itself. Successful team functioning will be more than desirable; it may be absolutely essential for success in the twenty-first century. This chapter teaches how to build those successful teams.

**chapter ■ sixteen**

Chapter Sixteen, "Motivating People," succinctly overviews the accepted models of motivation and discusses both traditional and nontraditional methods that companies can use to develop and maintain high levels of employee motivation. From Taylor's scientific management to present-day job sharing, flextime, and job enrichment, motivation is shown to be at the heart of employee performance.

**chapter ■ seventeen**

Chapter Seventeen, "Getting Results through Effective Leadership," begins by clearly distinguishing between leadership and management, while extolling the virtues of each. The chapter discusses each major model of leadership in sufficient depth so that students will know how and when to apply different types of leadership behavior, as well as what traits to look for in successful leaders. This chapter closes with an overview of specific behaviors required for transformational leaders, those most needed in today's rapidly changing business environment.

**chapter ■ eighteen**

Chapter Eighteen, "Communicating in Organizations," concisely gives the student a complete understanding of the forms and functions of interpersonal communication in organizations. It overviews the factors that affect communication and leaves the reader with a clear understanding of the importance and varied nature of the communications process in organizations, as well as how communication is used in various organizational settings to permit successful organization management.

**chapter ■ nineteen**

Chapter Nineteen, "Organizational Change and Development," offers the view that, in the new business environment, the only constant is change. It discusses the major models of and approaches to change, as well as how to design, initiate, implement, and sustain different kinds of organizational change, from major structure and strategy changes to less far-reaching changes in human and technical processes. This chapter is enriched by a multitude of examples of change behavior and programmatic change efforts that have occurred in today's businesses.

**chapter ■ twenty**

Chapter Twenty, "Managing Operations and Increasing Productivity," defines operations management and identifies the activities associated with it. The chapter describes the elements involved in planning and designing an operations system and specifies some of the techniques that managers use to manage inventory. The importance of quality in the operations management process is emphasized. Finally, the chapter examines the importance of productivity and ways to improve it.

**chapter ■ twenty-one**

Chapter Twenty-One, "Managing Information Systems," explains why managers need information as well as the characteristics that information must possess to be useful. It describes a management information system and identifies the basic factors that determine an organization's information needs. The chapter summarizes the uses of computers in management information systems, including executive information systems, networks (including the Internet), and communications. It also describes and distinguishes among the basic types of management information systems. Finally, the impact of information technology on people, organizations, and information is described.

**chapter ■ twenty-two**

Chapter Twenty-Two, "Management Control Systems," explores the importance of management control. It describes the process through which managers develop and implement control, and differentiates among its various forms. It also discusses the elements of effective control, as well as ways to overcome resistance that is sometimes encountered with managerial control. Finally, signs of inadequate systems and methods of evaluating an organization's control program are detailed.

# PEDAGOGY

*Management: Comprehension, Analysis, and Application* provides numerous features to foster student learning:

- Learning objectives at the beginning of each chapter inform students what should be achieved by reading the chapter.

- An opening vignette sets the scene for the issues discussed in the chapter.

- "Dynamics of Diversity," "Ethics Encounter," "Going Global," "Magnifying Management," and "Quest for Quality" boxes spotlight real, often recognizable, issues and particular company events to help students gain practical experience about management.

- A "Business Dilemma" box in each chapter gives students an opportunity to think creatively in applying chapter concepts to hypothetical situations that could occur in the real world.

- "Careers Corner" boxes provide information about career planning and management career opportunities.

- End-of-chapter materials include a "Summary and Review," which addresses chapter learning objectives; "Key Terms and Concepts," including the page number where they appear in text; "Ready Recall" questions to test and reinforce understanding; and "Expand Your Experience" questions to challenge students to apply and expand on the concepts learned in the chapter.

- A comprehensive, challenging case at the end of each chapter tests the students' judgment and decision-making skills.

- A "Strengthen Your Skills" exercise at the end of each chapter gives students an opportunity to build critical skills through a variety of self-tests and other exercises.

- End-of-book materials include a glossary of key terms in alphabetical order.

- Name, company, and subject indexes at the end of the book aid in finding key people, companies, and topics.

# SUPPLEMENTAL MATERIALS FOR INSTRUCTORS AND STUDENTS

The *Management: Comprehension, Analysis, and Application* package includes several useful ancillary materials available to facilitate teaching the material.

The *Annotated Instructor's Edition,* developed by Marilyn Helms of the University of Tennessee at Chattanooga, is a special version of the text with introductory material explaining the content of the text and the supplements available for the course, as well as marginal notes to the instructor. It includes detailed suggestions for teaching with the complete package and marginal notes containing examples, teaching notes, comments on boxes, and critical thinking challenges.

The *Instructor's Manual,* also prepared by Marilyn Helms, includes an overview of how to use the manual, alternate instructional approaches, and sample course lesson plans. For each chapter, the *Instructor's Manual* provides a chapter overview; learning objectives; chapter outline; key terms from the text; answers to "Ready Recall" questions; a summary of each boxed feature; a synopsis of the "Strengthen your Skills" exercises, and the case and answers to case questions. Teaching notes are also provided for each of the selected transparency masters.

The *Test Bank*, developed by Gary Gardiner of the Smith Collins Company, provides, for each chapter, 75 multiple-choice questions (including 15 skill and ability questions, some of which are taken from the box material), 20 true/false questions, and 5 short essay questions.

*Transparency Acetates* are available for adopters. In addition to the transparency masters included in the *Instructor's Manual*, instructors are also provided with all-new four-color transparencies and teaching notes. These colorful acetates will provide instructors with a choice of interesting material to supplement their classroom lectures and activities.

A *Study Guide*, developed by Corinne Livesay of Belhaven College, includes learning objectives, a chapter outline, chapter recap, key terms, review questions and answers, and a student exercise with answers in each chapter.

A computer diskette is included with the *Study Guide* that allows students to take sample exams. The disk includes true/false and multiple-choice questions from each chapter. The student can take a sample quiz from each chapter or simulate a test by choosing multiple chapters. The student can select a multiple-choice exam, a true/false exam, or a combination of each. A self-study scoring system keeps track of the scores on each exam for up to ten separate attempts, allowing the student to measure his or her improvement and mastery of the subject.

Finally, the *Management: Comprehension, Analysis, and Application* package includes a video program, with one video for each chapter. Each video is accompanied by a video guide that provides instructors with teaching notes to support their use of videos in the classroom. The video program is also available on laserdisc.

## ACKNOWLEDGMENTS

We would like to acknowledge a number of individuals who contributed to the research and writing of this text. Gwyneth M. Vaughn assisted as the developmental editor of this project. Her dedication and hard work helped craft our work into a highly readable, student-friendly text. Barbara Gilmer provided editorial support and technical assistance. Corinne Livesay developed the "Strengthen Your Skills" exercises at the end of each chapter and served as a consultant and coordinator on several aspects of the project. Bill Schoof, president of Austen Press, and John Weimeister, Austen Press acquisitions editor, conducted research and provided guidance on this project. Kurt Messersmith, with Richard D. Irwin, Inc., provided support and direction for the distribution of our book. Special thanks to Elm Street Publishing Services, Inc., for design and production provided by Phyllis Crittenden, Karen Hill, Kelly Spiller, Kathy Mitchell, Sue Langguth, Nancy Moudry, and Doris Milligan. Graduate students at the University of Memphis who provided various types of assistance include Kathy Janowicz, Kristin Prien, Timothy Pett, and Terry Gabel. Susan Hanlon of the University of Akron, John Parnell of North Carolina Central University, Donna Bush of Middle Tennessee State University, Todd Palmer of Pennsylvania State University at Erie, and Barbara Carlin of Southern Methodist University are also acknowledged for their contributions in the writing of chapters and cases.

We would also like to thank the following reviewers and survey participants:

## Reviewers

Meg Birdseye
*Augusta College*
Mark Butler
*San Diego State University*
Claudia Daumer
*California State University*
Ken Dunegan
*Cleveland State University*
Karen Froelich
*North Dakota State University*
Robert Insley
*University of North Texas*
Allen Jedlicka
*University of Northern Iowa*
Marvin Karlins
*University of Southern Florida*

Robert Nale
*Coastal Carolina University*
Richard Paulson
*Mankato State University*
Pat Saunders
*Howard University*
Mel Schnake
*Valdosta State College*
Herman Theeke
*Central Michigan University*
James Walker
*Moorhead State University*
Stephen Winter
*Orange County Community College*

## Survey Participants

Dave C. Anderson
*California State University*
Robert Anthony
*Western Montana College*
Barry Armandi
*State University of New York*
Rodrigo Arrioja
*University of Colorado*
Debra A. Arvanites
*Villanova University*
Peter Bacalles
*Corning Community College*
Gail Ball
*University of Nevada*
David N. Bateman
*Southern Illinois University*
Schon Beechler
*Columbia University*
Sandra Bennett
*Southwest Institute of Merchandising
and Design*
Meg Birdseye
*Augusta College*
Jim Brakefield
*Western Illinois University*
Duane Brickner
*South Mountain Community College*
Monica Briendenbach
*DeVry Institute of Technology*

James B. Bross
*Central Wesleyan College*
Carl W. Buckel
*College of the Canyons*
Gabriel Buntzman
*Western Kentucky University*
Allen Bures
*Radford University*
Bill Burtis
*De Anza College*
Mohammad Busaliah
*Glendale Community College*
Mark C. Butler
*San Diego State University*
David Cadden
*Quinnipiac College*
Robert Callahan
*Seattle University*
James Carey
*Onondaga Community College*
Lawrence Carroll
*Elmhurst College*
Kathleen Carter
*Harcum Jr. College*
Chan S. Chang
*Lander College*
Arnold Charitan
*Los Angeles Harbor College*
Don Chatman
*University of Wisconsin*

Peter Checkovich
*Shepherd College*
Barbara Ching
*Los Angeles City College*
Elizabeth Cohee
*Harrisonburg, VA*
Roland Cousins
*La Grange College*
Sam Crowley
*DeVry Institute of Technology*
William Cullen
*Troy State University*
Carol Cumber
*South Dakota State University*
Jim Dahl
*Millikin University*
Claudia Daumer
*California State University*
Tim R. V. Davis
*Cleveland State University*
Gerald De Moss
*Blue Mountain Community College*
Linda Dell'osso
*California State Polytechnic University*
Gordon Di Paolo
*City University of New York*
Dale L. Dickson
*Mesa College*
Rolf Dixon
*West Texas State University*
Ken Dunegan
*Cleveland State University*
Robert Eberle
*Iona College*
Regina Eisenbach
*California State University*
H. Richard Eisenbeis
*University of Southern Colorado*
Patrick G. Ellsberg
*Lower Columbia College*
Dawn Elm
*University of St. Thomas*
William L. Enslin
*Glassboro State College*
Peter Fairweather
*College at New Paltz*
David Feldman
*Katharine Gibbs School*
Dave Fewins
*Neosho County Community College*
Betty Foster
*Danville Community College*

Donald Foster
*Columbia College*
Lowell Frame
*Indiana Business College*
Charles Franz
*University of Missouri*
Alan J. Fredian
*Loyola University*
Cherie Fretwell
*Troy State University*
Karen Froelich
*North Dakota State University*
Patricia Gallagher
*University of Massachusetts*
Margaret Galligan
*Pennsylvania State University*
Richard Gardner
*West Virginia University*
Eugene Gonzales
*Ag & Tech College of New York*
Martin Gonzales
*Pensacola Jr. College*
Delmar G. Good
*Goshen College*
Mark S. Goodenow
*South Dakota State University*
Leonard R. Graziplene
*College at Buffalo*
Bill Greenwood
*Northern Montana College*
Tom Gwise
*Florida Southern College*
David Hamm, CPA
*Ohio Valley College*
M. Hammington
*Mount St. Mary's College*
Donald A. Hantula
*St. Joseph's University*
Lorraine Hartley
*Barry University*
Robert Hawkes
*Bakersfield College*
Warren E. Helmstedter
*Bakersfield College*
Brian Helper
*Pennsylvania State University*
Richard Herden
*University of Louisville*
Jack Herlihy
*California State Polytechnic University*

Eldra Hernandez
*University of the Sacred Heart*
Catherine Hinchey
*Antioch University*
Robert Hollis
*Peralta C Laney College*
Floyd Huiatt
*College at Potsdam*
Frank R. Hunsicker
*West Georgia College*
Paula L. Irwin
*Reading Area Community College*
Henry J. Jackson
*Delaware County Community
College*
Dorothy Jeanis
*Fresno City College*
Allen Jedlicka
*University of Northern Iowa*
Tom Jones
*Greensboro College*
Richard J. Judd
*Sangamon State University*
Jay Kahn
*Keene State College*
Marvin Karlins
*University of South Florida*
Nancy Kaufman
*University of North Carolina*
Edward Keidat
*Phildelphia College of Textiles and
Science*
Daniel Kemper
*Lindenwood College*
Robert R. Kemp
*Peralta C Laney College*
Jeff Kilgore
*Norwich University Military College
of Vermont*
Jerry Kinard
*Francis Marion College*
Lori Kravets
*Ottawa University*
Steve Kresky
*Brown Mackie College*
Danny Lam
*Seton Hall University*
Connie Laury
*Park College*
Grant L. Learned
*Defiance College*

Bob Ledman
*Maryville College*
Youngho Lee
*Howard University*
Chad Lewis
*Everett Community College*
Sharon Lewis
*Utah State University*
Barbara Libby
*Niagara University*
Bryan Macolm
*University of Mississippi*
Jim Mahony
*Central Wesleyan College*
Barbara Mandeville
*Western Kentucky University*
Maurice R. Manner
*Marymount College*
Dan McCallister
*University of Nevada*
Michael McCormick
*Jacksonville State University*
James McElroy
*Iowa State University*
Kenneth McKenzie
*Texas Wesleyan College*
Mary McNally
*Eastern Montana College*
Bonita H. Melcher
*Baldwin Wallace College*
Hank Metzner
*University of Missouri*
James Michael
*Upsala College*
Pam Mickelson
*Morningside College*
Herff L. Moore
*University of Central Arkansas*
Zarzad Moussavi
*University of Northern Iowa*
Robert Nale
*University of South Carolina*
Thomas A. Natiello
*University of Miami*
Wayne Nelson
*Central Missouri State University*
Aldo Neyman
*Tri-State University*
Inge Nickerson
*Barry University*
James Nimnicht
*Central Washington University*

John N. O'Del
*State University of New York*
Michael J. O'Keefe
*St. Peter's College*
Howard Oden
*Nichols College*
Dan Panda
*Delaware State College*
Joseph Paolillo
*University of Mississippi*
Joseph Papenfuss
*Westminster College*
Thomas A. Pascarella
*Hiram College*
Allison Paul
*St. Joseph's University*
Stephen H. Paul
*Temple University*
C. Richard Paulson
*Mankato State University*
Sheila Pechinski
*University of Maine*
Monique Pelletier
*San Francisco State University*
Peter B. Petersen
*Johns Hopkins University*
Don Phillips
*Clayton State College*
Danny H. Pogue
*North Carolina Agricultural and
Technical State University*
Keramat Poorsoltan
*Frostburg State College*
Philip Quaglieri
*University of Massachusetts*
Richard Randall
*Nassau Community College*
Ellen Reynolds
*Pasadena City College*
Rick Ringer
*University of Colorado*
Anthony Rizzi
*Central Missouri State University*
George Rohr
*Central Washington University*
Walter F. Rohrs
*Wagner College*
Gary Ross
*College of the Southwest*
Robert Roth
*City University*

Hal Rumsey
*Washington State University*
John T. Samaras
*University of Central Oklahoma*
Joseph Santara
*Essex County College*
Nick Sarantakes
*Austin Community College*
Stuart M. Schmidt
*Temple University*
Mel Schnake
*Valdosta State College*
Susan Schneider
*Endicott College*
Elliott Ser
*Barry University*
Eldon Shafer
*Pennsylvania State University*
Arthur Shanley
*Milwaukee School of Engineering*
Del Shenas
*San Diego State University*
Allen Shub
*Northeastern Illinois University*
Ed Sibley
*Western Iowa Technical Community
College*
W. Jack Skaggs
*Oklahoma Christian University*
Jonathan Slesinger
*California State University*
Ron Stone
*Lincoln Memorial University*
Mario Sverdlik
*University of Puerto Rico*
Sherrie Taylor
*Texas Woman's University*
Herman Theeke
*Central Michigan University*
Walter Tymon
*Villanova University*
Mary Uhl-Bien
*University of Alaska*
Martha Valentine
*Regis University*
John J. Vitton
*University of North Dakota*
Jim Walker
*Moorhead State University*
Gary R. Weaver
*Pennsylvania State University*

Jim Welch
*Kentucky Wesleyan College*
Kathleen White
*MacMurray College*
Ellen Whitener
*University of Virginia*
William White
*Alvernia College*
Fred Whitman
*Mary Washington College*

Bill Wilcox
*Northwest College*
Steve Williams
*Michigan Christian College*
J. Clay Willis
*Oklahoma Baptist University*
Andrew Zacharakis
*University of Colorado*

Robert D. Gatewood
*Athens, Georgia*

Robert R. Taylor
*Memphis, Tennessee*

O.C. Ferrell
*Memphis, Tennessee*

*January 1995*

# ABOUT THE AUTHORS

**Robert D. Gatewood**

Robert D. Gatewood is the Chairman of the Department of Management at the University of Georgia. He received his Ph.D. in Industrial Psychology from Purdue University. Bob teaches undergraduate and graduate classes in Human Resource Management, Quantitative Methods, and Organizational Behavior. In addition, he has taught numerous management development seminars and has been a consultant to several organizations including Westinghouse, PPG, Ford Motor, IBM, and Gulf Power. He has written approximately 70 books, chapters, papers, and articles. These have been published in both academic and practitioner journals such as *The Academy of Management Journal, The Academy of Management Review, Personnel Psychology, Journal of Applied Psychology, Human Resource Planning,* and *The Personnel Administrator.* In addition, Bob's textbook, *Human Resource Selection,* written with Hubert Feild, has recently been published in its third edition. He has also been quite active in professional organizations such as the Academy of Management, Southern Management Association, and the Society for Industrial and Organizational Psychology.

**Robert R. Taylor**

Robert R. Taylor is Associate Professor of Management at the University of Memphis. He received his Ph.D. in Social-Industrial Psychology from Louisiana State University in 1979. After directing the Organizational-Industrial Psychology program at the University of West Florida in Pensacola for four years, he joined the Department of Management at the University of Memphis in 1983. Bob presently teaches undergraduate, masters, and doctoral courses in Organizational Behavior and has taught Human Resource Management and Organizational Change and Development. He strives to maintain an integrated balance between teaching, research, and professional consulting, training, and service. His list of consulting clients includes such prominent companies as International Paper, FedEx, Kroger, Kellogg, Sedgwick James Insurance, First Tennessee Bank, St. Regis Paper, Hardee's, LeBonheur Children's Hospital, Mallincrodt Medical, and Memphis Light Gas & Water. Both his business application and teaching interests are reflected in his research and in more than 40 publications in academic proceedings and such journals as *Group and Organizational Management, Personnel Journal, Journal of Management Education,* and *Case Research Journal.* In 1992, Bob won the prestigious Distinguished Teaching Award given by the University of Memphis.

**O.C. Ferrell**

O.C. Ferrell is the Interim Dean of the Fogelman College of Business and Economics at the University of Memphis. He received his Ph.D. from Louisiana State University and has held positions at Southern Illinois University, Illinois State University, and Texas A&M University. O.C. has taught undergraduate and graduate classes in marketing, marketing strategy, business policy, social issues, and business ethics. He has taught numerous management development seminars for organizations such as General Motors, Army and Air Force Exchange System, American Society of Florists, Central Illinois Light Company, and the Dallas Market Center. O.C. was the cofounder of a successful specialty printing company that has more than 75 employees and serves national markets. He has published approximately 45 refereed journal articles. O.C.'s major research interest has been business ethics, and he has coauthored a textbook, a tradebook, and over 20 refereed articles on this topic. This is the fifth textbook that he has coauthored. His other textbooks include *Marketing: Concepts and Strategies, Strategic Marketing Management, Business Ethics: Ethical Decision Making and Cases,* and *Business: A Changing World,* the latter also published by Austen Press.

# Brief Contents

## Note to the Instructor

Austen Press texts are marketed and distributed by Richard D. Irwin, Inc. For assistance in obtaining supplementary material for this and other Austen Press titles, please contact your Irwin sales representative or the customer service division of Richard D. Irwin at (800) 323–4560.

# Contents

# Foundations *of* Management

*chapter* ■ *one*

# The
# Essence
## *of*
# Management

**After reading this chapter, you will be able to:**

- Define management and describe its purpose in organizations.
- Determine the effect that management actions have on the manager and others in the organization.
- List the major functions of managers.
- Explain the importance of decision making in management activities.
- Describe the many roles managers play in an organization.
- Specify why different managers perform different job activities.
- Review what you can reasonably learn from a textbook about how to perform management activities.
- Evaluate a small business owner's management skills and propose a future course of action for the firm.

© Tom Tracy for Dreyer's Grand Ice Cream, Inc.

# Managing Ice Cream— Dreyer's and Edy's

In 1977, Rick Cronk, Gary Rogers, and their venture capital backers bought Dreyer's Grand Ice Cream for $1 million. At that time it was a small-market, private, San Francisco Bay Area firm with an excellent reputation. Presently, it is a public company, with an international market, annual sales of approximately $500 million, over 1,800 employees, and an even better reputation. Its goal is to become the largest premium ice cream company in the country.

The organization produces under two names: Dreyer's Grand Ice Cream, west of the Rockies and in the Pacific Rim, and Edy's Grand Ice Cream, east of the Rockies and in Europe. Cronk and Rogers have obviously been extremely successful in managing a small business into a very large one in less than 20 years. In this time they have designed and implemented numerous innovations and changes in the company. A few of their most important management activities have been:

• Product Innovation—More than 50 percent of the ice cream sold today is from products that were created since 1988. Dreyer's was first to market "light" ice cream and frozen yogurt. Among its other innovations are a no-sugar-added ice cream, fat-free ice cream, lactose-reduced ice cream, ice-cream-on-a-stick, and frozen juice novelties. It has a pilot plant in Union City, California, to develop and test new flavors and products.

• Direct-Store Delivery System— By offering direct-store delivery rather than warehousing, Dreyer's has better control of both quality and the appropriate product-mix for each store. As part of this effort, Cronk and Rogers oversaw the development of a costly information system that allows delivery personnel to use hand-held computers both to provide consumer information to central data files and to manage inventory on their trucks. The result is shelf stocking designed for each retail outlet and better information about customer consumption patterns.

• Work Group Teams—The company has two production plants in California and one in Indiana. All are operated by work teams that are in charge of quality and sanitation checks, meeting business goals, and internal scheduling, as well as training, discipline, and wage schedules. To support these activities, Dreyer's has developed an extensive training and orientation program and a monthly incentive system.

• Distribution Ventures—More than 40 percent of the company's profits are derived from its distribution business. Dreyer's delivers other companies' ice cream products to retail outlets. Among these products are Con Agra's Healthy Choice, Mocha Mix, Dolly Madison, and Steve's Homemade Ice Cream. Even more interestingly, Dreyer's manufactures ice cream that is sold by other brands. Ben & Jerry's Homemade is the biggest customer. In early 1989, the two companies signed a three-year agreement under which Dreyer's produced at least 5 million gallons at its Indiana plant for Ben & Jerry's. In 1992, Dreyer's produced over 40 percent of Ben & Jerry's product.

• Expanding Territories—Dreyer's is steadily increasing the geographic size of its market. It continues to move eastward in the United States and, through joint ventures with Nissho Iwai, has established a Dreyer's of Japan. Through this organization, small packages of ice cream (quarts, pints, and cups), which fit the limited freezer space of Japanese households, are sold throughout Japan.

Both Cronk and Rogers see only further growth for Dreyer's.

Even consumer health-consciousness isn't regarded as a major problem. As Rick Cronk has said, "People speak of wanting to be concerned with their weight … but when they want ice cream, they want a big bowl."

*Sources:* Diana B. Henriques, "Ben & Jerry's—and Dreyer's?" *The New York Times,* June 16, 1991, Sec. 3, Col. 2; Gail Rosenbaum, "Onward & Upward: Dreyer's Aims for Elusive Number One Slot," *Dairy Foods* 93 (June 1992): 48–51; and "A Triple Scoop of Innovation," *Cal Business,* Spring 1994, 11–15.

*introduction*

This brief history of Dreyer's illustrates the diversity in management activities, which is one reason why management seems difficult to teach and learn. There do not seem to be general principles or concepts that can be applied to all these different activities. Not surprisingly, our purpose is to show you that there are such general principles, which are important for understanding and learning management.

Our basic idea in this chapter is that, in order to understand what management is, it is necessary to know how it is similar and different across organizations. There are a number of similarities. All managers make decisions about the use of organizational resources to reach organizational goals; engage in the same basic activities of planning, organizing, leading and controlling; and act in the same general roles for their organizations. On the other hand, the specific task activities of managers can vary greatly due to differences—such as size and industry—in the characteristics of the organization to which they belong.

**Example:** McDonald's Corporation must plan for raw material needs as well as human resource needs just like a local hamburger restaurant. In addition, management at McDonald's corporate headquarters must consider language, culture, and taste differences when planning menus and making staffing decisions for international locations.

**management**
A set of activities designed to achieve an organization's objectives by using its resources effectively and efficiently.

**effectively**
Having the intended result.

**efficiently**
Accomplishing objectives with a minimum of resources.

**managers**
Individuals who make decisions about the use of the organization's resources and are concerned with planning, organizing, leading, and controlling the organization's activities in order to reach its objectives.

**organizations**
Groups of individuals who work together to achieve desired objectives.

## THE NATURE OF MANAGEMENT

**Management** is a set of activities designed to achieve an organization's objectives by using its resources effectively and efficiently in a changing environment. Resources are used to accomplish the manager's intended purpose. **Effectively** means having the intended result; **efficiently** means accomplishing the objectives with a minimum of resources. Both are part of good management—reaching objectives with a minimum of cost. One factor that makes management difficult is that the work situation constantly changes. That is, such factors as employees, technology, competition, and cost vary greatly. **Managers** are individuals who make decisions about the use of the organization's resources, and are concerned with planning, organizing, leading, and controlling the organization's activities so as to reach its objectives. (See Figure 1.1.)

Although it may seem that management activities are quite diverse, they share some common characteristics. First, all activities occur within the context of an organization. As we will discuss in more detail in Chapters 12 and 13, **organizations** are groups of individuals who work together to achieve the goals or objectives that are important to these individuals. For example, the Boston Red Sox is an organization that tries to win baseball games; the organization known as Domino's Pizza serves food to customers; LOMA, Life Office Management Association, provides management consulting assistance to association member insurance companies. All three organizations have managers who are essential to their success.

**FIGURE 1.1**

**Common Characteristics of Management Activities**

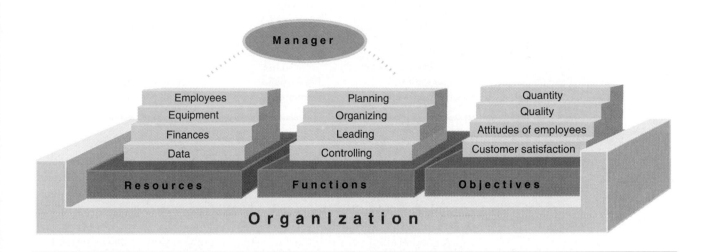

Second, managers are in charge of the organization's **resources**—people, equipment, finances, data—and of using these resources to help the organization reach its objectives. How well a manager coordinates the firm's activities and uses its resources determines not only how well the organization accomplishes its objectives but also how he or she will be judged in terms of job performance.

**resources**
The people, equipment, finances, and data an organization uses in order to reach its objectives.

## THE IMPACT OF MANAGEMENT

The management practices of an individual affect more than the person himself or herself. Management is characterized by interaction with others, decision making, and completing work tasks. Because such activities are not carried out in isolation, management reaches several different groups connected with the organization. Moreover, management's effect is not neutral. If management is done well, it has a positive impact on these groups; if management is done poorly, it has a negative effect. Finally, it is important to recognize that all management decisions have consequences.

As shown in Table 1.1, the three groups most affected by management activities are the manager, the manager's immediate subordinates, and the manager's organization. This table illustrates some of the effects on all three of these groups, and you can probably think of others, based on your own experiences. From the manager's perspective, those who manage well are distinctly successful. Successful managers will be given the opportunity to manage more resources and asked to make decisions that have even more impact on the organization.

Obviously, a manager's subordinates are directly affected by his or her actions. If the work process is organized well, everyone performs better, which is reflected in the performance appraisals of individual workers. Good performance appraisals often result in increased financial rewards and advancement opportunities. Research also suggests that employees' relationships with their manager strongly affect their work attitudes, such as commitment, satisfaction, and work involvement.[1]

**Critical Thinking Challenge:** Have students list reasons why clear goals and directions are important to subordinates. Have them list some of the disadvantages or problems that could result if managers do not provide proper direction to employees.

**TABLE 1.1**

**The Impact of Management**

| The Manager | Subordinates | Organization |
| --- | --- | --- |
| Self-esteem | Work attitudes | Productivity |
| Career development | Self-esteem | Quality |
| Time allocation | Performance | Customer service |
| Relationship with others | Career development | Environment |

Finally, by its very nature, management affects the number and the quality of the organization's goods and services. As we have said, managers coordinate the organization's resources to help it reach organizational objectives. If the manager coordinates poorly or makes poor decisions, the organization's objectives will not be met as well or as quickly.

A good example of the impact of management decisions is an operation that we all are familiar with—an auto repair shop. Customers are dramatically affected by a number of decisions: the quality of parts used, the maintenance of repair equipment, and the extent to which leading technology is utilized. Even more noticeable to most customers is how the manager handles disputes. The extreme ranges from the shop redoing questioned work at no expense to refusing to adjust any but very obvious mistakes. Employees are greatly affected by other types of decisions: the extent of training that is company sponsored, the compensation system used, and the maintenance of the physical facilities.

## THE FUNCTIONS OF MANAGEMENT

All management activities can be classified into four major functions: planning, organizing, leading, and controlling. We will discuss these separately, but they usually occur simultaneously in management activities.

### Planning

**Planning** involves determining what the organization will specifically accomplish and deciding how to accomplish these goals. How to use the resources at the command of the manager is the object of planning. For example, after the manager of the Boston Red Sox baseball team determines which opposing team is next on the schedule, he plans which pitchers and players to use in the line-up to try to win the game. At Domino's, an individual store manager plans ahead by anticipating the next week's demand for food, which may be affected by variables such as weather and holidays. She then plans a work schedule of employees, orders supplies, and inspects all equipment, including delivery vehicles, to try to meet that demand. A manager of training at LOMA examines employee records to determine how many employees have had training in selection interviewing, identifies an instructor who has done this training well in the past, schedules the seminar facilities, and designs the brochure that advertises the seminar. We will take a closer look at the planning function in Chapter 9.

---

**Example:** The popular mail-order outdoor and sporting goods company L.L. Bean has made a conscious management decision to work toward total customer satisfaction. It is open 24 hours a day and will take customer returns with no questions asked. Customers have even been given credit for hiking boots owned for more than 25 years!

**planning**
The process of determining what the organization will specifically accomplish and deciding how to accomplish these goals.

Southwest Airlines CEO Herbert Kelleher (hand extended), shown here at an employee dinner, knows how to lead employees to perform at their best. LUV is not only the airline's stock exchange symbol, it's also the theme of the company's employee and customer relationships. By treating employees with genuine care and respect, Kelleher motivates them to treat customers the same way. As a result, Southwest rates highest in customer satisfaction and employee productivity of any major U.S. airline.

*Source:* © 1994 Louis Psihoyos/MATRIX.

## Organizing

**Organizing** refers to the activities involved in designing jobs for employees, grouping these jobs together into departments, and developing working relationships among organizational units/departments and employees to carry out the plans. Some organizing activities, such as forming and closing committees, developing work teams, and staffing for special projects, occur frequently. Others are periodic. For example, the departmental structure that results from the organizing function is retained until something suggests that a change in structure is needed. Within the Boston Red Sox organization, for instance, there may be departments for scouting, player development, and travel arrangements. The Red Sox manager can use all three departments to carry out his plans for the upcoming series.

Not long ago IBM undertook a reorganization and a restructuring, resulting in a change in the arrangement of its various administrative divisions and departments. High-level managers of IBM determined that the company's past structure was not helping it achieve its goals and decided to develop different organizational departments and employee working arrangements to implement the company's plans and reach its goals. We will discuss organizing in more detail in Chapters 12 and 13.

**organizing**
The activities involved in designing jobs for employees, grouping these jobs together into departments, and developing working relationships among organizational units and employees to carry out the plans.

**Critical Thinking Challenge:** Form students into small groups of 4 or 5 people. Ask each group to form a company, choosing its industry and market. Once the decisions have been made, have them design the organizational units and departments required. Have students present their organization to classmates for critique and discussion.

## Leading

**Leading** refers to influencing others' activities to achieve set goals. As we will discuss in Chapters 14 through 18, leading is based on knowledge of the principles of human behavior. Basically, a manager attempts to organize the work environment to obtain high work performance from employees. Even though there is much more to be learned, we already understand a lot about how to influence individuals' performance. For example, there are ample data to indicate that selection, training, communication, goal-setting levels, compensation, and work design are among the organizational factors that managers can use to significantly affect an employee's job performance.[2] The manager of the Red Sox, for example, must lead and motivate highly publicized athletes who often earn millions of dollars. On the other hand, employees at a Domino's restaurant, for the most part, are students working part time for minimum wage, who do not view the work as part of their careers. A training manager at LOMA deals with employees who are well-educated specialists concerned with long-term professional careers. In each organization, the

**leading**
The act of influencing others' activities to achieve set goals.

manager attempts to influence the level of employees' work performance by applying principles of human behavior.

## Controlling

**controlling**
Those activities that an organization undertakes to ensure that its activities lead to achievement of its objectives.

The management activities that we have described so far establish future goals, specify how to reach these goals, and attempt to motivate organizational members to work toward the attainment of these goals. If all these functions are carried out properly, goals should be attained. However, we've all heard the expression, "the best-laid plans of mice and men." The management function of **controlling** refers to those activities that an organization undertakes to ensure that its actions lead to achievement of its objectives. It involves collecting and analyzing information about work performance and taking corrective action if this information indicates that performance is not contributing to goal achievement.

Returning to the Red Sox baseball team, the manager will examine batting averages, pitching records, and other data and make changes in the line-up accordingly to try to win more games. The LOMA manager will look at written evaluations of instructors gathered from students of the training class, as well as the students' test scores at the end of class, to determine how well the instructor is doing. We will discuss controlling in several places, especially in Chapter 21.

## MANAGEMENT DECISION MAKING

Along with the four basic management functions, all managers engage in the decision-making process—gathering information, using information to reach a decision, and implementing the decision (Figure 1.2). Each of the four management functions requires a manager to make decisions. Planning, for example, requires gathering information about future objectives, assessing the organization's ability to reach those objectives, and drawing up specific actions needed to guide the organization toward achievement of its objectives. In essence, processing the appropriate information is the key to planning. John Scully, former CEO of Apple Computer, puts it this way, "The issue is how do I get all the information I want without getting all the other junk that is out there."[3]

**Teaching Note:** In the move to ensure customer satisfaction, many organizations hire "mystery shoppers" who pose as typical customers and evaluate employee performance, cleanliness, etc., to report to management. Such information is used to make changes to enhance customer service. This reflects decision making in the context of the controlling function.

As another example, leading—influencing employees' performance—also requires a lot of information gathering. The manager must understand the principles of human behavior and the factors that positively and negatively influence performance. He or she must also be familiar with employees' characteristics such as job skills, desire for achievement, and work commitment because these are linked to individual work performance. Moreover, the manager should know what characteristics of the work situation influence performance, such as the level of difficulty of operating the technology and time allowed for completing each task. Obtaining this information should precede the manager's evaluation of what alternatives are available in a particular situation, as well as implementation of the chosen alternative.

While this decision-making process may sound easy to carry out, it is very difficult. The difficulty lies in the complexity of the information gathered and the uncertainty of the decision process and the methods of implementing the decision. For example, account managers in computer software firms have a number of important decisions to make with very little certain information. Typically the account manager comes in after the sales representative has made the sale and has promised services and programs to the new client. In a short time, the account manager must prepare a service plan that includes a schedule of events such as

**FIGURE 1.2**

**An Example of Management Decision Making:  Influencing Employees' Performance**

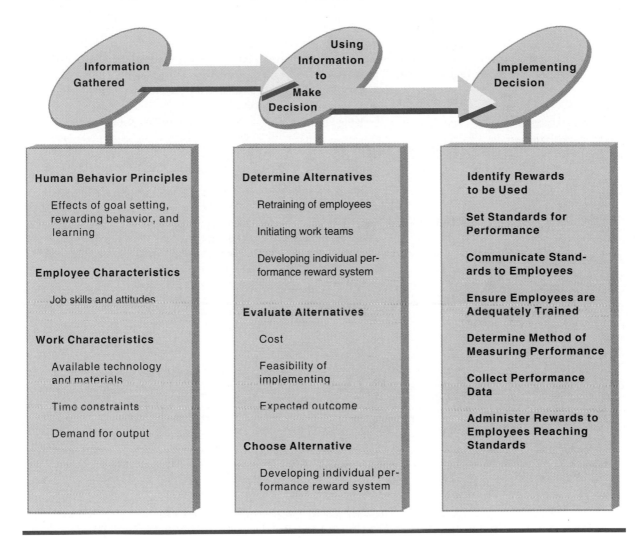

training, on-site visits, trials of the software programs, and quality-control test runs. To do this, the account manager must make specific commitments of personnel, products, and equipment. These commitments, in turn, become the milestones upon which the software company is judged by the client. Yet, these decisions are often made with only limited data about the expertise of the client's employees, the condition of the necessary company data and records, and the accuracy of the client's own judgment of needs.

## MANAGEMENT ROLES

Another aspect common to all managers is the role that management activities serve within organizations. By *role*, we mean a set of similar or organized activities that serve a specific purpose for the organization. Henry Mintzberg, a noted management

**TABLE 1.2**

**Mintzberg's Ten Management Roles**

| General Role Category | Specific Role | Example Activity |
|---|---|---|
| Interpersonal | Figurehead | Attending award banquet |
| | Liaison | Coordinating production schedule with supply manager |
| | Leadership | Conducting performance appraisal for subordinates |
| Informational | Monitor | Contacting government regulatory agencies |
| | Disseminator | Conducting meetings with subordinates to pass along policy changes |
| | Spokesperson | Meeting with consumer group to discuss product safety |
| Decisional | Entrepreneur | Changing work process |
| | Disturbance Handler | Deciding which unit moves into new facilities |
| | Resource Allocator | Deciding who receives new computer equipment |
| | Negotiator | Settling union grievance |

professor, has published several reports about what managers do and how they go about doing it. He actually followed managers for a number of days and took detailed notes about whom they met with, what they did, and the purpose of their activities.[4]

We have already grouped management activities into planning, organizing, leading, or controlling, all of which emphasize the work process for which managers are responsible. Mintzberg described ten specific roles that managers perform, which, in turn, can be grouped into three larger categories—interpersonal, informational, and decisional (Table 1.2). While Mintzberg's roles also categorize management activities, they describe more specific categories of work, activities with individuals external to the organization, and activities that support work activities. As such, Mintzberg's roles provide additional information for understanding management. His ten categories, taken together, also underscore our previous point that gathering information, making decisions, and implementing decisions are the critical processes of management. Mintzberg's ten roles identify ten sets of activities used to carry out decision making.

## Interpersonal Roles

**interpersonal roles**
Activities that involve interacting with others who may be external or internal to the organization and at a higher or lower level than the manager.

**Interpersonal roles** refer to activities that involve interacting with others who may be external or internal to the organization and at a higher or lower level than the manager. These roles allow the manager to gather information for the decisions that must be made. The first of the interpersonal roles, *figurehead,* describes the formal activities in which the manager acts as a public official for the company. These activities may range from award banquets to ribbon-cutting ceremonies for the opening of new offices. In this role, managers often deal with people external to the organization, and the activities are not directly related to the work process.

Top managers of Britain's Grand Metropolitan PLC perform the figurehead role during the rededication ceremony of Burger King's Miami headquarters, where an employee's car was embedded in the building by Hurricane Andrew. During the ceremony, the managers praised Burger King employees for their volunteer work in helping the community recover from hurricane damage. Shown, left to right, are Sir Allen Shepard, GrandMet chairman; Jim Adamson, chief executive of Burger King; and George Bull, group chief executive.

*Source:* Courtesy of Burger King Corporation.

In the *liaison* role, the manager interacts with peers outside of the organization. This role is, therefore, composed of a network of relationships. The manager gives information to get information. For example, managers from Ford, GM, and Chrysler have formed ten consortiums to research a variety of topics from low-polluting paint to more humanlike crash dummies.[5] Each consortium shares information collected from the three automobile rivals as a base from which to expand the knowledge of each of the three.

As we have already mentioned, the *leadership* role requires actions that define and direct the work activities of employees. This role naturally requires the manager to obtain information concerning the status of the work activities of members of the organization. In this role, Kent Nelson, CEO of United Parcel Service, decided to refocus the work activities of managers within the company. After reviewing department performance records, he sent 500 managers to one-week classes at Michigan State University, where they were coached to think in terms of customer service, using new technology for tracking packages and contacting customers about their reactions to service.[6]

**Example:** The purchasing function is a liaison role. Purchasing employees must work with other internal employees to identify raw material and supply needs, then work with external vendors and suppliers to identify and procure quality suppliers and materials.

## Informational Roles

The second category of roles includes activities that Mintzberg regarded as focused almost exclusively on the transmission of information. **Informational roles** are activities—including reporting, preparing data analyses, briefings, delivering mail, and making telephone calls—that focus on obtaining data important for the decisions the manager needs to make. In describing these roles, Mintzberg referred to the manager as being the "nerve center" and the "focal point" of information for the organization. For example, a manager of a securities investment group receives information from the company's research division regarding both securities that are expected to do well in the future and those that are not, and passes this information on to the brokers in the group. The brokers, in turn, gather information about their clients' attitudes concerning the economy and about purchasing various types of securities. They feed this information back to the manager.

As *monitor,* a manager seeks information to detect problems or opportunities, build general knowledge about the work situation, and make necessary changes.

**informational roles**
Activities, such as reports or briefings, that focus on obtaining data important for the decisions the manager needs to make.

**Example:** Managers gather informal information from numerous sources including professional meetings. The National Association of Purchasing Managers (NAPM) is an organization providing monthly speakers, networking opportunities for managers, as well as recognized certification programs for continuing education in the purchasing field.

While much of this information comes from formal mechanisms such as reports, news media, and public forecasts, more comes from informal conversations with both organization members and those external to the organization. Managers use this information in two ways: (a) to review performance and plan for changes in the work process and (b) partly to pass on to others in the manager's informational roles of disseminator and spokesperson.

As *disseminator,* the manager sends information from external sources to various parts of the work group, and information from internal sources to others both internal and external to the organization. This information is of two types: facts and value. Factual data are of observable events that can be checked for accuracy, such as production figures, contract specifications, and so on. A United Way manager, for example, will tell the volunteer fund raisers how close to the goal is the total amount raised. Value information is about preferences—that is, the opinions and attitudes of others about "what ought to be" or the present condition of the work or products. Customer judgments of product safety are one example.

In the *spokesperson* role, the manager provides information about the work group to those outside the group. Two parties are of special concern. One is the manager's own immediate superior, because the manager's boss is also involved in planning, coordinating, leading, and controlling and must have as much information as possible to perform those functions. For example, a regional sales manager needs to know the correct sales performance of all the groups in the region before planning an upcoming sales campaign. The second is the organization's "public," which includes customers, suppliers, trade organizations, government agencies, consumer groups, and the press. Because of the manager's position in the work unit, he or she becomes the expert and the logical contact person for all information about the unit. For this reason Craig Weatherup, CEO of Pepsi-Cola North America, made six personal appearances on morning and evening television news shows to explain that a syringe could not possibly be placed in a can of Pepsi during bottling operations. This was in response to charges made by four individuals who claimed to have found syringes in cans of Pepsi they had purchased. The FBI later arrested all four for making false claims about a product.[7]

## Decisional Roles

**decisional roles**
Activities that deal primarily with the allocation of resources in order to reach organizational objectives.

Mintzberg describes decisional roles as the most crucial part of the manager's work. **Decisional roles** are activities that deal primarily with the allocation of resources in order to reach organizational objectives. Managers use the information gathered in the interpersonal and informational roles to make judgments that affect both the short- and long-term well-being of the firm. In the role of *entrepreneur,* the manager acts as the initiator and designer of changes within the work group. These changes may be in employee skills, work redesign, information reports, and goods or services provided, and the decisions require as much factual data as possible. For example, productivity reports, customer satisfaction surveys, consumer buying patterns, trends in the cost of raw materials, and educational and training statistics are some of the data that can be used. In this role, Cherrill Farnworth, CEO of TME Inc., a magnetic resonance imaging service for hospitals, ordered extensive training for 18 marketing employees after reviewing the company's performance and the employees' skills. In Farnworth's words, "We have high energy, intelligent people who don't look for traditional promotion situations. The goal is ... institutional insecurity." The training addressed financial statistics, margins, business plans, forecasting, and time and stress management.[8]

While the entrepreneur role deals with voluntary change by the manager, the role of *disturbance handler* deals with change forced on the manager by other factors. The manager acts because it is a necessity—a disturbance occurs and a solution must be found. There are three types of disturbances: conflicts among individuals, interaction difficulties between one unit and another, and conflicts over resource losses. Examples of conditions that may cause such disturbances are the departure of an employee, damage to the physical facility, the loss of an important customer, a sudden rise in price of labor or raw materials, or a disagreement between subordinates. For the most part, these disturbances require quick action and temporary solutions to the problem. More long-term adaptations are subsequently developed.

Another decisional role is that of *resource allocator,* which both protects and uses the unit's assets: money, time, material and equipment, human resources, data, and reputation. Control systems are used to protect resources such as cost of travel, materials, and training; such control systems are the result of decisions to conserve resources.

The final role is that of *negotiator,* which focuses on reaching agreement with others outside the work group on work-related issues or materials, such as labor union contracts and leasing agreements concerning machinery and vehicles. This role includes agreements with other units within the organization regarding arrival and quantity of necessary goods, use of common equipment, and exchange of personnel with rare skills. It can also include reforming and restructuring companies. For example, Eli Broad, head of both SunAmerica Inc., an insurance company, and Kaufman and Broad Home Corporation, a construction company focusing on homebuilding, built both companies in a series of negotiated agreements. Many of these involved buying assets from financially crippled institutions.[9]

Mintzberg's description of roles provides important information about the specific activities that managers perform in carrying out the planning, organizing, leading, and controlling functions. In addition, it also provides more detail about specific activities involved in the management process of collecting information, making decisions, and implementing them. All of this information is intended to present the clear idea that management is not "the ability to work with others" or a function of the "personality" of the manager. Rather, management is a complex set of activities that use extensive skills, knowledge, and abilities to perform—many of which can be learned.

**Example:** Other management fundamentals include: Lead by bringing out the best in others; personally care about your customers, employees, and company; collaborate with everyone affected by your decisions; and share information openly and honestly.

## MANAGEMENT SKILLS

In a general discussion of management such as this, it is useful to describe what skills are necessary to operate successfully as a manager. Given the complexity of management, it is not possible to list all of the necessary skills; instead, we will discuss a representative sample of the general and specific skills that managers need.

### General Skills

One way to categorize skills managers need is as interpersonal, technical, and conceptual.[10]

**Interpersonal Skills.**   Many of the ten management roles described by Mintzberg involved interacting with others inside and outside of the organization. The success of these interactions depends directly on a manager's **interpersonal skills,**

**interpersonal skills**
Those management skills, such as communication, conflict resolution, and leading, that are necessary to work with others.

**Example:** Surveys of managers continue to reveal the importance of interpersonal skills. Executives were asked what skills they needed more training on while in school. The most popular response was communication and interpersonal skills for working with others.

those skills such as communication, listening, conflict resolution, and leading that are necessary to work with others.

Interactions with others take many forms. Within a work unit, for example, a manager might select and set up new word-processing equipment, review an employee's work performance, or try to determine if an employee's poor performance is a result of drug or alcohol addiction. Activities outside the work unit are equally varied, and may include responding to hostile consumer or environmental groups concerning the use of chemicals or natural resources; lobbying members of a local or state legislature to provide better roads, water systems, or sewage facilities for manufacturing; or discussing a customer's complaint about a perceived deficiency in a good or service. In each of these instances, the manager's interpersonal skills in clearly presenting his or her viewpoint, extracting information from the others, and arriving at a mutually acceptable agreement become essential to the organization's well-being.

**Technical Skills.**    Most managers work within a specific department or administrative unit of an organization, and, in most cases, such departments handle a specialized portion of the firm's work. Therefore, there are accounting managers, research and development managers, sales managers, scheduling managers, and so on. These managers use their departments' resources to plan, organize, lead, and control the work of the unit.

**technical skills**
The knowledge and ability to accomplish the specialized activities of the work group.

To manage their departments' work, managers must have **technical skills,** that is, the knowledge and ability to accomplish the specialized activities of the work group. For example, the accounting manager must know current tax reporting regulations, how to apply accounting systems to new products, and how to compile financial reporting data. If the manager lacks these skills, he or she will not be able to make correct decisions or answer employees' questions about job tasks. Obviously, the more complex and advanced the work of the department becomes, the more technical skill the manager requires. For example, financial managers in investment firms frequently are concerned with only one investment area such as futures, bonds, or international money markets. Therefore, these managers must be extremely knowledgeable about the particular investment area they are managing. In many organizations, a manager's career track is within one technical area until he or she reaches the very highest levels of management. While he was CEO of Apple Computer, John Scully summarized the importance of technical skill in this way, "... leading Apple without knowing much about technology was like trying to do brain-surgery in the first year of medical school. ... I really didn't know enough in those early years to have a strong point of view in terms of where the industry was heading."[11]

**Example:** As procedures become more complex and demand for additional knowledge increases, technical skills are becoming more important in organizations. The Krystal Company, a Tennessee-based hamburger chain, requires all managers to have hands-on experience as restaurant managers before they can progress through upper management levels.

**conceptual skills**
The intellectual abilities to process information and make accurate decisions about the work group and the job task.

**Conceptual Skills.**    Earlier, we said that a key part of management is gathering information and making and implementing decisions. **Conceptual skills,** the intellectual abilities to process information and make accurate decisions about the work group and the job tasks, are essential to this process. First, a manager must be able to understand and retain a large amount of data, obtained while carrying out his or her informational role. Second, he or she must analyze these data in various ways in order to understand their meaning. Some analyses are statistical, such as forecasts of consumer demand based on past buying patterns. Other analyses are essentially judgmental, such as estimating consumer demand by taking into account expected changes in the local economy. Third, the manager must use an

## BUSINESS DILEMMA

*You're the Manager ...What Would You Do?*

THE COMPANY:  Mrs. Acres Homemade Pies

YOUR POSITION:  Owner

THE PLACE:  Ames, Iowa

As a child growing up in the Midwest, Shelly Acres learned how to make pies from her mother and grandmother—rhubarb, boysenberry, apple, almost any variety you can imagine. The pies were always praised and never lasted long enough to cool off. When Acres graduated from Iowa State University with a business administration degree, she decided to take some big risks and enter the world of business by making and marketing specialty pies. She had to plan, organize, and control the business with limited experience.

Acres and a supportive friend bought a commercial oven from a bakery that had gone out of business and purchased used food processors to knead the pie crusts. She converted one of the machine sheds on her family's farm into a small pie factory. To support the business and convert the shed, Acres borrowed $25,000 from a local bank. As she was unable to get the loan on her own financial merit, her parents had to cosign the note and put up their home as collateral. They cosigned because they believed in their daughter's skills and vision in organizing the venture.

Acres's conservative business plan for Mrs. Acres Homemade Pies was to sell them initially through local supermarkets and select family restaurants. This required communicating with customers about the quality of the product. The company name sprang from the notion that the image for the pies should be that of a grandmother, not a 23-year-old college graduate. The image was further extended to incorporate the use of all natural ingredients, the fact that the pies were "homemade," and the unique variety of flavors available.

In the first six months, Acres and a few part-time employees made 100 pies per day at a gross profit margin of $1.70 for each pie. The reception to the pies was extraordinary: Restaurants began to produce table promotional pieces featuring the local pies, and production could not keep up with demand. Acres made a profit of nearly $3,500 per month in the first half year. Local magazines and newspapers approached her for interviews and recipes for these "hot"

pies. She seemed to have the ability to control daily operations and continue expansion.

Acres began expanding operations, borrowing an additional $10,000. The staff increased from three part-time to four full-time employees, and sales increased from 100 to 400 pies per day. All the employees were loyal friends whom she knew growing up in Iowa. Profits soared to $18,000 per month. The key to success for Mrs. Acres Pies was Acres's close supervision, the strong support and motivation of her employees, a profit-sharing plan that spurred productivity and innovation for new recipes/flavors of pies, and keen business sense. Her employees began to feel they were part owners of the business.

Currently demand has again accelerated beyond supply and Acres is faced with several options. She can expand present facilities and add more staff, possibly beyond her inner circle of friends. She can lease or purchase new facilities; with higher production and lower distribution costs, the gross margin could be increased. A national frozen pie company has suggested a joint alliance to make pies for national supermarket chains under her name, recipes, and guidance, and she would not have to continue to manage production. A breakfast chain has also proposed a joint venture for production and marketing of her pies under a licensing arrangement that would give her a percentage of each pie sold with minimal involvement on her part.

### Questions

1. What management skills has Acres used to make Mrs. Acres Homemade Pies successful?
2. What challenges does she face as she evaluates these options?
3. What is your recommendation for the future of Acres's business?

analysis to select a course of action among several options. If consumer demand is expected to increase over the next six months, for example, should the firm run a sale to attract a lot of consumer attention early in the period or should it conduct an intensive advertising campaign? These steps require the conceptual skills of reasoning, information processing, and evaluation.

**Example:** As managers move up in organizations, the need for conceptual skills increases faster than the need for technical skills. Strategic planners must process information about the company and demographic, social, political, and environmental trends.

## Specific Skills

For many years, organizations have been trying to identify the specific skills that are related to managerial job performance. Following are a few that researchers have identified across several different organizations.

• *Job knowledge:* Knowing the facts about equipment, materials, and the work process, as well as the relationships among all parts of the work operation. Example: Knowing about personal computers and software programs.

• *Oral communication:* Verbally presenting information to others in such a manner that the information means the same to everyone. Example: Communicating work objectives to all members of a work team.

• *Persuasiveness:* Influencing others who have different viewpoints to reach agreement on an acceptable plan of action. Example: A committee member explaining a position on future group actions.

• *Problem analysis:* Determining why a situation does not conform to standards and deciding what to do about it. Example: Determining why a group of products has failed final inspection.

• *Cooperativeness:* Working easily and well with others in group projects. Example: The interaction of members of a strategic planning committee.

• *Tolerance of stress:* Continuing work performance in adverse or hostile circumstances. Example: Multiple projects coming to completion at approximately the same time.

• *Negotiation:* Arriving at mutually acceptable joint decisions. Example: Agreeing with a supplier as to a mutually acceptable price for raw materials.

• *Assertiveness:* Clearly and consistently expressing a point of view on a topic being discussed. Example: Individual performance review with a subordinate who has a deficiency in work activities.

• *Initiative:* Determining what work activities must be pursued and starting them. Example: Determining what must be done to successfully operate new production equipment.

These are only a few of the skills research has identified as necessary for successful managerial work. Hopefully, the relationship between these specific skills and the general categories of technical, interpersonal, and conceptual skills is obvious: These specific skills are subparts of the general categories. They all involve interacting with others, evaluating the work process, or making decisions.

## SITUATIONAL DIFFERENCES IN MANAGEMENT ACTIVITIES

The main emphasis of this chapter so far has been on the similarities of management activities across organizations. However, if you were to observe the activities of several managers, you would probably be impressed with how different their specific tasks are, even though these tasks address the same management process and functions. In this section we will explore some of the characteristics of organizations that cause these differences in management activities: level of management, area of management, organizational size, organizational culture, industry, and whether the organization is profit or nonprofit (Figure 1.3).

**FIGURE 1.3**

**Factors in Organizations That Cause Differences in Management Activities**

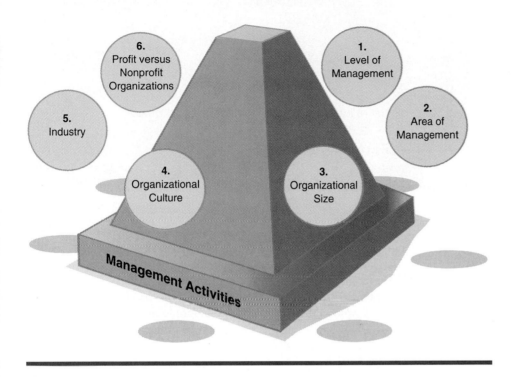

## Level of Management

Managers may be classified according to their level or position within the organization. We commonly categorize managers as being in lower, middle, or upper levels of management; however, these terms generally apply only in organizations large enough to have specialization. **Upper managers** spend most of their time planning and leading because they make decisions about the overall performance and direction of the organization. Therefore, they are usually involved in the development of goals and strategies to achieve those goals. Conceptual and interpersonal skills are especially important. Chief executive officer (CEO), chief financial officer (CFO), chairman, president, and executive vice president are common titles at this level. **Middle managers** are those managers who receive broad statements of strategy and policy from upper-level managers and develop specific objectives and plans. They spend a large portion of their time in planning and organizing activities. Conceptual and technical skills underlie these activities. Examples of the titles of middle managers are product manager, department head, plant manager, and quality control manager. **Lower or first-line managers** are those concerned with the direct production of items or delivery of service. These actions require leading and controlling. Because first-line managers train and monitor the performance of their subordinates, technical skills are especially important. Common titles are supervisor, sales manager, loan officer, and store manager. Middle- and upper-level managers coordinate the activities of specialized, lower-level managers.

**upper managers**
Those who make decisions about the overall performance and direction of the organization.

**middle managers**
Those who receive broad statements of strategy and policy from upper-level managers and develop specific objectives and plans.

**lower (first-line) managers**
Those concerned with the direct production of items or delivery of service.

Sears sales managers use the technical and interpersonal skills needed by first-line managers when they conduct "ready meetings" for sales associates. Sales managers hold these meetings in each department before a store opens. During the meetings, managers give associates updated sales information that helps them deliver better service to customers.

*Source:* © Mark Joseph for Sears, Roebuck and Co.

**Example:** As president of McDonald's USA, Edward H. Rensi is responsible for strategic decisions. McDonald's only venture outside the fast-food business and into children's indoor entertainment centers was recently sold to Blockbuster Entertainment Corporation. A stakeholder in Discovery Zone, Inc., Mr. Rensi made the decision to concentrate on the company's core fast-food business.

**human resource managers**
Managers concerned with developing and carrying out programs used to make decisions about employees, such as selection, training, and compensation.

**marketing managers**
Managers who develop programs that provide information about the company's goods or services and encourage potential customers to purchase these.

**finance managers**
Managers concerned with the value of the organization's assets and various investment strategies that would increase net worth.

**production and operations managers**
Managers who schedule and monitor the work process that turns out the firm's goods and services.

In terms of differences in activities necessary for performance, upper-level managers have numerous contacts with people external to the organization, such as when they negotiate agreements or provide information about organizational activities. Middle-level managers often associate with other managers of the organization to collect information and plan how to implement programs. Lower-level managers generally work with the nonmanagerial employees on technical tasks.

## Area of Management

We will discuss functional units, or areas of organization, in Chapter 12. For now we will refer to these functional areas in terms of jobs with similar technical content. Human resource management, marketing, and production could all be functional areas of one organization, and managers in each of these areas must gather information, make decisions, and implement programs that are appropriate for their area. For example, **human resource managers** are concerned with developing and carrying out systems that are used to make decisions about employees such as selection, training, and compensation. **Marketing managers** develop programs that provide information about the company's goods or services and encourage potential customers to purchase these. **Finance managers** are concerned with the value of the firm's assets and various investment strategies that would increase net worth. **Production and operations managers** schedule and monitor the work process that turns out the goods or services of the organization.

Although each of these managers engages in planning, organizing, leading, and controlling, these functions take different forms due to the different technical information among them. The human resource manager may plan an instructional program on sexual harassment, while a marketing manager may plan a national television sales campaign. Both programs are developed to provide information to others. However, how the two proceed and the activities that they perform are quite different.

## Organizational Size

Generally, the larger a firm the more specialized will be its managers' activities. The owner of a small business, for example, often functions as the chief executive

Rallies that recognize the achievements of Mary Kay Cosmetics' saleswomen are an integral part of the company's culture and key to its success. Depending on the level of their sales, women win crowns, badges, jewelry, trips, and pink Cadillacs, won by the sales directors shown here. Revered as their hero, Mary Kay inspires rally participants with stories of her experiences in the corporate world, why she left it, and how she invested her life savings of $5,000 to start her own company that would treat women right by rewarding them for their hard work.

*Source:* Nina Berman/SIPA.

officer, chief financial officer, marketing director, and production manager. On the other hand, large firms tend to employ managers who have the specialized training and experience required to work in a narrow range of activities.

Large organizations are also characterized by more formalized rules, procedures, and policies, essential to coordinating the work activities of a large number of employees. Formalization affects a manager's activities in many ways, including the requirement of much more paperwork and reporting forms—such as work schedules, selection procedures for hiring new employees, and production or quality reports. Many interactions between manager and subordinates are also formalized, such as grievance and discipline meetings, performance evaluation sessions, and salary adjustment discussions. Small firms frequently have much less formalization, and coordination of employees is achieved through daily interaction. Often the only reports or forms a small business manager must complete are those necessary for legal compliance or financial reporting.

**Critical Thinking Challenge:** Have groups of students interview local managers in a small organization and in a large organization. Ask them to gather information on formalization of interactions and the presence of formalized rules and policies. Have each group report its findings.

## Organizational Culture

**Organizational culture** refers to the values, beliefs, traditions, philosophies, rules, and heroes that are shared by members of the organization. The culture of an organization distinguishes it from others and shapes the actions of its members. For example, by providing necessary time and resources, 3M encourages individuals to experiment with the development of products. Much latitude is given an individual to pursue projects that initially do not look promising. As an example, Post-it brand notes were developed from a glue that failed in its initial purpose. The glue was not able to bond items together very well. However, over time, this inadequate glue became the critical feature of a multimillion dollar product. Other organizations have cultures that use financial data as the primary basis of decision making. A manager at 3M might engage in actions that encourage an employee to develop a potential product, but at another company, the manager may order the employee to cease all activities because of the cost.

There are four main components of culture. The first of these is values, which are the basic beliefs that define success of employees in the organization. For example, many state universities value academic journal publications. Others demand high student evaluations and additional signs of teaching excellence.

**organizational culture**
The values, beliefs, traditions, philosophies, rules, and heroes that are shared by members of the organization.

Heroes, the second component, are individuals who personify the company's values and serve as role models to other employees. Lee Iacocca is a hero at Chrysler. His hard work, determination, and attention to the public helped turn around Chrysler's financial picture.

The third component, rites and rituals, are routines or ceremonies that the company uses to show employees what to do or to call attention to those who have succeeded. The annual, lavish convention of sales representatives of Mary Kay Cosmetics awards pink Buicks and Cadillacs to leading sellers. Finally, the cultural network is the informal means of communication within an organization that is the carrier of corporate stories of both heroes and those who have failed. It is difficult, if not impossible, to understand the organization without being familiar with this network.

## Industry

The industry that an organization operates in determines the knowledge and skills its managers must possess. A manager in an oil-refining company needs knowledge of manufacturing, chemistry, and environmental laws, whereas a banking manager needs knowledge of investments, currency exchange rates, and securities laws. There are major differences in the activities of managers with the same titles but operating in different industries. For example, a regional marketing manager for a consumer package goods company may deal extensively with planning advertising and sales promotions. On the other hand, a regional marketing manager for an industrial equipment manufacturing company may spend little time with such activities, and instead communicate directly with current and potential clients to determine specifications and the uses of equipment for the future.

## Profit versus Nonprofit Organizations

**for-profit companies**
Companies owned either privately by one or more individuals or publicly by stockholders.

**nonprofit organizations**
Institutions such as governments, churches, and universities that cannot retain earnings over expenses, do not have equity interests, and cannot be bought or sold.

**Example:** A nonprofit organization, the Metropolitan Museum of Art depends on donations from patrons, the city of New York, and funds generated from admissions and museum shops. Competition for limited city funds as well as trends in tourism and leisure activities affect the scope of the museum's activities.

**For-profit companies** are owned either privately by one or more individuals or publicly by stockholders. These organizations must pay taxes on profits and may be bought and sold. **Nonprofit organizations** are institutions such as governments, churches, and universities that cannot retain earnings over expenses, do not have equity interests, and cannot be bought or sold.

There are two differences between these two types of organizations that affect management activities. First, nonprofit organizations frequently have several groups of individuals who have a major influence in setting the goals of the organization. For example, state universities are influenced by legislators, university administrators, faculty, staff, students, and state taxpayers in determining their goals and operations. Often, these groups have conflicting opinions as to what is desirable. For example, faculty may wish for fewer classes and more time allocated for research. State legislators often ask for more classes and less time for research. In contrast, for-profit organizations, such as Microsoft, the computer software organization, ordinarily have closer agreement as to their goals and activities.

The second difference is in how funds are generated and what may be done with them. Nonprofit organizations generally raise part of their necessary funds from the sale of goods or services; often the remainder is from governmental support or charitable contributions. Profit organizations exist primarily on the sale of goods and services and, secondarily, on investments of corporate assets. These differences affect, among other things, the planning and organizing activities of managers in the two types of organizations.

## AN EMERGENCY ROOM MANAGER'S JOB

I have three basic areas in which I make a lot of decisions. First, I initiate changes in policy or organization that will help my staff better serve the patients; second, I manage personnel; and third, I manage budgets. With the exception of hiring ER [emergency room] physicians, I am responsible for all aspects of the emergency room.

With respect to initiating organizational change, one of the most common problems at any ER is the long wait that most patients experience. I recently decided to divide our emergency room into an ambulatory (those who can walk) section and an emergency section. Since emergency patients have priority over ambulatory patients, ambulatory patients can easily feel slighted by the system. By separating them, this perception was removed. Additionally, I decided to hire two patient assistants to circulate among all patients and families in the waiting rooms. These assistants keep the patients who are waiting informed of when to expect treatment. They also try to take care of any needs that the patients may have while in the waiting room. If the patients are kept

informed about when they can expect treatment, they tend to have a better experience here.

I also decided to establish a bereavement counseling center, which assists families of those who die in the ER. This has been a very effective program not only for the families but also for training our staff in dealing with grief. I must also anticipate trends that will affect the types of service we deliver and decide what to do in the future. For example, as the population ages, we must be increasingly prepared to handle the types of medical emergencies common to older people.

To keep abreast of these trends, I rely primarily on my network of colleagues both inside and outside the

hospital. I have several people that I interact with regularly to keep up-to-date on latest trends. Trade journals also provide me with an opinion of what forces will shape the ER of tomorrow. We also conduct a follow-up telephone survey of 10 percent of our patients to see what they thought of our care. All this information helps me make decisions. However, once all the information is in, the decision is rarely obvious. Intuition from experience is critical in this field and often makes the difference between good and bad choices.

*Source:* Personal interview with Anita Lewis, emergency room manager at Athens (GA) Regional Hospital, conducted June 1993.

---

## An Example

In the "Magnifying Management" box, a manager describes her activities. Her description demonstrates that a manager is constantly involved in obtaining information, making decisions, and implementing those decisions, as well as planning, organizing, leading, and controlling.

**Comment on Box:** Have students discuss how each of the manager's activities illustrates one of the functions of management. Have students also discuss how the actions of the manager are related to improved customer service for the patients and their families.

## CAN YOU LEARN MANAGEMENT IN A MANAGEMENT CLASS?

The answer to this, not surprisingly, is "Sure!" If the answer were no, what would we do with the rest of the book? You can certainly learn valuable aspects of management in a college or university class. As evidence, many organizations develop or require formal training in management that is very similar to the topics of this text and the format of your class.[12]

We have discussed that management is a process of collecting information, making decisions, and implementing decisions about how to use the organization's resources to reach its objectives. Formal classes like this one are valuable for

# Careers Corner

## What's Ahead in the 1990s

If you've been reading business news over the last several years, you may be a bit skeptical about management as a career choice. Indeed, many companies have reduced their management layers significantly, especially middle-level managers. However, this information, by itself, can be misleading.

Management is, and will continue to be, one of the most crucial functions in the survival and growth of every business. So, the good news is that companies will continue to recruit and offer positions to candidates with training and experience in how to manage capital and human resources.

The U.S. Department of Labor reports that, as a group, executive, administrative, and managerial occupations will grow by 27 percent from 1990 to 2005. This growth will be due to the increasing complexity of business operations, the globalization of markets, and more extensive laws and regulations. In terms of trends, general managers and top executives currently account for 35 percent of managerial jobs, but because firms are expanding areas of responsibility rather than creating new positions, the growth among this group will be average. Higher-than-average growth is anticipated for marketing, advertising, and public relations managers, along with those in engineering and the natural sciences. Below-average managerial growth will characterize governments; agriculture, forestry, and related industries; construction; precision production; assembly; and unskilled labor.

A few of the high growth–specific occupations include the following:

### Hotel/Restaurant

The travel and tourism industry is the world's largest job generator. Large growth is expected in the last part of this decade. Lodging employers alone are expected to boost payrolls by 30 percent.

### Health Care

The health service industry will employ nearly 10 percent of all U.S. workers by 2005. Job growth will be driven by an insistence on better care, an aging population, and breakthroughs in medical technology.

### Public Relations

The increasingly complex business environment, along with the need to maintain a squeaky-clean corporate image, is prompting a job boom for PR executives. Of special importance is assisting employers in managing crises and addressing new government regulations.

### Forensic Accounting

Business fraud is so widespread that accounting investigators who can help organizations chase paper trails in order to determine criminal wrongdoing will remain in demand for years to come. Because federal laws hold executives liable for employees' actions, many organizations will develop their own fraud-detection programs.

### Employment Training

By 2000, at least 65 percent of all employees will require some education and training beyond high school—as a result, primarily, of the introduction of technology into the workplace. Independent consulting groups will be in high demand.

*Sources:* "Managing Your Career, The College Edition of The National Business Employment Weekly," *The Wall Street Journal,* Spring 1994; Jeffrey M. Humphreys, "The Occupational Outlook During the 1990s," *Georgia Business and Economic Conditions* 51 (March–April 1991); U.S. Department of Labor, *Occupational Outlook Handbook,* Bureau of Labor Statistics, May 1992, Bulletin 2400.

**Comment on Box:** Have students select a possible career choice and use library resources to research the long-term projections for this career. Share the findings on various careers with the class and discuss possible reasons for the rate of growth for the chosen professions.

learning what data sources and types of information are useful for making specific decisions. Classes can also point out the relationships among variables used in decision making. For example, you will learn about the relationship of organizational rewards to the employees' job performance in a later chapter. Knowing this relationship will be useful in deciding how to use rewards within the organization.

In addition to presenting factual data and relationships among data, formal classes can help you develop conceptual and analytical skills, which are needed by all managers. The vignettes, cases, and boxes in the chapters of this text describe work situations that can be valuable in helping you develop these skills. Finally, the discussion of organization and human behavior principles should serve as an important basis for the managerial activities associated with leading.

However, there are two aspects of management that cannot fully be taught in an introductory management textbook or class. The first is the job knowledge necessary to be successful as a manager in a specific functional area of an organization; you must acquire this knowledge from your other courses and job experience. If you are interested in being a financial manager, for example, you must acquire the basic knowledge from your finance courses and perhaps from internships or other employment in the finance industry; if your interest is in marketing management, this job knowledge must come from your marketing courses as well as from experience as a consumer and employee.

The second aspect that cannot be fully taught is implementation of decision making. We will discuss how managers go about getting their plans and decisions carried out within organizations. Simulations, role plays, and exercises can help you reproduce and develop these skills. However, these teaching techniques frequently lack the long-term, repetitive interaction that characterizes management; for being taught this, some form of on-the-job training is a more appropriate vehicle.

What will this text do for you? The first three chapters provide a framework of what management is. Included in this is the historical development of principles of management and a discussion of the many factors that affect management activities. In Chapters 4 through 8 we address many contemporary issues of management, ethics, global competition, diversity in the work force, an emphasis on quality, and the development of small businesses. Chapters 9 through 13 describe details of the essential processes of planning, management decision making, and organizing. The human behavior and motivational issues associated with leading are addressed in Chapters 14 through 19; we discuss the various interpersonal roles of the manager in detail. The following three chapters, 20 through 22, treat the principles necessary for the delivery of a good or service. In this book, we thoroughly present principles that are critical for management activities, and we are confident that you will benefit from them.

## SUMMARY AND REVIEW

- **Define management and describe its purpose in organizations.** Management is concerned with using the resources of the organization to reach the organization's objectives. Its purpose is to use these resources effectively and efficiently so that the objectives of the organization are achieved with a minimum of cost.

- **Determine the effect that management actions have on the manager and others in the organization.** Because management is essentially a decision-making process, it affects others. The consequences of a manager's decisions may have either a positive or negative effect on the manager, the manager's subordinates, and the organization, as well as other groups.

- **List the major functions of managers.** The four management functions are planning (determining what the organization will specifically accomplish and deciding how to accomplish these goals); organizing (designing jobs for employees, grouping these jobs together into departments, and developing working relationships between organizational departments and employees to carry out the plans); leading (influencing others' activities to achieve set goals); and controlling (ensuring that an organization's actions lead to achievement of its objectives).

- **Explain the importance of decision making in management activities.** Because managers must use resources to reach the organization's objectives, they must continuously make decisions about how to best use these resources. The manager must gather important data to be considered and, based on the data, make and then implement the decision required. A correct decision can be useless if it is not implemented appropriately.

- **Describe the many roles managers play in an organization.** Henry Mintzberg described ten specific roles that can be placed into three broad categories. Interpersonal roles involve interaction with others who are external or internal to the organization, at the same level as the manager or at higher or lower levels. Informational roles focus on obtaining data that are important for the decisions made by the manager. Decisional roles deal primarily with the allocation of resources in order to reach organizational objectives. Mintzberg's detailed description of each of the specific roles provides valuable descriptions of management tasks.

- **Specify why different managers perform different job activities.** Management is similar across all organizations in that managers are all involved with planning, organizing, leading, controlling, and decision making; their activities may also be described in terms of common roles they play within their organizations. However, the specific job activities of managers differ greatly both among and within organizations because of differences in the level of management, functional area, organizational size and culture, and industry.

- **Review what you can reasonably learn from a textbook about how to perform management activities.** Some aspects of management can be learned in formal classroom situations. Most organizations teach management to their employees through training programs that are similar in format to college classrooms. Learning management in this format can assist your understanding of sources of information and relationships among variables, basic principles to use in decision making, and the fundamentals of how to implement decisions. However, job knowledge relevant for specific functional areas of an organization and the requisite interpersonal skills can most effectively be learned in one's unique working environment.

- **Evaluate a small business owner's management skills and propose a future course of action for the firm.** The "Business Dilemma" box presents a question for the owner of the firm. Should you continue to expand your own work or form a joint venture with large companies for expansion? Your assessment of the owner's skills and ability to manage rapid expansion will determine your answer.

## Key Terms and Concepts

management *4*
effectively *4*
efficiently *4*
managers *4*
organizations *4*
resources *5*
planning *6*
organizing *7*
leading *7*

controlling *8*
interpersonal roles *10*
informational roles *11*
decisional roles *12*
interpersonal skills *13*
technical skills *14*
conceptual skills *14*
upper managers *17*
middle managers *17*

lower or first-line managers *17*
human resource managers *18*
marketing managers *18*
finance managers *18*
production and operations managers *18*
organizational culture *19*
for-profit companies *20*
nonprofit organizations *20*

## Ready Recall

1. Define management; indicate what its principal purposes are and why managers are essential to organizations.
2. What are the resources of the organization? How are these used in management decision making?
3. What are the four functions of management? How are they related to the work process?
4. Describe the steps in management decision making. What are the difficulties in making management decisions?
5. Discuss the three general roles of management. What are the purposes of these roles? What specific roles fall under each general role?
6. Discuss the general skills necessary to be successful in management. How do these relate to both the management roles and management decision making?

7. How do management activities differ across organizations? Describe the specific effects of organization size, industry type, organizational culture, and profit vs. nonprofit organizations on these differences.
8. How do management activities differ within an organization? Describe the specific effects of level of management and functional specialty on these differences.
9. Discuss the impact that management decisions have on others.
10. Discuss how management may be learned in a classroom setting.

## Expand Your Experience

1. Interview a small sample of managers. Discuss the specific, major tasks that these managers perform. Relate these tasks to the management functions of planning, organizing, leading, and controlling.

2. Obtain descriptions of recent decisions made by managers in specific organizations as reported in sources such as *The Wall*

*Street Journal.* Discuss what information would be useful to know before making the decisions. Also discuss how accessible and accurate such information may be.

3. Obtain job descriptions of various management positions. Discuss the specific skills that are necessary to perform the tasks of these job descriptions.

---

**CASE**

# *Managing the Olympics:  A Herculean Task*

So you think it would be great to manage the Olympics? Well, so does Billy Payne, president of the Atlanta Committee for the Olympic Games (ACOG). However, he tempers his enthusiasm with the realities of the job that he is doing.

The first thing Payne has had to contend with is the certainty of going out of business as soon as the event is over. The ACOG was formed in 1990 after the International Olympic Committee (IOC) named Atlanta host of the 1996 Olympics. To the host falls the task of organizing everything—deciding where to locate the various events, constructing the necessary buildings, staging the events, and, most importantly, generating the financial support—and then dismantling everything as soon as the Olympics are over to reduce costs. To do this, Billy Payne became the president of an organization large enough to be in the middle of the *Fortune* 500 and to stage the equivalent of three Super Bowls a day for sixteen days.

Of the diverse management activities Payne has performed, perhaps the most crucial task was generating the money necessary to stage the games. ACOG's aim was not only to make the Olympics self-supporting but also to generate several million dollars of profit that could be used for the development of future Olympic athletes. Although such a goal had been reached before—the 1984 Olympics in Los Angeles netted a profit of $215 million—most other games have been substantially supported by government funds. Montreal, host of the 1976 Olympics, which lost $1 billion, is still paying off its bills. The Spanish government underwrote many of the costs of the 1992 games staged in Barcelona, especially those for construction of highways and housing. The Atlanta games are estimated to have a price tag of $1.38 billion.

ACOG raised a great majority of the necessary funds through the sale of the broadcasting rights to worldwide television outlets and the sale of Olympic sponsorship for advertising to corporations. The original budget called for $549 million to be raised from television rights. The greater part of this revenue came from the European Broadcast Union, which paid $250 million, and NBC in the United States, which bid $456 million. ACOG received 60 percent of this money. The additional income was generated from cable and other global networks. One of the most valuable incentives was extending the games from 16

to 17 nights. Beginning one day earlier than originally scheduled gave television networks one more prime-time evening for which to sell advertising. Payne announced this plan three weeks before negotiations began with the three major U.S. television networks for contract rights.

The most interesting challenge regarding corporate sponsors was to enlist 12 corporations to be official Olympic sponsors at $40 million each. To understand the strategy that Payne used, it is helpful to know a little about Olympic sponsorship history. The 1980 Winter Olympics in Lake Placid, New York, had 357 official sponsors, including an official banana and an official lip balm, which produced a measly $14 million. The result was humorous from the public's viewpoint and ineffective from that of the corporate sponsors. The large number of sponsors, many not widely known, prevented large amounts of advertising by a single corporation. Moreover, having so many sponsors devalued the concept to consumers and made the Olympics easy game for "ambush advertising," which occurs when an Olympic sponsor's competitor airs advertising presenting itself as a corporate sponsor even though the organization has not paid for such a privilege. For example, VISA paid approximately $20 million to be a sponsor for the 1992 Winter Games in Albertville, France. Even so, American Express Co., a nonsponsor, ran advertisements with an Olympic motif. In contrast to the chaos at Lake Placid, the organizers of the 1984 Los Angeles Games limited sponsorship to 35, at a cost of $4 million each. This selectivity enhanced the value of the official status for corporations.

The ACOG's strategy was to carry the idea of selectivity even further to an exclusive group of 12 "partners," each of whom paid $40 million for U.S. marketing rights. The cost was obviously very high. Lesa Ukman, editor of *IEG Sponsorship Report*, a Chicago newsletter that tracks event marketing, pointed out a number of limitations to organizations. For one thing, the figure was the same as the figure that the International Olympic Committee (IOC) was charging its sponsors for worldwide rights. "It's not logical," she said, "that the U.S. would be worth the same as the U.S. plus the rest of the world." (It should be noted that the IOC and the ACOG divided up sponsor groups so as not to overlap. For example, the IOC could get a soft-drink sponsor, but the ACOG could not.) Further, Ukman estimated that for the $40 million, a company could sponsor every state fair, marathon, jazz festival, and Fourth-of-July celebration in the country and still have $30 million left over.

To make the investment of corporate sponsorship worthwhile, Payne put together a number of features. Perhaps the most important was an aggressive plan to prevent ambush marketing: One ploy was to immediately expose and publicly embarrass the guilty parties. Second, within Atlanta itself, Payne has spoken with billboard companies, owners of high-rise buildings, city and county officials, rental-car companies, and the Federal Aviation Administration (which monitors hot air balloons) to prevent nonsponsors from buying space in order to hype their products before and during the games. In addition, a group of law firms in the ten largest media markets has agreed to help quash companies who give the appearance of being corporate sponsors when they aren't.

As further incentives, the ACOG made available to sponsors access to 400 hotel rooms, 800 tickets for the opening and closing ceremonies, as many as 1,600 tickets for daily use, and a "Platinum VIP Hospitality Package" that included chauffeured sedans. Hospitality villages were built so that sponsors could entertain guests. Also, the ACOG has produced three 1-hour tele-vision specials with spots that thank each corporate sponsor. It has also provided office space in the city, seminars, newsletters, and a "Look for the Rings" public relations campaign to encourage consumers to purchase products from official sponsors. These incentives, coupled with the very large TV market that is generated broadcasting from the eastern time zone of the United States (in comparison with the other three time zones), proved successful in enlisting the desired number of sponsors.

The result of all these activities was to generate enough revenue to develop and stage the 1996 Atlanta Olympics as Payne had originally intended.

*Sources:* Glenn Ruffenach, "Olympic Trials: An Atlanta Attorney Sprints to Pull Off 1996 Summer Games," *The Wall Street Journal,* June 11, 1993, 1A, 4A; Glenn Ruffenach, "Olympic Backers Will Pay Atlanta Plenty for Exclusivity and Ambush Protection," *The Wall Street Journal,* June 4, 1992, B1; Glenn Ruffenach and Daniel Pearl, "Warming Up for 1996 Summer Olympics, Atlanta Finds Field of Financial Hurdles," *The Wall Street Journal,* January 29, 1993, B1; Melissa Turner, "'96 Games Officials Hope to Score Big with TV Deals in Foreign Countries," *Atlanta Constitution,* August 20, 1993, F1.

## Questions

1. Discuss the planning and organizing issues that must be addressed in preparing for the Olympics.
2. What managerial roles do you think Payne played in developing and implementing the strategy of enlisting a few corporate sponsors for $40 million each?
3. Discuss organizing and planning activities that you think were part of Payne's efforts to sell television rights.

## STRENGTHEN YOUR SKILLS
### *Flexibility*

As was pointed out in the "Management Skills" section of this chapter, many management experts agree that flexibility is essential for managing in today's business environment. Flexibility will be your ally in dealing with the unexpected problems that are a regular part of a manager's day.

The following self-assessment will help you find out how flexible you are. Select the response that most accurately describes your behavior by placing a ✔ in the appropriate box. Be as candid as possible so that you can get feedback that will be helpful in improving your flexibility.

| | Almost Always | Sometimes | Rarely | Never |
|---|---|---|---|---|
| 1. It is important for me to have a place for everything. | | | | |
| 2. I make strong demands on myself. | | | | |
| 3. I feel uncomfortable when I have to break an appointment. | | | | |
| 4. When leaving home I find that I have to check and recheck doors, lights, windows, stove, etc. | | | | |
| 5. It bothers me when people do not put things back exactly as I left them. | | | | |
| 6. I think it's a good idea to plan and schedule activities very carefully. | | | | |
| 7. I get upset if things do not go as planned. | | | | |
| 8. After completing a task, I have doubts about whether I did it right. | | | | |
| 9. I do certain things over and over even though I know it is pointless to do them. | | | | |
| 10. I don't dwell on my problems too long. | | | | |
| 11. I worry about a lot of things. | | | | |
| 12. I react quickly to unexpected situations. | | | | |
| 13. I am meticulous and orderly with most of my possessions. | | | | |
| 14. I strive for perfection in what I do. | | | | |
| 15. I don't care if people laugh at my ideas. | | | | |
| 16. I feel I miss out on a lot of opportunities because I don't act quickly enough. | | | | |
| 17. I find time to relax and simply do nothing. | | | | |
| 18. I move, walk, and eat rapidly because I don't like wasting time. | | | | |
| 19. I go back and forth searching for the right decision. | | | | |
| 20. I'm very punctual. | | | | |
| 21. Stress makes me disorganized. | | | | |
| 22. I like to make lists of my daily tasks and activities. | | | | |

| | Agree | Disagree |
|---|---|---|
| 23. I often feel anxious or apprehensive even though I don't know what has caused the worry. | | |
| 24. I frequently get angry or annoyed at others for not keeping on schedule with plans we've made. | | |
| 25. I seldom act without thinking. | | |
| 26. I sometimes get a kick out of breaking the rules and doing things I'm not supposed to do. | | |
| 27. I tend to dwell on things I did but shouldn't have done. | | |
| 28. I'm frequently tense or nervous. | | |
| 29. There is frequently a discrepancy between the way I want to behave and the way I actually behave. | | |
| 30. My work tends to pile up so much that I have difficulty completing it. | | |

Add up your points using the numbers provided in the chart below:

| Number | Almost Always | Sometimes | Rarely | Never | Your Score |
|:------:|:-------------:|:---------:|:------:|:-----:|:----------:|
| 1 | 5 | 3 | 2 | 1 | |
| 2 | 6 | 4 | 2 | 1 | |
| 3 | 4 | 3 | 2 | 1 | |
| 4 | 6 | 4 | 2 | 1 | |
| 5 | 6 | 4 | 2 | 1 | |
| 6 | 7 | 4 | 2 | 1 | |
| 7 | 6 | 4 | 2 | 1 | |
| 8 | 5 | 3 | 2 | 1 | |
| 9 | 5 | 3 | 2 | 1 | |
| 10 | 1 | 2 | 4 | 6 | |
| 11 | 7 | 5 | 2 | 1 | |
| 12 | 1 | 2 | 4 | 6 | |
| 13 | 6 | 3 | 2 | 1 | |
| 14 | 7 | 4 | 2 | 1 | |
| 15 | 1 | 2 | 4 | 7 | |
| 16 | 6 | 3 | 2 | 1 | |
| 17 | 1 | 2 | 4 | 7 | |
| 18 | 7 | 4 | 2 | 1 | |
| 19 | 7 | 4 | 2 | 1 | |
| 20 | 6 | 3 | 2 | 1 | |
| 21 | 7 | 4 | 2 | 1 | |
| 22 | 5 | 3 | 2 | 1 | |

| Number | Agree | Disagree | Your Score |
|:------:|:-----:|:--------:|:----------:|
| 23 | 6 | 1 | |
| 24 | 5 | 1 | |
| 25 | 6 | 1 | |
| 26 | 1 | 6 | |
| 27 | 7 | 1 | |
| 28 | 6 | 1 | |
| 29 | 6 | 1 | |
| 30 | 6 | 1 | |
| **Total Points for 1–30** | | | |

**Interpreting Your Score**

In order to get an interpretation of your performance on this self-assessment, your instructor will tell you what your score indicates based upon the following point categories. Circle the category in which your score falls:

    30–52          53–84          85–132          133–182

**How to Increase Your Flexibility**

Because flexibility is something you can learn, here are some steps you can follow:

1. **Take more risks.** People who successfully achieve their goals often do so by going out on a limb. It's a self-reinforcing cycle of improvement. Taking a risk and venturing into uncharted territory forces you to become more flexible—and opens up a wider range of opportunities for fulfillment. As a result, you develop a greater sense of self-worth, which in turn breeds self-confidence. And the competitive edge that self-confidence brings emboldens you to take even greater risks. That in turn breeds more success and a sense of control over your career destiny.

   Identify a risk you can take this week: _____

   What's the best-case scenario if your risk-taking succeeds? _____

   What's the worst case scenario if you fail? _____

   Is it worth the risk to go out on a limb and make it happen? _____

2. **Make a deliberate change in your routines.**

   Identify a routine you have that you can change today: _____

3. **Make a point of being in touch with people who are completely different from you.**

   Identify three people who are completely different from you with whom you can spend at least a half hour this week: _____
   _____

Ironically, avoiding risk and clinging to the predictable doesn't always reduce fear and uncertainty. It often creates worries, increases frustration, and throws up barriers to action. Flexibility arms you for the future—whatever it may be.

*Source:* Eugene Raudsepp, "Are You Flexible Enough to Succeed?" First appeared in *Working Woman,* October 1990: 106 107. Reprinted with the permission of *WORKING WOMAN* magazine. Copyright © 1990 by WORKING WOMAN, Inc.

# The
# Development
*of*
# Management
# Thought

**Outline**

**After reading this chapter, you will be able to:**

- Specify the major cultural changes that preceded the development of modern management practice and thought.

- Explain the major theories within the classical approach to management.

- Examine some of the major contributions to the development of the behavioral approach to management.

- Describe the systems approach to management theory and identify the early contributors to this perspective.

- Relate the significance of the contingency approach within the study and practice of management.

- Summarize how current management knowledge and practices are a result of the work and ideas of many management scholars and practitioners over the past century.

- Apply the management theories discussed in this chapter to a manager's efforts to revitalize a small business.

# Business Maxims, Circa 1890

The following maxims are typical of the simple and straightforward advice for the practice of good management that prevailed over a century ago.

1. Your first ambition should be the acquisition of knowledge pertaining to your business.
2. Above all things acquire a good, correct epistolary style, for you are judged by the business world according to the character, expression, and style of your letters.
3. During business hours attend to nothing but business, be prompt in responding to all communications, and never suffer a letter to remain without an answer.
4. Never fail to meet a business engagement, however irksome it may be at that moment.
5. Lead a regular life, avoid display, and choose your associates discreetly, and prefer the society of men of your own type.
6. Avoid litigation as much as possible, study for yourself the theory of commercial law, and be your own lawyer.
7. Never run down a neighbor's property or goods and praise up your own. It is a mark of low breeding and will gain you nothing.
8. Never misrepresent, falsify, or deceive; have one rule of moral life, never swerve from it, whatever may be the acts or opinions of other men.
9. Watch the course of politics in national affairs, read the papers, but decline the acceptance of political positions if you desire to succeed in a certain line of business. Never be an office seeker.
10. Be affable, polite, and obliging to everybody. Avoid discussions, anger, and pettishness. Interfere with no disputes that are the creation of others.
11. Never form the habit of talking about your neighbors, or repeating things that you hear others say. You will avoid much unpleasantness, and sometimes serious difficulties.
12. Never sign a paper for a stranger. Never sign a paper without first reading it carefully.
13. Goods well bought are half sold, and goods in store are better than bad debts.
14. Write in a good, plain, legible hand.
15. Never gamble or take chances on the Board of Trade.
16. Keep your word as good as a bank.

*Source:* J. L. Nichols, *The Business Guide; or Safe Methods of Business*, 18th ed. (Cleveland: Lauer & Mattill, 1890).

*introduction*

Hundreds of thousands of students will complete some sort of formal undergraduate or graduate course in management this year, and next year, and probably the next. Every day, millions of people go to work and perform some sort of managerial job. However, the large-scale study and practice of management, as we know it today, has not always been the case. There was a time in history when not only was management not commonly practiced and studied, but those people who engaged in commerce and trading were considered lower class and denied the right to vote.[1] The development of management as a widely accepted body of knowledge, formally studied and taught as it is today, is the topic of this chapter. Further, it may be interesting for you to learn why you are attending a Principles of Management class when your grandparents or great-grandparents probably did not have the opportunity.

In this chapter, we will consider two major aspects of the history of management thought. One is the major developments within the history of Western civilization that stimulated the evolution of the practice and study of management. The other is the development of major perspectives of management thought and some of the important contributors to the various perspectives.

## A CULTURAL FRAMEWORK FOR THE DEVELOPMENT OF MANAGEMENT THEORY

To understand the evolution of the study and teaching of management principles and concepts, we need to establish a general cultural framework of the social, economic, and political forces that have influenced our ideas about management. **Social forces** refer to the relationship of people to each other within a particular culture. **Economic forces** refer to the relationship of people to resources, and **political forces** refer to the relationship of individuals, their rights, and their property to the state.[2] Four major developments in Western culture set the stage for the systematic study and teaching of management that began during the late 1800s and early 1900s: (1) the Protestant ethic, (2) capitalism and division of labor, (3) the Industrial Revolution, and (4) the productivity problem.

### The Protestant Ethic

Between the fall of the Roman Empire and the Renaissance, from about A.D. 600 to A.D. 1500, was a period of time known as the Middle Ages. Frequently described by historians as the "Dark Ages," this was a time of almost complete stagnation of education and scientific and literary progress. Poverty and ignorance were the principal characteristics of the masses of society, and the primary concern of individuals was to protect themselves against murder, robbery, and violence.[3] During this period, the church's promise of an afterlife was virtually the only consolation for bearing the hardships and bleakness of life on earth. This promise required that people think only of salvation from this life and moving on to the next world, and little thought was given to how life on earth might be improved.

A challenge to this philosophy of life was led by Martin Luther and John Calvin, who believed that each person should consider himself or herself part of the "elect," those who would be treated well in the afterlife. As a member of this

**social forces**
The relationship of people to each other within a particular culture.

**economic forces**
The relationship of people to resources.

**political forces**
The relationship of individuals, their rights, and their property to the state.

Martin Luther (1483–1546) modeled the Protestant ethic of working hard and leading a self-denying life. A priest, professor of philosophy and theology, leader of the Protestant Reformation, and organizer of the Lutheran Church, Luther wrote more than 400 works and developed a new system of church government. He was one of the first leaders to promote public support of schools and libraries. This painting shows Luther (seated at desk) working on his translation of the Bible. An enormous undertaking, Luther's translation was an important contribution to German literature.

*Source:* The Bettmann Archive.

elect, each individual was urged to fulfill the obligations of his or her earthly calling. This notion of everyone being worthy and having a calling on earth, as opposed to the Dark Ages belief in the calling of only a royal few, led to a new interpretation of the purpose of life—referred to as the Protestant ethic. The **Protestant ethic**, or work ethic, held that instead of merely waiting on earth for release into the next world, people should pursue an occupation and engage in high levels of worldly activity so that they could fulfill their calling.[4] Society interpreted the Protestant ethic as a mandate for people to work hard, to use their wealth wisely, and to live self-denying lives. This created a new age of self-determination, self-control, and individualism.[5]

**Protestant ethic**
An interpretation of the purpose of life, stating that, instead of merely waiting on earth for release into the next world, people should pursue an occupation and engage in high levels of worldly activity so that they could fulfill their calling.

## Capitalism and Division of Labor

Another major societal change that occurred following the Middle Ages was the move from feudalism to capitalism and division of labor. After the fall of the Roman Empire, slavery in Europe became uneconomical. Feudalism prevailed in place of slavery as serfs tilled plots of land owned by lords in exchange for military protection. Feudalism resulted in a society of rigid class distinctions in which all rights of ownership and wealth, and control of all markets, were assigned to the government, the church, and a small privileged class of people. The masses had no such rights.

In the 1700s, this rigid system of allocation of resources was challenged by the ideas set forth in the economic theory of capitalism. As described in economist Adam Smith's *The Wealth of Nations*, the basic tenets of **capitalism** are the following:

1. Natural laws of supply and demand and free competition within the marketplace will efficiently regulate the flow of resources within a society.
2. All individuals should have the right to accumulate wealth.
3. All individuals should have the right to private ownership of property.
4. Division of labor would lead to great gains in productivity.[6]

**Division of labor**, also called specialization, is the simple idea of breaking an entire job into its component parts and assigning each specific task to an individual worker. This contrasts with the traditional craft approach to production in

**Teaching Note:** Remind students that Scottish-born Adam Smith had never experienced capitalism for himself and was raised and educated in the socialistic system of government.

**capitalism**
An economic system wherein the natural laws of supply and demand and free competition within the marketplace will efficiently regulate the flow of resources within a society.

**division of labor**
The idea of breaking down an entire job into its component parts and assigning each specific task to an individual member; also called specialization.

which one craftsman performs all the component tasks required to produce an entire product from beginning to end. Smith described in detail the outcome and advantages of division of labor in the first three chapters of *The Wealth of Nations*.[7] Increased output would result due to increased expertise by each worker (because each is concentrating on a smaller component of the task), time saved from not repeatedly switching from one task to another, and the invention of specialized machines for each component of the overall job. Smith also acknowledged that the dysfunctional aspect of division of labor was that a lifetime spent doing a very specialized, narrow job could result in boredom, and lack of intellectual and/or social development.[8]

**Critical Thinking Challenge:** Plan a tour to a local manufacturing organization in your area. Look for examples of the division of labor in the chosen production environment. Have students discuss the reasons for the division of labor.

## The Industrial Revolution

The final development needed to launch the world toward large-scale business and industrialization was the refinement of the use of the steam engine and the ensuing Industrial Revolution in England and America. In 1765 James Watt developed the first workable steam engine and twelve years later began manufacture of the engines for industrial use.[9] Power-driven machinery gave rise to the factory system where people came together under one roof to manufacture products rather than working in their homes. This was necessary because even though power-driven machinery lowered production costs, capital requirements were increased to the point where few individuals could buy and install machinery at home. Instead, workers had to travel to the machine's home—the factory.[10]

Techniques for mass-production of standardized products, made from interchangeable parts in a factory system using steam-powered machines, were the hallmarks of the American manufacturing system in the late 1800s.[11] By the turn of the twentieth century, the possibilities of manufacturing seemed endless. Lower production costs led to lower prices and expanded markets. Innovation led to countless new inventions. Inventions and expanded markets led to large-scale production, which resulted in an abundance of material goods such as the world had never seen.

## The Productivity Problem

These major developments in Western culture led to an age of great technological advancement and creation of individual wealth, but these gains did not come about easily. Instead of steady progress, a certain degree of chaos existed in industry at the dawn of the twentieth century due to changes in philosophies of life, economic structures, and manufacturing systems. Businessmen and politicians perceived the chaos in terms of a national "productivity problem." Frustration with the inefficiencies of manufacturing practices of the day and concern over the "question of national efficiency"—waste of natural resources and human effort—was widely expressed.[12] Three issues formed the basis of the productivity problem.

First, there was the technical and behavioral problem of meshing workers and machines. With so many new machines available, there was confusion as to how best to use them in the workplace. Moreover, widespread fear of machines existed among factory workers. People feared that substituting machine power for human energy would result in the elimination of their jobs, and they were often physically afraid of large, dirty, noisy, and dangerous factory machines.

A second obstacle to the improvement of efficiency was general inexperience in the operation of organizations and factories of the size needed to achieve the

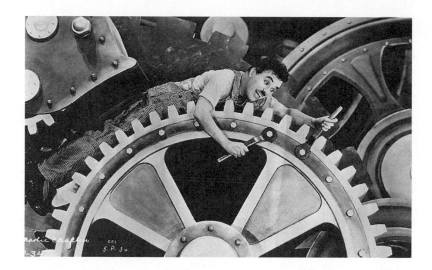

Charles Chaplin's portrayal of a factory worker in the 1936 silent film *Modern Times,* which Chaplin also wrote, directed, and produced, illustrates the technical and behavioral productivity problem of meshing men and machines. Armed with two wrenches, Chaplin's job of tightening nuts on steel plates that move on a conveyor belt drives him berserk. He uses a squirting oil can as a weapon to wreak havoc in the factory, is captured, and sent to a mental hospital for treatment. Chaplin's man-eaten-by-machine theme stemmed from an experience he had at 12 as an apprentice in a London print shop where he was terrified of an enormous printing press he feared would devour him and from reports of Detroit's automotive assembly lines.

*Source:* The Bettmann Archive.

economies of scale inherent in mass production and distribution (that is, making large volumes of a product to lower the cost per item). With the exception of the church and military, large organizations did not exist. Few owners and employees were accustomed to working in groups much larger than an extended family. Size brought with it a need for different authority structures, standardized operating procedures, and overall depersonalization of the workplace. These phenomena were new to most people and not welcomed by many.

Finally, the third and most critical issue was the widespread lack of both management and trained managers. Slowly the realization occurred that further progress in industry depended on systematic management rather than on the charismatic talents of a few extraordinary men—the so-called "captains of industry." With this realization came the need to define the role of management and managers as a unique and necessary factor of production. Bringing the first three factors of production—raw materials, capital, and labor—together on a large scale with power-driven machines could no longer be accomplished without the presence of management. Management was the missing link to future productivity gains, and it was now time to begin its formal, systematic study and teaching.

## THE DEVELOPMENT OF MANAGEMENT THEORIES

A **management theory** is a systematic statement, based on observations, of how the management process might best occur, given stated underlying principles. However, there is no single universally accepted and practiced management theory—instead, there are many. Although the practice of management has existed in its most basic forms since ancient times, the systematic study and teaching of management has existed on a widespread basis for only the past 60 to 80 years. Relative to other areas of study such as mathematics and literature, this makes management a young discipline.

One commonly accepted system of grouping management theories, which we will follow in this chapter, categorizes the major perspectives from which to study management as the (1) classical approach, (2) behavioral approach, (3) systems approach, and (4) contingency approach (see Figure 2.1). Our main concern in this chapter is to establish the major categories of management theories and how they came to exist in the development of management thought.

**management theory**
A systematic statement, based on observations, of how the management process might best occur, given stated underlying principles.

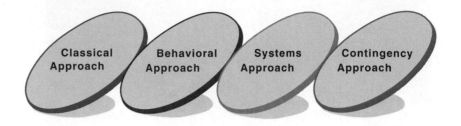

**FIGURE 2.1**

**The Major Management Theories**

## THE CLASSICAL APPROACH

**classical approach**
An approach to management that stresses the manager's role in a formal hierarchy of authority and focuses on the task, machines, and systems needed to accomplish the task effectively.

The **classical approach** to management stresses the manager's role in a formal hierarchy of authority and focuses on the task, machines, and systems needed to accomplish the task efficiently. This approach to management thought has two components: scientific management and administrative management. The theories included in the classical approach—the first well-developed frameworks of management—emerged in the late 1800s and early 1900s.

### Scientific Management

**scientific management**
A theory within the classical approach that focuses on improvement of operational efficiencies through the systematic and scientific study of work methods, tools, and performance standards.

**Scientific management** is a theory within the classical approach that focuses on improvement of operational efficiencies through the systematic and scientific study of work methods, tools, and performance standards. The development of scientific management began as a movement to define management as a separate and systematic factor of production.

In 1886 Henry Towne (1844–1924) presented a paper to the American Society of Mechanical Engineers (ASME) in which he stated that the time had come to blend the study and functions of engineering with those of business economics into one field and function. He labeled this function the "management of works" or "shop management" and argued that it was such an important industrial function that ASME should form a separate division for the recording and sharing of experiences related to shop management.[13] It is important to note that, like Towne, most of the first management writers were engineers by training, which explains much of the overall emphasis of early management theories on machines, tools, work methods, and costs of production, rather than on the people doing the work.

**Critical Thinking Challenge:**
Have students select a professional management periodical and identify the backgrounds of the management writers. What is their training? How has the emphasis of today's managers changed since the time of Henry Towne?

The notion of shop management developed into an entire new science mostly due to the efforts of Frederick W. Taylor, who is often called the "father of scientific management." As a result of time spent in the steel mills of Philadelphia, first as a laborer and later as an engineer, Taylor concluded that the productivity problem of the day was due to lack of attention given to management of men and their work. This was contrary to the beliefs of many businessmen of the day, who chose to blame the productivity problem on the pure laziness of common laborers. Taylor's drive to develop principles and methods of management based on logic, reason, and the scientific method of experimentation and observation was based mainly on his observations of "soldiering" among steel mill laborers.

Beyond the natural tendency of humans to "take it easy and work at a slow, easy gait," **soldiering** is the systematic slowdown in work by laborers with the deliberate purpose of keeping their employers ignorant of how fast the work can be done.[14] Taylor said that soldiering existed in factories because employers did not know how much work could be done; laborers believed that if they worked too fast, they would work themselves and others out of jobs, and workers did not know how to do their jobs efficiently. Consequently, Taylor argued that the lack of productivity was management's fault, not labor's.[15]

**soldiering**
The systematic slowdown in work by laborers, with the deliberate purpose of keeping their employers ignorant of how fast the work can be done.

**Principles of Scientific Management.**   After almost 26 years of investigating the problems of low productivity, Taylor devised the principles of scientific management. According to these scientifically derived principles, the role of management is to:

1. Develop the "one best way" to perform any task.
2. Scientifically select, train, teach, and develop each worker.
3. Cooperate with workers and provide an incentive to ensure that the work is done according to the "one best way."
4. Divide the work and the responsibility equally between management and the workers.

The first principle refers to the idea that, for every task, there exists one way to do the job that will result in the highest rates of output and the highest rates of earnings for the laborer, and will not totally physically drain the laborer. The manager will develop the one best way based on reason, logic, and scientific observation and experimentation. It will include the movements and motions of the laborer as well as the correct tools and placement of machines within the work area.

The second principle states that it should not be up to the worker to pick the job he or she wants to do and then learn it through trial and error. Rather, it is the manager's job to select people for jobs based on their mental and physical traits and abilities and to place only those individuals best suited for a particular task in the job. Then it is the manager's job to continue to train and develop the selected employee until he or she is successful at the task.

Principle three implies that it is the manager's job to devise methods and rates of pay that will make it in the workers' best interests to perform their jobs according to the one best way they have been taught to do the job for which they were selected. Overall, this principle also means that it is the manager's job to look after the best interests of his or her employees as well as the best interests of the firm.

The last principle states that managers must take over all the work for which they are better prepared than the worker (the planning or primarily mental aspects of work). In the past, almost all work—physical and mental—and the greater part of responsibility for getting the work done were thrown on the workers. In other words, Taylor was conveying that workers will not be able to, and should not be expected to, perform to the fullest extent unless management has already determined the best way to do the job, selected and trained the best people for each job, and provided adequate rewards for work done well.

**Example:** Organizations still look for methods of operation that yield higher output and efficiency with minimal effort. The scoop used by McDonald's Corporation to place hot french fries into the paper containers was designed using these principles. It is easy and safe to use and its efficiency requires minimal effort by the employee. Training time is also minimized for this operation.

**Assumptions of Scientific Management.**   The assumptions of Taylor's scientific management, for which he was later criticized, related to his view of the nature of people. The first assumption was that employers and employees had mutual interests associated with economic gain. Taylor believed that it was possible for employees to get what they wanted—high wages—at the same time that employers got what they wanted—low costs. He philosophized that a "mental revolution" had to occur among employees and employers whereby both groups would come to believe that mutual interests did exist and could be achieved through mutual cooperation.

A second assumption was that man is a rational being and economically motivated. Taylor assumed that people would follow any work methods and system based on reason and logic if it would allow them to fulfill their economic needs.

The last assumption Taylor made was that, for every man willing to work hard, there was a job for which he was ideally suited according to his mental and physical traits and abilities. If placed in this job, he could be a "first-class-man," one who performed better than most at his job and earned higher than average wages for his work at that job.

**Criticisms and Contributions of Taylor.**    Frederick Taylor and scientific management became quite well known throughout the country in 1910, when newspapers reported expert testimony before the Interstate Commerce Commission that railroads should not be allowed to raise their rates, but should instead reduce their costs through the use of scientific management. Scientific management achieved even more notoriety in 1911–1912, when a congressional investigation was held to determine if scientific management was abusive to workers. This was in response to strikes that had occurred over the use of Taylor's methods and philosophy. The investigation found no concrete evidence of abuse, but the negative publicity was devastating to Taylor. He was quite impatient with critics, who were often not well informed, and who argued that the use of scientific management's efficiency methods led to exploitation of workers by getting them to produce more and causing large reductions in the work forces of companies using scientific management. Years after his death, Taylor's critics have said that he failed to give credit to others for the work they did and that perhaps some of the data reported in his studies of various jobs may have been fabricated to some extent.[16]

Despite the criticisms, there is much evidence that Taylor's ideas about management and methods of studying work remain in use today. His strong support of the use of science and precise measurement methods prevails currently in the areas of management study and practice known as the quantitative approach, management science, and production/operations management. The **quantitative approach** emerged several decades later, during World War II, as a viewpoint of management that emphasizes the application of mathematical models, statistics, and structured information systems to support rational management decision making. **Management science** has developed into the field of management that includes the study and use of mathematical models and statistical methods to improve the effectiveness of managerial decision making. Production/operations management, which we will explore in great detail in Chapter 20, is a somewhat more narrow branch of the quantitative approach that focuses on managing the process of transforming materials, labor, and capital into useful goods and/or services.[17]

**The Gilbreths.**    Frank Bunker Gilbreth (1868–1924) and Lillian Moller Gilbreth (1878–1972) were perhaps the first "dual-career couple," and they are known for their contributions to the scientific management movement. Through his careful study of bricklaying, Frank was able to reduce the number of motions necessary to lay bricks by 89 percent and increased the number of bricks laid from 120 to 350 per hour. His methods are still used by modern bricklayers.

Frank Gilbreth met and married Lillian Moller in 1904. She pursued formal studies in psychology in the belief that it would help in her husband's work. Her

**quantitative approach**
A viewpoint of management that emphasizes the application of mathematical models, statistics, and structured information systems to support rational management decision making.

**management science**
The field of management that includes the study and use of mathematical models and statistical methods to improve the effectiveness of managerial decision making.

Frank and Lillian Gilbreth used many of their scientific management techniques and theories to increase the efficiency of household routines and to raise their 12 children. From a private laboratory in their home, they offered motion study instruction to business managers. After Frank died at the age of 56, Lillian carried on their work, lecturing at schools of engineering and business and becoming professor of management at Purdue University. Lillian applied the techniques of motion analysis to design special household equipment adapted to the needs of the handicapped. This 1923 photograph shows the Gilbreth family breakfasting outside on Nantucket Island, Massachusetts.

*Source:* The Bettmann Archive.

thesis was published as a book, *The Psychology of Management*, which stands in management literature as one of the first contributions to understanding the human implications of scientific management.[18]

Another of Frank Gilbreth's innovations was the use of motion picture technology to analyze the motions used in a job. Gilbreth attached small lights to an employee's hand, while he was filmed performing a manual task, to trace the movements of the lights through time exposure (called a cyclegraph). The findings of these studies resulted in a classification of 16 basic work motions Gilbreth called therbligs.[19]

Based upon their time and motion studies, the Gilbreths made many specific recommendations for means of reducing fatigue. Examples of these include improved footrests and chairs, comfortable shoes and clothing, rest periods and comfortable rest rooms, elimination of unnecessary bending and twisting of the body, and proper heating and cooling of the work area.[20]

**Example:** Students interested in the work of the Gilbreths may want to read the book *Cheaper by the Dozen* or watch the Disney movie of the same title. The title comes from the fact the Gilbreths had 12 children because Frank found all products, like eggs, to be cheaper by the dozen.

**Henry Gantt.**    If not for Henry L. Gantt (1861–1919), scientific management might have been lost in a storm of criticism. He spent many years as a mechanical engineer and consultant making it plain that scientific management was more than just inhuman attempts to speed up labor. Though he is best known for creating the Gantt chart—a simple graph method of scheduling work according to the amount of time required instead of the quantity of work to be performed—his real claim to fame lies in his role as passionate advocate of workplace democracy and humanitarian management.

Gantt took every opportunity to humanize scientific management, such as inventing a task and bonus system that offered foremen a bonus for every worker who succeeded, which motivated foremen to show interest in their employees and help them achieve as much as they could. Gantt's concern for devotion to service in the business system, and his call for "morality in the habits of industry," made him a pioneer in the area of business ethics and corporate social responsibility as they are studied in management today.[21]

**Morris L. Cooke.**    Morris Llewellyn Cooke (1872–1960) was one of the four men originally authorized to teach Taylor's management methods. He is remembered as a true "radical" of his time for his role as a militant proponent of conservation, public power, and regional planning. Cooke's unique contribution to scientific management lies in his relentless attempts to apply the gospel of efficiency in higher education, in government agencies, and in the management of World War I. As the appointed management expert to the Carnegie Foundation for the Advancement of Teaching, Cooke compiled a report on the efficiency of university management practices that was considered a "bombshell." The gist of the report was that universities did not follow a single principle of scientific management and that there was an alarming lack of cooperation among professors, which resulted in intolerable levels of inefficiency. Cooke went so far as to suggest that college professors be paid based on their efficiency and that the system of life-long tenure should be scrapped.[22]

## Administrative Management

**administrative management**
The universality of management as a function that can be applied to all organizations.

Another component of the classical approach to management theory is **administrative management**, which emphasizes the universality of management as a function that can be applied to all organizations—large, small, for-profit, not-for-profit, political, religious, or any other. This contrasts with scientific management's emphasis on the role of a manager in the efficient use of resources primarily in industrial organizations. Administrative management theories focus on the need to organize and coordinate the workings of the entire organization instead of dwelling on organizing the work of individual workers, as in scientific management. Two important contributors to administrative management are Henri Fayol and Max Weber.

**Henri Fayol.**    Henri Fayol (1841–1925) was well-educated and had a long and distinguished career as an engineer and manager in a large mining company in his native France. Fayol's work as a philosopher of administration, done mostly during the last ten years of his life, earned him a place of respect and importance in French history similar to that held by Frederick Taylor in the United States. His theories were originally published in a monograph, *General and Industrial Management,* in 1916. Although Taylor and Fayol were contemporaries, writing at about the same time, Fayol's work did not become well known in the United States until the 1950s because translation of his work into English was slow and did not begin until 1930.

One of Fayol's main contributions to management thought is that he devised what has become known as the *functional definition of management,* which states that management is "to forecast and plan, to organize, to command, to co-ordinate and to control...."[23] You will recognize that this definition of management is similar to our own and forms the basis of the organization for this text—and almost all Principles of Management books—with major sections about planning, organizing, leading (commanding and coordinating), and controlling.

Another of Fayol's major contributions was the development of a comprehensive list of general principles of management (Table 2.1). Fayol referred to this list as an indispensable code needed for the management of business, industry, politics, religion, war, or philanthropy, in addition to religious and moral codes already in existence.

Fayol's final contribution to the development of management thought is his ideas about the possibility and necessity of teaching management. He believed that the education available for future managers in his day was much too oriented

**TABLE 2.1**

## Fayol's General Principles of Management

| | |
|---|---|
| Division of Work | The object of division of work is to produce more and better work with the same effort. It reduces the number of things one has to pay attention to and is applicable to all work involving a considerable number of people. |
| Authority and Responsibility | Authority is the right to give orders and the power to exact obedience. A manager must have both personal and official authority. Responsibility is the natural consequence of authority and accepting responsibility requires courage. Fear of responsibility must be reduced in both managers and subordinates. |
| Discipline | Discipline is basically respect of agreements between the firm and its employees. It is absolutely necessary for the smooth running of a business and it requires good leaders at all levels, clear and fair agreements between the firm and its employees, and penalties for disobedience fairly applied. |
| Unity of Command | An employee should receive orders from one superior only. If it is violated, authority is undermined, and discipline, order, and stability are threatened. |
| Unity of Direction | Activities with the same purpose should have one plan with one person in charge. |
| Remuneration of Personnel | Pay should be fair and as satisfying as possible to both employees and the firm. A method of payment should encourage and reward good performance, it should not lead to overpayment, and it may include rewards other than just money. |
| Centralization | Everything that increases the importance of subordinates' roles is decentralization; everything that reduces it is centralization. Every organization will naturally have some degree of centralization; however the exact degree must vary according to different cases, with an objective of optimum utilization of all talents/skills of personnel. |
| Scalar Chain | The scalar chain is the chain of authority ranging from the top to the bottom of the organization. This is the route by which all communication should flow except in cases requiring quick action. In this case communication between peers is appropriate as long as all managers in the chain are kept informed. |
| Order | All material things should have a well-chosen place and be kept in that place. All people should be carefully selected and placed in well-organized positions—the right person in the right place. |
| Equity | In order to ensure devotion and loyalty from employees they must be treated with kindness and justice. |
| Stability of Tenure of Personnel | Managerial personnel must be given enough time to get to know their jobs and to succeed in doing the job well. Turnover is expensive and has negative effects on the firm. |
| Initiative | Managers should encourage all members of the organization to develop and implement plans. The manager who encourages initiative on the part of employees and allows the exercise of initiative is a superior manager. |
| Esprit de Corps | Managers should try hard to create harmony and unity among the employees of a firm. Toward this end managers should encourage the use of oral communication between employees as opposed to written communication, and managers must take care not to create jealousy between workers. |

*Source:* Henri Fayol, *General and Industrial Management* (London: Sir Isaac Pitman & Sons, Ltd, 1949).

toward mathematics and engineering, and that managers needed to know much more about how to read and write than about mathematics. Further, Fayol strongly advocated experience—in the shop and at home, through the management of family affairs—as an important component of management education.[24] In Table 2.2 we share some interesting facts about Fayol, Taylor, the Gilbreths, and others discussed throughout this chapter.

**TABLE 2.2**

**Did You Know...**

- Frank and Lillian Gilbreth had 12 children, and a book and movie, *Cheaper by the Dozen*, depicts their life and attempts to apply their ideas about elimination of wasted motion to everyday family life?
- Frederick Taylor and a partner won the U.S. Doubles Tennis Championship in 1881?
- Chester Barnard failed to receive an undergraduate degree from Harvard University because he completed all requirements except for the lab portion of a science course, which he was "too busy" to take?
- One of W. Edwards Deming's first jobs in the 1920s was at Western Electric's Hawthorne Plant in Chicago, where the famous Hawthorne Experiments took place?
- Lillian Gilbreth's doctoral dissertation was published under the name L. Gilbreth, as a means of disguising the fact that it was written by a woman?
- Frederick Taylor never accepted a penny of pay or traveling expense reimbursement for any of his lectures at Harvard or other places?
- Henri Fayol had intended to write two more parts to his book, *General and Industrial Management*, but died before they could be completed?

**Max Weber.**   German philosopher Max Weber (1864–1920) spent most of his life as a student and scholar in a broad range of areas such as sociology, religion, economics, and political science. He focused all of his education with his observations of industry in both Germany and the United States to form a theory of how large organizations might operate more efficiently. Weber saw the issue of size as the major challenge to the progress of industry. He felt that the only means of operating large organizations efficiently was to design and operate them as rationally as possible. Toward that end, he devised a pure form of organization based on rationality called bureaucracy (from the German word *buro*, meaning office).

According to Weber, **bureaucracy** is a theory of management by office or position, rather than by person, based on rational authority. In bureaucracy, it matters not who (from what family or class) you are, but instead it matters what (job or position within the organization) you are, where matters of authority and value are concerned. Due probably to his academic rather than practitioner background, Weber never intended for his very theoretical ideas of the ideal—but probably not attainable—form of organizations to be used as guidelines for practicing managers; rather he intended them as food for thought as to a new basis for authority.

Weber envisioned an organization developed around a set of impersonal and logical rules, routine, clear divisions of labor, selection based on technical qualifications, and strict adherence to a clear chain of command. He felt that observance of these disciplines would allow for orderly and systematic management of large groups of people that was not possible when personal preferences, which were likely to be illogical, and loyalty to individuals were the basis for operation.[25]

Indeed, many of us cringe at the word bureaucracy, as it brings to mind frustration, waste, and red tape. It is interesting to note that this would not have surprised Weber. He expressed his own doubts about the overuse of his model when he said, "It is horrible to think that the world could one day be filled with nothing but those little cogs, little men clinging to little jobs and striving towards bigger ones... . A passion for bureaucracy ... is enough to drive one to despair."[26]

**bureaucracy**
A theory of management by office or position, rather than by person, based on rational authority.

**Example:** Because organizations want to eliminate as much as possible of the bureaucracy that limits effective work, some even give rewards to employees who find and suggest ways to eliminate bureaucracy. FedEx Corporation, a leader in expedited package delivery, gives employees monetary rewards for reducing "red tape" within the organization.

## Contributions of the Classical Approach to Management Theory

As indicated by the label "classical," the theories we have explored in this section are those that have formed the main roots of the study and practice of management as we know it today. Within the classical approach we find the very definition of management as it had to be initially carved out as a separate and distinct function from economics, sociology, and engineering in the late nineteenth and early twentieth centuries. Often the main criticism of the classical theories is that they focused too narrowly on the work, machines, authority structures, and efficiency, and that they ignored the human aspect of work. However, while these theories certainly emphasized the work and getting it done efficiently, you should not forget the basic purpose behind each theory: to improve the standard of living and quality of life for all members of the organization and society in general.

# THE BEHAVIORAL APPROACH

Classical management theories are broadly based on the assumption that work is a rational endeavor pursued for almost purely economic reasons, and, consequently, that the behavior of people at work will be fairly predictable and easy to understand. However, when you realize that this assumption often does not hold true—that often work is not a rational, logical, or reasonable process and, moreover, that to many people work is more than just a means of satisfying economic needs—the need to study and understand human behavior becomes very important. The theories of management beginning to develop during the early 1900s that looked at the role of management in this light, as well as the effects of machines, authority, and systematic management on human behavior, are referred to as the behavioral approach to management theory. The **behavioral approach** is a view of management that emphasizes understanding the importance of human behavior, needs, and attitudes within formal organizations. In our study of this approach we will discuss the ideas of Mary Parker Follett, the conclusions of the Hawthorne Experiments, and the contributions of Abraham Maslow and Douglas McGregor.

**behavioral approach**
A view of management that emphasizes understanding the importance of human behavior, needs, and attitudes within formal organizations.

## Mary Parker Follett

Mary Parker Follett (1868–1933) was not an engineer, psychologist, or manager of any sort, yet she has been credited with making contributions to the development of management thought that are as important as those made by Taylor and Fayol.[27] Follett was one of the earliest management thinkers to advocate a break from the classical management school and to view effective management as based on the self-control of groups of workers, and cooperation.

Follett's strong views on the importance of society "learning to live together" and group efforts as solutions to problems of both business and society in general grew out of her political science education, and her experiences in social work.[28] In addition to many published papers and lectures given during the early 1930s, Follett's best known works were two books she wrote: *The New State,* published in 1918, and *Creative Experience,* first published in 1924.

One of Follett's contributions to the behavioral approach to management was her ideas about the importance of groups to managing work situations. She argued that work groups are one of the primary sources of influence on worker behavior— more so even than management's control and reward systems. In fact, she believed

**Example:** Today's organizations are working to improve the functioning of groups. Group processes are even more important in the total quality management environments of work teams and quality circles. Teams are so important to Roper Corporation, a North Georgia appliance manufacturer, it allows current team members to interview potential new team members and make hiring decisions.

that groups of workers had the ability to control themselves, and she advocated a group-oriented process of shared self-control based on group members' power *with* each other rather than power *over* each other.[29] This idea is currently considered "innovative" relative to the use of self-regulating or self-managing groups, as will be explained in Chapter 15. Follett's ideas of shared power and human cooperation earned her an international reputation as a political and business philosopher. She viewed business leaders, rather than political leaders, as the hope for the future.[30]

## The Hawthorne Studies

**Hawthorne studies**
A group of studies that provided the stimulus for the human relations movement within management theory and practice.

One of the most often told—some would say "mistold"—stories concerning management history is that of the Hawthorne studies. The **Hawthorne studies** provided the stimulus for the human relations movement within management theory and practice. The story began at Western Electric Company's Hawthorne plant in Cicero, Illinois, in 1924. It was there that a series of experiments were begun to try to answer scientifically a fairly simple question: What is the effect of workplace lighting on workers' output?

To answer this seemingly simple question, researchers from MIT came to the Western Electric plant and began a series of experiments with several different groups of factory operators. After three years of experimentation, careful observation, and record keeping, the researchers concluded that productivity rose regardless of whether the level of lighting was increased or decreased. Something other than lighting was affecting worker output to a great degree.[31]

George Pennock, the assistant works manager, had been following the studies and was very interested in the notion that something other than the lighting changes had caused worker output to increase. So, beginning in April 1927 and continuing until May 1933, Western Electric conducted more experiments, involving a group of six female telephone relay assemblers. Every few weeks, the company made some change related to hours worked, rest periods, incentive pay, hot lunches, etc.[32]

According to published reports, output bounced up and down throughout the manipulations with an overall trend toward greater output than before the experiments began. No clear relationships between any of the varied factors and worker output could be detected. It became clear that something unusual was occurring. Pennock sought professional advice from two professors, Claire Turner of MIT and Elton Mayo of Harvard University.[33]

Upon joining the research team, Mayo conducted a phase of the Hawthorne Experiments known as the *interviewing program.* During interviews with members of the research team, employees were given an opportunity to talk freely in complete confidence about anything, personal or work related, of concern or interest to them. Mayo observed that the employees seemed to lose their shyness and fear. In short, the relay room workers came to trust and feel valued by their coworkers, supervisors, and the company.[34] After studying all the data and conducting even more experiments, Turner and Mayo both concluded separately that the rise in output was due to workplace factors related to the social relationships among the workers themselves and between the workers and their supervisors.

**Contribution of the Hawthorne Experiments.**    The general conclusion drawn from the Hawthorne studies was that human relations and the social needs of workers are a crucial aspect of business management. This gave factory management a social dimension as well as an economic dimension. From this point on, employees would be viewed as members of informal groups of their own, with their own leadership and codes of behavior, instead of as just unrelated individual workers assigned to perform individual tasks. This change in direction of management theory and practice is often referred to as the **human-relations movement.**

Nothing as well known as the Hawthorne studies could go without criticism. Scholars have criticized the studies as having too many uncontrolled variables to permit valid conclusions.[35] Others have (1) criticized the interpretation of the data as having been biased toward pushing for support of the importance of the social and human relations aspects of work, (2) said that the results have been overstated, and (3) said that reanalysis of the data does not support the conclusions that physical and economical factors did not affect workers' output.[36]

Regardless of the actual experimental results, the fact remains that the Hawthorne Experiments were the first set of lengthy tests conducted in the workplace to study actual worker behavior. Many, including Mayo, see their main contribution as stimulating thinking and research about the nature and significance of human behavior, feelings, and attitudes at work, and the role of the informal group in formal organizations.

**human-relations movement**
A practice whereby employees came to be viewed as informal groups of their own, with their own leadership and codes of behavior, instead of as unrelated individual workers assigned to perform individual tasks.

## Abraham H. Maslow

Psychologist Abraham H. Maslow (1908–1970), an early humanist psychologist, developed one of the most widely recognized needs theories of human motivation. He is best known for his hierarchy of human needs theory, published in 1943, in which he proposed that humans have five needs: psychological, safety, social, self-esteem, and self-actualization needs. (We will explore this theory in Chapter 16.)

Maslow advocated a humanistic approach to management, which did not mean simply being nice and maintaining good human relations. It required taking the basic innate nature and needs of human beings into account in management theories and practices. Maslow proposed that people's behavior at work could be explained by a need for something beyond the money essential for their basic existence. This differed from classical management theories, which emphasized the role of pay as the sole source of employee motivation. Maslow also stated that after an employee's basic survival and security needs were fulfilled by money, other needs would become important as a source of continued motivation to work. The top rung and ultimate need of all humans was self-actualization, the need to fulfill one's full potential. Work could be a major source of fulfillment of this need.

## Douglas McGregor

Douglas McGregor (1906–1964) spent most of his career teaching and conducting research at MIT. As president of Antioch College he came to realize, as a practicing manager, that effective management required a thorough understanding and consideration of human nature and human behavior. Like Maslow, McGregor advocated a humanistic approach to management.

McGregor is best known for Theory X and Theory Y, as presented in his book, *The Human Side of Enterprise* (1960). He felt that managers' individual assumptions about human nature and behavior determined how they managed their employees. How managers treated employees then led to how employees behaved. **Theory X** is the assumption that people are naturally lazy, must be threatened and forced to work, have little ambition or initiative, and do not try to fulfill any need higher than security needs at work. Theory X assumptions represented traditional

**Theory X**
The assumption that people are naturally lazy, must be threatened and forced to work, have little ambition or initiative, and do not try to fulfill any need higher than security needs at work.

## Magnifying Management

### GYP THE BOSS, GYP YOURSELF

Worthington Industries, based in Columbus, Ohio, is no glamorous, high-tech, "touchy-feely" company. It is a player in the very traditional, highly competitive, cyclical steel business. In terms of performance, however, Worthington is indeed glamorous, with strong earnings growth and high return on equity in an industry that has been producing staggering losses in both jobs and dollars during the past decade. What is its secret?

Company founder and chairman John H. McConnell says there is no secret. He and his managers simply run the business like entrepreneurs, not bureaucrats. In one sentence he describes the philosophy of the business for the past 38 years: "Pay people well, treat them like people and expect them to work a bit harder than people who regard the boss as an antagonist."

McConnell once worked in an auto plant, where he was chewed out by a coworker for finishing his work in five hours instead of making it last eight. This was madness, he thought. By gypping the boss, workers were gypping themselves, because such a firm cannot pay good wages and remain profitable for very long.

When he began his own company, he was determined to establish a climate in which the workers would find it in their own best interests to be productive. He also was determined to treat his workers with respect and to demonstrate that he trusted them to do their best work for the good of the company and themselves. To this end, he removed all time clocks from the plant, as well as first-level supervisors. Worthington does not give its more than 6,000 workers coffee breaks, either. However, it does provide free coffee to be enjoyed when an individual feels it is appropriate. Also, using their own judgment, workers may refuse to ship a product if they feel its quality is below standard.

Worthington pays all employees a salary. Basic pay is relatively low, but bonuses and profit sharing bring Worthington wages up to union levels. A typical production employee received $11,200 in cash bonuses in 1993 and $1,200 to $3,000 more in deferred profit sharing. When the company suffers, so do the employees, because so much of their pay is tied to the firm's performance. This means that workers automatically take pay cuts when orders drop, but because they own a large chunk of the business, the workers are less resentful because they know the decline in their pay is helping to protect their long-term investment in the company.

*Source:* "Labor Relations at Minimills Proven Successful," *Iron Age,* July 1993, 26–27; "You Have to Trust the Workforce," *Forbes,* July 19, 1993, 78–81.

---

**Theory Y**
The assumption that people naturally want to work, are capable of self-control, seek responsibility, are creative, and try to fulfill higher-order needs at work.

management views of direction and control. **Theory Y** is the assumption that people naturally want to work, are capable of self-control, seek responsibility, are creative, and try to fulfill higher-order needs at work. Theory Y assumptions represented a new view of integration of human and organizational needs and goals. Theory X and Y are intuitively simple and easy-to-understand concepts that are still widely applied today. The "Magnifying Management" box highlights one company that has accepted Theory Y.

**systems approach**
An approach to management theory that views organizations and the environments within which they operate as sets of interrelated parts to be managed as a whole in order to achieve a common goal.

**system**
An arrangement of related or connected parts that form a whole unit.

## THE SYSTEMS APPROACH

The **systems approach** to management theory views organizations and the environments within which they operate as sets of interrelated parts to be managed as a whole in order to achieve a common goal.[37] A **system** is an arrangement of related or connected parts that form a whole unit. As systems, organizations consist of inputs, transformation processes, outputs, and feedback (see Figure 2.2). Contemporary system theorists find it helpful to analyze the effectiveness of orga-

**FIGURE 2.2**

## Organizations as Systems

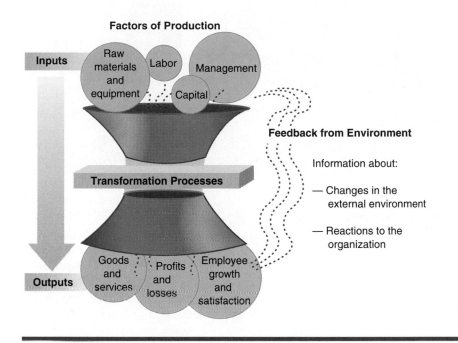

**Factors of Production**

**Inputs**

Raw materials and equipment    Labor    Management    Capital

**Transformation Processes**

**Feedback from Environment**

Information about:

— Changes in the external environment

— Reactions to the organization

**Outputs**

Goods and services    Profits and losses    Employee growth and satisfaction

*Source:* Adapted from Katheryn M. Bartol and David C. Martin, *Management* (New York: McGraw-Hill, 1991), 63.

**Critical Thinking Challenge:** Have students identify as many subsystems as possible of an organization, the larger system. Have student teams compete against others on identifying the most. Subsystems can include production, accounting, human resources, purchasing, warehousing, finance, and marketing.

nizations according to the degree to which they are open or closed. A **closed system** interacts little with its external environment and therefore receives little feedback from or information about its surroundings. An **open system**, on the other hand, continually interacts with its environment and therefore is well informed about changes within its surroundings and its position relative to these changes.

A **subsystem** is any system that is part of a larger one. **Entropy** is the tendency of systems to deteriorate or break down over time. **Synergy** is the ability of the whole system to equal more than the sum of its parts.[38] In other words, when we view organizations as systems, we must understand that there is a natural tendency for the organization to become less effective over time unless feedback and information from the environment are integrated into the system. The ultimate advantage of forming an organization is that it allows us to achieve more together than all of us as individuals could achieve separately. Management is indeed just one component of an organization that must be carefully attuned to the other components. In this section we will consider two systems theorists, Chester Barnard and W. Edwards Deming.

**closed system**
An organization that interacts little with its external environment and therefore receives little feedback from or information about its surroundings.

**open system**
An organization that interacts continually with its environment and therefore is well informed about changes within its surroundings and its position relative to these changes.

**subsystem**
Any system that is part of a larger one.

**entropy**
The tendency of systems to deteriorate or break down over time.

**synergy**
The ability of the whole system to equal more than the sum of its parts.

## Chester Barnard

Chester Barnard (1886–1961) rose through the ranks to become president of New Jersey Bell, then a division of American Telephone and Telegraph (AT&T). Barnard was a self-made scholar whose ideas have influenced the development of the systems approach, the behavioral approach, and the field of organization or administrative theory that is an aspect of the classical approach to management theory.[39]

W. Edwards Deming's systems approach to management focused on methods for continually improving the quality of goods and services. Deming taught managers that they should view their organizations as systems using the knowledge and skills of all employees to improve quality. In this photo, Deming shares his quality philosophy with both large- and small-business owners during a seminar sponsored by the Greater Philadelphia Chamber of Commerce.

*Source:* Courtesy of Philadelphia Area Council for Excellence (PACE).

**Cooperative Systems.**    In the early pages of his book, *The Functions of the Executive,* Barnard expressed the need for a universal theory of management that would guide managers in effectively adjusting the workings of the organization to a constantly changing external environment.[40] Towards this end, he devised a theory of managing organizations as cooperative systems. Barnard's basic premise is that formal organizations—within which we all work and by which we are all educated and governed—are necessary so that individuals can accomplish tasks that they could not accomplish working on their own. An important factor in cooperation is the recognition of each individual's special abilities. Barnard cautions that cooperation requires the acceptance and adoption of a group, not a personal, purpose. He wrote that members of an organization are more willing to cooperate when they believe in the organization's purpose or goal. Getting them to believe is a major function of a manager.[41]

**Acceptance Theory of Authority.**    Barnard stated that the major means of ensuring cooperation of individuals was through communication. He even defined authority relative to communication:  Authority is the degree to which an organizational member accepts communication directed at him or her as something that should govern his or her actions. The **acceptance theory of authority** states that, in formal organizations, authority flows up, because the decision as to whether an order, or communication, has authority lies with the person who receives the communication. Organization members will accept communications (orders) as authoritative if four conditions are met:  (1) they could and did understand the communicated order; (2) they believed that the order was consistent with the organization's purpose at the time of their decision; (3) they believed that the order was compatible with their personal interests as a whole; and (4) they were mentally and physically able to comply with the order.[42]

**acceptance theory of authority**
The theory that, in formal organizations, authority flows up, because the decision as to whether an order, or communication, has authority lies with the person who receives the communication.

**Example:** In Japanese organizations, authority is pushed down to the lowest level for decision making. A popular Japanese noodle bar in London, England, Wagamama uses teams of employees to design the menu and layout and oversee operations. Customers order by menu number and wait personnel use a tool belt to hold placemats, napkins, and chopsticks for efficiency.

## W. Edwards Deming

W. Edwards Deming (1900–1993) has been credited with transforming Japan's postwar economy more than 40 years ago. During his lifetime he was desperate to get his dual message of continuous improvement of the system and zero defects through to American managers, workers, government officials, and educators.[43] (We will explore Deming's management theory and methods in depth in Chapter 7.)

For now it is important for you to learn that Deming's work is appropriately classified as a systems theory of management.

One of Deming's major contributions was to integrate emphasis on quantitative methods and efficiency (relative to the classical approach) with emphasis on the psychological and social dimensions of the work environment (relative to the behavioral approach) into an approach in which all dimensions of the formal organization and its environment are considered as part of one system. Some have referred to Deming as a capitalistic revolutionary who transformed our notions of quality into a driver of profits instead of a cost of doing business.[44]

## THE CONTINGENCY APPROACH

During the 1960s a new phrase, "it depends," began to appear regularly in management literature. This signaled a move by theorists to yet another perspective of management that was noticeably different from the "one best way" approach followed by previous management theorists. The phrase "it depends" characterized the **contingency approach** to management theories, which emphasizes identifying the key variables in each management situation, understanding the relationships among these variables, and recognizing the complex system of cause and effects that exists in each and every managerial situation.[45] For example, an organization with a highly unstable operating environment should be structured and organized quite differently than one operating in a very stable environment. This is in contrast to Weber's idea of a pure bureaucracy as the one best way of organizing. Further, managers should use a different degree of supervision and control on employees who are very willing and able to do a job than on those who are not willing or able to perform their jobs.

The contingency approach is especially common in areas of management such as strategic planning, leadership styles, use of technology, design of reward systems, and organizational design. Generally, it is considered to be an outgrowth of the systems approach. While criticized as being inadequate as a true theoretical basis, the contingency approach has inspired research and understanding relative to how the gap between theory and practice may be bridged.

**contingency approach**
An approach to management theories that emphasizes identifying the key variables in each management situation, understanding the relationship among these variables, and recognizing the complex system of cause and effects that exists in each and every managerial situation.

**Critical Thinking Challenge:** Because contingency plans are just as important for individuals as for organizations, have students discuss their contingency plans for after graduation. Possibilities can include return to school for an advanced degree, choose a job outside their major, work as a co-op student or intern, or try to win the lottery.

## MANAGEMENT THEORY:  PAST, PRESENT, AND FUTURE

This chapter has been about beginnings, the individuals who pioneered these beginnings, and the times in which the beginnings occurred. Within the ideas of those before us lie our directions for the future. If we include the beginnings of history theory and practice in our ideas and behaviors, then our journey through organizations may be a little smoother and more meaningful. Each major approach to management theory that we have examined has added significantly to our current knowledge about management. The ideas embedded in each approach have also changed, in some respects, the way managers think and act. Contemporary managers and managers of the future benefit most from understanding and applying selected aspects of each approach.

The classical approach is still very evident today in our continued emphasis on the importance of efficient methods of operations and the use of quantitative methods in basic administrative principles of authority and division of labor, and in the prevalence of bureaucracy in our formal organizations. The behavioral approach is evident in the importance placed on people as the most valuable

## BUSINESS    DILEMMA

*You're the Manager ...What Would You Do?*

THE COMPANY:   **RMS Corporation**

YOUR POSITION:   **Owner**

THE PLACE:   **Portland, Oregon**

When Jim Keller took over RMS Corporation, a linen and bedding manufacturer, the company was near bankruptcy and employee morale was at an all-time low. RMS was losing $2 million a year and was plagued with high absenteeism, employee turnover, and accidents. At his first meeting with employees, Jim saw a level of apathy and abandonment that spurred his determination to revitalize the plant and its employees. He realized that the only way to save the company was to rekindle the employees' interest in its survival.

Jim, along with key employees, developed the "Initiative," a program he designed to get employees interested in the plant and to raise productivity. He set simple goals for product quality, safety, cleanliness of work spaces, and productivity. When the employees attained 100,000 hours with no recordable accidents, he closed the plant for a day and everyone celebrated with a "Barbecue Bash." When Jim had the departments compete against one another for a trophy, production increased dramatically. As a result of the company's setting measurable performance goals and offering rewards, employees began to care about the company's fate. After just four months, RMS showed a profit for the first time in years.

Keller improved the "Initiative" by offering all employees a full range of business courses—accounting, plant auditing, purchasing, etc.—to help them understand RMS's production reports and financial situation. The goal was to get employees to understand the huge amount of data required to monitor the firm's performance. Keller wanted employees to be able to gauge the impact of their activities on the plant and set their own performance standards to help improve the company.

Employees were given constant reminders of how they were doing. An electronic message board running continuous production reports was installed in the cafeteria. Employees who exceeded their production quotas were given a bonus under a plan known as "Output is sunny ... now give us some money." Employees also received bonuses for ideas that improved the company's operations. The employees were motivated to make RMS succeed because they understood not only the physical aspects of their jobs, but also how the company was doing and what needed to be done for success. When the company did well, so did they. Jim Keller's efforts and plans were enormously successful.

### Questions

1. What schools of management thought is the owner applying to revitalizing RMS?
2. What other management theories could you apply in the revitalization effort?
3. Contrast these actions against those that a factory manager of the early 1900s might have taken.

assets of organizations, and in the increasing attention paid to creating a working environment in which all our human needs are addressed, as well as the overwhelming emphasis placed today on the importance of effective work groups and teams and means of improving them. Evidence of the systems approach to management theory is quite apparent in attempts to manage organizations so that they meet the needs and challenges of the external environment and in the strong interest in total quality management methods. Finally, evidence of the influence of contingency approaches to management is found in the unique and varied success stories we hear every day from managers in many different and complex managerial situations.

Contemporary views of management that are in the process of being tested and evaluated today are fundamentally based on some aspect of theories we have considered in this chapter. For example, the eight attributes of excellence described by consultants Thomas Peters and Robert Waterman in their book, *In Search of Excellence,* are all in some way just new, unconventional terminology for

**FIGURE 2.3**

## A Time Line of the Development of Management Theory

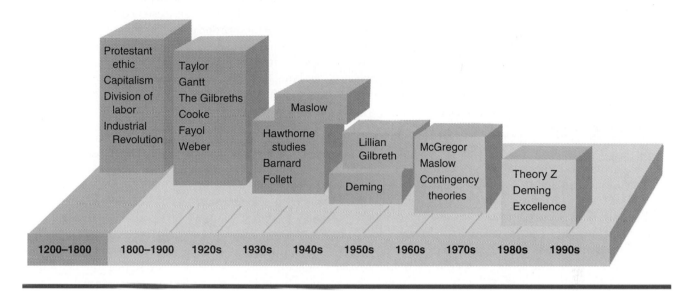

conventional management concepts and practices. Their attribute, "productivity through people," expresses all the beliefs and principles offered through the decades by the behavioral approach to management theory. More than anything else, Peters and Waterman remind managers that they must pay attention to the basics of customers, employees, and ideas.[46] Their mandate to encourage creativity and innovation is quite consistent with McGregor's concept of Theory Y management. For more than a decade, this line of management thought has been popular and well received by managers. However, with the passage of time, some of the "excellent companies" have indeed lost their excellent status. This is a good example of the complex, contingent, and dynamic nature of management.

Another relatively recent perspective on management is William Ouchi's idea of how Japanese and American management practices and philosophies should be combined into one integrated approach. This results in what Ouchi has labeled **Theory Z**, and it involves increased concern for quality of work-life, job security, group decision making, cooperation between groups, informal control mechanisms, and concern for work-family issues.[47] Obviously, Ouchi's contribution to management theory is consistent with theories of cooperation and self-control espoused nearly six decades ago by Follett and Barnard, and with theories of human needs for autonomy, respect, and meaningful work put forth by Maslow and McGregor.

Nothing stays the same. Remember we said that what we have studied in this chapter, although it spans a time period of nearly a hundred years (Figure 2.3), is only the beginning. Management theories and the study of management will continue to change today and tomorrow. While the changes are bound to be many and to be varied, they are likely to revolve around our efforts to compete in a global economy and our need to simultaneously increase productivity (benefits to the firm) and quality of work-life (benefits to the individual). These are important challenges for which we will be well prepared if we follow the ideas of the past, present, and future.

**Teaching Note:** After students have had time to review and discuss Figure 2.3, have them brainstorm about what the problems of the future may be and what possible management theories may be developed to cope with the problems of 2000 and beyond. To get students started ask them to first identify key problems facing business today.

**Theory Z**
A management theory involving increased concern for quality of work-life, job security, group decision making, cooperation between groups, informal central mechanisms, and concern for work-family issues.

**Example:** Nohria and Berkley in the January 1994 *Harvard Business Review* criticize management of the last 15 years because market shares in key U.S. industries declined. They call for "pragmatism" and believe pragmatic managers are sensitive to their company's context, are open to uncertainty, focus on outcomes, and are willing to make do.

## SUMMARY AND REVIEW

- **Specify the major cultural changes that preceded the development of modern management practice and thought.** Major cultural changes that preceded the evolution of modern management practice and thought were the development of the Protestant ethic, capitalism, and the Industrial Revolution. These changes culminated in a period of industrial chaos and low productivity, which gave rise to the definition and development of management as a critical factor of production.

- **Explain the major theories within the classical approach to management.** The classical approach to management stresses the manager's role in a formal hierarchy of authority and focuses on the task, machines, and systems needed to accomplish the task efficiently. The major theories that developed within this approach were Taylor's scientific management, Fayol's administrative theory, and Weber's theory of bureaucracy. Scientific management's overall emphasis was the systematic study of and experimentation with workers' tasks, methods, and tools as a means of improving worker efficiency. It had many contributors in addition to Taylor, including Frank and Lillian Gilbreth, Henry Gantt, and Morris L. Cooke. Fayol's theory was broader than scientific management and was directed at defining management as a universal process composed of four functions, and at developing principles needed to coordinate all the activities of the entire organization. Weber's ideas about bureaucracy added the concept of rational authority and management by position to classical management theory.

- **Examine some of the major contributions to the development of the behavioral approach to management.** The behavioral approach to management thought emphasizes the importance of human behavior, needs, and attitudes within organizations. Some management theorists and researchers who made major contributions to the development of the behavioral approach were Mary Parker Follett, those associated with the Hawthorne studies, Abraham Maslow, and Douglas McGregor. Follett had strong views on the importance of integrative unity, shared power, and human cooperation. She looked to managers as the means for improving society. The Hawthorne studies, through a long series of different experiments, brought to managers' attention the critical nature of the social needs of workers and led to the development of the human-relations movement. This signaled the beginning of the joining of management with psychology.

Maslow proposed that people's behavior at work could be explained by human needs for something beyond the money earned for basic existence. Self-actualization was the highest-order need identified by Maslow, and management practices directed toward satisfying this need pointed to a new direction for management theory and practice. McGregor labeled and explained such a nontraditional approach as Theory Y, in contrast to the traditional approach of Theory X.

- **Describe the systems approach to management theory and identify the early contributors to this perspective.** The systems approach to management theory views organizations and the environment within which they operate as sets of interrelated parts to be managed as a whole in order to achieve a common goal. Cooperative systems and the acceptance theory of authority were two aspects of Barnard's view of how organizations must be managed so that they can adjust effectively to a constantly changing external environment. Deming was a contemporary contributor to the systems approach whose work began in the 1940s.

- **Relate the significance of the contingency approach within the study and practice of management.** Within the study and practice of management, the contingency approach is significant because it has helped bridge the gap between theory and practice. It emphasizes identification of key variables in each management situation and as such maintains that there is no one best way to manage. The contingency approach is widely followed in areas of management such as strategic planning, leadership, and organization design.

- **Summarize how current management knowledge and practices are a result of the work and ideas of many management scholars and practitioners over the past century.** Widespread attention placed on job redesign and the use of technology that will result in efficiency and meaningful work that will fulfill individuals' higher-order needs is based on the theories of the classical and behavioral approaches. The overwhelming emphasis on team-building and implementation of total quality management is consistent with and based on the theories found in the systems and behavioral approaches. Finally, the emerging sense of experimentation and innovation found in small and large organizations indicates the influence of the contingency approach to management.

- **Apply the management theories discussed in this chapter to a manager's efforts to revitalize a small business.** The "Business Dilemma" box describes the steps a manager took to revitalize a failing small business. You should be able to assess and apply the schools of management thought that Keller applied to the situation and understand why he chose those theories over others.

## Key Terms and Concepts

social forces *32*
economic forces *32*
political forces *32*
Protestant ethic *33*
capitalism *33*
division of labor *33*
management theory *35*
classical approach *36*
scientific management *36*
soldiering *37*

quantitative approach *38*
management science *38*
administrative management *40*
bureaucracy *42*
behavioral approach *43*
Hawthorne studies *44*
human-relations movement *45*
Theory X *45*
Theory Y *46*
systems approach *46*

system *46*
closed system *47*
open system *47*
subsystem *47*
entropy *47*
synergy *47*
acceptance theory of authority *48*
contingency approach *49*
Theory Z *51*

## Ready Recall

1. What cultural changes led to the emergence of management as the fourth factor of production? What are the other three factors of production?
2. Compare and contrast the various approaches to management theory.
3. What are the principles and assumptions of scientific management?
4. What contributions to scientific management were made by people other than Taylor?
5. On what type of authority is bureaucracy based?

6. What four things should managers do to ensure that their authority will be accepted by subordinates?
7. What were the unexpected results of the Hawthorne studies and what conclusions were drawn from these results?
8. What issues formed the basis of the productivity problem at the turn of the twentieth century?
9. What were Fayol's main contributions to management thought?
10. What are the various characteristics of systems?

## Expand Your Experience

1. Do you think too much emphasis is placed on human relations within the work environment? too little emphasis? What direction do you think should be taken in the future relative to emphasis on human relations? Why?
2. What events and trends in society, technology, and economics do you think will shape management theory in the future?

3. View the video *Cheaper by the Dozen* and report on how the Gilbreths tried to incorporate their passion for efficiency into their family life.

---

**CASE**

## *How Business Schools Began*

---

Oh, but for the good old days when everything you needed to know to be a successful business manager could be contained in one book! Such was the case in 1890 when J. L. Nichols, principal of the North-Western Business College in Naperville, Illinois, published *The Business Guide; or Safe Methods of*

*Business.* He recommended his book as a "cheap form of full information as to methods of doing business." Or perhaps, instead of a minimum of four years of college education, you could have educated yourself completely by studying *How To Do Business.* Published in the late 1890s, this comprehensive text contained in one volume every topic of business considered important from banking, letter writing, grammar, and mechanic's arithmetic to business geography (see the opening vignette).

The notion of the formal study of business as a separate, fully developed curriculum of undergraduate education began to take shape in 1881 with the formation of the Wharton School of Finance and Economy at the University of Pennsylvania in Philadelphia. It was the desire of Joseph Wharton, a successful financier and iron manufacturer, that with his initial $100,000 endowment the University of Pennsylvania develop a program of college education that would "fit for the actual duties of life … men other than lawyers, doctors and clergymen." Wharton's plan was that the $6,000 in interest earned by the $100,000 endowment plus $150 a year in tuition fees from each of 40 students would provide funds to pay the $3,000 salary of the dean of the business school and a $1,500 salary for each of five professors, with $1,500 left over to buy books and provide student research grants.

The school opened with 13 students enrolled in a three-year program taught by one full-time and one part-time professor. Enrollment rose to 113 by 1894, and the curriculum was expanded to four years. By 1911, all U.S. universities housed a total of 30 undergraduate business programs, and by 1925 there were 164 colleges of business. By 1960 the count was 860, with an estimated student population of 600,000 in 1970.

When the Wharton School of Business was founded in 1881, the U.S. labor force included 17 million workers, and over half of them had agriculture-related jobs. Employers of that time expressed the need for employees with a little knowledge of bookkeeping, some commercial geography, mathematics, and the ability to write clearly.

World War I was a turning point for business degrees. The war created more work as well as demand for greater business acumen. The economy shifted from an agricultural base to a manufacturing one. An example of this shift is the automobile industry. Automobile production became a big industry in urban areas and caused people to leave farms for the higher paying manufacturing jobs. Consequently, to handle these more complex jobs, education became more important.

After WWI, emphasis shifted from basic, bottom-line ideas to overall business environment issues. Personnel practices, marketing, and the further development of accounting beyond just crunching numbers became important issues for effective managers. Schools were then forced to adjust to this shift in focus, as well as to the increase in the number of students interested in business. By 1940, there were 18,549 undergraduate degrees awarded in business, 1,139 master's, and 37 doctorates.

The makeup of students also affected what was taught in business schools. In the 1940s and 1950s, because of WWII veterans returning to the classrooms, students were older and more interested in courses that covered more complex issues. Schools responded by hiring professors with diverse backgrounds. Business schools, striving for prestige, became more broad in nature, teaching a variety of topics to attract even more students.

The 1970s brought a reversal of this trend, back to the more specific courses. Statistics, production management, and decision making were now specific tracks within the business discipline. Enrollment among the 18- to 24-year-old group increased during this time, leading schools to develop programs that covered the full range of business subjects, from the basics in economics and business law to the more advanced issues such as specific courses of action for different industries.

In the 1980s and 1990s, business became the most popular degree to pursue. Forty percent of all degrees awarded were business related; M.B.A.s were turned out by the tens of thousands every year. Today, employers are once again changing their definitions of what a business degree should entail. Current issues such as cultural diversity, global business, and the economic situation will force schools and students to rethink their approach to business once again. This dynamic nature of business will cause the content of business degrees to change constantly. The challenge will be for industry and academic institutions to work together and be flexible so that students will know what they need to know and be able to adjust quickly once they earn that all-important degree.

*Source:* Paul S. Hugstad, *The Business School in the 1980s: Liberalism versus Vocationalism* (New York: Praeger Publishers, 1983); *The Association of Collegiate Schools of Business: 1916–1966* (Homewood, Ill.: Richard D. Irwin, Inc., 1966); "Famous Firsts: How Business Schools Began," *Business Week,* October 12, 1963, 114–116.

## Questions

1. What do you think about going back to the "good old days" when business education was less formal and more general? Have our business schools become too specialized and quantitatively oriented?

2. What changes do you think will occur within business schools in the next 10 to 20 years? What will be the basis for these changes?

3. How are business school students of today different from those in the past? What difference does this make?

## Thinking

To conclude this chapter on the development of management thought, you will look at brain lateralization to help you understand your own thoughts, or thinking style. *Brain lateralization* is the term used to describe how the human brain is split into two halves, with each having its own special abilities. The following table summarizes the basic underlying ideas of the brain lateralization studies conducted at the California Institute of Technology by Nobel Prize winner Dr. Roger Sperry and his associates.

|  | **Characteristics of Dominant Brain Hemisphere** | **Problem-Solving Style** | **Gathering Information** |
|---|---|---|---|
| *Left-brain thinkers* (Those who rely more on their left hemispheres) | Active, verbal, logical, rational, and analytical; tend to process words and numbers in a linear, ordered way; capable of cataloging and analyzing information quickly | Adept at solving problems that call for planning and organization; excel in working with and analyzing sets of numbers; develop an understanding of a problem or situation by concentrating on its details | Often impose a system or concept on how information should be arranged and weighed; tend to start with a conceptual framework, then look for facts to fit it |
| *Right-brain thinkers* (Those who rely more on their right hemispheres) | Intuitive, creative, primarily nonverbal; deal in three-dimensional forms, images, and gestalts (see the forest versus the trees); perceive relationships in complex configurations and structures; create metaphors, analogies, and new combinations of ideas | More comfortable with problems that are complex, ambiguous, and difficult to define; often more resourceful and ingenious in solving problems with incomplete data; can come up with a number of different scenarios, trust their hunches, and don't act until they've considered multiple alternatives; often see mental images, alternatives, and possibilities that left-brain thinkers can't | Digest and ponder facts and clues first, then develop a theory around them |

A thick cable or core of nerve fibers called the corpus calossum connects the left and right hemispheres. Its main function is to transmit memory and learning between the two. Therefore, in the creative process, both hemispheres work together. The right brain devises the idea; and the left brain finds the appropriate tools to express it, whether in words, colors, sounds, or movement. For example, novelists may use right-brain inspiration to generate plot outlines. They engage in left-brain processes to manipulate dialogue, scenes, and characters that tell the finished stories.

The following brain dominance and thinking styles inventory will help you determine and clarify which side of the brain you rely on more when thinking and solving problems. You will use the results of this inventory in the exercise at the end of Chapter 3 to help you decide what job you'd enjoy most.

**Brain Dominance and Thinking Styles Inventory**

**Directions:**

Examine each set of four statements below and rank each of the statements from 1 to 4 in terms of your preferences, with

4 = most preferred
1 = least preferred

Make sure your ranking in each set uses all four numbers—1, 2, 3, and 4.

# Brain dominance and thinking styles inventory

Examine each set of four statements below and rank each of the statements from one to four in terms of your preferences, with four being your most preferred response and one your least preferred response. Make sure to rank order statements in each set.

\* \* \*

1. I would like to be involved in work situations that deal with:
   ___ a. Doing detective work on hard-to-solve problems.
   ___ b. Setting realistic and practical goals, then helping to achieve them.
   ___ c. Helping the people I work with to grow and progress.
   ___ d. Coming up with innovative ideas which will improve the organization.

2. I consider information to be good if it provides:
   ___ a. Usefulness.
   ___ b. Facts.
   ___ c. Meaning.
   ___ d. Hidden possibilities.

3. The most exciting times for me occur when:
   ___ a. I can communicate with someone with whom I've had past difficulties.
   ___ b. I discover a unique breakthrough solution for a chronic, long-standing problem.
   ___ c. I put together a step-by-step procedure for implementing an important plan.
   ___ d. I can quantify and therefore truly understand some difficult choices.

4. During the first five years in a new job I would like to:
   ___ a. Launch new, innovative ventures.
   ___ b. Help improve the quality of people's working lives.
   ___ c. Plan for and manage a task force responsible for improving an organization's performance and profits.
   ___ d. Be a resource person and technical consultant for solving day-to-day problems.

5. If I were to be tested or examined for a job, I would prefer:
   ___ a. Developing methods to apply in concrete situations.
   ___ b. A discussion or debate with other candidates for the position.
   ___ c. Objective, problem-oriented questions on how I would solve a particular problem.
   ___ d. An opportunity to make a visual-oral presentation of my knowledge on the subject.

6. I am most likely to believe something if it:
   ___ a. Fits in with the other things I believe.
   ___ b. Makes sense and is logical.
   ___ c. Gives me a new insight into something I took for granted.
   ___ d. Has been shown to have worked in practice.

7. When I have to make an important decision, I rely mostly on:
   ___ a. Orderly sequencing of all the pros and cons.
   ___ b. My past experience.
   ___ c. My feelings of rightness or wrongness.
   ___ d. My hunch or intuition.

8. When I wish to persuade another person about the soundness of my suggestion or idea, I:
   ___ a. Demonstrate in a step-by-step fashion how the details and principles would work out in reality.
   ___ b. Construct a logical rationale that would be difficult to refute.
   ___ c. Picture the benefits and personal satisfaction the adoption of my idea would bring to that person.
   ___ d. Emphasize the unique features of my idea which would open up new opportunities.

9. When it comes to problem solving, I prefer to:
   ___ a. Discuss the problem with others in order to get different feelings and opinions about the situation.
   ___ b. Come up with a number of innovative solutions to the problem.
   ___ c. Implement the agreed-upon solution.
   ___ d. Research the facts and/or figures in order to define the problem.

10. I find a theory to be useful if it:
    ___ a. Shows me a new way to think about something.
    ___ b. Serves to clarify my own feelings about something.
    ___ c. Leads to a practical and concrete application.
    ___ d. Can systematically shed light on a number of situations.

11. When starting to work on a group project, I would first like to:
    ___ a. Determine how to organize and implement it.
    ___ b. Understand how it would benefit each member of the group.
    ___ c. Determine exactly how the group should be doing the project.
    ___ d. Understand what further opportunities it might open up for the future.

12. The magazine articles I prefer to read in my leisure time are:
    ___ a. Descriptions of how someone resolved a personal or interpersonal problem.
    ___ b. Accounts of technical or scientific research.
    ___ c. Descriptions of historical events.
    ___ d. Humorous depictions of events or humorous people.

13. I prefer dealing with people who know how to:
    ___ a. Plan and successfully implement each step necessary to get a job done.
    ___ b. Make decisions and set priorities.
    ___ c. Get support from others.
    ___ d. Generate new ideas and alternative solutions.

14. People who know me well would describe me as:
    ___ a. A person who implements and follows through on plans.
    ___ b. A person who uses sound logic in arriving at decisions.
    ___ c. A good listener able to empathize with other people's feelings.
    ___ d. An imaginative person who sees new possibilities.

15. If I strongly disagree with another person, I would:
    ___ a. Seek the most agreeable compromise with the least fuss.
    ___ b. Outline the unique features and ideas of my position.
    ___ c. Argue out the differences in value, principle or policy.
    ___ d. Show in a logical fashion how I arrived at my position.

16. I experience great difficulties communicating with people who:
    ___ a. Don't seem to grasp what I'm trying to say.
    ___ b. Are insensitive to the feelings I'm trying to express.
    ___ c. Constantly jump from one subject to another.
    ___ d. Don't make much sense and are illogical.

17. My major source of enjoyment during leisure time comes from:
    ___ a. Competing with other people in a challenging situation and moving ahead.
    ___ b. Doing things with close friends and family that make me feel good.
    ___ c. Working on complex puzzles and problems that require careful thought.
    ___ d. Expressing myself and my personal values in some imaginative way.

18. I am especially good at:
    ___ a. Motivating others.
    ___ b. Strategic planning.
    ___ c. Creative problem solving.
    ___ d. Organizing projects.

19. I would rather be considered:
    ___ a. Reliable.
    ___ b. Practical.
    ___ c. Cooperative.
    ___ d. Resourceful.

20. I feel it is a worse fault to be considered:
    ___ a. Unreasonable.
    ___ b. Illogical.
    ___ c. Unsympathetic.
    ___ d. Unimaginative.

21. Which of the following statements applies mostly to you:
    ___ a. I prefer doing things with others rather than alone.
    ___ b. I like to come up with new ideas.
    ___ c. I enjoy supervising and directing others.
    ___ d. I like to work according to a well-thought-out plan.

22. After reading a book of fiction, I best remember:
    ___ a. The further possibilities or alternatives the author could have used.
    ___ b. The feelings and emotions the story evoked in me.
    ___ c. Portions of the book I liked and/or didn't like.
    ___ d. The development of the story line.

23. I prefer to spend my time in surroundings that:
    ___ a. Are neat and orderly.
    ___ b. Provide warm and friendly conversations with other people.
    ___ c. Are appropriate to the task at hand.
    ___ d. Stimulate and excite my imagination.

24. People whose abilities I admire the most are:
    ___ a. Teachers and doctors.
    ___ b. Engineers and economists.
    ___ c. Artists, writers and philosophers.
    ___ d. Business and government leaders.

25. The quote that provides me with most comfort and guidance is:
    ___ a. Learn from the mistakes of others since you can't live long enough to make them all yourself.
    ___ b. Balloonists have an unsurpassed view of the scenery, but there's always the possibility that it may collide with them.
    ___ c. The wealth of a soul is measured by how much it feels, its poverty by how little.
    ___ d. I'll not listen to reason since reason always means what someone else has to say.

**Scoring yourself:**

1. Copy your rank orderings for each question in each set (A, B, C, D).
2. Total each column. The four totals should add up to 250. If they don't, go back and check your rank orderings on the test and whether you copied them correctly in each column.

| | A<br>Upper Left | B<br>Left Right | C<br>Right Right | D<br>Right Left |
|---|---|---|---|---|
| 1. | a. | d. | c. | b. |
| 2. | b. | d. | c. | a. |
| 3. | d. | b. | a. | c. |
| 4. | d. | a. | b. | c. |
| 5. | c. | d. | b. | a. |
| 6. | b. | c. | a. | d. |
| 7. | a. | d. | c. | b. |
| 8. | b. | d. | c. | a. |
| 9 | d. | b. | a. | c. |
| 10. | d. | a. | b. | c. |
| 11. | c. | d. | b. | a. |
| 12. | b. | c. | a. | d. |
| 13. | a. | d. | c. | b. |
| 14. | b. | d. | c. | a. |
| 15. | d. | b. | a. | c. |
| 16. | d. | a. | b. | c. |
| 17. | c. | d. | b. | a. |
| 18. | b. | c. | a. | d. |
| 19. | a. | d. | c. | b. |
| 20. | b. | d. | c. | a. |
| 21. | d. | b. | a. | c. |
| 22. | d. | a. | b. | c. |
| 23. | c. | d. | b. | a. |
| 24. | b. | c. | a. | d. |
| 25. | a. | d. | c. | b. |
| Totals | | | | |

**Interpreting your scores:**

You will interpret your scores when you complete the exercise for Chapter 3.

# Environmental Factors *of* Management

**Outline**

**After reading this chapter, you will be able to:**

- Define the term *environment*.
- Formulate the components of the general environment, task environment, and internal environment.
- Examine the major factors in the general environment.
- Analyze the major factors in the task environment.
- Specify the major factors in the internal environment.
- Explain the stakeholder approach to viewing the environment.
- Distinguish the major ways that an organization can attempt to manage its environment.
- Specify why the external environment is important for organizations.
- Assess the environmental forces affecting business.

## "I Want My MTV"

**W**ith a heavy guitar riff and a beat you can dance to, MTV exploded on American cable systems in August 1981. With an attitude unlike anything ever seen on TV before, MTV quickly vaulted to the top of the American cultural scene. Besides providing teenagers the world over with the "wisdom" of Madonna, Sisters With Voices (SWV), and Pearl Jam, MTV has provided something more—profits. With a worldwide audience of more than 201 million homes, MTV's 1990 net profits were in excess of $85 million, making it one of the most successful of all cable operations. How did Robert Pittman, the 29-year-old founder of MTV, do it? Astute observation of the environment. He saw things and related them in ways nobody had before. In essence, MTV's success is a product of the unique way in which it views the world.

MTV observed the increased level of disposable income that teenagers possess. It noticed changes in the cable industry, most notably the expanded number of channels and the increased penetration rates of systems throughout America. It noted, as any parent will attest, that teenagers watch far more television than adults and listen to the radio a great deal more. Finally, it noted that, to promote rock acts, record companies were starting to distribute "videos," which they gave out for free to anyone willing to play them.

These videos became MTV's vehicle for presenting miniconcerts to its 18- to 34-year-old audience. For this audience, videos had the added advantage that they were usually only two to four minutes long, making it possible to see several different stars in a short period of time. As MTV demonstrated the popularity of videos, they markedly increased in sophistication and cost: Many videos now require as much staging and production as a live concert. As a result of the videos' increasing popularity and sophistication, MTV has become a major power in the careers of rock stars.

Exposure on MTV is usually an ingredient for success and sales of compact discs.

MTV continues to read its environment and develop in response. In 1987 it launched MTV Europe, which was switched on by Elton John from Amsterdam's Roxy Club. The main concept of MTV Europe was to address the lifestyle changes of young adults in Europe, especially in Central and Eastern Europe, whose fascination for rock music had long been known. Between 1987 and 1993, the number of household subscribers increased from 1.6 to 40 million. When the Berlin Wall separating East and West Germany fell, MTV preceded the event with a live feed into East Berlin two days before. Shortly afterwards, MTV began broadcasts into Poland, Czechoslovakia, Lebanon, Romania, and several parts of the former Soviet Union. A key strategy throughout this period has been for MTV Europe to imitate but not copy MTV. Although the network broadcasts videos of American performers, it has been careful to feature European stars.

In 1993, MTV announced the formation of another division, MTV Productions, to develop and produce feature films and network TV programs. In keeping with its youthful emphasis, the division was headed by Doug Herzog, MTV's 33-year-old senior vice president of programming. The division's purpose is to provide longer programs for the 18- to 34-year-old market.

*Sources:*   Elizabeth  Brown,  "Music Television Turns 10," *The Christian Science Monitor,* August 6, 1991, 10; Steve Clark, "Rock Conquers Continent," *Variety,* November 16, 1992, 35; Mike Hughes, "We Have Met the Future—and It Is MTV," *Gannett News Service,* July 29, 1991; "MTV Today, Tomorrow," *Variety,* June 7, 1993, 24; "MTV To Produce Movies," *The Los Angeles Times,* May 4, 1993, D1; Kevin Zimmerman, "Music Biz Targets Global Markets," *Variety,* March 22, 1993, 42.

*introduction*

Obviously, the pattern of demographic, economic, technological, and cultural trends presented an opportunity for MTV to become a very successful business; it was obvious, that is, to the company's founder. These trends were known to thousands, perhaps millions of people, but it took Robert Pittman and a group of colleagues to analyze them and, with the data, develop a successful enterprise. Pittman and his associates saw the world a little bit differently from others and, as a result, they are on a first-name basis with stars from all over the world.

MTV's success illustrates that knowledge of the environment in which a business operates is essential. In this chapter, we discuss the interaction between an organization and its environment, and we will answer the following questions: What is meant by the organizational environment? Why is it important to an organization? Are certain areas of the environment more pertinent than others? How do managers interact with the environment?

## THE NATURE OF THE ENVIRONMENT

Managers must constantly be aware of factors both inside and outside the firm that affect their decisions and actions. For example, the Civil Aeronautics Board deregulates the airline industry, creating cheaper fares and a more competitive market among airlines. The poor language and mathematical skills of many recent high-school graduate-employees leave many organizations feeling constrained in adopting new technology and work methods. Various consumer groups' protests about potential health risks associated with prepared foods are leading to many changes in the menus of fast-food restaurants and a more explicit presentation of ingredients on food packages. Such examples show that many factors affect managers and the actions they take. We consistently hear how organizations have succeeded or failed due to their adaptation, or lack thereof, to their environment. Managers must be able to determine what factors of the organization's world affect its operation and how these factors may be successfully addressed.

The **environment** refers to all those factors that affect the operation of the organization. It is inherently complex, with many individuals and groups affecting the firm. Many of these are constantly changing and difficult to control; however, this does not allow managers to ignore them. Managers must learn to perceive the environment accurately to deal effectively with these factors.

Figure 3.1 presents the components of the environment within which a manager must operate. As you can probably guess, the **external environment** refers to all the factors outside the organization that may affect its managers' actions. While such a definition is accurate, it is not very specific. Therefore, we divide the external environment into two parts. The first is the **general environment,**

**environment**
All of those factors that affect the operation of the organization.

**external environment**
All of the factors outside the organization that may affect its managers' actions.

**general environment**
The broad, complex factors that affect all organizations.

**FIGURE 3.1**

**The Organizational Environment**

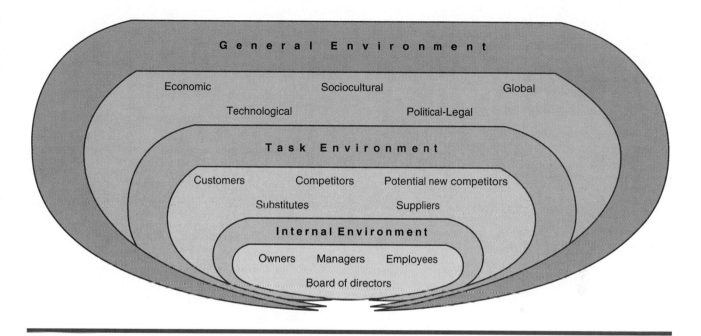

which refers to the broad, complex factors that affect all organizations. These factors include sociocultural, political-legal, technological, economic, and global influences. The makeup of and trends in each of these factors are the same for many companies. However, they affect organizations in different ways. Returning to our opening example, environmental factors that were positive for MTV were negative for the major television networks that had to figure out how to sell traditional programming to an increasingly nontraditional audience.

The second part of the external environment is the **task environment**, which is composed of those factors that have a direct effect on a specific organization and its managers, including customers, suppliers, competitors, substitutes, and potential new entrants to the industry. These factors usually vary in importance among organizations. However, there can be some factors that are common to several organizations, particularly those that are in the same industry.

Within the organization itself is a third element, the **internal environment,** which includes all factors that make up the organization, such as the owners, managers, employees, and board of directors. These factors, of course, directly affect actions that a manager may take.

**Critical Thinking Challenge:** Divide students into four groups and ask them to assume the role of one of PepsiCo's divisions —Pepsi, Pizza Hut, Taco Bell, and KFC (Kentucky Fried Chicken). Have students present factors in the general environment, task environment, and internal environment facing each.

**task environment**
Those factors that have a direct effect on a specific organization and its managers, including customers, suppliers, competitors, substitutes, and potential new entrants to the industry.

**internal environment**
All factors that make up the organization, such as the owners, management, employees, and board of directors.

## THE GENERAL ENVIRONMENT

The general environment refers to broad factors such as legal systems, population trends, economic conditions, and workers' educational levels. These forces influence all organizations, but they affect different organizations to different degrees. For example, the aging of the United States population may result in a potential decrease in consumption for soft drink bottlers but a potential increase for wineries. As previously stated, we can categorize general environment forces into five groups: sociocultural, political-legal, technological, economic, and global dimensions of the environment.

## The Sociocultural Dimension

The **sociocultural dimension** of the general environment includes the demographics and the values of the society within which an organization operates. This dimension is especially important because it determines the goods, services, and standards that society values.

Demographics are measures of various characteristics of the people and social groups who make up a society. Age, gender, and income are examples of commonly used demographic characteristics—often major determinants of consumer demand. For example, the increase in the median age of the population has resulted in the increased use of incontinence products such as Depends.[1] The recent growth in the Hispanic population in the United States has resulted in more radio stations adopting a Latino format.[2]

Values refer to certain beliefs that people have about different forms of behavior or products. Changes in how a society values an item or behavior can greatly affect a business. Changes in how society views "healthy" have had tremendous impact on the fast-food industry, for example, with the introduction of hamburgers that contain significantly less fat. However, our values concerning "healthy" continue to evolve. McDonald's introduced the "McLean" burger, a 91 percent fat-free hamburger, in 1991 to widespread acclaim and impressive sales. Yet, a few years later, the company was removing the product from the menus of many stores and generally deemphasizing it. Why the change? People were not buying the McLean, citing the taste or lack of taste.[3] Apparently, "healthy" is okay as long as it tastes good.

## The Political-Legal Dimension

The **political-legal dimension** of the general environment refers to the nature of the relationship between various areas of government and the organization. This dimension, composed of the political, legal, and regulatory elements, is important to organizations for several reasons.

**1.** It can constrain how a business operates. For instance, the Clayton Antitrust Act prevents many companies from creating alliances with other businesses. However, firms operating in other countries, such as Japan, have no such limitations and, as a result, can amass tremendous amounts of capital and resources that serve as advantages in international competition.

**2.** Manipulation of the political-legal processes can provide major competitive advantages to organizations. For example, U.S. tax law changes have boosted taxpayer demand for accounting and financial planning firms. Many people simply regard the Internal Revenue Service regulations as too difficult to address by themselves.

**3.** The political-legal dimension provides stability within which organizations can effectively plan and operate. The basis of most business relationships is the legal contract that spells out the obligations and duties of the respective parties. Failure to abide by such a legal document may result in a lawsuit that requires the offending party to pay damages to "make the other party whole." The recent col-

**TABLE 3.1**

## Business Political Action Committees and Political Contribution Levels

|  | Total Contributions | To Democrats | To Republicans |
|---|---|---|---|
| ARCO | $300,788 | $117,989 | $182,799 |
| Chrysler | 218,900 | 155,075 | 63,825 |
| FedEx | 756,950 | 478,450 | 278,700 |
| Marriott | 133,700 | 52,850 | 80,850 |
| Paramount | 114,050 | 84,250 | 29,800 |
| PepsiCo | 264,377 | 69,188 | 185,189 |
| Phillip Morris | 573,410 | 310,515 | 262,895 |
| UPS | 661,332 | 400,215 | 261,117 |

Source: Edward Zuckerman, *Almanac of Federal PACS 1992–1993* (Washington DC: Amward Publications, 1992).

lapse of communism in the former Soviet Union and the subsequent attempts by the Russian government to create a market economy illustrate the importance of contractual law. Because there are no legal traditions of binding contracts and enforcement mechanisms, most Western firms have been hesitant to establish businesses in Russia. There is no legal footing for building a stable relationship.[4]

The *political element* of the political-legal dimension refers to businesses' involvement in forming public policy. The past ten years have seen an explosion in the use of political action committees (PACs) by businesses and other groups trying to modify key pieces of legislation on both the national and local level. Table 3.1 lists some important business PACs and their recent contribution levels. In addition, businesses have increasingly had to contend with various interest groups, such as the National Association for the Advancement of Colored People (NAACP), the Sierra Club, and "Nader's Raiders," which have turned to the state and federal legislatures to promote their agendas.

The *legal element* is the use of the judicial branches of government to resolve disputes between parties. The traditional basis for litigation constituted contracts and torts (legal wrongs), such as negligence. However, recent developments in such areas as strict product liability and class-action suits have expanded the potential liability for a firm. Unsuccessfully pursuing a case in court may have unpleasant public relation effects as well as financial losses. GM, for example, has had to contend with a number of lawsuits concerning alleged poorly designed gasoline tanks in its pick-up trucks after the defect was judged to be responsible for the death of a driver.[5]

The third part of the political-legal dimension is the *regulatory element*. Table 3.2 lists some of the more prominent regulatory agencies applying federal regulations and laws that can greatly affect organizational operations. The Federal Trade Commission, for example, regulates trade practices and is empowered to investigate illegal activities.

Business organizations commonly view any government regulation negatively because complying with regulations increases the cost of doing business. Managers often think that regulation limits businesses' decision options. For example, equal employment laws can require organizations to employ a representative

**TABLE 3.2**

**Some U.S. Regulatory Bodies Affecting American Business**

Consumer Product Safety Division
Council on Environmental Quality
Council on Wage and Price Stability
Environmental Protection Agency
Equal Employment Opportunity Commission
Farm Credit Administration
Food and Drug Administration
Federal Communications Commission
Federal Deposit Insurance Corporation
Federal Energy Regulatory Commission
Federal Reserve Board
Federal Trade Commission
Interstate Commerce Commission
National Labor Relations Board
National Transportation Safety Board
Nuclear Regulatory Commission
Occupational Safety and Health Review Commission
Securities and Exchange Commission

mix of demographic groups; achieving this mix can mean extra costs of recruitment, selection, and training as well as compiling the paperwork required by the federal regulatory agency.

## The Technological Dimension

**technological dimension**
Within the general environment, the knowledge and process of changing inputs (resources, labor, and money) to outputs (goods and services).

The **technological dimension** of the general environment refers to the knowledge and process of changing inputs (resources, labor, money) to outputs (goods and services). An understanding of a business's technology component can have an important impact on its profitability and growth.

IBM's stance in developing the personal computer is a case in point. In the 1980s, IBM management thought that the most important technology was in the hardware—that is, the box, monitor, and keyboard. The company formed an alliance with Microsoft to use that company's DOS (disk operating system, which allows a user to issue commands to and run programs on a computer), which is absolutely critical to a computer's operation. In this business relationship, IBM permitted Microsoft to maintain control of DOS. This misreading of the technological base of the personal computer and the subsequent surrender of control of a vital component to another company was partially responsible for the severe financial difficulties of IBM.[6]

**Example:** Technological advances like the presence of cellular phones on airplanes have increased the productivity of business executives. Other advances like the fax machine, modem, pager, and portable computer are innovations that have changed the way business is conducted. Business offices now extend to an employee's home and car as mobile communication products proliferate.

Understanding the technological infrastructure in international transactions is of special importance to organizations. For instance, U.S. telephone companies are working to extend telecommunications in Eastern Europe basically through wireless technology. Why? The current telephone lines in Eastern Europe are too antiquated to support modern technologies, and it would be too expensive to replace them immediately. Cellular telephone technology allows a modern communication system to be erected efficiently and relatively inexpensively.[7]

Kodak employees manufacture imaging and health products for consumer, commercial, and medical customers on a worldwide basis. Kodak's global research, manufacturing, and marketing network allows each site to respond quickly to shifts in customer demand in any part of the world.

*Source:* Courtesy of Eastman Kodak Company.

## The Economic Dimension

The **economic dimension** reflects the overall condition of the complex interactions of economies the world over. Certain economic conditions of special concern to organizations include interest rates, inflation, unemployment rates, gross national product, and the value of the U.S. dollar against other currencies.

Changing economic conditions can greatly affect how organizations react. For instance, during times of high interest rates, the cost of borrowing money increases, making it more difficult for the firm to expand. Conversely, high unemployment rates mean that labor is more available at a lower price.

The general economic climate greatly affects the organization's prosperity and survival. During "boom" or growth periods, consumers are more likely to purchase the firm's products, and capital is easier to acquire, facilitating expansion and increased production. When growth slows, as in a recession, customers stop buying, unemployment rises, profit margins drop, and production declines.

One of the key economic issues in the U.S. economy in the 1990s is the expanding budget deficit. For many years, the government has spent more than it received in tax revenues, so it borrowed money to cover the difference. Many economists argue that this practice acts as a drag on the entire domestic economy. However, eliminating the deficit will require either an increase in taxes, spending cuts in government programs, or a combination of both. All options theoretically spell problems for businesses. Increased taxes take money out of the marketplace that could go toward the purchase of goods or services. Spending reductions could reduce the incomes of many recipients of government programs, thereby lowering the amount of goods they may buy.

**economic dimension**
The overall condition of the complex economies throughout the world.

## The Global Dimension

The **global dimension** of the general environment refers to those factors in other countries that affect the organization. (These factors will be discussed in detail in Chapter 5.) There is no doubt that the global dimension is becoming increasingly important to almost all aspects of business. U.S. firms engage in a variety of international trading relations. They may export or import products, license their trademarks or products to overseas companies, engage in joint ventures with foreign partners, or go international in the building of facilities.

**global dimension**
Pertaining to the general environment, those factors in other countries that affect the organization.

**Critical Thinking Challenge:** Have students brainstorm for possible differences in international environments. Write the list on the board for further discussion. Differences can include language barriers, currency fluctuations, type of government, attitudes toward business, holidays, social customs, and per capita income.

International business is a two-way relationship. American firms such as Boeing, Texaco, and AT&T have long-established international presences. Yet we are facing an expanding number of foreign companies entering the U.S. market, including Sony in consumer electronics, Hyundai in automobiles, and British Petroleum in gasoline, to name but a few.

When U.S. businesses venture abroad, they need to thoroughly understand the elements of the environment in which they will operate. Consumer buying habits abroad may be completely different from those in the United States. Governmental expectations toward business will be quite literally foreign. Expectations about cost and service may be quite different. We will look at these and other considerations in Chapter 5.

## THE TASK ENVIRONMENT

**Critical Thinking Challenge:** Have students select one of the following products: automobiles, soft drinks, computers, office furniture, or paint. Ask students to list suppliers for these products along with customers, competitors, substitute products, and potential new competitors.

The task environment includes a firm's competitors in industry as well as those parties that have a direct influence on the industry and firm. These include suppliers, customers, organizations that produce substitute goods or services, and current and potential new competitors. It is the overall impact of these five different factors which has a major effect on the overall profitability and competitive position of the firm within its industry.

### Suppliers

**suppliers**
Organizations and individuals who provide resources to other organizations.

**Suppliers** are organizations and individuals who provide resources to other organizations. They supply inputs such as products, raw materials, capital, labor, and information. Their power lies in their ability to control the flow of these inputs and thus set prices for them. Thus, the power of a supplier is related to the scarcity of its products. A business is at an advantage if it has many suppliers for a particular resource and at a disadvantage if it has only a few. A supplier may also be in a strong position if the cost of switching sources is high. For example, there is a certain cost involved when buyers switch from Apple Macintosh computers to IBM-compatible computers, because the two systems are largely incompatible in terms of both hardware and software.

**Example:** When McDonald's opened its first restaurant in Moscow, Russia, suppliers for raw materials were limited or nonexistent. Potato farmers from Canada trained Russian farmers, while suppliers of milk and dairy products were given training on sanitation and pasteurization to ensure a constant source of raw materials for the restaurant.

As another example, airlines have a limited number of manufacturers from which to buy aircraft, with Boeing and McDonnell-Douglas being the two main U.S. firms. These manufacturers can essentially determine the delivery time of most orders and limit the number of optional features that can be provided. When the airline industry was stronger economically and its members were enjoying high demand, the airplane manufacturers' ability to deliver new planes was a major factor in the strategic planning of carriers such as Delta and American Airlines. Moreover, the availability of planes limited future planning. On the other hand, for fast-food restaurants such as McDonald's, Wendy's, and Burger King, suppliers for potatoes are plentiful and relatively easy to change. They have very little control or power over restaurants and do not ordinarily limit the restaurants' planning or operation.

### Customers

**customers**
Those who purchase an organization's goods and/or services.

**Customers,** of course, are those who purchase an organization's goods and/or services. They may be individuals or other organizations. A customer may be the final

recipient (user) of the good or service or serve as an intermediary. Clothing stores, for example, are the customers of either manufacturers or distributors. These stores, in turn, sell the garments to their individual customers. Because of a need for products, we typically think of the customer as being dependent on the business. However, the customer is also a powerful force in an organization's operation. The power of the customer increases when:

- The firm's product is no different from that of its competitors. Many financial institutions, for example, offer MasterCard or Visa credit cards. The customer can easily change among these institutions, usually paying off the debt of the old card with the new card. Consequently, companies that issue these cards continually gather information about customer attitudes and needs for additional services. Customer influence on the organization's operations is very evident.

- The cost of the product is a significant expense for the customer. Consumers usually have more stringent standards of product features for automobiles, boats, and retirement investments than for magazines, shoes, and video games. They will more seriously attempt to negotiate a reduced price or special features for expensive items.

- The customer is a major buyer of the firm's total goods or services. Because of this, the firm actually depends on the buyer. Many small businesses are in this situation because of the small volume that they produce. One substantial order automatically makes that customer an important factor in the organization's operations.

**Example:** In the field of total quality management, employees are taught to think of the customer as the person at the next work station. This person is the next "customer" of your output and expects perfect quality. This thinking is perpetuated along the production chain to the ultimate final consumer of the product or service.

## Substitutes

**Substitutes** are goods or services that may be used in place of those furnished by a given business. Substitutes for a company's goods or services can limit how much it may charge. For example, if its price is low enough, plastic may be an attractive substitute for rubber—assuming it can be used for the same purpose.

Often substitutes come as a result of technological innovation. Compact discs (CDs) are substitutes for records and cassettes and have largely replaced LPs as the most important source of commercial recording.[8] Radial keratotomy, a surgical procedure for nearsightedness, has a growing impact on the market for contact lenses and eyeglasses, as the surgery is perfected and the price of the procedure drops. Similarly, today's microcomputers are capable of doing much of the processing of

**substitutes**
Goods or services that may be used in place of those furnished by a given business.

**Example:** The growth of the fast-food industry in the United States continues to slow due to both market saturation and substitutes for fast food including microwave meals, food counters in supermarkets, snacks in convenience stores, and competition from other restaurants.

**competitors**
Other organizations that produce similar, or in some cases identical, goods or services.

mainframe computers. Fax machines are substitutes for various types of mail-delivery services, and word processing units have greatly reduced the typewriter market.

Substitutes can have a very serious effect on a business by diminishing or eliminating consumers' demand for its products. Depending on the cost of the substitute, its effect can be quite rapid.

## Competitors

**Competitors** are other organizations that produce similar, or in some cases identical, goods or services. Many jewelry stores order their rings, pins, and earrings from the same limited number of suppliers. The only differences among jewelers may be in the (usually) small number of crafted items. Similarly, automobile dealers compete not only with other dealers who have the same vehicles but also with those who sell rival makes and models.

Competitors are often the most powerful force in a firm's operations. Prices, services, and support after sales are all directly compared with those of competitors. All companies attempt to gain an advantage on competitors in some part of the business operation, and they hope this advantage will result in increased sales. Companies are constantly monitoring others in the same field and trying to anticipate what they might do in the future. Sometimes, responses to competitors may actually be costly to the organization—for example, the fare wars among airlines. If one airline cuts ticket prices, most or all other carriers will usually follow or reduce fares even more. As evidenced by recent financial statements of many airlines, such fare wars have been disastrous to their profitability. However, each airline fears that losing customers will have even greater long-term consequences.

On the other hand, sometimes it is not apparent who a company's competitors are. For example, who are the competitors of Krispy-Kreme donuts? We can look first at other large national competitors such as Dunkin-Donuts. There may also be regional and local rivals, such as bakeries, and other businesses, such as supermarkets, that make donuts as part of their larger marketing efforts. In addition, Krispy-Kreme now has to contend with microwave donuts and prepackaged donuts from companies like Dolly Madison.

## Potential New Competitors

**potential new competitors**
Companies not currently operating in a business's industry but which have a high potential for entering the industry.

If an industry is profitable, it will attract the attention of other businesses seeking opportunities to expand, posing a threat to those already in the industry. **Potential new competitors,** then, are companies not currently operating in a business's industry but which have a high potential for entering the industry. Businesses must collect information concerning the probability of entry of these interested organizations. They must also ensure that their own operations are as efficient as possible and that their goods and services do not have any major weaknesses of which these potential new entrants could take advantage. The decision to enter an industry will depend, in part, on the barriers—the costs and difficulties—to entry. High barriers include the following:

• *High entrance costs.* These costs could be because of expensive equipment, location, or lack of availability of skilled employees. The automobile industry has large initial equipment costs.

• *Economies of scale.* This means that the cost per unit goes down as the organization produces more units. Existing organizations are probably already operating at a high volume. Any new entrant must have a large number of customers from the outset to be competitive with those companies already in the industry.

• *Lack of access to distribution channels.* If an organization cannot get its goods and services into the hands of customers, it may not succeed. Many U.S. firms complain that this is the reason they are unsuccessful in the Japanese marketplace. As a local example, Timex was unable to gain entry into the traditional distribution network for watches—jewelry stores—and was forced to use a different method—supermarkets and drugstores.[9]

• *Lack of technical expertise.* Each industry has a specific set of knowledge and skills necessary to deliver goods or services. Many industries, such as medicine and engineering, require high levels of technical expertise to be competitive.

**Example:** Blockbuster Video has established high barriers to entry. Its large selection, service, locations, special prices, and extended operation hours serve to deter smaller firms from entering the video-rental industry.

## THE INTERNAL ENVIRONMENT

The makeup of a firm's internal environment can vary greatly. We will discuss characteristics of this environment, such as job design, organizational structure, work teams, employee motivation, and human resource management programs, in detail in Chapters 12 through 18. Consequently, we will address only briefly some of the broad factors of the internal environment here. Regardless of organizational form, size, or scope, all firms have owners, managers, and employees. Additionally, state laws require all corporations to have boards of directors. Frequently, public institutions and nonincorporated businesses will have an equivalent group in the form of a board of trustees.

### Owners

Owners can have various degrees of influence and power within an organization. Small entrepreneurial firms normally have a very "hands-on" owner (or owners) who seeks to have control over all aspects of the firm. In corporations, ownership is held collectively by the stockholders. However, many stockholders see their possession of stock not as a form of ownership, but rather as a form of investment, and consequently they do not seek to exert control over management. This has led to a separation of ownership and control in many corporations.

A current trend involves large institutional investors, mostly pension funds, exerting increasing control over corporate management. Calpers, the California Public Employees Retirement System, and other such investors recently pressured GM and Westinghouse to oust their CEOs and implement changes to improve performance.[10] These institutional investors are demanding greater upper management accountability.

### Managers

In the smallest companies, the owner is the sole manager of the firm and fulfills all typical management tasks. As the organization expands and becomes more complex, however, the owner will normally bring in additional persons to act as managers.

For the purpose of interacting with the external environment, we can identify three types of managers:  strategic or institutional, technical, and operational.

Dana Corporation, a manufacturer and distributor of vehicle components, goes to great lengths to draw on the knowledge and skills of its employees. Dana asks each of its 36,000 employees for at least two ideas per month on how to improve his or her work and tries to implement 80 percent of the suggestions.

*Source:* Courtesy of Dana Corporation.

Strategic managers normally are involved with setting the overall direction of the organization. Usually from top management, they are concerned primarily with macroeconomic factors. Technical managers serve under the strategic managers and act to coordinate the various levels—that is, to serve as the middle managers. Operations managers are the ones who in some manner transform the organizational inputs into finished outputs; they are typically lower-level line managers or supervisors.

Recent trends in American business indicate that many organizations are "flattening" the organizational hierarchy and eliminating many of the technical managers. This has brought the strategic and operational levels into more immediate contact, and is intended to improve communication and bring the strategic managers "closer" to the customer.[11]

## Employees

One important way of classifying employees is as unionized and nonunionized. The difference between these two groups is important in terms of their effect on the internal environment. Unionized employees are represented by labor unions which, in essence, attempt to exert a strong influence on wages, working conditions, and job duties through a negotiation process with management called collective bargaining. Thus, the relationship between managers and unionized employees is quite different from that between managers and nonunionized employees. The former relationship is more formalized and dictated by the negotiated contract between the union and the organization.

Two general environmental factors, sociocultural and technological, are affecting the demands of management on employees. Changing demographics is creating an older and more culturally diverse work force, and technological change is forcing employees to acquire more complex skills. When these factors are coupled with an increase in the use of relatively low-paid, skilled foreign workers in countries such as China, tremendous challenges are arising for the American worker. Many organizations are trying to meet these challenges by increasing employees' skills through training, and then turning to employee involvement programs to take advantage of these skills.

**Critical Thinking Challenge:** Have students compare the internal environment of a union and a non-union employer. If possible, have students interview local employees of each and report the differences in attitudes toward management, benefits, and satisfaction.

## BUSINESS DILEMMA

*You're the Manager ... What Would You Do?*

THE COMPANY:   Amerigo Motors

YOUR POSITION:   Vice President of Operations

THE PLACE:   Detroit, Michigan

Amerigo Motors was founded in the late 1970s by two former engineers with Ford Motor Company in a joint venture with a French automaker. Amerigo focused on smaller automobiles before the "Big Three" (Chrysler, General Motors, and Ford) could shift their production focus to match consumer demand. Buyers were seeking smaller and more fuel-efficient automobiles in the 1980s, and Amerigo, along with several Japanese importers, was poised to meet that demand. Amerigo differentiated itself from the foreign competition by providing the domestic automobile alternative. Because almost everyone feels that hourly flat rates on automobile service are too high, Amerigo cut its dealerships' hourly service rates 25 percent below the average U.S. dealer rates. In so doing, Amerigo felt it had developed a superior benefit that consumers could readily identify in the car-buying process.

Amerigo Motors was successful through the mid-1980s, operating with a stable profit margin that allowed it to continue to grow and invest in research and development. The late 1980s, however, became a fierce competitive battlefield as American automakers had now produced independently and through joint ventures some of the more respected and critically acclaimed cars on the market. Amerigo's market share was not growing and for the first time in more than a decade the company was operating with a loss.

The dealership system was in trouble. Sam Evans, the vice president of marketing, felt that the lower rates charged in the service departments would add directly to the dealers' bottom line, but the vice president of finance, Joe Malone, said the margins on service department labor were not great enough to provide the desired profitability and that dealers needed a better product to survive. Malone indicated that his current sense of the service departments was that they, because of the original discount positioning on labor, operated more as nonprofit centers. Consequently, the dealers were in financial trouble.

Sam suggested that a quota system could enhance the service departments' profitability and productivity. Service consultants/advisors would have to sell a quota of service per four-hour time period. Joe felt the suggested system had merit. Joe and Sam felt the quota system would put the service departments in a more active role and increase the employees' motivation to check scheduled and nonroutine service and parts. This would increase their profits and keep them in business during a period of lower auto sales.

Joe and Sam schedule a meeting with you to discuss their plan. You are in a position to support, reorganize, or overrule their plan and provide suggestions of your own for their further consideration and development.

### Questions

1. What are the environmental issues influencing this situation?
2. What is your recommendation to Joe and Sam?
3. How could their plan positively/negatively affect the company?

**Comment on Box:** This exercise is a good way to review environmental issues facing organizations and to develop solutions based on environmental trends. Professors can call on students to report their recommendations for Joe and Sam as well as discuss the rationale behind their decisions.

## Boards of Directors

In corporations, the board of directors has the important task of representing the stockholders in their capacity as owners. Elected by the stockholders, the board is charged with ensuring that the corporation is being managed so as to increase stockholder wealth. The board is normally called on to approve major strategic decisions and to hire key personnel, most notably the chief executive officer (CEO).

In many corporations, however, the board seldom plays a major role. A board is often controlled by the CEO through his or her nomination of board members, and the CEO often manipulates the board through company perks and lucrative consulting contracts. As a result, critics argue that boards of directors do not exert the control they are legally obligated to provide. Recently, in several well-publicized

**FIGURE 3.2**

The Stakeholder View

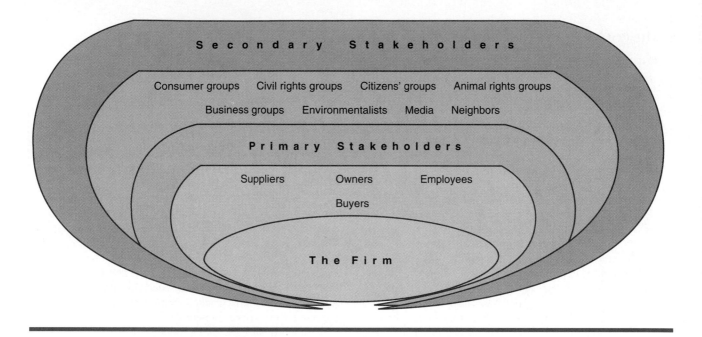

moves, the boards of several firms such as IBM, GM, Sears, and American Express have either fired the CEOs or strongly encouraged them to retire, following extended periods of low earnings.[12]

## STAKEHOLDER VIEW OF THE ENVIRONMENT

One way managers evaluate the environment is through the *stakeholder view*. A **stakeholder** is a person or a group which can affect, or is affected by, an organization's goals or the means to achieve those goals.[13] Stakeholders for a particular firm may include **primary stakeholders,** those who have a formal and/or contractual relationship with the firm, such as customers, suppliers, and employees. **Secondary stakeholders** are groups which have a less formal connection to the organization such as environmentalists, community activists, and the media. Figure 3.2 illustrates the stakeholder view of the environment.

In the stakeholder view, the firms and agents in the external environment are interrelated. Also external stakeholders may be related themselves—for example, consumer groups and broadcast media. Key to this view is that there is a two-way interaction between the stakeholder and the firm. The firm is at the center of a network of actors which the organization can hopefully identify and then manage.

### Identifying Stakeholders

The first step of interacting with the environment is to identify the specific individuals and groups which affect the organization. The manager is concerned with cre-

**stakeholder**
A person or group which can affect, or is affected by, an organization's goals or the means to achieve those goals.

**primary stakeholders**
Those who have a formal and/or contractual relationship with the firm, such as customers, suppliers, and employees.

**secondary stakeholders**
Groups which have a less formal connection to the organization, such as environmentalists, community activists, and the media.

**FIGURE 3.3**

Chester's Bar's Stakeholder Map, Day 2

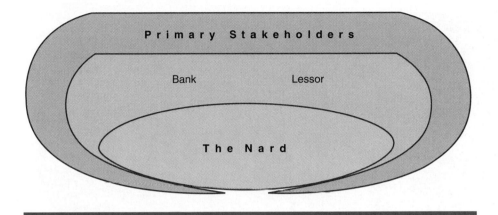

ating a **stakeholder map,** a representation of the organization's stakeholders and their stakes. A stake can be of three basic types: an equity interest, such as a stock-holder or lender may have; a market interest, which might be shared by buyers or suppliers; or an influencing interest, which may be represented by the government or an interest group.[14] The ability to visualize this universe through a stakeholder map is necessary for deciding how to manage the environment properly.

The following hypothetical illustration gives you an idea of how such a map may be derived.

**stakeholder map**
A representation of the organization's stake-holders and their stakes.

## Chester's Bar:  The Nard

Chester was a man with a dream, a dream to be an entrepreneur—but not just an ordinary entrepreneur. Chester, thinking back on his college days, recalled thoughts of the things that provided him the most comfort in those heady times—a letter from Mom, a warm and moving talk with Dad, a quip from his manage-ment professor—and decided to open a bar.

Chester immediately went down to his local bank, the Happy Bank, and secured a line of credit. Working on a tip from his banker, Chester signed a lease agreement in the town of New Paris, the home of the state's flagship university, Confusion State. At the end of the second day, Chester's stakeholder map looks like the one pictured in Figure 3.3.

The very next day, Chester rushed down to City Hall to get a permit to sell alcohol. But Chester was taken aback when he was informed that the city's zoning regulations placed his proposed bar in a G-1 zone (old, dilapidated downtown buildings) as opposed to a G-2 zone (old, dilapidated downtown buildings where you can sell liquor). Two days later Chester attended a zoning board meeting to seek a variance to these restrictions, when out of the back room came a group of citizens calling themselves CKSFHGT, Citizens to Keep Students From Having a Good Time. Citing the bar as a possible nuisance, the zoning commission reject-ed Chester's request. Three days later, Chester, with his attorney, I. Found Whiplash, appeared before the city council and persuaded it to overturn the zoning commission. Walking out of the room in victory, Chester was handed a list

**FIGURE 3.4**

Chester's Bar's Stakeholder Map, Day 8

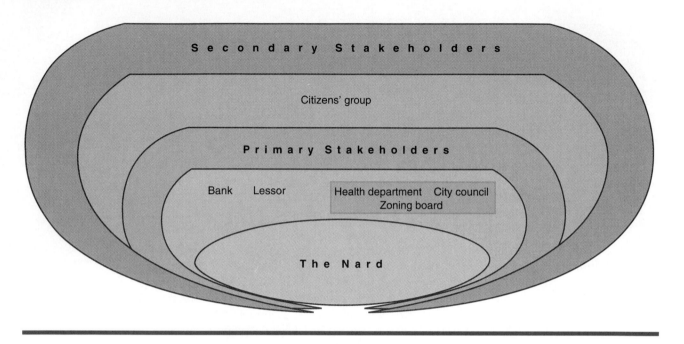

of violations by an inspector with the city's health department. At the end of eight days, then, Chester's stakeholder map looked like Figure 3.4.

Trying to get the bar in shape by the first day of the semester, Chester pressed onward. He contacted suppliers of food and alcohol. He hired his first employees, Ken Idrink, a bartender, and Mary Kokdbooks, an accountant who informed him that he would need to withhold income taxes and social security from his employees' wages if he wished to avoid the wrath of the IRS. On the first day of work, Ken slipped on a rug and filed a worker's compensation claim. At the end of 17 days, Chester's stakeholder map had grown into that shown in Figure 3.5.

Finally the big day arrived. Chester's bar, The Nard, which was named after his favorite management scholar, was open for business! His competitors were ready for him. Pete's Tofu Hut and Bar offered a two-for-one drink special. The Grilled Turkey expanded on its popular "Ladies Night" by requiring no proof of gender. The star reporter as well as the sales editor of the local paper, *The Semireliable Rumor Mill*, were there to write a story on The Nard's grand opening. Customer after customer poured in as a local band, the Outatunes, wailed away. What a great life, thought Chester. Just then a fight broke out among the Outatunes. The police arrived in minutes to break up the fight, and, on their way out, they handed Chester a ticket citing him for violating the city noise ordinance. Chester sighed as he looked at his stakeholder map in Figure 3.6.

## Gathering Information about Stakeholders in the Environment

Once the stakeholder map has been determined, the next step is to set up organizational processes for collecting information about the stakeholders. Such infor-

**FIGURE 3.5**

Chester's Bar's Stakeholder Map, Day 17

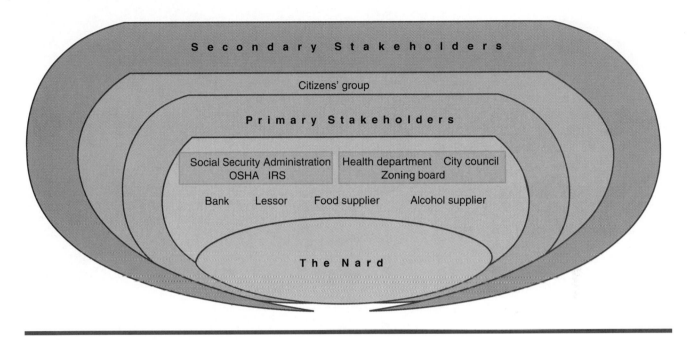

mation allows the organization to anticipate changes in its environment and develop plans to respond to these changes. This collection of information can be done informally, in a haphazard manner. However, there are a number of techniques that most organizations use to collect information more systematically and accurately.

**Customer Surveys.**    Customer surveys normally involve the use of interviews or written questionnaires to determine the opinions and attitudes of current and potential customers. Chester, for example, may interview his few customers on slow evenings or develop a list of individuals in the area to whom to mail questionnaires. He might try providing a price discount for completed questionnaires.

**Economic Forecasting.**    Economic forecasting creates a framework for predicting future movements in the economy by looking at past economic indicators. At the national level, forecasters use such data as the gross national product (GNP), disposable income, and the unemployment rate. Chester could use local measures such as the number of new business and housing starts, enrollment in the college, and the unemployment rate.

**Trend Analysis.**    Trend analysis develops models based on current trends and projects into the future. Chester could get information for each of the last five years on the number of liquor licenses granted by the city, the net population growth or loss, and the growth of fraternities and sororities.

**Delphi Method.**    The Delphi method uses the opinions of experts to form a statement of the external environment. Basically, the person gathering the information

**Example:** Not all stakeholders are desired by the organization. Some special interest groups or unwanted stakeholders cause organizations to change their focus. Mothers Against Drunk Driving (MADD) frequently boycotts the sale of alcoholic products. Because of the work of Gamblers Anonymous, many state lotteries must donate a portion of their revenues to gambling research and assistance.

## FIGURE 3.6

**Chester's Bar's Stakeholder Map, Opening Day**

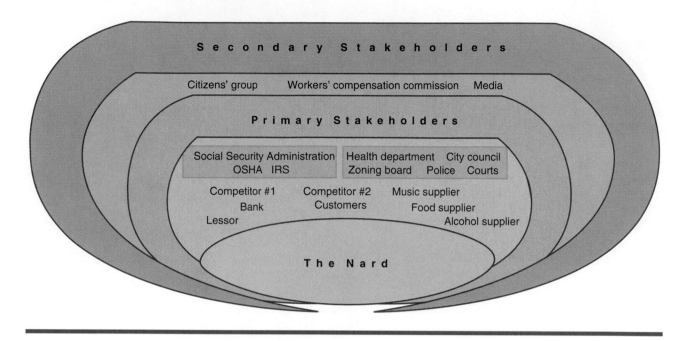

poses a series of questions to the experts, who are not in the same physical location. The experts provide answers that are circulated to the whole group. These answers can then be used in responses to additional rounds of questions. Questioning continues until the group arrives at a general consensus. This method is used extensively for forecasting political, sociocultural, and other forces in which past trends may not predict future trends. Chester can identify his bar's counterparts of the "Cheers" regulars and ask each of them to offer opinions on the future demand for hot wings, country music bands, and low-calorie beer.

### Techniques for Interacting with the Environment

After the manager has identified the relevant stakeholders and collected information about future trends involving these stakeholders, he or she must develop some means of interacting effectively with the environment. Through these interactions, the manager is trying to maximize well-being by gaining a competitive advantage or by blunting the negative effects that these stakeholders can have on operations.

Although there are numerous actions that the organization may take, some of the most common are the following.

**Teaching Note:** If possible, have a representative from the public relations office of your college or university speak to your class about his or her job, the role of the office, and the type of information released to the media.

**1.** Public Relations—Information that explains the firm's activities in a favorable manner is regularly transmitted to the public. Electric utilities, for example, provide information about the management of nuclear reactors, their benefits, and their low impact on the environment. Although the manager may release such information to the external environment, the information is also regularly used by groups in the internal environment. Chester could develop brochures describing the nutritional value of his menu.

**2.** Boundary Spanning—Representatives of the organization regularly meet with stakeholders, such as sales agents with customers or purchasing agents with suppliers, to present the current and future status of the organization and try to influence the stakeholder's immediate and future actions toward the company. At the very least, the representative attempts to gain information about the stakeholder's beliefs and attitudes about the organization. For example, Chester's serving staff, Marga Rita and Tom Collins, can regularly meet with local sorority and fraternity officers.

**3.** Lobbying—Members of the organization meet with government officials in an attempt to influence their votes on some policy that will affect the organization. For example, when President Clinton proposed a tax on energy and fuels, representatives from oil companies met with members of congressional staffs to explain that a high tax would be economically detrimental; they said it would result in the loss of jobs in the oil industries because the increased price of gasoline would lower demand. Physicians and educators have two of the most active lobby groups at both the federal and state levels. Chester exhibited lobbying behavior when he got the city council to overrule the zoning commission.

**4.** Negotiation—The organization arrives at a formal, legal agreement with stakeholders through a discussion that may include cost, time, and method of transportation. This technique is commonly used with both internal and external environmental forces. Labor contracts, sales agreements, and facility leases are examples. It is desirable for the organization to formalize the impact of the stakeholder so that it can predict with certainty what the stakeholder will do in the future, which makes planning much easier and more accurate. This is the reason sports teams agree to long-term contracts with their superior players. Chester uses negotiation to obtain contracts with local beer distributors that guarantee a certain volume at a certain price.

**5.** Alliances—The organization joins with other organizations, frequently competitors, to engage in an activity that promises great benefit. GM and Toyota, for example, have formed joint ventures to manufacture automobiles in the United States. The arrangement allows Toyota to produce automobiles that do not count against the voluntary export quotas of Japanese manufacturers, and it allows GM to improve its sales figures by producing automobiles that are in higher demand.[15] Other forms of alliances are takeovers, mergers, and acquisitions. In takeovers and acquisitions, one organization buys a competitor, supplier, or customer. (Often the organization is acquired against the wishes of its managers.) This happens through a direct offering to the company's stockholders, who make a profit on the sale of their stock. Mergers are the joining of two organizations to form a larger, combined firm. For example, the computer and data processing firms of Sperry Rand and Burroughs merged to form Unisys. Chester is thinking of joining with a friend of his who owns a laundromat to form a new business called Suds & Suds.

**6.** Organizational Restructuring—This involves changes in the organization's structure and the working arrangement among its internal parts. Frequently, these changes include laying off employees in an attempt to reduce the costs of doing business and to make the organization competitive against other organizations. In recent years, many individuals affected by layoffs have been middle-level managers. Chester is considering dismissing his bartenders and changing to a physical layout with automatic dispensers of beer and frozen daiquiris.

## THE IMPORTANCE OF THE EXTERNAL ENVIRONMENT

Our basic premise is that the external and internal environments must be compatible and appropriately linked to the organization's goals and objectives if the organization is to be successful. Both the external and internal environments present threats and opportunities to the organization—that is, factors that can either hinder or help future performance. Managers must perceive these threats and opportunities and react accordingly. The remainder of this chapter will focus on the importance of the external environment to the organization and its managers. Understanding this importance is essential for the material we present in Chapters 4 through 13. We will return to the internal environment in Chapters 14 through 18.

### Environmental Change: Two Stories

**Ford.**    All environments change, and there are many examples of businesses that failed to account for change and suffered the consequences for it. In the early part of this century, for example, Ford Motor Company was a giant of a firm whose founder, Henry Ford, knew exactly what the environment demanded early in the history of the automobile—inexpensive black cars—or so he thought. Working under the assumption that what consumers valued was cheap transportation, Ford perfected the technology that enabled the firm to produce mass quantities of reliable vehicles. But what Ford later failed to consider was that society was becoming more affluent and, in turn, demanding changes in its consumer goods. No longer were people satisfied with only basic items. Instead, they wanted a visible symbol of their success. "Keeping up with the Joneses" became the slogan for the emerging middle class. It was General Motors, not Ford, that first discerned this changing preference. GM, under the leadership of Robert Woods, created a process through which new models and changes were introduced each year, thus dating existing models. In addition, GM offered a variety of models in order to give customers the feeling that they could drive something different from their neighbors. Responding appropriately to changes in the environment resulted in GM surpassing Ford as the world's largest auto manufacturer.[16]

**McDonald's.**    The ability to perceive change and adapt or initiate action is important not only for large businesses but for small firms as well. Many "start-ups" begin in narrow market niches based on a certain set of environmental criteria. Many small ventures have become giants by correctly observing the environment and responding accordingly. Originally the fast-food industry had two basic customers: teenagers and people on road trips. In the 1950s McDonald's was a relatively small business operating like most other firms in its industry. Yet McDonald's was able to break from the pack because it saw both that the environment was becoming

Grandchildren not required.

McDonald's® isn't just for kids. We've also got lots for adults to enjoy. Now, if you're 60 or over, a small coffee or small soft drink is just 25¢. You can get it anywhere in the U.S. And no other purchase is necessary. So come on in, relax and stay a while. And if the kids want to know where you've been hanging out, get even. Don't tell them. **What you want is what you get.®**

Current prices and participation subject to independent operator decision. Prices may vary.

McDonald's takes advantage of growth opportunities by continually responding to changes in the sociocultural environment. Through ads such as this one, McDonald's targets older consumers, a large and fast-growing segment of the U.S. population.

*Source:* Courtesy of McDonald's Corporation, photographer, Tom Casalini.

even more automobile-oriented and that hurried families needed a place where they could obtain a quick meal. McDonald's, by concentrating on these environmental trends, began focusing its efforts in residential areas rather than on major thoroughfares. It vigorously courted families by standardizing almost every aspect of the restaurant's operation. Thus, parents knew exactly what McDonald's had to offer: inexpensive food with no surprises, and clean restrooms. The result? With fourth-quarter sales in 1992 of $5.71 billion, McDonald's was the biggest fast-food restaurant chain in the world.[17]

The "Magnifying Management" box presents yet another story about environmental change—that of Sears.

**Example:** Sara Lee's recent acquisition of Hanes has proved less than profitable. The environmental trend toward more casual days at the office means fewer women are wearing pantyhose to work, causing a loss of revenue for the hosiery division of Hanes.

## Constraints on Viewing the Environment

How difficult is it to gain an accurate view of the external environment? As you might guess, the answer is *"very* difficult." There is simply a large amount of changing information of which to keep track. This problem is worsened by the added difficulty of how to collect and process the information. The following are common problems in receiving and using information about the external environment.

**1.** *Limited Capability.* Although there is great variation among individuals, human beings are restricted in their cognitive ability to receive, process, and

Sears, Roebuck & Co. has been engaged in a gamble that will, undoubtedly, have a dramatic impact on its future success. The goal of the huge retailer is to make up for not responding very well to major changes in its consumer markets over the last 20 years. Its strategy also places it in highly competitive markets with retailers who have developed considerable experience over that same period.

Sears was incorporated in 1893 and, from the start, it was innovative in supplying consumers' needs. Its most visible and profitable vehicle was the "Sears Big Book," a merchandising catalog that brought "big city" fashion and goods to rural America. In 1897, the catalog was 500 pages long and went to 300,000 homes. It was targeted primarily at small communities that did not have retail stores with large numbers of items or variety within item lines. Thus, the Big Book became the equivalent of the modern mall, supplying almost all consumer needs relatively quickly and inexpensively. A brief litany of products clearly indicates this. Between 1908 and 1937, a consumer could order a home: Sears sold over 100,000 prefabricated homes complete with building plans. Before the Food and Drugs Act of 1906, the catalog listed a number of dubious medicines including laudanum, a notoriously addictive, opium-based headache remedy. Other items shown in the catalog included an automobile, pistols and rifles, models of military planes during WWII, manual-adjusting hospital beds, exercise equipment, and tanning beds. These were in addition to the standard household, clothing, and hardware items that made up the bulk of the products and profits.

# Magnifying Management

## THE SEARS BOUTIQUE?

The Sears marketing magic continued through the first half of this century as it added stores that showcased its catalog items. As Sears grew, however, it became increasingly resistant to change and to anticipating consumer demand. Perhaps the most major trend that it overlooked was the change from a rural society to an urban one. Over time, the catalog and stores were serving a smaller and less affluent group of customers. The items carried were functional, but no longer so fashionable or modern, and Sears became known primarily for its hardware and appliances. Also, it failed to keep pace with changes in retail marketing practices. For example, the catalog division did not provide an 800 number for placing customer orders until 1992. Also, Sears almost completely ignored the development of both discount houses and upscale specialty shops.

Currently, Sears is trying to upgrade its image and profitability by marketing such items as fine perfume, makeup, bath oils, and women's clothing. Managers hope the emphasis on feminine beauty products will provide highly visible merchandise that will attract customers as well as provide the sizable profits associated with these lines; the subsequent goal is that customers will be attracted to other departments of the store.

However, the marketing of these specialty items must address three important concerns. First, manufacturers of top product lines may have only limited interest in Sears as an outlet. Initial response from Chanel Inc. and Estee Lauder Inc., for example, was less than enthusiastic. Second, the display and sale of these products requires much more space and individual sales interaction than Sears has previously committed. Cosmetic centers must be expanded, better decorated, and staffed with more and better trained sales representatives. Third, Sears must convince women that it is the place to shop for these expensive status items. Somehow the image of the chic boutique clashes with the image of Sears as the home of the Die Hard battery and Road Handler tires. The success of Sears's new endeavor clearly depends on how well it addresses these issues.

*Sources:* Andrea Heiman, "Mourning the Passing of `Wish Book' Era," *The Los Angeles Times,* January 29, 1993, E3; Paul Gray, "An Ode to the Big Book," *Time,* February 8, 1993, 6, 66; Gregory Patterson, "Sears Makeover into a Department Store Calls for Enhancing the Role of Cosmetics," *The Wall Street Journal,* April 9, 1993, B1.

store information. When overloaded with information, we often use either just a small amount of the information or very basic decision rules when evaluating the information. Managers are increasingly using electronic means such as executive information systems (discussed in Chapter 21) to deal with these limitations. However, even these systems have limitations regarding how to collect and input data, models to be used for analysis, and how to test various scenarios that represent future alternatives of the organization and the environment.

**2.** *Lack of Information.* As you can guess, it is often difficult to obtain the information necessary to make thoughtful decisions. Either the information is simply inaccessible or the company lacks the structure and/or the systems to collect the data. This is particularly true for small firms. A small retail clothing store may want data about local residents' participation in various social and recreational events. Unfortunately, such data are not part of common records such as the U.S. Census or various economic measures. Most small businesses have neither the expertise nor the funds to conduct their own consumer surveys.

**3.** *Superfluous Information.* Sometimes the opposite may happen, the organization may receive too much information, especially in today's information-rich society. Managers are overwhelmed by all types of print and visual media, as well as specialized databases. Such databases may not be relevant to the problem at hand, however. For example, regional and national economic forecasts frequently assume that future patterns among economic variables will be the same as those of the past. In a changing economy, the data from these models may not be relevant for the organization's planning.

**4.** *Current Organizational Constraints.* The organization's current situation may prevent it from properly evaluating the environment. The firm's present view may bias its ability to perceive the environment as it is changing. The firm may have already spent resources that may be lost if new actions must be taken to conform with the changing view. IBM's failure to anticipate the change in the mainframe computer market due to the rapidly developing capacity of personal computers is such an example.[18]

Viewing the environment in order to anticipate change and respond accordingly is a skill that executives attempt to develop. Certain organizations pride themselves on their ability to develop such skills in their managers and actively work to remove any impediments to doing this. 3M, for instance, has had enormous success. It developed a glue that had an apparent flaw—it did not adhere very well. Given the environment in which glue is sold, such a discovery would normally wind up in a landfill. But one of 3M's employees saw a use for such a product: It could be applied to a small piece of paper that could be used as a marker on other documents. Out of such a sticky situation came 3M's hugely successful Post-it brand notes.[19]

## Dimensions of the External Environment

The ability to assess the external environment and match a firm's capabilities with perceived needs is the key to its ability to survive and prosper. Not doing this can mean the failure of the organization, not to mention an increase in fees paid to bankruptcy attorneys. Perceiving the external environment accurately and responding appropriately may result in a competitive advantage and success.

The external environment may be thought of as differing among organizations in two dimensions, homogeneity and change. The degree of homogeneity is the extent that the external environment varies from being relatively simple (having

## FIGURE 3.7

**Types of External Environments**

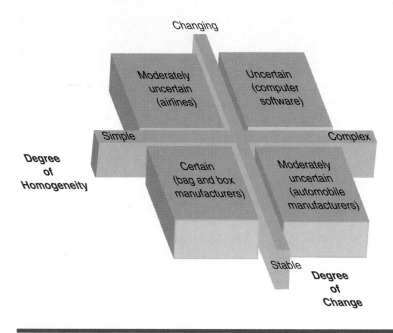

few elements that affect the organization) to relatively complex (having many elements that affect the organization). The degree of change refers to the extent that the external environment is relatively stable (change occurs slowly and/or predictably) or relatively dynamic (change occurs rapidly and/or unpredictably). The interaction of these two dimensions determines the extent of uncertainty that a business faces in its external environment (Figure 3.7).

While all environments have some uncertainty, the least amount occurs in simple, stable environments. Few factors affect the organization, and these factors change in a relatively slow or consistent manner. Bag and box manufacturers operate in such an environment; there are few competitors, and consumers' tastes in bags and boxes do not change dramatically over time. When the environment is high on one dimension and low on the other, a moderately uncertain environment exists for the organization. Airlines operate in a simple but dynamic environment; factors such as competitors, markets, and technology remain relatively constant for all, but fare prices are extremely changeable and unpredictable. On the other hand, automobile manufacturers exist in a complex but stable environment. While the number and combination of firms in the networks of suppliers, advertisers, distributors, and vendors are numerous, basic features of automobiles and competitors remain constant. Dynamic and complex environments are the most uncertain. The computer software industry is characterized by such an environment. New competitors are common, and customer needs change rapidly as does the technology that processes the software.

c   a   r   e   e   r   s

## Steps to Successful Career Planning

There are many factors that will affect your career, some of which you cannot fully anticipate or control. However, one factor that is totally dictated by you is the amount of planning you put into your career development. *Career planning* is the self-evaluation, exploration of alternatives, goal specification, and checking on progress that leads to informed and thoughtful decisions about work activities. The key here is the words "informed and thoughtful decisions." The philosophy of career planning is that it is better for a person to think ahead and make decisions about the future, based on systematically gathered information, than to continue haphazardly through life. Not all decisions that you make will turn out to have the results you hoped for. This often happens when an individual takes a career risk, such as starting a new business. However, it is generally better psychologically, physically, and financially to know why you made a decision than to have it made for you because of your lack of attention or because it seemed like a good idea at the time.

There are five parts to career planning.

1. Self-Evaluation—The initial step is gathering information about yourself. This information should include an assessment of your knowledge, skills, and abilities (what you can do) as well as your goals, needs, and interests (what you want to do). There are many self-help books for this purpose as well as professionally trained counselors.

2. Exploration of Alternatives—This involves gathering data about the various alternatives for work that are available to you. These alternatives should be related to the personal characteristics that you de-

termined in the previous step. For college students, this step would include examining various majors. For graduating seniors, exploration could take the form of identifying various industries in which your skills and interests would be appropriate.

3. Setting Goals—This involves both short- and long-term objectives. It includes such items as the type of position you wish to hold in five years, and how well you wish to perform your job during the next six months. Setting these objectives usually requires an evaluation of work vs. nonwork accomplishments. Everyone wishes to do particularly well in a job. Some individuals are willing to spend exceptionally long hours on work activities. However, others decide to spend more time on personal or family activities.

4. Planning—After setting goals, how do you get there? This includes setting deadlines, determining specific courses of action, personal contacts, training, and resource gathering. The goal of achieving two promotions within six years is going to require an entirely different set of actions than one of being the best employee in your current job four years from now.

5. Checking Progress—How well did you do? Why? If you set goals, then determining your accomplishments relative to these goals is straightforward. Some individuals engage in five-year planning in which each year they develop a plan for the next five years. Such planning requires a clear evaluation of how well previous goals were accomplished.

As we will point out in several subsequent chapters, the degree of uncertainty in the external environment affects many features of the internal environment, including the characteristics of structure, the degree of centralization of decision making, and the extent of formal policy and procedures. As you may be able to guess, increased uncertainty usually corresponds to fewer levels of management, more employees involved in decision making, and fewer policies and procedures. Another way of thinking about this is that an increased level of uncertainty requires a firm to gather and quickly process increased levels of information about the environment. This is necessary in order to read external factors accurately. The firm must be appropriately designed to collect and evaluate this necessary information.

**Teaching Note:** Assign the "Careers Corner" exercise for homework. Have students examine their strengths and weaknesses and then match these to the opportunities and threats of the chosen career. Have students report their findings and discuss possible changes in their career preparation strategy.

## SUMMARY AND REVIEW

- **Define the term *environment*.** The organizational environment includes all those factors that affect the operation of the organization. Its three main components are the general environment, the task environment, and the internal environment.

- **Formulate the components of the general environment, task environment, and internal environment.** The general environment refers to the external factors that affect all organizations, including economic, technological, sociocultural, political-legal, and global dimensions. The task environment includes the external factors that are specific to an organization, such as customers, suppliers, competitors, substitutes, and potential new entrants to the industry. The internal environment includes all the factors that make up the organization, such as the owners, managers, employees, and board of directors.

- **Examine the major factors in the general environment.** The sociocultural dimension of the general environment includes the demographics and the values of the society within which the firm operates. The political-legal dimension refers to the nature of the relationship between various areas of government and the organization. The technological dimension of the general environment refers to the knowledge and process of changing inputs (resources, labor, money) to outputs (goods and services). The economic dimension reflects the overall condition of the complex interactions of economies the world over. The global dimension of the general environment refers to those factors in other countries that affect the organization.

- **Analyze the major factors in the task environment.** Suppliers are organizations and individuals that provide resources to other organizations. Customers buy an organization's goods and/or services. Substitutes are goods or services that may be used in place of those of the business. Competitors are other organizations that produce similar, or, in some cases, identical goods or services. Potential new competitors are companies not currently operating in a business's industry but which have a high potential for entering the industry.

- **Specify the major factors in the internal environment.** Owners can have various degrees of influence and power within an organization. In the smallest organizations, the owner is the sole manager of the firm and fulfills all typical management tasks, but as orga-nizations expand and become more complex, more managers will be brought in. Managers may be divided into three types: strategic or institutional, technical, and operational.

  The relationship between managers and unionized employees is dictated by the negotiated contract between the union and the firm and is more formalized than is the relationship between managers and nonunionized employees. Changing demographics and technology are creating changes in the work force. In corporations, the board of directors has the important task of representing the stockholders in their capacity as owners.

- **Explain the stakeholder approach to viewing the environment.** The stakeholder view of the environment is concerned with those individuals or organizations that could affect the organization. Primary stakeholders have ongoing relationships with the organization through either formal contracts, ownership, or monitoring of a legal obligation of the organization. Secondary stakeholders do not have a formal connection to the firm but may affect it through public opinion. Some secondary stakeholders are environmental groups, community activists, and civil rights groups. The stakeholder view of the environment realizes that stakeholders, though external to the organization, constantly influence the organization. The nature of the relationship between the stakeholders and organization is dynamic, meaning that change is continual. Factors such as government regulation may be an advantage in some cases and a disadvantage in other cases.

- **Distinguish the major ways that an organization can attempt to manage its environment.** There are a number of ways in which the organization can interact with and manage its external environment. All involve attempts by the organization to lessen the threats and take advantage of the opportunities. By managing the environment, the organization reduces the uncertainty of the environment and makes it more predictable and controlled. Some common techniques are public relations, boundary spanning, lobbying, negotiation, forming alliances, and organizational restructuring.

- **Specify why the external environment is important for organizations.** The external environment presents threats and opportunities to the organization that must be addressed. Managers must perceive these threats and opportunities and react accordingly.

- **Assess the environmental forces affecting business.** The "Business Dilemma" box presents an opportunity for you to analyze the environmental forces affecting a business. An analysis of all the environmental factors affecting Amerigo Motors should enable you to make some recommendations about future directions for the company.

## Key Terms and Concepts

environment  *60*

external environment  *60*

general environment  *60*

task environment  *61*

internal environment  *61*

sociocultural dimension  *62*

political-legal dimension  *62*

technological dimension  *64*

economic dimension  *65*

global dimension  *65*

suppliers  *66*

customers  *66*

substitutes  *67*

competitors  *68*

potential new competitors  *68*

stakeholder  *72*

primary stakeholders  *72*

secondary stakeholders  *72*

stakeholder map  *73*

## Ready Recall

1. What is the external environment? How does it affect an organization?
2. Define and give examples of the sociocultural dimension of the external environment.
3. Why is the political-legal dimension of the external environment important for an organization?
4. What are some of the elements of the economic dimension of the external environment?
5. What are stakeholders? How are they related to an organization?

6. What are the elements of the task environment? Which of these are the most important to an organization?
7. Discuss briefly how suppliers and customers may have power over an organization.
8. Briefly describe some techniques that are used by organizations to interact with their environments.
9. What is meant by uncertainty in the external environment?
10. What do organizations try to accomplish when they attempt to manage their external environment?

## Expand Your Experience

1. Interview managers from both a profit and a nonprofit organization about the organizations' stakeholders. Draw a stakeholder map for each organization and compare the members of each map.
2. Interview managers from both a private and a public organization about the techniques each uses to gather information about the external environment and the techniques that are used to attempt to manage the environment. Compare the techniques used by the two different organizations.
3. Analyze the environmental factors affecting either your college or university or your place of employment. How does the organization gather information about these forces? Is it aware that some of these forces are changing? How is it responding to changes in its environment?

## CASE

# *Nike Knows*

Nike Inc. is one of the all-American business success stories. Founded in 1972 with the purpose of selling high-performance track shoes to high-performance athletes, Nike has become an international company by anticipating (some might say creating) the demands of its public.

Philip Knight, founder, current chairman, and CEO of Nike, was a middle-distance varsity runner for the University of Oregon's track team during the late 1950s. After graduation, he enrolled in Stanford University's MBA program. There, he wrote a paper on the start-up of an American running shoe company that designed and marketed shoes while farming out their production to low-cost Asian manufacturers. This concept would become the blueprint for Nike. After graduating from Stanford, Knight worked as an accountant until the mid-1960s.

At that time, he began a working partnership with his college track coach, Bill Bowerman, who had tinkered with track shoes for several years in an attempt to upgrade their quality for his athletes. Knight and Bowerman were employed by the Onitsuka Company of Kobe, Japan, which began incorporating Bowerman's ideas into its Tiger brand footwear. Knight spent his weekends visiting high school and college track meets attempting to sell the shoes, which he transported in the trunk of his Plymouth Valiant. Salesmen from Adidas and Puma, then the top-selling shoes, generally laughed at the "shops" set up on card tables. In the late 1960s, Knight began hiring other ex–collegiate runners who were looking for jobs that had flexible working hours to accommodate their track careers. The first of these, Jeff Johnson, came up with the name Nike for the sales company that Knight had started. He says the image of the Greek goddess of victory, Nike, came to him in a dream. The dream soon became reality.

Nike has always thought of itself as an organization that focuses on athletic performance first and fashion second. Anticipating the strong identification of the general public with star athletes, Nike's first national figure was distance runner Steve Prefontaine. Prefontaine was a free-spirited, world-class runner who often defied sports organizations by running with the word Nike printed on his shirt and shoes, which at that time violated rules concerning advertising. Nike customized Prefontaine's track shoes, and he attributed part of his success to the improved performance allowed by those shoes.

Anticipating the fitness craze of the American public, Nike happened into its future when Bowerman poured liquid latex into his waffle iron. The result was the famous waffle sole that helped promote running and jogging. The comfort and performance of Nike's running shoes with this type of sole was immediately noticeable even to nonathletes who wished to get into shape. The late 1970s were marked by steep growth, based on these running shoes, which reached $269 million in 1980 and allowed Nike to replace Adidas as the No. 1 athletic shoe company in the United States.

After this success, the early 1980s proved to be very difficult for Nike. The period might be characterized as a transition from the group of "athlete-managers," who started the firm and hustled it through its high growth, to the "professional-managers," who joined an established company. Jeff Johnson, the Nike-dreamer, left in 1983 and was shortly followed by several others who had been with Nike since its earliest days. All were multimillionaires due to their stock holdings in the original Nike company before it went public in December 1980. Original investments in the early 1970s of $5,000 were worth $3 million at that time and $30 million in 1993.

Perhaps partly due to this change in top-level managers, Nike slipped in the 1980s. The company chose to continue its emphasis on top athletes. In the 1984 Olympics, Nike athletes won 65 medals, and athletes at all levels favored Nike's products and image. Sales in track and running shoes continued to grow. However, this emphasis on premiere athletes helped blunt Nike's reading of the market. It erred seriously in underestimating the decline of interest in running and the growth of aerobics, especially among women. Nike continued to pursue its basic products with very little change. Reebok, on the other hand, became the Nike of the 1980s by appealing specifically to the aerobics market. By 1986, Nike had fallen to No. 2 behind Reebok in athletic shoe sales in the United States.

Learning from its mistake, Nike began to change its product line in the mid-1980s and became more attentive to the interests of various groups of consumers. It first anticipated the growth of NBA basketball. Signing the fledgling star, Michael Jordan, Nike put together a marketing campaign that blended Jordan's considerable athletic talents with an image created by national TV ads, the Nike logo, carefully coordinated colors, and a specially designed shoe, the Air Jordan. The shoe borrowed heavily from the knowledge gained by Nike of how to make runners' shoes lightweight but structurally advantageous. Literally banking on its reading of the interest of high school, college, and adult basketball players, Nike priced the shoe much higher than other basketball shoes. The response was immediate. Air Jordans were frequently redesigned, recreating a new market each time. In addition, the concept was divided into two additional styles. The Air Force segment was developed for and linked to Charles Barkley and David Robinson, who hit the floor hard. The Air Flight segment was targeted at those individuals who dreamed of playing with the lighter leaping ability of its star, Scottie Pippin. In each case, Nike attempted to project a distinct image of the player, the signature shoe, and the mood of the advertising. Sales were tremendous from the start. An important by-product of this campaign was the emphasis on the idea of a special shoe for each sport. This concept lead quite naturally to several new markets. For example, John McEnroe and Andre Agassi were used to promote lines of tennis shoes.

Nike is continually faced with competitive challenges. For example, teenagers and young adults flocked to the lower-priced Doc Marten clunky work boots and athletic sandals such as those produced by Tevas. In 1993, U.S. distributors of Doc Martens sold 2 million pairs, double the 1992 amount. Tevas expected revenue of $50 million, up from $1.3 million in 1988. All of this has taken place in a declining shoe market. These relatively cheap shoes are targeted at price-conscious individuals who feel that the work boots and sandals fit almost any occasion in which $100+ sneakers had been worn.

*Source:* Sara Collins, "Nike Goes to a Full-Court Press," *U.S. News and World Report,* April 19, 1993, 48–51; Jacqueline Gold, "The Marathon Man?" *Financial World,* February 16, 1993, 32–33; Donald Katz, "The Triumph of Swoosh," *Sports Illustrated,* August 16, 1993, 54–73; Joanne Lipman, "Nike Enters Management Field, Seeking Control Over Endorsers," *The Wall Street Journal,* September 22, 1992, B10; Reporter's Notebook, "Nike Wants to Become Global Household Word," *Footwear News,* October 5, 1992, 15; Gary Strauss and Martha T. Moore, "New Fashions Slam-Dunk Sneakers," *USA Today,* June 24, 1993, 1B–2B; and Lisa Williams, "Philip Knight," *Footwear News,* November–December 1989, 8–12.

## Questions

**1.** Discuss the consumer attitudes and other trends that Nike took advantage of during its growth.

**2.** What can Nike do to monitor and respond to new fashion trends?

**3.** What other projects might Nike undertake at the present time? Why?

---

**STRENGTHEN YOUR SKILLS**

## Deciding on Your Career

This exercise, in addition to the "Careers Corner" boxes throughout the text, is designed to provide you with information to help you make one of the most important decisions you will ever make. Everyone's idea of "enjoy," "decent income," and "successful" is probably different. However, most people would probably describe three goals they expect to achieve from their careers as doing something they enjoy, earning a decent income, and being successful at their jobs. You might expect that intelligence, strong motivation, and hard work would be all it takes to achieve these three goals. Career experts, however, indicate that more than you might imagine depends on your being suited to your career. This exercise is designed to give you some direction in answering the question: "How can I know which careers I'm suited for?"

When examining career options from the perspective, "What careers am I suited for?" some areas you should explore are (1) which career will best match my thinking and problem-solving style? (2) which job will best satisfy my primary motivational needs? (3) what occupational areas do I feel passionate about? This exercise will provide you with some information for answering the first question: "Which career will best match my thinking and problem-solving style?"

### Directions:

**1.** Using what you learned about "right-brain" and "left-brain" thinkers in Chapter 2's exercise, see if you and the others in your group can agree whether each career listed below is a left- or right-brain career choice. Transfer the letter for each career choice listed below to the appropriate column. There will be five answers in each column.

A. Psychology/Psychiatry
B. Arts/Design
C. Investment consulting
D. Public relations
E. Law/Attorneys
F. Marketing management
G. Sales
H. Military
I. Operations/Systems analysis
J. Training/Development

| Left-brain career choices | Right-brain career choices |
| --- | --- |
| | |
| | |
| | |
| | |
| | |

**2.** Refer to page 57, where you totaled your scores for the brain dominance and thinking styles inventory. Transfer your scores below:

Total points for A  _____
Total points for B  _____
Total points for C  _____
Total points for D  _____

A and D primarily represent the left-brain mode, while B and C primarily represent the right-brain mode. Your highest score indicates your strongest thinking style. The next highest is your secondary preference, and so on. If your scores are fairly equal, you show equal prowess in all four modes.

Your primary thinking style _____ (highest score—fill in A, B, C, or D)
Your secondary preference _____ (second highest score)

If your highest score is in A, you share the thinking and problem-solving attributes of people who are characterized as analytical, logical, rational, and critical and who often are talented in technical or quantitative areas.

If you scored highest in B, you're likely to be imaginative, innovative, intuitive, artistic, and visually oriented, and to do well in tasks calling for synthesizing ideas and conceptualizing.

A high score in C indicates that your strong suit is in participative, supportive, empathetic, interpersonal, idealistic, and emotional areas. Many who are dominant in C also are strongly musical and spiritual.

If you score highest in D, you're likely to be practical, pragmatic, decisive, realistic, organized, and detail-minded. Many in this category make excellent managers, planners, and implementers.

3. See the Career Choices chart for a list of careers best suited to your strengths. Highlight or circle the careers that match the primary/secondary letters you identified earlier. If your four scores (A, B, C, and D) are fairly equal, the good news is your thinking style fits a wide range of careers; the bad news is this inventory has done little in helping you narrow your decision field. Although this list does not include all career options, it can serve to steer you in a direction that indicates the type of work that best suits your natural abilities—and that needs to be one of your primary considerations when deciding on a career.

## Career Choices

| Left-brain | | Right-brain | |
|---|---|---|---|
| A | Statistics | B/A | Marketing/Advertising |
| A | Financial analysis | B/A | Library science |
| A | Accounting/Auditing | B/A | Architecture |
| A | Operations/Systems analysis | B/A | Entrepreneurship |
| A | Quality assurance | B/A | Writing |
| A | Economics | B/A | Personnel/Organizational development |
| A | Insurance | B/A | Inventing |
| A/B | Business analysis | B/A | Research science |
| A/B | Research and development | B/A | Editing |
| A/B | MIS/Data processing | B/C | Arts/Design |
| A/B | Engineering | B/C | Behavioral science research |
| A/B | Market research | C/A | Buying/Purchasing |
| A/D | Clinical medicine | C/A | Occupational therapy |
| A/D | Managerial science | C/A | Customer service |
| D | Law enforcement | C/B | Psychology/Psychiatry |
| D | Military | C/B | Sales |
| D/A | Production | C/B | Training/Development |
| D/A | Planning | C/B | Public relations |
| D/A | Marketing management | C/B | Music |
| D/A | Law/Attorneys | C/D | Teaching |
| D/A | Investment consulting | C/D | Nursing/Health care |
| D/A | Office management | C/D | Politics |
| D/C | Supervision/Management | C/D | Social work |
| D/C | Management consulting | C/D | Clergy |

# *The*
# Changing **World** *of*
# Management

## chapter four

# Management Ethics *and* Social Responsibility

**Outline**

**After reading this chapter, you will be able to:**

- Define business ethics and explain its importance to management.

- Detect some of the ethical issues that may arise in management.

- Specify how personal moral philosophies, organizational relationships, and opportunity influence decision making in management.

- Examine how managers can try to foster ethical behavior.

- Define social responsibility and discuss its relevance to management.

- Debate an organization's social responsibilities to owners, investors, employees, and consumers, as well as to the environment and the community.

- Determine the ethical issues confronting a hypothetical business.

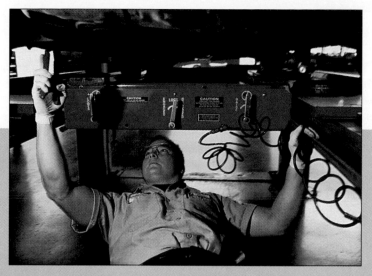

# The Sears Great Auto-Repair Ripoff

According to a poll of consumer protection agencies, auto repairs are the number-one consumer ripoff, with 71 percent of the 51 state and local consumer protection agencies surveyed reporting the most complaints in this area. Nonetheless, few would expect that Sears, Roebuck & Co., one of the nation's best-known businesses, would be responsible for what could be the major auto-repair scandal of the century.

After receiving a number of consumer complaints, the California Department of Consumer Affairs investigated and accused Sears of systematically overcharging its auto-repair customers and proposed revoking the company's license to operate 72 automotive centers in that state. The state conducted a year-long undercover investigation of billing practices at 33 Sears centers from Los Angeles to Sacramento, in which it found that its agents were overcharged nearly

90 percent of the time by an average of $233. After Sears was notified of the results of the investigation, a second undercover operation found that agents were still overcharged by an average of $100. Sears denied the charges, releasing a statement saying that the state's investigation was "very seriously flawed and simply does not support the allegations," adding that its performance was "in accordance with the highest industry standards."

The complaints against Sears began soon after the company implemented a new compensation plan for auto-repair center employees. California officials said that Sears established a quota for parts, service, and repair sales, and that employees were instructed to sell a certain number of shock absorbers or struts for every hour of work. Those who failed to meet their quotas had their hours reduced or were transferred out of the department.

Soon after California's investigation became public, Alabama, Florida, New Jersey, and many other states announced their own investigations of overcharging by

Sears auto-repair centers, and several class-action suits were filed against the company. Although Sears continued to deny that it deliberately schemed to recommend unnecessary repairs, it took action to resolve the issue. In an open letter to Sears customers, the company said it would replace the quota compensation system, conduct unannounced "shopping audits" of its centers, and help organize and fund an industry-consumer-government effort to review auto-repair practices. In 1992, the company agreed to a multimillion-dollar settlement with California and 41 other states that would provide refunds to customers.

A once-proud Sears, Roebuck & Co. was in deep trouble in terms of both consumer perceptions and financial standing. Sears's sales dropped 2 percent during the quarter that the overcharge allegations were made, while competitors such as Wal-Mart increased sales 8 percent during the same quarter.

*Sources:* Harriet Johnson Brackey, "Auto-repair Ripoffs Bane of Consumer," *USA Today,* July 15, 1992, 1A, 10A; Julia Flynn, "Did Sears Take Other Customers for a Ride?" *Business Week,* August 3, 1992, 24–25; Jonathan R. Laing, "Can You Count on Sears?" *Barron's,* May 18, 1992, 10–11, 25–26; News Release from Sears, Roebuck & Co., July 21, 1992; "An Open Letter to Sears Customers," advertisement appearing in *The Wall Street Journal,* June 25, 1992, C22; Gregory A. Patterson, "Sears Will Pay $15 Million, Settling Cases," *The Wall Street Journal,* September 3, 1992, A4.

*introduction*

Sears admitted that its managers "inadvertently created an environment in which mistakes have occurred."[1] After addressing ethical problems related to its pricing practices, Sears addressed other management issues and has achieved new levels of success. This chapter addresses ethics and social responsibility, two of the most important areas in establishing management trust and respect.

In the first half of this chapter we explore the role of ethics in management decision making. First we define business ethics and explain why it is important to understand the role of ethics in management. Next we explore a number of ethics issues to help you recognize such issues when they arise, and we discuss the process through which individuals make ethical decisions. Finally, we look at steps managers can take to improve ethical behavior in their organizations. The second half of the chapter focuses on social responsibility. First we describe the nature of social responsibility and its evolution. Next we explore some important social responsibility issues and the ways companies have responded to them. Finally, we discuss how organizations may manage their operations to fulfill their social responsibilities, including conducting social audits.

## WHAT IS BUSINESS ETHICS?

**business ethics**
Moral principles and standards that define acceptable behavior in business.

The term *ethics* refers to the study of morals and values and focuses on the standards, rules, and codes of conduct that govern the behavior of individuals and groups. **Business ethics** refers to moral principles and standards that define acceptable behavior in business. The public, government regulators, interest groups, competitors, and an individual's personal morals and values determine what is acceptable behavior in business. For example, we generally feel that ethical managers strive for success while being fair, just, and trustworthy.

This chapter does not prescribe a particular philosophy or process as the best or most ethical; it does not tell you how to judge the ethics of others. It will help you detect ethical issues and see how decisions are made within individual work groups as well as within the organization as a whole. Understanding *how* people make ethical decisions should help you improve your own ethical performance. Although we do not tell you what you ought to do, others—your superiors, coworkers, and family—will make judgments about the ethics of your actions and decisions. Learning how to recognize and resolve ethical issues is an important step in evaluating ethical decisions in management.

### Why Is Ethics Important in Management?

In Chapter 1, we said that making decisions is an important aspect of management. Ethical considerations exist in nearly all management decisions. The most basic ethical concerns have been codified as laws and regulations that encourage conformity to society's values and attitudes. At a minimum, managers are expected to obey these laws and regulations. Most legal issues arose as incorrect ethical choices that society deemed unacceptable. However, all actions deemed unethical by society are not necessarily illegal, and both legal and ethical concerns change over time.

You have only to pick up *The Wall Street Journal* or *USA Today* to see how truly difficult it is to deal with legal and ethical issues. For example, small inde-

While competitors accused Wal-Mart of unfair pricing practices, these citizens of a small Massachusetts town waged a successful campaign to prevent the discounter from building a store in their community. They charged that Wal-Mart's buying power and low prices would unfairly reduce competition by taking business away from small, local merchants.

*Source:* © Rick Friedman/Black Star.

pendent drugstores have filed suits against Wal-Mart, charging that the giant retailer has been selling more than 100 products below cost with the intent to shut its competitors out of the local market. Wal-Mart says that it is responding to competitors' prices and that its low administrative costs and great buying power allow it to offer the lowest prices.[2] While a court may decide whether Wal-Mart's activities are legal, this practice creates an ethical issue regarding whether the retailer is using its power unfairly to reduce competition, perhaps at the expense of consumer choice in the long run.

It is important to recognize that business ethics goes beyond legal issues; ethical decisions foster trust among individuals and in business relationships. Unethical decisions destroy trust and make the continuation of business difficult, if not impossible.[3] If you were to discover that a manager had misled you about company benefits when you were hired, for example, your trust and confidence in the company would probably diminish. If you learned that a colleague had lied to you about something, you would probably not trust or rely on that person in the future. From another perspective, mistakes may be unintended or events may alter a manager's intent or commitments. There may be miscommunication concerning promises in some cases. Therefore, business ethics involves many gray areas or borderline decisions about what is ethical or unethical. Martin Marietta, the United States's largest defense contractor, acknowledges the ambiguity in ethics training by having all its employees play a board game called "Gray Matters."

Well-publicized incidents of unethical activity strengthen the public's perception that ethical standards and trust in business need to be raised. American Home Products Corporation, for example, closed two major manufacturing plants and moved some of its operations to Puerto Rico. Although the company claimed that workers would not be harmed by the move, its employees' union, the Oil, Chemical and Atomic Workers International, filed a class-action suit against the company, claiming that the promise not to harm workers had been violated. The company agreed to a settlement, paying 1,180 workers more than $9,000 each.[4] Obviously, the workers questioned the ethics of the plant closing decision. In another instance, Arthur Andersen & Company agreed to pay $3.5 million after being charged with misleading investors of Colonial Realty Company and having improper ties with the Connecticut real estate company, which failed in 1990.[5] Often, questions that start as ethical conflicts turn into legal disputes when cooperative conflict resolution cannot be accomplished. On the other hand, companies sometimes take aggressive

**Example:** Total Quality Management programs in organizations also emphasize ethics and fairness to the consumer. Selling a faulty or poor quality product to consumers is considered unethical by many organizations that strive for zero defects in their products.

**Critical Thinking Challenge:** Have students gather recent examples of unethical or questionable business practices from *The Wall Street Journal, Fortune,* or *Business Week.* Discuss the ethical implications in class. Ask students how they would remedy the situation and why.

**FIGURE 4.1**

**Percentage of People Who Feel These Groups Have Good Moral and Ethical Standards**

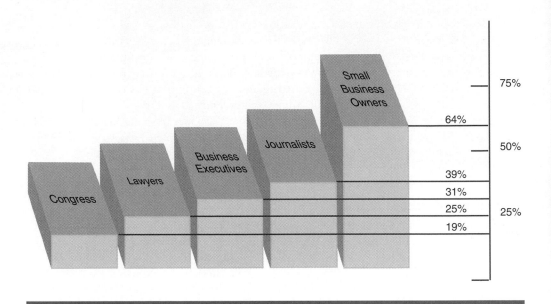

*Source:* Harris Poll of 1,258 adults, reported in *USA Today,* September 3, 1992, 1A.

actions to enforce their own ethical standards. For example, Levi Strauss & Co. severed ties with 30 of its foreign contractors for what the company cited as "pervasive violations of human rights."[6] Such examples support the notion that most decisions can be judged right or wrong, ethical or unethical.

Although they are often not so publicized, there are many ethical firms. Hershey Foods, for example, has built its leadership position as the number-one confectioner in the United States based on fairness, integrity, honesty, and respect. Chaparral Steel produces steel faster than any other mill in America, and it is well known for its openness and fairness to employees. Employees participate in almost all decisions, fostering a high degree of trust between workers and management. Trust goes beyond the absence of time clocks. There is a genuine human concern that employees sense and appreciate. Indeed, most organizations and managers do try to make ethical decisions; however, it is the unethical decisions that are publicized and result in public outcries for change. Figure 4.1 shows the results of a survey of the public's perceptions of the ethics of certain groups.

## RECOGNIZING ETHICAL ISSUES IN MANAGEMENT

Learning to recognize ethical issues is the most important step in understanding ethics in management. An **ethical issue** is an identifiable problem, situation, or opportunity that requires a person or organization to choose among several actions that may be evaluated as ethical or unethical. The "line" between an issue and an ethical issue is the point at which accepted rules no longer serve and the decision maker is faced with the responsibility for weighing moral rules and making a

**ethical issue**
An identifiable problem, situation, or opportunity that requires a person or organization to choose among several actions that may be evaluated as ethical or unethical.

choice. In management, the decision often requires weighing monetary profit or personal interests against what the individual, work group, or organization considers honest and fair.

A good way to judge the ethics of a decision is to look at the situation from several viewpoints: Should a manager pressure his employees into lowering product quality in ways the customer cannot detect in order to reduce costs? Should an engineer agree to divulge her former employer's trade secrets to ensure that she gets a better job with a competitor? Should a personnel manager omit facts about an employee's poor safety record to help the employee find a new job? Should a manager allow her company to discharge toxic chemicals into a nearby river to reduce disposal costs and increase profits for the owners? Such questions require the decision maker to evaluate the ethics of his or her choice.

Many business issues may seem straightforward and easy to resolve, but in reality, a person often needs several years of experience in business to understand what is acceptable or ethical. Many acceptable behaviors in your personal, private life may not be acceptable in business. For example, when does offering a gift—such as season basketball tickets—to a business associate become a bribe rather than just public relations? Obviously, there are no easy answers to such a question. But the size of the transaction, the history of personal relationships within the particular company, as well as many other factors may determine whether others will judge an action as right or wrong. For example, if you give your personal basketball tickets to a friend with whom there is no business relationship, the ethical issue vanishes.

Managers directly influence the ethical issues within an organization because they guide employees and direct the organization's activities. They should be especially concerned about ethical issues related to their organization's impact on the environment, the firm's ethical standards, plant closings and layoffs, employee discipline and benefits, discrimination, health and safety, privacy, and drug and alcohol abuse in the workplace, as well as the achievement of organizational objectives in an efficient and ethical manner. For example, the Texas Water Commission fined chemical company Elf Atochem $10 million after charging that managers at an Atochem plant knew their facility was leaking arsenic-tainted water into nearby lakes and creeks yet took no action to stop the pollution. According to the acting director of the Texas Water Commission, "Major corporations with substantial resources and an ethical conscience know what to do when confronted with information that demands prompt action to prevent a threat to their neighboring community."[7] (The fine was later reduced through negotiations between the company and the state, but negative feelings toward the company remain strong in the local community.) In this case, the state judged the plant managers' decision as unethical and took action on behalf of citizens harmed by that decision. This example also illustrates how an ethical issue can become a legal issue for a company.

Ethics is also related to the culture in which a business operates. In the United States, for example, it would be inappropriate for a businessperson to bring an elaborately wrapped gift to a prospective client on their first meeting: The gift could be viewed as a bribe. In Japan, however, it is considered impolite *not* to bring a gift. In Mexico, a small payment called *la mordida* (the "bite") may be considered necessary for doing business. In the United States such a payment would be considered a bribe. Experience with the culture in which a business operates is critical to understanding what is ethical or unethical. Understandably, there is considerable debate over whose ethics should apply in international business. U.S. managers need to respect other cultures, establish standards, and avoid violating U.S. or foreign laws when doing business globally.

**Critical Thinking Challenge:** Discuss with your class whether ethics can be taught. Discuss ways to increase ethical awareness and understanding and list these on the board for discussion.

**Example:** Smokeless tobacco products including snuff and chewing tobacco are not available for purchase in the United Kingdom. The products are said to cause both mouth and gum cancer as well as to harm teeth. These products are sold legally in the United States and other countries.

To help you understand ethical issues that perplex managers today, we will explore some ethical issues that may affect management decisions. Obviously, it is not possible to discuss every issue that may arise, but a discussion of a few can help you recognize the ethical decisions and issues that managers have to deal with daily.

## Ethical Issues in Management

As stated earlier, a decision becomes an ethical issue when accepted rules no longer apply and the decision maker must use his or her own moral principles and standards to decide what is right or wrong. Managers have an obligation to ensure that their ethical decisions are consistent with company standards, codes of ethics, and policies—as well as community and legal standards. The following represent some examples of ethical issues from different management areas.

**Organizational Relationships.**    Relationships with subordinates, coworkers, and superiors may result in ethical issues such as maintaining confidentiality in personal relationships; meeting obligations, responsibilities, and mutual agreements; and avoiding undue pressure that may force others to behave unethically. For example, ethical issues arise when employees are asked to lie to customers and other employees about the quality of a product, as when a supermarket employee is told to tell customers that the seafood is fresh when, in fact, it was previously frozen. A manager may ask employees to do things that are in conflict with their personal ethics, or the organization may provide only vague or lax supervision on ethical issues, providing the opportunity for unethical behavior. Managers who offer no ethical direction to employees create many opportunities for manipulation, dishonesty, and conflicts of interest.

**Example:** Employees who overstate their expense account purchases for meals and lodging or who turn in bogus receipts are committing an unethical act by stealing from their company.

**Operations and Communications.**    Many opportunities for unethical activity exist in the area of operations and communications. Surveys by the Michael Josephson Ethics Institute reveal that between 20 and 30 percent of middle managers have written deceptive internal reports.[8] When Beech-Nut began experiencing financial troubles in the early 1970s, it found a supplier that sold apple juice concentrate at 20 percent below market price. After it discovered that the apple juice concentrate was a chemical cocktail rather than real apple concentrate, the company covered this up because it was trying to lower production costs.[9] At first, it was just an ethical issue, but when employees lied to the government about the cover-up and destroyed records, they broke the law. Many companies have gotten into ethical trouble by covering up safety defects or by not being honest about the true quality of products. An ethical issue exists when a company is not truthful about important information related to product quality.

**Example:** Wal-Mart was recently questioned about the ethics of advertising products made in the USA when many were in fact manufactured and assembled outside the United States.

**Employee Relations.**    The area of human resource management is a minefield of ethical issues. The process of acquiring, developing, and compensating people to fill the organization's human resource needs generates many ethical issues. For example, testing procedures used in hiring personnel may violate an individual's rights. The disclosure of personnel records and personality tests represents an ethical issue when it violates workers' privacy. Performance appraisals are another ethical issue if appraisals are based on favoritism and political opportunism. Decisions regarding promotions, transfers, separations, and financial compensation that are not based on objective criteria will provide opportunities for conflicts.

## BUSINESS DILEMMA

*You're the Manager ...What Would You Do?*

THE COMPANY:    **Bingo's Pizza**

YOUR POSITION:    **Co-owner**

THE PLACE:    **Dallas, Texas**

Bingo's Pizza began delivering pizzas in 1969 when, with his sister, Jon McClanahan decided that customers would respond to having the pizza delivered for a small fee. Originally operating out of the Fort Worth area, Bingo's tested its delivery system and found that consumer response was overwhelming. Publicity for the company came quickly and easily as people were delighted and supportive of the delivery service. The company grew from one small store in Fort Worth to five, with an additional nine in the Dallas area, four in Waco, and two in Bryan/College Station, with negotiations beginning for units in Houston.

The success of the delivery concept brought on competition from the major pizza manufacturers who tried their hand at delivery. Jon's sister and partner Stephanie was a computer whiz, having majored in computer science at Texas A&M University. Stephanie thought that if they could develop an information database on computer, they could become more efficient and gain significant insights into consumer buying behavior and consumption patterns. Jon felt their current system could use improvement and instituted a test of the computerized ordering system. With this system, customers would call in and give their phone number. If they had ordered from Bingo's before, their address and previous order information would appear on the screen. The order taker could then ask if they wished to order the same kind of pizza. The system proved to be efficient, allowing for more accurate tracking of peak times and for ingredients to be ordered so as to maximize product freshness.

After successfully testing this system, Jon and Stephanie put the computerized order network in place in all of their restaurants. After three months of success, they wanted to gain some publicity for this new system, just as they had when they first instituted delivery service. After several days of attempting to write press releases, Stephanie had an idea. "I know we've only been running this system for a few months," she said. "But, let's give an award to the family that eats the most Bingo's pizza. McDonald's gave their best customer in Lubbock a card good for free McDonald's food and they received publicity across the country. We can use the giveaway as a springboard to talk about the computer system." Jon had not thought of that angle, and he liked the idea. He asked Stephanie to determine the "winner" and get back to him.

Stephanie found that the biggest consumer of Bingo's pizza worked outside Waco and had ordered a pizza every weekday for the past three months that the system had been in place. Stephanie put together a program to give him a nice prize—Bingo's gift certificates—and arranged for the newspaper to accompany her to make the award. You must decide how to proceed with this plan.

### Questions

1. Critique Stephanie's plan.
2. What are the potential ethical issues associated with this plan?
3. How would you proceed?

---

Ethical issues related to discrimination and prejudice affect business activities at many levels. Shoney's, Inc., the nation's third-largest restaurant chain, settled a lawsuit in 1992 charging that it discriminated against blacks in hiring and promotion. The company was required to set aside $105 million to compensate victims of discrimination.[10] Discrimination based on race, sex, age, or other identifiable characteristics is an ethical issue and can become a legal issue—when managers or company policy fails to control or prevent discrimination.

Strategies that management uses to develop human relations programs can also create ethical concerns. Strategies for motivating employees, such as methods of reward and punishment, can lead to unethical behavior. For example, if managers reward employees for achieving results without concern for how those results were achieved, they may send the wrong message to employees about

**Comment on Box:** As students critique the plan be sure to have them discuss privacy of information, ethics of maintaining such a detailed database on customers, and the possibility of the data being used by employees or others with access to the data for alternate reasons.

**Example:** Hooters Restaurant and Bar was recently sued by female employees over the tight T-shirts and shorts they were required to wear as waitresses. Many believe the uniforms led to harassment and were discriminatory against women.

**TABLE 4.1**

**Questions to Consider in Determining Whether an Action Is Ethical**

- How do other people in the organization feel about the action? Would they approve of your doing it?
- Does your firm have a specific policy on the action?
- Are there any industry trade groups that provide guidelines or codes of conduct that address this issue?
- Would this activity be accepted by your coworkers? Is it customary in your industry?
- Will your decision or action withstand open discussion with coworkers and managers and survive untarnished?
- How does the decision align with your personal beliefs and values?

what activities are acceptable and even encourage unethical actions to achieve results. In the vignette at the beginning of this chapter, for example, Sears's compensation plan may have encouraged employees to sell unnecessary repairs. Companies must consider the long-term effects of punishment/reward systems before selecting a policy. Issues such as long lunch breaks and the use of company resources are human relations issues that have ethical content.

## Making Decisions about Ethical Issues

Recognizing specific ethical issues can be difficult in practice. Whether a decision maker recognizes an issue as an ethical one often is determined by characteristics of the issue itself. Managers tend to be more concerned about issues that affect those close to them, as well as issues that have immediate rather than long-term consequences. Thus, the perceived intensity of an ethical issue may vary substantially, with only a few issues receiving scrutiny and many issues receiving less attention.[11]

Table 4.1 lists some questions you may want to ask yourself and others when trying to determine whether an action is ethical. While open discussion of ethical issues does not eliminate ethical problems, it does promote both trust and learning in an organization.[12] When people feel that they cannot discuss what they are doing with their coworkers or superiors, an ethical issue may exist. Once a person has recognized an ethical issue and can openly discuss it with others, he or she has begun the ethical decision-making process.

## THE ETHICAL DECISION-MAKING PROCESS

It is difficult for some people to believe that an organization can exert a strong influence on ethical behavior. In our society, we want to believe that we, as individuals, control our own destiny. However, ethical decisions within the organization are often made by work groups, not by individuals. Most new employees in highly bureaucratic organizations have almost no input into how things will be done in terms of basic operating rules and procedures. Employees may be taught management tactics and the way to resolve problems. Although many personal ethics issues may seem straightforward and easy to resolve, most managers make ethical decisions within the context of their organizations.

**Example:** In another example of ethics in marketing, Wal-Mart changed its advertising slogan to "Always Low Prices" from "Always the Lowest Price" when consumers questioned its pricing schemes.

**FIGURE 4.2**

**Factors Influencing Behavior**

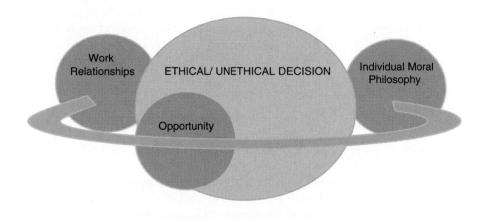

To better understand the significance of ethics in management decisions, it is helpful to examine the factors that influence how a person makes ethical decisions: an individual's moral philosophy, and relationships within the workplace, and opportunity (Figure 4.2).

## The Role of Moral Philosophies in Ethical Behavior

A **moral philosophy** is a set of principles that describe what a person believes is the right way to behave. People learn these principles by interacting with family members and social groups and in formal education. Individuals may be guided by different moral philosophies, however, and each has its own concept of what is ethical and rules for behavior. This, in turn, influences what a person identifies as ethical and how strongly he or she feels about those issues. Moral philosophies can be broken into two categories: utilitarian philosophies and ethical formalism.

Believers in the **utilitarian philosophy** seek the greatest satisfaction for the largest number of individuals. Utilitarians evaluate the ethics of an action or decision on the basis of its consequences for all affected persons. When confronted with an ethical issue, the utilitarian manager weighs the costs and benefits of the consequences of all possible alternatives, and then chooses the one that benefits the most people.

In contrast, **ethical formalism** focuses on human rights and values and on the intentions associated with a particular behavior. Ethical formalists judge an action by whether it infringes on individual rights or universal rules such as the Golden Rule. In business, ethical formalism is consistent with the idea that basic principles of acceptable conduct exist. A manager adopting a formalistic philosophy believes that he or she has a moral obligation to safeguard workers' health and safety and to make decisions that support individual rights without regard for the cost. A manager's decision to avoid discrimination in hiring is based on formalistic principles of equality.

Sometimes both ethical formalism and utilitarianism influence the same decision. For example, although Nike is headquartered in Oregon, which has only a

**moral philosophy**
A set of principles that describe what a person believes is the right way to behave.

**utilitarian philosophy**
A philosophy where believers seek the greatest satisfaction for the largest number of individuals.

**ethical formalism**
A philosophy that focuses on human rights and values and on the intentions associated with a particular behavior.

**Example:** A candy and confections maker purchased the mailing list of people enrolled in a weight-loss program. Sales of chocolate were highest to this group. The weight-loss program feels the marketing of candy to this group is unethical and now no longer sells its list to food products companies.

5 percent minority population, after a boycott by the African-American community, the company improved both its hiring of minorities and minority representation. Nike increased the percentage of minorities in its work force from 11 percent to 25 percent between 1990 and 1993.[13] It may be that Nike acted in its own interests, weighing the costs of having limited minority representation in its work force against its culturally diverse market. The benefits of being more culturally diverse may have outweighed the costs of implementing a minority hiring program. On the other hand, ethical formalism may have entered into the decision as a concern to avoid discrimination and a desire to have a fair representation of minorities. Regardless of the moral philosophy in operation, most people would agree that Nike just did "the right thing."

## Work Relationships

Successful managers achieve their company's objectives in part by influencing their employees' behavior. If the pressure to produce a result—such as increasing profits—is especially great, the pressure to perform is also strong. How an employee achieves goals is shaped by the moral climate of the organization, standards set by supervisors, and the conduct of coworkers.

The greater a person's exposure to unethical behavior, the greater is the likelihood that he or she will act unethically. Moreover, employees' perceptions of the ethics of their coworkers and managers are often a stronger predictor of behavior than what employees personally believe to be right or wrong.[14] For example, an employee who sees her coworkers regularly take home company supplies for personal use may engage in the same behavior even if she personally believes it is wrong. Thus, the overall moral climate in an organization sets the standards for employee conduct. Managers should keep this in mind.

The authority of an employee's superiors also affects ethical behavior. Powerful managers can affect employees' daily activities and directly influence behavior by implementing the company's standard of ethics. If managers act unethically, employees may feel that such activities are acceptable within that organization; if a manager asks an employee to do something unethical, the employee may feel pressured to perform the activity even though he feels it is wrong. For example, the ethical issues at Sears described in the opening vignette may have been due to management pressure. In addition to a major scandal relating to overcharges at Sears Automotive Centers in California and New Jersey, some insurance agents at the company's Allstate Insurance subsidiary say they felt pressured by management to cut corners, cheat, or ignore underwriting guidelines to keep their jobs. In a few instances, agents say they were fired for failing to meet quotas.[15] Consequently, the role of management is extremely important in fostering ethical behavior in an organization.

Managers who do not view ethics as important may encourage employees to act contrary to their personal ethics. Some employees succumb to organizational pressures rather than following their own values, rationalizing their decisions by maintaining that they are simply "following orders." This rationalization has several weaknesses, however:

1. People who work in organizations can never fully abdicate their personal, ethical responsibility when making business decisions. Claiming to be an agent of the corporation—"just following orders"—is not accepted as a legal excuse and is even less defensible from an ethical perspective.

2. It is difficult to determine what is in the best interest of the organization. Short-term profits earned through unethical behavior may not be in the long-run interest of the company.

3. A person in a business has a responsibility to parties other than the organization. Stakeholders and other concerned publics must be considered when making ethical decisions.[16]

Because employees' perception of the ethics of their coworkers influence their behavior, it should not be surprising that work groups within an organization have a strong impact on ethical behavior. In fact, work groups, or the perceived ethicalness of work groups, represent the most important factor affecting daily ethical decisions. High levels of conflict between employees may directly or indirectly influence the amount of unethical behavior within an organization.[17] The more conflict that exists within an organization, the lower the perceptions of the ethicalness of the work group. Because coworkers are so important in accomplishing daily business activities, it is important to support the ethics of the work group. If managers can provide direction and encourage ethical decision making, then the work group becomes a force to help the individuals make better ethical decisions. When managers allow greater participation with regard to the design and implementation of projects, conflict within the work groups is reduced and ethical behavior may improve.

**Critical Thinking Challenge:** Have students examine the mission statements of public corporations and report on the ethical issues discussed in the annual reports and missions. Most corporations today have added an ethical component to their mission. Have students compare and critique the selected mission statements.

## The Role of Opportunity

Opportunity refers to conditions that limit unfavorable behavior or reward favorable behavior. Thus, a person who is rewarded or is not punished for unethical behavior is likely to repeat the behavior; a person who receives no reward or is punished for behaving unethically probably will not repeat the action. For example, if a Texas Instruments Inc. employee is caught violating the company's ethical standards, as spelled out in its code of ethics, the employee may be reprimanded, placed on probation, suspended, or even fired. Such sanctions send a message to Texas Instruments employees that unethical or illegal behavior will not be tolerated and make it less likely that an employee will repeat the action that resulted in punishment.

The greater the reward and the smaller the punishment for unethical behavior, the greater is the likelihood that unethical behavior will recur. For example, huge rewards and lack of punishments created opportunities for some savings and loan association (S&L) managers to engage in fraudulent lending and accounting practices in the 1980s and probably encouraged other S&L managers to engage in unethical practices as well. Negligence and fraud in the savings and loan industry are believed to have contributed to the failures of a number of S&Ls, which the federal government has been attempting to salvage at an estimated cost of $500 billion. Indeed, opportunity to engage in unethical behavior has been found to be a better predictor of unethical behavior than one's personal beliefs or the beliefs of peers.[18]

## IMPROVING ETHICAL BEHAVIOR

Understanding how people choose their standards of ethics and what prompts a person to engage in unethical behavior can help improve ethical behavior in organizations. Establishing and enforcing ethical standards and policies can help

## THE CODE OF ETHICS OF IMPERIAL OIL

Imperial Oil Limited, based in Toronto, has sought to define its corporate values and to encourage ethical behavior among its employees. The company developed a 23-page booklet entitled *Our Corporate Ethics,* which delineates its values and addresses specific ethical issues arising from its business activities. Employees may use the booklet as both a guide to the values of Imperial Oil and its subsidiaries and a tool to justify their actions to others.

Imperial's code first establishes the company's core values: integrity; employee well-being; quality, excellence, and continuous improvements in company practices and products; and a stimulating work environment. The code next offers general guidance for Imperial's relationships with employees, customers, sales associates, competitors, the community, suppliers and contractors, and shareholders. It stresses the significance of each of these groups to the company and the importance of maintaining integrity in relationships with each group. For example, because Imperial Oil benefits from the Canadian free-market system, its code of ethics discourages anticompetitive activities, mandating instead the offering of goods and services of superior value.

Imperial's code of ethics then addresses some specific business issues

related to the environment, transactions with stakeholders, conflicts of interest, gifts and entertainment, confidential information, dealings with the government, insider trading, outside directorships, outside business activity, and Canadian competition. Regarding the environment, for example, the code specifies that the company and its subsidiaries incorporate environmental considerations into the design of products, facilities, and operations, as well as into all long-range planning, and that it support local environmental efforts, such as recycling. And, to help minimize conflicts of interest, employees are asked not to give or accept gifts and entertainment except where they are of modest value (generally, less than $25), infrequent, and appropriate.

Finally, the booklet provides an "Ethics Checklist" for employees to use when confronted with an ethical issue. Employees should attempt to

answer the following questions about their decision: Is it legal? Is it fair? Can I defend it? The code suggests throughout that employees who have questions about a particular activity should consult with their supervisor or a company ethics advisor.

Like most codes of ethics, Imperial Oil's code does not address every situation that may crop up in business. Rather, it attempts to provide guidelines for and values by which to judge actions taken in the name of the company. By delineating its corporate values and providing guidance in several general areas, Imperial Oil may foster greater ethical behavior by its employees.

*Source:* Adapted from *Our Corporate Ethics,* Imperial Oil Limited (111 St. Clair Ave. W., Toronto, Ont., M5W 1K3), March 1990.

---

**Comment on Box:** After discussing Imperial's code, have students discuss its merit. Why is every situation not included in the code? Should it be? Also discuss what training is needed for employees in ethical behavior and awareness.

**codes of ethics**
Formalized rules and standards that describe and delineate what the organization expects of its employees.

reduce unethical behavior by prescribing which activities are acceptable and which are not and by removing the opportunity to act unethically.

It is difficult for employees to determine what is acceptable behavior if a company does not have uniform policies and standards. Without such policies and standards, employees are likely to base decisions on how their peers and superiors behave. Professional **codes of ethics** are formalized rules and standards that describe and delineate what the organization expects of its employees. As an example, the "Ethics Encounter" box describes the code of ethics of Imperial Oil of Canada.

Codes of ethics and ethics-related corporate policy foster appropriate behavior by limiting the opportunity to behave unethically through the use of punishments for violations of the rules and standards. The enforcement of such codes and policies through rewards and punishments increases the acceptance of ethical

**TABLE 4.2**

## Ashland Oil's Code of Business Conduct

The mission of Ashland Oil, Inc., is to maximize the value of its shareholders' investment in the company. In pursuit of this goal, the company's employees will comply with this Code of Business Conduct. This Code applies to Ashland Oil, Inc., its divisions and all subsidiaries in which Ashland holds a majority interest. It also applies to the officers, employees, and agents of these entities. Anyone who violates the Code will be acting outside the scope of his or her employment and will be subject to disciplinary action.

The Code is based on the following general principles:

1. *Compliance with the Law*   Ashland and its employees will abide by the letter and the spirit of all applicable laws and regulations, and will act in such a manner that the full disclosure of all facts related to any activity will always reflect favorably upon the company.
2. *Adherence to High Ethical Standards*   Ashland and its employees will adhere to the highest ethical standards of conduct in all business activities, and will act in a manner that enhances Ashland's standing as a vigorous and ethical competitor within the business community.
3. *Responsible Business Citizenship*   Ashland and its employees will act as responsible citizens in the communities where the company does business.

*Source:* Ashland Oil, "Code of Business Conduct," 1994, 4.

standards by employees. Table 4.2 describes Ashland Oil Inc.'s Code of Business Conduct, which includes the directive that anyone who violates the code will be subject to disciplinary action.

Encouraging **whistle blowing**, when employees expose an employer's wrongdoing, is another way to foster ethical behavior. Typically, whistle blowers report wrongdoing to outsiders, such as the media or government regulatory agencies. Chester Walsh, for example, was awarded $13.5 million by the federal government for blowing the whistle on an Israeli bribery scheme involving General Electric. GE pleaded guilty in 1992 to charges connected to a plan to cheat the U.S. government out of $42 million from F110 engine and maintenance contracts with Israel. GE paid the government $62 million to settle the case. Walsh received his money, the largest such award ever, under a program the government maintains to provide incentives to whistle blowers connected to government contracts.[19] Increasingly, companies are establishing programs to encourage employees to report illegal or unethical practices internally so that they can take steps to remedy problems before they result in legal difficulties or generate negative publicity.

A survey of *Fortune* 1,000 companies conducted by Bentley College found that over 40 percent are holding ethics workshops and seminars, and about one-third have set up ethics committees. Some 200 major U.S. corporations have recently appointed ethics officers, usually senior managers of long experience, to serve as ombudsmen and encourage whistle blowing.[20] For example, Textron's Bell Helicopter has an ethics officer who addresses workers' complaints and questions, provides training sessions, helps coordinate meetings for a senior management ethics committee, and monitors broader corporate ethics issues.[21] Companies must develop open communication and trust in order to nurture ethical decisions. It is difficult without ethics training, clear channels of communication, and ethics

**whistle blowing**
The act of an employee's exposing an employer's wrongdoing; typically such reporting is to outsiders, such as the media or government regulatory agencies.

**TABLE 4.3**

## A Method to Make Ethical Choices

1. *Listen and learn.* Recognize the problem or decision-making opportunity that confronts your organization, team, or unit. Don't argue, criticize, or defend yourself—keep listening and reviewing until you are sure you understand others.
2. *Identify the ethical issues.* Examine how coworkers and consumers are affected by the situation or decision at hand. Examine how you feel about the situation and understand the viewpoint of those people who are involved in the decision or the consequences of the decision.
3. *Create and analyze options.* Try to put aside strong feelings such as anger or desire for power and prestige and come up with as many alternatives as possible before developing an analysis. Ask everyone involved for ideas about which options offer the best long-term results for you and the company. Which option will increase your self-respect even if, in the long run, things don't work out the way you hope?
4. *Identify the best option from your point of view.* Consider it and test it against some established criteria such as respect, understanding, caring, fairness, honesty, or openness.
5. *Explain your decision and resolve any differences that arise.* This may require neutral arbitration from a trusted manager or taking "time out" to reconsider, consult, or exchange written proposals before a decision is reached.

*Source:* Tom Rusk with D. Patrick Miller, "Doing the Right Thing," *Sky,* August 1993, 18–22.

advocates within the company to provide support throughout the organization. Some firms, including NYNEX and Martin Marietta, have set up ethics hotlines which employees can call in order to discuss ethics issues anonymously. Most calls do not result in action to deal with alleged ethical misconduct, but the employees are able to work through ethical problems. There is no substitute for individuals' thinking through ethical dilemmas and feeling comfortable with their choices. Table 4.3 provides a method for the individual to create an ethical choice.

If a company is to maintain ethical behavior, its policies, rules, and standards must encourage ethical decision making and be enforced through a system of rewards for proper behavior and punishments for unacceptable behavior.

To strengthen its long-standing ethics program and to ensure compliance with all legal requirements, Phillips Petroleum Company created a new Corporate Compliance and Ethics office. The office has a 24-hour, toll-free ethics hotline, giving employees and the public the opportunity to express their concerns in a confidential way.

*Source:* Courtesy of Phillips Petroleum Company.

**FIGURE 4.3**

**The Pyramid of Social Responsibility**

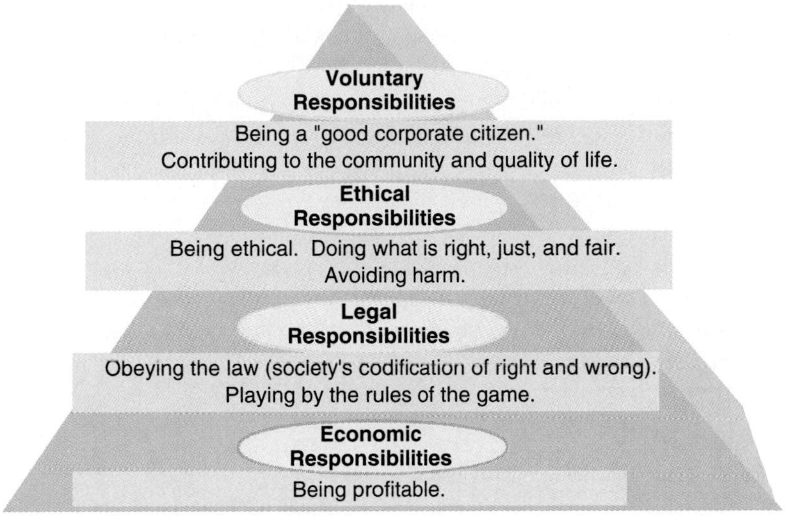

*Source:* Adapted from Archie B. Carroll, "The Pyramid of Corporate Social Responsibility: Toward the Moral Management of Organizational Stakeholders," *Business Horizons* 34 (July/August 1991):  42.

Reducing unethical behavior is a goal no different from increasing profits or cutting costs. The manager sets a goal—achieving greater ethical behavior among company employees—and measures the outcome. If the number of employees making ethical decisions regularly is not increasing, the manager needs to determine why and take corrective action through stronger enforcement of current standards and policies or by strengthening the standards and policies themselves. Ethical behavior occurs when a plan is developed and successfully implemented.

## THE NATURE OF SOCIAL RESPONSIBILITY

Many consumers and social advocates believe that businesses should not only make a profit but also consider the social implications of their activities. **Social responsibility** is the obligation a business assumes to maximize its positive impact and minimize its negative impact on society. While many people use the terms *social responsibility* and *ethics* interchangeably, they do not mean the same thing. Ethics relates to an *individual's* values and moral standards and the resulting decisions he or she makes, whereas social responsibility is a broader concept that concerns the impact of an *organization's* activities on society. From an ethical perspective, we may be concerned about a particular savings and loan officer's conflict of interest concerning specific properties or businesses; from a social responsibility perspective, we might be concerned about the impact that the operation of that savings and loan may have on the community's well-being. Thus, ethics is a component of social responsibility, because having a positive impact on society involves ethical considerations.

There are four dimensions of social responsibility:  economic, legal, ethical, and voluntary (including philanthropic) (Figure 4.3).[22] A business whose *sole*

**social responsibility**
The obligation a business assumes to maximize its positive impact and minimize its negative impact on society.

**Teaching Note:** Be sure to differentiate ethics and social responsibility as these terms are easily confused by students. Stress that social responsibility is a broader term with more serious implications for the organization. For example, the Exxon Valdez oil spill had far-reaching social responsibility effects on Alaska, its citizens, local wildlife, etc.

objective is to maximize profits is not likely to consider its social responsibility, although its activities will probably be legal. Profits are the economic foundation of the pyramid in Figure 4.3, and legal responsibilities are the next step. We have discussed ethical responsibilities, and voluntary responsibilities are additional activities that may not be required but which promote human welfare or goodwill. Legal and economic concerns have long been acknowledged, but voluntary and ethical issues are more recent concerns.

A business that is concerned about society as well as earning profits is likely to invest voluntarily in socially responsible activities. For example, Smith & Hawken, a mail-order gardening supply company, donates 10 percent of its pretax income to environmental causes.[23] Such businesses win the trust and respect of their employees, customers, and society by implementing socially responsible programs, and, in the long run, increase profits. Companies that fail to act responsibly risk losing consumers and may encourage the public and government to take action to restrict their activities. Most companies today consider being socially responsible a cost of doing business.

**Critical Thinking Challenge:** Have students discuss the strategic advantages of being socially responsible. List ways social responsibility can benefit an organization in the long term. Possibilities include goodwill, reputation, ability to attract better employees, long-term survival and profitability, etc.

## Arguments for and against Social Responsibility

Although the concept of social responsibility is receiving more and more attention, it is still not universally accepted. Among the arguments against social responsibility are the following.

1. It sidetracks managers from the primary objective of business—earning profits. Every dollar donated to social causes or otherwise spent on society's problems is a dollar less for owners and investors.

2. Participation in social programs gives businesses greater power, perhaps at the expense of particular segments of society.

3. Some people also question whether business has the expertise needed to assess and make decisions about social problems.

4. Many people believe that social problems are the responsibility of government agencies and officials, who can be held accountable by voters.

There are equally strong arguments for asking business to take responsibility for social issues, including the following:

1. Business helped to create many of the social problems that exist today, so it should play a significant role in solving them, especially in the areas of pollution reduction and toxic waste cleanup.

2. Businesses should be more responsible because they have the financial and technical resources to help solve social problems.

3. As members of society, businesses should do their fair share to help others.

4. Socially responsible decision making by business organizations can prevent increased government regulation.

5. Social responsibility is necessary to ensure economic survival: If businesses want educated and healthy employees, customers with money to spend, and suppliers with quality goods and services in years to come, they must take steps to help solve the social and environmental problems that exist today.

## Evolution of Social Responsibility

Before the twentieth century, businesses were largely responsible for defining how they would interact with society; their sole motivation was profit. Consumers could sue businesses that engaged in unscrupulous activities, but such action was expensive and the chances of winning slim. There were no consumer advocates or government agencies to protect consumers and society against deceptive advertising, defective products, or practices that harmed people and the environment. The rule for consumers was *caveat emptor*—let the buyer beware. Generally, consumers were so anxious for new products that they did not want government intervention. As more and more businesses entered the marketplace, however, competition grew fierce and abuses continued until it was inevitable that the government would have to intervene to protect consumers and workers.

Congress passed laws to reduce the monopolistic tendencies of big business and force companies to provide safer products and work environments. Federal agencies such as the Federal Trade Commission and the Securities and Exchange Commission were set up to protect consumers and police industry. Businesses gradually began to develop a sense of social responsibility when they realized that promotion, sales, and efficient production alone would not increase profits.

Finding that the key to increasing sales is to produce things that people want and need, by the early 1950s businesses began to ask customers what they needed and to develop products to meet those needs. At the same time, employees were demanding better working conditions, and management and owners began to listen to them. Companies also began to seriously address the public outcry for product safety and reliability.

The 1960s represented a decade of change on nearly every front. Civil rights abuses, deterioration of the environment, concerns about product safety, and the Vietnam War led Americans to reexamine their values and priorities. People began to recognize that manufacturing processes and waste-disposal methods were harming the environment, and that women and minorities had been denied their full rights in the workplace. The public began to demand that everyone— individuals, government, business—take greater responsibility for their actions. IBM, Levi Strauss, McDonald's, American Express, and other companies saw that the way to build a positive image with the public and to ensure future sales was to act in a socially responsible manner. This trend continues today, with more and more businesses adopting socially responsible management techniques, manufacturing processes, charitable donation policies, and otherwise trying to respond to the demands of society.

**Example:** TicketMaster, the seller of concert tickets, is being sued by both consumers and entertainers who feel the company has a virtual monopoly on setting ticket prices and handling fees for concert tickets.

## SOCIAL RESPONSIBILITY ISSUES

As with ethics, managers consider social responsibility on a daily basis as they deal with real issues. Among the many social responsibility issues they must consider are their organizations' relations with owners, investors, employees, customers, the environment, and the community. Social responsibility is a dynamic area with issues changing constantly in response to society's desires. This section highlights a few of the many social responsibility issues that managers face; as managers become aware of and work toward the solution of current social problems, new ones will certainly emerge.

**Example:** Dry cleaning establishments have been questioned about the disparity in pricing for women's and men's garments. Women, on average, pay more than men for having shirts dry cleaned. Department stores are questioned for providing free alterations on men's business suits, but charging for the same services provided to women.

## Relations with Owners and Investors

Businesses must first be responsible to their owners, who are primarily concerned with earning a profit or a return on their investment in a company. In a small business, this responsibility is fairly easy to fulfill because the owner(s) personally manages the business or knows the managers well. In larger businesses, particularly corporations owned by thousands of stockholders, assuring responsibility to the owners becomes a more difficult task.

A business's responsibilities to its owners and investors, as well as to the financial community at large, include maintaining proper accounting procedures, providing all relevant information to investors about the current and projected performance of the firm, and protecting the owners' rights and investments. In short, a business must maximize the owners' investment in the firm.

## Employee Relations

Another issue of importance to business is its responsibilities to employees, for without employees a business cannot carry out its goals. Employees expect businesses to provide them a safe workplace, to pay them adequately for their work, and to tell them what is happening within their company. They want employers to listen to their grievances and treat them fairly.

Congress has passed several laws regulating safety in the workplace, many of which are enforced by the Occupational Safety and Health Administration (OSHA). Labor unions have also made significant contributions to achieving safety in the workplace and improving wages and benefits. Most organizations now recognize that the safety and satisfaction of their employees are a critical ingredient in their success, and many strive to go beyond what is expected of them by the law. Healthy, satisfied employees supply more than just labor to their employers, however. Employers are beginning to realize the importance of obtaining input from even the lowest-level employees to help the company reach its objectives.

**Example:** In addition to day care for children, some organizations are providing elder care for the elderly parents of employees. Many women, in particular, in the "Sandwich Generation," have primary care responsibilities for both their children and their elderly parents.

A major social responsibility for business is providing equal opportunities for all employees regardless of their gender, age, race, religion, or nationality. Women and minorities have been slighted in the past in terms of education, employment, and advancement opportunities; additionally, many of their needs have not been addressed by business. For example, women—who continue to bear most child-rearing responsibilities—often experience conflict between those responsibilities and their duties as employees. Consequently, day care has become a major employment issue for women, and more companies are providing day-care facilities as part of their effort to recruit and advance women in the work force. Today, many Americans believe business has a social obligation to provide special opportunities for women and minorities to improve their standing in society.

## Consumer Relations

**Example:** To better address consumers, many companies, including Procter & Gamble, have added a 1-800 number to their product labels so consumers can reach company representatives.

**consumerism**
The activities undertaken by independent individuals, groups, and organizations to protect their rights as consumers.

A critical issue today is business's responsibility to customers. Consumers look to business to provide them with satisfying, safe products and to respect their rights as consumers. The activities undertaken by independent individuals, groups, and organizations to protect their rights as consumers are known as **consumerism**. To achieve their objectives, consumers and their advocates write letters to companies, lobby government agencies, make public service announcements, and boycott companies whose activities they deem irresponsible.

The spotted owl controversy symbolizes the difficulty in balancing economic development with resource preservation. Environmentalists want the government to protect the spotted owl's habitat in national forests under the Endangered Species Act as a way of preserving the ecosystem of the Pacific Northwest. Timber companies want to continue logging in national forests and blame environmentalists for the loss of at least 30,000 jobs since 1990 and the decrease in timber sales from public land.

*Source:* © Chris Pietsch/Register-Guard.

Many of the desires of those involved in the consumer movement have a foundation in John F. Kennedy's 1962 consumer bill of rights, which highlighted four rights. The *right to safety* means that business must not knowingly sell anything that could result in personal injury or harm to consumers. Defective or dangerous products erode public confidence in the ability of business to serve society. They also result in expensive litigation that ultimately increases the cost of products for consumers. The *right to be informed* gives consumers the freedom to review complete information about a product before they buy. This means that detailed information about ingredients, risks, and instructions for use is to be printed on labels and packages. The *right to choose* ensures that consumers have access to a variety of products and services at competitive prices. The assurance of both satisfactory quality and service at a fair price is also a part of the consumer's right to choose. The *right to be heard* assures consumers that their interests will receive full and sympathetic consideration when the government formulates policy. It also assures the fair treatment of consumers who voice complaints about a purchased product.

## Environmental Issues

Consumers want not only a multitude of products that improve the quality of life but also a healthy environment so that they can maintain a high standard of living over their lifetimes. Environmental responsibility has become a leading issue in the 1990s, as business and the public acknowledge the damage done to the environment by past generations. Today's consumers are increasingly demanding that businesses take a greater responsibility for their actions and impact on the environment.

**Animal Rights.**   One area of environmental concern in society today is animal rights. Probably the most controversial business practice in this area is the testing of cosmetics and drugs on animals who may be injured or killed as a result of the testing. Animal-rights activists say that such research is morally wrong because it harms living creatures. Consumers who share this sentiment may boycott companies whose products are tested on animals and take their business instead to companies such as The Body Shop and John Paul Mitchell Systems, which do not test products on animals. However, researchers in the cosmetics and pharmaceutical industries argue that animal testing is necessary to prevent harm to human beings who will eventually use the products.

Business practices that harm the habitats of endangered wildlife are another environmental issue. For example, a controversy has developed over the logging of old-growth forests on the west coast of the United States, the habitat of the endangered spotted owl. Animal rights activists argue that it is wrong to allow the extinction of any species, and that the spotted owl's habitat must be preserved at any cost. But workers at logging companies argue that logging in the spotted owl's habitat provides much-needed jobs in that area, as well as products essential to consumers. The federal government ended the debate by temporarily banning logging in the spotted owl's habitat, but similar controversies over the habitats of other endangered species continue around the world.

**Pollution.**    A major issue in the area of environmental responsibility is that of pollution. Surveys by the Roper Organization Inc. found that 62 percent of Americans believe that pollution is a very serious threat to their health and the environment, and 75 percent say that business should handle the cleanup.[24]

Water pollution results from the dumping of toxic chemicals and raw sewage into rivers and oceans, from oil spills, and from the burial of industrial waste in the ground where it may filter into underground water supplies. Fertilizers and insecticides used in farming and grounds maintenance also drain into water supplies with each rainfall. Water pollution problems are especially notable in heavily industrialized areas. Medical waste—such as used syringes, vials of blood, and AIDS-contaminated materials—has turned up on beaches in New York, New Jersey, and Massachusetts, as well as in other locations. Society is demanding that water supplies be clean and healthful to reduce the potential danger from polluting substances.

Air pollution is usually the result of smoke and other wastes emitted by manufacturing facilities, as well as carbon monoxide and hydrocarbons emitted by motor vehicles. In addition to the health risks posed by air pollution, when nitrous oxides and sulfur dioxides from the emissions of manufacturing facilities react with air and rain, acid rain results. Acid rain has contributed to the deaths of many valuable forests and lakes in North America as well as in Europe. Air pollution may also contribute to the "greenhouse effect," in which carbon dioxide collects in the earth's atmosphere, trapping the sun's heat and preventing the earth's surface from cooling. Chlorofluorocarbons also harm the earth's ozone layer, which filters out the sun's harmful ultraviolet light; this too may be a cause of the greenhouse effect. The greenhouse effect is highly controversial, however, and some scientists doubt its existence.

Land pollution results from the dumping of residential and industrial waste, strip mining, forest fires, and poor forest conservation. Manufacturers in the United States produce approximately 50 million tons of contaminants each year. Land pollution is tied directly to water pollution because many of the chemicals and toxic wastes that are dumped on the land eventually work their way into the water supply. Dumping of toxic wastes in Love Canal (near Niagara Falls, New York) caused later residents to experience high rates of birth defects and cancer before they were forced to abandon their homes by the U.S. government in the late 1970s and early 1980s. In Brazil and other South American countries, rain forests are being destroyed—at a rate of one acre per minute—to make way for farms and ranches, at a cost of the extinction of the many animals and plants (some endangered species) that call the rain forest home. Large-scale deforestation also depletes the oxygen supply available to humans and other animals.

Related to the problem of land pollution is the larger issue of how to dispose of waste in an environmentally responsible manner. Consumers contribute approximately 1,500 pounds of garbage per person each year to landfills, and landfill space

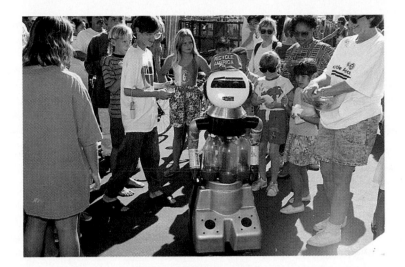

As part of its new national education initiative on recycling, WMX Technologies, Inc., is taking "Cycler," an interactive robot made of recyclable materials, to schools and community events to inform children about the importance of recycling. In another recycling initiative, WMX has informed its major suppliers that it wants to buy goods made with recycled materials and has developed a "Green Pages" guide for employees that lists sources of recycled goods.

*Source:* Courtesy of WMX Technologies, Inc.

is declining as old landfills are filled up before new ones can be developed. By the year 2005, 70 percent of the nation's landfills will be full.[25] Also compounding the waste-disposal problem is the fact that more than 50 percent of all garbage is made out of plastic, which does not decompose. Some communities have passed laws that prohibit the use of plastics such as Styrofoam for this reason.

**Response to Environmental Issues.**   Partly in response to federal legislation such as the National Environmental Policy Act of 1969 and partly due to consumer concerns, businesses are responding to environmental issues. Many small and large companies—from Smith & Hawken to Exxon, Walt Disney Co., Chevron, and Scott Paper—have created a new executive position, a vice president of environmental affairs, to help them achieve their business goals in an environmentally responsible manner.

Many firms are trying to eliminate wasteful practices, the emission of pollutants, and the use of harmful chemicals from their manufacturing processes. Sutter Home Wineries, E&J Gallo Winery, and other California vineyards, for example, are switching to organic farming methods that do not rely on pesticides or herbicides in the production of their wines.[26] Other companies are seeking ways to improve their products. Automakers from all over the world are trying to develop automobiles that run on alternative fuels—electricity, solar power, natural gas, and methanol.[27] Wal-Mart highlights products it deems environmentally responsible so consumers can readily identify them; it also sponsors recycling centers in the parking lots of some stores. Many businesses have turned to *recycling*, the reprocessing of previously used materials—aluminum, paper, glass, and some plastic—for new purposes. Kellogg's, for example, uses recycled paper in the packaging of its cereal products. Such efforts to make products, packaging, and processes more environmentally friendly have been labeled "green" business or marketing by the public and media.

It is important to recognize that, with current technology, environmental responsibility requires tradeoffs. Society must weigh the huge costs of limiting or eliminating pollution against the health threat posed by the pollution. Environmental responsibility imposes costs on both business and the public. Although people certainly do not want oil fouling beautiful waterways and killing wildlife, they insist on low-cost, readily available gasoline and heating oil. People

**Example:** In response to land pollution, many organizations are reducing the packaging component of their products or are packaging products in refillable or recyclable containers. As an example, laundry detergents like Tide and Cheer brands have developed smaller, more concentrated formulas of products to reduce packaging and waste.

do not want to contribute to the growing garbage-disposal problem, but oftentimes refuse to pay more for "green" products packaged in an environmentally friendly manner, to recycle as much of their own waste as possible, and to permit the building of additional waste-disposal facilities. Thus, managers must coordinate environmental goals with other social and economic ones.

## Community Relations

A final issue for businesses concerns responsibilities to the general welfare of the communities and societies in which they operate. Many businesses simply want to make their communities better places in which everyone can live and work. Although such efforts cover many diverse areas, some of their actions are especially noteworthy. The most frequent way that businesses exercise their community responsibility is through donations to local and national charitable organizations. Corporations contribute $6.1 billion annually to charitable organizations and social programs, about 1 percent of their pretax profits.[28]

After realizing that the current pool of prospective employees lacks many basic skills necessary to work, many companies have become concerned about the quality of education in the United States. Recognizing that today's students are tomorrow's employees and customers, firms such as Kroger, Campbell's Soup, Kodak, American Express, Apple Computer, Xerox, and Coca-Cola have donated money, equipment, and employee time to help improve schools in their communities and around the nation. They provide scholarship money, support for teachers, and computers for students, and they send employees out to tutor and motivate young people to stay in school and succeed. Although some members of the public fear business involvement in education, others believe that if business wants educated employees and customers in the future, it must help educate them now.

Business is also beginning to take more responsibility for the hard-core unemployed—some mentally or physically handicapped and some homeless. Organizations such as the National Alliance of Businessmen fund programs to train the hard-core unemployed so that they can find jobs and support themselves. Days Inns of America, a hotel chain, hires homeless people as reservations sales agents and allows them to stay in hotel rooms until they can afford their own housing. Some of Days Inns' formerly homeless employees have used the skills they learned there to go on to better, higher-paying jobs.[29] In addition to fostering self-support, such opportunities enhance self-esteem and help people become productive members of society.

## SOCIAL AUDITS

To determine whether it is adequately meeting the demands of society as well as its own social responsibility objectives, an organization can measure its performance through a voluntary social audit. (The term *audit* is derived from the Latin word that means "to listen.") The **social audit** is a systematic examination of the objectives, strategies, organization, and performance of the social responsibility function. In a social audit, managers evaluate a company's long- and short-term contributions to society to determine whether the firm's social responsibility approach is working. The social audit can also enhance a company's social responsibility efforts by helping management evaluate the effectiveness of current programs and recommend activities for the future. The "Ethics Encounter" box profiles Ben & Jerry's, which uses social audits to assist its efforts to be socially responsible.

---

**Example:** John Paul Mitchell Systems donates a portion of the sales from its hair care products to local zoos and wildlife parks in the United States. The company is against animal testing of any of its products and gives money to support animals and their health.

**social audit**
A systematic examination of the objectives, strategies, organization, and performance of the social responsibility function.

Ben Greenfield and Jerry Cohen opened their first ice cream shop in a converted gas station in Burlington, Vermont, in 1977, investing $12,000 in some secondhand equipment. Their rich, all-natural ice cream, full of sweet crunchy bits of cookies and candies, quickly became popular. Soon they were packaging more and more ice cream to sell in local restaurants and grocery stores, gaining shelf space in 150 stores across the state. By 1990, Ben & Jerry's Homemade Inc. topped $70 million in sales on 6 million gallons of ice cream. From the beginning, Cohen and Greenfield have incorporated a strong sense of social responsibility—to their employees, community, and the world at large—into their business.

When Cohen and Greenfield first went into business together, they wrote their own rules, including a corporate mission statement requiring the firm to initiate "innovative ways to improve the quality of life of a broad community—local, national, and international." But by the early 1980s, the two former "hippies" felt they were losing control of their wildly successful company—its growth, creativity, organization, and values; Jerry Greenfield even dropped out of the business for a time. When Cohen considered selling the company at one point, a friend pointed out to him that he could make it into whatever he wanted. Cohen soon developed the concept of "caring capitalism," which meant donating part of the company's profits to worthy causes, as well as finding creative ways to improve the quality of life of the firm's employees and the local community. Greenfield rejoined the company soon thereafter.

When Ben & Jerry's Homemade went public in 1984, Cohen first limited the sale of the company's stock to Vermont residents, with the idea that if local residents were part owners of the firm, the community would share in the success of the business. Then, in 1985, Cohen set up the Ben & Jerry's

# Ethics Encounter

## BEN & JERRY'S HOMEMADE BALANCES SOCIAL RESPONSIBILITY AND GROWTH

Foundation, which is dedicated to facilitating social change through the donation of 7.5 percent of Ben & Jerry's yearly pretax profits.

Ben & Jerry's social concern can be seen most clearly in some of the company's products. One of the firm's ventures is the Peace Pop, an ice cream bar on a stick, from which 1 percent of the profits are used to build awareness and raise funds for peace. To help preserve endangered rain forests, the company purchases rain forest nuts for its Rainforest Crunch ice cream, thus providing a market for goods produced by the rain forests. It also buys brownies made by homeless people for its Chocolate Fudge Brownie and Brownie Bars.

Ben and Jerry extend their social awareness to their own employees. A seven-to-one salary ratio at the firm limits the salaries of top executives to seven times those earned by the lowest-paid workers. This helps give all employees a sense of working together as a team. And when it seemed that the company was expanding too quickly (it grew from 150 people to 300 almost overnight), company executives made a conscious decision to slow growth in order to ensure that the plant's family atmosphere and the company's core values would not be lost. Employees also get three pints of ice cream a day, free health club memberships, and a partially subsidized company child-care center.

Ben & Jerry's continues to promote things and events of value to the community—instead of buying advertising on TV, on radio, or in newspapers. The company sponsors peace, music, and art festivals around the country and tries to draw attention to the many social causes it undertakes. One such cause is opposition to bovine growth hormone (a substance injected into cows to increase milk production), because Greenfield and Cohen fear that its use will drive small dairy farmers out of business. A local venture is the Giraffe Project, which recognizes people willing to stick their own necks out and stand tall for what they believe; local customers of Ben & Jerry's scoop shops nominate the recipients of Giraffe Commendations. And the company hopes to open a new scoop shop in the Soviet Republic of Karelia, from which the profits will be used to fund cultural exchanges between Americans and Soviets.

Each year, Ben & Jerry's asks someone to conduct a social audit to measure whether the company is fulfilling its self-stated obligations. The company will likely continue to struggle in its efforts to balance growth and profits with social responsibility, and its customers—mostly 25- to 45-year-olds—will probably continue to buy its ice cream so that they may feel that they are doing something good for society.

*Sources:* Erik Larson, "Forever Young," *INC.* 10 (July 1988): 50–62; Maxine Lipner, "Ben & Jerry's: Sweet Ethics Evince Social Awareness," *COMPASS Readings,* July 1991, 22–30; and Eric J. Wieffering, "Trouble in Camelot," *Business Ethics* 5 (January/February 1991): 16–19.

# Corner

## Planning a Career in Business Ethics and Social Responsibility

As a prospective employee, you should be concerned not only about opportunities for jobs in the areas of ethics and social responsibility, but also how to make the right choices in your daily decisions. Part of the challenge in getting a job is selecting a company that matches your own personal value system and which will treat you fairly. Some companies are known for their ethical and socially responsible approaches to doing business. One such company is FedEx, which offers an unusual challenge—a grievance procedure that involves a trial by the employee's peers. Called the Guaranteed Fair Treatment (GFT) approach, it is a part of the culture of the company. GFT provides an opportunity for an employee who feels he or she has been treated unfairly to appeal a manager's decision.

Approximately one-third of *Fortune* 1,000 firms have an ethics officer, a position most companies have created only in the last five years, who is usually responsible for:

- meeting with employees, the board of directors, and top management to discuss and provide advice about ethics issues;

- disseminating a code of ethics;

- creating and maintaining an anonymous, confidential service to answer questions about ethical issues;

- taking actions on possible ethics code violations; and

- reviewing and modifying the code of ethics.

Many career opportunities are emerging today in the field of business ethics and social responsibility. Don't look for specific titles such as director of ethics and social responsibility if you are interested in a specific job in this area. Titles range from director of ethics to ombudsman to vice president. Job descriptions vary as widely as job duties, falling sometimes within the legal department and, in some companies, human relations, labor relations, or even accounting. Most of the people holding such ethics/social responsibility positions probably never had a formal college course in the area.

There are entry-level jobs that provide an opportunity for advancement in ethics departments. Companies need competent employees to manage hotline services, help individuals interpret codes of ethics, and generally counsel and advise others on how to do the right thing. For example, NYNEX, which employs 81,900, received as many as 2,700 calls to its ethics hotline in a recent year. Fifty percent of the callers were seeking information or clarification about corporate codes of ethics while only 10 percent of the calls dealt with wrongdoing. The remaining 40 percent involved human interaction issues such as how to talk to a superior.

To prepare yourself for a career in the area of business ethics and social responsibility, there are several suggestions. Take courses in business ethics, legal environment, and business and society. Some elective courses in moral philosophy or sociology may also be useful. Subscribe to a magazine such as *Business Ethics*, a popular trade journal that provides information about companies that have ethics programs or are involved with socially responsible activities. By learning more about how the ethics/social responsibility function is being performed within organizations, you will be prepared to apply for a job and be knowledgeable in matching your interests with a company's needs. Although there are a small number of jobs available today in this emerging area, you could be in the forefront of a developing concern that has much potential for career advancement. If you prepare yourself properly, especially if you can get a part-time job or internship in a large firm with an ethics department, you will greatly enhance the probability of developing a career in business ethics and social responsibility.

*Sources:* Susan Gaines, "Holding Out Halos," *Business Ethics* 8 (March/April 1994): 21; Judith Kamm, "Ethics Officers: Corporate America's Newest Profession," *Ethics: Easier Said Than Done,* Summer 1993, Josephson Institute, 38; Robert Levering and Milton Moskowitz, *The 100 Best Companies to Work for in America* (New York: The Penguin Group, 1994), 123.

Managers should conduct a social responsibility audit on a regular basis—perhaps annually—to develop a good benchmark of where the company has been and where it is going. Conducting the audit involves five fundamental activities:

1. Identifying ongoing and new programs that support socially responsible actions and programs,

2. Determining the resources and the cost of resources that are required to support the programs and the benefits that have been achieved to date,

3. Identifying organizational objectives and making certain that social responsibility activities support those objectives,

4. Defining the reasons for undertaking particular social responsibility programs or supporting certain causes, and

5. Evaluating the success of each social responsibility program undertaken and identifying benchmark goals for future involvement.

The concept of auditing implies an official examination of social responsibility activities; however, these audits are often designed to occur informally. Most of the problems that arise in an audit can be attributed to the fact that there are few standards for evaluating social responsibility. The resulting information from the audit should be as quantitative and accurate as possible, depicting both the positive and negative findings.

A social audit can indicate to a firm whether it is living up to the expectations of society. It can pinpoint areas where the firm can take additional steps to maximize the positive effect of its activities as well as to minimize their negative impact. Used effectively, the social audit provides a tool for managers to help their firms become better citizens by contributing positively to society.

## SUMMARY AND REVIEW

- **Define business ethics and explain its importance to management.** Business ethics refers to moral principles and standards that define acceptable behavior in the world of business. Ethical considerations exist in nearly all management decisions. Ethical decisions foster trust among individuals and in business relationships; unethical ones destroy trust and make the continuation of business difficult, if not impossible.

- **Detect some of the ethical issues that may arise in management.** An ethical issue is an identifiable problem, situation, or opportunity requiring a person or organization to choose from among several actions that must be evaluated as ethical or unethical. Managers should be concerned about ethical issues related to their organization's impact on the environment, the firm's ethical standards, plant closings and layoffs, employee discipline and benefits, discrimination, health and safety, privacy, and drug and alcohol abuse in the workplace, as well as the achievement of organizational objectives in an efficient and ethical manner.

- **Specify how personal moral philosophies, organizational relationships, and opportunity influence decision making in management.** People are guided by different moral philosophies (a set of principles setting forth what is believed to be the right way to behave), each having its own concept of rightness or ethicalness and rules for behavior. Two categories of moral philosophies are utilitarian and ethical formalism. Organizational relationships—including the influence of managers, coworkers, and the work group—are important factors in ethical decision making. The greater a person's exposure to unethical behavior by managers and coworkers, the greater is the likelihood that the person will behave unethically. Opportunity is a set of conditions that punish unfavorable behavior or reward favorable behavior. A person who is not rewarded or is punished for unethical behavior is not likely to repeat the behavior.

- **Examine how managers can try to foster ethical behavior.** Managers can change the organizational environment to promote ethical behavior by employees by limiting opportunity. Formal codes of ethics and policies reduce the incidence of unethical behavior by informing employees what is expected of them and providing punishments for those who fail to comply. Additionally, managers can work to minimize conflict and tensions within work groups and try to create an environment in which ethical decisions will be made.

• **Define social responsibility and discuss its relevance to management.** Social responsibility is the obligation an organization assumes in order to maximize its positive impact and minimize its negative impact on society. Socially responsible businesses may win the trust and respect of their employees, customers, and society, and in the long run increase profits. There are strong arguments both for and against social responsibility by businesses.

• **Debate an organization's social responsibilities to owners, investors, employees, and consumers, as well as to the environment and the community.** Organizations must be responsible to their owners and investors, who expect to earn a profit or a return on their investment in the company. Businesses must maintain proper accounting procedures, provide all rel-

evant information to investors about the current and projected performance of the firm, and protect the owners' rights and investments. In relations with employees, businesses are expected to provide a safe workplace, pay employees adequately for their work, and treat employees fairly. Consumerism refers to the activities undertaken by independent individuals, groups, and organizations to protect their rights as consumers. Consumers' basic rights are spelled out in John F. Kennedy's 1962 consumer bill of rights: the right to safety, the right to be informed, the right to choose, and the right to be heard. Increasingly, society expects business to take greater responsibility for the environment. Among the issues of environmental responsibility are animal rights, and water, air, land, and noise pollution. Many businesses engage in activities to make the communities in which they operate a better place in which everyone can live and work.

• **Determine the ethical issues confronting a hypothetical business.** The "Business Dilemma" box presents an ethical dilemma at Bingo's Pizza. Using the material presented in this chapter, you should be able to analyze the ethical issues present in the dilemma, evaluate the McClanahans' plan, and develop a course of action for the firm.

## Key Terms and Concepts

business ethics *92*
ethical issue *94*
moral philosophy *99*
utilitarian philosophy *99*

ethical formalism *99*
codes of ethics *102*
whistle blowing *103*
social responsibility *105*

consumerism *108*
social audit *112*

## Ready Recall

1. Define business ethics. What groups determine whether a business activity is ethical?
2. What is an ethical issue?
3. Distinguish between the utilitarian philosophy and ethical formalism. Supply an example of a business that has used each to make a decision.
4. How does opportunity contribute to unethical decisions in business?
5. What is a code of ethics? How can managers reduce unethical behavior in business?
6. Distinguish between ethics and social responsibility.
7. List and discuss the arguments for and against social responsibility by business. Can you think of any additional argu-

ments (for or against)? Can you take a position (for or against) and defend it?
8. What responsibilities does a business have toward its employees?
9. What responsibilities does business have with regard to the environment? What steps have been taken by some responsible businesses to minimize the negative impact of their activities on the environment?
10. What is a social audit? How can a social audit help a business improve its social responsibility activities?

## Expand Your Experience

1. Discuss some recent examples of businesses engaging in unethical practices. Why do you think the business chose to behave unethically? What action might the business have taken?
2. Discuss with your class some possible methods of increasing ethical standards in business. Do you think that business should regulate its own activities or should the federal gov-ernment establish and enforce ethical standards? How do you think businesspeople feel?
3. Find some examples of socially responsible businesses in newspapers or business journals. Explain why you believe their actions are socially responsible. Why do you think a given company chose to act as it did?

---

**CASE**

# *Bootleg and Counterfeit Recordings*

---

Many look-alike counterfeit products can be difficult to distinguish from the originals. It has been estimated in the United States that more than $8 billion worth of counterfeit and bootleg music recordings are sold each year. Even more annual sales of counterfeit movies ($18 billion) and counterfeit computer software (over $39 billion) occur. Often, counterfeit recordings—illegal copies of major-label releases—are sold at flea markets or by street vendors as original or factory seconds for two to three dollars less than retail. The piracy potential is enormous and growing because consumers want rare, unreleased recordings as well as lower-priced "bootlegs" of current hit recordings. There are three categories of recording piracy: bootlegging, counterfeiting, and piracy. Bootlegging involves the unauthorized sale of previously unreleased recordings, such as concert performances and studio outtakes. Counterfeiting is the duplication of previously released sound recordings as well as of the original packaging. Piracy is the manufacture and sale of previously released recordings, often in foreign markets, in order to bypass established distribution channels.

Federal and state laws about illegal record sales include federal copyright and trademark statutes, state consumer protection and trade statutes, and unfair competition laws. With respect to bootlegging, a 1971 federal statute makes it illegal to sell or distribute an unauthorized recording. However, such a recording can be owned for private collecting purposes. This means that selling bootlegs is copyright infringement, punishable by up to five years in prison and $250,000 in fines; however, individuals currently owning bootleg records and CDs for their private enjoyment are not in violation of federal laws.

While the United States has tight laws against music piracy, European laws allow the sale, without the artist's consent, of unreleased concert and studio material more than 20 years old. As a result, music pirates manufacture the albums overseas and then ship them into the United States. The Beatles, Rolling Stones, The Who, and Elton John are a few of the artists whose concerts and alternate recordings are available in large quantities.

The Recording Industry Association of America (RIAA) is continually lobbying for stricter laws and regulations against those who sell unauthorized recordings. The RIAA works closely with the United States Customs Service to enforce regulations on imported recordings. Money laundering, smuggling, and copyright infringement charges can be brought against anyone caught shipping unauthorized recordings.

During the past three decades, the FBI, CIA, and the RIAA have tried to control the sales of bootleg and counterfeit recordings in the United States. In fact, in the last few years, seizures of unauthorized recordings have reached new levels. As many as 100,000 duplicated, counterfeit recordings have been seized in some raids. Counterfeit cassettes and albums from unauthorized sources have often been third- or fourth-generation copies with poor sound quality. However, the emergence of compact disc technology permits high-quality digital reproduction, making it very difficult to distinguish between the original and the counterfeit.

With the explosion of compact disc bootlegs on the market, the RIAA was formed to protect the rights of recording companies, who say that music pirates rob them of profits. Because illegal counterfeits and pirates duplicate already-released albums and are sold at a cheaper price, recording companies fear that consumers will purchase these illegal products instead of legitimate releases, perhaps not even realizing they are buying fakes. The RIAA points out that consumers pay when recording companies and retailers raise prices to make up for business lost to counterfeiters. Inasmuch as counterfeiters pay no royalties to performers and do not incur any of the normal costs associated with the development of hit recordings, the RIAA says that counterfeiters are cheating performers of royalties and may also be contributing to the disappearance of less popular artists by squeezing companies' financial resources and decreasing their profit margins. Big-name artists may represent only 15 to 16 percent of a company's total performers, but their profits subsidize less profitable music such as classical and jazz.

Recording companies also fear that illegal copies of their albums will be sold in countries where they do not have widespread distribution. For example, to increase interest in an upcoming concert by LaToya Jackson in Poland, her agents wanted to distribute her albums there. However, they discovered she was already known and very successful. Music piracy is common in Poland (along with many other less developed countries), and Jackson's albums are pirated by street vendors and shopkeepers. The imported legitimate recording would cost $15 while the pirated recording sells for only $1.

While record companies are concerned about losing profits, musical artists are concerned with bootleggers making money from recordings not chosen for release. Bruce Springsteen, who once thought that bootlegs formed a bond with his fans, has now changed his mind and helps the RIAA prosecute bootleggers. Many artists believe that it is acceptable for people to hear the bootlegs or even to trade them, but they do not condone other people profiting illegally from their recordings. Even strong advocates of bootlegging have heard such poor copies of certain recordings that they question some operators' motives.

Counterfeiters, pirates, and a few collectors claim that counterfeiting and pirating are ethical, which raises more complex questions concerning bootlegging. Consumers want to collect live recordings and studio outtakes. If someone made an inferior copy of an actual album and sold it at a lower price, it would be illegal counterfeiting—a form of stealing. But what about alternative recordings made at live concerts? "What about the rights of collectors?" asked one bootlegger recently arrested during a police sting operation. Many bootleggers argue that because the albums they distribute are not legitimately released by a recording company, they cannot be accused of taking profits away from recording companies and musical artists. They claim that if these recordings were available through sanctioned channels they would buy them. Often the prices they pay for a bootleg recording far exceed what a legitimate record company would charge. A bootleg copy of Paul McCartney's 1989–1990 concert tour sold in record shops in Illinois for $75 for a two-CD set—a high price by any standard!

As for consumers buying bootlegs instead of the legitimate releases, most collectors are avid fans of the artists they collect, so they purchase all the legitimate releases. When they want still more recordings by the artist, they turn to bootlegs. Other bootleggers compare themselves with historians trying to preserve music's heritage. "In the Middle Ages, the church controlled all the artists. If some work of art didn't fit in with their religious doctrines, the church would put it away or destroy it. That's what record companies are doing—destroying history," says one boot-

legger who has pirated such things as outtakes of John Lennon and live concerts of Prince and Miles Davis. Many fans believe that studio outtakes and concerts represent more of the artist's true talent without the intervention of sampling, synthesis, sound enhancing, overdubbing, voice layering, etc.

There are several different sources for bootlegged music—radio simulcasts, television specials, DAT (digital audio tape), and recordings by audience members—which still represent the main source of live concert recordings. However, there are more illegal ways of getting recordings of rare songs. Many times someone working for the artist or even a band member makes recordings that are later bootlegged. Reportedly, many of Paul McCartney's studio session tapes were stolen by a former member of one of his post-Beatles backup bands. However, the majority of bootlegs come from deals struck between bootleggers and collectors who have rare masters of songs.

A new ethical issue has emerged, as Garth Brooks—top-selling country music recording artist of the 1990s—has refused to sell his CDs to any record chain that carries used CDs. Brooks claims that it is an endless sales loop that excludes artists, writers, and publishers, who get no royalties from used CDs. The issue surfaced when Wherehouse Records started selling used CDs.

While many believe counterfeiting and pirating to be wrong, there is much disagreement on whether bootlegging and selling used CDs should be legal or illegal. Should the United States continue to expend law officials' time and legal costs to prosecute bootleggers? Most experts do not think anything as potentially profitable as piracy will be stopped. Nevertheless, recording companies and musical artists in the United States believe that piracy reduces profits and harms the integrity of the artists' musical work.

*Source:* This case was derived from one written by Linda Ferrell and Brett Nafziger, based on sources from: "Entering CD Fray," *The (Memphis) Commercial Appeal,* July 1, 1993, A12; Mike Hennessey, "Superstar Slips Thru Protection Gap in Germany," *The Billboard Review,* August 8, 1992, 1; Ed Moyer, "Quality Is Job None with Fakes," *USA Today,* March 9, 1993, 2B; "Poland's Pirate Pop," *The Economist,* November 10, 1990, 81; Jeffrey Ressner, "Bootlegs Go High-Tech," *Rolling Stone,* May 30, 1991, 15–16; and Stan Soocher, "He's the #1 Bane of Pirates; CD Copies Worry the Music Business," *The National Law Journal,* June 19, 1989, 1.

## Questions

1. What are the ethical issues related to recording piracy, bootlegging, and counterfeiting?
2. If an individual records an artist at a concert and shares that recording with friends, is the artist harmed? If not, is this practice ethical?

3. What are the ethical issues and concerns related to the selling of used CDs, books, and computer software? Does Garth Brooks have an ethical argument in restricting his CDs to stores selling only new CDs?

## STRENGTHEN YOUR SKILLS
## *Making Decisions about Ethical Issues*

You've read in this chapter about the ethical decision-making process. Now's your chance to try out what you learned.

**Instructions:**

1. You and the rest of the class are managers at Martin Marietta Corporation, Orlando, Florida. You are getting ready to do the group exercise in an ethics training session. The training instructor announces you will be playing *Gray Matters: The Ethics Game.* You find out that *Gray Matters,* which was prepared for Martin Marietta employees, is also played at 41 universities, including Harvard University, and at 65 other companies. There are 55 scenarios in *Gray Matters,* so you will have time during this session to complete only the five scenarios that your group draws from the stack of cards.

2. The training instructor asks you to form into groups of four to six managers and to appoint a group leader who will read the case to the group, conduct a discussion of the case, obtain a consensus answer to the case, and then be the one to report the group's answers to the training instructor. You will have five minutes to reach each decision, after which time all groups will discuss their answers, and the instructor will give the point values and rationale for each choice. Then you will have five minutes for the next case, etc., until all five cases have been completed. Keep track of your group's score for each case; the winning team will be the group scoring the most points.

3. Since this game is designed to reflect life, you may believe that some cases lack clarity or that some of your choices are not as precise as you would have liked. Also, some cases have only one solution, while others have more. In still others there is no good answer, and you must choose the answer that is the best of those presented. Each choice is assessed points to reflect which answer is the most correct. **Your group's task is to select only one option in each case.**

Your group draws cards 5, 12, 20, 31, and 51.

---

### 5
### MINI-CASE

A defense program has not yet been formally approved nor have the funds been allocated. Nevertheless, because it all looks good and you need to get started in order to meet schedule, you start negotiating with a supplier. What do you tell the supplier?

#### POTENTIAL ANSWERS

A. "This is a 'hot' program for both of us. Approval is imminent. Let's get all the preliminary work under way."

B. "The program is a 'go.' I want you under contract as soon as possible."

C. "Start work and we will cover your costs when we get the contract."

D. "If you want to be part of the team on this important, great program, you, like us, will have to shoulder some of the start-up costs."

---

### 12
### MINI-CASE

Your price is good on a program contract you are bidding, but you think it will take you several months longer than your competitor to develop the system. Your client, the U.S. Army, wants to know the schedule. What do you say?

#### POTENTIAL ANSWERS

A. Tell the Army your schedule is essentially the same as what you believe your competitor's will be.

B. Show the Army a schedule the same as what you believe your competitor's is (but believing you can do better than what your engineers have told you).

C. Explain to the Army the distinct advantage of your system irrelevant of schedule.

D. Lay out your schedule even though you suspect it may cause you to lose points on the evaluation.

## 20
### MINI-CASE

You work in finance. Another employee is blamed for your error involving significant dollars. The employee will be able to clear himself, but it will be impossible to trace the error back to you. What do you do?

#### POTENTIAL ANSWERS

A. Do nothing. The blamed employee will be able to clear himself eventually.

B. Assist the blamed employee in resolving the issue but don't mention your involvement.

C. Own up to the error immediately thus saving many hours of work.

D. Wait and see if the matter is investigated and at that time disclose your knowledge of the case.

## 31
### MINI-CASE

A close relative of yours plans to apply for a vacancy in the department that you head. Hearing of this, what would you say to that person?

#### POTENTIAL ANSWERS

A. "Glad to have you. Our organization always needs good people."

B. "I would be concerned about the appearance of favoritism."

C. "It would be best if you did not work for me."

D. "If you get the job, expect no special consideration from me."

## 51
### MINI-CASE

A current supplier contacts you with an opportunity to use your expertise as a paid consultant to the supplier in matters not pertaining to your company's business. You would work only on weekends. You could:

#### POTENTIAL ANSWERS

A. Accept the job if the legal department poses no objection.

B. Accept the job.

C. Report pertinent details to your supervisor.

D. Decline the position.

*Source:* Permission granted by the author of *Gray Matters,* George Sammet, Jr., Vice President, Office of Corporate Ethics, Martin Marietta Corporation, Orlando, Florida, to use these portions of *Gray Matters: The Ethics Game* © 1992. If you would like more information about the complete game, call 1-800-3ETHICS.

# Managing *in a* Borderless World

## Outline

## After reading this chapter, you will be able to:

- Analyze the factors within the global trade environment that influence business.

- Specify the different levels of organizational involvement in international trade.

- Summarize the various trade agreements and alliances that have developed worldwide and how they influence business activities.

- Determine how global business affects management.

- Assess the opportunities and problems facing a small business considering expanding into international markets.

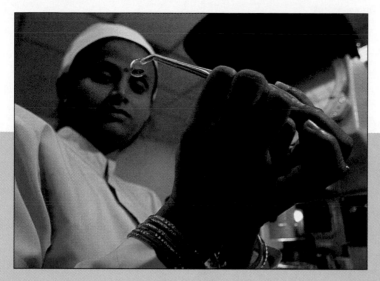

# The American Dream in Asia

While struggling both at home and in stagnant major export markets such as Japan and Western Europe, many major American consumer companies are increasingly turning their attention to developing Asian markets such as India, Indonesia, and even China, potentially the largest consumer market in the world. Demand for American products such as Procter & Gamble detergents and shampoos and Ray-Ban sunglasses is increasing faster than even the rapidly improving economic conditions and standards of living in many emerging Asian nations. As a result, the branded products of many well-known American marketers are commanding huge premiums over inferior local competitors in these developing markets.

Two critical factors—increased domestic competition and vast market potential abroad—appear to be driving this geographical shift in marketing emphasis. Increased competition from private-label "store" brands, such as Sam's Choice, President's Choice, and Equate products at Wal-Mart stores across the nation, has cut deeply into sales and profits for many U.S. consumer brands. In 1992, sales of private-label products in U.S. grocery stores accounted for over 18 percent of all goods sold, with the category as a whole growing at twice the rate of national manufacturer brands. Such competition has led consumer products giants such as Procter & Gamble and Johnson & Johnson to announce massive employee layoffs, factory closures, and economic setbacks—Procter & Gamble lost $1.2 billion in just one quarter of 1993—as well as altered marketing strategies in order to retain market share.

Combined with stagnant sales in the U.S. market, rapidly increasing standards of living for literally billions of potential customers who are increasingly receptive to Western ways and products have also served to drive American brands into Asia. For example, nearly one-quarter of the world's population lives in China, a nation of 1.2 billion people becoming more and more open to Western influence. In 1992 Procter & Gamble had sales of about $130 million in the country, up 50 percent from the previous year. The company's Whisper-brand sanitary napkins are so popular with Chinese women that they sell for roughly ten times the price of competing local products. Familiar Johnson & Johnson brands such as Johnson & Johnson Baby Shampoo and Band-Aid brand bandages sell for as much as five times the price of their counterparts of Chinese origin. In Indonesia, a nation of 180 million people where U.S. exports increased by 47 percent in 1992, Bausch & Lomb, marketer of Ray-Ban sunglasses, has been selling its popular eyewear at much higher prices than in the domestic market. The company is also now producing and selling its products—contact lenses and sunglasses—in India, another rapidly developing consumer market with huge potential for American brands.

The citizens of most developing Asian nations are enjoying increased levels of disposable income, thus allowing them the luxury of American brands. What they see in these brands is often nothing less than a better way of life. For many Asian consumers, American brands represent not only the highest-quality products available, but also a piece of the American Dream itself, which they can now increasingly afford.

*Sources:* Rahul Jacob, "Asia, Where the Big Brands Are Blooming," *Fortune,* August 23, 1993, 55; Valerie Reitman, "Enticed by Visions of Enormous Numbers, More Western Marketers Move Into China," *The Wall Street Journal,* July 12, 1993, B1; Valerie Reitman, "U.S. Firms Turn to the Developing World," *The Wall Street Journal,* August 4, 1993, A2; Eben Shapiro, "Price Lure of Private-Label Products Fails To Hook Many Buyers of Baby Food, Beer," *The Wall Street Journal,* May 13, 1993, B1; Gabriella Stern, "P&G Reports Fiscal Fourth-Period Loss Of $1.22 Billion After Taking a Charge," *The Wall Street Journal,* August 11, 1993, A2; and Elyse Tanouye, "Another Job Reduction Set In Drug Industry," *The Wall Street Journal,* August 12, 1993, A3.

**global business (globalization)**
A strategy in which organizations treat the entire world or major regions of it as the domain for conducting business.

**international business**
The buying, selling, and trading of goods and services across national boundaries.

*introduction*

**G**lobal business (globalization) is a strategy in which organizations treat the entire world or major regions of it as the domain for conducting business. It includes management decisions about business activities for the whole world, including the United States, rather than focusing on trade between countries. **International business** is a narrower concept defined as the buying, selling, and trading of goods and services across national boundaries. Falling political barriers and advancing communications and transportation technology are enabling many companies to sell their products overseas as well as in their own countries. And, as cultural and other differences among nations narrow, the trend toward the globalization of business is becoming increasingly important.

Already, consumers around the world can drink Coca-Cola and Dr Pepper; eat at McDonald's and Pizza Hut; see movies from Mexico, France, Australia, Japan, and China; and watch Cable News Network (CNN) and MTV on Toshiba and Sony televisions. The products you consume today are just as likely to have been made in Korea or Germany as in the United States. Similarly, consumers in other countries buy Western electrical equipment, clothing, rock music, cosmetics, and toiletries, as well as computers, robots, and earthmoving equipment. Brands such as Coca-Cola, Sony, British Petroleum, and Levi Strauss seem to make year-to-year gains in the global market.

Turner Broadcasting System, Inc., is capitalizing on global television programming opportunities resulting from satellite technology, political change, and emerging consumer markets. TBS is expanding its news and entertainment networks, with the option of customizing them for specific countries and regions of the world. Its TNT Latin America provides 24-hours of film and cartoon entertainment in English, Spanish, and Portuguese to more than 2.6 million homes in Central and South America, as well as the Caribbean.

*Source:* TNT Latin America is a trademark of Turner Network Television, Inc.

In this chapter we explore management in this global market. First, we examine the sociocultural, political-legal, and economic environment of global business, which managers must understand to carry out their functions. Next, the levels of organizational involvement in international business are addressed. Then we look at some important regional trade alliances and agreements and the impact of foreign investment in the United States. Finally, we briefly discuss how global business affects management decisions on planning, organizing, leading, and controlling.

# THE GLOBAL BUSINESS ENVIRONMENT

Managers considering international business must research a country's social, cultural, political, and legal background and obtain information about how to deal with its tariffs, quotas, and currency as well. Such research will help the company choose an appropriate level of involvement and operating strategies.

**Teaching Note:** To encourage students to think more internationally, assign each student a different country to research. Have each student make a 10-minute presentation on the location, history, development, and status of the chosen country.

## The Sociocultural Environment

Most businesspeople engaged in international trade underestimate the importance of social and cultural differences, but these differences can create nightmares for managers. Culture can be defined as a sort of blueprint of acceptable behavior in a society that is passed from one generation to the next. Unfortunately, cultural norms are rarely written down, and what is written down may well be inaccurate.

Cultural differences include variations in language and body language. Although it is possible to translate words from one language to another, the true meaning is sometimes misinterpreted or lost. For example, General Motors successfully marketed the Chevrolet Nova in the United States for many years, but GM had some problems selling the car abroad. In English, *nova* means "bright star," an acceptable name for a car. In Spanish, however, *nova (no va)* means "it does not go," which certainly does not convey a positive image for the car. Similarly, *Esso* in Japanese translates to "stalled car," so not surprisingly the Japanese were reluctant to fuel up with Esso gasoline. Americans found a German chocolate confection particularly unappetizing: It was marketed under the name Zit.[1] While such examples are humorous, they also illustrate the difficulties of conducting business in other languages and cultures.

**Example:** When the Snicker's candy bar was first introduced in the United Kingdom, the name was changed to Marathon because the company felt the word *snickers* rhymed with the word for women's undergarments—"knickers."

Differences in body language and personal space are another aspect of culture that may affect international trade. Body language is nonverbal, usually unconscious communication through gestures, posture, and facial expression. Personal space is the distance at which one person feels comfortable talking to another. Americans tend to stand a moderate distance away from the person with whom they are speaking. Arab businessmen tend to stand face to face with the object of their conversation. Additionally, gestures vary from culture to culture, and gestures considered acceptable in American society—such as pointing—may be considered rude in others. Such cultural differences may generate uncomfortable feelings or misunderstandings when businesspeople of different countries interact.

The people of other nations quite often have a different perception of time as well. Americans and Germans value promptness: A business meeting scheduled for a specific time seldom starts more than a few minutes late. In Mexico and Spain, however, it is not unusual for a meeting to be delayed half an hour or more.

**Example:** Business hours and meal times also vary by country. In Mexico and Spain, for example, most restaurants do not open for the evening meal until 8:00 p.m., with most people eating between 9:00 and 10:00 p.m.

**Example:** Holidays vary internationally and affect business operating hours. For example, the Fourth of July and Thanksgiving are U.S. holidays not celebrated in other parts of the world.

**Example:** McDonald's had to change the name of its Quarter Pounder to the "Hamburger Royal" for countries on the metric system.

**Example:** Electrical appliances made for the United Kingdom have a three-pronged electrical plug and must run on 220 voltage, not 110 voltage like in the United States.

Such a late start might produce resentment in an American negotiating in Spain for the first time.

Companies engaged in foreign trade must observe the national and religious holidays and local customs of the host country. In many Islamic countries, for example, workers expect to take a break at certain times of the day to observe religious rites. In Thailand and many other countries, public displays of affection between the sexes are unacceptable in advertising messages; in many Middle Eastern nations, showing the soles of your feet is considered an insult. Because India's Hindu population considers it taboo to eat beef, McDonald's will market hamburgers without beef there; it will likely offer lamb or vegetarian burgers.[2] Table 5.1 lists additional cultural variations that may affect business discussions.

Different countries may have different customs regarding respect for authority, as well. In Scandinavia, Great Britain, and the Netherlands, managers tend not to be too intimidated by their superiors, which enables companies such as British Petroleum (BP) to encourage managers to provide feedback on their own superiors' performance. However, in countries such as Turkey, Greece, and France, there is a strong tradition of deference toward superiors, so managers in those countries may feel uncomfortable commenting on their superiors' actions.[3]

With the exception of the United States, most nations use the metric system. This lack of uniformity creates problems for both buyers and sellers in the international marketplace. American sellers, for instance, must package goods destined for foreign markets in liters or meters, and Japanese sellers must convert to the English system when they plan to sell a product in the United States. Tools also must be in the correct system if they are to function correctly. Hyundai and Honda service technicians need metric tools to make repairs on those cars.

The literature dealing with international business is filled with accounts of sometimes humorous but often costly mistakes that occurred because of a lack of understanding of the social and cultural differences between buyers and sellers. Such problems cannot always be avoided, but they can be minimized through research on the cultural and social differences of the host country. IBM, Motorola, and many other large companies now employ consultants to help train managers being transferred to other countries to understand cultural differences and how to solve problems related to these differences.[4]

## The Political-Legal Environment

**The Political Environment.** Like social and cultural customs, political considerations are seldom written down and often change rapidly. In the 1980s, disapproval of South Africa's policy of apartheid led Eastman Kodak, General Motors, and many other American firms to sell their holdings there, though companies are returning since apartheid was overturned and Nelson Mandela was elected president in 1994. Many world governments levied economic sanctions against the former Yugoslavia in the early 1990s to protest atrocities committed in that country's civil war. While these were dramatic events, political considerations affect international business daily as governments enact tariffs, embargoes, or other types of trade restrictions in response to political events.

Managers engaged in international trade must consider the relative stability of the countries in which they wish to do business. While countries such as Canada, Great Britain, and Japan are relatively stable, political unrest in other countries may create a hostile or even dangerous environment for foreign businesses. Civil war, terrorism, and frequent changes of government make it difficult

**TABLE 5.1**

## A Sampling of Cultural Variations

| Country/ Region | Body Motions | Greetings | Colors | Numbers | Shapes, Sizes, Symbols |
|---|---|---|---|---|---|
| Japan | Pointing to one's own chest with a forefinger indicates that one wants a bath. Pointing a forefinger to the nose indicates "me." | Bowing is the traditional form of greeting. | Positive colors are in muted shades. Combinations of black, dark gray, and white have negative overtones (black and white are the colors of mourning). | Positive numbers are 1, 3, 5, 8. Negative numbers are 4, 9. | Pine, bamboo, and plum patterns are positive. Cultural shapes such as Buddha-shaped jars should be avoided. |
| Europe | Raising only the index finger signifies a person wants two items. When counting on one's fingers, "1" is often indicated by the thumb, "2" by the thumb and forefinger. | It is acceptable to send flowers in thanks for a dinner invitation, but not roses (associated with sweethearts) or chrysanthemums (associated with funerals). | Generally, white and blue are considered positive. Black often has negative overtones. | The numbers 3 and 7 are usually positive. 13 is a negative number. | Circles are symbols of perfection. Hearts are considered favorably at Christmas time. |
| Latin America | General arm gestures are used for emphasis. | The traditional form of greeting is a hearty embrace followed by a friendly slap on the back. | Popular colors are generally bright or bold yellow, red, blue, and green. | Generally, 7 is a positive number. Negative numbers are 13, 14. Numerical rating scales are not used. | Religious symbols should be respected. Avoid national symbols such as flag colors. |
| Middle East | The raised eyebrow facial expression indicates "yes." | The word "no" must be pronounced three times before it is accepted. | Positive colors are brown, black, dark blues, and reds. Pink, violets, and yellows are not favored. | Positive numbers are 3, 5, 7, 9. Negative numbers are 13, 15. | Round or square shapes are acceptable. The 6-pointed star, raised thumb, and Koranic sayings are to be avoided. |

*Source:* James C. Simmons, "A Matter of Interpretation," *American Way,* April 1983, 106–111; "Adapting Packaging to Cultural Differences," *Business America,* December 3, 1979, 3–7; *Business Week,* December 6, 1976, 91-92; and Carlos E. Garcia, "Hispanic Market Is Accessible If Research Is Designed Correctly," *Marketing News,* January 4, 1988, 46, as appeared in *Business: A Changing World* by O.C. Ferrell and Geoffrey Hirt. © 1993 Richard D. Irwin, Inc./Austen Press.

for managers to plan for the future and may even expose a firm's employees to danger. In Spain and Great Britain, for example, terrorists have bombed tourist attractions; clashes between different ethnic groups in India could endanger businesspeople working there; business executives have been murdered and kidnapped in Peru by revolutionaries.[5] In Russia, foreign managers, of whom 16 were murdered in 1993, often have to hire bodyguards.[6] And a sudden change in power can result in a regime that is hostile to foreign investment. A major risk is nationalization—when a government takes over a company's facilities, usually without reimbursing the company for the loss of its property. When Fidel Castro came to power in Cuba, for example, he nationalized many American businesses. Whether they like it or not, companies are often involved directly or indirectly in international politics.

Political concerns may lead a group of nations to form a cartel to generate a competitive advantage in world markets. A **cartel** is a group of firms or nations that agree to act as a monopoly and not compete with each other. One successful cartel is the De Beers Central Marketing Organization, which markets industrial and gem-quality diamonds for South Africa, Russia, Zaire, and Botswana. Probably the most famous cartel is OPEC, the Organization of Petroleum Exporting Countries, founded in the 1960s to increase the price of petroleum throughout the world and to maintain high prices. By working to ensure stable oil prices, OPEC hopes to enhance the economies of its member nations.

**The Legal Environment.**    Unlike social, cultural, and political barriers, laws are written down and usually are quite explicit. A firm that decides to enter the international marketplace must contend with the laws of its own nation, international laws, and the laws of the nation with which it will be trading.

The United States has a number of laws that affect domestic firms engaged in international trade. The **Webb-Pomerene Export Trade Act**, passed in 1918, allows selected American firms desiring international trade to form monopolies in order to compete with foreign cartels. However, these firms are not allowed to limit free trade and competition within the United States or to use unfair methods of competition in international trade. The **Foreign Corrupt Practices Act**, passed in 1978, outlaws direct payoffs to and bribes of foreign governments or business officials by American companies. An American company is allowed to make small gifts where they are customary but may not make large payments or offer bribes to influence the policy decisions of foreign governments. This act specifies penalties for both the company and the individuals involved. The United States also has a variety of friendship, commerce, and navigation treaties with other nations. These treaties allow business to be transacted between citizens of the specified countries.

The laws of the other nations are often different from those of the United States. Many of the legal rights that Americans take for granted do not exist in other countries, and a firm doing business abroad must understand and obey the laws of the host country. Many nations forbid foreign nationals from owning real property outright; others have copyright and patent laws that are less strict than those of the United States. They may also have strict laws limiting the amount of local currency that can be taken out of the country and the amount of foreign currency that can be brought in. Table 5.2 lists some restrictions on advertising in Europe. If a business wishes to succeed in another country, its managers must pay careful attention to their activities to ensure that it remains within that country's laws.

**Tariffs and Trade Restrictions.**    Tariffs and other trade restrictions are part of a country's legal structure but may be established or removed for many political reasons. An **import tariff** is a tax levied by a nation on goods bought outside its borders and imported into the country. A *fixed tariff* is a specific amount of money levied on each unit of a product brought into the country, while an *ad valorem tariff* is based on the value of the item. Most countries allow citizens traveling abroad to bring home a certain amount of merchandise without paying an import tariff. A U.S. citizen may bring $400 worth of merchandise into the United States duty-free. After that, U.S. citizens must pay an ad valorem tariff based on the cost

**cartel**
A group of firms or nations that agree to act as a monopoly and not compete with each other.

**Webb-Pomerene Export Trade Act**
Legislation allowing selected American firms desiring international trade to form monopolies in order to compete with foreign cartels.

**Foreign Corrupt Practices Act**
Legislation outlawing direct payoffs to and bribes of foreign governments or business officials by American companies.

**Critical Thinking Challenge:** Ask student groups to consider the type of training an expatriate manager and his or her family would need before taking an expatriate assignment. Have students present their rationale for their choices.

**import tariff**
A tax levied by a nation on goods bought outside its borders and imported into the country.

**TABLE 5.2**

**European Restrictions on Advertising**

| Country | Restriction | Justification |
| --- | --- | --- |
| France | No tourism advertising is allowed. | This minimizes the public's spending outside the country. |
| | No TV commercials for supermarket chains are permitted. | Small grocers should not be driven out of business by the larger chains. |
| Germany | Comparative advertising is heavily discouraged and must pass rigorous fairness tests. | Comparative advertising is often felt to be misleading and deceptive. |
| | Children cannot talk about product benefits or be appealed to in an ad. | Children are not to be exploited or taken advantage of. |
| Great Britain | Product categories banned from TV advertising: undertakers, the Bible, matrimonial agencies, fortune tellers, private detectives, contraceptives, and pregnancy tests. | Whenever the independent Broadcasting Authority receives ten or more complaints about an ad/product, it is banned. |
| Switzerland | People cannot be used in print and TV ads for alcoholic beverages. | The consumption of alcohol should not be depicted as glamorous. |
| Spain | Tobacco and alcohol (excluding wine and beer) are banned from TV. | These products are not viewed as beneficial to the public. |

*Source:* Laurel Wentz, "Local Laws Keep International Marketers Hopping," *Advertising Age,* July 11, 1985, p. 20, as appeared in *Business: A Changing World* by O.C. Ferrell and Geoffrey Hirt. © 1993 Richard D. Irwin, Inc./Austen Press.

of the item and the country of origin. Thus, identical items purchased in different countries might have different tariffs.

The use of protective tariffs, which raise the price of foreign goods, has become a controversial topic, as Americans become increasingly concerned over the U.S. trade deficit. Protective tariffs allow more expensive domestic goods to compete with foreign ones. Many advocate the imposition of tariffs on products imported from Japan, particularly automobiles, audio components, and computers. However, Congress fears economic reprisals from Japan if the tariffs are levied specifically on Japanese products.

Critics of protective tariffs argue that their use inhibits free trade and competition. Supporters of protective tariffs say they insulate domestic industries, particularly new ones, against well-established foreign competitors. Once an industry matures, however, its advocates may be reluctant to forego the tariff that protected it. Tariffs also help when, because of low labor costs and other advantages, foreign competitors can afford to sell their products at prices lower than those charged by domestic companies. Some Americans argue that tariffs should be used to keep domestic wages high and unemployment low.

**Exchange controls** are restrictions on the amount of a particular currency that may be bought or sold. Some countries control their foreign trade by forcing

**exchange controls**
Restrictions on the amount of a particular currency that may be bought or sold.

businesspeople to buy and sell foreign products through a central bank. If John Deere, for example, receives payments for its tractors in a foreign currency, it may be required to sell the currency to that nation's central bank. When foreign currency is in short supply, as it is in many Third World and Eastern European countries, the government uses foreign currency to purchase necessities and capital goods and produces other products locally, thus limiting its need for foreign imports.

**quota**
The maximum number of units of a particular product that may be imported into a country.

A **quota** is the maximum number of units of a particular product that may be imported into a country. A quota may be established by voluntary agreement or by government decree. The United States has imposed an import quota on some Japanese cars and trucks in an effort to reduce the amount of dollars leaving the country.

**embargo**
The suspension of trade in a particular product by the government.

An **embargo** is the suspension of trade in a particular product by the government. Embargoes are generally directed at specific goods or countries and may be established for political, health, or religious reasons. For example, the United States forbids the importing of cigars from Cuba for political reasons. In 1991 the United States placed an embargo on sales of all American goods to Iraq as a political protest against that country's invasion of Kuwait. Health embargoes prevent the importing of various pharmaceuticals, animals, plants, and agricultural products. Muslim nations forbid the importing of alcoholic beverages.

**dumping**
The sale of products, by a country or business firm, at less than what it costs to produce them.

One common reason for setting quotas is to prohibit dumping. **Dumping** occurs when a country or business firm sells products at less than what it costs to produce them. Korean firms accused of dumping computer chips in the United States in the early 1990s were threatened with import tariffs on their products. The United States requires that a product be sold for not less than its production costs plus 10 percent for overhead and 8 percent for profit. Nonetheless, American auto manufacturers have accused Japanese manufacturers of dumping small pickup trucks in the United States.

A company may dump its products for several reasons. Dumping permits quick entry into a market; it sometimes occurs when the domestic market for a firm's product is too small to support an efficient level of production. In other cases, technologically obsolete products that are no longer salable in the country of origin are dumped overseas. Dumping is relatively difficult to prove, but even the suspicion of it can lead to the imposition of quotas.

## The Economic Environment

When considering doing business in another country, managers must look at its level of economic development as well as exchange rates.

**Economic Development.**    The degree of economic development varies from country to country, and American businesspeople must recognize that they cannot take for granted that other countries offer the same things as the United States. Many countries in Africa, Asia, and South America, for example, are, in general, poorer and less economically advanced than those in North America and Europe. These countries are often called *less-developed countries (LDCs),* characterized by low per capita income (income generated by the nation's production of goods and services divided by the population). LDCs represent a potentially huge and profitable market for many businesses. More economically advanced countries, such as the United States, Japan, Great Britain, and Canada, are often referred to as *industrialized nations.* Table 5.3 illustrates one measure of economic development among countries, the percentage of household spending on food.

### TABLE 5.3

**Percentage of Household Spending on Food**

| | |
|---|---|
| United States | 10% |
| Germany | 12% |
| Singapore | 19% |
| Poland | 29% |
| Thailand | 30% |
| Mexico | 35% |
| Iran | 37% |
| Kenya | 38% |
| India | 52% |

*Source:* Ricardo Sookdes, "The New Global Consumer," *Fortune*, Autumn/Winter 1993, 68-77.

A country's level of development is determined largely by its **infrastructure**, the physical facilities that support its economic activities, such as railroads, highways, ports, air fields, utilities and power plants, schools, hospitals, communication systems, and commercial distribution systems. When doing business in LDCs, for example, a business may need to compensate for confusing distribution and communications problems, or even a lack of technology, in order to achieve its goals.

**infrastructure**
The physical facilities that support a country's economic activities, such as highways, utilities, schools, hospitals, communication systems, and commercial distribution systems.

**Exchange Rates.**   The ratio at which one nation's currency can be exchanged for another nation's currency or for gold is the **exchange rate.** On June 16, 1994, one British pound could be exchanged for $1.52, one German mark for $.61, and one Japanese yen for less than one American cent (Figure 5.1). Familiarity with exchange rates is important in international trade because a business seeking to import goods from another country often must obtain the other country's currency to complete the trade. A Kuwaiti company that wants to buy oil-field equipment from a U.S. company, for example, will have to exchange its dinars for American dollars—at the current exchange rate—to complete the purchase.

**exchange rate**
The ratio at which one nation's currency can be exchanged for another nation's currency or for gold.

## International Trade Facilitators

Although the sociocultural, political-legal, and economic environments may seem like daunting barriers to international trade, there are facilitators of international trade that can help managers get involved in and succeed in global markets. These include the General Agreement on Tariffs and Trade, the World Bank, and the International Monetary Fund. Additionally, individual countries may offer incentives to promote import and export trade, such as loans and free trade zones.

**General Agreement on Tariffs and Trade (GATT).**   During the Great Depression of the 1930s, nations enacted so many protective tariffs covering so many products that international trade became virtually impossible. By the end of World War II, there was considerable international momentum to liberalize trade and minimize the effects of tariffs. The **General Agreement on Tariffs and Trade (GATT)**, signed by 23 nations in 1947, provides a forum for tariff negotiations and a place

**General Agreement on Tariffs and Trade (GATT)**
Legislation, first signed by 23 nations in 1947, providing a forum for tariff negotiations and a place where international trade problems can be discussed and resolved.

## Foreign Exchange Rates on June 16, 1994

# CURRENCY TRADING

## EXCHANGE RATES

**Thursday, June 16, 1994**
The New York foreign exchange selling rates below apply to trading among banks in amounts of $1 million and more, as quoted at 3 p.m. Eastern time by Bankers Trust Co., Dow Jones Telerate Inc. and other sources. Retail transactions provide fewer units of foreign currency per dollar.

| Country | U.S. $ equiv. Thurs. | U.S. $ equiv. Wed. | Currency per U.S. $ Thurs. | Currency per U.S. $ Wed. |
|---|---|---|---|---|
| Argentina (Peso) | 1.01 | 1.01 | .99 | .99 |
| Australia (Dollar) | .7305 | .7300 | 1.3689 | 1.3699 |
| Austria (Schilling) | .08715 | .08693 | 11.47 | 11.50 |
| Bahrain (Dinar) | 2.6522 | 2.6522 | .3771 | .3771 |
| Belgium (Franc) | .02980 | .02973 | 33.56 | 33.64 |
| Brazil (Cruzeiro real) | .0004394 | .0004474 | 2276.04 | 2235.04 |
| Britain (Pound) | 1.5203 | 1.5220 | .6578 | .6570 |
| 30-Day Forward | 1.5195 | 1.5212 | .6581 | .6574 |
| 90-Day Forward | 1.5182 | 1.5199 | .6587 | .6579 |
| 180-Day Forward | 1.5167 | 1.5184 | .6593 | .6586 |
| Canada (Dollar) | .7194 | .7194 | 1.3900 | 1.3900 |
| 30-Day Forward | .7186 | .7186 | 1.3916 | 1.3916 |
| 90-Day Forward | .7166 | .7166 | 1.3954 | 1.3954 |
| 180-Day Forward | .7133 | .7133 | 1.4019 | 1.4019 |
| Czech. Rep. (Koruna) | | | | |
| Commercial rate | .0346224 | .0344732 | 28.8830 | 29.0080 |
| Chile (Peso) | .002423 | .002423 | 412.64 | 412.64 |
| China (Renminbi) | .114943 | .114943 | 8.7000 | 8.7000 |
| Colombia (Peso) | .001201 | .001201 | 832.90 | 832.90 |
| Denmark (Krone) | .1564 | .1563 | 6.3919 | 6.3969 |
| Ecuador (Sucre) | | | | |
| Floating rate | .000465 | .000465 | 2149.01 | 2149.01 |
| Finland (Markka) | .18272 | .18230 | 5.4728 | 5.4854 |
| France (Franc) | .17976 | .17936 | 5.5630 | 5.5755 |
| 30-Day Forward | .17956 | .17916 | 5.5692 | 5.5817 |
| 90-Day Forward | .17931 | .17891 | 5.5768 | 5.5893 |
| 180-Day Forward | .17915 | .17875 | 5.5819 | 5.5944 |
| Germany (Mark) | .6131 | .6116 | 1.6310 | 1.6350 |
| 30-Day Forward | .6128 | .6113 | 1.6319 | 1.6359 |
| 90-Day Forward | .6124 | .6109 | 1.6328 | 1.6368 |
| 180-Day Forward | .6127 | .6112 | 1.6322 | 1.6362 |
| Greece (Drachma) | .004053 | .004049 | 246.75 | 246.95 |
| Hong Kong (Dollar) | .12935 | .12936 | 7.7310 | 7.7305 |
| Hungary (Forint) | .0096993 | .0096581 | 103.1000 | 103.5400 |
| India (Rupee) | .03212 | .03212 | 31.13 | 31.13 |
| Indonesia (Rupiah) | .0004613 | .0004613 | 2168.02 | 2168.02 |
| Ireland (Punt) | 1.4899 | 1.4902 | .6712 | .6711 |
| Israel (Shekel) | .3277 | .3277 | 3.0520 | 3.0520 |
| Italy (Lira) | .0006231 | .0006260 | 1604.90 | 1597.42 |
| Japan (Yen) | .009689 | .009744 | 103.21 | 102.63 |
| 30-Day Forward | .009707 | .009762 | 103.02 | 102.44 |
| 90-Day Forward | .009750 | .009806 | 102.56 | 101.98 |
| 180-Day Forward | .009819 | .009876 | 101.84 | 101.26 |
| Jordan (Dinar) | 1.4599 | 1.4599 | .6850 | .6850 |
| Kuwait (Dinar) | 3.3568 | 3.3568 | .2979 | .2979 |
| Lebanon (Pound) | .000594 | .000594 | 1682.50 | 1682.50 |
| Malaysia (Ringgit) | .3848 | .3851 | 2.5985 | 2.5970 |
| Malta (Lira) | 2.6178 | 2.6178 | .3820 | .3820 |
| Mexico (Peso) | | | | |
| Floating rate | .2979294 | .2973978 | 3.3565 | 3.3625 |
| Netherland (Guilder) | .5473 | .5462 | 1.8271 | 1.8310 |
| New Zealand (Dollar) | .5901 | .5875 | 1.6946 | 1.7021 |
| Norway (Krone) | .1411 | .1409 | 7.0883 | 7.0984 |
| Pakistan (Rupee) | .0327 | .0327 | 30.61 | 30.61 |
| Peru (New Sol) | .4694 | .4694 | 2.13 | 2.13 |
| Philippines (Peso) | .03765 | .03765 | 26.56 | 26.56 |
| Poland (Zloty) | .00004408 | .00004408 | 22686.00 | 22686.00 |
| Portugal (Escudo) | .005895 | .005895 | 169.62 | 169.63 |
| Saudi Arabia (Riyal) | .26667 | .26667 | 3.7500 | 3.7500 |
| Singapore (Dollar) | .6521 | .6524 | 1.5335 | 1.5327 |
| Slovak Rep. (Koruna) | .0307314 | .0307314 | 32.5400 | 32.5400 |
| South Africa (Rand) | | | | |
| Commercial rate | .2750 | .2761 | 3.6358 | 3.6218 |
| Financial rate | .2103 | .2096 | 4.7550 | 4.7700 |
| South Korea (Won) | .0012402 | .0012402 | 806.30 | 806.30 |
| Spain (Peseta) | .007399 | .007427 | 135.16 | 134.64 |
| Sweden (Krona) | .1273 | .1271 | 7.8541 | 7.8693 |
| Switzerland (Franc) | .7302 | .7299 | 1.3695 | 1.3700 |
| 30-Day Forward | .7302 | .7299 | 1.3695 | 1.3700 |
| 90-Day Forward | .7306 | .7304 | 1.3687 | 1.3692 |
| 180-Day Forward | .7319 | .7316 | 1.3663 | 1.3668 |
| Taiwan (Dollar) | .036958 | .036958 | 27.06 | 27.06 |
| Thailand (Baht) | .03971 | .03971 | 25.18 | 25.18 |
| Turkey (Lira) | .0000324 | .0000316 | 30870.10 | 31665.32 |
| United Arab (Dirham) | .2723 | .2723 | 3.6725 | 3.6725 |
| Uruguay (New Peso) | | | | |
| Financial | .202429 | .202429 | 4.94 | 4.94 |
| Venezuela (Bolivar) | | | | |
| Floating rate | .00607 | .00607 | 164.80 | 164.80 |
| SDR | 1.42596 | 1.42334 | .70128 | .70257 |
| ECU | 1.17680 | 1.17800 | | |

Special Drawing Rights (SDR) are based on exchange rates for the U.S., German, British, French and Japanese currencies. Source: International Monetary Fund.
European Currency Unit (ECU) is based on a basket of community currencies.

*Source: The Wall Street Journal,* June 17, 1994, C11.

where international trade problems can be discussed and resolved. Currently, more than 100 nations abide by its rules.

GATT has sponsored rounds of negotiations aimed at reducing trade restrictions. Two of the most successful of these sessions were the Kennedy and Tokyo Rounds. President John F. Kennedy was granted authority by the Trade Expansion Act of 1962 to call for a round of negotiations to reduce tariffs on more than 60,000 items. In this round, tariffs were reduced by an average of 40 percent by 50 members of GATT. The Tokyo Round (1973–1979) involved 100 nations. It reduced many tariffs by 30 percent, and the negotiators were able to eliminate or ease nontariff trade restrictions such as import quotas, red tape in customs procedures, and "buy national" agreements. The Tokyo Round also worked to increase the availability of foreign currency.

The Uruguay Round (1988–1994) further reduced trade barriers for most products and provided new rules to prevent dumping. In the United States, manufacturers of large equipment, toys, paper, scientific instruments, aluminum, furniture, steel, liquor, and medical equipment, as well as apparel retailers, will

The Uruguay Round of GATT eliminates tariffs on most of the construction equipment products made by Caterpillar, making it better able to compete with other global manufacturers. Caterpillar's strategy for global growth includes expanding sales to the Commonwealth of Independent States, China, and other developing regions of the world with significant growth potential. Here, Caterpillar ships tractors to Russia from the Port of Milwaukee.

*Source:*  Courtesy of Caterpillar Inc.

benefit from tariff reductions. Japan, however, may experience an adverse effect, at least in the short run. Japan's steel, agricultural, processed food, and dairy businesses have enjoyed a high degree of protection through substantial tariffs placed on imports to Japan and closed markets. With such barriers eliminated, these industries will face outside competition. Some U.S. industries are also dissatisfied with the Uruguay Round because they face continued barriers. The motion picture industry had hoped to gain greater access to European markets, while pharmaceutical companies are concerned about the additional ten years that developing countries will be given to pirate drugs. Moreover, GATT will initially cost revenue to participating countries as a result of the loss of tariffs. Economists estimate that $12 to $13 billion will be lost over the next five years, but that as exports grow because of an expanded GATT, tax revenues should eventually rise due to higher corporate profits.[7]

Each of the previous GATT rounds has reduced trade barriers and has been followed by a period of strong economic growth. By the year 2002, falling trade barriers are expected to add $250 billion to the value of goods and services worldwide, which translates into an 8 percent boost in the global domestic product.[8] It is hoped that, by reducing trade barriers, nations will develop closer relationships and, as this happens, global markets should become more efficient.

**World Bank.**    The **World Bank**, formally known as the International Bank for Reconstruction and Development, was established and supported by the industrialized nations, including the United States, in 1946 to loan money to underdeveloped and developing countries. It loans its own funds or borrows funds from member countries to finance projects ranging from road and factory construction to the construction of medical and educational facilities. The World Bank and other multilateral development banks (banks with international support that provide loans to developing countries) are the largest source of advice and assistance for developing nations. The International Development Association and the International Finance Corporation are associated with the World Bank and provide loans to private businesses and member countries.

**International Monetary Fund.**    The **International Monetary Fund (IMF)** was established in 1947 to promote trade among member nations by eliminating trade

**World Bank**
Financial organization established and supported by the industrialized nations to loan money to underdeveloped and developing countries; formally known as the International Bank for Reconstruction and Development.

**International Monetary Fund (IMF)**
Organization established to promote trade among member nations by eliminating trade barriers and fostering financial cooperation.

barriers and fostering financial cooperation. It makes short-term loans to member countries that have balance-of-payment deficits and provides foreign currencies to member nations. If Peru, for example, wants to purchase machine parts from a German company but lacks German marks, IMF will loan the marks to Peru. Peru will repay the loan with gold or with various currencies from other transactions.

# LEVELS OF ORGANIZATIONAL INVOLVEMENT IN GLOBAL BUSINESS

**Critical Thinking Challenge:** Have each student select a company and research and present its involvement in international business issues. You may want to rank the companies on the board from the least to the most global.

Businesses engage in international trade at many levels—from a small Kenyan business that occasionally exports African crafts, to a huge multinational corporation such as Shell Oil that sells products around the globe. The degree of commitment of resources and effort required increases according to the level at which a business involves itself in global trade. In this section we examine exporting and importing, trading companies, licensing and franchising, contract manufacturing, joint ventures, direct investment, and multinational corporations. The "Going Global" box discusses Colgate-Palmolive's international involvement in some specific countries.

## Exporting and Importing

Many companies first get involved in international trade when called upon to supply a foreign business with a particular product. **Exporting**—the sale of goods and services to foreign markets—enables organizations of all sizes to participate in global business. A small software company may boost sales by exporting a computer program to buyers in other countries, in addition to selling within the United States.

**exporting**
The sale of goods and services to foreign markets, enabling organizations of all sizes to participate in global business.

**importing**
The purchase of goods and services from a foreign source.

**countertrade agreements**
The bartering of a product for other products instead of for currency.

**Importing** is the purchase of goods and services from a foreign source. For example, a grocery store chain may import bananas from Honduras and coffee from Colombia. The United States imports a variety of raw materials and manufactured goods from foreign companies, including petroleum, platinum, industrial diamonds, chrome, and bauxite. Table 5.4 lists the leading purchasers of U.S. exports and the leading suppliers of U.S. imports. It is interesting to note that 17 out of the top 20 export buyers are also on the import suppliers list.

Exporting sometimes takes place through **countertrade agreements**, which involve bartering products for other products instead of for currency. Such arrangements are fairly common in international trade, especially between Western companies and Eastern European nations. PepsiCo, for example, has an agreement with Russia to barter Pepsi concentrate for ships and Stolichnaya vodka. In Rumania, PepsiCo trades syrup for wine, marketing the wine in the United States under its Monsieur Henri label.[9] An estimated 30 percent or more of all international trade agreements contain countertrade provisions.

A company may export its wares overseas directly or import goods directly from their manufacturer, or it may deal with an intermediary, commonly called an export agent. Export agents seldom produce goods themselves; instead, they usually handle international transactions for other firms. Export agents either purchase products outright or take them on consignment. If they purchase them outright, they generally mark up the price they pay and attempt to sell the product in the international marketplace. They are also responsible for storage and transportation.

# Going Global

## COLGATE-PALMOLIVE: SPREADING SMILES WORLDWIDE

Founded in 1806 by William Colgate, New York–based Colgate-Palmolive Company is a truly multinational enterprise, deriving nearly two-thirds of its business from international sales. The company has marketed its products internationally for over 75 years, and its well-known brands such as Colgate, Palmolive, Ajax, Irish Spring, Fab, and Mennen Speed Stick are sold in more than 150 countries. In the global arena, the company has been particularly interested in expanding into Mexico, the former East Germany, and Poland, as well as in continuing its association with Operation Smile.

To better understand Mexico's large and diverse population, Colgate-Palmolive conducted a "video anthropological study" of the rapidly expanding consumer market. An independent team of researchers set out across the country, compiling some 60 hours of videotaped discussions with consumers. That research directly influenced both new product development and the advertising campaigns for existing products in the Mexican market. When the research identified problems related to the scarcity of water for many Mexican consumers, for example, marketing managers developed new laundry care products that use less water, as well as advertising messages that show how Colgate-Palmolive products can be used in situations where little water is available.

Colgate-Palmolive was one of the first companies to gain a foothold in East Germany shortly after the fall of the Berlin Wall. The company's early success there was attributed not only to its being positioned for easy entry by virtue of existing operations in neighboring countries, but also to the fact that East Germans were eager to try Colgate products, many of which they had seen in advertisements on West German television stations but had been unable to cross the border to buy. After just three years of Colgate's doing business in the region, 35 percent of its total German toothpaste business comes from the east side of the crumbled Berlin Wall, even though that region accounts for but 25 percent of the total German population.

To expand into Poland, by far the largest potential market in Eastern Europe with a population of some 38 million, Colgate formed a joint venture with a local entrepreneur experienced in consumer product sales and distribution. Initially, the company planned to offer only a limited line of its top products—Colgate toothpaste, Palmolive soap and shampoo, and Ajax scouring powders—through the partner, which was entrusted with the responsibilities of both manufacturing and marketing the goods. To facilitate the joint arrangement, Colgate appointed as its general manager for the region a Polish native who had previously served the company in a variety of senior marketing management positions in both Belgium and France.

Colgate-Palmolive's operations in many developing nations in Latin America and Africa are aided by its ongoing affiliation with Operation Smile, a volunteer organization of doctors, dentists, and corporate sponsors that travels the world performing reconstructive surgery on children who suffer from cleft palates and lips, and facial deformities of the mouth and nasal region. Although these disorders are fairly common and the corrective surgery is not considered complicated by American medical standards, many children in developing or Third World nations either cannot afford such surgery or find that it is not available in their areas. Thus, Operation Smile goes to the patient and performs the surgery free of charge. Since its inception in 1982, the program has performed reconstructive surgery or specialized dental treatment on well over 5,000 children, while at the same time teaching the corrective procedures to local doctors so that the surgery can be performed on a regular basis in their particular region. Colgate-Palmolive's involvement with Operation Smile includes not only organizing and funding of corrective surgeries, but also extensive oral education programs for children in many less-developed nations of the world.

*Sources:* Colgate-Palmolive Company, 1992 Annual Report; Colgate-Palmolive Company, Corporate Video Documentaries: "The Colgate World Report," June 1992; "The Colgate World Report," October 1991; "The Colgate World Report," December 1990; "Consumer View—The Evolutionary Use of Video in Mexico," November 1990; and *Hoover's Handbook of American Business 1993*, Gary Hoover, Alta Campbell, and Patrick J. Spain, eds. (Austin, TX: The Reference Press, Inc., 1993), 204.

**TABLE 5.4**

**Top Twenty U.S. Export Buyers and Import Suppliers**

| Export Buyers | Import Suppliers |
|---|---|
| Canada | Canada |
| Japan | Japan |
| Mexico | Mexico |
| United Kingdom | Germany |
| Germany | Taiwan |
| South Korea | United Kingdom |
| France | South Korea |
| Netherlands | China |
| Taiwan | France |
| Belgium/Luxembourg | Italy |
| Australia | Saudi Arabia |
| Singapore | Singapore |
| Italy | Hong Kong |
| Hong Kong | Venezuela |
| Spain | Brazil |
| Brazil | Nigeria |
| Switzerland | Switzerland |
| China | Thailand |
| Saudi Arabia | Malaysia |
| Malaysia | Netherlands |

Source: U.S. Department of Commerce, *U.S. Foreign Trade Highlights* (Washington DC: Government Printing Office, 1991), 11–18.

An advantage of exporting through an agent is that the company does not have to deal with foreign currencies or the red tape (paying tariffs and handling paperwork) of international business. A major disadvantage is that because the export agent must make a profit, either the price of the product must be increased or the domestic company must provide a larger discount than it would in a domestic transaction.

## Trading Companies

**trading company**
An organization that acquires goods in one country and sells them to buyers in another country.

A **trading company** acquires goods in one country and sells them to buyers in another country. Trading companies handle all activities required to move products from one country to another, including purchasing the products outright. They offer consulting, marketing research, advertising, insurance, product research and design, warehousing, and foreign exchange services to companies interested in selling their products in foreign markets. Trading companies are similar to export agencies, but their role in international trade is larger. By linking sellers and buyers of goods in different countries, trading companies promote international trade.

## Licensing and Franchising

**licensing**
A trade agreement in which one company (the licensor) allows another country (the licensee) to use its company name, products, brands, trademarks, raw materials, and/or production processes in exchange for a fee, or royalty.

**Licensing** is a trade arrangement in which one company—the licensor—allows another company—the licensee—to use its company name, products, patents, brands, trademarks, raw materials, and/or production processes in exchange for a fee, or royalty. In a royalty agreement, the licensee agrees to pay the licensor a fixed percentage of the profits on each unit manufactured or sold. Coca-Cola and PepsiCo frequently use licensing as a means to market their soft drinks in other countries. Licensing is a way for a company to enter the international marketplace without spending large sums of money abroad and hiring or transferring personnel to handle overseas affairs. It also minimizes problems associated with shipping costs, tariffs, and trade restrictions.

Another advantage of licensing is that it allows the firm to establish goodwill for its products in a foreign market. This goodwill will help the company if it decides to produce or market its products directly in the foreign country at some future date. There are potential disadvantages to licensing as well. If the licensee does not maintain high standards of quality, the product's image may be hurt; therefore, it is important for the licensor to monitor its products overseas and to enforce its quality standards.

**Franchising** is a form of licensing in which a company—the franchiser—agrees to provide a franchisee a name, logo, methods of operation, advertising, products, and other elements associated with the franchiser's business, in return for a financial commitment and the agreement to conduct business in accordance with the franchiser's standard of operations. KFC (Kentucky Fried Chicken), Wendy's, McDonald's, and Holiday Inn are well-known franchisers with international visibility.

**franchising**
A form of licensing in which a company (the franchiser) agrees to provide a franchisee elements associated with the franchiser's business, in return for a financial commitment and the agreement to conduct business in accordance with the franchiser's standard of operations.

## Contract Manufacturing

A firm that does not wish to get involved with licensing arrangements may try **contract manufacturing**, which occurs when a company hires a foreign company to produce a specified volume of the firm's product to specification; the final product carries the domestic firm's name. Spalding, for example, relies on contract manufacturing for its sports equipment; Reebok uses Korean contract firms for the manufacture of many of its athletic shoes. Marketing may be handled by the contract manufacturer or by the original company.

**contract manufacturing**
Occurs when a company hires a foreign company to produce a specified volume of its product to specification.

## Joint Ventures

Many countries, particularly the less-developed ones, do not permit direct investment by foreign companies or individuals. Or, a company may lack sufficient resources or expertise to operate in a particular country. In such cases, a company that wants to do business in another country may set up a **joint venture** by finding a local partner (occasionally, the host nation itself) to share the costs and operation of the business. For example, General Electric and Hungary's Tungsram have formed a joint venture to manufacture light bulbs in Budapest. Even small companies can form ventures to gain a foothold in a foreign market: Blue Sky Natural Beverage Company signed an agreement with the Japanese firm Cheerio Kansai, which uses its knowledge of Japanese customers to distribute and market Blue Sky's all-natural sodas in Japan. Japanese sales now contribute 10 percent to the Santa Fe, New Mexico, company's revenues.[10]

A **strategic alliance**, a relatively new form of international joint venture, is a partnership formed to create competitive advantage on a worldwide basis. In some industries, such as automobiles and computers, strategic alliances are becoming the predominant means of competing. International competition is so fierce

**Critical Thinking Challenge:** Assign students to present recent examples of international joint ventures, franchising, licensing, exporting, or importing to the class for further discussion.

**joint venture**
An agreement by which a company that wants to do business in another country may find a local partner (occasionally, the host nation itself) to share the costs and operation of the business.

**strategic alliance**
A relatively new form of international joint venture formed to create competitive advantage on a worldwide basis.

Joint ventures are part of General Electric's strategy of global expansion. GE strengthened its position in Japan by forming a joint venture with Hitachi, providing export opportunities for GE plants in North America and Europe. The joint venture serves the Japanese lighting market through some 100 distributors that supply about 10,000 Hitachi retail outlets.

*Source:* Photo by Caroline Parsons—Liaison International for GE.

and the costs are so high that few firms have the individual resources to go it alone. Thus, individual firms that lack the resources essential for international success may seek to collaborate with other companies.[11] An example of such an alliance is the agreement between IBM and Apple Computers to cooperate in the development of computer chips, which the two companies believe will give them greater power in world computer markets.

## Direct Investment

**direct investment**
The purchase of overseas production and marketing facilities.

Companies that want more control and are willing to invest considerable resources in international business may consider **direct investment**, the purchase of overseas production and marketing facilities. With direct investment, a company may control the facilities outright, or it may be the majority stockholder in the company that controls the facilities. Many firms have direct investments in production plants and companies around the globe. Ford Motor Company and 3M, for example, own subsidiaries and manufacturing facilities in many foreign countries. Japanese-owned Nissan owns a plant in Smyrna, Tennessee, as well as other facilities internationally.

**outsourcing**
A form of direct investment that involves transferring manufacturing or other functions to countries where labor and supplies are less expensive.

   **Outsourcing,** a form of direct investment, involves transferring manufacturing or other functions (such as data processing) to countries where labor and supplies are less expensive. Many American computer, apparel, and athletic-shoe makers, for example, have transferred production to Asian countries, where labor costs are lower than in the United States. Many companies have transferred certain operations to Mexican plants under the *maquiladora* system, under which U.S. companies supply labor-intensive assembly plants, called *maquilas,* with components for assembly, processing, or repair. The Mexican plant returns the finished products to the United States for further processing or shipment to customers. The company pays a U.S. tariff only on the value added to the product in Mexico. U.S. businesses benefit from Mexico's close proximity, low labor rates, and relatively cheap peso, while Mexico benefits from the increased economic development and the creation of new jobs.[12] *Maquilas* are not limited to those associated with U.S. firms; increasingly, firms from Japan and other countries are outsourcing to Mexico.

## B U S I N E S S    D I L E M M A

*You're the Manager …What Would You Do?*

THE COMPANY:   Audiotech Electronics

YOUR POSITION:   Sales Manager

THE PLACE:   Birmingham, AL

Audiotech Electronics was founded in 1959 by a father and son working out of their garage to manufacture television station control consoles. Today, Audiotech employs 75 and currently operates a 35,000-square-foot factory in Birmingham, Alabama, and has two wholly owned subsidiaries. The company now manufactures control consoles for television and radio stations and recording studios. The company's products are used by all the major broadcast and cable networks, including Cable News Network (CNN).

When Audiotech began, its custom-made consoles for recording studios were not widely available. Within a few years, the company switched from custom manufacturing to larger production to reduce the costs of its consoles and expand into new markets more rapidly. The company is involved in every facet of production—designing the systems, installing the circuits in its computer boards, and even manufacturing and painting the metal cases housing the consoles. The success of the metal-working division led to it being spun off as a separate subsidiary that does complete metal stamping, finishing, and painting. The second subsidiary manufactures tape playback cartridge machines and accessories for radio stations.

Audiotech consoles have unique features designed to meet specific customer needs. The Xenon series television console, for example, was the first marketed specifically for television stations. High-tech consoles modified for use in television

stations can cost $300,000, but the Audiotech model costs less than half that amount. The Xenon models incorporate features traditionally found in recording systems, producing more sophisticated sound quality. The firm's newest products allow television correspondents to simultaneously hear and communicate with their counterparts in different locations. Such specialized products are potentially useful in every country with radio and television stations and recording studios.

Sales of Audiotech consoles have historically been strong in the United States but recently have stabilized, and little growth is occurring. Key personnel in the company are investigating the possibility of expanding the market for their product internationally. Even though Audiotech is a small, privately owned firm, they believe they should evaluate and consider global expansion.

### Questions

1. What are they key considerations you should evaluate as sales manager in determining global expansion?
2. Do you think that a joint venture should be considered? What about the use of a contract sales force from the country you are entering?
3. What are some of the unique problems that a small business might face in global expansion that larger firms would not?

## Multinational Corporations

The most committed or highest level of international business involvement is the **multinational corporation (MNC)**, a corporation, such as IBM, Exxon, and Citicorp, that operates on a worldwide scale, without significant ties to any one nation or region. MNCs are more than simple corporations. They often have more assets than some of the countries in which they do business. General Motors, Exxon, Ford Motors, and General Electric, for example, have sales that are higher than the gross national product of many of the countries in which they operate.[13]

Initially, most multinational corporations were American firms that had increasing international commitments. Now, a growing number of MNCs have their headquarters in some nation other than the United States. Nestlé, with headquarters in Switzerland, operates more than three hundred plants around the world and receives revenues from Europe; North, Central, and South America; Africa; and Asia. The Royal Dutch/Shell Group, one of the world's major oil

**multinational corporation (MNC)**
A corporation, such as IBM or Exxon, that operates on a worldwide scale, without significant ties to any one nation or region.

**Comment on Box:** Have students discuss the "Business Dilemma" box and refer to the variables presented in the chapter. Discuss why it is difficult for a small business to consider global expansion. List some of the problem areas Audiotech must consider.

NAFTA is a boon to small business exporters like Wendy Wigtil, president of Barnyard Babies, which makes cloth designs for children to color. Wigtil exports her toys to Japan, France, and Canada. NAFTA makes it easier for Wigtil to expand exports to Canada, where tariffs on toys will be reduced to zero over the next 10 years.

*Source:* © Ken Touchton. All Rights Reserved.

producers and another MNC, has its main offices in The Hague and London. Other MNCs include BASF, British Petroleum, Cadbury Schweppes, Matsushita, Mitsubishi, Siemens, Texaco, Toyota, and Unilever.

## REGIONAL TRADE ALLIANCES AND AGREEMENTS

Although managers are increasingly viewing the world as one huge marketplace, various regional trade alliances and specific markets have created both difficulties and opportunities for organizations engaging in global business. In this section we focus on the North American Free Trade Agreement, the European Economic Community, the Pacific Rim markets, and Eastern Europe and the Commonwealth of Independent States (the former Soviet Union).

### The North American Free Trade Agreement (NAFTA)

The North American Free Trade Agreement (NAFTA), which went into effect on January 1, 1994, effectively merged Canada, the United States, and Mexico into one market of about 374 million consumers. NAFTA eliminates most tariffs and trade restrictions on agricultural and manufactured products among the three countries over a period of 15 years, although some tariffs could be reimposed temporarily if necessary. It is estimated that output for the North America trade area is $7 trillion.

NAFTA liberalizes U.S. investment in Mexico and Canada, providing for intellectual property rights (of special interest to high technology industries); expands trade and services by requiring equal treatment of U.S. firms in both countries; and simplifies country-of-origin rules, which hinders Japan's use of Mexico as a staging ground for further market penetration into U.S. markets. Although most tariffs on products to the United States will be eliminated, duties on more sensitive products such as household glassware, footware, and some fruits and vegetables will be phased out over the 15-year period. Additional agreements have been made concerning labor and the environment. A side agreement is provided for environmental issues and enforcement of federal and international environmental laws.

Canada's 27 million consumers are affluent, with a per capita gross domestic product (GDP) of $19,400. Canadian exports are worth about $130 billion, not including services, almost $100 billion of which goes to the United States. Around $90 billion in goods goes to Canada, making it the United States's largest export market. Currently, exports to Canada support approximately 1.5 million U.S. jobs.

Although Mexico has a low per capita GDP of $3,200, the average Mexican spends approximately $450 annually on U.S. products, as compared to only $385 by the Japanese.[14] Seventy cents of every dollar spent on exports is for U.S. products. In 1992, the United States imported more than $30 billion worth of products from Mexico and exported $40 billion back.[15] The Institute for International Economics estimates that exports to Mexico currently support 700,000 U.S. jobs, and that number is expected to grow to over 1 million by 1995 under NAFTA.[16] Mexico's membership in NAFTA also gives the United States a bridge to other Latin American countries in Central and South America. Many American firms, including Kmart, Sears, Arby's, and PepsiCo, have manufacturing facilities in Mexico. NAFTA provides the opportunity for integration of trade by all nations in the Western Hemisphere.

Most experts believe NAFTA will enable firms in all three countries to compete more effectively against Asian and European rivals, create more jobs in the United States, increase U.S. exports, and decrease illegal immigration to the United States by raising Mexicans' standard of living.[17] However, opponents of the trade pact fear that American jobs will be lost to Mexico, which generally has lower wages. Additionally, environmental groups such as Greenpeace and the Sierra Club oppose the pact on the grounds that Mexico has a poor record on environmental issues.[18] Thus, NAFTA has been highly controversial in all three countries, negotiations have been lengthy, and the future of the trade pact remains unresolved. In the United States, nearly as many citizens are undecided about the pact as are for or against it.[19]

## The European Economic Community

One of the oldest regional alliances, the European Economic Community, or Common Market, was established in 1958 to promote the movement of resources and products among member nations. The first six members were Belgium, France, West Germany, Italy, Luxembourg, and the Netherlands. In 1991 East and West Germany merged into one nation, and by 1992 the United Kingdom, Spain, Denmark, Greece, Portugal, and Ireland had joined as well (Austria is expected to follow in 1995). Until 1992, each nation functioned as a separate market, but at that time, the twelve nations merged into one of the largest single world markets—the European Community (EC), with more than 340 million consumers.[20]

One of the objectives of the EC is to create an economic force capable of competing with Japan, the rest of the Pacific Rim, and North America. The long-run goals are to eliminate all barriers for trade within the EC, improve the efficiency of the EC industries, stimulate economic growth, and thus make the EC economy more competitive in global markets.

Before completely free trade can be established, however, many barriers remain to be overcome. Nationalism and a global recession during the early 1990s have hindered the EC from accomplishing all the objectives related to unification. Some businesspeople and economists believe that because of inconsistencies between the administrations of member states—for example, VAT levels, tax systems, and laws—1992 was only a symbolic date. In reality, there is likely to be continued discussion between member states over outstanding issues of this type, and it will be many years before the EC is truly a single deregulated market.[21]

**Example:** Another benefit of the EC is the harmonization of international quality standards. ISO 9000 represents a group of international standards for product quality and documentation that member countries must meet to sell goods in the EC markets.

## The Pacific Rim Nations

Companies of the Pacific Rim nations—Japan, China, South Korea, Taiwan, Singapore, Hong Kong, the Philippines, Malaysia, Indonesia, Australia, and Indochina—have become increasingly competitive and sophisticated in global business in the last three decades. The Japanese, in particular, have made tremendous inroads in world consumer markets for automobiles, motorcycles, watches, cameras, and audio and video equipment with well-known brand names such as Sony, Mitsubishi, Toshiba, and Toyota. Managers from other nations study and imitate Japan's highly efficient management and manufacturing techniques.

However, Japan's marketing muscle has not been without criticism. The United States and Europe rely on Japan's informal trade restraints on its exports of cars, textiles, steel, and audio and video consumer products. Also, the United States has been critical of Japan's reluctance to accept imports from other nations, such as beef and rice. Trade negotiations have been aimed at increasing access to Japan's markets in autos and auto parts, insurance, and government purchases of medical and telecommunications equipment. Economists have estimated that if Japan imported goods at the same rate as other major nations, the United States would sell $50 billion more to Japan a year. In 1993, the value of U.S. goods shipped to Japan was $60 billion less than the value of Japanese goods shipped to the United States. Searching for a way to avoid possible U.S. trade sanctions over the trade imbalance, Japanese leaders have drafted legislative measures aimed at opening the nation's markets to foreign goods and services.[22]

**Example:** China represents an untapped growth market for many U.S. products. Also because of China's favorable feelings toward the United States, many feel this is the next key world market.

The People's Republic of China, a country of 1.2 billion people, has been moving slowly toward economic reform. Although there have been a few setbacks, such as the suppression of a 1989 student pro-democracy uprising in Beijing, its gross domestic product increased 13 percent in both 1992 and 1993, and it is expected to grow at that rate again in 1994. Per capita annual income is still only $420, but a middle class is emerging. Development of privately operated light industry—such as factories that make toys, clothing, and shoes—is encouraged. Most experts on the Pacific Rim are optimistic about China's pace of change toward capitalism. The potential of China's consumer market is so vast that it is almost impossible to measure. As managers at Nike say, "There are two billion feet in China."[23]

South Korea has become very successful in world markets with familiar brand names such as Samsung, Daewoo, and Hyundai. Less-visible Pacific Rim countries such as Singapore, Taiwan, and Hong Kong have become major manufacturing and financial centers. Hong Kong, however, faces an uncertain future after it reverts from British to Chinese control in 1997. Taiwan may have the most promising future of all the Pacific Rim nations. It has a strong local economy, has lowered many import barriers, and has begun to privatize some state-run organizations. Firms from Thailand and Malaysia are also blossoming, carving out niches in the world markets for a variety of products from toys to auto parts. And, in 1994, President Clinton lifted a 19-year U.S. trade embargo against Vietnam, giving U.S. businesses an opportunity to participate in one of Asia's fastest growing markets.

## Eastern Europe and the Commonwealth of Independent States (CIS)

The Commonwealth of Independent States (formerly the Soviet Union) and other formerly communist nations of Eastern Europe—Poland, Hungary, then–East Germany, Yugoslavia, Rumania, the former Czechoslovakia (now split into the Czech Republic and Slovakia), and Bulgaria—have experienced monumental political and economic changes. Widespread measures have been implemented to improve their economic development by making their economies more responsive to the forces of supply and demand. Among the reforms in the former Soviet Union are efforts to privatize state-owned enterprises and farms—replacing them with independent businesses leased or owned by workers, shareholders, cooperatives, and joint ventures. For example, the Ust Ilimsk Wood Industrial Complex, one of the largest lumber mills in the country, will be sold to stockholders, who include among them the firm's 12,000 employees.[24] In addition, the reformers of the Russian, Polish, and Hungarian economies want to reduce trade restrictions on imports and offer incentives to encourage exports to, and foreign investment in, their countries. There is even speculation that some Eastern European nations will ultimately join the EC, allowing for freer trade across all European borders.

The dramatic changes in Eastern Europe have not been easy. Russia, in particular, has experienced a serious economic setback due to a lack of coherent economic strategy in its attempt to become more market-oriented. Political instability has had clear effects on its economy. In 1993, Russia's GDP shrank 12 percent while in 1992, GDP shrank 19 percent. Annual inflation reached 900 percent in 1993.[25] Russia has tried to switch from communism to capitalism in a single leap. It cut state assistance to many aging, uncompetitive factories, which led to the collapse of many businesses and created high levels of unemployment. These events have reduced the country's standard of living and left many Russians ambivalent toward further reform efforts.

On the other hand, the countries of Eastern Europe had a history of free enterprise before World War II and, despite the difficulties, are making significant progress toward becoming market-oriented. Because of economic and political reforms, productivity in Eastern Europe and Russia is expected to increase as workers are given more incentives and control, raising the possibility that Eastern Europe will eventually become an economic powerhouse.

Because of the changing economic conditions in Eastern Europe and the Soviet Union, there are many business opportunities in these countries for American, European, and Asian firms. Monsanto, Hewlett-Packard, Honeywell, Reebok, Philip Morris, RJR Nabisco, Coca-Cola, Bristol-Myers Squibb, McDonald's, Pizza Hut, and many other companies have already established themselves in the former Soviet Union, through either joint ventures or direct ownership. However, because of the swift and uncontrolled nature of the changes taking place in Eastern Europe and the Commonwealth of Independent States, firms considering doing business in these countries must carefully monitor events and proceed cautiously. For example, civil war broke out in Bosnia-Herzegovina, Yugoslavia, in 1992, making that country unsafe for foreign businesspeople; political instability remains a major obstacle to business in Eastern Europe.

**Example:** While many U.S. companies have entered the CIS market, some question the ethics of sending Coca-Cola, McDonald's, and Barbie dolls when the country needs basic foods, medicines, and infrastructure. Some companies, like TamBrands, makers of feminine hygiene products, have been so successful in Russia they have had to do little if any advertising.

## MANAGING GLOBAL BUSINESS

Competing in an increasingly global economy provides both challenges and opportunities for today's managers as they engage in the planning, organizing, leading, and controlling functions.

Planning in a global economy requires managers to understand the sociocultural, political-legal, and economic environment of the countries in which they operate. Before moving outside their own borders, managers must conduct environmental analyses to evaluate the potential of and problems associated with various markets and to determine how best to penetrate those markets. Failure to do so may result in losses and even negative publicity. If McDonald's, for example,

## Managing in a Global Environment

The composition of the workplace is changing dramatically as minorities and immigrants working in the United States bring a culturally diverse perspective. Since the 1980s, U.S. manufacturers have been increasingly willing to move their assembly operations to foreign countries where workers are amenable to lower wages, a trend that has shifted many blue-collar jobs out of the United States. Advancing technology and growing sophistication among low-cost foreign work forces are fueling a similar migration of some white-collar office jobs. On the other hand, passage of NAFTA has created more opportunities for U.S. firms to sell their products in Canada and Mexico. In fact, economic studies conclude that because of new opportunities for U.S. products to be exported to Mexico, NAFTA will result in a net gain of 200,000 new jobs in the United States by 1995. In addition, communications technology and increasing global trade are linking more and more parts of the world and reducing barriers to trade. These diverse trends will certainly affect your career opportunities in management. There are few jobs, if any, that are not influenced by the new borderless and culturally diverse global economy.

The successful manager in the twenty-first century will need to be globally aware, looking beyond his or her own region or country to the whole world. Being globally aware requires objectivity, tolerance, and knowledge. Objectivity is crucial in assessing opportunities, evaluating potential markets and opportunities, and resolving problems. Tolerance of cultural differences does not mean you have to accept, as your own, the cultural ways of other countries, but it does mean that you must permit others to be different and equal. Managers should accept the differences that may exist between cultures and make use of that understanding to relate effectively. Finally, a globally aware person will stay informed about social and economic trends because a country's prospects can change, sometimes seemingly overnight, as social, political, and economic trends shift direction or accelerate.

This increasingly borderless world is creating many career opportunities, and most new jobs will have at least some global component as managers make strategic decisions about foreign markets. Students looking for more direct involvement in global trade may consider import or export jobs in a variety of firms, both large and small. An export manager is responsible for managing all of a large company's exporting activities and supervises the activities of foreign sales representatives who live and work abroad. Export sales managers process foreign customers' orders and draw up contracts and arrange shipping details; export credit managers review the customers' financial status and arrange credit terms. For importing tasks, a company generally employs a support manager to handle the purchase of foreign goods and raw materials and to supervise the work of buyers, who live and work abroad. Instead of hiring their own import and export workers, companies may elect to engage the services of export brokers, who sell companies' goods abroad for a commission, or import merchants, who sell products from foreign countries in this country. A company may also sell its goods to export commissionhouse brokers, who are speculators who buy domestic goods outright and then sell them in foreign countries. Import and export workers can advance to management and executive positions. Buyers and foreign representatives sometimes advance by going into business for themselves as export brokers or import merchants.

While the likelihood of your receiving a foreign assignment when you get your first management job is low at this time, the possibility of developing and implementing global strategies is high. Today many colleges and universities are encouraging study in international business, foreign languages, cross-cultural communication, and related areas in order to be prepared for the borderless world. In the future, you can expect that it will be a requirement, not an option, to have global management skills.

*Sources:* Philip R. Cateora, *International Marketing*, 8th ed. (Homewood, Ill.: Richard D. Irwin, 1993), 25-26; *Global Exchanges*, T. Bettina Cornwell, ed. (Boston: Allyn and Bacon, 1993), 61-63; "The NAFTA: Exports, Jobs, Wages, and Investment," *Business America*, October 18, 1993, 3; and *VGM's Handbook of Business & Management Careers*, Annette Selden, ed. (Lincolnwood, Ill.: VGM Career Horizons, 1993), 43-44.

had failed to research the Indian market and had decided to introduce its regular all-beef patty menu there, its revenues in India would likely have been quite low and it may even have experienced resistance from the Hindu population. Some companies rely on local managers to gain greater insights and faster response to changes within a country. Managers today need to "think globally, act locally," that is, while constantly being aware of the whole picture, they must adapt their firms' strategies to accommodate local markets.

Organizing a business operating in the global marketplace is also challenging. It is difficult enough to organize a domestic business to operate effectively and efficiently; the task is considerably more complex for a business with facilities and subsidiaries around the world. How much decision-making authority and responsibility will local managers have? What organizational structure is most appropriate for the firm? The answers to such questions depend on the firm's resources, the abilities of its managers, and the countries in which it does business. We will take a closer look at organizing considerations in Chapters 12 and 13.

Leading is an especially complex task for managers working outside their own country. Managers must learn to deal not only with different languages, but also with different customs, values, and work ethics. Moreover, what motivates an employee from the United States to work hard may not have value in another country with a different work ethic. How much supervision is acceptable in a certain country? How much participation should employees have? How should a manager discipline an employee for unacceptable behavior? Managers must learn to respect and accommodate the needs of their employees regardless of what country they are in.

Issues such as productivity, quality control, information systems, and more are just as important in overseas facilities as they are at home. Clearly, when a business fails to meet its goals in overseas markets, managers must determine why and take corrective action. Such action may involve altering strategies for a particular market or abandoning it altogether—both very costly alternatives.

As we've pointed out in this chapter, many past political barriers to trade have fallen or been minimized, opening and expanding new market opportunities. Managers who can meet the challenges of planning, organizing, leading, and controlling effectively and sensitively in the global marketplace can help lead their companies in meeting these opportunities. Multinational corporations such as General Electric and Ford, which derive a substantial portion of their revenues from international business, depend on savvy managers who can adapt to different cultures. Small businesses, too, can succeed in foreign markets when their managers have carefully studied those markets and prepared and implemented appropriate strategies. Being globally aware is therefore an important quality for today's managers and will become a critical attribute for managers in the twenty-first century.

**Example:** Even in the EC, McDonald's must use local sources for beef and assure customers that beef is EC approved. Some European customers prefer not to eat hormone-treated U.S. beef products.

**Example:** FedEx Corporation had to change its air express operations in the United Kingdom. Because the United Kingdom is a geographically concentrated market with efficient rail delivery of the Royal Mail twice per day, the need for express shipments was minimal. Instead, in the United Kingdom the company concentrates on forwarding shipments to other world markets.

## SUMMARY AND REVIEW

- **Analyze the factors within the global trade environment that influence business.** The sociocultural environment includes culture, language, body language, local customs, time perception, religious considerations, and more. The political environment may relate to the stability of a country, while the legal environment establishes rules and regulations for conducting business in a certain country. Trade restrictions are part of the legal environment of a country, but their imposition may be politically motivated. The economic environment of a country affects how business may be conducted there and includes the level of economic development, what infrastructure exists, and exchange rates. Trade facilitators such as GATT, the World Bank, and International Monetary Fund foster global business by working to reduce trade restrictions and loaning money to developing nations.

- **Specify the different levels of organizational involvement in international trade.** A company may be involved in international trade at several levels, each requiring a greater commitment of resources and effort. Exporting is the sale of goods and services to foreign markets; importing is the purchase of goods and services from a foreign source. Countertrade agreements involve bartering products for other products instead of currency. At the next level, a trading company links buyers and sellers in different countries to facilitate trade. In licensing, one company agrees to allow a foreign company the use of its company name, products, patents, brands, trademarks, raw materials, and production processes, in exchange for a flat fee or a royalty. Franchising is a form of licensing in which a franchiser agrees to provide a franchisee a name, logo, methods of operation, advertising, products, and other elements associated with the franchiser's business, in return for a financial commitment and the agreement to conduct business in accordance with the franchiser's standard of operations. Contract manufacturing occurs when a company hires a foreign company to produce a specified volume of the firm's product to specification; the final product carries the domestic firm's name. A joint venture is a partnership in which companies from different countries agree to share the costs and operation of the business. The purchase of overseas production and marketing facilities is direct investment. Outsourcing, a form of direct investment, involves transferring manufacturing or other tasks to countries where labor and supplies are cheap. A multinational corporation is one that operates on a worldwide scale, without significant ties to any one nation or region.

- **Summarize the various trade agreements and alliances that have developed worldwide and how they influence business activities.** There are many important regional trade alliances and agreements that create both difficulties and opportunities for business. These include the North American Free Trade Agreement, the European Economic Community, Pacific Rim markets, and Eastern Europe and the former Soviet Union.

- **Determine how global business affects management.** Competing in an increasingly global economy provides both opportunities and challenges for today's managers and affects how they engage in planning, organizing, leading, and controlling.

- **Assess the opportunities and problems facing a small business considering expanding into international markets.** The "Business Dilemma" box presents a small business looking to expand to international markets. Using the material provided in the chapter, you should develop a plan for taking the business international; the planning process should include evaluating specific markets, anticipating problems, and analyzing methods of international involvement.

## Key Terms and Concepts

global business (globalization) *124*
international business *124*
cartel *128*
Webb-Pomerene Export Trade Act *128*
Foreign Corrupt Practices Act *128*
import tariff *128*
exchange controls *129*
quota *130*
embargo *130*
dumping *130*

infrastructure *131*
exchange rate *131*
General Agreement on Tariffs and Trade (GATT) *131*
World Bank *133*
International Monetary Fund (IMF) *133*
exporting *134*
importing *134*
countertrade agreements *134*

trading company *136*
licensing *136*
franchising *137*
contract manufacturing *137*
joint venture *137*
strategic alliance *137*
direct investment *138*
outsourcing *138*
multinational corporation (MNC) *139*

## Ready Recall

1. How do social and cultural differences create barriers to international trade? Can you think of any additional social or cultural barriers (other than those mentioned in your text) that might inhibit international business?
2. How do political issues affect global business?
3. What is an import tariff? A quota? Dumping? Why can dumping result in the imposition of tariffs and quotas?
4. What effect does a country's economic environment have on global business?
5. How does the General Agreement on Tariffs and Trade (GATT) facilitate trade?

6. At what levels might a firm get involved in global business? What level requires the least commitment of resources? What level requires the most?
7. Compare and contrast licensing, franchising, contract manufacturing, and outsourcing.
8. Discuss the opportunities that have arisen from the various regional trade alliances and agreements discussed in this chapter. Discuss the difficulties.
9. How does global business affect the four managerial functions? Why is being globally aware so important a quality in managers today?

## Expand Your Experience

1. If the United States were to impose additional tariffs on automobiles imported from Japan, what would happen to the price of Japanese cars sold in the United States? What would happen to the price of American cars? What action might Japan take to continue to compete in the U.S. automobile market?

2. Study the recent Uruguay Round of GATT from the perspective of the U.S. motion picture industry. What had that industry hoped to gain from the GATT negotiations and why was it not able to achieve that hope? What does the future hold for the U.S. motion picture industry in foreign markets?

3. Identify a local company that is active in international trade. What is its level of international business involvement and why? Analyze the threats and opportunities it faces in foreign markets, as well as its strengths and weaknesses in meeting those challenges. Based on your analysis, make some recommendations for the business's future involvement in international trade. (Your instructor may ask you to share your report with the business.)

**CASE**

# Danek Goes Global

The Danek Group, Inc., is a Memphis-based firm involved in producing and marketing a wide variety of spinal implant devices. Founded by several former executives of a rival orthopedics company, Danek was established in 1983 as Biotechnology, Inc., in Warsaw, Indiana, where the company continues to operate its primary production facilities. By 1987, annual sales had climbed to nearly $5 million. Three years later, the company officially became known as the Danek Group, Inc.

Spinal implant devices such as those produced and marketed by Danek are used in the surgical treatment of degenerative diseases and deformities—such as scoliosis, a sideways curvature of the spine—and to increase stability during the healing of spinal injuries. Often, these products function by linking two or more vertebrae in the spine itself. Although the spinal implant products constituting Danek's TSRH product line account for nearly 85 percent of its sales, the company also manufactures and markets both metal plates and screws used to fixate bones, as well as wiring products used in surgical procedures of the spine. Additionally, the company engages in contract manufacturing, building highly specialized equipment according to individual customer specification.

Danek continued to prosper throughout the early 1990s, marketing its products primarily in the United States and eventually becoming the market leader. However, Danek managers realized that the company would need to increase its level of international involvement—recognizing the fact that the market for their products had become global in nature—and that Danek would have to expand its operations beyond its domestic boundaries in order to ensure continued growth. This realization was, in part, due to the fact that the company had grown somewhat frustrated with the relatively slow and costly process of introducing new products in its domestic market. This difficulty, one experienced by many medical products companies regardless of national origin, was due to higher levels of testing required for product use in the United States as opposed to other major countries.

In 1992, Danek made international expansion a top corporate priority, opening its first two international sales offices. The new locations—in Japan and Germany—contributed to an 88 percent increase in international sales, which as a whole accounted for nearly 10 percent of total corporate revenues. That same year, the company posted record sales and income of $76 million and $13 million—up from $41 and $7 million—respectively. Also in 1992, Danek was recognized by *Business Week* as one of the top ten small corporations in the United States.

Danek's international expansion continued in 1993, with the announcement of the company's merger with French competitor Sofamor, S.A. Danek's new partner was recognized as a leader in the innovation and development of spinal implant devices, having gained this reputation by, among other things, actively training surgeons in product use, a practice believed to have led to increased use of spinal implant devices worldwide. As a result of the merger, the newly formed organization emerged as the world's largest developer and marketer of spinal implant products, with an estimated 40 percent share of the global market.

Headquartered in France, Sofamor had established a strong international presence in both the European Community and Pacific Rim nations with subsidiaries in Spain, Hong Kong, Italy, and Germany. Like Danek, Sofamor had built up a satisfied network of surgeons using its products with whom the company worked very closely to improve ongoing research and development, as well as customer satisfaction. Also like its U.S.-based partner, Sofamor had developed sales and distribution practices specifically tailored to the cultural and industry peculiarities of the many markets in which its products were sold. Sofamor estimated that its products were used in 45 different countries and that 60 percent of its 1992 sales of $46 million (in U.S. dollars) were accounted for internationally.

In general, marketing strategies for spinal implant devices can be globalized, that is, one basic strategy can be used for all markets. This is due to the fact that spines, as well as spinal diseases, deformities, and injuries, are essentially the same regardless of geographical market, which makes it possible to use identical products worldwide. Where customization becomes a factor, however, is in regard to how the product is sold, inasmuch as customer preferences—primarily of surgeons and hospitals—differ due to deep-seated social and cultural forces found within individual markets. For example, in marketing in Japan, it is necessary to focus on the development of long-term relationships with both hospitals and subdistributors, as these parties have more of a role in the buying process than in many other markets.

For the several years prior to 1992, demand for spinal implant devices had been growing rapidly due to several distinct factors. In the United States, for example, which is the largest market for such products, the aging of the population, combined with more active lifestyles across all age groups, led to the occurrence of more back injuries, as well as to degenerative diseases and deformities that could possibly be corrected through implant use. Also, global trends such as innovations in product technology, growing evidence of the benefits of implant use, and an increasing number of spinal surgeons trained to use the devices were also responsible for this steady increase in demand.

As a result of this growing demand, other medical products companies have been entering the spinal implant market, a trend expected to continue for some time to come. Many of these new entrants are subsidiaries of corporations much larger—and with more resources—than either Danek or Sofamor. For example, Bristol-Myers Squibb, one of the largest pharmaceutical and medical-products companies in the world with 1992 sales and profits of $11.8 billion and $2.0 billion respectively, recently entered the market.

In early 1994, Sofamor Danek announced it had signed patent agreements regarding two innovative spinal implant technologies to be incorporated into its products. Specifically, the company signed agreements concerning both a group of technologies used to stabilize the spine during spinal fusion and disectomy, as well as one covering implants, instruments, and methods for simultaneously removing a damaged disc and implanting a device in a single laparoscopic-type procedure. Products incorporating the new technologies were expected to be available worldwide by mid- to late 1994.

As the newly formed Sofamor Danek Group prepared to venture out into the highly competitive global spinal implant marketplace, officials with the company expressed confidence in their union. Industry analysts shared this optimism, with annual sales estimates for the newly formed multinational enterprise as high as $295 million by 1995.

*Sources:* Laurel Campbell, "Danek Buys French Concern," *The (Memphis) Commercial Appeal,* June 22, 1993, B3; Laurel Campbell, "Danek to Merge, Erect New Quarters," *The Commercial Appeal,* March 30, 1993, A1; Laurel Campbell, "Sofamor Danek Signs 2 Patent Agreements," *The Commercial Appeal,* January 15, 1994, B5; Danek Group, Inc., 1992 Annual Report; Danek Group, Inc. Notice of Annual Meeting of Shareholders, June 1993; "Guide to the Global 500," *Fortune,* July 26, 1993, 187; *Hoover's Handbook of Emerging Companies 1993,* Patrick Spain, Alta Campbell, and Alan Chai, eds. (Austin, TX: The Reference Press, Inc., 1993); and Scott Shepard, "Sofamor/Danek Merger Gives Firm Backbone," *The Memphis Business Journal,* July 12–16, 1993, 1.

## Questions

1. From a global expansion perspective, what potential benefits might have motivated Danek to merge with Sofamor? Similarly, why would the merger with Danek have seemed advantageous to Sofamor?
2. Discuss the nature of Danek's increasing level of international involvement. Specifically, in addition to the merger with Sofamor, what has the company done to ensure successful international expansion?
3. What additional strategic moves pertaining to its level of international involvement might the Danek Group consider implementing to increase its competitiveness in the growing global spinal implant market?

## STRENGTHEN YOUR SKILLS
## *Learning about Other Cultures*

Many forces in recent years have contributed to "shrinking" our globe. Two of the more dominant forces are the growth of the world economy and the explosion of electronic media that link the world—media such as newspapers, televisions, fax machines, computers, and satellite communication systems. As trade barriers crumble and international trade continues to escalate, more and more Americans will be doing business face to face, both here and abroad, with people from different cultures.

One characteristic often attributed to Americans traveling around the globe—whether for business or for pleasure—is they offend the natives in the country they're visiting by expecting them to think, talk, act, eat, do business, and behave the "American way." "You mean you don't speak English here?" "Where's the ice machine?" "Why do they keep me waiting?" "Don't they have any normal food around here?" "Why doesn't she look me in the eye when she talks to me?"

When your job requires you to deal with people from other parts of the world, you need to adopt an attitude of "Here is my way. Now what is yours?" The more you see that you are part of a complex world and that your culture is different from, not better than, others, the better you will communicate and the more effective you will be in a variety of situations. It takes time, energy, understanding, and tolerance to learn about and appreciate different cultures. Naturally you're more comfortable doing things the way you've always done them. Remember, however, that that fact will also be true of the people from different cultures with whom you are doing business.

One training tool that companies such as Allstate Insurance, Kraft General Foods, 3M Company, and Procter & Gamble are using to help their employees understand people from other cultures is the board game *DIVERSOPHY*™— *Understanding the Human Race.* The game contains, among many other features, a set of 60 *diversiSMARTS*™ cards that develop your knowledge of facts about other cultures. (The "Strengthen Your Skills" exercise at the end of Chapter 6 will give you information on other features of the game.)

Here are five questions taken from the *diversiSMARTS*™ cards. See how many you know:

1. In Hispanic families, one of the highest values is placed on:
   A. achievement
   B. money
   C. being on time
   D. respect for elders

2. In group sessions, some Japanese find it hard to share their feelings and ideas because:
   A. the Americans do all the talking
   B. they are a very shy people
   C. they feel it's inappropriate to tell personal experiences in public

3. People from Spanish-speaking countries may tend to _____ differences between people related to age, status, or gender.
   A. emphasize
   B. ignore
   C. minimize

4. If the world could be reduced to the size of a village in which there were 546 Asians, 210 Europeans, 86 Africans, and 80 South Americans, proportionately how many North Americans would live in the village?
   A. 60
   B. 124
   C. 92

5. In most Asian-American cultures, respect for another person is indicated by:
   A. looking them in the eye
   B. looking down and avoiding eye contact
   C. turning one's body in order to look to the side

Check your answers with your instructor.

Whether you got all five answers correct or whether you got all five wrong, you should have an interest in learning more about other cultures. The more you learn, the more effective you will function as a citizen of our global economy. The list that follows presents some ways you can increase your knowledge and understanding of different cultures. In a class discussion, select one of the items that you have done and relay to the rest of your class how it helped you learn more about another culture. Consider selecting one of these items you've never tried and see if you can use it to help you learn more about another culture.

- Be alert to and take advantage of opportunities to talk to and get to know people from other races and ethnic groups. You can find them in your neighborhood, in your classes, at your fitness center, at a concert or sporting event—just about anywhere you go. Take the initiative to strike up a conversation and show a genuine interest in getting to know the other person.
- Select a culture you're interested in and immerse yourself in that culture. Read novels, look at art, take courses, see plays.
- College students often have unique opportunities to travel inexpensively to other countries—for example, as a member of a performing arts group, or a humanitarian mission group, or as part of a college course studying abroad. Actively seek out travel opportunities that will expose you to as many cultures as possible during your college education.
- Study a foreign language.
- Expand your taste buds. The next time you're going to go to a restaurant, instead of choosing that old familiar favorite, use the Yellow Pages to find a restaurant that serves ethnic food you've never tried before.
- Many large metropolitan cities sponsor ethnic festivals, particularly in the summertime, where you can go and take in the sights and sounds of other cultures. Take advantage of these opportunities to have a fun time learning about cultures that are different from yours.

*Source:* © 1992 MULTUS INC., 46 Treetop Lane, Suite #200, San Mateo, CA 94402 (415) 342-2040. Permission granted to adapt this material from *DIVERSOPHY*™—*Understanding the Human Race.*

*chapter* ■ *six*

# The
# Dynamics
*of*
# Diversity

**Outline**

**After reading this chapter, you will be able to:**

- Define cultural diversity and explain why it has become so important in business.

- Examine some of the significant cultural groups in the American work force and discuss some issues of concern to each.

- Determine the benefits and problems associated with cultural diversity in the work force.

- Assess different organizational approaches to managing work-force diversity.

- Explain how work-force diversity is created, maintained, and valued by a truly multicultural organization.

- Propose a plan for turning a company into a multicultural organization.

# U S West Seeks Strength from Cultural Diversity

**B**elieving there is strength in cultural diversity, U S West, Inc., a Denver-based telecommunications company, is trying to employ more Native American Indians and other minorities. The firm already employs nearly 650 American Indians—about 1 percent of its work force—but wants to raise that figure. CEO Richard McCormick says American Indian participation in U S West's work force is important, in part, because half of the American Indians in the United States live and work within the 14-state area his company serves.

U S West has not resorted to quotas to boost its representation of American Indian employees, nor lowered its standards to "let" minorities gain employment. Instead, the company tries to develop for each position a pool of potential candidates, relying on every possible resource to ensure that minorities are included and have a chance to gain those positions.

To boost employment of Native Americans, the company developed the American Indian Leadership Initiative (AILI). AILI has much support from the company's top executives, which is critical if the company wants to show current employees that it values cultural diversity.

Externally, AILI focuses on recruiting new employees from tribal colleges. The company sends American Indian employees, including Denise St. Cyr, director of human resources and a member of the Nebraska Winnebago tribe, to talk with students about what it is like being an American Indian in the corporate world and to provide information about U S West. Although the company initially focused its recruiting efforts on six tribal colleges, it has also donated $1.3 million to the American Indian College Fund as well as to 21 tribal colleges. U S West also supports minority student organizations at many colleges and universities and funds scholarships for minority students as well as programs that help colleges and universities attract more minority high school students.

Internally, the company holds workshops to help Indian employees recognize and deal with cultural differences, learn to be more competitive in the corporate world, and find the right career path. The company also has a support group for its Indian employees, the Voice of Many Feathers. The group gave CEO McCormick the Lakota Sioux name *Wambli Ohitika,* or "Eagle Who Cares about People," in a traditional naming ceremony. They also gave him a painted buffalo pelt illustrated by artist Dawn Little Sky, which depicts his life story from birth to his appointment as "chief" of U S West. The pelt includes illustrations depicting the development of communications from smoke signals to telegraph lines, which the Lakota tribe once called "singing wires."

The American Indian Leadership Initiative and other programs developed by U S West demonstrate the company's commitment to cultural diversity. By providing opportunities for American Indians and other minorities who live in its operating area, U S West is helping to ensure that it has quality human resources for the future—valuable employees who can help it meet the needs of a culturally diverse customer base.

*Sources:* "CEO of U S West Is Eagle Who Cares," *Fortune,* February 10, 1992, 141; telephone interview with John Graboski, director of university relations at U S West, February 21, 1992; and telephone interview with Denise St. Cyr, director of human resources at U S West, February 24, 1992.

*introduction*

As we move toward the twenty-first century, the U.S. work force is becoming increasingly diverse. Once dominated by white men, today's work force includes significantly more women, blacks, Hispanics, and other minorities, as well as handicapped and older workers. While the proportion of these groups within the work force is increasing, the overall growth of the U.S. labor force has declined to less than 2 percent a year. To have sufficient human resources to remain competitive and meet the needs of an increasingly diverse customer base, companies such as U S West are expending more effort to recruit, retain, manage, and motivate workers of different cultures.

In this chapter we focus on the increasing importance of cultural diversity in the work force. First we define cultural diversity and examine several important cultural groups in the American work force. Next we discuss the benefits and problems associated with a culturally diverse work force. Finally, we look at the ways organizations can manage their diverse human resources more effectively.

## WHAT IS CULTURAL DIVERSITY?

The U.S. Labor Department estimates that, between now and the year 2005, 50 percent of all new entrants into the work force will be women, and one-third will be Hispanics, blacks, and other minorities.[1] Already, minorities and immigrants hold more than 22 percent of all jobs in the United States. By 2000, minorities and immigrants will hold 26 percent of all jobs, and women will hold 47 percent.[2] Table 6.1 shows how the American work force has changed over the years.

Additionally, the work force of tomorrow will become increasingly older as the American population ages. This is due in part to the aging of the "baby boom" generation. By 2000, one in three workers will be over age 45.[3] These older workers will be more concerned with issues such as medical benefits, profit sharing, and retirement accounts as well as job security. It is possible that with people living longer, elder care will have a greater impact on the workplace than child care.[4] The number of people 85 and older who rely on their children will nearly double by 2030 and more than triple by 2050. The U.S. Census Bureau indicates that families provide 80 percent of needed long-term care. Elder care remains largely

**TABLE 6.1**

### The Changing American Work Force

|  | 1966 | 1980 | 1990 |
|---|---|---|---|
| Women | 35.0% | 42.0% | 45.0% |
| Blacks | 6.5% | 9.4% | 10.1% |
| Hispanics | NA | 5.6% | 7.5% |
| Asians | NA | 1.0% | 2.6% |

*Source:* U.S. Department of Labor, Bureau of Labor Statistics, 1991.

*Note:* NA = Not Available.

**Critical Thinking Challenge:** After studying Table 6.1, have students discuss the implications changing diversity patterns will have on organizations. Focus on both human resource implications as well as marketing and promotional issue changes.

**TABLE 6.2**

## Percentage of Population in Each Cultural Group, by Age

| Age | White | Black | Hispanic | Asian/Pacific Islander | Native American | Other Races |
|---|---|---|---|---|---|---|
| 0–9 | 74.8 | 15.0 | 12.6 | 3.3 | 1.1 | 5.9 |
| 10–19 | 75.1 | 15.1 | 11.6 | 3.3 | 1.1 | 5.4 |
| 20–29 | 77.3 | 13.1 | 11.5 | 3.3 | 0.8 | 5.5 |
| 30–39 | 79.9 | 12.0 | 8.9 | 3.3 | 0.8 | 4.0 |
| 40–49 | 82.9 | 10.4 | 7.1 | 3.1 | 0.7 | 2.9 |
| 50–59 | 84.4 | 10.1 | 6.4 | 2.6 | 0.6 | 2.3 |
| 60–69 | 87.4 | 8.8 | 4.8 | 1.9 | 0.5 | 1.5 |
| 70–79 | 89.3 | 7.9 | 3.5 | 1.4 | 0.4 | 0.9 |
| 80+ | 90.4 | 7.5 | 3.2 | 1.0 | 0.3 | 0.8 |
| All ages | 80.3 | 12.1 | 9.0 | 2.9 | 0.8 | 3.9 |

*Source:* U.S. Bureau of Census, 1990.

*Note:* Hispanics may be of different races; hence, the percentages do not equal 100 percent.

undiscussed at most companies and is a hidden issue that causes stress for many employees who disrupt their service to take care of aging parents.[5]

These changes mirror those taking place in the United States as a whole. The U.S. Census Bureau estimates that by the year 2050, the percentage of whites will decline to 53 percent from the current 75 percent, while the projected U.S. population of 383 million will be 21 percent Hispanic, 15 percent black, 10 percent Asian, and 1 percent Native American.[6] One reason for this change is that birthrates among some minority groups are high, as seen in Table 6.2. Immigration into the United States is at an all-time high, and a new law passed in the early 1990s increased immigration limits from 560,000 to 700,000 per year. The result could be more middle-class minorities, changing the stereotypes on which racism is based. Today, minorities already form majorities in 51 large cities.[7]

With the changes taking place in the U.S. population, it is not surprising that organizations are facing challenges in effectively managing this increasingly diverse work force. To remain competitive in tomorrow's marketplace, today's organizations must accept, value, *and* manage their culturally diverse work forces.

## Understanding the Characteristics of Cultural Diversity

**Cultural diversity** refers to differences in age, gender, race, ethnicity, nationality, and ability. Understanding cultural diversity means recognizing and accepting differences. When managers speak of culturally diverse work forces, they are generally referring to differences in gender and race, and while gender and race are important characteristics of cultural diversity, others are also important, as shown in Figure 6.1. In the inner circle of Figure 6.1, age, gender, race, ethnicity, abilities, and sexual orientation represent **primary characteristics of diversity**, which are inborn characteristics that cannot be changed. They define our

**cultural diversity**
Differences in age, gender, race, ethnicity, nationality, and ability.

**primary characteristics of diversity**
Inborn characteristics, such as age, gender, race, ethnicity, abilities, and sexual orientation, that cannot be changed.

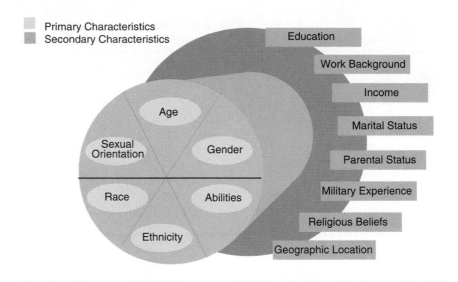

*Source:*  Marilyn Loden and Judy B. Rosener, *Workforce America! Managing Employee Diversity as a Vital Resource* (Homewood, IL:  Business One Irwin, 1991), 20. Used with permission.

**secondary characteristics of diversity**
Characteristics, such as work background, marital status, and education, that can be changed.

self-image and shape our thoughts, feelings, and behaviors. Because they cannot be changed, we cannot escape their impact.

In the outer circle of Figure 6.1 are eight **secondary characteristics of diversity**—work background, income, marital status, military experience, religious beliefs, geographic location, parental status, and education—that can be changed. We acquire, change, and discard them as we progress through our lives.[8] While these attributes are not part of our core identity, they do add to our self-image, thoughts, feelings, and behaviors. Sometimes they can be as powerful in shaping behavior as the primary attributes.

Dividing characteristics of cultural diversity into primary and secondary components facilitates our understanding, but we must remember that each person is defined by the interrelation of all characteristics. In dealing with diversity in the work force, managers must consider the complete individual, not one or a few of a person's differences. In the next section, we look at some specific cultural groups in the American work force and how their different characteristics create issues for American business.

**Example:** With the growing emphasis on Americans with disabilities and the ADA (Americans with Disabilities Act) some organizations have hired workers in wheelchairs to provide suggestions on ways to arrange and configure office furniture to meet the needs of the disabled.

## CULTURAL GROUPS IN THE AMERICAN WORK FORCE

Although federal laws such as the Equal Pay Act of 1963 and the Civil Rights Act of 1964 prohibit discrimination in hiring and compensating workers, inequities still exist in the workplace. Minorities, women, and the disabled have traditionally been denied the opportunities for experience in organizations that would enable them to assume leadership roles in corporate America.

**FIGURE 6.2**

## The Wage Gap: Blacks versus Whites

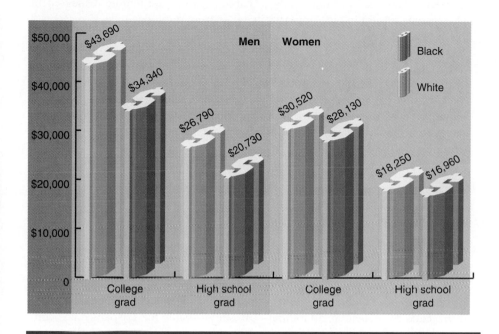

*Source:* U.S. Census Bureau, 1993.

## Minorities

Blacks (also called African-Americans), Hispanics, Asians, and Native Americans all face equality issues in the workplace. Hispanics, for example, have an unemployment rate of 11.4 percent; blacks, an unemployment rate of 14.1 percent. In contrast, the unemployment rate for whites is only 6.5 percent.[9] And, just as they hold fewer jobs than whites, members of these minority groups also tend to earn less money—a fact that often perpetuates their economic status because they cannot afford better educations to merit higher-paying jobs.

**Blacks.**    During the 1980s, the black population grew by 13.2 percent, faster than the U.S. population as a whole. The black population is concentrated in the southeastern United States, with significant groups scattered elsewhere around the country.[10] In general, blacks have experienced higher rates of unemployment and lower wages than whites. They also tend to have less education. Even with a college education, blacks still earn less than whites: White males ages 25 and older earn 27 to 29 percent more than black men with similar levels of education.[11] Figure 6.2 illustrates the black-white income gap. The gap is smaller for women but affects high school and college graduates equally. White women ages 25 and older who work full time earn 7 to 8 percent more than black women.[12]

Some blacks have risen to positions of power. Noteworthy examples are General Colin Powell, former Chief of Staff of the U.S. Armed Services; Erroll Davis, CEO of WPL Holdings and the first black chief executive to be named in *Business Week* magazine's list of the CEOs of the *Business Week* 1000 companies[13];

the late Reginald Lewis, former CEO of TLC Corporation; Bill Cosby, entertainer and philanthropist; and Jesse Jackson, an African-American political leader and head of the Rainbow Coalition. Such successful black leaders inspire other blacks to strive for success, but the reality is that few get beyond middle management. The reasons for limited job opportunity range from prejudice to lack of access to job networks.

Even at the lowest levels of business, black workers may face prejudice and discrimination from their coworkers and superiors—which lower their self-esteem, satisfaction, and morale. In a much-publicized instance, Marge Schott, owner of the Cincinnati Reds baseball team, was accused of making racist slurs and, consequently, was fined, had her ownership privileges revoked, and experienced extensive negative publicity.[14] Such an example indicates the prejudice that remains a problem in the 1990s.

**Hispanics.**    Hispanics represent the fastest growing minority group in the United States, particularly in California, Texas, Florida, New York, and Illinois. According to the U.S. Census, over 17 million people in the United States speak Spanish, and 54 percent of these do not speak English at home. Many are recent immigrants from Mexico and other Latin American countries. Like blacks, Hispanics generally have higher unemployment rates, lower wages, and less education. Consequently, few Hispanics reach middle and upper levels of management in the United States; a notable exception is Roberto Goizueta, a Cuban immigrant who now heads the Coca-Cola Company. Business issues for Hispanics are compounded by a language barrier because many new immigrants, as well as some long-time U.S. residents, speak little or no English. Consequently, they not only face discrimination and prejudice, but also may have difficulty communicating their needs, wants, and ideas in the workplace.

Additionally, Hispanics bring different religious and cultural values to the workplace, which may bring them into conflict with coworkers and superiors. In general, Hispanics place a high value on religion and family, which may generate conflict when managers or coworkers expect them to place work issues ahead of the family and church. Other workers may inadvertently or deliberately discriminate against Hispanic coworkers and subordinates by failing to recognize differences in values and/or to deal with language problems in the work force. Hispanics may find it harder to break into the communication network and gain information necessary for career advancement.

**Asians.**    Immigrants from Japan, China, Vietnam, Korea, Singapore, the Philippines, and other Asian countries, along with their descendants, make up another significant cultural group in the U.S. work force. Like Hispanics, Asian Americans often bring to the workplace different languages and cultural and religious values, which may lead to discrimination by, and conflict and misunderstandings with, coworkers and managers. Asians generally place a high value on education and work; consequently, Americans of Asian ancestry have generally achieved a higher level of education, enabling some Asians to gain more business ownership and upper management positions. As a whole, Asian Americans have also gained more relative wealth and more white-collar jobs than have other minority groups. However, like other minority groups, Asian Americans remain outside the highest levels of corporate America in all but a tiny group of companies.

**Examples:** Studies have shown that some tests discriminate against African-Americans and women. In particular, the SAT (Scholastic Aptitude Test) has been shown to generate lower scores for these groups as it doesn't consider the cultural diversity of women and African-Americans.

**Example:** Conversely, the presence of Hispanics in the United States creates opportunities to market products to these groups. Organizations have developed advertisements for Spanish language publications. Television stations targeting these markets have also emerged.

**Native Americans.**    Native Americans include members of the Navajo, Sioux, Mohawk, Seminole, Apache, Comanche, Cherokee, Hopi, Tlingit, and many other tribes. Although Native Americans make up only a tiny percent of the U.S. population, awareness of past harsh treatment and current problems of different tribes has been heightened in recent years with the environmental movement, movies such as *Dances with Wolves* and *Thunderheart,* and other events. Entrepreneurship among Native Americans is on the rise, but they continue to face problems similar to those of other minority groups: lack of education, very high unemployment, low wages, and language and cultural differences.

While all Native Americans do not live on the tribal reservations scattered throughout the United States, the majority who do face some unique problems. Job opportunities on reservations are limited, restricting most tribal members to jobs in government, tourism, and the arts. Unemployment on many reservations often exceeds 50 percent. Health care, education, and utilities on reservations are often lacking. Few corporations locate facilities on the reservations; those that do often must form joint ventures with the tribe itself. More recently, many Indian tribes have been involved in parimutuel gambling operations. Most Indian reservations are considered sovereign states, which means they cannot be regulated directly by state government. This has allowed some tribes to attain some degree of prosperity from gaming activities in states that otherwise do not allow gambling.[15]

Tribal customs and ceremonies may result in conflict with other tribes and other cultural groups when members do find work in off-reservation businesses. For example, a medicine man may have difficulty taking eight days off from his off-reservation job to conduct a healing ceremony, which helps his tribe retain its cultural identity. Additionally, government policies may contribute to the cycle of poverty and poor education among Native Americans, denying them the motivation to succeed as entrepreneurs and employees.

## Women

Women, too, are underrepresented and underpaid relative to men, despite the fact that they are entering the work force in record numbers (see Figures 6.3 and 6.4). Women tend to be concentrated in low-paying clerical, sales, and teaching jobs, and in general do not have as much formal education as do men. The average pay for a woman with a high school diploma is about $17,500 a year—$28,300 a year for a woman who has graduated from a four-year college. The earnings gap between college-educated women and those with high school diplomas is expected to keep widening.[16] According to the U.S. Census Bureau, on average, women currently earn 70 cents for every $1 earned by men. (In 1981, the gap was 59 cents per $1; in 1939, 58 cents per $1.[17]) The situation for minority women is even bleaker, with black and Hispanic women earning 62 cents and 54 cents, respectively, for every $1 earned by white men.[18]

Like minority group members, women have trouble getting through the so-called glass ceiling to reach upper-level management in larger companies. Women are outnumbered by men at the executive vice-president level by nearly three to one.[19] Women own just 18 percent of franchises according to the International Franchise Association, a leading trade group, which says franchisors still view women as extensions of their husbands. In addition, pressure to succeed can be greater on women because they are not encouraged to take risks.[20] Elizabeth Dole, who heads the American Red Cross; Janet Reno, U.S. Attorney General;

**Example:** Organizations are recognizing the importance of women in the workplace. Particularly in quality circles, the input of women in decision making has been critical for growth strategies and new product development.

## The Wage Gap: Women's Earnings as a Percentage of Men's

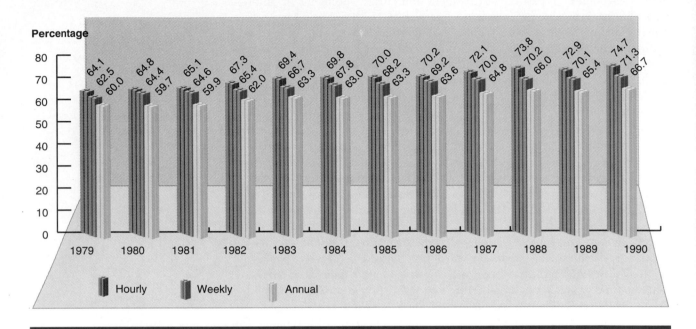

*Source:* "Facts on Working Women," U.S. Department of Labor, Women's Bureau (Washington D.C.: Government Printing Office, October 1991), 1, 2.

Linda J. Wachner, CEO of Warnacho Group; and Carol A. Bartz, CEO of Autodesk Inc., are exceptions who have broken through the glass ceiling. Former U.S. Labor Secretary Lynn Martin has argued that the glass ceiling is the product of companies failing to nurture women and minorities who have the potential to lead—because they have different attitudes and threaten the status quo. In limiting women's career paths, companies prevent them from reaching the top, where they could motivate other women and cater to the needs of women customers.[21]

**Example:** Organizations have developed four-day workweeks, flextime arrangements, and other scheduling adjustments to better meet the needs of working women.

A major issue for women in the workplace relates to the fact that they may need time off from work to have children and care for them. Figure 6.5 shows the number of women of childbearing age who stay in the work force. Federal law requires companies to give women a minimum of six weeks' unpaid maternity leave and a comparable job upon their return, but most companies have few provisions for dealing with working mothers. Moreover, leaving the work force to have children may damage a woman's career. Anne Bernstein, chairwoman of the maternity and medicine task force of the American Medical Women's Association, says that, in her profession, an employer "immediately takes for granted that you're not dedicated to your career if you take an extended leave."[22] Consequently, some businesswomen feel pressured never to have children or to leave the work force altogether if they opt to have children. Mothers who take extended time off from work are finding it hard to return because it is the view of potential employers that they have lost contacts, earning power, and, in some cases, skills. Further, a woman who chooses to quit will cost her organization its investment in her training and exper-

**FIGURE 6.4**

## Percentage of Jobs Held by Women

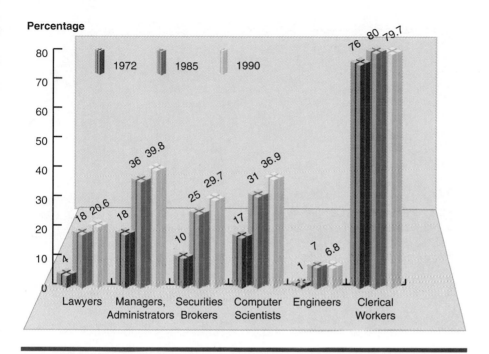

*Source.* U.S. Department of Labor, Bureau of Labor Statistics, 1991.

tise, a fact that some firms use to justify continued discrimination against women.[23] Table 6.3 presents the costs of not integrating women into the work force.

The Campbell Soup Company, Mellon Bank, Digital Equipment Corporation, and other companies are developing alternative programs that allow women to strike a balance between advancing their careers and their responsibilities as mothers. These so-called "mommy track" programs permit mothers to work part time or to work at home when their children are young, and then to resume their careers when they are ready.[24] Other companies permit working parents more flexible working hours. Still other companies provide on-site day-care programs so that working moms can spend more time with their children. Although many working mothers want to take advantage of such programs, the mommy track concept has been controversial. Feminists argue that the mommy track perpetuates discrimination against women, and businesses dislike the expense of maintaining a separate career track for working mothers.

## Persons with Disabilities

As with cultural minority groups, the nearly 15 million people with disabilities face barriers to entry and success in the work force.[25] Their barriers are physical rather than cultural, however. Mentally and physically disabled persons are frequently left out of the work force altogether because companies cannot or will not accommodate their unique needs. Wheelchair-bound workers may find they cannot get to work because of parking and mobility problems. The blind need special equipment

**FIGURE 6.5**

### Percentage of Women of Childbearing Age Staying in the Work Force

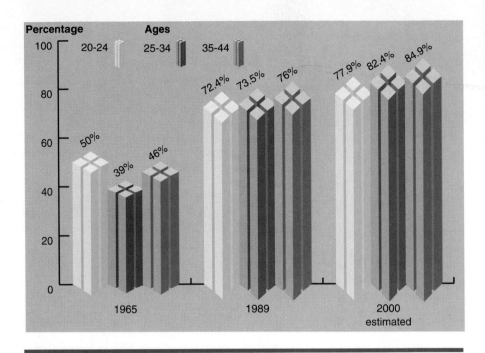

*Source:* U.S. Department of Labor, Bureau of Labor Statistics, 1991.

to give them access to information and to participate in decision making. The deaf may need translators when superiors and coworkers do not know sign language. Mentally disabled people face additional discrimination when businesses do not feel they are sufficiently competent to hold even the most menial jobs. Additionally, these same barriers prevent many disabled persons from getting more than a basic education, which further restricts their employment opportunities.

**TABLE 6.3**

### The Cost of Not Integrating Women into the Work Force

1. Not hiring or promoting the best individuals for the top levels in the organization
2. Not maintaining optimal quality at every level
3. Treating women who are hired as "dead weights" by not giving them the same promotion and training opportunities as those available to men
4. Minimizing the value of women's contribution by having them, at times, report to less competent bosses
5. Psychologically undervaluing women because of their role in childraising and domestic responsibilities
6. Wasting recruiting and training funds because women hired are often treated differently after childbirth and consequently leave the company
7. Failing to create role models for future female employees
8. Overall failing to achieve a representative work force to match the diverse consumer market

*Source:* Adapted from Felice N. Schwartz, "Women As a Business Imperative," *Harvard Business Review* 70 (March/April 1992): 105–113.

Small business owner Mike King (left), president of Mari-Mann Herb Company, Inc., provides employment opportunities for people with disabilities. About 80 percent of King's employees have a mental or physical disability. King accommodates the special needs of employees with disabilities including those with learning disorders, epilepsy, and severe visual and hearing impairments.

*Source:* © 1993 John Zich.

Some businesses—American Express, McDonald's, and FedEx, for example—have taken steps to provide greater access and opportunities for disabled workers and customers, but it is the Americans with Disabilities Act (ADA), passed in 1990, that has forced businesses to address some of the problems of the handicapped. The ADA prohibits discrimination against people with disabilities and requires that they be given the same opportunities as people without handicaps. The law requires that businesses provide access and specialized equipment to ensure that handicapped workers can participate. At Du Pont, for example, visually impaired Tom Tufano uses special computer software to help him read the papers and memos he uses in his job as a director of research in experimental photography. Pizza Hut instituted a program called Jobs Plus to recruit, train, and employ nearly 3,000 handicapped workers.[26] Such programs not only provide employment opportunities, they also enhance the self-esteem of handicapped persons and enable them to support themselves instead of living off Social Security and welfare.

## BENEFITS AND PROBLEMS OF DIVERSITY IN THE WORK FORCE

Managers are beginning to recognize that cultural diversity is a fact of life that cannot be changed. As we shall see, effectively managing cultural diversity in the work force involves cultivating and valuing its benefits and minimizing its problems.

### The Benefits of Cultural Diversity

As the U.S. population becomes increasingly diverse, serving the disparate needs of different cultural groups will become particularly important. Who better to serve the needs of culturally diverse customers than a culturally diverse work force that truly understands their individual needs? This philosophy has been put to good use by the Avon Corporation. Faced with extremely low profits in its inner-city markets, Avon made personnel changes, giving black and Hispanic managers more authority over inner-city operations. This helped Avon increase sales in inner-city markets dramatically, and today, these markets are among Avon's most profitable.[27]

Honeywell values diversity as an asset that gives the company a competitive advantage in the global marketplace. Honeywell's diverse global work force includes employees who speak 29 languages and represent 47 cultures and 90 ethnic backgrounds. Diversity Councils such as the one shown here help Honeywell managers and employees identify and resolve common issues on an ongoing basis. Honeywell has councils for American Asians, blacks, Hispanics, American Indians, employees with disabilities, older workers, Vietnam veterans, women, and those concerned with balancing work and family.

*Source:* © Jim Sims, Sims/Boynton Photography.

**Critical Thinking Challenge:** After discussing the benefits of valuing diversity, have students brainstorm other examples to add to the list.

There are a number of benefits to fostering and valuing work-force diversity, including the following:

1. More productive use of a company's human resources

2. Reduced conflict among employees from different cultural groups as they learn to respect each other's differences

3. More productive working relationships among employees from different culture groups as they learn more about and accept coworkers of "different" cultures

4. Increased commitment to and sharing of organizational goals among culturally diverse employees at all organizational levels

5. Increased innovation and creativity as employees of different cultural groups bring new, unique perspectives to decision-making and problem-solving tasks

6. Enhanced ability to serve the needs of an increasingly diverse customer base.[28]

In the area of productivity and innovation, for example, organizations that nurture their culturally diverse employees have a positive effect on their employees' perception of equity, which increases their morale, effort, and performance. This is borne out by studies that have shown that heterogeneous groups (composed of people of various races, values, backgrounds, etc.) are more productive than homogeneous groups, while other studies have shown that employees who feel valued and supported by their organizations are more innovative.[29]

A company must make a substantial commitment of energy and resources to gain these benefits, however. Thus, it is important to recognize that the benefits of cultural diversity are long term in nature and will come only to those organizations willing to make the commitment. One such company is *USA Today*, owned by Gannett News Media. Nancy Woodhull, president of Gannett, firmly believes that the national newspaper's success can be attributed to the presence of people from a wide variety of cultural backgrounds in daily news meetings. In fact, cultural diversity was envisioned as a part of the paper's daily management and organization.[30] It helps the newspaper meet the needs of a varied group of customers around the nation. Another company with such a commitment is Auto Zone, a

Memphis-based national retailer of auto parts, which has been extremely successful in developing blacks and women for managerial positions.

As cultural diversity becomes a valued organizational asset, companies spend less time managing conflict and more time accomplishing tasks and satisfying customers. Organizations willing to meet the challenge of valuing work-force diversity are likely to benefit from reduced organizational conflict, increased employee morale, lower turnover, greater innovation and productivity, and an enhanced ability to meet customer needs.

**Critical Thinking Challenge:** Assign students the task of interviewing an employee from a local organization. Ask students to gather information on the benefits provided to employees as well as the mechanisms in place for dealing with work-force diversity.

## Problems Associated with Cultural Diversity

While the benefits of work-force diversity are realized in the long run, they bring with them short- or long-term problems, depending on how management approaches cultural diversity. When an organization recognizes the benefits to be gained from valuing diversity and moves in that direction, the problems are likely to be short term and can be overcome if the organization makes the necessary commitment of time, effort, and resources. However, if the organization fails to recognize and accept the benefits of work-force diversity, then problems are likely to be long term. The most significant problems associated with cultural diversity include prejudice, discrimination, and conflict.

**Prejudice and Discrimination.    Prejudice** is negative attitudes and feelings toward others because of their membership in a different cultural group. Beyond prejudice is **discrimination**, negative behaviors toward people from other cultural groups. Discrimination also refers to organizational practices that purposely or accidentally disadvantage members of different cultural groups. Because prejudice is an attitude rather than a behavior, it is more difficult than discrimination for an organization to change.

Prejudice and discrimination affect business activities at many levels. Among individual employees, for example, racial slurs and gestures, sexist comments, and other behaviors by coworkers harm the individuals at whom such behavior is directed. In such cases, members of different cultural groups may feel hurt, depressed, or even threatened and suffer from lowered self-esteem, all of which harm their productivity and morale. Such minority employees may simply leave the firm, wasting the time, money, and other resources spent on hiring and training them. When discrimination comes from a supervisor, employees may also fear for their jobs. The "Dynamics of Diversity" box discusses the issue of sexual harassment in the workplace. A study of 439 top-ranking women in the country's largest industrial and service companies found that 59 percent reported being sexually harassed at some point in their careers.[31]

When prejudice and discrimination so pervade a company that employees come to view it as acceptable, the entire company suffers. A reputation for discrimination may harm the firm's ability to recruit employees, particularly those who are members of minority groups. Without employees of different backgrounds who can bring unique perspectives to the company's decisions and activities, the company's competitiveness may suffer. A reputation for discrimination may also result in boycotts by minority consumers, as well as lawsuits. For example, Shoney's Inc., the third largest restaurant chain in the United States, is struggling to resolve a reputation for prejudice and discrimination against blacks. Until the late 1980s, the company hired few blacks and employed none in management

**prejudice**
Negative attitudes and feelings toward others because of their membership in a different cultural group.

**discrimination**
Negative behaviors toward people from other cultural groups.

**Example:** In addition to Shoney's, other restaurants have been accused of discrimination. Denny's Restaurant chain has been said to discriminate against African-Americans, taking longer to serve them and in some cases refusing service. Cracker Barrel Restaurants was also found to discriminate against homosexuals in its hiring practices.

In the fall of 1991, workplaces across the United States were abuzz over allegations of sexual harassment that lawyer Anita Hill made against Supreme Court nominee Clarence Thomas, who had been her supervisor ten years before. Although Thomas eventually gained the seat on the nation's highest court despite the charges, his conflict with Hill sparked a national debate on the issue of sexual harassment in the workplace.

## SEXUAL HARASSMENT IN THE WORKPLACE: WHERE'S THE LINE?

Although everyone, it seems, has an opinion about sexual harassment, few can provide a useful definition that companies can use to create a more satisfying environment for female employees. It is obvious that sexual harassment has occurred when a supervisor threatens to fire an employee if she does not have sexual relations with him, but other situations are fuzzier. Is it harassment when a man displays photos of nude women or tells off-color jokes in the presence of women colleagues? What about when a woman repeatedly refuses a coworker's request for a date, but he won't give up? The issue is complicated by the fact that men and women have different attitudes about what constitutes sexual harassment. One study found that while most men would be flattered to be propositioned at work, a majority of women said they would be offended by such behavior from men.

Despite the lack of definition, the issue is no longer taken lightly. The New England Patriots and three of its football players were fined for making lewd gestures and remarks to a female reporter in their locker room. The majority leader of Florida's House of Representatives lost his position for allowing an atmosphere of sexual innuendo on his staff. Two Long Beach, CA, female police officers won $3.1 million in a lawsuit after three years of sexual taunts from colleagues. Indeed, employers are just beginning to realize the pervasiveness of the problem. A poll by the National Association for Female Executives revealed that 53 percent of the 1,300 members surveyed had been sexually harassed or knew someone who had. Another poll found that half the men surveyed admitted having done something that a woman might view as harassment.

The controversy surrounding sexual harassment has reaffirmed changes already made at companies such as Du Pont, Corning, and Digital Equipment; these companies have made combating sexual harassment a top priority not only to recruit and retain their female employees but also to avoid lawsuits. Other companies are seeking the advice of consultants on how to set up grievance procedures or expand training sessions.

Experts advise that companies should focus on prevention. They recommend that employers develop and distribute policies that precisely define unacceptable conduct and the punishment for violating the policy. Companies should hold training seminars that sensitize workers to the issue through videos, lectures, and role-playing exercises. Finally, companies should set up dispute-resolution procedures that permit confidential complaints of harassment that circumvent immediate supervisors, who often are the harassers.

*Sources:* Michele Galen, with Joseph Weber and Alice Z. Cuneo, "Sexual Harassment: Out of the Shadows," *Business Week,* October 28, 1991, 30–31; Ted Gest and Amy Saltzman, with Betsy Carpenter and Dorian Friedman, "Harassment: Men on Trial," *U.S. News & World Report,* October 21, 1991, 38–40; and Zachary Schiller, with Mark Landler and Julie Flynn Siler, "Ending Sexual Harassment: Business Is Getting the Message," *Business Week,* March 18, 1991, 98–100.

**Comment on Box:** After discussing the facts presented, have students identify issues that should be included in an organization's sexual harassment policy. What types of training should be provided? How can the training be effectively implemented?

positions or such white-collar jobs as mail clerks, secretaries, or data processors at the company's headquarters in Nashville. Some former managers say they were discouraged from hiring blacks at all; others say the company's former chairman used racial epithets to refer to blacks.[32] The company agreed to settle a lawsuit by paying up to $105 million to as many as 10,000 who could show that the company discriminated against them, by promoting more blacks to management positions at both the outlet and headquarter level, and by buying out its founder, Raymond Danner, and his affiliates. In addition, Danner will not be eligible for reelection to the board of directors. Danner, who was accused of promoting the culture of bias, funded 83 percent of the settlement by contributing Shoney's stock.[33]

**Conflict.** Another problem related to work-force diversity is conflict between members of different culture groups. **Cultural conflict** refers to the tension or friction between culture groups that stems from a lack of understanding by one group of the values, attitudes, and behaviors of the other. While ethnic or racial conflict in the workplace is seldom as violent as the riots in south-central Los Angeles in 1992 or the civil wars in Bosnia, such examples illustrate how underlying tensions among different cultural groups can trigger conflict. Conflict in the workplace most often arises when minority culture groups question the values and attitudes of the dominant group. In many cases, conflict can arise from personal prejudice against a particular group, or from discriminatory hiring and promotion practices within the organization. Conflict harms work-group relationships and decision making, which minimizes a company's competitiveness.

> **cultural conflict**
> The tension or friction between culture groups that stems from a lack of understanding by one group of the values, attitudes, and behaviors of the other.

# APPROACHES TO MANAGING WORK-FORCE DIVERSITY

Whether an organization realizes benefits from a culturally diverse work force depends on how it manages that work force. Integrating men and women of different races, nationalities, ages, and abilities into a coherent organization that pulls together to achieve its objectives is an important aspect of managing work-force diversity. Over the years, businesses have tried three different approaches to managing cultural diversity: assimilation, affirmative action, and the development of a truly multicultural firm.

> **Example:** To promote awareness and understanding of culture and diversity, Chattanooga State Technical Community College has sponsored educational and entertainment programs to educate workers about the benefits of diversity. Programs including music and festivals of other countries have fostered cultural awareness.

## Assimilation

**Assimilation** refers to organizational practices that force minority groups to accept the norms and values of a majority group. In some U.S. businesses, this translates to activities that require women, Hispanics, and other minority groups to adopt and act according to the standards and values of white men. Assimilation is based on several assumptions:

1. Diversity is an organizational weakness.
2. Diversity is a threat to the organization's effectiveness.
3. Minority groups who are uncomfortable with the majority group's values are oversensitive.
4. Members of minority groups want to be and should be more like the majority group.
5. Equal treatment of employees means the same treatment for all employees.
6. Managing work-force diversity means changing the people, rather than the organization.[34]

> **assimilation**
> Organizational practices that force minority groups to accept the norms and values of a majority group.

Businesses relying on these assumptions generally do not value minority groups for what they can contribute to the organization. Though the strength of diversity lies in the differences between groups, firms using assimilation try to eliminate the differences, seeing them as a threat to their existence.

Businesses using assimilation as a cultural-diversity approach generally have little or no integration of minority groups. Members of different cultures do not mix formally within the organization or even informally in social relationships. The work force contains mostly white men, with very few women or minorities in management positions.

Within organizations using assimilation, conflict is minimal because all employees are expected to hold the same norms and values. While reduced conflict is certainly beneficial, other characteristics of assimilation are not. Because these organizations do not value members of different cultural groups, they often have high levels of prejudice and discrimination. Additionally, women and minorities generally have a hard time feeling that they belong in the organization. Because they do not fit in with the white male–dominated culture, women and minorities rarely feel that they contribute to the organization.

Perhaps the most positive comment on assimilation is that many American businesses began to move away from it during the 1960s and 1970s. Social changes, including the civil rights and women's liberation movements, led businesses to recognize that assimilation wasn't working to fully integrate members of different cultures into the work force.

## Affirmative Action

**affirmative action programs**
Policies designed to increase job opportunities for minority groups through analysis of the present pool of workers, identification of areas where women and minorities are underrepresented, and establishment of specific hiring and promotion goals along with target dates for meeting those goals.

In the last three decades, many organizations have moved from assimilation to affirmative action programs to reduce inequality and integrate more minority groups into the work force. **Affirmative action programs** are designed to increase job opportunities for minority groups through analysis of the present pool of workers, identification of areas where women and minorities are underrepresented, and establishment of specific hiring and promotion goals along with target dates for meeting those goals. In many companies, these policies have generated work forces in which minority groups make up more than 20 percent of the total.

Affirmative action began in 1965 as Lyndon B. Johnson issued the first of a series of presidential directives. It was designed to make up for past hiring and promotion prejudices, to overcome workplace discrimination, and to provide equal employment opportunities for blacks and whites.[35] Since then, minorities have made solid gains. For example, the percentage of blacks in the American work force has increased 50 percent since 1965. Most of these gains were made by southern blacks and black women. The percentage of black managers in U.S. companies rose five-fold between 1962 and 1989, to 5 percent.[36]

The biggest gains from affirmative action have gone to women. Today, women make up over 45 percent of the American work force, up from 35 percent in 1966. Over the last 20 years, women have made great advances within corporations, especially in professional occupations. For example, nearly 20 percent of all American lawyers are women, up from 5 percent in 1970.[37]

However, there are growing signs that affirmative action programs do not go far enough. Compared with whites, blacks still hold far fewer managerial and administrative positions and far more service and laborer jobs. While women and minorities often make up 20 percent or more of the work force, these same groups hold only 5 to 12 percent of management positions, as shown in Figure 6.6. Though the use of affirmative action is a plus, these organizations often do not allow women and minorities to become full participating members.

Another sign of the ineffectiveness of affirmative action is the difference in pay between men and women and blacks and whites. As of 1989, white men averaged about $28,000 per year while white women averaged about $20,000. Black men averaged about $18,000 and black women about $16,000. Salaries for women

FIGURE 6.6

**Percentages of Blacks and Whites in Selected Job Categories**

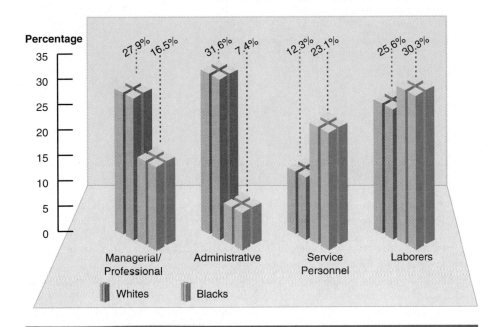

*Source:*  U.S. Bureau of Labor Statistics, 1991.

and blacks have risen slightly since the late 1960s, but a huge gap still remains between their salaries and the salaries of white men.

While affirmative action programs help to minimize prejudice and discrimination, they tend to create a great deal of group conflict within the organization. Many white men began to resent affirmative action policies because they felt they were having to pay for management mistakes of the past. This problem reveals the irony of affirmative action. When companies go out of their way to compensate for past inequalities and discrimination, they often do so at the expense of white male workers, resulting in reverse discrimination. **Reverse discrimination** occurs when a company's policies force it to consider only minorities or women instead of concentrating on hiring the person who is best qualified. Reverse discrimination may cause tension between white male workers and minority workers, as well as conflict between white workers and management.

While affirmative action represents a great advance over assimilation in managing cultural diversity, it still falls short in many respects. First, white men remain the dominant majority group. Second, organizations using affirmative action programs may still stifle the innovation and creativity brought about by diversity because they practice assimilation to ensure that all members of the work force share the same norms and values. Finally, as with assimilation, women and minorities continue to have trouble identifying with, or feeling that they belong in, the organization. In short, affirmative action accepts diversity without valuing it. Because of these problems, many businesses are beginning to move toward a third approach to managing cultural diversity, creating multicultural organizations.

**reverse discrimination**
The result of a company's policies that force it to consider only minorities or women instead of hiring the person who is best qualified.

**Example:** Many white males in the United States feel they are victims of reverse discrimination. With more women and minorities in the workplace competing for limited jobs, the white males as a group are facing limited job opportunities.

---

**TABLE 6.4**

**Differences between Affirmative Action Programs and Multicultural Organizations That Value Work-Force Diversity**

| Affirmative Action | Valuing Diversity |
| --- | --- |
| Government initiated | Voluntary |
| Legally driven | Productivity driven |
| Quantitative | Qualitative |
| Problem focused | Opportunity focused |
| Uses assimilation | Uses integration |
| Reactive | Proactive |

---

## Multicultural Organizations

**multicultural organizations**
Companies that value their culturally diverse employees as assets, and that develop and implement policies designed to promote cultural diversity and equality.

More and more firms are trying to become **multicultural organizations**—companies that value their culturally diverse employees as assets, and which develop and implement policies designed to promote cultural diversity and equality. Such organizations have come to realize the many benefits to be gained from creating, managing, and sustaining a culturally diverse work force. Within multicultural organizations, different cultural groups are encouraged to share and adopt the norms and values of other groups. Members of different cultural groups can be found throughout the organization, in both formal and informal relationships. Employees identify with the company and truly feel that they belong and have something of value to contribute. Prejudice and discrimination do not exist. These characteristics greatly minimize conflict among members of different groups within the organization.

Multicultural organizations go beyond affirmative action programs in managing diversity, as shown in Table 6.4. They build on affirmative action programs by focusing on the quality of the work environment and the improvement of skills for *all* employees. However, unlike affirmative action programs, valuing cultural diversity is a voluntary process based on the need for innovation. In fully integrating diverse culture groups, the multicultural organization values the contributions of all employees.

**Example:** McDonald's is a U.S.-based organization that uses local nationals as employees and managers in its restaurants around the world.

Multicultural organizations never question the value of work-force diversity. Instead, they operate on a set of assumptions that differ markedly from those used in the assimilation approach. These assumptions are based on the recognition that diversity has many potential benefits.

**Example:** To meet the diverse tastes of the region, McDonald's alters its menu to appeal to local tastes. In Japan rice, soups, and teriyaki burgers are on the menu. In France beer is available. In Prince Edward Island, Canada, a McLobster sandwich is present, and in London, England, Fish McNuggets are a popular item.

1. Work-force diversity represents a competitive advantage in meeting the needs of an increasingly diverse customer base and in recruiting the best-qualified employees.
2. Because deriving benefits from diversity is a long-term process, the organization is in a constant state of transition.
3. Valuing diversity involves changing the organization to adapt to the changing needs of people, rather than changing the people.[38]

While the truly multicultural organization is still largely hypothetical, it represents the latest phase in the evolution of managing a culturally diverse work

## BUSINESS DILEMMA

*You're the Manager ...What Would You Do?*

THE COMPANY:  Stoneware, Inc.

YOUR POSITION:  Director of Human Resources

THE PLACE:  Bethesda, MD

Stoneware, Inc., is one of the largest manufacturers of dinnerware, both nationally and internationally. Founder Herb Crammer has created a highly profitable company that shares the wealth with both its stockholders and its employees. Stoneware has been rated as one of the best companies to work for in terms of compensation, benefits, work environment, and promotion opportunities. Recently, however, this positive work environment has suffered some setbacks: Women and minorities have been leaving the company in excess of the normal attrition rate. Managers became aware of the situation due to the increased hiring and training expenses, approaching $5 million a year, within the company over the past 2 years.

To determine the cause of the turnover, managers have conducted exit interviews and contacted former employees by phone to find out their reasons for leaving the company. Because there have been few personnel problems in the company, such exit interviews had never been conducted before. The interviews and calls revealed that both women and minorities felt their career opportunities were limited at Stoneware. Beyond the consideration of offering an equal opportunity workplace, Stoneware is concerned about the situation because the changing demographics in the United States make it even more important to recruit and retain more women and minority employees.

The CEO of the company immediately initiated a task force to address the turnover problem in general and more specifically the problems pinpointed through interviews with former employees. Further review of complaints by former women employees targeted specific issues such as a lack of career support and child-care programs, unequal pay, and cases of sexual harassment. Minority complaints revealed a slower rate of promotion, unequal pay, incidents of ridicule and harassment, and situations where tasks performed exceeded the extent of the job description.

As director of human resource management, you have been asked to develop a companywide program to deal with the problems addressed by the task force. You are considering several approaches:  establishing child-care programs or subsidies for outside child-care services, offering employees the opportunity to work flexible schedules, providing diversity training, and working to develop educational materials that address sexual harassment in the workplace. You are in the process of developing a comprehensive program to support the concerns of women and minorities and implementing the program at all levels in the organization.

### Questions

1. As human resource manager, how do you defend the investment in the training and development area for Stoneware, Inc.? What are the potential benefits?
2. What type of plan would you provide for the organization? Specifically address programs, materials provided, and who should participate.
3. Anticipate problems in developing and implementing the new policies and programs to deter harassment and disparate treatment of employees.

force. Many companies—Avon, American Express, Levi Strauss, Digital Equipment, Monsanto, Corning, and many others—have already begun to adopt and incorporate these assumptions into their corporate policies. In the next section, we look at how these and other companies can move toward a truly multicultural organization—one that succeeds with the help of its diverse employees.

## CREATING THE MULTICULTURAL ORGANIZATION

Managing cultural diversity involves recruiting, managing, and retaining highly qualified employees from an increasingly diverse pool of workers. It also requires

After learning about diversity issues expressed by women and minorities, top managers of GE Silicones set the stage for transforming its traditional, white-male-oriented culture to one that values the benefits of recruiting and promoting culturally diverse employees such as Diana Yoshimura, quality engineer, and Lesly Regis, manager of quality assurance, shown here. Managers committed resources and became personally involved in initiating diversity programs and policies, including a mentor program for women and minorities, and were the first at GE to attend training workshops that explored individual attitudes toward diversity.

*Source:* Courtesy of GE Silicones, Waterford, NY.

effectively structuring communication with employees to embrace a wide variety of cultural backgrounds. Managers need to be able to motivate employees whose backgrounds are dissimilar. Finally, business must create organizational climates that value all employees for the many talents and perspectives they have to offer. In short, successful management of work-force diversity involves not only recognizing that diversity exists but also valuing diversity for the benefits it brings to the organization.

Going beyond affirmative action plans to a multicultural organization that creates and values work-force diversity involves a series of complex and integrated steps: setting the stage, educating and implementing, and maintaining diversity.[39]

## Step One:  Setting the Stage

This first step in creating a multicultural organization is critical because it becomes the basis on which all other efforts are developed. It creates early interest in valuing diversity by emphasizing the benefits of cultural diversity. This step includes four important actions: getting the support and involvement of top management, going beyond affirmative action programs, upholding diversity through communication, and adopting and communicating a pluralistic vision.[40]

**Critical Thinking Challenge:** Have students discuss other ways to gain the support and involvement of top management. Also discuss the reasons this support is needed.

**Getting Support and Involvement from Top Management.**    Cultural diversity cannot succeed without the support and commitment of top management. This support is necessary to gain the backing and involvement of other managers, as well as of all employees within the organization. At Levi Strauss & Company, for example, top managers teach classes in valuing diversity that are open to all managers. Levi executives also participate in workshops that encourage open dialogue about diversity issues. Part of managers' bonuses is tied to meeting goals established in Levi's "Aspiration Statement," which, among other things, asks employees to aspire to appreciate diversity.[41] In this role, top managers motivate other managers and employees to inspire commitment and interest in the organization's efforts at creating a culture of diversity.

**Going Beyond Affirmative Action Programs.**    As indicated in Table 6.4, there are many differences between affirmative action programs and the programs of multicultural organizations. The primary distinction is that affirmative action programs are mandated by federal laws, while valuing cultural diversity is voluntary. Affirmative action has produced measurable changes in the composition of the American work force, but it has had little effect in changing organizational cultures and their accompanying beliefs and values regarding diversity. Thus, valuing cultural diversity goes beyond correcting past discrimination to include a complete change in organizational culture.

**Upholding Diversity through Communication.**    Having top management support diversity as well as understanding how valuing diversity differs from affirmative action are important first actions in setting the stage. However, upholding diversity through communication to employees is critically important. Organizational leaders must endorse the goal of cultural diversity by enthusiastically promoting the benefits it brings to the organization. Promoting diversity involves more than communicating to employees. Organizational leaders must also uphold diversity through public means, such as through advertising and public relations campaigns.

**Adopting and Communicating a Pluralistic Vision.**    Adopting a pluralistic vision means looking toward the future, a future in which employees of different cultural groups are allowed to express themselves and to participate fully in decision making. In charting the future of the organization, top managers must emphasize how cultural diversity relates to the organization's goals and mission. In this sense, the potential benefits of cultural diversity are recognized as important aspects of the organization's future success. Additionally, a pluralistic vision serves as a guide to all employees by showing them how they fit into the company and where the company is heading. This vision shows employees what the organization will be like when it becomes truly multicultural, when all employees can contribute their unique values and perspectives to the success of their company.

## Step Two:  Education and Implementation

Step one set the stage for changing the organizational culture; step two implements these changes. While the first step involves actions by upper-level managers, the second step focuses on lower-level employees. This step includes five important activities:  awareness training, developing employee support, diversifying work groups and providing coaching, altering benefit packages and tying rewards to behaviors, and creating a structure that supports diversity.

**Awareness Training.**    The fastest-growing technique companies use to address problems raised by a culturally diverse work force is awareness training.[42] Awareness training involves open discussions with employees about the benefits of achieving a culturally diverse work force. Through workshops, meetings, retreats, and other training sessions, employees are encouraged to speak openly about personal values, stereotypes, and prejudices that affect their work and their relationships with other employees. Top managers and training leaders can then explain how many of these factors impede the cultural change process and limit organizational success. In addition, employees talk about how diversity affects them as the organization moves toward such a culture. For example, Pacific Gas & Electric (PG&E) conducts awareness training programs, where employees, under the supervision of carefully trained "diversity awareness trainers," can talk openly

Diversity training at Price-Waterhouse includes playing a board game called *The Diversity Game*, played here by the company's human resource managers. Board games are effective employee awareness training tools because they provide players with information on diversity issues and promote informal discussion about personal values, stereotypes, and prejudices.

*Source:* Courtesy of Price-Waterhouse.

about race, religion, discrimination, stereotyping, and other cultural diversity issues.[43] Sharing experiences this way helps to eliminate the cultural barriers between coworkers and breaks taboos against talking about such topics at work. The end result of awareness training is an increased appreciation of other cultures and a decrease in culture clashes.

### Developing Employee Support.
The best way to gain employee support is to involve workers in the company's effort to foster cultural diversity and develop a multicultural organization. This often involves the use of formal and informal networks of employees to spread the message to other employees. As at Pacific Gas & Electric, employees can serve as awareness training leaders to convince others of the benefits to be gained from valuing diversity.

**Critical Thinking Challenge:** Have students interview the human resources manager of a local company. How have worker diversity patterns changed over time? Ask students to report on the change in the number of women, minorities, and nontraditional jobs.

### Diversifying Work Groups and Providing Coaching.
It is one thing for an organization to talk about diversity, but another thing entirely to actually practice it. To demonstrate their commitment to cultural diversity, businesses must integrate work groups at all levels and in all departments. Integration can be measured by examining the number of women and other minorities in nontraditional jobs such as executive positions. This increased integration can produce many benefits, ranging from increased innovation and teamwork to work-group productivity.

Coaching diverse work groups is important in fostering teamwork and interpersonal relationships, especially in the beginning. Coaching helps everyone in the work group ease into newly defined roles by providing assistance in handling the change process. Through technical assistance, interpersonal feedback, and personal attention to employee needs, coaching increases employee comfort, reduces tension and conflict, and increases overall work-group performance.

### Altering Benefit Plans and Tying Rewards to Behaviors.
Altering employee benefits (vacation and sick leave, insurance, pension plans, and so on) to reflect diversity requires an understanding of the different needs of various culture groups within the organization. For example, some employers have begun to offer extended-

hour child care to those employees who work overtime and evenings. In addition, different culture groups often have different health care needs. Blacks and American Indians, for example, may need programs that address diabetes; women may require programs relating to childbirth and maternity care. Unfortunately, recent increases in health care costs nationwide have led organizations to cut back on employee health benefits. Nonetheless, health care and other benefits remain a positive means through which companies can attract and retain the best employees.

As cultural change progresses within an organization, reward systems must also change to reflect the new emphasis on cultural diversity. It is not enough simply to train managers and employees to understand diversity; nor is it enough to develop employee commitment to the organization's diversity efforts. All employees must be held accountable for valuing each other if the effort is to produce benefits. Employees should be rewarded for respecting other cultures, cooperating in diverse work groups, and supporting diversity as an organizational philosophy. Employees who exhibit these behaviors are more likely to work effectively within diverse work groups and to reach higher performance levels. These employees are also more likely to be effective managers when they are promoted.

**Example:** Three- and four-week vacations or holidays are common and expected in Europe and the United Kingdom. Expatriates from these areas to the United States are surprised to learn that only two-week vacations are the norm and many expect additional leave time for personal vacations.

**Creating a Structure That Supports Diversity.** Changing the organizational structure to support cultural diversity can be accomplished on either a formal or informal level. On the informal level, for example, companies can use employee networks. As previously discussed, these networks serve to increase employee commitment to and involvement in the organization's efforts at valuing diversity. Such networks also act as support groups by providing educational resources and feedback to their members.

A more formal way to change organizational structure is to create an office or position to oversee the firm's efforts at achieving cultural diversity. A vice president of cultural diversity, for example, could encourage open communication among culture groups and between employees and management about diversity-related issues. In addition, a cultural-diversity manager can manage the overall change process as the organization's diversity efforts expand. The University of California at Los Angeles (UCLA) has created a diversity council that reports directly to the university president. Its main task is to ensure that employees of all culture groups are equally represented in all campus and academic activities.[44]

## Step Three: Maintaining Diversity

Once a business has set the stage for change and implemented policies to promote cultural diversity, it must strive to maintain it. As with any business policy, this requires following up to ensure that cultural diversity remains a high-priority organizational value. Follow-up activities may include:

1. Continuous monitoring of recruitment, hiring, and promotion activities to maintain the organization's commitment to cultural diversity

2. Periodic cultural audits that examine organizational practices, values, goals, and norms to determine whether current diversity efforts are effective

3. Periodic employee opinion surveys to identify emerging diversity issues.[45]

By following up with these activities, a company can monitor its cultural-diversity efforts and make changes, if needed. Additionally, the company must also

**Critical Thinking Challenge:** Have student teams draft a possible survey to use to measure diversity issues in a typical organization. Compare team questionnaires and discuss the reasons for the inclusion of the chosen questions.

## Diversity Training for Success in Business

Many companies are taking steps to manage diversity through human resource activities. In some cases, companies are hiring work-force diversity managers for their human resource departments to elevate the importance of diversity management and ensure the benefits associated with a multicultural organization. Pacific Gas & Electric (PG&E) believes that "managing diversity improves its competitive advantage in recruiting and training employees and that it increases productivity, quality, creativity, and morale." PG&E trained and certified 100 line and staff employees as diversity-awareness trainers, who in turn will train the firm's 27,000 employees to help create an environment in which cultural diversity improves the organization's competitive advantage in such areas as productivity, customer service, employee recruitment, and employee retention.

Many firms have developed diversity programs, which often create opportunities for women and minorities. Although there is no consensus on the degree of opportunity for advancement for women and minorities who go into diversity training, some believe that diversity training and the human resources area are more involved in strategic planning and thus eventually will be in the inner circle of decision making.

Many entrepreneurial opportunities abound for minorities, women, and immigrants. Currently, women own 18 percent of franchises, according to the International Franchise Association, while minorities make up just 9.5 percent of franchise owners. Today, women are launching small businesses at twice the rate of men. The traditional obstacles to women, minorities, and persons with disabilities in starting any new business, franchise or not, have been lack of management experience and difficulty raising funds. To overcome some of these problems, small business development centers sponsored by the Small Business Administration (SBA), usually at colleges and universities or chambers of commerce, provide advice.

Some franchisors have targeted specific target markets. For example, Computertots provides hands-on computer enrichment classes for 3- to 5-year-olds in day care centers and nursery schools. All of its franchisors are women, and 79 percent of its franchisees are women. Accent Hair Salons are mall-based salons specializing in care for the African-American market. Currently, all its franchisors are African-American. All the franchisees of Kinderdance, which provides dance and exercise classes to 3- to 5-year-olds in day care centers and nursery schools, are women. Seventy-five of the franchisees for Manchu Wok, an oriental fast-food chain, are Asian. McDonald's Corporation offers qualified franchisees a short-term lease of an existing restaurant through a women and minority franchise association.

Cultural diversity is changing the nature of business strategies. While the work force is becoming more diverse, so are consumer markets. Companies are beginning to realize that they must have a very diverse work force in order to serve heterogenous markets. As the concept of the multicultural organization is accepted, opportunities for people of different races, ages, cultural and geographic origins, abilities, and genders should increase.

*Sources:* Ronita B. Johnson and Julie O'Mara, "Shedding New Light on Diversity Training," *Training and Development,* May 1992, 26; Mark L. Mathis and John H. Jackson, *Human Resource Management,* 7th ed. (Minneapolis-St. Paul: West Publishing Co., 1994), 30; Ronaleen R. Roha, "Wanted: Women and Minorities," *Kiplinger's Personal Finance Magazine,* March 1994, 123-124; "Training to Meet Skills Shortages May be Wrong Focus for Tomorrow's Jobs," *The Wall Street Journal,* February 22, 1994, A1; "What's the Future of HR Careers for African Americans?" *Black Enterprise,* February 1994, 140.

make a commitment to train new employees as they enter the work force. In short, valuing work-force diversity is a never-ending process. To truly value its culturally diverse employees, the company must move beyond where it is today to find where it is going tomorrow. When valuing cultural diversity becomes the norm, companies will see the benefits of using all the abilities of all employees, and they will achieve the success that cultural diversity can bring.

# SUMMARY AND REVIEW

- **Define cultural diversity and explain why it has become so important in business.** Cultural diversity refers to differences in age, gender, race, ethnicity, nationality, and ability. Businesses need to encourage and manage cultural diversity to ensure that they have sufficient human resources to remain competitive and to gain a work force that better matches and understands the increasingly diverse customer base.

- **Examine some of the significant cultural groups in the American work force and discuss some issues of concern to each.** Minorities (primarily African-Americans, Hispanics, Asians, and Native Americans), women, and the disabled are three major cultural groups in the work force. Together, they face discrimination and prejudice from the white male majority because of their differences in attitudes and values. As a consequence, they generally have higher unemployment rates, lower compensation, and less education. They also may experience problems associated with different cultural and religious values, different languages, and physical barriers that prevent their full participation in the work force.

- **Determine the benefits and problems associated with cultural diversity in the work force.** The benefits of valuing and effectively managing a culturally diverse work force include more productive use of human resources, reduced conflict, better work relationships among workers of different cultures, increased commitment to and sharing of organizational goals, increased innovation and creativity, and enhanced ability to serve culturally diverse customers. Problems related to work-force diversity include prejudice, discrimination, and conflict; to avoid these problems, companies must manage their diverse work forces carefully.

- **Assess different organizational approaches to managing work-force diversity.** Businesses have tried three different approaches to managing the culturally diverse work force: assimilation, affirmative action, and developing multicultural organizations. Assimilation refers to organizational practices that force

minority groups to accept the norms and values of a majority group. Organizations using assimilation do not value cultural diversity, have little integration of cultural groups, have high levels of prejudice and discrimination, and have minority employees who do not feel that they belong.

Affirmative action programs are designed to increase job opportunities for minority groups through analysis of the present pool of workers, identification of areas where women and minorities are underrepresented, and establishment of specific hiring and promotion goals along with target dates for meeting those goals. Affirmative action programs help to reduce prejudice and discrimination but create more conflict.

Multicultural organizations are those that value their culturally diverse employees, and which develop and implement policies designed to promote cultural diversity and equality.

- **Explain how work-force diversity is created, maintained, and valued by a truly multicultural organization.** Managing cultural diversity involves recruiting, managing, and retaining highly qualified employees from an increasingly diverse pool of workers. It also involves effectively structuring communication to include a wide variety of cultural backgrounds, motivating employees whose backgrounds are dissimilar, and creating organizational climates that value all employees for the many talents and perspectives they have to offer. Developing a multicultural organization that creates and values cultural diversity involves three steps: setting the stage, educating and implementing, and maintaining diversity.

- **Propose a plan for turning a company into a multicultural organization.** The "Business Dilemma" box presents a scenario in which a company must address high turnover among women and minority employees. You, in the role of the human resources manager, have the task of designing a program to reduce this turnover and create a multicultural organization that values all its employees.

## Key Terms and Concepts

cultural diversity *153*
primary characteristics of diversity *153*
secondary characteristics of
  diversity *154*

prejudice *163*
discrimination *163*
cultural conflict *165*
assimilation *165*

affirmative action programs *166*
reverse discrimination *167*
multicultural organizations *168*

## Ready Recall

1. Define cultural diversity. Why is it becoming so important in business?
2. List the primary and secondary characteristics of diversity. How do they define an individual? Which ones can be changed?
3. List the various cultural groups discussed in the text and discuss how their workplace needs and desires differ from those of white male workers.
4. What are the benefits of having a culturally diverse work force?
5. What problems are associated with having a culturally diverse work force?

6. Compare and contrast the three approaches businesses have used in dealing with cultural diversity. Which approach has the least conflict? the least prejudice and discrimination? In which approach are all employees likely to feel a sense of belonging and contribution?
7. Define a multicultural organization. What assumptions does the multicultural organization rely on in managing its human resources?
8. What steps and activities does a company have to pass through on its way to becoming a multicultural organization?

## Expand Your Experience

1. Using a large company in your area, analyze the company's human resource pool. What percentage of women, minorities, and disabled persons make up the company's work force? Do these figures match the population of the local community? In what approach or phase is the company with regard to cultural diversity? What are its future plans and goals with regard to its work force?

2. Find some examples of companies that value their culturally diverse work forces, perhaps some of the companies mentioned in the chapter. In what ways have these firms derived benefits from promoting cultural diversity? How have they dealt with the problems associated with cultural diversity?

## CASE

# *Dealing with Racial Discrimination at Denny's*

Based in Spartanburg, South Carolina, TW Holdings is one of the largest food-service companies in the United States, with nearly 130,000 employees in 49 states. The company has been very successful, posting 1992 revenues of $3.7 billion from its franchise restaurant operations, which include Denny's, Canteen, El Pollo Loco, Hardee's, and Quincy's Family Steakhouse. However, since 1993, after allegations of racial discrimination by Denny's managers, the company has had to take steps to salvage its reputation.

The first problem developed on March 24, 1993, in San Jose, California, when 32 African-Americans filed suit against Denny's—a nationwide chain of 1,460 restaurants known for 24-hour service and reasonably priced meals—alleging a pattern of racial discrimination in Denny's 330 California restaurants. They cited as evidence such practices as black customers being required to pay a cover charge to enter Denny's restaurants, having to pay for meals in advance, and being charged for items and services usually given free to white customers, such as birthday meals and dinner rolls. Additionally, the suit alleged that Denny's managers had made derogatory, sometimes threatening, racial remarks toward black patrons, as well as having them forcibly removed from the restaurants. Finally, "racial coding" was allegedly employed by the company's managers to indicate

situations in which too large a proportion of customers in a given restaurant were black. (This alleged racial coding bore a striking similarity to charges brought in November 1992 against Denny's chief competitor—Shoney's—which had been accused of engaging in discriminatory hiring practices. The Shoney's case resulted in a $105 million settlement.)

In response to a Justice Department investigation that substantiated allegations of bias against blacks brought about by the San Jose suit, Denny's agreed to take measures to ensure the fair treatment of all customers, regardless of their race. Spokespersons for TW Holdings denied the alleged pattern of discrimination in California, but admitted that the company had identified isolated areas of concern. They stated that these situations had arisen out of late-night security measures enacted in response to customers leaving without paying for their meals. Denny's assured all parties involved in the dispute that any time racially motivated discriminatory activity is brought to the attention of company management, it is dealt with harshly.

One day after the California suit was filed, Denny's signed a consent decree with the Justice Department in an effort to settle the dispute. Although negotiations regarding settlement of the suit itself continued, Denny's agreed to take corrective action to, among other actions, provide cultural diversity training to restaurant employees, include nondiscrimination statements in all newspaper and television advertisements, and hire a "civil rights monitor" to oversee operations and ensure against racial discrimination for a four-year period, during which time "spot testing" of Denny's restaurants would occur. In addition, Denny's pointed out that it had already implemented a program in 1992 with goals of improving minority hiring and employee promotions, as well as increasing the number of black franchisees in the Denny's system (only 1 out of 163 Denny's franchisees was black).

On the same day the signing of the consent decree was announced, however, a former Denny's manager in San Jose filed a separate suit against the company alleging racial discrimination regarding hiring and promotion practices. This former manager was represented by the same New York-based law firm that had represented both the plaintiffs in the Shoney's case, as well as the 32 individuals filing the original suit against Denny's.

Then, in May 1993, a Denny's manager in Annapolis, Maryland, was fired for failing to report complaints lodged against the restaurant by a group of six black Secret Service agents. Just hours before the firing, the group had filed a racial discrimination suit in U.S. District Court in Baltimore. The new charges alleged that the group had entered the restaurant with a group of white Secret Service agents for breakfast, and that although the white agents were served within 10 minutes of ordering, the black agents had to wait some 45 minutes before their food arrived, too late for them to have time to eat. Ironically, this incident took place on the very day—April 1—that Denny's settled the original suit brought against it in California.

Eventually, both the noted civil rights leader Reverend Jesse Jackson and the National Association for the Advancement of Colored People (NAACP) became involved in negotiations with Denny's. Company chairman Jerome Richardson stated that Denny's was in need of help and that it had turned to the civil rights agency for just that. To show his continuing opposition to the alleged discrimination practices, however, Jackson announced plans to participate in a scheduled June 5 protest march on the Annapolis Denny's where the incident with the black Secret Service agents had taken place. In addition, Reverend Jackson stated that he would attempt to prevent Richardson's bid to bring a National Football League (NFL) expansion team to Charlotte, North Carolina, to which Richardson responded by vowing to give blacks the opportunity to invest in the NFL franchise should it become a reality.

In mid-June, the company announced that it had hired Norman J. Hill to head human resource operations for Denny's parent company, newly named Flagstar Companies (formerly TW Holdings, the name change being effective the previous week). Hill, an African-American and the former vice president of human resources for competitor Perkins Family Restaurants, vowed to bring a different perspective and greater sensitivity to the situation. He told reporters that he felt that Chairman Richardson was committed to solving Denny's problems and that he himself was eagerly looking forward to the impending challenge.

In late June, Denny's announced completion and scheduling of a television commercial designed to help repair its deteriorating public image. To combat the allegations of racial discrimination, the company—in collaboration with its advertising agency—chose the theme, "You Are Welcomed." The 60-second commercial features appearances by Chairman Richardson and a series of racially diverse Denny's employees, all of whom assure the viewer that, although mistakes were made, they were isolated and not indicative of the Denny's chain as a whole. The advertisement takes the form of a pledge by Denny's to the viewer to provide fair and equal treatment of all customers. Denny's announced plans to run the commercial for at least two weeks in all 41 major market areas in which it does business.

Before Denny's officials could themselves view the finished commercial, the company was sued again, this time by five current and former black employees in Cleveland, Ohio. The suit charged the restaurant chain with racial bias and harassment.

Many companies hold the view that the fair and ethical treatment of employees and customers is a responsible approach for business. On the other hand, Denny's is not the only firm to experience problems in implementing this ideal. As previously mentioned, Shoney's, a major competitor of Denny's operating restaurants throughout the Sun Belt, has also had problems of alleged discrimination. These firms must depend on culturally and racially diverse employees with their own, often deeply ingrained personal biases to implement company philosophy regarding fair and equal treatment of customers.

*Sources:* Laura Bird, "Denny's TV Ad Seeks to Mend Bias Image," *The Wall Street Journal*, June 21, 1993, B4; Laurie Campbell, "New Denny's Exec Relishes Challenge: Facing Firestorm," *The (Memphis) Commercial Appeal*, June 20, 1993, C1; "Denny's to Settle Federal Bias Charge," *The Commercial Appeal*, March 27, 1993, B2; "Denny's Fires Annapolis Manager," *The Commercial Appeal*, May 25, 1993; James Harney, "Civil Rights Leaders Divided Over Denny's," *USA Today*, June 4, 1993, 2A; Benjamin A. Holden, "TW Holdings' Denny's Restaurants Unit Signs Consent Decree in U.S. Bias Case," *The Wall Street Journal*, March 26, 1993, A6; Julia Lawlor, "Denny's Vows to Fix Unequal Treatment," *USA Today*, March 26, 1993, 2B; Andrew E. Serwer, "What to Do When Race Charges Fly," *Fortune*, July 12, 1993, 95-96; and Amy Stevens, "Denny's Agrees to Alter Practices in Bias Settlement," *The Wall Street Journal*, March 30, 1993, B9.

## Questions

1. Why do you think Denny's has been the subject of so many charges of racial discrimination?
2. What impact do you think the allegations of racial discrimination toward customers have on Denny's employees?
3. Suggest a strategy for Denny's to use in implementing a fair and equal service policy toward customers and employees.

# Using Good Judgment

Reviewing the statistics in Tables 6.1 and 6.2 as well as the information in Figure 6.1 will reinforce one thing you learned from reading this chapter: The American work force is very diverse and becoming increasingly more diverse. The challenges that accompany these demographic trends require managers to use good judgment in handling the many situations that arise from a diverse work group. Very few managers in the 1960s and 1970s would have had to deal with the situations presented in this exercise. Today, these represent common managerial situations.

One training tool that companies such as Herman Miller, McDonald's Corporation, Miami Herald Publishing, and Philip Morris Corporation are using to challenge their employees to handle encounters with people different from themselves is the board game *DIVERSOPHY™—Understanding the Human Race*. This game addresses such broad diversity issues as race, gender, age, sexual orientation, and physical abilities by providing four types of challenges.

- The green *diversiSMARTS™* cards develop your knowledge and awareness of other people. (The "Strengthen Your Skills" exercise in Chapter 5 and the exercise in the *Study Guide* that accompanies this text, gave you a chance to try some of the *diversiSMARTS™* cards.)
- The yellow *diversiCHOICE™* cards put you in everyday work situations and help you learn how to choose culturally appropriate behaviors.
- The blue *diversiSHARE™* cards provide a forum to dialogue and share personal background and experiences.
- The red *diversiRISK™* cards allow you to experience situations of cultural diversity.

In *DIVERSOPHY™* players take turns rolling dice and moving game pieces around a multicolored board that has a pattern resembling a racetrack. Colored squares along the paths correspond to colored cards. When landing on these squares, players read a corresponding card and follow directions.

This exercise will give you a chance to sample four of the sixty cards available in the *diversiCHOICE™* category. (Besides a multitude of corporations using *DIVERSOPHY™* to train their employees on diversity issues, many universities and colleges are using the game as well.)

## Instructions

1. Stand with your textbook open to this page and something to write with. You will remain standing throughout this 25-minute exercise.

2. Get in a group of 3 to 5 other students where you will have five minutes to discuss the **first question only** and reach a consensus as a group as to what choice in each situation

reflects your best collective judgment. Mark the answer that your group decided on in your book.

3. After five minutes, your instructor will announce it is time for everyone to quickly move to form new groups of 3 to 5 students. This new group will discuss and reach a consensus on the **second question only**. Mark that answer in your book.

4. You will continue this process of forming a new group of 3 to 5 students every five minutes and discussing only **one question**, marking your answer and moving to a new group when your instructor announces time.

5. After the final question has been answered and you have recorded the fourth group's decision, go back to the first group you were in and compare answers 2 to 4 among the members of your first group. If any of you have questions with different answers, share with one another the reasoning your other groups used in reaching your decision.

6. Your instructor will lead a discussion, giving you the answers provided on the back side of the *diversiCHOICE™* cards from the *DIVERSOPHY™—Understanding the Human Race* game.

Here are the four questions, representing one each from the diversity issues of race, gender, age, and physical abilities taken from the *diversiCHOICE™* cards.

1. One of your Latin American counterparts speaks at length, seems to go in circles, and is slow getting to the point. When working or negotiating with this person, it might be useful to:

   A. Listen for subtle nuances and check out what you read between the lines.
   B. Help the person be clearer by asking such things as, "So, what's the bottom line?"
   C. Set deadlines to force your counterpart to be brief and to the point.

2. Your female colleague is being constantly interrupted in conversation by a male coworker. You should:

   A. Call him on being insensitive.
   B. Tell her "off line" to take some assertiveness training.
   C. Interrupt him yourself and insist that your colleague be allowed to finish.

3. A 61-year-old employee asks you to approve him/her for a leadership training program. Normally it takes seven years for the employee to advance to the intended management position. You should:

   A. Acknowledge the employee's right to participate and enroll him/her.

B. Reject the application.

C. Discourage the applicant and get him/her to voluntarily withdraw.

4. A stockroom assistant must be able to move heavy boxes. The first applicant to enter your office this morning is wearing a back brace. During the interview you:

A. Ask, "Have you ever been treated for a bad back?"

B. Ask, "This job asks you to lift 40-pound boxes every day. Can you do it?"

C. Say nothing at all about the requirement, assuming the applicant knows what he/she is doing in applying for a job of this kind.

*Source:* © 1992 MULTUS INC., 46 Treetop Lane, Suite #200, San Mateo, CA 94402 (415) 342-2040. Permission granted to adapt this material from *DIVERSOPHY™—Understanding the Human Race.*

*Note:* MULTUS Inc. has also introduced two additional sets of 180 cards each. One set is on gender, sexual harassment, and sexual orientation; the other is on global negotiation.

# Managing for Total Quality

## Outline

## After reading the chapter, you will be able to:

- Define total quality management and trace its development.
- Summarize the TQM philosophies of Deming, Juran, and Crosby.
- Explain how quality relates to consumers through the marketing function.
- Discuss the relationship between quality and strategy in the organization.
- Examine some of the tools available to help improve quality.
- Recommend how managers can implement the TQM philosophy in their organizations.
- Compare the Japanese approach to quality with the American approach.
- Describe the importance of national and international awards for quality improvements.
- Propose a course of action for a small business that has just won a prestigious quality award.

# Quality Service at Walt Disney

**G**uests at the Walt Disney World Resort—including the Magic Kingdom Park, EPCOT Center, Disney-MGM Studios Theme Park, resorts, and recreational facilities—often comment on three aspects of Disney's service: the cleanliness of the theme park, the quality of the shows, and the friendliness of the employees. Quality service at Disney can be traced back to the opening of Disneyland in 1955. Today, Disney has over 32,000 employees (called "cast members") who perform more than 1,400 different jobs for millions of guests each year. Disney employees are known for their propensity to smile, even under stress, in crowds, and in the summer's typical 98-degree weather.

The emphasis of the Disney approach is simple: Make people happy. But beyond that simplicity is a strategy based on hard work, attention to detail, and exceeding customer expectations. The Disney University puts all new employees

through an intensive three-day training program to familiarize them with Disney practices, the company's history, its mission and objectives, and its emphasis on quality service.

Disney recognizes that it has an energetic, loyal audience with high expectations, and meeting these expectations requires more than just adherence to a policy manual. Disney executives recognize that supervision of all employees at all times is not possible, so quality must be ingrained in the organization's culture. Quality service becomes a way of life in the company; employees follow the guidelines implicit in the culture. As evidence, Disney employees routinely converse using the Disney language of "guests," "cast members," "on stage" (working), and "off stage" (not working).

Disney's secret to quality service is no secret at all: Since 1986, it has built a business sharing advice with other companies. In fact, Disney has been so successful with its approach to quality service that more than 3,000 executives from 1,200 companies have attended seminars at Disney University in Orlando to

learn the Disney philosophy. Seminar instructors teach that four principles designed to fulfill this goal can be adapted by any company.

First, know your customers. Disney maintains guest information in areas such as demographics, evaluation of current marketing strategies, attraction evaluations, payment preferences, price sensitivities, and the economy. The more than 600,000 letters Disney receives from guests each year are summarized for top management, which then takes corrective action to resolve any problems. Disney also hires professionals to attend the theme parks and evaluate the service they receive.

Second, empower your employees and treat them with care. Create a descriptive vision for the future and sell that vision to each member of the "cast." In other words, a positive work environment makes happy employees; happy employees enjoy providing quality service.

Third, build delivery systems to ensure quality service. At Disney, front-line employees have the authority to resolve customer problems. And when they have questions, employees can turn to one of the many telephones in the park for an immediate connection to a centralized question-and-answer line.

Finally, create a service theme so simple that it can be understood by everyone. Disney's theme is "We create happiness by providing the finest in family entertainment."

As a result of its total quality orientation, Disney is very profitable and growing fast. From 1984 to

1989, sales rose from $1.5 billion to $4.6 billion, profits increased from $98 million to $703 million, and earnings per share increased ten times. Worldwide growth continues in the 1990s.

*Sources:* Rick Johnson, "A Strategy for Style," *The Journal of Business Strategy* 12 (September/October 1991): 38–43; Gareth R. Jones, "Michael Eisner's Disney Company," in Charles W.L. Hill and Gareth R. Jones, *Strategic Management: An Integrated Approach* (Boston: Houghton Mifflin, 1991), 784–805; and Jeanne C. Meister, "Disney Approach Typifies Quality Service," *Marketing News,* 24 (January 1990): 38.

## introduction

B usiness leaders have long been seeking the "formula" for success in the global marketplace. During the past two decades, the quality crisis in the United States and the apparent decline in international competitiveness of many U.S. firms have become hot topics. The business community is being inundated with apocalyptic calls for change to improve the quality of American goods and services.

**Quality** reflects the degree to which a good or service meets the demands and requirements of the marketplace. It is an elusive concept whose definition differs according to the type of organization involved.[1] To an appliance manufacturer, for example, quality might mean that a very high percentage of the appliances produced meet predetermined specifications. To an appliance repair business, quality might mean that products are repaired correctly and within stated cost and deadline parameters. To a food-service firm such as McDonald's, quality applies to both the food itself (taste, freshness, and so on) and the service (length of time to be served, friendliness of the cashier, cleanliness of dining room, and so on).

In this chapter we highlight one approach to improving the quality of goods and services in an organization—total quality management. The first section in the chapter traces the development of the total quality management concept and then relates quality to the consumer and strategy. Next, we outline recommendations for implementing an effective total quality management approach. Finally, we look at some of the Japanese innovations that sparked the renewed American emphasis on quality, as well as efforts to reward quality in American and Japanese organizations.

**quality**
The degree to which a good or service meets the demands and requirements of the marketplace.

**Teaching Note:** Ask students to compare the definition of quality in the following industries: automobile tires, stereo equipment, computers, pest control services, and pizza restaurants. What variables are common to all industries?

## WHAT IS TOTAL QUALITY MANAGEMENT?

**total quality management (TQM)**
A management view that strives to create a customer-centered culture which defines quality for the organization and lays the foundation for activities aimed at attaining quality-related goals.

**Total quality management (TQM)** is a management view that strives to create a customer-centered culture which defines quality for the organization and lays the foundation for activities aimed at attaining quality-related goals.[2] TQM is not merely a technique, but a philosophy anchored in the belief that long-run success depends on a uniform commitment to quality in *all* sectors of the organization. The concept of TQM rests largely on five principles: quality work the first time, focus on the customer, strategic holistic approach to improvement, continuous improvement as a way of life, and mutual respect and teamwork. TQM is an outgrowth of an emerging American perspective on quality that can be traced to changes in Japanese management practices immediately following World War II.

# The Evolution of the TQM Concept

Quality departments in U.S. companies began to evolve in the late 1940s. During World War II, many U.S. industries made a concerted effort to minimize waste and improve productivity for the war effort, changes that resulted in a strengthening of the economy immediately after the war. When Japan began its own postwar rebuilding process, many of its companies had been all but destroyed, and they were therefore forced to adopt even more stringent productivity measures to survive. This marked the beginning of a newfound commitment to quality in Japan. While Japanese companies embraced quality in production and service, U.S. firms were more interested in quality control, an end-of-the-line evaluation orientation.

During the 1950s and 1960s, quality champions such as Joseph M. Juran and W. Edwards Deming, shunned by American business leaders, spent considerable time in Japan. There, many of their ideas, such as building quality into processes and using line-workers to solve process problems through the use of applied statistics, enjoyed an overwhelming reception. U.S. companies largely ignored Juran's and Deming's concepts during this time, relying instead on quality-control departments as the primary means of ensuring quality. Under the quality-control approach, one department within an organization inspected products for quality, while other departments conducted business as usual. This was the only form of quality control that most American managers felt their companies needed to achieve quality objectives.

The systems of the 1970s were not customer-focused, emphasizing only the manufacturing processes and embracing such techniques as zero defects, or **error-free production**, a manufacturing process consisting of maintaining machinery and equipment, quality inspection checks, and well-trained employees. Managers believed that quality was high if their firm's products were suitable for shipment to customers, even if the products did not meet the customers' specific demands. They measured quality by examining the costs absorbed by the factory when it built defective products.[3] However, these quality management systems had drawbacks of their own. While they represented a greater commitment to quality by top management, participation by nonmanagement employees was quite limited. Managers were unwilling to relinquish much of their authority in the pursuit of quality, and quality was still an end-of-the-line measure.

By the 1980s, the American conception of quality had changed. Many consumers began to purchase products manufactured in Japan because they perceived Japanese products to have higher standards. Consequently, quality became more critical as American managers sought ways to involve quality considerations in more areas of the company—not just in production and manufacturing—to become more competitive. This perspective required all areas of the organization responsible for providing goods and services to internal and external customers to be concerned with quality. This emphasis on total quality management provided a new partnership between managers, employees, customers, and suppliers of the organization.

The TQM philosophy extended the American definition of quality to other functional areas, including marketing, distribution, and strategic management. Although changing the workplace was not easy, companies applying TQM began to design both products and the processes that produce and deliver them to meet specific standards. They began to focus more attention on the consumer through better service and product guarantees. They began to listen to consumers' wants and needs and to deliver products or services that fulfilled them. The definition of "consumer" was even expanded to include any person within or outside the company to whom an employee passed his or her work.

**error-free production**

A manufacturing process consisting of maintaining machinery and equipment, quality inspection checks, and well-trained employees.

## BUSINESS DILEMMA

*You're the Manager …What Would You Do?*

THE COMPANY:  Ace Manufacturing

YOUR POSITION:  Human Resource Manager

THE PLACE:  Harrisburg, PA

Ace Manufacturing is a small producer of pipes, valves, and fittings for the oil and gas industry. The company has been family owned and operated for nearly 50 years. Its success stems from the close control and involvement of family members and key management personnel. Ace has 200 employees, 12 of whom are family members. Major changes in the company's operations are occurring as a result of winning the Golden Crest Award, a prestigious national quality award. Very few companies have been honored with such recognition, and Ace is the smallest company ever to win the award.

Ace was considered for the award because of its strong organizational culture, which supports quality, commitment, and cooperation among employees. The company stresses teamwork to achieve organizational goals. Team planning and decision making are facilitated by customer-focused databases that employees can access through the company's computer system. They are further assisted by 12 statistical process control coordinators, who chart trends, conduct analyses to isolate problems, and evaluate progress toward quality objectives. This decentralization and teamwork have been important to Ace's strategy to improve quality. Employees are referred to as "Aces" and operate with special privileges and autonomy. They even play competitive card games at company outings with special "Ace" awards and gifts given to the winners.

The results of Ace's programs can be seen in reduced turnover, absenteeism, and work-related injuries. The company's regional market share has increased from 8 percent in 1990 to 18 percent in 1993. On-time delivery of parts increased from 72 percent to 92 percent, with a goal of 97 percent for next year. Not only has the volume of business increased, but the customer base has increased as well. Profitability has not yet increased due to the costly nature of the programs implemented to support the quality initiative.

Having won the Golden Crest Award, Ace is now entrusted with helping to spread the word about how to implement quality programs successfully. This will take some investment on the part of the company, but family members are excited and look forward to the travel and correspondence, as well as extended visibility and publicity. In addition, select organizations will be permitted to tour Ace's facilities and obtain information on its quality programs.

However, some company members are concerned because internal projections indicate the oil and gas industry may suffer depressed prices due to a national oversupply of crude oil. As human resource manager, you are evaluating next year's employment plans for the owners.

### Questions

1. Evaluate your organization's quality-improvement initiative.
2. How would you, as the manager, describe Ace's corporate culture to potential new employees?
3. How would you proceed with respect to the company's activities and resources associated with the Golden Crest Award? Speculate as to its impact on your organization.

**Comment on Box:** Students should have a favorable impression of the quality-related activities at Ace. However, the emphasis may change as new employees are added. Spend time on the issues that all employees must know, initially, to perpetuate the quality culture. While the Golden Crest Award is excellent, sharing it with others and continuing to emphasize it may take needed energy from further quality improvements.

# THREE MASTERS OF QUALITY: DEMING, JURAN, AND CROSBY

Today, the three most widely cited "masters" of quality are W. Edwards Deming, Joseph M. Juran, and Philip Crosby. Although each has promoted the importance of a quality emphasis, their ideas and backgrounds are not always consistent. Juran and Crosby continue to teach the various strands of the TQM philosophy today (Figure 7.1).

## W. Edwards Deming

Dr. W. Edwards Deming (1900–1993), known as the "Father of TQM," was a statistician. His early work employed statistical techniques to measure production

**FIGURE 7.1**

**An Advertisement for a Seminar by Dr. J. M. Juran**

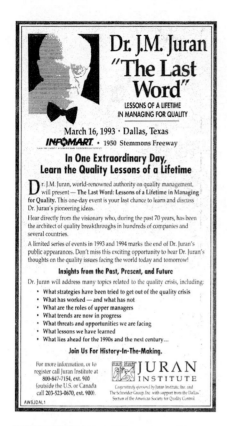

quality and identify changes necessary to improve quality. In the late 1930s, Deming worked at the National Bureau of the Census, where the first widescale application of his concepts improved productivity as much as 600 percent.[4]

After World War II, General Douglas MacArthur invited Deming to visit Japan as an advisor to the Japanese census. Deming's teachings on quality control resulted in future invitations to lecture on statistical methods for industry. At this time, his ideas had not yet taken hold in the United States. Although lower-level managers were receptive to his ideas, top managers were not yet willing to commit their organizations to them. In Japan, Deming requested and received opportunities to speak directly with top executives of Japanese companies, who not only embraced Deming's ideas, but also became committed to implementing them in their companies. As a result, Japanese firms began to experience remarkable improvements in both productivity and competitiveness.

Most of the applications of Deming's ideas in the 1950s and 1960s occurred in Japan. It was not until 1978 that Ford executives on a visit to Japan became aware of Deming's teachings. In 1981, Deming began his work with Ford. By the early 1990s, Ford was hailed as a model of American quality management, and Deming was the most sought-after speaker on quality in the world until his death.

Deming taught Ford that an important part of quality improvement is determining customer needs and wants and using this information in designing useful and dependable products. This recent Ford advertisement illustrates Ford's customer-focused approach to quality.

*Source:*   Courtesy of Ford Motor Company.

Deming's approach to quality was philosophical, based on continuous improvement toward the perfect ideal. With this approach, Deming believed that a commitment to quality requires transforming the entire organization. His philosophy is based on a system known as the "Fourteen Points," which were the basis for his lectures to American managers.

**Teaching Note:** Ask students to examine the issues associated with Deming's 14 points, and discuss what each point means. You can have students discuss the points in small groups, and assign a production major to lead each group discussion.

1. Create and publish to all employees a statement of the aims and purposes of the company or other organization. The management must demonstrate constantly their commitment to this statement.

2. Learn the new philosophy, top management and everybody.

3. Understand the purpose of inspection, for improvement of processes and reduction of cost.

4. End the practice of awarding business on the basis of price tag alone.

5. Improve constantly and forever the system of production and service.

6. Institute training.

7. Teach and institute leadership.

8. Drive out fear. Create trust. Create a climate for innovation.

9. Optimize toward the aims and purposes of the company the efforts of teams, groups, staff areas.

10. Eliminate exhortations for the work force.

11a. Eliminate numerical quotas for production. Instead, learn and institute methods for improvement.

   b. Eliminate M.B.O. (management by objectives). Instead, learn the capabilities of processes, and how to improve them.

**12.** Remove barriers that rob people of pride of workmanship.

**13.** Encourage education and self-improvement for everyone.

**14.** Take action to accomplish the transformation.[5]

About 600 or more managers attended each of Deming's four-day seminars. However, Deming projected that only a few will ever implement the 14 points due to the difficulty in changing an organization's ingrained culture. The implementation process, if undertaken, is costly and requires great commitment and sacrifice. For example, Torrington Brass and Steel invested 2,000 hours in management training for three-day seminars, in addition to numerous quality improvement exercises. According to Torrington president John Murphy, internal communication processes have improved considerably, thereby reducing distribution errors. However, the long-term benefits remain to be seen.[6]

## Joseph Juran

Dr. Joseph Juran (1904– ) believes that statistical techniques are useful tools in helping to achieve quality goals, but he argues that quality must move well beyond statistical analysis. According to Juran, if managers are to recognize the importance of improving quality, new measures have to be developed to attract their attention.[7] Juran emphasizes customer perceptions of quality rather than statistical techniques. He defines quality as "fitness for use," meaning that a product should perform so as to satisfy a customer need.[8] His flexible approach to attaining high quality takes into account every stage of a product's life cycle.

Juran developed "The Juran Trilogy," which focuses on quality planning, quality control, and quality improvement as a means of managing finance and quality. This trilogy emphasizes the cost effectiveness of pursuing quality. To measure the costs associated with striving for a given level of quality in production, Juran developed a **cost-of-quality (COQ) accounting system**, which permits managers to calculate precisely the costs and savings associated with their quality efforts. This system relates quality costs to the costs "associated solely with defective products— the costs of making, finding, repairing, or avoiding defects."[9] Juran points out that managers notice how important quality improvement is when product failure costs are presented as a percentage of sales or profits.

Juran identified three elements of a quality program: (1) Top management must be in charge; (2) employees have to be trained in quality management; and (3) quality needs to be improved at a faster rate.[10] Top management must also fully support the quality program and monitor it on an annual basis to ensure that improvements are occurring.

**cost-of-quality (COQ) accounting system**
A system that permits managers to calculate precisely the costs and savings associated with their quality efforts.

## Philip Crosby

Philip Crosby (1926– ) left ITT in 1979 and wrote his book, *Quality Is Free,* in which he argued that dollars spent on quality and the attention paid to it always return greater benefits than the costs expended on them. Whereas Deming and Juran emphasized the sacrifice required for a quality commitment, Crosby takes a less philosophical and more practical approach, asserting instead that high quality is relatively easy and inexpensive in the long run.

Crosby is a true practitioner—the only American quality expert without a doctorate. He is responsible for the **zero defects** program, which emphasizes "doing it right the first time," with 100 percent acceptable output. Unlike Deming and

**Teaching Note:** Be sure to differentiate between the textbook concept of zero defects and the actual practice in industry. While few firms, if any, ever reach zero defects, the term is an excellent motivator and mission to work toward. It serves to focus all organizational employees on the total quality objectives.

**zero defects**
A program that emphasizes "doing it right the first time," with 100 percent acceptable output.

Through continuous improvement and people empowerment, MagneTek plans to realize its vision of becoming the best electrical equipment company in the world. Important elements of T.E.A.M. (Total Excellence At MagneTek) include Crosby's quality concepts of conformance to requirements, prevention, zero defects, and price of nonconformance. T.E.A.M. action groups meet regularly to identify and eliminate work process problems.

*Source:* © MagneTek, Inc.

**Teaching Note:** In discussing conformance to specifications, have students compare other examples. For example, compare a room at Motel 6 to one at Holiday Inn, or a fish dinner from Hardee's to one from Red Lobster. Remind students that all can be quality products as long as they conform to the requirements and expectations of the customer.

**Teaching Note:** Have students compare Crosby's 14-point program to Deming's 14 points. For example, Deming is against recognition, posters, slogans, and other forms of "cheerleading," while Crosby encourages recognition and a day to honor zero defects. Have students find other differences and similarities.

Juran, Crosby argues that quality is always cost effective. Like Deming and Juran, Crosby does not place the blame on workers, but on management.

Crosby also developed a 14-point program, but his program is more practical than philosophical. It provides managers with actual concepts that can help them manage productivity and quality.[11] His program is built around four "Absolutes of Quality Management."[12]

Crosby's first absolute is that quality must be viewed as conformance to specifications. If a product meets design specifications, then it is a high-quality product. For example, an Escort that meets Ford's requirements for an Escort is as much a high-quality product as a Cadillac that conforms to Cadillac requirements.[13]

Second, quality should be achieved through the "prevention" of defects rather than inspection after the production process is complete. According to Crosby, this traditional quality control approach taken by American firms is not cost effective. Instead, production workers should be granted the authority and responsibility to ensure that quality goods or services are produced at every step of the process.

Third, managers need to demonstrate that a higher standard of performance can lead to perfection through zero defects. Crosby believed that the goal of any company should be zero defects.

Fourth, quality should be measured by the price of nonconformity. It has been demonstrated that it costs less to produce quality than not to produce it. Crosby contends that the costs associated with achieving quality should be a part of a company's financial system.

Crosby provides two tools to help managers identify and understand their quality problems: (1) quality-costing measures that help companies attain the fourth absolute, and (2) five quality awareness stages for self-assessment. Once a company recognizes its existing strengths and weaknesses related to quality, it can use Crosby's 14-point program to improve its quality efforts:

1. Management commitment
2. Quality improvement teams
3. Quality measurement
4. Cost of quality evaluation
5. Quality awareness
6. Corrective action
7. Zero defects planning

8. Supervisor planning
9. Zero defects day
10. Goal setting
11. Error cause removal
12. Recognition
13. Quality councils
14. Do it all over again.[14]

This program emphasizes prevention and focuses on changing an organization's culture through leadership and commitment. By "doing the process all over again," commitment is renewed among old employees and new ones are made part of the process.

## QUALITY AND THE CONSUMER

In developing TQM or any other quality program, it is imperative that companies understand how consumers define quality in both the goods and services offered. If the company pays more attention to quality in the production process, there will be fewer problems later when the product is in the consumer's hands. Customers include not only those who purchase the final product (external customers), but also suppliers and other employees within the company (internal customers), as discussed in the "Quest for Quality" box. One way to measure product performance and quality is through customer surveys, which can help managers discover design or manufacturing problems.

According to quality consultant Armand V. Feigenbaum, quality is best defined by the end user. Hence, the concept of quality must be expanded to include not only "objective" measures of the good or service, but also the "subjective" interpretations of buyers.[15] Consumer perceptions have to be changed if a company wants to change a product's quality image. This has often been accomplished through extended service programs and improved warranties. For example, Whirlpool Corporation promises that parts for all models will be available for 15 years, while Mercedes-Benz provides technical roadside assistance after dealer service hours.[16]

In the pursuit of customer-based quality enhancements, many companies have developed customer-driven quality programs. Caterpillar, for example, conducts two customer surveys after the purchase of a product, one after 300 hours of use and the other after 500 hours of use.[17] By developing customer service programs, companies can build long-term business through increased customer loyalty.

Toyota has integrated total customer satisfaction into all of its processes. The prime goal and focus of its marketing strategy are to satisfy customers' needs and expectations. Toyota began with a commitment from top management, realizing that everyone in the company must have the same goal of customer satisfaction. The company's "The Toyota Touch" is a commitment to excellence, concern for superior quality, and caring for people based on communication, cooperation, and consideration.[18] Through this plan, Toyota can ensure that the customer is first and that the quality of its service matches the quality of its products.

One means of ensuring a commitment to quality "after the sale" is the product or service guarantee. Wal-Mart is known for its no-hassles return policy for any product—with or without a receipt. Mail-order house L.L. Bean has replaced a pair of hunting boots purchased ten years earlier with new boots.[19] Saturn automobile

**Example:** Wal-Mart selectively phones customers who have returned an item to inquire about their return experience and the helpfulness of the return employee. Lawn and garden departments of stores including Kmart and Lowes invite customers to return any plants that do not live at least one year for a full refund or replacement.

## TQM AND THE INTERNAL CUSTOMER

TQM has always been considered a customer-oriented philosophy, with companies focusing on providing high quality and value to the consumer while minimizing costs. This notion of TQM suggests that only those members of the organization who have direct or indirect contact with consumers need to incorporate the philosophy.

Recently, however, the boundaries of TQM have expanded to include relationships within the organization. In this new thinking, consumers include not only the end users of the company's goods and services, but also every member of the organization, because each individual provides some sort of good or service to someone else in the company. This broadening of the focus makes TQM *everyone's responsibility,* not only sales representatives' and production operators', but also payroll and maintenance workers'.

Consider that behind every product stretches a chain of internal customers and suppliers. Applying TQM internally means that each employee must consider all the others who depend on him or her for internal supplies or services as customers. In other words, if you never come face to face with the people who pay for your company's goods or services, then your customers get their paychecks from the same company you do.

Companies start applying TQM internally by determining how their customers and potential customers define quality. Surveys, focus groups, and other traditional approaches are fine, as long as the approach is customer-centered. Then members of the organization measure processes that lead to quality output as defined by its customers. Efforts are made to ensure that each process within the organization contributes to the final goal of total quality. Success or failure is measured in the same way quality was originally explored—through the eyes of the customer.

In a restaurant, this means establishing a supplier-customer relationship between food servers and food preparers. The cooks' customers are the waiters and waitresses; and the vague, indirect line of responsibility from cook to patron is replaced by clear, direct lines from cook to waiter or waitress, and from waiter or waitress to patron. In a production firm, the supplier-customer link is between those who deliver components to the manufacturing site and those who begin the production process. As a result, each member of the company stays focused on quality and remains fully aware of his or her contribution to it and responsibility for it.

To date, companies such as Westinghouse, McCormick & Company, Inc., and AT&T have adopted an internal customer philosophy and have reported solid gains in the quality of internal service within their organizations.

*Source:* Chris Lee, "The Customer Within," *Training* 28 (July 1991): 21–26.

**Comment on Box:** Have students discuss other ways to measure quality. Because most students have some work experience or knowledge, poll them on ways quality is measured in their jobs. Share with students various ways teaching quality is measured at your school—student evaluations, peer review, committee decisions, etc.

retailers provide total refunds for vehicles within 30 days if the customer is not fully satisfied. One Saturn commercial features a representative traveling all the way to Alaska to replace a defective seat in a customer's vehicle. However, many companies are not willing to incur the short-run costs associated with such guarantees.

## QUALITY AND STRATEGY

A study by the Forum Corporation revealed two main reasons why organizations embrace a quality strategy. One reason is that a company's founders typically hold strong views concerning the importance of quality. A classic example is Honda's founder, Soichire Honda, who upheld quality as a primary focus of the company. Honda's corporate philosophy and strategy for quality have not changed in 45 years.[20]

The Pacific Eagle Express shown here symbolizes Union Pacific Railroad's commitment to satisfying customers with reliable, on-time service performance. The train leaves Chicago five nights a week, with guaranteed delivery to Los Angeles 52 hours later. The quality dimensions of reliability and performance give UPRR a competitive edge as the number one intermodal carrier in the railroad industry.

*Source:* Courtesy of The Union Pacific Corporation, Photographer, Ovak Arslanian.

The second reason is that many companies respond to economic downturns or competitive pressures by adopting a customer-focused strategy. These companies realize that environmental pressures act as a stimulus for change, and managers focus on such factors as loyalty, satisfaction, and changes in the demand structure.

## A TQM Strategy Begins at the Top

To be effective, the TQM philosophy must begin at the top. From the board of directors to the hourly line employees, TQM must be supported at all levels if the firm is to realize any real improvements in quality. Specifically, if top management does not fully support it, other employees may see TQM as mere symbolism and not substance, and therefore not be as inclined to support it.[21]

## Obstacles to Effectively Adopting TQM

With the increased availability of international goods and services, U.S. consumers have more choices than ever before. Such global pressures are forcing more companies to incorporate TQM into their business strategies. Moreover, those companies using TQM successfully are realizing a decrease in long-run costs by building a more satisfied customer base. However, because short-run costs for new equipment, materials, and additional labor are sometimes required to implement TQM processes, many companies are hesitant to adopt TQM.

Time is another deterrent to the adoption of TQM. Many companies do not want to wait the two to ten years typically required to gain initial benefits from TQM. However, some payoffs can be realized in only a month's time. For example, improved customer service through surveys and improved employee relations with management are two areas where results can be achieved from the onset.

## TQM and Commitment

A commitment to quality can become a key element of any company's strategy. There are eight dimensions of quality that serve as a framework for strategic analysis:

**Example:** Saturn automobile company has emphasized quality continually. When the company has experienced problems, like a defective seat mechanism, Saturn kept the public informed and even communicated how the problems were being corrected and eliminated. These measures emphasize a quality commitment.

**Teaching Note:** Explain to students that TQM initiatives can start with a small pilot project. Simple steps like adding a phone number to product labels so customers can call for customer service, or developing a survey to gather customer opinions on products are easy projects for a beginning TQM team.

**FIGURE 7.2**

**An Example of a Flowchart for a Morning Routine**

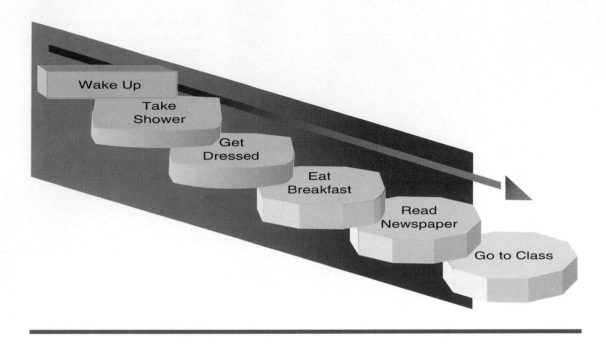

1. Performance
2. Features
3. Reliability
4. Conformance
5. Durability
6. Serviceability
7. Aesthetics
8. Perceived quality.[22]

**Example:** While Steinway has a higher perceived quality in grand pianos, Kawai, the Japanese competitor who manufactures grand pianos using advanced production techniques, has an equal performance quality. Often perceived differences exist only in the minds of the customer.

Different products are evaluated in different dimensions, which do not have to be pursued simultaneously. For example, Tandem Computers has achieved a reputation for superior reliability, whereas Steinway & Sons has been the "tone" quality leader in pianos—but not other products—for many years.[23] Companies may focus on a selective quality niche to gain competitive advantage because few firms are equipped to excel in all dimensions simultaneously.[24] This niche should be based on the product's characteristics and the organization's goals and unique resources.[25]

## TOOLS FOR IMPROVING QUALITY

Once a company determines that it wants to improve quality and develops a strategy to achieve that goal, it must next establish quality improvement processes. There are seven major tools and techniques that can help a company accomplish this goal.

**FIGURE 7.3**

**Example of a Cause-and-Effect (Fishbone) Diagram**

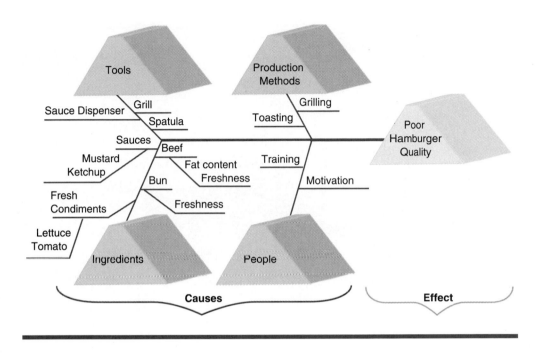

One such tool is the **flowchart**, which simply diagrams a process from start to finish, identifying those aspects of the process that need improvement (Figure 7.2). A flowchart can be used in administrative or staff functions as well as in manufacturing functions. Flowcharts help identify improvements, help employees to understand the process better, and improve communication between all levels of employees.[26] Flowcharts can be simple or very specific: The degree of specificity should be determined by the process being diagrammed. Simple flowcharts promote an understanding of a general process, as shown in Figure 7.2. On the other hand, a detailed flowchart helps delineate a more intricate process, such as assembling an automobile engine.

Another tool for accomplishing quality goals is the **cause-and-effect diagram**—also known as fishbone analysis—a method for analyzing process dispersion that relates causes and effects (Figure 7.3).[27] The cause-and-effect diagram graphically depicts the effects of TQM activities. Developed in 1943 by Ishikawa at the University of Tokyo, the cause-and-effect diagram is best suited for team applications. This tool "fosters team work, educates users, identifies lowest-level issues on which to work, helps show a true picture of the process, guides discussion, and can be used for any issue a business might face."[28]

The third tool is the histogram, which was developed in France in 1833 by A. M. Guerry. A **histogram** is a graphic summary of data that enables a user to interpret patterns that are difficult to see in a simple table of numbers (Figure 7.4).[29] Histograms provide information about processes that is easily understood by managers and employees responsible for the processes. Histograms do not alter or

**flowchart**
A tool that diagrams a process from start to finish, identifying those aspects of the process that need improvement.

**cause-and-effect diagram**
A method for analyzing process dispersion that relates causes and effects; also known as fishbone analysis.

**Example:** Another way the Japanese identify the causes of a problem is to ask "why." They believe that by asking "why" seven times they will discover the root cause of a problem.

**histogram**
A graphic summary of data that enables a user to interpret patterns that are difficult to see in a simple table of numbers.

**FIGURE 7.4**

**Example of a Histogram**

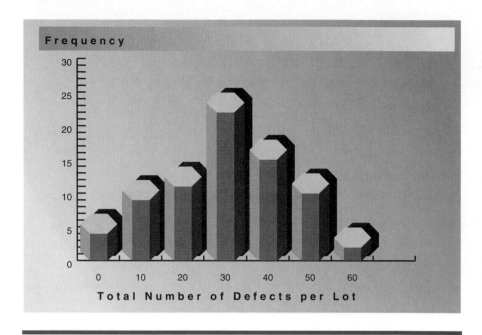

manipulate data but merely provide an illustration to aid in comprehending the data.

**Pareto chart**
A diagram that graphically illustrates the frequencies of key factors that contribute to poor quality.

The **Pareto chart**, developed by Juran in 1950, graphically illustrates the frequencies of key factors that contribute to poor quality. The Pareto principle suggests that most negative effects stem from relatively few causes. In other words, "80 percent of the problems come from 20 percent of the machines, raw materials, or operators."[30] The Pareto chart highlights the critical 20 percent that should be addressed (Figure 7.5). After drawing a Pareto chart, the company first tackles the most frequent problem identified. Then the Pareto chart is redrawn and the process repeated with the next most frequent problem, and so on. The Pareto chart helps managers and team members focus on problems that have the greatest impact on quality.

**control charts**
Diagrams that display data over time as well as computed variations in those data.

**Control charts** display data over time as well as computed variations in those data (Figure 7.6). The charts visually depict when the data fall outside a previously set acceptable range of quality. Managers can then more closely examine the special causes of variation during those time periods so that they can develop improvement plans.

**scatter diagrams**
Illustrations allowing management to evaluate the relationship between two variables, using one variable to make a prediction about another variable or characteristic.

**Scatter diagrams** allow management to evaluate the relationship between two variables, using one variable to make a prediction about another variable or characteristic. Each data point on a scatter diagram represents measures of the two variables at a given time. The distribution of the data on the diagram can help managers infer relationships between two variables (Figure 7.7).

**checksheets**
Data-recording forms that have been designed to allow managers to enter data on the form and simultaneously analyze trends in the data.

**Checksheets** are data-recording forms that have been designed to allow managers to enter data on the form and simultaneously analyze trends in the data (Figure 7.8). Checksheets help managers tally the frequency of critical events,

**FIGURE 7.5**

**Example of a Pareto Chart**

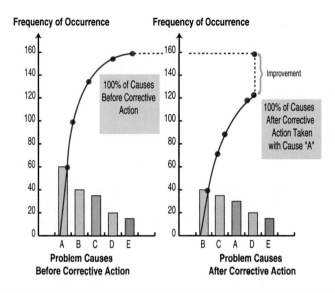

such as different product defects, to provide data critical to statistical analysis. As such, checksheets are best suited for simple questions or problems that require an immediate response.

## IMPLEMENTING AN EFFECTIVE TQM PROGRAM

After a company determines those areas or processes most in need of quality improvement programs, it needs to implement the programs immediately. Managers must take an active role in changing an organization to a total quality management system. They need to understand how different quality tools work so they can be committed to continuous improvement. This will help build better relationships between management and employees, as well as promote the pursuit of quality within the organization.

**Example:** Many TQM programs fail because top management is not actively involved or does not initiate the program. Simply paying lip service to the project is not enough.

### The Implementation Process

Many managers have successfully implemented total quality management principles or systems in their companies. However, before quality efforts can be successful, top management must develop a plan that will help them achieve their quality goals. Juran's approach—one of the three facets of the Juran Trilogy—is known as quality improvement, or the "breakthrough sequence." According to Juran, an organization must go through the following seven steps to implement quality improvements effectively:

1. Achieve a breakthrough in attitudes. Organizations should collect data to demonstrate the extent of the current problems and conduct cost-benefit analyses to illustrate the need for change.

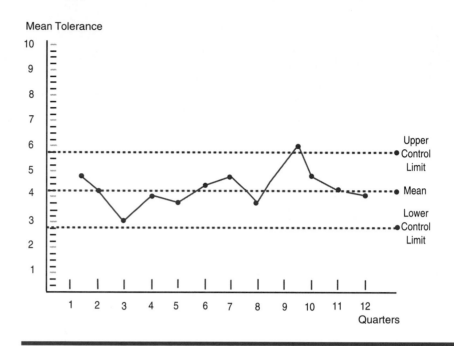

**FIGURE 7.6**

**Example of a Control Chart**

**2.** Identify a few key projects. Organizations should not attempt to tackle too many problems at once.

**3.** Organize for a breakthrough in knowledge. The steering group, composed of people from different departments, defines the problem, suggests possible causes, helps overcome resistance to change, and implements the solution.

**4.** Conduct the analysis. The diagnostic group typically consists of quality experts and line managers and is responsible for analyzing the problem.

**5.** Design a plan to overcome the resistance to change. Participation of all relevant parties is critical.

**6.** Institute the change. Organizations should not overlook the need to cultivate commitment among key departments, as well as to recognize any needs that may exist for additional training.

**7.** Institute controls to monitor the results. Establish benchmarks to help track the company's progress in the quality improvement program.[31]

From the beginning phases of planning strategy to continuously improving and modifying quality programs, management must be fully committed and involved in every step. Virtually all managers claim to be concerned about quality, but total commitment and involvement—not just lip service—sends a message to employees that the company is serious about quality improvement. For example, Bob Galvin, chairman of Motorola and architect of its quality efforts, responds to one customer complaint a day, in an effort not only to satisfy the customer, but also to remedy the situation that led to the dissatisfaction.[32]

## FIGURE 7.7

**Example of Scatter Diagrams**

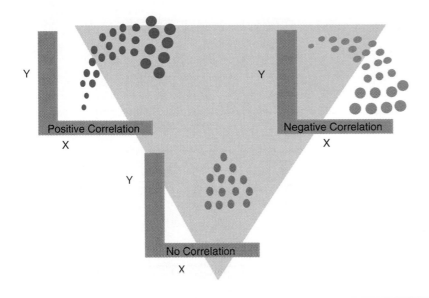

Positive Correlation

Y

X

Negative Correlation

Y

X

No Correlation

Y

X

## Quality by Listening

Quality improvement programs give human resources "bottom line" importance, with the potential to add value to the company. Managers can utilize their human resources by fostering an environment that is open to suggestions and creativity. By allowing employees a certain degree of flexibility and authority in decision making in their jobs, productivity and quality can improve. On the other hand, if employees do not respond to the quality challenge, the organization will lose the resources invested in the program, with no benefits to show for it.[33]

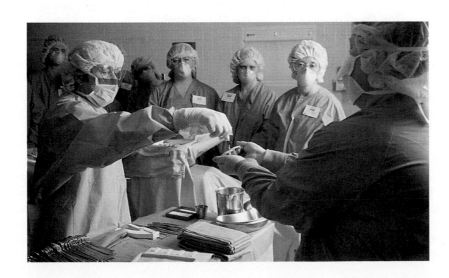

To get a close understanding of customer needs, wants, and quality expectations, employees (with name tags) from a 3M medical and surgical products plant, from production-line workers to senior executives, put on scrubs and observe how doctors and nurses use their products in the operating room. The face-to-face interaction gives employees the chance to learn about customer complaints and suggestions for product improvements.

*Source:* © Sandy May.

**Example of a Checksheet**

| Defect Type | Defect Count | Sub Total |
|---|---|---|
| Low Tolerance | ＨＨＴ ＨＨＴ ＨＨＴ ＨＨＴ ＨＨＴ ＨＨＴ Ｉ | 31 |
| Bent | ＨＨＴ Ｉ | 6 |
| Chipped | ‖ | 2 |
| **Grand Total:** | | **39** |

Product:  Component 211B    Date:       9/7/94
Lot:       7               Examiner:  J. Charles
Total Examined:            450
Signature:  _J. Charles_

**Example:** As part of the TQM programs, some companies have implemented suggestion boxes where employees can recommend changes. Organizations even share cost savings resulting from employee suggestions.

Companies must also listen to suggestions and complaints from customers, whether they are internal or external to the company. One way to measure the success of quality programs, aside from increased profits or decreased defects, is through customer satisfaction. Managers need to determine their customers' wants, needs, and quality expectations. By listening to customers, companies can design quality into a product, and the processes involved, that will lead to less waste and fewer defects, as well as enhanced customer satisfaction.

## Generating Quality throughout the Organization

Once management and employees are involved and customers and suppliers have been considered, quality can be implemented into all areas of the company, or into certain areas that have been identified by management, such as production or distribution. Managers and employees must determine which approach is best suited to meet the needs of customers and the resources of the company. The appropriate tools and techniques can help improve performance in processes and human resources.

Quality programs need to be continuously improved to meet the changing needs of the organization and its customers once they have been implemented. Management must remember that achieving excellence through quality is a long-term effort that requires performance measurements. Implementing and maintaining quality processes can be costly in terms of both human resources and capital requirements, depending on how extensive the required changes are. However, investment in quality programs can help achieve long-term improvements in productivity, quality, and organizational performance.

# QUALITY IN JAPANESE FIRMS

Japanese firms are responsible for many of the most important advances in quality management. Indeed, many Japanese companies are known for quality in their respective industries. The Japanese "design in" the quality of goods or services instead of "inspecting out," as has been typically the case with American firms.[34]

## Genichi Taguchi

A key Japanese contributor to the quality revolution in Japan is Dr. Genichi Taguchi (1924– ), an international consultant and past director of the Japanese Academy of Quality. Taguchi emphasizes designing products that will achieve high quality despite environmental fluctuations, while improving the process design of the manufacturing process rather than the process-control technologies.[35] Taguchi's approach is also built on the **quality loss function (QLF)**, the idea that a product that fails to meet consumer expectations results in a measurable loss to society. Through continuous improvements in the design phase of a product, both consumers and manufacturers benefit through higher-quality products at lower costs.

The Ford Motor Company was one of the first U.S. companies to apply Taguchi's ideas, in the 1980s, followed by ITT, Bell Laboratories, Xerox, and General Motors. The 3M Company reported $2 million in annual savings after implementing Taguchi's techniques.[36]

## Quality Function Deployment

**Quality function deployment (QFD)**, which originated in 1972 at Mitsubishi's Kobe shipyard, is a set of planning and communication routines that focus and coordinate skills within an organization, first through design, then through the manufacturing and marketing of products.[37] Under QFD, products should be designed to reflect consumer demands, requiring the collaboration of all areas of the company from the design engineers to the marketing department.

## Quality Circles

A popular application seen in Japanese firms are **quality circles**, which are groups of managers and employees, representing production tasks, who meet periodically to discuss proposals to seek continuous improvements in the production system. After his ideas were largely rejected by U.S. executives, W. Edwards Deming taught Japanese managers the principles of quality circles in the early 1950s. Although the employee-involvement tool proved very successful in Japan, it did not return to the United States until the 1970s. American firms hesitated to embrace the concept until signals such as falling market share, large inventories, reduced profitability, and a changing attitude among consumers indicated that U.S. companies were losing the economic war against Japan. By 1985, more than 90 percent of *Fortune* 500 firms had instituted quality circle programs.[38]

One reason for this widespread application of quality circles is the benefits reported by Japanese companies that have used them. For example, Toyota Motor Company and Nippon Electric Corporation each reported that quality circles resulted in savings of $10 million.[39] Thus, quality circles help improve employee development and involvement while improving a company's competitiveness in the

---

**Teaching Note:** Explain the difference between total quality management and quality control. Quality control is a reactive or after-the-fact check that does nothing to improve the process. It only screens for defects, usually in the final product. TQM, on the other hand, is proactive and looks to identify and correct the causes of poor quality at all stages of the production process.

**quality loss function (QLF)**
The idea that a product that fails to meet consumer expectations results in a measurable loss to society.

**quality function deployment (QFD)**
A set of planning and communication routines that focus and coordinate skills within an organization, first through design, then through the manufacturing and marketing of products.

**quality circles**
Groups of managers and employees, representing production tasks, who meet periodically to discuss proposals to seek continuous improvements in the production system.

**Example:** Quality circles are less than successful in the United States because workers are not familiar with working in teams, like Japanese workers. Individual rewards also limit group participation. Even middle management fears giving power for decision making to groups because many feel their jobs would no longer be needed.

marketplace. The quality circles movement in the United States was not as successful as manufacturers had hoped, largely because many quality circles were implemented without the full acceptance of the TQM philosophy and supporting cultural and managerial practices.

## Training of Japanese Employees

Training of the labor force is very important in implementing quality processes throughout Japanese companies. Many firms have realized the importance of employee development and have responded by implementing extensive training programs. Most Japanese companies prepare new assembly-line workers by training them for all jobs on the line. It takes approximately six months to properly train a worker in many firms.

In contrast, American workers typically receive only a few hours' to a few days' training, and many are trained to perform only one task. They also receive little information about the product or adaptations to their outputs that take place within the plant or on the line. Today, many American companies have realized that an employee's inexperience on the line and lack of familiarity with the products produced contribute to high defect rates.[40]

Although times are changing, many Japanese companies continue to provide their employees with lifelong employment. Once workers are trained by a particular company, it is assumed that they will stay with that company for the rest of their lives. It is believed that this concept of permanent employment improves quality, reduces the number of defects, and results in lower absenteeism and turnover because the workers feel that they are an integral part of the company. American firms have been slow to adapt the lifetime employment philosophy, instead often arguing that cultural differences would seriously hamper the process.

## NATIONAL AND INTERNATIONAL RECOGNITION OF QUALITY

There are several key awards made to American and Japanese firms to recognize their quality improvement efforts. One such award, the Malcolm Baldrige National Quality Award, was created by Congress in 1987 to recognize quality improvement efforts by U.S. companies and to foster greater competitiveness in the areas of excellence and high standards. The purpose of the Baldrige award is "to promote quality awareness, recognize quality achievements of U.S. companies and to publicize successful quality strategies."[41] Among the companies that have won the award are IBM Rochester, FedEx, Cadillac, Globe Metallurgical, and the Wallace Company.

**Critical Thinking Challenge:** Have student groups discuss both the advantages and disadvantages of quality awards, contests, and other recognition programs. Possible advantages: reward workers, stimulate interest in the company, motivate ongoing quality programs, increase business, etc. Possible disadvantages: take time away from improvements, emphasize quality exclusively, etc.

Companies competing for the award are judged on seven integrally related quality criteria: (1) leadership, (2) information and analysis, (3) strategic quality planning, (4) human resource development and management, (5) management of process quality, (6) quality and operational results, and (7) customer focus and satisfaction.[42] A possible 1,000 points can be awarded, but companies usually score around 500 points. No more than two companies can receive the Baldrige award in each of the three categories—manufacturing, service, and small business.

The Deming Prize, named to honor the American statistician, is given to business quality leaders in the United States and Japan. The purpose of the Deming Prize, as stated in the award guidelines, is to "award prizes to those companies which are recognized as having successfully applied company-wide quality

For its commitment to constantly improving the total quality of its business and products, such as the duplicating equipment shown here, Xerox Corporation is the only company in the world to win all three of the world's major quality awards—The Malcolm Baldrige National Quality Award, The European Quality Award, and the Deming Prize. Xerox has also received awards for quality in Canada, France, England, China, Mexico, Australia, Belgium, Holland, Colombia, and Hong Kong.

*Source:* Courtesy of Xerox Corporation, photographer, Ted Kawalerski.

control principles based on statistical quality control and which are likely to keep up with it in the future."[43]

Judging criteria for the Deming Prize are based on ten categories: (1) policy and objectives, (2) organization and operations, (3) education, (4) assembling and disseminating information, (5) analysis, (6) standardization, (7) control, (8) quality assurance, (9) effects, and (10) future plans.[44] The Deming Prize is awarded to those companies that meet a previously established standard for quality. However, achieving the standard for companywide quality control principles is very difficult, as evidenced by the small number of companies that pass the standard.

Five years after a company wins the Deming Prize, it can qualify to win the Japan Quality Control Award. This award was created in 1969 and is given only to companies that have won the Deming Prize and have proceeded to attain a higher level of excellence and quality.[45]

Another award that can be given to a U.S. or Japanese firm is the Shingo Prize for Excellence in Manufacturing. This award was established in 1988 and is given in large and small business categories. Globe Metallurgical is the only company that has won both the Malcolm Baldrige Award and the Shingo Prize for Excellence in Manufacturing.[46]

## QUALITY IN THE TWENTY-FIRST CENTURY

As U.S. firms move toward the coming century, they must integrate a quality emphasis into all aspects of their operations, not just in their mission statements and objectives. Although elaborate mission statements and expressed commitments to quality can help, managers should emphasize tangible quality improvements, not just slogans.[47]

Europeans are showing a renewed interest in American products, and companies such as Lands' End, Goodyear, and Walt Disney are beginning to see a tremendous growth potential.[48] The market potential for automobiles in the former Soviet Union and China has also captured the interest of the big three automakers.[49] Amidst all these international opportunities, however, one question remains: Will American firms seek competitive advantage by emphasizing quality, or will they rely solely on marketing expertise for success?

# orner

## Pursuing a Career in TQM

Career opportunities in TQM-related fields are quite diversified and attractive for both quality experts and those seeking to integrate quality with another chosen field. There are two reasons why quality-related positions will likely continue to be very strong in years to come.

First, businesses have begun to emphasize both production efficiency and high quality in their goods and services. Today's consumers demand both high quality and competitive prices. Hence, organizations must pay greater attention to how their quality efforts are implemented throughout the organization to remain competitive. When companies emphasize value—quality at a competitive price—everyone in the organization must become more quality-conscious. Delivering value to the customer becomes a function of all departments. To provide value, company recruits for positions in all divisions should be well-versed in the principles of total quality. Even quality-oriented candidates in a variety of fields such as sales, finance, and human resources have the potential to play key roles in the integration of quality throughout the organization.

The second reason for bright career opportunities is the ongoing movement toward universal quality standards, especially in the international arena. Since 1993, companies selling goods and services in Europe have been required to provide evidence of an approved quality management system. European firms can reject goods or services from sellers that do not have registered quality systems.

The International Standards Organization's ISO 9000 series of quality standards was the first quality system to meet European Economic Area directives. The ISO 9000 series guidelines aim to ensure that each company continuously meets quality standards for its products

that are acceptable to its managers, customers, and end users. ISO 9000 certification enhances a firm's worldwide recognition, eliminates expensive, time-consuming audits by prospective customers, often reduces costs, empowers employees, and ultimately improves quality.

The universal quality standards movement is not limited to the European market. In the United States, many organizations—including 3M, Du Pont, Eastman Kodak, Kellogg, Union Carbide, and even the U.S. Department of Defense—have obtained ISO 9000 series certification and now require their suppliers to meet ISO 9000 quality standards. As a result, companies have experienced difficulty recruiting graduates who understand the design and implementation of TQM systems.

For these reasons, all students are encouraged to "think quality" when preparing for a business career. For those who pursue advanced study in TQM in either an undergraduate or graduate program, the prospects for employment and career advancement in the field is promising.

*Sources:* T. E. Benson, "Quality Goes International," *Industry Week,* August 19, 1991, 54–57; A. F. Borthick and H. P. Roth, "Will Europeans Buy Your Company's Products?" *Business Credit,* November/December 1992, 23–24; S. J. Harrison and R. Stupak, "Total Quality Management: The Organizational Equivalent of Truth in Public Administration Theory and Practice," *Public Administration Quarterly* 6 (1992): 416–429; C.W.L. Hart and P.E. Morrison, "Students Aren't Learning Quality Principles in Business Schools," *Quality Progress* 25 (January 1992): 25–27; and D. Marquardt, "Vision 2000: The Strategy for the ISO 9000 Series Standards in the 90's," *Quality Progress* 24 (May 1991): 25–31.

**Teaching Note:** Because most cities have a chapter of the American Production and Inventory Control Society (APICS) or the American Society for Quality Control (ASQC), ask a local manufacturing manager to address your class on both careers and trends within the production/ operations area. Also tour a local manufacturing organization if possible.

While efforts at improving quality have been significant, many companies continue to depend on political pressure and "Buy American" campaigns to spur sales domestically, and slick marketing campaigns to succeed internationally.[50] With global markets continuing to open and passage of the North American Free Trade Agreement (NAFTA), battles for new markets will continue to intensify. In this environment, quality—not just superior marketing—will likely determine the winners and losers in the coming century.

# SUMMARY AND REVIEW

- **Define total quality management and trace its development.** Quality reflects the degree to which a good or service meets the demands and requirements of the marketplace. Total quality management is a management view that strives to create a customer-centered culture that defines quality for the organization and lays the foundation for activities aimed at attaining quality-related goals. The concept of TQM rests largely on five principles: quality work the first time, focus on the customer, strategic holistic approach to improvement, continuous improvement as a way of life, and mutual respect and teamwork.

  When Japan began its post–World War II rebuilding process, many of its companies had been all but destroyed, and they were forced to adopt stringent productivity measures to survive. While Japanese companies began to embrace quality in production and service, U.S. firms were more interested in quality control, evaluating quality level of finished products. During the 1950s and 1960s, quality champions such as Joseph M. Juran and W. Edwards Deming introduced to Japan ideas such as building quality into processes and using line-workers to solve process problems through the use of applied statistics. U.S. companies largely ignored their concepts during this time, relying instead on quality control departments as the primary means of ensuring quality. The systems of the 1970s emphasized only the manufacturing processes and embracing such techniques as zero defects, or error-free production, a manufacturing process consisting of maintaining machinery and equipment, quality inspection checks, and well-trained employees. When they realized they were not competing effectively with the more efficient Japanese, U.S. companies began applying quality considerations throughout their organizations rather than just to production.

- **Summarize the TQM philosophies of Deming, Juran, and Crosby.** W. Edwards Deming, a statistician known as the "Father of TQM," encouraged the use of statistical techniques to measure production quality and identify changes necessary to improve quality. He argued that a commitment to quality requires a transformation of the entire organization, and he developed a 14-point system to achieve that commitment.

  Joseph Juran believes that while statistical techniques are useful tools in helping to achieve quality goals, quality must move well beyond statistical analysis. He emphasizes instead consumer perceptions of quality, defining it as "fitness for use."

Philip Crosby takes a more practical approach, asserting that high quality is relatively easy and inexpensive in the long run. Crosby is responsible for zero defects programs that emphasize "doing it right the first time." He also developed four "Absolutes of Quality Management": (1) Quality must be viewed as conformance to specifications; (2) it should be achieved through the "prevention" of defects rather than inspection after the production process; (3) management needs to demonstrate that a higher standard of performance can lead to perfection through zero defects; and (4) quality should be measured by the price of nonconformity.

- **Explain how quality relates to consumers through the marketing function.** In developing quality-improvement programs, companies need to understand how both internal and external customers define quality. If the company pays more attention to quality in the production process, there will be fewer problems later when the product reaches the consumer. One way to measure product performance and quality is through customer surveys, and a means of ensuring a commitment to quality "after the sale" is the product or service guarantee.

- **Discuss the relationship between quality and strategy in the organization.** There are two main reasons why organizations embrace a quality strategy. One is that a company's founders typically hold strong views concerning the importance of quality. A second is that many companies respond to economic downturns or competitive pressures by adopting a customer-focused strategy. A commitment to quality can become a key element of any company's strategy.

- **Examine some of the tools available to help improve quality.** The flowchart, which diagrams a process from start to finish, identifying those aspects of the process that need improvement, can help identify refinements, better understand the process, and improve communication between all levels of employees. The cause-and-effect or fishbone diagram is a method for analyzing process dispersion that relates causes and effects. A histogram is a graphic summary of data that enables a user to interpret patterns that are difficult to see in a simple table of numbers. A Pareto chart graphically illustrates the frequencies of key factors that contribute to poor quality and highlights the most frequently occurring problems that need immediate attention. Control charts display data over time as well as computed variations in those data. Scatter diagrams allow managers to evaluate the relationship between two variables, using one variable to make a prediction about another variable or characteristic. Checksheets are data-recording forms that have been designed to allow managers to enter data on the form and analyze trends in the data at the same time.

- **Recommend how managers can implement the TQM philosophy in their organizations.** Managers must take an active role in changing an organization to a total quality management system. They need to understand how different quality tools work so they can be committed to continuous improvement. Before quality efforts can be successful, top managers must develop a plan that will help them achieve their quality goals. Juran identified seven steps through which a company must go to implement quality improvements effectively: (1) Achieve a breakthrough in attitudes; (2) identify a few key projects; (3) organize for a breakthrough in knowledge; (4) conduct the analysis; (5) design a plan to overcome the resistance to change; (6) institute the change; and (7) institute controls to monitor the results. Managers can utilize their human resources by fostering an environment that is open to suggestions and creativity. Companies must also listen to suggestions and complaints from customers, whether they are internal or external to the company. Quality programs need to be continuously improved to meet the changing needs of the organization and its customers once they have been implemented.

- **Compare the Japanese approach to quality with the American approach.** Japanese firms are responsible for many of the most important advances in quality management. Genichi Taguchi emphasizes designing products that will achieve high quality despite environmental fluctuations, while improving the process design of the manufacturing process rather than the process-control technologies. Taguchi's approach is also built on the quality loss function (QLF), the idea that a product that fails to meet consumer expectations results in a measurable loss to society. Quality function deployment (QFD) is a set of planning and communication routines that focus and coordinate skills within an organization, first through design, then through the manufacturing and marketing of products. Quality circles consist of managers and employees who meet periodically to discuss proposals to seek continuous improvements in the production system. Most Japanese companies prepare new assembly-line workers by training them for all jobs on the line, and it takes approximately six months to properly train a worker in many Japanese firms. In contrast, American workers typically receive only a few hours' to a few days' training, and many are trained to perform only one task. Many Japanese companies also provide their employees with lifelong employment with the idea that it improves quality, reduces the number of defects, and results in lower absenteeism and turnover because the workers feel that they are an integral part of the company.

- **Describe the importance of national and international awards for quality improvements.** The Malcolm Baldrige Award promotes quality awareness, recognizes quality achievements of U.S. companies, and publicizes successful quality strategies. Japan's Deming Prize is awarded to those companies recognized as having successfully applied companywide quality control principles based on statistical quality control and which are likely to keep up with it in the future. Five years after a company wins the Deming Prize, it can qualify to win the Japan Quality Control Award, which is given only to companies that have won the Deming Prize and have proceeded to attain a higher level of excellence and quality. The Shingo Prize for Excellence in Manufacturing is given in large and small business categories to Japanese and U.S. companies. Awards such as these may encourage businesses to aspire to higher standards of quality and to implement quality-improvement programs.

- **Propose a course of action for a small business that has just won a prestigious quality award.** In the "Business Dilemma" box, you are faced with several decisions after winning a national quality award, which will require employees' time and resources to support. The award supports the quality initiatives and culture of the organization but may prove costly, especially in light of lower productivity in the oil and gas industry. As the manager you need to defend your decisions with a strong rationale.

# Key Terms and Concepts

quality *182*
total quality management (TQM) *182*
error-free production *183*

cost-of-quality (COQ) accounting
   system *187*
zero defects *187*

flowchart *193*
cause-and-effect diagram *193*
histogram *193*

## Ready Recall

1. Compare and contrast Deming's 14-point program with Crosby's 14-point program.
2. How are the teachings of Deming, Juran, and Crosby similar? How are they different?
3. What is Juran's cost-of-quality accounting system? Why is it important?
4. Explain Crosby's four "Absolutes of Quality Management." Are they philosophical or practical? Explain.
5. What is a quality circle? Why have quality circles become popular in the United States in the past two decades?
6. What awards are made to U.S. and Japanese firms for their quality improvements? How are companies judged in these competitions?
7. What are the seven major tools and techniques that can help companies establish quality improvement processes? How do these tools aid decision makers in the pursuit of quality?
8. How does Armand V. Feigenbaum define quality? What implications does his view have for organizations seeking to improve the quality of their goods or services?
9. According to Juran, what seven steps are necessary to effectively implement quality improvements in an organization?

## Expand Your Experience

1. How would you measure quality at your college or university? Do you think your task would be easier than measuring quality in a manufacturing organization? Why or why not?
2. Recall the last restaurant you patronized. How would you measure the quality of the food you received? How would you measure the quality of the service you received? Would you be more likely to complain to management about poor food quality or poor service quality? Why?
3. List all of the factors you would consider in planning an enjoyable extended vacation. How many of these factors are contingent on a quality production process (e.g., a reliable automobile)? How many are contingent on a quality service (e.g., maintenance of the automobile)? Did you list more goods or services? What does this tell you about the potential for applications of TQM in manufacturing and service industries?

## CASE

# *Total Quality Management at Saturn Corporation*

By the early 1980s, imported vehicles had made significant inroads into the United States automobile market and General Motors' response—the "J car" design introduced in 1982 as the Chevrolet Cavalier, Pontiac 2000, Oldsmobile Firenza, Buick Skylark, and Cadillac Cimarron—did nothing to slow its continued erosion in the small-car market. Then-CEO Roger Smith decided to start from scratch, considering the best production technology and labor-management techniques from around the world in pursuit of total quality in the automotive industry. In 1982, Smith initiated a project to innovatively design and manufacture small cars in the United States that were competitive with imported vehicles.

Ninety-nine United Auto Workers (UAW) members, GM managers, and staff personnel from 55 plants joined to form the "Group of 99" to make plans for pursuing this goal. Together, this group was given the task of identifying and recommending the best approaches to integrate people and technology in order to competitively manufacture a small car in the United States.

In 1985, GM formed Saturn Corporation as an independent, wholly owned subsidiary. In 1987, construction began on Saturn's manufacturing, assembly, and training and development operations facility, now covering 4 million square feet and located on 2,400 acres in Spring Hill, Tennessee. By early 1988, Saturn began recruiting the first of 3,000 workers for the plant from 136 GM/UAW facilities in the United States. Smith and UAW President Owen Bieber drove the first Saturn vehicle off the final assembly line on July 30, 1990. Today, Saturn employs approximately 8,500 team members on three shifts. The Spring Hill facility is currently producing about 250,000 vehicles; an additional 100,000 can be added to reach full capacity. Vehicle quality and satisfaction rates rival or exceed those of many of Saturn's Asian competitors. Saturn has embarked on a distinctively different course of automotive success.

Saturn drafted the following mission to guide its goal setting and all other activities:

> *Market vehicles developed and manufactured in the United States that are world leaders in quality, cost and customer satisfaction through the integration of people, technology and business systems and to transfer knowledge and experience throughout General Motors.*

The company also adopted five corporate values to support its commitment to be one of the world's most successful car companies:  commitment to (internal and external) customer enthusiasm, commitment to excel, teamwork, trust and respect for the individual, and continuous improvement.

Saturn promotes the use of self-directed, integrated teams of six to fifteen members that manage their own work and contribute to decisions that affect them. Decisions are made not by voting, but by consensus. Applicants for new team member positions must complete a detailed 12-page assessment that asks for specific information on skills, attitudes, and behaviors. There are no time clocks, no privileged parking spots, and no private dining rooms at Saturn. Dress is casual, and all employees are on salary. Words such as "manager" and "executive" are not frequently used.

A key tenet of Saturn's strategic approach to operations is the flexible assembly system. Specifically, Saturn's system is flexible enough to assemble up to 12 different transmission and engine combinations, along with accessories such as air conditioning and power steering. Flexible assembly plays its most important role in assembly of the engine and transmission, where heavy components can be readily rotated and repositioned for a variety of assembly operations. Such flexible assembly systems are helping manufacturers like Saturn cut production costs, improve quality, increase factory output, and build different versions of a product while on the same production line, saving more than 40 percent of floor space.

Perhaps the most compelling example of how Saturn has used team-member involvement in its operations design is the skillet-system method of assembly. Under the traditional chain-and-drive system, workers move along the line to complete production tasks. A group of Saturn engineers and team members sought a more effective system, given four primary parameters: ergonomics, quality, member utilization, and cost-effectiveness. After two years of research and teamwork, the skillet system was recommended. The skillet system can be described as a moving sidewalk; workers step on the skillet, perform their necessary operations, and step off when done. The vehicle continues to travel on the skillet to other workers. The result, according to Saturn officials, is a more user-friendly system that requires fewer team members and is consistent with Saturn's world-class quality mission.

Saturn also seeks just-in-time (JIT) partnerships with suppliers to improve efficiency and reduce storage costs associated with excess inventories. Just-in-time (JIT) management, also called *kanban,* is an approach that focuses on acquiring supplies when they are needed, or "just in time." Saturn also employs JIT principles in the production facility, where the inventory created at any stage of production may supply the next stage for two hours or less.

Today, Saturn's quest for total quality appears to be paying off. Saturn's sales accounted for approximately 2 percent of the U.S. car market in 1992. Further, J.D. Power and Associates reported that Saturn customer satisfaction (a score of 160) trailed only Lexus (179) and Infinity (167), while ranking ahead of industry leaders Acura (148), Mercedes-Benz (145), Toyota (144), Audi (139), Cadillac (138), and Jaguar (137), as well as the industry average (129).

At a time when layoffs are common at GM facilities, automobile sales are declining, and losses are mounting, Saturn reported its first operating profit in 1993. But in late 1993, sales began to level off, and vehicle inventories rose to an all-time high of about 90 days at the typical Saturn retailer. While Saturn has embarked on a distinctly different course for automobile excellence, the challenge of sustaining success remains.

*Sources:* J.D. Power and Associates, *The Saturn Way* (New York: J.D. Power and Associates, 1992); L. O'Connor, "Flexible Assembly:  Saturn's Road to Success," *Mechanical Engineering,* November 1991, 30–34; J. O'Toole and J. Lewandowski, "Forming the Future:  The Marriage of People and Technology at Saturn," *Stanford University Industrial Engineering & Engineering Management,* March 29, 1990; J.B. White, "GM Saturn Unit Trumpets Profit Turned in 1993," *The Wall Street Journal,* January 6, 1994, A4.

## Questions

1. What factors are responsible for Saturn's initial success and rapid growth in the automobile industry?
2. How does Saturn's approach to human resources and decision making contribute to the quality of its automobiles?
3. Should Saturn maintain or change its quality emphasis in the future? Why or why not?

## *Listening*

You learned that managers can improve customer satisfaction by listening to their customers to determine their wants, needs, and quality expectations. You also learned the seven quality criteria for the Malcolm Baldrige National Quality Award. The category worth the most points (300 out of a total of 1,000 for all seven categories) is *customer focus and satisfaction.*

This exercise will give you a chance to practice your listening skills to determine customer quality perceptions that can provide management with information on areas needing improvement.

### Instructions

1. Break up into pairs throughout the class.

2. Select two businesses (local restaurants, retail stores, etc.) that you are both frequent patrons of and/or employed by and are both fairly well acquainted with.

3. For the first business, one of you will role-play the "manager" and the other will role-play the "customer." You will reverse roles at the second business you selected.

4. As "managers" at your respective locations, you are to prepare a list of five questions you will ask the "customer" during the role play. The questions you prepare should be designed to get the "customer's" viewpoint on how good customer service is at your business. If one of your responses leads to a problem area, you may need to ask a follow-up question to determine the nature of the dissatisfaction. For example, if the customer says, "No" when you ask, "Were you satisfied with the level of knowledge the salesperson had in helping you determine which brand/model would best suit your needs?" you should ask, "What information would you have liked the salesperson to give you that you didn't get?"

Prepare one main question and a follow-up question if necessary for each of the five dimensions* of service quality listed below:

*Reliability*—the ability to provide what was promised, dependably and accurately
*Assurance*—the knowledge and courtesy of employees, and their ability to convey trust and confidence
*Tangibles*—the physical facilities and equipment, and the appearance of personnel

*Empathy*—the degree of caring and individual attention provided to customers
*Responsiveness*—the willingness to help customers and provide prompt service.

5. Begin the two role plays. When it is your turn to be the "manager" (listener), remember to practice effective listening skills when your partner gives answers to your prepared questions. You need to get information on how to improve the quality of customer service at your company. You will achieve this by identifying the problem areas (weaknesses) that need attention.

6. After completing both role-play situations, fill out the form below for the role play where you were "manager" (listener). (This chart is one way to structure the feedback you received; you may not have gathered information to fill in all these boxes. For example, for some categories, the "customer" may have had only good things to say; for others, the comments may have all been negative.) Be prepared to share this information with the rest of the class.

I role-played the "manager" at (location) _____.

After listening carefully to the "customer's" responses to my five questions, I determined the following strengths and weaknesses as they relate to the five dimensions of service quality.

| Dimension | Strength | Weakness |
|---|---|---|
| Reliability | | |
| Assurance | | |
| Tangibles | | |
| Empathy | | |
| Responsiveness | | |

*The five dimensions of service quality are taken from A. Parasuraman, V. A. Zeithaml, and L. L. Berry, "A Conceptual Model of Service Quality and Its Implications for Future Research," Report 84–106, Marketing Sciences Institute, Cambridge, MA, 1984.

# Entrepreneurship *and* Small Business

## Outline

## After reading this chapter, you will be able to:

- Define entrepreneurship and small business.
- Summarize the importance of small business in the U.S. economy and the reasons certain fields attract small business.
- Analyze why small businesses succeed and fail.
- Specify how you would go about starting a small business and what resources you would need.
- Determine why many large businesses are trying to "think small."
- Critique a small business's strategy and make recommendations for its future.

Courtesy of Starbucks Coffee Company.
Photographer, Vincent Ricardel.

## Bringing the *Total Coffee Experience* to America

Seattle-based Starbucks Coffee Company actually began in 1971 as a single retail outlet selling packaged coffee beans. However, during a trip to Italy in 1983, Howard Schultz was inspired by the ancient piazzas of Milan as he strolled the city streets late one evening and was struck with an idea that transformed Starbucks into the thriving chain of gourmet coffee bars and retail shops it is today. Named after the adventure-loving first mate in Melville's classic, *Moby Dick,* Starbucks was named among the 40 fastest growing companies in the United States by *Fortune* magazine in 1992. Schultz himself was named "Entrepreneur of the Year" by *Inc.* magazine in both 1992 and 1993. In its first year of public availability, Starbucks stock swelled from $17 to $54 a share, as eager investors scrambled to cash in on the company's skyrocketing growth.

What Schultz observed in Milan was a "total experience" built around the enjoyment of coffee in the city's cheerful espresso bars, an experience he contrasted to the typical American coffee-drinking scene—functional and habitual consumption of coffee in unappealing surroundings. Schultz was certain that the concept of coffee drinking as a pleasurable social event would find success in America. He decided to rebuild Starbucks on the assumption that there were a significant number of American consumers who wanted and would pay for something better. The Starbucks strategy would be to create and deliver this "total coffee experience."

To build Starbucks on the basis of this guiding vision, the company's first concern was to create an atmosphere in which the company's own employees would be thoroughly satisfied. To this end, Starbucks offers all of its workers one of the most attractive, supportive benefits packages in the country. The company's stock option plan—"Bean Stock"—allows all company employees, even part-timers, a chance to share in the company's profitable growth. Schultz believes that such a keen focus on meeting the needs of Starbucks's personnel serves both to satisfy and motivate current employees, and to allow the company to attract the highest quality people in the job market, something that makes effective implementation of its strategies all the more likely.

Between 1982 and 1994, Starbucks grew from four locations to more than 400 attractive, well-managed outlets now employing a total of more than 6,000 people. The company had sales of $163 million in 1993—up from $93 million the previous year—and expects to reach more than $250 million by the end of the 1994 fiscal year. Although currently concentrated in ten primary West Coast cities in the United States, Starbucks coffee bars can now be found in Denver, Chicago, Washington, DC, and Vancouver (Canada) among other cities.

Many young retail organizations choose to promote growth through franchising, in which independent managers working within guidelines set by the parent company are responsible for the success of their individual locations. However, franchising is out of the question at Starbucks, because CEO Schultz fears that quality might be sacrificed. Now the leading specialty coffee retailer in the United States, Starbucks sees no reason to risk compromising itself. The high standards of quality set by the company based on Schultz's initial entrepreneurial vision will remain those on which the company continues to grow in coming years.

*Sources:* Dawn Gusch, "Benefits Leverage Hiring and Retention Efforts," *Personnel Journal,* November 1992, 90; Charles McCoy, "Entrepreneur Smells Aroma of Success in Coffee Bars," *The Wall Street Journal,* January 8, 1993, B2; Judith Schroer, "Is Pricey Starbucks Stock Addictive?" *USA Today,* August 18, 1993, 3B; Andrew E. Serwer, "America's 100 Fastest Growers," *Fortune,* August 9, 1993, 40; and *Hoover's Handbook of Emerging Companies 1993-1994,* eds. Patrick Spain, Alta Campbell, and Alan Chai (Austin, TX: The Reference Press, Inc., 1993), 332.

*introduction*

Although many management students go to work for large corporations upon graduation, others may choose to start their own business or find employment opportunities in small businesses with 500 or fewer employees. There are approximately 17 million small businesses operating in the United States today, each representing the vision of its entrepreneurial owners to succeed by providing new or better products. Small businesses are the heart of the U.S. economic and social system because they offer opportunities and express the freedom that people have to make their own destinies. Today, the entrepreneurial spirit is growing around the world, from Russia and China to Germany, Brazil, and Mexico.

In this chapter we examine the world of entrepreneurship and small business. First we examine several definitions of small business, the role of small business in the American economy, and industries that provide small-business opportunities. Then we analyze why small businesses succeed or fail. Next, we discuss how an entrepreneur goes about starting a small business. Finally, we look at entrepreneurship in larger businesses.

## THE NATURE OF ENTREPRENEURSHIP AND SMALL BUSINESS

**entrepreneur**
A person who creates a business or product, manages his or her resources, and takes risks to gain a profit.

**entrepreneurship**
The process of creating and managing a business to achieve desired objectives.

An **entrepreneur** is a person who creates a business or product, manages his or her resources, and takes risks to gain a profit. **Entrepreneurship** is the process of creating and managing a business to achieve desired objectives. In the past, entrepreneurs were often inventors who brought all the factors of production together to produce a new product. Thomas Edison, whose inventions include the record player and light bulb, was an early American entrepreneur. Entrepreneurs have been associated with such uniquely American products as Levi's 501 blue jeans, Dr Pepper, and Apple Computers. More recent entrepreneurial ventures have included Lone Star Steakhouse and Saloons, Gateway Computers, and Bombay retail furniture stores. Of course, smaller businesses do not have to evolve into such highly visible companies with large market shares to be successful, but those entrepreneurial efforts that result in rapidly growing businesses become more visible with their success. Notably successful recent entrepreneurs are Michael Dell and Bill Gates.

The entrepreneurship movement is accelerating, with many new smaller businesses emerging. Computing power that was once available only to the largest firms can now be acquired by a small business for less than $2,000. Technology—including printers, voice mail, computer bulletin boards and networks, faxes, copiers, and even overnight delivery services—enables small businesses to be

**Example:** Japanese companies have achieved success with companies much smaller than U.S. companies. These small companies form a profitable strategic syndicate called a *kiretsu.*

more competitive with today's giant corporations. Small business can also develop alliances with other businesses to produce and sell products in domestic and global markets.[1] Indeed, John F. Welch, Jr., chairman of giant General Electric, says, "Size is no longer the trump card it once was in today's brutally competitive world marketplace—a marketplace that ... demands value and performance."[2]

## Defining Small Business

What *is* a small business? This question is difficult to answer because size is relative. For example, Spartan Motors, a small Charlotte, MI, manufacturer of vehicle chassis, has sales of $153.4 million a year, enough to rank the company number 92 on *Business Week* magazine's list of 250 "Companies on the Move."[3] But that figure is small in comparison to General Motors' annual sales of approximately $130 billion. On the other hand, Spartan is certainly not small compared to a neighborhood auto repair shop.

While there is no generally accepted definition, research has shown that the average person uses the term *small business* to refer to an owner-managed business that employs a handful of people—usually not more than 20 or 25. A White House conference defined a small business as one with 400 or fewer employees.

In this book, we define a **small business** as any business that is not dominant in its competitive area and does not employ more than 500 people. A local Mexican-food restaurant may be the most patronized Mexican-food restaurant in your community, but because it does not dominate the restaurant industry as a whole, it can be considered a small business. This definition is similar to the one used by the **Small Business Administration (SBA)**, an independent agency of the federal government that offers managerial and financial assistance to small businesses. Table 8.1 shows additional standards that the SBA uses to determine which businesses qualify to receive its help.

**small business**
Any business that is not dominant in its competitive area and does not employ more than 500 people.

**Small Business Administration (SBA)**
An independent agency of the federal government that offers managerial and financial assistance to small businesses.

## The Role of Small Business in the American Economy

No matter how you define small business, one fact is clear:  Small businesses are vital to the soundness of the American economy. Ninety-nine percent of all U.S. firms are classified as small businesses, and they account for over 40 percent of the U.S. gross national product (GNP). Small businesses are largely responsible for fueling job creation, innovation, and opportunities for minorities and women.

**Job Creation.**   The energy, creativity, and innovative abilities of small-business owners have resulted in jobs for other people. Cognetics Inc., a Cambridge, MA, consulting firm, says that small and midsize companies created all of the 5.8 million new jobs from 1987 to 1992 (while companies employing 500 or more employees lost 2.3 million jobs).[4] Small businesses are expected to generate 80 percent of all new jobs for new college graduates in the 1990s in the United States. Table 8.2 indicates that businesses employing fewer than 20 people account for 86.69 percent of all businesses, and 99.75 percent of all businesses employ fewer than 500 people.

Many small businesses today are being started because of encouragement from larger businesses. Hyatt Hotels, for example, has tried to help creative employees start businesses by becoming their first customer. Hyatt believes that helping a supplier become successful will encourage that supplier to be more

**Example:** Most of the new technological innovations and inventions come from small businesses. Usually the invention is commercialized by larger corporations, however.

**Critical Thinking Challenge:** Using the criteria and standards discussed in Table 8.1, have students provide local examples of small businesses.

**TABLE 8.1**

**Small Business Administration Standards for Small-Business Size for Selected Industries**

| Type of Business | Size of Business |
| --- | --- |
| *Manufacturers* | *Employing fewer than* |
| Petroleum refining | 1,500 people |
| Electronic computers | 1,000 |
| Macaroni and spaghetti | 500 |
| House furnishings | 500 |
| *Wholesalers* | *Employing fewer than* |
| Sporting goods | 100 people |
| Furniture | 100 |
| Paints and varnishes | 100 |
| *Retailers* | *Earning sales of less than* |
| Grocery stores | $13.5 million a year |
| Automobile dealers | 11.5 |
| Restaurants, noninstitutional | 3.5 |
| *Services* | *Earning sales of less than* |
| Hotels and motels | $3.5 million a year |
| Advertising agencies | 3.5 |
| Radio and television repair | 3.5 |
| Doctors' offices and clinics | 3.5 |

*Source:* National Archives and Records Administration, "Standard Industrial Classification Codes and Size Standards," in *Code of Federal Regulations* (Washington DC: GPO, January 1, 1991), 351–364.

loyal and responsive to the needs of Hyatt.[5] Many jobs are being created by big company/small company relationships. Whether through formal joint ventures, supplier relationships, or producing or marketing cooperative projects, the rewards of collaborative relationships are creating many jobs for small-business owners and

**TABLE 8.2**

**Number of Companies by Employment Size**

| Employees per Firm | Number of Firms | Percentage of All Firms |
| --- | --- | --- |
| 1,000 plus | 6,000 | 0.10 |
| 500 to 999 | 10,000 | 0.16 |
| 100 to 499 | 122,000 | 1.98 |
| 20 to 99 | 684,000 | 11.08 |
| Less than 20 | 5,354,000 | 86.69 |

*Source:* U.S. Bureau of the Census, *Statistical Abstract of the United States, 1993,* 113th edition (Washington DC: GPO, 1993), 538.

*Note:* Percentages may not total 100 percent due to rounding.

Coca-Cola Company, J.C. Penney, Lockheed Aeronautical Systems, Anheuser-Busch, and many other large companies rely on small-business owner Edith Hammond and her seven-employee firm, Hammond Enterprises, to supply them with hats, mugs, T-shirts, and other promotional items with their corporate logos. Shown here with Hammond are Brian Head (left) of Lockheed and Floyd Lewis of Anheuser-Busch.

*Source:* © Michael Pugh.

their employees.[6] Some publishing companies, for example, contract out almost all their editing and production to small businesses. Elm Street Publishing Services is a small editing/production house in Hinsdale, Illinois, that provides the services to turn a manuscript into a bound book.

**Innovation.**   Perhaps the strength of small businesses is their ability to innovate and bring significant changes and benefits to customers.[7] Ensoniq Corporation, a small manufacturer of musical instruments, overcame Japanese competition with a quality-improvement program that provided greater reliability and durability than did its larger rivals.[8] Small businesses are also important because they contribute innovation, which further stimulates the economy. A recent study shows that small companies produce 2.4 times as many innovations as larger ones, despite their more limited resources.[9] According to the U.S. Office of Management and Budget, more than half the major technological advances of the twentieth century —including air conditioning, the ballpoint pen, the instant camera, insulin, the zipper, and xerography—were developed by individual inventors and entrepreneurs. Polaroid, Xerox, Ford Motor, Procter & Gamble, Levi Strauss, and Apple Computer all began as innovative small companies and grew into multibillion-dollar enterprises. Not all companies start small, of course; Saturn Corporation started as a major new General Motors subsidiary.

Successful firms are built on innovation, which takes many forms. For example, Little Calgene Inc., based in Davis, CA, developed the Flavr Savr, a tomato that is genetically engineered to stay fresh longer.[10] Small businessman Ray Kroc found a new way to sell hamburgers and turned his ideas into one of the most successful fast-food franchises in the world—McDonald's. Small businesses have become an integral part of our lives. They provide fresh ideas and usually have greater flexibility to change than large companies.

**Opportunities for Minorities and Women.**   Small businesses also provide opportunities for minorities and women that are sometimes unavailable in larger firms because of prejudice and other factors (see Chapter 6). Historically, immigrants to the United States found that starting their own business was the best way to enter the American mainstream. Asians are the most likely to own businesses,

Breaking into the male-dominated tool-manufacturing business challenged Hillary Sterba and Nancy Novinc when they used their combined 26 years of experience in the industry to start their own company, S&N Engineering. Finding prospective customers was especially difficult, since they were denied membership in a local trade association. To build a customer base, they contacted customers and colleagues they had dealt with at their previous jobs, who gave them advice on leads to customers.

*Source:* © 1994 Roger Mastroianni.

followed by Hispanics and blacks.[11] The last survey of minority-owned enterprises by the Census Bureau found almost 850,000 businesses (5 percent) owned by nonwhite persons.[12]

For example, entrepreneur Russell Simmons owns Rush Communications, the second-largest black-owned entertainment company, which includes five record labels, several management companies, a film and television branch, a radio production company, and a clothing line. Artists such as LL Cool J and Public Enemy have propelled Simmons's firm to sales of $34 million.[13] Small businesses also provide opportunities for immigrants such as Jung Pack to thrive in the United States. Jung gave up a white-collar career in his native South Korea to come to the United States in 1982, where he opened the Virginia Market, a grocery store in Washington DC.[14]

Women own or control roughly 6.5 million small businesses (about one-third) and are starting new small businesses at twice the rate of men.[15] One of these women, Sheri Poe, founded Ryka Inc., based in Norwood, MA, when she discovered that athletic shoes for women were designed without the narrow heel or the high arch typical of women's feet.[16] Although most women-owned businesses are retail or service firms, in the 1990s women are increasingly entering construction and manufacturing. Nancy Novinc and Hillary Sterba, for example, formed S&N Engineering, a tool-engineering company, after they were laid off from Cleveland Twist Drill Co.[17]

Women and minority small-business owners often face problems associated with lack of experience and education. This is being addressed by a number of government, industry, professional, and collegiate groups that offer managerial and financial assistance as well as training programs for women and minority entrepreneurs. For example, the Small Business Administration has organized an Office of Women's Business Ownership, and there is a National Association of Women Business Owners. Additionally, the Women's Business Ownership Act of 1988 established a training and assistance program for businesswomen, while banning discrimination against women applying for business loans. Such programs are helping to boost minority business ownership as well as enhancing the opportunities minorities have to thrive in the world of business.

**Critical Thinking Challenge:** Invite a local small-business owner to participate in a question-and-answer session with your class. Ask him or her to discuss the unique problems of a small-business owner. You can also contact your local Small Business Administration office for suggestions on possible speakers.

## Industries That Attract Small Business

Small businesses are found in nearly every industry, but retailing, wholesaling, services, and manufacturing are especially attractive to entrepreneurs because they

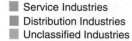

### The Relative Proportion of Small Business by Industry

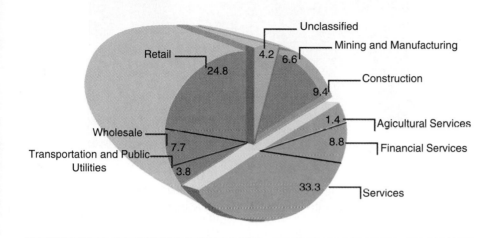

- Service Industries
- Distribution Industries
- Unclassified Industries
- Production Industries

Unclassified

Mining and Manufacturing

Retail — 24.8

4.2  6.6

Construction

9.4

Agicultural Services  1.4

Financial Services  8.8

Wholesale — 7.7

Transportation and Public Utilities — 3.8

Services  33.3

*Source:* U.S. Bureau of the Census, *Statistical Abstract of the United States, 1993,* 113th edition (Washington DC: GPO, 1993), 538.

are relatively easy to enter and require low initial financing. Small-business owners also find it easier to focus on a specific group of consumers in these fields than in others, and new firms in these industries suffer less from heavy competition, at least in the early stages, than do established firms. Figure 8.1 shows the relative proportion of small businesses by industry.

Traditionally, small businesses have been strongest in low-technology areas such as retailing and wholesaling. But the growth of small businesses in computer and information processing, scientific measurement equipment, medical goods, electronic components, and chemical and allied products suggests that small business is moving into the high-technology area at a rapid pace.[18]

**Retailing.**   Retailers acquire goods from producers or wholesalers and sell them to consumers. Main streets, shopping strips, and shopping malls are lined with independent compact disc stores, sporting-goods shops, dry cleaners, boutiques, drugstores, restaurants, caterers, service stations, and hardware stores that sell directly to consumers. Greg Boyd, for instance, converted his love of farming into a small business, selling fresh produce in Memphis. He raised the money to open his store—called Top Banana—through years of selling fruits and vegetables from the back of his truck.[19]

Retailing attracts entrepreneurs such as Boyd because gaining experience and exposure in retailing is relatively easy. Additionally, an entrepreneur opening a new retailing store does not have to spend the large sums of money for the equipment and distribution systems that a manufacturing business requires. All that a new retailer needs is a lease on store space, merchandise, enough money to sustain the

**Example:** In Chattanooga, Tennessee, a small business called "Cookie Bouquet" achieved growth by selling fresh-baked cookies arranged in a flower pot on tall sticks like flowers. These bouquets became popular gifts for birthdays, anniversaries, etc.

Comedians Jerry Saslow and Mollie Allen use their performing skills to provide a unique service to large moviemakers. As partners in Saslow and Allen Film Crowd Entertainers, they entertain extras on movie sets between takes as well as explain what's happening on the set and what reactions are required of the extras and when.

*Source:* © 1994 Ilene Ehrlich.

business, knowledge about prospective customers' needs and desires, the ability to use promotion to generate awareness, and basic management skills.

**Wholesaling.**    Wholesalers supply products to industrial, retail, and institutional users for resale or for use in making other products. Wholesaling activities range from planning and negotiating for supplies, promoting, and distributing (warehousing and transporting) to providing management and merchandising assistance to clients. Wholesalers are extremely important for many products, especially consumer goods, because of the marketing activities they perform. Although it is true that wholesalers themselves can be eliminated, their functions must be passed on to some other organization such as the producer, or to another intermediary, often a small business.

Success in today's highly competitive global economy requires finding the right partners to warehouse, transport, track inventories, communicate, and deliver products. Many small businesses have the flexibility to solve distribution problems for large businesses. When Brother International needed help locating suppliers and market information, the company formed an arrangement with Illinois-based EMD Technologies, Inc., a seven-person company. This small business could make a decision over lunch that might take a larger company longer to make because of many layers of management.[20] Such partners become an indispensable link in the distribution and supply chain. Moreover, small businesses are often closer to the final customers and know what it takes to keep them satisfied. Some smaller businesses start out in manufacturing, but find their real niche as a supplier or distributor of larger firms' products. Management Logistics Inc., for example, started out as a small computer-terminal repair service, but today over half its 200 employees are focused on distribution and warehouse support for companies such as American Express.

**Services.**    Services include businesses that do work for others but do not actually produce tangible goods. They represent the fastest growing sector of the U.S. economy, accounting for 60 percent of the nation's economic activity and employing nearly 70 percent of the work force. Real-estate and insurance and personnel

## FIGURE 8.2

**Companies with Fewer than 100 Employees with the Following Equipment**

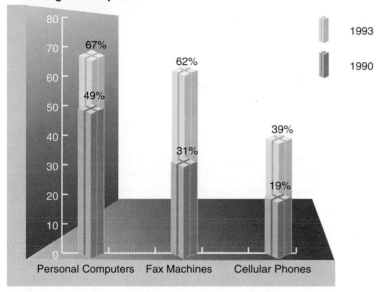

Percentage of Companies

67% 49% 62% 31% 39% 19%

1993
1990

Personal Computers   Fax Machines   Cellular Phones

*Source:* Peter Coy, "Start with Some High-Tech Magic," *Business Week/Enterprise 1993,* Special Issue, 32.

agencies, barbershops, banks, television and computer repair shops, copy centers, dry cleaners, and accounting firms are all service businesses. Services also attract individuals—such as beauticians, morticians, jewelers, doctors, veterinarians—whose skills are not usually required by large firms. Many of these service providers are also retailers because they provide their services to ultimate consumers.

One of the best-known examples of a small service business that expanded dramatically is H&R Block, Inc., the tax preparation company. With $5,000 borrowed from an aunt, Henry W. Bloch started United Business Services with his younger brother Richard after World War II. The firm provided bookkeeping, management advice, and income tax preparation for small businesses. By 1954, the bulk of the business was tax preparation, so in 1955 the brothers dissolved United Business Services and formed H&R Block, Inc. The company now prepares more than 10 million tax returns and is valued at more than $500 million.[21]

**Manufacturing.**   Manufacturing goods can provide unique opportunities for small businesses, which can often customize products to meet specific customer needs and wants. Such products include custom artwork, jewelry, clothing, furniture, and computer software. Marlowe Industries, for example, makes customized thermoelectric devices that heat, cool, or stabilize the temperature of electronic equipment. The winner of a Malcolm Baldrige National Quality Award, Dallas-based Marlowe now has 160 employees and sales of $12 million, including exports to other countries.[22]

"Small" is often equated with responsiveness and flexibility in production. Moreover, technological developments have made it possible for small businesses to compete with larger companies. Figure 8.2 shows the growing use of technology in small businesses. Computer-control devices help maintain quality, while computerized databases give small businesses access to information resources comparable to those of large firms with extensive research and development departments. Electronic networks can allow small firms to interact with other firms to exchange information and expertise. Finally, computers and advanced software allow smaller firms to perform computer-aided design, which was available only to large firms with significant resources a few years ago.[23]

## REASONS FOR SMALL-BUSINESS SUCCESS

There are many reasons why small business entrepreneurs succeed. Entrepreneurs are often obsessed with their vision of success and are willing to work hard and long hours. The ever-present risk of failure may place a degree of excitement and concern on each decision. The small business is more flexible in responding to the marketplace through innovative products and staying close to the customer. Small businesses usually have only one layer of management—the owner(s)—so they can make decisions without consulting multiple levels and departments within the organization. Flexibility and rapid decision making mean that new product development can occur more rapidly in small businesses than in larger ones. The "Ethics Encounter" box describes a company that sets itself apart from the competition with an environmental focus.

Entrepreneurs go into business for themselves for many reasons, but most say it is so that they can use their skills and abilities, gain control of their life, build for their family, and simply enjoy the challenge. Other reasons include being able to live in a location of their choosing, gain respect and recognition, earn lots of money, and fulfill others' expectations. Others say that it was the best alternative available at the time.[24] Small businesses sometimes emerge because of a distinctive competency to meet a consumer need not being addressed by other firms. For example, Merry Maid took a simple service (housecleaning) and offered standardized service in cities across the country. Table 8.3 shows some of the reasons entrepreneurs start their own businesses; many of these reasons provide a strong drive to succeed.

### Independence and Autonomy

Independence and autonomy are linked to success and probably are the leading reasons that entrepreneurs choose to go into business for themselves. Being a small-business owner means being your own boss. Many people start their own businesses because they believe they will do better for themselves than they could do by remaining with their current employer or by changing jobs. They may feel stuck on the corporate ladder or feel that no business would take them seriously enough to fund their ideas. Sometimes people who venture forth to start their own small business are those who simply cannot work for someone else. Such people may say that they just do not fit the "corporate mold." More often, small-business owners just want the freedom to choose whom they work with, the flexibility to pick where and when to work, and the option of working in a family setting.

Many small businesses start in the entrepreneur's home and then expand to a separate office or facility. Working out of the home has accelerated in popularity as a result of the explosion of telecommunications technology and the

**Critical Thinking Challenge:** Have students compare a job in a small business to one within a larger organization. Discuss the lifestyle of an individual in each environment and the pros and cons of working for each.

# Ethics Encounter

## THE DELUXE CORPORATION "THINKS GLOBALLY, ACTS LOCALLY"

Deluxe, Inc., a small business in College Station, Texas, has a strong commitment to ethics and social responsibility, particularly environmental concerns. It owns and operates two restaurants—Cafe Eccell and Rosalie's Pasta. The company has previously owned a Mexican restaurant and a diner-style hamburger bar but changed formats or sold these restaurants. One reason behind the restaurants' success is the owners' adherence to the environmentalist credo, "Think Globally, Act Locally."

The company's owners, Don and Cheryl Anz, are longtime members of the Sierra Club, so it is only natural that they bring an environmentally conscious outlook to their business. Concerned about declining landfill space for garbage and the amount of waste that restaurants contribute to landfills, the Anzes began a recycling program to minimize the negative impact of their restaurants on the environment. They soon learned that recycling not only helps reduce the amount of garbage going into landfills but also saves energy and cuts down on pollution.

All paper from the company office is sent to a recycling facility, as are paper and cardboard packaging and glass containers from the restaurants. The office staff even recycles photocopy paper by using both sides. Menus are printed on recycled paper, and no Styrofoam packaging is used for take-out meals. All glass drinking bottles are recycled behind the restaurant and the company uses recycled products in the restaurants wherever possible. Take-out containers, for example, are made of recycled paper plates with aluminum foil as a cover. The firm is also trying to eliminate the use of as many toxic materials as possible. The company even composts food scraps from the kitchen, using the compost on the landscaping and herb gardens surrounding its two restaurants.

In the past, the Anzes encouraged members of the community to bring recycled garbage to bins placed behind the restaurants. The Anzes made no money from the recycling program because they had to pay employees to sort and handle the recyclable materials. Local participation increased as community members became aware of the importance of being environmentally responsible. Eventually, the recycling site became so big that it was moved and turned over to a local nonprofit organization that employs mentally and physically handicapped persons.

Don Anz says his efforts have given his restaurants extra exposure in the community and have been some of the best advertising he's ever done. Indeed, many customers say they frequent the restaurants because of their environmental efforts. While the Anzes have had major competition hurt the sales in some of their restaurants (when their Mexican restaurant was closed it was turned into the pasta house), the commitment to recycling has continued in new restaurant formats. They firmly believe their environmental efforts provide them with a competitive advantage and give them an identity in the local restaurant market. Finally, Don Anz says he would not stop recycling and other environmentally responsible efforts even if they hurt his profits, because he believes that his company has a responsibility to the environment.

*Source:* Contributed by Gwyneth M. Vaughn and O.C. Ferrell, based on personal interviews with Don Anz, co-owner and president of Deluxe, Inc., August 14, 1990, and May 4, 1994.

downsizing of many major companies. The development of the home office, with computer, copy machine, telephone, and fax machine, has fostered the development of many home-based businesses. Not all people are suited to working at home, however: there are often complaints of a sense of isolation and missing interaction with coworkers. Other complaints relate to overworking—not being able to confine work activities to normal hours, family problems, and an inability to generate the increased productivity expected. Nonetheless, the home work environment provides the autonomy that many successful small business owners desire.[25]

**Comment on Box:** In using this example, bring out ethical issues as well as entrepreneurial concepts. Have students discuss other ways small businesses can create a niche by emphasizing ethics.

**TABLE 8.3**

**Reasons Entrepreneurs Start Businesses**

| Biggest Reason for Starting Business | Overall | Among Those Who Were Successful |
|---|---|---|
| Wanted the autonomy and independence | 32% | 54% |
| Had identified a market opportunity | 37% | 33% |
| Wanted to make more money | 9% | 8% |
| Wanted to use knowledge and experience | 11% | 0% |
| Wanted to show they could do it | 2% | 0% |
| Other (to learn, needed a job, to be creative, to provide jobs, etc.) | 9% | 5% |

*Source:* Alessandra Branch, "New Businesses," *Inc.,* July 1993, 47.

## Taking Advantage of Market Opportunities

Table 8.3 indicates that identifying a market opportunity ignored by larger firms is a major reason behind many small business start-ups as well as a factor in predicting success. Small businesses that utilize industry databases, conduct market surveys, and develop a marketing plan are more successful in business. Learning allows the business entrepreneur to see opportunities. Success in finding a market opportunity is often attributed to luck, but successful entrepreneurs review alternatives and capitalize on their discoveries, not random events. In other words, even with a limited budget, entrepreneurs engage in "luck-shaping market strategies" because they do their homework well. They pay attention to facts, assess surprises, and notice patterns that increase the chance that something predictable will happen.[26]

# CAUSES OF SMALL-BUSINESS FAILURE

Despite the importance of small businesses to our economy, there is no guarantee of small-business success. According to the Small Business Administration, 24 percent of all new businesses fail within two years, and 63 percent fail within six years.[27] Neighborhood restaurants are a case in point. Look around your own neighborhood, and you can probably spot several restaurants that have gone out of business.

Small businesses fail for many reasons. A poor business concept—such as insecticides for garbage cans (research found that consumers are not concerned with insects in their garbage)—will produce disaster nearly every time. Expanding a hobby into a business may work if a genuine market niche exists, but all too often people start such a business without identifying a real need for the goods or services. Other notable causes of small-business failure include the burdens imposed by government regulation, insufficient funds to withstand slow sales, and vulnerability to competition from larger companies. However, three major causes of small-business failure deserve a close look: undercapitalization, managerial inexperience or incompetence, and poor control systems.

**Example:** While some small businesses fail, almost every business starts out as a small business. FedEx Corporation started out with founder Fred Smith working on a card table in an airplane hangar.

## BUSINESS DILEMMA

*You're the Manager ...What Would You Do?*

THE COMPANY:   Signet Marketing Consultants

YOUR POSITION:   Owner and Chief Executive Officer

THE PLACE:   Wilmette, IL

Signet Marketing Consultants was founded by Dan Signet, an engineering major and graduate of the Minnesota State University MBA program. It publishes promotional calendars and business planners. The company originated as a printing firm where Dan could use his education to provide creative, high-quality printing services. To differentiate and grow, Dan decided to specialize in customized desk-pad calendars imprinted with promotional advertising for a company or product. The company sells these calendars directly to businesses for use in their own promotion.

The company grew and, through its success, Dan made major financial commitments to add a new, large, high-speed press and to purchase, redesign, and rebuild a specialized collating machine to further automate the assembly process. The sophistication of the company's marketing efforts improved dramatically. Signet began identifying customers by their Standard Industrial Code (SIC) number and sales volume. It also installed a toll-free phone line to encourage direct calls from potential customers. Customers who call to inquire about Signet's services receive a sample calendar with alternative advertising ideas related to their area of business and a follow-up phone call within several days after they receive the materials.

Realizing that the commercial printing business had matured and that competition was increasing, Signet decided to sell his printing operations and focus all his efforts on the marketing of these specialty calendars. A long-term contract with the buyer of the printing plant assured Signet the opportunity to maintain production at that plant. Now Signet could focus all of his energy on creating and selling new calendar products.

Dan revised his customer base in order to aggressively pursue *Fortune* 500 service companies. He expanded the product line to include wall planners, pocket calendars, and diaries. In addition, more aggressive marketing efforts were developed. Signet built new office facilities and eventually grew to a staff of nine full-time employees. Between 1985 and 1990, the business grew rapidly and profits were very high.

After carefully assessing the characteristics of the calendar buyers, Signet identified a new market opportunity. Signet had historically worked closely with marketing/advertising people within large companies who distributed the calendars to customers through their sales forces. Managing and implementing such a calendar program required extensive time on the part of the company initiating it. Therefore, Signet developed and marketed a "Total Service Package" as an option for customers. Signet employees handled the entire calendar promotion, including conception, design, production, and delivery. Of course, the process for Signet employees became very stressful and time consuming, and required great attention to detail and approval-seeking from the client. Dan has been lucky to have such a loyal, productive, and cohesive group of employees. In many ways, their culture has been like that of a small family.

The "Total Service" program has been enormously successful, with Signet shipping to some 20,000 locations for single customers. The only problem facing Dan Signet and his employees is that they are outgrowing their facilities. He wonders if he should hold business at its current level or sell the current building and purchase a new, larger facility and hire and train additional staff.

### Questions

1. What do you perceive as the key to Signet's success?
2. As owner of Signet, do you feel that selling the printing portion of the business was the correct decision in helping the company achieve its objectives?
3. Evaluate Signet's opportunity and the considerations involved in expansion of its operations to grow its overall sales.

## Undercapitalization

The shortest path to failure in business is **undercapitalization**, the lack of funds to operate a business normally. Thirty to fifty percent of small businesses close within five years, most often because they are undercapitalized. Too many entrepreneurs think that all they need is enough money to get started, that the business can survive on cash generated from sales thereafter. But almost all businesses

**undercapitalization**
The lack of funds to operate a business normally.

Undercapitalization posed a threat to the expansion of Critical Care Associates, Inc., a service firm owned by Beverly Zeiss that provides critical-care nurses to hospitals. Her capital-intensive business pays nurses each day they work, but CCA must wait anywhere from a month to a year to be repaid by its hospital customers. Zeiss's bank turned down her request for expansion financing because her firm wasn't in business for three years. To keep her fledgling but successful business going, Zeiss borrowed $92,000 on 19 credit cards.

*Source:* © Alan Dorow 1993.

**Example:** Cash flow is a problem for many small businesses. Some owners, unable to obtain financing from banks, use their own credit cards—the most expensive form of debt financing.

suffer from seasonal variations in sales, which make cash tight, and few businesses make money from the start. Adriana's Bazaar is a case in point. Located on one of Manhattan's busiest thoroughfares, the gourmet foods and spices/ethnic take-out food/exotic gift store has won great reviews, good publicity, and daily revenues of $1,100. But owner Rochelle Zabarkes is still broke, constantly trying to scrape together enough funds to meet the store's debts and placate creditors, even defaulting on a loan. She vows she will do whatever it takes to keep her business alive, but admits she will need at least $100,000 to pay off her bills and finance the growth of her store.[28] Without sufficient funds, the best small-business idea in the world will fail.

## Managerial Inexperience or Incompetence

Poor business management results in many business failures. Just because an entrepreneur has a brilliant vision for a small business does not mean he or she has the knowledge or experience to manage a growing business effectively. A person who is good at creating great product ideas and marketing them may lack the skills and experience to make good management decisions in hiring, negotiating, finance, and control. Moreover, entrepreneurs may neglect those areas of management they know little about or find tedious, at the expense of the business's success. Some businesses fail when their owners "burn out." To manage a small business takes significant time, effort, and planning. The stress and strain can lead to closure or sellout.

While many entrepreneurs successfully learn these skills on the job, they may still find that, as the company grows, it is necessary to give up some control by bringing in more experienced managers to run the company. The founders of many small businesses, including those of Gateway and Dell Computers, found that they needed to bring in more experienced managers, in specific areas, to help manage their companies through intense growing pains.

## Poor Control Systems

Businesses large and small have met their downfall through inadequate control systems. The brightest visions and hard work do little good if they do not contribute to the achievement of the organization's objectives. Like all managers, small business owners must collect and analyze information about work performance and take corrective action if this information indicates that performance is not contributing to goal achievement. If the firm's control systems do not alert the manager that there are such problems as cash flow, excess inventory, high defect rates, or declining sales, it may be difficult or impossible to survive. For example, managers of the Wallace Company, a Houston-based industrial distributor which won a Malcolm Baldrige National Quality Award in 1990, may have let the award distract them. While company officials were busy going around the country making presentations about the quality-improvement program that helped their company win the award, they failed to respond to declining sales during a recession. After losing nearly $1 million in 1991, the company declared Chapter 11 bankruptcy.[29]

## STARTING A SMALL BUSINESS

To start a business, an entrepreneur must first have an idea. Sam Walton, founder of Wal-Mart stores, had an idea for a discount retailing enterprise and spawned a global retailing empire that changed the way traditional companies look at their business. Next, the entrepreneur needs to devise a business plan to guide planning and development. Finally, decisions must be made as to the form of ownership, the financial resources needed, and whether to buy an existing business, start a new one, or buy a franchise.

### The Business Plan

A key element of business success is a **business plan**—a meticulous statement of the rationale for the business and a step-by-step explanation of how it will achieve its goals. The business plan should include an explanation of the business, an evaluation of the competition, estimates of income and expenses, and other information. It should establish a strategy for acquiring sufficient funds to keep the business going. Indeed, many financial institutions base their decision of whether or not to loan a small business money on its business plan. However, the business plan should act as a guide and reference document, not a shackle to limit the business's flexibility and decision making.

Table 8.4 presents the fundamental components of a small business plan. The summary outlines the main focus of the plan. It should be two to three pages in length and consist of an introduction, the major aspects of the plan, and implementation considerations.

The situation analysis examines the difference between the firm's current performance and past stated objectives. In a brand new firm, it assesses where the entrepreneur is now in his or her development. The situation analysis may also include a summary of data relating to the creation of the current business situation obtained from both the firm's external and internal environment. Depending on the situation, details on the composition of the target market segment, marketing objectives, current marketing strategies, business trends, sales history, and profitability may also be included.

In the analysis of strengths, weaknesses, opportunities, and threats, the business plan must address both internal and external elements. Internally, the firm must look at the strengths and weaknesses of its major functional areas: operations, finance, management, and marketing, as well as the opportunities and threats of

**business plan**
A meticulous statement of the rationale for the business and a step-by-step explanation of how it will achieve its goals.

**Critical Thinking Challenge:** Form students into small groups. Assign them the task of developing a business plan for a small business. They can pick their own business or suggest a restaurant, automobile repair shop, lawn service, or aerobics studio. Focus students to create action plans addressing all business functional areas.

**TABLE 8.4**

## The Components of a Business Plan

I. Summary
II. Situation Analysis
    A. Nature of the business
    B. Target market
    C. Measures of performance
III. Strengths, Weaknesses, Opportunities, and Threats
    A. Operations
    B. Financial
    C. Management
    D. Marketing
    E. Political, legal, and regulatory forces
    F. Economic factors
    G. Competitive factors
    H. Technological factors
IV. Business Resources
    A. Financial
    B. Human
    C. Experience and expertise
V. Financial Projections and Budgets
    A. Delineation of costs
    B. Estimate of sales and revenues
    C. Expected return on investment
VI. Controls and Evaluation
    A. Measures of performance
    B. Monitoring and evaluating performance

those elements in the business's operating environment. Externally, the plan describes the current state of the business environment, including the political, legal and regulatory, economic, competitive, and technological factors. It should also make predictions about the future directions of those forces and their possible impact on the implementation of the business plan. Because of the dynamic nature of these factors, managers need to periodically review and modify this section of the plan to adjust for changes.

A business's human and financial resources, as well as its experiences and expertise, are major considerations in developing a business plan. Therefore, the business plan outlines the human, financial, and physical resources available for accomplishing goals and describes resource constraints that may affect implementation. This section also describes any distinctive competencies that may give the firm an edge, and it takes into account strengths and weaknesses that may influence the firm's ability to achieve implementation.

The financial projections and budgets section outlines the returns expected through implementation of the plan. The costs incurred are weighed against the expected revenues. A budget must be prepared to allocate resources in order to accomplish business objectives. It should contain estimates of the costs of implementing the plan.

The controls and evaluation section details how the results of the plan will be measured. Next, a schedule is developed for comparing the results achieved with

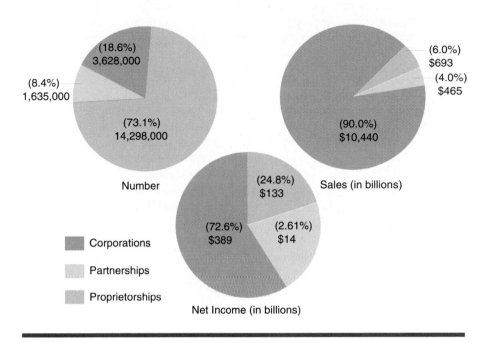

**Comparison of Sole Proprietorships, Partnerships, and Corporations**

*Source:* U.S. Bureau of the Census, *Statistical Abstract of the U.S., 1993*, 113th ed. (Washington DC: Government Printing Office, 1993), 531.

*Note:* Percentages may not total to 100 percent due to rounding.

the objectives set forth in the business plan. Finally, guidelines may be offered out-lining who is responsible for monitoring the program and taking remedial action.

## Forms of Business Ownership

While developing a business plan, the entrepreneur also has to decide on an appropriate legal form of business ownership, of which there are three basic ones: sole proprietorship, partnership, and corporation.

**Sole Proprietorships.**   **Sole proprietorships,** businesses owned and managed by one individual, are the most popular form of business organization. Common examples include most restaurants, barbershops, flower shops, dog kennels, and independent grocery stores. Indeed, many sole proprietors focus on services—small retail stores, financial counseling, appliance repair, child care, and the like—rather than on the manufacture of goods, which often requires large amounts of capital not available to sole proprietors.

Sole proprietorships are typically small businesses employing fewer than 50 people. There are more than 14 million sole proprietorships in the United States (73 percent of all businesses, 82 percent of all small businesses), but they account for just 6 percent of total business sales and 25 percent of total net income (Figure 8.3). This means that proprietorships account for more profits as a per-centage of sales than do corporations or partnerships.

**sole proprietorships**
Businesses owned and managed by one individual; the most popular form of business organization.

Sole proprietorships have the advantages that they are easy and inexpensive to form; they permit a high degree of secrecy; all profits belong to the owner (taxed as the owner's personal income); the owner has direct control over the business; there is minimal government regulation; and the business can be easily dissolved. Disadvantages are that sole proprietors generally must use personal assets to borrow money, often find it difficult to obtain external sources of funds, and generally must be jack-of-all-trades managers to handle diverse activities. Moreover, the survival of the business is tied to the life of the owner and his or her ability to work.

**partnership**
An association of two or more persons who carry on as co-owners of a business for profit.

**general partnership**
A complete sharing in the management of a business, with each partner having unlimited liability for the business's debts.

**limited partnership**
An association of at least one general partner, who assumes unlimited liability, and at least one limited partner, whose liability is limited to his or her investment in the business.

**Partnerships.**    The Uniform Partnership Act defines a **partnership** as "an association of two or more persons who carry on as co-owners of a business for profit." There are three basic types of partnership. A **general partnership** involves a complete sharing in the management of a business, with each partner having unlimited liability for the business's debts. Professionals such as lawyers, accountants, and architects often join together in general partnerships. A **limited partnership** has at least one general partner, who assumes unlimited liability, and at least one limited partner, whose liability is limited to his or her investment in the business. Limited partners are barred from participating in the management of the business but share in the profits in accordance with the terms of a partnership agreement. Limited partnerships exist for risky investment projects where the chance of loss is great, such as oil-drilling and real-estate ventures. The third type of partnership is a joint venture, established for a specific project or for a limited time. The partners in a joint venture may be individuals or organizations, as in the case of the international joint ventures discussed in Chapter 5. Control of a joint venture may be shared equally, or one partner may control decision making. For example, the Picuris Pueblo, a tribal village in New Mexico, entered into a joint venture with the private owners of the Hotel Santa Fe. As owner of a 51 percent stake in the hotel, the Pueblo will receive 51 percent of its profits, help make decisions about running the hotel, and gain employment opportunities for tribal members.[30]

**Critical Thinking Challenge:** Have students compare the advantages and disadvantages of the three forms of business ownership. List and discuss these.

Partnerships offer the advantages of being easy to organize and having higher credit ratings because of the partners' combined wealth. Additionally, partners can specialize; partnerships can make decisions faster than large businesses; they are subject to few government regulations; and profits are paid directly to owners. However, partnerships have the following disadvantages:  General partners have unlimited liability for the debts of the partnership; partners are responsible for each others' decisions; it is difficult to sell a partnership interest at a fair price; the distribution of profits may not reflect the amount of work done by each partner; partnerships cannot find external sources of funds as easily as corporations; and the death of a partner terminates the partnership.

**corporation**
A separate legal entity, or body, created by the state, having assets and liabilities which are distinct from those of the owners of the corporation.

**stock**
Shares of a corporation that can be bought, sold, given as gifts, or inherited.

**Corporations.**    A **corporation** is a separate legal entity, or body, created by the state. Its assets and liabilities are distinct from those of the owners of the corporation. As a legal entity, a corporation has many of the rights, duties, and powers of a person, including receiving, owning, and transferring property. Corporations can enter into contracts with individuals or with other legal entities. They can sue and be sued in court. The owners own shares of **stock** in the corporation, which can be bought, sold, given as gifts, or inherited.

The corporate form of business boasts several advantages:  The owners are not responsible for the firm's debts and have limited liability; ownership (stock) can be easily transferred; corporations usually have a perpetual life; external capital is more easily raised than in other forms of business; and expansion into new busi-

## Sources of Capital for Entrepreneurs (billions of dollars)

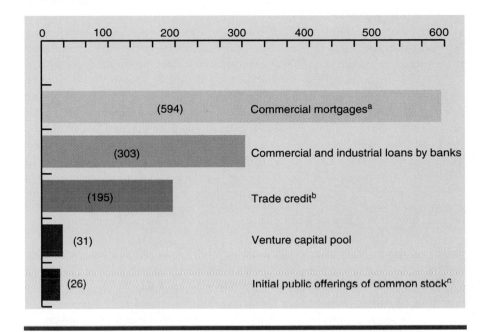

*Source:* Adapted from *The State of Small Business: A Report of the President* (Washington DC: GPO, 1990), 170.

[a] For nonfarm, noncorporate businesses only
[b] Total estimated by the Federal Reserve Board
[c] The total estimated cumulative value of initial public offerings of common stock for the period 1976–1987

nesses is simpler because of the company's ability to enter into contracts. Corporations also have disadvantages: The company is taxed on its income and stockholders pay a second tax on any profits received as dividends; forming a corporation can be expensive and complicated; much information must be made available to the public and to government agencies; and owners and managers may be different individuals with diverse goals.

## Financial Resources

To make money from a small business, the owner must first provide or obtain money to get the business started and to keep it running smoothly. Even a small retail store will probably need at least $50,000 in initial financing to rent space, purchase or lease necessary equipment and furnishings, buy initial inventory of merchandise, and use as working capital. Often, the small-business owner has to contribute a significant percentage of the necessary capital. Few new business owners have the entire amount, however, and must look to other sources for additional financing. Many small-business owners combine funds from a variety of sources to finance their business ventures. Figure 8.4 shows where entrepreneurs turn when they don't have sufficient resources to start their businesses.

**venture capitalists**
Persons or organizations that agree to provide some funds for a new business in exchange for an ownership interest, or stock.

**Equity Financing.**    The most important source of funds for any new business is the owner. Many owners include among their personal resources ownership of a home or the accumulated value in a life-insurance policy or a savings account. A new business owner may sell or borrow from the value of such assets to obtain funds to operate a business. Additionally, the owner may bring useful personal assets, such as a typewriter or computer, desks and other furniture, or a car, as part of his or her ownership interest in the firm. The owner can also provide working capital for the business by reinvesting profits or simply by not drawing a full salary.

Small businesses can also obtain financing by finding investors for their operations. They may sell stock in the business to family members, friends, employees, or other investors. **Venture capitalists** are persons or organizations that agree to provide some funds for a new business in exchange for an ownership interest, or stock. Venture capitalists hope to purchase the stock of a small business at a low price, and then sell the stock for a profit after the business has grown successful. Although these forms of equity financing have helped many small businesses, they require that the small-business owner share the profits of the business, and sometimes control as well, with the investors.

**Debt Financing.**    New businesses sometimes borrow over half of their financial resources. In addition to financial institutions, they can also look to family and friends as sources for loans of long-term funds or to other assets such as a computer or automobile that are exchanged for an ownership interest in a business. In such cases, the business owner can usually structure a favorable repayment schedule and sometimes negotiate an interest rate below current bank rates. If the business fails, however, the emotional losses for all concerned may greatly exceed the money involved. Anyone lending a friend or family member money for a venture should state the agreement clearly in writing.

The amount a financial institution is willing to loan depends on its evaluation of the business's likelihood of success and of the entrepreneur's ability to repay the loan. The institution will often require the entrepreneur to put up collateral, a financial interest in the property or fixtures of the business, to guarantee payment of the debt. Additionally, the small-business owner may have to offer some personal property as collateral, such as the owner's home, in which case the loan is called a mortgage. If the small business fails to repay the loan, the lending institution may eventually claim and sell the collateral (or the owner's home, in the case of a mortgage) to recover its loss.

Banks and other financial institutions can also grant a small business a line of credit—an agreement by which a financial institution promises to lend a business a predetermined sum on demand. A line of credit permits an entrepreneur to take quick advantage of opportunities that require a bank loan.

Small businesses may obtain funding from their suppliers in the form of trade credit—that is, suppliers allow the business to take possession of the needed goods and services and pay for them at a later date or in installments. Occasionally, small businesses engage in bartering—trading their own products for the goods and services offered by other businesses. For example, an accountant may offer accounting services to an office supply firm in exchange for computer paper and diskettes.

Additionally, some community groups sponsor revolving loan funds to encourage the development of particular types of businesses. State and local agencies may guarantee loans, especially to minority businesspeople or for development in certain areas.

On the federal level, the Small Business Administration offers four types of financial assistance to qualifying businesses:  direct loans, usually made only to businesses that do not qualify for loans from financial institutions; guaranteed loans, which ensure that a direct loan made by an institution to a qualified small business will be repaid; participation loans, a combination of guaranteed loans and direct loans in which the SBA guarantees an institution's loan for part of the firm's needs and makes up the balance in a direct loan; and Minority Enterprise Small Business Investment Companies (MESBICs), which are financing companies partially funded by the SBA that make loans to minority-run businesses. In 1992, the SBA loaned $6 billion to small-business owners, $808 million of that to minority-owned businesses.[31] However, the SBA makes loans only to businesses that have been in operation for three years. It does not offer start-up money for new ventures.

## Approaches to Starting a Small Business

### Starting from Scratch versus Buying an Existing Business.   Although entrepreneurs often start new small businesses from scratch much the way we have discussed in this section, they may elect instead to buy an existing business. This has the advantage of providing a network of existing customers, suppliers, and distributors and reducing some of the guesswork inherent in starting a new business from scratch. However, an entrepreneur buying an existing business must also deal with whatever problems the business already has.

**Critical Thinking Challenge:** Have students examine small businesses for sale listed in local papers. Discuss types of businesses available and the possible disadvantages associated with the businesses.

### Franchising.   Many small-business owners find entry into the business world through franchising. A license to sell another's products or to use another's name in business, or both, is a **franchise.** The company that sells the franchise is the **franchiser**. Dunkin' Donuts, McDonald's, and Jiffy Lube are franchisers with national visibility. The "Magnifying Management" box profiles another franchiser: Back Yard Burgers. The purchaser of a franchise is the **franchisee**.

The franchisee acquires the rights to a name, logo, methods of operation, national advertising, products, and other elements associated with the franchiser's business in return for a financial commitment and the agreement to conduct business in accordance with the franchiser's standard of operations. Depending on the quality of the franchise, the initial fee and start-up costs can range from $1,000 to more than $2 million. Table 8.5 shows the initial start-up costs for *Entrepreneur* magazine's top 20 franchisers. In addition, the franchisee pays the franchiser a monthly or annual fee based on a percentage of sales or profits. In return, the franchisee often receives building specifications and designs, site recommendations, management and accounting support, and, perhaps most importantly, immediate name recognition.

The practice of franchising first began in the United States when Singer used it to sell sewing machines in the nineteenth century. It soon became commonplace in the distribution of goods in the automobile, gasoline, soft-drink, and hotel industries. The concept of franchising grew especially rapidly during the 1960s, when it expanded to more diverse industries, particularly restaurants; growth slowed in the 1970s, but franchises again grew steadily throughout the 1980s. During this period, many U.S. franchises, including McDonald's, Kentucky Fried Chicken (KFC), and Holiday Inn expanded internationally.

Franchises continue to grow at a fast pace today. In 1991, sales of goods and services at more than 542,000 franchise outlets reached $758 billion. The largest franchising sectors, ranked by sales, are automobile and truck dealers (46.8 percent), gasoline service stations (18.9 percent), restaurants (11.3 percent), and

**franchise**
A license to sell another's products or to use another's name in a business, or both.

**franchiser**
The company that sells a franchise.

**franchisee**
The purchaser of a franchise.

## BACK YARD BURGERS: FRESH GOURMET FOOD FAST

Since its modest inception in 1987 in Cleveland, Mississippi, as a single outlet, Back Yard Burgers has grown into a significant competitor in the fast-food industry in the southern United States. The company moved its headquarters to Memphis in 1990 and went public in 1993, by then operating more than 40 outlets in 12 states. Early investors were optimistic about the company's chances for long-term success, boosting the price of its stock to nearly twice its initial price in the first day of over-the-counter trading. By the end of 1993, there were over 50 Back Yard Burgers locations and plans for even more rapid expansion in coming years.

Back Yard Burgers founder Lattimore Michael created the company on the premise of introducing an upscale product—gourmet hamburger and chicken-filet sandwiches—into an industry typically characterized by standard products. Back Yard Burgers' menu features competitively priced, made-to-order grilled ⅓-pound and ⅔-pound "Back Yard Burgers"; seven types of ⅓-pound "Gourmet Burgers," including Hawaiian, Blackened, Barbecue, and Mushroom varieties; and five kinds of charbroiled chicken-filet sandwiches. Back Yard Burgers sells these "alternative" fast-food products primarily through compact double-drive-through facilities with a "backyard barbecue" theme. Thus, the company brought this nonstandard product offering into what was then the fastest-growing segment of the fast-food industry—double-drive-through restaurants.

Like other fast-food service establishments, Back Yard Burgers also emphasizes speed of service, with a typical order delivery time of just 40 seconds, faster than fast-food competitors often serve pre-made food items. The company achieves this exceptional service through use of a computerized point-of-sale order-taking system, which also assists in both inventory and labor-cost control. Unlike many of their competitors, Back Yard Burgers restaurants offer, with but a few exceptions, no indoor seating, preferring instead to place limited seating facilities outside the building adjacent to a walk-up window for nondrivethrough orders, all in an effort to promote the "backyard barbecue" theme. The restaurant buildings themselves are less than one-quarter the size of typical fast-food hamburger chain restaurants and require approximately one-third to one-half the land area, offering great flexibility in site selection. As a result, Back Yard Burgers restaurants can be constructed at minimal cost and in much less time than customary fast-food establishments.

As of the start of 1994, about 85 percent of Back Yard Burgers locations were franchised, managed by independent franchisees who pay a fee to operate the restaurants and share in the operating profits. Although the predominance of franchised outlets served the company well during its initial stage of growth by providing much-needed, readily accessible financial resources, Back Yard Burgers' corporate management hopes eventually to increase the percentage of company-owned facilities from 15 to 50 percent in order to have more direct control over the operations of its individual restaurants.

Following Lattimore Michael's vision of bringing upscale products to the most rapidly growing segment of the fast-food industry, Back Yard Burgers has quickly established a name for itself across the southern United States. While most industry competitors continue to give customers competitively priced standard products, Back Yard Burgers gives them something more— a menu that is a step above typical fast food—and a good value at the same time.

*Sources:* "Back Yard Adds 51st Location," *The (Memphis) Commercial Appeal,* January 6, 1994, B5; Laurel Campbell, "Back Yard Burgers To Buy Back Franchises," *The Commercial Appeal,* September 11, 1993, B4; Laurel Campbell, "Burger Stock Sales Keep Growth Sizzling," *The Commercial Appeal,* August 15, 1993, C1; Charles Conner, "Backyard Burger Sizzles in Initial Public Offering," *The Commercial Appeal,* June 26, 1993, B3; Laurel Campbell, "Back Yard Burgers To Offer Stock," *The Commercial Appeal,* April 21, 1993, B4; and Franklin-Lord, Inc., "Back Yard Burgers, Inc.: Preliminary Prospectus," April 20, 1993.

## TABLE 8.5

### The Top 20 Franchises in the United States

| Company | Business | Minimum Start-Up Costs |
|---|---|---|
| 1. Subway | fast food | $ 32,400 |
| 2. McDonald's | fast food | 610,000 |
| 3. Jani-King | commercial cleaning | 6,500 |
| 4. Little Casaer's Pizza | pizza | 117,000 |
| 5. Hardee's | fast food | 694,280 |
| 6. Chem-Dry | cleaning services | 3,800 |
| 7. Arby's | fast food | 525,000 |
| 8. Electronic Realty Associates | real-estate services | 1,110 |
| 9. Kentucky Fried Chicken (KFC) | fast food | 150,000 |
| 10. Jazzercise | fitness centers | 2,000 |
| 11. Service Master | commercial cleaning | 8,700 |
| 12. Intelligent Electronics | computer products and services | 150,000 |
| 13. Domino's Pizza | pizza | 76,500 |
| 14. Budget Rent a Car | auto rentals | 150,000 |
| 15. Dairy Queen | ice cream | 375,000 |
| 16. Midas International | auto repair | 182,000 |
| 17. Burger King | fast food | 333,600 |
| 18. H&R Block | income-tax services | 5,000 |
| 19. Coverall North America | commercial cleaning | 350 |
| 20. Choice Hotels International | hotels, motels | 76,000 |

*Source:* Based on *Entrepreneur* magazine's ranking of company age, number of units, start-up costs, and growth rate as reported in "Magazine: Subway Is Top Franchise," *USA Today*, January 10, 1991, 12B.

nonfood retailing (4.1 percent).[32] Women owned more than 10 percent of all franchise outlets in 1991, and male-female partnerships accounted for ownership of another 20 percent.[33] Figure 8.5 shows the growth in franchise units and sales from 1970 to 1990. The average franchiser owns 2.6 units, and approximately 20 percent own more than one franchise—for instance, a Jiffy Lube and a McDonald's (Figure 8.6).[34]

**Example:** Subway is the fastest growing franchise in the United States. Its growth stems partly from finding creative locations for its business. The company has entered school cafeterias, hospitals, and small strip shopping centers.

## Help for Small-Business Managers

Because of the crucial role that small business and entrepreneurs play in the U.S. economy, a number of organizations offer programs to improve the small-business owner's ability to compete. These include entrepreneurial training programs and those sponsored by the Small Business Administration. Such presentations provide small-business owners with invaluable assistance in managing their businesses, often at little or no cost to the owner.

Entrepreneurs can learn critical marketing, management, and finance skills in college classrooms and seminars from Harvard to the University of Washington. Knowledge, experience, and judgment are necessary for success in a new business. While knowledge can be communicated and some experiences can be simulated in the classroom, good judgment must be developed by the entrepreneur. Local chambers of commerce and the U.S. Department of Commerce offer information

**FIGURE 8.5**

## The Growth in Franchise Units and Sales

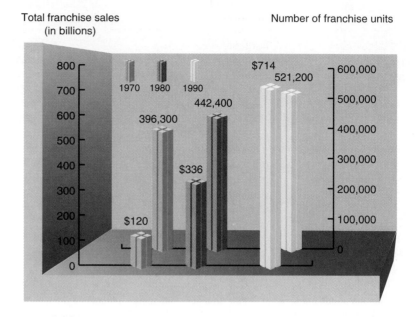

Total franchise sales
(in billions)

Number of franchise units

*Source:*  U.S. Bureau of the Census, *Statistical Abstract of the United States, 1993,* 113th edition
(Washington DC:  GPO, 1993), 780.

and assistance helpful in operating a small business. Additionally, many urban areas—such as Chicago, Jacksonville, FL, Portland, OR, St. Louis, and Nashville—have a weekly business journal/newspaper that provides stories on local businesses as well as on business techniques that a manager or small business can use.

For small firms that want to tap overseas markets, the Small Business Administration sponsors conferences that bring together U.S. manufacturers with export companies. During these matchmaker conferences, the SBA conducts workshops to inform small-business owners how to export their goods overseas. Through its Office of International Trade, the SBA also provides a variety of finance services for exporters, including its international trade loan program, an export working-capital guarantee program for short-term financing, and a business loan-guarantee program for medium-term working capital and long-term, fixed-asset financing.

*Source:*  Courtesy of The Port Authority of New York and New Jersey.

**FIGURE 8.6**

**Retail Sales Breakdown**

Total retail sales = $758.5 billion

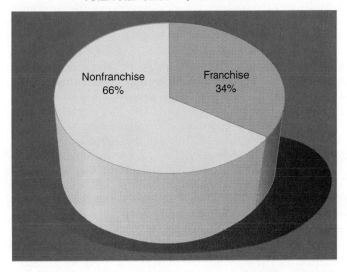

*Source:* Carol Steinberg, "Multi-unit Owners: They're Hooked on Franchising," *USA Today,* September 9, 1993, 9B.

The Small Business Administration offers many types of management assistance to small businesses, including counseling for firms in difficulty, consulting on improving operations, and training for owner/managers and their employees. Among its many programs, the SBA funds Small-Business Development Centers (SBDCs). These are business clinics, usually located on college campuses, that provide counseling at no charge and training at only a nominal charge. SBDCs are often the SBA's principal means of providing direct management assistance.

The Service Corps of Retired Executives (SCORE) and the Active Corps of Executives (ACE) are volunteer agencies funded by the SBA to provide advice for small firms. Both are staffed by experienced managers whose talents and experience the small firms could not ordinarily afford. Together, SCORE and ACE have about 12,000 counselors working out of 350 chapters throughout the country. The SBA has also organized Small Business Institutes (SBIs) on almost 500 university and college campuses in the United States. Seniors and graduate students and faculty at each SBI provide on-site management counseling.

## ENTREPRENEURSHIP IN LARGE BUSINESSES

The continuing success and competitiveness of small businesses through rapidly changing conditions in the business world have led many large corporations to take a closer look at what makes their smaller rivals tick. More and more firms are emulating small businesses in an effort to improve their own bottom line. Beginning in the 1980s and continuing through the present, the buzzword in business has

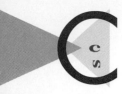

careers corner

## Getting Started with Small Businesses

Business success is not something you can learn easily. It is an outgrowth of knowledge and experience. All kinds of life experiences—with family and friends, as an employee, as a student, as a partner, in sports and art, as a consumer—are valuable. "The things you know and love and see opportunities in—you ought to pick your business based on that," says Bill Gates, founder of Microsoft, on being an entrepreneur.

Someone with a B.S. in business from a university and a $50,000 inheritance from a rich aunt will not succeed as an entrepreneur without good judgment. A person with no college degree and $2,000 in savings may end up wealthy because of good business judgment. Steven Jobs and Steve Wozniak started Apple Computer with a few thousand dollars and developed the first mass-market personal computer. Michael Dell, another high-tech entrepreneur, started Dell Computers in his University of Texas dorm room. So great was their success that IBM and other large corporations created new products to compete with Apple and Dell.

Whatever you call it, "good business sense," "shrewdness," "savvy," "being ahead of your time," or "having a good head on your shoulders," the challenge is to demonstrate good judgment. Translating experience into business sense is not easy. If it were, almost everyone would be successful in business.

In the 1980s and 1990s, many of the largest industrial companies have reorganized, downsized, and laid off employees. Intense competition in the global arena has led many businesses to cut back on hiring. IBM, for example, planned to cut 12 percent, or 50,000 jobs; Sears cut 14 percent of its work force and closed 113 stores. Many such businesses are downsizing in an effort to emulate the flexibility and rapid decision making that contribute so much to small-business success. Many of the layoffs are the result of structural changes, whereby companies are responding primarily to global competition, not to economic conditions of the 1990s.

Consequently, it has become more difficult to find a good job in corporate America in the 1990s, and you and your classmates will be entering a highly competitive job market. To gain an edge in that market, you will need to know what characteristics recruiters look for and how to present your skills and achievements effectively. It has been estimated that 80 percent of new jobs for college graduates will be found in small businesses. Therefore, knowing about successful small businesses may be the first step in assessing job opportunities. Reading *Inc.* or *Entrepreneur* magazine provides a good start in learning more about small business.

*Sources:* "How Can Somebody Not Be Optimistic," *Business Week/Reinventing America 1992*, Special Issue, 185; Mark Memmott, "Cutbacks Create Fierce Undertow," *USA Today*, October 20, 1993, B1.

**Teaching Note:** Contact your alumni office to determine if any local alumni are also small-business owners. See if they will address the management class on small-business careers. Poll the class to determine any small-business aspirations and ideas for a creative small business.

**intrapreneurs**
Individuals who, like entrepreneurs, take responsibility for, or "champion," developing innovations of any kind within the larger organization.

been to *downsize*, reduce management layers and corporate staff, and to focus work tasks to make the firm more flexible, resourceful, and innovative like a smaller business. Many well-known U.S. companies, including IBM, General Dynamics, Apple Computer, General Electric, Xerox, and 3M have downsized to improve their competitiveness, as have German, British, and Japanese firms. Other firms have sought to make their businesses "smaller" by making their operating units function more like independent small businesses, each responsible for its profits, losses, and resources. Of course, some large corporations, such as Southwest Airlines, have acted like small businesses from their inception—with great success.

In an attempt to capitalize on small-business success in introducing innovative new products, more and more of even the largest companies are trying to instill a spirit of entrepreneurship. In these large firms, **intrapreneurs**, like entrepreneurs, take responsibility for, or "champion," developing innovations of any kind *within* the larger organization.[35] Often, they use company resources and time to develop a new product for the company. At 3M, for example, an employee who develops an idea for a new product forms a team of interested coworkers from technical, operations, marketing, and finance areas. The team designs the product and develops a plan to manufacture and market it. If the new product achieves sales of $5 million, the intrapreneur who developed it is promoted to project manager for the product. Such intrapreneurship has contributed to the development of Post-it Notes, light pipes, and Scotch-Brite scrubbing sponges, all successful products for 3M.[36] Xerox spins off potentially successful employee ideas into small businesses that it partly owns. Of 12 startups begun this way, only two have failed.[37] Hyatt Hotels, mentioned earlier, also encourages creative employees to spin off businesses that ultimately benefit Hyatt.[38] A company can foster intrapreneurship by supporting employees, letting employees learn from failures, rewarding innovation, breaking down barriers to internal communication, employing teams for long-term projects, and eliminating paperwork and red tape that may hinder timely action.

> **Teaching Note:** Have students discuss the importance of intrapreneurship. The innovation experienced in small businesses is essential to all organizations. Have students discuss ways to encourage creativity in organizations.

## SUMMARY AND REVIEW

- **Define entrepreneurship and small business.** An entrepreneur is a person who creates a business or product and manages his or her resources and takes risks to gain a profit; entrepreneurship is the process of creating and managing a business to achieve desired objectives. A small business is one that is not dominant in its competitive area and does not employ more than 500 people.

- **Summarize the importance of small business in the U.S. economy and the reasons certain fields attract small business.** Small businesses are vital to the American economy because they provide products, jobs, innovation, and opportunities. Retailing, wholesaling, services, and manufacturing attract small businesses because they are comparatively easy to enter, require relatively low initial financing, provide an opportunity to focus on a specific group of consumers, and may experience less heavy competition.

- **Analyze why small businesses succeed and fail.** Small businesses often succeed because of their owners' vision and hard work; independence and autonomy; ability to pinpoint market opportunities overlooked by other firms; and the flexibility, innovation, and rapid decision making afforded by small size. Small businesses fail for many reasons: undercapitalization, management inexperience or incompetence, neglect, disproportionate burdens imposed by government regulation, and vulnerability to competition from larger companies.

- **Specify how you would go about starting a small business and what resources you would need.** First, you must have an idea for developing a small business. Next, you need to devise a business plan to guide design and development of the business. Then you must decide what form of business ownership to use: sole proprietorship, partnership, or corporation. Small-business owners are expected to provide some of the funds required to start their businesses, but you can also obtain funds from friends and family, financial institutions, other businesses in the form of trade credit, investors (venture capitalists), state and local organizations, and the Small Business Administration. In addition to loans, the Small Business Administration and other organizations offer counseling, consulting, and training services. Finally, you must decide whether to start a new business from scratch, buy an existing one, or buy a franchise operation.

- **Determine why many large businesses are trying to "think small."** More large companies are emulating small businesses in an effort to make their firms more flexible, resourceful, and innovative like a smaller business, and generally to improve their bottom line. This effort often involves downsizing (reducing management layers, laying off employees, and focusing work tasks) and intrapreneurship, in which an employee takes responsibility for (champions) developing innovations of any kind within the larger organization.

- **Evaluate a small business's strategy and make recommendations for its future.** As the manager of Signet Marketing Consultants (described in the "Business Dilemma" box), you should be able to analyze your company's strategy, including its strengths, weaknesses, threats, and opportunities, and make recommendations for the future.

## Key Terms and Concepts

entrepreneur 210
entrepreneurship 210
small business 211
Small Business Administration
  (SBA) 211
undercapitalization 221

business plan 223
sole proprietorships 225
partnership 226
general partnership 226
limited partnership 226
corporation 226

stock 226
venture capitalists 228
franchise 229
franchiser 229
franchisee 229
intrapreneurs 234

## Ready Recall

1. Why are small businesses so important to the U.S. economy?
2. Which fields tend to attract entrepreneurs the most? Why?
3. What elements contribute to the success of small businesses?
4. What are the principal reasons for the high failure rate among small businesses?
5. What decisions must an entrepreneur make when starting a small business?
6. List the advantages and disadvantages of each form of small-business ownership.

7. What types of financing do small entrepreneurs typically use? What are some of the pros and cons of each?
8. List the types of management and financial assistance that the Small Business Administration offers.
9. Describe the franchising relationship.
10. Why do large corporations want to become more like small businesses?

## Expand Your Experience

1. Interview a local small-business owner. Why did he or she start the business? What factors have led to the business's success? What problems has the owner experienced? What advice would he or she offer a potential entrepreneur?
2. Write a business plan for a small-business idea that you have, using Table 8.4 as a guideline.

3. Using business journals, find an example of a large company that is trying to emulate the characteristics that make small businesses flexible and more responsive. Describe and evaluate the company's activities. Have they been successful? Why or why not?

## CASE

# *Dell Computer: From Dorm Room to Desktops Worldwide*

Dell Computer Corporation founder and chairman Michael Dell pioneered the direct-mail approach to personal computer (PC) marketing when he moved what would eventually become the company out of his college dorm room and into offices of its own in 1984. The story of Dell's venture, based in Austin, Texas, is one of the most intriguing tales of entrepreneurial success in recent U.S. business history.

Michael Dell was a successful businessman by the age of 13, at which time he ran a mail-order stamp-trading business from his parents' home in Houston that grossed over $2,000 just a few months after start-up. At 16, Dell sold newspaper subscriptions to the *Houston Post,* and at 17, bought his first BMW. Shortly after arriving at the University of Texas in 1983, Dell

ventured into the computer business by selling RAM (random-access memory) chips and disk drives for IBM PCs. He bought the goods that he then resold through local newspaper ads—and later national computer reseller magazines—from local IBM dealers. He was able to buy the goods at cost because the dealers were then required to order larger-than-needed monthly quotas of equipment from IBM and were often left with excess stock, which then had to be liquidated at bargain-basement prices. The prices that Dell charged for his computer equipment were often 10 to 15 percent less than those IBM charged for the identical products.

By the time Michael Dell moved his thriving operation out of his UT dorm room in 1984, it was bringing in about

$80,000 in profits per month. Shortly thereafter, he was selling his own "clones" of IBM PCs under the brand name PC's Limited. At a time when most PC marketers were selling their products through retail computer stores, Dell instead sold his products directly to end-users through the mail. By cutting out the intermediary—the retailer—PC's Limited machines sold for about 40 percent less than comparable machines made by IBM.

Using a toll-free 24-hour order and customer-service hotline, Dell's mail-order clone PC operation experienced exponential growth. The company posted profits of roughly $1 million on sales of $34 million in 1985. The next year, the company, now renamed the Dell Computer Corporation, grew by nearly 93 percent, with sales reaching $70 million. Sales more than doubled again in 1987, with profits tripling to $9 million. By this time, Dell Computer had established several international offices and expanded its marketing efforts to include direct sales—through its own outside sales force—to both government and large corporate accounts.

In 1992, Dell Computer posted profits of $92 million on sales of $2.3 billion. And, although the company then employed nearly 3,000 employees and had built a large client base in some 70 foreign markets, it still retained many of the entrepreneurial qualities responsible for its initial rise to prominence. For example, its extensive and innovative customer-service programs were recognized by *Fortune* magazine as the best in the computer industry in 1992. That same year, despite its relatively large size, Dell Computer was also listed by *Fortune* as still being among the 100 fastest growing companies in the United States, having experienced a 62 percent annual rate of growth for the year.

Dell Computer's rise from a dorm-room mail-order operation into one of the top computer companies in the world did not come without its share of growing pains. The company's rapid ascent to the top of the computer world came to a screeching halt in 1993. Caught in the middle of a fierce price war that spelled the end of the road for competitors such as Everex Systems and CompuAdd Computer, Dell found itself facing potentially debilitating problems. An inadequate system of sales forecasting caused the company to overestimate consumer demand and therefore produce far more computers than necessary, thus leaving its warehouses packed with unsold equipment. Dell was forced to sell so many of these units below cost that it lost nearly $20 million due specifically to this forecasting error. The company also suffered from an ill-fated foray into notebook computers, then one of the hottest markets in the computer industry, as well as badly slumping European sales. All this, coupled with the fact that it was locked in the midst of fierce price competition that cut deeply into already dwindling profit margins, caused Dell to lose some $80 million in just one three-month period of 1993. Some industry analysts speculated that the $2.3 billion company had outgrown the entrepreneurial mold in which Michael Dell—already a multimillionaire yet to reach his 30th birthday—had cast it less than a decade before.

To its credit, Dell Computer admitted that it had lost touch with its customers in the midst of both rapid internal growth and cutthroat industry competition. As a result, it undertook an extensive marketing research campaign to find the causes of and solutions to its problems. After carefully analyzing the extensive telephone-customer database it had compiled over the years, Dell went to work contacting customers to find out what they really wanted in computing equipment. The research showed that even though consumers were considerably more sophisticated and knowledgeable than expected, many were still intimidated by computer technology. Dell also found that many customers were confused with the multiplicity of seemingly similar PCs then on the market. Moreover, Dell learned that its "one-size-fits-all" marketing strategy of merely adding features to its basic PC was no longer appropriate given the current state of the PC marketplace and the stated product preferences of both current and prospective customers.

On the basis of its marketing research, Dell redesigned its line of products around four basic types of customers—after finding that its existing products did not offer the features and capabilities desired by these individuals. For example, for that segment of customers it defined as "techno-criticals"—high-end corporate purchasers interested in advanced features and enhanced productivity—Dell designed the OptiPlex, a unit built around Intel's 486 processor and featuring built-in network circuit cards. Putting itself into head-to-head competition with Apple Computer (also hurting as a result of the ongoing price war), Dell designed for "techno-wizards"—highly sophisticated computer users who were known to order "hot" components from computer magazines—the $2,999 Dimension XPS featuring ultrafast graphics, enhanced video and audio capabilities, and a built-in CD-ROM player.

Although Michael Dell's achievements cannot be overstated, the growth pains eventually experienced by the company point to the fact that the entrepreneurial spirit must sometimes be tempered with patience and a willingness to give up some measure of control. As Dell himself stated in 1993, "If I could do it over again, I would have hired more talented personnel in areas like systems and finance earlier on."

*Sources:* Fred J. Eckert, "Michael Dell's Two-Billion-Dollar Dream," *Reader's Digest,* March 1994, 115-119; *Hoover's Handbook of American Business 1993,* eds. Gary Hoover, Alta Campbell, and Patrick J. Spain (Austin, TX: The Reference Press, Inc., 1993), 235; Scott McCartney, "Dell Programs New Products, Sales Strategy," *The Wall Street Journal,* August 2, 1993, B1; Charles McCoy and Ken Yamada, "Apple's Woes Renew Worries About Price War's Bite," *The Wall Street Journal,* June 10, 1993, B1; Kyle Pope, "Dell Computer Expects a Loss In 2nd Quarter," *The Wall Street Journal,* July 15, 1993, A3; Kyle Pope, "Dell Computer Posts Loss for Quarter, Backs Away From Forecast of Rebound," *The Wall Street Journal,* August 18, 1993, B10; Patricia Sellers, "Companies That Serve You Best," *Fortune,* May 31, 1993, 74-88; and Andrew E. Serwer, "America's 100 Fastest Growers," *Fortune,* August 9, 1993, 40-56.

## Questions

1. How did Dell's initial entrepreneurial success lead to Dell Computer's eventual problems as a large global corporation?

2. Did Dell Computer grow too fast or just too large? Or both? What can entrepreneurs do to guard against manage-rial problems such as those encountered by Dell Computer in 1993?

3. What lessons—both positive and negative—can be learned from the example of Dell Computer?

---

### STRENGTHEN YOUR SKILLS
## *Creativity*

The entrepreneurial success stories in this chapter are about people who used their creative abilities to develop innovative products or ways of doing something that became the basis of a new business. Of course, being creative is not just for entrepreneurs or inventors; creativity is an important tool to help you find the optimal solutions to the problems you face on a daily basis. Managers, in particular, rely heavily on their creativity skills to help them solve daily workplace problems.

According to brain experts, the right brain hemisphere is the source of creative thinking (see the "Strengthen Your Skills" exercise for Chapter 2), and the creative part of the brain can "atrophy" from lack of use. This two-part exercise will help you examine how much "exercise" you're giving your right brain hemisphere. Part One will allow you to assess your creativity quotient; Part Two will give you some mental aerobic exercises to strengthen your creative thinking.

### Part One:  Assess Your Creativity Quotient[39]

Instructions:

1. Take the following self-test to check your Creativity Quotient.

2. Write the appropriate number in the box next to each statement according to whether the statement describes your behavior always (3), sometimes (2), once in a while (1), or never (0).

|  | Always 3 | Sometimes 2 | Once in a While 1 | Never 0 |
|---|---|---|---|---|
| 1. I am a curious person who is interested in other people's opinions. |  |  |  |  |
| 2. I look for opportunities to solve problems. |  |  |  |  |
| 3. I respond to changes in my life creatively by using them to redefine my goals and revising plans to reach them. |  |  |  |  |
| 4. I like to examine assumptions, biases, or preconceived beliefs for loopholes and opportunities. |  |  |  |  |
| 5. I would describe myself as a trend spotter. I actively monitor changes in my environment to spot opportunities early. |  |  |  |  |
| 6. I am good at being alert to concepts I can borrow from one field to apply to another. |  |  |  |  |
| 7. I am willing to develop and experiment with ideas of my own. |  |  |  |  |
| 8. I rely on my hunches and insights. |  |  |  |  |
| 9. I can reduce complex decisions to a few simple questions by seeing the "big picture." |  |  |  |  |

| | Always 3 | Sometimes 2 | Once in a While 1 | Never 0 |
|---|---|---|---|---|
| 10. I am good at promoting and gathering support for my ideas. | | | | |
| 11. I think farther ahead than most people I associate with by thinking long term and sharing my vision with others. | | | | |
| 12. I dig out research and information to support my ideas. | | | | |
| 13. I am supportive of the creative ideas from my peers and subordinates and welcome "better ideas" from others. | | | | |
| 14. As an innovative networker, I have people with whom I share creative ideas for feedback and support. | | | | |
| 15. I read books and magazine articles to stay on the "cutting edge" in my areas of interest. I am fascinated by the future. | | | | |
| 16. I believe I am creative and have faith in my good ideas. | | | | |
| Subtotal for each column | | | | |
| GRAND TOTAL | | | | |

**3.** Check your score using the following scale:

41–48   High creativity. You will find the mental aerobic exercises helpful in maintaining and improving your creative capacity.

36–40   Average creativity. Use the mental aerobic exercises as a starting point to explore and expand more of your creative potential.

30–39   Low creativity. You will realize some improvements in using creativity in your daily life if you will try these mental aerobic exercises.

0–29   Undiscovered creativity. You have yet to uncover your creative potential. Use the mental aerobic exercises to help you learn more about your creative potential.

### Part Two:  Creativity Conditioning (Mental Aerobic Exercises)

Instructions:

**1.** Between now and the next class session, select three items from the list of mental aerobic exercises presented below.

**2.** At the next class session, report in one of the following formats the results of your creativity conditioning.

**a.** Write a 2- to 3-paragraph paper for your instructor where you highlight some positive/negative results of your "mental workouts."

**b.** Take a few minutes at the beginning of class for several students to describe the results of their participating in these mental conditioning exercises.

**c.** Break into groups of 3 to 4 students and share some outcomes of your participation in this exercise.

### Mental Aerobic Exercises

- If you're right-handed, try using your left hand to do things. If you're left-handed, switch to your right for a while.
- Do a jigsaw or crossword puzzle.
- Try a new way of expressing your creativity (cook something you've never made before, paint a picture, write a poem, throw a party that has an interesting theme).
- Guess at measurements rather than using a ruler, tape measure, or measuring cup. Then measure and see how close you were.
- Watch three-quarters of a movie on video, stop the tape, and think of your own ending.

- Stretch your thinking beyond what might be your typical approach to solving problems. See if you can solve one of these brain teasers (your teacher has the answers):

  1. Arrange the letters below into one word:
     NEW DOOR

  2. Change the Roman numeral that represents the number 9
     IX
     into a 6 by using only one line.

  3. Determine in what order the numbers below are arranged.
     8, 5, 4, 9, 1, 7, 6, 3, 2, 0

- Go to the library and look up an article or find a biography about a famous creative person (Thomas Edison, Walt Disney, Steven Spielberg, etc.) and spend 20 minutes skimming the book or reading the article, looking for insights into the creative process. For example, Thomas Edison is considered to be the most prolific inventor the world has ever seen. Among his inventions are the incandescent light, the phonograph, and the motion picture projector. One quotation attributed to Edison is "[Creative] genius is 99 percent perspiration and 1 percent inspiration."

- Go to a day-care center and spend a half hour observing 2-, 3-, and 4-year-olds at play. Jot down any "creative" things you observe the children doing. ("Tests show that a child's creativity plummets 90 percent between ages 5 and 7. By the age of 40 most adults are about 2 percent as creative as they were at 5."[40])

# Planning *and* Organizing

# Developing
# Organizational
# Plans

**After reading this chapter, you will be able to:**

- Discuss the benefits that planning can bring to an organization.
- List the steps in planning.
- Describe the nature of an organization's mission and goals and how they influence planning.
- Recognize and enumerate the various types of goals that an organization tries to meet.
- Determine the various levels of plans that organizations develop and explain how these levels are related.
- Formulate actions that managers can take to improve the effectiveness of planning.
- Describe management by objectives and explain how it can be used to coordinate planning within the organization.
- Evaluate the goals and plans of a business.

# Diamonique Has Never Glittered So Brightly

Home shopping is growing up. Once thought to be the preferred shopping outlet for lower-middle-class women, home shopping channels such as QVC and the Home Shopping Network (HSN) are now appealing to a more affluent crowd. Even Gabe Dopplet, the editor-in-chief of *Mademoiselle,* is an avowed home shopping fan, purchasing knick-knacks and clothes, and wearing her cable ensembles at the office. This transformation has been the result of careful planning by HSN and QVC. With a firmly established goal of increasing revenues, both firms realized that the strategy to pursue was to go after the hearts and wallets of upscale viewers.

Once specializing in such items as costume jewelry (Diamonique is the brand name of a popular cubic zirconium jewelry line), these firms have broadened their focus through their planning. They reached a major milestone in attracting choice viewers in spring 1993 when Saks Fifth Avenue "starred" in its own program and generated over $1 million in sales. This spurred retail giants such as Nordstrom and Bloomingdale's to seriously consider entering your living room via television. Even venerable Macy's announced plans for its own 24-hour channel, TV Macy's.

Home shopping via television was a $2 billion industry in 1992. Although it represents only a small percentage of total retail sales, it is growing at 20 percent per year. When compared to traditional retailing, home shopping offers some significant cost advantages. As Alan Milstein, a retail consultant, states, "The three biggest expenses for a retailer are rent, sales help, and advertising." Home shopping appears to be an ideal alternative.

One indicator of the expected glittery future of home shopping is recent acquisition attempts. In 1993 QVC and HSN discussed a merger that would have created a network reaching over 60 million viewers. After this failed, Ted Turner of Turner Broadcasting Inc. became interested in HSN in Spring 1994. This proposed takeover also failed. About the same time, CBS Television failed in its attempt to purchase QVC. Finally, Comcast Corp. and Liberty Mutual Corp. (a subsidiary of TeleCommunication Inc.) agreed to purchase QVC for $1.42 billion. At the time of this printing, this acquisition was still being pursued.

In such a highly competitive, changing industry, good planning is essential, and planning tends to be quite long term and strategic in nature. One problem that these planners are having is trying to forecast possible future scenarios. How do you divine what type of technology will be prevalent in ten years, much less how people will react to and use it?

Although home shopping is a relatively tiny industry right now, the potential is enormous. The ability to exploit these opportunities, however, will depend on the quality of the networks' planning, in both the formulation and implementation stages. So what will it be? Will it be cubic zirconium or 14-carat diamonds? Stay tuned to your local cable network.

*Sources:* Laura Zinn, Gail De George, Rochelle Shoretz, Dori Jones Yang, and Stephanie Edward Forest, "Retailing Will Never Be the Same," *Business Week,* July 26, 1993, 54; Paul Farhi, "QVC Shopping Network Sold to TCI and Comcast," *Washington Post,* August 5, 1994, v 117, B3.

*introduction*

Whether you are Barry Diller contemplating ways to expand home shopping or a Keebler elf concocting a new chocolate chip cookie, planning is an essential element in the recipe for successful management. Planning establishes the means to achieve the future. It requires that the manager or the organization specify where it wishes to go in the future and how to get there.

In presenting this important topic, we will discuss the general steps of planning, the nature of goals, and the various types of plans used in organizations. In this chapter we will emphasize that the various types of plans should be related and that part of planning is implementing the plan.

## THE NATURE OF PLANNING

**plan**

A set of activities intended to achieve goals, whether for an entire organization, department, or an individual.

A **plan** is a set of activities intended to achieve goals, whether for an entire organization, department, or an individual. Planning involves determining what the organization will specifically accomplish, deciding how to accomplish these goals, and developing methods to reach the goals. At the most basic level, a plan is a road map that answers the fundamental question, "How do we get there from here?" Almost everybody agrees that a map is important; however, organizations differ greatly in how they create that map. These range from formalized, detailed steps that produce a set of written procedures to be followed, to informal discussions that result in general verbal agreements. Continuing the analogy of a map, this is like comparing a U.S. Geographical Survey map prepared by trained cartographers to a map drawn by your Uncle Bud on the back of an old envelope. Both are maps but they differ greatly in the information that they provide. As it is with any organizational action, the quality of the result—in this case, implementation of the plan—will vary depending on the quality of the planning process.

**Teaching Note:** Stress that while planning does not guarantee success, research shows that companies who participate in strategic planning outperform those who do no planning.

Planning does not necessarily guarantee success. As we shall see, many things can go wrong with plans. However, companies and managers who develop specific plans should have a definite head start in reaching goals and a distinct advantage over those who do not adequately plan. Let's consider two hypothetical national rumor magazines, *All-Lies* and *Make-It-Up*. Both magazines have planning processes, yet there are important differences. *All-Lies* requires managers to submit their plans for the next year as part of their performance review. These plans include the deployment of reporters in anticipation of events of major importance. Every year senior- and middle-level managers at *All-Lies* have a weekend retreat dedicated to planning. Moreover, all employees are expected to participate in the planning process at their job level. *Make-It-Up* magazine, on the other hand, lives up to its name. Its plans are for the immediate future, made at the last minute, and usually involve just a few employees. Which magazine do you think will have the best chance of having one of its reporters at the next sighting of Elvis flying his UFO to a hamburger stand in Michigan? Of course, *Make-It-Up* may get lucky and have a reporter eating in the hamburger stand because she is covering the story of a 102-year-old giving birth to quintuplets. However, because of its planning, we would expect that *All-Lies* would have reporters who regularly tour this state of past Elvis sightings and, all else being equal, would have significantly increased the magazine's chances of capturing this important story.

Implicit in our definition is that planning has a future orientation. All managers are concerned with some aspect of the future, but different levels or types of man-

Planning is a systematic, ongoing process of the Zoological Society of San Diego. Gorilla Tropics, shown here, is the result of a long-term strategic plan the Society began in 1984 to lead it to its 75th anniversary in 1991. One goal of the plan was to develop integrated animal, plant, and natural habitat exhibits. It took years of planning to coordinate the construction, fund raising, and operation of the 2 ½-acre simulation of an African rain forest. The Society continues its strategic planning process to carry it into the 21st century.

*Source:* © Zoological Society of San Diego. All Rights Reserved. Photo by Ron Garrison.

agers will be more concerned with different time frames. Typically, the top management of a firm, the chief executive officer for instance, is concerned with the firm's long-term future, while first-line supervisors focus on daily and weekly planning. Lou Hughes, president of General Motors Europe, for example, is concerned with purchasing trends in 25 different countries where customers' tastes continue to differ; a manufacturing system spread across Europe that includes Great Britain, Portugal, Hungary, Turkey, and Sweden; and well-organized labor unions in each country.[1] A GM factory foreman may be only slightly interested in the long-term future, but is greatly concerned about how the next quarter's demands affect his current manufacturing processes.

**Example:** All organizations are concerned with the future. Rolls Royce forecasts potential markets for its airplane engines. Strategic planners research the growth of markets as well as the fleet age of existing airlines.

## THE BENEFITS OF PLANNING

Among the several benefits that arise from planning, some are economic in nature: For instance, the firm may receive a higher return on investment. Yet it should be noted that planning is not a "cure-all." A company may have excellent planning and still not do well. It may have made the wrong assumptions about the environment, for instance, or it may have been incorrect in evaluating its own strengths. It is also possible to overplan—that is, to spend so much time and money formulating plans that little of either resource remains to actually accomplish anything. This warning aside, planning can benefit organizations by forcing them to focus, helping to coordinate activities and people, and motivating employees and managers.

### Focus

Planning is an excellent tool for getting a company's managers to consider seriously its present status and the environment in which it operates. Forcing managers to ask basic questions about the firm's operations and customers can greatly benefit the firm. "Are we doing this operation the best way?" "How does this fit with our other business activities?" and similar queries can help individuals in an organization gain a common understanding of the firm and its purposes.

This forced focusing can be especially important for large companies with many different businesses. General Electric is a multinational corporation with thousands of employees and a multitude of products ranging from locomotives to the NBC television network. It is often difficult for managers and employees to obtain a common consensus on what *is* GE. However, the firm has developed and implemented a number of plans that add focus and "bring good things to light."

## Coordination

One of the major tasks of management is to coordinate the activities of groups and individuals. Proper planning provides a mechanism for meshing these different segments of the organization. For example, in many consulting companies, it is important that experts in different business areas—for example, management information systems and production—coordinate work activities. Without planning, each consultant is likely to concentrate on his or her own activities. The management information systems consultant may emphasize the need to develop sophisticated databases, while the production consultant may be more interested in tracking current product flow. Proper planning takes into account these differing organizational priorities.

## Motivation

Planning can help create an environment conducive to properly motivating managers and employees. Frequently, the effects of focus and coordination arising from planning can lead to higher performance levels, as organizational members recognize the firm's overall goals.

In a related manner, planning is often used to get organizational members to contribute their particular knowledge and opinions to a decision. For instance, top management may have very good reasons for banning smoking on the premises (lower health insurance, productivity, and so on). Given this goal, the company could implement a ban on smoking by erecting "No Smoking" signs and by putting special smoke detectors in the restrooms. However, a better approach may be to get organizational members involved by including them in planning. In this case, it would be especially important to include smokers, who would feel particularly threatened by such a ban. Thus, the reactions of various groups can be anticipated and included in the final plan. Finally, we know that performance of individuals and groups in an organization is directly influenced by the specificity and difficulty of goals that are set. Planning is an excellent way of designing goals that maximize the performance of employees.

## STEPS IN PLANNING

Figure 9.1 presents the steps in planning for an organization. Although these planning steps are the same as those taken by an individual manager, the specifics, such as the nature of the goals, are different. Because planning is meant to increase the probability that the organization will achieve its objectives, the process should start with the organization's mission statement. Next the firm needs to assess how it is doing relative to its mission. Third, it should state its specific

## The Steps in Planning

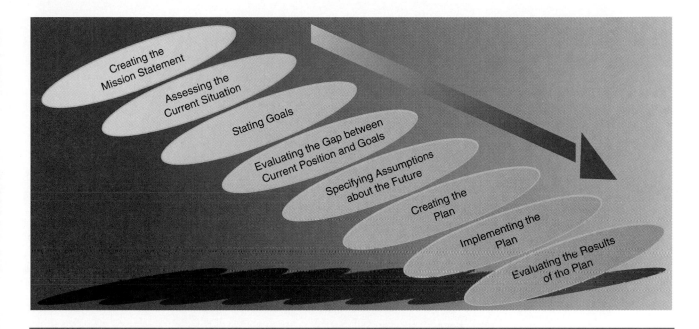

goals, which should be logically related to its mission. Then, it should evaluate the gap between the goals and the current status of the organization and specify assumptions about the future. These form the basis for the next step, the creation of the plan. The last two steps in planning are implementation and evaluation.

## Creating the Mission Statement

An organization's **mission** defines its fundamental purpose. It describes, in the most primary terms, the company's basic philosophy. It should answer the questions, "What are our values?" and "What do we stand for?" The values embodied in a mission will be the synthesis of the values of a number of important organizational stakeholders: managers, owners, employees, customers, government, and interest groups. A **mission statement** is a formal written declaration of the organization's mission that contains all, or at least most, of the following: the firm's philosophy, its primary products and markets, the intended geographic scope, and the nature of the relationships between the firm, its stakeholders, and society. Figure 9.2 is the mission statement of Duke Power Company, which illustrates these points.

In terms of planning, an important issue is the degree to which the firm has both defined and communicated its mission to its employees and other stakeholders. Many firms' mission statements are engraved, framed, hung in a prominent place in the lobby, and never looked at again. However, a clear understanding of the mission reduces the ambiguity that employees may have about where the organization is trying to go and how they can help it get there. Planning, especially implementing plans, becomes more straightforward and usually is accomplished

**Critical Thinking Challenge:**
Have students find a mission statement from a corporation's annual report. Ask them to critique the mission statement and discuss the key points. How could the mission statement be improved?

**mission**
A definition of an organization's fundamental purpose and its basic philosophy.

**mission statement**
A formal written declaration of the organization's mission; often includes the firm's philosophy, its primary products and markets, the intended geographic scope, and the nature of the relationships between the firm, its stakeholders, and society.

**FIGURE 9.2**

**Mission Statement of Duke Power Company**

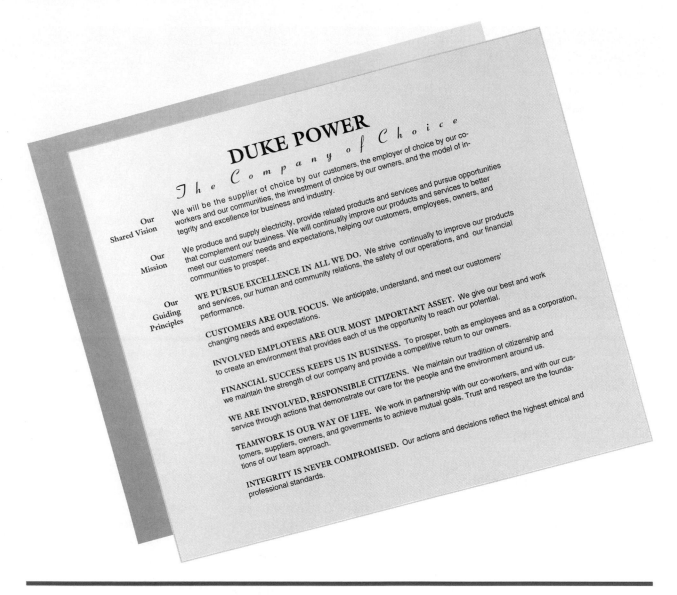

*Source:* Reprinted with permission from Duke Power Company.

more quickly if everyone understands what the organization values. Moreover, a firm's ability to communicate its mission to its customers and other stakeholders can give that firm a tremendous competitive advantage. Conversely, the inability to convey the mission effectively, either through the lack of communication skills or because the firm is unable to define its mission, can be an enormous handicap.

Compare two major retail store chains, Wal-Mart and Sears. When you hear the name "Wal-Mart," you may think of "everyday low prices," "made in the U.S.A.," and service, the embodiment of the values and philosophy of Wal-Mart and its founder, Sam Walton. Wal-Mart has had extraordinary success conveying its mission to both its employees and the buying public. Other retail stores have not been so successful. Sears, Roebuck and Co., for example, has gone from carrying a wide variety of low-priced consumer goods, even through catalog sales, to a more limited variety of competitively priced items, to being a more upscale marketer of items such as signature women's apparel. As a result, some employees and consumers may be relatively unsure as to what Sears values. Sears has recently begun a concerted effort to revise its mission—to feature "the softer side of Sears"—and convey it to the public. Time will tell if this critical task succeeds as the company hopes.

## Assessing the Current Situation

Where are we now? Before a company can make any plan, it must be aware of its present situation. This is mainly an evaluation of the current status of the internal organization. The first concern is determining the extent of the organization's resources: financial assets, employee skills, technology, and data about the work process. A second concern is the firm's working relationship with its suppliers, financial backers, and consumers.

Financial resources, employee skills, and current technology are important because they indicate the organization's strengths and weaknesses at the present time. If these factors are comparable to or better than those of other firms in the same markets, the organization has an advantage on which planning can be based. On the other hand, weakness usually indicates a less competitive position relative to other firms, a constraint that must be addressed in planning. Planning should not be based on goals that cannot feasibly be reached.

Data about the work process is of immediate importance in planning. Such data are necessary to obtain an accurate assessment of present production or service delivery capability. If the company has inaccurate or incomplete data to assess its present work operations, any plans based on these data will be suspect. An airline, for example, may keep precise records of fares and total dollars of sales. However, if it does not have records of ticket sales as a function of price of ticket, any plan for responding to a competitor's cut in fares may be more of a guess than a planned response. Matching the competitor's fare may not do anything but retain the same level of seats that would have been sold. The price may have to be reduced to $20 below the competitor's before enough volume can be generated to make up the lost revenue for the price cut. Thus, it should be apparent that information about financial assets, employee skills, and technology is necessary for the development of plans. These factors become the base from which the organization begins any change. It is necessary to know the current status of these factors to plan what the organization realistically can achieve.

In addition to evaluating the organization's status through its resources, it is also important to assess its relationships with suppliers, customers, and financial backers such as stockholders or financial institutions. These relationships may represent a potential limitation or a potential strength that should be addressed in planning. Consider Designs Inc., a retail store chain based in Chestnut Hill, MA, which sells any kind of apparel—as long as it is made by Levi Strauss & Company. The firm's management is fully aware of the problems in having a single supplier. Any change in production, distribution, or cost of Levi Strauss's items will directly affect Designs Inc. If, for any reason, Levi Strauss were forced to shut down for an extended time period, it might be necessary for Designs Inc. to close also or change its business drastically. On the other hand, the company enjoys a steady supply of top-quality clothing and spends relatively little time and money planning its buying activities. Moreover, the company has need for only limited marketing and advertising plans, further decreasing its costs. Most planning is thus concentrated in the daily operation and maintenance of the stores, which helps promote a positive image with customers. Management clearly believes that the benefits outweigh the disadvantages in this relationship.[2]

## Stating Goals

**goal**
The final result that a firm wishes to achieve.

Where are we going? A **goal** is the final result that a firm wishes to achieve. A company almost always has several goals that it is pursuing simultaneously, which reflects the complex nature of business. To be stated correctly, a goal must contain several components:

- the attribute sought—the topic being addressed, such as profits, customer satisfaction, or product quality;
- the target to be achieved—the specific amount or level, such as the volume of sales or the extent of management training, to be achieved;
- an index to measure progress—the unit that will be used to measure the target, such as dollars for sales volume or the number of individual managers for training; and
- a time frame—the time period in which the goal is to be achieved, frequently a specific date.[3]

In 1993, Compaq Computer Corp. expressed the goal to increase market share enough by the first quarter of 1996 to replace IBM as the leading seller of personal computers.[4] In this case, the attribute is market share and the time frame is the first quarter of 1996. The target is simply the share of market necessary to move past IBM; rather than being a fixed number, it depends on the performance of IBM. Information about all of these components is necessary in order to develop complete plans to achieve a goal. Simply put, it is necessary to know what is to be achieved, how much, when, and how it is to be determined whether the goal was reached or not.

Organizations set goals for a variety of activities that management thinks are essential for overall performance. Management scholar Peter Drucker suggests that the following areas should be considered.

**1.** Market standing—refers to the percentage of the market that the firm wishes to secure; e.g., what percentage of consumers buy Kodak film as opposed to its competitors' products.

**2.** Innovation—usually refers to the nature and amount of research and development the firm is committed to carry out. This is often measured as a percentage of R&D or sales.

**3.** Productivity—usually expressed in terms of the total output—such as number of units—of the firm or of a major part of the firm (such as a division or a plant).

**4.** Physical or financial resources—refers to the amount of dollars and other assets, such as stocks, land, or buildings, that the firm is committed to possessing.

**5.** Profitability—the amount of money remaining after the expenses of operating the business have been paid.

**Critical Thinking Challenge:** Have students continue to use information contained in a corporation's annual report to look for goals of the corporation. Ask students to find examples of attributes, an index, and a time frame for goals.

**Example:** Cadbury-Schweppes has a goal of expanding into China with its candy, confections, and soda products. The company is pursuing China for growth as well as increased market standing.

In launching GS Technologies, entrepreneur Ralph Grosswald set a goal of creating an innovative product that would require new technology. Grosswald, a vegetarian, spent six years and $2.5 million developing Vegicaps, a pharmaceutical capsule free of animal products. Grosswald achieved his goal, as Vegicaps is now sold in the United States, Canada, Europe, the Middle East, South America, Malaysia, India, and Australia.

*Source:* © 1994 Chris Stewart/Black Star.

**6.** Manager performance and development—performance refers to the level of productivity of individual managers or work groups; development refers to the additional skills a manager learns through either formal training or work experience.

**7.** Worker performance—level of productivity and the quality of activities of nonmanagerial employees.

**8.** Public responsibility—activities such as complying with laws in such areas as employment, product safety, and advertising; also includes areas that are not legislated, for example, work with civic groups and nonprofit organizations.[5]

The "Magnifying Management" box describes Hewlett-Packard's mission and goals.

**Types of Goals.**    Organizations develop three types of goals: strategic, tactical, and operational. While these three types are interrelated, they differ in terms of their content and the business operations that they address.

The firm's highest-level managers set **strategic goals**, which deal with such general topics as the firm's growth, new markets, or new goods and services. Strategic goals are developed for long periods of time, usually five or more years. These goals should be central to all of the organization's planning and activities. In other words, the strategic goals establish what the firm wants to achieve in the long-term future. Logically, all the organization's other plans and activities should focus on contributing to the achievement of the strategic goals.

Texas Instruments found in 1989 that it had dropped from a dominant first to seventh place in sales of computer chips. CEO Jerry Junkins met with his top 20 deputies to set strategic goals in order to reverse the slide and to make strategic plans that affected several areas of the company. TI formed joint ventures with companies in Europe and Asia to reach the goal of reducing its production costs. It dropped its initial plans to develop a direct market with consumers, returning to a focus on corporate customers. In addition, the company moved away from a catalog selling approach, appealing to several customers, to sales to big customers such as Sony and Sun Microsystems by designing products to fill their special needs.[6] In the next chapter, we will discuss strategic management in detail, including the activities developed to attain the strategic goals.

**Tactical goals**, the intermediate goals of the firm, are designed to stimulate actions necessary for achieving the strategic goals. As such, these goals are much

**strategic goals**
Goals set by upper managers that deal with such general topics as the firm's growth, new markets, or new goods and services.

**tactical goals**
The intermediate goals of the firm, which are designed to stimulate actions necessary for achieving the strategic goals.

# M agnifying anagement

$$HP = MC^2$$

**H**ewlett-Packard = Measurement, Computing, Communication might be just a slogan to some people, but to Lewis Platt, CEO of HP, it is the mantra that will guide his company into the twenty-first century. Platt is leading his firm through the digital revolution, seeking to create a unique niche in which HP may exploit its core technologies of networking, computers, and measurement instruments. HP's mission: to combine these three forms of technology to create entirely new types of products, products that will connect the user or viewer with the rest of the world, to make interactivity a reality.

Platt's goal is to make HP a tollbooth on the so-called digital information highway. This requires more than simply making computers, an area in which HP has flourished. It requires a unique vision of how people compute, communicate, and measure electronically. By viewing these needs and crossbreeding different categories of technology, HP is seeking new, innovative ways to address these needs. One example of such an applied technology is the auto analyzer that HP built for Ford. This is an advanced automobile diagnostic system that combines a personal computer, measuring instruments, and a "flight recorder." Other products currently in development range from a video printer that prints full-color images from your TV set to a health monitor that will measure a patient's vital signs and transmit that information directly to the doctor's computer.

As might be expected, planning and coordinating operations involving these different types of technologies represent a tremendous hurdle. One way HP is attempting to address this is by the creation of $MC^2$ Council, a group composed of people from all areas of the organization, that is identifying potential markets for HP to enter. Platt himself spearheads this coordination effort. So far he has held over 100 "coffee talks" with employees to enhance the planning process. Managers' bonuses are being tied to how well they respond to this new planning push.

In addition, HP is trying to increase the speed of planning, especially implementation. One way it is doing this is by entering into an increased number of partnerships to get new products out on the market quickly. For instance, HP teamed up with AT&T and the Citizen Watch Company to introduce a 1.3-inch disk drive. Although traditionally HP had built its disk drives solo, it significantly cut down on the time that it normally takes in the planning process.

HP is serious about its new strategy. It is spending about a third of its $137 million R&D budget in this area. The final result remains to be seen, but HP is hoping that it is placing itself in the fast lane on the information highway.

*Source:* Robert Hof, "Hewlett-Packard Digs Deep For A Digital Future," *Business Week,* October 18, 1993, 72.

**Comment on Box:** When presenting this case, point out how the company has integrated its planning process throughout the organization. The plan is supported with a vision, joint partnerships, and an emphasis on R&D. End the discussion by asking students how successful they think Hewlett-Packard will be in the future.

more specific than are strategic goals. Tactical goals are usually written by and directed to middle-level managers. They are stated for shorter time periods, usually one to five years, than are strategic goals because tactical goals must be completed before strategic goals can be fulfilled. Tactical goals become the basis for tactical planning about how to carry out the functional operations, such as operations, finance, and marketing. For example, a manufacturing firm's tactical goals for reducing costs may include closing two plants and introducing robots and computer systems to its other four plants within five years. In such a case, the human resources department would also have several tactical goals to implement the strategy. Among these might be to assess the technical and computer skill levels of the firm's employees within the next 12 months. Additionally, training programs in computer programming and operation must be developed within two years. The training itself must be completed for all appropriate employees within four years. For the closing of the two plants, it would be necessary to determine, within one year, a system for identifying those individuals who would be offered positions at

**FIGURE 9.3**

**Types of Goals**

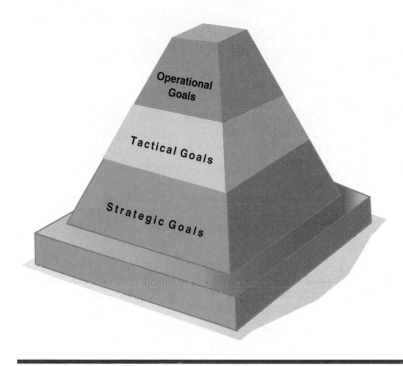

another plant and to set up an outplacement service for those employees who will be laid off at each plant within two years.

**Operational goals** are more specific and address activities that must be performed before tactical goals can be fulfilled. These are short-term goals that are addressed to first-line managers and usually apply to specific work operations that lead to the production of goods or services. Returning to the previous example, two of the operational goals of the human resource department would be to identify, within two weeks, the test battery that will be used to assess the skills of employees and to design the skill assessment program within seven weeks.

We can see that operational, tactical, and strategic goals and their accompanying plans are interrelated. Achieving the operational goals leads to fulfillment of the tactical goals, which leads to fulfillment of the strategic goals. One way of visualizing an organization's goal structure is through a framework like the one depicted in Figure 9.3. This framework starts with a broad view of the organization's strategy and works its way to a much narrower perspective. Each succeeding set of goals is related to the preceding ones, as are the plans that are developed and implemented in order to reach these goals.

**Difficulty of Setting Goals.**   On the surface, the basic question of planning, "Where are we going?" looks surprisingly easy to answer. But setting goals can be a difficult task in an organization. Recall our discussion of stakeholders in Chapter 3. Every organization has many groups of stakeholders, both internal and external, and each group has its own goals. Often different stakeholders' goals are in

**operational goals**
Those short-term goals that address activities that must be performed before tactical goals can be fulfilled.

**Teaching Note:** To reinforce the differences between tactical goals and operational goals, have students develop examples of each in small groups and discuss the differences using their examples. For example, a tactical goal might be to increase customer service while an operational goal might be to install a computerized inventory control system.

**Example:** Goals can be too stringent. Domino's Pizza had to discontinue its 30-minute pizza delivery guarantee when the goal caused automobile accidents and employee dissatisfaction.

It takes courage to compete against established fast-food giants McDonald's and Burger King, but Rally's managers took the risk in planning restaurants that offer customers superfast service—a burger, fries, and soft drink in just 45 seconds. Speedy service at double-drive-throughs and walk-up windows and a guarantee that "We get it right or you get it free" give Rally's a competitive advantage.

*Source:* © Falkenberg & Associates, Inc.

conflict with one another. Environmental groups such as the Sierra Club may contend that a chemical manufacturer's goal of cheaply disposing of chemical waste is socially irresponsible and should not be permitted. Internal stakeholder groups such as employees will almost always disagree with the firm's goal of reducing costs if implementing that goal involves laying off employees. The conflict in goals among stakeholders is a major issue in public organizations, especially governments. For example, citizens with children often wish to upgrade the school system by raising taxes to purchase better computers, school facilities, and supplies. Childless citizens, however, often object to raising the educational level and would prefer either to reduce taxes or devote the money to other services such as police and fire protection. Both elected and appointed managers in governments are confronted with the difficult task of representing both groups in terms of planning.

Another factor affecting an organization's ability to set goals is the nature of the environment. Rapidly changing external conditions may make it extremely difficult for the firm to plan because the environment may change in an unforeseen manner and make the plans impossible to carry out. In 1976, Sol Price invented the discount warehouse format with the inauguration of his Price Clubs. Yet 17 years later, Price Club was forced to merge with one of its competitors, Costco, due in part to its inability to set effective goals. One of Price Club's major goals was to be dominant in the southern California market on the premise that the California economy would continue its "boom" for an extended period of time. Of course, the boom eventually went bust and so did Price Club.[7] In general, companies operating in very dynamic external environments set goals for shorter periods of time and review their goals more frequently.

Another difficulty in goal setting has to do with organizational rewards. Many managers have a short-term focus; they are attentive to this quarter's productivity or this year's return on investment. This short-term orientation is reinforced by most organizations' reward structures. Bonuses, even for upper-level executives, are based on short-term performance, such as cost reduction for the upcoming quarter or the price of the company's stock within the next three years. To obtain the bonus, the manager must produce results within the time frame. However, these results may occur at the expense of long-term investments that would have had important benefits. A middle manager may reduce costs by eliminating management training for lower-level managers or reducing investments in maintenance. An upper manager may increase the profit statement of the firm by reducing research and development expenditures or the purchase of new technology. Often, such increased profitability will accelerate the demand for the stock and lead to a rise in the stock price.

Finally, good planning requires courage and risk taking. Often a firm's ability to develop a competitive advantage will depend to a great extent on making some plans that have a good deal of risk in their implementation. Managers of Rally's, a hamburger chain that sells only at drive-through windows, thought that a restaurant offering no sit-down service and only sparse menus could prosper. Managers devoted all their planning to implementing this idea, and as they approach store #500, it appears that they made the correct decision.[8] However, many managers are uncomfortable with risk and prefer the status quo. Planning in such a case involves a continuation of existing activities.

**Example:** Wells Lamont, a manufacturer of gardening gloves, planned and implemented changes to meet the changing demographics of homeowners. As more women and children are becoming involved in yard work, recycling, and gardening, the company has manufactured lines of gloves to fit smaller hands.

## Evaluating the Gap between Current Position and Goals

At this point in planning, the organization has assessed its present status and set goals for the future. The next step is to determine how much difference there is between the current situation and its goals, the gap between the actual and intended states. Are the changes needed to close this gap major or minor? Correspondingly, is it necessary to develop a plan that will require a dramatic amount of time, effort, and resources by the organization or merely an increase in the level of its present activities?

In many ways, it is much easier to develop a plan to increase present activities. For example, if a soft drink producer wishes to increase its market share, it could feasibly develop a plan that includes increasing production from its bottling plants, increasing marketing and sales promotion, and reducing prices. Obviously, the implementation of these requires the use of organizational resources. However, such activities are usually easier and less risky than those called for in plans that require a major shift for the organization. For example, the goal of Stan Shih, cofounder of Acer Computer, is to make his firm one of the top five computer companies in the world. Acer has quite a distance to go before it can achieve this goal. Its plans call for a change in focus from marketing its Acer brand name products—where it is completely overwhelmed by such companies as Dell and IBM—to building the hardware that is then sold by other companies under their own names. Acer is concentrating on its manufacturing skills and modular conversion, which allows it to "snap together" components as ordered.[9] Thus Acer has identified its gap between present and future states and has crafted a high-risk plan to bridge the gap.

## Specifying Assumptions about the Future

All planning involves making some assumptions about the future of both the organization itself and the external environment. Brooks Brothers has built a fortune on its reputation as a classy clothier of the older, affluent man. However, because of the aging of the "baby boomer" generation, with its emphasis on new styles, the managers of Brooks Brothers decided that the company could not continue to grow by basing its business on "a 55-year-old man who wears a three-button Brooks Brothers suit and only comes in twice a year." To pursue a more youthful market, they have started to emphasize sportswear and have updated their displays. In addition they are entering into unusual (for them) retail situations such as factory outlets.[10]

Generally, if the company can reliably assume that the organization and the external environment will remain relatively stable and similar to that of the recent past, planning is much easier because factors that may affect the appropriateness and the implementation of the plans can be anticipated with a great deal of accuracy. However, if the present status of the organization or its external environment can be expected to change in an unpredictable fashion, planning obviously becomes much more difficult and complex.

For example, planning for breweries has been relatively straightforward. Laws regarding legal drinking age, amount of alcohol permissible, consumption patterns, brewing techniques, and competitors' products have all been fairly constant in the recent past and can reasonably be assumed to remain so in the foreseeable future. Planning, for the most part, can be based on previous plans and data about the relationships among these factors. However, planning for companies that produce software for personal computers is an entirely different situation. Planners can assume that few elements of the organization or the external environment will remain constant in the future. Computer technology changes rapidly, often in unexpected directions. Competitors, their products, and their prices also change rapidly. Finally, the demand for software and systems fluctuates greatly, partially driven by the strength of the national economy. In general, organizations that cannot assume stability plan for shorter time periods and review and redesign plans more often than organizations that can make such an assumption.

**Example:** Walt Disney Corporation, recognizing changes in the age of the population, is planning future theme park attractions and resort and hotel complexes geared to the needs and desires of older individuals.

## Creating the Plan

How do we get there? The plan is the road map that shows how to get from the current state to the desired goal. If your goal is to become a chief executive officer, for example, your plan for achieving that goal will probably include getting an MBA as well as gaining management experience working at several different companies. For organizations, the plan is the document that designates methods, time frames, alternate procedures, and who is to implement it. The process of creating a plan can be broken down into four basic steps: determining alternatives, evaluating alternatives, selecting an alternative, and specifying the steps.

These steps are probably familiar to you because you use them to carry out your own personal plans and to make decisions. (We will take a detailed look at the steps in the decision process in Chapter 11.) However, here is a brief example of how these steps may work for a men's clothing store, Max Weber's Clothing ("Tailoring Clothes for the Distinguished Bureaucrat for Over 50 Years"), operating in a medium-sized university town. Max sells traditional styles and items for men, including medium-priced name-brand goods. With three children getting ready for college, Max has realized that he needs more money and must increase profits by 10 percent in each of the next four years. What should he do? First, Max decides that he will not change his basic mission—to sell quality goods at reasonable prices. What are his alternatives? He could open another store just like his present one in a neighboring town. He could increase marketing and reduce prices in the hopes of taking market share from his competitors. He could broaden the type and style of items he carries. Or, he could retain the men's clothing line as it is and introduce a women's line of apparel.

To evaluate these alternatives, Max estimates the cost of each. The opening of another store is the most expensive and costly to sustain because of the distance. Increasing marketing and sales promotions is relatively inexpensive and easy to do.

Expanding its product offerings is an important part of Blockbuster's goal to become a fully integrated global entertainment company. In its video stores, Blockbuster is designating special areas for the sale and rental of interactive game hardware, software, and accessories, where customers can sample the products. The company is also conducting a market retail test of CD-ROM products, shown here, in 57 video stores. The test includes more than 200 game, reference, and education titles from 35 software publishers on hardware from Philips, Panasonic, Sega, IBM, and Apple.

*Source:* BLOCKBUSTER and BLOCK-BUSTER VIDEO are registered trademarks of Blockbuster Entertainment Corporation, Ft. Lauderdale, FL 33301. © 1994 All Rights Reserved.

Broadening the type of menswear is slightly more costly but still relatively easy because he can purchase many of the new items from the same suppliers that he currently uses. Expanding into women's garments is somewhat more expensive because it involves new suppliers and more buying trips. In addition, Max would have to hire someone who knows more about women's clothing than he does.

In selecting among these alternatives, Max examines his previous records, gathers information about the demographic trends of the area, finds data from his professional association about the buying habits of various demographic groups, and estimates potential sales. He drops the opening-an-additional-store alternative because there are few traditional men in the neighboring town, which has a largely rural character, and the university professors who live there already shop at his store. He also discards the increased-advertising-and-sales-promotion option because his research suggests that his competitors will match what he does, and no long-term advantage will result. The same is true for adding more items to his men's line. Max judges that he will attract some college students but not enough to increase profits as much as he wishes. But the addition of women's clothing looks excellent. Max found out that women's garments are more expensive and have a higher profit margin than men's. Many of his sales are already to women who shop for their husbands or boyfriends. Finally, women spend a whole lot more on clothing than do men. That is the clinching argument.

To specify the steps for carrying out this alternative, Max first hires Mary Follett, who has worked for a large department store in the area but wishes to be in business for herself. Together the two of them draw up a list of specific activities, which includes who has authority over what purchases, who makes what decisions, the amount of space allocated for women's articles, the construction of new dressing rooms, and budgeting for buying trips and advertising. They even decide to sponsor a fashion show.

Creating a plan, as illustrated by Max Weber Clothing, shows that the process can be time consuming and involved, even for a small business. The methods used in creating the plan can be formal or informal. In this situation, Max's process is somewhere in the middle. A major force affecting the formality of a plan is the influence of outside stakeholders. Thus, in our example, if Max goes to a bank to obtain capital, the loan officer will probably require an extensive written document.

## Implementing the Plan

Implementation is carrying out the steps specified in the plan. It is where the organization goes from the "thinking" mode to the "doing" mode. Typically, the plan describes what steps are to be carried out but not how to carry them out, especially what decisions are to be made at each step and what information must be known to make the decision. At Max's clothing store, implementation calls for purchasing the items of women's clothing to be sold. How much? What specific items? What quality and style? As we discussed in Chapter 1, decision making is a major managerial task that requires, among others, technical and interpersonal skills. In addition, it also calls for the management activities of organizing, leading, and controlling.

The implementation stage is where many plans come undone. Many managers think of implementation as being merely "administrative" or "technical" and not worthy of full managerial involvement. Nothing could be further from the truth. A plan means nothing unless it is actually carried out and it contributes to the accomplishment of the organization's major goals. Thus, in our example, if Max creates a plan but Mary implements poorly—selecting poor quality clothing that Max's customers reject—then Max will not accomplish his goals. Max must ensure that the plan is implemented fully. This requires realistic decision making at each step of the implementation. Hasty decisions not based on facts are often very costly.

## Evaluating the Results of the Plan

Did we get there? Evaluating the results of planning is essential. A well-done assessment of the outcomes that resulted from the plan provides valuable feedback. The company can learn which goals are possible and which may not be, as well as which steps can be implemented easily and which cannot. Evaluation should, in most cases, be relatively easy and straightforward. Remember that goals should include information about how much of what should be accomplished, by when, and what is to be measured. Evaluation means that the information specified in the goal statement is gathered and compared against the results of the plan. For example, one year after introducing women's clothing, Max calculates his profit and realizes that it is 25 percent higher in total dollars than the previous year, even after giving Mary a commission on sales. His evaluation of the plan: "Wow! This is great! Do I really need to carry men's clothing?"

## LEVELS OF PLANNING

**strategic plans**
Plans that are intended to achieve strategic goals.

**tactical plans**
Plans that are designed to achieve tactical goals.

**operational plans**
Plans that are intended to achieve operational goals.

A variety of situations lead to a variety of plans, with differing attributes. One way to study the difference among plans is by looking at the level of the plan as it relates to the goals that it is developed to meet. **Strategic plans** are intended to achieve strategic goals; **tactical plans** achieve tactical goals; and **operational plans** achieve operational goals. As with goals, plans need to be interlocking. Thus, operational plans are needed to achieve operational goals, which are instrumental to the completion of tactical plans. Tactical plans have the same relationship to strategic plans. Thus, in evaluating each lower level plan, it is necessary for managers to ask themselves whether these plans are contributing ultimately to the realization of the firm's strategic goals. It is not uncommon for plans to take on a "life of their own" as functional areas adopt these plans and develop their activities around them. At some point, as the strategic goals change, the strategic, tactical,

## B U S I N E S S   D I L E M M A

*You're the Manager ...What Would You Do?*

THE COMPANY:    Flanagan Corporation

YOUR POSITION:    New Chief Executive Officer

THE PLACE:    Des Plaines, IL

Flanagan Corporation is a national manufacturer of ready-to-eat stews and casseroles. Originally, the business was family-run and operated, but it grew so very quickly that family members sold out their interest over 20 years ago. At that time, the company sought to diversify and purchased a national bakery and a canned vegetable manufacturer. Flanagan's stews now dominate the market with a 75 percent share, and its frozen casseroles are very popular and considered very competitive in the market. The company's reputation is based on using the highest quality ingredients and unique seasonings.

Twenty years ago, Flanagan was organized along two product lines: canned stews and frozen casseroles. Over the past several years, the company has adopted a more "consumer-oriented" organizational approach, developing or acquiring new products that reflect consumers' wants. The company has changed in many ways. It has added new product lines, streamlined operations, and taken more of a regional approach rather than nationwide mass-market advertising.

However, problems have arisen as the company's management was stretched thin trying to manage so many diverse units. Performance and profits declined. Jim Austerland, the chief executive officer, resigned under intense pressure from key employees and some large shareholders. Mark Johnston, with experience from a major competitor, has now taken over as CEO.

Johnston has set tough goals for the company and taken drastic steps to meet them, closing several factories and cutting 150 jobs out of corporate headquarters. He has redefined the company to focus exclusively on stews, frozen entrees, and canned vegetables. The bakery division was sold because its product did not fit in well with Flanagan's more successful product lines. These moves have limited the technologies that Flanagan will have to manage to produce heat-processed and frozen foods.

Under the previous CEO's leadership, each of Flanagan's units was headed by a single executive with total responsibility for it, from developing and marketing new products to manufacturing and logistics. While some managers enjoyed the diversity, others felt stress and strain from maintaining such a broad focus. Johnston has altered the organizational structure to more of a brand management approach, giving managers total responsibility for groups or lines of products. In addition, managers have more stringent goals for production and profitability. As CEO Mark Johnston, you are now implementing this reorientation of the company.

### Questions

1. What assumptions about future consumers' behaviors and attitudes are you making?
2. What role have goals played in your plans since arriving as CEO at Flanagan's?
3. What are some of the negative reactions you might have to face from employees and how would you deal with these?

and operational plans must be altered to accommodate the new strategic goals. Functional areas may hesitate to change their plans because they have invested much time and energy and thus feel a sense of ownership of them.

Because it is important to understand these three levels of plans and how they interrelate, we will discuss them extensively; Chapter 10 will examine how strategic plans are used in strategic management. In this chapter, we will look at the characteristics of tactical and operational plans.

**Comment on Box:** As students discuss the new structure, have them first develop a new mission along with goals and objectives for Flanagan. Also, discuss ways to minimize negative reactions from employees both before and after the changes.

## Tactical Plans

Of the several important characteristics of tactical plans, one is that, whereas strategic plans address general business actions, tactical plans are concerned with specific people, activities, and resources. For example, when an information

To support Whirlpool Corporation's growth strategy of becoming a global home-appliance leader, tactical planning of each functional area of the company—product development, engineering, manufacturing, marketing, sales, distribution, and procurement—focuses on identifying and responding to national and regional differences in consumer demand. From conducting marketing research in Asia, Whirlpool learned that for reasons of status and space, many Asians place their refrigerators in their living rooms. Whirlpool responded by developing compact refrigerators in bright colors, shown here on sale in Bangkok, Thailand.

*Source:* Krapit Phanvut/SIPA.

systems manager decides how many technicians to assign to developing an executive information system, he or she is implementing a tactical plan.

A second characteristic of tactical plans is that they are most commonly associated with the various functional areas of a business. That is, the planning has to do with how the activities and resources of such areas as marketing, operations, finance, R&D, and human resources may be used.

A third characteristic is that tactical plans are normally designed for a relatively shorter time period than are strategic plans. Tactical plans must be successfully completed for strategic plans to be successful. In this sense, tactical plans are stepping stones to strategic plans. If strategic plans are expressed for five-year time periods, then tactical plans must be expressed for shorter time periods so that the strategic time line can be met.

Finally, tactical plans are usually designed and implemented by middle-level managers. As strategic plans guide tactical planning, tactical plans guide operational planning. Middle-level managers are responsible for translating strategic plans into a form so that day-to-day plans can be related to them. They do this translation through tactical plans.

Let's look at tactical planning through the eyes of a hypothetical medium-sized company, Fayol's Safes, which for over 30 years has made wall safes for banks and other businesses. Five years of declining sales have prompted the company president, Henry Fayol, to set the strategic goal that the company should reinvent itself as a manufacturer of security systems, capitalize on its motto, "A Fayol Safe Never Fails," and have 50 percent of its sales from security systems within seven years.

To achieve this goal, the company develops strategic plans that identify potential markets, organizational resources to be developed, how these resources should be used, and what company strengths to emphasize. Once these plans are made, a number of supporting tactical plans are needed to bring Henry's visions to life. The finance department's planning is concerned with how the company may acquire capital to finance the venture. For instance, Henry's financial wizards must develop plans that address whether the company should pursue equity or debt financing.

The folks down in the marketing department are faced with the task of developing plans to sell a new product. Fayol's Safes were sold traditionally by word of mouth and a small sales staff. However, the security business appears to be much more competitive and seems to require a more aggressive marketing approach.

Because the technologies involved in safes and security systems are only marginally similar, the employees of the production department have their work cut out for them. Henry has decreed that since Fayol's reputation rested traditionally on its quality products, the company should keep the manufacturing of the security systems in-house. The department must, therefore, plan for entirely different production processes and contact different suppliers to fulfill materials requirements.

Thus, the number and scope of the plans supporting the strategic plans can be immense. The more radical the alterations in the organization's strategic plans, the greater is the resulting change in its tactical plans. The inability of management to create and implement corresponding changes in tactical plans may result in "Fayolure" for the entire strategy.

## Operational Plans

In operational plans, ultimately, "the pedal meets the metal." These are plans that serve to implement the tactical plans and which identify the basic footprints that the organization must follow at its service, delivery, or production levels. Operational plans may be classified by how many times they are used. A common way of categorizing such plans is by whether they are single-use or standing.

**Single-Use Plans.** As the name suggests, **single-use plans** are used one time and then discarded. The time frame for such a plan may be from no more than a few days or weeks to as long as several years, as is the custom in the aerospace industry.

Common types of single-use plans include programs, projects, and budgets. A **program** is normally an intermediate type of plan (longer than one year and shorter than five years) that encompasses a wide set of activities with a common focus. Boeing's decision to build the 777 was a major program for the company. A **project** is a subdivision of a program. Boeing's single-use projects included the building of the plane's structure and control mechanisms. A **budget** is a plan to allocate resources and expenses for a certain period of time. Such a document can be extremely important for an organization, division, or department. Budgets prioritize the firm's commitment to projects and resources in the international language of business—money. (We'll return to the topic of budgets in Chapter 22.)

**Standing Plans.** While single-use plans are created to deal with unique situations, **standing plans** deal with recurring actions. Standing plans save the firm time and money by acting as a standardized decision guide for members of the organization. By using standing plans, firm members do not have to "reinvent the wheel" when faced with common situations. Standing plans also promote fairness and equity within the organization.

Standing plans may be divided into policies, rules, and procedures. To illustrate, consider Stephanie Line, a hypothetical aspiring buyer, who has been presented by a supplier with two 50-yard-line tickets to see the Atlanta Falcons in the Super Bowl. (Remember this is a hypothetical example.) In order to determine if she can keep the tickets, Line may examine the firm's policy regarding gifts from those outside the company. A **policy** is a broadly stated standing plan that provides general principles or guidelines for making decisions in many situations. Usually, policies are interpreted as giving the manager who is employing the plan (in this case, Line's boss) considerable leeway in applying it. Therefore, Line's boss may

**single-use plans**
Plans that are used once and then discarded.

**program**
An intermediate plan that encompasses a wide set of activities with a common focus.

**project**
A subdivision of a program.

**budget**
A plan to allocate resources and expenses for a certain period of time.

**standing plans**
Those plans that deal with recurring, as opposed to unique, situations.

**policy**
A broadly stated standing plan that provides general principles or guidelines for making decisions in many situations.

| TABLE 9.1 |
| --- |

### Examples of Policies, Rules, and Procedures

*Policies*

Upholstery materials should be of strong enough construction to handle the wear and tear of heavy use. Tightly woven, flatly constructed nylons are preferred, but there are places, such as the cafeteria or labs, where vinyls perform best. Executive offices will have a richer appeal with wools or wool and nylon blends. "COM" fabrics may be used, provided the total list price including fabrics does not exceed the standard price list.

*Rules*

The use of the company golf course is governed by the following rules:
1. All players must sign register and pay fees in the Pro Shop before starting play.
2. Each player must have a minimum of seven clubs and a golf bag.
3. Driving range balls are prohibited on the golf course.
4. Fivesomes or more are prohibited. Singles have no standing on the golf course.
5. Attire
   Ladies: Abbreviated forms of attire are not allowed.
   Men:    Abbreviated forms of attire are not allowed; shirts with sleeves are required.

*Procedures*

Supplier representatives often contact individual departments as well as the Procurement Office. Should a representative, in contacting a department, suggest a demonstration of a particular good or service, the department should notify the Procurement Office since, in most instances, that good or service would be of interest to more than one department. The Procurement Office will:
1. Evaluate the need, if any, for the demonstration.
2. Establish a mutually beneficial time and, if the demonstration is to be held on-campus, place. Should the demonstration be held off-campus, the supplier will be responsible for acquiring the necessary space.
3. The supplier will be responsible for notifying departments of the time, place, and nature of the demonstration. All solicitation conducted for the purpose of generating sales should be by appointment.
4. Coordinate the demonstration with all concerned departments.

decide that, although the company's policy permits "small" gifts to employees, it did not envision that the employee should be allowed to accept valuable items such as Super Bowl tickets.

Stephanie Line's situation may not be covered by a policy, but rather by a **rule**, a specific plan that either condones or prohibits certain kinds of behavior. Therefore, a rule prohibiting all gifts over $10 would bar an employee from accepting Super Bowl tickets. Instead she could keep, for example, a coffee mug with the supplier's logo. Organizations have policies and rules that cover a wide range of activities and stakeholders.

**Procedures** are step-by-step descriptions that detail the action that firms or individuals undertake to carry out standing plans. Companies have numerous procedures covering all areas of the business such as personnel, payroll, manufacturing, and worker safety. Table 9.1 gives some examples of common policies, rules, and procedures utilized by businesses.

**rule**
A specific plan that either condones or prohibits certain kinds of behavior.

**procedures**
Step-by-step descriptions that detail the action that firms or individuals undertake to carry out standing plans.

# EFFECTIVE PLANNING

Certain approaches to planning can improve the chances that it will be successful. One of the major reasons why planning fails is that goals, plans, and actions are not constructively communicated. Sufficient information about all levels of planning—strategic, tactical, and operational—should be conveyed to organizational members. Many firms are establishing active communication programs and using technologies such as electronic mail (discussed in Chapter 21) to disclose more effectively the rationale behind the firm's plans.

It would be ideal if managers had stable environments in which to develop plans and implement them. But as we know, the environment sometimes changes between development and implementation. Assumptions on which plans are based change, and then the plan must be discarded or changed dramatically, often with little time for thought. Such issues can often be avoided by the development of **contingency plans**, which are alternate courses of action to be undertaken if certain organizational or environmental conditions change. For example, during the late 1970s and early 1980s, when interest rates were volatile and unpredictable, many large organizations developed alternative plans for growth, depending on the cost of borrowing money. Many organizations felt that they must know how to react quickly to a number of different cost scenarios. The best way of doing this was to develop several plans, each based on a different set of assumptions about interest rates and the difficulty of obtaining capital. Organizations that create contingency plans hopefully can react quicker and with greater thought than those that lack such plans.

Traditionally, planning was reserved for a few managers. Recently, however, it has been emphasized as appropriate for groups of managers and subordinates. One reason is that subordinates frequently have more technical knowledge about actual work steps, and are thus in a better position to evaluate the feasibility of alternative plans, saving time and cutting costs. Second, better planning frequently occurs when the managers and workers who will actually implement the plans are included in the process. This interaction permits consideration of more points of view and increases the likelihood of considering all valuable information. It also often increases the participants' understanding of the plan. They know why the plan has been designed and understand what is expected of them.

**Critical Thinking Challenge:** Relate the material on contingency plans to Chapter 2 and the contingency school of management. Have students hypothesize reasons why contingency plans are necessary.

**contingency plans**
Alternate courses of action to be undertaken if certain organizational or environmental conditions change.

# MANAGEMENT BY OBJECTIVES AND PLANNING

**Management by objectives (MBO)** is a management philosophy and systematic process through which managers of all levels communicate with subordinates in terms of goals and how specific activities of the subordinates can contribute to reaching these goals. MBO is based on the assumption that employees at all levels of the organization must be involved in goal setting and development and implementation of plans in order for the organization to most effectively conduct its business. It is generally thought that General Motors was the first organization to implement this philosophy. It was first fully described by management expert Peter Drucker.[11] According to the philosophy, MBO can be used to link together the three levels of plans we have discussed—strategic, tactical, and operational.

**management by objectives (MBO)**
A management philosophy and systematic process through which managers of all levels communicate with subordinates in terms of goals and how specific activities of the subordinates can contribute to reaching these goals.

## FIGURE 9.4

**Steps in Management by Objectives**

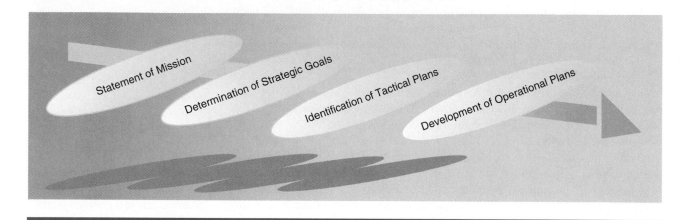

Statement of Mission

Determination of Strategic Goals

Identification of Tactical Plans

Development of Operational Plans

## Steps in the MBO Process

**Critical Thinking Challenge:** Ask students to assume the role of a vice president of PepsiCo in charge of Taco Bell. The goal for the fast-food chain is to continue intense promotional activities highlighting budget menu items. The organization is also concerned with cost-cutting and efficiency measures to lower food costs. Set objectives for all departments using MBO.

We will follow the steps shown in Figure 9.4 to illustrate the linking of the various levels of planning and the involvement of employees at all levels of the organization. Although there are several ways of structuring organizations, for the sake of this discussion, assume that we are discussing MBO in an organization with departments grouped according to function, such as production, research and development, marketing, and finance.

As we discussed previously, effective planning is based on the organizational mission. Logically, the mission must be the start of any organizationwide planning effort like MBO.

Strategic goals—the long-term objectives that the organization would like to achieve—are developed primarily through discussion and interaction among top executives who rely on information supplied by their immediate subordinates. All functional areas of an organization are usually represented in strategic planning to facilitate coordination and to benefit from the specialized knowledge of each area. Strategic goals established at this level become the foundation for the other parts of MBO.

The next step is to link the strategic goals to the planning of the administrative units that make up the organization. The head of each functional area, together with key staff, participated in the strategic planning and goal setting of the previous step. These individuals then meet with the next lower level of management in its functional area to transmit the strategic plans and goals and to use these as the framework within which all planning for the functional areas should be built. Thus, the strategic goals of the organization become the base for plans made by these managers. The purpose of planning is to develop tactical plans and goals that will allow the functional area to reach objectives necessary to fulfill the strategic plans and goals. This process is repeated at each lower level of management in the functional area. In other words, middle-level managers are identifying tactical goals and developing tactical plans that are linked to the strategic goals.

As the process continues to move down the organization, more individuals and those at lower levels of the organization become involved. In each case, the format for planning is the same. The goals and actions of the next highest level become the starting point for the planning of the present level. The purpose of planning is to anticipate and implement those actions that will allow the planning unit to achieve goals that will enable the next higher level to reach its broader goals. As you know, operational plans and goals are those that are specific to day-to-day work activities at the lower levels of the organization. As MBO reaches the final levels of the company, operational plans are, therefore, developed and closely linked with other plans.

## Effectiveness of MBO

Over the 40 years since its formal introduction, MBO has risen and fallen in use and popularity. There is much evidence of its effectiveness in terms of improving organizational performance. However, it is also a time-consuming process and its outcomes can be affected by future events. For example, a building construction firm may plan to develop a resort on Florida's Gulf Coast. However, if the national economy becomes substantially weaker or a major environmental issue such as pollution arises after planning has taken place, it may be difficult to revise the existing framework of plans. Even in cases in which major changes do not occur, common changes in the industry or the immediate business environment of the firm can affect MBO plans. Such events might include the entrance of new competitors, changes in consumer tastes, or the passage of local or state laws affecting the business. An additional issue in MBO is the heavy reliance on measurable results as an indication of reaching goals as well as the strict time frames that are developed because of the need to mesh activities with those of other units. Occasionally, this emphasis can lead to an inflexible approach to planning and business operations, which has detrimental effects in terms of adapting to necessary change.

## PUTTING PLANNING INTO PERSPECTIVE

There is an old saying among managers (or maybe it is a saying among old managers) that goes, "Failure to plan is planning to fail." What this means is that unless managers have a clear idea of their goals and have specified the means, resources, and activities that will be used to reach these goals, the chances of maintaining or improving performance are reduced.

The planning process should link all activities in the organization. That is, the work done in areas such as marketing, production, research, and human resources may be ineffective if it is not linked to the organization's plans, because it will probably not move the organization any closer to its goals. This linking of all activities becomes increasingly important as the company faces increasing competition. In highly competitive industries, every activity that does not directly relate to the organization's plans can increase the costs of business and lower the organization's competitive position.

We have discussed the steps in the general process of planning and described in detail planning at two levels, tactical and operational. In the next chapter we address strategic planning and strategic management. We will devote a whole chapter to these topics because of their complexity and importance to management actions.

**Critical Thinking Challenge:** Have students follow the strategic planning steps and develop a plan for their future including a mission, goals, objectives, contingency plans, implementation steps, and evaluation measures.

### Defining Your Interests

Before you can begin to plan your career, you should have a good idea about your own interests. Knowing about yourself is a logical prerequisite for planning your future and setting your career and personal goals. One method of finding out information about your occupational interests is to complete questionnaires that have been developed especially for this purpose and then have your answers interpreted for you by trained counselors. Most universities and colleges have counseling and testing centers at which students can complete these instruments and talk with trained personnel about their interests.

One of the most often used of such questionnaires is the *Strong Interest Inventory,* which contains 325 items requiring that the person respond by indicating either "Like," "Indifferent," or "Dislike." These 325 items ask about the following:

1. Occupations—131 occupations such as dentist, college professor, and stockbroker.

2. School subjects—36 items such as algebra, sociology, and public speaking.

3. Activities—51 items such as repairing electrical wiring, making statistical charts, and interviewing clients.

4. Leisure activities—39 items such as poker, symphony concerts, and preparing dinner for guests.

5. Types of people—24 items such as highway construction workers, high school students, and athletic people.

6. Preference between two activities—30 items such as having a few close friends versus having many acquaintances.

7. Your characteristics—14 items such as, "Usually start activities in my group," and "Can write a concise, well-organized report."

Scoring involves statistical analyses in which your answers are compared to the answer profiles of 48,238 people in 202 different occupations. Your counselor will then show you how your profile compares to others and tell you in which occupational groups your interests fit. The *Strong* has been used for over 50 years, and there is evidence that scores are related to satisfaction with occupational choice, tenure in occupation, and several other career outcomes.

Each respondent receives three types of scores. The first concerns general occupational themes and assumes that both individuals and occupations can be described as some combination of realistic, investigative, artistic, social, enterprising, or conventional. In general, the respondent's orientation is matched with occupations characterized by that orientation. The second scoring is on 23 basic interest scales—general occupational categories such as agriculture, mechanical activities, medical service, writing, merchandising, and business management. Each basic interest scale is illustrated by specific occupations that score high and low on that scale. The third scoring is of specific occupations, such as architect, athletic trainer, carpenter, credit manager, interior decorator, marketing executive, and psychologist. Usually, respondents find that they have interests similar to small groups of occupations.

*Source:* Jo-Ida C. Hansen and David P. Campbell, *Manual for the Strong Interest Inventory* (Palo Alto, CA: Consulting Psychologists Press, 1985).

## SUMMARY AND REVIEW

- **Discuss the benefits that planning can bring to an organization.** Planning can motivate employees to focus on the organization's present status and environment. It also provides a set of activities that coordinate the tasks of the various individuals and units. Finally, planning can help to create an environment conducive to motivating managers and employees. This can occur through the nature of the goals that are set and the process of participation in developing plans.

- **List the steps in planning.** The first step in planning is identifying the organization's mission. The second step is assessing the present status of the organization relative to its mission. Third is establishing specific goals. Fourth is evaluating how the organization is doing relative to its goals. Fifth is identifying the assumptions that must be made in planning, such as whether the environment will be stable or highly changeable. Sixth is developing the plan itself. The final two steps are implementing the plan and evaluating how well it achieved the goals for which it was intended.

- **Describe the nature of an organization's mission and goals and how they influence planning.** An organization's mission defines its fundamental purpose—what it values and how it wishes to conduct itself. An organization's goals are statements of what the firm wishes to accomplish in the future. The goals of an organization should reflect and correspond to the mission of the organization. A firm's plans should be made to attain its mission and goals.

- **Recognize and evaluate the various types of goals that an organization tries to meet.** Strategic goals are set by top managers and address the general activities of the organization for long periods of time. Tactical goals are the intermediate goals of the firm and are designed to carry out the strategic plans. Operational goals are the most specific and deal with daily activities. These are determined by lower-level managers and are used to carry out the tactical plans.

- **Determine the various levels of plans that organizations develop and explain how these are related.** There are three main levels of plans. Strategic plans focus on reaching the general, long-term strategic goals of the organization and usually address the organization's relationship to its environment. Tactical plans describe how the strategic plans may be implemented and are developed for each part of the organization. Operational plans are specific descriptions of actions that must be taken by a work group to carry out the tactical plans. The three levels of plans all address the same topics and are all related to attaining the organization's strategic goals. The strategic plans are the most general statements of actions, and the operational plans are the most specific.

- **Formulate actions that managers can take to improve the effectiveness of planning.** Of the several actions that can be taken to facilitate planning, one is to communicate goals and plans to all members of the organization so that they have an accurate idea of what the organization is attempting to accomplish. Second is to develop contingency plans, alternatives to the original plan that allow the organization to continue to function effectively in the face of change. Finally, involving many employees in planning is effective in achieving involvement throughout the organization.

- **Describe management by objectives and explain how it can be used to coordinate planning within the organization.** Management by objectives (MBO) is a management philosophy and systematic process through which managers at all levels communicate with subordinates in terms of goals and how specific activities of the subordinates can contribute to reaching these goals. It decentralizes goal setting and planning throughout the organization. This systematic process of planning maximizes communication about goals and the interaction of strategic, tactical, and operational goals.

- **Evaluate the goals and plans of a business.** Based on the materials presented in this chapter, you should be able to evaluate the planning and goal-setting efforts of the hypothetical company described in the "Business Dilemma" box.

## Key Terms and Concepts

| | | |
|---|---|---|
| plan *244* | strategic plans *258* | standing plans *261* |
| mission *247* | tactical plans *258* | policy *261* |
| mission statement *247* | operational plans *258* | rule *262* |
| goal *250* | single-use plans *261* | procedures *262* |
| strategic goals *251* | program *261* | contingency plans *263* |
| tactical goals *251* | project *261* | management by objectives (MBO) *263* |
| operational goals *253* | budget *261* | |

## Ready Recall

1. What is planning and how does it relate to an organization's mission?
2. Why is planning necessary for the organization?
3. What are the benefits of planning to the organization?
4. What are the various types of goals that an organization may have and how are they related?
5. Which groups of managers are responsible for strategic, tactical, and operational plans?
6. How might an organization or a manager evaluate a plan to determine if it has been effective?
7. Discuss the difference between single-use plans and standing plans.

8. What are some of the difficulties in planning in organizations?
9. How can an organization increase the successful implementation of its plans?

10. What is management by objectives (MBO) and how is it related to organizational planning?

## Expand Your Experience

1. Obtain copies of the mission statements of three different organizations in the same business or industry. Compare these statements in terms of what is important to the organization, how customers are addressed, and how employees are to be treated. Do you see any relationship between the mission statements and your opinion of these organizations?
2. Interview two managers about planning. Ask first if they do formal planning. If so, determine what steps they use to plan. Analyze this planning in terms of the steps described in this text. How do the two differ? If formal planning is not carried out, find out how future activities are anticipated. What are the risks of not having planning in this case?
3. Find the strategic plan of your college or university. Identify the strategic goals mentioned in this document. Discuss tactical plans that academic departments might develop to reach these goals. Also discuss operational goals and plans of faculty that may be useful in achieving tactical goals.

## CASE

# *Miramax Films and Disney:  Truth or Dare?*

The secret.

In 1992, moviegoers all over the United States were talking about the shocking twist of *The Crying Game.* In one memorable scene, the film's hero discovers the secret of his hairdresser girlfriend—she is a he. Coaxing critics and audience members not to reveal this, Miramax Film Corporation milked this startling plot twist to make it the most widely known secret in American movie history. And that cinematic payoff led to another type of payoff. With a domestic box office take of over $60 million, *The Crying Game* was the most profitable independent film venture ever. Miramax has long championed such controversial and erotic films as the nearly X-rated *Scandal* and *sex, lies, and videotape.* So the Walt Disney Company's acquisition in 1993 of Miramax Company raised a lot of eyebrows. Miramax and Disney? To many observers this makes about as much sense as putting Minnie Mouse in a Madonna video. (Miramax distributed Madonna's tell-all documentary, *Truth or Dare.*)

The marriage of this unlikely couple is raising a lot of questions in the film industry. Despite the fact that Disney has ventured into more adult entertainment in recent years, Miramax is light years ahead in dealing with mature themes. Even the most adult of Disney's movies look, well…Mickey Mouse, when compared to the films Miramax has distributed.

The contrast between the two companies is just as vivid when comparing their corporate structures and planning styles. Miramax is essentially a small family business whose owners make nearly all the decisions. And despite its preoccupation with mice, Disney is a behemoth with a massive organization containing a multitude of people and levels involved in planning and decision making.

The union of two such different companies raises several questions. Can scrappy Miramax continue its success under the control of its new owner? Will it be able to merge its own unique culture and planning styles with Disney? Will Disney ever build a theme park ride based on the Miramax hit, *Tie Me Up! Tie Me Down!*?

**Enchanted Miramax.**    Miramax is the brainchild of two brothers, Robert and Harvey Weinstein. Reportedly they got hooked on foreign films when, as teenagers, they went to see the French art classic, *The 400 Blows,* thinking that it was a porno flick; they left with a newfound appreciation for the cinema. This appreciation grew more focused as the brothers entered the entertainment business. In 1972, Harvey and a college friend (later joined by Bob) skipped their final exams, quit college, and soon began promoting concerts and opened a movie theater. In 1979, the brothers formed Miramax to distribute concert films. Their first big hit was a Monty Python project, *The Secret Policeman's Other Ball*, with a gross of over $6 million.

Flush with success and funds, the brothers decided to get into films in a much more direct way. They poured $2 million into the movie *Scandal.* The Weinsteins showed their marketing daring when, because of its sexually explicit material, the film was threatened with an "X" rating. The offensive scenes were ultimately toned down, but not before the Weinsteins made sure that the controversy received international press attention. When the film was released in video, the Weinsteins made certain that two versions were offered:  rated and unrated.

*Scandal* was followed by other remarkable films including *sex, lies, and videotape* and *My Left Foot* in 1989, *Cinema Paradiso* in 1990, and *The Grifters* in 1991. Each of these is considered a small film by Hollywood standards, with an average budget of $3 to $5 million compared with the industry average of four times that. Because of their relatively low costs, such films do not have to be blockbusters to make significant profits for the company. For instance, the Weinsteins spent only $1.1 million on *sex, lies, and videotape,* a film that eventually earned nearly $25 million. Their releases of both foreign and art films have earned 5 Academy Awards and 26 nominations.

**Disney and Miramax: Walking the Thin Blue Line.**
Disney's acquisition of Miramax is another step in its progression from Goofy to more adult-oriented films. In the last decade, Disney has created two production studios, Touchstone and Hollywood Pictures, to create and distribute films with mature attitudes and outlooks. In fact, the movie *Pretty Woman,* a Touchstone production about a prostitute, was the most popular film ever produced by Disney. Yet Touchstone and Hollywood Pictures, despite producing films with vivid language, are still very much Disney operations. Extensive planning was and still is a key part of the Disney mentality, and Disney executives are very much involved in all aspects of production. Tight planning has resulted in significant savings on cost, which has become a Disney trademark.

With the ascent of Michael Eisner as CEO in the early 1980s, all parts of the Disney company are seen as contributing to all other divisions. For example, when an animated cartoon is created, its characters are used as the basis for theme park rides and merchandising. Disney was one of the first of the major film studios to release its feature-length films in video format with relatively cheap prices. Children buying the video tend to buy character-inspired merchandise.

The acquisition has many people speculating on which of Miramax's attributes Disney wishes to capitalize. Miramax's main strength can be stated as its ability to market small films effectively, while it has shown little talent in creating its own. Furthermore, Miramax is thought of as a two-man show, and the Weinsteins have been described as abrasive and tough. Their flamboyant style lies in stark contrast to the conservatism of Disney. The gap between the entities is even more profound when you look at their operations. The Weinsteins operate Miramax as a personal kingdom. Planning tends to be approached informally and more from the short run as opposed to the long term. Decisions are more often based on the brothers' personal hunches and are generally not derived systematically.

On the other hand, Disney clearly wants the prestige of owning an entity such as Miramax. Under the terms of the contract, the Weinsteins will remain in control of Miramax, at least in the short run. But the question remains whether Disney will continue its hands-off policy and let Miramax be Miramax.

So how will it end? Will Miramax lose its independent streak? Will Disney force Miramax to adopt its management values, which favor more formalized planning? Will this merging of corporate cultures neuter Miramax's core competence? Will the *Miramax and Disney Story* get two thumbs up or two thumbs down? Check your local theater for listings.

*Sources:* Harry Berkowitz, "Harvey and Bob Weinstein Are Two Guys From the Queens; Is Disney Ready for Them? Miramax Films," *Newsday,* May 9, 1993, 80; Terry Pristin and James Bates, "The Climbing Game; Miramax Film Corp. Is Atop the Hollywood Heap, Thanks to 'The Crying Game.' The Brothers Who Run the Firm Are Legendary for Brilliant Promotion and Hardball—Some Say Ruthless—Tactics," *The Los Angeles Times,* March 29, 1993, A1; and Ronald Grover, "Crying All the Way to the Oscars," *Business Week,* March 15, 1993, 38.

## Questions

1. Discuss the strengths and limitations of Miramax's planning for the market it is in.
2. Discuss the strengths and limitations of Disney's planning for the markets it is in.
3. Do you think Miramax can be successfully operated using Disney's detailed planning? Why or why not?

## STRENGTHEN YOUR SKILLS
### *Setting Goals*

The December 6, 1993, issue of *Business Week* reported:

> [*Stephen R. Covey's*] Seven Habits of Highly Effective People, *still on* The New York Times *best-seller list after 144 weeks, has become a catechism of leadership, selling 3.5 million copies through 31 printings. ...Covey's seven precepts for success...urge followers to be proactive, establish clear-cut goals, think positively, and act ethically.*[12]

This exercise will elaborate on "establish clear-cut goals," mentioned in the quotation above. You learned by reading Chapter 9 the components a correctly stated goal will contain:

- attribute sought
- target
- index
- time frame.

Here again is the business example provided in the chapter to illustrate the four components:

*Maximize profitability (attribute sought) with a 7 percent increase (the target) in return on equity (the index) by the end of the fiscal year (the time frame).*

This exercise will help you apply these same principles to establish clear-cut goals for yourself, to help you start (or continue) practicing this habit of "highly effective people."

Here are two personal goals stated using the four components mentioned above.

*I will increase my physical fitness (attribute sought) by reducing my weight (the index) by 10 pounds (the target) by April 30 (time frame).*

*I will increase my savings account (attribute sought) by depositing 20 percent (the target) of my net paycheck (the index) into the bank beginning this Friday for the next eight weeks (time frame) so I'll have enough money to pay for my auto insurance when it comes due.*

You learned in the chapter that business-related types of goals are strategic, tactical, and operational. To help you in writing your personal goals in this exercise, here are some personal goal types: academic, career, family, financial, physical, social, and spiritual. A well-balanced person tries to have goals representing each of these categories.

**Instructions:**

1. In the space below write out four goals that are important for you to achieve during the remainder of this semester.

2. Some of the goals should be short term (maybe something you need to finish by the end of this week); others should have a longer time frame (maybe by the end of the semester).

3. Work to write your goal statement so you can check all four boxes (attribute sought, target, index, and time frame) as represented in your statement.

4. Your four goals should represent several different goal types (for example, academic, career, spiritual, family, financial, social, or physical goals).

5. After successfully achieving each goal, write the date in the FOLLOW-UP box next to the goal.

---

**Goal:**

| **FOLLOW-UP** |
| :---: |
| (when you've achieved this goal, write the date here) |

✔ **if statement contains:**    **Attribute Sought** ☐    **Target** ☐    **Index** ☐    **Time Frame** ☐

---

**Goal:**

| **FOLLOW-UP** |
| :---: |
| (when you've achieved this goal, write the date here) |

✔ **if statement contains:**    **Attribute Sought** ☐    **Target** ☐    **Index** ☐    **Time Frame** ☐

Goal:

**FOLLOW-UP**

(when you've achieved this goal,
write the date here)

✔ if statement contains:    **Attribute Sought** ❑    **Target** ❑    **Index** ❑    **Time Frame** ❑

---

Goal:

**FOLLOW-UP**

(when you've achieved this goal,
write the date here)

✔ if statement contains:    **Attribute Sought** ❑    **Target** ❑    **Index** ❑    **Time Frame** ❑

# Strategic

# Management

## Outline

## After reading this chapter, you will be able to:

- Define strategic management and strategy.
- Describe the steps involved in strategic management.
- Relate strategic management to the business environment.
- Differentiate among the major corporate strategies and tools that managers use to develop and implement strategies.
- Analyze several common business-level strategies.
- Evaluate the importance of strategy implementation.
- Assess a business's strategy and recommend alternative strategies.

## Strategy Guides PepsiCo Beyond the Cola Wars

When you mention PepsiCo, many people automatically think of the company that competes against Coca-Cola in the "cola wars." Although both companies do compete in the soft drink industry, as the world's number 1 and 2 competitors, PepsiCo's strategy for running its business is decidedly different from Coca-Cola's. Coca-Cola focuses primarily on the beverage industry in both domestic and international markets whereas PepsiCo views its market as the entire food and beverage industry. Besides its Pepsi-Cola beverage products, it also competes in the snack-food business as a result of a merger with Frito-Lay (1965), and in the restaurant and fast-food industries with the acquisitions of Pizza Hut (1977), Taco Bell (1978), and KFC (1986). Acquiring these companies gave PepsiCo not only an outlet for its beverage products, but also new markets for expansion,

expansion that has resulted in gains in market shares in both domestic and international markets. Currently, beverages make up about 35 percent of Pepsi's net sales, while the restaurants and snack foods contribute 37 percent and 28 percent, respectively, to total net sales.

To better compete in the international marketplace, Wayne Calloway, PepsiCo's CEO since 1986, has aggressively entered foreign markets and foreign agreements. In Poland, Calloway announced that PepsiCo will invest $500 million to satisfy the changing eating and drinking habits of Eastern Europeans. The company is also setting up bottling and processing plants in countries such as Spain, Mexico, and Argentina. An example of this international growth in the restaurant business can be seen by noting where the two largest restaurants are located, in Beijing (KFC) and Moscow (Pizza Hut). To better compete in the international market, Pepsi has developed a new sugar-free drink called Pepsi-Max in

an attempt to lure the growing health-conscious beverage drinkers of Europe who traditionally have been reluctant to purchase low-calorie or diet beverages.

Calloway is also changing the way PepsiCo operates in the domestic market. The fast-food outlets can now be seen on many street corners, competing against all types of restaurants. The snack foods have been aggressively competing for shelf space and have recaptured lost shelf space and market share. Even though the company is expanding, Calloway stresses that customers and product quality are still the primary concerns for PepsiCo.

PepsiCo's strategy for operating in different industries, like beverage and food, seems to be paying off. The company has experienced increased growth in sales from about $11 billion in 1987 to an estimated $25 billion for 1993, and net profits seem to be following: from $605 million in 1987 to an estimated $1.6 billion in 1993. So, the next time you think of PepsiCo, don't just think of the company that makes Pepsi.

*Sources:* Amy Barrett, "Indigestion at Taco Bell," *Business Week*, December 14, 1992, 66–67; Amy Barrett, "Pizza Hut? Aisle 5," *Business Week*, June 7, 1993, 82–83; Gary Hoover, *Hoover's Handbook of American Business 1994* (Austin, TX, The Reference Press, 1993); Seth Lubove, "Pepsi's New Strategy," *Forbes*, September 13, 1993, 216–224; and Patricia Sellers, "Eurofizz," *Fortune*, March 22, 1993, 15.

*introduction*

As the Pepsi vignette illustrates, strategy can play a major role in the success or failure of a business. You will remember from the previous chapter that a firm's top management sets strategic long-term goals that address such general topics as the firm's growth, new markets, or new goods and services. The firm's strategic plans determine what is needed to achieve its strategic goals. How a company carries out its strategic plans is the focus of strategic management.

In this chapter, we will define strategic management and strategy, and then look at the strategic planning process in the context of strategic management. Next, we will look at several levels of strategy—societal, corporate, business level, and functional. Then we take a more detailed look at corporate-level and business-level strategies. Finally, we discuss the implementation of strategy and some pros and cons of strategic management.

## STRATEGIC MANAGEMENT

**strategic management**

All the processes an organization undertakes to develop and implement its strategic plan.

**strategy**

A course of action for implementing strategic plans and achieving strategic goals; a general statement of actions an organization intends to take or is taking that is based on the fit of the organization with its external environment.

We can view strategic planning as determining how to fulfill the organization's mission and maintain its long-term growth and health. **Strategic management** is a more encompassing term that refers to all the processes an organization undertakes to develop and implement its strategic plan. These processes are the management activities of planning, organizing, leading, and controlling, which are necessary to achieve the strategic goals and carry out the strategic plan.[1]

Central to strategic planning and strategic management is the development of a **strategy**, a course of action for implementing strategic plans and achieving strategic goals. A strategy is a general statement of actions an organization intends to take or is taking that is based on the fit of the organization with its external environment. Goals are the specific end results the firm strives for, while strategies are the means through which these goals can be attained. The creation of a firm's strategy is an entrepreneurial activity that builds from the organization's mission and goals and responds to a rapidly changing business environment. Management expert Henry Mintzberg maintains that the strategic-planning and strategy-making processes should remain somewhat intuitive in the hands of top-level managers, not deferred to overly pragmatic or structured organizational planners.[2]

The purpose of a strategy is to take advantage of what the organization does well, or hopes to do well, which will have a benefit in the external environment.[3] The Gap, for example, employs numerous suppliers of high-quality, moderate-cost clothing items. It also provides a set of retail outlets situated in high-traffic areas that cater to a relatively youthful market. The Gap's growth strategy has been achieved by steadily increasing both its access to good suppliers and its number of stores nationwide.[4]

**Example:** Avon is an effective marketer of cosmetics and gifts through a catalog. When women entered the work force and were not home to buy door-to-door cosmetics, Avon representatives began taking the catalogs to offices. Avon also offers a mail-order service for ordering its products.

Strategies are the vital link as firms move from formulating to implementing, from thought to action. They provide the focus needed so that the firm's mission and goals can ultimately be translated into tactical and operational plans that work and make sense. Elizabeth Arden's strategy of offering a unique product at a premium price reflects its goal of being a leader in the prestige cosmetics market. This strategy was also the base for formulating and implementing the proper operational plans, in this case, to revamp packaging and promotions, emphasizing the needs of aging baby boomers. As a result, Elizabeth Arden is the fastest growing prestige cosmetic company in the United States.[5]

Trend analysis and consumer research help Rubbermaid expand by identifying consumer needs and opportunities for new product development. In 1993, Rubbermaid opened the Everything Rubbermaid laboratory store, the company's newest consumer research vehicle. Displaying 2,500 products, the store provides a laboratory setting for measuring customer reactions to everything from product price to color choices. Shown here in the store are Dr. William Hauser, manager of research services for the Home Products Div., and Ludwig Huck, vice president of new ventures for Rubbermaid Sales Corp.

*Source:* © 1993 Rubbermaid Inc., Wooster, Ohio. Used with permission.

To be complete, a strategy must have four components:  scope, resource deployment, synergy, and distinctive competence.

## Scope

Scope refers to the number of markets in which a company intends to compete or the number of products it intends to sell. A firm may have a broad or narrow scope. Compare, for example, Microsoft and WordPerfect, two premier software companies. While WordPerfect has essentially restricted itself to word processing software, Microsoft sells operating systems, as well as many types of application software, such as Word and Excel. Rubbermaid, *Fortune* magazine's most admired company of 1994, is possibly the leader when it comes to a broad scope. It produces over 5,000 products, puts a new product on the market on the average of one a day (365/year), and enters a new product category (for example, kitchen cabinets and garden sheds) every 12 to 18 months.[6]

## Resource Deployment

Organizations may invest their resources in a number of ways. For instance, one may choose to invest the majority of its funds in new manufacturing equipment or improved information systems. In a rapidly changing environment, priorities may have to be shifted and resources redeployed. With the growth of the computer industry and the increasing demand for more low-priced computers, many computer companies are finding it difficult to stay competitive. IBM, for example, finding it difficult to compete effectively at all levels of the computer industry, redeployed assets to the high-growth personal computer sector of the industry.[7]

## Synergy

Synergy refers to the cumulative, enhanced effect of a firm's strategies. The basic idea is that an organization's resources should be linked so that the combined performance of its subunits is greater than if those units were operating alone. Although all firms strive for synergy, many focus on creating synergy as a primary intended benefit of their strategies. The Japanese giant Sony purchased Columbia Pictures, in part, to attempt to create synergy between its consumer electronics division and the entertainment industry. Coca-Cola bought a small wine producer with the idea that it could distribute the wine through the same system through which it distributes soft drinks to grocery stores.[8]

## Distinctive Competence

**distinctive competence**
What a firm does well relative to its competitors.

**Example:** J.C. Penney ⋯lized its success as a moderately p⋯ed retailer of clothes and home fashions. Consequently it repositioned itself to differentiate its store from Sears, its nearest competitor. J.C. Penney is now successfully competing with more expensive department stores due to narrowing of its product lines.

A **distinctive competence** is what a firm does well relative to its competitors. The company focuses on this distinctive competence when developing its strategies. At the same time, however, it should not neglect other areas in which it is weaker relative to its competitors. Witness the plight of Apple Computers. Compared to its DOS-based competitors, Apple's distinctive competence has been its ability to create user-friendly software that is easier for the average computer buyer to use. To a certain extent, Apple focused less on higher-power machines and had a relatively higher cost structure. Enter Microsoft's Windows software, which attempts to replicate the ease of use found in Apple products by using recent advances in technology. Suddenly, Apple's distinctive competence, while not neutralized, is no longer so distinctive.[9]

## THE STRATEGIC MANAGEMENT PROCESS

A typical college student and an organization have at least one thing in common—they both have limited resources. Even the largest corporations have limits on the amount of physical, financial, and human resources they can expend. During the 1980s, for example, General Motors appeared to follow the philosophy that if something was wrong, throw money at it. Yet, even giant GM did not have the cash to postpone its problems indefinitely. The purpose of strategy is to use the organization's resources effectively to accomplish its strategic goals. In essence, strategy is working with what you have to get where you want to be.

The development and implementation of an organization's strategy is its way of effectively focusing its direction. The strategic management process (Figure 10.1) parallels the general planning process discussed in Chapter 9. It entails both formulation activities—which are the major focus of planning—and implementation activities—which carry out the strategy once devised. Strategic management differs from general planning mainly in its careful attention to the external environment and the long-term goals of the firm. In fact, we have defined strategy in terms of the fit or match between an organization's resources and its environment in order to achieve its goals. It should be no surprise, therefore, that the steps in the strategic management process are similar to those discussed previously with regard to general planning.[10]

## Identifying Mission and Goals

The first step in the strategic management process is determining the organization's mission and strategic goals, which we discussed in the last chapter. Remember that these goals are set by top management, address broad issues, and indicate where the company wishes to be in the long-term future.

**FIGURE 10.1**

**The Strategic Management Process**

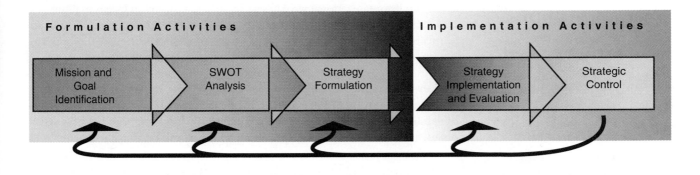

### Analyzing Strengths, Weaknesses, Opportunities, and Threats

From the firm's viewpoint, there are two overriding entities or forces—the organization and its environment. **SWOT analysis** means evaluating the organization's internal strengths and weaknesses and the opportunities and threats associated with the business's external environment. SWOT analysis emphasizes that the fit between a firm and its environment is of paramount importance, and the firm's strategy should be built around this match.

A strength is an ability or attribute that the company possesses which has the potential of giving it a distinctive competence. Potential strengths may rest in the firm's financial capability, its management skills, cost advantages, proprietary knowledge, and/or its marketing approaches, to name a few. Conversely, a weakness is a skill or attribute that the firm lacks or one that it has not developed and at which it performs poorly.

An opportunity is an environmental circumstance that is potentially beneficial for the firm. For example, the increasing proportion of older adults in the U.S. population provides an increasingly large market for organizations that offer health care and recreational services for seniors. A threat, on the other hand, is an environmental factor that could be potentially harmful to the organization. The increasing pressure from the U.S. Surgeon General's Office regarding the link between smoking and cancer, as well as other illnesses, has prompted several tobacco companies to diversify their products rather than rely mainly on one that is continually being attacked.

The quality of a company's SWOT analysis depends on its ability to effectively scan its environment. Environmental scanning is the collection and analysis of important data concerning trends in the environment. Once the firm has collected and analyzed this data, it can then use various quantitative and intuitive forecasting methods to predict future outcomes.[11]

### Strategy Formulation

Once the organization has developed its mission and goals and conducted a SWOT analysis, it can formulate a strategy. The formulation of a firm's overall strategy is done by top management, with input from lower level managers. Organizations formulate

**SWOT analysis**
The evaluation of the organization's internal strengths and weaknesses and the opportunities and threats associated with the business's external environment.

**Teaching Note:** Choose a popular company like McDonald's and divide the blackboard into 4 sections, each section representing one of the elements of SWOT. Have students perform SWOT analysis for the selected company. For example, McDonald's strengths include brand name; reputation for service, quality, value, and cleanliness; and market leadership. Have students continue to complete the list.

**Teaching Note:** Remind students that strengths and weaknesses are internal issues, while opportunities and threats are external issues to an organization. Also, stress that these categories can change as strengths not acted upon can become weaknesses, and missed opportunities can become threats.

their strategy by determining how they will compete at the corporate, business unit, and functional level. By formulating a strategy at all levels of the organization, the firm can improve the odds that the chosen strategy will be successful.

As a rule, a firm will formulate its strategy to capitalize on its greatest strengths and to keep its organizational weaknesses from being exploited by competitors and other factors in the environment. Opportunities and threats are often the same for all firms in an industry, but a successful strategy will better exploit the opportunities and limit the environmental threats than will competitors' less successful strategies. Ford formulated a new strategy that has given it a competitive advantage over other competitors, namely the Japanese auto makers. Ford capitalized on its own strengths in the streamlined manufacturing of mid- to large-sized automobiles and the opportunities in the market (that consumers wanted sedan automobiles at a reasonable cost) to become a world leader in the small-sedan market.[12]

## Implementing and Evaluating the Strategic Plan

Because strategy has to do with the mission and goals of the whole organization, the implementation of strategy must also involve the entire organization. This means that top management must coordinate all parts of the organization in their activities and ensure that all activities are focused on implementing the firm's strategy. Simply put, strategy implementation is the actual process of executing the strategy throughout an organization. This is what we have previously referred to as strategic management. When Sears decided to discontinue its catalog business, J.C. Penney implemented a new strategy in an attempt to fill the gap that Sears created; Penney's strengthened its catalog sales division by enhancing ordering systems, improving distribution centers, and increasing advertisements.[13] The "Going Global" box looks at how Nike implemented a strategy for expanding into international markets.

Evaluation is the same process that we discussed relative to general planning. In this case, it involves comparing the strategic goals with the results of the implementation of strategy. The major difficulty in such a comparison is the time needed to collect data for the comparison. Both strategic goals and strategy address the long-term future, making it impossible to evaluate strategy appropriately for several years. However, no organization can wait that long to determine whether it is benefiting or harming itself. Top managers therefore evaluate strategy by using short-term indicators that can be gathered and are thought to be related to the long-term goals. If the strategic goal of Ralston Purina is to become the dominant company in pet foods, it may examine the relative change in market share and the number of prize-winning poodles that use its products at shows.

## Strategic Control

After the strategy has been formulated and implemented, management needs to ensure that it is being followed. Strategic control is the feedback mechanism in the strategic management process; it compares the firm's actual performance to its intended performance. If the company fails to attain its goals, strategic control allows it to reevaluate the way the strategy was planned, formulated, and implemented. In so doing, the firm may find that a potentially successful strategy was formulated well but implemented poorly. Companies can establish a variety of control systems to analyze their performance, such as stock market valuation, market share fluctuation, or divisional goal attainment. Information used in this process can come from either external or internal sources.[14]

# Going Global

## CAN NIKE JUST DO IT?

Whenever people hear the name Nike, most think of that large U.S. company that sells athletic footwear and uses high-profile stars such as Michael Jordan, Charles Barkley, and John McEnroe in its advertising. The company has become the world's largest footwear producer, growing steadily to $4 billion in sales in 1992, but dropping to about $3.7 billion in fiscal 1994 with sagging U.S. sales.

Manufacturing of Nike footware products is actually carried out in various Asian countries, but most of the technology breakthroughs for which Nike has become famous occurred in its U.S. labs and offices, and two-thirds of all sales are from the United States. At least part of Nike's success can be attributed to a culture that gives individuals some freedom to make decisions and to be creative to come up with new ideas for marketing and product innovations. However, American consumers' tastes are shifting away from high-price footwear, and the recent barrage of advertisements from competitors has eroded Nike's domestic market share. These trends are forcing the giant athletic footwear producer to enter new markets abroad.

Founder and CEO Phil Knight believes that, in the near future, Nike will profit more from international sales than from domestic sales. Nike is therefore pushing for a new global strategy that targets new growth markets such as China, Mexico, Germany, and Japan. To help carry out this globalization strategy, Nike has bought up assorted distribution operations in these countries and is gearing up its advertising campaigns in these markets around the sports played within each. Nike's main concern is finding managers in these markets who have the same kind of creativity and independence that have always made up the company's corporate culture.

Nike distributes products to retailers through its "future system," which requires that retailers decide as much as eight months in advance of delivery the quantity of each shoe style they will want. This enables Nike to order the correct number of products from the Far East manufacturers and to ensure that each retailer gets the ordered products on time. The system creates just enough manufacturing inventory to meet orders. However, this system has created a problem in both Asian and European countries because retailers there are accustomed to having orders filled in weeks, not months, and contend that there is no way they can predict what customers will want eight months hence. The tremendous demand for Nike products has allowed U.S. retailers to live with this inconvenience because they know the shoes will sell if they order them. To overcome foreign resistance to the system, Nike bought various distribution channels in these countries to help reduce the time it takes to complete the "future" process. It also stepped up advertising in other countries to stimulate demand. Finally, it selected and trained foreign managers in the culture of Nike in hopes of duplicating the U.S. success over the last 30 years.

Nike is strategically planning the groundwork needed to be competitive in these markets. Included in this groundwork is the notion of becoming a more global competitor, while still keeping its culture, its "future system" of distribution, and its creativity intact. Nike's encouragement of creative independence has met with some limited success. The company has allowed the managers in various countries to develop products that might appeal to local consumers. In the Japanese market, for instance, managers developed a shoe that fits the smaller Asian foot better than any other product on the market. Still, Japanese sales have not been as strong as hoped. The same is true in Germany and France, where resistance to the "future" system has been strongest. In contrast, sales in Italy, Spain, and Great Britain are up.

Through strategic planning, Nike is becoming a more global force in the athletic footwear industry. The company has developed a plan based on the company's strengths and is attempting to take advantage of the potential opportunities that exist for a global competitor.

*Sources:* Dori Jones Yang, Michael Oneal, Charles Hoots, and Robert Neff, "Can Nike Just Do It?" *Business Week,* April 18, 1994, 86–90; Dori Yang, "Setting Up Shop in China: Three Paths to Success" *Business Week,* October 19, 1987, 74; and "Walking on Air at Nike," *Fortune,* January 1, 1990, 72.

Companies that have not attained their goals use the strategic control process as a means of feedback to help understand deficiencies in all stages in the strategic management process. This encourages a company to reevaluate its mission, goals, SWOT analysis, strategy formulation, and strategy implementation. The information also helps a company make improved decisions concerning all or part of the strategic management process. Even firms that have attained their goals can use the strategic control process as a means for improving their existing strategy. For example, although Intel has been very successful with its microprocessor chips, it continually evaluates its product performance and customer demands to determine how its products are performing relative to competitors'. As a result of this strategic control mechanism, the company has successfully maintained its high market share, with the introduction of the Pentium chip, even in the highly competitive computer industry.[15] Chapter 22 will examine control in greater detail.

## LEVELS OF STRATEGY

Crafting a strategy is essentially a matter of "how." How do we get there from here? How do we turn our mission and goals into action plans? How do we compete with our rivals? How do we allocate our resources? How do we reach our specified performance targets?

While "how" is at the essence of strategy making, a related matter of "who" arises. Who creates an organization's strategies? Many students (and some firms) would argue that it is only top managers who create strategy. This is too narrow a view of the concept of strategy, however. In fact, managers at all levels, not just the top, craft strategy. Because of the changing nature of all organizational environments, all managers face situations not expressly detailed in the company's "rule book." Strategy making is involved when a plant foreman responds to reports that his product output has an unacceptable amount of breakage. A sales manager is crafting strategy when she changes promotional efforts to attract new customers.

Thus, we can discuss strategy at a number of levels: societal, corporate, business, and functional. These are shown in descending order of scope of activities and part of the company addressed in Figure 10.2, which also depicts the overlapping nature of the different levels of strategies as well as which managers are usually associated with the various levels.

### Societal

The societal level of strategy addresses the question, "What does society expect of the organization?" Thus, this level is concerned with both the legal and ethical responsibilities that the community might impose upon the firm. Although all managers are involved in some aspect of societal strategy, it is primarily the domain of top managers. Societal strategy may be seen as the firm's response to a constraint imposed by society. An example of societal strategy has been Philip Morris's decision to limit its cigarette marketing efforts toward teenagers.

### Corporate

**Corporate strategy** is concerned with the enterprise as a whole. The basic question here is "What business or set of businesses should we be in?" Corporate

## FIGURE 10.2

### Levels of Strategic Management

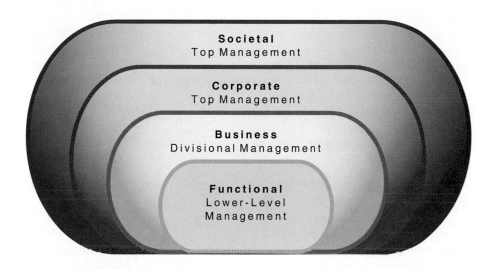

strategy deals chiefly with the scope and resource deployment components of strategy and focuses on determining what appropriate products/markets the firm should pursue. Corporate strategy is handled by top management for the entire organization. Specifically, at this level, firms make decisions about whether to create or acquire new businesses, get rid of existing ones, and establish funding priorities among their entire set of businesses. Philip Morris, for example, is a corporation whose primary business was cigarettes. Several years ago it purchased Kraft Foods in order to diversify its set of businesses and spread its economic risk. We will take a closer look at the topic of corporate strategy in the next main section.

**Example:** Kmart recently unveiled its new strategy, which includes plans to sell majority stakes in three of its four specialty divisions: OfficeMax, Sports Authority, and Borders/Waldenbooks. The strategic move will allow the firm to raise funds to revitalize the discount stores, which have been losing market share to Wal-Mart and Target.

Much of Tootsie Roll Industries' success results from a corporate strategy of making proven candy brands such as Tootsie Rolls and Tootsie Pops. Ellen Gordon, president, her husband, Melvin, CEO, and five top managers formulate corporate and business strategies. Part of the company's growth strategy is selective buying of brands, such as Charms, and Charleston Chew and Sugar Babies from Warner-Lambert. Recently, it opened a marketing and sales office in Hong Kong to tap growth opportunities in the Pacific Rim. *Forbes* magazine named the company one of "The Best Small Companies in America" and listed it on its honor roll of "the best of the best."

*Source:* ©Tootsie Roll Industries, Inc.

## Business

**business-level strategy**
The area of responsibility usually assigned to the divisional-level managers.

**Business-level strategy** is normally the area of responsibility for the divisional-level managers (unless the organization has only one business; in that case, corporate and business-level strategies would be carried out by the same group of managers). By focusing on the synergy and distinctive competencies components, business-level strategy attempts to answer the question, "Given our particular product/market, how do we best compete?" For example, managers of PepsiCo's beverage division began venturing beyond just cola drinks into fruit juices and even Lipton Iced Tea in the 1990s. However, when business fell off for Pepsi and Diet Pepsi, analysts questioned whether too much attention and advertising money had been diverted away from Pepsi's core business.[16] At Philip Morris, both tobacco and food products have their own distinctive business strategies. We will look closer at this topic later in the chapter.

## Functional

Narrowing their scope, organizations must also establish strategies for functional areas such as marketing, operations, research and development, finance, and human resource management—which are unique to a given business. Managers at the functional level will typically develop short-term goals and strategies but their primary purpose is to implement selected aspects of the firm's strategic plan. For instance, Philip Morris's tobacco business has, in recent years, concentrated its marketing efforts on increasing international consumption of cigarettes. For another example, consider that Southwest Airlines has an overall strategy of continued growth into different markets. However, at the functional level, say finance, Southwest is still concerned with a strategy of cost containment that can facilitate the growth process, in keeping with overall corporate strategy.[17]

## Integrating the Levels of Strategy

Each higher strategy level serves as a constraint on the activities of lower levels. Figure 10.2 illustrated how the societal strategy of an organization restricts corporate strategy, which restricts the business strategy, and so on. Thus, managers at the Taco Bell division could not decide, on their own, that they should go into a new business, say the oriental fast-food industry. The firm's corporate-level strategy, established by parent PepsiCo, effectively imposes limits on the business-level managers.

Another way of distinguishing among the levels is by looking at the fraternal twins of business decisions—effectiveness and efficiency. Effectiveness is "doing the right thing," and this is normally pursued at the corporate level and the business level. Efficiency is "doing things right" and tends to predominate activities at the functional level (see Figure 10.3). In the next sections, we will describe details of two of these levels in order to illustrate the information used, the decisions made, and the results of the strategy-making process. Because corporate-level strategy is usually the primary time-consuming focus of top management, our discussion will begin here.

## CORPORATE STRATEGY

Remember that corporate strategy is concerned with the enterprise as a whole. Company names, such as PepsiCo, often do not tell the full story of what products

FIGURE 10.3

**FIGURE 10.3**

**Strategy Levels and Business Decisions**

| Effectiveness: Doing the Right Thing | | Efficiency: Doing Things Right |
|---|---|---|
| Corporate-Level Strategy | Business-Level Strategy | Functional-Level Strategy |

a firm offers. Some may suggest that a more descriptive appellation for this firm may be "PepsiTacoBellKFCPizzaHutFritoLayCo," because it sells much more than just Pepsi. With the three major divisions of soft drinks, restaurants, and snack foods, PepsiCo is an organization with a deft grasp on its corporate strategy. It has identified what businesses it wishes to pursue and has provided an overall direction for them. All three of its divisions are vibrant and growing, each profitable and contributing to the success of the organization as a whole.

## Strategies for Dealing with Multibusiness Organizations

A diversified company (one with many businesses) provides a special challenge for corporate managers. It must develop a strategic plan for several businesses, each facing unique environmental circumstances. Such a company has three major strategic alternatives: diversifying into new businesses (either acquiring existing firms or starting up new ones), engaging in some type of partnership venture with other firms, or divesting itself of businesses it presently holds.[18] Of course, it could simply remain the same, but in our rapidly changing environment, maintaining the status quo could mean falling behind. Companies that do remain essentially the same often try to improve existing operations through organizational change and development activities or increased employee participation (see Chapter 19).

**Diversification.**    **Diversification** is a strategy of acquiring or developing other businesses, which must ultimately be justified by its ability to build stockholder wealth. That is, can the firm do a better job of building wealth for owners by creating a group of synergistically run companies than could an individual investor, with the same money, buying shares on the open market? A company that is contemplating diversification normally does so for one of two reasons: to gain a purely financial advantage through "playing the market" or to achieve synergy among businesses. The first reason reflects the belief that the company can buy and run an existing company, without major changes, better than the previous management group. The second reason reflects the belief that, through synergy, it will save money in certain cost areas for one or both operations. For example, when Kmart acquired OfficeMax as part of its growth strategy, it gained synergy in its operations by having multiple firms in similar industries and was able to use comparable resources, such as transportation and strategies.[19]

The reason behind the strategy decision will determine what type of diversification the company will use. A company that wants to develop synergy among its

**diversification**
A strategy of acquiring other businesses.

An Ocean Spray/Pepsi-Cola joint venture expands market opportunities for both firms. It gives Ocean Spray, the leader in canned and bottled juice drinks in supermarkets, access to Pepsi's million points of distribution serviced by 22,000 field service reps, making Ocean Spray single-serve bottles and cans more widely available in outlets such as convenience stores, drugstores, and vending machines. The alliance is important to Pepsi as a total beverage company, giving it instant entry in the juice drinks market.

*Source:* Courtesy of Ocean Spray Cranberries.

**related diversification**

A firm's acquisition of a business that has some connection with the company's existing businesses.

**unrelated diversification**
The action of diversifying into any business that is potentially profitable for the organization.

**conglomerates**
Firms that pursue unrelated diversification strategies.

**Example:** A joint venture example can be seen in the expansion of Doritos brand snack chips into the British crisps (their word for chips) market. British subsidiary Walkers Smiths Snack Food Ltd. will launch the corn tortilla chips in the United Kingdom with a $9 million advertising campaign. PepsiCo Inc. hopes the redesigned, thinner, flavored chips will be a success in the United Kingdom.

**divestment**
A strategy of selling off businesses that the company no longer wishes to maintain, either because they are failing or because the company has changed its corporate strategy and does not wish to be in those businesses any longer.

various parts will probably use a **related diversification**, acquiring a business that has some connection with the company's existing businesses. This combination of attributes can take a number of forms: similar marketing approaches, technologies, distribution systems, raw-material sources, or production facilities. When FedEx acquired Flying Tigers, for example, it effectively eliminated some of the competition in the industry. More importantly, this strategic move gave FedEx access to the Pacific Rim countries that it otherwise could not have attained.[20]

The rationale behind **unrelated diversification** is to diversify into any business that is potentially profitable for the organization. The acquired business need not be similar in any way to the existing businesses of the firm. Firms that pursue unrelated diversification strategies are normally referred to as **conglomerates.** Westinghouse, for example, is one of America's most prominent conglomerates, with businesses in such diverse areas as electric utility equipment, financial services, broadcasting, and defense systems.

**Joint Ventures.** Joint ventures, as you may remember from Chapter 5, are contractual partnerships with other organizations, in which each partner contributes to the enterprise while retaining a separate identity. A key element of such partnerships is that the partners bring unique skills to the venture, increasing the total value of the proposed endeavor. Joint ventures often provide a means for organizations to get into new markets or businesses that may be unavailable otherwise. KFC (Kentucky Fried Chicken), for example, entered into a joint agreement with Animal Production, a Chinese firm, in part, to gain access to the Chinese restaurant market, which was very difficult to enter at the time. France's Renault and Sweden's Volvo merged in 1994 so that complementary strengths could be utilized: Renault's expertise with small cars in Southern Europe and Volvo's expertise with larger cars in Northern Europe. The merger opened up a new market for the products of each without infringing on the other's primary market.[21]

**Divestment.** **Divestment** is a strategy of selling off businesses that the company no longer wishes to maintain, either because they are failing or because the company has changed its corporate strategy and does not wish to be in those businesses any longer. Among the reasons a company may choose to divest businesses are that the general or competitive environment has changed or that the expected synergy between business units never developed. IBM, for example, desiring to be more competitive in the personal computer industry, divested its Federal Systems division to Loral Industries for a record $1.6 billion.[22]

A strategy closely related to divestment is a **turnaround strategy**, in which the firm attempts to restore economic strength to a declining business. Generally this will involve moves such as cutting costs, enhancing quality, eliminating management positions, and altering product lines. Also, a company may divest itself of a poorly performing business in a turnaround. Turnaround strategies are often employed when the business is in an attractive industry and the firm wishes to retain it. Chrysler has successfully employed such a strategy. CEO Lee Iacocca, faced with declining market share and sales in Chrysler's automobile business, responded by reducing fixed and variable costs and by divesting some unrelated divisions, such as a corporate jet subsidiary.

A **liquidation strategy** is one in which the firm dismantles an operation and/or sells off parts that may be more valuable as separate entities than they were when combined in the business as a whole. As an example of dismantling, Sears liquidated its catalog division because the sales from the catalog division continued to slump and it became too unprofitable to keep the division going.[23] Frank Lorenzo, chairman of Texas Air, purchased Eastern Airlines and promptly began to dispose of the company's valuable assets, such as the Eastern Shuttle and its advanced reservation system. He believed, as most liquidators do, that the separate parts were worth more when sold than they would generate in profits if retained together. It should be noted that such a strategy does have considerable negative side effects, as many employees lose their jobs when liquidations occur.

## Portfolio Analysis

As firms move from single business entities to multibusiness organizations in a variety of industries, the complexity of the strategic planning process increases. As a firm grows, it becomes important to analyze each business unit as a separate company. A **strategic business unit (SBU)** is a separate division within a company that has its own mission, goals, strategy, and competitors. At PepsiCo, for example, Taco Bell, KFC, Pizza Hut, and the soft-drink division each function as separate companies within PepsiCo and thus are SBUs. Techniques have been developed to assist individual managers in developing and analyzing the quality of their corporate strategy.

One such technique is **portfolio analysis**, which allows managers to visualize their businesses as a set or portfolio using certain common criteria, such as profitability or growth potential. Using a matrix, managers can position their SBUs, assess their relative attractiveness, and determine appropriate strategies for each.

**Growth/Share Matrix.**    Figure 10.4 shows the four-square grid matrix first introduced by the Boston Consulting Group (BCG) as a tool for analyzing a company's SBUs. The axes for the matrix are market growth rate and relative market share, while each SBU is represented by a circle, the size of which indicates the percentage of total firm revenues attributed to the business. With such a matrix, it is possible for managers to more easily explore the relative strengths and weaknesses of each business, determining which ones deserve continued and perhaps greater funding and those that should be divested.[24]

---

**turnaround strategy**
A strategy in which the firm attempts, through such measures as cost-cutting, quality enhancement, or the elimination of management positions, to restore economic strength to a declining business.

**liquidation strategy**
A strategy in which the firm dismantles an operation and/or sells off parts that may be more valuable as separate entities than as part of the business as a whole.

**strategic business unit (SBU)**
A separate division within a company that has its own mission, goals, strategy, and competitors.

**portfolio analysis**
A technique allowing managers to visualize their businesses as a set or portfolio using certain common criteria, such as profitability or growth potential.

**FIGURE 10.4**

**Boston Consulting Group Matrix**

**Teaching Note:** To practice using the Boston Consulting Group matrix, have students choose a company and classify its products into the four categories. For example, considering McDonald's, cows include french fries and hamburgers; stars include Egg McMuffins and Chicken McNuggets; question marks might be breakfast burritos and McLean Deluxe; while a dog might be the McRib Sandwich.

**stars**
Those businesses that have high market shares and operate in industries experiencing major growth.

**question marks**
Those businesses that are viewed positively in the sense that they are located in attractive, fast-growing markets, but for which there is a question as to their ability to compete, given their low market share.

**cash cows**
Those businesses that tend to generate excess cash over what is needed for their continued growth due to their high market share in a slow-growing market.

**dogs**
Businesses that have only minimal profits or even losses due to their low market share in slow-growing markets.

Businesses in the upper left-hand quadrant of the matrix, called **stars**, have high market shares and operate in industries experiencing major growth. Stars represent the greatest potential opportunities for the firm, but also the greatest potential investment because increased resources are required to keep up with competitors in such rapidly expanding markets. Saturn, for example, represents a star business unit for General Motors, while it also represents a tremendous dollar investment for GM.

**Question marks**, located in the upper right-hand quadrant, are viewed positively in the sense that they are located in attractive, fast-growing markets, but there is a question as to their ability to compete, given their low market share. Because these businesses require large amounts of capital for the same reason as the stars do, corporate managers must determine if the business's potential earnings warrant this continued investment. An example of a question mark is the electric car, for which some experts believe the time has come.

**Cash cows**, in the lower left-hand quadrant, are so named because they tend to generate excess cash over what is needed for continued growth. This is due to their having a high market share and being in industries that have slowly growing markets. With a strong cash cow, the firm can use the excess funds to help support stars and question marks. An example of a cash cow is the minivan division of Chrysler Motors.

Finally, **dogs**, in the lower right-hand quadrant, are those businesses with low market share in slow growing markets. Because they are also low performers in their industries, these businesses have only minimal profits—sometimes even losses. Companies typically divest weaker-performing dogs because they act as a drag on the entire firm's earnings. An example of a dog was Sears's catalog division.

**FIGURE 10.5**

**GE Matrix**

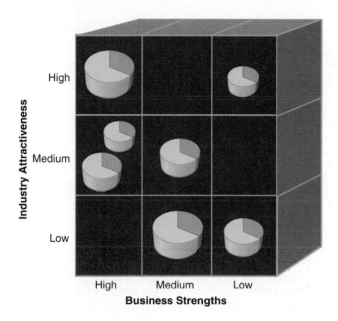

Several criticisms have been aimed at the BCG matrix. First, the labeling of businesses as stars, cash cows, question marks, and dogs tends to oversimplify the nature of these businesses. Many managers, hearing the term "dog," believe that such entities should be put to sleep. However, a firm might want to keep a dog that continues to generate profits. Second, and related to the first objection, is that a four-cell matrix neglects average-performing firms. Finally, the criteria used to classify the businesses, relative market share and market growth rate, may not be the best or only ones to apply when assessing businesses.

**Business Strength/Industry Attractiveness Matrix.**    Addressing such criticisms, many organizations, most notably General Electric, have developed newer portfolio assessment tools. The GE matrix, depicted in Figure 10.5, has nine cells. Each of its two main axes has three categories of high, medium, and low. Each axis is based on a number of different attributes. Industry attractiveness is a composite of such factors as market size, industry profit margins, and the ease of entry into the industry. Business strength is based on relative profit margins, cost position relative to competitors, and other factors. Each pie represents the relative size of each industry in terms of sales and the "wedge" indicates the firm's relative market share.

The GE matrix allows corporate managers to visualize their organizations as a basis for plotting strategy. Businesses in the three squares in the upper left-hand quarter of the matrix are ones that the firm may wish either to continue or to earmark for increased investment levels. These are relatively strong firms in attractive industries. The three cells in the lower right-hand corner include businesses that are relatively weak in less attractive industries—prime candidates for divestiture. The

**Teaching Note:** To better understand the differences between the Boston Consulting Group and the GE matrices, have students compare the two classification schemes. Both represent ways to look at the current products of an organization and its size and potential relative to the industry.

**Teaching Note:** Remind students that both the GE and the BCG models and matrices are descriptive. That is, they classify current products and markets. However, they are not prescriptive as they do not tell where new strategies or products should come from.

firms in the three diagonal cells from lower left to upper right are the ones that frequently require careful observation by corporate managers. They are usually marginal organizations on which a decision must be made either to continue funding or to divest the businesses and divert that funding to more promising ventures.

# BUSINESS-LEVEL STRATEGY

If corporate-level strategy is the overall plan for what all the businesses in an organization should be doing, then business-level strategy is the plan that identifies the specific actions an individual SBU should undertake to meet corporate strategy. These individual SBUs are all seeking an edge or advantage over their competitors by attempting to create "value" for their customers. But what good is an advantage if any one of the competitors can quickly adopt it and achieve similar results? Thus, it is important that the competitive advantage be sustainable and unique.

## Types of Business Unit Strategy

Each business strategy should be a response to the particular combination of the division's resources and environment. Despite the distinct nature of business strategies, however, it is useful to think about three major types of business strategy: cost leadership, differentiation, and focus. To be used successfully, each strategy requires different sets of skills, thought processes, and priorities.[25]

**cost leadership**
A business-level strategy aimed at achieving the overall lowest cost structure in an industry.

**Cost Leadership.**    **Cost leadership** is a business-level strategy aimed at achieving the overall lowest cost structure in an industry. The low cost is then used as a basis either for gaining market share or for undercutting competitors' prices. Cost leadership is normally attained through economies of scale, low raw materials cost, or low wages. (The latter is the factor used by many foreign competitors.) Typically, a low-cost structure is not the result of a single action, such as cutting employee wages, but rather the product of a corporate attitude that attempts to cut costs on all fronts.[26] Thus, Food Lion keeps a handle on costs in many ways, from using the excess heat from freezers to help heat the store to using packing crates to help display produce. Moreover, being the low-cost leader can provide a powerful competitive advantage for a business. For instance, despite Kmart's aim to keep prices low, Wal-Mart can still effectively undercut Kmart prices because Wal-Mart keeps such a tight handle on costs.

**Teaching Note:** Have students identify additional businesses basing their strategies on cost leadership. These can include discount stores and no-frills warehouse shops. Additional examples include Sam's Wholesale Club, OfficeMax, Home Depot, and Taco Bell.

**differentiation**
A business strategy in which the SBU offers a unique good or service to a customer at a premium price.

**Differentiation.**    **Differentiation** is a business strategy in which the SBU offers a unique good or service to a customer at a premium price. The underlying rationale behind this approach is to identify benefits that customers consider important and for which they are willing to pay extra. Differentiation can be based on image (Chanel No. 5), unique service (Mercedes offers 24-hour tow service), reliability (Maytag washers and dryers), high quality (BMW), and prestige (Rolex). In fact, almost any attribute that consumers value can be the basis of a differentiation strategy, from toilet paper that is extra soft (Charmin) to hot sauce that can raise blisters on your tongue (Tabasco). Note that although differentiation is based on selling unique attributes, the target market is still reasonably large. As a result, mass advertising plays an important role in persuading consumers to purchase goods and services that have a little something extra.

## MAKE THIS MOMENT MATTER.

When a young girl gets lost in a good book and falls in love with her doll, magic happens.

This is no time for toys with tasteless values that glamorize "growing up" at the expense of growing.

This is the time to plant dreams deep. The moment won't last. The dreams will.

THE AMERICAN GIRLS COLLECTION

Quality books and dolls for girls 7 and up.

For a free catalogue, call 1-800-845-0005.

PLEASANT COMPANY

Pleasant Company ads inform little girls and their parents about its special educational dolls and books that teach American history, family values, and self-reliance. Pleasant Rowland used a differentiation strategy in launching her mail-order company eight years ago to set her American Girls Collection of historical dolls apart from competitors like Mattel's Barbie. Customers are willing to pay a premium price, $82, for each of five dolls that represent different eras of American history. The company also markets a series of novels for each doll; historically accurate replicas of clothing, furniture, and memorabilia; and dresses for the doll's owner.

**Focus.**    **Focus** is a business strategy in which the business concentrates on one part or segment of the market and tries to meet the demands of that segment. Cannondale Corporation markets high-tech bicycles with super-light frames, rear shock absorbers, and front suspension for as much as $3,500. Its products are aimed not at a mass audience, but rather at serious and affluent enthusiasts with a need for top-quality bikes.[27] Cannondale is employing a focus strategy directed toward the needs of a distinctive market niche.

While some focus strategies, like Cannondale's, serve the needs of a niche market seeking benefits, not all focus strategies need to have a differentiation basis. Morris Air Service is a small airline, based in Salt Lake City, that offers only short-haul service with no inflight meals. The only way to get a ticket is to call Morris directly. It does not try to differentiate its service, but it does concentrate on a small market niche. Morris's niche market is the person in a small business who has a limited expense account and whose travel destination is in the Western United States.[28]

**focus**
A business strategy in which the business concentrates on one part or segment of the market and tries to meet the demands of that segment.

**Example:** Focus or niche strategies are followed by Sweden's Pharmacia, one of the 20 largest drug companies in the world, with sales in 1993 of $3.5 million. The drug company, unlike most giants who depend on a few blockbuster drugs to drive sales, makes money from different niche strengths, ranging from cancer therapy to allergy identification—making it more immune to price pressure.

## Product Life Cycle and Business Strategy

Pet rocks, mood rings, whale-bone corsets, leisure suits, hula hoops, and the VW Beetle all have one thing in common: They were introduced, they flourished, they reached a saturation point in the market, and they eventually succumbed to a lack of buyer interest. This cycle of birth, growth, and decline of a product is known as the **product life cycle**. It provides a useful framework for evaluating the changing phases of a product. It also provides strategists with useful information in crafting business-level strategy.

**product life cycle**
The cycle of birth, growth, and decline of a product.

### FIGURE 10.6

### The Product Life Cycle

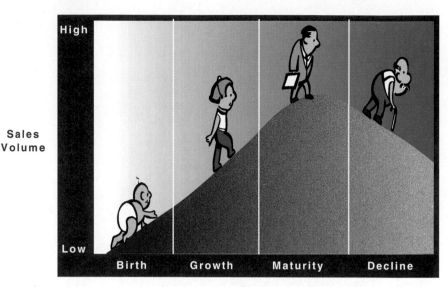

**Teaching Note:** To reinforce the product life cycle, have students position the following consumer audio products along the curve: record players (decline), 8-track players (decline), cassette players (maturity), compact disc players (growth), digital audiotape (birth).

**birth**
The initial stage when the product is introduced.

**growth**
The stage characterized by dramatic increases in the product's market share.

**maturity**
The stage when the product's market share either slows or has no growth.

**decline**
The stage marked by decreases in the product's market share.

Figure 10.6 illustrates the product life cycle as a function of time and market share. The initial stage, naturally enough, is **birth**. There the product is introduced, and for the most part, has slow growth, as the dominant design of the product is determined by the industry competition. An example of a product in the birth stage is the video telephone. The next stage, **growth**, is characterized by dramatic increases in market share. The wireless telecommunication industry is currently in a growth stage. Slowing or no growth is typical of the **maturity** stage. Automobiles are an example of a product in the maturity stage. Finally, the **decline** stage is marked with decreases in the growth rate. The typewriter is a product that definitely is in the decline stage.

Products are propelled through their life cycles by a number of factors. In some cases, technological change makes a product an anachronism. For example, with the advent of high-powered computers, the need for typewriters has declined. Often just changing consumer preferences will drive the life cycle. With consumers becoming more health conscious, caffeine-free and diet drinks are gaining in popularity. Also, political and legal events may shorten a product's life span or increase it. After the FDA ruled that smoking causes cancer, the demand for cigarettes declined, although the decline has been slow and bitterly fought by the tobacco industry.

Because of the vast number of catalysts, you should not be surprised to learn that the life cycles of different products vary tremendously. Products such as Nehru jackets (go ask your Dad) may have a life cycle, as a mass-market product, of less than a year. Other products, such as automobiles, which are currently in a mature phase, have much longer life spans.

The proper business strategy will be determined, in part, by the product life cycle. If a product is in the birth or introduction stage, the appropriate strategy may be one of focus, since at this point the price will be relatively high and the tech-

## B U S I N E S S   D I L E M M A

*You're the Manager ...What Would You Do?*

THE COMPANY:  Infinity Computers, Inc.

YOUR POSITION:  President and CEO

THE PLACE:  Palo Alto, CA

Infinity Computers, Inc., is a leading marketer of IBM-compatible laptop and notebook computers in the United States. The company not only sells notebook computers under its own Infinity brand name but also manufactures computers for direct-mail catalog companies and some retail computer stores under their private brand names. Infinity has pursued a niche strategy, specializing in quality notebook products. The firm engineers and assembles attractive, user-friendly computers employing components from the United States and Japan. In general, however, the product is not assembled on a low-cost basis and is not significantly differentiated on extra product-enhancing features. Recently, Infinity's performance has suffered as a result of a lack of applications software. Additionally, some buyers and trade critics have said its computers are "underpowered." Infinity's computers are powered by Intel chips, but some newer technology, including the Apple Power PC, represents a significant threat because of processing flexibility.

Infinity's strength has been its CEO and president, George Anderson. Declining sales and other signs indicate that there is a need to make the company more responsive to customers' needs and more competitive in the areas of technology, product quality, and service. The firm's weakness is having too many employees and too great a reliance on one product. Moreover, the Infinity Advanced 486 notebook computer is now technologically obsolete. The question is, "Should the firm focus on the cutting edge, highest quality, most expensive chip technology, such as Intel's Pentium chip, or focus on less advanced but effective technology at a lower

competitive price?" Additionally, what is the future of the notebook computer?

George Anderson now faces the problem of reorganizing the company to cut costs and be more competitive. It is obvious to him that the strategies that initially made the firm successful are no longer working effectively. Strategic management is needed to determine desired objectives and benchmarks as well as how to ensure that the desired future is achieved.

Many opportunities exist, but the threat of new technological developments and current competitive conditions could hurt or destroy Infinity. It may be necessary to reevaluate the firm's mission, establish strategic goals, and develop operating strategies. Anderson must make strategic choices to show at least modest sales growth over the next few years. Finally, changes in corporate strategy, along with cost cutting and monitoring of the changing competitive and technological environment, are necessary to make Infinity profitable.

### Questions

1. As president and CEO, conduct a SWOT analysis for Infinity Computers in preparation for developing new strategies.
2. Evaluate the current niche strategy and make suggestions for alternative strategies.
3. Develop an assessment of the prospects of Infinity, generating a successful strategy by which to compete over the next ten years.

---

nology may be unsettled. While in the growth stage, firms can compete with just about any strategy because of the potential for continued market share increases and because the exact number of competitors is unknown. The maturity stage normally favors a cost strategy because growth is sluggish and competitors will be competing primarily over price.[29]

## IMPLEMENTING STRATEGY

Long before he was pointing at charts on TV, billionaire businessman Ross Perot sold his company, Electronic Data Systems (EDS), to General Motors and went to work for GM. After some time spent exploring how GM works, Perot had this to say about how long it takes GM to make and implement a strategic decision:

**Comment on Box:** When teaching the Infinity Computer case in the "Business Dilemma" box, have students use the tools from the chapter, including the GE and BCG matrices, to analyze the position of the various products. Discuss the advantages and disadvantages of the various strategic alternatives including differentiation and focus/niche. Have students use case facts to justify their chosen alternative. Also, discuss implementation.

**FIGURE 10.7**

## McKinsey 7-S Framework

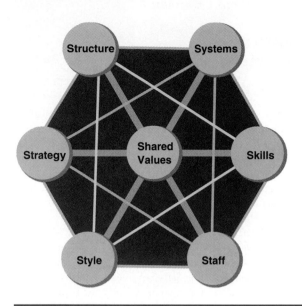

*Source:* Tom Peters and Robert Waterman, Jr., *In Search of Excellence* (New York: Harper & Row, 1982), 10.

> *The first EDSer to see a snake kills it. At GM, the first thing you do is organize a committee on snakes. Then you bring in a consultant who knows a lot about snakes. Third thing you do is talk about it for a year.*[30]

Implementation is important at all levels of strategy—societal, corporate, business, and functional. A firm can invest an impressive amount of time (sometimes too long, as in GM's case) and resources into planning and formulating, but it will not achieve its mission and goals unless it effectively and expeditiously implements these strategies. Unfortunately, many top managers believe that implementation is an "administrative process," something almost routinely accomplished. In reality, it is a process that should be driven by entrepreneurial instincts. Innovation is just as important in implementing strategy as it is in formulating it.

To better determine what factors lead to higher performance in a firm, Tom Peters and Robert Waterman developed the McKinsey 7-S framework in their book *In Search of Excellence.* The McKinsey 7-S framework (Figure 10.7) provides an excellent visualization of the components of a business that managers must consider when implementing strategy. Key to this framework is that all seven components must be managed during the implementation process. A change in any one component, say strategy, will result in the changing of the balance between strategy and the other six.[31]

**Example:** Implementation in Techmetals, a Dayton, Ohio, metal plater, is facilitated by using teams. The company began using teams in 1991 and its 80 employees now handle scheduling, delivery, and plant layout. The set-up makes it a more efficient company with better working conditions. Another benefit is a more educated work force, according to Lee Watson, director of improvements.

## Strategy

A change in a firm's strategy will result in a change in the balance between strategy and the other six "Ss." Managers must therefore reassess the entire management of the organization when contemplating a major strategic change. For example, when Lee Iacocca took over as CEO of Chrysler, not only did the leadership style change, but so did six other dimensions.

## Structure

Structure refers to a firm's hierarchy or pattern of organization, and a change in strategy will often require an adjustment of the firm's hierarchy. For instance, to become more competitive by getting closer to the customer, IBM has recently reorganized, giving each of its divisions (mainframes, PCs, etc.) much greater control over its destiny. By reducing corporate control, IBM hopes that these newly restructured business units can react more quickly to changing customer needs and competitors' moves. For more on organizational structure, see Chapters 12 and 13.

## Systems

In this context, systems are the procedures or guidelines that firms use in the course of doing business. To strike back at low-price rivals, Procter & Gamble has decided that it needs to get a better grip on costs. P&G managers recently studied the pit crews at the Indianapolis Speedway and applied their quick-change methods, in a fashion, to the firm's manufacturing procedures. In some cases, the new procedures reduced equipment changeovers from more than two days to two hours.[32]

## Skills

The skills of the organization's members primarily consist of their knowledge of the technical aspects of the business's goods or services and how to apply this knowledge, as well as general work abilities such as communication, planning, reading comprehension, and problem analysis. Employee skills often have to change in response to changes in business strategy. The firm may have to retrain its workers, or in extreme cases, lay off workers and procure employees with more relevant skills. As an example, in the past, the majority of AT&T's employees were either service workers or operators; relatively few people were involved in marketing, for instance. However, AT&T's transformation from a national telephone company to a global telecommunication firm has necessitated a change in the skills of its personnel. Recently the organization has more aggressively recruited people with marketing and international business skills.

## Staffing

Staffing involves finding and placing employees in jobs for which they have the appropriate skills. While this may sound easy, in practice it can be quite difficult. Many businesses have a wide variety of jobs with diverse knowledge and skill requirements. Staffing requires that new employees be assigned to work groups for which they have the necessary background. The difficulty is that most formal education in high school or college does not train individuals for particular jobs in particular organizations. Even previous work experience may not be a very good indicator of the required knowledge and skills because many jobs are specific to an organization and do not closely represent those in other organizations. Staffing for current employees calls for a planned system of career development, called succession planning, which involves determining what the knowledge and skills

**Example:** Structure at Country Cupboard, a truck-stop restaurant in Lewisburgh, Pennsylvania, has changed to include self-directed work teams. Carole Baylor-Hamm, the restaurant's co-owner, felt the business could be more effectively managed by turning budgeting and planning decisions over to the 350 employees.

AMP, a producer of 100,000 electrical/electronic connection devices, is gaining the commitment of over 28,000 employees at 175 facilities in 36 countries in implementing its Journey for Excellence continuous improvement program. Built on the basic principles of quality improvement, the Journey for Excellence is the foundation of AMP's strategy of product/market diversification and globalization. Implementing the program in AMP's international operations requires adapting it to many different national cultures. Here, AMP Mexico employees sign their commitment to a unique version of the program.

*Source:* Courtesy of AMP Incorporated.

of current employees are, what knowledge and skills will be needed in the future by these individuals, and developing appropriate training programs.

## Style

The leadership style of the firm's managers is an essential element in effective implementation. Managers who can communicate and stress the importance of strategies to employees and other stakeholders can make a tremendous difference in the implementation process. Managers with good leadership skills can better maintain the balance among the 7 Ss. For example, Bill Gates at Microsoft provides a dynamic, high-involvement leadership style that is consistent with the needs of his company, as well as with the demands of the rapidly changing computer software industry.

## Shared Values

**Critical Thinking Challenge:** As a written assignment, have students prepare a report on a leading *Fortune* 500 company using the 7-S framework as a guide to organizing the report and presentation of the findings.

You will remember from Chapter 1 that organizational culture is the set of values and beliefs shared by organizational members. A major part of the implementation process is to motivate managers and workers to "buy into" the strategy. If the formulated strategy taps into the values and beliefs of these people and reflects the organizational culture, the strategy is more likely to be implemented effectively. Frito-Lay's employees take great pride in their commitment to provide service to their customers. Supposedly, on any given day, Frito-Lay sales representatives will visit 99.5 percent of the supermarkets, convenience stores, and other outlets that carry their products to ensure that consumers have plenty of fresh Ruffles and Fritos. Frito-Lay employees have taken this level of service to heart and would probably reject any proposed strategy that threatens this shared value.[33] Thus, it is important for managers to identify core beliefs and build their implementation strategies around them.

## STRATEGIC MANAGEMENT:  PROS AND CONS

Much has been written, both good and bad, about strategic management. Some critics argue that strategic management is often all about planning, with little

## Personal Strategic Planning

Throughout this chapter, we discussed how strategic planning can better equip a company in making its long-range plans, based on various factors from its internal and external environment. Realistically, however, the likelihood of your being placed in a position to make such strategic decisions for a large corporation upon graduation lies somewhere between slim and none. Obviously, large companies depend on individuals who have a number of years' experience, often in several functional areas and frequently in several corporations. However, you can apply the process of strategic management to help plan your own career after graduation.

For example, suppose you want to start your own business after graduation; effective strategic planning can help you meet that goal. Although we generally think of strategic planning as a tool used primarily by large companies, it can help small-business entrepreneurs, too. Let's assume you want to open an advertising company. (Remember that strategic planning can be used in a similar manner for any type of business chosen.)

The reason you chose this particular business is that you first determined what your own strengths are relative to your weaknesses. Let's say your strengths include a keen sense for effective advertising—developed through your years working in summer jobs for a large advertising agency and through your education in college as a business major. Another strength is your mastery of various computer software packages that can be used to design new high-tech ads. Perhaps you were born with good technical abilities, which you honed by playing on the computer to design things (since your parents bought you your first computer at age eight). You enhanced your skill with several computer design classes in college. Finally, you have a strong internal desire to be your own boss and thus would not like working for anyone else. Your biggest weaknesses are a lack of capital to buy major equipment and the need for another creative computer specialist to help you with new ideas. Thus, you conducted an internal analysis of your strengths and weaknesses much like a corporation might conduct an internal analysis. Knowing that you just conducted part of a SWOT analysis, you move on to examine the external environment.

You conduct an external analysis to determine if you can match your strengths to the opportunities that exist in the market or the external environment. You already know that many small businesses are always looking for someone to develop advertising for them. Because the large firm you worked for in the summers always seemed to turn those small accounts away, you really can't recall ever seeing these firms use any type of sophisticated advertising. Further research into why these small firms seldom advertise suggests that it is because no firm specializes in providing advertising for smaller clients. Finally, those few firms that do complete advertising campaigns are always complaining that costs are rising and that the resulting ads lack the quality of those done for the larger companies. Your biggest perceived threat is that some major company will modify its strategy to include small advertisers—not likely because of the large organization's overhead expenditures—or that another small company will beat you to the market with the same service. You see a possible niche in the market in which a small firm could prosper.

Bringing this together, you have determined what your strengths are and believe that you can use those strengths to take advantage of the opportunities within the environment; further, you theorize that if you work quickly to find the right partner, you can minimize your own weaknesses and meet environmental threats successfully. To minimize your weaknesses you plan to approach another senior with similar ideas, as well as some capital, and together develop a well-thought-out business plan. This not only helps you minimize your weaknesses but also allows you both to share the risk. To keep the environmental threats to a minimum, you decide on targeting only those small firms in which the large agencies have little interest or who have been dissatisfied with larger ad agencies. Finally, you can develop a strategic plan based on this analysis and start implementing your chosen career.

This hypothetical example illustrates how aspects of strategy development can be used in career planning. Just as strategy planning is used in very large corporations to ensure long-term success, you, too, can use it to ensure the long-term future of your own career.

---

emphasis placed on implementation. It can be costly and time consuming for the organizational members involved. And many charge that its preoccupation with a long-term time frame is unrealistic, given the short-term expectations of stockholders and other financial stakeholders.

Despite these criticisms, strategic management, properly utilized, offers several benefits.

1. Strategic management involves managers at all levels of the organization and is group-based in its approach. This leads to more comprehensive inputs and, ultimately, better decisions.

2. This extended involvement by managers lessens resistance to contemplated changes reflected in the strategic plan.

3. Strategic management encourages managers to study and understand the organization's environment and resources. The systematic nature of the process promotes a more comprehensive analysis in these areas to secure an organization's fit with its environment.

4. Using the strategic management process helps to secure a more unified organization as organizational members understand what the firm stands for and the direction in which it is heading.

5. Strategic management as a process requires managers to be more proactive in planning and counteracts the tendency to be reactive.

## SUMMARY AND REVIEW

• **Define strategic management and strategy.** Strategic management is the processes (organizing, leading, and controlling) an organization undertakes to implement its strategic plan and achieve its strategic goals. Central to strategic planning and strategic management is the development of a strategy, the course of action for implementing strategic plans and achieving strategic goals.

• **Describe the steps involved in strategic management.** The first major step is to identify the organization's mission and strategic goals, what businesses it wishes to be in, and how the businesses should be doing. Secondly, the organization should conduct a SWOT analysis—identify the strengths, weaknesses, opportunities, and threats it faces. Based on this information, the organization develops a general strategy that positions it relative to its competitors. The final steps are implementing, evaluating, and controlling the strategic plan.

• **Relate strategic management to the business environment.** The purpose of strategic planning is to position the firm as advantageously as possible relative to its competitors in the business environment. In doing this, the organization must assess its strengths and weaknesses and those of its competitors. It also should know what the changes in the various components of its environment will be. Taking all this information into account, the organization develops plans for the long-term future.

• **Differentiate among the major corporate strategies and tools that managers use to develop and implement strategies.** Corporate strategy is con-

cerned with the organization as a whole, particularly which business or set of businesses the organization should be in. If the company operates many businesses, corporate-level strategy should account for the relationship among these. Three general corporate-level strategies are diversification (a strategy of acquiring other businesses), joint ventures (contractual partnerships with other organizations, in which each partner contributes to the enterprise while retaining its separate identity), and divestment (selling off businesses that the company no longer wishes to maintain either because they are failing or because the company has changed its corporate strategy and does not wish to be in those businesses any longer).

A major tool of corporate strategic planning is portfolio analyses. One such technique is the Boston Consulting Group's Growth/Share Matrix, a four-grid matrix that identifies strategic business units (SBUs) as stars, question marks, cash cows, and dogs, relative to the business's market growth rate and relative market share. The GE matrix places SBUs into one of nine cells of a matrix, depending on their industry attractiveness and business strength. These tools allow an organization to categorize its businesses and look at the relative performance and strength of each of these.

• **Analyze several common business-level strategies.** Business-level strategy refers to the actions that an individual strategic business unit should take to meet corporate strategy. These actions seek to gain an advantage relative to competitors. The major, general business strategies are cost leadership (attempting to achieve the overall lowest cost structure in an industry), differentiation (offering a unique good or service to a customer at a premium price), and focus (concentrating on trying to meet the demands of one part or segment of the market). The proper business strategy will be determined, in part, by the product life cycle.

- **Evaluate the importance of strategy implementation.** A firm will not achieve its mission and goals unless it implements its strategies effectively and expedi-

tiously. Changing one aspect of strategy can affect many parts of a business.

- **Assess a business's strategy and recommend alternative strategies.** The "Business Dilemma" box introduces a hypothetical business that needs to make some changes. Based on the concepts you've learned in this chapter, you should be able to engage in the strategic management process, including a SWOT analysis, to develop alternative strategies for Infinity Computers.

## Key Terms and Concepts

strategic management *274*
strategy *274*
distinctive competence *276*
SWOT analysis *277*
corporate strategy *280*
business-level strategy *282*
diversification *283*
related diversification *284*
unrelated diversification *284*

conglomerates *284*
divestment *284*
turnaround strategy *285*
liquidation strategy *285*
strategic business unit (SBU) *285*
portfolio analysis *285*
stars *286*
question marks *286*
cash cows *286*

dogs *286*
cost leadership *288*
differentiation *288*
focus *289*
product life cycle *289*
birth *290*
growth *290*
maturity *290*
decline *290*

## Ready Recall

1. How does strategic management relate to strategic planning? What is a strategy?
2. What is a distinctive competence? Give some examples of real companies' distinctive competencies.
3. List the steps in the strategic management process.
4. What is a SWOT analysis and why should a company conduct one?
5. Relate the four levels of strategy.

6. What corporate strategies can managers use? Give an example of a company using each.
7. What is portfolio analysis?
8. What is a strategic business unit? What business-level strategies can be applied to SBUs?
9. How does the product life cycle affect the strategy employed by an SBU?
10. Why is implementation so important to strategic management?

## Expand Your Experience

1. Do a SWOT analysis for a local small business—for example, a sporting goods store, restaurant, or clothing store. If such a store is not available, interview the manager of a small business to get information about the business and its environment. Based on the SWOT analysis, what strategic plan would you recommend to the owner?
2. Analyze the strategy of your college or university as if it were a business. Do a SWOT analysis for the school and discuss the appropriateness of its strategy and possible changes in strategy the school should consider. Determine the type of business strategy your school uses (cost leadership, differentiation, or focus) and compare it to that of schools in the surrounding area.
3. If your school is large enough to have separate colleges (business, engineering, arts and science, etc.), have some

fun using the Boston Consulting Group's matrix to determine which colleges are stars, question marks, cash cows, or dogs. Justify your answers.
4. Go to the local mall and list 10 to 15 businesses, from the largest to the smallest. For each business, note whether you think its business strategy is cost leadership, differentiation, or focus. Be able to justify your answer. Did you see any businesses that tried to combine strategies, for instance, differentiation with low cost? Explain.
5. Divide into groups of two or three students and have each group go test drive one Chrysler product and a comparable Ford, GM, or foreign-manufactured product. Discuss whether Chrysler is using a focus, differentiation, or cost strategy for that product. (Relate this to the end-of-chapter case.)

## CASE

# *Chrysler*

The new direction Chrysler has been attempting over the last ten years is finally starting to pay off. Newly appointed CEO Robert Eaton, Lee Iacocca's replacement, has Chrysler on the verge of making one of the most astonishing comebacks in U.S. manufacturing history. The company reported record profits of nearly $2 billion for 1993, more than General Motors and Ford combined, and a market share of nearly 15 percent. Chrysler's growth is due in part to three model years of new vehicles—the Jeep Grand Cherokee, the Intrepid, and the LH Sedan. The company continues to hold a high market share in the minivan market, which contributes about 25 percent of its net revenues. But a closer examination of the company's success reveals that it may be traced back to the strategic planning process Iacocca and his team did years earlier.

In the late 1970s and early 1980s, Chrysler hit rock bottom in the automobile industry when its market share and sales plummeted. To stay afloat, Iacocca masterminded the first and only loan guaranteed by the federal government for a private business—to the tune of $1.5 billion. Since that low point, the company has seen its profits and market share fluctuate. To deal with the turbulent environment, Chrysler revamped its organizational structure to make the company much more flexible and competitive.

Iacocca may have single-handedly saved Chrysler by his crisis-management intervention, but what did he and Eaton do to make the company what it is today? They divested and reorganized certain divisions within Chrysler, and they developed a new philosophy for the company's long-term survival. The company is made up of many different brands of automobiles under the Chrysler, Dodge, Eagle, Jeep, Plymouth, and Lamborghini names. It also owns and operates Chrysler financial services, as well as Thrifty, Snappy, Dollar, and General car rental agencies. Other units in unrelated businesses, such as Gulfstream Aerospace, were divested.

Within the auto industry, Iacocca and Eaton attempted to have each brand act as a distinct unit, unlike other manufacturers; however, technological, research, and development improvements are shared throughout the entire organization. The company implemented strict efficiency and quality standards with which all levels of managers and employees have to comply. Iacocca and Eaton both stressed the importance of these issues, even at the expense of lost revenues. The way in which Chrysler designs a car is also relatively new to U.S. automakers. Instead of having a team work on separate parts or sections of a car (for instance, engineers that work only on the transmission, body design, or chassis), an entire engineering team works from the raw materials stage to the finished product. This concept seems to be working quite well, especially given the recent success of the last three cars. The company faces another big test as it awaits the sales results for its new Neon line of small cars, which used this approach.

By going to a team or platform work-team technique, the company was able to reduce its work force and operations. Employees at all levels and areas helped in the development of new and innovative concepts for improving the cars' production time. Moreover, the employees began to realize the importance of their task to the success of the entire organization and openly offered more suggestions for improving the manufacturing process. Although not totally satisfied with the communication levels within Chrysler, Eaton likes the effects of the improvements made so far.

The company also implemented a cost-savings plan known as "just in time," an inventory control system widely used by many Japanese manufacturers that brings inventory to the plant just in time to be used. Under this program, Chrysler needed to work hand in hand with suppliers to ensure the quality and timeliness of the supplies. No longer will plant managers be able to stockpile costly inventory for emergency shortages. Those shortages are eliminated by having a coordinated effort between the divisions and the suppliers. Additionally, the company eliminated about 25 percent of its white-collar positions and effectively eliminated many of the redundant positions in middle and upper management.

While the other two U.S. manufacturers, Ford and GM, compete in a global market, Chrysler has taken a different road. It competes primarily in the highly competitive North American market and is currently looking at the feasibility of entering other markets in a broader capacity. Because Chrysler focuses its efforts primarily in North America, its profits are smaller and the competition more fierce than in any market in the world. Even given this difficulty, the company has finally succeeded in giving its consumers the products they demand at a price that they feel they can afford.

The success of Chrysler has been due in large part to the strategic planning of top management. The company has recently developed some top-selling, "hot" automobiles that have propelled it to new heights in sales and revenues. However, for the future, Chrysler is going to have to continually improve the customers' perceived quality of its products. It finally has the financial resources, distribution channels, and customer base to take on the other major automakers. Chrysler may even have all the necessary resources needed to become a true global competitor and increase revenues in the future.

*Sources:* Alex Taylor III, "Can Iacocca Fix Chrysler—Again?" *Fortune*, April 8, 1991, 51–54; Alex Taylor III, "Will Success Spoil Chrysler?" *Fortune*, January 10, 1994, 88–92; David Woodruff and Karen Lowry Miller, "Chrysler's Neon: Is This the Small Car Detroit Couldn't Build?" *Business Week*, May 3, 1993, 116–126; and Wilton Woods, "Iacocca's Last Stand at Chrysler," *Fortune*, April 20, 1992, 63–73.

## Questions

1. Discuss Chrysler's success using the McKinsey 7-S Framework. How has Chrysler changed its strategy and what has been the impact on the other six Ss?
2. Discuss Chrysler's corporate strategy and the business strategies for different cars. Do you think these strategies will be successful into the turn of the century? Why or why not?
3. Examine the different automobile models manufactured by Chrysler; which are cash cows, stars, question marks, and dogs?

---

### STRENGTHEN YOUR SKILLS
## *Strategically Planning Your Career*

To give you insights into strategically focusing your career, write answers to the following questions. Periodically thinking through such questions can keep your career from drifting.

1. What business are you in? What is your product (the service or value you create for others)? Who is your market (what type of employer or client is willing to buy your service)?

2. What are your strengths and weaknesses as an employee or self-employed provider of services? What are your core skills and competencies?

3. What external opportunities and threats do you anticipate? Where could you best use your competencies following graduation? What can go wrong in controlling your career?

4. What business should you be in? Where would you like your career to be, say, five or ten years from now? What vision do you value?

5. How do you reach your career vision? What actions do you need to undertake now to get there?

   a. What added education/training do you need?

   b. What organizational experiences do you need?

   c. What individuals are critical to your progress?

6. How do you know you are still on the right course? What milestones do you have for periodically checking up on your career progress?

*Source:* Robert E. Coffey, et al., *Management and Organizational Behavior* (Homewood, Ill.: Austen Press, 1994), 450. Reprinted with permission.

# Making

# Decisions

**After studying this chapter, you should be able to:**

- Define decision making and describe the types of decisions and conditions that may affect decision making.
- Specify the steps involved in decision making.
- Contrast the decision-making models.
- Examine the factors that may affect decision making.
- Summarize group decision techniques and the advantages and disadvantages of group decision making.
- Apply the decision-making models to a hypothetical situation.

## AT&T: Back and Better Than Ever!

In 1984, the U.S. government split the huge AT&T monopoly into seven regional operating companies. Since the split, AT&T has eliminated 140,000 jobs, lost nearly 30 percent of the long-distance market to new competitors such as MCI and Sprint, and struggled to prosper in the computer business. Has AT&T foundered, as many thought it would? Far from it! Today, in fact, AT&T is thriving, and many businesspeople believe the divestiture was the best thing that could have happened to the company. Although AT&T's sales have remained virtually flat since the breakup, its earnings per share set a record in 1992, and the stock has gained almost $30 billion in value since the breakup.

To what does AT&T—and others in the business world—attribute its success? For the most part, credit seems to go to Robert Allen, AT&T's chief executive officer (shown in the photo), and the decisions he has been instrumental in making since he assumed AT&T's top post in 1988. Some decisions that have proven successful under his leadership are the creation of a new organizational structure that encourages cooperation among otherwise independent business units; the development and promotion of a new set of company values; the recruitment of people outside the company to fill key executive posts; the forging of new ties with AT&T's unions, coupled with the proclamation that AT&T can no longer promise lifetime employment; and the investment in other companies that have critical technologies or attractive market positions.

Obviously, the decisions that AT&T has implemented over the last few years have had a tremendous impact on its competitiveness and ultimate success. While many large companies are struggling to remake themselves in the 1990s, AT&T appears to have succeeded in accomplishing one of the most remarkable makeovers in U.S. corporate history.

Although traditional long-distance service still accounts for 62 percent of its revenues, AT&T is no longer just a telephone company. In fact, AT&T is the nation's leading producer of electronic cash registers, as a result of its 1990 acquisition of NCR; the world's largest manufacturer of automated teller machines for banks; the third-largest issuer of credit cards, behind American Express and Citibank; a player in the field of multimedia, which consists of machines that combine text, graphics, sound, and video; an entrant in the video-game business, through a joint venture with Sega Enterprises and an alliance with Viacom, a cable-TV programmer; and a real competitor in the cellular market, due to its pending $3.8 billion purchase of 33 percent of McCaw Cellular Communications, the largest cellular company in the United States.

As CEO Allen is fond of saying, "This ain't Ma Bell." Instead of concentrating solely on telephone calls, AT&T has expanded its vision to include becoming a super player in the whole communication/electronic field. Through strategic decisions to acquire other companies, form strategic alliances and joint ventures, and develop its own new businesses, AT&T has transformed itself into one of the most formidable players in the field of information technology. Allen is pictured here with some of AT&T's new technology products.

*Sources:* David Kirkpatrick, "Could AT&T Rule the World?" *Fortune,* May 17, 1993, 55–66; Thomas McCarroll, "How AT&T Plans to Reach Out and Touch Everyone," *Time,* July 5, 1993, 44–46; and Shelley Neumeier, "Ringing Up Big Gains From Your Telecom Portfolio," *Fortune,* July 12, 1993, 19–20.

**introduction**

I t will be some time before it is clear to what extent the decisions of AT&T management have been in the best interests of the company. One thing is certain: Decisions that companies—actually managers—make can literally mean the difference between their success or failure. In fact, a recent study concluded that managers spend approximately 50 percent of their time dealing with the consequences of bad decision making.[1] Therefore, it is critical that any study of management include a discussion of decision making.

In this chapter we will discuss the essence of decision making by defining decision making, outlining the types of decisions that managers make, and analyzing conditions that affect decision making. We will outline the steps involved in the decision-making process and present several decision-making models. Finally, we will discuss factors that affect individual decision making and decision making in groups.

**Teaching Note:** Remind students that the strategic alternatives discussed in Chapter 10 also represent decision making; however, top managers usually select major strategies. All other managers and employees continually engage in decision making at all levels of the organization.

**decision**
A choice made from alternative courses of action in order to deal with a problem.

**problem**
The difference between a desired situation and the actual situation.

**decision making**
The process of choosing among alternative courses of action to resolve a problem.

**programmed decisions**
Decisions made in response to situations that are routine, somewhat structured, and fairly repetitive.

## THE ESSENCE OF DECISION MAKING

Making decisions is widely recognized as a key aspect of management, and many managers and academicians consider it to be the most crucial element of business management. So, what is decision making?

To begin with, a **decision** is a choice made from alternative courses of action in order to deal with a problem. A **problem** is the difference between a desired situation and the actual situation. Therefore, **decision making** is the process of choosing among alternative courses of action to resolve a problem.

### Types of Decisions

Managers make many different kinds of decisions, such as what hours to work, what employees to hire, what products to introduce, and what price to charge for a product. The "Magnifying Management" box, for example, describes a pricing decision made by the Philip Morris company. Of course, not all decisions that managers make are as critical as the pricing decision made by Philip Morris. Managerial decisions can range anywhere from simple to complex, routine to unique; in general, though, most decisions can be classified as either programmed or nonprogrammed decisions.

**Programmed Decisions.**    **Programmed decisions** are made in response to situations that are routine, somewhat structured, and fairly repetitive. Such situations enable managers to develop procedures that can be applied to resolving these problems when they recur in the future.[2] Examples of programmed decisions include deciding to reorder inventory when quantities fall below a certain level, deciding to renew the company's sponsorship of a youth softball team every spring, and establishing what skills/requirements are needed to fill certain jobs. Many business decisions about routine procedures and basic operations are programmed decisions.

Allstate Insurance Company is an excellent example of a company that has benefited from the application of programmed decisions to resolve routine, repetitive problem situations. Through the use of decision flowcharts, Allstate has devised step-by-step diagrams of the decision-making process that enable employees to more quickly and accurately handle the processing of insurance claims. In

## magnifying management

### PHILIP MORRIS CUTS PRICE OF MARLBOROS

In 1993, Philip Morris announced that it had decided to cut the price of Marlboro cigarettes by 20 percent, or 40 cents a pack. This move was Philip Morris's way of offsetting the overly aggressive pricing strategy that it had used for the last decade; the company had been increasing the price of Marlboros 10 percent a year, more than double the rate of inflation. By relying on continual price increases instead of value—improved quality at a reasonable cost—Philip Morris found itself in a bind. With smokers turning from the high-priced brands (like Marlboro) to the less profitable, deeply discounted cigarette brands (such as Philip Morris's own Basic brand), unit sales of the discount cigarettes grew to almost 15 percent of the domestic market at the expense of full-priced "premium" cigarettes, whose share fell to 70 percent in 1992. To reverse this downward trend, Philip Morris decided to slash the price of Marlboros—a decision that sent shock waves through the industry and started the "great cigarette war of 1993."

The ramifications of Philip Morris's price-cutting decision are far reaching: The company expects its U.S. tobacco operating profits to drop by as much as 40 percent, or $2 billion; its U.S. tobacco after-tax profits will be as much as $1.5 billion lower than Wall Street had expected; and the market value of the company's stock shares fell by $13.4 billion in a single day—with its stock plummeting from 64⅛ to 49⅜, the largest one-day decline by a single stock since October 19, 1987.

Philip Morris's decision has sparked an unprecedented debate. On the one side, many investors and industry specialists have denounced the price-cutting decision as "ill-conceived," "foolishly executed," and "dumb." Among these critics was Roger Enrico, head of Frito-Lay, who commented, "In the annals of business history, Philip Morris's action is bigger than New Coke. MBAs will study this decision for the next century."

On the other side, many in industry perceive the decision as "brilliant," "bold offensive strategy," and good foresight necessary for the long-term success of the company. Some in the industry view Michael Miles, Philip Morris's CEO from 1991 to 1994, as the company's savior, the one responsible for *not* letting Philip Morris follow a road to complacency and eventual decline. One analyst applauded the move as an effective way to combat the market-share decline. Among Philip Morris's supporters was

*Forbes* magazine, which declared that it "is willing to bet that when the smoke clears, Philip Morris will remain one of the world's biggest and most profitable makers of branded goods, and that its principal competitor, RJR Nabisco Holdings Corp., will have taken a beating." Kathleen Morris, a writer for *Financial World*, noted that the price-cutting strategy might take a while to succeed, but that "Miles's pricing decision will not be Philip Morris's Vietnam. Expect to see the company win this war."

*Sources:* Subrata N. Chakravarty, "Don't Underestimate the Champ," *Forbes*, May 10, 1993, 106–110; Michael Janofsky, "Sales Higher, Philip Morris Widens Cigarette Price Cuts," *The New York Times*, July 21, 1993, C1, D1; Kathleen Morris, "No Guts, No Glory," *Financial World*, May 25, 1993, 42–43; Patricia Sellers, "Fall for Philip Morris," *Fortune*, May 3, 1993, 68–69; and Laura Zinn, "Even Philip Morris Feels the Pull of Gravity," *Business Week*, February 15, 1993, 60–62.

Allstate's data entry operation, where 4,500 employees input information from insurance forms into computers, productivity increased 75 percent and quality jumped 90 percent when employees started using decision flowcharts to make routine, or programmed, decisions. Allstate estimates that these productivity and quality improvements will translate into savings of $35 million a year.[3]

**Comment on Box:** Stress that decisions are not always popular and that it takes time to see if some decisions are the right choice. Also, making decisions is difficult and some groups will always be unhappy.

**Nonprogrammed Decisions.** On the other hand, **nonprogrammed decisions** are made in response to situations that are unique, relatively unstructured, undefined, and/or of major consequence to the organization. No standardized procedures

**nonprogrammed decisions**
Decisions made in response to situations that are unique, relatively unstructured, undefined, and/or of major consequence to the organization.

**Teaching Note:** Have students brainstorm other examples of non-programmed and programmed decisions. Remind students that computer software is available to assist managers making routine or programmed decisions, freeing their time for unique issues and problems.

exist to resolve these situations because the problems have never arisen before, they are complex or uncertain, or they are of such significance to the organization that they require tailor-made decisions.[4] Examples of nonprogrammed decisions include deciding whether to build a new plant, close an old one, acquire another company, create a new position, enter into a strategic alliance with another company, invest in enhancing operations, or develop a new product.

Top managers at Frito-Lay, a unit of PepsiCo Inc., have successfully made and implemented many nonprogrammed decisions in response to lapses in product quality, prices that increased faster than inflation, and declining profits and market share, the latter due, in part, to fierce competition from Anheuser-Busch's Eagle Snacks. These decisions included drastically slashing prices of some key brands, eliminating 1,800 (or 60 percent of) management and administrative jobs, closing 4 out of 40 U.S. plants, dropping nearly 100 package sizes and flavors, reformulating the Doritos brand chip, repackaging and reformulating the Lay's and Ruffles potato chips, and investing heavily in catchy, star-studded advertising. These decisions have paid off with increasing profits for the company.[5]

## Conditions Affecting Decision Making

In an ideal business situation, managers would have all of the information they need to make decisions with certainty. Most business situations, however, are characterized by incomplete or ambiguous information, which affects the level of certainty with which a manager makes a decision. Generally speaking, there are three conditions that affect decision making: certainty, risk, and uncertainty.[6] In Figure 11.1, we can view decisions along a continuum of certainty.

**certainty**
The condition that exists when decision makers are fully informed about a problem, its alternative solutions, and their respective outcomes.

**Certainty.**    **Certainty** is the condition that exists when decision makers are fully informed about a problem, its alternative solutions, and their respective outcomes. Under this condition, individuals can anticipate, and even exercise some control over, events and their outcomes. Examples of decision making under the condition of certainty are scarce because business, like life, is filled with uncertainties. Even situations that seem certain, such as reordering supplies from the vendor who offers the best price and service, can be touched by uncertainty because of a back-order problem, a transportation breakdown, a change in personnel, or a quality lapse.

**risk**
The condition that exists when decision makers must rely on incomplete, yet reliable information.

**Risk.**    In the context of decision making, **risk** is the condition that exists when decision makers must rely on incomplete, yet reliable information. Under a state of risk, the decision maker does not know with certainty the future outcomes associated with alternative courses of action; the results are subject to chance. However, the manager has enough information to determine the probabilities associated with each alternative. He or she can then choose the alternative that has the highest probability of success. On the certainty continuum, the condition of risk means that a problem, its alternative solutions, and their respective outcomes lie between the extremes of being known and well-defined (certainty) and being unknown and ambiguous (uncertainty).

**uncertainty**
The condition that exists when little or no factual information is available about a problem, its alternative solutions, and their respective outcomes.

**Uncertainty.**    **Uncertainty** is the condition that exists when little or no factual information is available about a problem, its alternative solutions, and their respective outcomes. In a state of uncertainty, the decision maker does not have enough information to determine the probabilities associated with each alternative. In actuality, the deci-

## FIGURE 11.1

**The Continuum of Certainty in Decision Making**

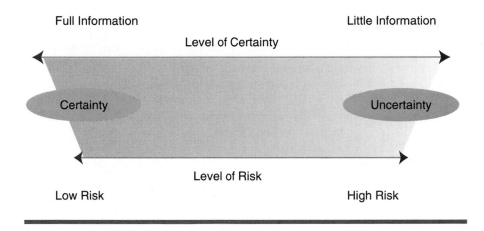

sion maker may have so little information that he or she may be unable even to define the problem, let alone identify alternative solutions and possible outcomes.

Making decisions under the condition of uncertainty is commonplace in today's business world. Managers must acquire as much relevant information as possible and then use logic, intuition, judgment, and experience to determine the best course of action to follow. Of the conditions affecting decision making, uncertainty is the condition under which managers are the least confident about their decision making and are the most prone to err.

Phil Ramos, owner and founder of Philatron International, a company that makes electrical wire and cable products, knows well what it is like to operate under uncertainty. In 1991, Philatron began producing a new kind of coiled air hose for use on tractor-trailer rigs. The product did well, selling 45,000 units in the first few months. Then the National Highway Traffic Safety Administration (NHTSA) ruled the product unsafe and ordered Philatron to stop selling it and to issue a recall. After months of discussion among Philatron, attorneys, NHTSA, members of Congress, and Small Business Administration officials, NHTSA agreed that there was no safety issue with the product and rescinded its order. Nonetheless, NHTSA said that Philatron still could not sell the hose until an outdated agency regulation was changed—a process that has dragged on for almost a year, with no end in sight. In the meantime, Philatron has lost a projected $5 million in potential sales and has been forced to lay off almost half of its work force. Ramos is planning a new line of consumer products; however, the shadow of the regulatory nightmare still hangs over the company, effecting a condition of uncertainty that is bound to influence decision making for a long time to come.[7]

**Example:** Uncertainty exists among the makers of five-gallon plastic containers used for detergent, wallboard joint compound, and paint. These containers are often reused and cause safety hazards to toddlers, who can drown in even a small amount of liquid. The manufacturers are considering warning labels and new designs and shapes. No performance standards exist yet for safer buckets.

## THE STEPS OF DECISION MAKING

Regardless of whether a decision is programmed or nonprogrammed, or of the state of certainty under which it takes place, experts view decision making as a process with six steps: (1) identifying the problem, (2) generating alternative courses of

**Teaching Note:** Compare the steps in the decision-making process to those used in strategic-planning and discuss the similarities. Remind students that these models are similar to the scientific reasoning process they may have studied in science or logic classes.

**Example:** Return to the hazardous five-gallon plastic container example. The industry manufacturers have identified the problem as a safety hazard for toddlers who don't weigh enough to turn the buckets over and consequently drown in their liquid contents.

**Example:** Because no industry standards exist, manufacturers must choose between labeling five-gallon containers with English- and Spanish-language warning labels, redesigning the containers, or changing to a lighter material. The U.S. Consumer Product Safety Commission has begun proceedings that could lead to a ban of the containers.

action, (3) evaluating the alternatives, (4) selecting the best alternative, (5) implementing the decision, and (6) evaluating the decision (Figure 11.2). All managers do not always go through all of these steps, as we shall see later in this chapter.

## Identifying the Problem

The first step in the decision-making process is identifying the problem. Earlier in this chapter, we defined a problem as the difference between an actual situation and a desired situation. We cannot put too much emphasis on this step in the process. In fact, problem identification is probably the most critical part of the decision-making process, for *it* is what determines the direction that the decision-making process takes, and, ultimately, the decision that is made.

In identifying a problem, managers should not confuse the symptoms of a problem with the problem itself:  Symptoms merely signal that a problem exists. For instance, a high level of absenteeism in a department is a symptom of a problem—not the problem itself. However, the symptom is significant because it lets the manager know that a problem exists. Then, through investigation and analysis of information, the manager can properly identify the problem. In the case of high absenteeism in a department, the issue might be that jobs in that department are not suitably designed, the rate of pay for jobs in that department is too low, or the supervisor in charge of that department has some managerial deficiencies.

## Generating Alternative Courses of Action

The second step in the decision-making process is generating alternative solutions to the problem. This step involves identifying items or activities that could reduce or eliminate the difference between the actual situation and the desired situation. For this step to be effective, the decision makers must allot enough time to generate creative alternatives as well as ensure that all individuals involved in the process exercise patience and tolerance of others and their ideas.

The importance of generating alternative courses of action is often overlooked because of the time and effort involved. In the pursuit of a "quick fix," managers too often shortchange this step by failing to consider more than one or two alternatives, which reduces the opportunity to identify effective solutions. Managers need to resist the urge to begin evaluating the proposed alternative solutions (Step 3) before completing the second stage. By holding off on alternative evaluation, the manager helps ensure the generation of as many alternatives as possible, increasing the likelihood that the "best" alternative will be among those considered as possible solutions.

Let's return to the previously discussed scenario about the department plagued with a high level of absenteeism. After investigating, upper management determines that the department's supervisor has poor interpersonal skills. Alternative solutions that might address this problem include (1) fire the supervisor, (2) transfer the supervisor to another position within the company, (3) demote the supervisor, (4) hire a new supervisor from outside the company, (5) promote an internal candidate to the position, (6) laterally move another supervisor from within the company to the position, or (7) train the supervisor in the interpersonal skill areas in which he has problems. It is important to realize that if decision makers do not give sufficient time to this alternative-generation phase, it could result in the supervisor being fired or transferred, when, in fact, the best alternative may be skills training.

**FIGURE 11.2**

**The Steps in the Decision-Making Process**

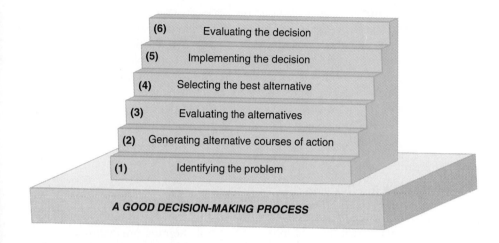

(6)   Evaluating the decision
(5)   Implementing the decision
(4)   Selecting the best alternative
(3)   Evaluating the alternatives
(2)   Generating alternative courses of action
(1)   Identifying the problem

*A GOOD DECISION-MAKING PROCESS*

## Evaluating the Alternatives

After generating a list of alternatives, the arduous task of evaluating each of them begins. Numerous methods exist for evaluating the alternatives, including determining the "pros and cons" of each; performing a cost-benefit analysis for each alternative; and weighting factors important in the decision, ranking each alternative relative to its ability to meet each factor, and then multiplying cumulatively to provide a final value for each alternative.[8] Regardless of the method used, it is during this third step of the decision-making process that the decision maker evaluates each alternative in terms of its feasibility (*can* it be done?), its effectiveness (how *well* does it resolve the problem situation?), and its consequences (what will be its *costs*—financial and nonfinancial—to the organization?).

Returning to the example of the departmental supervisor deficient in interpersonal skills, armed with information about potential supervisory candidates both inside and outside the company and available supervisory training programs, the decision makers evaluate the feasibility, effectiveness, and projected outcomes/consequences of each of the generated alternatives:  firing, demoting, laterally transferring, hiring, promoting, and training.

## Selecting the Best Alternative

After the decision makers have evaluated all the alternatives, it is time for the fourth step in the decision-making process:  choosing the best alternative. Depending on the evaluation method used, the selection process can be fairly straightforward. The best alternative could be the one with the most "pros" and the fewest "cons"; the one with the greatest benefits and the lowest costs; or the one with the highest cumulative value, if using weighting.

Yet, even with a thorough evaluation process, the best alternative may not be obvious. It is at this point that managers must decide which alternative has the highest combined level of feasibility and effectiveness, coupled with the lowest

**Teaching Note:** Continue the safer bucket example and have students evaluate possible alternatives as well as suggest other feasible alternatives. Remind students the CPSC feels the industry has not been aggressive enough in using warning labels, educating consumers about the drowning risks, or developing a performance standard for the product.

costs to the organization. Probability estimates often come into play at this point in the decision-making process. The decision makers can analyze each alternative in terms of its probability of success; then, they select the alternative with the highest probability of being successful.

In terms of the skill-deficient supervisor, an evaluation of the alternatives could reveal that the alternative with the highest probability of success—or, the highest level of feasibility and effectiveness with the lowest cost—is the one that proposes training the supervisor in the area of interpersonal skills to help him improve relations with the members of his department. This alternative affords the supervisor the chance to acquire the necessary skills at a reasonable financial cost to the organization. In addition, this alternative preserves stability in the supervisory ranks by not shuffling supervisors around and promotes the philosophy that the company values training (and employees) and will provide help when necessary.

## Implementing the Decision

This is the step in the decision-making process that transforms the selected alternative from an abstract thought into reality. Implementing the decision involves planning and executing the actions that must take place so that the selected alternative can actually solve the problem.

Implementation is a crucial step in the decision-making process, for the best alternative in the world cannot resolve a problem if it is not implemented properly. Many great ideas have been wasted because of breakdowns in implementation; too often managers lack the necessary resources, energy, ability, knowledge, leadership skills, or motivation to "make things happen." Successful implementation of a decision also depends on others' willingness to accept the decision and to work hard to ensure that it is carried out. Therefore, individuals affected by the decision need to be involved in the implementation stage, as well as in the rest of the steps in the decision-making process. Employee participation throughout the process engenders support for the decision and commitment to working to solve the problem.

In the scenario involving the departmental supervisor and the decision to provide training, implementation of the decision could involve enrolling the supervisor in a management development training program that focuses on interpersonal skills. Certainly the supervisor's superior would be involved in this process, along with possibly the human resource department.

**Example:** Implementation of self-directed work teams is catching on among small businesses after causing significant increases in the quality of goods and services offered at many large companies, according to Richard Wellins, a consultant and author on work teams in Bridgeville, PA.

## Evaluating the Decision

In evaluating the decision, the sixth and final step in the decision-making process, managers gather information to determine the effectiveness of their decision. Has the original problem identified in the first step been resolved? If not, is the company closer to the situation it desires than it was at the beginning of the decision-making process?

If an implemented decision has not resolved the problem, the manager must determine why the decision-making process failed.

1. Was the wrong alternative selected? If so, one of the other alternatives generated in the decision-making process might be a wiser choice.

2. Was the correct alternative selected, but implemented improperly? If so, attention should be focused solely on Step 5 to ensure that the chosen alternative is implemented successfully.

3. Was the original problem identified incorrectly? If so, the decision-making process would need to begin again, starting with a revised identification step.

4. Has management not given the implemented alternative enough time for it to be successful? If so, then more time—the true test of any solution—can be allotted to the process, and the decision can be reevaluated at a later date when it has had time to prove its worth.

Returning for the last time to the supervisor with poor interpersonal skills, the manager must evaluate the decision to train the supervisor through a management development training program. In this case, the manager has several means of evaluating the effectiveness of the decision: (1) personal observation of whether the supervisor's interpersonal skills have improved; (2) measurement of the level of absenteeism in the department, to see if it has dropped to an acceptable level; and (3) feedback from the supervisor's employees to see if they are happier with their supervisor's level of interpersonal skills.

# DECISION-MAKING MODELS

Having gained an understanding of the nature of decision making and the six steps involved in the decision-making process, it will be easier to understand the basic approaches to decision making. Management theory generally recognizes two major models of decision making—the classical model and the administrative model.

## The Classical Model

The **classical model of decision making** is a prescriptive approach that outlines how managers should make decisions. Also called the rational model, the classical model is based on economic assumptions and asserts that managers are logical, rational individuals who make decisions that are in the best interests of the organization. The classical model is characterized by the following assumptions:

1. The manager has complete information about the decision situation and operates under a condition of certainty.
2. The problem is clearly defined, and the decision maker has knowledge of all possible alternatives and their outcomes.
3. Through the use of quantitative techniques, rationality, and logic, the decision maker evaluates the alternatives and selects the optimum alternative—the one that will maximize the decision situation by offering the best solution to the problem.[9]

**classical model of decision making**
A prescriptive approach, asserting that managers are logical, rational individuals who make decisions that are in the best interests of the organization, that outlines how managers should make decisions; also known as the rational model.

**Teaching Note:** To develop familiarity with the decision-making models as well as an understanding of their definitions, have students provide personal examples of decisions they have made under each of the models and share them with the class.

## The Administrative Model

In contrast, the **administrative model of decision making** is a descriptive approach that outlines how managers actually do make decisions. Also called the organizational, neoclassical, or behavioral model, the administrative model is based on the work of economist Herbert A. Simon, whose research and findings in this area resulted in his winning a Nobel Prize in economics. Simon recognized that people do not always make decisions with logic and rationality, and he introduced two concepts that have become hallmarks of the administrative model—bounded rationality and satisficing.[10]

**administrative model of decision making**
A descriptive approach, recognizing that people do not always make decisions with logic and rationality, that outlines how managers actually do make decisions; also known as the organizational, neoclassical, or behavioral model.

**bounded rationality**
The idea that people have limits, or boundaries, to their rationality.

**Bounded rationality** means that people have limits, or boundaries, to their rationality. These limits exist because people are bound by their own values and skills, incomplete information, and their own inability—due to time, resource, and capability restraints—to process all of the information needed to make perfectly rational decisions. Because managers often lack the time or ability to process complete information about complex decisions, they usually wind up having to make decisions with only partial knowledge about alternative solutions and their outcomes. This leads managers to forgo the six steps of decision making in favor of a quicker, yet satisfying, process—satisficing.

**satisficing**
The decision maker's decision to choose the first alternative that appears to resolve the problem satisfactorily.

**Satisficing** means that decision makers choose the first alternative that appears to resolve the problem *satisfactorily*. Instead of going through the exhaustive process of generating and evaluating all possible alternatives in search of the best, or optimal, solution, managers are more likely to search only until they find an alternative that is satisfactory, or "good enough." Thus, satisficing suggests that managers tend to implement the *first* satisfactory alternative that comes to their attention, even if better alternatives are presumed to exist. In satisficing, managers decide that the time and expense involved in obtaining complete information are not justified.

The administrative model of decision making also has some basic assumptions:

1. The manager has incomplete information about the decision situation and operates under a condition of risk or uncertainty.

2. The problem is not clearly defined, and the decision maker has limited knowledge of possible alternatives and their outcomes.

3. The decision maker satisfices by choosing the first satisfactory alternative—one that will resolve the problem situation by offering a *good* solution to the problem.

## Applying Decision-Making Models to the Real World

So, which model is correct? As we said, the classical model of decision making is prescriptive, which means it describes how decisions *should* be made, not necessarily how they actually are made. Thus, it provides an example of decision making at its best—the "ideal" that managers can use to guide and enhance their own decision-making situations. However, the classical model is often too unrealistic and time consuming to be applied to real business situations.

The administrative model seems to describe accurately how managers actually make decisions—especially nonprogrammed ones and those under conditions of risk or uncertainty. In fact, a survey that included 200 CEOs of fast-growing private companies revealed that, when making decisions, only 40 percent of the companies surveyed considered alternative solutions other than the ones that were implemented.[11] For these companies, decision making was characterized more by the satisficing behavior described in the administrative model than by the maximizing behavior described in the classical model. However, while the administrative model is "realistic," it can promote shortsightedness and a willingness to settle for "OK" in lieu of striving for "the best."

The decision-making models are valuable because they help managers better understand the decision-making process. The classical model illustrates how managers can strive to be more rational and logical in their decision making. On the other hand, the administrative model illustrates how managers have limits to their rationality and how these limits affect their decision making. Thus, the informa-

Lee Iacocca relied on his intuition in deciding to champion Chrysler's development of the mini-van concept in the late 1970s, while competitors GM and Ford decided to shelve their minivan plans. Here, Iacocca introduces the new 1984 minivan, which immediately became a sales success. Against the opposition of all his top executives, Iacocca again relied on his intuition in commiting several hundred million dollars to expand the production of minivans after their first successful year. Thanks to Iacocca's gut instincts, the minivan is now Chrysler's cash cow, accounting for more than one-fourth of Chrysler's car and truck sales.

*Source:* Courtesy of Chrysler Corporation.

tion and insight provided by both models help pave the way for managerial understanding and growth in the all-important management function of decision making.

## FACTORS THAT AFFECT DECISION MAKING

When you are equipped with an understanding of the decision-making models, it is easy to see how many factors can get in the way of rational decision making. The administrative model points out the realities of managerial decision making—that situations can, and do, cause managers to "stop short" of making optimum decisions. This section will deal with some of the commonly recognized factors that affect decision making: intuition, emotion and stress, framing, escalation of commitment, and confidence and risk propensity. The "Dynamics of Diversity" box discusses the impact that cultural differences have on decision making.

### Intuition

A survey of over 2,000 top executives found that executives use intuition frequently in their decision making.[12] **Intuition** means immediately comprehending that something is the case, seemingly without the use of any reasoning process or conscious analysis. Whole books have been written about intuitive decision making, and there are researchers who view intuition as a rather rational skill that managers *should* use in making decisions.[13] Even though the steps of the intuitive process may be buried in the subconscious part of the brain—so that we may never understand them—most experts realize the existence and importance of intuition in managerial decision making and view it as a necessary area of study.

In lay terms, intuition is a hunch, a sixth sense, a flash of insight, something that "feels right," or a "gut" feeling. These descriptions could easily lead you to believe that intuitive decision making is irrational, arbitrary, or even somewhat mystical. However, such is not the case. While intuition refers to decision making without formal analysis or conscious reasoning, it is based on years of practice and experience that enable managers to identify alternatives quickly without conducting a systematic analysis of alternatives and their consequences. When making a decision using intuition, the manager recognizes cues in the decision situation

**intuition**
The immediate comprehension that something is the case, seemingly without the use of any reasoning process or conscious analysis.

## Dynamics of Diversity

### CULTURAL DIFFERENCES AND DECISION MAKING

There is no doubt that decision making, as well as every other aspect of organizational life, has been profoundly affected by the increasing cultural diversity that exists in today's business world. Due to changing work-force demographic trends and the increasing globalization of business, today's managers are realizing that being able to manage cultural differences is essential to the long-term success of their companies.

To understand cultural differences and their impact on decision making, managers must first acknowledge that people of different ethnic backgrounds have different attitudes, values, and norms that reflect their cultural heritages. One area of cultural difference that has been extensively researched is the issue of individualism versus collectivism. Understanding individualism and collectivism is important to understanding the effects of cultural differences on decision making because cross-cultural studies suggest that certain cultures tend to favor either individualism or collectivism. For example, North Americans and northern and western Europeans tend to be individualists, and Asians, Latins, and most east and west Africans tend to be collectivists. Additionally, there is evidence to support that African, Hispanic, and Far Eastern minorities in the United States tend to be collectivists.

Individualist cultures tend to place greater emphasis on the needs and goals of the individual over those of the group. Individualists consider their own beliefs and efforts of paramount importance, and they emphasize competition more than cooperation. In contrast, collectivist cultures place greater emphasis on the needs and goals of the group over those of the individual. Collectivists stress the importance of social norms, duty, and shared beliefs, and they emphasize the value of cooperation—not competition—with group members. When it comes to decision making, collectivists are more likely than individualists to sacrifice personal interests for the attainment of group goals.

Equipped with an awareness of such differences, today's managers will be better prepared to understand how decision making—both within their organizations and between different organizations (such as in joint ventures, strategic alliances, etc.)—is affected by diversity. Such an understanding of cultural diversity explains, for example, why over 90 percent of all large Japanese companies and most of the smaller ones use a deci-sion-making process called *ringi*. This system is based on the collectivist principle that decisions are made only when a consensus is reached among team members. Conversely, American companies, with their emphasis on individualism and independent action, do not see consensus as a necessity in decision making. Understanding this difference, and others, between Japanese and American cultures can only facilitate organizational decision-making processes.

*Sources:* Taylor Cox, Jr., "The Multicultural Organization," *Academy of Management Executive* 5 (May 1991): 34–37; Taylor H. Cox, Sharon A. Lobel, and Poppy Lauretta McLeod, "Effects of Ethnic Group Cultural Differences on Cooperative and Competitive Behavior on a Group Task," *Academy of Management Journal* 34 (December 1991): 827–847; Brian Mark Hawrysh and Judith Lynne Zaichkowsky, "Cultural Approaches to Negotiations: Understanding the Japanese," *European Journal of Marketing* 25 (1991): 40–54.

that are the same as or similar to those in previous situations he or she has experienced, rapidly conducts a subconscious analysis, and unconsciously makes a choice.

Managers rely on their intuition in decision making largely out of necessity. In today's complex, dynamic business environment, managers have to make a multitude of decisions, frequently with minimal information and under time and cost constraints. The collection and analysis of data and alternative solutions can be a laborious, time-consuming, expensive process that managers do not have the luxury to undertake. Consequently, intuitive decision making becomes a necessity for managerial survival. Of course, all managers, especially inexperienced ones, should be careful not to rely too heavily on intuition. Obviously, if rationality and analytical decision making are always ignored in favor of intuition, the odds are good that managers will make some faulty decisions. Thus, managers need to be aware of their own use of intuition and to be careful to moderate its use with logic and analysis.

Sam Walton, the late founder and chairman of Wal-Mart, exemplified the positive use of intuition. When he conceived the idea of building large discount retail stores in rural areas, he was told that the idea would never work. After all, Sears was a very successful large retailer whose success was based on stores located in urban areas. Nevertheless, Walton was sure his intuition was right … and the rest is history. In the early 1990s, Wal-Mart was the third largest company in the world, with a stock market value of $73.5 billion.[14]

## Emotion and Stress

Because most decision situations involve some element of risk, decision making invariably evokes anxiety, which leads to stress. Stress can, at times, derail people from following reasonable courses of action. All managers are susceptible to letting their emotions get in the way of rational decision making, and when emotions interfere with logic, managers can respond in nonproductive, even counterproductive, ways. These responses tend to be more common when decisions have to be made under time pressure.

**Example:** Komatsu officials from the Japan-based heavy equipment manufacturer evaluated locations in the Southeast United States for locating a plant. Examining transportation issues, labor supply, and distribution channels, they let emotion finally make the location decision. The Chattanooga area with its mountain and surrounding river reminded Japanese executives of their Osaka, Japan, home, and thus emotion was the basis for the expansion location

When you consider the powerful effect that emotions such as guilt, anxiety, and embarrassment have on individuals, it is easy to understand how managers could be driven to make decisions—even bad ones—in their need to relieve the feelings plaguing them. Due to the effects of emotions and stress, decision makers have been known to respond in some fairly predictable ways, all of which render their decisions less reasonable. Some typical responses to emotion and stress in decision making are defensive avoidance, which involves excessively delaying a decision; overreaction, making a decision impulsively to relieve anxiety; and hypervigilance, obsessively gathering more and more data in lieu of making a decision.[15]

Because the effects of emotions and stress on managers can result in faulty—even damaging—decisions, it is of paramount importance that managers realize when and how their feelings are affecting their decision making. It is during these stressful times that managers would be wise to devote time and resources to a logical decision-making process in an effort to ensure that the procedure is rational, not emotional.

## Framing

Framing is widely recognized as a factor that not only affects decision making, but also contributes to many decision failures.[16] Generally speaking, **framing** involves the tendency to view positively presented information favorably and negatively presented information unfavorably. It refers to how information is phrased, presented, or labeled. Labels create frames of reference that serve to bias judgment—or interpretation of information—which, in turn, influences behavior. The manner in which information about a problem or possible outcomes is presented can wield a tremendous amount of influence on a decision maker's evaluation of the situation and, ultimately, on his or her decision.

**framing**
The tendency to view positively presented information favorably and negatively presented information unfavorably.

For example, managers are more likely to view positively projects that have a 70 percent success rate than projects that have a 30 percent failure rate, even though these projects have the same probability of success. Because of framing, the projects presented as 70 percent successful probably seem more attractive to managers than the projects presented in terms of their failure rates.

Managers need to be aware of how easy it is to be overly influenced by the manner in which something is presented. Also, susceptibility to the power of framing is likely to increase when managers are making decisions under conditions of uncertainty. Thus, in the pursuit of sound decision making, managers must strive to analyze decision situations objectively, thereby reducing the chances that their decisions will be unduly influenced by framing.

## Escalation of Commitment

**escalation of commitment**
The tendency to persist with a failing course of action.

Another factor that affects decision making is an escalation of commitment to a chosen course of action. **Escalation of commitment** refers to the tendency to persist with a failing course of action.[17] In such cases, the decision makers become so immersed in their chosen course of action that they ignore or discount information that challenges the soundness of their initial decision. Caught up in the momentum of the situation, these managers lose their objectivity and seem unable to "call it quits," even though logic and rationality dictate that they should. Escalation of commitment is a decision-making trap often characterized by the following descriptions or scenarios: "throwing good money after bad," a preoccupation with "sunk costs," and "too much time and money invested to quit now."

There are several reasons why decision makers fall into the trap of escalating commitment. A primary reason is their unwillingness to admit—to others or themselves—that their original decision was incorrect. Coinciding with this is an unwillingness on the manager's part to accept that the resources—money, time, energy, and people—already committed to the course of action were allocated in vain. Therefore, in a need to reaffirm the wisdom of his or her original decision, the decision maker escalates his or her commitment by allocating even more resources to the attainment of the original goal. In addition, managers who have fallen into the trap of escalating commitment are often spurred to continue their seemingly faulty course of action by the feeling that the situation is bound to change for the better—because of the resources already invested, the projected favorable impact of additional resource allocation, their belief in and identification with the course of action, their unwillingness to give up or quit, and a sometimes unrealistic optimism that, despite evidence to the contrary, "things are bound to get better."[18]

Thus, managers must walk a fine line. On the one hand, they must be careful not to commit to an apparently faulty decision for too long, for to do so could be disastrous for the company. On the other hand, they must guard against bailing out of a seemingly faulty decision too soon—before time and resources have had a chance to render the course of action successful. Bailing out too soon can also be disastrous for the company, because of the risk that potentially successful courses of action would not be realized. Given the critical nature of escalating commitment in the decision-making process, managers should take steps to avoid the escalation trap. Some recommendations on how managers can avoid escalating commitment include the following:

1. Set limits on your involvement and commitment in advance and stick with them during the course of action. This gives the decision maker a better chance of remaining objective when evaluating the decision and subsequent course of action.

2. Don't look to other people to see what you should do. Because escalating commitment is a commonly observed behavior, it is easy to look around and see others who are escalating, too, making it easier to justify your own tendency to escalate.

3. Determine *why* you are continuing a course of action. If there are not sound reasons to continue, then don't.

4. Remind yourself of the costs involved. Consider the added costs of continuing the course of action—not just the costs already incurred—when making your decision.

5. Be vigilant in your awareness of the tendency to escalate. It is an easy trap to fall into, and managers must be aware of this phenomenon and continually reassess the costs and benefits of continuing any course of action.[19]

Examples abound in business and everyday life of escalating commitment, such as people who wait for an inordinately long time for a bus to take them somewhere instead of seeking other means of transportation to reach their destination; someone who stays in an unfulfilling job or career because that is the job for which he or she was trained, educated, and/or experienced; a couple who persist in continuing a souring romantic relationship; and a company that continues to pursue a failing venture.

The U. S. involvement in the Vietnam War is often cited as an example of escalation of commitment carried to the extreme. During the 1960s and 1970s, the United States committed enormous amounts of soldiers and money to the Vietnam War—even in the face of mounting evidence that U.S. involvement in the war was a losing proposition. The escalating commitment ceased in 1973 when President Richard Nixon terminated U.S. involvement in the war, which ended up costing over 50,000 American lives and billions of dollars. Conversely, President Jimmy Carter's decision in 1980 to abort a failed rescue attempt of American hostages held in Iran is an example of the avoidance of escalating commitment. When the military mission to rescue the hostages suffered accidents and misfortune that resulted in the deaths of eight Americans, Carter aborted the mission before even greater damage could occur. Faced with a failing venture that had already cost too much in terms of human life, Carter changed tack and instead worked feverishly through diplomatic channels to secure the release of the hostages, which occurred in January 1981.

## Confidence and Risk Propensity

Confidence and risk propensity are two factors that go hand in hand in affecting managerial decision making. **Confidence** means that a person has faith that his or her decisions are reliable and good. **Risk propensity** refers to a person's willingness to take risks when making decisions. Generally speaking, the higher your level of confidence in your decisions, the greater the likelihood that you will take risks in decision making.

Overconfidence is dangerous because it can lead decision makers to ignore the risks associated with a particular course of action. When this happens, organizations can become vulnerable to all kinds of negative exposure, including legal and financial exposure that can spell ruin. Thus, it is easy to see that an inappropriate confidence level can threaten successful decision making and implementation. Disaster is a common byproduct of poor decisions made with great confidence. Yet, by the same token, the potential benefits of a good decision may never be

**Teaching Note:** One cost of a course of action is waiting too long to make a decision and having the "window of opportunity" close. Competitors may make a more rapid decision and introduce a product first. Managers must learn to make both accurate and fast decisions.

**confidence**
A person's faith that his or her decisions are reliable and good.

**risk propensity**
A person's willingness to take risks when making decisions.

Confidence and risk propensity helped Sheri Poe decide to launch Ryka, Inc., a new athletic footwear manufacturer that would compete against name-brand, billion-dollar companies. A fitness enthusiast, Poe was dissatisfied with women's athletic shoes, which at the time were sized-down versions of men's shoes. She felt confident that women would buy her products because they are designed specifically for women's physiology. Poe risked everything to start her business, leveraging her house and borrowing money from family and friends. Poe's confidence and risk propensity, along with a well-conceived marketing plan, helped her company gain a successful foothold in a tough market.

*Source:* © John Alexanders/Black Star.

realized if the decision maker does not have, and does not project to others, enough confidence in the decision.

Similarly, there is a fine line to be walked when it comes to risk propensity. Managers who take too many and/or too great risks can lead companies to disastrous results; however, managers who are too risk averse may never lead their companies to their greatest potential. Like the other factors that affect decision making—intuition, emotion and stress, framing, and escalation of commitment—confidence and risk propensity must be scrutinized carefully to ensure that their contributions to the decision-making process are favorable and in the best interest of the organization.

Businessman Paul Reichmann offers an almost perfect example of the calamitous effects that overconfidence and risk propensity can have on an organization. During the 1970s and 1980s, Reichmann and two of his brothers created an empire of office buildings and natural resource companies, amassing a family fortune valued at $10 billion. However, the Reichmann family company, Olympia and York Developments Ltd., was forced to declare bankruptcy in 1992, and, by 1993, most of the company had been liquidated. The family's $10 billion fortune was also gone, drained by real estate speculation and disastrous stock market investments. By his own admission, the primary reason for the demise of the Reichmann empire was Paul Reichmann himself. He has said that his overconfidence and his ability to manage risk led to his downfall. In fact, in an almost uncanny parallel to this section's focus on confidence and risk propensity, it has been argued that "Paul Reichmann's taste for risk taking and his towering confidence in his own ability as a financier inevitably led to the destruction of the world's largest real estate company."[20]

**Example:** Risks can be seen in the pharmaceutical industry. According to Larry Feinberg, president of the investment firm Oracle Partners, 30% of all prescriptions are filled with generic drugs today. Within five years that figure could rise to 79%, representing a risk for brand-name pharmaceutical makers like Merck and American Cyanamid.

## DECISION MAKING IN GROUPS

All of the topics discussed thus far—types of decisions, conditions affecting decision making, steps of decision making, decision-making models, and factors that affect decision making—apply to decisions made by both individuals and groups. It is important to note, however, that in more and more organizations today, decisions are being made primarily by groups rather than individuals. In fact, in most organizations, it would be rare to find decisions being made regularly by one individual.

# B U S I N E S S    D I L E M M A

*You're the Manager ...What Would You Do?*

THE COMPANY:   J&G Chemical Company

YOUR POSITION:   Environmental Manager

THE PLACE:   Jacksonville, FL

J&G Chemical Company, one of the largest industrial chemical producers, has always been concerned about the safe and effective disposal of chemical waste. A year ago, CEO Ken Jones hired you as an environmental manager. In your brief time with the company, you have begun implementing a new, advanced program to ensure the safety of employees, the plant site, waste-disposal areas, and the general public.

Communication to line management concerning the new program has been extensive. All line managers involved in chemical-waste disposal have attended a series of informative, instructional workshops covering safety factors, disposal guidelines, and notification procedures in the event of a potentially harmful situation. A ten-step process for crisis intervention and handling was detailed. You have conducted drills individually with the line managers to determine their understanding of the new program and to ensure that they are following the new guidelines. The line managers have presented the same information to employees under their supervision, and drills with seven of the ten teams of employees have been held. Problems in the manufacturing processes employed by Teams 8, 9, and 10 have delayed their training and drills.

On September 5, Bill Smith, a relatively new employee, discovered a hairline crack in the chemical-waste containment unit controlled by Team 9. He immediately reported the problem to the line manager and returned to his work station. Contrary to the new guidelines, the manager did not shut down the manufacturing line, and the first-shift employees left for the day. Due to some personal problems, the line manager forgot to inform the incoming shift's manager of the problem. The second-shift employees continued to operate the line, sending the chemical waste into the damaged containment unit.

On September 6, Bill Smith missed work due to illness. Because Team 9 was shorthanded, and in their haste to meet a looming deadline, no one noticed the damaged containment unit until the second shift reported for work. By this time, the crack was substantially larger, and a small amount of chemical waste had begun seeping onto the surrounding platform and into a drain for treated, "clean" water. The pipes from this area empty into nearby Crystal Lake, known for its excellent fishing and bird watching. The employee who noticed the seepage reported the problem to the line manager, who disregarded the new guidelines and employed a stop-gap measure to allow the manufacturing process to continue.

By the time the first shift reported to work this morning, September 7, a crisis situation had developed. A disgruntled employee who learned about the leak called a local newspaper reporter known for her aggressive reporting on environmental issues. The reporter has asked to speak with you, demanding to know what J&G will do to correct the damage, if indeed environmental damage has occurred. You have politely informed her that she will be called as soon as more information is available on the situation. You have called a meeting of the line managers and asked for recommendations to defuse the crisis situation quickly, taking any necessary measures to contain environmental damage and minimize negative publicity concerning the event.

## Questions

1.  Trace the decision-making process you would use to handle the situation. What decision-making model would you use?
2.  How should decisions be made in such a crisis environment?
3.  Given the existing information, as environmental manager, what would you do?

---

The reasons for the prevalence of group decision making in organizations are varied. Today's complex, dynamic business world requires more specialized knowledge than just one person can usually possess. Thus, companies are almost forced to rely on groups of individuals to obtain sufficient information and expertise needed to make sound business decisions. Moreover, once a decision has been made, the success of its implementation depends, to a great extent, on the commitment of the individuals who must carry it out. It is proven that group participation throughout the decision-making process helps create acceptance of and commitment to the decision, which go a long way toward ensuring the successful

**Comment on Box:** Have students use each decision-making process and discuss how decisions would differ under each. Discuss how the safety problem was allowed to occur and have students outline policies and procedures, as well as training programs, to prevent such a problem in the future.

During brainstorming sessions, managers and employees of Haworth, Inc., an office-furniture manufacturer, use the technique of storyboarding to identify problems and suggest ideas to solve them. Originating with Walt Disney, storyboarding involves group members writing their ideas on movable cards that can be organized and reorganized on a bulletin board during idea analysis. Haworth used storyboarding as part of its efforts in applying for the Malcolm Baldrige National Quality Award.

*Source:* Courtesy of Haworth, Inc.

**brainstorming**
A technique in which group members spontaneously suggest ideas to solve a problem.

implementation of the decision. With groups such as teams, task forces, and committees becoming more commonplace in the realm of managerial decision making, it is appropriate to discuss both the techniques, as well as the advantages and disadvantages, of group decision making.

## Group Decision Techniques

There are several decision techniques that are helpful in group decision making. In this section, we will discuss three common ones: brainstorming, the nominal group technique, and the Delphi group technique.

**Brainstorming.**    **Brainstorming** is a technique in which group members spontaneously suggest ideas to solve a problem. Its primary purpose is to generate a multitude of creative alternatives, regardless of the likelihood of their being implemented. There are four basic rules for brainstorming:

1. Criticism is not allowed. Judgment or evaluation of ideas must be withheld until the conclusion of the idea-generation process.
2. "Freewheeling" is encouraged. The more novel and radical the idea, the better, for it is easier to "tame down" ideas than to think of them.
3. Quantity is desired. The greater the number of ideas, the greater the likelihood that a superior idea will be generated.
4. Combination and improvement are encouraged. In addition to contributing their own ideas, participants should suggest how others' ideas can be turned into better ideas, or how two or more ideas can be combined into yet another one.[21]

The object of brainstorming is to promote freer, more flexible thinking and to encourage group members to build on each other's creativity. By prohibiting criticism, brainstorming reduces inhibition and fears of ridicule or failure, which typically results in enthusiastic, involved participants. Brainstorming is considered to be a very effective technique for generating alternatives, the second step of the decision-making process.

**Nominal Group Technique.**    Unlike the highly interactive, unstructured brainstorming, the **nominal group technique** involves the use of a highly structured meeting agenda and restricts discussion or interpersonal communication during the decision-making process. While the group members are all physically present, they are required to operate independently. Specifically, the following steps occur in a nominal group:

**nominal group technique**
A process that involves the use of a highly structured meeting agenda and restricts discussion or interpersonal communication during the decision-making process.

1. Members meet as a group, but before any discussion takes place, each member independently writes down his or her ideas for possible problem solutions.

2. In round-robin fashion, each member takes a turn presenting a single idea to the group. This continues until everyone's ideas have been presented and recorded, usually on a flip chart or chalkboard. No discussion of the ideas occurs until all ideas have been recorded for general viewing.

3. The group then engages in an open discussion of the ideas for the purpose of clarification and evaluation.

4. A secret written ballot is then taken, with each member individually and silently ranking the ideas in priority order. The idea that has the highest aggregate ranking becomes the adopted decision.[22]

The nominal group technique is useful because it ensures that every group member has equal input in the decision-making process. It also avoids some of the pitfalls—such as self-censorship, pressure to conform, group member dominance, hostility, and conflict—that can plague a more interactive, spontaneous, unstructured forum such as one using brainstorming. The nominal group technique has been an effective tool in the generation and evaluation of alternatives, the second and third steps in the decision-making process.

**Delphi Group Technique.**    A more complex, time-consuming alternative, the **Delphi group technique** employs a written survey to gather expert opinions from a number of people without holding a group meeting. Unlike in brainstorming and nominal groups, Delphi group participants never meet face to face; in fact, they may be located in different cities and never see each other. The following steps take place in a Delphi group:

**Delphi group technique**
A technique employing a written survey to gather expert opinions without holding a group meeting.

1. The problem is identified, and members are asked to write down potential solutions through a series of carefully designed questionnaires.

2. Each member independently and anonymously completes the first questionnaire.

3. Results of the first questionnaire are compiled at a central location and then redistributed to the original respondents.

4. After reviewing the results, members are asked again for their solutions. This process usually triggers new solutions or causes amendments to the original position.

5. Steps 3 and 4 are repeated as often as necessary until a consensus is reached.[23]

The Delphi group technique has proven effective as a decision aid because group members can feel free to speak their minds with guaranteed anonymity. In addition, this technique offers the advantage of linking experts from all over the world without the expense and inconvenience associated with a group meeting at a central location. However, because of the repeated mailings and compilations

Faced with the decision whether to lay off some employees during a slow period, Ted Castle, president of Rhino Foods, a specialty-desserts maker, asked his employees to find an alternative solution that would save the company money yet minimize job losses. A group of employees formed a committee to study the problem. Their solution: lend employees to local businesses needing workers on a short-term basis. The group contacted 15 companies and found two that needed temporary workers and met Castle's criteria that the firms have a similar corporate culture and share Rhino's concern for social responsibility. By implementing the group's idea, Castle avoided the stress of layoffs and created a high level of trust among employees.

*Source:* © Alan Jakubek.

involved, the Delphi technique is extremely time consuming. Consequently, it is often not useful when quick decisions are required. Also, this method may not produce as many creative alternatives as brainstorming and the nominal group technique produce—due to the absence of the stimulation that can result from face-to-face interaction. Nevertheless, the Delphi group technique is an effective decision-making tool when it is used to combine expert opinions from different perspectives about an ambiguous problem.

## Individual versus Group Decision Making

Whatever technique is used, group decision making has clear advantages and disadvantages compared with individual decision making. Studies indicate that groups tend to make riskier decisions than would be advocated by individual group members prior to group discussion of the problem.[24] The results of dozens of individual versus group performance studies indicate that (1) groups tend to make higher-quality decisions than the *average* individual acting alone; and (2) *exceptional* individuals tend to outperform the group, particularly when the task is complex and the group is composed of relatively low-ability people.[25]

So, are two (or more) heads better than one? The answer depends on several factors, such as the nature of the task, the ability of the group members, and the form of interaction. Because managers often have a choice between making a decision by themselves or including others, they need to understand the advantages and disadvantages of group decision making.

**Advantages of Group Decision Making.**    Group decision making offers a number of advantages over individual decision making.

**1.** A group can bring much more knowledge and information to bear on a problem or decision than can an individual acting alone.

**2.** Individuals in a group bring different experiences, perspectives, and interests, which help the members see decision situations and problems from different angles.

**3.** Groups can typically generate and evaluate more alternatives than can one individual.

**4.** Within a group, discussion can serve to clarify vagueness and confusion, reduce uncertainty for those who are averse to risk, and provide an opportunity for intellectual stimulation that fosters creativity—all to a greater extent than would be possible with individual decision making.

**5.** People who participate in a group discussion about a decision are more likely to understand *why* the decision was made because they have heard the relevant arguments both for the chosen alternative and against the rejected alternatives.

**6.** Participants in group decision making are more likely to accept the decision ("it's 'our' decision") and, therefore, to be more committed to it, which translates into a greater motivation for ensuring successful implementation.

**7.** Our society values democracy, which the group decision-making process exemplifies. Thus, a group decision may be perceived by others as more legitimate than a decision made by a single individual.

**8.** Less-experienced participants in group interaction learn a great deal about group dynamics by actually being involved in the group decision-making process.

The advantages of group decision making can be readily seen in the automotive industry. In an effort to cut product development time and costs and improve product design and manufacturing, General Motors instituted a group decision-making technique in its redesign of the 1992 Buick LeSabre. Previously, product and process engineers had worked independently on car designs. With the redesign of the LeSabre, however, approximately 50 teams, averaging six members each, worked together throughout the project. The teams were composed of process and product engineers, financial experts, inside and outside suppliers, and assembly operators. The increased pool of knowledge, information, and perspectives afforded by the group decision-making process resulted in a car that surpassed all previous LeSabre models in almost every quantifiable category. According to GM's internal measurements, the ride quality (ride motions and smoothness) of the 1992 Buick LeSabre improved 45 percent over the 1991 model, car handling improved 14 percent, door-closing effort improved 20 percent, and trunk-lid closing effort improved 33 percent.[26]

**Disadvantages of Group Decision Making.**    Following is a list of the major disadvantages of group decision making.

**1.** Groups take more time to reach a decision than would a lone individual. Group assembly and interaction take time and can result in inefficiency and increased costs.

**2.** One or more group members may dominate the discussion and, therefore, exert undue influence on decision selection.

**3.** The desire by group members to be accepted and considered valuable to the group effort can result in participants feeling pressured to conform—or not to "rock the boat." Such pressure stifles the creativity of individual contributors and encourages conformity among viewpoints.

**4.** To avoid the time and inherent conflict typically associated with group decision making, participants may be willing to settle for a compromise, or satisficing, decision rather than pursue an optimizing, or maximizing, decision.

**5.** Because the group rather than any single individual makes the decision, there is no clear focus of decision responsibility. This ambiguity can result in confusion when it comes to decision implementation and evaluation.

**Example:** Group decision making is the norm at Charlie Leighton's CML Group, one of the nation's foremost seers of trends. Leighton gathers his presidents to brainstorm in thought-provoking settings four times each year.

areer

## Determining Your Decision Style

No matter what career you pursue, decision making will undoubtedly be a part of your job. Although the focus of this chapter has been on the decision-making process itself, it is also important to recognize that each of you has your own style of making decisions, which directly influences your own decision-making process. This manner of decision making, known as your *decision style,* reflects the way you *think* about certain situations.

To determine your decision style, refer to the "Strengthen Your Skills" exercise at the end of this chapter. Complete the decision-style inventory and score yourself as directed in the exercise. Upon completion of this exercise, you should have scores in the four basic decision styles: directive, analytical, conceptual, and behavioral. Your scores in these categories reflect the intensity of your preference for each. To help you understand the four decision styles and how they relate to "job fit," study the chart below in conjunction with the chart included in the "Strengthen Your Skills" exercise.

| Decision Style | Best Organizational Fit |
|---|---|
| Directive | Structured, goal-oriented, such as in bureaucracies, or where power and authority are important |
| Analytical | Impersonal; where planning or solving complex problems is important, such as in science, engineering, etc. |
| Conceptual | Loose, decentralized settings; open or organic organization |
| Behavioral | Well-designed, people-oriented, collegial settings |

Most people have multiple styles and are able to use them in combinations or patterns. Certain combinations of your decision styles reflect your likelihood for success in various fields of study, jobs, and careers. The following chart shows how varying combinations of the four decision styles relate to different careers. Compute your scores under column 1, "Pattern," using your scores from the decision-style inventory at the end of this chapter. Then mark the careers in column 3 to which your scores suggest you are most suited.

### *Does Your Decision Style Fit Your Job?*

| Pattern | Score | Typical of |
|---|---|---|
| Analytical + Directive | 165 or higher | Science, finance, law |
| Conceptual + Behavioral | 135 or higher | Psychologists, teachers, artists |
| Analytical + Conceptual | 170 or higher | Senior executives, leaders |
| Directive + Behavioral | 130 or higher | Supervisors, salespeople, athletes |
| Conceptual + Directive | 155 or higher | Entrepreneurs, crossover executives |
| Analytical + Behavioral | 145 or higher | Technical managers |
| Directive + Analytical + Conceptual | 245 or higher | Middle managers |

It is important to realize that decision styles and patterns are not definite predictors of job or career success; however, knowing this information is certainly useful when you are examining your career options.

*Source:* Alan J. Rowe and Richard O. Mason, "Decision-Style Inventory" from *Managing with Style* (San Francisco, CA: Jossey Bass, 1987), © 1987 Alan J. Rowe.

**6.** In groups, sometimes secondary considerations—such as winning an argument, making a point, saving face, defeating another's idea, or getting back at a rival—displace the primary goal of making an effective decision.

**7.** Groups may succumb to a phenomenon known as **groupthink**, which occurs when cohesive "in-groups" let the desire for unanimity, or consensus, override sound judgment in generating and evaluating alternative courses of action.[27] To avoid dissension, disagreement, and loss of "esprit de corps," group members may conform prematurely to poor decisions. A clear example of groupthink involved the space shuttle Challenger disaster. As NASA was preparing to

**groupthink**
A phenomenon occurring when cohesive "in-groups" let the desire for unanimity, or consensus, override sound judgment in generating and evaluating alternative courses of action.

launch the shuttle, numerous problems and questions surfaced. Nonetheless, decision makers repeatedly argued that everything was in order and that there was no reason to delay the shuttle launch. Tragedy struck when the shuttle exploded shortly after liftoff on January 28, 1986, killing all seven crew members.[28] (A more detailed discussion about groupthink appears in Chapter 15.)

Equipped with the knowledge of the advantages and disadvantages of group decision making, managers should be better able to determine whether individual or group decision making is most appropriate for a particular decision situation. If choosing group decision making, managers must realize that the success of the group—and, ultimately, the success of the decision—greatly depends on two factors: (1) the type of group technique used, and (2) how effectively the group capitalizes on the advantages and minimizes the disadvantages of group decision making.

## Using Computers in Group Decision Making

In concluding this chapter, it is important to mention the significant contribution that computer technology has made to the realm of decision making in recent years. Whether making individual or group decisions, programmed or nonprogrammed decisions, or decisions affected by one of the factors or conditions outlined earlier in this chapter, today's business managers have access to a wealth of computer information and technology that can aid and support their decision-making processes. In fact, this computer technology is becoming more advanced and sophisticated almost daily. For an in-depth discussion of computer-based support of decision making—including decision support systems, expert systems, and neural networks—refer to Chapter 21.

## SUMMARY AND REVIEW

- **Define decision making and describe the types of decisions and conditions that may affect decision making.** Decision making is the process of choosing among alternative courses of action to resolve a problem. Decisions may be programmed or nonprogrammed. Programmed decisions are made in response to situations that are routine, somewhat structured, and fairly repetitive. Nonprogrammed decisions are made in response to situations that are unique, relatively unstructured, undefined, and of major consequence to the organization. Three conditions affect decision making. Certainty exists when decision makers are fully informed about a problem, its alternative solutions, and their respective outcomes. Risk exists when decision makers must rely on incomplete, yet reliable, information. Uncertainty exists when little or no factual information is available about a problem, its alternative solutions, or their respective outcomes.

- **Specify the steps involved in decision making.** The decision-making process consists of six steps: (1) identifying the problem, the most critical step in the decision-making process; (2) generating alternative solutions—identifying items or activities that could reduce or eliminate the difference between the actual situation and the desired situation; (3) evaluating alternatives—determining the advantages and disadvantages of each alternative; (4) selecting the best alternative, based on each alternative's feasibility, effectiveness, and cost; (5) implementing the decision—the planning and instituting that must take place so that the selected alternative can actually solve the problem; and (6) evaluating the decision—gathering information so that managers can determine the effectiveness of their decision.

- **Contrast the decision-making models.** Management theorists typically recognize two major models of decision making: the classical model and the administrative model. The classical, or rational, model of decision making prescribes how managers should make decisions and asserts that managers are logical, rational individuals who make decisions that are in the best interests of the organization. In contrast, the administrative model of decision making describes how managers actually make decisions. Also called the organizational, neoclassical, or behavioral model, the administrative model includes the concepts of bounded rationality and satisficing. Bounded rationality means that people have limits, or boundaries, to their rationality, which lead them to forgo the six steps of decision making in favor of a quicker, yet satisfying, process—satisficing. Satisficing means that decision makers choose the first alternative that appears to satisfactorily resolve the problem situation.

- **Examine the factors that may affect decision making.** Many factors affect decision making, including (1) intuition—immediately comprehending that something is the case, seemingly without the use of any reasoning process or conscious analysis; (2) emotion and stress—feelings that can derail rational decision making and result in nonproductive or counterproductive behavior; (3) framing, which refers to how information is phrased, presented, or labeled and serves to bias judgment, or interpretation, of information; (4) escalation of commitment—the tendency of individuals and organizations to persist with failing courses of action; and (5) confidence and risk propensity—the notion that the higher your confidence level in your decisions, the greater the likelihood that you will take risks in decision making.

- **Summarize group decision techniques and the advantages and disadvantages of group decision making.** Brainstorming is a technique in which group members spontaneously suggest ideas to solve a problem. The nominal group technique involves the use of a highly structured meeting agenda and restricts discussion and interpersonal communication during the decision-making process. The Delphi group technique uses a written survey method for gathering expert opinions from a number of people, without holding a group meeting.

The major advantages that groups offer over individuals in decision making are that they (1) provide a greater pool of knowledge and information; (2) provide more approaches and perspectives; (3) are more likely to generate more alternative solutions; (4) clarify ambiguous problems, reduce uncertainty about alternatives, and increase intellectual stimulation; (5) foster greater comprehension of the decision; (6) foster increased acceptance of and commitment to the decision; (7) have increased legitimacy; and (8) provide a training ground. On the other hand, the major disadvantages of group decision making are that groups (1) are time consuming; (2) may be dominated by one or more group members; (3) are subject to social pressure; (4) may compromise decisions, or satisfice; (5) have ambiguous decision responsibility; (6) may experience goal displacement; and (7) are subject to groupthink.

- **Apply the decision-making models to a hypothetical situation.** Using the scenario presented in the "Business Dilemma" box, you should be able to apply the decision-making models and process described in this chapter to reach a decision, taking into account the factors and conditions affecting the situation.

## Key Terms and Concepts

decision *302*
problem *302*
decision making *302*
programmed decisions *302*
nonprogrammed decisions *303*
certainty *304*
risk *304*
uncertainty *304*

classical model of decision making *309*
administrative model of decision making *309*
bounded rationality *310*
satisficing *310*
intuition *311*
framing *313*
escalation of commitment *314*

confidence *315*
risk propensity *315*
brainstorming *318*
nominal group technique *319*
Delphi group technique *319*
groupthink *322*

## Ready Recall

1. Distinguish between the two main types of decisions, giving an example of each.
2. Describe the three conditions under which decision making may occur.
3. List the six steps of the decision-making process. Why is proper problem identification the most critical step in the decision-making process?
4. What are some of the reasons why breakdowns can occur during the decision implementation stage?
5. Contrast the two major models of decision making, outlining the assumptions associated with each.
6. Explain how the concepts of bounded rationality and satisficing affect the decision-making process.
7. Discuss five factors that affect decision making.

8. Compare and contrast the three group decision techniques presented in this chapter.
9. What are some of the advantages and disadvantages of group decision making?

10. Discuss the phenomenon of groupthink and how it affects group decision making.

## Expand Your Experience

1. The shipping department of a large pharmaceutical company is experiencing slumping productivity and an increase in order-fulfillment errors. Analyze this issue by working through the steps in the decision-making process.
2. A toy manufacturer makes *most* of its sales from a toy that has a *slight* safety issue. A product recall would result in the company going bankrupt. Discuss how such factors as intuition, emotion and stress, framing, escalation of commitment, and confidence and risk propensity could influence the company's decision making regarding this issue.
3. Think about decisions that you have recently made in your life or that you will need to make in the near future. Characterize

these decision situations as programmed or nonprogrammed and discuss how the conditions of certainty, risk, and uncertainty affect (or will affect) your decision-making process.

4. More and more businesses are using groups rather than a lone individual to make decisions. Think of three work situations that involve the need for decision making: one in which it would seem appropriate to utilize the brainstorming technique, one in which it would seem appropriate to use the nominal group technique, and one in which you would use the Delphi group technique. Discuss why each of these techniques was well suited to the particular decision situation at hand.

**CASE**

## *Difficult Decisions at Sears, Roebuck*

Born in 1886, Sears, Roebuck & Company ruled the world of retailing for the better part of the twentieth century. In 1962, Sears's sales were bigger than those of its next four rivals combined. A decade later, Sears was the sixth largest company *worldwide*, by stock market valuation, with a total market value of $18.2 billion. Then something happened. By 1982, Sears had declined from the sixth largest company worldwide to the thirteenth, with a total market value of $10.3 billion. Ten years later, Sears plummeted to the 81st spot on the list, with a total market value of under $16 billion, and the company suffered a loss of $3.9 billion—of which $3 billion was in the Merchandise Group. Sales for that group in 1992 were $32 billion, compared to Kmart's $38 billion in sales and $940 million in profits and Wal-Mart's $55 billion in sales and almost $2 billion in profits.

So, what happened to the retailing giant whose preeminence in the marketplace had seemed unassailable for so long? Armed with terrific store sites—many in flourishing malls—and economies of scale brought about from its purchasing power, Sears succeeded in surpassing Montgomery Ward and establishing itself as America's discount store ... that is, until the 1960s and 1970s, when Kmart and then Wal-Mart broke onto the discount scene and changed the course of discount retailing forever.

Content with its position and what it perceived as its predominance in the retailing industry, Sears seemed unaware of, or, at the very least, unthreatened by, the competition coming from Kmart and Wal-Mart. Sears seemed content to rest on its laurels and let whatever had made it great continue to guide the company. A kind of complacency seemed to envelop it, and as

Sears's managers looked inward and backward, Kmart and Wal-Mart blew right past them.

Obviously, Sears's leaders made some bad decisions, which resulted in the company's precipitous fall from the top. Will Sears be able to regain its might and magic? Sound decision making will certainly be a key factor in a turnaround. In 1992, when Sears dropped to 81st place on *Fortune*'s "world's largest companies" list, Wal-Mart had climbed to third place—just below Exxon and General Electric.

To begin its massive turnaround, Sears brought "new blood" into some key leadership posts in the organization. In 1992, the firm appointed Arthur C. Martinez, formerly of Saks Fifth Avenue, chairman and CEO of the Merchandise Group. Martinez, in turn, went not only outside Sears, but also outside the retail industry to fill the top marketing executive post for the Sears Merchandise Group with John H. Costello, former president and chief operating officer of Nielson Marketing Research USA. Martinez chose an outsider without retailing experience because he was seeking someone who could provide strategic thinking—incorporating multiple marketing disciplines—instead of the typical tactical thinking associated with retailers.

In one of its boldest moves, Sears announced in early 1993 that it had decided to discontinue its "Big Book," the Sears catalog. Although the 97-year-old catalog still had annual revenues of $3.3 billion, it had been losing money in the last few years. Discontinuing the catalog demonstrated how serious Sears was about changing its strategy for the 1990s. Long viewed as an American tradition, the Sears catalog had seemed sacrosanct.

During the first half of the 1900s, the Sears catalog was sometimes one of only two books that many Americans ever read; the other being the Bible. However, Sears's focus for the future is on retail stores, not mail-order retailing, so the "Big Book" became a chapter in Sears's long history.

Also in early 1993, Sears announced that it was closing 113 underperforming stores and eliminating 50,000 jobs. Nonmerchandise Sears businesses, such as stockbroker Dean Witter, the Discover credit card, and Coldwell Banker real estate operations, have been—or are in the process of being—sold. Sears is spending billions of dollars to remodel its stores. In addition, Sears has hired Young & Rubicam (Y&R) to handle the marketing and advertising efforts for its $40 million apparel account. Y&R's primary focus will be repositioning Sears as a more fashion-forward department store. Over the next five years, Sears will spend approximately $4 billion to reposition its retail division as a mall-based department store chain with a greater emphasis on apparel—along the lines of J.C. Penney Co.

Reviews are mixed on how successful Sears's restructuring decisions will be. Standard & Poor's Corporation (S&P) lowered its credit ratings on $17 billion of Sears securities, citing doubts about the revitalization plan. While recognizing that the store closings would probably result in better financial results for Sears in 1993 and 1994, S&P feared that intense competition in retailing and Sears's shift toward apparel might not produce the results needed to get Sears "out of the woods" for the long run. On the bright side, Sears posted a sharp jump in second-quarter 1993 profits—reflecting a faster payback than expected on its restructuring of retailing operations.

So, what will become of Sears? Will it become, as some have already speculated, a dinosaur? Or will it, again, become colossal—or at least be a contender—in the retailing industry? Time will tell if the decisions that Sears makes now and in the near future will render it vibrant … or extinct.

*Sources:* Barnaby J. Feder, "Sears Reports Strong Rise in Second-Quarter Earnings," *The New York Times,* July 21, 1993, D3; Kate Fitzgerald, "Sears Looks Outside Retail for Key Exec.," *Advertising Age,* March 15, 1993, 2; Carol J. Loomis, "Dinosaurs?" *Fortune,* May 3, 1993, 36–42; Cyndee Miller, "It Was the Worst of Times," *Marketing News,* March 15, 1993, 1–2; Standard & Poor's Corp., "Sears Ratings Are Lowered," *The New York Times,* March 18, 1993, C15; and "What Sears Must Do," *Advertising Age,* June 14, 1993, 16.

## Questions

**1.** What are some alternatives that Sears could have generated to address its problem of plummeting sales, profits, and market value?

**2.** From the information presented in the case, which of the factors that affect decision making seemed to affect Sears's decision making during the 1970s and 1980s?

**3.** Discuss the conditions that affect decision making as they relate to the Sears case.

---

### STRENGTHEN YOUR SKILLS
## *Making Decisions*

You—like everyone else—have a decision style that reflects the way you visualize and think about situations. Your style is determined from your patterns among predispositions, such as which situations you avoid, what kinds of jobs you enjoy, which things you dislike, how you communicate, how you approach problems, and how you make decisions.

The following decision-style inventory will help you identify your patterns and understand your style. After you have completed and scored the inventory, you will be provided with a brief explanation of the four basic decision styles.

### Instructions

**1.** Rank your response to the following questions using the ranking system provided:

Write a(n)  "8" next to the one you **most prefer**
     "4" next to the one you **consider often**
     "2" next to the one you **consider on occasion**
     "1" next to the one you **least prefer**

There are no right or wrong answers; therefore, your choices should reflect how you feel about the questions and what you prefer to do, not what you believe is correct or desirable. Some people find it easier to rank their "8" and "1" responses first before ranking their "4" and "2" responses.

1.    My prime objective is to:

_____A. Have a position with status.

_____B. Be the best in my field.

_____C. Earn recognition for my work.

_____D. Feel secure in my job.

2.    I enjoy jobs that:

_____A. Are technical and well defined.

_____B. Have considerable variety.

_____C. Allow independent action.

_____D. Involve people.

3.    I expect people working for me to be:

_____A. Productive and fast.

_____B. Highly capable.

_____C. Committed and responsive.

_____D. Receptive to suggestions.

4.    In my job I look for:

_____A. Practical results.

_____B. The best solutions.

_____C. New approaches or ideas.

_____D. Good working environment.

5.    I communicate best with others:

_____A. On a direct, one-to-one basis.

_____B. In writing.

_____C. In a group discussion.

_____D. In a formal meeting.

6.    In my planning I emphasize:

_____A. Solving current problems.

_____B. Meeting objectives.

_____C. Identifying long-range goals.

_____D. Developing people's careers.

7.    When solving a problem, I:

_____A. Rely on proven approaches.

_____B. Apply careful analysis.

_____C. Look for creative approaches.

_____D. Rely on my feelings.

8.    I prefer information in terms of:

_____A. Specific facts.

_____B. Accurate and complete data.

_____C. Coverage of many options.

_____D. Easily understood data.

9.    When not sure what to do, I:

_____A. Rely on intuition.

_____B. Search for facts.

_____C. Look for a compromise.

_____D. Wait before making a decision.

10.    Whenever possible, I avoid:

_____A. Long debates.

_____B. Incomplete work.

_____C. Numbers or formulas.

_____D. Conflict with others.

11.    I am especially good at:

_____A. Remembering dates and facts.

_____B. Solving difficult problems.

_____C. Seeing many possibilities.

_____D. Interacting with others.

12.    When time is important, I:

_____A. Decide and act quickly.

_____B. Follow plans and priorities.

_____C. Refuse to be pressured.

_____D. Seek guidance or support.

13.    In social settings I generally:

_____A. Speak with others.

_____B. Think about what is being said.

_____C. Observe what is going on.

_____D. Listen to the conversation.

14.    I am good at remembering:

_____A. People's names.

_____B. The places I've met people.

_____C. People's faces.

_____D. People's personalities.

15.    My work provides me with:

_____A. The power to influence others.

_____B. Challenging assignments.

_____C. Achievement of personal goals.

_____D. Acceptance by the group.

16.    I work well with those who are:

_____A. Energetic and ambitious.

_____B. Self-confident.

_____C. Open-minded.

_____D. Polite and trusting.

17.  When under stress, I:

_____A. Become anxious.

_____B. Concentrate on the problem.

_____C. Become frustrated.

_____D. Am forgetful.

18.  Others consider me:

_____A. Aggressive.

_____B. Disciplined.

_____C. Imaginative.

_____D. Supportive.

19.  My decisions typically are:

_____A. Realistic and direct.

_____B. Systematic or abstract.

_____C. Broad and flexible.

_____D. Sensitive to the needs of others.

20.  I dislike:

_____A. Losing control.

_____B. Doing boring work.

_____C. Following rules.

_____D. Being rejected.

**2.** Fill in your total scores for each letter response:

Total Points for A_____  (directive)

Total Points for B_____  (analytical)

Total Points for C _____  (conceptual)

Total Points for D _____  (behavioral)

**3.** Compare your scores with the averages in each style by transferring your score from each category as you have listed in #2 above and then subtracting your score from the average given. (Average scores based on a study of over 10,000 people.) For example, if your score in the YC column below for directive style were 70, your answer in the last column would be "5." If your score were 85, your answer in the last column would be "–10."

| Style | Average (A) | Your Score (YC) | A–YC = |
|---|---|---|---|
| Directive | 75 | | |
| Analytical | 90 | | |
| Conceptual | 80 | | |
| Behavioral | 55 | | |

**4.** Determine the level of dominance you show in each category. Transfer the four decision styles to one of the lines below based on the number you have written in the table above under the column labeled "A–YC =":

**Least preferred style(s)** +8 or higher _____

**Backup style(s)** –6 to +7 _____

**Dominant style(s)** –7 to –14 _____

**Very dominant style(s)** –15 or lower _____

**5.** To help you understand the four decision styles more thoroughly, study the chart on page 329. Both the "Careers Corner" on page 322 and the exercise in the *Study Guide* that accompanies this text will give you further insights into your decision style.

*Understanding Your Style*

| Style | Psychological Aspects | Major Criticism |
|---|---|---|
| Directive | Focuses on tasks and technical problems<br>Considers facts, rules, and procedures<br>Acquires information through hunches and by using short reports with limited data<br>Evaluates information by using intuition, experience, and rules<br>Has a low tolerance for ambiguity and needs structure | Rigid<br>Impersonal<br>Simplistic<br>Autocratic |
| Analytical | Focuses on tasks and technical problems, taking a logical approach<br>Considers every aspect of a given problem<br>Acquires information by careful analysis, using a large amount of data<br>Evaluates information through abstract thinking, avoiding incomplete data<br>Has a high tolerance for ambiguity and is innovative in solving problems | Dogmatic<br>Overcontrolling<br>Impersonal<br>Too careful, abstract, or mathematical<br>Sometimes too slow |
| Conceptual | Focuses on people and the broad aspects of a problem<br>Considers many options and possibilities<br>Acquires information by using intuition and discussion with others<br>Evaluates information by integrating diverse data and applying judgment<br>Has a high tolerance for ambiguity, takes risks, and is very creative | Dilettantish<br>Too idealistic, slow, indecisive<br>Difficult to control |
| Behavioral | Focuses on people and social aspects of the work situation<br>Considers the well-being of others<br>Acquires information by listening and interacting with others<br>Evaluates information by using feelings and instincts<br>Has a low tolerance for ambiguity | Too concerned about others<br>Wishy-washy<br>Can't make hard decisions<br>Can't say no |

*Source:* Alan J. Rowe and Richard O. Mason, "Decision-Style Inventory" from *Managing with Style* (San Francisco, CA: Jossey Bass, 1987), © 1987 Alan J. Rowe. Used with permission of Alan J. Rowe, Professor Emeritus, U.S.C., Management & Organization.

# Organizing:

# Designing Jobs

# *and*

# Departments

**Outline**

**After reading this chapter, you will be able to:**

- Discuss the concept of organizing and explain why it is important.
- Interpret an organizational chart.
- Explain why job specialization and division of labor are important for organizing.
- Assess the different approaches to grouping tasks into jobs and the advantages and disadvantages of each.
- Distinguish four different bases for grouping jobs into departments.
- Determine the relationships among authority, responsibility, and delegation.
- Define decentralization and describe what strengths it has for employee development.
- Critique a company's new organizational structure.

Courtesy of Volvo.

# Why Darwin Would Like Volvo

Since the late 1960s, the Swedish automobile manufacturer Volvo has been engaged in a continuous, deliberate evolution of its assembly worker jobs in an attempt to enhance the organization's productivity and improve the quality of work for its employees. Over the years, this evolution has led to a radical change in the activities of assembly workers and a demonstration of how jobs can change over time, even though the finished product has stayed basically the same.

Through the mid-1960s, the assembly jobs at Volvo were very similar to those in other automobile plants. Production was accomplished through an assembly line on which workers were given a single task to accomplish as the automobile passed through their work areas. It was not uncommon for one complete cycle of a worker's job to take no more than two minutes. The work day consisted of a continual repetition of these two-minute cycles.

The evolution of job activities began in the upholstery division of the Torslanda assembly plant, after absenteeism there increased steadily due to muscle fatigue and the monotony of single-task jobs. Management's early attempt to reduce these negative effects involved periodically rotating workers to other jobs in the assembly process. The workers appreciated both the change of tasks and the opportunity for increased social contact. Based on their response, Volvo initiated a new system in 1966 in which each worker learned all 15 jobs involved in the assembly of seats. All jobs were altered by combining previous one-task jobs to form longer cycle chains of activities for each of the 15 jobs. The results of this experiment were improved group spirit, fewer physical complaints, and higher quality. The final stage of evolution in the upholstery line occurred later when workers were formed into teams and given responsibility for planning the assembly assignments and checking the quality of materials that were used.

With this success as a basis, the use of independent work teams became an integral part of the work process of the Kalmar automobile assembly plant. The Kalmar plant was divided into about 20 functional areas, such as electrical assembly, brake systems, etc., with approximately 15 to 20 workers assigned to each area. Each work area became a craft shop that turned out a complete product with which the individual workers could identify. The actual work steps were carried out in two ways. The assembly approach used six work teams, each of which performed part of the assembly in a defined sequence. In the dock approach, two- or three-person teams did all the assembly in a defined work space. In both processes, the number of tasks that defined a job was definitely greater than those of traditional assembly-line production.

The latest stage of evolution of jobs took place at the Uddevalla plant. In this plant, highly automated material handling systems make just-in-time deliveries of engines, car bodies, and other parts to 40 teams of 10 workers. Each team is responsible for complete assembly of four cars per shift. In addition to this assembly, each work group interviews applicants and recommends specific training for itself.

Workers at Volvo turn out automobiles today just as they did in the 1950s. However, the jobs of individual workers and the way these jobs are organized are radically different and the quality has improved continuously.

*Sources:* Paul Bernstein, "The Learning Curve at Volvo," *Columbia Journal of World Business* 23 (Winter 1988): 87–95; Philip Burget, "Work-team Idea Meets Volvo's Goals," *Metalworking News*, July 9, 1990, 1; H. G. Jones, "Motivation for Higher Performance at Volvo," *Long Range Planning* 24 (October 1991): 92–104.

*introduction*

Almost any time that two or more people get together to work on a project, the issue arises of who should do what part. As Volvo demonstrated, this issue can have many solutions. Dividing work into parts, assigning these parts to individuals, and coordinating the activities of these individuals are examples of organizing. Organizing work, as we described in Chapter 1, is a major activity of management. As we will discuss in this chapter and the next, there are many ways to organize, each with its own strengths and weaknesses. One of the reasons that Volvo has changed the way it organizes work over the last 30 years is to take advantage of new technology and skills of its workers. It has done this by changing its jobs from single-task to multiple, complex-task assignments.

In this chapter, we will present the major approaches to organizing tasks into jobs and, in turn, jobs into departments. In presenting these major approaches, we will also discuss the strengths and weaknesses of each. The next chapter will address the third topic of organizing—how to organize departments into an organizational structure. In this way, you will become familiar with the various alternatives of organizing work.

## THE NATURE OF ORGANIZING

In Chapter 1, we defined an *organization* as a group of people working together to achieve goals or objectives that would be difficult or impossible for them to achieve individually. By this definition, Toyota is definitely an organization. Toyota's goal to build and market well-made, relatively inexpensive cars could have been developed by a small group of individuals or even by a single person. But to implement this vision, a virtual army of employees is necessary to complete the numerous tasks involved in making and selling an automobile. Similarly, the Girl Scouts of America is an organization in the sense that, acting as a group, the individual members can more easily accomplish their goals. These goals require them to interact and perform civic and individual assistance tasks at the local, national, and international levels.

Thought of in this way, an organization is a means of more easily performing the tasks that are essential for achieving an objective. Organizing is, therefore, the process of creating this organization. In Chapter 1, we defined organizing as the activities involved in designing an appropriate organizational structure, assigning employee duties, and developing working relationships among people and among tasks. Organizing addresses important questions such as: Who reports to whom? How are tasks linked together? Who is responsible for the completion of tasks? Who coordinates this group of people?

At the most basic level, people form organizations to implement their visions. Because the goals that managers often wish to pursue are difficult to reach and may encompass a number of subgoals, organizations are essential to provide certain advantages in reaching these goals.

## Reasons for Organizing

There are many reasons for organizing, the primary one being, as already stated, that it permits people to work together in order to achieve goals that would be difficult or impossible for them to achieve on their own. Other reasons include achieving synergy, avoiding duplication of resources, establishing lines of authority, and facilitating communication.

**Achieving Synergy.**    One reason to form organizations is to achieve synergistic effects. Synergy, which we talked about earlier in Chapter 2, is the ability of a whole system to equal more than the sum of its parts. If individuals or parts of an organization can specialize and thus gain greater knowledge and efficiency, and they are structured as a cohesive whole, then their results should be greater than if they did not specialize. In many companies, for instance, the human resources department is organized according to various activities. Some individuals specialize in recruitment, others in selection, and still others in compensation systems. Therefore, only the small number of employees in each activity are expected to master the various laws and techniques that are necessary to implement that activity. However, by having either an individual or a committee coordinate the activities of these three specialized teams, an organization can benefit both from having experts doing complex tasks as well as from having an integrated human resource program in which these activities complement one another.

**Avoiding the Duplication of Resources.**    A second reason for organizing, closely related to the first one, is to avoid duplicating resources. For example, General Motors uses the same engines for several different models of automobiles in its various divisions. Rather than have each division—such as Pontiac, Chevrolet, and Buick—manufacture its own engines, GM has plants that manufacture engines for all the divisions. This eliminates costs associated with building and maintaining duplicate engine manufacturing facilities and also reduces production costs through achieving economies of scale.

**Establishing Lines of Authority.**    A third reason for organizing is to establish lines of authority. As individuals are working, issues arise such as at what pace should each work, who does what, and what happens if materials are defective? To keep the work flowing, someone must make decisions, answer these and other questions, and tell others what specifically should be done and when. For each work group, someone or some method is charged with weighing alternatives and supplying direction for work assignments. Traditionally, one person acting as a supervisor or manager accomplished this. However, recent organizing efforts have established teams of workers that arrive at joint decisions. For example, the five work teams at Hannaford Bros. food distribution center in Schodack Landing, NY, schedule work, training, and discipline, and team members rotate as "star-points" or team leaders.[1] In these cases, the method by which the group arrives at a decision is usually specified. Therefore, organizing creates a basic blueprint that provides direction to employees in their work and interactions with others.

**Example:** Hospitality Franchise Systems is the franchiser of Days Inn, Howard Johnson, Ramada, and Super 8 motels. The company is responsible for advertising the brand names and has increased revenues for the franchisees under the umbrella of hotels and motels by working with service providers.

**Facilitating Communication.**   Finally, organizing fosters better communication. In large and even smaller companies, the number of people who must communicate may be formidable. Organizing creates formal channels of communication that permit the transmission of messages to large groups of people more efficiently and, hopefully, more accurately. For example, a vice president of sales may develop new procedures for collecting data about customer reactions to product use. She transmits these procedures to the ten regional sales managers. Each of these then passes on the information to the eight group sales managers who report to him or her. The group sales managers, in turn, communicate with the district sales managers. Finally, these district managers tell the retail salespersons what to do to collect the customers' reactions. If the communication channels were not in place, the vice president of sales would have to communicate with each of the retail salespersons herself. We should point out, however, that this communication function of organizing may be less important in the future as many organizations use information systems and networks for communication.

## Formal and Informal Relationships

**Formal Relationships.**   When we think of organizations we normally think of an organizational chart, like the one shown in Figure 12.1. An **organizational chart** is a pictorial display of the official lines of authority and communication within the organization. **Authority** is the right to give work orders to others in the organization, and is associated with a position within an organization, not with the individual occupying that position. The organizational chart shows the structure of the **formal organization**, which is the arrangement of positions that dictates where work activities are completed, where decisions should be made, and the flow of information.

The boxes in Figure 12.1 represent positions in the organization, in this case the food and beverage division of a large hotel. As you can tell, we have included the full set of positions for only two parts of this division: beverage and restaurant operations. The higher the level of the box in the chart, the higher the level of authority that position has within the organization. The solid lines between boxes at different levels represent lines of authority and formal communication. Positions at higher levels can give work orders to those positions at lower levels if they are connected by direct lines. Horizontal lines denote communication channels between positions that are at the same authority level.

According to the organizational chart for the food and beverage division, the president and managing director of the hotel and the vice president for food and beverage occupy the two highest positions. The vice president has direct authority over the directors of catering, culinary operations, stewards, and beverage and restaurant operations. These five positions share information as indicated by the horizontal line. In addition, these five directors have authority over one to six manager-type positions who report to each one of them. Notice that the titles of these manager-type positions vary, ranging from manager to steward. However, in all five operations the positions are equivalent in terms of level of duties. The managers who are connected on the chart by horizontal lines—the six restaurant managers, for example—share information and decision making. These six units are the gourmet restaurant, the specialty restaurant, the coffee shop, room service, take-out and deli bar, and the employee cafeteria. Four of these have assistant managers. However, these assistant managers within restaurant operations are not formally linked on the organizational chart and, therefore, have no formal interaction.

---

**organizational chart**
A pictorial display of the official lines of authority and communication within the organization.

**authority**
The right to give work orders to others in the organization; associated with a position within an organization, not with the individual occupying that position.

**formal organization**
The arrangement of positions, as shown on an organizational chart, that dictates where work activities are completed, where decisions should be made, and the flow of information.

**Teaching Note:** Discuss the organizational chart in Figure 12.1. Identify the various levels of authority within the chart. For example, ask students questions like who do the order takers report to? Who does the assistant manager/captains report to? The room service manager?

**FIGURE 12.1**

## Organizational Chart of the Food and Beverage Division of a Large Hotel

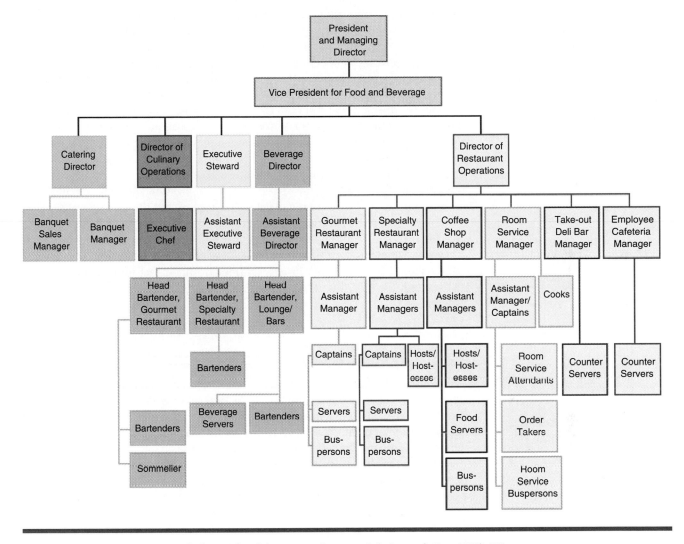

*Source:* Adapted from *Organizational Charts*, ed. Judith M. Nixon (Detroit: Gale Research, Inc., 1992), 220.

**Informal Relationships.**   The **informal organization** refers to the relationships among positions that are not connected by the organizational chart. These relationships occur either because the nature of the work forces the people occupying those positions to interact to complete the work more efficiently or because they have developed a friendship. The informal organization signals communication of information and decision making among positions without denoting organizational authority. As such, it is created by the employees to better accomplish their jobs.

Using the positions shown in Figure 12.1, we can describe an example of the informal organization that might develop in the food and beverage division. In reality, there is much information and decision making that occurs among all of the managers and assistant managers, because they are all affected by the same groups

**informal organization**
The relationships among positions that are not connected by the organizational chart.

**Teaching Note:** Discuss the benefits of the formal and informal organization. Ask students to discuss why the informal organization emerges and its benefits to organizational functioning. Friendships with other departments can create an informal organization and so expedite work.

of customers. For example, if the hotel books the national convention of the Academy of Management, with 3,500 attendees, the sequence of scheduled lunches, dinners, and cocktail parties affects all parts of the food and beverage division. When the convention has a served lunch meeting, the demand for food is increased for the banquet manager but is lessened for the other restaurant managers. Communication among all parties is used to order the appropriate amount of inventory and schedule the wait staff.

Communication and interaction are positive contributions of the informal relationships in the organization's operation. However, the informal organization can also have some negative effects, at least from the point of view of top management. In times of crisis or threat from external factors, the informal organization will communicate information about the seriousness of the crisis and possible responses by the organization. However, such information may not be accurate, particularly if it is based on incomplete or old data. This results in the rumors that frequently circulate in organizations. Moreover, the informal organization occasionally may not hold the same goals and values as the formal organization and may actually work at cross purposes. For example, workers on different shifts in a manufacturing plant may agree to restrict output to protest layoffs. Informal relationships are part of every firm and should be attended to by each manager within the organization. That is, the effect of the communication of the informal organization on work outcomes should be noted and directly addressed if incorrect information is being transmitted. We treat this in more detail when we discuss organizational grapevines in Chapter 18.

## The Process of Organizing

There is no one best way to organize. However, any organizing effort typically involves several activities:  grouping tasks into jobs, grouping jobs into departments, and determining authority and channels of communication. Let's return to the illustration of the hotel food and beverage division for examples of each of these activities before we discuss them in detail later in the chapter. Table 12.1 lists the major tasks the directors, managers, and assistant managers of the various units carry out. Top management usually identifies these tasks when the hotel initially opens and modifies them over time. We can see that directors perform several activities that have long-term effects on the unit's employees and customers. Managers report to directors and use the directions and information provided by the director to plan the operations of a particular hotel facility or service. For example, the gourmet restaurant manager will order supplies based primarily on the monthly forecasts of convention and meeting traffic provided by the director as well as on his or her own estimate of walk-in traffic. Assistant managers handle the majority of the daily operations of a particular unit. They schedule staff, inspect and maintain facilities, interact with customers, and address any work issues with the staff.

Figure 12.1 and Table 12.1 show us that within the food and beverage division, tasks are grouped into jobs based on similarity of activity:  long-term policies and planning (directors); operational policies and monitoring performance of a specific unit (managers); and daily operations of a specific unit (assistant managers). Jobs are grouped into departments according to either product (beverage), service (catering, restaurant operations), or group of employees (chefs and stewards). The authority and formal communication channels follow the solid lines of the organizational chart. The tasks associated with each job indicate the activities for which that job can make decisions. For example, the assistant manager for the

**Critical Thinking Challenge:** Have students draw a simple organizational chart of where they work (or of a previous employer, the university, or a familiar business). Have students discuss reasons for the structure. Was it effective? How did the informal organization work?

TABLE 12.1

## Grouping Tasks into Jobs in the Food and Beverage Division

*Director*

Determines operational policies and procedures of unit. Develops marketing and promotional campaigns both internal and external to hotel. Meets with representatives of convention groups to determine food/beverage needs. Forecasts monthly demand on unit for goods and services. Develops weekly cost and revenue statements for unit. Monitors overall service and quality of products provided by unit. Selects, trains, and reviews performance of unit's managers and assistant managers.

*Manager*

Reviews inventory, sales records, and costs of food or beverage products, equipment, and lines. Forecasts demand from both hotel conventions and guests as well as walk-in traffic. Maintains direct communication with vendors and distributors to determine quality and supply of items, places orders, and addresses all disputes between the unit and suppliers. Selects, trains, and reviews performance of assistant managers.

*Assistant Manager*

Directs the daily operations of the unit. This includes inspecting inventory for quantity and quality; maintaining and cleaning of all supplies and equipment; cleaning facilities, scheduling all unit personnel; and selecting, training, and reviewing performance of all personnel. Interacts with customers to determine reactions to service and resolve any complaints. Communicates information to manager concerning supplies, equipment, and personnel.

---

coffee shop can decide how to staff and serve food for that unit but not for the specialty restaurant.

The remainder of this chapter will explore various options and major areas of concern for each of these organizing activities.

## GROUPING TASKS INTO JOBS

If you needed a pair of shoes 300 years ago, you did not run to the mall to pick up a pair of Air Jordans. Instead you went to a rustic gentleman known as a cobbler, who would measure your feet and perhaps allow you to pick out the style of shoe you desired, although in most cases you really didn't have a choice. Once you left, his work would really begin. All alone (except for an elf or two), the cobbler might do literally all the activities involved in making you a pair of shoes, from tanning the leather and crafting the soles to dyeing the material and sewing the pieces together. This craft approach resulted in a pair of custom-made shoes that were expensive and required a long time to make. For the most part, craftsmen, such as cobblers, worked alone or in very small groups; there really was no reason to organize such a manufacturing operation because each craftsman performed all the activities.

That was the only way that shoes—and many other products—were made until the Industrial Revolution. Then, some businesses became concerned with producing many more products less expensively in order to deliver goods to the urban centers that were forming. They developed two basic principles of organizing during this time, which still influence present organizations: job specialization and

**job specialization**

The division of work into smaller, distinct tasks.

**job design**

The process of grouping tasks into jobs.

Example: At Nissan Motor Company in Spring Hill, Tennessee, automobiles leave the finished goods area of the assembly line at one car per minute due to the specialization and division of labor. How long would it take one worker to build a complete car? It might be an impossible task, but having various workers and procedures accomplishes the job quickly and easily.

**horizontal specialization**

The division of labor at the same level of the organization into simple, repetitive tasks.

**vertical specialization**

The division of labor at different levels of management into different tasks of planning, organizing, leading, and controlling.

**classical approach to job design**

The design of jobs based on the principles of division of labor and job specialization.

division of labor. **Job specialization** defines the division of work into smaller, distinct tasks. In the case of the hotel, examples of specialized tasks are making drinks, preparing meals, waiting on tables, and ordering food and supplies. Different individuals perform each of these tasks. Assigning these distinct tasks to different workers results in the division of labor.

**Job design** is the process of grouping tasks into jobs. A job is a set of tasks common to more than one worker. In this grouping, the manager must decide how many tasks to include in a job and how complex these tasks should be. In general, as more tasks are included and the complexity of these tasks increases, the job becomes more difficult to learn and perform and fewer workers have the necessary skills to do it successfully. There are, of course, several schools of job design, of which two are classical job design and behavioral job design.

## Classical Job Design

Classical job design is based on the assumption that increasing job specialization and division of labor increases an organization's overall productivity. The economist Adam Smith, in his book, *The Nature and Causes of the Wealth of Nations*, showed how, even in manufacturing something as simple as a pin, it was more efficient to divide the work into specialized tasks. One individual doing all the work could, at best, make a few pins a day. But if the labor was divided, 10 workers could produce 48,000 pins in a single day:

> One man draws out the wire, another straightens it, a third cuts it, a fourth points it, a fifth grinds it at the top for receiving the head; to make the head requires two or three distinct operations; to put it on, is a peculiar business, to whiten the pins is another; it is even a trade by itself to put them into the paper; and the important business of making a pin is, in this manner, divided into about eighteen distinct operations.[2]

Classical management specialists such as Frederick Taylor and Max Weber, whom we discussed in Chapter 2, further refined the principle of specialization. They advocated both **horizontal specialization**—the division of labor at the same level of the organization into simple, repetitive tasks—and **vertical specialization**—which applies the same principles to the various levels of management. That is, managers at different levels of the organization are assigned different tasks of planning, organizing, leading, and controlling. Thus, an ideal organization is one in which the managers perform all the planning and organizing tasks and nonmanagement workers perform all of the manufacturing tasks. Henry Ford carried the concepts of division of labor and specialization to their logical conclusion when he developed the assembly line for automobile production. The assembly line delivered the product so that each production worker did not have to waste time moving to the product. The worker stayed in a small, defined space that contained all the tools and materials necessary to complete the tasks.

When jobs are divided, they are reduced in complexity and operations until the activities of a single worker can be repeated with ease. As you can tell, the tasks Smith described in the making of a pin are very limited and simple, which greatly increased output.

This approach to job design was the hallmark of the Industrial Revolution and became the basis for the development of our modern production-based society. For that reason, the design of jobs based on the principles of division of labor and specialization is referred to as the **classical approach to job design**.

The results of Henry Ford's production assembly system were spectacular. After his moving assembly line was installed in 1913 at the company's Highland, Michigan, plant, assembly time for a Model T dropped from 12 hours 8 minutes to 2 hours 35 minutes. A year later, assembly time per car dropped to 1 hour 33 minutes, and 1,000 cars a day rolled off the line.

*Source:* The Bettmann Archive.

**Advantages of Specialization.**    The classical approach has a number of advantages. Because jobs are specialized, workers can develop and utilize unique skills and knowledge. Instead of having to know all the details of a large operation, a single individual has to know only a small part. Work therefore becomes more efficient and costs are easier to contain. The available labor pool for any job is large because many people can perform simple jobs, and a large labor pool, according to the law of supply and demand, reduces the wages that must be paid to workers for that job. Workers can quickly learn how to perform the tasks, reducing training costs. Moreover, the workers' skills can more easily improve over time, allowing them to become experts in their set of tasks. Finally, specialized equipment can be developed profitably for two reasons. First, larger markets result in larger amounts of products being sold, and the size of the market justifies the expense of developing machines. Second, dividing work activities into specialized tasks defines specific work operations for machines to do.

**Disadvantages of Specialization.**    However, management experts have learned that specialization has some detrimental effects on both the worker and the work being performed. Although task repetition can be seen as an advantage from the organization's point of view, from the workers' point of view, performing the exact same task over and over becomes boring. This affects quality when workers find it hard to concentrate and fail to notice variances from standard which often indicate poor quality goods. Moreover, workers often combat the monotony associated with their jobs by being absent and tardy more often. (Although it probably has not happened at your school, some academicians think that this may occur with college students as well.) One extreme reaction to monotony is industrial sabotage, in which material or equipment is deliberately damaged by the worker. Also, repetitive movements can result in fatigue injuries—for example, carpal tunnel syndrome.

Another major disadvantage of specialization arises from one of its advantages (from the company's point of view). Job specialization essentially reduces work to its common denominator, allowing the employer extreme flexibility in moving people around the factory floor because training costs will be relatively low. However, this often means insecurity for the worker, who can be easily replaced. In fact, the rise of labor unions can be traced, in part, to the fact that

**Critical Thinking Challenge:** Ask students to give examples of job specialization. If possible, tour a local service or manufacturing organization, or show a film based on a plant tour and discuss job specialization.

**Example:** Other examples of the disadvantages of worker specialization are eye strain, neck strain, and back problems associated with working at computers and video display terminals (VDTs) for long periods of time. These are especially common among order-entry, word-processing, and customer service jobs.

The goal of AT&T's job enlargement strategy is twofold: to increase fulfillment for employees and to increase its flexibility and global competitiveness. In a cooperative effort called Workplace of the Future, AT&T is working with employees and the unions to increase their involvement and input in challenging and stimulating tasks such as planning sessions and decision making in plants and at corporate headquarters. Here, a production associate and her coach review graphics of AT&T's Still-Image Phone produced at the company's Shreveport Works plant.

*Source:* © Frank Moscati.

job specialization allowed managers to replace workers fairly quickly and relatively inexpensively.

## The Behavioral Approach to Job Design

As the limitations to specialization became more apparent, both managers and researchers advocated new approaches to job design. These approaches were rooted in the idea that if a job could be made more compatible with an increasingly educated and trained work force, the negative effects could be avoided. Whereas the classical approach to job design thought of the worker as a part of the production process—much like machinery—the **behavioral approach to job design** views workers as independent parts of the production process whose individual characteristics should be taken into account in forming jobs. The behavioral approach to job design derives from the behavioral approach to management theories, which we discussed in Chapter 2. Of primary concern are individuals' needs to be engaged in work that is more complex, challenging, and less repetitive than that which resulted from classical job design. Behavioralists believe that if these needs are met, workers will be more efficient than those with classically designed jobs.

Several approaches to grouping tasks into jobs have been developed under the behavioral approach, including job enlargement, job rotation, and job enrichment.

**Job Enlargement.**    One strategy is **job enlargement**, which is aimed at increasing the number of tasks that comprise a job. Essentially, this is the reverse of horizontal specialization. By increasing the number of tasks, workers are, theoretically, assigned more challenging and stimulating jobs. For instance, instead of just typing, a clerical worker may also file, attend to the mail, answer the telephone, and schedule meetings and appointments. Over the years, several organizations have implemented job enlargement, including IBM, AT&T, and Maytag. While job enlargement has occasionally led to the anticipated improvements in worker attitudes and performance, the general result has not been consistently positive. To a large part, this is because the additional tasks change the overall characteristics of the job only minimally. The worker is doing a larger variety of tasks, but

**behavioral approach to job design**
The design of jobs based on the view that workers are independent parts of the production process whose individual characteristics should be taken into account in forming jobs.
**Example:** The Japanese management practices include assigning workers the freedom, authority, and responsibility to make decisions about their jobs and tasks. This practice, called "empowerment," is being used in teams, quality circles, and in work practices in the United States.

**job enlargement**
A behavioral approach to job design aimed at increasing the number of tasks that comprise a job.

all of these are about the same level in complexity and challenge. The employee is doing more of the same kind of activities.

**Job Rotation.**    A second behavioral job design strategy is **job rotation**, which involves a deliberate plan to move workers to various jobs on a consistent, scheduled basis. For instance, a warehouse worker may run a forklift for three months, check inventory the next three months, and load trucks for six months. Several organizations have tried this approach, including Ford Motor Company, Bethlehem Steel, and TRW. This strategy still uses the classical approach to job design:  The jobs consist of a few, specialized tasks. The only addition is that workers are rotated through several positions. From the organization's perspective, this is easy to implement because the jobs are both simplified and easy for new workers to learn.

The strategy has not been consistently successful as a counterbalance to the negative effects of specialization and division of labor. Presently, it is used in the cross-training of work teams that requires all members to be able to perform all the jobs of a work unit. The members of such work teams can successfully cover for one another during absences, or work together when equipment breakdowns slow a particular production step.

**Job Enrichment.**    Through **job enrichment**, jobs are designed to increase the number of similar tasks included and, more importantly, the number of tasks that require information processing and decision making. In this sense, job enrichment is a countermeasure to vertical specialization. Many of the team-building programs that have recently been started within organizations may also be regarded as job enrichment programs, because they increase the complexity of the team's jobs. For example, Development Dimensions International (DDI) uses teams that receive the training, authority, and responsibility previously reserved for managers.[3] Similarly, MasterCard implemented an automated point-of-sale program by empowering work teams to correct any operational problems they encounter.[4] The general results of job enrichment programs have been positive, although there is evidence that not all workers respond well. One intent of this approach is to increase the complexity, decision making, and responsibility of the job, and workers differ greatly in their needs for these components in their jobs. Clearly, those who have a high need respond more favorably to job enrichment programs. Job enrichment is discussed in more detail in Chapter 16.

# GROUPING JOBS INTO DEPARTMENTS

The grouping of jobs into departments is a second major activity required in organizing. **Departmentalization** means grouping related jobs to form an administrative unit—department, area, or center. Because the jobs in any one department are similar, for many purposes of the organization, each department can be considered to be a single piece of the organization. Departmentalization assists in the coordination of the jobs of an organization, and coordinating departments is easier than coordinating each job separately. Looking back at Figure 12.1, you can see that the food and beverage division has five departments:  catering, culinary operations, stewards, beverage, and restaurants. Jobs in each department are grouped because they deal either with the same product, service, or type of employee.

Departmentalization is also a normal stage in an organization's growth. Typically, a firm starts small, and the entrepreneur can exert a large amount of

**job rotation**
A behavioral approach to job design involving a deliberate plan to move workers to various jobs on a consistent, scheduled basis.

**Example:** Hallmark, the greeting card and social expression/gift company, has redesigned worker jobs so employees can participate in a variety of tasks throughout the year. They may begin the year working on Valentine cards, move to giftwrap, then to designing T-shirts and coffee mugs. This practice increases the workers' satisfaction as well as their potential.

**job enrichment**
A behavioral approach in which jobs are designed to increase the number of similar tasks involved, especially tasks that require information processing and decision making.

**departmentalization**
The grouping of related jobs to form an administrative unit.

## BUSINESS    DILEMMA

*You're the Manager ...What Would You Do?*

THE COMPANY:  **KBJ Beef Processing Equipment**

YOUR POSITION:  **President**

THE PLACE:  **Casper, Wyoming**

KBJ Beef Processing is one of the largest livestock equipment manufacturers in the United States. With the decrease in beef consumption over the past ten years, the company has remained successful through a redesigned organizational structure. Originally, KBJ operated with nine layers of management, which were reduced to three with the arrival of a new president, John Suede. The standing joke with employees when they learned of Suede's name and his reorganization plans was "Suede's going to turn our business inside out."

Suede's reorganization centered around the use of teams to accomplish tasks within the organization. The company established work teams and trained them to set their own production goals and schedules, communicate with the appropriate departments and levels, evaluate and report profitability, evaluate performance, address hiring needs, and determine raises. The autonomous, empowered work teams have proved to be one of the most successful strategies that Suede implemented.

KBJ also introduced flexible work schedules for its employees, allowing them to come in earlier or later as their individual needs warranted. The flexible schedules demonstrate KBJ's vote of confidence in its employees. Suede monitored the system during the first year after implementation and found abuse to be minimal. Employees want to be on the job, working in groups they enjoy and enhancing the company's performance.

The reorganization has also given managers great opportunity because each position in the organization can be held for no more than one and a half years. Even those employees who do not enter management positions are still compensated extremely well and given opportunities to rotate jobs and cross-train. Also, the company has made a concerted effort to eliminate jobs that it does not consider intrinsically satisfying within the corporate structure. Secretarial positions, for example, were eliminated, and all employees are now responsible for processing their own work, a step which required some computer training for a small number of the employees.

Employees like the new system and gain a far greater appreciation of their productivity through the comprehensive cost/output assessments they perform. Suede makes all financial summaries available on the computers that each work group has in its station. Everyone knows exactly how the company is performing; employees work hard and are rewarded for doing so. Employee surveys indicate they especially like the ability to solve problems on their own. Before, with all the layers of management and hierarchical reporting relationships, nothing was solved, settled, or fixed very quickly.

KBJ's new structure has allowed it to restore profitability and increase employee motivation and productivity in an increasingly pressured industry.

### Questions

1. What is the significance of reducing the layers of management in KBJ?
2. Evaluate the team approach implemented in KBJ versus the approach in existence when you (Suede) became president. What caused you to implement the new structure?
3. Why is it key to have employees responsible for most aspects of their job in the team setting? What is the role of communication?

**Comment on Box:** Poll students on how Suede used teams to accomplish tasks. Why were teams more effective? What were the advantages of reducing the layers? (Examples could include increases in communication, greater ownership of tasks, and greater worker satisfaction.)

control over all aspects of operations. But as the firm's product line and geographic base expand, the owner finds it increasingly difficult to coordinate the many facets of the growing firm, and usually forms departments to maintain control. However, this grouping is not done—should not be done—in a haphazard, disorderly manner. Departmentalization should have its basis in what the firm is trying to accomplish. Departments are formed to group jobs that should be linked in order for the organization to more easily reach its objectives.

Although a company's departmentalization serves its specific purposes and may be unique to that organization, we can talk about four basic types of departmentalization:  functional, customer, product, and geographic.

**FIGURE 12.2**

## Jobs within a Human Resource Management Department

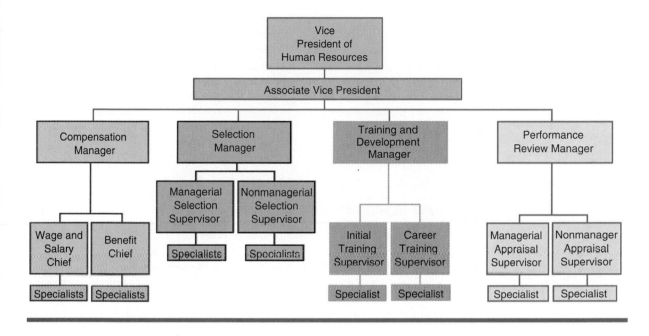

## Functional Departmentalization

One of the most common bases of departmentalization is economic function. **Functional departmentalization** is grouping jobs that perform similar functional activities, such as finance, manufacturing, and human resources. As an example, Figure 12.2 shows the jobs that may be found within a human resource management department. Organizations can create the number of functional departments that they perceive as important to compete effectively. Thus, in high tech computer software companies, a research and development department is a necessity, while in companies that sell commodity products, R&D may not be deemed important enough to have departmental status.

Functional departmentalization is often employed in smaller companies. It is also well suited to organizations that offer a limited number of goods or services. It has several advantages for these types of organizations. First, because functional departmentalization groups closely related activities and employees, it permits effective economies of scale. It allows workers with related knowledge and skills to work together on the same type of work issues. Marketing specialists, for example, work together to develop promotion and sales campaigns for each of the small number of products of the company. Second, functional departmentalization promotes the development of specialized skills and expertise in workers because they deal with the same issues over time. Third, managers have an easier time coordinating and planning because all the jobs that report to them are similar in content. AT&T Communications has departments of marketing, corporation human resources, and information systems.[5] Finally, this type of departmentalization is often intuitively simple to the persons involved in the organization in terms of their learning the lines of communication and authority.

**functional departmentalization**
The grouping of jobs that perform similar functional activities, such as finance, manufacturing, and human resources.

**Teaching Note:** Remind students that in a small business the manager/owner may perform all the functions. As a business grows, the typical first stage of development is to hire workers and group them into departments representing the functional activities.

A major disadvantage of functional departmentalization is that it often results in each department having a functional, as opposed to an organizational, perspective. This is because employees work on only one aspect of the business of the organization and, over time, begin to see the business only from that perspective. Sometimes this can lead to disagreements among members of different functional departments over allocation of resources and organizational direction. For example, a business slump for a clothing manufacturing company may be interpreted as calling for more advertising, by the marketing department, and for more efficient machinery, by the production department. Such perceptual differences are often difficult to resolve successfully. Related to this, managers often become so highly specialized in terms of expertise that they do not develop the necessary knowledge of other functions of the organization in order to be successful at top levels of management. Such management jobs require a broad set of skills to make decisions for the company as a whole.

## Customer Departmentalization

**customer departmentalization**
The grouping of jobs so that the job holders interact with a specific customer group or clientele.

An organization employing **customer departmentalization** groups jobs so that the job holders interact with a specific customer group or clientele. Figure 12.3 depicts such a departmental structure, a clothing store that has departments for men's, women's, boys', and girls' clothing. Each of these departments has a manager, assistant manager, clerk, buyer, inventory clerk, and sales clerks. However, the activities of those positions in any one department include only the clothing appropriate for its group of clients.

An obvious advantage of customer departmentalization is that it puts the organization in closer contact with its customers and should give the firm some advantage in addressing the needs of that particular clientele. For this reason many large advertising agencies are developing departments or even separate companies that serve one customer. For example, Omnicrom Group developed Merkley, Newman, & Harty to serve its huge WordPerfect account.[6] Structuring around the customer permits each department's employees to develop unique skills to address the customer's needs. In the case of the clothing store, each buyer specializes in clothing for only one group of customers—the men's buyer for men's clothes, the women's buyer for women's clothes, and so on. This allows the buyer to be knowledgeable about fabrics, fashion looks, and colors for that customer group rather than for all customers.

A disadvantage to customer departmentalization is that it can give the organization a perspective that perhaps grants too much leeway to customers. For instance, many have argued that, in the 1980s, loan officers of savings and loan institutions grew too enamored of their real estate developer customers. This resulted in officers approving loans that were not in the best interest of the institution or other customers. Also, customer departmentalization results in duplication of resources, as each customer department may have the same type of employees and equipment.

## Product Departmentalization

**product departmentalization**
The grouping of jobs or activities around a firm's principal goods and services.

Firms employing **product departmentalization** group jobs or activities around their principal goods and services. The hotel's food and beverage division shown earlier in Figure 12.1, for example, has different product departments for bever-

**FIGURE 12.3**

**Customer Departments within a Clothing Store**

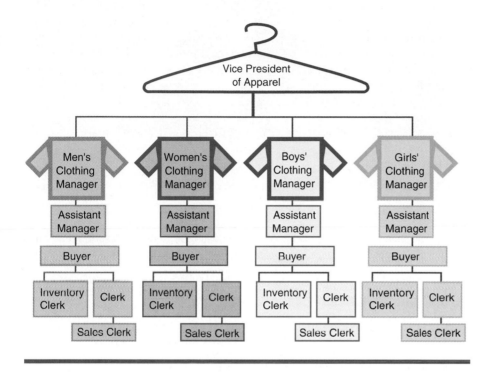

ages and restaurants as well as for catering. Many department stores—including Sears, Target, and other large retail chains—are organized on this basis, with departments for appliances, kitchen utensils, furniture, lighting fixtures, and sporting goods. Many large organizations that have several different products are similarly organized along product lines. For example, General Motors has product divisions associated with Pontiac, Chevrolet, GMC, Oldsmobile, Buick, and Cadillac. Also, as organizations grow, they often move from a functional to a product orientation for their structure. This is especially true if the firms produce or acquire a variety of products that may have some unique manufacturing, marketing, and distribution needs. For example, BellSouth Corporation has separate units for information systems, financial services, and mobile systems.

One advantage of organizing by product is that it permits the firm to adjust quickly to changes in market needs. NCR Corp., for example, has recently moved to develop departments based on its software products so that it can respond to the market.[7] Secondly, organizing by product provides good training for managers who may move into top management positions. The manager of a product department usually has to coordinate all the functional areas involved.

Problems associated with product departmentalization include an excessive amount of duplication in terms of functional efficiencies, costs, and effort. This is because a company may have parallel functional groups such as marketing and manufacturing for each product line. Also, there may be competition between the departments over organizational resources. Thus, even though product departments may be good training for future top managers, the managers in each department

**Teaching Note:** Have students interview the manager of a local department store, or ask such a manager to speak to your class on the organization and functioning of managers in specialty departments.

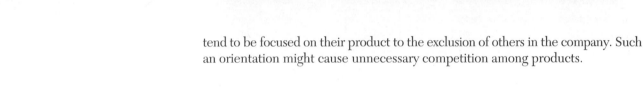

The Coca-Cola Company uses geographic departmentalization in organizing its international operations that extend to 195 countries. Its international geographic regions include European Community, Pacific, Northeast Europe/Middle East, Latin America, and Africa. Coca-Cola develops different marketing strategies for consumers in new markets, emerging markets, and established markets. In China, Coca-Cola is creating consumer awareness of its brands through outdoor signs, sports sponsorships, television advertising, and visibility in the marketplace.

*Source:* © 1993 Arthur Meyerson. All rights reserved.

**geographic departmentalization**
The grouping of jobs according to physical geography.

**Example:** NK Lawn and Garden Company sells packaged garden and flower seeds in large display racks to Kmart, Wal-Mart, and other retailers. Because of geographic variations, including weather, rainfall, and planting times, seeds are shipped earlier to Southern markets. The geographical differences also mean longer growing seasons, the need for more seeds, and larger racks for stores in Southern areas.

tend to be focused on their product to the exclusion of others in the company. Such an orientation might cause unnecessary competition among products.

## Geographic Departmentalization

**Geographic departmentalization** groups jobs according to physical geography. Many national organizations have regional offices, such as a northeast sales office and a southwest sales office. This departmentalization scheme is often used by firms with international operations requiring a special knowledge of or sensitivity to each particular nation or region. For example, Coca-Cola Inc. has divisions for Latin America, Europe, and the Pacific Rim. Departmentalization by geography can be based on any set of geographic parameters—for instance, area, state, or nation.

The advantages and disadvantages of geographic departmentalization are similar to those that were discussed for other forms of departmentalization. The primary advantage is that it allows the company to address needs or characteristics of consumers that are particular to that area. For this reason, the sales group of FourGen Technologies, a Seattle-based software developer, decided to change to geographical regions when sales growth slowed.[8] On a national level, different regions of the United States have different dining and eating patterns. Food distribution companies and restaurant chains organized on a geographic basis can vary their items according to location to better serve their consumers. In international companies organized by region or country, marketing for different countries can vary to accommodate cultural and national differences. The major drawback of geographic departmentalization is excessive cost through duplication. As we said of product departmentalization, this form leads to duplication of resources and employees, as each location usually has a full complement of functional areas.

## DETERMINING AUTHORITY RELATIONSHIPS

The third activity involved in organizing is determining authority relationships among employees. Usually these authority relationships flow down an organizational chart, from high positions such as president and vice presidents down to the lower levels of the organization. For this reason, this organizing activity is sometimes known as vertical or scaler organization. One major purpose of establishing authority relationships is to make it easier for the organization to achieve its goals. As we have discussed, one of the major tasks of managers is to direct the work of employees. For small companies, the manager can accomplish this through frequent interaction with the relatively small group of workers. As the organization matures and expands, however, this close contact is no longer possible. It usually is at this point that departments are formed. However, the organization still must coordinate and direct the activities of all employees. Therefore, all organizations must have authority and reporting relationships to specifically identify positions that serve to direct and coordinate the activities of other positions.

## Authority and Responsibility

Authority is bestowed by the organization. That is, the structure of the organization indicates that some positions have authority over others, and subordinate positions must report to higher-level ones. Authority, therefore, is related only to the structure of an organization, not to the individual who occupies a given position. Thus, the person who holds a position of authority gets that authority from his or her position. Going back to our earlier discussion of organization charts, authority is the right to give work directives to all directly connected lower positions in the organization.

As illustration, think of a classroom situation. The instructor has authority to give assignments and grades to the students. The instructor's ability to do these activities resides within the position held, as a duly authorized teacher of the university. Authority starts with the board of trustees and flows through the president, dean, department head, and finally, the instructor.

Authority is the legitimate use of power—that is, using power in areas deemed appropriate by the organization. An instructor is using legitimate power in directing students to write term papers, attend class, and complete examinations to earn credit for the course. When an organization gives one of its members authority, or the legitimate right to use power over others, it expects something in return. Authority always carries with it the burden of responsibility. **Responsibility** means being held accountable for attainment of the organization's goals.

Henri Fayol, discussed in Chapter 2, said that authority must accompany responsibility.[9] In other words, no one in an organization can be expected to be responsible for something over which he or she has no authority. For example, if workers on the assembly line are held responsible for their tools, then they need the authority to lock the tools up—they need power over or control of the tools. If a grocery store clerk is responsible for the accuracy of the till, then others in the organization cannot be given authority to use it, even if the store becomes very busy.

## Authority Relationships

As is true of the other topics in organizing, authority is a very complex issue. To whom the marketing specialist and the production specialist report is critical to the effective performance of the organization. These reporting relationships are partly defined by the type of departmentalization the organization uses. Under product departmentalization, for example, both of these specialists may report to the same position—the product manager—and thus attend many of the same planning and review meetings. Under functional departmentalization, these two specialists

**responsibility**
The individual's burden of accountability for attainment of the organization's goals.

would most likely report to a manager in their own areas, marketing and production, respectively. Under these circumstances, the two specialists may interact infrequently even if they are working on the same product. In addition to departmentalization, authority is affected by the span of control and the chain of command established by the structure.

**span of control**
The actual number of subordinates over which a position has authority.

**Span of Control.**    The **span of control** is the actual number of subordinates over which a position has authority. A broad span of control means that a manager supervises several subordinates; a narrow span of control means that she or he supervises only a few. Span of control is one of the older concepts in management and can be traced back to the early part of this century. Essentially, early theorists thought that a manager should never control more than a certain number of employees, normally five or six subordinates for higher-level managers and as many as thirty for lower-level managers. A basic assumption of such thought was that any one individual is limited in terms of available time and the amount of information that he or she can process. More subordinates mean more time demands and more information to process. However, if all subordinates are doing essentially the same job, as is the case with many lower-level managers, then more subordinates can be managed.

**Example:** The trend in organizations is to downsize or reduce the number of employees and layers in the organization, thus increasing a manager's span of control.

Over the years, many managers and researchers have criticized the notion of rigid adherence to any rule that prescribes exactly how many positions should report to another. Typically today, both groups would argue that the span of control should be determined by the particular circumstances involved. Factors such as complexity of the employees' jobs, the availability of information systems to keep track of performance data, the physical proximity of the workers, whether or not the task is self-directed, the workers' expertise, prevalence of standard operating procedures, and frequency of unpredictable problems should be addressed before determining the number of people whom a manager can effectively manage. For instance, in situations in which the work is relatively simple we would expect that a broader span may be appropriate. In scenarios in which the workers are geographically dispersed, such as convenience store managers, a narrow span may be the preferred choice.

The span of control may also be affected by managerial styles. A person who manages by forging close personal relationships would probably do better with a narrow span of control. On the other hand, a person who predominantly pays attention only to performance data and intervenes with subordinates only when performance is low could operate with a broad span of control. Recently, the use of computer systems has also affected the span of control of many organizations. Companies such as Purolator Courier, Ltd. employ telecommuting employees—those who are not in a company office but work through the computer system.[10] This practice usually adds many subordinates to the span of control because the amount of interaction between the telecommuting employee and the supervisor is reduced and the computer system keeps records of the employee's performance.

**Example:** The American Management Association's most recent survey of employment practices at 870 companies found that from 1992 to 1993 almost half had reduced their work forces. For two-thirds of those companies, this was at least their second year in a row of downsizing.

The number of subordinates directed by each position affects the overall structure of the organization. Commonly, when narrow spans of control are needed in an organization, there must be more managers, and thus more levels of management. The structure associated with a narrow span is usually referred to as a *tall organization,* while the structure associated with the broad span is referred to as a *flat organization.* The significance of these differences, which we will address in the next chapter, is that tall organizations frequently rely on higher-level managers for decision making, and communication usually takes longer to filter through the organization. Flat organizations disperse decision making and have fewer levels of management. Publix Super Markets, Inc., for example, recently changed its information systems unit into a simple group with a flat reporting structure.[11]

Quality control can also have a major effect on span of control. For example, at NASA, some tasks are considered so crucial that spans of control are one—the work of an employee is the sole supervisory task of another employee. The same is true for companies that make a number of heat-activated immunizations. If the product is not *perfect,* the result of receiving an immunization may be catastrophic; for example, a poor-quality polio vaccine might result in active polio rather than an immunity to polio. When quality control is crucial, the span of control tends to be narrower.

**Chain of Command.**    **Chain of command** is an organizing concept that ensures that all positions are directly linked in some way to top management. Such linkage means that all employees are coordinated in terms of work activities. The organizational chart depicts the chain of command.

Organizing specialists have developed a number of principles concerning the chain of command, which sound, not surprisingly, like dialogue from a John Wayne war movie.

**Unity of command** is the principle that a subordinate should report to only one immediate superior. Early practicing managers argued that if an employee reports to more than one boss, conflicting orders may be given. In addition, it will be difficult to convey organizational goals effectively. This has been a long-standing military axiom, but as we shall see in the next chapter, this principle has been effectively ignored by some organizations in order to operate in a highly changeable environment.

**Scaler chain** is the principle of organizing whereby authority should flow through the organization from the top down, one level at a time. This principle is concerned primarily with the need for precise information to be transmitted through the firm. If Sally skips her immediate subordinate, Rob, and talks directly to Rob's subordinate, Mel, about a work-related topic, Rob will miss information that may affect both immediate and future work activities of his group.

## Balancing Authority and Responsibility

Another issue that must be addressed in determining authority relationships is how to divide the authority among members of the organization or department. Another way of saying this is, "What work-related orders may be given by each position in the structure of the organization?" This is an especially critical issue for both growing businesses and those that are undergoing a major change in their organizational structure. The basic principle in this issue is that the top manager cannot be directly involved in all decisions. There simply is not enough time nor can any one individual know enough to do this. Therefore, decision making and authority must be spread throughout the members of the organization. There are two major methods of distributing authority:  delegation and decentralization.

**Delegation.**    **Delegation**, or empowerment, is the assignment of work activities and authority to an employee or work group. But this involves more than just saying, "Do it." Delegation is a deliberate attempt to create efficiencies. It is intended to speed the process of work operations by reducing the demands on any

**chain of command**
An organizing concept that ensures that all positions are directly linked in some way to top management.

**unity of command**
The principle that a subordinate should report to only one immediate superior.

**scaler chain**
The principle of organizing whereby authority should flow through the organization from the top down, one level at a time.

**delegation**
The assignment of work activities and authority to a subordinate.

---

**TABLE 12.2**

### Basic Issues in Delegation and Empowerment

- Include a complete set of work tasks—either a whole job or a definite part of a job.
- Set goals—the subordinate(s) should participate in developing definite end results that should be achieved.
- Include authority with responsibility—inform the subordinate and others that the subordinate has the right to make decisions for specific work activities.
- Provide information—subordinates must receive all data relevant to newly assigned job tasks.
- Communicate frequently—the subordinate should inform the manager of work on assigned job tasks. This is to provide the manager with necessary information, not to ask for direction.

---

one individual and therefore reducing delays in processing information, making decisions, and communicating these decisions to others. However, delegation is not a tactic to relieve managers of the responsibility for whether these work activities are performed well or not. A manager can only delegate work activities, not abdicate his or her responsibilities; therefore, it is in the manager's best interest to treat the delegation process as an important part of his or her job, one that requires careful attention and systematic review.

Essentially, delegation is something like a contract between persons. An exchange of work activities and authority is made by a manager and the subordinate. The manager obtains assistance for some work tasks and can therefore use the time that these tasks would take for other important activities. The subordinate, of course, has more to do but profits because the additional tasks are usually those that can provide experience in performing the activities of the next higher-level position. The subordinate is, therefore, benefiting from one form of career training. A new working relationship between the superior and subordinate is defined by this exchange.

Table 12.2 lists some basic issues that must be addressed in delegation. The manager must assign the work tasks to the subordinate with specific goals stated. Next, the manager must grant authority to the individual. This grant should also be communicated to people who work with him or her. The individual must accept responsibility for the task by agreeing to be accountable. Even though the employee is in control of the job activities, it is necessary for the two parties to meet frequently in order to keep the manager informed and to ensure that the employee has all relevant information. At this point, the manager has struck a new contract with the employee. However, this contract characterizes only the working relationship between the two people involved. The organization does not change its organizational chart or its formal authority relationships in light of delegation. As far as the organization is concerned, the manager is still ultimately responsible for the accomplishment of the delegated tasks. This is because it is possible to delegate authority, but not responsibility. Consequently, the manager will need to evaluate and control the individual's action.

Delegation has benefits for all involved. The manager is relieved of some of the daily activities necessary for getting a part of his or her work done. The employee often gets a chance to develop new skills and master additional tasks that will be assets in future career development. The organization benefits because the work process may be completed more efficiently and another employee gains skill in higher-level work assignments.

Despite these potentially favorable outcomes, delegation is not always used, possibly because of reluctance on the part of either the manager or the subordinate. A manager may not wish to delegate for a number of reasons. He or she may fear that the subordinate may do the job better and gain some notice in the organization. Another reason may be a lack of knowledge in how to properly organize the work to divide it between the two parties. A third is that the manager may fear loss of control and not wish to be responsible for anything not done personally. Many individuals, especially if new to the position, are reluctant to accept delegated tasks because they fear making a mistake and suffering the resulting criticism.

**Decentralization.**   An important question in the distribution of authority is to what extent authority should be spread across the organization. That is, should a few or many positions be given authority? **Centralization** is the pattern of concentrating authority in a relatively few, high-level positions. These positions must be involved in almost all decisions. As you can probably guess, **decentralization** is the opposite pattern, in which authority is dispersed to several positions at various levels in the organization.

In this sense, decentralization can be viewed as formalized delegation in the organization. Instead of being a personal working relationship between manager and subordinate, decentralization represents a systematic plan of the organization to spread authority. The advantages of decentralization are similar to those we have mentioned for delegation, except that these advantages accrue to the organization as well as to individuals. Information and decisions are processed more quickly because there are fewer levels of employees involved. Also more individuals receive training in how to make and implement managerial-type decisions. Bankers Trust Company decentralized its information systems operation in 1985, giving business units complete control over their information systems and resulting in systems that provide specific information necessary for decisions in each unit.[12] The "Magnifying Management" box discusses how decentralization has been beneficial for Hewlett-Packard.

Most organizations are neither completely centralized nor decentralized. In some firms, most decision making is centralized, with the exception of one or two departments that may have a great deal of decentralization, for example, quality control and customer service. In other organizations, only certain functions are centralized, such as manufacturing. The degree to which a firm will decentralize or centralize depends on a number of factors. Generally, if an organization's environment is highly dynamic, a decentralized approach may be preferred. It allows for the faster transmission of information to those who make decisions because there are fewer levels of management to go through to reach the appropriate decision maker. On the other hand, the degree of risk and the cost attached to a decision may affect a firm's position. Organizations will tend to be centralized if they are involved in decisions with high risk/high cost alternatives. A third factor is the skill and ability of the managers in the organization. Decentralization requires that managers be competent in the areas in which they are asked to assume authority. For this reason, decentralization is often accompanied by planned management development programs.

**centralization**
The pattern of concentrating authority in a relatively few, high-level positions.

**decentralization**
The pattern of dispersing authority to several positions at various levels in the organization.

**Example:** After using centralized planning, Sears mailed catalogs from its Illinois headquarters to Latin-American markets. Catalog sales were lower than projected and Sears discovered customers in this market were in opposite seasons and had different preferences for clothes and colors. As a result, planning was decentralized and a geographic organizational structure was adopted.

### HEWLETT-PACKARD DECENTRALIZES FOR SUCCESS

Hewlett-Packard Co. (HP) has prided itself on being the home of "groups of obstreperous, entrepreneurial, arrogant engineers running their shows," says management consultant and author Tom Peters. With that kind of employee, it is not surprising that decentralization has been characteristic of both HP's organization and its management philosophy. It is hard to imagine that a tightly controlled, centralized decision-making style would fit with the personalities of its engineers.

William Hewlett and David Packard have clearly been in control of the company since its beginning; however, they have not confused control with approval of all actions and projects. From its earliest days, these two owners made it a policy to divide any unit that grew to more than 1,500 employees. In 1969, for example, they divided a division making digital voltmeters and related products, including an early version of the hand-held calculator. They set up the calculator business as a separate unit and moved it 12 miles to another site in Colorado. As with all units within HP, it was endowed with its own management, engineering, marketing, and human resource staffs. The unit proved successful and has since developed into one of HP's computer divisions that now markets RISC-based workstations. The evolution has been based primarily on the decisions of the unit.

This separation of product units and decentralization of authority and decision making also explain the company's latest success—its dominance of the laser printer market for personal computers. In 1981, Richard Hackborn, a manager who had successfully advanced through HP, became familiar with a desktop printer powered by a small, totally contained engine. The inventor, the Japanese firm Canon, was not sure how to develop or market the product. Hackborn convinced HP management to allow him to leave the existing computer peripherals unit and sell desktop printers using the Canon technology. At the time, HP's only printer was a $100,000 mainframe machine sold by HP's sales force. The idea was radical for two reasons. First, the peripheral unit's purpose was to support HP's own computers, and the desktop printer did not fit that purpose. Second, it was based on a product developed by another company. Had HP been a traditional, integrated corporation, Hackborn's idea probably would have been turned down. Instead he was given the authority and resources to develop his idea. The result is a unit that now accounts for 40 percent of HP's income before interest and taxes.

Another example of putting decentralization into action occurred in the early 1990s. HP's stock value, like that of its rivals IBM and DEC, had dropped considerably. Bypassing their headquarters staff, Hewlett and Packard visited with small groups of low-level employees and concluded that the company had become too centralized and bureaucratic. They responded by moving people and power away from headquarters. For example, Lewis Platt, then head of HP's computer transfer systems group, was moved from the Palo Alto headquarters to Cupertino, CA. He used the move to develop a program to build a workstation on a very tight one-year schedule. The project was completed with little input from higher management.

The philosophy of decentralization is thoroughly ingrained in HP and thought by its employees to be necessary for its continued success. William Hewlett and David Packard's management philosophy seems to be successful.

*Source:* Julie Pitta, "It Had to Be Done and We Did It," *Forbes,* April 26, 1993, 148–152.

## SUMMARY AND REVIEW

- **Discuss the concept of organizing and explain why it is important.** An organization is a group of individuals working together to achieve goals or objectives that would be difficult or impossible for them to achieve individually. Organizing is the process of creating an organization. There are a number of reasons to organize.

One is to achieve synergy, the ability of a group of individuals to accomplish more than could the individuals working alone. Second, organizing reduces duplication of resources. Third, organizing creates lines of authority that facilitate coordination of job activities. Finally, organizing provides formal communication channels.

c   a   r   e   e   r   s

C
o
r
n
e
r

## Organizing Your Job Search

After you complete your college education, you will have learned a good deal and, probably, will be able to do a good deal. However, the problem almost everyone faces in looking for a job is how to contact employers and show them what you know and what you can do. Many students take a reactive approach to job search. That is, they react to published advertisements or leads supplied by friends. However, there is a better chance of success if you organize your efforts and become proactive as well as reactive. A proactive job search includes three parts: locating organizations that match your abilities and interests, preparing your résumé to fit the organization, and writing a cover letter that interests potential employers.

**Organizations.**    Jobs become available for many reasons. New technology, increased consumer demand, reorganization, new legislation, environmental challenges, social changes, plant relocation, and retirements are among them. There is much written in magazines, trade and professional journals, and newspapers about these and other topics in organizations. Read as much as you can to identify patterns of growth for chosen industries and particular companies. Pay careful attention to those that employ individuals in the same area in which you wish to work. Second, find the names of relevant companies in the geographic locations where you wish to work. Often, there are advantages in concentrating your efforts in one location. For example, you start building a network of people and reduce the expense and time of travel. There are many business directories in your college or local library that will provide essential information about specific organizations in specific locations.

**Résumé.**    Your résumé should provide an accurate and detailed advertisement of who you are. You must realize that, upon receipt, your résumé will be mixed with those of many other individuals. It is therefore important that it be distinctive and also accurately convey your characteristics. You should determine the main characteristic that you wish to convey to the readers of your résumé and make all aspects of it support that characteristic. Employers are usually looking for appli-

cants who can perform a specific function. Your résumé should provide enough detailed information so that the reader recognizes the match between your ability and the company's needs. A very general résumé that attempts to cover all jobs actually covers none very well.

**Cover Letter.**    Your letter of introduction to each organization should be written especially for that organization. Yes, this approach takes much more time, but it also distinguishes you from many other applicants. You should include the following points in your letter:

1. Address it to a specific individual by name. If possible, send letters to both the manager of the job you want and the human resource manager. Getting these names may require a library search and personal visits to the company.

2. Indicate in the first paragraph some particular features of the organization that are important to you; make it apparent to the reader that you are familiar with the company. This means more research from business news sources and company publications.

3. Communicate what you can do for the company. This should be logically related to the central point of your résumé. If you can work with information networks, for example, point that out in terms of the company's activities.

4. Request an interview and provide a specific range of days. Often this proves favorable because it reduces scheduling problems for the employer.

Looking for a job is a full-time job in itself. Very few individuals have companies seeking them. You also must realize that the large majority of your contacts are going to lead to a "no." Don't be unnecessarily discouraged. Organization and persistence are important to your final success.

*Sources:* Albert L. French, *How to Locate Jobs and Land Interviews,* 2nd ed. (Hawthorne, NJ: Career Press, 1993); and Tom Jackson, *Guerrilla Tactics in the New Job Market* (New York: Bantam Books, 1991).

---

- **Interpret an organizational chart.** An organizational chart is a pictorial display of the official lines of authority and communication within the organization. Vertical lines between positions indicate lines of authority; horizontal lines represent lines of communication. Positions at higher levels of the chart have authority over positions lower in the chart. The organizational chart shows the structure of the formal organization, which is the arrangement of positions that dictates which work activities are completed, where decisions should be made, and the flow of information, but does not designate the informal relationships.

- **Explain why job specialization and division of labor are important for organizing.** Division of labor refers to the breaking down of work activities into a number of distinct steps. Specialization is assigning individuals to work on each of these steps separately. These two concepts are closely related, and both are essential for making large quantities of goods efficiently. Workers assigned to only one small part of the work process can become very knowledgeable about that part very quickly. Specialized tools and equipment can be developed. The result is that more product can be made more quickly and for less cost.

- **Assess the different approaches to grouping tasks into jobs and the advantages and disadvantages of each.** Tasks can be grouped into jobs by using either the classical approach to job design or the behavioral approach to job design. The classical approach stresses making a job very simple by including a small number of job tasks. The behavioral approach takes into account the psychological makeup of the worker and attempts to increase the number of tasks in the job and to bring the challenge of worker interest to the job.

- **Distinguish four different bases for grouping jobs into departments.** Functional departmentalization groups jobs according to similarity of content. Firms employing product departmentalization group jobs or activities around their principal goods and services. Customer departmentalization brings together those jobs that have the same customer as their focus. Geographic departmentalization groups jobs according to their geographical similarity.

- **Determine the relationships among authority, responsibility, and delegation.** Authority is the right to give work orders to others in the organization. Responsibility refers to the accountability an individual or group is given for the attainment of goals. Delegation is the assignment of work activities and authority to a subordinate. Though the manager delegates work activities and the authority to complete them to a subordinate, the manager still is responsible for the subordinate's performance and the work activities themselves.

- **Define decentralization and describe what strengths it has for employee development.** Decentralization is the pattern of distributing authority beyond the top positions to various levels throughout the organization. Decentralization frees managers from some tasks, provides an opportunity for employees to develop new skills and master additional tasks such as managerial-type decisions, and speeds information processing and decision making because there are fewer levels of employees involved.

- **Critique a company's new organizational structure.** Using the principles in this chapter, evaluate the new organizational structure of the company described in the "Business Dilemma" box. Your evaluation should describe which approach to job design you used, what form of departmentalization you think would be best, the degree of employee responsibility/accountability, and the level of centralization the firm employs.

## Key Terms and Concepts

organizational chart *334*
authority *334*
formal organization *334*
informal organization *335*
job specialization *338*
job design *338*
horizontal specialization *338*
vertical specialization *338*
classical approach to job design *338*

behavioral approach to job design *340*
job enlargement *340*
job rotation *341*
job enrichment *341*
departmentalization *341*
functional departmentalization *343*
customer departmentalization *344*
product departmentalization *344*
geographic departmentalization *346*

responsibility *347*
span of control *348*
chain of command *349*
unity of command *349*
scaler chain *349*
delegation *349*
centralization *351*
decentralization *351*

## Ready Recall

1. What are the advantages of organizing over having individuals complete all work tasks?
2. Describe the relationships depicted in an organizational chart.
3. Define division of labor and job specialization. Why are these important for organizing?

4. Compare and contrast the classical and behavioral approaches to job design.
5. List and explain the four bases for grouping of jobs into departments. What are the advantages and disadvantages of each of the methods of forming departments?

6. What is meant by authority within an organization?
7. How are delegation and decentralization similar? How are they different?
8. What factors affect the span of control assigned to a position?

## Expand Your Experience

1. Obtain an organizational chart from a medium- or large-sized company, and discuss what bases it uses to departmentalize.
2. Interview the owner of a small business with several employees to find out how he or she delegates and whether the firm tends toward centralization or decentralization. What advantages and disadvantages does this offer the owner?

3. Interview a worker and his or her supervisor in a manufacturing company about their work activities. Describe the amount of specialization and division of labor in these jobs. What are the feelings of these two workers about their jobs and the organization?

## CASE

# GM's Saturn:  A Rocket or a Flare?

General Motors' compact car, Saturn, was to be the savior of the industrial giant's automobile business. Like other U.S. automobile manufacturers, GM had steadily lost market share and profits to foreign, especially Japanese, companies during the period from the late 1960s through the early 1980s. Industry analysts identified a number of reasons for the downslide: poor designs, poor employee-management relationships, too much centralized decision making, low worker involvement, and a minimal emphasis on quality. Thus in 1982, GM began to seriously think about how to end the decline. If it could not accomplish a turnaround, GM's role as a major part of the U.S. automobile market was in jeopardy. It had already laid off nearly 170,000 employees.

GM created an Advanced Project and Design Team to determine whether GM could build a high-quality, inexpensive subcompact to compete successfully with the imports. As had been true with its other projects, this team took a technological approach and began exploring new manufacturing methods such as lost-foam casting and high-speed machining. Simultaneously, a second group—composed of several executives from the Industrial Relations Staff and officials from the United Auto Workers Union (UAW)—began to explore new ways of designing and carrying out work activities. Because the two GM groups were really examining the same question from different viewpoints—technology versus employees—they quickly began operating jointly. Visiting 49 GM plants and 60 benchmark companies around the world, the joint group evolved a philosophy of work and manufacturing that was radically different from that which usually characterized automobile plants.

Underscoring the "new" approach to production, GM announced in January 1985 that Saturn Corporation would be a separate subsidiary of GM rather than another automobile division directly controlled by corporate headquarters. At the

heart of the Saturn approach is a team definition of tasks, jobs, and supervisor-worker relationships. Working relationships between union workers and Saturn managers are partnerships. At each managerial level from the president on down, and within each staff function, a UAW representative shares decision making with a Saturn manager. For example, the Strategic Action Committee includes the president of Saturn and the president of the local UAW union, as well as other executives and union officers.

All employees are part of at least one work team composed of six to fifteen workers. Each team functions as a self-directed work unit expected to discuss and reach unanimous agreement on all of the issues regarding its work activities. Underlying the development of these teams was extensive formal training, usually of about 500 to 700 hours. This amount of training was remarkable in light of the fact that the majority of workers were experienced automobile workers who had moved from other plants across the country. While the training covered technical job-skill topics, a large portion was devoted to work group interactions such as communication, conflict resolution, decision making, and goal setting.

Partnership was a central feature of the first Saturn employment contract signed between GM and the UAW in 1985. There were a number of features of this contract that were in pointed contrast to those of other GM plants. For one thing, the number of job classifications was sharply reduced. Saturn has one classification for production workers and five for skilled trades. This means that workers within the production group or any one of the skilled trades can easily be assigned to any task appropriate for that work group, creating enormous flexibility for work assignments. In other automobile plants, job tasks for specific workers are strictly defined and employees are prohibited by the labor contract from doing any task that is part of another employee's job. In large part, this strictness is an attempt to keep union members employed and avoid reduction in the labor force.

The Saturn contract also placed all employees on a salary rather than an hourly wage scale. However, this salary plan was designed to encourage continued high work performance. The base salary for all employees is approximately 80 percent of the average earnings of similar employees in other GM plants. Employees can earn additional bonuses after reaching production goals. These goals emphasize Saturn production, such as number of cars produced, overall quality of units, and productivity—not individual work group production. As a result, all plant employees receive the same percentage return for success. This bonus plan is designed to bring total compensation to at least the level of other plants and permits higher rewards if production goals are exceeded.

In addition, other traditional differentials between management and nonmanagement employees are minimized. No one wears ties or formal business clothing. There are no time clocks, privileged parking areas, or reserved dining rooms. The partnership atmosphere is intended for all employment activities. In return, Saturn has guaranteed lifetime employment for 80 percent of its employees, barring severe economic conditions or catastrophic events. Since union members are full partners in all decision making, the union will have a loud voice in determining whether such conditions exist or not.

The flexibility in job assignments forms the basis for the effective use of technology, which radically changes production. The Saturn facility is the largest single construction project in GM's history. The highly integrated plant contains a powertrain factory that casts, machines, and assembles the engines and transmissions; a plastic-molding plant; a shop for assembling the instrument panel and dashboard into a single unit; as well as the assembly and painting components. The few parts that are shipped in from other locations arrive at multiple unloading docks scattered throughout the site and close to where they are needed. All of this is in sharp contrast to other GM automobile plants in which many key components are manufactured at specialized facilities throughout the United States and shipped to each assembly plant. Saturn takes a great deal of pride in demonstrating that technology and work groups are mutual components of production.

The early results of the Saturn partnership are impressive. In 1991, Saturn sold more cars per dealer than any other manufacturer. The automobile has achieved the third highest customer satisfaction rating in the critical J.D. Power rankings, following two high-priced luxury cars, Lexus and Infiniti. In addition, Saturn has reached nearly all of the production and financial goals that GM set for it.

So, is the future one of higher flight for the GM Saturn? Despite its initial success, there is doubt about the future. A number of critical changes have occurred in the initial operating plan. For one, Saturn has agreed to employ only individuals who have been laid off from other GM plants. A large percentage of these come to Saturn with an initial distrust of management decisions and are apparently less favorable about the close working relationship between the union and management. In a referendum vote in January 1993, approximately 29 percent of the nonmanagement employees backed a shift toward traditional, arm's length labor relations rather than the partnership between the two groups. In addition, Saturn has greatly reduced the amount of training given to work teams, especially in non-job-skill components. This has been caused partly by Saturn's own success. The demand for automobiles has steadily risen, causing increased production goals that included the addition of a third shift in a short time period. In addition, GM's general economic slump has placed more demand on Saturn to become profitable quickly. Reducing training reduces costs and increases profitability. Finally, GM corporate officers are rethinking the Saturn Corporation's formal relationship to the rest of GM, considering ending its status as an independent company and rejoining it in some form to the GM Corporation.

*Sources:* Beverly Geber, "Saturn's Grand Experiment," *Training* 29 (June 1992): 27–35; "GM's Saturn Workers Vote to Keep Cooperative Pact," *The Wall Street Journal,* January 15, 1993, A3; Mary McGrory, "Enlightenment from Saturn," *The Washington Post,* December 1, 1992, A2; Kathleen Morris, "Sales: Saturn-GM," *Financial World,* April 14, 1992, 48; and David Woodruff, "Saturn: Labor's Love Lost?" *Business Week,* February 8, 1993, 122–124.

## Questions

1. Discuss the effects of Saturn's work teams on interactions among nonmanagement work-team members, work teams and managers, and necessary skills for work-team members.
2. Discuss possible effects of the recent trends at Saturn of reduced training for work groups and the employment of previously laid-off workers on the partnership of Saturn.
3. Discuss specific effects of Saturn's policies regarding lifetime employment, salary, and group decision making on the performance of work teams.

# *Negotiating*

You learned that one of Mintzberg's ten management roles discussed in Chapter 1 is that of negotiator. In the context of the material covered in this chapter, you can see how being a good negotiator would be a particularly helpful skill when you are involved in such activities as determining who will perform which tasks on a new project or when you are bargaining with other departments or upper management to obtain advantages for your own department.

*Distributive bargaining* and *integrative bargaining* are the two general approaches to negotiation that are compared for you in the following table:[*]

| Bargaining Variable | Distributive Bargaining | Integrative Bargaining |
|---|---|---|
| Available resources | Fixed amount of resources to be divided | Variable amount of resources to be divided |
| Primary motivations | I win, you lose | I win, you win |
| Primary interests | Opposed to each other | Convergent or congruent with each other |
| Focus of relationships | Short-term | Long-term |

Here is an exercise that will help you to understand the differences in these two approaches.

## Instructions

1. Someone in the class will volunteer to read the following story aloud as the rest of the class follows along:

### Who's to Blame?

*The tragic accident that ended the love triangle on the soap opera, "The Young and the Gutless," had its loyal audience of viewers around the country taking sides as to who was to blame for what happened. As the story began, Bolivia and Blake were engaged to be married and were planning a spring wedding. Bolivia's best friend, Bobbi Jo, secretly plotted to steal Blake from Bolivia and began her creative campaign to break up the two lovers and win Blake for herself.*

*Bobbi Jo made suggestive comments to Blake whenever Bolivia was out of earshot. She also never missed an opportunity to make negative remarks about Bolivia when Bolivia was not around to defend herself. Blake didn't seem to try to discourage Bobbi Jo's suggestive comments, and his feeble attempts to defend Bolivia when she wasn't around to do so herself didn't seem to slow down Bobbi Jo's continued efforts to undermine Bolivia. Even though Bolivia's Aunt Phoebe tried to warn her that Bobbi Jo was trying to steal her man, Bolivia chose to believe that Aunt Phoebe was imagining things and continued to encourage Bobbi Jo to spend time with her and Blake.*

*On the night before Blake's and Bolivia's wedding, Blake succumbed to Bobbi Jo's temptress scheme, and Bolivia saw Blake and Bobbi Jo together, unbeknownst to them, of course. With tears streaming down her face, she ran out of the house in the midst of a violent thunderstorm, got into her car, and drove away into the dark night. Completely devastated that her fiancé would betray her and that her*

*best friend could have deceived her so completely, she drove as fast as she could to get as far away from them as she possibly could. As she rounded a sharp curve, she lost control of her car and crashed into a tree, dying instantly.*

2. If you had been one among the millions of viewers who watched this complex plot unfold over the past two years you would recognize that all three characters contributed in their own way to the way things turned out. However, who would you say is *primarily* to blame for Bolivia's death? _____Why?_____
_____

3. Now that you have decided who you think is primarily to blame, you will have a chance to use your negotiating skills.

4. Your professor is offering $1,000 (in play money, of course; but this exercise is more fun if you can imagine it's real money) to the person in the class who can get the most people whose opinions are different from his or hers to agree to change their minds. For example, if you believe Blake is primarily to blame and you get someone who believes Bolivia is primarily to blame to switch to your viewpoint, you will have your first person to list under the next point.

5. Use the space below to write down the first name of each person who blames someone different than you blamed, but whom you convinced to switch to your viewpoint.

6. Your teacher will award the prize money at the end of five minutes of negotiating time.

[*]Table based on R. J. Lewicki and J. A. Litterer, *Negotiation* (Homewood, IL: Irwin, 1985), 280.

# Organizing:

# Designing *the*
# Overall Organization

**After reading this chapter, you will be able to:**

- Describe organizational structure.

- Detect four types of formal structures: functional, multidivisional, matrix, and networks/outsourcing.

- Specify three characteristics that define the latent structure of an organization.

- Summarize the contingency factors that influence the type of formal structure that is best for an organization.

- Describe the different types of coordinating mechanisms that can be used to support the organization structure.

- Distinguish among five organizational archetypes: simple structure, machine bureaucracy, professional bureaucracy, divisionalized form, and adhocracy.

- Assess an organization's structure.

## Bureaucracy versus The Salvation Army

As it has in every other city, big and small, in the United States, the problem of housing the homeless has hit New York City hard. The city of New York spends $500 million a year on the homeless, but the problem is far from solved. One of the skirmishes in the war to eradicate homelessness is telling both in its description of the difficulties faced and in the benefits to be realized from different types of organizational structure. How can organizational structure make a difference to the homeless? The difficulties faced by the Salvation Army in dealing with the city of New York will illustrate.

The city of New York runs a homeless shelter, Camp LaGuardia in Chester, New York, to which it buses the most serious of its homeless cases. The city recently decided to call for bids for an outside agency to take over the shelter. The Salvation Army, a religiously oriented organization whose purpose is to save souls by saving lives and livelihoods, submitted a bid to do just that. It is a nonprofit organization—and a most efficient one. Administrative and fund-raising costs for the Army's New York division are less than 10 percent of revenue. The city of New York cannot begin to approach that level of efficiency. The Salvation Army has a simple organization structure that emphasizes delegation of authority, distribution of decision making throughout the organization, and flexibility. New York City, on the other hand, is a highly bureaucratic, hierarchic organization with a fear of change and a desire to maintain the status quo.

The Salvation Army proposed to run Camp LaGuardia for $15 million a year. If the Army could run the shelter for less, the surplus would go back to the city: if costs were higher, the Army would swallow the deficit. It would seem that the city couldn't lose. But it did. "A unionized boss at LaGuardia, worried about his job, told [Army] staff: 'You're not welcome here.'" A year after the city called for bids, it still has not awarded contracts for Camp LaGuardia or five other shelters.

While a bureaucratic structure can be productive and efficient, it can also promote waste and inefficiency, as it does in New York City. Alternative structural forms, such as the more flexible, less bureaucratic one used by the Salvation Army, can promote efficiency. Why this is true and how various structures work are the subjects of this chapter.

*Source:* James R. Norman, "They Care About You," *Forbes*, January 3, 1994, 40-41.

In the last chapter, we discussed why organizations are formed and how they might be ordered. In this chapter, we are going to take this discussion one step further and consider the variety of ways that organizations can be structured and the circumstances that will dictate the form that is most suitable for any given organization. We will start by examining the types of formal structures that organizations can adopt and then we will consider the informal structures that arise as a matter of practice. Next we will consider extenuating factors that affect an organization's choice of formal structure and the coordinating mechanisms that are useful in helping organization members stay in contact with other elements of the company. Finally we will consider some general types of organizations, such as bureaucracies, professional organizations, and small, entrepreneurial organizations.

## STRUCTURING THE ORGANIZATION

We have already defined organizing as the process of creating an organization. **Organizational structure** is the result of that process, the way managers group jobs into departments and departments into divisions. Understanding the structure of an organization is important both for the survival of the organization and for the career success of an individual. Knowing who is in charge of which processes can be crucial to your career success in any company. One of the first things we learn as new employees is who is important in this company and who is not, and we learn these things by knowing the organizational structure.

In Chapter 12, we discussed how managers group tasks into jobs and jobs into departments. In very small organizations, as we will see, that may be sufficient. In larger organizations, however, departments may proliferate until there are too many to manage. In this case, departments are clustered together, much as jobs are clustered together, to form divisions. Much like departments, divisions can occur as functional, customer, product, and geographic structures. However, it is important to remember that some organizations will not have divisions, only departments; whereas others will have many divisions, giving them a multidivisional form. Other structures include the matrix structure, the network structure, and outsourcing. The following sections will describe the different ways that organizations can group departments into larger units, either divisions or projects.

**organizational structure**
The way managers group jobs into departments and departments into divisions.

### Functional Structure

When a company is relatively small or produces only one or several closely related goods or services, it usually finds that grouping jobs into departments provides as much structure as it needs. While such a company can organize its departments into any of the forms described in Chapter 12 (functional, customer, product, or geographic), the most popular form is the functional structure. As stated in the last chapter, a **functional structure** groups jobs according to similar economic activities, such as finance, production and operations, and marketing. The functional structure of the Southland Corporation, which operates 7-Eleven stores, can be seen in Figure 13.1. Southland makes use of a functional structure because it is involved in only one industry, convenience stores. The strengths and weaknesses of this structure are the same as those described for functional departmentalization in the last chapter.

**functional structure**
The grouping of jobs according to similar economic activities, such as finance, production and operations, and marketing.

## FIGURE 13.1

**Functional Structure:  Southland Corporation**

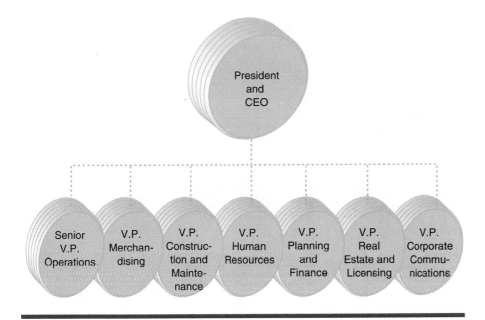

*Source:*  Southland Corporation 1992 Annual Report.

## Multidivisional Structure

A **multidivisional structure** groups departments together into larger groups called divisions. This usually occurs when a firm grows so large that functional departments become cumbersome. Growing companies often diversify, which can strain a functional structure, making communication complicated and difficult.[1] When the weaknesses of the functional structure—the "turf wars," miscommunication, and working at cross-purposes—exceed the benefits, growing firms tend to restructure into the divisionalized form. Just as departments might be formed on the basis of geography, customer, product, or a combination (hybrid), so divisions can be formed based on any of these methods of organizing.

**Product Divisions.**    When a company uses its different products as the basis for divisions, it is using a **product division structure.** This structure is useful when the firm's goods or services are specialized and require specific expertise for their manufacture and sale. It permits the organization to focus on its products rather than job specializations.

An example of the use of product divisions is The Walt Disney Co. Figure 13.2 shows that the corporation is divided into three divisions, Walt Disney Attractions, Walt Disney Studios, and Consumer Products. Each of these major divisions represents a different class of products. Walt Disney Attractions encompasses Walt Disney World, the Magic Kingdom in California, and the international parks in Tokyo and France (EuroDisney). The Walt Disney Studios division includes the movie production and TV studios, while the Consumer Product Division is in charge of producing and marketing assorted Disney-related merchandise. Each of

**multidivisional structure**
The organization of departments together into larger groups called divisions.

**product division structure**
The organization of divisions by product.

**Teaching Note:** When discussing product divisions, ask students why Walt Disney Co. chose to use this structure. Why would a functional structure be difficult to manage? Remind students that this is a large, mature company, and the divisions represent unique products, sold and marketed through differing channels and outlets.

**FIGURE 13.2**

**Product Divisional Structure: Walt Disney Corporation**

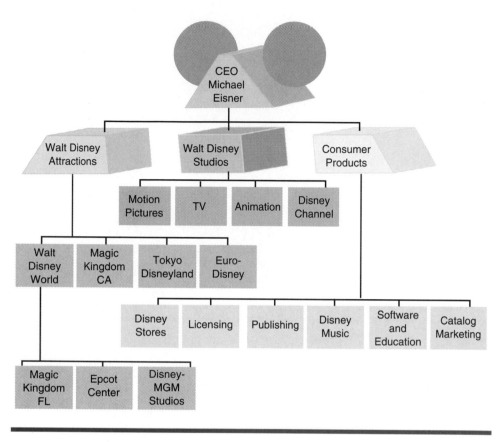

*Source:*  The Walt Disney Co., 1992 Annual Report.

these product types is separate and distinct and requires different job skills, expertise, and areas of familiarity.

**geographic division structure**
The organization of divisions by geographic region.

**Geographic Divisions.**   A firm with a **geographic division structure** creates divisions to support business operations in certain geographic regions. This structure is often used by multinational corporations because the needs of customers in different parts of the world can vary substantially. By clustering into one division those people, tasks, jobs, and departments that serve a particular geographic region, the company can address the specific characteristics of the region in the design, production, and marketing of the goods and services it plans to sell there. Such a structure permits those in the division to concentrate on the characteristics of the region rather than having their attention divided by the competing demands of providing products in a variety of widely different geographic areas.

An example is the MCI Corporation, shown in Figure 13.3, which is organized into a Central Division, Eastern Division, Southern Division, Western Division, and an International Division. Because MCI, as a long-distance telecommunications carrier, has to interact with the regional Bell telephone companies, this geo-

**FIGURE 13.3**

## Geographic Divisional Structure: MCI

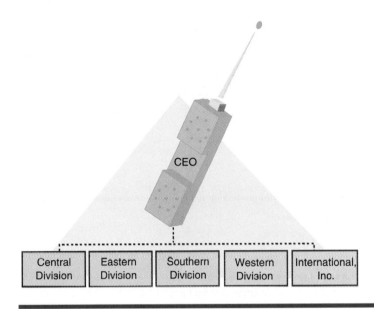

| Central Division | Eastern Division | Southern Division | Western Division | International, Inc. |
|---|---|---|---|---|

*Source:* MCI Communication Corporation, 1991 Annual Report.

graphic divisional structure permits each region to have close contact with its corresponding regional Bell company.

Typically, when a multinational firm uses a geographic divisional structure, the divisional headquarters of the region are located in that region, rather than in the United States. So, for example, a company with Asian, European, and African divisions may have head offices located in Tokyo, Paris, and Johannesburg. Furthermore, the majority of employees at these locations are likely to be regional citizens rather than Americans. This increases the likelihood of success in developing, manufacturing, and marketing products suited to the consumers of the region. Failure to accommodate to the needs of a different country can have consequences ranging from the failure of the product in that area to catastrophic events that threaten the health of the firm.

Consider the poor performance of the EuroDisney theme park, located in France. It has not made a profit since it opened, forcing Disney to make major changes in the park's operations, personnel policies, and pricing structures. Recently, Chairman Michael Eisner announced that Disney is considering several drastic options, including closing the park, if its "dreadful" financial performance does not improve.[2] As shown in Figure 13.2, EuroDisney is part of the Walt Disney Attractions division. Disney does not have a geographic divisional structure, and it built EuroDisney on the successful models in California and Florida. It now seems possible that theme parks that attract large numbers of visitors in the United States will not necessarily do so in Europe.

**Customer Divisions.**    When a firm organizes divisions by customer, it is using a **customer division structure.** As an example, consider the partial Motorola

**Example:** WordPerfect, the popular word-processing package, had to be redesigned for the United Kingdom. In the United Kingdom, the standard size A4 paper used in printers and copy machines is longer and narrower than the 8½ × 11-inch sheets used in the United States. The word-processing screens and printer commands were adapted for the geographic differences.

**customer division structure**
The organization of divisions by customer.

## FIGURE 13.4

### Customer Divisional Structure: Motorola

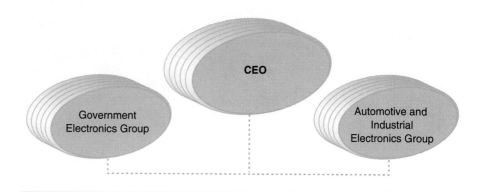

*Source:* Motorola Inc., 1992 Annual Report.

**Example:** Banks are also changing their organization to meet customer needs by entering 24-hour grocery stores to handle routine cash-withdrawal and deposit transactions. These mini-banks, along with automated teller machines, free bank employees at branches to better service commercial customers' specialized needs.

**holding company**
An organization composed of several very different kinds of businesses, each of which is permitted to operate largely autonomously.

organization chart depicted in Figure 13.4. Motorola has one division to produce products for the government and another to make products for the automotive industry. It does this because government contracts impose restrictions and paperwork requirements that are not present with other customer groups. By putting all government work in one division, the government's need for security, secrecy, and extensive paper controls can be met more easily and efficiently. Some companies may have one division for products for the private sector and another division for the public sector. Banks frequently organize their divisions to provide service to large commercial clients, small commercial clients, and individual accounts, such as personal checking or savings accounts.

**Holding Companies.**    A **holding company** describes an organization composed of several very different kinds of businesses, each of which is permitted to operate largely autonomously.[3] As we said in Chapter 10, a corporation that has diversified into a variety of unrelated businesses is known as a conglomerate. Each of the conglomerate's businesses (divisions) is operated independently because the knowledge and expertise needed to run one business may not apply to a different business—and may even be harmful. In this structure, the parent corporation is largely a coordinating office with few personnel; it usually tells each division what its profit contribution is expected to be, and each division has the freedom to meet these expectations as it sees fit.

The holding company form can also be used when the businesses are similar, as with the NationsBank Corporation (Figure 13.5). In each state, NationsBank operates as a separate entity, so there is a NationsBank of North Carolina, a NationsBank of D.C., a NationsBank of Georgia, etc. In all, NationsBank operates subsidiaries in 10 states. It also has a subsidiary that manages mortgages and a brokerage firm (NationsBank Securities). What is important in this structure is that each business be managed without the interference of the parent firm.

**hybrid structure**
A combination of several different structures; the most common form of organizational structure.

**Hybrid Structure.**    A **hybrid structure** is the combination of several different structures. It is fair to say that divisional hybrids are the most common form of

**FIGURE 13.5**

**Holding Company Structure: NationsBank**

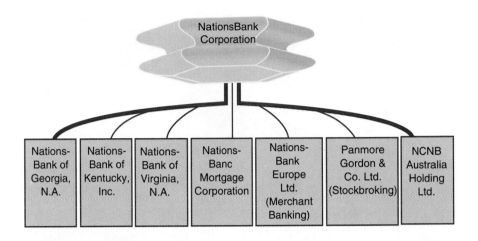

*Source:* NationsBank Corporation, 1991 Annual Report.

organization structure. An example of a hybrid form is PepsiCo Inc., shown in Figure 13.6, which uses both product and geographic divisions. Typically, in such a structure, each division is organized by function, so that within Pepsi-Cola International there is an accounting department, a personnel department, a marketing department, and so on. Hybrid structures can be any combination of multidivisional, functional, or holding company forms. The organization's environment, strategy, size, and primary technology all determine the best combination of structural forms to use. Later in this chapter we will discuss these factors in greater detail.

**Advantages and Disadvantages of a Multidivisional Structure.**   A multidivisional structure permits delegation of decision-making authority, relieving top management of the overwhelming burden of having to know everything about everything. It also permits those closest to the action to make the decisions that will affect them. Finally, it tends to promote loyalty and commitment among those lower-level members of the organization who are making important organizational decisions. Perhaps most importantly, these benefits lead to other benefits. Delegation of authority and divisionalized work mean that decisions are made faster and are more likely to be good decisions, and the work tends to be more innovative and creative. By focusing each division's attention on a common denominator (geography, product, or customer), each is likely to provide goods or services that are more closely aligned with the needs of its particular geographic area or customer.

The disadvantages of multidivisional forms are that top managers may feel they are losing power, even control of their company, when they delegate decision making to others. This fear may cause top management to centralize decision making which, in effect, eliminates some of the benefits of the multidivisional structure.[4] In addition, the divisional structure inevitably creates work duplication, which makes it more difficult to realize the economies of scale that result from grouping all functions together.

**FIGURE 13.6**

**Hybrid Structure: PepsiCo Inc.**

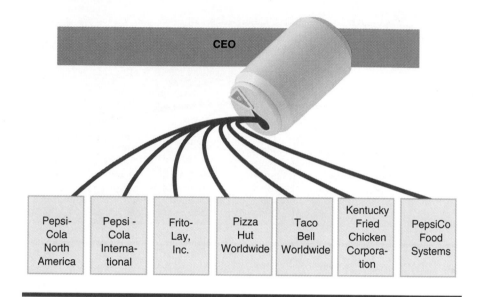

CEO

| Pepsi-Cola North America | Pepsi-Cola International | Frito-Lay, Inc. | Pizza Hut Worldwide | Taco Bell Worldwide | Kentucky Fried Chicken Corporation | PepsiCo Food Systems |

*Source:* PepsiCo, 1992 Annual Report.

For example, when each division has its own accounting department, the corporation probably employs more accountants than a centralized accounting department would require. Furthermore, a multidivisional organization may complicate consolidating the books because each division is likely to have its own unique accounting practices, some of which may be difficult to reconcile. Finally, such a structure allows each division some degree of latitude to "play" with the accounting figures, perhaps hiding some important, but negative, information from top management.

Other types of organizational structures, such as the matrix structure, arose in an attempt to address the disadvantages of the multidivisional form.

## Matrix Structure

**matrix structure**

A structure in which members of different functional departments are chosen to work together temporarily on a specific contract or project.

Critical Thinking Challenge: Have students interview a local business organization and gather information on the organizational structure employed and the possible reason for the use of this structure. Select students to present their findings to the class.

A **matrix structure** is utilized when members of different functional departments are chosen to work together temporarily on a specific contract or project. The groupings or temporary departments thus formed are called project groups or teams. The matrix structure is an attempt to capture the benefits of both the functional and multidivisional forms while eliminating the disadvantages.[5] Thus, matrix structures have both a functional and divisional form, which, when combined, looks like a matrix (Figure 13.7). Project groups are formed by pulling together employees from appropriate functional areas to work together to complete a specific project or assignment. These employees are under the supervision of both their functional supervisor and the project supervisor.

Matrix is the structure used when an organization engages in special projects. Large engineering firms such as Bechtel and Trammel Crow are examples. These

**FIGURE 13.7**

**Matrix Structure**

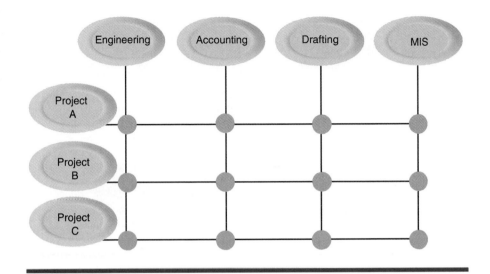

organizations are contracted to construct dams, to rebuild Kuwait, or to design and build large office buildings. Each of these contracts represents a project with a specific beginning and ending, and to manage these projects, the companies assemble project teams from appropriate functional areas. Matrix structures permit people who do similar functional work such as accounting, computer programming, or drafting to work together, but they also allow a subgroup of these specialists to work intensely together on a specific assignment. The matrix avoids the duplication of function that occurs with the divisional structure, and it prevents the "turf wars" and miscommunication of the functional structure.

However, the matrix structure has some weaknesses of its own. The biggest problem is that, because each team member reports to two bosses—the functional boss and the project boss—it violates the principle of unity of command described in the last chapter. This creates a good deal of ambiguity and confusion and can lead to conflicting demands being placed on team members. If not managed carefully, matrix structures can create more chaos than order.

## Network Organizations and Outsourcing

The structural forms just described have been in use in the United States for some time. Some of them (functional structures) have been used in one form or another for centuries. But the world is constantly changing, and new organizational forms are often needed to meet the challenges of a new environment. In his book, *Thriving on Chaos*, Tom Peters argues that the current organizational structures most favored by large corporations are stifling their ability to compete effectively. He proposes that radical new structures are needed to address the opportunities generated by the global economy.[6] One of the new forms that has arisen in recent years is the network form. A **network organization** is primarily a command unit and does not make a good or provide a service but instead coordinates agreements and contracts with other organizations to produce, distribute,

**network organization**
A structure, primarily a command unit, that does not make a good or provide a service but instead coordinates agreements and contracts with other organizations to produce, distribute, and sell products.

**FIGURE 13.8**

**Network Structure**

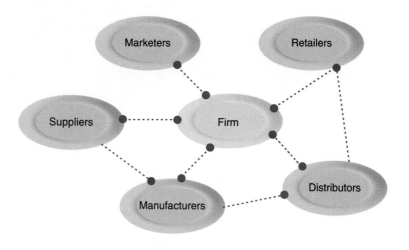

and sell products.[7] Network organizations utilize others to do the functional tasks involved in manufacturing and selling (see Figure 13.8).

A prominent example of a network structure is the Nike Corporation. Nike does not manufacture, distribute, or sell many of its shoes. It primarily designs shoes and then contracts with manufacturers in various parts of the world (usually the Pacific Rim) to manufacture the shoes according to Nike's specifications. It then contracts with distributors to ship the completed shoes, and it contracts with a variety of retail outlets to display, advertise, and sell the shoes.[8] Nike is, therefore, at the center of a complex network of organizations which together design, manufacture, distribute, and sell athletic shoes. This structure permits Nike to find the lowest-cost manufacturer that can meet its standards, the lowest-cost distributor, and so on. In short, Nike uses market competition to keep down its costs of doing business with suppliers.

A major disadvantage of the network structure is that it leaves Nike at the mercy of the other network members. If manufacturers cannot meet Nike's standards, if they suffer a strike or some other catastrophe, Nike has few alternatives. Further, because their relationship is contractual, Nike has less control over the work performed by its many partners. It can only negotiate with suppliers to improve the quality of the shoe, to increase the speed of delivery of the finished product, or to improve the marketing strategy used by retailers. Nike's solution to this vulnerability is to have multiple manufacturers, distributors, and sellers, but this increases the complexity of the network and the costs of managing it.[9]

Very recently, a variation on the idea of network structures has been used by large companies. Outsourcing, which we discussed briefly in Chapter 5, is a strategy whereby the organization manufactures critical components, but contracts with other organizations to manufacture less important parts. Other functional tasks, such as marketing and data processing, may also be outsourced. The intent is to trim the organization down to its essential components. The drawback is that outsourcing gives outsiders access to potentially valuable strategic information

### THE HORIZONTAL CORPORATION

As U.S. companies are continuing to lay off employees in their efforts to become leaner and more efficient, some of those companies are also reconsidering how the remaining employees should best be organized. The results, new forms suggested by both academics and corporate designers, eliminate the hierarchical form altogether. In the new structures, teams rather than individuals are the primary work units, and processes, not functions, are the core. In these new structures, the primary concern is not how to delegate authority downward through a "command and control" structure, but rather how to make teams the "owners" of processes and to provide the teams with the raw data needed to make decisions. To make such structures work, performance objectives would be based on customer satisfaction rather than profitability measures, and teams rather than individuals would be rewarded for work well done.

While these are very radical ideas, companies are considering making such massive transformations because the traditional hierarchical structures tend to get larger and more inefficient. Companies may lay off employees now, but they are likely to hire them back some time down the road as the bureaucracy grows and employees are needed just to manage the administrative chores. Companies are hoping that entirely new structures might permit them to become and stay efficient.

What do such forms look like? One scholar, James Brian Quinn, at Dartmouth University, thinks organizations will look more like starbursts in the future. Eastman Chemical Company has an organization chart that president Ernest W. Deavenport, Jr., calls "the pizza chart because it looks like a pizza with a lot of pepperoni sitting on it ... We did it in circular form to show that everyone is equal in the organization." PepsiCo uses an inverted pyramid to describe its structure in order to help employees remember to focus on the customer. However, it is unlikely that one form, or even one way of drawing the form (such as the organizational charts in common use today), will prevail in the future. Rather, it is more likely that structures will reflect the unique combination of processes and goals that makes up a company.

*Source:* John A. Byrne, "The Horizontal Corporation," *Business Week*, December 20, 1993, 76–81.

about the firm. More and more firms are turning to outsourcing as a way of making their organizations "lean and mean" and, hopefully, more competitive.[10]

The "Magnifying Management" box briefly describes another organizational structure that is evolving—the horizontal corporation. The horizontal structure deemphasizes hierarchy and emphasizes cross-functional teams. This results in a structure that is not as tall as the traditional organization.

## LATENT STRUCTURES:  WHAT THE ORGANIZATION IS REALLY LIKE

Up to now, we have described and discussed the formal ways in which an organization can structure itself. Chapter 12 discussed how organizational charts (such as those shown in Figures 13.1 through 13.8) display formal flows of authority and communication. However, although the organizational chart depicts the structure of the organization, it does not necessarily tell us who makes the important decisions, how specialized are its jobs, or how rigid are its rules. These things, together, describe more of what it is really like to work for an organization than does the

**Comment on Box:** After discussing the horizontal corporation, pass out blank sheets of paper to students. Assign them the task of drawing the new organizational structure of the future, considering current trends discussed in this chapter. After 20 minutes, have students share their new organizational "charts" and explain their logic to classmates.

Complementing its low degree of complexity, MCI Communications Corporation has a low degree of formalization. Most MCI offices are designed without doors to encourage employees to freely share ideas. MCI's formal and informal structure supports the company's strategy of maintaining the small-company entrepreneurship that helped it become the second-largest long-distance company in the United States.

*Source:* © 1993 Chris Usher.

**complexity**

The level of differentiation among structural units, including the specialization of jobs, geographical dispersion, and height of the firm.

**formalization**

The degree to which the organization's procedures, rules, and personnel requirements are written down and enforced.

**Teaching Note:** Remind students that as organizations mature along the life cycle and increase in size, formalization increases.

organizational chart. This is called the latent structure, which can be categorized according to degree of centralization, complexity, and formalization.[11]

We defined centralization in Chapter 12 as a pattern of concentrating decision-making authority in a relatively few, high-level positions. On the other hand, if decisions are made by the people confronted with the problem, regardless of their position in the hierarchy, then the organization is *decentralized.*

The degree of **complexity** describes how much differentiation there is between structural units; that is, how specialized are the organization's jobs, how geographically dispersed the organization is, and how tall it is. If the firm has many vertical levels and a high degree of division of labor, and is a multinational corporation, then it is a complex organization. Compare, for example, the organizational charts of MCI (Figure 13.3) and Walt Disney (Figure 13.2). The chart for MCI is relatively simple: There are two levels, and it appears that each division is like the other, only operating in different geographic areas. This suggests that differentiation is fairly low, because the company employs people doing the same thing only in different parts of the country. Walt Disney, on the other hand, has three levels and all the boxes suggest very different types of businesses. Disney is involved in amusement parks, movie and television production, music, computer software, and publishing. This tells us that jobs are very specialized and very different from one division to another. The organizational charts help us to visualize that MCI is not as complex an organization as Walt Disney.

**Formalization** refers to the degree to which the organization's procedures, rules, and personnel requirements are written down and enforced. A company that rigidly adheres to the chain of command and has a two-volume personnel handbook laying out in detail every moment of every employee's work life is a highly formalized organization.

Centralization, formalization, and complexity together describe an organization's latent structure.[12] There is a tendency for some of these characteristics to be found together. It is not hard to find centralized, highly formalized, and highly complex organizations; American Express is an example. This structure makes sense when you think about it. A very large company with extensive division of labor and many hierarchical levels (high complexity) can become chaotic very quickly, so it will tend to write down all the rules and procedures and try to reduce the demands on executive time by enforcing such things as the chain of command (high formalization). Furthermore, such an organization is likely to

## FIGURE 13.9

**Mechanistic/Organic Continuum**

want to preserve decision-making authority for those in command (centralization) to prevent all the disparate elements from running off into opposing directions. However, it is not a requirement that a complex organization also be formal and centralized. Indeed, some complex organizations are both informal and fairly decentralized, such as Apple Computer and Microsoft.

## Types of Latent Structures

Latent structures can be classified along a continuum (see Figure 13.9). **Mechanistic organizations** are highly formal, highly complex, and highly centralized; **organic organizations** are less formal, fairly simple, and decentralized.[13]

Mechanistic organizations tend to make decisions slowly and are easily bogged down in rules and procedures, but some employees prefer such environments because the rules are well known and well understood. A fast-food restaurant is a good example of a mechanistic organization.[14] A goal of most national fast-food chains is to have consistency at each restaurant. Customers of McDonald's, Burger King, or Arby's like to know that they will get the same sandwich prepared the same way whether they are in Miami or Anchorage. And one way to provide this consistency is to make sure everything is done exactly the same way in each restaurant. Hence, there are strict rules for preparing every item on the menu as well as stipulations regarding what the menu must offer. Employees are often provided with extensive on-the-job training to teach them how to prepare sandwiches, fries, and shakes in exactly the right way; creativity and innovation are discouraged. The city of New York, which figured in the opening vignette of this chapter, is another example of a mechanistic organization. The difficulties of managing a city as large and diverse as New York have resulted in a very large, very bureaucratic structure. Rules are specified for every transaction, whether they are pertinent to that particular situation or not. In such large bureaucracies, it is not uncommon to find employees more concerned with preserving the status quo than with fulfilling the mission of serving citizens.

Organic organizations, on the other hand, are ambiguous, make decisions quickly, experience rapid change, and can be uncomfortable places at which to work because the rules are not clearly known or understood. The NEXT Corporation is a good example of an organic organization. NEXT is the company Steve Jobs founded after his departure from Apple Computers. There are few formalized policies and procedures, and decision making is decentralized. Employees are encouraged to be innovative, and their opinions on strategy and other important issues are sought. Another example of an organic organization is the Salvation Army, depicted in the opening vignette. As an organization, it is significantly smaller than the government of New York City, and, as we shall see, it consequently does not need as complex a structure. This means that different

**mechanistic organizations**
Structures that are highly formal, complex, and centralized.

**organic organizations**
Structures that are less formal, fairly simple, and decentralized.

units of the organization are freer to take on new challenges, such as a new homeless shelter. Because its structure is less complex, it does not rely as much on written rules and procedures and can therefore create the procedures that will work best in a specific situation. The Salvation Army's ability to take on new tasks and to fulfill its mission regardless of the circumstances it faces is a hallmark of organic organizations.

Both the mechanistic and organic form are pure types, but most organizations fall in between. They can be decentralized, but very formal. They can be simple, but highly formal and centralized. An organization can implement a latent structure anywhere along the continuum from mechanistic to organic.

## Relating Formal Structures to Latent Structures

Any of the formal structures described at the beginning of the chapter can exhibit any combination of latent structures. However, it is not hard to imagine that an organization is likely to be more effective when its formal and latent structures are in harmony. For example, the purpose of using the multidivisional form is to delegate responsibility to others in the organization so that the top management team is not overwhelmed with the task of managing a very large organization. If an organization uses such a structure but then centralizes decision making and imposes overly rigid formalization, the benefits of the multidivisional structure are lost. In such a situation, the formal structure is intended to relieve those at the top of some of the burdens of management, but the latent structure puts the burden right back on them. The result is conflict, ambiguity, and, often, stagnation.

## FACTORS AFFECTING ORGANIZATIONAL STRUCTURE

Many things can affect the choice of appropriate structure for an organization. We will consider five such factors in this section: organization size, organization life cycle, strategy, environment, and technology.

## Organization Size

The larger an organization becomes, the more complicated its structure. As we noted in the last chapter, when an organization is small—such as a single retail store, a two-person consulting firm, or a restaurant—its structure can be simple. In fact, if the organization is small enough there probably isn't much of a structure at all.[15] A two-person consulting firm, for instance, probably has no organizational chart and no specified duties for either partner. They may have an accountant who does their taxes, and they may split the work between them according to tasks that each prefers or is most adept at doing (or dislikes the least). A restaurant, on the other hand, may not have an organizational chart but is likely to have a set of rather specific duties. There may be a hostess or maitre d', a cashier, wait staff, clean-up staff, chefs, cooking apprentices or assistants, and dishwashers. There may even be a rudimentary hierarchy, with the wait staff, clean-up staff, and cashier reporting to the hostess or maitre d'.

As an organization grows, it becomes increasingly difficult to manage without more formal work assignments and some delegation of authority. Thus, a company usually adopts a functional structure initially, but as it grows and diversifies, the weaknesses of the functional structure begin to outnumber and overwhelm the strengths and the firm shifts to a multidivisional structure.[16] Very large companies, such as the *Fortune* 500, use even more complicated structures such as hybrids, networks, and matrices. So, to a significant degree, the size of the organization dictates the structural forms that will be most effective. Stated another way, a small firm does not have enough members to form divisions while a very large organization would be too inefficient to survive if it used a functional structure.

## Organization Life Cycle

As organizations age, they tend to progress through stages, known as a life cycle. Two research scholars, Danny Miller and Peter Friesen, have found that the organization life cycle usually has five stages: birth, growth, maturity, revival, and decline. Each stage has characteristic features that have implications for the structure of the firm.[17]

**Birth.**    In the birth phase, a firm is just beginning. The founder is typically an entrepreneur who may not yet have identified precisely the appropriate market niche. An organization in the birth stage does not yet have a formal structure, and the informal structure is characterized by a high degree of centralization but a low degree of formalization and complexity. In such a young company, the founding entrepreneur usually calls all the shots, and because there are few employees, the founder does not delegate much authority.

**Growth.**    In this phase, the organization is trying to grow, in terms of both products offered and revenue. The emphasis in this stage is on becoming larger. The company shifts its attention away from the wishes of its founder/owner and toward its customers. It has become large enough to have a formal structure, usually functionally organized departments. This permits some delegation of authority, so the latent structure is marked by somewhat less centralization, but increasing complexity and some increase in formalization.

**Maturity.**    Once a firm has reached the maturity phase, it tends to become less innovative, less interested in expanding, and more interested in maintaining itself in a stable, secure environment. The emphasis is on improving efficiency and profitability. The formal structure is still a functionally based departmental form; the latent structure also remains much as it did in the growth phase. There tends to be more participation in decision making, but less delegation of authority. The lack of delegation of authority is probably because so little changes that decisions are repeatedly made by the same people.

**Revival.**    As might be imagined, if it persists long enough, the maturity phase could lead to decline. At some point, firms recognize that they are stagnating, usually when profit levels begin to decline, and they embark on a revival. The organization undergoes significant changes at this time. In current terms, a company may decide to *reengineer* itself—that is, its top managers reconsider what business the organization is in and how best to organize the work processes to achieve its goals. To achieve newly set goals, the company often launches a strategy to diversify its products and increase its size. To accommodate the rapid growth, the formal structure abruptly changes from a functional structure to a multidivisional one.

**Critical Thinking Challenge:** Have groups of students draw and develop organizational charts for all five stages of an organization's life cycle. Select one member of the group to report how the structure has changed over time and why the changes have occurred.

However, because the changes are so dramatic, top management tends to want to maintain a firm hand on the controls, resulting in a latent structure that is highly centralized, formalized, and complex. Because there is an inherent conflict in using a multidivisional formal structure and a centralized latent structure, organizations in this phase often make heavy use of coordinating mechanisms (discussed in detail in the following section) to resolve conflicts.

**Decline.**    Organizations in decline are slowly dying. The tendency toward efficiency that characterized the maturity phase may turn into stagnation. In their efforts to become more cost-effective, firms may reduce the amount of innovation they do, which results in old, stale products, which in turn results in sales declines and reduced profitability. Organizations in decline are in a vicious cycle, often attempting to improve the profit picture by reducing expenditures in the areas in which the firm most needs increased attention—R&D and new product development. In response to steady decline, companies tend to centralize their decision making even more and to become less complex but even more formalized. While the formal structure tends to stay the same, the latent structure changes, resulting in decreased communication among divisions and departments and between the organization and its environment. Decline, however, is not an inevitable stage. Firms experiencing decline may, in fact, institute the changes necessary to enter the revival stage.

**The Significance of the Organization Life Cycle.**    An organization may proceed sequentially through all five phases, but it does not have to. It may skip a phase, going directly from birth to maturity, for example, or it may cycle back to an earlier phase such as going from decline to revival. A company may try to change its position in the life cycle by changing its structure. A firm in the decline phase may try to spark a revival by changing to a different kind of multidivisional structure, such as going from a geographic divisional structure to a product divisional structure or even to something more dramatic such as a network structure. As the life-cycle concept implies, there is a relationship between organization age and size. As organizations age they tend to get larger, thus there is a parallel between the structural changes a firm experiences as it gets larger and the changes it experiences as it progresses through the life cycle. Of course, there is a limit to how large a firm can become, and it is common, especially in the 1990s, for firms to decide to become smaller.

*Example: Some firms go through all stages of a life cycle and then revive or revitalize and begin again. Other companies have a very long maturity stage, like Procter & Gamble with consumer laundry products.*

**Navistar:  An Example of Organization Life Cycle.**    In 1847, Cyrus McCormick incorporated McCormick Harvester Machine Company to manufacture and sell agricultural products. At that time, it was a modest company and made use of a simple functional structure. Growth was rapid, and by 1979, the company, then called International Harvester (IH), manufactured not only agricultural products, but construction products, engines, and medium- and heavy-duty trucks. It had sales of $8.4 billion and employed 95,000 people. The organization, by this time, was using a sophisticated form of the divisional structure, managing each major product line, such as engines, as a separate business.[18] Each business, in turn, had its own divisional structure.

By 1979, IH had progressed through the birth and growth stages and was surprised to find itself confronting a mature, very low-growth market. An honest assessment of International Harvester's condition in 1982 revealed that the company was actually experiencing organizational decline and facing bankruptcy. By not recognizing that its market had matured and that growth opportunities had substantially slowed,

To implement his product innovation strategy, Thermos CEO Monte Peterson (holding tongs) replaced the company's bureaucratic, functional structure with flexible, interdisciplinary teams. Team members shown here from marketing, engineering, manufacturing, and finance invented an entirely new electric cookout grill that gives food a barbequed taste, burns cleaner than gas or charcoal grills, and sports an award-winning design. Peterson plans to increase revenues by 13 percent each year by organizing teams to develop product innovations like the electric grill.

*Source:* © 1994 James Schnepf.

the company found itself burdened with enormous debt, high interest rates, and an employee strike. Further, the economy was undergoing a recession and the trucking industry was being deregulated. The future did not look bright, so to avoid death, the company saw the need to restructure itself, and thus entered the revival stage.

IH's revival was marked by the resignation of CEO Archie McCardell and the selection of Don Lennox to replace him. At the same time, the new management divested most of IH's businesses, including the construction equipment business and the solar turbine division. It also closed many plants and reduced staff. In 1984, the company even sold the agricultural product business, the business on which it had been founded, and with the business went the name. The resulting new firm, called Navistar, is a more focused company, producing trucks and engines. The major structural change that occurred with the advent of Navistar was to decentralize the decision making. While the company maintained a divisional structure, it emphasized the need for planning and decision making to occur at the lowest levels of the organization. In other words, it shifted from a mechanistic structure to an organic structure. Today, Navistar could be characterized as a company in a mature stage of the life cycle, but one that has learned how to avoid the decline phase by revitalizing itself.

## Strategy

The strategy an organization pursues will, to some degree, suggest a structural form. Similarly, the form an organization takes needs to be consistent with the strategy it intends to pursue. If the structure does not match the strategy, it will be very difficult, if not impossible, for the organization to implement its plan. Chapter 10 discussed some of the many different types of strategies an organization can pursue to attain its goals. A firm employing a diversification strategy, for example, will grow larger and more complex and require a more elaborate structure to manage its work effectively.

Another way to think of strategy is to think of how the organization is going to position itself in the market in terms of its product. There are two possible approaches: The company may decide always to be the first on the market with the newest and the best product (differentiation strategy), or it may decide that it will instead produce the same product more efficiently and thus more cost-effectively than its competitors (cost-leadership strategy). Each of these strategies requires a structure that will help the organization achieve its objective of either new product innovation or cost efficiency. Companies employing the cost-leadership strategy, for example, emphasize cost efficiency and generally find a functional structure most supportive of their goals. Production efficiencies are most likely achieved when job specialization is high and task variability low. Product innovation, on the other hand, requires a more flexible structure and greater coordination among organizational members. This is achieved with more complex structures such as the multidivisional or even matrix structures.

As an example of how strategy affects structure, consider the American automobile industry, especially Chrysler. Chrysler has suffered severe financial difficulties over the last two decades, nearly going bankrupt twice (once in the early 1980s and then again in the early 1990s). Much of that difficulty can be traced to both a strategy of focusing solely on defending its marketing niche as well as a structure that was not only functionally organized but also highly formalized, centralized, and complex. Chrysler, in short, did everything it could to isolate itself from its environment and to stifle any innovation or creativity among its employees. In desperation, in the early 1990s, Chrysler's chairman Lee Iacocca changed from a defensive strategy to a strategy emphasizing new and innovative products. To support the strategy, the company implemented a modified hybrid structure, putting together teams of designers, planners, engineers, and builders and letting them make their own decisions. The result was the new cab-forward design as well as best-selling new vehicles, including the Dodge Intrepid and Eagle Vision. These new cars brought Chrysler back from the edge of bankruptcy.[19]

## Environment

The environment, you may remember from Chapter 3, is the world in which the organization operates, including its stakeholders—customers, suppliers, competitors, substitutes, owners, managers, employees, and board of directors—as well as the communities in which the organization maintains facilities, and special interest groups. A healthy organization needs to know what expectations each stakeholder holds. While companies tend to formulate plans and strategies to deal with each stakeholder group separately (for example, marketing plans to attract customers, purchasing plans to negotiate the best supplier arrangement, public relations plans to respond to the needs of the community), taken as a whole, these disparate elements can be categorized according to whether they are beneficial or harmful and whether they are relatively predictable or not.

If there is a large market for the organization's products, if the funds needed to continue operations are readily available, and if other stakeholder groups are satisfied or pleased with an organization's performance, then the organization is said to be operating in a **munificent environment.**[20] An example of a munificent environment is the video-game industry, in which there is high demand for the product, it is relatively easy to enter the industry, and capital is readily available. If the opposite is true—money is tight, the market is stagnant or declining, or stakeholder groups are making conflicting and difficult demands—then the organization is operating in a **scarce environment.** An example of a scarce environment is the baby food industry. The consumer base (birth rate) is declining in the United States, substitutes for prepared baby foods are readily available, government regulation is high, and consumer watchdog groups are abundant.

**munificent environment**

An environment in which the organization has a large market for its product and has funds needed to continue operations readily available, and other stakeholder groups are satisfied or pleased with the organization's performance.

**scarce environment**

An environment wherein money is tight, the market is stagnant or declining, or stakeholder groups are making conflicting or difficult demands.

**FIGURE 13.10**

**FIGURE 13.10**

**Environmental Characteristics**

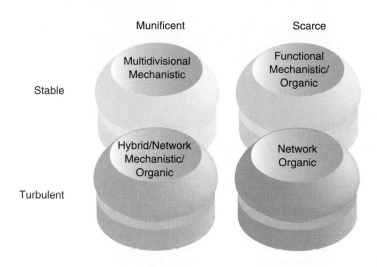

Similarly, if stakeholder demands, and specifically customer desires, are well understood and relatively stable over time, the organization has a **stable environment.**[21] An example of a stable environment is the machine tool industry. While subject to economic fluctuations, it is sensitive to little else. The market is well understood and readily predictable. If customer or other stakeholders' demands are continuously changing or the primary technology of the company is constantly being improved and updated, then we are describing a **turbulent environment.** An example of a turbulent environment is the electronics industry. Not only is the technology changing just about daily, but so are consumer preferences.

Organizations deal with environments that are more or less munificent (or scarce) and more or less turbulent (or stable). These features, then, occur along a continuum, and together, they have a lot to say about the types of organizational structures that will be effective. As shown in Figure 13.10, these features can be depicted as a 2 × 2 matrix.

If the environment is scarce (few resources) but stable, a company must be efficient with its resources. The stable market means that the company probably does not have to respond quickly to changes. In such an environment, a functional structure may be appropriate, as it is the most efficient and should be effective in an environment where market demands are well understood. The Southland Corporation (Figure 13.1) faces such an environment. The market for convenience stores is saturated, meaning there are many competitors for the same customer, but it is a well-understood industry that doesn't face many changes. Consequently, Southland's functional structure suits both its corporate needs and the constraints of the environment.

If the environment is both turbulent (rapidly changing) and scarce (few resources), then an organization may use a network structure or may make heavy use of outsourcing. In such an environment, the organization faces many changing demands and few resources with which to respond to those changes. Therefore, the organization must be both flexible and efficient. Network structures permit

**stable environment**
An environment in which stakeholder demands, and specifically customer desires, are well understood and relatively stable over time.

**turbulent environment**
An environment wherein customer or other stakeholder demands are continuously changing or the primary technology of the firm is constantly being improved and updated.

**Example:** Tobacco products manufacturers are operating in an increasingly turbulent environment. With increased health warnings against smoking, consumer demand for healthier, nonsmoking restaurants and public buildings, and increased excise taxes on the products, future industry growth is unlikely. Even Chrysler is eliminating ashtrays and cigarette lighters on some new car models due to public demand.

Dell Computer Corporation adapts to the nanosecond changes in the turbulent PC industry by operating as a network organization. To avoid the huge costs and inflexibility of manufacturing computers, Dell leases two small factories where employees assemble computers from outsourced parts, as shown here. The network structure allows Dell to concentrate on what it does best—marketing and service.

*Source:* © 1992 Steven Pumphrey. All Rights Reserved.

organizations to be both. They are flexible because it is faster to negotiate new contracts that entail new specifications with, possibly, new suppliers, than it is to retool a factory. They are efficient because those best equipped to do the work are doing it; the organization does the one thing it does best and the rest is done by contract providers. An example is the Dell Computer Corporation in Austin, Texas. The personal computer industry is both very turbulent and relatively scarce. Many competitors are vying for a share of a low-growth market that seems to change on almost an hourly basis. Dell responds to these challenges by operating largely as a network. It buys computer components from a variety of vendors and puts them together in configurations that match customer specifications. This structure permits Dell to be flexible, responding rapidly to new technological advances. Dell products are available by phone order and at Sam's Club, Price Club, and CompUSA.

If the environment is munificent (many resources) and stable (few changes)—the best of all possible worlds—the organization is likely to use a multidivisional or hybrid structure. Because there are many resources, it is likely that the company will become rather tall because it can afford to have many layers. It needs neither to conserve resources nor to worry about rapidly changing market conditions. This was the circumstance for many defense contractors through the period of the 1980s. There were many government contracts available for the production of defense systems, and the desires of the Pentagon were well understood by the corporations. Consequently, corporations such as Lockheed, Northrop, General Dynamics, and others became very large and had many levels of management. These companies have been hard hit by the need to reduce their administrative staffs and to lay off thousands of employees as the less munificent period of the 1990s progresses. The fall of communism—a surprising and wonderful event for the rest of the world—has made the environment less munificent for defense weapon manufacturers.

If the environment is munificent (many resources) but turbulent (rapidly changing), the form used may well be a hybrid or a matrix. If there are sufficient resources, the costs of a matrix (ambiguity) may be easily absorbed by the organization, but the form will provide the company with the flexibility needed to respond to rapidly changing market requirements. An example of such an environment is the telecommunications industry. The great need for communications facilities has provided a munificent environment for telephone, telecommunications, and cable companies. However, as the United States attempts to build an "information superhighway," the technology is changing rapidly. Many companies are not changing their organization structures so much as they are adding new structural elements in the form of complex interrelationships with partners who will help them achieve their goals. As an example, Microsoft has entered a $9 billion partnership with McCaw Cellular Communications to build and deploy a satellite network that will provide infrastructure for the "information superhighway."[22] Such partnerships often offer the flexibility of matrix structures with not quite as much ambiguity.

## Technology

In Chapter 3, we said that technology is the process and knowledge of transforming inputs into outputs. At Chrysler, for example, the technology is the method through which steel, plastic, computer chips, and glass are assembled into a minivan. Service providers also rely on technology: In a bank, computers and electronic communications technology help transfer money between accounts and keep track of it. There are three basic levels of technology, each of which influences an organization's structure: small-batch production, mass production, or continuous production.

In **small-batch technology**, the firm makes small numbers of goods in response to a specific customer request. Many defense contractors use small-batch production, as their contracts may specify a small number of missiles, satellites, or planes. Another example is *haute couture*, where small numbers of designer dresses are produced.

Firms using **mass technology** produce large numbers of the same product. A typical mass-production operation employs an assembly line, with the product traveling down a conveyer belt and employees processing it at each station on its journey. A wide variety of products are made or processed using mass-production technology: automobiles, computers, integrated circuit chips, shoes, chicken, and even candy. One of the most famous episodes of a popular TV show, "I Love Lucy," involved the comedienne and her friend desperately trying to package candy as it moved down an accelerating assembly line. This image has remained in the popular imagination as the prototypical assembly line.

In **continuous technology**, raw materials flow continuously through a system that transforms them into finished products. For example, oil refineries use continuous production to transform oil (raw material) into gasoline.

A British researcher, Joan Woodward, first identified these three technology types. She noted the importance of an organization's structure being consistent with its type of technology. She found that both small-batch and continuous-process technologies achieved higher performance when used in organizations with an organic latent structure, whereas mass-production technology was best used in firms with mechanistic latent structures. This is because work is customized and specialized in small-batch firms, so the specialists doing the work need to make the decisions about the work they are doing. Decision-making freedom is also necessary in continuous production because the tasks are so complex that problems are best handled at their source. Mass production, on the other hand, employs standardized technology using well-known procedures, allowing formal routines and centralized decision making.[23]

## Putting It Together

As we have said, size, life cycle, strategy, environment, and technology affect the type of structure an organization might use. What makes the choice particularly

---

**Example:** Kinko's uses small-batch technology and has a number of general purpose machines in its retail photocopying stores. Customers request a particular job, and Kinko's responds by renting computers, making copies, binding reports, printing flyers, etc.

**small-batch technology**
The production of small numbers of goods in response to a specific customer request.

**mass technology**
The production of large numbers of the same product.

**continuous technology**
A method of production in which raw materials flow continuously through a system that transforms them into finished products.

## BUSINESS DILEMMA

*You're the Manager ...What Would You Do?*

THE COMPANY:  Aerodyne Motors

YOUR POSITION:  Strategic Planning

THE PLACE:  Round Rock, TX

Aerodyne Motors is a new division of Wright Motors Company, which is a traditionally structured multinational automaker and fourth largest in the United States. Wright Motors developed Aerodyne as an upstart division that does not suffer from the built-in bureaucracy and overhead of its parent company. Aerodyne represents an experimental approach for Wright Motors, and, if successful, could reorganize the entire organization.

Formed in 1990, Aerodyne manufactures cars in Round Rock, Texas. Texas was chosen due to the opportunity to develop a nonunionized work force. The company's first model will be introduced in 1996. The entire facility, from research and development to production, operates out of one facility. Over 50 percent of the production process will be automated, significantly reducing the fixed cost of each car.

The company initially plans to position its products as very high-quality, very efficient, compact to mid-sized cars. The cars, which will sell for from $15,000 to $25,000, will not be discounted because of low margins on each car. Aerodyne will sell its cars through Wright Motors dealerships, but as a result of this unique pricing structure, salespeople will be less involved in the process. Computerized information booths will be available to give potential buyers information about the cars, the pricing of options, and availability. A booth can also operate on an interactive basis whereby a potential buyer can talk with an expert from the Round Rock office. Research suggests that this approach will be successful because customers don't want to be pressured by salespeople, and they want the most accurate information possible. Buyers can order cars through the computerized system and receive credit approval in one-fourth the time it would take to work through traditional channels. The only interaction the buyer has with the dealership is in test driving the vehicle and taking delivery. Because of margins and limited involvement, dealers receive smaller margins on the Aerodyne cars than for traditional Wright Motors autos. Dealerships are already promoting the upcoming line of cars through early promotional brochures and teaser advertising campaigns.

In comparison to the organizational structure for Wright Motors, Aerodyne operates a much leaner organization. It has no decentralized regional offices. Distribution occurs through the established Wright Motors dealerships across the country. Dealerships are linked to Aerodyne through a computer network that provides electronic mail as well as the computerized information and order booths. Dealers are supportive because they have longed for a product that could compete directly against newer companies such as General Motors' Saturn division.

### Questions

1. How would you compare the organizational structure of a large multinational firm such as Wright Motors to Aerodyne?
2. What are the potential benefits and risks in structuring an organization such as Aerodyne? What is the role of control and communication in this structure?
3. Speculate as to the success of the Aerodyne company.

**Comment on Box:** The Aerodyne Motors case makes a good quiz to use to test students' knowledge and understanding of the concepts presented in Chapter 13. It can be used in class and should take less than 30 minutes to complete individually.

complicated is that each organization needs to consider all of these factors simultaneously. In some cases, the needs of one factor may contradict the needs of another. For example, a small company may be trying to implement a differentiation strategy in a scarce/stable environment using a highly complex, expensive, and flexible technology. The functional structure that would work best for small/scarcity/stability will not work well with the technology used or the strategy to be implemented.

## COORDINATING DIFFERENT PARTS OF THE ORGANIZATION

Managers intending to design an organization, or more likely, to redesign an organization, certainly have many things to consider. Not only do they have to think of the strengths and weaknesses of all the formal structural choices facing them, but they have to consider the factors of size, organization life cycle, strategy, environment, technology, and the characteristics of the latent structure such as centralization, complexity, and formalization. In short, a designer has to coordinate many different things to derive an organizational structure that is going to be both effective and efficient.

When you start thinking of all the things that must be considered, it becomes apparent that different structural elements might well create conflict. Fortunately, designers have a variety of tools they can use to help them coordinate such a complicated entity as an organization. **Coordination** links jobs, departments, and divisions so that all parts of the organization work together to achieve goals. Coordination is critical to all organizations. It must be formalized and ingrained into the structure of large organizations. In small businesses, on the other hand, coordination can frequently be directed by the owner/manager of the business, who is in charge of all activities.

Coordination can be divided into two types. **Vertical coordination** is the integration of succeeding levels of the organization. An example would be using divisions to coordinate departments. **Horizontal coordination** describes linking subunits on the same level—for instance, coordination between the marketing and legal departments.

**coordination**
The linking of jobs, departments, and divisions so that all parts of the organization work together to achieve goals.

**vertical coordination**
The integration of succeeding levels of the organization.

**horizontal coordination**
The linking of subunits on the same level.

## Coordinating Mechanisms

Managers have developed a number of ways to help coordinate aspects of the organization, both vertically and horizontally. The goal is to link those people who must interact in the work process. For example, it is important that product development personnel talk to sales personnel so that the salespeople do not find that they have been trying to sell a product that cannot be produced. The major agents of coordination are the organizational hierarchy, rules and procedures, committees, task forces, and liaison personnel.

### Organizational Hierarchy.
The organizational hierarchy itself serves to coordinate subunits and employees. Managers are given the authority to make work-related decisions for those positions that report to them. At the very least, this authority allows for the coordination of the jobs held by employees. In other cases, this authority allows the coordination of departments that the employees manage. Managers coordinate authority and communication in the organization.

### Rules and Procedures.
Often a major coordination question confronting managers is one of priority. If two subunits need access to the same resources at the same time, which gets access first? Rules and procedures address such priority issues. Thus in a hospital, standard operating procedures dictate that using ambulances to transport severely injured people to hospitals for emergency treatment takes precedence over the use of ambulances by the radiology department to transfer patients to another hospital that has specialized testing equipment. Rules and procedures are usually intended for commonly occurring situations in work operations. The organization cannot develop rules that will cover each possible situation, however. As mentioned earlier, the degree to which a company attempts to document every rule and procedure is the degree to which the organization is formalized.

**Teaching Note:** Bring a copy of your university's handbook to class. Share various examples of rules and procedures with your class. For example, read the university honor code to class. Discuss reasons for these results and procedures.

**Committees.**   Committees are formal, permanent groups of people brought together to monitor and keep track of ongoing situations. They usually address nonroutine work situations that cannot be covered by rules and procedures. For example, corporate boards of directors usually have permanent committees on executive compensation, employee benefits, and capital expenditures. Committee membership may change over time, but the purpose of the committee remains fairly stable.

**Task Forces.**   A task force is a temporary group of employees responsible for bringing about particular change. Task force members are usually chosen for their expertise in specific areas. For example, the White House established a task force, chaired by Hillary Rodham Clinton, to develop a plan to redesign health care in the United States. The task force members include health policy specialists, economists, representatives from the insurance industry, financial experts, and health care consumers. Each member of the task force was expected to contribute knowledge and experience to the task of devising a solution to the problem of health care in the United States. Once a plan was developed and presented to the president, the task force was dissolved. We will take a closer look at task forces and committees in Chapter 15.

**Liaison Personnel.**   Liaison personnel coordinate the efforts of different people in the organization. A hospital, for example, may employ a patient advocate to coordinate the efforts of physicians, nurses, technicians, and specialists in the provision of care to a particular patient. Another type of liaison may be a systems analyst whose task is to ensure that those who will eventually use a computer system are communicating effectively with the system's designers and programmers. Liaison roles usually serve the purpose of enhanced communication. A liaison person can "speak the language" of a variety of different job specializations and can thus act as translator when specialists need to communicate with one another.

### How Coordinating Mechanisms Work

Each of these coordinating mechanisms works by bringing together people from different parts and levels of the organization to solve a problem or accomplish a task that requires the cooperation of a diverse group. Such mechanisms are useful in correcting weaknesses in a particular organizational structure. In a company with a formalized, centralized functional structure, for example, management may feel that certain products are not changing as fast as consumer preferences. Such a structure lacks flexibility, making rapid change difficult. Thus management may choose to create product teams, where specialists are brought together to manage the product. This would introduce some flexibility into an otherwise inflexible organization.

## CONFIGURATIONS OF STRUCTURAL TYPES

Given all of the structural options and coordinating mechanisms available to organization designers, is there any guidance to help them make sound choices for their organization? As it happens, researchers have found, by examining many successful organizations, that companies tend to organize using one of five general archetypes.[24] While there are, in reality, an infinite number of ways a company can structure itself, in fact this amazing variety tends to cluster into five general types,

The manufacturing division of Merck & Co., Inc., the world's largest pharmaceutical company, formed a Global Facilities Optimization Task Force to examine the company's global network of chemical and pharmaceutical plants. The task force is helping Merck to create production and packaging centers that focus on a core technology of Merck's product line. Each center will achieve an optimal balance of technological resources, inventory levels, capital utilization, and manufacturing costs. The Ballydine, Ireland, plant shown here will be the worldwide source for *Fosamax*, Merck's new osteoporosis medicine.

*Source:* Courtesy of Merck & Co., Inc. Photographer: Michael Sheil/Black Star.

which, according to Professor Henry Mintzberg, are the simple structure, machine bureaucracy, professional bureaucracy, divisionalized form, and adhocracy.[25]

## Simple Structure

A **simple structure** is one with few departments, arranged by function, headed by an entrepreneur/owner, and with few technical support staff. An organization is likely to use a simple structure when it is small, probably very young, and therefore entrepreneurial. The firm has few employees and little job specialization or formalization. If there are enough people to have a formal structure, it will be functional. The organization is usually in the birth or early growth phase of the life cycle and does not yet have a specific strategy. Austad, a Sioux Falls, South Dakota, mailorder company that markets a Gopher golf ball finder, is a small business with a simple structure.[26]

**simple structure**
A structure with few departments, arranged by function, headed by an entrepreneur/owner, and with few technical support staff.

## Machine Bureaucracy

A **machine bureaucracy** is a highly structured, formal organization that emphasizes procedures and rules. The formal structure is functional, and the latent structure emphasizes complexity, formalization, and centralization. The machine bureaucracy is a classic mechanistic organization, where everything is done "by the book." It is of medium size, its environment is stable, and its favored technology is mass assembly. American car companies prior to the 1970s were classic machine bureaucracies. Current examples include most government agencies, such as public schools.

**machine bureaucracy**
A highly structured, formal organization that emphasizes procedures and rules, has a functional formal structure, and contains a latent structure emphasizing complexity, formalization, and centralization.

## Professional Bureaucracy

The **professional bureaucracy** is like the machine bureaucracy, but with some distinct differences. Like the machine bureaucracy, it has a functional structure, is medium sized, and works best in stable environments. It differs from the machine bureaucracy in that most of its employees are professionals, and it provides nonroutine services. Because the employees are professionals, the latent

**professional bureaucracy**
An organization that has a functional structure, is medium sized, and works best in stable environments, but has primarily professional employees and a decentralized latent structure.

structure tends to be decentralized, allowing those closest to the work to make the necessary decisions. Examples of professional bureaucracies include large law firms, medium-sized accounting firms, universities, and group medical practices.

## Divisionalized Form

**divisionalized form**
A multidivisional structure or hybrid; typically a very large corporation that has organized its departments into divisions.

The **divisionalized form** is essentially the multidivisional structure or a hybrid. It is typically a very large corporation that has organized its departments into divisions. The latent structure, however, tends to be decentralized, allowing each division to make the decisions needed for its effective operation. The level of formality and complexity may vary from division to division depending on the circumstances faced. Similarly, because each division faces its own product market or geographic region, the level of environmental turbulence/stability and munificence/scarcity varies from division to division. Since each division is responsible for the production of its own goods or services, the technology can also vary substantially from one division to the next. Examples of organizations with the divisionalized form include Procter & Gamble, Time Inc., and Chrysler.

## Adhocracy

**adhocracy**
A centralized, informal, but complex organization which tries to maintain flexibility in the face of rapid environmental changes by using a matrix or network formal structure.

An **adhocracy** is a decentralized, informal, but complex organization that tries to maintain flexibility in the face of rapid environmental changes by using a matrix or network formal structure. It is a medium-sized firm operating in a highly turbulent environment requiring flexibility and ease of change. To accomplish this, the organization tends to delegate authority and does not overload itself with rules and procedures. Such firms are usually involved in complex, state-of-the-art technology and are pursuing new product strategies. Examples of adhocracies include many pharmaceutical firms, those doing business in the electronics industry, and, often, hospitals.

## How Best to Structure the Organization

While organizations tend to fall into one of the five archetypes of structure just described, in reality the structures used are unique to each and every company. There are so many factors that a company must account for and so many alternate methods it may use in order to facilitate its becoming more efficient and effective that no two companies ever share exactly the same structure.

Furthermore, new structural forms are being tried all the time. It is usually true that when a company is not doing as well as expected, the first thing management does in an effort to improve performance is to change the organization's structure—to reorganize. So, companies do not choose a structure and then stay with it forever. In fact, organizational structures change almost continually, always evolving to meet the needs of changing strategies, technologies, environments, and phases of the life cycle. To remain vital and profitable, a company must be prepared to shed its skin and try on something new periodically. It must be prepared to change.

c  a  r  e  e  r  s

## Flexibility and Adaptability

Typically, business school students major in marketing, finance, accounting, management information systems, or general management. Upon graduation, they generally expect to be hired by a company to do more of whatever it is they were trained to do as a business school student. So, an accounting major expects to be an accountant, perhaps for one of the Big 6 accounting firms. A marketing major may anticipate a career as a market researcher or sales representative. A finance major may be hoping for a career on Wall Street or perhaps in a prestigious bank. How are these choices of career affected by the structure of the hiring organizations?

If you are hired by a large divisionalized company, you might expect to practice your profession among many others doing the same or similar tasks. You are likely to be involved only with the business of the division to which you belong, often not learning much, if anything, about any of the other businesses in which the company may be involved. For example, as a management information specialist working for a large company, say American Express, you might be asked to write computer programs or to help develop systems to improve customer relations between the company and its cardholders. So, you might be involved in developing information systems that will allow management to identify cardholders who spend large amounts of money on airline tickets, or on electronic equipment, or in restaurants to help the marketing department develop better marketing approaches. However, you are likely to be completely unaware of what information specialists do when they work for the Traveler's Cheque Division or for Travel Services or for Money Orders. You may learn one part of the business fairly well, but be completely uninformed about other parts of the business. A wise employee in this situation will learn to request occasional transfers to other divisions in order to learn all aspects of the corporation to improve his or her usefulness

to the company and thereby improve his or her own promotion chances.

On the other hand, if you gain employment in a very small company, or in one that is heavily decentralized, you may find that you are expected to do more than merely the tasks for which you were trained. As an information systems specialist, for example, if you were to become an employee of a small savings and loan, you may find that you not only are expected to develop information systems but may also be expected to participate in customer relations and other marketing efforts. In very small organizations, employees are often expected to wear multiple hats in order to make the organization more efficient. It can come as a shock to students to discover that, in addition to doing some accounting, they are also doing bookkeeping, secretarial work, and public relations.

Similarly, employees in organizations that are experimenting with new structural forms and which are making heavy use of teams and decentralized decision making may find that the company expects more of them than the skills learned in school. To be an effective team member, you may find that you will not only contribute your skill and expertise, perhaps in financial analysis, but you may also be expected to learn some engineering, computer science, and marketing to be able to understand the needs and constraints of the other members of the team. An employee who wishes only to practice what he or she was trained to do would probably be happier in a more traditional organization. However, be warned that traditional structures seem to be adapting to the use of teams and that it may be difficult in the future to anticipate spending a career of 40 years as just an accountant. Organizational flexibility requires individual flexibility, and those employees willing to take on new domains and challenges will be the employees who survive and prosper in the future.

**Comment on Box:** After discussing "Careers Corner," ask students which organizational structure they would prefer and why. Ask them to consider the management styles, interests, expertise, and any other factors influencing their decision.

# SUMMARY AND REVIEW

- **Describe organizational structure.** Organizational structure is the result of the process of creating an organization—the way managers group jobs into departments and departments into divisions. The formal structure is depicted in organization charts, while the latent structure is understood but not explicitly described by organizational members.

- **Detect four types of formal structures: functional, multidivisional, matrix, and networks/outsourcing.** An organization with functional departments, such as the accounting department, the marketing department, and the engineering department, has a functional structure. The functional structure is efficient and is useful for capturing economies of scale, but it can make communication across departments difficult and costly. In a multidivisional structure, the organization groups all the activities involved with a specific product, geographic region, customer, or some other common denominator together into a division. This facilitates communication across functional areas but creates duplication of effort, and it can be difficult to realize economies of scale. A matrix structure brings together employees from different functional areas to act as a team in order to complete a specific project. This avoids duplication of effort and has the efficiencies of the functional structure, but it means that each employee has two supervisors. Network organizations do not make products themselves, but contract to others the tasks of producing, transporting, and selling the product according to their designs and plans. Outsourcing means that the organization makes critical components, but contracts to others less important manufacturing or other internal tasks. Outsourcing allows the organization to stay small and simple and therefore efficient and highly flexible, but it leaves the organization heavily dependent on others, over whom it has little or no control, for work that is crucial to its success.

- **Specify three characteristics that define the latent structure of an organization.** The latent structure describes what the organization is really like, that is, its degree of complexity, formalization, and centralization. Complexity refers to the degree of job specialization, vertical levels in the organization, and diversity of tasks the organization is involved in. Formalization is the degree to which the company makes use of written rules and procedures. Centralization describes an organization in which all the decision making is done in the higher echelons.

- **Summarize the contingency factors that influence the type of formal structure that is best for an organization.** What structure is best for an organization depends on its size, strategy, environment, and technology. The larger the organization, the more complex the structure tends to become. Different types of strategy are more effectively implemented with different structures. Different structures also respond in different ways to varying levels of environmental munificence/scarcity and turbulence/stability. The more scarce and/or turbulent the organization's environment, the more organic the organization structure should become. Technology also affects the type of structure an organization should use.

- **Describe the different types of coordinating mechanisms that can be used to support the organization structure.** Coordinating mechanisms are tools that can be used to help reduce the disadvantages of any given organizational structure design choice. Task forces are temporary groups of employees brought together to try to solve a specific problem or dilemma. Committees are more permanent groups that work on longer-range issues. Liaison personnel are people whose skill is in communicating across various functional and hierarchical levels.

- **Distinguish among five organizational archetypes: simple structure, machine bureaucracy, professional bureaucracy, divisionalized form, and adhocracy.** Simple structures are used by new, small firms with too few employees to require a more complex organization. The machine bureaucracy is the classic bureaucratic structure, used by medium-sized organizations in stable environments using mass-production technology. The professional bureaucracy applies to organizations whose work force is made up of professionals, such as hospitals, universities, and law firms. The divisionalized form is used by very large, very complex organizations that need to separate their businesses into divisions. Adhocracy organizations, which may use network or matrix structures, are highly complex, highly decentralized, and fairly informal.

- **Assess an organization's structure.** After reading the "Business Dilemma" box, you should be able to evaluate the organizational structure of Aerodyne Motors and make suggestions for improving it if you think the structure is unsuitable.

## Key Terms and Concepts

## Ready Recall

1. What is the difference between departments and divisions? Can the terms be used interchangeably? Why or why not?
2. Describe three different types of multidivisional structures. Do companies use only one of the types or can they be mixed?
3. What are the advantages and disadvantages of using the matrix structure? If you were the CEO of a small bicycle manufacturing company would you use a matrix structure? Why or why not?
4. Is it true that the more formalized the corporate rules and procedures the better? Why or why not?
5. What is meant by organic structure and how does it differ from a mechanistic structure?

6. A company in the decline stage of the corporate life cycle will always ultimately go out of business. True or false? Defend your answer.
7. What kind of latent structure would be best for a company in the mature stage of the life cycle?
8. The ABC Widget Company is using a cost-efficiency strategy. What formal structure is likely to work best to support that strategy? Why?
9. How is a professional bureaucracy different from an adhocracy? How are they alike?
10. Why would a company need coordinating mechanisms such as task forces or committees?

## Expand Your Experience

1. Find General Motors' organizational structure prior to 1992 and after 1992. What are the differences? What do you think those differences were meant to accomplish? Do you think the changes will help GM to become more competitive? Why or why not?
2. Talk to some of your teachers and determine the chain of command in a university or college. How many levels are in your school? What do you think your school's environment is like? Why? What structure is your school using? Is that the best structure it could use? Why or why not?

3. Study a local small business and then analyze its organizational structure. Is the structure appropriate for the organization's size, strategy, industry, environment, etc.? If not, make some recommendations for what structure you believe would be most appropriate, defending your choice. How can the owner implement this structure? Your professor may require you to make your analysis available to the business owner.

**CASE**

## *Thermos Grills Up a New Look*

Many of us ate and drank our lunches from Thermos products as we were growing up, and Thermos will forevermore remind us of the halcyon days of our youth. Despite such warm memories, however, Thermos was not firing up Wall Street with its lukewarm growth and financial performance. In 1990, Monte Peterson be-

came CEO and he decided that Thermos needed a change of structure and a change in culture in order to be revitalized.

When Peterson took over the company, Thermos had a standard functional structure, with departments for marketing, manufacturing, engineering, and so forth. It had also become highly bureaucratic, highly centralized, highly formalized, and highly predictable. Peterson believed that the most immediate market of concern was the barbecue grill market, which accounted for a significant portion of Thermos's revenue and promised opportunity for expansion. Peterson assessed the environment as relatively turbulent in that Thermos faced many competitors such as Sunbeam, Char-Broil, and Weber. While not a scarce environment, it was not exactly munificent either. The industry was in the mature stage of the life cycle and appeared to be likely to stay there.

It seemed that what Thermos needed was a strategy of new product development that would expand the opportunities available in a mature market. However, Thermos's bureaucratic structure was likely to prevent the implementation of any such strategy. So, Peterson changed the structure. He replaced the functional departments with teams composed of people from all departments and even from outside the company. For example, about 10 employees of Fitch Inc., an industrial design company, were members of the team that was to design a new barbecue grill. The team leader rotated depending on the stage of product development. While doing market research, a member of marketing was the team leader. But when it came time to make use of the research results, a member of the design department became leader. In this way, no one department or concern dominated the development process.

By having all those who would eventually be involved with the product engaged from the very beginning, costly mistakes were avoided. For example, the designers originally wanted the new grill to have tapered legs. But manufacturing noted that such legs would have to be custom-made at great expense, perhaps increasing the eventual price of the product beyond what the market would bear. The designers therefore decided to use straight legs on the new product.

The end result of Thermos's new structure was both a new organizational culture and a new barbecue grill. Because the structure encouraged and even required decisions to be decentralized, and because it eliminated the "chain of command" as it is typically implemented, participants in the project felt freer to submit ideas, to point out flaws, and to become more innovative in designing the product. The result was a new electric grill that made use of insulating properties (with which Thermos is so familiar from its Thermos bottles) to correct the problems associated with conventional electric grills. The new grill can become hot enough to sear food, giving it the desired barbecue taste while not forcing the chef to cope with clumsy gas or messy charcoal. Further, the electric grill made barbecuing a possibility for apartment residents who are typically prohibited from grilling because of the danger of fire. The new product has been a major success, and Peterson predicts a 13 percent increase in Thermos revenue in 1994.

*Source:* Brian Dumain, "Payoff From the New Management," *Fortune,* December 13, 1993, 103–110.

## Questions

1. Should Thermos make use of this new structure throughout the company? Why or why not?
2. What drawbacks are there in the use of teams instead of functional departments?

3. Do you think the use of such a structure would benefit any company? Why or why not?

---

**S T R E N G T H E N  Y O U R  S K I L L S**
## *Politicking*

Even if your work experience is limited, you no doubt have seen politicking occur in a setting such as a club or sports team. That's because politicking is used by those who want to influence or at least try to influence who gets or does what in an organization. From an organizational perspective, research and work experience support the fact that many managers fail because they are:

- unwilling or unable to perform the political tasks associated with their jobs
- naive about the political structure and activities in their organization
- incompetent at politicking.

Understanding the formal and latent structure where you work serves as an important foundation to politicking. This exercise will allow you to relate to organizational structure the nine general politicking guidelines listed and briefly described on the next page. In each blank, answer one of the following two questions:

- How can your knowledge of the organizational structure where you work help improve your politicking effectiveness as it relates to this guideline?
- Can you think of an example from work or another setting with which you are familiar of how you or someone else has used or not used this guideline? What outcomes did you observe?

### Nine General Politicking Guidelines

1. **Frame arguments in terms of organizational goals.** Those who appear to be promoting their self-interests above the interests of the organization are likely to lose influence.

   _____

   _____

2. **Develop the right image.** As you work to project the kind of image that fits in with your organization's culture and with what the organization expects from its managers in terms of dress, associations, behaviors, etc., you will be attending to an important subjective element affecting politicking. _____

   _____

   _____

3. **Gain control of organizational resources.** Two examples of important resources to control are knowledge and expertise because they make you more valuable to the organization. Usually the more valuable you are, the more receptive your audience will be to your ideas. _____

   _____

   _____

4. **Make yourself appear indispensable.** The decision makers will most likely work harder at meeting your desires and keeping you satisfied if you are perceived as someone who is not easily replaced. _____

   _____

5. **Be visible.** Your boss and those in power need to be made aware of your contribution. Some strategies to achieve this without coming across as a braggart are to lobby to get assigned to projects that will increase your visibility, send progress reports to your boss and others, attend and be seen at social functions, and be active in your professional associations. _____

6. **Get a mentor.** The more visible you are, the more likely someone higher up will take an interest in becoming your mentor. A mentor is someone who can help and encourage you and from whom you will be able to learn a great deal.

   _____

   _____

7. **Develop powerful allies.** In addition to having a mentor, you need to cultivate relationships with potentially influential people above you, at your level, and in the lower ranks. These allies can sometimes provide you with information unavailable through the formal communication channels, and they can also be a basis of support in those situations where there is strength in numbers. _____

   _____

8. **Avoid "tainted" members.** Your effectiveness can be diminished if you are closely associated with those perceived on the fringe of the organization whose performance and/or loyalty is in question._____

9. **Support your boss.** Since your boss evaluates your performance and is the most important influence on your immediate future with your organization, find out the criteria your boss will be using to evaluate your performance. You can keep your boss on your side by helping him or her succeed. Never speak negatively about your boss to others, nor should you undermine your boss. Do everything in your power to support your boss and to make him or her look good.

   _____

   _____

_Source:_ Stephen P. Robbins, _Training in Interpersonal Skills: TIPS for Managing People at Work_ (Englewood Cliffs, NJ: Prentice-Hall, Inc., 1989), 172–174.

# Directing *and* Staffing

# Managing Human Resources

## Outline

## After reading this chapter, you will be able to:

- Discuss the term *human resource management* and its activities.

- Summarize how managers may plan for human resource needs.

- Specify how organizations recruit new employees.

- Explain how companies use application forms, interviews, and tests in selecting new employees.

- Formulate the information used in designing effective training programs.

- Describe the types of performance appraisal.

- Explain the purposes of compensation systems and the basic steps in setting up these systems.

- Summarize some of the major laws that affect employment decisions.

- Assess an organization's attempts to select, train, and appraise its employees with an improved human resource management program.

H. Armstrong Roberts, Inc.

# Magnavox Trains for Business Literacy

Illiteracy in the U.S. work force is an increasing problem as companies shift to new technology or develop self-directed work teams. Experts estimate that as much as one-half of the adult work force does not read, write, or compute well enough to perform their jobs satisfactorily. Moreover, many of these employees have become skillful at hiding their problems by mimicking the behaviors they see around them. Their limitations are major issues for the organization that must be addressed by human resource management training specialists.

One organization that has recently dealt with this issue is Magnavox Electronic Systems Company. The company suspected illiteracy problems for several reasons: meeting announcements failing to gather workers, numerous misunderstandings about written assignments, increasing scrap and rework costs, and an unsuccessful attempt to implement statistical process control to improve product quality. To diagnose the problem, Magnavox purchased and administered the Test of Adult Basic Education to a sample of its employees. The company also drew a representative sample of work-related materials, including manufacturing instructions, routing cards, charts, and blueprints, and analyzed them to identify the grade levels at which they were written.

Magnavox determined that employees should be able to read at the eighth grade level and comprehend mathematics at a sixth grade level in order to understand the workplace documents. Unfortunately, many workers tested below these levels. The company concluded that of its hourly workers, 52 percent were functionally illiterate in reading and 36 percent in math. After considering various options, the company decided to use a federal funding program that was available through the Carl D. Perkins Vocational Education Act. Because illiteracy is an issue that is well suited for cooperative work between business and educational institutions, Magnavox developed a partnership with the California State Department of Education and the Torrance Adult School to carry out a training program.

The first step in the training program was to hire a consulting firm to conduct a literacy audit of work activities. This audit identified the exact reading, writing, listening, speaking, and arithmetic skills that employees needed to use work materials and documents, and formed the basis of the instructional program. Learning objectives were written and sequenced according to a logical order of learning and difficulty level. An instructor from the Torrance School was selected to conduct the classes.

The name of the class was "Process Improvement and Communications" to avoid the stigma of having "illiteracy" in its title. One of its first activities was the administration of the test, which served as a baseline against which to compare later learning. The program was divided into three six-week sessions and included English as a Second Language, a native language literacy class for English-speaking employees, and classes in math and communication skills.

After completing the program, Magnavox evaluated its effect in several ways. Reading skills increased 1.1 grade levels and mathematical skills 1.4 grade levels. Job performance showed steady improvement, as did students' monthly efficiency ratings. In addition, scrap and rework costs noticeably declined. While activities in addition to the literacy program affected these results, Magnavox strongly believed that its program was a major contributing factor.

*Sources:* Donald J. Ford, "Toward a More Literate Workforce," *Training and Development* 46 (November 1992): 52–54; Donald J. Ford, "The Magnavox Experience," *Training and Development* 46 (November 1992): 55–57.

*introduction*

If an organization is to be successful, it must have employees who have the appropriate skills for their jobs. Magnavox illustrates how one human resource program, training, can be used to develop necessary skills. Other programs can be similarly used. Ensuring that the firm has sufficient employees with the appropriate skills is the domain of human resource management.

In this chapter, we will explore the role and functions of human resource management. We will begin by defining the term and discussing its importance to organizational success. Next, we will explore some human resource management programs, including planning, recruiting, selecting, orientation and training, performance appraisal, compensation, and promotions, transfers, and terminations. Finally, we will look at some of the laws that affect human resource management.

## THE NATURE OF HUMAN RESOURCE MANAGEMENT

**human resource management (HRM)**
All activities that forecast the number and type of employees an organization will need and then find and develop employees with necessary skills.

**Teaching Note:** Students may still be familiar with the term "personnel" for human resource management. Explain that the new term is preferred because it focuses on employees as key resources or components of the organization.

**Human resource management (HRM)** includes activities that first forecast the number and type of employees an organization will need and then find and develop employees with necessary skills. For example, human resource planning, recruiting, and selecting are programs concerned with bringing the appropriate individuals into the organization. Orientation and training programs develop the skills required by employees to carry out the work of the company. Performance appraisal evaluates work accomplishments, while compensation can reward those who perform at high levels. Compliance with the law is also important, but such compliance is not the major reason for developing sound human resource programs. The primary reason is to ensure a sufficient number of employees who have the appropriate skills to meet the organization's needs. If these HR programs are appropriately designed and implemented, the organization will have an efficient work force that serves as a primary strength in competitive markets.

### The Importance of Human Resource Management

Organizations use HRM programs to make work-related decisions about employees. These decisions have become increasingly important to companies in recent years for several reasons, the most important of which is that industries have become more and more competitive, and many face foreign competitors that have low labor costs. Companies with relatively high labor costs can compete by having well-skilled employees who are rewarded for high performance. HRM addresses these issues.

Another important reason for the increased importance of HRM is that a number of federal and state laws affecting employment decisions have been intro-

**TABLE 14.1**

## A Partial List of Tasks and KSAs for the Position of Regional Sales Manager

*Job Tasks*

1. Use data from last year's sales, the present state of the economy, and the number of competitors in the region to develop a sales forecast for each product item for the next six months.
2. Interview applicants for sales positions and, together with the district sales manager, decide which applicants to select. Use training and experience forms, ability tests, and performance tests.
3. Develop promotion and sales campaigns using data from the sales forecast, recent sales, company-sponsored market surveys, and competitors' promotion and sales practices.

*Knowledge, Skills, and Abilities Needed*

Knowledge of algebra
Ability to use situational interviewing for selection of sales staff
Ability to design a promotion campaign for each product for a six-month time period
Skill in use of personal computer for word processing and development of mathematical tables for sales forecasting

---

duced in the last 30 years. Many of these laws are very complex in their interpretation and implementation. HR specialists are concerned with how an organization can both comply with these laws and meet its needs for an effective work force.

A third reason concerns the increasing use of new technology in business operations. Such technology, of course, requires operators who are skilled in its use, maintenance, and repair. The task of finding these skills in the general work force and developing these in current employees falls primarily to human resource managers.

**Critical Thinking Challenge:** Have students use Table 14.1 to develop a job analysis profile for a cashier in a fast-food restaurant. Combine student profiles into a complete job analysis recorded on the board.

## Information Needed for Human Resource Management

A basic activity of HR managers is collecting information to use in making job-related decisions about individuals. Most HR programs use some combination of three types of information: job characteristics, worker qualifications, and job performance. **Job analysis** is the systematic process of gathering information about important work-related aspects of a job. It identifies the first of two types of information, which includes the tasks that make up a job; the worker knowledge, skills, and abilities (KSAs) needed on the job; the information, equipment, and materials used; and the working conditions. Table 14.1 provides some example task statements and KSAs that are appropriate for the position of regional sales manager. Performance appraisal, discussed in a later section, is the process of collecting the third type of information, job performance of individual employees.

**job analysis**
The systematic process of gathering information about important work-related aspects of a job.

## HUMAN RESOURCE PLANNING

**Human resource planning** involves forecasting the organization's future demand for employees, forecasting the future supply of employees within the organization, and designing programs to correct the discrepancy between the two. It serves the same purpose for human resource management as strategic planning does for other management activities. The purpose of human resource planning is to

**human resource planning**
The forecasting of an organization's future demand for employees and the future supply of employees within the organization, and the designing of programs to correct the discrepancy between the two.

**Teaching Note:** Remind students that just as we must use the tools of strategic planning to prepare for changes in industry and customer needs, we must also plan for the future human resource needs that are necessary to support new strategies.

ensure that, in the future, the firm has enough employees with the appropriate skills so that it can accomplish its long-term goals.

The starting point of human resource planning is the organization's strategic plans and goals. Let's use a hypothetical example. Hubert Spotswood presently owns a successful jewelry store. Hubert has read that, because of the cost of building new homes, economic forecasters are predicting that individuals will choose to remodel their existing homes rather than buy new ones. He has therefore decided that in six years he wishes to be the largest jewelry and tool marketer in the area. His strategic plan is to open a large discount store, Jewels & Tools, which will carry watches and other jewelry as well as tools for household repair and maintenance. In addition, he wishes to have three upscale boutiques for each of the two product groups, to be called Pretty Things and Puttering Things. He knows that implementing these plans will necessitate more employees with different skills than those he presently employs. Hubert does not have the time to handle all the details of the strategic plan, so he has hired Diana Taylor as a human resource manager. Diana, because she did well in her management courses, knows that she must start by drawing up a human resource plan that will be implemented over the next six years.

## Forecasting Demand for Employees

Forecasting demand for employees involves predicting how many employees the firm will need in specific jobs in the future. There are two types of forecasting methods: quantitative and qualitative.

**Quantitative Forecasting Methods.** Quantitative methods, as you can probably guess, use statistical techniques. Two of the most often used techniques are the productivity index and regression analysis. The productivity index is the ratio of employees to unit of output. Returning to our hypothetical example, Diana goes through Hubert's records for the last ten years and calculates that each salesperson accounts for $85,000 in yearly sales. If she can find out the amount of sales in the strategic goal, Diana can determine the number of salespersons that will be needed. Regression analysis uses data about a number of variables that are correlated to predict sales and numbers of employees. In this case, Diana uses population of the area, number of competitors, economic strength of the community, and the number of students enrolled in the local building and trade school to determine the number of salespersons needed.

**Critical Thinking Challenge:** Have student teams develop a list of business conditions and social, political, and economic trends that would signal the need for a change in the number of human resources for an organization.

**Qualitative Forecasting Methods.** Qualitative forecasting methods rely primarily on the judgments of experts. These methods are used when planners cannot gather historical data to develop statistical forecasts or when they think that future business activities will be quite different from those of the past. Quantitative forecasts usually assume that what has occurred in the past will continue in the future. For example, if one salesperson produced $85,000 in sales for the last five years, then this should happen in the next five. However, if more competitors start up, or the economy weakens significantly, or the firm introduces many different products, this forecast will not be accurate. In such a case, moving to qualitative methods, planners consult experts in the business operation who have a good idea about the future environment of the business, and who can provide useful judgments. One technique for gathering information from these experts is through the Delphi method, which we discussed in Chapter 3. Another is nominal grouping,

Beginning in 1990, the U.S. Army began planning for a massive "peace reduction" downsizing to decrease its size from 710,000 active-duty soldiers to about 495,000 soldiers by 1997. To meet this challenge, the Army developed an outplacement program that includes 55 job-assistance centers worldwide, a pool of 286 job counselors, and a computer database linked to some 11,000 U.S. employers. Part of the outplacement counseling program are seminars, workshops (shown here), and individual training that equip soldiers with job-search skills such as preparing résumés and cover letters for networking and interviews.

*Source:* U. S. Army.

which divides a large group into smaller ones, and then structures the exchange of information among the groups.

## Forecasting Supply of Employees

Forecasting the supply of employees involves two predictions. The first estimates how many employees there would be in the organization in specific jobs if the human resource programs currently in place continue. As with forecasting demand, both quantitative and qualitative techniques can be used. The most-used quantitative technique is Markov Modeling, which uses historical records to determine the probabilities, in one year, of employees in a specific job either staying in that job, moving to another job in the company, or leaving the company. These are known as transition probabilities and are calculated for each job. By using these probabilities in computer simulations, planners can determine how many individuals should be in each position at any year in the future.

The second prediction is how many individuals in the external labor market would have the necessary skills for employment in the organization at a specific time in the future. As an example of using a qualitative forecasting technique, Diana Taylor could gather experts in a Delphi situation and collect several rounds of data concerning population trends, education levels of specific age groups, and the demand for employees by other companies. She could then use these data to estimate the number of individuals available in the external labor market. The results from both predictions will provide an estimate of the total supply of individuals with appropriate skills.

## Planning Programs

After HR planners have made forecasts of both future demand and supply, the next step is to compare the two forecasts. If they are similar, the planners may conclude that continuing current HRM programs will provide sufficient employees to meet the organization's future demands. If there is a discrepancy between the two forecasts, then managers must redesign HRM programs either to reduce or increase the supply of employees to meet future demand. In the case of Jewels &

Tools, the two forecasts will be different because of the growth that Hubert plans. Diana will, therefore, design the HRM programs of recruiting, selecting, training, and compensating to bring more individuals into the organization over the next six years and to develop their appropriate skills.

Many organizations in the real world have recently faced the opposite situation. Many have made strategic plans to reduce business costs and, therefore, their demand for employees is less than the supply. Depending on the size of the difference between supply and demand, they can employ various programs. If the difference is small, perhaps reducing recruitment and selection programs will suffice. Or the HR manager can design an early retirement program to increase the number of senior employees who will leave the organization voluntarily. If the difference between demand and supply is great, the company will be forced to develop systematic termination programs. Such programs frequently include outplacement activities in which the organization assists those employees who have been laid off in preparing for and carrying out job searches.

To work well, HRM programs must be appropriately designed and implemented. The next sections of this chapter will therefore discuss some of the most important HRM programs, pointing out the appropriate features of each.

# RECRUITING

**recruiting**
The process of attracting potential new employees to the organization.

**Recruiting** is the process of attracting potential new employees to the organization. This HR program is closely related to selection, which we will discuss next, because it supplies a pool of qualified applicants from which the organization can choose those best suited for its needs.

## The Purposes of Recruiting

Recruiting serves three purposes. The first is to provide enough applicants from which to select future employees. If there are too few applicants, the company's chances of hiring the best employees will be limited. The worst case occurs when the number of applicants is equal to or less than the number of available positions, possibly causing the organization to hire all the applicants regardless of their level of skills and abilities or not to fill all the open positions. The opposite problem can also occur—too many applicants are recruited. This happened at a paper mill in Duluth, Minnesota, when 10,000 individuals applied for 300 operator positions. In such cases, the time and cost involved in gathering applications and reviewing applicants are considerable and may delay the schedule of hiring. Generally, selection specialists think that five to ten applicants for each available position is appropriate. This number is small enough to process easily and yet should provide a large enough pool to identify potentially excellent employees.

The second purpose, really an extension of the first, is to attract at least minimally qualified applicants. It does little good to have a number of applicants if most are not suited for the open positions. The processing of such applicants wastes time and resources.

The third purpose of recruiting is to attract a demographically and culturally diverse applicant pool. For example, it is difficult to achieve a diverse work force in the organization if the recruitment process uses sources such as schools, media, or mailing lists that are dominated by one or a few demographic groups. The "Dynamics of Diversity" box describes Nike's efforts to achieve a diverse work force.

## NIKE JUST DID IT

Minorities make up only about 5 percent of Oregon's population, making it difficult for companies located there to employ a diverse work force. That difficulty dealt Beaverton-based Nike a public relations blow in 1989 when a group of African-American activists threatened to boycott the company's products unless it improved its minority hiring. The $4 billion shoemaker responded by calling on minority friends and black leaders from across the country to verify that it has consistently supported minority programs. The threatened boycott was quickly halted, but the criticism alarmed Nike managers, and drove them to make some changes in their hiring practices.

In 1989, Nike implemented a number of minority recruiting programs both inside and outside the company. To increase access to minorities, Nike goes to National Urban League conferences, sponsors a summer minority internship program for college students, and recruits graduates from a variety of universities around the country. The company's recruiting efforts are targeted to ensure that it hires employees with the right skills for very specialized jobs. Additionally, during the hiring process, the company separates résumés and other application forms from documents that may identify an applicant's race to ensure a "blind process."

To address women's issues, Nike created a task force of women employees to focus on management training and development, and brought in a facilitator from the Families and Work Institute. Based on the task force's findings, managers developed broad policy recommendations. Liz Dolan, vice president for communications, says that because the organization had grown so fast, managers had not been taught how to manage. Women didn't know what career paths were available.

In 1991, human resource managers also began to collect companywide data on minority hiring so that they could track hiring trends. If those trends become worrisome, Cheryl Nickerson, employee relations manager in charge of affirmative action programs, can go to each division's human resource manager and recommend changes. Additional, broader recommendations come from an internal advisory board, formed in 1990, to review termination, hiring, and promotion activities.

Nike's efforts to improve diversity in the workplace have been successful. The company has doubled the percentage—from 11 to 22 percent—of minorities in its global work force in the last three years. Nike's work force is now 13 percent black, 2.8 percent Hispanic, 5.4 percent Asian, and .73 percent American Indian. At its Beaverton headquarters in Oregon, where 3,100 of the company's 5,300 workers are located, the proportion of minority employees has more than doubled—to 14 percent from 6.9 percent. However, the company now faces some corporate "belt-tightening" and layoffs in the face of slow sales and profits. Dolan says that the company has focused on positions rather than people to ensure that no one group is affected more than others.

*Source:* Jo McIntyre, "They Just Did It: Nike's Crusade for Diversity," *Business Ethics* 8 (March/April 1994): 14.

## Fulfilling Recruiting Purposes

The company controls three ways of fulfilling these purposes of recruiting: the sources through which potential applicants are contacted, the information given to applicants, and the contacts between the applicants and the company. Although all three affect the number and types of applicants, companies cannot totally control recruiting. Individuals often contact companies on their own, especially well-known ones such as the Coca-Cola Company and General Electric. However, some firms refuse to respond to such applications because of the cost in staff time and resources that such responses would require.

HR managers may recruit externally or internally. External sources include newspapers, broadcast media, employment agencies, educational institutions, and brochures, flyers, and signs. Internal sources include posted notices within the organization as well as formal programs that encourage current employees to recommend that friends and family members in the job market apply to the organization. These various external and internal sources differ greatly in terms of the number of individuals and the demographic groups they attract and the costs involved. For example, AMP Incorporated, the world's largest manufacturer of electronic interconnection products, installed a telephone-based job-posting system that decreased recruiting costs from $311,000 in 1991 to $87,000 in 1992.[1]

The second factor, the information conveyed to applicants during the recruiting process, is important because applicants use this information to decide whether to pursue further contact with the company. Research has shown that, at the initial stage of recruiting, lengthy ads providing relatively large amounts of information attract more applicants than do shorter ads. Announcements that describe specific job tasks and necessary KSAs also increase the percentage of appropriately qualified applicants while reducing the total number who apply. Another recruiting tactic is providing applicants with realistic job previews (RJPs), accurate descriptions about the job and the organization, positive points as well as negative ones. This gives any applicants who do not think the position is appropriate for them a chance to drop out of the process on their own. Utilizing RJPs benefits the company because it is better to lose such individuals before the company has invested considerable time and effort in them.

Several aspects of contact between the organization and applicants are important. One is the promptness with which the firm gives information to the applicant, such as how quickly it schedules interviews after initial contact, when it provides information promised by recruiters, and how soon it gives evaluation messages after interviews. Another aspect is the attention given to arranging for on-site visits. Sometimes applicants are expected to find the hotel or the company's office with very little instruction, or the details of schedules are not provided or are changed without notice. A third aspect is the interaction between recruiters and applicants. Applicants generally react favorably to the organization when there are frequent contacts, the company is receptive to visits, and recruiters are viewed as being representative of the employees of the company. NCR, for example, feels that it benefits because its recruiters maintain an unusually strong presence on many college campuses. They attend job fairs, play active roles in campus groups, organize job-search courses, and arrange for student groups to tour NCR facilities.[2]

## SELECTING EMPLOYEES

**selection**
The process of collecting systematic information about applicants and using that information to decide which applicants to hire.

**Selection** is the process of collecting systematic information about applicants and using that information to decide which applicants to hire. The major purpose of the various devices of selection—application form, interviews, testing, and reference checking—is to gather information about the applicants' job-related skills. A very important principle used in developing selection devices is that the content of the questions should reflect the activities of the job to be filled.

### The Application

Traditional application forms ask information about educational and work history, avocational interests, and honors. However, such forms have limitations. In the

**TABLE 14.2**

## Job Behavior–Based Interview Questions for Selection of Managers

*Interview Questions*

1. Describe a situation in which you had to convince another person to change his or her opinion about how to perform a task. What arguments did you use? What points did the other person bring up? How did you respond to these?
2. Describe a situation in which you had to tell an individual that he or she had performed a task incorrectly. What did you tell the person? What did the person say in response? How did you end the conversation?
3. You are scheduled to attend a training session tomorrow. That night you receive a telephone call that a close relative is seriously ill. What do you do?

---

majority of cases, they have limited space, so the applicant can supply only basic information such as the names of schools attended, major, dates of attendance, and previous job titles and dates of employment. Such superficiality of information often does not give the manager sufficient detail to make sound judgments about the applicant's skills and abilities. A second limitation is that a large percentage of respondents falsify the information that they report. Such falsification is easy because often all that is requested is brief information such as job title and major. A company can use one of several devices in addition to or instead of the application form to minimize these limitations.

One device that has been used successfully is a **training and experience form**, which presents a small number, for example five, of the important tasks of the job. The form asks applicants to indicate whether they have ever performed or been trained in each of the activities. If they answer yes, they are then asked to describe briefly how to perform the activity. Thus, the questions relate directly to the major tasks of the job, satisfying the principle that the content of the questions should reflect the activities of the job to be filled. It is also more difficult to falsify answers because it is necessary to have some knowledge of the activity to respond to these questions; inaccurate answers can usually be easily detected.

**training and experience form**
An application device that presents a small number of the important tasks of a job and asks the applicants whether they have ever performed or been trained in each of the activities.

## The Interview

The interview is, perhaps, the most often used selection device. The purpose of the interview is to allow at least one member of the organization to interact with each applicant and assess that applicant's job-related KSAs. As an example, Gates Rubber uses a series of three interviews in its Siloam Springs, Arkansas, plant. The first two are conducted by different human resource representatives and the third by a panel of employees from different parts of the plant. Gates strongly believes that these interviews have helped reduce its annual turnover rate, which is 8 percent versus 100 percent in a comparable plant in town.[3]

Two aspects of the interview format are especially important. First, the interview should be structured, meaning that the interviewer asks the same set of job-related questions of each candidate. This ensures that the interviewer gathers full information from each applicant, and it makes comparisons among applicants easier because they all are evaluated on the same characteristics. The second aspect of format is the nature of the questions. Questions about job-related behaviors have proven to be quite useful. Table 14.2 provides some examples of such questions. The idea behind them is that gathering information about behaviors that

**Critical Thinking Challenge:**
Divide students into pairs. Assign one student the role of interviewer and the other the role of job candidate for an entry-level management position. Using the questions in Table 14.2 have the interviewer poll the applicant. Reverse roles after 15 minutes. Summarize effective answers to the questions.

Will Knecht (left) uses personality testing in hiring employees such as master craftsman Ty Thompson at Wendell August Forge, a small, family-owned firm that crafts metal giftware it sells through direct mail and two retail stores. Knecht also uses personality test results in promoting, training, team forming, and other personnel decisions. Results help him manage the firm's 75 employees, including craftsmen, artists, salespeople, and customer-service people, so each worker can be most productive.

*Source:* © 1994 Scott Goldsmith.

are performed on the job is useful in making selection decisions. The interviewer must evaluate the accuracy or completeness of the response.

Training for interviewers usually is concerned with how to conduct a job interview and how to evaluate applicants. In training for conducting interviews, topics such as legal issues, physical barriers to interaction, guiding the interview, and how to establish rapport with the applicant are important. In training for making evaluations, interviewers can be asked to make decisions about individuals who are role playing applicants. The use of various types of information in making these decisions is then discussed.

## Tests

**ability tests**
Paper-and-pencil quizzes, usually multiple choice, that measure an applicant's knowledge of specific work content or cognitive ability.

**performance or work-sample tests**
Examinations that verify an applicant's ability to perform actual job behaviors identified from a job analysis.

**assessment center tests**
Programs that typically simulate managerial tasks.

**integrity tests**
Tests that measure an applicant's attitudes and opinions about dysfunctional behaviors such as theft, sabotage, physical abuse, and substance abuse.

**personality inventories**
Programs that measure the thoughts, feelings, and behaviors that define an individual and determine that person's pattern of interaction with the environment.

Many organizations use tests during the selection process to identify those applicants who have the specific KSAs needed for the available positions. Human resource managers can use many kinds of tests. The most common are the following:

- **Ability tests** are paper-and-pencil quizzes, usually multiple choice, that measure an applicant's knowledge of specific work content or cognitive ability.

- **Performance or work-sample tests** verify an applicant's ability to perform actual job behaviors identified from a job analysis. Perhaps the oldest example is a typing test.

- **Assessment center tests** are programs that typically simulate managerial tasks. One of the most often used simulations is the *In-Basket*, which simulates 20 to 30 office memos, complete with an organizational chart and relevant company policy statements.

- **Integrity tests** measure an applicant's attitudes and opinions about dysfunctional behaviors such as theft, sabotage, physical abuse, and substance abuse. Companies generally use paper-and-pencil, multiple-choice tests that ask about the applicant's thoughts and reactions to a number of illegal or unethical situations.

- **Personality inventories** measure the thoughts, feelings, and behaviors that define an individual and determine that person's pattern of interaction with the environment. Two general types of personality tests have been used in selection. One is a multiple-choice questionnaire. The second type of personality test is the projective test, which asks an applicant to write a story about ambiguous pictures or to finish partially completed sentences.

• **Physical examinations** test individuals for placement in manually and physically demanding jobs. The Americans with Disabilities Act of 1990 states that physical exams can be given only after an offer for employment has been made to the individual. This also applies to testing for the AIDS virus.

**physical examinations**
Tests that qualify an individual's placement in manually and physically demanding jobs.

There is much evidence that tests can significantly improve selection decisions. Franciscan Health System of Dayton recently found that a three-test battery reduced turnover and increased productivity, resulting in annual savings of more than $300,000.[4] Similarly, Burger King Corp. estimated that selection tests have resulted in a savings of $2 to $3 million per year.[5]

## Reference Checks

A company considering hiring a particular applicant often contacts previous employers or others who know him or her well to verify the information previously obtained. Reference checks can be handled in three ways. The first, and most often used, is through telephone conversations, in which previous supervisors of the applicant are contacted. Other ways include in-person visits and mail inquiries. The organization may also obtain reference information from investigative agencies, credit bureaus, and public documents.

While checking references is popular among managers, there is very little evidence to support its use in selection. There are, in fact, a number of reasons why this information would not be useful. First, when an applicant names an individual as a reference, the company assumes that the reference meets a number of criteria: that the reference has observed the applicant in situations similar to those of the job being filled, is competent to make an evaluation, wishes to give frank and honest statements, and is able to express himself or herself adequately. Obviously, many references do not meet these requirements. This is especially true for references supplied by the applicant, which are usually chosen because of prior favorable interaction and anticipation of a positive recommendation.

Another issue is the possibility of legal action being brought by the applicant against a reference who makes negative comments. If the reference provides opinions that are not substantiated by official records, a charge of defamation of character is possible. In the case of True v. Ladner, for example, True, a high school teacher, won a libel and slander suit against Ladner, the school superintendent, after Ladner told a prospective employer that True was not a good mathematics teacher, was more concerned with living up to his contract than going the extra mile, and was not able to "turn students on." The jury found that Ladner's reference statements were given with "reckless disregard of their truth or falsity."[6]

For all these reasons, when asked to supply a reference, many human resource departments will only verify factual data of employment, such as dates and job title, and organizations often inform employees of such policies in the event they are asked directly for business references for present or former associates.

## ORIENTATION AND TRAINING

Once the firm has chosen the best applicants and offers have been accepted, new hires must be oriented to the organization and trained to do their jobs.

Lazarus Department Stores uses touch-screen multimedia training for new-hire orientation and point-of-sale (POS) instruction. The training program first orients new sales and support employees to the company's philosophy and mission; history; organizational structure, policies, and procedures; sales and service concepts; and customer service expectations. In the POS portion of the program, new hires use a replica POS keyboard to simulate actual sales transactions. Multimedia training gives Lazarus a consistent orientation and training format across all its stores in Ohio, West Virginia, Indiana, Kentucky, and Pennsylvania.

*Source:* Courtesy of Lazarus Department Stores; Deborah Friedman, Director, Federated Corporate Training.

## Orientation

**orientation**

The process of familiarizing newly hired employees with fellow workers, company procedures, and the physical properties of the organization.

**Teaching Note:** Because many of your students will have work experience, call on various students to share their orientation experiences with the class. What typical steps are included in most orientations? Which ones are unique to the job or industry?

**Orientation** is the process of familiarizing newly hired employees with fellow workers, company procedures, and the physical properties of the organization. Orientation generally includes a tour of the buildings; introductions to supervisors, coworkers, and subordinates; and distribution of manuals describing the firm's policy on vacations, absenteeism, lunch breaks, company benefits, and so on. Many companies now show videotapes featuring procedures, facilities, and key personnel to facilitate orientation.

Many companies regard orientation to be a valuable socialization device. For example, The Walt Disney Company considers the most important day of training to be Day 1—attending the seminars entitled *Traditions I.* This initial orientation program is "… where pride in the company is developed."[7]

## Training

**training**

The process of instructing employees in their job tasks and socializing them into the organization's values, attitudes, and other aspects of its culture.

**Training** is the process of instructing employees in their job tasks as well as socializing them into the organization's values, attitudes, and other aspects of its culture. There are several reasons why training is an important human resource program. First, as we have already mentioned, it develops new employees' job skills and attitudes. Second, because jobs frequently change in organizations, especially those in which technology plays a large role, employees are frequently in need of additional training even if they remain in the same position. For example, during the 1980s almost every secretary had to learn how to use a personal computer and at least one word-processing program to continue in the same job. Third, as successful individuals move up to different positions, they need training to learn requisite new tasks. For example, when nonmanagers are promoted to managerial positions, they need to master many of the topics presented in this book as part of their formal training programs. Fourth, the current organizational trend to downsize and reduce managerial layers has shifted many of the survivors to new positions, often increasing the range of tasks and requiring additional training.

The steps in training are straightforward. First, the trainer determines the employee's needs, then develops a training program to meet these needs. Finally, the trainer performs an evaluation to determine if the training was successful. These steps were used by Magnavox in the training program described in the opening vignette for this chapter.

### Training Needs.

There are two basic ways of identifying training needs. For new employees or employees moving to new positions, the job analysis is the place to start because it states the job's tasks and KSAs. Training programs are developed to teach these. For example, the job of a bank loan officer may require knowledge of the bank's loan procedures, of how to interview loan applicants to acquire all necessary information, and of how to analyze applicants' financial information to determine their loan risk. These activities become the subject of the training program.

To determine training needs for employees who remain in the same job, it is necessary to know whether there are any substantial changes in the job and/or if the employee's job performance has declined. Changes in the job are always accompanied by new tasks, which frequently require at least minimal initial training. However, if job performance is significantly lower than before the change, extensive training may be required.

After assessing training needs, the trainer develops a detailed statement of what knowledge and skills are required and what specific objectives should be attained. For example, in training the loan officer, suitable training objectives might be (a) to know the tax laws concerning the purchase, holding, and resale of municipal tax-free bonds and (b) to be able to gather, through the interview and the application form, all information concerning an applicant's financial status. The statement of such objectives is important because they define what should be included in the training program.

### Developing the Training Program.

A number of techniques are used in training. One group of training methods includes variations of **on-the-job training**, in which the employee learns the job tasks while actually performing the job. In such cases, the manager or an experienced worker conducts the training. For example, a new Pizza Hut store employee may learn how to prepare and cook pizzas by watching and then assisting an experienced cook. Frequent difficulties with this type of training are that trainers may not be well versed in how to teach, and they must continue to do their own jobs while they train the new employee. As a result, the employee often has to learn through trial and error or by carefully observing others. Also, if a particular situation does not arise during the training period, the trainee will be unprepared for this situation when it occurs on the job.

Another group of methods involves off-job educational programs conducted by outside individuals hired by the company. Often these individuals are experienced instructors who have a wide variety of materials they can use in training. However, it is sometimes difficult for the employee to translate the instruction directly into job actions because the nature of the learning situation is different from the work situation. On the other hand, Bell Helicopter Textron recently demonstrated that this type of training can be successful. It developed three-month programs to prepare 240 high-school graduates who were applicants for work in either structural aircraft assembly or electrical aircraft assembly. Ninety-five percent of these trainees were hired.[8]

A third group of methods makes use of computer instruction. As computers become more powerful and less expensive, it is likely that they will become increasingly essential to training. Many different job skills can be taught through

**on-the-job training**
A technique in which the employee learns the job tasks while actually performing the job.

**Example:** Training was an important factor in BMW's new plant in Spartanburg, South Carolina. BMW contracted out training efforts. Through exposure to instructors using the latest technologies like robotics and state-of-the-art electronics, employees are able to increase their flexibility on the job. Additional team training, held in Germany and the United States, prepares employees to react quickly to changes in production.

computers. Job knowledge through the presentation of text material and subsequent testing is commonplace. Canada's Hudson's Bay Co., for example, uses a computer-based course to train sales associates. The company thinks that its system can deliver content in 30 percent less time than classroom instruction and cover many more sales situations.[9] Recently 3-D simulations have been developed to instruct workers in how to operate machinery, and both airline pilots and surgeons have been trained with such simulations.

There are a number of training methods that are used primarily for training managers. Among the most frequent are:

- *Coaching*—Senior managers help guide the decisions and actions of new managers. For example, the senior manager may provide advice about how to conduct a disciplinary session. Such senior managers are sometimes referred to as mentors.

- *Committee assignments*—Organizations assign inexperienced managers to either a permanent committee or a single-project committee. The inexperienced manager interacts with others and benefits by observing how successful managers plan, organize, and direct the project.

- *Job rotation*—Companies often have a specified plan of assignments for new managers that includes jobs in various parts of the organization or department. The purpose of such training is to have the manager develop a broad knowledge of the work operations. The "Going Global" box discusses how Colgate-Palmolive uses job rotation in its efforts to train employees to function effectively in a global marketplace.

- *Role playing*—Managers demonstrate how they would carry out a specific activity in the presence of others. For example, the manager might be asked to conduct a performance appraisal of an employee who has specific, deficient areas of job performance. In role playing, the "employee" is also a manager going through the training.

- *Case study*—The manager reads written descriptions of events in an organization and must make decisions about what to do next. For example, the description may be of the initiation and administration of a TQM program. Based on the presented information, the manager makes specific statements about such actions as training.

**Example:** In many organizations committee leadership positions are increasing in importance. They are ways for employees to get management experience as well as mechanisms to groom employees for future advanced managerial positions.

### Evaluation of Results of Training.

Managers often assume that exposing employees to training means that they have learned the material and can effectively perform the job. However, training should be directly measured to determine how well employees have, in fact, learned the material. If any deficiencies are apparent, training can be repeated. One method of evaluation is to ask employees what they thought about the training, such as whether the instructor was competent and what they think they learned. However, this has limited value because the answers may simply indicate the instructor's ability to interact with the trainees.

A better method is to give a formal test at the end of training. This could be a written questionnaire based on knowledge, or a demonstration performance of what was covered in training. Usually the instructor grades the trainees on these tests. This information can provide a very good basis for judging an individual's readiness to perform the job. A third method is to have the supervisor appraise the employee's performance shortly after the completion of training. This can also be useful in identifying job tasks for which further training is needed.

## COLGATE-PALMOLIVE GLOBALIZES ITS HUMAN RESOURCE PROGRAM

While the globalization of the marketplace has generally afforded companies more opportunity for growth and profitability, its impact on human resource programs has provided definite challenges. Recruiting and selection practices, in particular, have undergone major changes. New decisions, complicated by the size and scope of the business, must be made, such as: How will overseas operations be staffed? When is it most effective to rely on expatriates vs. local nationals? Who is the best to send abroad? What personal and professional qualities lead to success? What about the host country employees? And, how do corporations develop a team of global managers?

Companies such as Colgate-Palmolive have been active in the global marketplace for decades. However, it wasn't until the early 1990s that Colgate designed a global human resource strategy that directly affects staffing. "Global competencies are the centerpiece of the HR strategy," says Brian Smith, Colgate's director of global staffing and HR strategy. "They're grounded in business needs."

Colgate-Palmolive's global competencies have three major components. First there is a technical/functional focus which includes acquiring the necessary skills to be proficient in working with technological resources, consumer insight, and creative excellence. The second competency area is managerial/planning, where presentation skills, planning from a global perspective, and local execution are driving forces. Here communication becomes critical. Finally, the individual may move into the leadership/strategic focus, emphasizing strategy, vision, teamwork, and long-term planning.

Colgate's Global Marketing Program is another example of the company's commitment to recruiting and staffing globally. The program takes approximately 15 high-potential recent MBA graduates and rotates them through various departments for 18 to 24 months. Recruits learn about the sales process, experience the global business development group, and get exposed to manufacturing and technology. After their stint at company headquarters, they're deployed overseas. "The whole objective of the program is to generate that international cadre of management to run the business," says Smith. "These are the future leaders of the company." The rotation of individuals early in their careers helps people learn quickly whether they can handle this kind of duty. If they can, it is not unusual for someone to move functionally from finance to marketing to human resource management, and

physically from continent to continent before returning to New York headquarters several years later.

The Global Marketing Program is a powerful recruiting tool. More than 15,000 people line up for the slots every year. Typically, participants have master's degrees, speak at least one foreign language, and, either through past experiences or personal travels, demonstrate an interest in living abroad. As the company looks to move these individuals up the global ladder, it examines three general criteria: to what extent the person has developed functional competencies, how sensitive he or she is to diverse cultures, and the range of his or her personal experiences of living abroad.

About half the company's marketing recruitment is through this program, which does not target just U.S. nationals but attracts candidates worldwide. Also, high-potential workers early in their careers are encouraged to participate in the program.

*Source:* Charlene Marmer Solomon, "Staff Selection Impacts Global Success," *Personnel Journal* 73 (January 1994): 88–101.

## APPRAISING PERFORMANCE

**Performance appraisal** is a formal measurement of the quantity and quality of an employee's work within a specific period of time. Usually, performance appraisal occurs once, or at most, twice a year. There are several methods of performance appraisal, which differ in what aspects of performance are measured and how the measurement is made.

**performance appraisal**
A formal measurement of the quantity and quality of an employee's work within a specific period of time.

## Objective Measures

Objective performance measures count tangible products of work performance. These could be measures of quantity—such as the dollar amount of sales or the number of garments sewn—or quality—such as the amount of scrap or the number of defect-free garments. For example, bank loan officers are evaluated on the dollar amounts of loans or the time required to process loan applications. Professional athletes are appraised variously on batting average, tackles made, points served, and minutes played.

Many organizations prefer objective measures because they appear to be unbiased, direct gauges of work performance. This is not always true, however. One reason is that these measures are influenced by environmental conditions. Sales volume, for example, may be affected by the number of competitors, the economy, and the size of the territory. Not all salespersons are comparable in regard to these factors, so comparisons are not quite equitable. Another limitation of objective measures is that they cannot always describe all aspects of the job. For example, it is difficult and expensive to obtain measures of customer service, such as by contacting customers and asking their opinions as to how well employees have interacted with them. Equipment maintenance is another measure that is often difficult to gather. Thus, using objective measures exclusively often means that only part of the job is appraised. Moreover, very often this results in workers devoting most of their time to the parts of their jobs that are measurable and virtually ignoring the other parts.

## Subjective Measures

Subjective measures are judgments about how an employee is performing. Generally, the supervisor is the one who makes such judgments, although in some instances, they may be gathered from coworkers and subordinates as well. Judgments can be made about either workers' traits or workers' behaviors, as shown in Table 14.3.

**trait appraisal**
A subjective evaluation of an employee's personal characteristics such as attitude, motivation, cooperation, and dependability.

**Trait Appraisals.**   A **trait appraisal** evaluates an employee's personal characteristics such as attitude, motivation, cooperation, and dependability. Although companies commonly use these measures, they are problematic and not generally recommended as performance measures because they do not directly affect job activities.

One of the main difficulties with using trait appraisal is that there are no clear definitions of many traits. For example, some managers may define "cooperative" in terms of whether the employee assists fellow workers in completing work assignments. Other managers may define the trait as how willingly the employee does what the manager tells him or her to do. If traits are not clearly defined, managers find it difficult to utilize trait appraisal simply because they are not certain as to what to evaluate.

**behavior-based appraisal**
A subjective evaluation of the way an employee performs job tasks.

**Behavior-Based Appraisals.**   A second type of subjective measure, **behavior-based appraisal**, evaluates how the employee performs job tasks. The items used in this appraisal must come from the job analysis. Table 14.3 lists examples of three types of behaviors used by a technical service firm in appraising its managers. These behavior appraisals were developed by teams of both managers and nonmanagers.[10] Notice that the dimensions to be evaluated are described in terms

**TABLE 14.3**

**Trait- and Behavior-Based Dimensions of Performance Appraisals**

*Trait-Based Appraisals*

Evaluate the employee on each of the following characteristics:
    Cooperation
    Attitude
    Enthusiasm
    Job knowledge
    Motivation
    Dependability

*Behavior-Based Appraisals*

1. *Directing*. Provides clear and timely instructions on specific assignments and responsibilities; is accessible to staff and allows ample time to answer questions; provides necessary guidance on other resources; reviews work on a timely basis; provides regular performance feedback to the project team.
2. *Scheduling/Controlling*. Understands and prepares plans to meet customer needs and expectations; accurately defines scope of project, having clear end-products and tasks; develops workable budgets using input from others; communicates project progress; controls budget and resources; promptly identifies any change in scope to customer.
3. *Customer Communications*. Establishes rapport with customer; develops logical report outlines; composes clear written presentations; delivers persuasive oral presentations; identifies potential problems or sources of conflict promptly and brings to a successful resolution.

*Source:* Sandra O'Neal and Madonna Palladino, "Revamp Ineffective Performance Management," *Personnel Journal* 11 (February 1992): 93–102.

of either activities or results. The complete appraisal form contains behaviors necessary for project management, business development, customer satisfaction, and financial performance.

## Advantages and Disadvantages of Subjective Measures.

Subjective performance measures provide several advantages. First, they can permit the supervisor to judge all aspects of the employee's work. Even those aspects that do not result in a finished product, such as the job task, "providing information to answer customers' questions about various bank services," can be evaluated by a supervisor who monitors the interactions between the receptionist and the bank's customers. Secondly, the evaluation of job behaviors makes it much easier to identify deficient performance and to determine specific methods of correcting deficiencies.

The disadvantages of the use of subjective performance appraisal generally relate to the errors that supervisors may make in judging performance. For example, *leniency errors* refer to rating all employees very highly; *severity errors* result in rating all employees very low; and *central tendency errors* result in all employees being rated as average. A *halo error* occurs when the supervisor judges that, because an employee is performing very well in one job behavior, he or she is performing well in others and evaluates the employee highly in all aspects even if this is not the case. However, these errors generally can be overcome through training.

**Teaching Note:** Using the trait-based appraisal characteristics listed in Table 14.3, have student groups list ways to objectively measure cooperation, attitude, enthusiasm, knowledge, motivation, and dependability. Discuss ways to limit the subjectivity of these appraisals.

**Teaching Note:** Invite a representative from the human resources department of your university to address your class on the employee evaluation techniques used. Ask the manager to focus on the types and frequency of the performance measurements and appraisals used.

---

## BUSINESS DILEMMA

*You're the Manager ... What Would You Do?*

THE COMPANY: **Turner Industries**

YOUR POSITION: **Human Resource Manager**

THE PLACE: **Jackson, Mississippi**

Turner Industries, a family-operated carpeting manufacturer, was started 49 years ago just outside Jackson, Mississippi. Today, the company is the third largest producer of carpeting in the United States. With revenue over $1 billion, Turner employs over 6,000 workers at this now-massive facility.

Five years ago, Turner developed an "Employee Initiative" program to instill commitment to customer satisfaction throughout the company. The company's employees play a vital role in this program. A flat organizational structure gives employees, working in self-managed teams, significant authority and autonomy. Production work teams can undertake training, schedule work, and determine individual performance objectives. Any production process can be halted if an employee believes that quality is suffering or safety is jeopardized.

Teams form the core of Turner's quality-improvement efforts. The company formed 25 "Proactive Teams" to address specific manufacturing and production challenges. In addition, select teams work on ways to enhance the relationship between Turner and its suppliers. The teams, in general, respond to customers' comments, work on developing new products, and create activities that bring employees together in social situations (sporting activities, picnics, and fund-raising efforts for employee-supported charities). With diverse opportunities to affect the company, the teams demonstrate a fundamental commitment to customer satisfaction—even creating marketing opportunities that generate additional revenue.

Management and motivation of the work force require special care on the part of Turner's management. Training and recognition is key. In a single year, the company invests $1,600 per employee in training. Recognition comes in the form of participation in teams, leadership opportunities, and interaction with top management.

Turner's efforts at improving its management and human resource practices have allowed it to reduce the number of managers; lower its overall defect rate; and increase quality, efficiency, and customer satisfaction. Revenues have increased significantly over the last four years. As a result of the focus on employees' and customers' needs, Turner has won over 20 quality awards and was voted the outstanding employer in the South in a regional competition. The company has been written about in the *Top 200 Employers in the U.S.*, and its efforts to involve employees in determining the firm's direction have been very successful, enhancing customer satisfaction and improving business performance.

### Questions

1. As human resource manager, what employee characteristics might be used in the selection of team members?
2. How might performance appraisal be done? Can team members be involved in the review of other members?
3. Identify training needs at Turner. Do you believe a company can spend too much money training employees? Why?

---

**Comment on Box:** As you discuss the program implemented by Turner, remind students of the advantages of teams. Also, ask them to recall job enlargement and the benefits of supervising themselves. Are there any tasks that should not be delegated to teams? Discuss.

**compensation system**
The basis on which an organization gives money, goods, or services to its employees in exchange for their work.

For example, the Forest Division of Temple-Inland Forest Products Corporation trained both managers and subordinates extensively before it introduced a new performance-based appraisal and compensation system. The result was that in the first year of operation the appraisal system was favorably received by all employees.[11]

## COMPENSATING EMPLOYEES

A **compensation system** is the basis on which an organization gives money, goods, or services to its employees in exchange for their work. This system is important to an organization because it serves to attract, motivate, and retain employees. If properly designed and implemented, a compensation system can help a firm reach its strategic goals and serve as a competitive advantage relative to other firms in the same industry. It can also help to motivate employees to perform at their highest levels. This was demonstrated by the city of Englewood, Colorado, which changed its compensation system to reward employees who have mastered skills and abilities and who have demonstrated performance and achieved specific goals. Since the city implemented the new system, the number of employees seeking added responsibility has increased, as has the number passing state certifications and attending educational programs.[12] These behaviors are not common in those governments in which compensation is based mainly on seniority.

## Determining Compensation

To set up a compensation system, a company must gather two sets of data. For one, it must determine, through wage and salary surveys, what comparable organizations pay some specific jobs. Second, by using a job evaluation method, the organization must determine the worth of each job to the organization itself. Individual employees are then paid according to the worth of the job to the organization, how much comparable firms pay the same job, and how well or how long they have done that job.

### The Wage and Salary Survey.
A **wage and salary survey** tells the company how much compensation comparable firms are paying for specific jobs that the firms have in common. For example, a small manufacturing firm in Seattle that recruits its work force from the Seattle metro area may exchange information on a regular basis through wage and salary surveys with other firms—usually in the same industry—that employ workers with the same skills and are within geographic regions that would allow employees to relocate or commute.

The wage and salary survey gathers information about key jobs—that is, jobs that are stable over time, are similar among the companies participating in the survey, and are at various levels in the organization. Although questions used in wage and salary surveys vary, they usually ask about direct wages, benefits, other forms of compensation, regular hours worked, and number of overtime hours. As a result of this survey, participating firms obtain data about pay in their relevant labor markets which they can use to determine compensation for their own employees.

**wage and salary survey**
A study that tells the company how much compensation is paid by comparable firms for specific jobs the firms have in common.

### Job Evaluation Methods.
A major principle in setting up a compensation system is that jobs, rather than the individuals who work in the jobs, are the primary basis for compensation. Some jobs, such as that of a vice president, are more valuable to the company than others and therefore are compensated at higher levels. **Job evaluation methods** determine the value of an organization's jobs and arrange these jobs in order of pay according to their value.

Although there are many job evaluation methods, the three most often used are ranking, the point method, and the job grading method. Ranking, used mainly in small companies, involves a committee of managers and compensation specialists reviewing the information gathered from job analyses and ranking each job according to its overall worth or criticalness to the company. The point method evaluates jobs quantitatively, assigning points to jobs depending on how much of certain factors a job requires. For example, jobs may be assigned 50, 100, or 150 points depending on how much education is necessary to do the work. The points a job is assigned indicate its worth to the organization. The job grading method, used primarily by governments, groups all jobs into grades depending on the complexity of the job duties. Grades with more complex job duties are more highly compensated than grades with less complex job duties.

**job evaluation methods**
Techniques that determine the value of an organization's jobs and arrange these jobs in order of pay according to their value.

In most compensation systems, similar jobs are grouped together and treated similarly in terms of compensation. For example, in the job grading method, all jobs within the same grade receive similar compensation. In the point method, all jobs with similar points receive the same compensation. For example, in the point system, the jobs of research technician and computer specialist may be placed in a job group that has a pay range of $25,000 to $35,000 a year.

**Compensation for Individuals.**    The pay range for a group of jobs defines the upper and lower limits of how much every employee who has one of those jobs can earn. In our previous example, all research technicians and computer specialists would earn between $25,000 and $35,000. The compensation within this range for any one employee usually depends on either seniority or performance. Seniority is the basis for differential pay in most government and unionized systems. Those individuals in a job grade who have more tenure usually earn more than those individuals with less tenure. Many private companies, however, try to use performance as the basis for differential pay by giving larger raises to those who receive higher performance appraisals.

A third way of paying individuals differently is skill-based pay plans, which have been introduced by both public and private institutions. Essentially, skill-based pay links jobs together into hierarchies of related but increasingly difficult tasks. As a worker learns to perform more tasks, compensation increases. Procter & Gamble has such plans in 30 plants, and Polaroid is becoming the first corporation to pay almost all employees with this system.[13]

## Benefits

Among the fastest-rising costs in organizations are those associated with benefits for employees. In the 1940s, benefits accounted for approximately 5 percent of the compensation given to employees. By 1990, the cost of benefits was approximately 40 percent of compensation. Although benefits vary among organizations, the major categories are mandatory protection programs, pay for time not worked, optional protection programs, and private retirement plans.

**Mandatory Protection Programs.**    Mandatory protection programs are those required by federal law. For many employers, Social Security is the most expensive benefit. In 1994, employee and employer each contributed 7.65 percent of each employee's earnings. Of this percentage, 1.45 percent goes toward Medicare, and 6.20 percent to old-age survivors and disability. The 6.20 percent applies to the first $60,600 of earned income, and the 1.45 percent to all earned income. A related benefit is unemployment compensation, which is funded by employers through a tax on a portion of the total compensation of a company's employees. A third mandatory benefit is workers' compensation, which provides prompt benefits for workers who are injured on the job regardless of fault.

**Critical Thinking Challenge:** Have students interview a local manager and gather information on holidays, vacation, sick leave, and personal leave policies. Discuss the range of pay for time not worked. What unique or creative benefits (family leave time, personal holidays, birthday pay, etc.) were discovered?

**Pay for Time Not Worked.**    This benefit includes pay given employees for holidays, vacation, sick leave, and personal leave. This can total up to 45 days per year, depending on the organization's policies.

**Optional Protection Programs.**    Optional protection plans are benefits not mandated by law but offered to make the organization competitive in the labor market.

A major program is health insurance. The features of such programs vary widely among employers, such as the amount paid by the employee, the limits of coverage, and the extent of inclusion of dental services and mental health care. Employer-provided health-insurance programs may undergo some changes in the next few years as politicians debate changes in the United States's health care delivery system; the nature and extent of those changes continue to be the subject of great political debate. Additionally, companies may elect to offer benefits such as stock-ownership and other profit-sharing plans, wellness or exercise programs, educational assistance, child care, and counseling for drug or alcohol abuse.

**Private Retirement Plans.**    In most cases, employees and employers share the cost of funding pension plans. In rare exceptions, the employer bears the total cost. There are two major types of pension plans:  Under the defined benefit plan, the retirement payment depends on a formula that includes length of service and average income. Under the defined contribution plan, regular contributions are made to an investment fund, with the retirement benefits a function of the value of the investments.

# PROMOTING, TRANSFERRING, AND TERMINATING EMPLOYEES

A major HRM concern is the movement of employees after they have been selected and trained to perform their initial job with the organization. **Promotion** is the advancement of a current employee to a higher-level job within the organization. Generally, the new position is more complex, has more responsibility, and receives more compensation. A **transfer** is the reassignment of a current employee to another job at the same level as the original job. Although the individual may receive more compensation as a result of the transfer, usually the responsibility and complexity of the new job are roughly equal to that of the original one. **Termination** is the separation of an employee from the organization. This process is used by firms when they close facilities, reduce their work force, or respond to continued poor performance.

**promotion**
The advancement of a current employee to a higher-level job within the organization.

**transfer**
The reassignment of a current employee to another job at the same level as the original job.

**termination**
The separation of an employee from the organization.

## Promotions and Transfers

We can think of promotion and transfer as being essentially the same process we discussed previously as selection because the central focus of all three is to match an individual's KSAs to the requirements of a job. There is one important difference, however; the nature of the data collected for transfers and promotions is different from that collected in selection because candidates for promotion or transfer already work for the organization. Consequently, managers can gather data from previous performance appraisals as well as opinions from current and former supervisors, with an emphasis on job activities that are similar to the activities of the new job.

Promotions and transfers that require geographical relocation are more difficult to arrange now than previously because social trends such as two-career couples, single parents with joint child-custody rights, and employees with multigenerational responsibilities present difficulties in physical relocation.[14] As a result, companies are providing services such as career counseling for spouses, legal counseling for child-custody questions, and financial and family counseling in connection with making such a change.

## Termination

There are two major types of termination: for cause and layoffs.

**For-Cause Terminations.**    Termination for cause occurs when an individual's job behavior is unacceptable. For example, an employee may be fired for poor performance or violations of the company's rules and policies. This is a complex activity that is difficult for both the company and the individual.

Well-managed terminations for cause have three distinct stages. Often, particularly in unionized firms, these three stages are part of a formally stated policy. First, the manager notifies the employee, often during the performance appraisal, that his or her work behavior is unacceptable. The manager should discuss specific aspects of performance and describe the deficiencies or problems in detail. The second stage begins with the development of a program to improve the work performance. This may include additional training, regular monitoring of performance by the supervisor, and frequent feedback concerning the quality of work. If performance does not improve even after additional training and feedback, the third stage begins when the company decides that the individual is incapable of performing adequately on the job and that it is in the best interests of both the organization and the individual to terminate the relationship. The manager should record in writing all information from these stages, give a copy to the employee, and place additional copies in the employee's file. This will provide necessary data concerning the poor performance as well as attempts to improve any deficiencies in case the termination is legally contested.

**Example:** When David Sokol and his partner invested in California Energy, a firm selling power to utilities, they found the previous managers had hired so many unnecessary staff members that earnings were only $5 million on revenues of $90 million. Because profits were so far below the industry average, the new management was forced to let 150 people go.

**Layoffs.**    The second type of termination is a reduction-in-force, or layoff, which ends the employment of groups of individuals or, in extreme cases, closes a complete plant or part of the organization. Layoffs are usually attributable to poor economic performance of the organization rather than the performance of the individuals involved. Many firms—IBM, General Dynamics, GM, Apple, Boeing, McDonnell Douglas, and Sears Roebuck—laid off tens of thousands of employees during the 1990s to reduce costs even though those individuals may have performed their jobs very well.

There are a number of specific actions a company can take to reduce its work force. Among them are:

**1.** Attrition—The organization stops recruiting and selecting new employees and allows retirements, voluntary resignations, and individual termination to reduce the number of employees. Usually, this option requires a long time to achieve a large reduction.

**2.** Early retirement programs—The organization offers a variety of incentives for senior employees to retire, such as bonuses and nearly full retirement pay for otherwise unqualified employees.

**3.** Job sharing—Two employees each work part time at a job that would require only one employee on a full-time basis.

**4.** Group dismissal—A group of employees is terminated. This may be a complete office, department, or division. Terminated employees are often, but not necessarily, given severance pay and some assistance in searching for another position.

There are no definite guidelines as to when it is appropriate to use each of these options. To a large extent, the choice depends on the severity of the economic crisis, the expected duration of the crisis, the presence of employee unions, and the relationship between the organization and the employees. Most organizations attempt to use a variety of these options, but usually use group dismissal as a last resort.

Hewlett-Packard provides an example of actions in which it is possible to retain many of the affected employees in other parts of the organization. While the organization as a whole was strong, HP decided to reduce its Loveland, Colorado, facility by 400 employees. With the intention of finding replacement jobs, HP developed a number of programs to redistribute these 400 employees to other facilities. Among the programs were giving these individuals priority in selection, temporary reassignment programs for employees, a draft of employees by other plants, and reclassification to lower-paying jobs.[15]

## Legal Aspects of Termination

There are a number of legal issues that affect organizations' prerogative to terminate employees. Traditionally, the legal principle of *employment-at-will* prevailed, which holds that an employment contract is a legal agreement between free agents in which the government should not interfere, and either party may break the contract at any time. Under strict interpretation of this principle, an organization need not show any evidence or reason to justify termination. Recently, however, a number of factors have served to limit employment-at-will.

Equal employment laws provide protection for a number of demographic groups against disproportionate termination. That is, terminations should not affect larger percentages of these groups than others. Union contracts have given some protection to union members. Often these negotiated agreements between employees and the organization limit the number of individuals who can be terminated during the life of the contract. Also these contracts ensure that a pattern of procedures must be completed by the organization before termination. Wrongful discharge identifies four instances that are exceptions to employment-at-will: (1) the employee was discharged for reasons that contradict a fundamental principle of public policy; (2) there is an expressed or implied guarantee of employment; (3) the employer's conduct violates the concepts of "good faith dealing"; and (4) other conduct interferes with a legitimate employment contract.

# THE LEGAL ENVIRONMENT OF HUMAN RESOURCE MANAGEMENT

Over the last 50 years, regulation of human resource activities has increased in terms of both areas covered and the number of laws passed. Table 14.4 contains a brief description of some of the important laws affecting employment decisions. These are just a few of the many that affect HRM; the list is certainly not complete.

The equal employment opportunity laws are designed to protect individuals from unfair discrimination in employment decisions. Unfair discrimination generally can take two forms: (1) an individual is negatively affected because of a certain demographic characteristic, such as when an applicant is denied a job because she is female, or (2) the demographic group is more negatively affected than other groups, for example, a much smaller percentage of Hispanic applicants is hired than of other groups. The Civil Rights Acts of 1964 and 1991 prohibit employment discrimination on the basis of race, color, religion, national origin, and

**Example:** The National Football League has been criticized for not hiring minorities in management and leadership positions. African-Americans, for example, are represented on teams as players, but not as coaches and managers.

**TABLE 14.4**

## Federal and State Laws That Affect HRM

*Equal Employment Opportunity Laws*

| | |
|---|---|
| Title VII of Civil Rights Act of 1964 & Civil Rights Act of 1991 | Prohibits discrimination based on race, color, religion, sex, national origin. |
| Age Discrimination in Employment Act of 1967 (amended 1978) | Prohibits discrimination against individuals 40–70 years. |
| Americans with Disabilities Act of 1990 | Prohibits discrimination based on physical or mental disabilities. |

*Health and Safety Laws*

| | |
|---|---|
| Occupational Safety and Health Act of 1970 | Establishes safety standards, inspections of workplaces, and citations for violations of standards. |
| Workers' Compensation | Provides for payments to workers due to injury or illness, regardless of fault. Also covers rehabilitation and income loss due to death. |

*Labor-Management Laws*

| | |
|---|---|
| National Labor Relations Act of 1935 | Establishes the right to organize and declares that certain employer actions are unfair labor practices. |
| Labor Management Relations Act of 1947 | Establishes that certain union actions are unfair labor practices, and permits state right-to-work laws that make union membership nonmandatory. |
| Fair Labor Standards Act of 1938 | Establishes a minimum wage, requires overtime pay, and provides standards for child labor. Classifies employees as exempt (executive, administrators, professionals, and outside salespersons) or nonexempt (all others) relative to overtime pay regulations. |

sex. The Age Discrimination in Employment Act of 1967 prohibits age discrimination against individuals between 40 and 70 years of age. This law has had serious implications for companies' termination and selection decisions relative to cost-cutting goals. For example, the U.S. Court of Appeals, Fifth Circuit, affirmed a jury verdict of $3.4 million to a 59-year-old executive of Monarch Paper Co., whom Monarch reduced from assistant vice president to sweeping floors and cleaning the employee cafeteria even though he had routinely received merit raises and performance bonuses for his work.[16] In another case, a U.S. District Court concluded that an employer's refusal to consider job applicants who have extensive experience may unfairly screen out older individuals. In this case, a 63-year-old with 30 years of experience was denied employment partly because it was assumed that he would be too expensive to employ.[17] The Americans with Disabilities Act of 1990 prohibits discrimination against individuals with mental or physical disabilities (including AIDS and alcoholism) that substantially limit one or more life functions.

Another set of laws are devoted to issues of employment health and safety. The Occupational Safety and Health Act of 1970 requires that organizations comply with safety standards and eliminate all hazards that affect health and safety, even if there are no existing standards. The Occupational Safety and Health Administration (OSHA) is the government agency that can set standards, inspect organizations for compliance with these standards, and issue citations for violations. State workers' compensation laws cover a number of issues that result from injury or illness, such as partial payment for income loss from partial or total disability,

c    a    r    e    e    r    s

## Cost of Living and Wonderful Places

As you know, all cities in which you may wind up working after graduation are not alike. Two ratings of cities may provide valuable information when you start your job hunt and make your final decision of where to relocate. The first of these is the City-by-City Index computed by the American Chamber of Commerce Researchers Association. This index compares the cost of living in various cities based on housing, transportation, health care, and various consumer items—but not taxes. The following list provides the ratings of select cities for the first quarter, 1994.

| | |
|---|---|
| Phoenix, AZ | 102.3 |
| Los Angeles, CA | 126.7 |
| Denver, CO | 106.9 |
| Washington, DC | 135.1 |
| Orlando, FL | 99.0 |
| Atlanta, GA | 98.4 |
| Indianapolis, IN | 97.3 |
| New Orleans, LA | 94.4 |
| Baltimore, MD | 106.9 |
| Boston, MA | 142.1 |
| Detroit, MI | 116.6 |
| Minneapolis, MN | 102.5 |
| St. Louis, MO | 96.7 |
| New York, NY | 208.7 |
| Charlotte, NC | 101.6 |
| Cleveland, OH | 109.1 |
| Philadelphia, PA | 127.5 |
| Dallas, TX | 104.4 |
| Norfolk, VA | 100.6 |
| Seattle, WA | 116.2 |

You can use the index to estimate the salaries necessary to live equivalently in two different cities by using this formula:

$$\frac{\text{City 1 Index} \times \text{City 2 Starting Salary}}{\text{City 2 Index}} = \text{Salary in City 1}$$

For example, what salary in Boston would be equivalent to $25,000 in Atlanta?

$$\frac{\text{Boston } 142.1 \times \$25,000}{\text{Atlanta } 98.4} = \$36,102.64$$

Another set of ratings of cities that you might find useful is the *Places Rated Almanac,* which should be available in your college or local library. This book rates every metropolitan area with more than 50,000 people in the United States and Canada, according to quality of life. This rating takes ten factors into account: cost of living, job outlook, housing, transportation, education, health care, crime, the arts, recreation, and climate. Each city is rated on each of these ten and all ratings are combined into one overall evaluation. The top 15 metropolitan areas, in order, are:

1. Cincinnati, OH
2. Seattle-Bellevue-Everett, WA
3. Philadelphia, PA
4. Toronto, ON
5. Pittsburgh, PA
6. Raleigh-Durham-Chapel Hill, NC
7. Washington, DC
8. Indianapolis, IN
9. Salt Lake City-Ogden, UT
10. Louisville, KY
11. Vancouver, BC
12. Atlanta, GA
13. Portland, OR
14. Knoxville, TN
15. Cleveland-Lorain-Elyria, OH

*Source:* Stacey Slaughter Miller, "Cost-of-Living Comparisons," in "Managing Your Career," Special Edition of *National Business Employment Weekly,* Spring/Summer 1994, 31; and David Savageau and Richard Boyer, *Places Rated Almanac* (New York: Prentice Hall Travel, 1993).

medical expenses, rehabilitation expenses, and death benefits. Because payments are funded by both the federal and state governments, the amount of payment differs among states.

Labor laws address union organization and conditions of employment. The National Labor Relations Act of 1935 (Wagner Act) established the right of workers to organize unions and bargain collectively with employers over wages, hours, and terms and conditions of employment. This act also set up the National Labor Relations Board (NLRB), a federal agency empowered to enforce labor-management regulations. The Labor Management Relations Act (Taft-Hartley Act) of 1947 provided further protection to organized labor by prohibiting employers from interfering with organization efforts by either implicit or overt threats, from dominating a union by providing financial assistance, or from discriminating against union members or those who file charges of labor contract violations. Another important law, the Fair Labor Standards Act of 1938, is critical for compensation. Among many items, it establishes a minimum wage and determines which types of employees are entitled to overtime pay.

The challenge for human resource managers is to understand the complex information that comes from laws and court cases and to translate it into HRM practices. Human resource management, then, is understanding both the laws and the decisions of courts as well as using this information to design and monitor HRM programs to ensure that they comply with the law and serve the organization's goals.

## SUMMARY AND REVIEW

- **Discuss the term *human resource management* and its activities.** Human resource management includes those activities that forecast the number and type of employees that the organization will need and then design and implement programs that provide those individuals with necessary skills. The main programs are human resource planning, recruiting, selection, orientation and training, performance appraisal, compensation, promotion, transfer, and termination. To perform these activities, HR managers need to conduct job analyses, which identify (1) the tasks that make up a job; (2) the worker knowledge, skills, and abilities (KSAs) needed to perform the job; (3) the information, equipment, and materials used; and (4) the working conditions.

- **Summarize how managers may plan for human resource needs.** Human resource planning involves forecasting the organization's future demand for employees, forecasting the future supply of employees for the organization, and designing programs to correct the discrepancy between the two forecasts. Quantitative methods of forecasting rely on empirical data, while qualitative methods use experts' opinions and judgment to estimate the appropriate numbers. If the forecast for demand for employees exceeds the supply, the organization must alter its human resource programs of recruitment, selection, and training to increase the number of employees available in the future. If the demand for employees is smaller than the supply, the

organization must set up procedures in order to reduce its number of employees.

- **Specify how organizations may recruit new employees.** Recruiting is the process of attracting potential new employees to the organization. Companies may recruit using internal (job postings within the organization) or external sources (employment agencies, media and broadcasting, brochures and pamphlets, college visits, and word of mouth involving current employees).

- **Explain how companies use application forms, interviews, and tests in selecting new employees.** Application forms, interviews, and tests should be designed so that they employ questions that gather information actually related to the behaviors that comprise the available job.

- **Formulate the information used in designing effective training programs.** Two basic types of information are needed to determine training needs and to design training programs. The first is a description of the tasks and the necessary knowledge, skills, and abilities of the job. The second is information about how well the employee can currently perform the job. This information should be gathered for specific aspects of the job; any part that indicates poor or marginal performance could be the basis on which to develop training programs to correct these deficiencies.

- **Describe the types of performance appraisal.** Two major types of performance appraisal are objective and subjective measures. Objective measures count tangible products of work performance such as dollar amount of sales, the number of garments sewn, or the amount of scrap produced. Subjective measures rely on the opinion of either the supervisor, coworkers, or subordinates to form a judgment about the employee's work performance. Judgments can be made about the worker's traits or specific job behaviors.

- **Explain the purposes of compensation systems and the basic steps in setting up these systems.** Compensation systems attract, motivate, and retain employees. To set up a compensation system, a company must determine what comparable firms pay specific jobs, through wage and salary surveys. Also, the company must determine how much each job should be paid through job evaluation. Individuals are then compensated according to how well or how long they have done that job.

- **Summarize some of the major laws that affect employment decisions.** Among the most important federal laws are the Civil Rights Act of 1964, the Americans with Disabilities Act, the Occupational Safety and Health Act, and the Labor Management Relations Act.

- **Assess an organization's attempts to select, train, and appraise its employees with an improved human resource management program.** You should be able to evaluate the success of the human resource program described in the "Business Dilemma" box, including its ability to select, train, evaluate, and retain employees and give the company a competitive edge.

## Key Terms and Concepts

human resource management (HRM) *394*
job analysis *395*
human resource planning *395*
recruiting *398*
selection *400*
training and experience form *401*
ability tests *402*
performance or work-sample tests *402*

assessment center tests *402*
integrity tests *402*
personality inventories *402*
physical examinations *403*
orientation *404*
training *404*
on-the-job training *405*
performance appraisal *407*
trait appraisal *408*

behavior-based appraisal *408*
compensation system *410*
wage and salary survey *411*
job evaluation methods *411*
promotion *413*
transfer *413*
termination *413*

## Ready Recall

1. What are human resource management programs intended to do for the organization?
2. What information do job analyses provide and why is this information important for HRM programs?
3. What is human resource planning?
4. Define recruitment and the two major sources for recruiting.
5. What is selection? Also, what is meant by a performance test?
6. What is the purpose of training and what are the major steps in training?
7. What purpose does the performance appraisal serve? Describe what is meant by objective and subjective performance measures.
8. What is a compensation system and what purpose does it serve within an organization?
9. What is meant by promotion, transfer, and termination of employees?
10. List some of the laws that affect human resource management. To which HRM programs do laws apply?

## Expand Your Experience

1. Interview a human resource manager who selects both management and nonmanagement employees. Identify the differences in the selection instruments that are used for the two types of positions, including what information about the applicants is sought.
2. Obtain a job description and a performance appraisal form from a human resource manager. Discuss whether the form directly measures essential job behaviors.
3. Interview a human resource manager about the content of a training program in his or her company for entry-level managers. Discuss the completeness of this training program from the perspective of points in the text.

**CASE**

# Levi Strauss & Company

Levi Strauss & Company (LS&CO) has been known as "a great place to work" for years. One reason for its reputation is its Aspiration Statement, developed in 1987, which records the ideals by which every operation, department, and employee is evaluated. The Aspiration Statement is not simply words on paper, according to top management, but it is woven into every aspect of the workplace:

> We all want a Company that our people are proud of and committed to, where all employees have an opportunity to contribute, learn, grow and advance based on merit, not politics or background. We want our people to feel respected, treated fairly, listened to and involved. Above all, we want satisfaction from accomplishments and friendships, balanced personal and professional lives, and to have fun in our endeavors.
>
> When we describe this kind of LS&CO we want in the future, what we are talking about is building on the foundation we have inherited: affirming the best of our Company's traditions, closing gaps that may exist between principles and practices, and updating some of our values to reflect contemporary circumstances.

LS&CO has identified six types of "aspirational" leadership behavior needed to carry out the company's overall mission. Every manager is evaluated on these behaviors; for senior managers, the behaviors are weighted more heavily.

1. **Diversity:** Leadership that values a diverse demographic work force (age, gender, ethnic group, etc.), diversity in experience, and diversity in perspectives.

2. **New Behaviors:** Leadership that exemplifies directness, openness to influence, commitment to the success of others, willingness to acknowledge our own contributions to problems, personal accountability, teamwork, and trust.

3. **Recognition:** Leadership that provides both financial and "psychic" recognition for individuals and teams that contribute to LS&CO's success.

4. **Ethical Management Practices:** Leadership that represents stated standards of ethical behavior, providing clear expectations and enforcing these standards through the corporation.

5. **Communication:** Leadership that is clear about what is expected of workers, providing workers with timely and honest feedback on their performance and career aspirations.

6. **Empowerment:** Authority and responsibility for those closest to products and customers. Managers need to actively push responsibility, trust, and recognition into the organization.

How are these "ideals" integrated into the everyday work lives of LS&CO employees? Instead of top management "set-

ting" HR policies and practices, employees have both the opportunity and responsibility to communicate what they need and to share what they think are good ideas for the future. For instance, during Aspirations training, employees challenged the company to define its commitment to balanced personal and professional lives. A task force promoted by Bob Haas, CEO and great-great-grandnephew of founder Levi Strauss, was created to identify broad issues facing all levels of employees in different parts of the United States. More than 17,000 workers completed a 27-page survey, which resulted in awareness training throughout the firm to communicate management's commitment to creating a comfortable work-and-family environment; flexible work hours; a new time-off-with-pay program (TOPP) to replace separate vacation, sick leave, and floating holiday plans; child-care leave expanded to include leave to care for other family members or significant others; a corporate child-care fund ranging from infant care to after-school programs, based on worker needs; a child-care voucher system for hourly workers in field locations; and expansion of employee-assistance program services in the field.

Besides actively seeking employee input, the human resource staff at LS&CO has an overall guiding philosophy that employee "niches" are important. "One thing I learned a while back is that you really have to pay attention to the little niches," says Reese Smith, director of employee benefits. Whereas most companies design benefits for the majority of employees, LS&CO tries to say "OK, we've made 90 percent of the people happy, but what about the other 10 percent? What about the niches within that 10 percent?" A relevant example is that of providing domestic partner benefits for unmarried couples. After an employee presented Smith with a written proposal on the subject, a consulting firm was contacted, and cost estimates and plans were gathered. Top management then approved the plan. Smith says, "It all boils down to aligning our practice of nondiscrimination with our policy. We say that we don't discriminate because of marital status, so we had to change our practice to coincide with our policy." Now the company offers unmarried couples and their dependents the same medical and dental benefits as those offered to married couples.

Overall, LS&CO has adopted the view that employees are responsible adults. The company has no dress code because it assumes that employees will look professional. If problems arise, it is up to management to coach the person. Trust in the employees' good judgment ties in with the concept of empowerment, one of the six aspirations. For example, TOPP was developed to give employees a choice about how to use their time away from work, and a flextime plan, even for workers in sewing and finishing facilities, allows the employee and manager to figure out what his or her 40-hour week will be.

Recognition comes in two major forms, financial and psychic. LS&CO's total compensation package is designed to include a savings plan (the company matches up to 10 percent of pay), pension, short- and long-term disability, profit-sharing, and a choice of five medical options including dental and vision. The company has about 100 applicants for every open position. The psychic aspect of recognition comes primarily in the form of fun, according to Donna Goya, senior vice president for personnel, who encourages people to explore their fun in different ways including performing plays "poking fun at management programs or policies," or dressing up for Halloween.

But with superior compensation also comes responsibility—lots of it. At Levi's 27 U.S. manufacturing plants, workers participate in a team process called Alternative Manufacturing System (AMS), which ties compensation and incentives to team goals. Under AMS, sewing machine operators sit in a horseshoe configuration that allows them to see what everyone else is doing, where work is piling up, etc. If a backlog occurs, employees decide how to manage the problem. Managers are team leaders who train their own teams, usually composed of 35 workers. Employees get 80 to 150 hours of training in AMS, which includes communication, teamwork, problem identification, brainstorming, and conflict resolution. Production, budgeting, work-flow, and product-mix training is also provided. Under AMS, teams have to solve problems "or the work doesn't get done, and nobody goes home," as one worker explains. Teams can choose their own schedules within the number of hours a facility is open. The result of AMS has been encouraging so far. Plants have had lower inventories, shorter lead times, better quality, decreased absenteeism and turnover, and fewer injuries.

*Source:* Jennifer J. Laabs, "HR's Vital Role at Levi Strauss," *Personnel Journal* 71 (December 1992): 34–46.

## Questions

1. Given LS&CO's apparent success with its HR programs, why don't most companies adopt a similar strategy? (What are basic requirements or resources of an organization in order to do what LS&CO has done?)
2. Envision yourself as a sewing machine operator for LS&CO. What would make you want to remain an employee? Is there anything you would not care for in terms of the policies, practices, or the job itself?
3. Envision yourself as an HR vice president for a company. What are the advantages of actively soliciting employee input and implementing those ideas? What are the disadvantages?

## STRENGTHEN YOUR SKILLS
### Learning to Learn

From a human resource management perspective, the foundation for an individual employee's success, and thus for your organization as well, is that each worker possess the ability of knowing how to learn. With knowledge doubling every two years and change in technology occurring every one and one-fifth years, the skill that is in greatest demand by employers, according to the U.S. Department of Labor, is the ability of employees to learn.

*Once an individual learns how to learn, he or she can achieve competency in all other basic workplace skills. Learning skills are required in order to respond flexibly and quickly to technical and organizational change; to make continuous improvements in quality, efficiency, and speed; and to develop new applications for existing technologies, goods, and services.*[18]

The exercises presented in Part Four (Chapters 14–19) will build on the skill of learning to learn:

*Individuals must be able to demonstrate skill in the cognitive domain by organizing, relating, recalling, and evaluating knowledge; moving from knowing to understanding and applying knowledge; understanding how to think logically, divergently, critically, and intuitively; understanding alternative learning strategies and tools ... [B]ecause learning in applied settings often involves interacting with others, employees must have a complementary set of interpersonal learning skills, including giving and receiving feedback, learning collaboratively, and using others as learning resources.*[19]

Because the six exercises in Part Four build on one another, it is essential that you understand the principles presented in this exercise before the remaining exercises in Part Four will be meaningful for you.

**FIGURE 14.1**

## The Way Things Work in Most Organizations

### Instructions for Square Wheels™ One Exercise[20]

1. Figure 14.1, Square Wheels™ One, illustrates the way things work in most organizations. Using the cognitive skills discussed in the previous quotation, you and the others in your group are to brainstorm for five minutes in completing step 2 of the exercise.

2. Break up into groups of five to seven people. Based upon your collective experiences—jobs you've had, committees or other groups you've been part of, reading about organizations, hearing about others' workplace experiences, etc.—list as many ideas as your group can come up with for these questions:

- Who might be represented by the person at the front?_____

   _____

- Who are the people at the rear of the wagon? _____

   _____

- What might be represented by the wagon itself?_____

   _____

- What is represented by Square Wheels? _____

   _____

- What might be represented by the rope at the front?_____

   _____

- What might be represented by the pushers' hands? _____

   _____

- What might the round wheels represent? _____

   _____

   _____

3. As a class, share the collective knowledge of each group to discuss the meaning of the illustration. The metaphors you develop here will guide you in the rest of the Part Four exercises.

## chapter fifteen

# Building Successful Groups and Teams in Organizations

## Outline

## After reading this chapter, you will be able to:

- Distinguish between the terms *group* and *team*.
- Summarize a general model of group effectiveness, including its primary components.
- Describe the types of groups that exist in organizations.
- Specify five stages of group development.
- Discuss how group size, norms, cohesiveness, and trust affect group performance.
- Determine different roles that members can play in a group.
- Relate some of the problems associated with group functioning.
- Analyze a business's use of teams.

Courtesy of Electronic Data
Systems Corp. (EDS).

# Teamwork Makes EDS an Information Powerhouse

Are teams and teamwork important? Don't ask that question of the folks at Electronic Data Systems (EDS) or they will laugh you out of the building! Management guru Tom Peters describes EDS as the world's largest project organization in the world's zaniest industry: 72,000 smart people in bands of 10 who generate over $7 billion a year in revenues ($8.6 billion in 1993), while working in the information business, or more specifically, the business of extracting, integrating, and applying knowledge. EDS assists client organizations in the development of computer information systems designed to address and solve business problems. The firm's client organizations run the full gamut of types and sizes, including a $712 million contract with the Army, Navy, and Defense Logistics Agency for a "small multi-user computer project." You may have noticed its unique advertisements during the 1994 World Cup Soccer playoffs, depicting its involvement in those games.

EDS consists, at any one time, of hundreds of project teams organized roughly into 38 strategic business units designated according to industry served (transportation, health care, electronics, etc.). In other words, EDS is just a big collection of loosely connected project teams, each containing normally 8 to 12 programmers and systems experts and lasting for a period of 9 to 18 months. What's fascinating about EDS is not so much that it is big and profitable, but that it runs effectively and efficiently with little hierarchy. The key seems to be a lot of informal communication within and between highly empowered, accountable, independent teams.

The EDS organization has a number of interesting characteristics: Its "murky" formal team structure consists of individual performers, subproject team leaders, and formally designated team leaders, all of whom tend to report to one another; promotions and advancement happen informally through team member evolvement; members move on and off teams informally according to project needs, as project managers bid for, negotiate for, and "raid" members from other teams; communications and the spread of knowledge throughout the organization are also very informal; teams epitomize the "close to the customer" concept with team members working physically within the client organizations.

EDS has developed a successful blend of teamwork and team coordination that is the envy of project-oriented organizations in many fields of endeavor.

*Source:* Tom Peters, *Liberation Management: Necessary Disorganization for the Nanosecond Nineties* (New York: Alfred A. Knopf, 1992).

*introduction*

Although EDS is unusual in its size and level of success, it is not so rare in its use of teams. It began using them from its inception 30 years ago, while other organizations have only recently begun to apply their tremendous power. Although a survey of 476 *Fortune* 1000 organizations notes that about 7 percent of the work force is currently organized into self-managed teams, management professor Charles Manz estimates that as much as 40 to 50 percent of the work force may be managing itself through such teams by the turn of the century.[1] Jerry Junkins, CEO of Texas Instruments, says, "No matter what your business, these teams are the wave of the future."[2] Being able to manage in a team environment—and to direct groups in general—has therefore become an important skill for today's managers.

In this chapter, we will examine aspects of group behavior in organizations with an emphasis on understanding how work groups develop and function, what potential pitfalls they can face, and how managers can make groups function more like teams. First, an important distinction should be made between groups and teams.

**Examples:** Scores of service companies like FedEx and EDS have boosted productivity up to 40% by adopting self-managed work teams.

## THE NATURE OF GROUPS AND TEAMS

Although some management experts do not make a distinction between groups and teams, in recent years there has been a gradual shift to an emphasis on teams and managing them to enhance individual and organizational success. Some experts now believe that the highest productivity results occur only when groups become teams. They see the two concepts as conceptually different, with groups being the more general of the two.[3] All teams are groups, but not all groups are teams. Let's take a closer look.

A **group** has traditionally been defined as two or more individuals who communicate with one another, share a collective identity, and have a common goal. Thus, a group can be virtually any size above one, as long as the members engage in some form of communication, maintain that they are a group, and have some common objective, be it weakly or strongly held. The United States Congress is a group, although few would call it a team. A **team** is a "small number of people with complementary skills who are committed to a common purpose, set of performance goals, and approach for which they hold themselves mutually accountable."[4]

**group**
Two or more individuals who communicate with one another, share a collective identity, and have a common goal.

**team**
A small number of people with complementary skills who are committed to a common purpose, set of performance goals, and approach for which they hold themselves mutually accountable.

### Groups versus Teams

Table 15.1 points out some important differences between groups and teams. One major difference revolves around how work gets done. Work groups emphasize individual work products, individual accountability, and even individual-centered leadership. In contrast, work teams share leadership roles, have both individual and mutual accountability, and create collective work products. In other words, a work group's performance is a function of what its members do as individuals, while a team's performance is based on collective products, what two or more workers accomplish jointly. Regardless of the team designation and platitudes of teamwork, the sales force at Gwatney Chevrolet in Memphis is still a group because its members are responsible solely for their own performance, they are managed individually, they are paid for individual performance, and there is minimal, if any, collaboration in serving customers. Because of the nature of the busi-

**Teaching Note:** Ask students to provide examples of groups and teams in which they are involved. Have them compare the differences. For example, they may be in a discussion group on the Internet or in a group related to a hobby.

**TABLE 15.1**

**Differences between Groups and Teams**

| Work Group | Team |
|---|---|
| Has strong, clearly focused leader | Has shared leadership roles |
| Has individual accountability | Has individual and group accountability |
| Has the same purpose as the broader organizational mission | Has a specific purpose that the team itself delivers |
| Creates individual work products | Creates collective work products |
| Runs efficient meetings | Encourages open-ended discussion and active problem-solving meetings |
| Measures its effectiveness indirectly by its effects on others (e.g., financial performance of the business) | Measures performance directly by assessing collective work products |
| Discusses, decides, and delegates | Discusses, decides, and does real work together |

ness, this working group may still be successful without being a real team. Contrast these salespersons to the EDS project teams discussed in the opening vignette, which indeed are teams. They must use their complementary skills in a highly collaborative fashion to solve customer problems. They share leadership and are evaluated almost totally on the final performance of the overall team effort. Without a common purpose, common objectives, and an agreed-upon common approach, they could not be successful, no matter how good they might be as individual performers.

One useful way to picture any work group is the extent to which it functions like a team. If you were to draw continuous lines between items in the left and right columns in Table 15.1, you could then treat the items as continuous dimensions along which groups could vary, from very individualistic groups, such as a company's geographically dispersed salespersons, to collective teams, such as EDS's highly interdependent professionals. Throughout this chapter, we will discuss factors that influence the effectiveness of groups and teams wherever they fit on this continuum.

## Benefits of Teams

So what is all the excitement over teams? In the rapidly changing, highly competitive environment businesses face today, teams contribute to the bottom line in a number of ways.

**1.** *Teams help to motivate workers.* Teams motivate by providing both internal rewards in the form of an enhanced sense of accomplishment for employees as they achieve more, and external rewards in the form of praise and certain perks. At Chrysler Corporation's Newcastle Industrial plant, for instance, team members run many aspects of plant operations including assigning tasks, altering work hours, and confronting slow performers. Over a five-year period, absenteeism dropped from 7 to 2.9 percent and union grievances dropped from more than 1,000 a year to 33 in 1991.[5]

**2.** *Teams can be a major part of the quality effort.* In that same Chrysler plant, defects per million parts dropped from 300 to 20 in three years.[6] Teams

**Example:** Boeing used teams to cut the number of engineering hang-ups on its new 777 passenger jet by more than half.

Teamwork at Unocal helps the company save money. Team members, shown here in a delivery truck, solved a scheduling problem that occurred when service stations weren't ready to receive a shipment of gasoline. By improving communications between dealers, drivers, and the terminal, the cross-functional team is saving the company from $8,000 to $12,000 a month.

*Source:* © Jeff Corwin for UNOCAL.

helped decrease defect rates at Corning's new specialty cellular ceramics plant from 1,800 parts per million to 9 parts per million, and at Volvo Corporation's Kalmar facility by 90 percent.[7]

**3.** *Teams help companies be innovative.* Komatsu, for example, uses off-line project teams to determine creatively how to meet rigorous goals and deadlines.[8] 3M introduced teams into its respirators and safety equipment division to enhance new product development. By 1990, that division was one of 3M's fastest-growing and most innovative divisions.[9]

**4.** *Teams enhance productivity and cut costs.* Shenandoah Life Insurance Companies in Roanoke, Virginia, introduced teams and reduced staff, saving $200,000 per year in salaries and increasing productivity 33 percent. Westinghouse Furniture Systems increased productivity 74 percent in three years by using teams.[10]

**5.** *Teams can enhance worker involvement, information sharing, and perceived task/job significance.* Research comparing traditional workers with those in self-directed work teams, where workers manage the team largely without supervision, found the latter to be higher in all of these dimensions, as well as in innovation.[11]

**Example:** Professor Henry Sims at the Maryland Business School cautions not to use teams when they are not needed and to analyze the work before a team is formed. Does the work require that people interact with each other? Can it be done faster alone? Teams require time and energy to establish. For example, insurance sales reps and long-haul truckers need not work in teams.

In a general sense, teams tend to have and use greater knowledge than individuals, and when working together they create a greater number of approaches to problems than individuals. Furthermore, team participation enhances employee acceptance of, understanding of, and commitment to team goals.[12] Because so much organizational activity occurs in groups, managers need to understand how groups develop and operate if they are to realize these benefits and help their organizations function efficiently and effectively.

## A MODEL OF WORK GROUP EFFECTIVENESS

Figure 15.1 shows that organizational context and group structure and processes interact to influence the effectiveness of work groups and are influenced, in turn, by the groups' results through feedback.[13] Obviously, factors within the organization itself—culture, task design/technology, mission clarity, autonomy, level and type of feedback mechanisms, reward and recognition systems, training and con-

FIGURE 15.1

## Model of Work Group Effectiveness

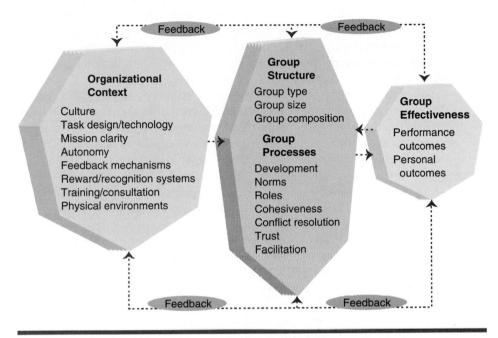

*Source:* Adapted from Eric Sundstrom, Kenneth P. DeMeuse, and David Futrell, "Work Teams: Applications and Effectiveness," *American Psychologist* 45 (February 1990): 120–133.

sultation, and physical environments—will have an influence on the effectiveness of work groups. However, the primary focus of this chapter is factors within the group or team—structure and processes—because we discuss organizational context elsewhere. Still, it is important to see how organizational context influences other group variables.

The factors that influence the effectiveness of work groups most directly are those found within the group or team itself: structure and process. Structural factors include team or group type, size, and composition of skills and abilities. Group processes include stages of development, norms, roles, cohesiveness, and interpersonal processes such as trust development, facilitation, influence, leadership, communications, and conflict resolution.[14]

Effectiveness is demonstrated by performance and personal outcomes. Performance outcomes may be measured by products made, number of ideas generated, customers served, number of defects per thousand items produced, overtime hours, items sold, or customer satisfaction levels. Personal outcome measures include employee satisfaction, commitment, and willingness to stay on the team. Both are important for the long-term viability as well as the short-term success of a team.

## STRUCTURAL INFLUENCES ON GROUP EFFECTIVENESS

The type, size, and composition of groups and teams are structural factors that influence their effectiveness, so we will take a closer look at them now.

## Types of Groups

We can classify groups along a number of dimensions, including how they develop, what parts of the organization they draw their members from, as well as their purpose, duration, and even level of **empowerment**—the extent of their authority and ability to make and implement work decisions. The type of groups an organization develops depends on the tasks it needs to accomplish and other contextual variables already noted. How successfully these groups will function depends on a number of other structural and process characteristics.

Groups may be formal or informal. Most groups or teams with a title or group designation are **formal groups** created by the organization as part of its formal structure and generally having their own formal structure as well. **Informal groups** arise naturally from social interaction and relationships and are usually very loosely organized. A friendship group or a clique is an example of an informal group. A departmental athletic team, although titled, often grows informally out of social relationships. Organizations such as Hewlett-Packard and EDS encourage considerable informal communication throughout their organizations to enhance the dissemination of knowledge.

Groups can also be functional or cross-functional. **Functional groups** (sometimes called command groups), as the name suggests, perform specific organizational functions, with members from several vertical levels of the hierarchy. Accounting, personnel, and purchasing departments are examples of functional groups. **Cross-functional groups** (sometimes called horizontal groups) cut across the firm's hierarchy and are composed of people from different functional areas and possibly even different levels. While functional groups are usually permanent, cross-functional groups are often temporary, lasting for as little as a few months to as long as several years, depending on the group task being performed.

Most groups can also be classified as having one of three purposes: (1) Some groups recommend things, for instance by making suggestions to improve quality; (2) some groups make or do things, such as teams formed for product development; and (3) some groups run things, such as functional groups that conduct business in their area of operations.[15] Obviously the latter two group types would tend to be more autonomous than the first.

Given these general categorizations, we can now examine the nature of some specific kinds of groups and teams: task forces, committees, project teams, product-development teams, quality-assurance teams, and self-directed work teams.

**Task Forces.**    A **task force** is a temporary group of employees responsible for bringing about a particular change. They may be formed within a functional area, but are most frequently cross-functional, temporarily pulling workers from throughout the organization. For example, Mary T. Inc., a 600-person Minneapolis company, formed a task force to implement a smoke-free workplace within an 18-month period.[16] Task force membership is usually a function of someone's expertise rather than hierarchical position.

**Committees.**    A **committee** is usually a permanent formal group that does some specific task; it may be functional or cross-functional. A loan committee in a bank, for instance, may have members from several areas besides the loan department to help provide outside expertise. A grievance committee resolves grievances in a union environment, while a graduate studies committee in a university determines the graduate curriculum. Because committees often make formal deci-

---

**empowerment**
The extent of a group's authority and ability to make and implement work decisions.

**formal groups**
Groups created by the organization that generally have their own formal structure.

**informal groups**
Groups that arise naturally from social interaction and relationships and are usually very loosely organized.

**functional groups**
Groups that perform specific organizational functions, with members from several vertical levels of the hierarchy.

**cross-functional groups**
Groups that cut across the firm's hierarchy and are composed of people from different functional areas and possibly different levels.

Critical Thinking Challenge: Have student teams interview managers from a local organization. What are its formal groups? Informal groups? Which of the groups are cross-functional? Which represent a task force?

**task force**
A temporary group of employees responsible for bringing about a particular change.

**committee**
A permanent formal group that does some specific task; may be either a functional or cross-functional group.

sions, they usually have official members of the formal hierarchy as part of the group, unlike a task force.

### Project Teams.

**Project teams** are similar to task forces, but usually they are responsible for running their operation and are totally in control of a specific work project. They are often cross-functional and almost always temporary, although a large project, such as designing and building a new airplane at Boeing Corporation, may last for years. Project teams, such as those at Boeing or EDS, are often the guts of the organization or the central business function.

**Product-development teams** are a special type of project team formed to devise, design, and implement a new product. Masters Industries Inc., an Arsonia, Ohio, plastic-injection molding company, employs a cross-functional product-development team that consists of the manager of mold building, the manager of quality control, the engineering manager, and the production chief.[17] Sometimes product-development teams exist within a functional area—research and development—but now they more frequently include people from numerous functional areas and may even include customers to help ensure that the end product meets the customers' needs. At EDS, for instance, a client company typically works hand in hand with an existing project team to create a new information system to meet the client's need.

### Quality-Assurance Teams.

**Quality-assurance teams** are generally fairly small groups formed to recommend changes that will positively affect the quality of the organization's products. Quality circles are the most common form of quality-assurance team. Recall from Chapter 7 that quality circles (QCs) are groups of workers brought together from throughout the organization to solve specific quality, productivity, and service problems. Although the "quality circle" term is not as popular as it once was, the quality movement and total quality management are stronger than ever. The use of teams to address quality issues will no doubt continue to increase throughout the business world.

### Self-Directed Work Teams.

A **self-directed work team (SDWT)** "is an intact group of employees who are responsible for a 'whole' work process or segment that delivers a product or service to an internal or external customer."[18] Sometimes called self-managed teams or autonomous work groups, SDWTs are designed to give employees a feeling of "ownership" of a whole job. At Tennessee Eastman, a division of Eastman Kodak Company, teams are responsible for whole product lines, including processing, lab work, and packaging.[19] With shared team responsibility for work outcomes, team members often have broader job assignments and cross-train to master other jobs, permitting greater team flexibility.

The defining characteristic of an SDWT is the extent to which it is empowered by management. At Xerox, for example, empowered teams of plant assembly-line operators can shut down an assembly line, when a severe problem arises, and then solve the problem themselves.[20] Figure 15.2 shows a hypothetical continuum of team empowerment with approximate amount of responsibility/authority shown in increments of 20 percentage points. A team empowered at 20 percent, for instance, might do its own housekeeping, have members who train each other, repair and maintain equipment, and perhaps schedule production. A team takes on additional functions normally reserved for managers, professionals, and other specialists as the level of empowerment increases. For example, a team empowered

**project teams**
Groups similar to task forces, but usually responsible for running an operation and in control of a specific work project.

**product-development teams**
A special type of project team formed to devise, design, and implement a new product.

**Example:** Boeing's 777 project resembles a traditional organizational pyramid, but instead of layers of management, it has three layers of teams. There are over 200 cross-functional teams, each made up of people from various departments including engineering, manufacturing, and finance.

**quality-assurance teams**
Generally small groups formed to recommend changes that will positively affect the quality of the organization's products.

**self-directed work team (SDWT)**
An intact group of employees who are responsible for a *whole* work process or segment that delivers a product or service to an internal or external customer.

**Teaching Note:** If a work team has the authority to make decisions about how the daily work gets done, it's properly described as a self-managed or high-performance team. Common tests for a self-managed team are whether it can change the order of tasks and whether it has budgets.

**FIGURE 15.2**

**Team Empowerment Continuum**

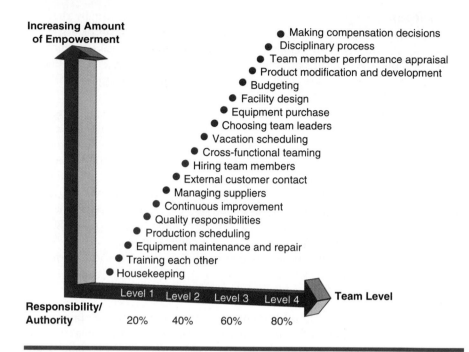

*Source:* Adapted from Richard S. Wellins, William C. Byham, and Jeanne M. Wilson, *Empowered Teams: Creating Self-Directed Work Groups That Improve Quality, Productivity, and Participation* (San Francisco: Jossey-Bass Publishers, 1991), 26.

at 60 percent might also manage suppliers, schedule vacations, hire new employees, choose team leaders, and even be responsible for the purchase of new equipment. Naturally, the functions and their order will vary across organizations and teams. The lack of a 100 percent level indicates that some leadership roles still exist even in the most highly empowered teams.[21] When Frances Hesselbein took over the Girl Scouts, she threw out the organizational chart and developed a circular structure, including a corporate management team to make strategic decisions, although she still maintained her role as a strong facilitator of this team.[22]

We pay special attention here to self-directed work teams because so many organizations today are desperately searching for ways to cut costs and to adjust to changes in our highly competitive and increasingly global marketplace. Work teams hold the promise for meeting these challenges. SDWTs reduce the need for extra layers of management and thus can help control costs. They also provide the flexibility, through facilitation of communications and reduction of bureaucracy, to change rapidly in order to meet the competition or respond to customer needs.

## Size of Groups

Much of the earlier research into group decision making suggested that the ideal group size is about seven. Fewer members might make faster decisions but are less likely to have the optimum mix of skills and abilities. With much larger groups, decisions can get bogged down with too many inputs, or individual contributions are minimized or lost entirely.

Recently, more flexibility is being seen in group size, with as many as 12 members being viewed as a desirable number for most of the types of teams discussed thus far. Johnsonville Foods, a Wisconsin sausage-making firm, has self-managed teams of about a dozen. Titeflex, a Springfield, Massachusetts, manufacturer of fluid and gas holding systems, uses six- to ten-person de facto "small business teams or manufacturing cells" to make its products. Recall that EDS project teams usually have eight to twelve members.[23] Traditional work groups performing fairly routine, repetitive tasks requiring little coordination might function well with only one supervisor for a group of 50 to 75 employees. However, groups of this size tend to break naturally into smaller, informal groups, whether the formal structure dictates such a break or not.

In fact, for most groups trying to function as teams, 20 may be about as many members as the team can use effectively. Motivation may wane as meetings drag on and even the difficulty of finding an adequately sized meeting space makes larger teams less effective. A major problem in larger groups is **free-riding**, the tendency for some individuals to perform at less than their optimum in groups, relying instead on others to carry their share of the workload. Free-riding tends to increase as group size increases.[24]

## Composition of Groups

Regardless of the type or size of a group, none will be successful without the right mix of skills and abilities. Ensuring that group members have the necessary technical skills to perform a job may be one of a manager's or group leader's most important functions. At EDS, project leaders invest considerable time and effort working through both formal and informal channels to attract skilled team members to their teams. The accomplishment of this task is one of the key success factors of team leaders.[25]

In team-oriented work environments, ensuring optimal team composition can be a massive task, and some organizations have put their computers to work to assist in the process. Cypress, a San Jose, California, computer chip maker, has developed a computer system that keeps track of all 1,500 employees as they crisscross between different functions, teams, and projects. Apple's Spider system instantly tells a manager whether an employee is available for a project, what his or her skills are, and where he or she is located in the company.[26] EDS has a similar system, although the project team leaders seem to prefer the informal over the formal system of soliciting members.

Although the right mix of talents is important, in general, the more heterogeneous a group, the better it is likely to be able to solve problems. Groups with diverse membership may take longer to become cohesive, but are likely to be more productive in the long run.

## PROCESS INFLUENCES ON GROUP EFFECTIVENESS

How a team functions once it is formed largely determines its likelihood of success. The most highly talented sports teams must "gel" or they won't be successful. The same holds true for teams in business. Their success depends on how they develop, the norms that evolve in the group, the roles that members perform, and how well they perform a number of important group processes.

**Teaching Note:** Ask students to share experiences about teams and team projects they have worked on. Were there free-riders? How did they work with the dysfunctional group members? How did they evaluate these members' performance?

**free-riding**
The tendency of some individuals to perform at less than their optimum in groups, relying instead on others to carry their share of the workload.

**Example:** Boeing has over 200 work teams that have responsibility for specific parts of its new 777 plane. These work teams are typically cross-functional groups of five to fifteen workers. Examples of teams include a wing team, a flap team, and a tail team.

## BUSINESS DILEMMA

*You're the Manager ...What Would You Do?*

THE COMPANY:   Pass the Pizza

YOUR POSITION:   Director of Operations

THE PLACE:   Madison, WI

The success of home-delivered pizza companies led Jane Jones to open the first Pass the Pizza store in 1988. Pass the Pizza has grown rapidly and now has annual sales of more than $1.5 billion, 1,200 corporate-owned stores, and additional franchise stores. Such success created a need for effective employee training and a system for maintaining quality. Jones maintains that training is the responsibility of each person in the organization. Store managers shoulder the task of making sure their employees are successful by serving as a resource for them.

Promotions at Pass the Pizza are based not only on successes but also on each employee's ability to train someone to take over his or her position. The hourly positions at the store level include order taker, pizza maker, oven tender, router, and driver. Most store managers cross-train their employees to compensate for absences and expected, as well as unexpected, rushes. Pass the Pizza supplements on-the-job training with MTV-style videos demonstrating pizza making and safety, service, and security tips. Employees are well rewarded for their successes and implemented suggestions. Thus, Pass the Pizza gains the benefit of creative ideas, and employees are encouraged to be constructive and independent.

Because Pass the Pizza offers and promotes "the fastest delivery service in town," driver-safety training has become an important focus in the overall training program. Last year, 20 drivers for a major competitor were involved in accidents, and an Indiana teenager was killed while making a delivery for a competitor.

There is growing concern that there has been an overemphasis on performance for employees who work together in self-managed work teams. In the highly competitive home-delivery pizza industry, customers want quality and speedy delivery. The major advantage of getting employees to work together in teams is quick response time. The team's self-regulating nature allows for greater error detection, and, through supportive team relationships, corrections are possible as the order moves through the hands of the hourly employees. On the surface, it appears that the teamwork allows one employee to compensate for another employee's weakness. In the case of Pass the Pizza, top management is concerned that the close, cohesive work teams have achieved high efficiency but not other organizational goals. An overemphasis on speed of delivery may create legal, ethical, and social responsibility concerns and problems for the organization.

### Questions

1. As director of operations, how would you describe the type of groups that exist at Pass the Pizza? What is the relationship between informal or friendship groups and the formal organizational structure?
2. How is the work group utilized at Pass the Pizza to increase product quality, including delivery speed?
3. Discuss the possibility of work groups becoming so internally focused and concerned with efficiency that legal, ethical, or social responsibility issues emerge. What are the legal, ethical, and/or social responsibility issues you face in this situation?

## Stages of Group Development

Groups, like people and even organizations, have life cycles. They are born, they develop, and most, eventually, are terminated. During this progression, groups pass through certain stages, although the stages may vary in duration from one situation to another, and sometimes even the sequence may be changed. Understanding how groups progress can give a manager insight into behaviors needed to help the group function successfully at each stage. Although there are several models of group development, emphasizing different types of behaviors and orientations, one very useful depiction of the process includes five phases: forming, storming, norming, performing, and adjourning.[27] The leader's role is to help facilitate task and social interactions throughout the stages.

**Forming.**   Group members meet for the first time or two in the **forming stage** and become acquainted with each other and familiarize themselves with the group's task. They may "test" others for potential friendships and mutual interests and see how others approach the task at hand. Emerging leadership functions and interdependencies are often a concern here. A formal group leader might encourage some informal interaction among group members at this stage. Many groups start, even within the first minute of group interaction, to form a strategy for addressing the group's task. This strategy often lasts through the first half of the group's allotted time to deal with the task.[28] The manager or team leader can sometimes facilitate this task approach by giving some thought and preliminary work to the task before the group meets, and by withholding the setting of the formal agenda for a period of time.

**forming stage**
The stage when group members meet for the first time or two, become acquainted, and familiarize themselves with the group's task.

**Storming.**   Conflict generally occurs during the **storming stage** as group members begin to assert their roles, jockey for leadership positions, and make known their feelings and thoughts about the task. Some members may challenge the leader's position or show hostility to those with whom they disagree or have personality clashes. Others may psychologically withdraw from the group. Cliques may form and subgroups may argue over task or relationship issues. The group leader should strive to keep everyone involved and communications lines open, thus emphasizing the importance of reasonably sized groups. He or she should also encourage members to manage and resolve conflict constructively rather than allowing it either to escalate or be subdued only to rise again later. If member roles and group norms are not successfully negotiated during the storming stage, then the group may never advance to a more productive level of functioning. It is during this stage that the groundwork for having a true team is laid because interaction patterns start evolving at this time.

**storming stage**
The stage when conflict usually occurs and in which group members begin to assert their roles, jockey for leadership positions, and make known their feelings about a task.

**Example:**  If teams seem to be less than optimal, it may be due to clashing personalities. Robert Baugh, a workplace specialist at the A.F.L.-C.I.O., asks: "How do you get people who have been at each other's throats for years to start to cooperate?"

**Norming.**   Conflicts are largely resolved and harmony ensues during the **norming stage**, sometimes to the detriment of giving full consideration to minority opinions, as we shall see later. In this stage, a sometimes tenuous balance of interpersonal forces is achieved. Members accept their roles, divide work tasks, have largely resolved leadership issues, and mostly share mutual expectations. The leader must promote a balance between maintaining harmony and continuing to strive to achieve the task at hand. The danger for a group at this time is that members may feel good about themselves but not be getting the job done. Most of the time, groups move through this stage fairly quickly.

**norming stage**
The stage when conflicts are largely resolved and harmony ensues.

**Performing.**   A group reaches the **performing stage** when members have reached a level of maturity that facilitates total task involvement. Members concentrate on solving the problem or performing the task, and they listen and provide important inputs and feedback on issues. They are not afraid to offer suggestions, and they help other group members express their opinions. Conflicts at this stage are over legitimate task concerns rather than petty personality or power issues. Issues are confronted, not ignored. Members are clear on the goals of the group and the means for accomplishing the goals. During this stage, the leader should concentrate on task-oriented behaviors, while maintaining relationships through encouragement, reward, and positive communication. Many groups never fully reach the performing stage. Research has found that, in temporary groups with designated time frames, the group starts "performing," or

**performing stage**
The stage in which members have reached a level of maturity that facilitates total task involvement.

Improving the safety of utility work to provide 100 percent fall protection was the central value binding members of Duke Power Company's Fall Protection Team. After a 58-foot fall from a transmission tower paralyzed a Duke Power line technician who was wearing a safety belt, a supervisor investigated the accident and formed a team to find a way to avoid similar accidents. Team members included line technicians and other employees whose jobs required them to climb. Not satisfied with equipment available from national manufacturers, the team worked with national and international equipment firms to develop new safety belts and rewrote the safety procedures.

actually making good progress on the task, at almost exactly the midway time point on the task regardless of how much time is allotted.[29]

**adjourning stage**
The stage in which task forces, project teams, or committees complete their task and disband.

*Critical Thinking Challenge:*
Have students share examples of experiences at the various stages of group development. Most students, even those with little or no work experience, have had to work on class or project teams.

**norms**
Prescriptions for appropriate behavior of group members that help reduce the disruption and chaos that would ensue if group members didn't know how to act.

**Adjourning.**    The **adjourning stage** occurs when task forces, project teams, and committees complete their task and disband. At this stage, heightened emotions and some depression over separation from the group and its members are accompanied by positive feelings associated with task accomplishment. The leader may want to commemorate this stage with a ceremony to recognize not only the group's accomplishments, but also the positive associations and friendships. This emphasis on the positive should help promote future cohesiveness should the team or some of its members be reunited.

## Group Norms

Group **norms** are important because they prescribe appropriate behavior for group members and help reduce the disruption and chaos that would ensue if group members didn't know how to act. Groups enforce norms to facilitate group survival, establish what behavior is expected of group members, help the group avoid embarrassing interpersonal problems, express the central values of the group, and clarify what is distinctive about the group.[30] Norms can influence nearly all aspects of group functioning, from how members carry out a task to how they dress, eat, and talk to the boss.

Norms can be very positive in that they can support the goals, mission, and success of the organization. At EDS, for example, completing all projects on time is a widely accepted norm that helps keep the organization successful. At most Ritz Carlton hotels, a widely held norm is that a customer's problem or request is "owned" by the person who receives it regardless of whose job it might involve. The employee will strive to resolve the problem within ten minutes of receiving it. This norm of customer service makes the Ritz Carlton distinctive among major hotel chains and helps ensure its success.

However, norms can also be negative by encouraging dysfunctional behavior. Occasionally some group members may form a subgroup, called a shadow organization, that has norms contrary to those of the greater group or organization.[31]

For example, workers may establish standards of production far below what is possible or desired by management.

### Levels of Norms.
Norms tend to be of three levels: pivotal, relevant, and peripheral.[32] **Pivotal norms** are critical for success within a group. If a group member rejects a pivotal norm, then his or her stay in the organization is likely to be very limited. When Microsoft founder and CEO Bill Gates meets with a product-development team, he asks some very pointed questions about both the technical and financial aspects of the project. Team leaders and members must be prepared to answer these questions or they may not last long at Microsoft. Thus, being prepared is a pivotal norm at Microsoft.

**Relevant norms** are fairly important, but not as critical as the pivotal norms. It is generally important for a salesperson to be on time for work (relevant norm) but with productivity (pivotal norm) tops in the department, he or she might be able to come in late more often with minimal repercussions.

A **peripheral norm** is one that some people accept, but which is not important for success in an organization. Managers in one engineering company meet every Friday after work for a beer at a nearby pub. Although most show up all the time, some seldom show up and a few never go at all. Status at work is not affected by this peripheral norm.

Of course, what is peripheral in one group may be relevant or pivotal in another. For managerial success in most Japanese organizations, the kind of after-work "schmoozing" the engineers were doing is absolutely essential. At some companies, such as Levi Strauss & Company, mode of dress is peripheral because the norm for even the top executive team is—you guessed it—Levis jeans. At other firms, such as IBM or Procter & Gamble, dress code is more likely to be a relevant norm.

### The Development of Norms.
Figure 15.3 shows four methods through which norms develop over time.[33] One way is through the explicit statements of group leaders. The founder of Mars Candy Co. once brought to a meeting of his top executives a box of stale Mars candy bars he had found at a store. He went around the room, threw a candy bar at each team member, and told them he would hold each of them responsible if he ever found another stale Mars candy bar in a store. However, most explicit statements are not as extreme. For instance, a dean's comment to a faculty member that he stopped by during office hours and did not find him there might be enough to enforce a norm that professors are expected to honor office hours.

A second way norms develop is through some critical event in a group's history. The Mars example above could be one. Another is a common tale about Ray Kroc, the founder of McDonald's. Kroc once ordered the backs of the chairs of McDonald's store managers to be cut off to remind them that their job was to be out in the restaurant managing, not lounging in their offices. A university ethics committee's vote to sanction a faculty member for having an affair with a student sends a message that lasts for years about the values and norms the group holds.

Sometimes the first behavior pattern that emerges in a group sets group expectations for subsequent ones. If, during the first meeting, a team leader cracks a joke and asks for every member's opinion about an issue, then the norms of casual interaction and full participation may be initiated within the team.

The final method through which norms may evolve is through a carryover from past experiences. EDS project team members know most of the team norms

**pivotal norms**
Standards that are critical for group success.

**relevant norms**
Norms that are important, but not as critical as the pivotal norms.

**peripheral norms**
Norms that are accepted by some, but are not important for organizational success.

**Example:** Allina, a company that runs 17 nonprofit hospitals in Minnesota, had to close one of its hospitals. To avoid leaving employees without jobs, it formed a team that set up an employment center, placing 95% of the employees in other positions at Allina or in other companies. This gesture set the norm for teams in the company and raised morale. It also saved the company in severance costs.

## FIGURE 15.3

**Development and Socialization of Group Norms**

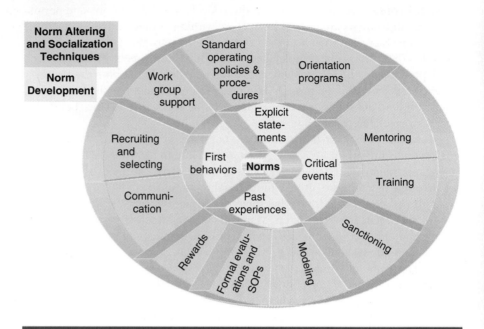

*Source:* Adapted from Daniel C. Feldman, "The Development and Enforcement of Group Norms," *Academy of Management Review* 9 (1984): 47–53; and Edgar H. Schein, "Organizational Socialization and the Profession of Management," The Third Douglas Murray McGregor Lecture of the Alfred P. Sloan School of Management, Massachusetts Institute of Technology, reprinted in David A. Kolb, Irwin M. Rubin, and James M. McIntyre, *Organizational Psychology: Readings in Human Behavior in Organizations,* 4th ed. (Englewood Cliffs, NJ: Prentice-Hall, Inc., 1984).

because they have participated on similar EDS project teams in the past. Even new EDS employees may know some norms from project work in other organizations. You and your instructor know the basic norms for your management class simply from having been participants in previous classes.

**Socializing and Modifying Norms.**    Regardless of how norms are established, it is the manager's job to help new employees learn the group's norms and values. This is called **socialization**, the process by which an individual learns the norms, values, goals, and expectations of an organization. The manager must also support prevailing positive norms and try to change dysfunctional or negative ones. Figure 15.3 depicts some techniques managers can use to maintain, change, and teach organizational norms. These include providing a formal and informal orientation program; establishing a mentoring system; conducting training (which communicates norms as well as develops skills); modeling the desired behaviors; sanctioning positive behaviors and weakening negative ones, through speech and action; using formal evaluations to support positive norms; using the rewards system to reinforce norms, such as paying for performance; using informal and formal communication and feedback to discuss norms and how well group members are meeting the norms; recruiting and selecting individuals who already have exhibited positive norms; gaining the support of the group's informal leaders to promote

**socialization**
The process by which an individual learns the norms, values, goals, and expectations of the organization.

FIGURE 15.4

## The Role-Taking Process

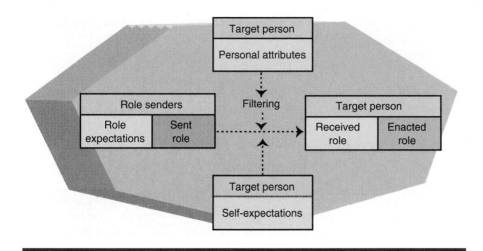

*Source:* Adapted from Daniel Katz and Robert L. Kahn, *The Social Psychology of Group Behavior*, 2nd ed. (New York: John Wiley & Sons, 1978).

positive norms; and developing standard operating policies and procedures that clarify and support desired norms.[34] Because teams need to be adaptable, these techniques should be used to socialize members to the pivotal norms, but not to stifle their creativity by forcing them to conform to every relevant and peripheral norm the group may hold.

## Group Roles

While norms relate to rules and expectations shared by all group members, a **role** is the behaviors expected of a specific person in the group. A work team, for instance, may share a norm related to quality customer service, but individual group members may engage in different behaviors relative to that norm. Some may interact with customers on a daily basis, while others serve the customer behind the scenes. Problems can result if roles are not clear in a group. It is a manager's job to ensure that necessary roles are performed, that people understand their roles, and that resolutions are reached when role behaviors come into conflict.

Figure 15.4 shows how a person's role behaviors are derived. *Role senders,* who may include a person's boss, fellow group members, customers, suppliers, and even the formal organization through a job description, send messages about what they expect from the *target person.* The target person perceives (filters) this *sent role* and develops the *received role,* what she thinks others want her to do. She mixes this role with her own personal attributes and self-expectations to determine the role behaviors in which she will engage.

These role concepts are easy to see in sports teams. The coach, teammates, fans, and even the position description send role expectations. In baseball, the pitcher is the only position expected to throw the ball to batters, while all players share the common role behavior of catching the ball. Everyone bats, but expectations vary as to how they will perform. Historically, Babe Ruth and Hank Aaron

**role**
A description of the behaviors expected of a specific group member.

**TABLE 15.2**

**Group Role Behavior**

| Task-Specialist Role | Group-Maintenance Role | Antigroup Role |
|---|---|---|
| Initiating activity | Encouraging | Blocking |
| Giving information and opinions | Harmonizing | Seeking recognition |
| Seeking information and opinions | Setting group standards | Dominating |
| Summarizing | Gatekeeping | Avoiding |
| Elaborating | Tension relieving | |
| Consensus testing | Testing group feelings | |

played the role of home-run hitters, as do present-day stars Barry Bonds and Cecil Fielder. Their personal attributes and self-expectations allowed them to develop special role behaviors. If Bonds and Fielder don't perform their respective roles or they do them poorly, then their teams are not likely to be successful and their fans will be disappointed.

The same kinds of phenomena occur in work groups, although they may be less obvious. Some role behaviors are apparent. The team leader, for example, sets the agenda, calls the group to order, and directs the discussion by calling on various members. Each member also may perform certain behaviors dictated by her or his job title: welders weld, accountants tally numbers, and so on. Other less apparent role behaviors evolve in a group and are particularly relevant during meetings and discussions. Two important roles are leadership roles and boundary-spanning roles.

**Leadership Roles.**   Two kinds of roles emerge in groups: task-specialist roles and group-maintenance roles.[35] Although these are often called leadership roles, this is somewhat of a misnomer in a group because these roles are performed by all group members at various times. **Task-specialist roles** are behaviors oriented toward generating information and resolving problems. These include initiating activity to get the group started, giving information and opinions, seeking information and opinions from others, summarizing the group's inputs in concise form, elaborating on others' inputs to facilitate comprehension, and testing group consensus. These roles are obviously aimed at getting the job done. **Group-maintenance roles** help the group engage in constructive interpersonal relationships and help members fulfill personal needs and derive satisfaction from group participation. These behaviors include encouraging inputs from all members, harmonizing to deal with conflict, setting standards of group operation, gatekeeping to ensure that everyone has a chance to speak, relieving tension through suggesting breaks or using humor, and testing group feelings. Note that these two roles are aimed at the two primary effectiveness outcomes in the general model of groups in Figure 15.1. Some group members tend to be task specialists while others tend toward maintenance roles. Unfortunately, some tend to perform dysfunctional roles called antigroup behaviors. The characteristics of each of these roles are shown in Table 15.2.

**Antigroup roles** include behaviors that disrupt the group, draw attention to individual rather than group functioning, and detract from positive interactions. These include blocking the discussion of others, seeking recognition through

**task-specialist roles**
Behaviors oriented toward generating information and resolving problems.

**group-maintenance roles**
Behaviors that help the group engage in constructive interpersonal relationships, and help members fulfill personal needs and derive satisfaction from group participation.

**antigroup roles**
Behaviors that disrupt the group, draw attention to individual rather than group functioning, and detract from positive interactions.

Hewlett-Packard facilitates group cohesiveness by encouraging employees to work together and by giving them the resources and freedom to solve problems. At HP's Inkjet Components Division, self-directed teams of highly focused engineers called "seam teams" (named because their work crosses the "seams" of different organizations such as paper and ink suppliers) are empowered to address technically and organizationally complex issues that satisfy a customer need. Seam team members share a common mission. The sole mission of one team was to find a solution to paper that came out of the printer curled at both ends.

*Source:* Courtesy of Hewlett-Packard Company.

side discussions or inappropriate joking, dominating the conversation, or avoiding group interaction entirely. When antigroup role behaviors are present, leaders and others must utilize the task and maintenance behaviors to get the group back on target.

**Example:** Some teams are less than successful. The CEO of a Western manufacturing company suddenly announced that everyone would be in a team. The next day absenteeism soared.

**Boundary-Spanning Roles.**   **Boundary-spanning roles** involve interacting with members in other units of the organization or even outside the organization. The group leader who acts as a link with upper-level bosses is in a boundary-spanning role. Many members in quality teams go visit and work with client organizations to help learn how to serve the client better. Some group members act as liaisons with other teams or have membership on other teams and, thus, share information across the boundaries among the groups. As the use of teams grows, change accelerates, and demands for customer service and quality become even more pronounced, such boundary-spanning roles will become ever more important. The increase in the use of cross-functional teams is a reflection of these changes.

**boundary-spanning roles**
Group behaviors involving interaction with members in other units of the organization or outside the organization.

## Group Cohesiveness

**Cohesiveness** refers to the tendency of group members to unite in their pursuit of group goals and to be attracted to the group and each other. This definition includes both an individual element—members attracted to each other and the group itself—and a group element—members united in pursuit of a goal, reflecting a "synergistic" effect of the cohesive group possibly being greater than the sum of its parts.

How groups get to be cohesive and how managers can facilitate that process has been a topic of interest to researchers and practitioners for some time. The more opportunities group members have to interact and communicate with one another, the better they will get to know each other and the more likely they will develop close relationships. Having to work together on tasks also tends to promote

**cohesiveness**
The tendency of group members to unite in their pursuit of group goals and to be attracted to the group and each other.

group cohesiveness. Thus, if a group is too large or geographically dispersed, such opportunities will be minimized. If the members see themselves as similar in attitudes, values, and personal characteristics, initial attraction to the group may be stronger and can foster cohesiveness. In more diverse groups, a manager may have to identify and promote similarities to speed along the bonding process. One extremely important method of doing this is developing agreement around a common goal. The more specific and clear the goal and the more it can be shown to fulfill important member needs, the greater the likelihood that cohesiveness will occur. Agreeing on a common mission, such as the customer service mission of the Ritz Carlton, or the "absolutely positively overnight" delivery mission of FedEx enhances cohesiveness.

**Example:** Professor Ed Lawler agrees quality circles are losing appeal because they operate parallel to the work process and not within work functioning. Lawler believes that they are good for solving minor quality problems, but because they don't accompany changes in the way work is done, they can't bring about rapid leaps in productivity.

Sometimes that goal can be directed externally in the form of competition against another group. Pitting one group against another is a potent force promoting internal solidarity. On the other hand, "competition" within the group tends to damage cohesiveness. In sports, it is often the case that the stronger the opponent, the greater the team's desire to work together to beat it. In business, the exhortation to "beat the competition" is used to motivate and foster team cohesiveness. Moreover, if external groups and others within the broader organization recognize its success, the team becomes more cohesive. In football, the Oakland Raider franchise is a strongly united and successful team. Its players take pride in the fact that other teams see them as fierce competitors, even the hated black sheep or rebels of the league. Management uses this to promote the "us against them" mentality.

Understanding group cohesiveness is important because of the direct impact it has on a group's functioning and work output. In general, research has shown a positive relationship between overall productivity and group cohesiveness.[36] Moreover, highly cohesive groups tend to engage in more internal social interaction and communication; have more positive, cooperative, and friendly interactions; exert greater influence on their members; have greater member satisfaction; and be more effective in achieving goals they set for themselves.[37]

Figure 15.5 demonstrates the interaction between group cohesiveness and performance norms. Groups tend to be most productive when they are highly cohesive and have high performance norms. Members agree on a specific goal of high performance and their cohesiveness helps them accomplish it. A group with high norms but low cohesiveness is moderately successful because individual members are striving for success but may not be working together as a team. Groups with low performance norms and high cohesiveness may provide the most severe challenge for a manager, because they have set low standards and members are strongly in agreement on the production level due to their cohesiveness. The manager must try to raise standards, possibly through a pay-for-performance system or through interpersonal intervention in the group, such as by establishing relationships and gradually modeling high productivity. If these attempts fail, the manager could reduce the work interdependency of team members or even break up the group on certain tasks. If the group is complacent, then competition within the group could have a positive impact. All of these techniques may be resisted by the cohesive group, but without some action the group has little chance for improvement.

## Additional Interpersonal Processes

A number of interpersonal processes influence the effectiveness of groups. Processes such as open communications, power and influence, leadership, and

**FIGURE 15.5**

**Effect of Group Cohesiveness and Norms on Performance**

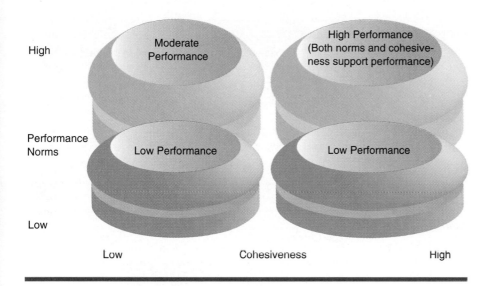

change are discussed in some detail in other chapters of this text. Three other processes that seem particularly important are managing conflict, building trust, and group facilitation.

**Conflict Resolution.**    Although conflict has traditionally been viewed as negative, the more modern view is that conflict is both inevitable and in many cases desirable if properly managed.[38] Managing conflict is an essential skill for team success because conflict has the potential to immobilize virtually any group. Conflicts grow almost naturally out of individual interaction and can be defined as antagonistic interaction in which one person blocks the goals, intentions, or behaviors of someone else. Conflicts can be caused by different individual goals, scarce organizational resources such as money or personnel, power and status differences, personality clashes, personal aggressiveness, ambiguous roles or job boundaries, faulty communications, differences in values or perceptions, inadequate authority or power, and even management's oppressive behavior.

Management experts generally recognize five major styles for dealing with conflict, although subtle variations may be observed. These styles evolve from different levels of the individual attempting to satisfy both his or her own goals or concerns and those of the other person (see Figure 15.6).

**1.** The **competing style** involves a stance of high assertiveness with low cooperation. A person using a competing style wants to get his or her way or to win, and doesn't care much about the other person's feelings or about a long-term relationship. You might adopt this style when negotiating your best deal on a car purchase.

**2.** The **avoiding style** displays low assertiveness and low cooperation. Here the individual is not much concerned about personal goals and may not care enough about the larger goal to fight about it. This style might be appropriate on

**competing style**
A management style involving a stance of high assertiveness with low cooperation.

**avoiding style**
A style displaying low assertiveness and low cooperation.

## FIGURE 15.6

### Conflict Management Styles

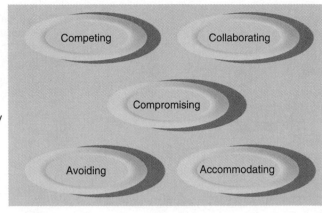

High Assertiveness

Competing    Collaborating

Assertiveness
(Party attempts to satisfy
own concerns or goals)

Compromising

Avoiding    Accommodating

Low Assertiveness

Low Cooperation          High Cooperation

Cooperation
(Party attempts to satisfy the other party's concerns or goals)

*Source:* Adapted from Kenneth Thomas, "Conflict and Conflict Management" in *Handbook of Industrial and Organizational Behavior,* Marvin D. Dunnette, ed. (New York: John Wiley, 1976), 900.

**accommodating style**
A style exhibiting low assertiveness and high cooperation.

**compromising style**
A style that reflects a moderate concern for both your goals and the other person's goals.

**collaborating style**
A style displaying both high assertiveness and high competition.

**Critical Thinking Challenge:** Have students compare the various styles of dealing with conflict. How would each affect the functioning of a work team?

trivial matters and when there is little chance of winning the conflict. This could be a good strategy for dealing with the company "know-it-all."

**3.** The **accommodating style** exhibits low assertiveness and high cooperation. You allow the other person's needs to be satisfied at the expense of yours. This is a good strategy when the relationship is more important than your needs—for instance in discussing a mother-in-law's visit with a spouse!

**4.** The **compromising style** reflects moderate concern for both your goals and the other person's. You both give up something in order to reach agreement and, at least partially, to attain desired outcomes. This strategy is common when goals are diametrically opposed and no resolution appears to be otherwise attainable—for example, the case of what department will receive what percentage of a travel budget. Some experts disdain too ready a willingness to settle for compromise because each party loses something in the exchange.

**5.** The **collaborating style** shows both high assertiveness and high cooperation. Both parties win as they work through issues and reach an optimal solution that meets everyone's needs to the fullest. This style is appropriate for most important organizational decisions where goals are important and relationships must be maintained.

Conflicts over important issues generally can have a beneficial outcome when everyone collaborates. Team members should care enough about their own goals, the goals of others, and certainly the overall organizational goals to work through problems.

Problems abound where conflicts have not been successfully worked through and negative consequences resulted. An excellent example of poorly handled conflict in the sports world occurred in events leading up to Coach Jimmy Johnson's resignation from the Dallas Cowboys football team in 1994. To outside observers, it appeared that a clash of dominant personalities—Johnson's and team owner Jerry Jones's—and conflicting thoughts over who should run the team were not worked through. After several years of conflicts, neither appeared willing to collaborate, compromise, or accommodate to resolve their differences, and a separation was the inevitable result.

This example points out the negative side of conflict. It can result in restricted communication, personal attacks, dysfunctional organization behaviors, an inappropriate test of wills, and disrupted groups. Handled properly, though, conflict can result in enhanced creativity and innovation as well as improved organizational efficiency as issues are resolved. It can keep people motivated and involved as they meet the challenges of team functioning.

**Trust.**   Trusting someone is not only believing that he or she is honest, straightforward, and sincere but also believing in that person's ability to perform.[39] Trust underlies the entire concept of empowerment and self-directed work teams. Managers must trust that employees will honestly and capably handle the increased responsibility given them. Employees must believe that management truly cares about them, trusts them, has faith in them, and will not undermine their empowered efforts. When Jon Simpson took over the hose maker Titeflex, he handed over customers to employees on the shop floor, empowering his employees to solve the problems the customers were having with their products. He opened the books to employees, conferred with unions, dumped first-line supervisors, started self-managed teams, and turned the company around in 90 days.[40]

Because management has the power, managers are the ones who must establish relationships of trust. They cannot expect trust or demand it from employees, but they can do some things to facilitate and earn it: Communicate information openly and honestly; listen; be consistent in feelings, expressions, words, deeds, and missions; demonstrate sincere regard and concern for self and others; treat others fairly; be consistent and predictable with others; show respect for employees by empowering them through delegation and listening to their opinions and suggestions; demonstrate competence and trustworthiness as a given.[41] When Will Potter came to Preston Trucking in 1978, he announced he would run the company based on trust and respect. Blaming management for the company's poor past performance, he opened the books, gave employees keys to the operation, and asked them to solve problems. Now, Preston is highly successful and judged by outsiders to be one of the 100 best companies in America to work for.[42]

**Group Facilitation.**   The team environment in which managers find themselves in modern organizations calls for a new kind of leadership. No longer can a manager be the highly directive, all-knowing autocrat or straw boss. Because knowledge is widely shared and decisions are being made in groups, managers must also be **facilitators**, helping the group overcome internal obstacles or difficulties so that it may achieve desired outcomes efficiently. In the role of facilitator, managers or group leaders focus the group's energy on defining and accomplishing goals; help the group communicate efficiently; foster an atmosphere that encourages all team members to participate; encourage group decision making at every appropriate opportunity to ensure member support and commitment; anticipate emergencies

**Example:** Unions have been reluctant to trust work teams in unionized organizations. The National Labor Relations Board struck down employee-involvement teams at Electromation and Du Pont. Since then the Association for Quality and Participation has established a list of suggestions to help its members keep their teams within the law. For example, teams must avoid making decisions on mandatory bargaining subjects such as conditions of work, wages, and benefits.

**facilitators**
Leaders who help the group overcome internal obstacles or difficulties so that it may achieve desired outcomes.

Facilitators leading interdisciplinary quality teams at The George Washington University Medical Center in Washington, D.C., help resolve conflicts among nursing, pharmacy, and other units to better serve patients. Facilitator Dr. Robert S. Siegel (center), medical director of the Oncology Department, led a team to improve service to patients who had to wait an average of 11 hours between being admitted and receiving their chemotherapy treatment. The team cut patient waiting time to less than 2 hours by asking doctors to fax chemotherapy prescriptions to the hospital 24 hours before the patient's arrival and by preparing admissions paperwork and a room before check-in.

*Source:* © 1993 Terry Ashe.

**Teaching Note:** Many firms hire outside consultants as facilitators to assist in establishing work teams. For example, in firms moving to a total quality management perspective, many use consultants trained in implementing systems developed by Dr. W. Edwards Deming.

requiring rapid decisions and establish procedures to handle them so that group support is maintained; and encourage self-discovery and experimentation by protecting group members and their ideas from attack so they can feel secure in sharing and exploring new ideas, proposals, thoughts, and opinions.[43]

Remember that it is possible, and even desirable, that all members of the group share in the facilitation responsibilities to ensure a group works successfully. The "Magnifying Management" box provides some specific ways to facilitate success of meetings.

## CONTEXTUAL INFLUENCES ON GROUP EFFECTIVENESS

A number of factors within the overall organization and environment have a major impact on how groups function. These factors include culture, task design/technology, mission clarity, autonomy, feedback mechanisms, reward and recognition systems, training and consultation, and physical environments. Of these, culture, organizational missions, and training are discussed elsewhere. The "Quest for Quality" box on page 448 describes how Motorola's training and reward systems have helped its teams boost quality and profits. The other characteristics warrant a brief discussion due to their impact on group and team functioning.

The nature of the task determines to a large extent whether a group or team is called for. A claims adjuster at State Farm Insurance, for example, is largely independent of other adjusters in working directly with clients. The position requires some information sharing, but not a high degree of coordination. On the other hand, basketball's Chicago Bulls, in winning their third straight NBA championship in 1993, required constant task interdependence. Without tremendous teamwork, even Michael Jordan could not have carried his team to victory. Technology has affected group behavior, as well. With teleconferencing capabilities and computer-aided decision making, even geographically dispersed workers can function more like a team.

The level of autonomy in decision making fostered by top management also influences group functioning. If top managers have centralized decision making, then using empowered or self-managed work teams will be virtually impossible. As we discussed in Chapter 7, many of the early failures of quality circles resulted

## MAKING MEETINGS WORK

If you have ever participated in a poorly run group meeting, you probably understand the expression, "a camel is a horse designed by a committee." Many hours, resources, and dollars are wasted in poorly run meetings. If you look at meetings in terms of the cost of the participants' time, a meeting with 10 participants who each earn $25,000 a year costs $240 per hour. Multiply that by the thousands of employees in large companies and the thousands of meetings they attend yearly, and the cost is staggering. Yet, a number of fairly simple actions on the part of the leader and participants before, during, and after the meeting can help make meetings more productive.

*Preparing for the Meeting:* (1) Make sure a meeting is really necessary; don't call a group meeting if the issue can be resolved more quickly via the telephone, face-to-face individual meeting, e-mail, fax, or memo. (2) Ensure that the right people are at the meeting; that is, the ones who have relevant information, need to hear the information discussed, have a stake in a decision, or have the position and authority to implement the group's decisions. (3) Determine the purpose of the meeting (e.g., information dissemination and discussion, idea development, alternative consideration, decision making) and communicate it to the participants ahead of time. (4) Help prepare participants by providing them with important background

papers, telling them what they should bring of their own, and explaining what general or specific roles they will be asked to play. (5) Prepare and distribute an agenda that specifies the topics to be discussed, the desired outcomes of the discussions, whose specific inputs will be needed, and the time frame of each discussion. (6) Set up the room to enhance the activity: straightforward seating for one person to share information with the group, circular or U-shaped for full group discussion. Make sure necessary equipment is present.

*During the Meeting:* (7) Start on time and keep the discussion of specific topics within the time frames allotted. Schedule breaks and meals to facilitate informal discussion of important topics brought up in the meeting. (8) Play the facilitator role: Encourage feedback and full participation of group members, keep the group on the task, and avoid time robbers (excessive joking, rambling, side discussions). (9) Pace the meeting. Get to each issue on the agenda

if possible, but remember that a decision postponement may be appropriate at times. (10) Acknowledge the contributions of members as you go and in summary at the end. Make sure key leaders have a chance to comment. (11) Do not use your role as meeting leader to control others and impose your point of view. (12) Close the meeting with a summary of what took place and what is expected of participants after the meeting. Where appropriate, reach a conclusion on when follow-up activities will be completed and when the next meeting will convene.

*Following up the Meeting:* (13) Send a meeting summary with key decisions and assignments, and dispense dates to each participant. Seek feedback from participants about how future meetings can be improved.

*Sources:* Arthur H. Bell, *Mastering the Meeting Maze* (Reading, MA: Addison-Wesley Publishing Company, Inc., 1990); and Thomas A. Kayser, *Mining Group Gold* (El Segundo, CA: Serif Publishing, 1990).

from a perceived lack of real impact on the problems considered, due to top management's required approval of all changes. The increasing use of self-directed work teams requires that teams have greater autonomy to carry out their tasks and goals.

Feedback mechanisms—the amount and nature of information that individuals and teams receive about their performance—affect team functioning in a number of ways. Feedback may indicate that groups are not sufficiently cohesive to sustain commitment and retain employees, or customer satisfaction measures may indicate that project teams are not advancing rapidly enough through the stages of development to be performing adequately. Feedback mechanisms may be informal, such as casual chats with customers, or they can be quite sophisticated.

**Comment on Box:** After discussing the points on making meetings more effective, ask students to share examples of both successful and unsuccessful meetings. Have them add additional suggestions to the list, or let them interview managers about meeting effectiveness.

## MOTOROLA FOSTERS TEAM SPIRIT

Motorola Inc., based in Schaumburg, Illinois, produces a wide variety of products, including communication systems—primarily two-way radios, cellular phones, and pagers—semiconductors, and equipment for defense and aerospace applications, data communications, information processing, and automotive and industrial uses. The company employs 107,000 workers in more than 50 major facilities worldwide. Motorola's 1993 profits of $1.02 billion on sales of $17 billion are evidence of its strong reputation for quality in markets worldwide. Indeed, the company was the first large corporation to win the prestigious Malcolm Baldrige National Quality Award, in 1988. Motorola estimates that it saves about $2.2 billion annually from quality programs that in recent years have increasingly emphasized teamwork.

Motorola relies on teams at plants all over the world to help it meet its quality objectives, reduce waste, speed up product development, and satisfy customers. For example, "away teams" helped the company open its MOS-11 memory chip plant in Austin, Texas—which makes some of the most sophisticated chips in the world with circuit lines measuring $\frac{1}{200}$ the width of a human hair—in just eighteen months, compared to the three or four years generally required. Team members went to plants around the world to gain expertise on the equipment that would fill their Austin plant. Their efforts worked:  After MOS-11 opened, it set a company record for output of good chips in just its third lot.

Training is critical for Motorola's team approach. The company already spends 4 percent of its payroll on training, providing all employees with at least 40 hours of training per year, one of the heaviest commitments in U.S. industry. A new lifelong learning program to boost employee skills will quadruple that level by the year 2000. Most team members receive some training at Motorola University, a training center in Schaumburg (with 14 branches around the world) with a budget of more than $120 million. The return on Motorola's training dollars has been high:  Productivity has increased sharply, with sales per employee rising from more than $60,000 in 1987 to more than $120,000 in 1993.

To recognize significant team efforts and to foster motivation, the company holds an annual Total Customer Satisfaction Team Competition, a sort of all-day Olympics in which award-winning teams make presentations to the whole company and receive awards. For example, the B.E.A.P. (Back End Automated Process) Goes On team from Boynton Beach, Florida, where Motorola makes its top-selling Bravo pagers, explained how changes they made in the equipment and procedures used to test products coming off the assembly line had increased the production rate by 50 percent. These changes saved the company from spending $4.2 million on a new production line, improved safety and product quality, and accomplished operating savings of $100,000 a month. A team from the company's semiconductor plant in Manila demonstrated how Motorola, without spending millions on new machinery, eliminated more than 99 percent of the problems with a 30-year-old molding process that had been producing more than 5,000 errors per million operations. The competition not only rewards team efforts, but gives contestants an opportunity to share their experiences with other parts of the huge multinational firm and to collect ideas to take back to their own plants, for the benefit of all employees.

*Sources:* Barnaby J. Feder, "At Motorola, Quality Is a Team Sport," *The New York Times,* January 21, 1993, D1, D7; Kevin Kelly, with Peter Burrows, "Motorola: Training for the Millennium," *Business Week,* March 28, 1994, 158–163; and U.S. Department of Commerce, "Malcolm Baldrige National Quality Award, 1988 Award Winner."

Hewlett-Packard, for example, developed a system it calls a "Return Map" that graphically represents all team members' contributions to the development and sale of a new product in terms of time and money. Product team leaders track product development from initial idea, through development, and into the manufacturing and sales stages to determine break-even time and various return-on-investment ratios over the product's life cycle. The company uses this information to examine the effectiveness of various team activities and to indicate necessary operational changes.[44] If feedback mechanisms are inadequate, then teams can flounder for months or even years without realizing that change is required.

Reward and recognition systems also determine group functioning. Some experts point out that individuals and departments are expected to interact frequently and meaningfully with other individuals and departments, yet are rewarded totally on the basis of individual accomplishments rather than for their interdependent performance—which diminishes interaction and mutual aid.[45] Players for the Chicago Bulls, for example, would probably be very reluctant to pass the ball to a teammate, even if he had an easier shot, if all of their rewards, even their future on the team, were based solely on their scoring averages at the end of the season. Thus, reward systems should encourage team efforts, not hinder them.

A final factor often neglected in examining work group functioning is the physical environment. Office arrangement and layout can influence work and communication flow or send powerful messages about organizational values and norms. At CNN, the fast-paced decision making required by a 24-hour news operation is facilitated by the fact that all the chief decision makers create a highly flexible environment around a central control room. Vice president Ed Turner (no relation to company president Ted Turner) and his staff have small offices by the control room, but they spend the vast majority of their time in the control room, making decisions in two minutes that the big three networks might take two hours to make.[46] In this case, task design and office layout combine with strong norms to create an environment that supports instantaneous change. Such rapid decisions could not be made with offices and people spread throughout a ten-story building. At Union Carbide, all managerial-level employees were assigned offices of equal size when they moved to their new headquarters to emphasize the importance of equality. Similarly, in Procter & Gamble's new office, only open office plans with few walls were provided so that employees would clearly recognize the importance of teamwork at P&G.[47]

## PROBLEMS IN GROUPS

Obviously, groups and teams can be powerful forces for satisfying employee needs and accomplishing organizational goals. However, there are difficulties associated with groups and teams that can derail organizational success. Some of these have been discussed already—problems with role ambiguity and role conflict; difficulties in establishing positive group norms consistent with the organizational culture; hardships in getting the right mix of skills, abilities, and traits; free-riding; and various antigroup behaviors. Other problems in groups that must be worked through are personality clashes and other conflicts over jurisdiction, scarce resources, or power and status differences. In completing this chapter, we will explore some additional problems that may occur in group interaction.

### Conformity and Agreement

One common problem many teams face is dealing with the related issues of conformity and agreement. In the context of a group, **conformity** means adherence to the group's norms, values, and goals. While member acceptance of pivotal norms is important for both individual and group success, too much conformity—

**conformity**
Adherence to the group's norms, values, and goals.

especially to the point of blind adherence even to all peripheral norms—can result in reduced creativity and objectivity in addressing issues and solving problems. For example, in a set of experiments in which subjects were asked to judge whether three lines were equal or different in length, many individuals conformed to the consensus of a group, judging lines that were obviously different in length to be the same just because the rest of the group said they were.[48] This kind of conformity, when applied to work situations, can detract from the generation of new ideas and from appropriate disagreements with inappropriate behaviors the group might be demonstrating.

Experts have identified two special cases of group conformity. We defined the concept of groupthink in Chapter 11 as a condition in which poor decision making occurs because the desire to maintain group cohesiveness precludes the critical evaluation of alternative courses of action.[49] For example, to avoid "rocking the boat" or upsetting the positive shared feelings of group solidarity, members may withhold information or opinions that would go against an apparent group consensus. The result is decisions made and implemented without considering all possible alternatives, or the alternatives offered being given less than full examination.

Irving Janis, who coined the term *groupthink*, identified eight symptoms of the phenomenon:

1. Illusion of invulnerability—members become convinced that they are invincible, and their overconfidence results in a willingness to take great risks.

2. Illusion of morality—members believe that whatever they do is good, ethical, and morally correct, when, in fact, it may not be.

3. Illusion of unanimity—members falsely believe they are all in agreement.

4. Collective rationalization—members justify any concerns about the value of what they are doing or challenges to their decisions.

5. Mindguarding—some members protect the group by preventing adverse information from being presented.

6. Shared stereotypes—members negatively stereotype outsiders who may present a threat to the group and its decisions.

7. Self-censorship—members consider disagreement with the group inappropriate, so they don't speak out.

8. Direct pressure—members who voice objections to the apparent group consensus are pressured by other members to conform.[50]

Figure 15.7 illustrates these symptoms in the context of a meeting of a pharmaceutical company's board of directors discussing the introduction of a new weight-loss drug. These groupthink symptoms can be prevented through specific techniques, including assigning the role of critical evaluation to everyone in the group, appointing a specific individual to be a "devil's advocate" to challenge the group consensus, breaking the group into smaller subgroups to discuss issues, having the leader withhold his or her opinion about the issue, and bringing in outside experts to challenge the group's thinking. Within the broader organization, ways to preclude groupthink include establishing an organizational culture that encourages original thinking and challenge, training leaders, and conducting organizational development activities such as team building and creative problem solving. It is important that leaders establish cohesive groups with norms that encourage rather than discourage critical evaluation of ideas.[51]

A special case of groupthink called the **Abilene Paradox**—a term derived from originator Jerry Harvey's family's unwanted, but agreed upon, automobile trip

---

**Example:** According to Professor Edward Lawler at the Center for Effective Organizations at the University of Southern California, people are naive about how easy it is to establish a team. According to Lawler, "Teams are the Ferraris of work design. They're high performance, but high maintenance and expensive."

---

**Abilene Paradox**

A situation occurring when members of a group publicly agree on a course of action even though there is an underlying consensus agreement that an alternative course is preferred.

## FIGURE 15.7

### Demonstration of the Symptoms of Groupthink

Board of Directors Meeting of a Pharmaceutical Company Discussing the Marketing of a New Weight-Loss Drug

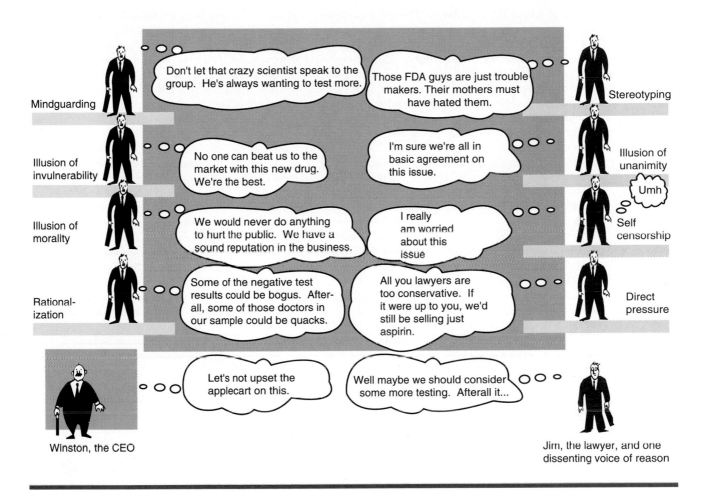

Source: Adapted from film Group Dynamics: Groupthink (CRM Films, 1982).

to Abilene—occurs when members of a group publicly agree on a course of action even though there is an underlying consensus agreement that an alternative course is preferred.[52] Each person incorrectly assumes that everyone else wants the publicly chosen alternative. An example would be when an executive team continues to approve expenditures for a project that each member privately believes ought to be scrapped. The unwillingness of members to bring up their true feelings and beliefs results in an escalating commitment to a bad decision. This phenomenon can result from some combination of the desire not to "step on someone's toes" or to humiliate the original project advocate, negative fantasies and fear of rejection or exclusion from the group, and insecurities in one's own point of view.

# sorner

## Team Leaders

We've all heard the expression, "I've got good news and bad news." The bad news, according to management guru Tom Peters, is that "middle managers, as we have known them, are cooked geese." Almost everyone knows that many organizations are downsizing and eliminating layers of middle management. That's bad for existing middle managers—especially those who cannot adapt to different jobs—and it's bad for those aspiring to become traditional middle managers. These people are in for a hard time.

The good news, and there are actually two pieces of good news, is that there is an emerging new position taking the place of the middle manager, and there is a totally new job position needed in many organizations. Although middle managers are on the way out, in many organizations they are being replaced by team leaders or team facilitators. One young woman in the finance department of a Memphis manufacturing company relates that she was moved from a supervisory position to departmental team leader. She was struggling to figure out what to do in her new role when she talked to one of the authors of this text. Her plight is not atypical.

What's happened is that the old environment required managers who dictated orders and followed up to see that they were obeyed. They either made all the decisions or passed down the decisions made by upper-level managers. They emphasized the "control" role and generated a culture of conformity from subordinates and repressed thoughts, feelings, and often good new ideas. New team leaders, however, emphasize the "learner" role by encouraging continual skill and intellectual upgrading in themselves and others. They must foster a culture of innovation, idea generation rather than suppression, openness of thoughts and feelings, and willingness to challenge across authority boundaries. The person might be a functional area expert, such as an accountant or operations manager, or a generalist specifically trained in team-leading skills. That ex-

pertise can come from traditional college education programs and both in-house and external management development programs. What's certain is that this person can no longer act the part of the "kick butt, and take names" straw boss.

Such a person may be an external organizational development (OD) expert (see Chapter 19) who specializes in team-building, but is even more likely, with the current emphasis on cost consciousness in companies, to be a permanent in-house employee. With companies moving toward team management, someone must teach team leaders how to lead effectively and members how to be good team participants. They will train organizational members how to develop team incentives, manage boundary activities with customers, suppliers, and other managers, make decisions, engage in brainstorming, create measures of group performance, encourage innovation, and facilitate the process behaviors discussed in this and other chapters. This person may have a management degree with a human resource or organizational behavior emphasis and may have a degree, or at least considerable coursework, in psychology, communications, education, sociology, or counseling.

Over $45 billion is spent nationwide on training each year. One expert believes that it is reasonable for a company to have from 10 to 15 in-house trainers while some may even have more. With the new team emphasis, no doubt many of these dollars will be spent on trainers to develop team interaction skills.

*Sources:* Deborah Harrington-Mackin, *The Team Building Tool Kit* (AMACOM, a division of the American Management Association, New York, 1994); Larry Hirschhorn, *Managing in the New Team Environment* (Reading, MA: Addison-Wesley Publishing Co. Inc., 1991); J.J. Laabs, "Team Training Goes Outdoors," *Personnel Journal* 70 (June 1991): 56-63; and Tom Peters, *Liberation Management* (New York: Alfred A. Knopf Inc., 1992), 758.

## Politics

**politics**
The maneuvering by an individual to try to gain an advantage in the distribution of organizational rewards or resources.

Yet another problem endemic to groups is **politics**, which in this context refers to maneuvering to try to gain an advantage in the distribution of organizational rewards or resources. Although most people view this pursuit of self-interest at work negatively, many see it as necessary for individual success.[53]

Political maneuvering is considered negative because it consumes valuable time better spent on productive matters, often subverts organizational goals, diverts human energy, and can result in the loss of valuable employees who cannot or do not wish to "play the game." Such maneuvering includes a full range of activities, from the fairly benign and acceptable—such as helping others to gain favor and developing a network of positive relationships—to the dastardly and dangerous—such as backstabbing. Other common political tactics include generating destructive competition, using ingratiating language, spreading rumors, using scapegoats, leaking confidential information outside the group, blaming others, sabotaging others' projects, circumventing a boss, playing it safe by not being associated with projects that might fail, playing dumb, and even intentionally escalating commitment to a collapsing project so that immediate failure will not be acknowledged. A full list of political behaviors is almost endless, but the point is clear. Playing politics in most cases is negative and should be avoided if possible.[54]

As a manager, you can minimize the effects of politics by establishing a trusting and honest communication climate, promoting team goals and rewards, discouraging competition for limited outcomes, rewarding those who help others instead of competing with them, basing performance evaluations on productivity and not personalities, reducing favoritism, using job rotation and highly interdependent tasks to promote group member cooperation; and having upper management model nonpolitical behavior.

Despite the costs and problems associated with teams, their benefits can far outweigh any negatives. Harnessing the power of the group will likely be the management imperative far into the twenty-first century.

# SUMMARY AND REVIEW

- **Distinguish between the terms *group* and *team*.** A group is two or more persons who communicate, share a collective identity, and have a common goal. A team is a small group whose members have complementary skills, as well as a common purpose, goals, and approach, and who hold themselves mutually accountable. The major distinction is that individual performance and outcomes are most important in groups, while collective work group performance and outcomes are what count most in teams.

- **Summarize a general model of group effectiveness, including its primary components.** Effectiveness is measured by performance outcomes, such as units produced, as well as personal outcomes, such as member satisfaction and commitment to the group. These outcomes are influenced by group structure—including the group type, size, and composition of skills and abilities—as well as the processes of group development, cohesiveness, norms, roles, conflict management, trust, and facilitation. Also important are aspects of the organization itself, such as

culture, task design and technology, mission clarity, autonomy, feedback mechanisms, reward and recognition systems, training and consultation, and the physical environment.

- **Describe the types of groups that exist in organizations.** The many types of groups and teams in organizations vary by composition, duration, degree of autonomy, development, and function. Special kinds of groups include task forces, committees, project teams, new-product development teams, quality-assurance teams, and self-directed work teams.

- **Specify five stages of group development.** Groups tend to develop through the stages of forming, storming, norming, performing, and adjourning.

- **Discuss how group size, norms, cohesiveness, and trust affect group performance.** Work teams function best when limited to between 7 and 20 members, but the optimal number depends on the circumstances. They also function better when expectations about appropriate behavior within the group—

norms—are positive and clear, when members trust one another, and when they are cohesive.

- **Determine different roles that members can play in a group.** Roles are the behaviors expected of and demonstrated by specific individuals in groups. Some members emphasize task-oriented roles, some group-maintenance roles, and others roles that span the boundaries of the group.

- **Relate some of the problems associated with group functioning.** Difficulties associated with groups and teams include role ambiguity and role conflict; problems in establishing positive group norms consistent with the organizational culture; problems getting the right mix of skills, abilities, and traits; free-riding; personality clashes; conflicts over jurisdiction, scarce resources, or power and status differences; and various antigroup behaviors. Other problems relate to excessive conformity to group norms, which can reduce creativity and objectivity in addressing issues and solving problems. Groupthink and the Abilene Paradox are two examples. Another problem in groups is politics, maneuvering to try to gain an advantage in the distribution of organizational rewards or resources, because it consumes time, may subvert organizational goals, diverts energy, and can result in the loss of valuable employees.

- **Analyze a business's use of teams.** In the "Business Dilemma" box, you encountered a hypothetical business having difficulties with its team environment. You should be able to analyze the teams' effectiveness, using the model presented in this chapter, and make recommendations for a future course of action.

## Key Terms and Concepts

## Ready Recall

1. Explain the difference between groups and teams.
2. What are some of the assets of teams?
3. What are the two outcomes in the group effectiveness model? What factors affect these outcomes?
4. What are self-managed work teams and what tasks might they perform that traditionally are performed by managers?
5. How are norms formed and taught or altered in an organization or group?
6. How are team cohesiveness, norms, and performance related?
7. What major roles do group members perform?
8. Discuss the way teams develop over time.
9. What are some problems that may crop up in groups and teams?
10. What are the symptoms of groupthink and how can team leaders prevent it from happening?

## Expand Your Experience

1. If teams are being used in any of your classes this term, try to identify the stage of development each of the teams is in. Describe each team in terms of cohesiveness, trust levels, and norms.
2. In your fraternity, sorority, school athletic team, or workplace, see if you can identify instances of political behavior.

Have these behaviors had positive or negative effects on group functioning?
3. Interview the department chairperson in charge of one of the academic departments in your college or university. Using Table 15.1 as a guideline, explore whether the professors function more like a group or a team. Contrast what

you find here with what you see on your school's basketball, football, or baseball team.

4. Find and interview the owner of a local small business or the manager of a fairly large department in a larger company.

Ask this manager to describe some of the norms operating in the organization and the methods used to ensure that new individuals are socialized to the norms. See how they fit the model in Figure 15.3.

## Work Teams at Rubbermaid

At Rubbermaid, innovation is a way of life. Thirty-three percent of the firm's revenues come from products introduced during the past five years. Indeed, Rubbermaid has set a goal of entering a new market area every 12 to 18 months. The company produces over 360 new products every year. The result is a new product nearly every day at Rubbermaid. Many of Rubbermaid's successes have been new products, such as recycling bins. But other new products have been simple improvements to well-known consumer products. For example, how do you improve a mop pail? Rubbermaid did, by adding comfortable handles to make it easier to carry the pail. Unlike most other firms, Rubbermaid's new products succeed in an increasingly competitive marketplace. According to CEO Wolfgang Schmitt, 90 percent of all new Rubbermaid products succeed. The company's successes and overall innovation strategy are paying off for stockholders: Sales have grown at 14.6 percent annually since 1982, while earnings per share have grown 18 percent over the same time period. Moreover, during the same ten years, both dividends and stock appreciation have contributed to an average 25 percent return to stockholders.

How does Rubbermaid do it? Schmitt has a clear vision of the firm's strategy—to be a low cost, innovative producer. Many firms have a clear strategy, but Rubbermaid also has the philosophy, the culture, and the processes necessary to implement the strategy. For an outside observer, the question might be, just how does Rubbermaid keep coming up with new ideas and how does it keep track of (and succeed at) all of this innovation?

A big part of the answer lies with the company's product development teams. There are 20 "business teams," each responsible for a "specific product line." Each of these teams includes five to seven associates from marketing, manufacturing, finance, sales, and research and development (R&D). At Rubbermaid, the folks who get a paycheck at the end of the week are called "associates," not "employees." This seemingly trivial departure from other companies emphasizes the equality that must exist if the teams are to succeed. It also reflects the company's commitment to employee empowerment.

Each team has the knowledge necessary to take a product from a designer's imagination to your kitchen. Team members are responsible for a product line from start to finish, from product development to bottom-line profits. Team members test new products themselves, rather than suffering the delays (and possible exposure to competitors) of market testing. The result is new products that meet customers' needs, address their

concerns, and make it to the customers quickly. For example, growing environmental concerns prompted Rubbermaid teams to design and introduce a lunchbox with built-in food containers to eliminate excessive plastic or paper garbage. Recycling bins are also new products designed to appeal to the environmentally conscious. In fact, Rubbermaid typically discontinues products before customer demand dies down. The key is that the company stays immediately responsive to shifts in customer attitudes and preferences. New products immediately follow or even anticipate demand, but, on the other hand, the firm doesn't risk having an inventory of outdated products.

There is also a considerable sense of partnership among employees and teams, resulting in a degree of idea communication seldom seen in the business world. If one team comes up with a good idea, other teams or even individual employees are encouraged to make use of that idea. For example, the combination tool box and stepladder developed by one team became the inspiration for another team's combination toy box and stepstool.

Although product development is important at Rubbermaid (14 percent of net profit goes to R&D), teamwork isn't limited to the product development teams. Schmitt believes that the firm should also be in partnership with customers, suppliers, stockholders, and the community, as well as with its associates. To maintain contact with the retailers who actually see and sell to the customers, Rubbermaid gets sales information directly from retailers' point-of-sale computer systems. In overseas marketing, the company often collaborates with customers—the retail stores. Rubbermaid asks suppliers for their ideas, too. Finally, the company takes its public and community obligations seriously, as shown by its top rating on community and environmental responsibility in *Fortune* magazine's surveys of corporate reputations.

These partnerships have several benefits beyond the obvious. Product teams, of course, facilitate the process of developing, manufacturing, and marketing a new pail or dishpan. But what advantage is there for including outsiders as partners? For example, good working relationships with the firm's customers, the retail stores, encourage retailers to give Rubbermaid products a generous allocation of scarce shelf space.

In the 1990s companies are finding that survival depends on meeting customers' needs. Moreover, the flexibility needed to meet customers' needs in a dynamic environment can best be attained through teamwork. At Rubbermaid, teamwork includes all of the firm's stakeholders—stockholders, management, employees, customers, and the communities in which the firm operates. This expanded vision of teamwork produces extraordinary results for all of the stakeholders.

*Sources:* Erik Calonius, "Smart Moves by Quality Champs," *Fortune,* Spring/Summer 1991, 24–28; Alan Farnham, "America's Most Admired Company," *Fortune,* February 7, 1994, 50–54; Kate Fitzgerald, "GE, Rubbermaid Plan Green Intros," *Advertising Age,* January 14, 1991, 6; Seth Lubove, "Okay, Call Me a Predator," *Forbes,* February 15, 1993, 150–153; Dana Milbank, "As Stores Scrimp More and Order Less, Suppliers Take on Greater Risks, Costs," *The Wall Street Journal,* December 10, 1991, B1; Michael K. Ozanian and Alexandra Ourusoff, "Never Let Them See You Sweat," *Financial World,* February 1, 1994, 34–38; Zachary Schiller, "At Rubbermaid, Little Things Mean a Lot," *Business Week,* November 1, 1991, 126; Wolfgang R. Schmitt, "The Ethics of Partnerships," *Executive Excellence,* November 1993, 15–16; Richard Tompkins, "Low Tech, High Yield: Richard Tompkins on How Rubbermaid Became a Corporate Hero," *Financial Times,* March 11, 1994, 11; Tricia Welsh, "Best and Worst Corporate Reputations," *Fortune,* February 7, 1994, 58–66; and "Why Rubbermaid is the Best Consumer Stock," *Money,* October 1993, 67.

## Questions

1. How else might Rubbermaid choose to implement a strategy of product innovation? Would other approaches be as successful?
2. What makes Rubbermaid's product development teams *teams*, rather than just *work groups*?
3. Is it possible for a company to have both employee empowerment and a strong top management team? Why or why not?

---

## STRENGTHEN YOUR SKILLS
### *Teamwork*

You will use the illustration presented in Figure 15.8 to complete this exercise. Keep in mind the metaphors you established in Chapter 14's exercise and adapt them for this exercise. For example, where you may have decided that the guy holding the rope was the boss in Chapter 14's exercise, it would be more appropriate in this exercise to think of him as the team leader.

**FIGURE 15.8**

**Teamwork**

## Instructions

1. Break into groups of four people per group. Decide among yourselves which character in the illustration each of you will be to complete this exercise. If you have more than four people in your group, then more than one person will have to play each character (or, if you'd prefer, somebody can be the horse). If you have fewer than four people in your group, one of your group members will have to play the role of two of the characters.

2. As a group, create your own story about what happened to lead up to the events in the illustration and decide how your character behaved in the time leading up to what you see occurring in this illustration. Be creative and have some fun in making up an interesting story about your team. Instead of referring to the characters as "the guy holding the rope" or "the one who's sweating," give each character a name. The names can be fictitious, or maybe you'd prefer to give them your names.

3. Once your group has agreed on the story and how each team member in the picture performed, you will use those assumptions to complete the following team self-evaluation. Each member is to evaluate the team independently, using his or her own form.

### *How Well Are We Working Together?*

|  | Strongly Disagree | Disagree | Neither Agree Nor Disagree | Agree | Strongly Agree |
|---|---|---|---|---|---|
| 1. The team knows exactly what it has to get done. | ① | ② | ③ | ④ | ⑤ |
| 2. Team members get a lot of encouragement for new ideas. | ① | ② | ③ | ④ | ⑤ |
| 3. Team members freely express their real views. | ① | ② | ③ | ④ | ⑤ |
| 4. Every team member has a clear idea of the team's goals. | ① | ② | ③ | ④ | ⑤ |
| 5. Everyone is involved in the decisions we have to make. | ① | ② | ③ | ④ | ⑤ |
| 6. We tell each other how we are feeling. | ① | ② | ③ | ④ | ⑤ |
| 7. All team members respect each other. | ① | ② | ③ | ④ | ⑤ |
| 8. The feelings among team members tend to pull us together. | ① | ② | ③ | ④ | ⑤ |
| 9. Everyone's opinion gets listened to. | ① | ② | ③ | ④ | ⑤ |
| 10. There is very little bickering among team members. | ① | ② | ③ | ④ | ⑤ |

### Scoring and Interpretation

To find your total score, add the numbers in the circles. _____

To find your average score, divide the total score by 10. _____

If your average score is 4 or higher, teamwork is strong. If your average is between 3 and 4, teamwork is healthy, but there's room for improvement. If your average is 2 or lower, something is getting in the way of teamwork. Whatever the score, discussing these issues together with an open mind is likely to improve teamwork.

4. Compare evaluations and identify which of the ten items your team agreed were strengths of the team (ratings of 4 or 5) and those that you agreed were weaknesses (ratings of 1 or 2). Discuss what the team needs to do to work more effectively together.

*Source:* Table from John H. Zenger, et al., *Leading Teams: Mastering the New Role* (Homewood, IL: Business One Irwin, 1994), 97. Used with permission.

# Motivating

# People

## Outline

## After reading this chapter, you will be able to:

- Define motivation and explain its importance to managers.
- Compare and contrast the content theories of Abraham Maslow, Frederick Herzberg, and David McClelland.
- Analyze the various process theories relating to how managers can motivate employees, including equity theory, expectancy theory, and the Porter-Lawler expectancy model.
- Determine how managers may use reinforcement theory to motivate employees to behave as expected.
- Explain how goal-setting theory can be used to enhance employee motivation.
- Specify how managers may design jobs or apply strategies to motivate employees.
- Evaluate a company's efforts to motivate its sales team.

The Ritz-Carlton photograph was provided by The Ritz-Carlton Hotel Company. Ritz-Carlton is a federally registered trademark of The Ritz-Carlton Hotel Company.

# Pioneers in Motivation

When John D. Rockefeller, Jr., and Charles Schwab were young men at the turn of the century, few managers were concerned about their employees' needs or morale; production and output was their primary focus. Rockefeller and Schwab, who became "captains of industry" of their time, were two managers who attributed their success to a highly motivated work force.

When Charles Schwab took over Bethlehem Steel in 1904, he realized he could not buy imagination, loyalty, or productivity from his employees. Schwab set up incentive systems to motivate his employees: "Do so much and you get so much; do more and you get more—that is the essence of the system." Schwab paid the highest salaries in the steel industry in order to foster creativity and loyalty in his employees. He started a new practice in the industry by taking 15 men out of the steel mill and making them partners in the business. Many managers criti-

cized Schwab's policies, but the policies worked. Sales at Bethlehem Steel went from $10 million in 1904 to $230 million in 1916. During the same period the company's stock rose from $20 to $600 per share.

John D. Rockefeller, Jr., sought the same goal at Standard Oil as had Schwab at Bethlehem Steel—getting more work and productivity from employees. Rockefeller motivated through example, frequently joining his men at work even in rough manual activity such as loading wagons in the oil fields. Rockefeller also offered high salaries, generous bonuses, and praise for and recognition of a job well done. He tried not to reprimand workers, but when criticism was required, he tempered it with praise for what had been done right. Rockefeller recognized and encouraged ideas from employees. Additionally, he allowed managers to take time off with pay (a practice unheard of in this time period). Standard Oil's workers were loyal, and the company was rarely plagued by the labor unrest that affected many companies of this era. Rockefeller's ideas, though rad-

ical for the time, allowed him to recruit and keep the best employees in the oil business. His emphasis on respect for, and good relations with, his employees built Standard Oil into one of the largest companies in the early twentieth century.

Charles Schwab and John D. Rockefeller, Jr., managed their employees with common sense and empathy. Both men recognized that employees who fulfill their needs are more likely to be happy and productive in the long run. Both also understood that motivating employees requires respect for and faith in them and recognition in the form of financial rewards and praise. Although we think of the practices of Schwab and Rockefeller as common today, they were revolutionary for their time. A manager today who shows insight into management and motivation of employees is Horst Schulze, president of The Ritz-Carlton Hotel Company. Schulze provides employees 100 hours of training each year, which works to change employees' attitudes about their place in the organization and focuses on the importance of teamwork. Schulze has successfully linked his total quality strategy with employee motivation to produce unequaled service.

*Sources:* Burt Folsom, *Administrative Radiology* 6 (November 1987): 80–82; Patricia A. Galagan, "Putting on the Ritz," *Training and Development* 47 (December 1993): 41–45.

Because employees have the ability to influence the achievement of organizational goals, most top managers agree that employees are an organization's most valuable resource. To achieve organizational objectives, employees must have the ability (appropriate knowledge and skills), the tools (proper training and equipment), and the motivation to perform their jobs. Ensuring that employees have the appropriate knowledge, skills, and the proper training is the subject of Chapter 14; this chapter is concerned with employee motivation. Managers who understand how to motivate their employees can help them be more productive and thus contribute to the achievement of organizational goals.

In this chapter we examine a number of theories regarding motivating employees. First we define motivation and discuss its importance and how managers have traditionally viewed it. Next we discuss several theories that attempt to identify what motivates employees, followed by several theories that look at how employees' motivation is directed and controlled. Finally, we explore how managers may design jobs to better motivate employees.

## WHAT IS MOTIVATION?

**motivation**
An inner drive that directs behavior toward goals.

**Teaching Note:** Have students give examples of needs and goals. For example, they may have a need to complete their degree in business to get a better job. A goal to help them fulfill this need would be to receive a passing grade in this class along with other business classes.

**Motivation** is an inner drive that directs behavior toward goals. A need—the difference between a desired state and an actual condition—is a major influencer of motivation and thus a component of many motivation theories. A goal is a desired end result that, when attained, may help satisfy a need. Both needs and goals can be motivating. Motivation explains why we do what we do; at times, a lack of motivation explains why we avoid doing what we should do. If you feel that you can afford to get a D on the final for this class and still have a B average overall, you may be less motivated to study for the test. A person who recognizes or feels a need will be motivated to take action to satisfy that need and achieve a subsequent goal (Figure 16.1).

Consider a mother who needs money to pay for her child's medical expenses. Because of the difference between her current pay and the amount of money she requires in order to pay for the additional expenses, she recognizes a need. To satisfy the need and achieve the goal of gaining more money, she may ask for a raise, work harder to differentiate her performance in order to gain a promotion, seek a higher paying job, or even steal from the company. Human resource managers, and all managers in general, are concerned with the needs of employees, their goals and how they try to achieve them, and the impact of these needs and goals on job performance.

**morale**
The sum total of employees' attitudes toward their jobs, employer, and colleagues.

**Example:** John Deere has made labor force innovations to increase morale. It has begun an experimental program in which a small number of hourly workers' pay raises are tied to completing technical courses at a local community college and then demonstrating their new skills on the job.

One important individual characteristic that affects motivation is **morale**, the sum total of employees' attitudes toward their jobs, employer, and colleagues. Low morale may cause high rates of absenteeism and turnover. For instance, after Caterpillar Tractor Company's negotiations with union officials broke down and its union employees went on strike in the 1980s, Caterpillar executives said that all striking union employees could easily be replaced with nonunion employees. After the strike was over and union employees returned, morale at Caterpillar was at an all-time low. Caterpillar employees went on strike again in 1994. Conversely, high morale can lead to high levels of productivity and employee loyalty. When Cadillac won the Malcolm Baldrige Award for quality, employees' pride in the organization and the quality of the cars they made rose. Respect, appreciation,

## FIGURE 16.1

**The Motivation Process**

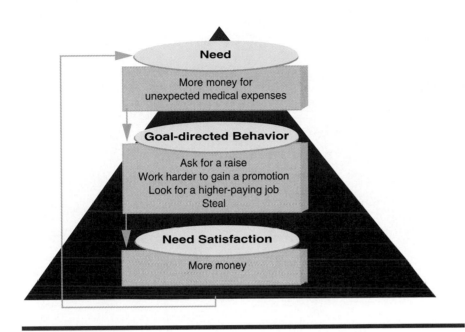

adequate compensation, involvement, promotion opportunities, a pleasant work environment, and a positive organizational culture are all potential morale boosters and can influence motivation.

## The Importance of Motivation

A major goal of management is to help employees satisfy their needs in ways that benefit both the individual and the organization. The impact of dissatisfied employees can be costly, through decreased productivity and possibly high turnover. The cost to hire and retrain individuals is high in many firms.

Motivation is more than a tool that managers can use to foster employee loyalty and boost productivity. It is a process that affects all the relationships within an organization and influences many areas such as pay, promotion, job design, training opportunities, and reporting relationships. Fundamentally, employees are motivated by the nature of the satisfying relationships they have with their supervisors, by the nature of their jobs, and by characteristics of the organization (Figure 16.2). In particular, supervisor qualities that support motivation include honesty, supportiveness, empathy, accessibility, fairness, and openness. Companies can motivate employees by paying equitably, rewarding dedication, and recognizing exceptional performance and creativity.[1] These elements are in turn influenced by the nature of employees' motivation in a dynamic relationship.

Efforts to motivate employees should consider organizational and individual needs to be successful. A recent trend has been to empower or give employees greater autonomy in decision making within the organization. Many employees enjoy the challenge and vote of confidence such decision autonomy can bring. However, research has found that certain occupations, such as service representatives

## Internal Employee Motivation

Satisfying relationships between the employee and supervisor, the job, and the company lead to motivation.

**Teaching Note:** Have students study Figure 16.2 and discuss the relationships of these four characteristics. Call on students to discuss their relationship with a supervisor, a job, and an organization in terms of how each influences their motivation for work performance.

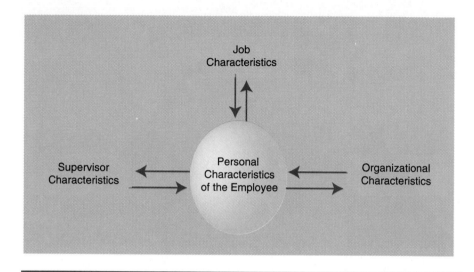

*Source:* Adapted from Carolyn Wiley, "Create an Environment for Employee Motivation," *HR Focus* 69 (June 1992): 14–15.

**Example:** Quad/Graphics Inc., a fast-growing printing company headquartered in Pewaukee, Wisconsin, boasts a long list of training courses, an on-site sports center, and a stock-ownership program. It also sets up every press crew as an autonomous profit center, responsible for its own operations. These actions serve to improve morale and productivity.

(for example, hotel personnel), dislike increased empowerment.[2] Perhaps these employees have found that with increased decision-making autonomy comes increased responsibility that they do not want.

Managers certainly recognize the importance of motivation. In a survey, top business executives were asked to rank their top company concern: Service quality and product quality ranked at the top. Of those surveyed, 85 percent felt that product quality could be enhanced by improving employee motivation.[3] The "Quest for Quality" box describes how one company is using humor to try to motivate employees to be more productive and boost quality. The current economic environment and financial pressure have firms looking for more creative methods to motivate their employees. Many public relations and advertising firms, for example, are offering employees who would otherwise be given raises the opportunity to work with an experienced and respected practitioner in lieu of a salary increase.

Efforts to motivate employees may have negative effects on the organization. When Sears Auto Centers in California implemented an incentive system tied to sales quotas, the result was that employees tried to meet their quotas by selling customers more repair service and parts than requested or warranted. The resulting scandal not only harmed Sears's image, but cost it $8 million to settle a class-action lawsuit as well as an additional $1.5 million to finance automobile repair training programs at community colleges throughout the state.[4] What seemed a straightforward link between pay and performance to motivate employees failed,

You may recognize John Cleese from his roles in "Monty Python's Flying Circus" or "Fawlty Towers," or the hit movies *Monty Python and the Holy Grail* and *A Fish Called Wanda,* or his Emmy Award–winning appearance on "Cheers." An accomplished comedian, actor, writer, and producer, Cleese is also the cofounder of Video Arts, Ltd., Britain's leading producer of industrial training films. The company sells and rents films to over 100,000 companies, in 30 countries, in 20 languages to use in their training programs. The company has sales in excess of $20 million and operates offices in London and Chicago. Video Arts' films teach managers how to manage and communicate with their employees effectively—sometimes through the use of examples of how *not* to manage—while making them laugh. Not a bad use of Cleese's law degree from Cambridge University.

Cleese entered the training film business because of two curiosities: how to encourage individuals to work in groups and enjoy doing so, and what makes our mind function the way it does? The combination of these two questions led Cleese to produce humorous, effective training films that deal with fundamental management issues and help companies achieve current service and quality goals. The key to effective implementation of total quality strategies is the ability to do the fundamentals correctly (communication, motivation, evaluation, and training of employees), which many of the films address.

Cleese says the problem with most training films is that they are boring. In fact, he believes that most workplaces are far too serious and that a sense of fun and playfulness is needed to build

## TOTAL QUALITY MANAGEMENT WITH A SMILE, JOHN CLEESE STYLE

the confidence needed to manage effectively. Cleese advocates the relaxing effect of humor and the end result of greater spontaneity and creativity. Empowered employees need a certain amount of creativity and confidence to accomplish organizational goals. Cleese also believes in the positive motivational impact of training through use of negative examples rather than confronting someone directly and saying "Don't ever do that again."

This philosophy guides each Video Arts training film. In one of the company's best-known productions, "The Unorganized Manager," Cleese plays St. Peter. He denies entry to heaven to an unorganized businessman who died of a heart attack brought on from the stress of being disorganized. In a humorous way Cleese shows the man the error in his ways and gives him an opportunity to make things right. The key issues in the film are establishing priorities, managing time effectively, and delegating responsibility. In "Managing Problem People," Cleese plays Moaning Minnie, Silent Sam, and Rule-bound Reggie, and other problem employees so that managers can learn to recognize and deal with such people. Cleese and guest star Prince Charles deal with environmental issues in "Grime Goes Green."

Video Arts now has a library of 125 such training films using well-known actors, directors, producers, and writers. The films run half an hour and include humorous skits that demonstrate lessons on customer and employee relations, the art of management, and basic workplace issues including quality. The reason the films have been so successful is that the humor works. In allowing businesspeople to laugh and learn—from John Cleese's mistakes—Video Arts helps its clients motivate their employees to work toward quality goals.

*Sources:* Nancy Croft Baker "E-Trainers Mix Carrots and Sticks," *Environment Today* 4 (May 1993): 1, 10; Paul B. Brown, "Laughing All the Way," *Inc.* 10 (April 1988): 18; Paula Dwyer, "John Cleese's Flying Business Circus," *Business Week,* June 21, 1993, 104–109; Jeffrey Ferry, "Funny Business," *Continental Profiles* 2 (April 1988): 3, 72, 74, 76, 81; Bob Filipczak, "An Interview With John Cleese," *Training* 30 (November 1993): 37–41; Eva Innes, "Basil Fawlty's Video Training Film Flourishes," *Financial Post Daily,* May 5, 1988, 17; Jo McHale, "Screentest," *Personnel Management,* November 1993, 51; and Alvin P. Sanoff, "Now for Something Completely Different...," *U.S. News and World Report,* October 16, 1989, 105.

in part, because the quotas imposed were higher than could readily be obtained in normal service situations. Thus, managers need to evaluate all motivation plans carefully to ensure that they are realistic and will generate the desired results.

This child-care center is one of many family benefits John Hancock Mutual Life Insurance Company provides for its employees. John Hancock supports its belief that employees are the company's greatest asset by helping to satisfy their needs. It has an on-site fitness center, an elder-care hotline, lunchtime seminars on issues such as health care, and a cafeteria program that allows employees to buy well-balanced, prepared meals on their way home from work. Such benefits make employees feel good about the company and motivate them to be more productive.

*Source:* Courtesy of John Hancock Financial Services.

## Historical Perspectives on Motivation

Our current understanding of motivation comes from three distinctive historical approaches:  the traditional approach, the human relations approach, and the human resources approach. The contributor of each has uniquely shaped our current philosophy.

**The Traditional Approach.**   Frederick Taylor, the "father of scientific management," was one of the first to address formally the issue of worker motivation. As we discussed in Chapter 2, scientific management was concerned with analyzing job tasks to develop more efficient and productive workers. Taylor's approach to employee motivation was based on the principle of hedonism, which maintains that people are motivated to seek pleasure and avoid pain. He suggested that incentives would provide pleasure and motivate employees to be more productive. Punishments were also common in the Taylor system. Taylor and his peers believed that work was generally distasteful to employees and that earning money and avoiding punishment were the employees' primary goals. The concepts that emerged from this time include incentive pay systems, which are quite visible today in many organizations.

**The Human Relations Approach.**   In contrast with Taylor's output-driven theories, Elton Mayo, who developed the human relations approach to management, felt that giving employees feedback and some level of self-esteem and appreciating their performance would best motivate them. Mayo's Hawthorne studies at the Western Electric plant (discussed in Chapter 2) showed that social needs are of great importance in motivating employees. The evolution of personnel departments has been attributed to Mayo. As the belief was established that the social environment influences general employee satisfaction and therefore work satisfaction, personnel departments arose to systematically address workers' needs and desires.

**The Human Resource Approach.**   The human resource approach encompasses, yet goes beyond, the traditional and human relations approaches. It considers both the

**Teaching Note:** Remind students of Taylor's "one best way" approach. Because Taylor believed employees had to be constantly motivated to work and produce quotas, his use of monetary incentives emerged.

**Teaching Note:** Remind students that in Chapter 2 we learned from the Hawthorne studies at the Western Electric plant that worker output improved even under very dim lighting conditions. Workers enjoyed the attention and thus worked harder.

economic and social needs of the individual as well as the need to feel like a positive contributor to an important undertaking. This perspective views workers as complex entities who are valuable resources to the organization as well as important in their own right. It maintains that the maximum utility for both the company and the workers lies in using as much of the employee's skill and ability as possible to accomplish organizational goals. Companies' efforts to provide benefits beyond stock options and health insurance address such needs. Many companies, for example, are providing on-site day care for children, flexible scheduling, and company-paid health club memberships or on-site health clubs, to name a few additional benefits. Employee trust, loyalty, commitment, and productivity can be influenced by a firm's efforts to consider what the employees might actually want and need to function optimally in the work environment. This motivates employees to do their best for the organization while satisfying the maximum number of employee needs.

**Example:** Pro Fasteners, an industrial parts distributor based in San Jose, California, buys a set of San Francisco 49ers tickets every year, along with a set of tickets to concerts and performances. Employees put in preferences for dates, and everyone is assured of attending at least one event. While this benefit costs the company a few thousand dollars a year, the value to employees is high.

# CONTENT THEORIES OF MOTIVATION

Throughout the twentieth century, researchers have sought ways to motivate workers to increase productivity. Their studies have generated theories of motivation that have been applied with varying degrees of success. Among these are the **content theories**, a group of theories that assume that workers are motivated by the desire to satisfy needs and that seek to identify what those needs are. In other words, content theories try to determine the content of activities or rewards needed to motivate individuals. Taylor's traditional view of motivation, for example, suggests that money to satisfy financial obligations motivates employees. In this section, we discuss the content theories of Abraham Maslow, Frederick Herzberg, and David McClelland.

**content theories**
A group of theories that assume that workers are motivated by the desire to satisfy needs and that seek to identify what their needs are.

## Maslow's Hierarchy of Needs

Psychologist Abraham Maslow theorized that people have five basic needs: physiological, security, social, esteem, and self-actualization.[5] **Maslow's hierarchy of needs** shows the order in which people strive to satisfy these needs (Figure 16.3).

*Physiological needs* are the essentials for living—water, food, shelter, and clothing. According to Maslow, people devote all their efforts to satisfying these physiological needs until they are met. For example, if you are struggling to get a job to provide food and shelter for your family, you will probably be concerned more with a job's pay than with whether the employees are nice or the company has an exercise facility. Only when physiological needs are met do people focus their attention on satisfying the next level of needs—security.

*Security needs* relate to protecting yourself from physical and economic harm. Examples of actions that a person may take to satisfy security needs include reporting a dangerous workplace condition to management, maintaining safety equipment, and purchasing insurance with income protection in case the person becomes unable to work. Once security needs have been satisfied, people strive for social goals.

*Social needs* include love, companionship, and friendship—the desire for acceptance by others. To fulfill social needs, a person may try many things—making friends with a coworker, joining a professional organization, volunteering at a charity, or throwing a party. Once their social needs have been satisfied, people attempt to satisfy their need for esteem.

**Maslow's hierarchy of needs**
The order in which people strive to satisfy the five basic needs as theorized by Maslow—physiological, security, social, esteem, and self-actualization.

**FIGURE 16.3**

**Maslow's Hierarchy of Needs**

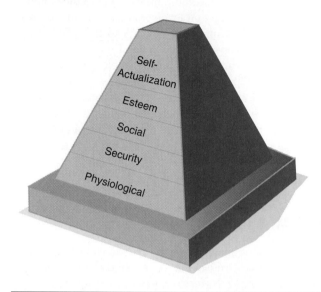

*Source:* Adapted from Abraham H. Maslow, "A Theory of Human Motivation," *Psychology Review* 50 (1943): 370–396.

*Esteem needs* relate to respect—both self-respect and respect from others. One aspect of esteem needs is competition—the need to feel that you can do something better than anyone else. Competition often motivates people to increase their productivity. For example, a department may hold a contest promising that the associate with the highest sales will be treated to dinner by the store manager; such a competition may inspire all the salespeople to work harder. Esteem needs are not as easily satisfied as the needs at lower levels in Maslow's hierarchy because they do not always provide tangible evidence of success. However, these needs can be realized through rewards and increased involvement in organizational activities. When people feel they have achieved some measure of respect, self-actualization becomes the major goal of life.

*Self-actualization needs* derive from a desire to be the best you can be, to maximize your potential. A self-actualized person feels that she or he is living life to its fullest in every way. For actress Meg Ryan, it might mean winning an Oscar; for Nigel Mansel, it might mean winning the Indianapolis 500 to follow his success as a Formula One driver. Although such milestones reflect the need to self-actualize, Maslow believed that this need is never fully realized. Rather, it represents an ongoing lifelong striving for self-improvement that not all individuals desire to achieve.

Maslow's theory suggests that people must satisfy the needs at the bottom of the hierarchy before working toward higher-level ones. Thus, people who are hungry and homeless are not very concerned with obtaining respect from their colleagues. Only when physiological, security, and social needs have been more or less satisfied do people seek esteem. This theory also suggests that if a low-level need such as security is suddenly reactivated, the individual will try to satisfy that need rather than higher-level needs. For example, many workers laid off by General Motors, IBM, Apple, Boeing, and numerous other firms in the early 1990s prob-

**Example:** Pitney Bowes, Quaker Oats, Nike, Salomon Brothers, and others are asking employees to restructure benefit plans. Most start by probing workers' fears, needs, and desires in focus groups and through surveys. Employees often express worries about not being able to buy a house, send children to college, or care for elderly parents.

**TABLE 16.1**

**Herzberg's Maintenance and Motivational Factors**

| Maintenance Factors | Motivational Factors |
|---|---|
| Company policy | Achievement |
| Supervision | Recognition |
| Working conditions | Work itself |
| Relationships with peers, supervisors, and subordinates | Responsibility |
| Salary | Advancement |
| Security | Personal growth |

ably shifted their focus from striving to satisfy high-level esteem needs to the need for security. Managers should learn from Maslow's hierarchy that employees will be motivated to contribute to organizational goals only if they are able first to satisfy their physiological, security, and social needs through their work.

Maslow's hierarchy, although intuitively appealing and frequently used in management training, has not found widespread support from management researchers. Beyond the first two basic needs, people vary in their need emphasis. Some may seek social-need satisfaction, while others may emphasize esteem needs or even self-actualization. Thus, each individual may respond differently to organizational characteristics. Moreover, the steps in Maslow's hierarchy are not necessarily experienced in a sequential manner: People can have more than one need at the same time. Situations dictate which needs are most important at a given point in time. If a woman is pregnant, for example, and knows she will be taking a maternity leave from her job, causing money to be tight, she is likely to be more conscious of security and physiological needs, whereas before, with two well-paying jobs, she and her husband had no financial concerns. Because of the overly simplified nature of Maslow's model, it provides little to help managers motivate employees. Instead, it functions best in enhancing managers' awareness of individuals' needs and the complex and broad nature of these needs.

## Herzberg's Two-Factor Theory

In 1959, psychologist Frederick Herzberg proposed a theory of motivation that focuses on the job and on the environment where work is done. In his study, Herzberg asked engineers and accountants to relate what job-related issues made them feel good about their jobs and which ones made them feel bad. He also asked them to describe the conditions that led to these positive or negative feelings. From this, Herzberg identified two categories of job factors, which he called maintenance factors and motivational factors (Table 16.1).

Herzberg's **maintenance factors**, which relate to the work setting, include adequate wages, comfortable working conditions, fair company policies, and job security. These factors do not necessarily motivate employees to excel, but their absence may be a potential source of dissatisfaction, low morale, and high turnover. Many people feel that a good salary is one of the most important job factors, even more important than job security and the chance to use one's mind and abilities. However, a recession and general trend toward downsizing during the early 1990s, which resulted in layoffs of both blue- and white-collar workers at many companies,

**maintenance factors**
Those aspects of a job that relate to the work setting, including adequate wages, comfortable working conditions, fair company policies, and job security.

may have led some of those people to place security ahead of salary as they feared for their jobs and the ability to support themselves and their families. Salary and security, two of the maintenance factors identified by Herzberg, make it possible for employees to satisfy the physiological and security needs identified by Maslow. However, the presence of maintenance factors is unlikely to motivate employees to work harder.

**motivational factors**

Those aspects of a job that relate to the content of the work, including achievement, recognition, the work itself, involvement, responsibility, and advancement.

**Example:** IBM has set up a new compensation program that rewards top managers for company-wide performance rather than an individual unit's performance.

**Motivational factors** relate to the content of the work and include achievement, recognition, the work itself, involvement, responsibility, and advancement. They promote higher levels of performance. The absence of motivational factors may not result in dissatisfaction, but their presence is likely to motivate employees to excel. Danbury Plumbing Supply in Danbury, Connecticut, uses motivational factors to encourage employees to reduce costs. Danbury managers post a chart showing the company's sales and expenses every month and put 15 percent of the company's profits into a bonus pool. Bonuses are distributed to the employees on the basis of their seniority and salary level. The bonuses and the increased involvement in company activities motivate employees to close doors and turn out lights (reducing expenses) and to increase sales (increasing profits). This involvement ultimately fattens the bonuses, which are a tangible reflection of their higher achievement levels.[6] Thus, the higher-level goals in Maslow's hierarchy and the motivational factors identified by Herzberg are important factors in motivating employees to work harder.

Herzberg's theory is not without criticism. One is that initial interviews for the study are subject to multiple interpretations and conclusions. Another is that the original study was limited to professional engineers and accountants and that the results may not be generalizable to blue-collar workers.[7] Subsequent studies by Herzberg and other researchers conducted on a variety of blue- and white-collar jobs have yielded inconsistent results.[8] Still another criticism is that the theory oversimplifies the nature of the relationship between motivation and sources of job satisfaction or dissatisfaction.[9] Nevertheless, Herzberg's ideas have had a significant impact on the practice of management by making managers aware of the importance of motivation.

Herzberg's motivational factors and Maslow's esteem and self-actualization needs are similar. Workers' low-level needs (physiological and security) have largely been satisfied by minimum-wage laws and occupational-safety standards set by various government agencies and are therefore not motivators. Consequently, to improve productivity, management should focus on satisfying workers' higher-level needs (motivational factors) by providing opportunities for achievement, involvement, and advancement and by recognizing good performance. Many companies combine both motivational factors and maintenance factors to maximize employee motivation. By combining employee participation (motivational factor) with employee stock ownership plans (maintenance factor), studies show that companies have grown 8 to 11 percent faster than those without such plans.[10]

## McClelland's Achievement Motivation Theory

Psychologist David McClelland identified different needs than those examined by Maslow and Herzberg: achievement, affiliation, and power. The need for achievement refers to an individual's desire for goals that are well-defined and moderately difficult, include employee participation, and provide feedback. People with a high need for achievement are motivated, show great initiative, and are goal-oriented. How do you increase employee need for achievement and instill characteristics valuable to the organization? McClelland suggests a training course called "total push," within which employees are given role models with a high need for achievement to emulate. Short-term work goals are set, and exercises and techniques are provided to encourage employees to analyze their hopes, aspirations, fears, successes, and failures.[11]

The need for affiliation is the desire to work with others in the organization rather than alone. Individuals with a high need for affiliation want to interact with others, guide others, and learn from those with whom they work. The need for affiliation relates to the social needs identified by Maslow. Employees with a high need for affiliation would probably be most effective working in an environment with peers rather than working at home alone.

The need for power is a function of the influence and control an individual has over others. What people are able to contribute in the organization is often limited or constrained by the organizational environment that allocates power. To successfully utilize power within the organization, the individual must be accepted, forceful, and capable.

# PROCESS THEORIES OF MOTIVATION

Whereas content theories try to determine "what" motivates employees, the **process theories** try to determine "how" and "why" employees are motivated to perform. This group of theories attempts to describe the processes that motivate behavior. For example, the idea that working hard may result in a promotion comes from process theory. Process theories differ from content theories in that they attempt to determine the reasons employees are motivated, whereas content theories look only at what motivates the individual. Process theories include equity theory, expectancy theory, and the Porter-Lawler expectancy model.

**process theories**
A set of theories that try to determine "how" and "why" employees are motivated to perform.

## Equity Theory

Equity theory developed from the research of J. Stacy Adams, who suggested that individuals strive to engage in equitable exchanges or relationships.[12] According to **equity theory**, how much people are willing to contribute to an organization depends on their assessment of the fairness of the rewards they will receive in exchange. In an equitable situation, a person receives rewards proportional to the contribution he or she makes to the organization. In practice, equity is a subjective notion.

According to equity theory, each of us regularly develops a personal input-outcome ratio, taking stock of our contribution (inputs) to the organization in time, effort, skills, and experience and assessing the rewards (outcomes) offered by the organization in pay, benefits, recognition, and promotions. We then compare our ratio to the input-outcome ratio of some other person—a "comparison other," who may be a coworker, a friend working in another organization, or an "average" of several people working in the organization.

**equity theory**
A theory stating that the extent to which people are willing to contribute to an organization depends on their assessment of the fairness of the rewards they will receive in exchange.

$$\frac{\text{Inputs (Self)}}{\text{Outcomes (Self)}} = \frac{\text{Inputs (Other)}}{\text{Outcomes (Other)}}$$

If the two ratios are close, then we will probably feel that we are being treated equitably.

Consider two salespersons, one who earns $26,000 per year and the other $32,000. The lower-paid salesperson has less experience in sales and generates

Mayflower Transit's pay-for-performance approach to driver compensation illustrates Vroom's expectancy theory. Mayflower compensates its van operators according to their performance ratings on safety, on-time delivery, claims, and customer satisfaction, which is gauged directly from customer evaluations on survey forms. Pay for performance motivates van operators to give customers exceptional service during the stressful moving process.

*Source:* Courtesy of Mayflower Transit, Inc.

**Example:** Chattanooga State Technical Community College in Chattanooga, Tennessee, has two Salary Equity Committees. The faculty committee is made up of faculty representatives, and the Staff Committee includes employees from professional, nonfaculty, clerical, and support staff. The committees determine whether salary recommendations are equitable and fair to others in the institution within the same pay grade.

lower volume than the one earning $32,000; therefore, she is likely to perceive overall equity as fair. As she gains experience and brings in greater sales, there should be increases in her salary. If the higher-paid salesperson were to decrease her productivity over a sustained period, her salary should not increase and possibly should even decrease to maintain equity within the organization.

Because of the subjective and comparative nature of the evaluation, a person will feel either equitably compensated, overcompensated, or undercompensated. The result of this perception will be one of several outcomes. The person may increase performance or productivity to remedy the perception of overcompensation, decrease performance or productivity to remedy the perception of undercompensation, or do nothing if the situation is perceived as being equitable. Unfortunately for managers, workers often have trouble communicating their feelings of inequity and instead decrease the quantity or quality of their work or increase their absenteeism.

Because almost all the issues involved in equity theory are subjective, they can generate problems. Managers should try to avoid equity problems by ensuring that rewards are distributed on the basis of performance and that all employees clearly understand the basis for their pay and benefits.

## Expectancy Theory

**expectancy theory**
A theory stating that motivation depends not only on how much a person wants something but also on the person's perception of how likely he or she is to get it.

Psychologist Victor Vroom developed **expectancy theory**, which says that motivation depends not only on how much a person wants something but also on the person's perception of how likely he or she is to get it.[13] A person who wants something (a particular outcome) and has reason to think he or she will actually get it by putting effort toward performance will be strongly motivated (Figure 16.4). Consider, for example, a salesperson at a BMW dealership who has been told that if he can increase his average sales over the previous three months by 30 percent, he will receive double the commission on his overall sales. But because he knows that sales are usually much slower in this quarter, and thus increasing his sales would be nearly impossible, he does not change his selling behavior or effort to achieve the goal. A more realistic goal would have the salesperson attempting to maintain his sales average in a period in which he generally sells less. Such a goal is more realistic, attainable, and has motivational potential for the employee.

**FIGURE 16.4**

**Expectancy Theory**

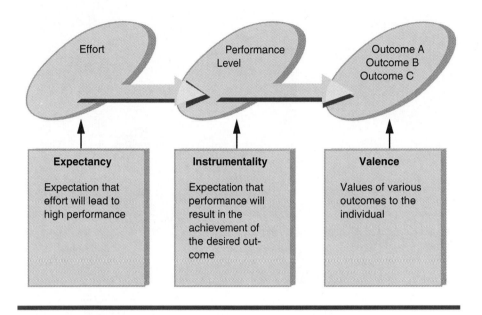

Expectancy theory is illustrated in Figure 16.4. **Expectancy** refers to a person's expectation that effort will lead to high performance. If the car salesperson believes that extra effort will help him attain a bonus or increased commission, then he will probably be motivated to strive for that goal. On the other hand, if the salesperson lacks the ability or the opportunity to reach high performance, his expectancy will be low and so will his motivation.

**Instrumentality** is a person's expectation that performing a task will lead to a desired outcome. If the salesman believes that studying competitive cars (performance level) will increase his ability to sell cars (outcome), he will probably be more motivated to do so. But if he believes that BMW buyers are highly educated and have conducted extensive research themselves, then he may not be motivated to investigate the competition.

Each potential outcome has a value or **valence**, which describes its importance to the individual. Employees are likely to be more motivated to perform at higher levels if they consider the resulting outcomes valuable; conversely, they are less likely to work hard to achieve outcomes that hold little value to them. If our BMW salesman is trying to put his daughter through college, for example, he may be quite motivated to try to sell more cars to gain double the commission on his overall sales despite a slow quarter, but he may be less motivated to perform if the outcome of his efforts will merely be a certificate of appreciation from his employer. Each individual places different valences on each potential outcome, so an outcome desired by one employee may hold little interest for another.

Expectancy theory suggests that managers can influence an employee's motivation in three ways—first, by helping the employee to believe he or she can achieve successful performance, second, by having faith in the employee, and third, by providing needed support such as training and guidance. In addition, it is important to determine the kinds of outcomes that have high valence for different

**expectancy**
A person's expectation that effort will lead to high performance.

**instrumentality**
A person's expectation that performing a task will lead to a desired outcome.

**valence**
The importance of each potential outcome to the individual.

**FIGURE 16.5**

**The Porter-Lawler Expectancy Model**

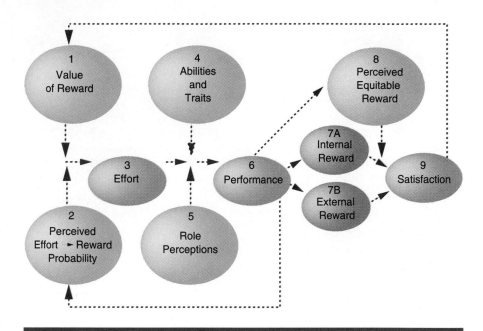

*Source:* Adapted from Craig C. Pinder, "Valence-Instrumentality-Expectancy Theory," in Richard M. Steers and Lyman W. Porter, *Motivation and Work Behavior* 5th ed. (New York: McGraw-Hill,): 151.

**Example:** 83% of young adults believe they need more formal training or education to maintain or increase their earning power in the years to come, according to a survey conducted by the Gallup Organization for the National Career Development Association. These adults will seek additional training or education at a four-year college or university; through their employer; through community colleges; and through business, technical, or trade schools.

**Porter-Lawler expectancy model**

An extension of the expectancy theory stating that satisfaction is the result rather than the cause of performance and that different levels of performance lead to different rewards, which, in turn, produce different levels of job satisfaction.

individuals, recognizing employee diversity. Finally, managers should relate outcomes to performance.

## The Porter-Lawler Expectancy Model

Lyman Porter and Edward Lawler extended the expectancy theory with their own. Their **Porter-Lawler expectancy model** suggests that satisfaction is the result rather than the cause of performance and that different levels of performance lead to different rewards, which, in turn, produce different levels of job satisfaction (Figure 16.5).[14] Additionally, employees can be motivated by the intrinsic satisfaction that comes from performing a task. Internal (intrinsic) rewards are intangible and occur simultaneously as the task is performed. For example, a nurse who successfully assists a doctor in surgery may have an enormous feeling of accomplishment and satisfaction. If the hospital's chief of surgery takes the same nurse out to dinner, then the behavior receives a more tangible external (extrinsic) reward. External rewards could include raises, promotions, additional benefits, or time off. According to the Porter-Lawler model, performance results in both internal and external rewards. The worker perceives the equity of the rewards relative to the effort put forth and the level of performance attained. If he or she perceives the rewards to be equitable, then he or she is satisfied.

Factors that affect this balance include the employee's skill, knowledge, and ability for the job held. Recognition and compensation must also reflect equity

## B U S I N E S S   D I L E M M A

*You're the Manager …What Would You Do?*

THE COMPANY:   **Eagle Pharmaceuticals**

YOUR POSITION:   **Director of Sales**

THE PLACE:   **St. Louis, MO**

Eagle Pharmaceutical is the second-largest prescription drug manufacturer in the United States. The St. Louis-based company has recently been recognized for its innovative and effective techniques for motivating its sales force. The "Touchdown," which uses many analogies from sports, highlights the salesperson who has been the most successful during the previous quarter. Besides being named in the company newsletter, the employee receives a football jersey with the company name and logo on the front and his or her name on the back, and an engraved plaque. The employee also receives $1,000 worth of Eagle stock.

Beyond the recognition and gifts, Eagle tries to capture some of the successful tactics and strategies the winning salesperson has used with a video conference hook-up between the winner and the managers of the other four regional offices. The regional managers summarize the ideas and then discuss them with the salespeople they manage.

Sales managers feel strongly that programs such as this are important and that, by sharing strategies and tactics with one another, they can be a successful team. The direct selling area does not heavily use such a team orientation because of the individualized nature of goals, objectives, and performance. Thus, Eagle has worked hard to break down the barriers and have employees communicate freely with one another through their voice mail system or at biannual meetings. Vice president Hal Brenner says, "When the team scores, the individual scores. We recognize the individual and allow him (or her) to share his success with everyone else.

That's how we succeed. The employees like it and the stock prizes give them an even greater incentive to make the company a success."

Other programs Eagle uses to motivate employees include a "Superbowl Club" for those employees who reach or exceed their sales goal. And the top 20 salespeople (in terms of goal achievement, not in comparison to one another) each year (out of a sales force of 250) win a "Heisman Award," which includes an all-expense-paid vacation to the Caribbean. Excellence in performance is acknowledged by top management. In addition, Eagle gives its employees great autonomy in decision making, empowering salespeople and district managers. This has led to higher-quality work, increased productivity, and lower turnover for the company.

### Questions

1. From the sales manager's perspective, what is the importance of getting employees to compete against a goal instead of against one another?
2. What do you think are the most effective motivational rewards Eagle uses? Critique the practices currently used.
3. As sales manager, if you had to go to a university Introduction to Management class and talk about the use of motivational theories in your company's practices, which would you discuss and why?

with others in the organization. Some people say that chief executive officers' high compensation reflects a belief in higher levels of performance tied to reward measures such as salary, bonuses, benefits, and stock options. Others criticize the pay and reward systems of many CEOs, suggesting there is no way to tie an $88 million compensation package to one individual's performance. In addition, the fact that some CEOs consistently get high compensation packages regardless of their firms' performance can actually be demotivating to the CEO and limit problem-solving activities.

The salesperson responsible for your using this textbook may be more intrinsically satisfied with the independent nature of the direct-selling position, the autonomy, and the scheduling flexibility than with the salary or benefits. If the salesperson finds that each year his sales goals are related to his previous year's performance, he may be less motivated to achieve exceptional levels. For example, the

**Example:** According to data covering about 250 companies a year, there have been at least 227 cases, since 1987, in which a corporate executive made more than $5 million a year and 77 cases in which an executive made more than $10 million per year. Executive compensation has been the subject of critical attention especially in light of recent terminations, corporate takeovers, and downsizing.

employee who achieves 120 percent of his sales goal will have to do at least that well next year to succeed in the company—a hard goal to achieve; therefore, he may strive just to hit the goal, not exceed it.

# REINFORCEMENT THEORY

**reinforcement theory**
A process theory which assumes that behavior may be reinforced by relating it to its consequences.

**behavior modification**
An application of reinforcement theory, which involves changing behavior and encouraging appropriate actions by relating the consequences of behavior to the behavior itself.

**Reinforcement theory** is a type of process theory which assumes that behavior may be reinforced by relating it to its consequences. The most widely discussed application of reinforcement theory is **behavior modification**, which involves changing behavior and encouraging appropriate actions by relating the consequences of behavior to the behavior itself. The concept of behavior modification was developed by psychologist B. F. Skinner, who showed that there are two types of consequences that can modify behavior: reward and punishment. Skinner found that behavior which is positively reinforced, or rewarded, will tend to be repeated, while behavior that is punished will tend to be eliminated.

## Types of Reinforcement

**positive reinforcement**
The act of strengthening a desired behavior by rewarding it or providing other positive outcomes.

**Example:** Allstate of Tennessee employees receive longevity pay after three years of service. For each year of service up to 25 years, employees receive $100. This motivates employees to remain in their jobs and reduces turnover and recruiting expenses.

There are four types of reinforcement: positive reinforcement, negative reinforcement or avoidance, punishment, and extinction. **Positive reinforcement** strengthens a desired behavior by rewarding it or providing other positive outcomes. Traditional employment rewards include praise and recognition, raises, bonuses, and promotions for doing a good job; such rewards reinforce behavior because the desirable consequences encourage employees to continue the behavior. For example, one Massachusetts manufacturing firm implemented a "100 Club" to foster team spirit within the company. To become members of the club, employees had to accumulate 100 points by favorable work behavior (attendance, punctuality, performance, and attitude). The concept was quite successful, generating $1.6 million in financial benefits, primarily from a decrease in quality-related mistakes. Attendance improvements alone accounted for $90,000 in savings.[15] Such programs can have extensive impact on organizational performance and profitability by motivating employees effectively.

**avoidance**
The act of strengthening a desired behavior by allowing individuals to avoid negative consequences by performing the behavior.

**Avoidance** strengthens a desired behavior by allowing individuals to avoid negative consequences by performing the behavior. For example, employees are likely to come back from lunch on time to avoid being reprimanded or docked for taking long lunch breaks.

**punishment**
The act of weakening or eliminating an undesired behavior by providing negative consequences.

**Punishment** weakens or eliminates an undesired behavior by providing negative consequences. An employee who uses work time to deal with personal matters, for example, may be reprimanded, have his or her pay reduced, or even be fired if the situation becomes severe enough. Unfortunately, more managers have access to methods of punishment than access to rewards; consequently, punishment activities are more prevalent. At Las Casuelas Terraza restaurant in Palm Springs, CA, for example, an employee who is chronically late or does not sell enough has to stay and polish the wood and brass fixtures.

**extinction**
Weakening an undesired behavior by not providing positive consequences.

**Extinction** weakens an undesired behavior by not providing positive consequences. It occurs when positive reinforcement is withdrawn from a previously positively reinforced behavior. When the behavior is not reinforced, it will subside and eventually stop. A manager faced with an employee who complains needlessly and endlessly may reduce the complaints by ignoring the behavior.

Xerox manager Frank Pacetta stands next to a ship captain's bell he installed at a sales office as a positive reinforcement tool. When members of his team of 70 sales reps complete a sale, he asks them to ring the bell to signal their achievement. Pacetta also uses praise, hugs, and testimonial dinners to reward employees' good performance. Pacetta punishes weak performance by putting an ugly troll on the desks of poor performers. Salespeople who don't improve their performance after three consecutive visits from the troll are fired.

*Source:* © 1994 David Graham.

## Schedules of Reinforcement

According to reinforcement theory, the timing of reinforcement is just as important as what kind of reinforcement is used. A **fixed-interval schedule** provides reinforcement at specified periods of time, regardless of behavior. The time between reinforcements does not change. The weekly paycheck is an example. However, this method does not provide a great deal of incentive because employees know they will receive the paycheck regardless of the level of work performance. A **variable-interval schedule** varies the period of time between one reinforcement and the next. The boss who brings donuts for the office staff from time to time, but on no set schedule, and not related to performance, is using a variable-interval schedule of reinforcement. Although this act may help morale, it does little to motivate work behavior because it is not tied to performance.

Two additional reinforcement schedules are based on the frequency of behavior rather than time. A **fixed-ratio schedule** offers reinforcement after a specified number of desired performance behaviors, regardless of the time elapsed between the behaviors. Piece-rate pay systems are examples of fixed-ratio schedules of reinforcement. Another example is giving salespersons a bonus for every fourth sale made. The fixed-ratio schedule is a strong motivator because the reward is linked directly to the performance behavior.

A **variable-ratio schedule** varies the number of behaviors required for each reinforcement. For example, praising an employee after completing the third, eighth, fourteenth, and twentieth circuit boards completed is an example of using a variable-ratio schedule. While it is difficult to keep track of when and whether employees have been rewarded, the variable-ratio schedule can be quite a powerful motivator. An interesting application of a variable-ratio schedule of reinforcement is using the poker card game to improve workplace attendance. Employees who are at work on time each day can draw a card from a deck. By Friday, each employee with perfect attendance has a poker hand, and top hands can win prizes. The fun of playing and potentially winning are all reinforcers randomly tied to desired performance behavior.

**fixed-interval schedule**
A pattern of reinforcement at specified periods of time, regardless of behavior.

**variable-interval schedule**
A pattern whereby the period of reinforcement varies between one reinforcement and the next.

**fixed-ratio schedule**
A pattern offering reinforcement after a specified number of desired performance behaviors, regardless of the time elapsed between them.

**variable-ratio schedule**
A pattern whereby the number of behaviors required for reinforcement is varied.

## Applying Reinforcement Theory

Managers who want to motivate employees to behave appropriately should carefully consider the long-term effects of punishment and reward before selecting a policy. Punishing unacceptable behavior provides quick results but may lead to undesirable long-term side effects such as employee dissatisfaction and increased turnover. Consequently, punishment must occur only in certain situations in which the nature of the offense is so serious, dangerous, or in violation of corporate codes of ethics that a message must be sent to all employees. Punishment tells the person what not to do, but does not prescribe appropriate behavior. Recent research does suggest that punishment can be used in the workplace without undesirable side effects. In the long run, however, rewarding appropriate behavior will generally be more effective in modifying behavior.

To encourage employees to behave appropriately, most firms use internal or external rewards. For example, Avon sales representatives who exceed their sales goals receive praise from their supervisors and become eligible for cruises and gifts. Successfully managing employees requires balancing internal and external rewards in making the job challenging enough and acknowledging the appropriate behavior with external rewards.

One company manager found an alternative to punishment that motivates employees to admit to their mistakes and provides a lesson to the rest of the staff. Steve Ettridge, CEO at Temps & Co. in Washington, DC, offers $250 to any employee who admits to a mistake. Ettridge figures that if an employee confesses to a $2,000 error in judgment in front of 20 other employees, the error becomes a lesson worth $100 a person. Ettridge himself won the $250 when he admitted to running out of gas while driving an important prospect to the airport.[16] The key concern in implementing such a program is that managers reinforce the admission of errors, not the act of causing errors. This motivational technique can increase productivity because the employees know that most of their mistakes will be used as a learning experience and not as grounds for dismissal.

**Example:** Harry Pearce, executive vice president of General Motors, commented on GM's old system of incentive compensation: "Executives were thankful they got a big bonus but often didn't know why. If you want to design a system that's set up just to hand out gratuities to people you like, that's the way you'd set it up."

# GOAL-SETTING THEORY

**goal-setting theory**
A theory which recognizes the importance of goals in improving employee performance.

One of the most discussed theories in management has been **goal-setting theory**, which recognizes the importance of goals in improving employee performance. In other words, goals can act as motivators by focusing employees' efforts on specific activities. Thus, employees operating with goals outperform those without goals. The particular advantages of goals include directing attention and action, mobilizing effort, creating patterns of persistent behavior, and developing strategies for goal attainment.[17]

The biggest barrier to getting employees to attain organizational goals is merging the individual's and the organization's needs. Employees ask such key questions as "Will this benefit just management, or will it benefit me?" "Is this behavior rewarded?" "Do I have the support, equipment, facilities, time, budget, and staff to attain this goal?" For goals to motivate effectively, these issues must be addressed. Researchers have found five key characteristics that improve employees' commitment to and acceptance of goals: specificity, difficulty, feedback, participation, and competition.[18]

Goal specificity means goals should be clear and well-defined. They should serve as a call to action, a preferred outcome, a deadline, and a budget. For example, goals for an advertising manager might be to launch a new microwavable frozen pizza in national supermarket chains, and establish market presence with a 2 percent share of the frozen pizza market within one year on a budget of $5 million. The advertising manager will obviously need more information to achieve the goal, but the broad considerations—inputs and outputs—have been established and provide a starting point for goal achievement.

Difficulty of goals refers to challenge. Easy goals do not motivate employees because they provide no challenge. At the other extreme, impossible goals discourage and frustrate employees. Goal difficulty must be assessed by looking at the individual's (or group's) skills, knowledge, and ability.

Feedback on goals may occur at varying times in the process of achievement. You can receive feedback on your plan for goal achievement, or on an ongoing basis throughout the process and upon completion of the goal(s). Feedback can both motivate the employee and assist in effectively achieving the goal. If an employee is "off track," he or she needs feedback as soon as possible.

Participation in the process of setting goals gives employees insights and control and deepens their commitment. Competition in goal attainment can involve pitting one individual against another (as in individual sales goals) or pitting one group against another (as in cost-efficiency for one team or division versus another). Competition, however, can have negative side effects if employees engage in unethical behavior or behavior that could harm the organization in the long run.

## MOTIVATION AND JOB DESIGN

The various theories on motivation have helped managers develop strategies for motivating their employees to achieve organizational objectives and for boosting morale within their organizations. Many of these techniques involve job design, which applies motivational theories to the structuring of jobs in order to increase productivity and morale.

Herzberg identified the job itself as a motivational factor. Managers have several strategies that they can use to design jobs and thereby promote employee motivation. Among these strategies are job design techniques such as job rotation, job enlargement, and job enrichment, which we discussed in Chapter 12. In this section, we will look at a job characteristics model, flexible scheduling strategies, and paying for performance.

### Hackman and Oldham's Job Characteristics Model

J. Richard Hackman and Greg Oldham took a different approach to job design by trying to identify how managers can motivate workers by helping them to achieve more of their higher-level needs.[19] They first identified five job characteristics that determine a job's potential to motivate (Figure 16.6):

1. *Skill variety* is the number of diverse activities and skills an employee performs in a job. Jobs perceived as challenging are probably high in variety.

2. *Task identity* is the degree to which an employee performs a complete job with a recognizable beginning and ending. When workers perform only one part of the entire job, as is common with specialization, they may fail to feel a sense of completion or accomplishment. Expanding the job's tasks may both help workers gain that sense of completion and increase task identity.

**FIGURE 16.6**

**The Job Characteristics Model**

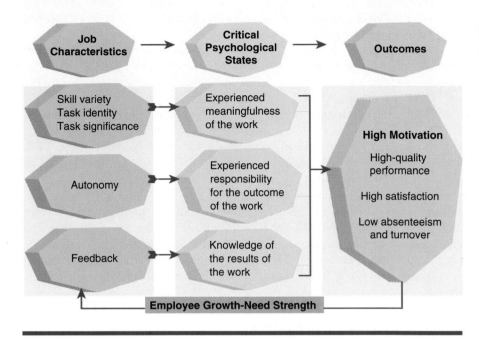

*Source:* Adapted from J.R. Hackman and G.R. Oldham, *Work Redesign* (Reading, MA: Addison-Wesley, 1980): 83.

**Example:** John Deere has provided skill variety through nontraditional work patterns and provides feedback to employees through customer contact and supplier meetings. In partnership with the UAW, Deere assigns employees to jobs in customer service and dealer training to diversify their skills. To improve quality, hourly workers visit farms to meet customers and see how they use the equipment. Deere also organizes sessions between suppliers and assembly-line workers to help suppliers cut costs and improve delivery time.

3. *Task significance* is the degree to which an employee perceives the job as important and having an impact on the company or consumers. Feeling that they are doing something worthwhile is important to most people.

4. *Autonomy* is the degree of control (freedom and discretion) employees have in performing the job. It fosters a sense of responsibility.

5. *Feedback* is the extent to which employees know how well they are performing the job. People need to know how they are doing so that they can modify their performance appropriately.

Oldham and Hackman's theory suggests that the more of these five characteristics managers can design into jobs, the higher will be employees' motivation.

The job characteristics model also identified three psychological states that affect workplace motivation. When any of these psychological states is low, so is employee motivation.

1. *Experienced meaningfulness* is the degree to which employees perceive their work as satisfying and rewarding. If you feel, for example, that soldering circuits onto circuit boards is a trivial task, your motivation to perform that task won't be very high, regardless of how much responsibility or feedback you get from that task. Experienced meaningfulness is influenced by skill variety, task identity, and task significance.

2. *Experienced responsibility* is the extent to which employees feel personally responsible for the quality of their work. It is influenced by autonomy.

**3.** *Knowledge of results* is the extent to which employees receive feedback about their performance. It is influenced by feedback.

The influence of the five job characteristics on employees' psychological states results in high work motivation, high work performance, high satisfaction, and low absenteeism and turnover.

Additionally, Oldham and Hackman identified *growth-need strength,* the extent to which an employee desires a job that provides personal challenges, a sense of accomplishment, and personal growth. Different individuals bring different needs to the workplace. One employee may need to satisfy only low-level needs, while another may need to satisfy the highest-level needs. Managers need to identify employees' needs and design jobs accordingly; this is particularly important when dealing with a culturally diverse work force. For those employees with high growth-need strength—those who are seeking the greatest challenges and personal growth—job enrichment programs may enhance motivation. Conversely, for those employees with low growth-need strength, such job enrichment programs may frustrate rather than motivate.

## Flexible-Scheduling Strategies in Work Design

While many Americans continue to work a traditional 40-hour work week—consisting of five 8-hour days with fixed starting and ending times—many companies are turning to flexible-scheduling strategies as solutions to motivation issues as well as to meet the needs of an increasingly diverse work force. These strategies include flextime, compressed work weeks, job sharing, part-time work, and working at home.

**Flextime** allows employees to choose their starting and ending times as long as they are at work during a specified core period (Figure 16.7). Understandably, flextime does not reduce the total number of hours that employees work; rather, as its name suggests, it gives them flexibility in selecting the hours they work. Employees are free to schedule their work around core times in which all employees must be present. A firm may specify that employees must be present from 10:00 A.M. to 3:00 P.M. One employee may come in at 7:00 A.M. and leave at the end of the core time, perhaps to attend classes at a nearby college after work. Another employee may come in at 9:00 A.M. in order to have time to drop off children at a day-care center and commute by public transportation to the job. Aetna Life & Casualty is one of many companies that have adopted flextime to meet the needs of their employees.[20] The percentage of eligible employees who actually use flextime is 24 percent.[21]

The **compressed work week** is a four-day (or shorter) period in which an employee works 40 hours. Under such a plan, employees generally work ten hours per day and have a three-day weekend. The compressed work week reduces an organization's operating expenses because its actual hours of operation are reduced. It is also a benefit to parents who want to have more days off to spend with their families.

**Job sharing** occurs when two people do one job. For example, one person may work from 8:00 A.M. to 12:30 P.M., and the second person would come in at 12:30 P.M. and work until 5:00 P.M. Job sharing gives both people the opportunity to work and time to fulfill other obligations, such as parenting or education. With job sharing, the company has the benefit of the skills of two people for one job, often at a lower total salary cost than one person working eight hours a day would be paid.

Two other flexible scheduling strategies in increasing use are allowing full-time workers to work part time for a certain period and allowing workers to work at

**flextime**
A work schedule that allows employees to choose their starting and ending times as long as they are at work during a specified time period.

**compressed work week**
A four-day (or shorter) period in which an employee works 40 hours.

**job sharing**
A working arrangement whereby two employees do one job.

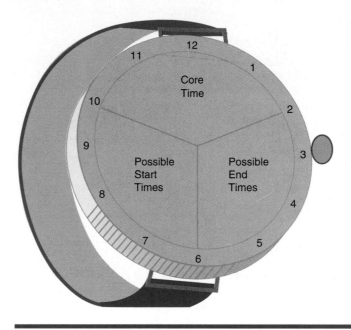

**FIGURE 16.7**

**Flextime, Showing Core and Flexible Hours**

home. Some firms, including CitiCorp, are allowing employees to work only part time for six months or a year so that they can care for a new baby or an elderly parent or just slow down for a little while to "charge their batteries." When the employees return to full-time work, they are usually given positions comparable to their original full-time position. Other firms are experimenting with having employees work at home part time or even full time. In fact, companies now have some 7.6 million employees working at home.[22] These employees, usually in management, sales, or other nonassembly positions, are frequently connected to their workplace through computers, fax machines, and telephones. Some full-time computer programmers at CIGNA Corp., for example, are permitted to work at home two days a week.[23] While many employees ask for the option of working at home to ease parenting responsibilities, some have discovered that they are more productive at home without the distractions of the workplace. Others, however, have discovered that they are not suited for working at home. Work-at-home programs do help reduce overhead costs for businesses, but they may cause problems when the absence of home-bound employees slows operations.

**Critical Thinking Challenge:** Have students poll managers at a local company about their work schedules and policies. Do they use flexible schedules or job sharing? Why did they adopt the policy? How long has it been in use? Have students report their findings to the class and discuss the benefits of the varied work schedules.

Companies are turning to flexible work schedules to give more options to employees who are trying to juggle their work duties and family responsibilities. A Hewitt Associates survey of 259 companies found that 56 percent offered some sort of flexible scheduling options. Of these firms, 42 percent offered flextime; 36 percent permitted part-time employment; 17 percent offered job-sharing programs; 13 percent employed compressed work schedules; and 9 percent allowed employees to work at home occasionally.[24] Because flexible scheduling plans are fairly new, it is difficult to evaluate their effectiveness. Preliminary results, however, indicate that they increase job satisfaction, and greater job satisfaction, in turn, may lead to increases in productivity.

A flextime program at Quill Corporation, a direct marketer of office products and computers, helps employees juggle their work and family responsibilities. Quill employee Lisa Cokefair uses the company's flextime option to schedule her work hours around those of her firefighter husband, Jon. With Lisa on flextime, the Cokefairs avoid having to hire a babysitter for their two daughters. Instead, they can coordinate their work schedules so one parent can be with the children when the other is working.

*Source:* © John Zich.

Flexible-scheduling strategies are among the benefits that certain employees value more than others. Companies are hearing that employees are not necessarily aware of the value of many of their basic benefits. Communicating the value of employee benefits can reduce the pressure to increase the benefits package, reduce turnover, increase employee motivation, and increase overall productivity and profits.[25]

## Paying for Performance

How much and how employees are compensated for their performance obviously has some influence on their motivation and effort, but the issue of how much pay motivates may cause problems for managers seeking ways to enhance motivation. Maslow and Herzberg show that pay (money) enables an employee to satisfy his or her basic needs. While Herzberg sees money as a maintenance factor that does not necessarily motivate an employee to perform at higher levels, his theory indicates that low or inadequate pay may result in dissatisfied, unmotivated employees. Equity theory suggests that employees must be paid at least fairly, that they need to perceive that they are earning what their efforts are worth. Skinner's behavior modification theory shows that employees need to be rewarded for their efforts, but suggests that the weekly paycheck (a fixed-interval positive reinforcement) may not be as effective at motivating employees as other methods of reinforcement.

With this in mind, managers can create pay plans that motivate if they (1) show employees that good performance leads to high levels of pay, (2) minimize any negative consequences of good performance, and (3) create conditions that provide desired rewards other than pay for good performance.[26] So-called merit pay, which rewards employees according to their performance contributions, is a natural product of expectancy and reinforcement theories because it links pay increases to work performance. IBM has developed a program whereby 60 percent of employees' compensation relates to the profitability of an order and 40 percent is based on customer satisfaction determined by customer surveys. IBM is tying pay to performance and customer satisfaction—two of its goals.[27]

Companies today are increasingly striving to relate pay to performance at both the hourly and managerial level. For example, a Quaker Oats plant in Lawrence,

**FIGURE 16.8**

**Integration of Motivation Theories**

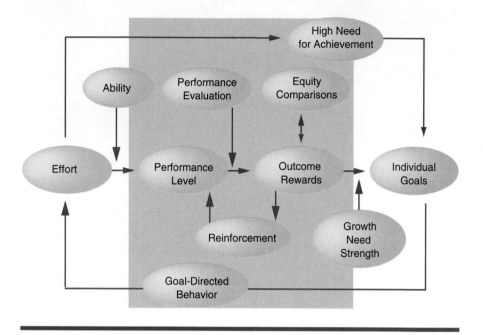

*Source:* Adapted from Marc Siegall, "The Simplistic Five: An Integrated Framework for Teaching Motivation," *Organizational Behavior Teaching Review* 12 (1987/1988): 141–143.

Kansas, has developed a compensation plan that ties employees' pay raises to the plant's performance. The company determines the extent to which the plant has achieved its objectives and it groups company performance goals such as financial, safety, quality, sanitation, focus, and division performance so employees can see the impact of their efforts. The plan promotes greater communication and participation among employees as well as the perception of equity between pay and organizational performance.[28] When IBM brought in Louis V. Gerstner (formerly chairman of RJR Nabisco) as its new chairman and CEO, it gave him not only a base salary, but also the chance to earn large bonuses if he achieves specific objectives.[29]

"Competition cannot continue to rely on traditional job-based pay, job evaluation systems, and individual performance criteria," says Dick Dauphinais, founder of Strategic Compensation Partners.[30] Noncash incentives include merchandise, travel, recognition, and status. Such incentives endure longer for employees through the creation of a memory or ongoing benefit (a Hawaiian vacation or wide-screen TV, for example). Noncash rewards can be related to the goal; for example, if an employee is the top salesperson in a region, a new luxury car would reinforce the sales contribution to the organization.

## INTEGRATION OF MOTIVATION THEORIES

To understand motivation, it is best to look at all the theories of motivation we have discussed in conjunction with one another. Many of the ideas and relationships are

c   a   r   e   e   r   s
c
o
r
n
e
r

## Utilizing Motivational Techniques

Students interested in the field of motivation can apply their interest to many jobs and careers. All good managers must develop skills and knowledge with regard to motivation. The most direct use of motivation in management would be as a motivational speaker who lectures employees or trains them in a specific area. With new technology, techniques, and processes, communication to employees can involve the use of external management consultants or internal training experts to facilitate change. Management consultants can deal with many different topic areas. Their function is to assess the firm's current situation or problem and recommend courses of action. Many management consultants operate on an independent or freelance basis and generally earn salaries from $28,000 to $50,000. But exceptional students, probably with graduate degrees, hired by large organizations can earn significantly higher salaries.

Office managers also need motivational skills. In many businesses, office managers are responsible for overseeing the day-to-day operations of the office—interacting with accounting and payroll, human resource management, secretaries and clerical staff, as well as other functional areas in the organization. Because of the supervision and control function in this position, as well as the coordination of staff employees, an understanding of motivational techniques contributes to suc-

cess as an office manager. The salary range for office managers is $15,000 to $45,000.

Human resource managers obviously make use of many motivational techniques. The human resource manager is responsible for implementing and dealing with many of the personnel policies of the organization, including recruiting, hiring, training, developing wage scales, conducting outside surveys, and developing and administering benefit programs, as well as numerous other functions. Human resource managers deal with everyone in the organization at some point in time. Often they are trying to assess needs (training), assess compensation levels (internal and external equity), and administer what in large organizations can be a diversified and complex employment program. Human resource managers try to determine how to help the organization best achieve its goals, which involves understanding what motivates employees within the organization. Growth is anticipated in this field as companies continue to focus on the development of their human resources. The salary range in this area is $19,000 to $65,000.

*Sources:* Annette Seldon, *VGM's Handbook of Business and Management Careers* (Lincolnwood, IL: NTC Publishing Group, 1993), 55–56, 64–66, 68–70.

---

similar from model to model, and the ultimate benefit comes from their synergy. Expectancy theory provides the foundation for an integrated model of motivation (see Figure 16.8). Effort, on the left-hand side of the model, directly affects performance and is directly affected by goals. Performance will be high if employees perceive a relationship between their performance level and rewards. Although effort directly affects performance, ability has a moderating effect: The more training, experience, or raw talent, the greater the performance level.

According to expectancy theory, performance level is directly related to outcome rewards. Performance evaluation must be fair and equitable (equity theory) for employees to view the outcome rewards favorably. The rewards serve to reinforce the behavior or performance level. Inequitable or low-level rewards may inhibit maximum productivity of employees.

Individual goals and McClelland's need for achievement determine how goal-directed the individual is. These factors also take into account equity theory and reinforcement. The higher the employee's need for achievement, the greater his or her goals and the more defined his or her goal-directed behavior. The need for achievement is an internal drive, and individual goals may also take into account external needs, such as a larger home or a new car.

**Comment on Box:** Invite an HRM of a local company, or even the HRM manager from your college or university, to speak to your class. Ask him or her to focus on pay and motivation issues as well as key changes in the field of HRM.

Reinforcement theory acknowledges the importance of the interaction between performance level and the outcome rewards. It becomes a self-fulfilling prophecy. The more appropriate the level of rewards, the higher the levels of performance. Growth-need strength (Hackman and Oldham) moderates the relationship between outcome rewards and individual goals. This integrated model provides insights identifying key areas to address in increasing employee motivation.

# SUMMARY AND REVIEW

- **Define motivation and explain its importance to managers.** Motivation is an inner drive that directs behavior toward goals. It is more than a tool managers can use to foster employee loyalty and productivity; it is a process that affects all the relationships within an organization and influences many areas.

- **Compare and contrast the content theories of Abraham Maslow, Frederick Herzberg, and David McClelland.** Abraham Maslow defined five basic needs and arranged them in the order in which they must be satisfied: physiological, security, social, esteem, and self-actualization. Frederick Herzberg identified two types of factors that relate to motivation. Maintenance factors, such as adequate wages and comfortable working conditions, relate to the work environment; they must be present for employees to remain in a job. Motivational factors—recognition, responsibility, advancement, and the job characteristics—relate to the work itself; they encourage employees to be productive. Herzberg's maintenance factors can be compared to Maslow's physiological, security, and social needs; motivational factors may include Maslow's esteem and self-actualization needs. David McClelland identified three needs: achievement, affiliation, and power.

- **Analyze the various process theories relating to how managers can motivate employees, including equity theory, expectancy theory, and the Porter-Lawler expectancy model.** Equity theory suggests that how much people are willing to contribute to an organization depends on their assessment of the equity of the rewards they will receive in exchange. Each person develops a personal input-outcome ratio of the rewards (outcomes) offered by the organization divided by his or her contribution (inputs) to the organization. The worker then compares his or her ratio to the input-outcome ratio of some "comparison other" and adjusts effort accordingly.

Expectancy theory states that motivation depends not only on how much a person wants something but on the person's perception of how likely he or she is to get it. Expectancy is a person's expectation that effort will lead to high performance. Instrumentality is a person's expectation that performing a task will lead to one or more desired outcomes. Valence is the value a person sets on these outcomes. Expectancy theory suggests the entire set of outcomes of any given act, and the person's subjective probability of attaining these outcomes, determines motivation.

The Porter-Lawler expectancy model extends expectancy theory by suggesting that satisfaction is the result rather than the cause of performance and that different levels of performance lead to different rewards, which, in turn, produce different levels of job satisfaction.

- **Determine how managers may use reinforcement theory to motivate employees to behave as expected.** Reinforcement theory assumes that behavior may be strengthened by relating it to its consequences. Behavior modification involves changing behavior and encouraging appropriate actions by relating the consequences of behavior to the behavior itself. Four types of reinforcement are positive reinforcement, negative reinforcement or avoidance, punishment, and extinction. Four schedules of reinforcement are fixed-interval schedule, variable-interval schedule, fixed-ratio schedule, variable-ratio schedule. Managers who want to motivate employees should consider the long-term effects of punishment and reward.

- **Explain how goal-setting theory can be used to enhance employee motivation.** Goal-setting theory recognizes the importance of goals in improving employee performance. Specificity, difficulty, feedback, participation, and competition improve commitment to and acceptance of goals.

- **Specify how managers may design jobs or apply strategies to motivate employees.** To motivate workers, managers frequently employ job-design strategies that relate the consequences of behavior to the behavior itself. Job rotation, job enlargement, and job enrichment are some job-design strategies managers may use. Hackman and Oldham's job characteristics model takes a different approach to job design by trying to identify how managers can motivate workers by helping them to achieve more of their higher-level needs. It identified five core job characteristics that determine a job's potential to motivate—skill variety, task identity, task significance, autonomy, and feedback—which lead, in turn, to three psychological states that affect workplace motivation: experienced meaningfulness, experienced responsibility, and knowledge of results. Growth-need strength is the extent to which an employee desires a job that provides personal challenges, a sense of accomplishment, and personal growth.

It determines whether or not a more enriched job will actually motivate a worker. Managers may also employ flexible scheduling strategies (flextime, compressed work weeks, job sharing, work sharing, part-time work, working at home) and design effective pay-for-performance strategies.

- **Evaluate a company's efforts to motivate its sales team.** You should be able to apply the various theories discussed in this chapter to evaluate the effectiveness of the manager described in the "Business Dilemma" box and make recommendations for future programs to maintain morale.

## Key Terms and Concepts

motivation *460*
morale *460*
content theories *465*
Maslow's hierarchy of needs *465*
maintenance factors *467*
motivational factors *468*
process theories *469*
equity theory *469*
expectancy theory *470*

expectancy *471*
instrumentality *471*
valence *471*
Porter-Lawler expectancy model *472*
reinforcement theory *474*
behavior modification *474*
positive reinforcement *474*
avoidance *474*
punishment *474*

extinction *474*
fixed-interval schedule *475*
variable-interval schedule *475*
fixed-ratio schedule *475*
variable-ratio schedule *475*
goal-setting theory *476*
flextime *479*
compressed work week *479*
job sharing *479*

## Ready Recall

1. Why do managers need to understand the needs of their employees?
2. Describe the motivation process.
3. Explain Maslow's hierarchy of needs. Why is it important?
4. What are Herzberg's maintenance and motivational factors? How can managers use them to motivate workers?
5. Differentiate between the content and process theories of motivation. Which do you think are most useful to managers looking for ways to motivate their employees?
6. Compare and contrast equity theory and expectancy theory. How can managers apply these theories to promote higher levels of motivation?

7. Explain the significance of behavior modification in motivating employees.
8. Describe the four types of reinforcement. Which do you think would be most effective at eliminating a problem behavior? Which of the four schedules of reinforcement do you think would be most effective at motivating employees to work harder?
9. Discuss some of the job-design strategies mentioned in the chapter. How can managers use these to increase motivation of shop-floor employees?
10. Name and describe some flexible-scheduling strategies. Why would a business use a flexible-scheduling strategy?

## Expand Your Experience

1. Consider a person who is homeless: How would he or she be motivated and what actions would that person take? Use the motivation process to explain. Which of the needs in Maslow's hierarchy are likely to be most important? Least important?
2. Look at your college or university's football or other athletic team and interview managers and players. What is its level of morale? How does the team currently motivate

players to perform? Based on the theories you've learned in this chapter, recommend changes to enhance motivation and morale.
3. Visit a local business and interview managers and employees there. What is the level of morale? How does the firm currently motivate employees to work toward company goals? Based on the theories you've learned in this chapter, recommend changes to enhance motivation and morale.

## CASE

# Motivating Employees at Chaparral Steel

Chaparral Steel Company was formed in Midlothian, Texas, in 1975 by Texas Industries, Inc. (TXI) and Co-Steel International of Canada. Texas Industries eventually bought out its Canadian partner and is now sole owner. Since 1975, Chaparral has more than doubled in size with an annual capacity of more than 1.2 million tons of steel. (In comparison, Bethlehem Steel, the nation's number-two steel producer, produces more than 10 million tons annually.) Chaparral Steel employs just 930 employees, no two of whom receive the same wage. Administering a human resource program that takes seniority, experience, education, and training received into consideration is complex to implement, but employees heartily approve.

The steel industry has been hard hit by a slow economy and tough competition in the 1990s. Bethlehem Steel eliminated 4,200 jobs to improve its overall profitability, and USX, the nation's largest steel manufacturer, experienced losses as great as $750 million in the early 1990s. Legal and political problems also plague the industry; USX was found guilty of price fixing and fined $630 million in damages. USX and five other steel manufacturers filed a suit against low-cost, subsidized foreign steel manufacturers. In the face of low-cost foreign competition, Chaparral initiated its export operations through unheralded efficiency in production. The industry average of work hours per ton of steel is 1.95, but Chaparral has cut its rate to 1.6 work hours per ton. Such a rate can be attributed to the use of unique management techniques not previously utilized in the steel industry.

Chaparral differs from its competitors in other ways, as well. It is a lean, flexible, and responsive organization with few barriers between the plant floor manager and management. The plant's employees are receptive to change, unlike competitors. Chaparral's open management structure allows employees to cross-train—move from job to job in the organization, broadening their understanding of the entire mill's production process and capabilities. Chaparral also offers higher pay for individuals who take training courses and/or cross-train within the organization.

Also setting Chaparral apart from the competition is its nonunion labor force. Texas Industries believes it can better represent the needs and interests of its employees than can an outside group. The company hires most of its employees from nonindustrial areas. In particular, Chaparral tries to hire young college graduates who have an interest in learning the steel business. The lower employment rates for college graduates make this strategy more readily achievable than might be the case with higher employment rates in a stronger economy. The company's willingness to invest in additional schooling and training for some employees makes it an attractive employer. The expense of providing education pays off because the employees usually stay with Chaparral, giving the company the benefit of their increased expertise and productivity.

Another interesting approach used by Chaparral is to make every employee a member of the sales department. Management took this step because it believes that every employee should be familiar with customer needs. In return, management offers employees benefits in the form of stock options and gives managers direct involvement in the production process.

Chaparral offers a sabbatical plan for its front-line managers, which further sets it apart from the competition. The sabbatical program helps to prevent job burnout and to generate renewed interest and excitement about work. Managers on sabbatical are given special projects such as researching a new technology, or visiting other steel mills and customers. While a manager is on sabbatical, another employee acts as the substitute foreman and other workers are shifted around. This rotation of employees has increased both productivity and motivation.

Chaparral does not have a research and development department or a laboratory. Instead, management views the whole plant as one big laboratory, trying out new ideas right on the production floor. The production employees are responsible for keeping production processes at the leading edge of technology. They visit other companies and customers to find new ideas and technology that might help their own jobs or Chaparral as a whole. Employees have gone not only to Pittsburgh and Chicago, but to Japan and Germany as well. The company also works with universities on research projects to stimulate new ideas and ways of doing business.

The company has an extremely well-trained and experienced human resource management department. Although the department consists of only two employees, they are responsible for initial screening of employees and a few clerical duties. Chaparral's plant supervisors do all their own hiring and training. And, because there are no quality inspectors, the supervisors and their employees are responsible for product quality. In addition, Chaparral has no time clocks: the company demonstrates its trust in its employees in the form of a liberal flextime system.

Chaparral Steel has used innovative management and personnel practices to make a name for itself in an industry traditionally dominated by significantly larger competitors such as USX and Bethlehem Steel. Chaparral's management understands that its people are just as important to the steel-making process as its physical plant and equipment. The company understands that employee needs go beyond the desire for money and tries to accommodate and fulfill those needs. As a result, labor costs at Chaparral are only 10 percent of sales (average labor costs for the whole industry are around 40 percent). Chaparral's understanding of human relations and motivation have allowed it to achieve something that even its bigger competitors have not—growth and prosperity despite a troubled time in the industry. Chaparral Steel's insights could be applied to many firms that are facing a period of economic uncertainty and downsizing.

*Sources:* Gary Hoover, Alta Campbell, and Patrick Spain, *Hoover's Handbook of American Business 1994* (Austin, TX: The Reference Press Inc., 1993), 268–269, 1092–1093; Alan M. Kantrow, "Wide-Open Management at Chaparral Steel," *Harvard Business Review* 64 (May–June 1986): 96–97, 99–102; Lisa M. Keefe, "Forward March," *Forbes,* April 20, 1987, 104–105; Robert Levering and Milton Moskowitz, *The 100 Best Companies to Work for in America* (New York: Plume, 1994), 60–64; and George Melloan, "Making Money Making Steel in Texas," *The Wall Street Journal,* January 26, 1988, 29.

## Questions

1. How would you describe Chaparral's style of management? What are the successful elements?
2. Describe the benefits of the communication system utilized at Chaparral Steel. Identify the specific impact on product quality and productivity.

3. What are some of the advantages a smaller company would have in implementing Chaparral's motivational policies? Identify some of the ones you think would be applicable in a larger company such as USX and Bethlehem.

## STRENGTHEN YOUR SKILLS
### *Motivating*

You will use the four illustrations presented in Figures 16.9 through 16.12 to complete a story in pictures and words about motivation. The title for each picture and the script for the first picture are provided. You and your group will write the script for the remaining three pictures in the motivation story. Your team of scriptwriters is to base the script on what you have learned about motivation and your collective experiences about how motivation works.

**FIGURE 16.9**

**Square Wheels One™**

*Source:* © Performance Management Company, 1993, 1994. All Rights Reserved. 800–659–1466.

It is a day just like any other day at Gubernautics International. The workers show up for work. And even though they rarely see their boss, they assume he must be around somewhere doing whatever it is bosses do. They decide they had better get to work just in case the boss comes by to check up on them. They do their jobs, just like every other day, recognizing the inefficiencies of the systems that surround them. Even though they have great ideas about how to improve things when they talk among themselves, no one else seems to listen to their ideas—or, for that matter, to even care that they do have ideas. So they "park their brains at the door" and start pushing … just like every other day.

**FIGURE 16.10**

**Visions from the Front of the Wagon**

**FIGURE 16.11**

**The View from the Back**

**FIGURE 16.12**

**Shared Visions and Missions**

Conclude the exercise with one member from each group reading the group's motivation story to the rest of the class.

*through* Getting Results

Effective

# Leadership

**After reading this chapter, you will be able to:**

- Differentiate leadership from the process of management.
- List the sources of power leaders use to influence others' behavior.
- Distinguish successful leaders from less successful leaders and nonleaders, according to their traits.
- Compare and contrast the major dimensions of leadership behavior used in the behavioral theories.
- Summarize the contingency factors covered in Fiedler's contingency theory, Blanchard's situational leadership theory, and path-goal theory.
- Determine what may neutralize, or substitute for, leadership behavior.
- Specify the leadership practices that can contribute to successful transformational leadership and that distinguish it from transactional leadership.
- Evaluate a leader's efforts to manage a crisis situation.

## America's Best CEO?

The cover of the May 2, 1994, issue of *Fortune* magazine asked, "Is Herb Kelleher America's Best CEO?" accompanied by a wacky looking picture. Kelleher, CEO of Southwest Airlines, is the jokemeister of the airline industry and the consummate free spirit who loves to sit up all night drinking Wild Turkey while exchanging bawdy tales with anyone and everyone from other airline executives to one of his own mechanics. He's considered the industry's most outrageous and funny speaker. When other airlines lost billions and Southwest Airlines remained slightly profitable, he related that "it was like being the tallest guy in a tribe of dwarfs."

All jokes aside, Herb Kelleher is arguably America's best CEO. One security analyst described him as "brilliant, charming, cunning, and tough." In an industry racked by billion-dollar losses and bankruptcies, Kelleher has led Southwest through 20 straight years of making a profit. Southwest's debt-to-capitalization ratio of 60 percent is remarkable compared to American's 83 percent and United's 98 percent. Southwest stock is still rated a buy by almost every stock analyst, and its bonds are the only airline bonds not described as "junk" by one Standard & Poor's bond analyst.

Kelleher has achieved such success by being extremely hard nosed on costs—personally approving any expenditure over $1,000—and keeping his highly efficient work force to a minimum. Compare his work force of 81 employees per aircraft to Delta's 134 or Northwest's 127, and imagine the cost savings. At the same time, though, Kelleher (just Herb to his employees) is one of the most employee-oriented inspirational leaders of America's big businesses. He is most proud of Southwest's family atmosphere and the concern for people that the company demonstrates, remarkable considering that it is 80 percent unionized. Says one longtime observer of the airline industry, "At other places, managers say that people are their most important resource, but nobody acts on it. At Southwest, they have never lost sight of the fact." Kelleher is the heart of his company and he reigns over his 12,000 employees "like some sort of manic father." He's so proud of his company and his employees that he relishes the forthcoming assault the other airlines will probably level on Southwest, as they try to emulate its operational efficiency and consider moving into Southwest's markets. Regardless of the outcome of these airline battles, Herb Kelleher will likely remain the star of the industry and its most unique spokesperson. As one writer notes, "In the dictionary under 'one of a kind' there should be a picture of Herb Kelleher grinning."

*Source:* Kenneth Labich, "Is Herb Kelleher America's Best CEO?" *Fortune,* May 2, 1994.

Leadership is one of the most fascinating and discussed aspects of management, and characters like Herb Kelleher make it easy to see why. Max DePree, leadership expert and CEO of the Herman Miller Company, views leadership as an art, "more tribal than scientific, more a weaving of relationships than an amassing of information."[1] Because of its almost mystical nature, writers and practitioners have been interested in leadership for centuries; scientists have been studying it for at least the last 80 to 90 years. The number of approaches to and definitions of leadership are nearly as numerous as the writers who have delved into the process.

In this chapter, we will define leadership and distinguish it from management, and then examine different sources of leadership power. Next, we will explore several theories that attempt to determine what makes an effective leader. We will conclude with a discussion of some of the newer approaches in the study and practice of leadership.

## THE NATURE OF LEADERSHIP

**Leadership** is the process of influencing the activities of an individual or a group toward the achievement of a goal. This definition reflects three elements: the leader, the followers, and the process of influencing goal-directed behavior. Sam Walton, the late founder of Wal-Mart stores, and General Norman Schwarzkopf, who led U.S. troops during the Persian Gulf War, are examples of strong leaders who influenced different kinds of groups of followers to accomplish goals.

### Leadership versus Management

Management is a broad concept that encompasses activities such as planning, organizing, staffing, and controlling, as well as leading—as we have seen throughout this book. Leadership, on the other hand, focuses almost exclusively on the "people" aspects of getting a job done—inspiring, motivating, directing, and gaining commitment to organizational activities and goals. Leadership accompanies and complements the management functions, but it has more to do with coping with the dynamic, ever-changing marketplace, with rapid technological innovation, increased foreign competition, and other fluctuating market forces. In short, management influences the brain, while leadership encourages the heart and the spirit.[2] Table 17.1 highlights some of the basic distinctions between leadership and management.

Organizations need both management and leadership, and some leaders, like Herb Kelleher, can provide both. Others manage but cannot lead, while still others seem born to lead, but cannot manage. Unfortunately, most U.S. companies today appear to be overmanaged and underled.

When Fred Smith founded the Federal Express Co., he was acting as a leader. His vision of overnight package delivery represented a quantum leap forward in the industry, and he had to inspire acceptance of and commitment to that vision by all employees, customers, and investors. Now FedEx has grown into a gigantic organization, with hundreds of complex systems. Smith and the company's executives spend much of their time managing these systems in order to provide stability and avoid chaos. Smith still spends time communicating his vision to his workers by emphasizing the need for quality and service to meet the competition.

---

**leadership**
The process of influencing the activities of an individual or a group toward the achievement of a goal.

**Teaching Note:** Before you begin the chapter, have students list traits of leaders. List the traits on the board or on an overhead projector and discuss why these traits are chosen and how they support leadership.

**Teaching Note:** Spend some time on Table 17.1 and be sure students can differentiate between management and leadership. Have students provide examples of personal experiences with managers and with leaders.

**TABLE 17.1**

**How Leaders and Managers Differ**

| Activity | Management | Leadership |
|---|---|---|
| Organizational emphasis | Developing stability in response to complexities of large, chaotic organizations | Developing an action orientation in response to the volatility of a rapidly changing organizational environment |
| Setting an agenda | Planning and budgeting: Involves setting goals, establishing detailed action steps, and allocating resources | Setting a direction: Developing a vision of the future and strategies for producing changes required by that vision |
| Developing human linkages to achieve the organizational agenda | Organizing and staffing: Managers organize and staff human systems to implement a plan by structuring jobs, establishing hierarchical structures, training, delegating authority, setting up rewards systems—all very logical processes | Aligning people: Leaders communicate with many constituents to help them understand and commit to the vision; they establish the credibility of the vision and empower followers to action |
| Execution of the plans | Controlling and problem solving: Spotting discrepancies in the plan, controlling the process logically, solving problems that arise | Motivating people: Inspiring bursts of energy by satisfying basic human needs; aiding in overcoming political and organizational barriers by involving people in decision making |
| The results | Establishing a culture of stability with predictable results and moderate, incremental improvements | Establishing a culture of leadership where risk taking is encouraged and learning from mistakes is acceptable; change, often in quantum leaps, is possible to meet competitive demand |

*Source:* Adapted from John B. Kotter, "What Leaders Really Do," *Harvard Business Review* 68 (May–June 1990): 103–111.

## The Sources of Power

Understanding leadership requires insight into the possession and use of power. **Power** refers to a person's capacity to influence the behavior and attitudes of others. We can think of it as an ability attributed to a person—potential but unused. Bosses can fire employees but seldom do on a regular basis. We can also think of power as attempts to influence someone to do what you want—power in action. A boss actively directing an employee's behavior represents the use of power.

In either case, power is inherent in a relationship between two people and is based on one's ability to satisfy or deny satisfaction of some need of the other. That ability may be based on a formal contractual relationship between an organization and an individual, called **organizational power**, or it can be based on an interpersonal relationship between individuals or on one's personal characteristics, called **personal power.**[3] There are eight major sources of power: legitimate, reward, coercive, expert, referent, charisma, information, and affiliative.[4]

**Legitimate Power.**   **Legitimate power** comes from a person's formal position in an organization and the authority that accompanies that position. The contractual relationship between employees and managers, for example, grants managers legitimate power to influence certain kinds of behavior. However, this kind of power may be limited by the formal contract—for example, when an employee refuses to

**power**
A person's capacity to influence the behavior and attitudes of others.

**organizational power**
A person's ability to satisfy or deny satisfaction of anothers' need, based on a formal contractual relationship between an organization and the individual.

**personal power**
A person's ability to satisfy or deny satisfaction of anothers' need, based on an interpersonal relationship between individuals or on his or her personal characteristics.

**legitimate power**
The influence that comes from a person's formal position in an organization and the authority that accompanies that position.

As founder and chairman of Nike, Philip H. Knight uses his organizational power in leading employees to achieve the company's corporate goal of "enhancing people's lives through sports and fitness." Through his personal power, Knight has created a corporate culture that stands for sports, performance, and the free-flowing spirit of the athlete. After employees learn Nike's culture, Knight trusts his creative team to carry out the corporate slogan "Just Do It" in designing athletic footwear. Under Knight's leadership, Nike has grown from a start-up in 1972 to a worldwide company with nearly $4 billion in sales.

*Source:* © 1994 Alan Levenson.

do anything more than what the specific job description dictates. Thus, using a "do it because I'm the boss" approach may limit a manager's capacity to lead.

**reward power**
Organizational power that stems from a person's ability to bestow rewards.

**Reward Power.**    **Reward power** stems from a person's ability to bestow rewards. This, too, is an organizationally based source of power because companies generally grant managers the right to assign formal rewards, such as bonuses, days off, and promotions. Managers can also use social rewards, such as praise and recognition. Effective leaders learn that the creative use of informal rewards along with formal ones enhances their ability to lead. For example, at Buckman Laboratories, an international chemical producer, managers have a formal financial bonus system they can use to reward good performance. They also have "small-wins boards" in each department where employees can post a note of thanks or recognition for the help they received or the good job someone did.

**coercive power**
An organizationally based source of power derived from a leader's control over punishments or the capacity to deny rewards.

**Coercive Power.**    **Coercive power**, another organizationally based source of power, is derived from a leader's control over punishments or the capacity to deny rewards. Leaders who demote, berate, withhold an expected pay increase, or threaten someone with a poor job assignment are using coercive power. Physical coercion was common in many businesses prior to the turn of the century, while psychological and emotional coercion are more commonly used forms of negative influence today. Linda Wachner, CEO of clothing manufacturer Warnaco and one of *Fortune* magazine's toughest bosses, once called a group of executives "eunuchs" in a business meeting, and told the new company president he had to fire some people "so they'll understand you're serious."[5] Although regulations and laws limit a leader's ability to use coercive power, it is still all too common in many business settings. However, the use of punishment to gain compliance has the negative side effect of creating hostility and resentment toward the punisher and possibly reduced dedication to an organization. While some still cling to the model of the hard-nosed executive boss, many CEOs see the use of coercion diminishing in favor of more positive sources of power.[6]

**expert power**
Power or influence derived from a person's special knowledge or expertise in a particular area.

**Expert Power.**    **Expert power** is derived from a person's special knowledge or expertise in a particular area. The mechanic fixing a piece of equipment would prob-

An employee-centered leadership style helps Pam Del Duca succeed in the tough business of small retailing. Del Duca is CEO and president of The Delstar Group, a successful specialty gift and fashion apparel retailer whose profit margin is well above the 2 percent industry average. Her philosophy is "when we grow people, we grow the business." Del Duca provides ongoing employee training in product knowledge and customer service. She sets individual sales goals for each employee and rewards those who meet or exceed their goals. Her 16 store managers are loosely supervised and allowed to buy merchandise within their budget and without seeking higher approval. Here Del Duca leads her managers on a river raft trip during an off-site meeting.

*Source:* © Don B. Stevenson.

ably have more expert power in that technical area than would a CEO. Professors and researchers rely mostly on expert power. Managers who wish also to be leaders learn to develop and use this personal source of power more than the formal sources. Bill Gates has tremendous expert power because of his computer knowledge, in addition to the formal, legitimate power he has as CEO of Microsoft.

**Referent Power.**    **Referent power** results when one person identifies with and admires another. Referent power cannot be granted by organizations; it is a personal source of power you develop on your own. Through friendly communication, sharing of information, and mutual rewarding, close interpersonal relations and even friendships develop. In such relationships, the employee may want to please the manager or some other person simply because it gives both of them pleasure or satisfaction. We do things for our friends, simply because we like them, that we won't do for others.

**referent power**

Personal power that results when one person identifies with and admires another.

**Charisma.**    People with **charisma**, another personal source of power, seem to inspire admiration, respect, loyalty, and a desire to emulate, based on some intangible set of personality traits. Charismatic leaders are often distinguished by two characteristics: They are usually excellent communicators, the proverbial "silver-tongued devils," and they make people feel more secure and more powerful in themselves. Martin Luther King, Jr., and Malcolm X made their followers feel strong enough to resist racism and segregation. John F. Kennedy beseeched U.S. citizens to "ask not what your country can do for you, ask what you can do for your country." These charismatic leaders empowered their followers to serve their causes. Like referent power, charisma cannot be granted by an organization.

**charisma**

The ability to inspire admiration, respect, loyalty, and a desire to emulate, based on some intangible set of personality traits; a personal source of power.

**Information Power.**    **Information power** requires having access to important information that is not common knowledge, or having the ability to control the flow of information to and from others. The information may come from formal organizational sources or informal reciprocal relationships. People at all levels of an organization can have this source of power; indeed, it is not uncommon for a CEO's secretary to be one of the most influential and powerful employees in the company. Information power may be organizational or personal.

**information power**

Power that is a result of having access to important information that is not common knowledge, or of having the ability to control the flow of information to and from others.

**TABLE 17.2**

**Reactions to Different Power Sources**

| Source | Commitment | Compliance | Resistance |
|--------|-----------|-----------|-----------|
| Legitimate | Possible | Likely | Possible |
| Reward | Possible | Likely | Possible |
| Coercive | Unlikely | Likely | Likely |
| Expert | Likely | Possible | Possible |
| Referent | Likely | Possible | Unlikely |
| Charisma | Likely | Possible | Possible |

*Source:* Adapted from Gary Yukl and Tom Taber, "The Effective Use of Managerial Power," *Personnel* 60 (March–April 1983): 37–49.

**affiliative power**

Power that is derived by virtue of a person's association with someone else who has some source of power.

**Affiliative Power.**   **Affiliative power** comes by virtue of a person's association with someone else who has some source of power. It is "borrowed" from that person and works only when those being influenced are aware of the association and recognize the power of the person from whom the power is being "borrowed." For example, First Lady Hillary Rodham Clinton, though powerful in her own right, also gains power by virtue of her affiliation with her husband, President Bill Clinton.

## The Use of Power

Managers and leaders exercise power to gain an appropriate response from others. Responses from subordinates fall into three major categories: commitment, compliance, or resistance. Table 17.2 shows the likelihood of the different reactions to the use of each of the power sources. Commitment means the subordinate does what the leader wants because he or she really wants to and is committed to successfully fulfilling the request. Commitment comes about because of a desire to please the other person (referent power), respect for the leader's knowledge and the belief that the desired action is the best thing to do (expert power), or the inspiration or empowerment to engage in what might be perceived as a noble behavior (charisma power). Compliance means the subordinate does only what is required and nothing more. Compliance is the likely response when a manager exercises the formal authority of his or her position (legitimate power), offers special inducements contingent on fulfilling the request (reward power), or threatens punishment (coercive power). Resistance can take many forms, from the subtle (such as working slowly) to the obvious and extreme (such as destroying products or personal belongings and systematic employee theft). Although resistance is possible with any of the sources of power, it is least likely with the personal power sources and very likely when coercion is used. Information and affiliative power (not in Table 17.2) may have various effects, depending on how they are exercised.

The implications of Table 17.2 are profound. If managers want to foster employee commitment to tasks, they should develop and use personal sources of power as the primary means of influencing their employees' behavior. Organizational power sources—particularly legitimate and coercive—should be used selectively, as when there is little time to explain rationally or encourage com-

**TABLE 17.3**

**Leadership Traits and Skills Most Frequently Found in Successful Leaders**

| Traits | Skills |
| --- | --- |
| Adaptable to situations | Clever (intelligent) |
| Alert to social environment | Conceptually skilled |
| Ambitious and achievement-oriented | Creative |
| Assertive | Diplomatic and tactful |
| Cooperative | Fluent in speaking |
| Decisive | Knowledgeable about group task |
| Dominant (desire to influence others) | Organized (administrative ability) |
| Energetic (high activity level) | Persuasive |
| Persistent | Socially skilled |
| Self-confident | |
| Tolerant of stress | |
| Willing to assume responsibility | |

*Source:* Gary A. Yukl, *Leadership in Organizations* (Englewood Cliffs, NJ: Prentice Hall, 1989), 176.

mitment or when the dangers of noncompliance are severe. Personal sources of power are essential when extra effort is required, when close surveillance is impossible, and when the manager has no legitimate authority or control over rewards and punishments.

# TRAIT APPROACH TO LEADERSHIP

The earliest approaches to the study of leadership focused not on the process of influencing others, but on the personal characteristics of the leaders themselves. Philosophers and researchers alike tried to determine what traits—physical, intellectual, and personal—distinguish leaders from followers (sometimes called "The Great Man" approach). Early studies revealed a perplexingly large number of traits related to leadership success. Researchers have analyzed over 300 of these studies and found a few traits to be fairly consistent characteristics of leaders[7] (Table 17.3). However, because researchers found no single small set of traits that consistently predicts leadership success in a variety of situations, the trait approach lost credibility in the 1950s and 1960s. Experts now recognize that certain traits increase the likelihood that a person will be an effective leader, but they do not guarantee effectiveness, and the relative importance of different traits depends on the nature of the leadership situation.[8] The trait approach has not fully died out, but the focus has shifted more to what leaders do to be successful, rather than what kinds of personalities or physiques they might have.

A recent published analysis of leadership traits condensed the important primary ones into six core-trait categories:

1. *Drive:* Leaders desire to achieve and are ambitious about their work; they take initiatives and show energy and tenacity in accomplishing chosen goals.

2. *Motivation:* Leaders want to lead; they possess a socialized or positive need for power and are willing to take charge.

3. *Honesty and Integrity:* The best leaders are honest and truthful, and they do what they say they will do.

4. *Self-Confidence:* Leaders project their confidence by being assertive and decisive and taking risks. They admit mistakes and foster trust and commitment to a vision. They are emotionally stable, rather than recklessly adventurous.

5. *Cognitive Ability:* Leaders tend to be intelligent, perceptive, and conceptually skilled, but are not necessarily geniuses. They show analytical ability, good judgment, and the capacity to think strategically.

6. *Business Knowledge:* Leaders tend to have technical expertise in their businesses.[9]

## BEHAVIORAL MODELS OF LEADERSHIP

As the trait approach waned, researchers began trying to identify the behaviors that distinguish effective from less-effective leaders. Two major dimensions of leader behavior emerged from this body of research: One deals with how leaders get the job done and the other deals with how leaders treat and interact with their subordinates. In this section, we will discuss three models that developed from this research: the Ohio State model, the University of Michigan model, and the leadership grid model.

### The Ohio State Studies

**consideration behaviors**
Patterns of being friendly and supportive by listening to employees' problems, supporting their actions, "going to bat" for them, and getting their input on a variety of issues.

**initiating-structure behaviors**
Defining and structuring leader-employee roles through activities such as scheduling, defining work tasks, setting deadlines, criticizing poor work, getting employees to accept work standards, and resolving problems.

In an effort to describe what leaders actually do, researchers at Ohio State University analyzed the results of questionnaires they administered to a sample of leaders and followers. From this, they concluded that leadership behavior consists of two broadly defined dimensions they labeled "consideration" and "initiating structure."[10] **Consideration behaviors** involve being friendly and supportive by listening to employees' problems, supporting their actions, "going to bat" for them, and getting their input on a variety of issues. **Initiating-structure behaviors** involve defining and structuring leader-subordinate roles through activities such as scheduling, defining work tasks, setting deadlines, criticizing poor work, getting employees to accept work standards, and resolving problems. The dimensions seem to be relatively independent of each other, so leaders may rank high on one dimension and low on another at the same time.[11] Herb Kelleher obviously engages in both consideration and initiating-structure behaviors.

Early studies found that "Hi-Hi leaders," those ranking high in both dimensions, are most effective, although results were inconsistent. Subsequent research found that there may not be a simple relationship between the two dimensions and effectiveness. The only reliable finding has been that leaders exhibiting consideration behaviors tend to have more satisfied subordinates. Relationships between the two dimensions and effectiveness appear to depend on the situation. That "Hi-Hi" leaders are always the best leaders appears to be myth.[12]

### The University of Michigan Studies

At about the same time the Ohio State studies were being conducted, researchers at the University of Michigan were also studying leadership effectiveness from a

## Going Global

### DIVERSE LEADERSHIP THE KEY TO GLOBAL SUCCESS

Four of the United States's ten most admired companies may have a leg up on the competition when it comes to both diversity and globalization issues. The CEOs of J.P. Morgan, Rubbermaid, Coca-Cola, and 3M were all born in foreign countries and have extensive international experience.

J.P. Morgan's Dennis Weatherstone came to the United States on the QEII from London in 1971, supposedly for a four-year stint at Morgan's headquarters. Needless to say, he found a permanent home. At least he did not face much of a language barrier. Wolfgang Schmitt spoke no English when he moved from Germany with his parents at age 10 and settled near the Wooster, Ohio, site of his eventual employer, Rubbermaid. Coca-Cola's Roberto Goizueta was a chemical engineer for Coca-Cola in Havana, Cuba, before the revolution. Livio DeSimone grew up in Canada and joined 3M Canada just out of

college before coming to the United States three years later. All four express a certain sense of pride and consider themselves fortunate to have such international perspectives.

Wolfgang Schmitt notes an advantage of his heritage: "It gives you a certain empathy for minorities, because you've been one." Goizueta relates that working in so many countries for Coca-Cola left him with more of a corporate identity than a national one. He says, "I suppose I am of the Coca-Cola culture." DeSimone

says that two thirds of 3M's top 100 managers have spent three or more years outside the United States. "They are comfortable anywhere."

The four CEOs' global perspective, intense company culture, tolerance of others, and comfort level in any location suggest that a global management team may be another wave of the future.

*Source:* Alan Farnham, "America's Most Admired Company," *Fortune,* February 7, 1994, 50–56.

---

behavioral perspective. They too compared effective leaders to less-effective leaders and came up with two dimensions of leadership behavior, which they labeled "task-oriented behaviors" and "relationship-oriented" behaviors.[13] The researchers found that effective managers engage in **task-oriented behaviors** such as planning and scheduling work, coordinating employee activities, and providing necessary supplies, equipment, and technical assistance—all designed primarily and specifically to get tasks completed and goals met. This task-oriented behavior appears to correspond to the initiating-structure dimension identified in the Ohio State studies.

The researchers also found that effective managers employ **relationship-oriented behaviors**, such as being considerate, supportive, and helpful to subordinates by showing trust and confidence, listening to employees' problems and suggestions, showing appreciation for contributions, and supporting employees' careers. These relationship-oriented behaviors correspond to the consideration behaviors of the Ohio State research. The "Going Global" box highlights several managers whose diversity enables them to be particularly empathetic as well as successful.

Rensis Likert, a management theorist and leader of the Michigan Institute for Social Research, summarized the research by concluding that the most effective managers engage in both dimensions of leadership behavior by getting employees involved in the operation of their departments or divisions in a positive and constructive manner, setting general goals, providing fairly loose supervision, and recognizing their contributions. He called these managers **employee-centered leaders.**

**task-oriented behaviors**
Behaviors—such as planning and scheduling work, coordinating employee activities, and providing necessary supplies, equipment, and technical assistance—designed primarily and specifically to get tasks completed.

**relationship-oriented behaviors**
Behaviors such as being considerate, supportive, and helpful to employees by showing trust and confidence, listening to employees' problems and suggestions, showing appreciation for contributions, and supporting employees' concerns.

**employee-centered leaders**
The most effective managers, who engage in both dimensions of leadership behaviors by getting employees involved in the operation of their departments or divisions in a positive and constructive manner, setting general goals, providing fairly loose supervision, and recognizing employees' contributions.

**FIGURE 17.1**

**The Leadership Grid**

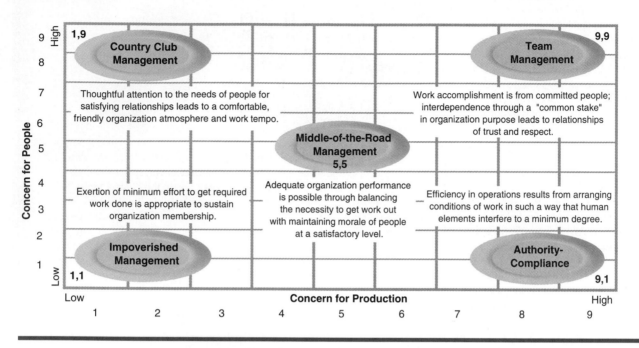

*Source:* The Leadership Grid® Figure from *Leadership Dilemmas—Grid Solutions,* by Robert R. Blake and Anne Adams McCanse, Houston: Gulf Publishing Company, 29. Copyright © 1991, by Scientific Methods, Inc. Reproduced by permission of the owners.

**job-centered leaders**

Less-effective managers, who are mostly directive in their approaches and more concerned with closely supervising employees, explaining work procedures, and monitoring progress in task accomplishment.

**Teaching Note:** Spend time discussing the various leadership styles in Figure 17.1. Remind students the Japanese approach to team or consensus management by using worker participation and organizing around quality circles has proved very successful. Many U.S. companies as well as international organizations are using team management with positive results.

Less-effective managers are mostly directive in their approaches and more concerned with closely directing employees, explaining work procedures, and monitoring progress in task accomplishment; these he called **job-centered leaders.**[14]

## The Leadership Grid

The leadership grid grew out of the two-dimensional behavioral approach to leadership. Developed originally as a managerial grid by consultants Robert Blake and Jane Mouton, this model builds on the Ohio State and Michigan studies and depicts a leader's style as a position in or on a $9 \times 9$ grid, as shown in Figure 17.1.[15] Concern for production, which parallels task-oriented behavior and initiating structure, is a continuum on the horizontal axis, while concern for people is shown as a continuum on the vertical axis. Blake and Mouton emphasize five major styles reflected by differing levels of the two leadership behaviors and different positions on the grid.

*Impoverished management* (1,1 on the grid) is a management style somewhat devoid of purpose, with the manager showing little concern for getting the job done or meeting the needs of the employee. *Country club management* (1,9) places most of the emphasis on satisfying employee needs, often to the detriment of work-goal accomplishment. *Authority-compliance management* (9,1) emphasizes production accomplishment with little concern for the needs or involvement of employees. An intermediate approach (5,5) is called *middle-of-the-road management*, reflected by moderate emphasis on both styles. *Team management* (9,9) is often considered the ultimate style. The team manager is maximally concerned for both production and people. Goals are accomplished through the joint efforts of managers and employees working closely together for the good of the company and of all employees. Team managers strive to have everyone committed to team goals and to feel a sense of ownership of outcomes. Note how the 9,9 team management approach parallels the Hi-Hi leadership style discussed in the Ohio State studies.

Two additional styles of leadership, not shown in the grid, are paternalism and opportunism. *Paternalistic* or "father knows best," management uses a high level of concern for people to reward for compliance, or punish for rejection. The paternalist strives for high results. The *opportunistic* or "what's in it for me?" management style describes a leader who uses whatever grid style needed to obtain selfish interests and for self-promotion. These managers adapt to situations to gain maximum advantage. Performance by the manager occurs according to a system of exchanges, and effort is given only for an equivalent measure of effort from employees.

The grid approach has as an underlying assumption that one approach (team management) is best. The contradictory results of the research into the Hi-Hi style, however, suggest that some flexibility is needed in the application of this and other models.

# CONTINGENCY THEORIES OF LEADERSHIP

Neither the trait nor the early behavioral approaches to leadership were able to identify conclusively a single best style of leadership. In fact, the most effective leadership style depends on the situation a leader faces. Whether to be task- or people-oriented, or job- or employee-centered, or even how much employees should be allowed to participate in decision making is contingent on certain situational characteristics. In this section, we will examine several leadership models that address contingency factors, including situational leadership theory, Fiedler's contingency theory, path-goal theory, and the Vroom-Yetton-Jago participation model.

## Situational Leadership Theory

Probably the most popular leadership model, and the one most frequently applied in leadership development and training, was originally developed by consulting and training gurus Paul Hersey and Ken Blanchard as the "life cycle theory of leadership."[16] It evolved through several versions into the **situational leadership theory**, the premise of which is that a leader's style should be contingent on subordinates' competence and commitment.[17]

To understand situational leadership theory, we must define several concepts. *Directive behaviors* involve telling a subordinate the how, what, when, and where of a task and closely supervising task accomplishment. *Supportive behaviors* entail listening to subordinates, supporting and encouraging their progress, and involving them in decision making. As with the leadership grid, levels of directive and supportive behaviors can be shown on the horizontal and vertical axes of a matrix (Figure 17.2), with a leader's style (S1 to S4) falling into one of the four quadrants of the matrix. Hersey and Blanchard suggest that the levels of directive behavior (akin to task-oriented or initiating structure behaviors) and supportive behavior (akin to people-oriented or consideration behaviors) that a leader uses should depend on the development level of the subordinates. *Development level*

**situational leadership theory**
A leadership model whose premise is that a leader's style should be contingent on subordinates' competence and commitment.

**FIGURE 17.2**

## Situational Leadership Theory

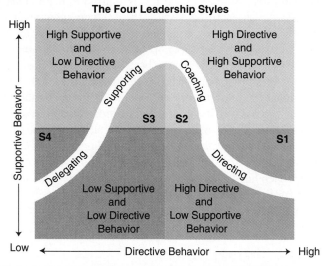

*Source:* Adapted from Kenneth Blanchard, Patricia Zigarmi, and Drea Zigarmi, *Leadership and the One Minute Manager* (New York: William Morrow and Company, Inc., 1985), 68.

refers to a subordinate's competence in setting and attaining goals related to a specific task and commitment to accepting responsibility for those goals.

According to situational leadership theory, managers assess an employee's development level on a continuum, such as the one shown in the bottom of Figure 17.2, then move up to that part of the curved line above that development level to ascertain the appropriate levels of directive and supportive behaviors—that is, the leadership style. Employees at position D1 on the continuum are high in commitment, but low in competence—for example, the new employee who is excited about the job, but knows little initially about how to perform. For that employee, the manager must employ a primarily *directing leadership style* (S1), telling the employee what to do and when, where, and how to do it, to guide the employee in properly carrying out the task. College freshmen might also be considered to be on a D1 level, excited but somewhat lacking in competence. Level D2 employees have gained some, but not full competence in their tasks but have low commitment. College sophomores may also be at D2, going through the "sophomore slump." They need a *coaching leadership style* (S2) that provides fairly high levels of direction as well as a high level of support to deal with their waning commitment.

After employees and college students have been around awhile (level D3), they know what they are supposed to do (competence) but their motivation and desire to perform (commitment) vary over time. These employees require a mostly *supporting leadership style* (S3) from the manager, who may listen to complaints, show support, and help talk through personal issues, but seldom needs to provide direction in task areas. Finally, the most highly developed employees (D4) are both fully competent and fully committed. For these employees, a *delegating leadership style* (S4) is appropriate, allowing the subordinates full rein to determine how to perform their tasks. Because these employees/students know what to do and readily accept responsibility for accomplishing their tasks, they do not require significant direction or support.

Bill Walsh, former coach of football's San Francisco Forty Niners, notes that, out of ten players, two will be superstars and require little coaching. In Blanchard's framework these represent D4s. Six players (maybe the D2 and D3 players) will perform well enough, with the right motivation and direction, to help the team, and two will waste your time (D1s with not quite enough ability). Walsh says to spend most of your time coaching the middle six in order to be successful in football.[18]

Application of the situational leadership model is not easy. Managers must first observe and communicate with employees to determine their level of development. Managers must also be flexible in applying direction and support because employees vary from one to another, as well as within themselves, over time and from task to task. Some managers tend to be inflexible in their leadership style. Moreover, employees may not initially agree with a manager's assessment of their development level, thus requiring a leader's skill in arriving at an assessment consensus and an agreed-upon leadership style, a process called **contracting for leadership style**. It is also important for a leader to be constantly aware of the need to develop team members by gradually moving ahead of them on the leadership curve and pulling them along the development continuum. Yet another difficulty with the model is that it deals with only one aspect of a situation, the subordinates, and ignores other possibly important factors.

## Fiedler's Contingency Theory

While Blanchard's theory calls for leaders to adjust their behaviors to meet the situational needs of subordinates, Professor Fred Fiedler took a different approach in his earlier **contingency theory**, suggesting that successful leadership requires matching leaders with primarily stable leadership styles to the demands of the situation.[19] If a leader's style does not match the situation, then either the situation should be changed or another leader should be found who does match the situation.

**Leadership Style.**    A major, often controversial aspect of Fiedler's theory is how he characterizes and measures leadership style. Fiedler asserts that a leader tends to be either relationship-oriented (similar to the consideration or employee-centered styles) or task-oriented (comparable to the initiating structure and directive styles). He considers a leader's style, like a trait, to be rooted in his or her personality and to be stable regardless of the situation. Task-oriented leaders consistently emphasize getting the job done without much concern for their subordinates' feelings; relationship-oriented leaders are most concerned about their people across all kinds of tasks. However, Fiedler's critics counter that people are capable of learning and changing their behaviors, even leadership behavior.[20]

To measure a leader's style, Fiedler devised a **least preferred coworker (LPC) scale** consisting of a series of adjective continuums. Low-LPC leaders view and describe their least preferred coworkers negatively and are thought to

---

**Example:** Carlos Slim is a directing CEO with a hands-on, no-frills management style. He owns more than 65% of two organizations: Group Carso, with $3.2 billion in 1993 sales and a market value of $9.9 billion, and Group Financiero Inbursa, Mexico's fourth largest financial group.

**contracting for leadership style**
A process whereby employees may not initially agree with a manager's assessment of their developmental level, thus requiring a leader's skill in arriving at an assessment consensus and an agreed-upon leadership style.

**contingency theory**
The suggestion that successful leadership requires matching leaders with primarily stable leadership styles to the demands of the situation.

**least preferred coworker (LPC) scale**
A measurement of a leader's style consisting of a series of adjective continuums.

be task-oriented. High-LPC leaders view even their least preferred coworker in a relatively favorable light and are thought to be relationship-oriented. Fiedler's LPC scale to measure leadership style is also controversial, with some researchers questioning the scale's validity.[21]

**Situational Contingencies.**    Whether a relationship-oriented or task-oriented leader will be successful depends on the favorability of the situation—that is, the extent to which the situation gives the leader control over subordinate behavior. Favorability is defined by three aspects of the situation:

1. *Leader-member relations*—the extent to which the leader is accepted by group members and has their support, respect, and goodwill is the most important determinant of favorability.

2. *Task structure*—the degree to which a task is well defined or has standard procedures for goal accomplishment. Creative or ambiguous tasks would be less structured.

3. *Position power*—the extent to which a leader has formal authority over employees to evaluate their work, assign tasks, and administer rewards and punishment.

By combining these three situational variables, we can derive eight different situations, called octants (Figure 17.3). The most favorable situation (octant 1) is one in which leader-member relations are good, the task is structured, and the leader has strong position power. The least favorable situation (octant 8) is one where a leader has poor relations with subordinates, an unstructured task, and little formal power.

**Style Effectiveness.**    In his research, Fiedler found that task-oriented leaders tended to be most effective (have higher group productivity) in the three most favorable and the very least favorable situations (octants 1, 2, 3, 8), while relationship-oriented leaders were most effective in the situations of moderate favorableness. If the leader's style does not match the situational demands, Fiedler would advise the leader to alter the situation, perhaps by restructuring the task or seeking more position power.

There has been considerable research on Fiedler's model, generating both support and criticism for his ideas. Criticisms of the model include its neglect of leaders who score in the middle on the LPC scale, the use of the LPC scale itself, the fact that many leaders can and do change their behaviors, and the relative lack of consideration of other situational characteristics related to the followers.[22] Nonetheless, Fiedler's contingency theory was one of the first to recognize the importance of the situation to leadership effectiveness, and it sensitized managers and researchers alike to the ineffectiveness of the one-best-way approach to leadership.

## Path-Goal Theory

**path-goal theory**
A model concerned with how a leader affects employees' perceptions of their personal and work goals and the paths to goal attainment.

Another contingency model of leadership was developed by management professor Robert House as an outgrowth of the expectancy theory of motivation discussed in Chapter 16. **Path-goal theory** is so named because it is concerned with how a leader affects subordinates' perceptions of their personal and work goals and the

## FIGURE 17.3

### Fiedler's Contingency Model

The left-hand side of the figure indicates the contingency characteristics of the situation, which are combined to determine the favorableness of the situation and whether a task-oriented or relationship-oriented style is preferred.

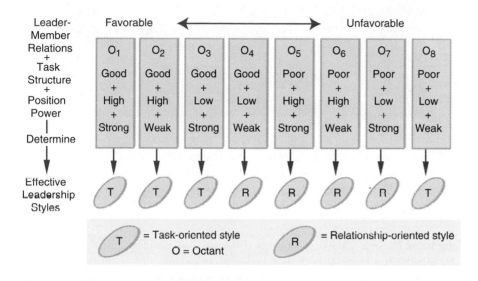

Source: Adapted from Fred E. Fiedler, *A Theory of Leadership Effectiveness* (New York: McGraw-Hill, 1967); and Fred Fiedler and M.M. Chemers, *Leadership and Effectiveness Management* (Glenview, IL: Scott, Foresman, 1974).

paths to goal attainment. It considers leaders effective to the degree that their behavior increases employees' attainment of goals and clarifies paths to these goals. What behaviors will help to accomplish these positive results depend on two aspects: leader behavior and situational factors.[23]

**Leader Behavior.**    Path-goal theory recognizes four major types of behavior:

1. *Directive Leadership:*  As with situational leadership theory, directive behaviors include giving task guidance, scheduling work, maintaining standards, and clarifying expectations.

2. *Supportive Leadership:*  Leaders concentrate on being approachable, showing concern for employees' well-being, doing little things to make the work environment more pleasant, and helping to satisfy employees' personal needs.

3. *Participative Leadership:*  Leaders consult with subordinates, solicit suggestions, and seriously consider their input when making decisions.

4. *Achievement-Oriented Leadership:*  Leaders set challenging goals, expect high performance, constantly seek improved performance, and show confidence in employees' ability to accomplish goals.

While attending a corporate leadership and team management training program, Levi Strauss sewing plant manager Tommye Jo Daves (right) learned "you can't lead a team by just barking orders." Since the training, Daves has changed her leadership behavior from directive to participative. She now involves all 385 employees in making plant operating decisions from organizing supplies to setting production goals. Daves's participative leadership has increased employee commitment to improve product quality and speed response to customer orders. Her plant has reduced flawed product by a third, decreased the time from order to shipment by ten days, and shrunk the time a pair of jeans spends in process from five days to one.

*Source:* © 1994 Michael A. Schwarz.

At different times and under different conditions, any of these leader behaviors may be most effective. Unlike Fiedler's model, path-goal theory assumes that leaders can adapt their styles to meet the demands of the situation or needs of subordinates to gain favorable outcomes from them.

**Situational Factors.**    Path-goal theory proposes that two classes of situational factors affect what leadership behaviors are appropriate: (1) employees' personal characteristics, and (2) environmental pressures and demands with which the employee must cope to accomplish the goal.

One important personal characteristic is an individual's locus of control (LOC), the extent to which a person believes he or she has control over what happens to him or her in life. Individuals who have an internal locus of control believe they largely control what happens to them; those with an external LOC believe that their lives are more controlled by fate, luck, chance, or significant other people. Consider Sarah, who has done poorly on a management test. If Sarah has an internal LOC, she will probably say her poor grade is due to not studying hard enough, but if she has an external LOC, she may attribute the poor grade to bad luck or an unfair professor. An individual with an internal locus of control may require less directive behavior than one with an external LOC.

Another personal factor is an employee's belief in his or her own ability to perform the task at hand. People with low confidence in their ability would likely respond better to directive behavior.

Environmental characteristics include (1) the nature of the task structure, (2) the formal authority of the situation, and (3) the nature of primary work groups. Although there are many propositions concerning how situational characteristics, personal characteristics, and leader behaviors interact to influence employees, the general premise of the path-goal theory is that the leader should apply whatever behavior helps to provide more positive rewards for employees, strengthen their belief that their effort will lead to goal accomplishment and positive rewards, or make rewards more contingent on goal accomplishment. Table 17.4 demonstrates several ways in which this may happen.

Path-goal theory has been very beneficial by pointing out a number of important situational contingency variables not covered in other theories; it also points

**TABLE 17.4**

**Path-Goal Theory of Leadership**

| Situation | Leader Behavior | Impact on Subordinates | Possible Outcome |
|---|---|---|---|
| Role or task is ambiguous; subordinate has external LOC | Directive behavior | Strengthens likelihood subordinate sees effort leading to goal accomplishment | Performance effort increases |
| Task is highly structured, but boring and repetitive; work group provides little support | Supportive behavior | Goal-related behaviors are more tolerable | Subordinate satisfaction increases |
| Task is unstructured and subordinates are internals who value autonomy | Participative behavior | Roles are clarified, leading to stronger effort-goal beliefs | Effort increases and satisfaction increases |
| Task is easy and not challenging | Achievement-oriented behavior | Higher goals are set | Performance effort increases |

*Source:* Adapted from Gary A. Yukl, *Leadership in Organizations,* 2nd edition (Englewood Cliffs, NJ: Prentice Hall, 1989), 98–104.

out the important motivational consequences of leader style on subordinate attitudes, beliefs, and behaviors.

## Vroom-Yetton-Jago Participation Model

One of the most important leadership behaviors involves employees in managerial decision making. The **Vroom-Yetton-Jago (VYJ) participation model**, developed by leadership experts Victor Vroom and Philip Yetton, and later modified by Vroom and Arthur G. Jago, provides a set of rules for employee participation in decision making.[24] Table 17.5 summarizes five decision-making styles for a "group-related problem." They include two autocratic styles (AI and AII), two consultative styles (CI and CII), and one group style (GII). Vroom and Jago provide five slightly different styles for problems involving only the leader and one other group member, that is, "individual problems." These five styles reflect that leaders are not just participative or autocratic, but act in different ways in getting employee involvement.

Which style to use depends on eight different situational characteristics related to the problem itself or the problem's impact on subordinates. These characteristics are depicted in the form of eight questions the leader answers in order. Depicted graphically, the eight questions form a flowchart or "decision tree," like the one shown in Figure 17.4. To use the decision tree, start at the left and answer the first question. The answer determines whether you take the top or bottom branch on the tree to the next question. Follow through until all relevant questions have been answered, and the most appropriate decision style to use will be indicated.

Vroom and Jago indicate that four different decision trees are appropriate: one for groups with time pressures, one for group problems with no time pressure, one for individual problems with time pressure, and one for individual problems with no time pressure. Figure 17.4, for example, shows a decision tree for a group problem with time pressures, used for determining how much participation the

**Vroom-Yetton-Jago (VYJ) participation model**
A model that provides a set of rules for employee participation in decision making.

## Decision Styles in the Vroom-Yetton-Jago Model

| Decision Style° | Definition |
| --- | --- |
| AI | Manager makes the decision alone. |
| AII | Manager asks for information from subordinates but makes the decision alone. Subordinates may or may not be informed about what the situation is. |
| CI | Manager shares the situation with individual subordinates and asks for information and evaluation. Subordinates do not meet as a group, and the manager alone makes the decision. |
| CII | Manager and subordinates meet as a group to discuss the situation, but the manager makes the decision. |
| GII | Manager and subordinates meet as a group to discuss the situation, and the group makes the decision. |

*Source:* Victor H. Vroom and Philip W. Yetton, *Leadership and Decision Making* (Pittsburgh: University of Pittsburgh Press, 1973).

° A = autocratic; C = consultative; G = group.

work group should have. General Electric's Jack Welch described how his leadership team, under time pressure, went into GE's failing appliance complex in Louisville and got the employees—management and union alike—involved in solving its problems. This CII and GII approach was required because the problem was important and unstructured, employees had much of the needed infor-

## VYJ Model Decision Tree for a Group Problem Under Time Pressure

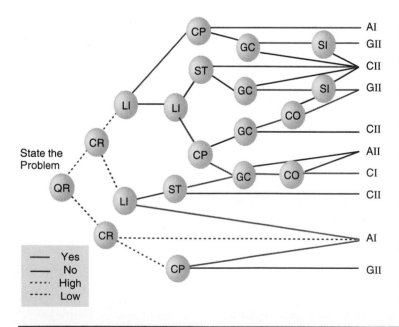

| | |
| --- | --- |
| **QR** | Quality requirement: How important is the technical quality of this decision? |
| **CR** | Commitment requirement: How important is subordinate commitment to the decision? |
| **LI** | Leader's information: Do you have sufficient information to make a high-quality decision? |
| **ST** | Problem structure: Is the problem well structured? |
| **CP** | Commitment probability: If you were to make the decision by yourself, is it reasonably certain that your subordinate(s) would be committed to the decision? |
| **GC** | Goal congruence: Do subordinates share the organizational goals to be attained in solving this problem? |
| **CO** | Subordinate conflict: Is conflict among subordinates over preferred solutions likely? |
| **SI** | Subordinate information: Do subordinates have sufficient information to make a high-quality decision? |

*Source:* Victor H. Vroom and Arthur G. Jago, *The New Leadership* (Englewood Cliffs, NJ: Prentice-Hall, 1988).

## BUSINESS    DILEMMA

*You're the Manager ...What Would You Do?*

THE COMPANY:    **Academy Oil**

YOUR POSITION:    **Base Commander**

THE PLACE:    **Altus, OK**

Academy Oil is a small oil production company owned and operated by the U.S. Army. The facility supplies the oil to a major petroleum refinery and receives credit toward future purchases. The oil production facility has been in operation for 25 years. Recently, a crisis occurred when a storage tank ruptured while being filled. Thousands of gallons of crude oil eventually spilled into a local river, the major source of drinking water for the area. The oil spill had immediate negative effects on wildlife, fish, and local residents.

The military base assembled a crisis management team to go to the scene of the incident and direct the clean-up operation. The Army had created such crisis management teams to deal with just such disasters. The teams plan worst-case scenarios that might occur, analyzing past public relations and other problems in prior incidents and assessing what could have been done to improve the situation. The team knows how to disseminate information and serves as a center for outside sources to contact. In this disaster, the base's commander, Col. Jim Briggs, did not make a public statement until he had collected enough information and had enough support activities engaged to honestly assure the public that everything possible was being done.

The situation worsened when clean-up efforts failed to contain the oil spill. Already fearful city residents were warned that the city's water systems would be shut down and they would be without water for several days. Reporters on the scene collected enough information to levy some fairly serious charges against the base's managers. They found inadequate training procedures and some old, ill-maintained equipment, including the 25-year-old tank that had ruptured.

Briggs then held a press conference with the media in which he acknowledged that problems had existed at the base in operating the oil production facilities, apologized, and took full responsibility. He also indicated that an oil company would be purchasing the oil production facilities and rights and the base would no longer be involved in the oil business.

The crisis team worked to get volunteers from major oil companies to donate their efforts to help clean up the spill. The team also worked closely with the media to keep them informed, as did Col. Briggs. Briggs brought water tankers into city areas to provide emergency water supplies. The spill was contained and water service reconnected in the area within three and a half days.

### Questions

1. Evaluate your (Briggs's) effectiveness in managing the crisis.
2. What type of leadership skills did you use in this situation?
3. Describe the function of the crisis team and how this assisted you in dealing with the public in this situation.

---

mation upper management did not have, and employee acceptance was essential if the effort was to be successful.[25]

Although the participation model appears complicated at first to many managers and students, its premises are very straightforward. First, analyze the situation according to eight important variables, and then apply the best of five different levels of participation. The questions and variables reflect good common sense. For example, if you don't have the necessary information to make a decision, it makes no sense to use an autocratic style. Overall, the model provides an excellent guide for determining employees' involvement levels in decisions. To help managers use the model, its authors have developed a computer program to facilitate answering the questions and generating a style. This program gives managers feedback about which styles they tend to use so that they can modify their behavior to make more effective decisions. Research provides strong support for the validity of the model in enhancing the quality and acceptance of decisions.[26]

**Example:** Ideo Product Development, the high-tech products designer in Palo Alto, California, uses employee involvement in decision making along with participation. The company allows career changes and short-term team leadership within a matrix-style organization. Peer reviews gauge individuals' progress and employees even choose their own reviewers.

## CURRENT TRENDS IN THE STUDY AND PRACTICE OF LEADERSHIP

Although the contingency approach has not died out, a number of other approaches to the study of leadership have been introduced in recent years. In this section, we will discuss the leader substitute approach, leader-member exchange theory, charismatic leadership, and transactional and transformational leadership, none of which totally abandons the contingency approach.

### Leadership Substitutes Theory

The contingency models discuss conditions that call for certain leadership behaviors. Some situational aspects have an even greater effect by severely limiting the ability of a leader to influence outcomes. Two such situational factors have been identified as substitutes and neutralizers.[27] Some other situational aspects actually have a positive impact on the leader behaviors; hence, they are called enhancers.

**leadership substitutes**
Aspects of the task, subordinates, or organization that act in place of leader behavior and thus render it unnecessary.

**Leadership substitutes** are aspects of the task, subordinates, or organization that act in place of leader behavior and thus render it unnecessary. For example, unambiguous, routine tasks or employees' knowledge, ability, and experience can substitute for task-oriented or directive behaviors (see Table 17.6). Employees in the FedEx hub and UPS distribution centers in Memphis, Tennessee, once trained, require little task structuring in their respective sorting and truck-loading jobs. Their supervisors therefore concentrate on keeping them motivated by engaging in supportive or consideration-oriented behavior, such as praise or other rewards, that help overcome the tedium of their routines.

The interesting possibility exists that leaders may not be necessary at all in some situations. If a cohesive work team of trained professionals performs structured tasks in a highly formalized environment, then little direct supervision and involvement by a leader may be warranted. Indeed, the understanding and creative use of leadership substitutes may be integral to the success of self-managed work teams, as discussed in Chapter 15.

**leadership neutralizers**
Aspects of the task, subordinates, or organization that have the effect of paralyzing, destroying, or counteracting the effect of a leadership behavior.

**Leadership neutralizers** are aspects of the task, subordinates, or organization that have the effect of paralyzing, destroying, or counteracting the effect of a leadership behavior. For example, if employees, such as those at FedEx and UPS, are indifferent to organizational rewards, then a supervisor engaging in the supportive leadership behavior of praising and rewarding would likely have little positive effect on employee satisfaction or motivation. In such a situation the supervisor may have to stick to task-oriented behaviors, try other supportive (but nonreward-oriented) behaviors, or replace these employees with ones who will work within the system.

**leadership enhancers**
Aspects of the task, subordinates, or organization that amplify a leader's impact on employees.

In some situations, other changes might be made that enhance the effectiveness of a leader's behavior. **Leadership enhancers** are aspects of the task, subordinates, or organization that amplify a leader's impact on employees. For example, if a nonperformance-based reward system is neutralizing a leader's impact, then changing the system to give the leader more power to influence rewards can make the same leadership behavior more effective. Likewise, having team-building exercises as part of a training program may aid in fostering positive group norms and values that help employees accept the task-oriented behaviors of a fairly directive leader. The creation of leadership enhancers can work very well when a leader has the necessary skill and appropriate organizational goals but is prevented by one or more neutralizers from being effective.[28]

**TABLE 17.6**

## Substitutes, Neutralizers, and Enhancers for Task Structuring and Consideration Leadership Behaviors

| Substitute Neutralizer | Supportive Leadership | Instrumental Leadership |
|---|---|---|
| *Employee Characteristics* | | |
| Experience, ability, training | | Substitute |
| "Professional" orientation | Substitute | Substitute |
| Indifference toward rewards offered by organization | Neutralizer | Neutralizer |
| Employees with external locus of control | | Enhancer |
| Employees with low self-efficacy | | Enhancer |
| *Task Characteristics* | | |
| Structured, routine, unambiguous task | | Substitute |
| Feedback provided by task | | Substitute |
| Intrinsically satisfying task | Substitute | |
| *Organization Characteristics* | | |
| Cohesive work group | Substitute | Substitute |
| Low position power (leader lacks control over organizational rewards) | Neutralizer | Neutralizer |
| Formalization (explicit plans, goals, areas of responsibility | | Substitute |
| Inflexibility (rigid, unyielding rules and procedures) | | Neutralizer |
| Leader located apart from employees with only limited communication possible | Neutralizer | Neutralizer |
| Leader with increased control over both rewards and resources | Enhancer | Enhancer |
| Leader given increased influence outside of work | Enhancer | |
| Crisis requiring immediate action | Enhancer | Enhancer |
| External competition with another group | | Enhancer |
| Leader given important responsibilities as an "in-house champion" to increase his/her image | Enhancer | Enhancer |
| Team building | Enhancer | Enhancer |

*Sources:* Summary based on Jon P. Howell, David E. Bowen, Peter W. Dorfman, Steven Kerr, and Phillip M. Podskoff, "Substitutes for Leadership: Effective Alternatives to Ineffective Leadership," *Organizational Dynamics* 19 (Summer 1990): 21–38; and Steven Kerr and John M. Jermier "Substitutes for Leadership: Their Meaning and Measurement," *Organizational and Human Performance* 22 (December 1978): 375–403, appearing in Gary Yukl, *Leadership in Organizations*, 2nd ed. (Englewood Cliffs, NJ: Prentice Hall, 1989).

In general, understanding how substitutes, neutralizers, and enhancers influence the effectiveness of leadership behavior can help an organization when a leader cannot be changed for political, financial, ethical, or other practical reasons, or when leadership is in transition. When Stanley Gault of Rubbermaid retired in 1991, the company got two new CEOs in 18 months—one retiring amid controversy—yet never missed a beat. The highly successful cross-functional team structure continued to churn out new products and thus substituted for the leadership from above that may have been lacking during the transition.[29]

## Leader-Member Exchange Theory

The **leader-member exchange (LMX) theory** describes how leaders develop "unique" working relationships with each of their subordinates, based on the nature of their social exchanges.[30] Each leader-subordinate relationship differs in

**Example:** Leadership substitutes and enhancers can be seen in the Hollywood marketing team of Buffy Shutt and Kathy Jones. These two women are heads of marketing at Universal pictures and are effective and experienced players in selling films to moviegoers. They collaborate and both say they are equals who make decisions together.

**leader-member exchange (LMX) theory**
A description of how leaders develop "unique" working relationships with each of their employees, based on the nature of their social exchanges.

Nelson Mandela exemplifies the traits of a charismatic leader. He devoted his life to working to achieve his vision of ending apartheid and creating a democratic and free society in South Africa. Imprisoned and prepared to die for his cause, Mandela inspired millions of South Africans to rally behind him. His leadership power as head of the African National Congress led to his triumph as the first black president of South Africa. For his undying commitment to the cause of racial equality, Mandela won a Nobel Peace Prize.

*Source:* © Louise Gubb/JB Pictures.

terms of both the feelings present and the behaviors demonstrated. Higher-quality relationships are reflected by more positive attitudinal statements, closer emotional ties, and stronger mutual commitment and loyalty, as well as more employee influence and autonomy.[31] Based on these relationships, leaders tend to develop *in-groups*—those subordinates who are part of their "team"—and *out-groups*—those who aren't.

Research has found that in-group members perform better, have higher levels of satisfaction, tend to be promoted more quickly, and have lower turnover rates. This implies that employees should try to be in the in-group if they desire more rewards. Managers need to be aware that these two distinct groups can develop, with both positive and negative consequences. If the in-group includes virtually every employee, then all workers will be more likely to receive these positive outcomes. Out-group members, though, will often feel disenchanted and resentful and lose their team identification and commitment.

Although the theory is somewhat vague on how leader-member exchange relationships develop, some recent research suggests that friendship and the process of forming friendships may parallel the LMX relationship development process and have similar effects. Simply becoming and remaining friends on the job may be the essential element of positive LMX relationships and may assist the leader in motivating employees.[32]

## Charismatic Leadership

**Example:** At Nynex Corporation, executive vice president Robert J. Thrasher is a leader with a history of breaking rules. At 5 feet, 3 inches, he is a bundle of energy and is completely committed to the company. He wants to be known as the "agent of change" and has the vision to make hard choices to improve service and reduce costs to stay competitive.

Much has been written about charismatic leaders in nearly all phases of public life. Lee Iacocca, formerly of Chrysler; Bill Gates of Microsoft; Michael Jordan and Bobby Knight of basketball fame; George Steinbrenner, shipbuilder turned baseball team owner; and Ross Perot, industrial giant turned politician—all are examples of charismatic leaders. Charisma has become even more important because of companies' need to inspire employees to higher levels of performance to meet stiff competition. If we can find out what makes a leader charismatic, then we may be able to advance our organizations and motivate employees like never before. Thus, a closer look at charisma is warranted.

Charismatic leaders tend to inspire followers to a higher plane of performance or existence, instill confidence in leader and self, empower, and generate tremendous devotion and often unquestioned obedience.[33] They are sometimes viewed as saviors, as in the case of Lee Iacocca at Chrysler, or virtual cult leaders, as with Southwest's Herb Kelleher. Charismatic leaders have a strong sense of dominance, self-confidence, a need to influence, and a belief in the value and righteousness of their causes.[34] They are typically good speakers who can eloquently express a vision or ideology that often borders on or exceeds the hazardous or the revolutionary.[35] John DeLorean, for example, was revolutionary in his automobile designs, but unfortunately was also reckless with financial resources.

For our purposes, it is more important to know what charismatic leaders actually do, especially in the business world. They tend to promote causes that deviate greatly from the status quo, yet still fall within the realm of acceptance by followers. They take personal risks that often appear heroic and engage in unconventional behavior to achieve the changes they desire. They assess the environment realistically and implement innovative strategies when the environment appears favorable. Finally, they engage in self-promotion to inspire employees or followers, often by presenting the status quo as negative and their vision and themselves as the solution. They exert personal power (expert and referent) that may involve elitist, entrepreneurial, and exemplary behaviors that position them as reformers, rather than administrators or managers.[36] Finally, charismatic leaders maintain intensely personal relationships with their followers, based on emotional rather than rational grounds.

Contrary to traditional beliefs, not only can many of these behaviors be learned, but they represent a separate dimension of leadership behavior, distinct from consideration or initiating structure, that enhances employees' task performance and satisfaction. Charismatic leadership may help convey the importance of a given task, while initiating structure conveys the orderliness of the task, and consideration expresses the shared responsibility (supportiveness) for the task.[37]

## Transactional versus Transformational Leadership

The discussions of leader-member exchanges and charismatic leadership highlight the contrast between two major leadership styles currently being discussed by leadership experts: transactional and transformational leadership.[38]

**Transactional leadership** is more traditional, with managers engaging in both task- and consideration-oriented behaviors in an exchange manner—you do things for me and I'll do things for you. Transactional leaders get things done by promising and providing recognition, praise, pay increases, and advancements in return for higher performance. They also impose punishments on workers who perform poorly. Some managers actively engage in these types of transactions by seeking out opportunities to take action to improve performance and thus reward employees. Other less-effective managers use a more passive management-by-exception approach and often concentrate on punishing nonstandard performance.[39] Although the active-reward approach has shown better results than the passive-punishment approach, both can result in mediocre performance. In a path-goal fashion, these two approaches require the manager to clarify subordinate roles, define subordinate needs, and clarify how those needs will be met in exchange for valued outcomes. The leaders' effectiveness is limited in many cases by lack of control over organizational rewards and punishments as well as the inability to excite, inspire, or foster commitment in employees.[40]

**Transformational leadership** goes beyond mere exchange relationships by inspiring employees to look beyond their own self-interests and by generating

**transactional leadership**
A more traditional approach in which managers engage in both task- and consideration-oriented behaviors in an exchange manner.

**transformational leadership**
A style that goes beyond mere exchange relationships by inspiring employees to look beyond their own self-interests and by generating awareness and acceptance of the group's purposes and mission.

Stanley Gault (left) is a transformational leader. As CEO of Rubbermaid, he transformed the company from a little-known maker of consumer goods with sales of $300 million into one of the most admired companies in the United States, with sales of $1.5 billion. After retiring from Rubbermaid, Gault was hired as CEO to rejuvenate Goodyear Tire and Rubber. Gault leads firms to profitability by trusting employees and involving them in the process of change. He gives personal attention to employees by listening to their problems and ideas and inviting them to call him Stan. Here, Gault visits with a Goodyear tire store employee.

*Source:* © Steven Rubin/JB Pictures.

awareness and acceptance of the group's purposes and mission. Transformational leaders often appeal to higher ideals and moral values such as justice, humanitarianism, peace, and equality or to baser emotions such as fear or hatred. Consequently, some transformational leaders, such as Adolf Hitler, or religious cult leaders Jim Jones and David Koresh can have extremely negative effects on their followers.[41] Transformational leaders in business, though, excite employees to perform beyond what they thought they were capable of doing, doing so to satisfy the higher-order needs identified in Maslow's hierarchy. Examples would be Lee Iacocca, who rescued Chrysler from the brink of bankruptcy; Jan Carlzon, who turned around Scandinavian Airlines in little over a year; and Wal-Mart's Sam Walton, who pumped up his employees to be service-oriented even in a low-cost retail business.

A number of characteristics seem to distinguish transformational leaders from the more traditional transactional leaders:

1. *Charisma:* Transformational leaders provide a vision and sense of mission and instill a sense of trust and respect in followers. Charisma is a necessary condition for transformational leadership, but it is insufficient without the remaining traits.

2. *Inspiration:* Transformational leaders communicate through images, conveying a simple yet powerful message that inspires followers to a higher purpose.

3. *Intellectual Stimulation and Empowerment:* They stimulate their followers' intellectual process by promoting rationality and problem solving. They are willing to take risks and get their followers thoroughly involved in their purpose.

4. *Individual Consideration:* They give individualized and personal attention to followers. They act as coaches, developers, and supporters, admonishing when necessary, but emphasizing the positive.

5. *Change Facilitation:* They recognize the need for and promote change. They see themselves as agents of change who are willing to commit themselves and their subordinates' involvement to the future they envision.

6. *Integrity:* They promote the higher-order values noted above and model honesty and integrity with their own behavior.[42]

Transformational leadership, although not common in business and government, is certainly not a mystical phenomenon found only in a few "born" charismatics. Moreover, research has found that transformational leadership exists at all levels of organizational hierarchies and is positively related to a number of different performance criteria in an extremely broad range of organizations: senior U. S. Navy officers, business and industry leaders in many countries, educational administrators, and religious leaders.[43] Perhaps the most exciting aspect of transformational leadership is that there is increasing evidence that it can be learned. In the next section, we present a set of behavioral practices that leaders of all kinds in all types of situations can develop in themselves and help to develop in others.

**Example:** General Electric, under chairman John F. "Neutron Jack" Welch Jr., was known for its tough-as-nails attitude toward employees in the lower ranks. Now Welch wants managers who can make transformations through empowering others. This includes worker involvement and trust.

## The Leadership Challenge

James Kouzes and Barry Posner, two California educators and trainers, list five major leadership practices, each with two behavioral subcategories, that they found present in successful leaders.[44] These five practices are quite similar to the characteristics of transformational leadership and, moreover, are behaviors that nearly any manager (or aspiring manager) can learn. Kouzes and Posner challenge managers to become true leaders by:

**Challenging the Process.**    Leaders act as pioneers by changing the status quo through searching out opportunities to change, grow, and improve, as well as experimenting, taking risks, and learning from their mistakes. They actively look for things to change, and they encourage subordinates not to fear taking a calculated risk with them. Nicholas Hayek challenged the process when he turned around the Swiss watch industry with the Swatch watch. He proved, contrary to popular belief, that being innovative and attending to detail could build a high-quality, high-value, mass-market consumer product in the highest-wage country in the world at low cost.[45]

**Inspiring a Shared Vision.**    Leaders begin to inspire by envisioning the future—perhaps a new facility, a major process innovation, or a new product or market. They then enlist others in the common vision by appealing to their values, interests, hopes, and dreams. They paint a picture with language, using metaphors and symbols to give life to their vision and attract others to it. Bill Gates, Sam Walton, and Ross Perot all epitomize the visionary leader.

**Enabling Others to Act.**    Leaders build successful teams and make others feel like owners of the vision by fostering collaboration and strengthening others. They encourage collaboration by emphasizing cooperative, instead of competitive, goals, by seeking integrative solutions, and by building relationships based on trust, mutual respect, and individual dignity. They empower others by involving them in planning and decision making, and granting autonomy and discretion.

**Modeling the Way.**    Leaders epitomize what they want others to do, and they encourage them to do it. First they set the example, by developing a set of values and then by reflecting those values in decisions they make and actions they take. They also plan small wins, by dividing tasks into smaller chunks and experimenting frequently, giving people a sense of choice and accomplishment along the way.

## Career's Corner

### Leadership Training Programs

The old view about teaching leadership was about the same as the view about teaching sex. "If you really need lessons, well…." With the demise of the trait approach, that view has changed, at least about teaching leadership, and leadership training has become a burgeoning industry over the last two decades. Over 600 academic institutes offer some sort of formal approach to leadership development, as do several hundred independent institutes and training organizations. For the person who wishes to specialize in leadership development, an attractive and financially rewarding career could await. For example, Tom Peters, coauthor of *In Search of Excellence* and the reigning leadership guru, charges $65,000 for a one- or two-hour lecture, or $80,000 per day, and he speaks about six times a month. His training income is supplemented, as if he needs it, by royalties from books, training materials, videos, and other programs his company sponsors. Although you may not become the next Tom Peters, you still might do very well by finding a niche for yourself in one of the four major categories of leadership programs described in McGill University professor Jay Conger's recent book, *Learning to Lead.*

The "feedback" approach to leadership development involves enhancing self-awareness of the student's leadership skills through videotaped observation and feedback by experts, or through surveys of his or her coworkers, bosses, and subordinates (what some call a 360-degree evaluation). The Center for Creative Leadership in North Carolina epitomizes this approach to leadership development, but it hires primarily Ph.D.s in psychology, other behavioral sciences, and organizational behavior.

The "personal growth" approach teaches leadership and team building by challenging the student's limits, often through physical activities such as rock climbing or "ropes" courses. Places like Outward Bound and the Pecos River Learning Center offer programs of various length and difficulty. To work for such a program, your degree could vary from business to education, but experience or training in physical education or recreation can also be helpful.

"Skill-building" approaches attack specific aspects of leadership—often through exercises and experiential learning—and operate with the philosophy of "practice makes perfect." An example of an exercise might involve giving an inspirational speech to help develop your transformational leadership skills. The Blanchard Learning Center (Ken Blanchard, author of the *One Minute Manager*) and the Tom Peters Group are leaders in this type of training, but many others offer skill-building programs. Although it helps, you can still work as a trainer in some of these companies without a Ph.D. Business degrees in HRM and degrees in education or psychology, as well as some good work experience, prepare you to provide this type of training.

The final approach is the "conceptual awareness" orientation, with the underlying philosophy that if you grasp the concept you can act on it. This is the most intellectual approach, utilizing case studies and exercises, and is offered largely through academic institutions such as Harvard and Stanford. Primarily, only Ph.D.s need aspire to these types of training careers.

All of these approaches have been adapted for in-house training programs in some major U.S. companies, and thus offer additional career opportunities. Whether or not you aspire to a graduate education, a career in leadership training may be just the one for you.

*Source:* John Huey, "The Leadership Industry," *Fortune,* February 21, 1994, 54–56.

---

They build commitment to the goal and the process. Bill Gates models the work ethic of Microsoft by working long hours himself.

**Encouraging the Heart.**    Leaders make people feel good about what they are doing by recognizing contributions and celebrating accomplishments. Effective leaders use a variety of rewards and strive to link them to performance. At Cooper Tire, Ivan W. Gorr has developed an innovative pay system in which hourly workers get paid more for more production, and executive compensation can be raised or cut 30 percent based on company performance, as compared to benchmarks.[46] Leaders who encourage the heart also cheerlead, have public ceremonies and rituals, stay personally involved, and build caring social networks. They give heart to others. Vince Lombardi said that love—which he defined as loyalty and team-work—was at the core of his success as a coach.

Managers who engage in these leadership practices are more likely to be perceived as leaders and to gain the personal sense of achievement that accompanies the accomplishment of important goals through people.

## SUMMARY AND REVIEW

- **Differentiate leadership from the process of management.** Leadership is the process of influencing the activities of an individual or a group toward the achievement of a goal. While leadership involves inspiring and motivating change in people through a shared vision, management involves organizing processes logically to achieve goals by adding stability.

- **List the sources of power leaders use to influence others' behavior.** Power is a person's capacity to influence the behavior and attitudes of others. Leaders can use several sources of power to gain commitment and/or compliance from followers, while not generating resistance: legitimate authority of their position, expertise, charisma, referent relationships, rewards, punishments, information they possess, or their affiliations with other powerful people.

- **Distinguish successful leaders from less successful leaders and nonleaders, according to their traits.** Leaders tend to be higher than followers in many trait areas, such as intelligence, sociability and even height, but the differences are often small. Recent research has found that leaders tend to possess six core traits: drive, motivation to lead, honesty and integrity, self-confidence, cognitive ability, and business knowledge in their disciplines.

- **Compare and contrast the major dimensions of leadership behavior used in the behavioral theories.** The behavioral theories of leadership all include two major dimensions of leadership behaviors. In each, one dimension involves getting the job done by directing employees, scheduling, monitoring and controlling work, and providing resources. The other dimension involves maintaining good leader-subordinate relationships, employee commitment, and satisfaction by listening, supporting, praising, and involving subordinates in work decisions. The Ohio State studies labeled these two dimensions "initiating structure" and "consideration," while the Michigan studies called them "task-oriented behaviors" and "relationship-oriented behaviors." Many other major leadership theories and models, such as situational leadership theory, Fiedler's contingency theory, and the leadership grid, use some form of these two behavioral dimensions.

- **Summarize the contingency factors covered in Fiedler's contingency theory, Blanchard's situational leadership theory, and path-goal theory.** Situational leadership theory, Fiedler's contingency theory, and path-goal theory all maintain that the appropriate leadership style depends on, or is contingent upon, certain characteristics of the situation, usually related to the nature of the followers, the leader-follower relationship, or the nature of the task environment. Situational theory contends that the competence and commitment of the followers are the key variables. Fiedler's theory says the quality of leader-member relations, the level of task structure, and the position power of the leader are key. Path-goal theory maintains that such things as employees' locus of control, task structuring, the leader's formal authority, and the nature of the work group should determine leader behavior.

- **Determine what may neutralize, or substitute for, leadership behavior.** Leadership substitutes are aspects of the task, subordinates, or organization that act in place of leader behavior and thus render it unnecessary. Leadership neutralizers are aspects of the task, subordinates, or organization that have the effect of paralyzing, destroying, or counteracting the effect of a leadership behavior.

- **Specify the leadership practices that can contribute to successful transformational leadership and that distinguish it from transactional leadership.** Transactional leadership is more traditional, with managers engaging in both task- and consideration-oriented behaviors in an exchange manner. Transformational leadership inspires employees to look beyond their own self-interests and generates awareness and acceptance of the group's purposes and mission. Good leaders challenge the process, inspire a shared vision in followers, enable others to act by fostering collaboration and empowering others, model the way by epitomizing the values they encourage in others, and encourage the hearts of their followers by recognizing their contributions and celebrating their accomplishments.

• **Evaluate a leader's efforts to manage a crisis situation.** You should be able to evaluate the effectiveness of the manager described in the "Business Dilemma" box, applying the various management theories discussed in this chapter.

## Key Terms and Concepts

leadership *492*
power *493*
organizational power *493*
personal power *493*
legitimate power *493*
reward power *494*
coercive power *494*
expert power *494*
referent power *495*
charisma *495*
information power *495*
affiliative power *496*

consideration behaviors *498*
initiating-structure behaviors *498*
task-oriented behaviors *499*
relationship-oriented behaviors *499*
employee-centered leaders *499*
job-centered leaders *500*
situational leadership theory *501*
contracting for leadership style *503*
contingency theory *503*
least preferred coworker (LPC) scale *503*
path-goal theory *504*

Vroom-Yetton-Jago (VYJ) participation model *507*
leadership substitutes *510*
leadership neutralizers *510*
leadership enhancers *510*
leader-member exchange (LMX) theory *511*
transactional leadership *513*
transformational leadership *513*

## Ready Recall

1. Discuss how leaders and managers differ. Do you think a person can be a successful leader and manager at the same time? Why?
2. What are the different sources of power a manager can use? Which tend to be the best? Why?
3. Discuss the five major leadership styles in the leadership grid.
4. What are the contingency variables or situational characteristics in the situational leadership theory, Fiedler's contingency theory, and the Vroom-Yetton-Jago participation model?
5. What are the four leadership styles used in the situational leadership theory and when should they be used? What are some of the difficulties associated with applying the model?

6. What are the four major types of leader behaviors discussed in the path-goal theory of leadership?
7. Name some personal and situational factors that can enhance or neutralize the effect of a leader's actions or can in some cases substitute for his or her action.
8. Contrast transactional and transformational leaders.
9. How do path-goal theory and leader-member exchange theory parallel transactional leadership?
10. Name the five leadership practices that Kouzes and Posner challenge managers to develop within themselves and within subordinate managers and supervisors.

## Expand Your Experience

1. Take any local leader in business, politics, or education (your school's president may be a good one) who appears frequently in the newspaper. Peruse whatever articles you can find on this individual and, using Kouzes and Posner's five categories, discuss whether this person qualifies as a transformational leader.
2. Listed below are some political, military, and business leaders, sports and entertainment personalities, characters in TV shows, and other well-known personalities. For each person that you recognize, list in rank order the three most prominent sources of power you believe the person possesses. Use the number corresponding to the source of power. Sources of Power: 1 = Expert 2 = Legitimate 3 = Referent 4 = Reward 5 = Charisma 6 = Coercive 7 = Affiliative 8 = Information

Bill Gates (founder of Microsoft)  _____ _____ _____

U.S. President Bill Clinton  _____ _____ _____

First Lady Hillary Rodham Clinton  _____ _____ _____

Civil rights leader Martin Luther King, Jr.  _____ _____ _____

Ann Richards, former Texas governor  _____ _____ _____

Joe Montana, famous football quarterback  _____ _____ _____

Nazi leader Adolf Hitler  _____ _____ _____

John F. Kennedy, late U.S. president  _____ _____ _____

Barbara Walters, journalist  _____ _____ _____

Michael Jordan, basketball star  _____ _____ _____

Ross Perot, businessman/politician  _____ _____ _____

James Bond, fictional spy  _____ _____ _____

U.S. General Norman Schwarzkopf  _____ _____ _____

U.S. General George Patton  _____ _____

Madonna, singer, actress  _____ _____ _____

Perry Mason, fictional attorney  _____ _____ _____

Jim Bakker, TV evangelist and ex-convict  _____ _____ _____

Bill Cosby, entertainer  _____ _____ _____

Jackie Joyner Kersee, Olympic track star  _____ _____ _____

Roberto Goizueta, CEO of Coca-Cola  _____ _____ _____

3. Below are listed, on the left, nine societal and business trends that may present problems for managers now and into the twenty-first century. On the right are listed the ten leadership behaviors that make up the five major behavioral practices presented by Kouzes and Posner in their book, *The Leadership Challenge*. For each trend, rank the three most important leadership behaviors that managers may need to use to deal with it by marking the number of the three practices in the space provided.

A. Globalization of business competition  _____ _____ _____

B. Rapid change  _____ _____ _____

C. Cost consciousness/downsizing  _____ _____ _____

D. Quality emphasis  _____ _____ _____

E. Rejection of tacit formal authority  _____ _____ _____

F. Eroding Protestant work ethic/survival motive  _____ _____ _____

G. Self-importance/me generation  _____ _____ _____

H. Work-force diversity/changing role of women  _____ _____ _____

I. Demoralization of spirit  _____ _____ _____

**Challenging the Process**
1. Search for opportunities
2. Experiment—take risks
**Inspiring a Shared Vision**
3. Envision the future
4. Enlist others
**Enabling Others to Act**
5. Foster collaboration
6. Strengthen others
**Modeling the Way**
7. Set the example
8. Plan small wins
**Encouraging the Heart**
9. Recognize contributions
10. Celebrate accomplishments

# Bill Gates: America's Richest 800-Pound Gorilla

You may have heard the old joke "Where does an 800-pound gorilla sit?" The answer: "Anywhere it wants." That's how *Time* magazine referred to Bill Gates, founder of Microsoft, the computer software giant. He's that powerful. *U.S. News & World Report* called him the next Rockefeller, and *Fortune* named him the United States's richest person, with a personal wealth—mostly from shares in his company's stock—valued at well over $6 billion. Whether you call him an 800-pound gorilla, the next Rockefeller, the $6 billion man, or the country's foremost computer "nerd," there is no doubt that Bill Gates is successful. The key to his success is not only his computer genius, but even more so his business acumen and leadership skills.

In 1975, when he was 19 years old, Gates founded Microsoft with his friend Paul Allen. Gates dropped out of Harvard soon after because he could not wait to start his entrepreneurial career. In 1979 Gates moved Microsoft to its present location in Seattle, where it was discovered by IBM. Big Blue introduced its standard-setting personal computer in 1981, using a Microsoft operating system (the foundation software that enables users to issue instructions to their computers) and the microprocessor furnished by Intel (that's a different success story). Actually, Gates licensed the operating system, MS-DOS, from someone else and improved it. IBM erred by allowing Gates to sell MS-DOS to other companies. Hundreds of small companies quickly "cloned" IBM's PC, and nearly every one of the millions of IBM compatibles, as they are often called, ran on MS-DOS. Every computer requires an operating system, and MS-DOS is the operating system in an estimated 140 million PCs, or between 80 and 90 percent of those existing in the world today.

Since Microsoft went public in 1986, its annual revenues have exploded from $198 million to $2.8 billion in 1992, with a net profit margin of 25.7 percent. One hundred shares of Microsoft, bought for $2,100 in 1986, were worth about $77,850 in 1993. Even in an era of downsizing, Microsoft has increased its work force 700 percent since 1986 to over 14,000 employees in 1993.

How Bill Gates has been able to accomplish so much is a testament to his ability to manage a company and motivate people. Although Gates is admittedly frugal with company funds and doesn't pay people exceptionally well by industry standards, he is generous with company stock options. In fact, an estimated 2,000 of his employees are millionaires because of their ownership of Microsoft. Gates has managed to make his employees feel like, and actually be, his partners in the firm. He expects and gets a high degree of loyalty from them, very few of whom leave the company. There is also a strong Microsoft work ethic. Rather than gloating over their successes, Gates and his followers are relentlessly industrious. They work extremely hard and often very long hours.

Gates serves as the model for this culture. He typically works 13 hours a day and Saturdays, and spends half his time on the road, visiting subsidiaries and talking to clients. He also has a fierce management style, resulting in a relentless assault on every objective. He reads voraciously the various reports, product information, and market analyses; challenges his employees in product-development meetings; and expects them to be able to respond under fire. He is very willing to listen and give way when he believes someone else has a better point, but he makes employees prove their positions. He also hires only the best and brightest young programmers, hotly recruiting them from the top schools and treating them well with personal offices and a couple of computers each on their oak desks.

Gates also has tremendous resilience and persistence. He predicted in 1984 that Windows would be the wave of the future. Windows is a computer program that enhances DOS to allow PCs to emulate the more graphical-oriented Apple Macintosh. When Windows flopped in its mid-1980s debut, his advisers pleaded with him to drop it. Besides, many PC companies were lining up to purchase IBM's new OS/2 operating system. When OS/2 came out in 1988, it was sluggish and used too much memory, rendering it questionable for many existing, and even the newer, personal computers. Windows, having improved through four versions, finally took off. It now sells about as many copies a month as the still viable MS-DOS.

What anchors Bill Gates's decisions and his management actions is a clear vision, not only for his company, but even for the future of the computer industry. He once said that his goal is to have a computer in every home in America, each running Microsoft software. Although only about 15 percent of homes now have computers, he hasn't abandoned that dream; in fact, he has built on it. In a recent annual meeting, he articulated his vision, including such things as computer-based multimedia, interactive TV, and even a wallet PC. He envisions TV-PCs made so simple that even computer phobics will enjoy using them.

To realize Gates's vision, Microsoft spends $350 million on R&D, or 13 percent of revenues (compared to 11 percent for Merck or 10 percent for IBM). His 20 or more business units have already ventured into numerous new software areas, CD-ROM information storage and retrieval, and new operating systems that run large mainframe computers and allow them to work in conjunction with the PCs. Although Microsoft is not always ahead of the competition in these efforts—with extremely strong rivals in specific niches—Gates views each area as a potential leadership position for Microsoft.

One of Gates's greatest accomplishments has been to establish a culture that allows Microsoft to remain highly competitive and move rapidly in a business area that seems to change by the minute. Microsoft has even had to fight off a Federal Trade Commission investigation because of accusations that it has developed a monopoly and engages in unfair practices. Gates meets these challenges by keeping himself and his people sharp. As one sales executive notes, "Don't get complacent," is etched into the minds of every employee. They have a "siege" mentality that everyone is out to get them. The recent FTC investigation lends credence to that notion.

In spite of all the pressure, Gates has developed a work atmosphere that makes Microsoft "the" technology company to work for. He keeps business units small and leanly staffed to maintain the small-company atmosphere. Microsoft's modest buildings and grounds outside of Seattle are like a college campus, with employees who look and act like students. There is virtually no dress code, and some employees come to work wearing outrageous clothes or no shoes. Employees decorate their work areas as they see fit, and they relax their minds by taking breaks to play, such as having water pistol fights or playing in makeshift bands. One engineer even brings his boa constrictor to work. Gates tries

to operate with a "nerdy" humor, once addressing a computer convention dressed in Star Trek uniform and sporting Mr. Spock ears. Yet this casual atmosphere does not mask the key pivotal norm or standard of high productivity. Project teams relentlessly gather all available information about their competition and constantly strive to be number one in their respective niches.

Bill Gates is one of the few entrepreneurs who has been able to mesh technological genius with the management and leadership expertise necessary to be a true winner. He may well be the epitome of the type of leader needed to carry U.S. business into the twenty-first century.

*Sources:* William J. Cook, "The Next Test for Bill Gates," *U.S. News & World Report*, February 15, 1993, 70, 72; William J. Cook with David Bowermaster, "The New Rockefeller," *U.S. News & World Report*, February 15, 1993, 64–69; Alan Deutschman, "Bill Gates' Next Challenge," *Fortune*, December 28, 1992, 30–41; "Is Microsoft Too Powerful?" *Business Week*, March 1, 1993, 82–90; and "The Next 800 lb. Gorilla," *Time*, May 20, 1991.

## Questions

1. Analyze Bill Gates's leadership style using the Ohio State, Michigan, and leadership grid terminology.
2. What sources of power does Bill Gates have and use? Explain.

3. Use the Kouzes and Posner categories and assess whether or not Bill Gates qualifies as a transformational leader.

## STRENGTHEN YOUR SKILLS
### *Leading*

As you will recall from reading the chapter, James Kouzes and Barry Posner's research identified five major leadership practices in successful leaders. Here again is the leadership practice described in the chapter as "Enabling Others to Act":

*Leaders build successful teams and make others feel like owners of the vision by fostering collaboration and strengthening others. They encourage collaboration by ... seeking integrative solutions and building relationships based on trust, mutual respect, and individual dignity. They empower others by involving them in planning and decision making, and granting autonomy and discretion.*

To continue using the Square Wheels™ language that you have been using in the "Strengthen Your Skills" exercises in Part Four (Chapters 14 to 16), look at Figure 17.5.

Here are some questions for you to consider (either as a class or in groups of 4 to 6 people):

1. Describe what this manager's "bright idea" is. (Refer to Figure 14.1 in the "Strengthen Your Skills" exercise on page 422 if you have forgotten what the wagon looked like originally.) _____

_____

**A Desk Is a Dangerous Place from Which to View the World**

*Source:* © Performance Management Company, 1993, 1994. All Rights Reserved. 800–659-1466.

**2.** Is this manager's behavior characteristic of the behavior described in the opening Kouzes and Posner quotation? Why or why not? _____

_____

_____

**3.** Review the other four characteristics described by James Kouzes and Barry Posner in the chapter section titled "The Leadership Challenge." List any of these four practices ("Challenging the Process," "Inspiring a Shared Vision," "Modeling the Way," "Encouraging the Heart") you think this manager is using and why you think she is using the one(s) you listed. _____

_____

_____

The second illustration, in Figure 17.6, shows the results of the manager's "bright idea" being implemented. She and the accounting manager appear pleased with the results.

**FIGURE 17.6**

**One Less Bump per Revolution**

As you and your group continue your discussion, consider these ideas related to the second illustration:

- If the person/people involved in trying to improve a process have a perspective that is too narrow, the "solution" can miss some important factors. Implementing changes without a real understanding of how things really work can be costly.
- There can be unanticipated side effects from some efforts to improve the organization. Leadership must be sensitive to the impacts on people and quality.
- Limited views from any perspective are dangerous. The best leaders solicit ideas from cross-sections of people and then help them get implemented.

Think of examples from your work experience or any situation in which you have participated where you have observed the leadership principles you've discussed during this exercise. Share the situation/problem, the leader's behavior, the results, and the impact on people and quality.

# Communicating *in* Organizations

**Outline**

**After reading this chapter, you will be able to:**

- Define communication and explain its importance to managers.

- Describe the communication process and the factors that affect it.

- Compare and contrast the various communication forms and channels and the "richness" of each.

- Distinguish between formal and informal communication in an organization.

- Determine how groups and teams communicate.

- Detect the barriers to effective communication and specify potential ways to overcome them.

- Critique an organization's communication efforts.

H. Armstrong Roberts, Inc.

# Spiegel

Through an employee survey, Spiegel Incorporated learned that many of its employees were dissatisfied with their benefit plan, a plan that Spiegel had prided itself in offering. The survey results suggested to Spiegel's benefits managers that employees did not fully understand the benefits package. In response, Spiegel launched an aggressive $40,000 communications campaign to provide employees a better understanding of their benefits and to show them how to use their benefits more effectively.

To begin with, Spiegel reevaluated the value of its benefits with the assistance of benefits consultants Hewitt Associates of Lincolnshire, Illinois. Spiegel revamped the benefits program into a cafeteria-style offering which allowed employees to choose from three different levels of coverage. In addition, the new benefits package included a preferred provider organization (PPO) network, dental insurance, and spousal life insurance. The real challenge was to communicate the value of the new plan to employees.

Communication efforts began three months before the plan was officially introduced. First, Spiegel sent employees a packet of printed material explaining the benefits package. Next, it held several meetings with benefits officers and small groups of employees. In addition to an oral presentation, employees watched a slide presentation about the new benefits plan and were given the chance to ask questions. Employees also received a printed handout on the plan and enrollment materials.

When the new benefits went into effect, Spiegel provided each employee with a "personalized employee statement" that summarized the options the employee had chosen and recapped how each worked. The company also instituted an annual fall benefits meeting (small-group sessions with the benefits staff) in which new changes would be presented and discussed. According to Michael Talaga, Spiegel's benefits and compensations director, "Benefits is a marketing issue and it really is a matter of having employees understand the product."

It is easy to see from this example the vital role that communication can play for both managers and employees alike. It is also apparent that critical misunderstanding can occur if the two parties do not effectively communicate with one another. For instance, if Spiegel had initially made concerted efforts toward communicating the worth of the benefits package, then perhaps employees would not have been dissatisfied.

*Source:* Kay Robbins, "A Case Study: Spiegel Saves $1 Million with Plan Redesign," *Business & Health,* October 1992, 54–55.

*introduction*

A s the opening vignette illustrates, communication is of vital importance. If we were unable to indicate that we were hungry or in serious danger, for instance, our survival could be at stake. The role of communication is also critical for an organization and its managers. Most managerial activities—meetings, phone calls, and talking with employees and customers—involve communication skills. Indeed, research has found that managers spend over 75 percent of their time communicating in some way.[1] Thus, management and communication go hand in hand.

For managers to become effective communicators, they must first understand what communication is and that it is subject to misunderstanding and distortion. Thus, in this chapter, we will explore the concept of communication by discussing the communication process, identifying the various types and forms of communication, and exploring some common barriers to effective communication—as well as possible ways to overcome them.

## WHAT IS COMMUNICATION?

**communication**

The process through which information and meaning are transferred from one person to another.

**Critical Thinking Challenge:** Have students list various ways they have engaged in communication in the past week. How effective was each of the means of communication in conveying the intended message or information? How could each of the incidents have been improved?

Some may think of communication as one person telling another person something, either orally or in writing, but it entails much more. **Communication** is the process through which information and meaning are transferred from one person to another. The information and meaning can be transferred in various forms (such as written or oral), and the methods used to transfer the information and meaning can vary (for example, face to face, telephone, memo, or report) as well. A combination of methods may even be used to help ensure that a message is received properly. Your supervisor, for example, may choose to have a face-to-face meeting concerning your promotion and then follow up with a written memo that reiterates the main points of the meeting.

In general, people communicate because they want to achieve a goal, satisfy a personal need, or improve their immediate position.[2] It is very important to note that real communication has not occurred until the person for whom a message is intended has both received and understood the information sent. In other words, it is not enough simply to send a message. Let's say, for example, that your professor is writing the answer to a complex mathematical problem on the chalkboard, but offers neither a verbal explanation for how he arrived at the answer nor the opportunity for questions. In this instance, the professor has sent a message (via the chalkboard); however, the chances are very good that many students do not fully understand what the message means. Thus, communication has not taken place. Therefore, communication is a process of "sharing," rather than simply sending, information.

In the business world, this sharing of information allows companies to accomplish diverse goals. For example, several semiconductor companies asked their customers to share their perceptions of those firms through customer satisfaction surveys. The companies used the resulting information to maintain a competitive advantage in their industry.[3] Allied Signal used open communications with employees to maintain morale during a turbulent time created by acquisitions and divestitures.[4]

### The Importance of Communication

Communication is of vital importance to managers because it allows them to engage in the planning, organizing, leading, and controlling functions. Managers

**FIGURE 18.1**

**The Communication Process**

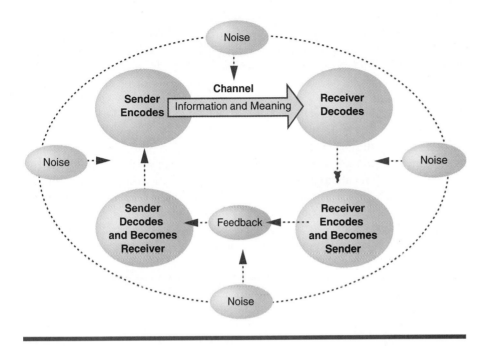

must be able to communicate their visions, goals, and directions to others, and others must be able to communicate back to managers to let them know whether goals and objectives are being achieved. For instance, a goal in connection with covering this chapter is to enrich your understanding of communication. However, the professor who does not allow questions to be asked or does not ask questions of you cannot be sure that this goal has been attained. Research shows that both organizational and individual performance improve when managerial communication is effective.[5] Indeed, communication competency is a fundamental aspect of job performance and managerial effectiveness.[6] Most human resource executives who have managed to climb the corporate ladder to top management positions attribute a great majority of their success to "good communication skills."[7]

## The Communication Process

We can think of communication as a process consisting of a chain of identifiable links, with the ultimate objective being to influence behaviors, attitudes, and beliefs. And, like a chain, it is only as strong as its weakest link. A baseball team, for example, can consist of many strong hitters, but if there are no good pitchers, the team is not likely to win many games. Each position on a baseball team is critical, just as is each element of the communication process, which consists of definite and identifiable components: the sender, encoding, channel, the receiver, decoding, and feedback (Figure 18.1).

The **sender**, the person who wishes to relay or share particular information and meaning, initiates the communication process. For example, let's say your friend missed today's management class, in which the professor announced that the

**sender**
The person who wishes to relay or share particular information and meaning, and initiates the communication process.

**encoding**
The process of transforming information into understandable symbols, typically spoken or written words or gestures.

**channel**
The medium or method used to transmit the intended information and meaning, such as by phone or in person.

**receiver**
The person to whom the information and meaning are sent.

**decoding**
The process of interpreting and attaching personal meaning to the message.

**feedback**
The receiver's response to the sender's communication.

**noise**
Anything acting as an information filter, such as knowledge, attitudes, and other factors, that interferes with the message being communicated effectively.

**Critical Thinking Challenge:** For each of the communication interactions students can identify, use the vocabulary words here to identify each component.

next test has been moved up by one class period. To communicate that important information to your friend, you assume the role of sender and initiate the communication process. First, you perform the process of **encoding**, or transforming your information into understandable symbols, typically spoken or written words or gestures. Next, you choose an appropriate **channel**—the medium or method used to transmit the intended information and meaning (such as leaving a message on your friend's answering machine or telling her face to face). The **receiver**, the person to whom the information and meaning are sent—in this case, your friend—then attempts to "decode" the sender's message. **Decoding** is the process of interpreting and attaching personal meaning to the message. In other words, during the decoding process the receiver attempts to understand what the encoded symbols mean.

**Feedback**, the receiver's response to the sender's communication, is another important component of the communication process. For example, if you choose to communicate to your friend about the test by leaving a message on her answering machine, she may later provide feedback in the form of a verbal "thank you" for the information. Feedback can be thought of as sort of a return message that lets the sender know the message has indeed been received, as when a colleague requests an RSVP for a business luncheon.

The processes of encoding and decoding are potential sources for communication errors. In the translation of symbols to meaning, knowledge, attitudes, and other factors can act as information filters and create **noise**, anything that interferes with the message being communicated effectively. Noise can be of various types. Differences in educational level, experience, and culture can impede the communication process. For example, much of the difficulty encountered when U.S. managers try to implement traditional American management styles (autocratic leadership) in foreign countries is due to cultural differences. Physical noise (such as loud equipment or loud talking) can also inhibit effective communication, as does being preoccupied with another thought (as with a supervisor who is too rushed to meet a deadline). We will look at ways of overcoming noise later.

Effective communication, therefore, can be defined as the process of sending a message in such a way that the message received is as close in meaning as possible to the message intended. The process is cyclical in nature. Once a message is decoded into meaning by the receiver, some sort of response is often desired. Then, a new message is sent by the receiver (now the sender) to the original sender (now the receiver) and the process starts over again. Restated then, effective communication requires (1) the message to be encoded into symbols that will accurately convey it to the receiver (a good rule of thumb is to keep symbols simple, relevant), (2) the message to be conveyed in a well-organized manner, and (3) distractions to be eliminated.[8] For example, when a supervisor discusses a performance evaluation with an employee, the supervisor should do so in a quiet, private place with no disruptions, and should both strive to use language the employee can understand and explain the evaluation clearly.

Many factors affect the communication process, including the form and channel of communication chosen, perception, and the state of communication within organizations, topics we will explore in the rest of this chapter.

## FORMS OF COMMUNICATION

Essentially you can think of the way in which a message is communicated as being two-dimensional. One dimension has to do with the form of communication

In its annual report, Home Depot, a home improvement retailer, explains its communications philosophy: "Our company does not manage by memo or edict. It's done primarily on a one-to-one basis." Senior officers and managers spend much time in stores, working with, teaching, and listening to store associates. Shown here are Home Depot president Arthur Blank (center left) and CEO Bernard Marcus on the set of the company's live quarterly broadcast, "Breakfast with Bernie and Arthur." During these shows, the company founders speak directly to all employees, informing them about sales and profits, briefing them on new developments, and taking call-in questions.

*Source:* Co Rentmeester.

you choose—verbal, written, or nonverbal. The second dimension has to do with the medium or channel of communication employed. Within each form, there are several channels of communication from which to choose. For instance, verbal communication may take place face to face, over the telephone, or over a two-way radio. When choosing the form and channel of communication, it is important to keep in mind the ultimate objective of the communication. If your goal is to reduce the uncertainty of a particular situation, for example, then you should choose a communication form and channel that permit and encourage information exchange, such as face-to-face verbal communication.[9] In this section, we will first take a closer look at the different forms of communication and then move to a more detailed discussion of the various channels of communication.

## Verbal Communication

We can think of **verbal or oral communication** as words spoken to convey information and meaning. Verbal communication can take place through various channels (such as face to face or over the telephone) and can take place on different levels (individually, in a group). Verbal communication is a significant part of a manager's job. For example, most managers hold meetings, talk on the telephone, and give speeches. Research has found that managers spend as much as 90 percent of their total communication time involved in oral communication.[10]

Verbal communication offers both benefits and drawbacks. Among its greatest benefits are that it encourages immediate feedback—through questions or verbal confirmation—and allows the integration of nonverbal communication, such as head nodding and voice tone. In addition, verbal communication tends to be easier to use than other forms of communication. It does not require the complex skills that are needed in writing a report or typing a memo on a word processor. Among the drawbacks of verbal communication are that incorrectly chosen words invite inaccuracies. Such is the case when your professor tells you that you are doing "OK" in the course. Does this mean that you have a low C average, or a high C average, or perhaps even a B? Leaving out important information (the sender) or forgetting or "selecting out" part of the message (the receiver) are other disadvantages. Noise is another, more prevalent problem in oral communications. Additionally, oral communication does not accommodate the need for

**verbal or oral communication**
Words spoken through various channels to convey information and meaning.

**Example:** Levi's CEO, Robert B. Haas, encourages verbal communication in supporting diversity. The company supports in-house networking groups of blacks, Hispanics, lesbians, and gay men. A Diversity Council, made up of two members of every represented group, regularly meets with Levi's executive committee on raising awareness of diversity issues.

formal documentation or written records, which might be needed in a court dispute covering an employee's termination, for instance.

## Written Communication

**Written communication**, information and meaning transferred as recorded words—such as memos, reports, and electronic mail—tends to be more accurate than verbal communication, as senders take more time to collect, organize, and send the information. Written communication also has the benefit of providing a permanent record of communication, an important consideration in the business world. For example, when an employee needs to be informed of a new policy, it is often done in a written form. However, written communication also has its serious drawbacks. It tends to inhibit immediate feedback and exchange and is more difficult, complex, and time consuming than is oral communication, in most cases.

## Nonverbal Communication

In general, **nonverbal communication** refers to information conveyed by actions and behaviors rather than by spoken or written words. Nonverbal communication plays a critical role in shared understanding and meaning because it influences messages sent and received. In fact, most shared understanding comes from nonverbal messages, such as facial expressions, voice, hand gestures, and even clothing worn. If verbal and nonverbal communication contradict one another, the receiver is likely to become confused and give more weight to the nonverbal communication. Nonverbal communication also conveys the emotional state of the sender, which can often be the most important part of the message. If your boss claims not to be angry, but is turning red, has clenched fists, and is standing tense and stiff as a board, you may want to walk softly, because the nonverbals express extreme anger.

Much nonverbal communication is unconscious or subconscious. In fact, quite a bit of information sharing can take place without a word ever being spoken. Assume, for example, that you are in your management class trying to hear the lecture. However, you cannot hear very well because there is a group of students just behind you talking about a party (noise). The professor notices the distraction and throws a nasty glare at the talking students, who immediately stop. A message was sent (stop talking) and received (the students stopped) without a word being spoken. Far too often we think that effective communication requires the written or spoken word, but in reality, neither is required.

Research suggests that managers typically send two types of nonverbal communication.[11] One type of nonverbal communication is sent by the setting or the physical properties of the context in which the message is sent. These properties include such things as boundaries, how familiar the area is to the sender and receiver, or whether or not it is "home turf." For example, many executives place visitors in front of their desks while they sit behind them. The desk serves as a boundary beyond which the guests are not to go. The second and most popular form of nonverbal communication is **body language**, the broad range of body motions and behaviors—from facial expressions to the distance one person stands from another—that send messages to a receiver. For instance, hourly employees may stand farther away from their company president in an elevator than from each other, indicating that the employees feel more comfortable with one another than with the company president. The distance maintained can also be a reflection of the power or status of the boss relative to others.

**FIGURE 18.2**

## A Continuum of Channel Richness

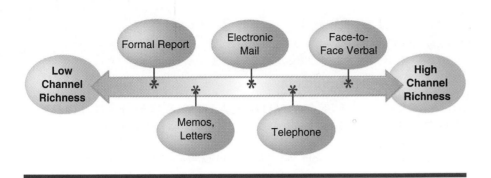

Because nonverbal communication has such a dramatic influence, managers should pay close attention to their nonverbal actions and behaviors when communicating. In particular, they should ensure that their nonverbal messages agree with their verbal or written messages. Managers should also pay attention to the nonverbal messages sent by others; research suggests that the more effective managers tend to be those who are sensitive to nonverbal cues.[12]

## Communication Channels

As stated earlier, choosing the appropriate channel (face to face, the telephone, written reports, etc.) is an important consideration when communicating information. One critical aspect of choosing an effective channel is **channel richness**, a channel's ability to transmit information. Channels differ in their ability to handle multiple cues simultaneously, to encourage immediate feedback, and to focus personally on the receiver. We can view communication channels as falling along a continuum of richness (Figure 18.2), with face-to-face communication the richest medium and, of course, impersonal written communications, such as reports, the least rich.[13] The "Quest for Quality" box describes a novel communication channel, interactive technology.

The face-to-face channel is the richest medium because it can handle many cues simultaneously (for example, the spoken word, facial expression, and voice tone), prompt immediate feedback, and create and maintain personal focus on the communication. For instance, a one-on-one conversation between you and your supervisor concerning your work performance allows you to ask specific questions and allows the supervisor to better determine where your particular strengths and weaknesses lie. The telephone medium is not quite as rich as face-to-face communication because it does not permit the communicators to see each other's body language. Communicating over the telephone tends to prompt greater immediate feedback than written channels, but not as much as face-to-face communication. Like face-to-face communication, the telephone is a personally focused channel. Although written channels can be personally focused, they can handle only one cue (e.g., no body language, no voice tone). Because written channels can convey only the message on paper or computer terminals, they are slow to prompt feedback. For instance, it is easy to allow a memo that requires a response to be buried underneath a stack of other papers, all the while thinking, "I'll respond to that later."

**channel richness**
A channel's ability to transmit information, including the ability to handle multiple cues simultaneously, encourage feedback, and focus personally on the receiver.

**Example:** Manco Inc., a Westlake, Ohio, distributor of duct tape and materials, has charts on its cafeteria walls to track revenue growth, productivity changes, and up-to-the-minute sales figures. It uses a multitude of channels of communication such as weekly gatherings to share ideas and update sales reports on territories. Monthly meetings for all employees review the company's profit and loss statements. The extensive communication helps people do their job better.

### INTERACTIVE COMMUNICATIONS TECHNOLOGY HELPS MANAGERS IMPROVE QUALITY

Technological advancements in communications have allowed many businesses to reap the benefits of expert information concerning quality. For example, in small towns such as Sioux Center, Iowa, a Midwestern town of about 5,000, both managers and employees can listen to live presentations given by quality management experts via satellite technology. In addition, questions can be asked of these quality experts. Currently, such presentations are provided by the U.S. Chamber of Commerce in Washington, DC., at several hundred sites in most states and Canada.

Various businesses in Sioux Center are taking advantage of this new way of transmitting information and knowledge about total quality management. For example, Link Manufacturing, Ltd., a 60-person company that makes components for the heavy-truck industry, sent three to four of its employees to each of the ten satellite seminars on quality management offered by the U.S. Chamber of Commerce's Quality Learning Services division.

John M. Franken, the president of JESCO Wholesale Electrical Supplies, a family-owned firm with 45 employees at five locations in Iowa,

Nebraska, and Minnesota, has also attended these seminars. One seminar that Franken attended was on "Customer Satisfaction and Loyalty," in which Christopher Fay, vice president of the Juran Institute, a quality-management consulting firm, spoke on the critical differences between customer satisfaction and customer loyalty. Fay and a panel of experts then took fax and telephone questions from sites all over the country. JESCO has realized significant quality improvements and won back lost customers by implementing suggestions offered in the seminar.

The purpose of these seminars is not to provide "cookbook" solutions but rather to stimulate awareness of quality issues and help businesses, particularly small ones, give shape

and direction to their quality efforts. These satellite presentations are not only helping to improve quality in the businesses that attend the seminars, they are also allowing participating businesses to form a viable network.

Such interactive communications technology makes it possible to bring together experts, like total quality management experts, and various businesses in need of specific information. The seminars allow managers to enhance their awareness and sharpen skills concerning particular issues such as quality.

*Source:* Michael Barrier, "Quality Via Satellite," *Nation's Business,* December 1993, 71–72.

The message and the particular situation, not the sender's whim or preference, should guide the selection of a particular channel. Like decisions, communications can be classified as routine or nonroutine. Routine communications tend to be more simple, straightforward, already agreed upon, and well understood. Therefore, routine messages can be effectively communicated through less rich channels, such as written memos. Nonroutine communications are characterized by ambiguity, time pressure, and surprise. Because nonroutine communications have a high potential for misunderstanding, they should be communicated through richer channels that can handle more cues simultaneously and encourage immediate feedback. For example, a contract negotiation between a company and its union representatives is an example of a nonroutine communication. There are many subtle issues that make such communications ambiguous, so they should be done face to face. On the other hand, the daily production numbers in a plant are often simply posted on a chart on the bulletin board or sent to various managers' offices on computer printouts.

# PERCEPTION AND DISTORTION

**Perception**, the process through which we receive, filter, organize, interpret, and attach meaning to information taken in from the environment, is an important behavioral component of the overall communication process. Physical systems (for example, our eyes and ears) take in and filter information, while our mental processes further filter, organize, interpret, and attach meaning to that information. **Distortion** occurs when there is a deviation between the sent message and the received message. In major distortions, the received message may bear little resemblance to the actual message. Because the perception process involves so many manipulations of incoming information, it is common for distortions to result from our perceptions.

Filtering or screening, often referred to as **perceptual selection**, involves choosing stimuli from the environment for further processing. Perceptual selection has to do with a person's willingness or unwillingness to receive information. It may occur for three basic reasons: (1) The receiver is uncomfortable with the information; (2) he or she does not want to bother with the information; or (3) there is simply too much information to process fully, a condition called "information overload." Unfortunately, managers often ignore certain information (for example, a downturn in sales figures) because they do not want to hear it or they "hope" things will change. Also, managers may engage in perceptual selection because they discern a threat. Managers who sense a threat may display "defensive behavior," which inhibits the communication process because it requires that they defend themselves rather than concentrate on the communication at hand. Consider, for example, the manager who just learned that he received a very poor evaluation from his employees and in ten minutes is having a conference with one of those employees concerning her performance evaluation. Often in this undesirable situation, the offensive sender has sent multiple cues and the defensive listener distorts what he has received.[14]

The process of organizing, interpreting, and attaching value to the selected stimuli is called **perceptual organization**. This is a natural and essential process that handles the information we take in more efficiently and effectively. By organizing diverse information into fewer conceptual categories, we can better understand and capitalize on the information. Sometimes, though, such categorizing can have negative effects. One all-too-familiar form of perceptual organization is **stereotyping**, which occurs when we categorize people into certain groups based on an attribute such as race, sex, or education level and then make generalizations about them according to their group membership. For example, many people assume that men are better at performing mathematical exercises than women. A manager might therefore view men as being better at number-oriented tasks than women in the organization, when in fact the women may be better. Managers must be particularly sensitive to perceptual organization, as it can inhibit open and honest communication because of the distortions it might cause at any point in the communication process.

Managers have an enormous amount of information to deal with, especially with the ever-increasing use of computers and computer information systems. To be more effective, managers and decision makers need to understand how people select and organize this information.

# COMMUNICATING IN ORGANIZATIONS

Communication within an organization can flow in a variety of directions and from a number of sources, each using both oral and written forms. In addition,

---

**perception**
The process through which we receive, filter, organize, interpret, and attach meaning to information taken in from the environment.

**distortion**
A deviation between the sent message and the received message.

**perceptual selection**
The choosing of stimuli from the environment for further processing; also known as filtering or screening.

**Teaching Note:** To illustrate the presence of distortion, play the popular childhood communication game in class. Start a message at the front of the room with one student and have him or her whisper the message to the next person and continue around the room. Remind each person to pass on the message just as he or she has heard it, and have the last person repeat the message out loud. How was the final message different? Was it distorted?

**perceptual organization**
The natural and essential process of organizing, interpreting, and attaching value to the selected stimuli.

**stereotyping**
A type of perceptual organization in which we categorize people into groups based on certain characteristics such as race, sex, or education level, and then make generalizations about them according to their group.

organizational communication comes in many forms, such as plans, performance appraisals, future projections, open-door policies, reports, meetings, and compensation packages.[15] Traditionally, formal communication patterns in an organization were classified as vertical and horizontal. More recently, with the increased use of matrix structures and various types of teams, formal communication may occur in a number of patterns. There are also informal communication patterns used by managers as well as employees.

## Formal Communication

Formal channels of communication are intentionally defined and designed by the organization. They represent the flow of communication within the formal organizational structure. Typically, communication flows in three separate directions: upward, downward, and horizontally, though diagonal communications have become common more recently (Figure 18.3).

**upward communication**
Communication flowing from lower to higher levels of the organization, such as progress reports, suggestions, inquiries, and grievances.

**Upward Communication.**    As indicated, **upward communication** flows from lower to higher levels of the organization. Examples of upward communication include progress reports, suggestions for improvement, inquiries, and grievances. Researchers have found that upward communication is more often subject to distortion than downward communication. For example, workers are more likely to distort or even withhold information that may make them look bad. This tendency increases as the receiver's status increases or distrust in the receiver increases.[16]

**downward communication**
The traditional flow of information from upper organizational levels to lower levels, such as job directions, assignment of tasks, performance feedback, and information concerning the organization's goals.

**Downward Communication.**    **Downward communication** refers to the traditional flow of information from upper organizational levels to lower levels. Typically, this type of communication involves job directions, assignment of tasks and responsibilities, performance feedback, and certain information concerning the organization's strategies and goals. Speeches, policy and procedure manuals, employee handbooks, company leaflets, managerial telecommunications, and job descriptions are all examples of downward communication.

The main problem with downward communication is that, as information gets passed from one level to the next, message content may be distorted or lost, usually more through natural filtering than through the intentional distortion that characterizes some upward communication. A major problem with managers and downward communication is their assumption that employees don't need or want to know much about what is going on. For instance, many times after an acquisition has taken place, management tends to neglect explaining to employees what they can expect next. Jean Keffeler, company president and entrepreneur, maintains that employees, especially during times of change (as with acquisitions, for example), have a tremendous need to know what is going on. She urges managers to communicate a lot and pull no punches, to be as honest and forthright as possible.[17]

**horizontal communication**
The exchange of information among individuals on the same organizational level, either across or within departments.

**Horizontal Communication.**    **Horizontal communication** involves the exchange of information among individuals on the same organizational level, such as across or within departments. Thus, it generally involves colleagues and peers. Horizontal information informs, supports, and coordinates activities both intradepartmentally and interdepartmentally. At times, the organization will formally require horizontal communication among particular organizational members, as is the case with task

**FIGURE 18.3**

## The Flow of Communication in an Organization

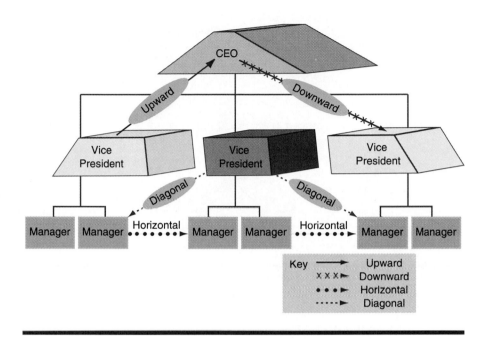

forces or project teams. In general, horizontal communication should be increased when tasks are nonroutine and high in uncertainty. However, when tasks are more routine in nature, communication is typically more formal and follows the chain of command.

**Diagonal Communication.**    Some organizational structures, particularly matrix structures, employ teams comprised of members from different functional areas, even different levels of the hierarchy. When these individuals from different units and organizational levels communicate, it is **diagonal communication.** With more and more firms reducing the number of management layers and increasing the use of self-managed work teams, many workers are being required to communicate with others in different departments and on different levels to solve problems and coordinate work. At 3M, for instance, a team might be formed of workers from all functional areas (accounting, marketing, operations, and human resources) to work on a specific product project to ensure that all points of view are considered. Diagonal communication will likely continue to increase in importance.

## Informal Communication Channels

Informal communication channels are not deliberately designed and, therefore, do not abide by the formal organizational hierarchy or chain of command. In this section, we will look at two types of informal communication channels: the grapevine and the process of "management by walking around."

**diagonal communication**
The flow of information, often in matrix structures, between individuals from different units and organizational levels.

**Example:**  At McKinsey and Co., Inc., a management consulting firm, new MBAs complete a grueling and intense interview process in which they are asked to solve problems. The firm requires a comprehensive training program in which new employees learn communication skills as well as team-leadership training in addition to client-relationship skills.

## FIGURE 18.4

### Two Common Grapevine Chains

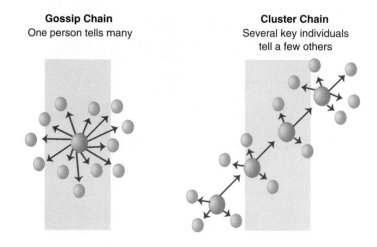

**Gossip Chain**
One person tells many

**Cluster Chain**
Several key individuals
tell a few others

*Source:* Based on Keith Davis and John W. Newstrom, *Human Behavior at Work,* 8th ed. (New York: McGraw Hill, 1989).

**grapevine**
Informal communication channels, found in virtually all organizations.

**gossip chain**
The spreading of information by one person to many others.

**cluster chain**
An exchange in which one person or a selected few share information with only a few others.

**The Grapevine.**    Informal communication channels are typically referred to as the **grapevine**, which exists in virtually all organizations. Research has identified two common types of grapevines, shown in Figure 18.4. In a **gossip chain**, one person spreads information to many other people. A **cluster chain** involves one person or a selected few people exchanging information with only a few others. In other words, the information and its exchange "clusters" around a selected few, rather than many, individuals.[18]

In the past, the accuracy of grapevine information was of great concern, particularly to managers. However, researchers have found that grapevine information is surprisingly accurate—perhaps as much as 75 to 95 percent.[19] Today, many managers view the quality of communication through formal organizational channels as being poor. A national survey of middle managers found that 62 percent did not agree that the quality of the information they received was good, but these managers agreed that informal communication channels (the grapevine) were frequently a much better source of good and accurate information than formal channels.[20] Thus, the grapevine can serve dual purposes for a manager: (1) The manager can receive accurate information from grapevine sources, and (2) the manager can use the grapevine to communicate information to organizational members.

Attempts to eliminate an organization's grapevine are useless. In fact, informal communication is increasing.[21] A more practical way to deal with an organization's grapevine is to accept it and control it where and when possible. For example, maintaining open communication channels throughout the organization can help determine what is being said on the grapevine, as well as the information's accuracy. Managers can also use the grapevine to their advantage—as a "sounding device" for possible new policies, for example. Therefore, managers can obtain valuable information from the grapevine that could improve decision making.

Wal-Mart CEO David Glass manages by walking around. He spends from two to three days a week away from company headquarters in Bentonville, Arkansas, visiting managers and associates (the terms the company uses instead of *employees*) of Wal-Mart stores and warehouses. With notebook in hand to record what he learns, Glass talks directly with associates, asking them about sales in their department, if their work is challenging, and if they have any suggestions for doing things differently. Glass's walking around also includes visiting competitors' stores.

*Source:* © Nicole Bengiveno 1994/ MATRIX.

**Management by Walking Around.**    A more recent form of informal communication that has evolved is "management by walking around" (MBWA), in which managers informally interact and exchange information with employees by simply circulating around the office or plant on a regular basis.[22] MBWA involves managers (at all levels) developing positive relationships with employees and talking with them directly to find out about their particular jobs, departments, or divisions. MBWA also allows managers to utilize the richest communication channel (face-to-face verbal communication), while breaking down some of the common barriers to communication, such as distance and formality.

## Communication in Groups and Teams

People tend to communicate differently in group or team situations than they do individually.[23] With the current trend of using groups to aid in decision making and greater focus on team management, today's managers must know and understand these special communication patterns and behaviors.

Three basic communication patterns within groups have been observed (Figure 18.5). The *wheel pattern* is highly centralized, with all communication in the group flowing through one person. In other words, one person distributes necessary information to group members and, in turn, all group members must communicate through this one person to make decisions or solve problems. The *Y pattern* is a little less centralized in that two persons tend to be the focal points of communication processes. The most decentralized pattern is the *network pattern*, in which communication flows freely among all group members and all group members participate equally.

The nature and degree of task complexity play an important role in determining which communication pattern is more effective. The centralized pattern seems to be more effective when group tasks are simple, routine, and require very little interdependency, as is the case with a traditional assembly line. On the other hand, tasks that are highly interdependent, nonroutine, and complex—such as when a management team analyzes potential companies for acquisition—tend to require a more decentralized group communication pattern.[24]

**Example:** During a recent assignment for ITT, a pair of McKinsey & Co. consultants were placed on a team with six or seven ITT managers at each of the company's nine corporate and division headquarters. The consultants were there to challenge the status quo with "what if" questions while ITT employees counteracted these questions with real-world experiences.

**FIGURE 18.5**

**Group Communication Patterns**

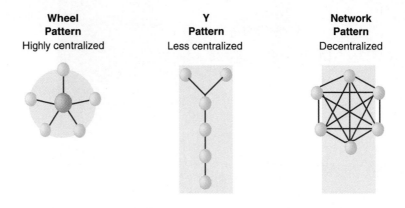

| Wheel<br>Pattern<br>Highly centralized | Y<br>Pattern<br>Less centralized | Network<br>Pattern<br>Decentralized |

Each pattern of group communication has unique benefits and drawbacks. A centralized pattern, due to the dominance of one person, tends to discourage members from contributing input and discourages openness and honesty. By the same token, a decentralized pattern may create confusion and ill will and be too time consuming because everyone participates equally. Of course, seldom in the real world do all individuals participate exactly equally, even in a fully decentralized work team.

Managers should be alert to the concerns of group communication and attempt to structure the communication pattern appropriately. Computer technology can help address some of these concerns. For instance, group decision support systems, discussed in Chapter 20, combine communication and computer technology to facilitate group decision making. Such systems can help manipulate communication patterns among group members so that information flows more effectively. Research shows that computer information systems are improving communication flow and efficiency.[25] In fact, technology is increasingly changing the way in which group members communicate. A poll by the International Air Transportation Association found that many international leaders and managers expect communications technology—such as fax machines—to replace a noticeable share of their face-to-face communication (which requires them to travel extensively).[26]

## BARRIERS TO EFFECTIVE COMMUNICATION

To be effective, managers need not only to understand the communication process, but also to understand and strive to overcome the barriers to effective communication. Communication barriers occur at three levels: personal, organizational, and environmental.

### Personal Barriers

Personal communication barriers are often the result of differing individual characteristics, semantics, channel selection, consistency of signals, credibility problems, and incrimination.

**B U S I N E S S   D I L E M M A**

*You're the Manager …What Would You Do?*

THE COMPANY:   Star Quest Manufacturing

YOUR POSITION:   Vice President of Production

THE PLACE:   Bismarck, ND

Like many manufacturers in the United States, Star Quest (SQ) took a hard look at the techniques used by Japanese firms to gain dominance in world markets. As one of the few manufacturers of microwave ovens in the United States, SQ saw firsthand the importance of the total quality process and other strategies American factories used to compete against the Japanese. So, in 1993 SQ developed a quality program for its Iowa plant. From the beginning, SQ saw communication as a vital element of the quality drive.

SQ launched a new program called "Intracommunication Leadership Initiative," which gave employees tasks once handled by first-line managers. At first, however, employees viewed the program as just another management fad. Therefore, the company had to do some "damage control," reemphasizing top management's commitment to the new program and the potential benefits to employees. Once employees got the message, their attitude toward the program changed quickly.

The fundamental purpose of the Intracommunication Leadership Initiative program was to flatten the layers of management. Instead of having a supervisor overseeing many employees, the system relies on teamwork and peer pressure to accomplish the plant's goals. Employees who handle similar tasks meet regularly with each other and the manager who has ultimate responsibility for their duties. For example, SQ's human resource manager meets weekly with the 17 employees assigned the task of human resources for their groups. Employees make all decisions within the boundaries of their responsibilities, ranging from electing representatives to changing jobs. One team was given the task of replacing the policies and procedures handbook with a one-page list of guiding principles. Another team reviews ethics-related issues and makes recommendations to management. Yet another team evaluates ways to improve on-the-job safety.

Employees who are not self-motivated team players or who cannot get used to their peers' authority have difficulty within this system. Also, the remaining upper-level managers face additional stress and frustration; in addition to their regular management duties, they must also train workers to supervise themselves.

By improving communications and empowering workers to take control of more and more aspects of their jobs, the company not only motivates them to work harder but also saves money on supervisory expenses. All employees are now highly knowledgeable about what is going on within their group as well as how their group is linked to the total quality processes and strategies SQ has adopted in its efforts to compete against Japanese microwave oven manufacturers.

**Questions**

1. At Star Quest, how is the communication process linked to a desire to improve product quality? What could have happened had you, as vice president of production, and other upper-level managers not reacted quickly to employees' initial negative attitude toward the program?

2. Within each work group, an employee is elected, drafted, or persuaded to assume one of the supervisory duties. What techniques or skills do you look for in individuals to achieve the appropriate communication with and motivation of the work group?

3. What are the communication problems you face in dealing with many team representatives who are being trained to supervise themselves?

---

**Individual Characteristics.**   Individual characteristics that affect communication have to do with personality, background, basic beliefs and attitudes, and even mood. These elements not only affect how a person chooses to communicate, but may cause a person to misunderstand, distort, or even block out a message. For instance, if your professor is in a really bad mood when you ask for an extension on a project deadline, she may ignore your request or blast you for procrastinating, rather than waiting for you to explain that someone has stolen your car, which contained your paper.

Several dimensions of personality may affect communication. For example, if you are an extrovert, then you probably prefer face-to-face communication, where-

**Comment on Box:** Why is top management's commitment so critical to total quality processes, or any change initiative in organizations? What training should be provided to employees before they become involved in teams?

Dennis Longstreet, president of Ortho Biotech, learned from employees that communication barriers tied to cultural and other personal differences among employees were hindering the teamwork and flexibility needed for the company to succeed in the fast-paced biotech pharmaceutical industry. Longstreet used intense, organized communication to help employees overcome stereotyping and prejudices. He listened to problems and aspirations of different employee groups—African-American men; Asian women; gay, lesbian, and bisexual men and women; white men; and single people. Through open communications with employees, Longstreet built an effective team that shares a common vision. Shown here are members of Ortho's diverse work force.

*Source:* © Brian Smale.

**Example:** In Spain and Latin America, the perception of time is different from that in the United States. People may acceptably arrive thirty minutes to one hour late to meetings, but punctuality is expected in the United States.

**Example:** In Japan, when business cards are exchanged, the recipient is expected to carefully hold the card and read both sides thoroughly, then place it carefully in a coat pocket. The card represents an extension of the person and should be treated accordingly.

as an introverted person may prefer written forms of communication. Another personality dimension is "sensing types" versus "intuitive types." A sensing type prefers to deal with concrete facts and details, and has a here-and-now orientation, whereas an intuitive type favors broader overviews and general information while having a future orientation.[27] From a communication perspective, a sensing-type person is likely to send very detail-oriented messages; however, an intuitive type will probably tend to send, and prefer to receive, only the essential general information and its implications. In addition, a sender who has a "feeling" type personality would be much more concerned with how a message affects the receiver than would one leaning toward the "thinking" personality type. Thus, our basic core personality significantly influences the way in which we send and receive information.

Our ethnic, national, and cultural backgrounds also affect how we communicate: Words and symbols have different meanings. For example, it is perfectly acceptable for heterosexual males to kiss each other in France, but this practice is not as readily acceptable in the United States. Another example is the use of the word *diet*. In most European countries, the term is strictly prescriptive or medicinal in nature. In the United States, though, the term can be used both prescriptively and to mean reduced calories. Consequently, U.S. beverage producers do not use the word *diet* on labels of products exported to some countries to indicate reduced calories, but instead use the word *light*. Thus, a person's background can influence how he or she perceives a communicated message.

Another important individual characteristic that influences communication is social background, which plays a critical role in the formation of attitudes and beliefs. For example, our particular social background tends to determine how we stereotype other people or groups (occupations, genders, races, departments, customers, employees). If, for instance, employees have the attitude that customers are a "pain in the neck," then they will probably perceive information received from customers as "complaining" or "whining," instead of as valuable feedback on which to base product-change decisions. In addition, managers who believe that employees are lazy and need to be told what to do (Theory X managers) will communicate quite differently with employees than will managers who believe that employees want to work and need autonomy (Theory Y managers). For example, a Theory X manager may use more written communication in the way of rules and policies than a Theory Y manager.

Finally, even a person's mood at the time of the communication can influence its effectiveness. For example, the division sales manager who has just had an argument with a spouse is not likely to receive a quarterly sales report showing a downturn in sales with much sensitivity or to be open to explanations as to why sales are low. However, it is possible that, with time to cool off, the manager will be more willing to listen to reasons for poor sales. Mood, as indicated earlier, involves a time element, as people's moods change over time.

**Semantics.**  **Semantics**, which refers to the different uses and meanings of words, also influences the effectiveness of a message. For example, the word *successful* has different meanings for different people. For some, a successful career means having a prestigious job title and making lots of money; for others, it may mean having a job they really enjoy and plenty of personal time to spend with family and friends. Some words have numerous denotations, and the meaning a person or group attaches to a particular word may differ according to circumstances and individual and group characteristics. On hearing that a particular person is "cool," members of one generation may take it to mean the person is fun to be around, while members of an earlier generation may believe it means that the individual is unemotional and insensitive. Managers should be aware of such differences and take steps to ensure that receivers understand the intended meaning of their communications.

**semantics**
The different uses and meanings of words, often influencing the effectiveness of a message.

**Channel Selection.**  Communication channels can be personal barriers in that some individuals always seem to lean toward a particular channel even though a more effective one exists. Consider, for example, a supervisor who uses a written memo to let you know about the recent denial of a promotion. The more effective channel in this case might have been a face-to-face meeting in which you could ask questions. However, the supervisor, perhaps uncomfortable in one-on-one situations, chose the written memo. It is also possible that the organization itself dictates the use of certain channels over others. At most universities, professors are notified of their tenure status via a written letter, even though a meeting with the tenure-peer committee might be a more appropriate channel to allow the professor to ask for additional information and elaboration on the group decision. Managers who desire to communicate effectively should be aware of their own communication channel preferences, as well as the organization's, which may or may not be the best to use in a given situation.

**Critical Thinking Challenge:** Have students interview a local company about the types of communication it regularly uses as well as the channels selected for communication. How effective are the channels? Why were these modes of communication chosen over others?

**Consistency.**  It is important to ensure that communication symbols and signals are consistent. If the words chosen to communicate a message do not match the sender's body language, the potential for misunderstanding and confusion increases. Inconsistency may even cause the receiver to mistrust the sender and the message being sent, which gives rise to credibility issues. For example, if a supervisor assures an employee of a high performance rating, but the employee later learns that a request for a raise in pay was denied because of a low performance rating by the supervisor, the employee most likely will not trust the supervisor in the future.

**Credibility.**  A sender's credibility plays an important role in how a message is received and understood. If the receiver does not consider the sender trustworthy or knowledgeable about the subject being communicated, he or she will most likely be reluctant even to listen to the message. For example, if you learn that your professor has no practical management experience, you may feel that she has little knowledge concerning the area of management and, thus, place little weight on anything she tells you concerning the subject. Likewise a sender may limit what he or she communicates to a receiver who is not considered trustworthy. For instance, if an employee offers an idea for a more efficient way to perform a job and his supervisor takes credit for it, then the employee is more likely to withhold future information from the supervisor, as he will probably not trust the supervisor with such information.

**Incrimination.**    Finally, we should point out that there are times when people may be apprehensive and, therefore, reluctant to transmit information because it is likely to anger a supervisor or make the transmitter look bad. Such reluctance will increase if the sender believes that the incriminating information will not be acted upon appropriately or sensitively. Managers need to be aware of such situations and make adjustments accordingly.

## Organizational Barriers

Organizational characteristics can also inhibit effective communication. The more prominent of these are power and status problems, goal and priority differences, and organizational structure.

**Power and Status.**    People in the upper areas of the organization's hierarchy, those who have more status and power, may be hesitant to listen to those individuals lower in the hierarchy, feeling, for example, that people of lower status and power do not possess any useful information. By the same token, individuals of lower status and power may be reluctant to share information because they believe that people with higher status and power will not listen. One way Duane Hartley, the general manager of Hewlett-Packard's microwave instruments division, is trying to overcome this problem is by holding informal "chats" between senior management and employees on topics such as profitability and personal contribution.[28] The informality of these meetings helps to break down the status and power difference barriers.

**Goal and Priority Differences.**    Goal and priority differences among organizational functions, departments, or divisions may influence how effectively a message will be sent and/or received. Obviously, each department or unit will view problems and concerns from its own perspective. For example, operations managers want workers with certain levels of physical strength and may not fully understand the human resources department's need to hire more women. Consequently, neither department is very receptive to the other's messages. The use of cross-functional decision making or project teams helps overcome this barrier.

**Organizational Structure.**    Finally, the structure of the organization can dramatically influence the effectiveness of communication. For example, if the firm's organization does not provide sufficient upward, downward, and horizontal communication channels, then not only the quality, but the quantity of information sharing could be reduced. The structure can also influence which channels are used. A more centralized structure, for example, tends to make greater use of written communications, whereas a more decentralized structure encourages more face-to-face communication. In recent years, there has been a trend toward eliminating middle-management layers, and a by-product of this trend has been improved communication effectiveness. This is because centralized structures—those with several layers between top management and first-line supervisors—tend to inhibit effective communication flow from the bottom of the organization up. Companies are also restructuring to facilitate communications between and among organizational units and/or divisions and to overcome communication barriers. Merrill Lynch, for example, plans to merge its Mortgage-Backed Securities (MBS) divisions and its Asset-Backed Securities (ABS) division into one unified structure so that communication between the two will be more open and free-flowing.[29]

**Example:** As more companies flatten their hierarchies, command and control in management are becoming more consensual. Team building and efficient information transfer require more sophisticated communication skills than the mere ability to give and take orders.

## Environmental Barriers

Factors inherent in the environment in which a message is transmitted can disrupt the communication process. These factors include noise, information overload, and physical barriers within the environment.

Earlier, we defined noise as anything that interferes with the message being communicated effectively. A mother who works at home, for example, may find her efforts to communicate with clients on the telephone distracted by an active toddler.

**Information overload** refers to the condition of having too much information to process, as is the case when a worker is given too many jobs to perform. The implication is that individuals can effectively process only a certain amount of information. An example would be if your professor gave you too much information, too quickly, concerning a term paper's requirements or if a manager gave an employee too much information at one time about a report's requirements. In either situation, the receiver probably does not receive the entire message. Managers need to be aware of the potential for information overload and to make appropriate adjustments, such as providing written instructions to back up verbal instructions.

**Information overload**
The condition of having too much information to process.

Additionally, there are physical structures in the environment that can inhibit effective communication. For example, firms that locate managers' offices on floors separate from where employees are working tend to reduce communication flow between the two. Likewise, a large desk that separates students from a professor tends to inhibit open and honest communication. In an effort to overcome these kinds of communication obstacles, many companies are locating managers' offices in the middle of employee work areas and even having managers eat lunch in the employee cafeteria; many professors now lecture to students who are sitting in circularly arranged desks.

## Overcoming Communication Barriers

There is no sure way to guarantee effective communication, but there are several techniques available for improving the chances that it will occur. These include listening, providing feedback, being aware of cultural diversity, choosing an appropriate channel, structuring the organization appropriately, and improving interpersonal relationships.

**Listening.**   Unfortunately, ours is not a society that practices good listening skills, and many communication breakdowns can be attributed to poor listening. Listening involves accurately receiving and understanding information. Many

**Teaching Note:** Have a communications professor from your university speak to your class on ways to overcome communication barriers as well as tips for better listening.

factors both inside and outside organizations demonstrate that today's managers need to acquire good listening skills. For example, currently many organizations are decentralizing, which means that information is flowing upward much more so than in more traditionally structured organizations. And, as new technology develops, customers' preferences change, societal concerns intensify, and more companies globalize, receiving accurate information is critical to survival. Such changes require that managers become better listeners.

Many organizations are recognizing the increased importance of good listening habits. Consider, for example, the alert salesperson who recognizes that listening often involves sorting out complex relationships in a client company. Only by listening can he or she determine the one person or department who is the key in the final purchasing decision.[30] In addition, auditors are now being taught that success depends not only on technical proficiency but also on mastering certain people skills such as effective communication and listening.[31]

**Teaching Note:** Have students make up additional examples or use examples from their own personal experiences for each of the four levels of listening and responding presented in Table 18.1.

In general there are four levels of listening and four levels of related responses, as illustrated in Table 18.1. The first level is *unrelated listening and responding,* when the receiver does not listen to anything the sender says. Consequently, the response is completely different or unrelated to the message. The second level is *tangential listening and responding,* where the receiver hears a small portion (perhaps a word or two) of the sender's message and then goes off on a tangent. The amount of the message actually heard, however, is not enough to provide a fully appropriate response. At the third level, *furthering listening and responding,* the sender is encouraged by the receiver (either verbally or nonverbally) to continue with his or her message. In other words, the receiver is actively listening; however, full understanding of the message has not been attempted. At the fourth level, *feeling listening and responding,* the receiver attempts full understanding of the information and meaning. He or she focuses not only on the words but also on the feelings or emotions being expressed or implied. Often the receiver will express his or her own feelings while acknowledging the feelings of the sender. Acknowledging these levels of listening and responding should demonstrate that, for communication to reach its maximum effectiveness, good listening requires being sensitive to others' feelings.[32] After all, successful communication requires points both to be made and to be learned.

Perhaps the most important asset to effective communication is *active listening,* which involves giving and receiving feedback concerning the information contained in the message. Characteristics of active listening include asking questions, showing interest, paraphrasing, making direct eye contact, and consciously eliminating noise. In short, active listening allows for two-way communication. To help make sure that you are an active listener, try going through the following steps:

1. Maintain frequent eye contact
2. Be sensitive to nonverbal messages (body language)
3. Know yourself (your perceptions and biases)
4. Eliminate both physical and mental noise
5. Remain open-minded and sensitive.

**Providing Feedback.**   Closely related to listening well is the ability to give effective feedback. The tendency to pass judgment or evaluate others is a common cause of communication breakdown. It can cause the receiver to become defensive or resentful, which may distort the sender's message and intentions (noise). Effective feedback enhances and facilitates the communication process. Effective feedback

**TABLE 18.1**

## Levels of Listening and Responding

*Level 1    Unrelated Listening and Responding*

Receiver does not listen to sender's message.
Example:    *Sender:*  I had a car accident this morning.
                 *Receiver:*  Have you heard that Mary and Charlie are getting divorced?

*Level 2    Tangential Listening and Responding*

Receiver listens to a small portion of sender's message.
Example:    *Sender:*  I had a car accident this morning.
                 *Receiver:*  Cars can really be a pain. I put mine in the shop twice last week.

*Level 3    Furthering Listening and Responding*

Receiver signals the sender that he or she is listening and encourages the sender
to continue with the message.
Example:    *Sender:*  I had a car accident this morning.
                 *Receiver:*  Where did it happen?

*Level 4    Feeling Listening and Responding*

Receiver fully attempts to understand the message.
Example:    *Sender:*  I had a car accident this morning.
                 *Receiver:*  I'm so sorry! Were you or anyone else hurt?

1. Focuses on description, not judgment; managers should describe the situation, for instance, rather than label a person.

2. Focuses on behavior, not personality; managers should talk about what a person actually does rather than what they think or imagine the person is like.

3. Incorporates the receiver's needs; in other words, managers should provide beneficial, not harmful, feedback.

4. Addresses behavior that the receiver can do something about or has control over.

5. Is asked for, not imposed.

6. Involves sharing information, not making demands.

7. Is given at the appropriate time, preferably as soon as possible.

8. Does not result in information overload. Managers should think in terms of how much information can be used, rather than how much they would like to give.

9. Is concerned with *what* actually happened rather than *why* it happened. In other words, managers should not assume they know someone else's intentions or motivations.[33]

**Being Aware of Cultural Diversity.**    Communicators should also be aware of the increasingly diverse nature of today's work force, as discussed in Chapter 6. Recognizing and being sensitive to others' needs and perspectives can help reduce semantic problems and noise, increase objectivity, and generally enhance communication.

**Example:** Providing feedback is the job of Diane McFerrin Peters, director of new ventures at Rosenbluth Travel, a Philadelphia-based company with $1.5 billion in revenues. At the company, managers undergo "vertical interviews" at least once a year. Employees are asked to be fair and honest in their evaluation of managers. According to Peters, just asking for feedback sends a positive message to employees.

**Example:** While quality circles have been successfully implemented within the Japanese culture, working in teams is new and somewhat difficult for an American culture used to individual rewards and activities. Groups and teams must be implemented carefully to be successful in the United States. Often additional communication and training are necessary.

## Sharpening Your Communication Skills

As we suggested in this chapter, communication is a skill that is integral to most every profession, particularly that of management. Thomas Delan, president of the American College of Healthcare Executives (ACHE), says that communication skills are going to become even more important to CEOs as they become heavily involved in public policy issues, such as health care changes, at the state and national levels.

Nonmanagement employees, too, are going to need to become more proficient in their communication skills. According to one source, employees must take more initiative and responsibility for their career success, including: (1) knowing themselves, (2) aligning their personal needs with those of the organization, and (3) effectively communicating those needs to management.

Two seemingly popular career areas that directly relate to the communication field are public relations and sales. Results of a recent survey suggest that the best un-

dergraduate preparation for public relations is to minor in public relations and major in some other communication field such as journalism. Additionally, the survey revealed that writing communication skills are most important, which may indicate that a minor in English might be beneficial as well. With respect to a sales career, perhaps a major in communication and a minor in marketing (sales management) should be considered.

*Sources:* Carol Gelatt, "How to Motivate Employees When Promotion Is Unlikely," *Human Resources Professional* 4 (Winter 1992): 33–36; Mary Grayson, "CEOs in the 1990s," *Hospitals,* January 20, 1993, 32–35; Donald F. Schwartz, J. Paul Varbrough, and Shakra M. Therese, "Does Public Relations Education Make the Grade?" *Public Relations Journal* 48 (September 1992): 19–21, 24–25.

**Comment on Box:** Ask a local sales representative to speak to your class on the importance of communication to his or her job. How is communication used each day? What skills are most important? How can business students best prepare for the communication demands they will face in their jobs?

**Choosing an Appropriate Channel.**   Different channels of communication have advantages and disadvantages, and certain types of information warrant specific types of channels. Firing an employee, for example, should be done face to face. Thus, choosing an appropriate communication channel can be conducive—even essential—to effective communication.

**Structuring the Organization for Communication.**   Organizations can take specific steps to enhance the communication process. For example, providing employees with proper communication training should benefit the communication processes within the organization. Fostering a climate of trust and openness should also encourage frequent and open communication. Moreover, the communication process can be facilitated by ensuring that formal communication channels are available in all directions (upward, downward, horizontal, diagonal). Finally, the use of multiple channels should be encouraged, including both formal and informal communications. Thus, the structure of the organization should fit the communication needs of its members.

Many organizations are responding to tough times by focusing on improving internal communications. AEB Company, the manufacturing division of a *Fortune* 100 company, developed and implemented two-way channel mechanisms in settings where communication between management and employees was infrequent and ineffective. The company took this action in response to a survey in which 67 percent of AEB employees said they felt uninformed about company goals; that figure fell to 23 percent after the two-channel mechanisms were put in place. An interesting side benefit of the changes was that management's credibility increased dramatically.[34]

**Improving Interpersonal Relationships.**    Perhaps one of the most important ways to improve the communication process is to view it as a people process.[35] This improves interpersonal relationships and reduces defensive communication. Suggestions for improvements in this area include not using judgmental language or behaviors, regarding the sender or receiver as being an equal, not trying to control the sender or receiver (for example, by imposing certain values or points of view), not having hidden motives (being open and honest at all possible times), not using gimmicks or tricks, being spontaneous, showing empathy (not neutrality), and approaching every communication situation with an open mind.[36]

One of the most important messages in this chapter is the critical nature of communication. Communication is vital both personally and professionally. It is particularly vital to managers, as it is integral to every part of a manager's job and responsibilities. Additionally, the very success of the entire organization hinges on effective communication, both internally and externally.

## SUMMARY AND REVIEW

- **Define communication and explain its importance to managers.** Communication is the process through which information and meaning are transferred from one person to another. Managers must communicate in order to perform their organizational roles and the functions of planning, organizing, leading, and controlling. Communication is necessary for managers to convey their goals and visions to employees and to see if employees correctly understand, accept, and are achieving those goals and visions.

- **Describe the communication process and the factors that affect it.** The communication process can be thought of as a chain of identifiable links with the ultimate objective of influencing behaviors, attitudes, and beliefs. It consists of a number of distinct components: A sender encodes a message that is sent across some channel to a receiver who decodes the message and sends a return message, called feedback, letting the sender know the message was received and how it was interpreted. Many factors, called noise, can interfere with the process, including differences in educational level, experience, and culture as well as various types of physical noise such as machinery running or background talk. Other factors that may influence the communication process include perception, perceptual distortions, and the form and channel of communication used.

- **Compare and contrast the various communication forms and channels and the "richness" of each.** Three major forms of communication are verbal, written, and nonverbal. Various channels can be utilized for each form. Verbal communication may be face to face, over the telephone, and even on two-way radios.

Written channels include letters, memos, reports, and electronic mail. Nonverbal communication consists of messages sent by actions or behaviors, rather than by spoken or written words. Ideally the nonverbal, verbal, and written messages should be consistent to prevent receivers from becoming confused. Channels vary in richness, or the ability to transmit information. Face-to-face verbal communication is the richest medium because verbal, visual, and even other sensory cues can be used during communication. Written channels are the least rich.

- **Distinguish between formal and informal communication in an organization.** Formal communication is intentionally defined and designed by the organization and represents the flow of communication throughout the formal hierarchy. Formal communication may be upward, downward, horizontal across functional areas, or even diagonal across functions and hierarchical levels, but is usually within the context of formal organizational functioning. Informal communication channels—the grapevine—are not deliberately designed and do not abide by formal organizational hierarchy or other arrangement.

- **Determine how teams and groups communicate.** Within groups, individuals develop specific patterns of communication, depending on how centralized or decentralized the communication is. In a wheel pattern, the messages flow only through a centralized person or "spoke." This highly centralized pattern contrasts sharply with the decentralized network pattern, in which communication flows freely among all group members. The pattern of group communication should reflect the complexity of the issue being discussed or decision being made.

• **Detect the barriers to effective communication and specify potential ways to overcome them.** Barriers to effective communication may be classified as personal, organizational, and environmental. Personal barriers include individual characteristics, semantics, inappropriate communication channel, inconsistent symbols and signals, and credibility issues. Organizational barriers include power and status, goal and priority differences, and organizational structure. Environmental barriers include noise, information overload, and physical barriers. Techniques to overcome these barriers include listening, providing more effective feedback, being aware of cultural differences, making better channel choices, and certain organizational actions such as worker-communication training, and improved interpersonal relationships.

• **Critique an organization's communication efforts.** Evaluate the communications process at Star Quest, as described in the "Business Dilemma" box. Your evaluation should include a discussion of how the firm's unique structure dictates communications.

## Key Terms and Concepts

communication *526*
sender *527*
encoding *528*
channel *528*
receiver *528*
decoding *528*
feedback *528*
noise *528*
verbal or oral communication *529*

written communication *530*
nonverbal communication *530*
body language *530*
channel richness *531*
perception *533*
distortion *533*
perceptual selection *533*
perceptual organization *533*
stereotyping *533*

upward communication *534*
downward communication *534*
horizontal communication *534*
diagonal communication *535*
grapevine *536*
gossip chain *536*
cluster chain *536*
semantics *541*
information overload *543*

## Ready Recall

1. Define communications and explain its importance to management.
2. Describe the communication process.
3. Give examples of how perceptions might influence the communication process.
4. What is meant by "defensive" communication? Give personal examples.
5. Compare and contrast formal versus informal communications.
6. How do groups/teams communicate differently than individuals?
7. List some barriers to effective communication and discuss ways managers can minimize them.
8. Discuss the characteristics of effective feedback.
9. Explain the concept of "good listening."
10. Discuss how "information overload" can inhibit effective communication.

## Expand Your Experience

1. Divide into groups of two. Have one person give and one person receive at the four different levels of listening and responding. Have the receiver describe his or her feelings. Then reverse the roles.
2. Explain the statement, "The communication process can be thought of as being a chain, made up of definite and identifiable links—and like any chain is only as strong as its weakest link."
3. Go to a local organization and interview the person most responsible for the company's public relations. Find out the various forms and methods of communication used and report them back to your class.
4. Interview local businesspeople at various organizational levels concerning their communication roles and responsibilities. In addition, ask them to describe their view of communication and how it may change in the future. Report these findings to the class.

## CASE

# GM and Daewoo: The Missing Link

In 1976, General Motors Corporation formed a joint venture with the Daewoo Group of South Korea. This venture represented GM's second attempt at entering the markets of East Asia. The first, with Shinjin Motor Company, dissolved after a short time when GM became extremely unhappy with Shinjin's management. GM was initially hesitant to enter into a joint venture with Daewoo, which was better known at that time for its textile and trading operations than for its experience in the automobile industry, but that resistance was soon put to rest by Kim Woo Choong, Daewoo's chairman. Eventually, the two companies established the venture, called Daewoo Motors, with high hopes of effectively mixing GM's engineering and marketing know-how with Daewoo's cheap labor in producing cars for domestic and foreign consumption.

Unfortunately, the venture was plagued by communication problems. To begin with, early on in the venture, Daewoo negotiated a deal to sell 7,000 of its cars to Eastern Europe, putting the Daewoo cars in direct competition with GM's Opel automobiles. GM officials were enraged by Daewoo's decision to enter the Eastern European market (which GM regarded as its own) without even consulting them.

Another major problem came in 1991 when the two firms could not agree on how to handle poor sales of the Daewoo-made LeMans. In fact, the two firms even disagreed as to the reason for the car's sluggish sales. GM blamed the problem on Daewoo's lack of attention to quality. The cars made in the Daewoo plant were plagued with electrical and brake problems. And, even though both sides agreed that GM should handle efforts to redesign the car's brakes, GM engineers had a very difficult time explaining the new brake design to Korean suppliers and assemblers because of language barriers. Daewoo, however, attributed the poor sales to GM's poor marketing. The LeMans was marketed through GM's Pontiac division and was often used by dealers as a low-priced promotion to entice customers into the showroom.

In addition, the two partners could not agree on how to respond to the venture's increasingly poor financial performance. Kim Woo Choong ordered that the company's slipping market share (which had fallen from 31.5 percent in 1987 to 19.3 percent in 1991) be reversed. As a result, Daewoo began manufacturing more cars, and stepping up overtime from a 44-hour work week to a 58-hour work week ... even though stocks of unsold cars were increasing. In an effort to reduce the rising number of unsold cars, Daewoo introduced a concessionary finance program, allegedly without informing GM. The program offered loans to potential buyers at very attractive rates. GM loudly objected to such concessions, calling it foolhardy to pay "24 percent for money and then loan it out at zero interest." GM believed that the key was to build cars better, not to build more cars. This disharmony pointed to a fundamental difference in strategy and corporate ethos. Daewoo insisted that domestic market share should take precedence while GM insisted on the bottom line.

In 1992, GM and Daewoo announced the dissolution of their 15-year joint venture. Even then, the two companies could not agree as to whether the venture had even been profitable. Applying Korea's liberal accounting standards, Daewoo found the venture had a profit of $13.6 million for the 1991 fiscal year. GM, using American accounting standards, showed the venture had a loss of $1.3 million in the same year. Eventually, the two firms agreed that Daewoo would buy out GM's share of the business for $100 million (a significant loss considering that GM poured $200 million into the venture). Ironically, the dissolution came at a time when many aspects of the joint venture appeared to be improving. For instance, a 25 percent increase in productivity and throughput had been realized over the prior two years and quality had markedly improved.

*Sources:* Mark Clifford, "Wheels Off the Wagon," *Far Eastern Economic Review,* January 23, 1992, 44–45; Damon Darlin and Joseph White, "Failed Marriages: GM Venture in Korea Nears End, Betraying Firm's Fond Hopes," *The Wall Street Journal,* January 16, 1992, A1, A12; James B. Treece and Karen Lowry Miller, with Richard A. Melcher, "The Partners," *Business Week,* February 10, 1992, 102–107.

## Questions

1. In what stages of the communication process did communication break down for GM and Daewoo?
2. What barriers to communication are at work here?
3. What could GM and Daewoo have done initially and during the venture that might have avoided the communication problems and perhaps have saved the venture?

*Communicating in Groups*

**FIGURE 18.6**

**Square Wheels™ One**

Looking at the *Square Wheels™ One* illustration in Figure 18.6 above, use these analogies when talking about the cartoon.

- The *person at the front of the wagon* represents the administration at your college/university.
- The *people at the rear of the wagon* are the faculty and the students at your school.
- The *wagon* represents _____ (fill in the name of your college/university).
- The *square wheels* represent the way things are done around your school—the old ways of doing things, the systems and procedures that don't work all that well, the ways the school has always done things.
- The *rope at the front* represents the administration's tendency to be somewhat isolated from what is really happening to the wagon.
- The *pushers' hands* belong to the faculty and students, who feel every thump and bump encountered.
- The *round wheels* represent ideas for improvement that exist but aren't being used.

**3-5-3 Fast Networks**

Procedure:

1. As a class discuss what some of the *Square Wheels™* are at your school. Maybe students grumble about the way the cafeteria is run, or you might discuss ways to solve problems with the living conditions in the dorms. Perhaps registration

isn't run as smoothly as the students think it should be, or the student activity center needs some changes. Select three *Square Wheels™* that your class would like to try to solve in this exercise and write the three problems down in one sentence each following a question format. For example:

- What are some best ideas to improve the school's library?
- What are some best ideas to increase participation and involvement in student government on campus?
- What are some best ideas to improve service at the campus bookstore?

Write down the three questions your class decides to address:

_____

_____

_____

2. Break into groups of 4 to 6 people. Your instructor will help you determine which of the three questions is your group's responsibility. Remember these general rules when your group brainstorms for ideas:

- Every idea gets written down
- No negative discussion allowed—focus on the positives
- Generate ideas, not results
- Everybody participates
- Try to "think out of the box"—you need to generate new, creative ideas for improvement

**3.** Your instructor will let you know when to begin each phase of **3-5-3 Fast Networks**:

- **Phase One:** Each team has **3 minutes** to generate ideas that apply to your question.
- **Phase Two:** Your team will have **5 minutes** to move around the classroom talking to people from other teams asking them for their best ideas *on your question.* You will probably also have to give them your best idea on their question also.
- **Phase Three:** Your team then has **3 minutes** to summarize the ideas into your **3 best ideas.**

**4.** Your instructor will call on all groups assigned to the first question and have one representative from each group read each group's 3 best ideas. Of all the ideas read (depending on how many groups are assigned to each question), the class will decide on the best of the best and create a final listing of 3 best ideas.

**5.** Follow this procedure for each of the three questions.

**6.** Time permitting, each group should take the best-of-the-best ideas for their question and spend 10 additional minutes generating ideas for their implementation plans.

Remember the **3-5-3 Fast Networks** method of group communication when you're a member of a workplace team that needs to generate ideas/solutions. This method creates a high level of group involvement and participation in a minimal amount of time. It is structured to generate time pressures and specific challenges to perform, while encouraging group ownership of *all* the ideas, thus decreasing resistance to change.

*Source:* Adapted with permission from Scott J. Simmerman, *The Book of Square Wheels: A Tool Kit for Facilitators and Team Leaders,* 3rd ed. (Taylors, SC: Performance Management Company, 1994), 49–51.

## chapter nineteen

# Organizational Change and Development

## Outline

## After reading this chapter, you will be able to:

- Define organizational change and explain the dimensions and types of change.
- Interpret three models of change, particularly the steps involved in the comprehensive model of change.
- Determine the major causes of resistance to change and recommend how managers can deal with change resistance.
- Explain organization development (OD) and summarize the major OD interventions.
- Assess an organization's change program.

## Can Corporate Dinosaurs Evolve?

**W**hat happens when successful companies become gigantic bureaucracies? Do they become dinosaurs—difficult to change, if not doomed to failure? Three of the United States's once most successful companies have often been called dinosaurs. The word is a stretch because they are not extinct, just painfully and wheezingly short of breath. The three dinosaurs are IBM, General Motors, and Sears, Roebuck, all in the top six companies in stock market valuation in 1972. IBM was the value leader at $46.8 billion, while GM was third at $23.2 billion, and Sears was sixth at $18.2 billion. By 1992, none of the three was in the top 10 or even top 20 in market valuation.

What happened to these models of American market dominance can best be explained by their inability to change as needed to maintain their positions of strength. All three had a history of strong leaders who saw opportunities, then captured the day against strong opponents, and rose to the top. They were decisive and driven by a common vision. Then each succumbed to failure for a number of reasons, including, if not most importantly, a failure of management. As management guru Peter Drucker says, "Every failure is a failure of a management." Their successors lacked the vision to lead the companies to new heights during times of prosperity. They lacked the decisiveness to make the tough decisions to change their organizations to meet changes in their business environments. Perhaps the biggest problem was their perception that there was no need to change. These leaders saw their roles as caretakers of invulnerable giants. They ignored the signs their environments sent them, possibly drugged by their own successes.

The most important environmental sign missed by these three was the emergence of new and formidable competition. GM—unable to perceive the Japanese as worthwhile competitors who could build quality cars—virtually ignored the Japanese challenge. Sears thought of itself as America's discount store and ignored the new discount franchises, Kmart and Wal-Mart. IBM failed to recognize the importance of a competitive product, the personal computer, for which, ironically, it invented the technology. Instead, IBM kept the large mainframe computer as the center of its strategy and ultimately lost business to the personal computer producers.

The dinosaurs also were overcome by debilitating bureaucratic cultures that stymied quick and effective decision making. One GM executive decried GM's maddening "inability to execute." The Sears bureaucracy became so stifling that it had a bulletin that spelled out how to handle every problem someone could face. Said one Sears executive, "God forbid there should be a problem that comes up for which there isn't a bulletin. That means the problem is NEW!" IBM lost the ability to take calculated risks because of a bureaucracy determined to maintain the status quo. One business partner of IBM said that trying to get action out of IBM was like swimming through "giant pools of peanut butter."

The inability to recognize customer attitude changes, confront competition successfully, streamline their bureaucracies, hasten decision making, and overcome the debilitating effects of their own perceived self-importance and invulnerability has turned these companies into dinosaurs, by hampering their ability to change as the world around them changed.

*Source:* Carol J. Loomis, "Dinosaurs?" *Fortune*, May 3, 1993.

*introduction*

I f we look closely at what happened to the American dinosaurs discussed in the opening vignette, we can see that their declines were fairly gradual and perhaps even predictable given increasing competition, general economic conditions, and rapidly changing technologies. Some changes, though, are shockingly rapid. In July 1992, *Fortune* magazine labeled Northern Telecom Canada's most successful multinational company, and its CEO Paul Stern was lauded on the magazine's cover as the new "High Tech Star." Only half a year later, however, Stern had resigned, and half the company's stock value had evaporated.[1] In the business world, change is inevitable; in many cases, as with Northern Telecom, it can be both rapid and devastating. Change is influenced by a number of forces, both inside and outside of companies, and companies' ability to deal with and shape these forces determines their ultimate success. Jean B. Keffeler, an organizational change consultant, says that American companies can be either agents or victims of these changes: "We will either choose change or chase it."[2] Our industrial dinosaurs did not choose to change rapidly enough and are now chasing it. And even choosing change will not guarantee success, but ignoring it will almost surely guarantee failure.

This chapter deals with the process of organizational change. We will discuss briefly some of the major forces influencing organizational change and delve into the steps and techniques managers may use to deal with the process of planned change. We will conclude with a brief overview of some of the people-oriented approaches to planned change that have collectively been labeled organizational development.

## THE NATURE OF ORGANIZATIONAL CHANGE

**organizational change**
Any modification in the behaviors or ideas of an organization or its units.

**Organizational change** can be defined as any modification in the behaviors or ideas of an organization or its units. The "Magnifying Management" box describes ten things a manager can do to begin changing his or her organization. One important aspect of organizational change is that such modifications don't just happen: Something causes them to occur. To understand change and how best to manage it, we must be aware of some of the major forces causing change.

### Forces Causing Organizational Change

In Chapter 3, we explored the various internal and external environmental forces that may affect an organization. You will remember that external forces include technological, economic, sociocultural, political-legal, and international influences, as well as customers, suppliers, competitors, substitutes, and potential new entrants to the industry. The internal forces include the owners, managers, employees, and board of directors. How managers respond to these forces may determine the success or failure of their entire business enterprise. A few examples of the pervasive impact of these forces will demonstrate the importance of responding to change.

**External Forces.**    Examples of the influence of technology on business organizations abound. In the early 1970s, the Swiss watch industry dominated the world and held 90 percent of the market for high-quality mechanical watches. When the

---

Ten things CEOs can do immediately if they want to change their organization:

**1.** Visit ten customers personally in the next month to ask "How are we doing?" and "What can we do better?"

**2.** Visit ten plants or offices in the United States in the next four months and five plants abroad in the next twelve months that you've heard are doing unusual and good things. Ask lots of questions.

**3.** Announce next week that in the next two years you want the entire organization organized around "teams," especially cross-functional teams.

**4.** In the next year, install a gain-sharing compensation system. Build it around employee involvement.

**5.** Create in the next six months an improved measurement system that focuses on productivity and quality. Disseminate the system widely throughout the organization and use it in your budget, performance appraisal system, compensation system, and reporting system.

# Magnifying management

## BUT WHAT DO I DO ON MONDAY MORNING?

**6.** In the next four months, launch a quality improvement program involving the entire organization. Plan to apply for the Malcolm Baldrige Award by the fifth year.

**7.** Triple your training budget in the next 12 months and do that each year until it's 5 percent of payroll.

**8.** Tear down most of the interior walls of the building in the next six months. Move those who work together closer and mix line and staff people, professionals and operational people.

**9.** Focus not on "cost reduction" but on "eliminating waste." Set a goal of cutting waste (of materials, people, space, time, motion,

etc.) by 100 percent in the next 12 months.

**10.** Change yourself. Learn new things. Practice them. Set a goal to learn three new areas in the next twelve months; read three books you wouldn't otherwise read; do one "outrageous" thing you've never done in the organization to make a point. Do most things with "emotion" that others can see—be hot, not cool.

*Source:* C. Juckson Grayson, Jr., "... But What Do I Do on Monday Morning?" *Academy of Management Executive* 3 (Fall 1989): 239.

---

digital technology was demonstrated, ironically by the Swiss themselves, at an international trade show, Seiko and Hewlett-Packard picked up on it, and within a few years had virtually eliminated the Swiss from the marketplace. The more recent Swiss success story has grown out of innovations with digital technology, mass manufacturing, and the marketing of such pop-culture staples as the Swatch watch.[3] The concept of television home shopping is revolutionizing the retail industry with sales increasing by 20 percent a year. Within just a few years, digital technology will let viewers ask for information and place orders on their TV screens.[4] Failure to respond to a technological change almost cost the Swiss their entire watch industry, while successfully responding to new digital communications technology may spur on an entire new industry in rapid home shopping.

Government and political actions have had a radical impact on a number of industries. When AT&T was ordered by judicial decree to divest itself of local telephone operations, six new "Baby Bells" were formed, each not only providing basic telephone service, but also becoming an independent manufacturer, developer, and provider of new equipment. No longer under "Ma Bell's" wing and direction, Bell Atlantic has been forced to become a telecommunications "entrepreneur" in order to meet the challenges of competitors from all over the world who joined in battle for a share of the giant market for telephone equipment systems.[5] When

**Comment on Box:** For each of the ten items described in the "Magnifying Management" box, have students discuss how organizations will be changed. How should these changes be effectively implemented? How will these actions change the organization for the better?

**Example:** IBM's new chairman, Louis V. Gerstner, Jr., has combined change and technology at IBM. He has set up a new technology-assessment system in which teams from around the company will come together to make judgments about technology.

the Cold War ended and the Berlin Wall fell, inventor Charlie Kaman, CEO and founder of Kaman Industries, moved from producing nuclear weapons and anti-submarine technology to selling, among other things, commercial helicopters that can haul logs and other nonhuman payloads. His strategic change has been a direct function of political forces.[6] In both Bell Atlantic and Kaman Industries, an effective response to a governmental or politically induced change has meant survival and, hopefully, success.

Yet another example of external forces comes from the cola industry where a customer complaint spurred a change in a major company. Craig Weatherup, PepsiCo president, cites as a major influence for change a meeting he had with David Glass, CEO of Wal-Mart, an important Pepsi customer. Glass told him bluntly, "There is nothing about the way your company does business with us that I like."[7] Such customer complaints spurred Weatherup to reorganize PepsiCo with a new quality service orientation.

**Internal Forces.**    The major internal forces for change are owners, top management, and employees, primarily through internal feedback mechanisms. These forces, although powerful in their own right, often respond to what is happening in the external environment. Often the combination of external forces, in concert with internal forces, generates tremendous impetus for change.

Sometimes a top manager notices something in the internal operation of the business or in the external environment, and exerts tremendous forces for change. Management professor Noel Tichy says, "All corporate revolutions are started from the top. It's crucial to form from the beginning a small, tight group of people 100 percent dedicated to implementing the plan."[8] Even with annual returns of 15 percent on shareholders' equity, and a virtual telecommunications monopoly in the Midwest, William Weiss, CEO of Ameritech, one of the most profitable Baby Bells, sensed a need for his company to change or die. He foresaw competitive pressures based on the introduction of technological innovations, a forecast that not everyone agreed with. Weiss pulled out four top executives who were in tune with his need for change, and they proceeded to restructure Ameritech around a focus on customer needs and internal efficiency.[9]

Sometimes the collective actions of workers, as in a strike, can start the machinery for change rolling. When the United Steelworkers Union went on strike at Globe Metallurgical, managers and a skeleton crew of replacement workers ran the plant, from working on the maintenance crew—as did then president Arden Sims—to running a furnace. Without the structure imposed by union rules and because of the labor shortage, Sims and his team had to be innovative in finding a more efficient way to run the plant. Within a few weeks of the strike, production had actually increased 20 percent. Self-managed work teams developed; the first-line supervisor position became unnecessary; the company began making a profit; and within a year, the plant was operating with just 120 workers, about a third of the prestrike total. All of these changes grew out of the necessity caused by the union walkout.[10]

Sometimes internal feedback mechanisms, as monitored by different organizational members, can signal that the organization needs to change in response to one or more environmental forces. Attitude surveys, performance data, employee performance evaluations, and grievances may indicate that there is a gap in performance, requiring that behaviors or activities need to be changed to close it. A **performance gap** is the difference between an organization's desired and actual performance levels. One of the best approaches to change is to set demanding

**Example:** Differences in management practice and behavior can lead to misunderstanding, miscommunication, and internal resentment. When feelings get hurt, communication channels break down and a host of organizational illnesses grow including absenteeism and alcoholism. If these differences are unchecked, productivity, profits, and morale will deteriorate.

**performance gap**
The difference between an organization's desired and actual performance levels.

The internal force of change at Globe Metallurgical Inc.—an 18-month strike—caused a complete change in the way the company operates. To maximize customer and employee satisfaction and boost profits, Globe adopted TQM principles, removed time clocks, and rewrote job descriptions; broadened its focus from the declining steel industry to the foundry, chemical, and aluminum industries; and hired a new top management team. These changes helped Globe become 50 percent more productive. Today, Globe produces 1,100 tons of material per worker-hour, compared with the industry average of 450 to 500 tons, and export sales now account for 20 percent of sales, up from 2 percent before the strike.

*Source:* © 1993 Laura Elliott.

standards of performance for all operations, measure performance against those standards, and hold managers accountable to them. At PepsiCo, President Craig Weatherup set a 20 percent profit as the standard and has held his managers accountable to it. Although this may seem obvious, organizations often have both poor measures of actual performance and a weak understanding of what demanding standards should be or look like, as we will discuss later in the chapter.

## Dimensions of Organizational Change

Organizations change in a number of different ways, along several different dimensions that often relate to one another. When examining any organization that is experiencing a performance gap, these dimensions—extent of planning, degree of change, degree of learning, target of change, and amount of organization being emphasized—can help provide useful guidelines along which to diagnose causes and then to structure a change program.

**Degree of Planning.**   Organizational change varies along a continuum with regard to the extent to which it is planned. At one end is **reactive change**, which occurs when organizational members react spontaneously to external and internal forces but do little to modify these forces or their behaviors. At the other end, **planned change** involves the deliberate structuring of operations and behaviors, often in anticipation of environmental forces. Most organizations fall somewhere in the middle. Businesses are too complex to have totally planned change, but at least some planning for change occurs in all organizations or the ensuing chaos would quickly destroy them.

Experts differ about how much change can be planned, and examples can be found at many points on the continuum. Globe Metallurgical's president, Arden Sims, made the point that most of the changes at his company were either specific reactions to forces out of the company's control or trial-and-error learning experiences gleaned from facing real problems.[11] On the other hand, PepsiCo's Craig Weatherup orchestrated a detailed plan of programmed meetings involving successively greater numbers of employees in information dispersal and training.[12]

**Example:**  Performance gaps can exist when senior executives lose sight of customers. Top-level managers at some industrial companies must spend a day in the life of key customers in their distribution channels. Unless senior executives make market focus a personal, strategic priority, they will not be motivated to initiate organizational change. There is no substitute for senior executives' instincts, imagination, and personal knowledge of the market.

**reactive change**
A situation in which organizational members react spontaneously to external and internal forces but do little to modify these forces or their behaviors.

**planned change**
The deliberate structuring of operations and behaviors, often in anticipation of environmental forces.

Some research suggests that many managers are fooling themselves in their belief that they can truly plan major organization transformations. However, it is still important that managers take steps to set up conditions that permit and even encourage necessary change to occur.[13]

Managers can take specific steps to facilitate change, and these steps can be learned; however, there are no guarantees that any specific action will always result in successful change. In any event, planned change increases the odds of success for a manager and is, thus, the focus of this chapter.

**incremental change**
A relatively small change in processes and behaviors within just one or a few systems or levels of the organization.

**Degree of Planned Change.**    Planned change also differs along another continuum, that of degree of change. Changes may range from incremental to quantum.[14] **Incremental change**, relatively small change, involves fine-tuning processes and behaviors within just one or a few systems or levels of the organization. It occurs within the context of the organization's current structure, strategy, and culture. For example, Rader Co., a Memphis-based lumberyard equipment maker, underwent training to improve the communication and leadership skills of top managers. The workshops involved interviewing employees about manager strengths and weaknesses and then feeding back the information to managers in structured open meetings. Because no major organizational restructuring occurred, this resulted in only incremental change. **Quantum change**, or large-scale planned change, involves significantly altering how the firm operates, usually by altering multiple organization levels and several of the dimensions of structure, culture, reward systems, strategy, and work design.[15]

**quantum change**
A large-scale planned change in how the firm operates.

**Example:** Quantum change can be seen in the downsizing of corporate America. In 1993, a record 615,186 layoffs were made. Even in the midst of an economic recovery, big companies continue to shed workers. In the first quarter of 1994, staff reductions of 192,572 were announced—more than 3,100 per day.

**Degree of Organizational Members' Involvement in Learning How to Change.**    A third dimension deals with the degree to which organizational members are actively involved in learning how to plan and implement change while engaging in solving an existing problem. Author Peter Senge describes the "learning organization" as engaged in continuous experimentation and feedback in an ongoing examination of the way it goes about addressing and solving problems.[16] In contrast, some organizations focus on solving immediate problems without examining the appropriateness of current learning behaviors. Using the company examples already cited, Globe Metallurgical probably comes closest to a learning organization because of its strong learn-as-you-go orientation.

**Target of Change.**    Organizational change programs—systematic planned change efforts—can also vary with respect to the hierarchical level or functional area at which the change is targeted. Some changes are designed to influence top managers, such as the one at Memphis Light, Gas, and Water, where consultants interviewed subordinates of the top 15 managers and gave each feedback about his or her leadership style strengths and weaknesses. Other change programs might involve basic skills learning, such as customer service techniques, for lower-level employees only. Others could involve restructuring a marketing or R&D division without any planned change in other areas. Changes planned for one level or area, though, often have an impact on other parts of the organization, as we will discuss shortly.

**Amount of Organization Being Emphasized.**    Finally, organizational change can differ with regard to the extent of "organization" being emphasized or how reg-

Under the leadership of new CEO Eckhard Pfeiffer (in photo), Compaq Computer completely changed its product and marketing strategy. Compaq had an excellent reputation for producing high-priced computers mainly for the business market. Pfeiffer embarked on a new low-price, high-volume strategy by designing desktop and notebook computers, printers, and other new products for consumers and small-business customers. To reach these customers, Pfeiffer expanded distribution from 3,300 to 8,300 outlets worldwide by selling products through computer superstores and mass merchandisers.

*Source:* © Peter Schinzler/Agentur Anne Hamann, Munich.

ulated and structured its activities may be. Some organizations are overly organized and bureaucratized and need "loosening up," while others suffer from poor coordination and may be underorganized. Fairly young and rapidly growing organizations often suffer from underorganization and may need to emphasize structure, rules, and stronger norms to lend stability to the chaos. When John Scully joined Apple Computer, it already had innovation but needed increased structure and a more closely managed culture. Scully helped stabilize a somewhat loose operation.[17]

## Types of Organizational Change

There are also several major types of planned change that vary according to the area of emphasis for the change: changes in strategy, organizational structure or design, technology, and human processes and culture. Note that these categories are not mutually exclusive.

**Changing Strategy.**   Changing a company's strategy involves changing its fundamental approach to doing business (see Chapter 10)—the markets it will target, the kinds of products it will sell, how they will be sold, its overall strategic orientation (cost, differentiation, etc.), the level of global activity, and its various partnerships and other joint-business arrangements. Changing strategy involves an attempt to align a company's resources with the various environmental forces recently discussed.

Many examples abound in which companies have made major strategic change. Polaroid, in response to stiff foreign competition, announced in 1993 a shift from its traditional photography business to electronic imaging systems for printing X-rays and other electronics products.[18] Compaq Computer Co. still sells the same product for which it was established, but has expanded its distribution to include direct sales to customers through mail order, rather than just through retailers. This strategic marketing change is aimed directly at the market share of competitors Dell Computer Corporation and Gateway, who have a large market in the direct-mail computer business.[19] These strategic changes reflect differences in extent as well as in the nature of the initiated change.

**Example:** After a study of its long-term strategy, Frito-Lay dismissed nearly one-third of its corporate headquarters staff and completed a reorganization of the company.

**Example:** Borden Inc.'s chief executive, Ervin R. Shames, and a cadre of new managers face the daunting task of trying to breathe life into the companies that remain under the Borden banner. The company is trying to remake itself as a viable smaller company by slashing costs, boosting marketing, and shedding money-losing businesses such as its $800 million domestic snack unit.

**Changing Structure and Design.**    When a company alters its structure, it may change its departmentalization, hierarchical reporting relationships, line-staff relationships, and overall design. Chapters 12 and 13 discussed various structures and designs and the benefits of each. One frequent reason for restructuring in today's environment is to meet customer needs more effectively. William Weiss broke a monolithic, hierarchically oriented Ameritech into twelve businesses, each focused on a different kind of customer or customer need—small, large, and residential customers.[20] The quality revolution in America, increased competition, and cost consciousness will likely result in continued downsizing and streamlining of larger business, resulting in even more structural changes.[21]

**Changing Technology.**    Many companies are introducing technological changes in their manufacturing or service operations to keep pace with massive environmental changes and competitive challenges. Computers, for example, have radically changed the very nature of business, even in very small operations, by speeding up routine activities and providing fast access to huge amounts of information. Robotics is another area that is helping many large manufacturers improve efficiency. Manufacturing firms in the United States, Asia, and Europe are using robot technology to build Toyotas, Oldsmobiles, BMWs, and Fiats.[22]

Sometimes new technology is the focus of the business—the product itself—and not just a way to improve making a good or speed up a service. Xerox CEO Paul Allaire has totally restructured his company to balance independent business divisions with integrated research and technology. Xerox now concentrates on computerized digital information processing technology as it stands alone or merges with its traditional electro-optical devices. Xerox's focus is now on helping customers store, retrieve, and utilize their "documents," in whatever form they may take, rather than simply reproducing paper documents. New technologies and competitors have resulted in massive strategic and structural changes at Xerox.[23]

**Changing People Processes and Culture.**    Changing people processes involves changing the processes of communicating, motivating, leading, and interacting in groups. It may entail changing how problems are solved, how people learn new processes and skills, and even the very nature of how they perceive themselves, the organization, and their jobs. Major organizational change may involve altering the organization's entire culture.

Some people changes may involve only incremental changes or small improvements in a process. For example, many organizations undergo leadership training, which might teach managers how to communicate more openly with employees, use praise and other rewards to motivate performance, resolve interpersonal conflicts and deal with disruptive employees, and encourage more employee participation. Other programs might concentrate on team processes by teaching both managers and employees how to work together effectively to solve problems. Still other programs might strive to enhance union-management relations or to learn how to deal with an organization's existing power structure, which makes up what is often called the informal organization. We will take a closer look at some of these approaches later in this chapter.

**Example:** Louis Gerstner, chairman of IBM, has changed people and culture particularly in the management structure. Gerstner set up a new 11-member executive committee to promote greater corporate cooperation and formed a 34-member worldwide management council to discuss operating results, company practices, and problems.

Major organizational change could entail dealing with all the people processes as well as changes in such human resource systems as rewards and compensation, training and development, selection, and performance appraisal. For major change to succeed, fundamental alterations must occur in three areas: (1) coordination or teamwork, including coordination between departments and between labor and management; (2) commitment to a high level of effort, cooperation, and planned actions; and (3) competencies, meaning improved conceptual, analytical, and interpersonal skills in both labor and management. Most planned change programs target only one, or at best, two of these areas, while all three are essential for major change to occur.[24]

There are numerous examples of major change programs that have focused on changing the way people function. At Bell Atlantic, Raymond Smith had his people learn to think "the Bell Atlantic Way," or for the good of the overall organization. Smith changed the culture from one of an "implementation" mentality—just doing what AT&T corporate headquarters dictated—to one of innovation, customer service, productivity, accountability, and mutual support. Smith also emphasized the key role that management played as models for essential behaviors—what he called "the shadow of the leader"—and the necessity for everyone to learn new entrepreneurial skills. His change program has all three elements of coordination, commitment, and competency.[25]

# MODELS OF PLANNED CHANGE

Managers who want to plan organizational change may find it helpful to have a model of how the change process works. In this section, we will briefly review two basic models of change, discuss some implications of each, and then delve more deeply into a comprehensive model that could encompass most change programs.

## Lewin's Model of Change

One of the earliest and most fundamental models of change was provided by behavioral scientist Kurt Lewin. Lewin viewed the change process as a modification of the forces that keep a system's behaviors stable. He depicted the level of any behavior or attitude existing at a given time as a function of "driving forces," which are pushing for change in behavior, and "restraining forces," those striving to maintain the status quo. When these forces are about equal, Lewin said a state of quasi-stationary equilibrium exists. He devised a technique called "force field analysis" that depicts the driving and restraining forces—the real conditions of people, organization, or environment—in a situation that keeps it stable. Figure 19.1 provides an example of a force field analysis of the forces that may have kept the attitudes and behavior of automobile industry executives stable in the 1970s when they should have been changing.

Lewin's model of major change grew out of this force field concept. He describes change as consisting of the following three phases (see Figure 19.2):

1. **Unfreezing** involves disrupting the forces maintaining the existing state (state A) or level of behavior. This might be done by introducing new information to show discrepancies between state A and one desired by the organization—that is, a performance gap. The performance gap for the American car manufacturers got so big that the "Big Three" finally were unfrozen.

2. **Moving** entails a transition period (state B) during which the behaviors of the organization or department are shifted to a new level (desired state C). It involves developing new behaviors, values, and attitudes

**unfreezing**
The disruption of forces maintaining the existing state (state A) or level of behavior.

**moving**
The transition period (state B) during which the behaviors of the organization or department are shifted to a new level (desired state C).

## FIGURE 19.1

### Sample Force Field Analysis for the Automobile Industry of the 1970s

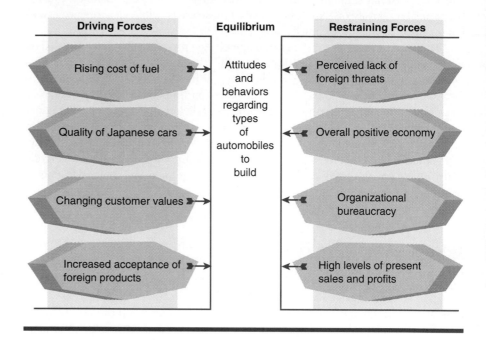

through changes in structure, technology, strategy, and human processes. The auto manufacturers finally adjusted their strategies and through TQM have even changed many of their processes.

3. **Refreezing** stabilizes the organization at a new state of behavioral equilibrium (state C). This is accomplished through the use of supporting mechanisms that reinforce the new organizational state, such as culture, norms, policies, and structures.[26] Making TQM teams a part of standard operating procedures would exemplify refreezing.

**refreezing**

The phase in which the organization is stabilized at a new state of behavioral equilibrium (state C).

**Critical Thinking Challenge:** Have students bring an organizational change example to class and use Lewin's model to discuss the three phases of change as exhibited by the chosen organization. Have students present their findings. Why was it necessary to refreeze the change?

## FIGURE 19.2

### Lewin's Model for Implementing Change

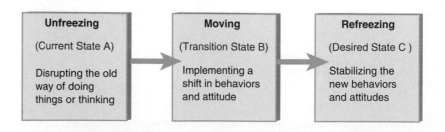

*Source:* Adapted from Thomas G. Cummings and Edgar F. Huse, *Organization Development and Change,* 4th ed. (St. Paul: West Publishing Co., 1989).

**FIGURE 19.3**

## Congruence Model of Change

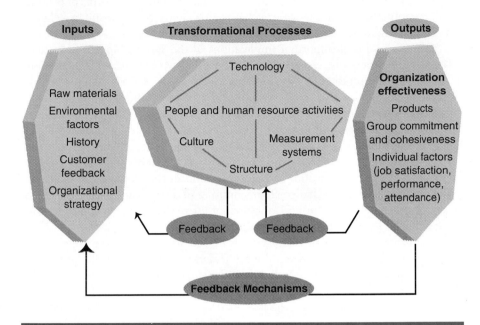

*Source:* Adapted from Thomas G. Cummings and Christopher G. Worley, *Organization Development and Change,* 5th ed. (St. Paul: West Publishing Co., 1993).

Thus, Lewin viewed change as the adjustment of driving and restraining forces in order to facilitate movement to a new equilibrium state which is then reinforced and stabilized. This model, therefore, suggests that managers should find ways to unfreeze the existing equilibrium before any change will occur.

## Congruence Model of Change

The **congruence model of change**, an outgrowth of the systems approach to organizational theory, emphasizes the interrelationships between the various parts of an organization and how change in one part will cause reactive changes in other parts. You may remember from Chapter 2 that the systems theory depicts organizations and their environments as sets of interrelated parts to be managed as a whole in order to achieve a common goal, with each system consisting of inputs, transformation processes, outputs, and feedback (see Figure 2.1 in Chapter 2). In the congruence model, inputs may include raw materials, environmental factors, history, customer feedback, and the organization's strategy. Processes consist of technology, human resource activities, culture, structure, and measurement systems. Outputs are all those things that reflect the firm's effectiveness: its finished products, group commitment and cohesiveness, and such individual outcomes as job satisfaction, personal performance, and attendance (Figure 19.3).[27]

The key aspect of the congruence model is that system elements, both inputs and processes, interact with one another such that changes in one part of the

**congruence model of change**
An approach that emphasizes the interrelationships between the various parts of an organization and how change in one part will cause reactive change in other parts.

system can cause radical changes in another part of the system. For example, a change in the nature of raw materials or other inputs into the system may necessitate a change in the organizational and job structures, as well as in human resource processes, and may ultimately influence the outputs in terms of product quality or job satisfaction. Likewise, a change in technology may result in a change in culture, structure, and any or all of the other transformation processes.

There are several important implications of the systems approach to diagnosing and implementing change. Managers need to recognize that changes in one area may cause unintended changes in another, as the overall system seeks to regain equilibrium. Also, because systems tend to seek equilibrium, managers can expect that some changes may be resisted or even nullified by a lack of change in the rest of the system. For example, taking managers offsite for training in participative management may not result in actual change back on the job if the structure, the informal organization, and human resource systems and culture remain unchanged. A major implication is that, for significant change to occur, managers may have to intentionally change all or a number of the transformational processes simultaneously and in support of one another so that the new configurations work in harmony to exact improved outputs.

A number of the organizations we have discussed thus far have attacked the change process while recognizing the interrelationship of change variables. For example, Raymond Smith, at Bell Atlantic, changed his company's strategy to become more entrepreneurial in aggressively seeking telecommunications business opportunities. He also changed the leadership patterns managers were modeling and the whole culture of the company around a quality imperative and a mutual support philosophy. The company was restructured and downsized, and the ways information was passed and rewards administered were also changed.[28] Bell Atlantic's change process reflects an attempt to reach congruence between the various processes as they are all being changed at once.

## COMPREHENSIVE MODEL OF PLANNED CHANGE

**comprehensive model of planned change**
A step-by-step plan for implementing major change.

The **comprehensive model of planned change**, a step-by-step plan for implementing major change, encompasses all of the facets of change discussed thus far and more.[29] It includes a set of activities managers must engage in to manage the change process effectively: recognizing the need for change, motivating change, creating a vision, developing political support, managing the transition, and sustaining momentum for the change (Figure 19.4).

### Recognizing the Need for Change

The change process begins with someone recognizing a need for change after scanning the organization's environment. We have already discussed some of the forces that may prompt a need for change, as well as some of the feedback mechanisms that may suggest needed directions for change. Recognition of the need for change may occur at the top management level or in peripheral parts of an organization, but experts disagree on where the change is most likely to start. Once the need for change is recognized, the manager must motivate change by preparing people for the changes they will face and overcoming their natural resistance to change.

**FIGURE 19.4**

**Comprehensive Model of Planned Change**

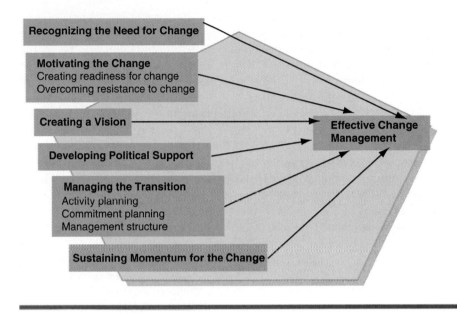

**Recognizing the Need for Change**

**Motivating the Change**
Creating readiness for change
Overcoming resistance to change

**Creating a Vision**

**Developing Political Support**

**Managing the Transition**
Activity planning
Commitment planning
Management structure

**Sustaining Momentum for the Change**

**Effective Change Management**

*Source:* Adapted from Thomas G. Cummings and Christopher G. Worley, *Organization Development and Change,* 5th ed. (St. Paul: West Publishing Co., 1993), 155.

## Creating Readiness for Change

Preparing people for change is similar to Lewin's unfreezing step. It entails primarily bringing dissatisfaction with the current state to the surface. PepsiCo's Craig Weatherup acknowledged that change was uncomfortable and that the company might even fail, but kept pushing the idea that change was absolutely necessary. Customer dissatisfaction, competition, and economic demands could no longer be denied.[30] CEO Mike H. Walsh of Union Pacific says that the biggest enemy of progress is "happy talk." He pushed for change, even after the company had reported its biggest earnings year ever, by continually showing his managers how the company was gradually but inevitably dying under its present practices.[31]

Preparing people for change requires direct and forceful feedback about the negatives of the present situation, as compared to the desired future state, and sensitizing people to the forces of change that exist in their environment. Managers can make themselves more sensitive to pressures for change by surrounding themselves with "devil's advocates," using networks of people and organizations with different perspectives and views, visiting other organizations in order to be exposed to new ideas, and using external standards of performance, such as a competitor's progress or benchmarks.[32]

**Example:** After having to make temporary layoffs, Rhino Foods president Ted Castle asked employees in his $5-million Burlington, Vermont, specialty dessert business to think of alternatives. They suggested contracting out idle workers to other local businesses.

## Overcoming Resistance to Change

When change occurs, there will almost always be resistance, and understanding why resistance occurs can give managers some insight into how to deal with it.

### Sources of Resistance to Change.

Some of the most common reasons for resisting change include uncertainty and insecurity, reaction against the way change is presented, threats to vested interests, cynicism and lack of trust, perceptual differences, and lack of understanding.

People need a certain amount of stability and security in their lives, and change can present unknowns that produce anxiety. Employees may worry about their ability to meet new job demands or even fear losing their jobs. Given the recent era of company downsizing, it is logical and understandable that most employees view change negatively. They may believe they will be unable to learn new required skills, or they may simply have personalities that cause them to dislike ambiguity. Change often results in altered work practices and work group relationships. Workers may resist restructuring attempts and continue to conduct business as they did before if the fabric of their social relationships is threatened.

Resistance to change may grow out of a reaction against being controlled or loss of autonomy. If a change seems arbitrarily imposed or unreasonable, if management uses little tact in implementing or announcing it, or if it is poorly timed, negative reactions may result. If a company had encouraged participation and empowerment but stopped because of a tough economy or bad business cycle, that kind of change is likely to be severely resented.

Some changes may result in employees losing their positions of power; labor union situations provide an excellent example of concern over such loss. Alan Wilgus of Inland Steel described the painstakingly slow progress in trying to implement a TQM program at his company as the United Steelworkers scrutinized every move management tried to make to improve operations.[33]

Employees who have been treated unkindly or at best indifferently by management over the years are likely to face any change with skepticism. At Inland Steel, workers were cynical because they were accustomed to hearing management pay "lip service" to employee empowerment without seeing any meaningful change. Years of traditional hierarchical management may cause workers anywhere to be very skeptical when management proposes moving into more progressive organizational practices, such as TQM and empowerment.

Sometimes people resist change because they perceive the situation differently from those trying to institute the change. They may perceive that no change is warranted or that a different type of change would be more effective, based either on a different diagnosis of a problem or a different opinion about what should be done. Employees and supervisors in one large manufacturing plant told their corporate engineers that the new design for a production line would not work. The company spent nearly $300,000 changing the line anyway and, sure enough, the new line did not work. Managers should recognize that workers' perceptions of a situation may be more accurate than their own because of their proximity to it. In some cases, resistance to a bad change can ultimately save the company much in time and money.

Finally, resistance may stem from a lack of understanding of the change, including its need, nature, or implications for individuals. When the change process is not clearly presented, people tend to fill in the information gaps with rumors and speculation, often assuming the worst in terms of personal impact.

### Reducing Resistance to Change.

Research has identified a number of different strategies that managers may apply to deal with resistance to change, including education and communication, participation and involvement, facilitation and support, negotiation and agreement, manipulation and co-optation, and coercion

**Example:** Wellex, an award-winning contractor with annual revenues of $13.5 million and clients like IBM and Sun Microsystems, implemented a Japanese-type employee suggestions system with cash rewards of at least $15 for ideas that saved the business time or money. This program overcame resistance to change and got employees involved in the growth of the company by valuing their input.

**TABLE 19.1**

## Methods for Dealing with Resistance to Change

| Approach | Commonly Used in Situations | Advantages | Drawbacks |
|---|---|---|---|
| Education and communication | Where there is a lack of information or inaccurate information and analysis. | Once persuaded, people will often help with the implementation of the change. | Can be very time-consuming if lots of people are involved. |
| Participation and involvement | Where the initiators do not have all the information that they need to design the change, and where others have considerable power to resist. | People who participate will be committed to implementing change, and any relevant information they have will be integrated into the change plan. | Can be time-consuming if participators design an inappropriate change. |
| Facilitation and support | Where people are resisting because of adjustment problems. | No other approach works as well with adjustment problems. | Can be time-consuming, expensive, and still fail. |
| Negotiation and agreement | Where someone or some group will clearly lose out in a change, and where that group has considerable power to resist. | Sometimes it is a relatively easy way to avoid major resistance. | Can be too expensive in many cases if it alerts others to negotiate for compliance. |
| Manipulation and co-optation | Where other tactics will not work, or are too expensive. | It can be a relatively quick and inexpensive solution to resistance problems. | Can lead to future problems if people feel manipulated. |
| Explicit and implicit coercion | Where speed is essential, and the change initiators possess considerable power. | It is speedy and can overcome any kind of resistance. | Can be risky if it leaves people mad at the initiators. |

*Source: Harvard Business Review.* An exhibit from "Choosing Strategies for Change" by John P. Kotter and Leonard A. Schlesinger (March–April 1979). Copyright 1979 by the President and Fellows of Harvard College; all rights reserved.

(Table 19.1). Managers try to match a strategy to the demands of a situation to overcome resistance or to manage it with minimal disruption. Factors worth considering are the amount and type of change being attempted; the power of the resisters; the nature, cause, and form of the resistance; and the short- and long-term effects of the strategy.

One of the primary tactics used to help people deal with the anxiety of change is education and communication. Consultant Jean Keffeler says that "the amount of communication required to allay organizational anxiety in times of unusual change, even if the change is perceived as positive, is enormous. People have an insatiable need to hear what's going on and what it means to them."[34] Craig Weatherup spent a tremendous amount of time communicating in various-sized groups the necessity of PepsiCo changing to a customer-oriented culture.

In the long run, getting employee participation in change decisions and increased involvement in all aspects of the change may be the single best method to overcome resistance. Participation increases understanding of the change process, enhances feelings of control and autonomy, and provides for employee input that can make the change work better. It reduces uncertainty and often allows for the maintenance of social relationships during the change. Once the change is finally complete, a sense of ownership discourages resistance and increases commitment to making the change successful. When Paul Allaire took over

**Teaching Note:** Have a local middle manager speak to your class about change in his or her organization. Which of the approaches outlined in Table 19.1 has the organization used to manage change? How was it successful? What are the organization's future plans for change?

At Union Carbide's industrial chemicals division, plant and equipment maintenance accounted for 30 percent of costs. Top managers decided work processes needed to be redesigned to reduce these high costs. They set cost-reduction goals and then asked employees to develop new work processes. Employees took ownership of the project by setting up new work shifts and designing new procedures for repair and cleaning jobs. By involving employees, Union Carbide increased employee commitment to making the change successful. Plant employees shown here with their new work design saved the company more than $20 million, 50 percent more than the goal set by management.

*Source:*    John   Chiasson/GAMMA LIAISON.

**Example:** As organizations move to a more culturally diversified staff, white males feel threatened and feel they have little job security. Some white males feel powerless and are worried about their futures. Listening, counseling, and even career coaching can be helpful.

**Example:** In the course of its continuing restructuring, IBM eliminated more than 100,000 jobs over the past four years. A former marketing vice president with 20 years experience with the struggling computer maker discusses the organization change: "Every year we'd call it something different—early retirement, reorganization, re-engineering," she recalls. "It was a slow water torture."

Xerox, he appointed a six-person "Future Architecture" team of managers to examine what kind of structure and practices Xerox needed to be successful. The team involved 75 more managers over a 15-month period in a participative process of gathering information and suggestions for restructuring. Another team—called an Organization Transition Board—was appointed to work out the details of the new division structure and help implement it, even to the point of designing a new evaluation system for the selection of division managers. This high level of involvement, besides encouraging intellectual inputs, generated maximum acceptance and maximum understanding of the restructuring.[35]

When anxiety and fear cause resistance, management can offer support in the form of stress counseling, special training, and simply good listening. Unfortunately, most organizations do a bad job with respect to stress counseling and listening. Managers should acknowledge the legitimacy of the anxiety and discomfort, whereas many managers intensify anxiety by acting startled that employees would not readily accept a change. Accepting employees' discomfort and helping them deal with it can help management gain commitment to the change. Training in change management, coping mechanisms, stress management, and career self-management will facilitate the change process.[36]

Sometimes management can negotiate an exchange of something in return for acceptance of a change. Making concessions in an area not related to the change, or distributing perks that help make the change easier can help overcome resistance. Because of strong union resistance, changes at Inland Steel were negotiated at almost every phase of change and over nearly all issues related to job design, work team design, the compensation system, and even transition team make-up. Although changes took longer under these conditions, management recognized the real power of the union to undermine any change attempt of which it disapproved, as well as the union's power to help change occur. Negotiation and participation slowly overcame some of the resistance.[37]

Manipulation and co-optation are sometimes used when other tactics will not work or have been tried unsuccessfully. Manipulation occurs when information and decisions are selectively distributed to control the perception of a change. Co-optation involves having resistant individuals join the change team—specifically to reduce their power to resist, rather than to truly participate. If employees recognize the manipulation or co-optation, however, even greater resistance can occur and ultimately make the change even more difficult. In universities, it is a common practice for deans to appoint faculty "troublemakers" to advisory committees in areas where they might resist a dean's proposed change. This co-opting makes the resisters part of the change process and minimizes their impact, but keeps them from complaining about not being involved or about their loss of autonomy. There is sometimes a fine line between participation in the change process and co-optation. A real danger occurs with this tactic if it is obvious or superficial. Imagine the reaction if John or Bobby Kennedy had tried in 1963 to co-opt the resistance of Martin Luther King, Jr., by offering him a government job during the civil rights movement.

Coercion is sometimes used when managers will not or cannot take the time to implement less authoritarian tactics. The obvious danger with the use of real or implied threats or punishment is the antagonism and further resistance that are generated—sometimes very subtly—and the damage that it can do to the relationship between the change agent and those resisting the change. Many progressive managers reject the use of coercion, as well as manipulation and co-optation, on moral and ethical, as well as practical, grounds. These techniques are not consistent with the more open, ethical, and positive climates their companies are trying to create.

## Creating a Vision

Managers can facilitate change by clearly defining and communicating their vision of where their firms are headed. Applying Lewin's model, this means knowing what the desired future state C will look like. That mental picture can be fairly general—perhaps being a lean, flexible organization—or it can be quite specific—such as one multinational company's vision of having sales forces of a certain size placed on each of five major continents by the year 2000.

AT&T Chairman Robert E. Allen has a very clear vision of AT&T's future as captured succinctly in its slogan "anywhere, anytime." That means "a pervasive high-tech communications system that will actually track people down and deliver a phone call or a fax whether they're in the office, on a ski lift, or sitting in an airplane."[38] AT&T already has most of the elements in place to give it a strategic advantage in this all-encompassing communication vision. Moreover, its vision is clear enough to guide its decisions regarding acquisition of other businesses needed to fulfill its strategy. Finally, the visual image of a skier receiving a phone call on a ski lift is a compelling and inspirational symbol for everyone to see. Allen also represents a key requirement for successful major change: leadership. Transformational leaders, you will remember from Chapter 17, inspire with their visions of the future. John F. Kennedy said in 1961 that we would reach the moon in that decade, inspiring a space program and a nation. Martin Luther King, Jr.'s, "dream" of equality in his lifetime inspired an entire race.

A research study that surveyed several hundred change agents (those who initiate or foster change) found that the single most positive facilitator of a change program is "creating a shared vision with employees of what the organization will look like when the program is completed."[39] The ability to visualize and communicate the desired future state is therefore crucial to planned change. Helpful mechanisms include a clear mission statement, a specific statement of desired performance and human outcomes, a clear explanation of processes that will facilitate the outcomes (for example, rewards being based on performance), and midpoint goals to keep motivation high and to provide feedback.[40]

**Example:** Digital Equipment Corporation suffered a $183 million loss in 1993. Enrico Resatri now has the responsibility of reshaping the company. Resatri has outlined a dramatic $1 billion restructuring plan that cuts jobs, and focuses on key groups. He plans for the new DEC to emerge as a Procter & Gamble-like array of units, each with its own functions of engineering, manufacturing, and marketing.

**Example:** Robert Carlson, a former Pratt and Whitney CEO, uses his retirement to help transfer business skills to Russia. He lives in a cramped hotel room in Nizhnii Novgorod, a provincial city on the Volga River. Because of his vision for change, he spends his days helping factory directors in Russia devise restructuring plans. He also scouts business opportunities for Western investors.

Frank Fulkerson (center), owner of Vortex Industries, a small firm that repairs and replaces warehouse doors, used activity planning to achieve his goal of improving customer service. Rather than having each employee perform one task, Fulkerson organized employees into teams and asked each member to master several skills. Most employees resisted the change. To overcome resistance, Fulkerson rewarded employees by initiating a profit-sharing plan that returned 25 percent of each month's profits to them. He instituted weekly "communication meetings" to allow employees to express problems adjusting to the change. Fulkerson also sent employees to seminars in sales, management, and customer service.

*Source:* © 1994 Patricia Lanza.

## Developing Political Support

We can picture organizations as political systems composed of different groups competing for power. Managers of different functional areas compete for resources and influence, so each develops his or her own sources of power. Workers compete with management over who will determine the structure of jobs and overtime and other work issues. For change to be successful, leaders of change must identify key stakeholders and then develop support within the key political groups.[41] They can use various sources of power and the change strategies noted in Table 19.1 to generate support from these players. Once the key leaders are brought on board, they can in turn generate energy in support of a change. Raymond Smith used the term "shadow of the leader" at Bell Atlantic to depict the role of leaders who were to cast their shadows over the organization by modeling desired behaviors. PepsiCo's Weatherup trained a small group of top executives in his new vision of PepsiCo, who each then trained another group of managers and so on until all management and supervisory personnel were trained in the new customer-oriented philosophy by which the organization was to operate.[42]

Leaders can also use symbols and language to facilitate change. Researchers are now exploring the importance of the use of metaphors to diagnose organizational functioning.[43] For example, picturing a top executive group as "a basketball team that sometimes plays together, but often has one player hog the ball," can help the group understand a problem it may be having with one strong member dominating the group and its subsequent effects on other group members. Using symbolic team names can also help people focus on change. Allaire's use of the Future Architecture team and Xerox's Organizational Transition Board helped focus attention on the participative nature of their transitions, and kept powerful leaders in tune with and supportive of the change.

## Managing the Transition

**transition state**
The period during which the organization learns the behaviors needed to reach the desired future state.

While the organization moves from the current state to its desired future state, it will go through a period of change, or "moving" in Lewin's terminology. This **transition state** is the period during which the organization learns the behaviors needed to reach the desired future state. This can be a period of extreme disruption and must be effectively managed, or chaos can occur and the desired future state never met. During the transition, the organization needs to develop and use feedback mechanisms to ensure that changes really are happening as planned. These can include surveys, sensing groups, and consultant interviews, as well as existing informal communication channels. Three major activities are required during the transition:  activity planning, commitment planning, and management structures.[44]

**Activity Planning.**   Activity planning refers to designing the road map and noting specific events and activities that must be timed and integrated to produce the change. Change expert David Nadler says that, at this stage, change leaders should use "multiple and consistent leverage points." Growing out of systems theory and the congruence model, his idea is that a number of different processes (leverage points) must be changed so that they support one another and the overall desired state.[45] If greater customer service is the goal, then the organizational structure might be changed to empowered teams. Team members could be sent to visit key customers personally to assess their needs, and reward systems could be changed to encourage new ideas for customer service and to reduce defects that cause customer dissatisfaction. Such activities must be sequenced and integrated to form a consistent system. Using Lewin's terminology, this would mean reducing many of the "restraining forces" and increasing the "driving forces" all at once or in the proper sequence. Paul Allaire at Xerox emphasizes that there must be a "fit" or "alignment" of these key processes.

**Commitment Planning.**   Commitment planning starts with identifying key political powers in the organization. It also entails planning specific ways to get them involved in the transition activities in order to gain their support. Being assigned to Xerox's Transition Board got key members involved in redesigning the division structure and evaluation systems.

**Management Structures.**   Management structures (such as individual appointees, teams, or ad hoc committees) must be used to help run things during the transition, plan the direction of the changes, and keep ongoing operations running smoothly as the change occurs. Management structures for handling the transition can include the chief executive officer or other top manager, a project manager to coordinate the transition, representatives of major constituencies involved in the change, natural leaders who have the confidence and trust of large numbers of affected employees, a cross-section of people representing different functions and levels, and/or a cabinet, representing people with whom the chief executive consults and in whom the CEO confides.[46]

Our example companies have used different structures. At Inland Steel, joint management and union committees have managed the change. Allaire, at Xerox, was good at using natural leaders from different functions and levels on his Organization Transition Board. It is interesting that Allaire was able to get these individuals to dismiss self-interests and organize a new structure without regard to where they personally would fit into the structure.

## Sustaining the Momentum of the Change

Once a change has begun, initial excitement can dissipate rapidly in the face of everyday problems. However, managers can help sustain the momentum for

**Example:** Karl R. Wyss, chairman of Lear Siegler Inc., took over the company two years after the conglomerate was taken private. For years managers thought they were making money in a significant product line, but Wyss found they were losing money as well as market share. He relocated the plant to take advantage of cheaper labor and reengineered the product to cut manufacturing costs.

**Example:** McKinsey & Co., a management consulting firm, advises its clients to provide a new framework for change in the twenty-first century. It advocates a flatter, more horizontal, and cross-functional structure for organizations instead of the traditional vertical hierarchical organization.

## BUSINESS DILEMMA

*You're the Manager …What Would You Do?*

THE COMPANY: Preston County Transportation Department

YOUR POSITION: Transportation Director

THE PLACE: Portland, Oregon

Preston County Transportation was a highly centralized organization with authority concentrated at upper levels. Low-level employees had to go through their superiors and fill out reams of paperwork to accomplish anything. Even simple repairs took days or even weeks, and, as a result, morale was very low. Maintenance on the county's buses was substandard, in part due to employee apathy because mechanics were not held accountable for the condition of the buses. Poor maintenance led to low-quality service with high levels of pollution, poor internal seating and conditions, and breakdowns.

The county brought in a retired military general, Jim Barnes, as the new transportation director to assess the problems and provide a detailed recommendation of how to change the situation. After weeks of study and interviews, Barnes suggested decentralizing the department and delegating responsibility to the lowest levels of the organization. He recommended creating maintenance teams and giving team members responsibility for the maintenance of all buses under their control. Barnes also suggested moving maintenance teams to several locations throughout the county to provide greater accessibility to major routes and bus traffic. The key to Barnes's plan is creating a feeling of personal interest and pride in each team's success.

The county decided to accept and implement Barnes's plan. The results were outstanding. Teams developed very strong identities and began to compete with each other for safety and duration awards, indicating length of time between major service problems. The plan made maintenance and lower-level employees feel important and necessary for the success of the organization.

With morale, involvement, and performance improving, Barnes next set out to address the problem of the mounds of paperwork required to accomplish anything in the department. Bus repairs had been slowed because upper-level authorities had to approve all major work. This system was changed by giving employees greater opportunity to make repair decisions and greater access to parts (inventories were dramatically expanded). Microcomputers were used to list available parts at each repair facility and vans were utilized to shuttle parts to needed locations. After the reorganization, parts could be shipped to most locations within one hour.

Finally, Barnes ordered that all county transportation facilities be painted and completely cleaned and refurnished, and that new uniforms be provided for employees. This was intended to enhance employees' pride in working for the county bus system.

### Questions

1. As new transportation director, evaluate your plans to change this organization.
2. What are the inherent benefits and risks with decentralization?
3. What do you see as your long-term priorities in managing this new system? How do you maintain morale and productivity?

**Comment on Box:** After completing the chapter, assign the "Business Dilemma" box as an outside assignment. Have students bring their answers to class and divide the class into groups of 5 to 6 students. Have them discuss their recommendations and after 20 to 30 minutes, have a representative from each group discuss the group consensus on each of the questions. Put suggestions for maintaining morale and productivity on the board for further discussion.

change by providing resources, developing new competencies and skills, reinforcing new behaviors, and building a support system for those initiating the change. Extra resources may be needed for training, consultation, data collection and feedback, special meetings (even off-site retreats), and to provide a financial buffer if performance drops during the transition period. Managers usually underestimate both the time and extra resources needed to execute a major change. Changes often require new skills of organizational members: problem-solving skills for group members, interpersonal skills for line workers suddenly asked to talk to customers, and computer skills for employees using new technology. The new skills employees are required to learn and new resources go hand in hand.

The entire organization must reinforce not only the learning of new behaviors, but also those persons initiating the new learning. When top managers are the agents of change, the reinforcement and support must come from the network of persons who understand and support the change. An internal consulting group or external consultant can reinforce the executives and provide a sounding board for their decisions. New organizational structures may have to be devised for support. Top management must reinforce lower-level managers and workers by linking formal rewards to the desired behaviors. Ford, for instance, in trying to improve quality, links 40 to 60 percent of its managers' bonuses to product quality. Recognition, encouragement, and praise are informal rewards that can be tied quickly to desired behaviors. Even the good intrinsic feeling associated with achievement of goals can help maintain momentum when early successes are built into the change program.[47] Linda Wachner, CEO of underwear maker Warnaco, and, according to *Fortune* magazine, one of the country's toughest bosses, has Friday-night meetings with her management team to discuss and celebrate the week's successes. David Johnson at Campbell's Soups puts tremendous pressure to perform on his employees, but frequently has what he calls "wingdings" to celebrate their performance improvements.[48]

# ORGANIZATIONAL DEVELOPMENT

One general approach to planned change that has gained prominence over the last 30 years or so focuses primarily on people processes as the target of change. This approach—called organization development—is grounded largely in psychology and other behavioral sciences, although more recently it has evolved into a broader approach encompassing such areas as organizational theory, strategy development, and social and technical change.

## The Nature of Organizational Development

**Organizational development (OD)** can be formally defined as "a systemwide application of behavioral science knowledge to the planned development and reinforcement of organizational strategies, structures, and processes for improving an organization's effectiveness."[49] This definition reflects several important features of organizational development. First, OD deals with whole systems (company, department, work group) as opposed to a single individual or a single function within a system. Second, OD uses behavioral science knowledge, as in the areas of leadership, motivation, team functioning, rewards, conflict resolution, and change. This distinguishes it from such things as computer-systems or operations-research types of change approaches. Third, OD involves planned change, but not in the more rigid sense of organizational planning. Rather, it involves more of an adaptive, flexible, ongoing process of diagnosing and solving people-related problems. Fourth, it involves the creation and reinforcement of change with all the implications we have discussed thus far. Fifth, it can encompass strategy, structure, and process changes—although, traditionally, OD has focused on the people processes almost exclusively. Finally, OD focuses on improving organizational effectiveness, in terms of both productivity and quality of work life. An important aspect of the practice of OD is that effectiveness implies that organizations learn to solve their own problems and ultimately deal successfully with issues without the help of an outside consultant who specializes in OD.

    Organizational development is often carried out with the aid of a consultant, either from outside the company or from within, who is separate from the team or group being assisted. An OD practitioner, often called a change agent, facilitates

**organizational development (OD)**
A systemwide application of behavioral science knowledge to the planned development and reinforcement of organizational strategies, structures, and processes for improving an organization's effectiveness.

## FIGURE 19.5

## Organizational Iceberg

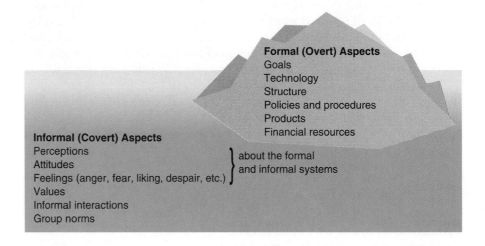

**Formal (Overt) Aspects**
Goals
Technology
Structure
Policies and procedures
Products
Financial resources

**Informal (Covert) Aspects**
Perceptions
Attitudes
Feelings (anger, fear, liking, despair, etc.)
Values
Informal interactions
Group norms

} about the formal and informal systems

*Source:* Wendell L. French and Cecil H. Bell, Jr., *Organization Development: Behavioral Science Interventions for Organization Improvement,* 2d ed. (Englewood Cliffs, NJ, Prentice-Hall, 1978), 14–19.

the change process by structuring learning experiences, diagnosing problems, helping to generate and implement solutions, and encouraging certain types of interaction processes. The actions of these agents of change are generally referred to as interventions because they attempt to hinder the erosion of the organization's effectiveness by modifying the ways its members function. Although OD practitioners usually have specialized training in the behavioral sciences, many have supplemented that expertise with training in other areas to give them the broader perspectives that are useful in facilitating change in today's complex organizations.

The focus of OD is often the hidden or more subtle features of an organization as reflected in Figure 19.5. Although an OD intervention might change more visible features, such as structure, formal authority relationships, policies, and technology, OD tacitly recognizes the impact of the more hidden, informal organization and deals with many of these features to promote organizational effectiveness.

**action research**
An approach to change that involves an ongoing process of joint (with clients) problem discovery, diagnosis, action planning, action implementation, and evaluation.

Most OD interventions use an **action research** approach to change, which encompasses and further defines the steps of the Lewin change model (see Figure 19.6) and involves an ongoing process of joint (consultant with clients) problem discovery, diagnosis, action planning, action implementation, and evaluation. The evaluation uncovers further problems on which to focus, using the action steps again. As problems are successfully addressed, the organization, over time, learns the skills necessary to properly conduct the action research process without an OD practitioner's assistance, and the client-consultant relationship is eventually terminated. This model provides the basic format through which a number of varied OD interventions are implemented.

**FIGURE 19.6**

## Comparison of Action Research Model to Lewin's Change Model

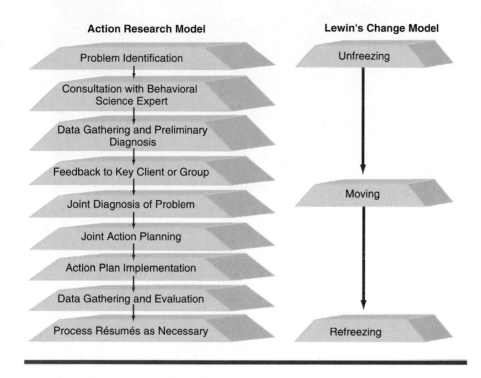

## OD Interventions

The following overview of OD interventions, although not exhaustive, reflects the varied nature of the OD approach to change, as well as the different levels at which change might be targeted. Many OD interventions use some combination of these different approaches, with the number and variety of techniques, tools, and facilitative experiences being limited only by the art, skill, and imagination of the many practitioners.

**Survey Feedback.**    **Survey feedback** involves gathering data through questionnaires and/or personal interviews. The data are tabulated, organized, and returned to the surveyed group by the change agent in anonymous summarized form and used as a vehicle to stimulate discussion about problem areas that the group should address. The content or focus of the survey is usually the behavioral processes that make up this section of your management textbook (leadership, motivation, and so on) although other problems that surface may also be addressed. Data may consist of facts, perceptions, attitudes, and opinions, but tend to be most helpful when they are specific, accurate, limited, relevant, important, and inspiring. How the data are used is as important as the nature of the data itself. Data must be fed back to the client group in such a way as to be accepted as valid, cue the group into important areas, stimulate movement or change, promise a reward if behavior is successfully changed, and generate present and future learning.[50]

**survey feedback**
The gathering of data through questionnaires and/or personal interviews and the return of that data to employees in a structured form to facilitate discussion and problem solving.

Germany's automaker Porsche used process consultation in an effort to reverse the declining sales of its expensive cars. From 1987 to 1993, orders for Porsche cars dropped from 53,000 to 12,500. Porsche CEO Wendelin Wiedeking hired a team of Japanese consultants to observe production work processes, diagnose problems, and implement changes. The process consultants helped assembly workers improve processes by reducing faults by almost 22 percent and by reducing assembly time from 85 hours per unit closer to the Japanese norm of 10 hours per unit. Shown here is a Japanese consultant teaching the Porsche employees how to raise their productivity.

*Source:* VISUM/Jo Röttger/Manager Magazin.

An example of survey feedback occurred in a 15-year-old engineering company whose president felt that some top managers and key employees resisted attempts to make necessary changes, seemed to lack a sense of urgency about performance, and in general did not function well as a team. A consultant (one of the authors of this text) conducted personal interviews with the top managers and discovered that the president's authoritarian and often sarcastic leadership style was a root cause of many of the symptoms the president had perceived. These data were presented during an off-site retreat exercise in which the president was allowed to listen to and to seek clarification of the summarized data but not to defend reported actions. The employees' perceptions were accepted as valid, verified during the exercise, and treated as important. The group, with the consultant's help, designed a program to help the president improve in key interpersonal areas. This example, as well as a number of the other techniques discussed below, should emphasize the importance of the behavioral science training of the change agent. The potential damage, for individuals and the overall organization, is severe if these activities are not planned, structured, and implemented with skill and understanding. Untrained amateurs have no business engaging in this type of endeavor.

**process consultation**

A technique in which a consultant focuses on the dynamic task-related processes and assists the client organization in diagnosing how to enhance these kinds of processes.

**Process Consultation.**    During **process consultation**, a consultant focuses on the dynamic task-related processes—how a client or group sets goals, gathers information, solves problems, and allocates work—and assists the client organization in diagnosing how to enhance these kinds of processes. Again, such areas as communication, conflict resolution, leadership, and decision making may be examined and targeted for improvement. A key difference between process consultation and survey feedback is that the consultant is involved in more direct behavioral observation in the former, while asking others about their perceptions, attitudes, and feelings in the latter.[51] Feedback, diagnosis, action planning, implementation, and evaluation are still a part of both interventions.

**team building**

The use of structured group experiences to help ongoing work teams function more effectively through better decision making, goal setting, and intragroup communications.

**Team Building.**    **Team building** involves using structured group experiences to help ongoing work teams function more effectively through better decision making, goal setting, and intragroup communications. It may also deal with group leadership patterns, roles members perform in the group, and group norms and values. Team building may be part of process consultation or grow out of a diagnosis conducted through the survey-feedback process. Owens Corning's Jackson, Tennessee, plant opened in 1994 with a work force composed mainly of four self-managed work teams. Before the opening, the teams participated in a day-long set of physical-activity challenges designed to enhance communication and problem-solving skills under stress.

**Intergroup team building** is designed to facilitate functioning between two or more groups by helping the groups understand and deal with areas of conflict; debilitating interaction patterns; perceptual discrepancies; norm, goal, and value differences; and lack of coordination. Certain exercises in the Owens Corning training program brought the teams together to work on larger problems requiring group interactions.

> **intergroup team building**
> A set of activities designed to facilitate functioning between two or more groups by helping the groups understand and deal with areas of conflict.

## Role Negotiation.
**Role negotiation** entails structuring interactions between interdependent persons or groups to clarify and negotiate role behaviors and expectations. Role negotiation helps groups and individuals know what their responsibilities are, what actions they should take at different times in dealing with certain issues, and, in general, how they are to work together. This intervention can be a primary focus in itself or part of a broader team building or intergroup team building program.

> **role negotiation**
> The structuring of interactions between interdependent persons or groups to clarify and negotiate role behaviors and expectations.

## Life and Career Planning.
**Life and career planning** involves the use of structured counseling and group discussions, often accompanied by skill and interest testing, to assist employees in planning career paths and integrating life and career goals. These activities can be planned and combined with an overall education and employee development program.

> **life and career planning**
> The use of structured counseling and group discussions to assist employees in planning career paths and integrating life and career goals.

## Third-Party Peacemaking.
**Third-party peacemaking** involves a consultant who facilitates conflict resolution between two individuals. It may entail structuring meetings, facilitating discussions, interpreting communications, pacing interactions, and suggesting compromises or integrative solutions.[52]

> **third-party peacemaking**
> A process in which a consultant facilitates conflict resolution between two individuals.

## Techno-Structural Redesign.
**Techno-structural redesign** is a large-scale intervention that involves redesigning the organizational structure—reporting relations, division of labor, departmentalization, functions, and the like—to better address environmental contingencies and better utilize information and process technologies. A self-designing organization intervention involves employees in the ongoing process of self-examination and redesign to meet rapid environmental changes.

> **techno-structural redesign**
> A large-scale intervention that involves redesigning the organizational structure to better address environmental contingencies and better utilize information and process technologies.

## Job Redesign.
Job redesign, you will remember from Chapter 12, focuses on changing the nature of how tasks are performed and often entails job rotation, job enrichment, and/or job enlargement. Job redesign attempts to enhance not only productivity, but also job involvement and organizational commitment.

## Grid OD.
**Grid OD** is a six-phase overall organization intervention that comprehensively and systematically attempts to enhance personal management style, team functioning, intergroup problem solving, overall organizational functioning, and the ability of the organization to continually improve how it solves its own problems, resolves conflicts, and makes decisions.

> **grid OD**
> A six-phase organization intervention that comprehensively and systematically attempts to enhance personal management style, team functioning, intergroup organizational functioning, and the organization's ability to improve its method for solving problems, resolving conflicts, and making decisions.

# Careers in Organizational Development and Organizational Change

In contrast to such occupations as medicine and law, organizational development is an emerging profession. It is still developing a common body of knowledge, educational requirements, accrediting procedures, a recognized code of ethics, and rules and methods for governing conduct. Yet it is a challenging field, wide open for the individual who has certain skills related to interpersonal interaction and understanding human behavioral processes.

OD practitioners generally are external consultants, internal consultants, or managers who have developed skills in OD interventions (see the types of OD interventions in the chapter). All have common training, skills, and experience in the social processes of organizations (for example, group dynamics, leadership, communication, etc.) and a concern for organizational effectiveness, competitiveness, and bottom-line results. Although behavioral science training (in psychology, organizational behavior, and sociology educational programs) has been the traditional focus of training, the more recent expansion of the OD profession has made it accessible to those skilled in technical, structural, and strategic aspects of organizations.

The term OD practitioner applies to people who act as change agents in a number of ways in organizations. External consultants are generally highly skilled professionals with advanced degrees—doctorates in most cases. They have faculty positions at universities, run their own consulting practices, or work for large consulting firms. Some may specialize in subfields like management development and, more recently, total quality management.

Internal OD consultants often have somewhat lower academic credentials. They may have master's degrees and are often managers with specialized training from specialized organizations, such as the OD Institute, National Training Laboratories, or University Associates. Individuals who aspire to be external con-

sultants often start as internal consultants to learn more about the discipline. Internal consultants assist managers in their own work organizations and implement planned change.

The third category of OD practitioners is line managers. These are individuals who have training in management or a specialized business area (human resources, finance, etc.) but who have developed OD skills through on-the-job experience as well as with off-site training companies who specialize in OD. They have developed a knack for intervening in interpersonal process areas and are willing to implement planned change on their own or in conjunction with an internal or external consultant.

The person aspiring to be an OD practitioner needs a broad-based background in the behavioral sciences, as well as in management. Courses in all aspects of management—and in particular human resources management—should be supplemented with courses in psychology, sociology, communication, anthropology, and even political science. Specialized training in TQM, strategy, operations research, statistical quality control, and even economics and finance may prove helpful, since the field has expanded to encompass a broad range of intervention areas in recent years.

OD practitioners earn very good salaries, but they have been observed to experience burnout if they stay in the profession for many years. They must constantly deal with ambiguous situations that involve interpersonal problems as well as personal difficulties that generate a high level of stress. For the person with the skills and temperament, the OD practitioner job can be one of the most rewarding of the helping professions.

*Source:* Thomas G. Cummings and Christopher G. Worley, *Organization Development and Change,* 5th ed.(St. Paul: West Publishing Co., 1993).

**Comment on Box:** Ask a local consultant to speak to your class on his or her career and to share experiences managing and instigating change in organizations. Students will probably have many questions about careers in consulting.

**Using OD Interventions Successfully.** The success of OD interventions depends on matching the correct intervention to the organizational need, the skill of the OD practitioner at implementing the program, and the readiness of the client organization to accept the intervention. Because OD emphasizes joint diagnosis and action planning, acceptance of the process and the ultimate change strategies is often very high.

It should be apparent from the information presented in this chapter that organizational change is both a complex and pervasive phenomenon. Understanding the process of planned change and developing skills in various change techniques and processes will likely be a key competency for successful managers of today's intricate business organizations.

## SUMMARY AND REVIEW

- **Define organizational change and explain the dimensions and types of change.** Organizational change refers to modifying the behaviors or ideas of an organization or its units. Organizational changes are often a result of reactions to internal or external environmental forces. Organizational change varies in how extensively it is planned (reactive to planned change), how extreme the change is (incremental to quantum change), how much members are involved in learning how to conduct future change, where the change is targeted (level and/or functional area), and in whether the organization needs to be loosened up or more highly organized. Different types of change reflect an overall focus on different features of organizational functioning. Strategy changes focus on the nature of how the organization will conduct its business and meet its market demands. Organizational structure and design changes deal with how work will be organized, delegated, and managed. Technology changes focus on changing machinery or equipment that enhances either the products of the company or its means of producing the product or service. Human process changes focus on the interpersonal processes and overall cultural components that influence or make up the way people interact in the organization.

- **Interpret three models of change, particularly the steps involved in the comprehensive model of change.** Kurt Lewin's model of change views change as a process of "unfreezing" the forces that keep an organization functioning at a certain level (state A), "moving" or changing to new behaviors (state B), and then "refreezing" the behavior into a new equilibrium or behavioral level (state C). The congruence model characterizes change as an interrelated set of transformational processes and structures that turn organizational and environmental inputs into organization, group, and individual outputs.

  The comprehensive model of planned change involves a sequence of management activities that are important for quantum change. Managers first must recognize a need for change by scanning the internal and external environments. Then they must motivate the

change by preparing people for change (unfreezing) and overcoming the resistance to change that inevitably arises. Managers must also create and communicate a vision of the future that inspires commitment to the change process and the desired future state, and develop political support for change with powerful constituencies. The transition must also be successfully managed through activity planning, commitment planning, and use of management structures to control the process. Finally, momentum for the change must be maintained by providing resources for the change, developing new competencies and skills, reinforcing new behaviors, and building support for the change agents.

- **Determine the major causes of resistance to change and recommend how managers can deal with change resistance.** Resistance to change may occur because of uncertainty and insecurity, reaction to the way change is presented, threatened vested interests and real loss, cynicism and lack of trust, perceptual differences, and a simple lack of understanding. Specific tactics for addressing resistance include education and communication, participation and involvement, facilitation and support, negotiation and agreement, manipulation and co-optation, and, when all else fails, explicit and implicit coercion.

- **Explain organizational development (OD) and summarize the major OD interventions.** Organizational development is a systemwide application of behavioral science knowledge to the planned development and reinforcement of organizational strategies, structures, and processes for improving an organization's effectiveness. OD often involves the use of change consultants or practitioners who help the organization implement an action research approach to change by jointly discovering and diagnosing problems, developing and implementing action plans, and evaluating results and repeating the process. Specific OD interventions that typically use the action research approach include survey feedback, process consultation, team and intergroup development, role negotiation, life and career planning, third-party peacemaking, techno-structural redesign, job design, and grid OD.

- **Assess an organization's change program.** Based on what you've learned in this chapter, you should be able to assess the change program implemented in the "Business Dilemma" box and project future actions for the department.

## Key Terms and Concepts

organizational change *554*
performance gap *556*
reactive change *557*
planned change *557*
incremental change *558*
quantum change *558*
unfreezing *561*
moving *561*

refreezing *562*
congruence model of change *563*
comprehensive model of
  planned change *564*
transition state *570*
organizational development (OD) *573*
action research *574*
survey feedback *575*

process consultation *576*
team building *576*
intergroup team building *577*
role negotiation *577*
life and career planning *577*
third-party peacemaking *577*
techno-structural redesign *577*
grid OD *577*

## Ready Recall

1. What external forces necessitate changes in the way companies do business? What internal forces can cause a change in the way a company does business? Supply examples of how these forces prompt change.
2. Explain the five dimensions of change along which organizations can be analyzed to determine causes and solutions to problems.
3. Name and briefly explain four different types of organizational change.
4. Compare and contrast Lewin's model of change with the congruence model of change.

5. What are the major steps in the comprehensive model of planned change?
6. What are the major sources of resistance to change in organizations? List six major strategies for overcoming resistance to change.
7. What is organizational development (OD)?
8. List and explain at least seven major types of OD interventions.

## Expand Your Experience

1. Think about the external and internal forces that have affected your college or university in the recent past, are affecting it now, and will affect it in the not-too-distant future. What changes have you seen and what ones do you think will be necessary in the future in the areas of strategy, structure and design, technology, and people processes or culture to deal with these forces of change?
2. Find and interview the owner of a fairly small business (25 to 75 employees) in your community that has been in existence for at least ten years. Discuss the major changes he or she has made in the business and analyze how the changes came about and how they were implemented and sustained.

Compare and contrast these changes to the models of change discussed in your text—in particular, the comprehensive model of planned change. (This would be a good project to do with one or two fellow classmates.)

3. Many employees in business have been asked to undergo radical changes in how they do their jobs. Find an employee who has faced a major change (it could be a friend, relative, classmate, etc.) and discuss his or her resistance to the change, including why he or she felt resistance. How was it overcome? How did the company try to overcome resistance? Think of a similar change you've been asked to make and analyze your own sources of resistance to change.

**CASE**

# Organizational Change at General Electric

Although other megafirms, such as General Motors and IBM, have fallen on hard times in the 1990s, General Electric thrives. Over the past 15 years, net income has "nearly tripled" and in the past 5 years, it has doubled. Since 1981, CEO John F. Welch (also known as "Neutron Jack") has led GE through a dramatic change, even a "corporate revolution."

When Welch became CEO in 1981, GE wasn't in financial trouble, but its growth in earnings and productivity was, at best, only average. The firm's entrenched bureaucracy made decisions slowly, never finding new answers. Innovation was nonexistent. Increased competition and limited growth opportunities spurred the need for change.

In the first phase of the corporate revolution, GE refocused its business strategy. New CEO Welch announced that GE's goal is to have each of its businesses "rank first or second in its global market." The company achieved this goal by 1987 by concentrating on its core strengths and eliminating bureaucratic obstacles to change.

As part of its change in business strategy, Welch knew that more than products had to be changed—people had to change as well. Thus, since 1981, GE has also undergone a planned change in organization culture. The change process included three phases, "Awakening," "Envisioning," and "Re-architecting." That is, the company had to *awake* to the need for change, *envision* what that change would be, then *re-architect* or *rebuild* the company according to that vision. According to Welch, there is a set of basic values that drive GE:

1. Create a clear, simple reality-based customer-focused vision and communicate it straightforwardly to all constituencies.

2. Understand accountability and commitment.

3. Have a passion for excellence.

4. Have the self-confidence to empower others and behave in a boundaryless fashion.

5. Have the capacity to develop global brains and global sensitivity.

6. Stimulate and relish change.

7. Have enormous energy and the ability to energize and invigorate others.

Once these values were derived, both the values themselves and the need to adopt them were communicated, widely and frequently, to all employees. Naturally, this process of value change did not happen overnight. Technological barriers, political barriers, and cultural barriers all hindered change. People were used to doing things a certain way and were fearful of change. But, change did happen. Sudden breakthroughs occurred, often succeeding periods where there was no apparent change. But, according to Welch, it was during these periods of no apparent change that trust, confidence, and teams were growing.

The change GE underwent was without boundaries, involving "the ability to work up and down the hierarchy, across functions and geographies, and with suppliers and customers." Without boundaries, communications could take place faster and with less resistance. Decisions could be made quickly, giving GE the ability to respond to the dynamic external environment. As Welch says, "If you're not flexible enough to handle rapid change and make big decisions, you won't win."

GE looks quite different now. Layers of middle managers are gone, as is much of the paperwork those managers were responsible for. With fewer managers, employees have the opportunity to try out new ideas and to learn from their failures—without a manager looking over their shoulder. However, employees are held more accountable than before. In GE's 360-degree evaluations, employees receive their performance appraisals from peers, subordinates, and even customers, as well as from their superiors. According to Welch, these are the "roughest evaluations you can get." He says you may be able to hide weak performance from your boss, but you can't hide weak performance from those with whom you work on a daily basis.

The increased emphasis on communications, in all directions, is also an integral part of the revolution. In "Work-Out" meetings, employees from all levels of the organization are given the chance to see the connection between their work and GE as a whole. Problems are brought out and addressed. For example, in one session (lasting five days), managers expressed concerns about teamwork and problem solving. The results were that participants left, having signed contracts committing them to specific steps to resolve these issues.

In the new GE, employees are empowered and encouraged to adopt an entrepreneurial spirit and contribute their ideas to GE's success. For example, management, unions, and employees collaborated to return a GE appliance factory to profitability, to the benefit of both GE and the employees (who would otherwise have lost their jobs). Reward systems have been redesigned so that employees' salaries and bonuses are tied to their performance.

GE certainly isn't the only organization to have launched a change process. But at GE, change isn't seen as a special project or a one-time process. Rather, GE has incorporated the idea of constant change and adaptation to change into its day-to-day operations. For example, GE has redesigned its manufacturing processes so that *customers'* changing needs can be met with a minimum of time and expense.

But, can change be painless? It certainly wasn't for the GE employees who were laid off in the 1980s. The remaining 291,000 GE employees have had to abandon their old tried-and-true ways of doing things and learn new approaches to their work. Those that couldn't, didn't last. According to Jack Welch, "We've had managers at GE who couldn't change, who kept telling us to leave them alone. They wanted to sit back, to keep things the way they were. And that's just what they did—until they and most of their staffs had to go." Business researchers constantly tell companies such as GE that they must learn to adapt and change and constantly innovate and improve. GE certainly seems to have taken this advice to heart.

*Sources:* Lawrence A. Bossidy, "Why Do We Waste Time Doing This?" *Across the Board* (May 1991): 17–21; Charles R. Day, "Leaders, We Hardly Knew Ye," *Industry Week,* April 18, 1994, 7; Robert Frigo and Robert Janson, "GE's Financial Services Operation Achieves Quality Results Through "Work-Out" Process," *National Productivity Review* (Winter 1993/1994): 53–61; "A Master Class in Radical Change,"

*Fortune,* December 13, 1993, 82–90; Stephen W. Quickel, "CEO of the Year: Welch on Welch," *Financial World,* April 3, 1990, 62–70; Thomas M. Rohan, "Factories of the Future," special section, *Industry Week,* March 21, 1988, 44; Noel M. Tichy, "Revolutionize Your Company," *Fortune,* December 13, 1993, 114–118; Noel Tichy and Ram Charan, "Speed, Simplicity, Self-Confidence: An Interview with Jack Welch," *Harvard Business Review* (September–October 1989): 112-120; Michael Vesperel, "When Change Becomes the Norm," *Industry Week,* March 16, 1992, 35–38; John F. Welch, Jr., "The Speed and Spirit of a Boundaryless Company," *Executive Speeches* (June/July 1993): 37–39; and John F. Welch, Jr., "Working Out of a Tough Year," *Executive Excellence* (April 1992): 14–16.

## Questions

1. What was the purpose of organizational change at GE? Would other organizations have the same motivation to change?
2. Is organizational change an easy or painless process? Should it be? Can it be? Who might be most affected by organization change? Who might adjust best to change?

3. Compare GE's model of change to the Lewin model and to the transition state model of change. What differences do you see? What similarities exist between the three models?

---

### STRENGTHEN YOUR SKILLS
## *Managing Change*

This is the final exercise of Part Four where you will use the *Square Wheels*™ theme to help you learn more about management. This is a simple exercise to help you think about some of the issues involved when change occurs in an organization.

### Best Practices

Because everyone is so busy pushing and pulling the wagons in organizations, it can be difficult to find time to share ideas and perspectives. To overcome this inherent roadblock to managing change successfully, managers need to make an effort to recog-

nize, share, and celebrate throughout the organization when one part of the organization successfully implements change. The success of one department can serve as positive pressure toward more change. Also, managers can avoid a great deal of frustration if they understand two important principles of change: (1) Many people will, by nature, resist change; and (2) managing change is a gradual process involving many steps—with both successes and failures along the way.

The following series of illustrations tells a story of change in pictures (you will provide the words following the instructions on page 584):

**FIGURE 19.7**

**Best Practices**

Caption 1: _____

Caption 2: _____

Caption 3: _____

Caption 4: _____

Caption 5: _____

The captions with explanations for each of the five cartoon illustrations are scrambled below. You will write the words to this story by transferring the correct caption under each of the five illustrations.

### Collaboration and Celebration

As organizations learn to share Best Practices effectively and efficiently, performance will improve throughout the whole wagon train.

### Put on the Skids

Someone will always be resisting the change. Sometimes the resistance will come at the front of the train from a leader who has not been actively involved by the change effort.

### The Wagon Train Can Go Only As Fast As the Slowest Wagon

In most work groups, better ideas have already been implemented in an individual or small work-group basis. Top performers are already doing things differently, but the organization is too busy to see the differences. The need for perspective, celebration, and collaboration exists throughout the organization, and groups must look for ways to share Best Practices effectively and efficiently throughout the organization.

### Innovation Explosion

The group will eventually progress faster and faster, and innovation will begin to stimulate more innovation.

### Change:  Incremental, Discontinuous, Random, and Slow

Implementation of change across departments is incremental and discontinuous, and the improvement process occurs somewhat randomly. It's usually slower than management would like.

*Source:*  Adapted with permission from Scott J. Simmerman, *The Book of Square Wheels: A Tool Kit for Facilitators and Team Leaders,* 3rd ed. (Taylors, SC: Performance Management Company, 1994), 41–42, 68, 79.

# Operations *and* Control

# Managing Operations *and* Increasing Productivity

## Outline

## After reading this chapter, you will be able to:

- Define operations management and identify the activities associated with it.
- Determine the elements involved in planning and designing an operations system.
- Specify some of the techniques that managers may use to manage inventory.
- Assess the importance of quality in the operations management process.
- Define productivity, explain why it is important, and propose ways to improve it.
- Evaluate operations issues in a franchise operation.

## Toys 'R' Us Competes with a New Twist

Michael Goldstein, chairman of Toys 'R' Us, believes that if his company is to maintain its competitive advantage, its operations must focus on four main factors: service, selection, low prices, and fun. Toys 'R' Us has managed to capture and hold 21 percent of the United States's $17-billion-a-year toy market. However, Toys 'R' Us cannot ignore tough competitors such as Wal-Mart—which has grabbed 10.4 percent of the U.S. toy market—as they are always ready and willing to capitalize on the weaknesses and shortcomings of competitors. To stay ahead of the competition, Goldstein believes that Toys 'R' Us must change the way in which it offers its services. According to Goldstein, the com-pany already offers good prices and a huge selection, but it must go a step further by making shopping entertaining for customers. In other words, shopping should be fun and customers should really like shopping at Toys 'R' Us.

One step Toys 'R' Us has taken to help adult customers enjoy their shopping experience more has been the addition of employees called "Geoffrey Helpers" (named after the giraffe character used in advertisements). These employees, who wear smocks that say "ask me" on the back, patrol the aisles, particularly areas with big-ticket items such as bicycles and baby furniture. Also, the company has installed UPC scanners in aisles so that customers can check shelf prices for themselves.

To make shopping more fun for younger customers and to make use of every inch of each Toys 'R' Us store, the company is opening Books 'R' Us sections. These are mini-bookstores which have been carved out of excess backroom space that has been freed by improved inventory management. Books 'R' Us sections are plushly decorated with carpeting, sharp presentation, and bright lighting (this type of decor contrasts with the decor in the rest of the Toys 'R' Us store); designing and furnishing costs tend to run between $20,000 and $30,000 per section. Each section will carry approximately 1,900 book titles. In addition to making shopping more fun for kids and using capacity more efficiently, Toys 'R' Us hopes that these book and reading sections will send the message to kids that reading can be fun!

Toys 'R' Us takes "fun shopping" very seriously and continues to find new and inventive ways to enrich the shopping experience for its customers. The company is currently testing in-store formats dedicated to Lego building blocks, party supplies, and stuffed animals.

*Source:* Susan Caminiti, "After You Win the Fun Begins," *Fortune,* May 2, 1994, 76.

*introduction*

As the opening vignette illustrates, the operations function of an organization should not become stagnant. Environmental changes (for example, in consumer demand) make it necessary for the operations function to change as well. Frequently, these environmental changes will affect the resources the organization needs to attain its goals. In all societies, there is a limited supply of resources such as land, labor, capital, knowledge, time, and raw materials. Using these resources efficiently is critical not only to fulfilling social needs and demands (such as education and health care) and maintaining competitiveness, but also to sheer survival. These conditions also hold true for businesses and other organizations. If a company uses its resources wastefully, more efficient competitors are likely to gain an advantage in the marketplace and possibly even put the less efficient company out of business. Within an organization, the operations function is responsible for ensuring that the firm uses resources as effectively and efficiently as possible.

In this chapter we discuss the role of operations management in acquiring and managing the resources necessary to create goods and services, in planning the processes that will transform those resources into finished products, in overseeing the transformation process, and in ensuring that the products are of the quality expected by customers. Additionally, we look at the way technology has changed production and operations and the increasing importance of productivity.

## THE NATURE OF OPERATIONS MANAGEMENT

As we have said before, the three main functions within a business are finance, marketing, and operations. **Operations management (OM)** is the development and administration of the activities involved in transforming resources into goods and services. Operations managers oversee the transformation process, the planning and designing of operations systems, and the managing of inventory, quality, and productivity. Operations management is the "core" of most organizations because it is responsible for the creation of the organization's products.

**operations management (OM)**
The development and administration of the activities involved in transforming resources into goods and services.

### The Transformation Process

At the heart of operations management is the transformation process through which **inputs** (resources such as labor, money, materials, information, energy) are converted into **outputs** (goods, services, and ideas). The transformation process combines inputs in predetermined ways using different equipment, administrative procedures, and technology to create a product (Figure 20.1).

Transformation may take place through one or more processes. In a business that manufactures oak furniture, for example, inputs pass through several processes before being turned into the final outputs—furniture to sell to customers (Table 20.1). The furniture maker must first strip the oak trees of their bark and saw them into appropriate sizes—one step in the transformation process. Next, the firm dries the strips of oak lumber, a second form of transformation. Third, the dried wood is routed into its appropriate shape and made smooth. Fourth, workers assemble the wood pieces, then treat, and stain or varnish the piece of assembled furniture. Finally, the completed piece is stored until delivery can be made.

**inputs**
Resources such as labor, money, materials, information, and energy that are converted to outputs in the transformation process.

**outputs**
Goods, services, and ideas that are converted from inputs in the transformation process.

FIGURE 20.1

## The Transformation Process of Operations Management

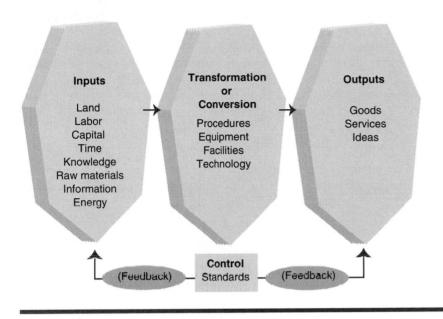

Different types of transformation processes take place in organizations that provide services, such as banks, colleges, and most nonprofit organizations. A bank transforms inputs such as employees, time, money, and equipment by way of processes such as filling out loan applications and repayment agreements, cashing checks, and accepting deposits. Outputs of these processes include automobile loans, home mortgages, checking and savings accounts, and other financial products. In your college or university, inputs such as information, classrooms, and teachers are used to produce well-educated students, hopefully, who possess the necessary skills and qualifications to successfully enter the professional job market. In this setting, transformation processes include lecturing, textbook reading, and computer simulations. Transformation processes occur in all organizations,

**Teaching Note:** Have students compare Figure 20.1 to Figures 19.3 and 19.4 in the previous chapter on organizational change and development. Remind students that this model of transformation works for people as well as organizational systems.

TABLE 20.1

## Inputs, Outputs, and Transformation Processes in the Manufacture of Oak Furniture

| Inputs | Transformation | Outputs |
|---|---|---|
| oak trees | cutting or sawing | oak furniture |
| labor | routing | |
| information/knowledge | measuring | |
| stain or varnish | assembling | |
| router and saw | staining/varnishing | |
| warehouse space/time | storing | |

regardless of what they produce or their objectives. For most organizations, the ultimate objective is for the produced outputs to be worth more than the combined costs of the inputs.

Note, in Figure 20.1, that the operations manager is concerned with all activities that directly relate to the production of outputs. To ensure that this process takes place within acceptable standards of quality and rate of output, managers control the production process by taking measurements (feedback) at various points in the transformation process and comparing them to previously established standards. If there is any deviation between the actual and desired outputs, the manager may wish to take some sort of corrective action.

## Historical Perspective

Historically, operations was known as "production management," or "manufacturing," primarily because of the view that operations was limited to the manufacture of physical goods. The focus was on methods and techniques required to operate a factory efficiently. The change from "production" to "operations" represents a broadening of the discipline to include the increasing importance of service organizations. Additionally, the term "operations" reflects managers' interest in viewing the operations function in its totality—including procedural considerations—rather than simply as an analysis of inputs and outputs.

Today, OM includes a wide range of organizational activities and situations outside of manufacturing, such as health care, food service, banking, entertainment, retailing, education, transportation, and government. Thus, we use the terms **manufacturing** and **production** interchangeably to represent the activities and processes used in making *tangible* products, whereas we use the broader term **operations** to describe those processes used in the making of *both tangible and intangible products.*

**manufacturing**
The activities and processes used in making tangible products; interchangeable with production.

**production**
The activities and processes used in making tangible products; interchangeable with manufacturing.

**operations**
Those processes used in the making of both tangible and intangible products.

## Operations in Service Businesses

Manufacturers and service providers are similar, yet different. For example, both types of organizations must make design and operating decisions. An automobile manufacturer must determine where to locate its factory and how large the factory should be; a bank must determine where to locate its main office and how large a building is required. Manufacturers and service providers must both schedule and control operations as well as allocate necessary resources. Though manufacturers and service providers often perform similar activities, they also differ in several respects. We can classify these differences in five basic ways.

First, manufacturers and service providers differ in the nature and consumption of their output. For example, the term *manufacturer* implies a firm that makes tangible products, such as radios, basketballs, or watches. A service provider, on the other hand, produces intangible outputs such as airline travel or photo processing. The very nature of the service provider's output requires a higher degree of customer contact than does the output of the manufacturer. Also, the actual performance of the service typically occurs at the point of consumption. When you go to a doctor for an illness, for example, you must be physically present for the doctor to make the exam and issue a diagnosis and prescription. Ford and other automakers, on the other hand, can separate the production of a truck from its actual use. Consequently, manufacturing can occur in an isolated environment, away from the customer; whereas service providers, due to their need for customer contact, are often more limited than manufacturers in selecting work methods, assigning jobs, scheduling work, and exercising control over operations.

A second way to classify differences between manufacturers and service providers has to do with the uniformity of inputs. Manufacturers typically have more control over the amount of variability of inputs than do service providers. For example, each customer entering a bank is likely to require different services due to differing needs and wants, whereas many of the tasks required to manufacture a truck are the same across each unit of output, such as painting the truck or putting tires on it. Because of this variability, the products of service organizations tend to be more "customized" than those of their manufacturing counterparts. Consider, for example, a haircut versus a bottle of shampoo. The haircut is much more likely to incorporate your specific desires (customization) than is the bottle of shampoo.

Manufacturers and service providers also differ in the uniformity of their output. Because of the human element inherent in providing services, each service tends to be performed differently. Not all bank tellers, for example, wait on customers in the same way. Therefore, a service output tends to have high variability. If a barber or stylist performs fifteen haircuts in a day, it is unlikely that any two of them will be exactly the same. In manufacturing, the high degree of automation available allows manufacturers to generate uniform outputs; thus, the operations are more smooth and efficient.

A fourth point of difference is the amount of labor required to produce an output. Service providers are generally more labor-intensive (require more labor hours) because of the high level of customer contact, perishability of the output (must be consumed immediately), and high degree of variation of inputs (customization). A manufacturer, on the other hand, is likely to be more capital-intensive because of the machinery and technology used in the mass production of highly similar goods.

The final classification of differences between service providers and manufacturers involves the measurement of productivity for each output provided. Manufacturers find measuring productivity much more straightforward because of the tangibility of the output and its high degree of uniformity. For the service provider, variations in demand (for example, higher demand for home loans in some months than in others), variations in service requirements from job to job, and the intangibility of the product make productivity measurement more difficult. Consider, for example, how much easier it is to measure the productivity of employees involved in the production of 100 automobiles as opposed to serving the needs of 100 bank or barbershop customers.

It is convenient and simple to think of organizations as being either manufacturers or service providers, as we have been doing here. In reality, however, most organizations are a combination of the two, with both tangible and intangible qualities embodied in what they produce. For example, automobile manufacturers provide customer services such as toll-free hotlines and warranty protection, while banks may sell checks and other tangible products that complement their primarily intangible product offering. Thus, we consider "products" to include both tangible physical goods as well as intangible service offerings. It is the level of tangibility of its principal product that tends to classify a company as either a manufacturer or a service provider. From an OM standpoint, this level of tangibility greatly influences the nature of its operational processes and procedures.

# PLANNING AND DESIGNING OPERATIONS SYSTEMS

Before a company can produce any output or product, it must first decide what it will produce and for what group of customers. It must then determine what processes it will use to make these products as well as the facilities it needs to produce them. These decisions make up operations planning. Although planning was once the sole realm of the production and operations department, today's more successful companies involve all departments within an organization, particularly marketing and research and development, in these decisions.

## Planning the Product

Before making the product, a company must determine what consumers want and then design a product to satisfy that want. Most companies use marketing research to determine the kinds of goods and services to produce and the features they must possess to satisfy consumers. Marketing research can also help gauge the demand for the product and identify how much consumers are willing to pay for it. Once management has developed an idea for a product that customers will buy, it must then plan how to produce the product.

**Example:** Planning the product became easier at Boeing Co. as it used a team approach to group experts in design, manufacturing, maintenance, and finance to speed new-product development.

Within a company, the engineering or research and development department is charged with turning a product idea into a workable design that can be produced economically. In smaller companies, a single individual (perhaps the owner) may be solely responsible for this crucial activity. Regardless of who is responsible for product design, planning does not stop with a blueprint for a product or a description of a service; it must also work out efficient production of the product to ensure that enough is available to satisfy consumer demand. How does an automobile company transform steel, aluminum, glass, and other materials into a new car design? How does a day care center use toys, educational materials, and human labor to teach and care for children while their parents work? Operations managers must plan for the types and quantities of materials needed to produce the product, the skills and quantity of people needed to make the product, as well as the actual processes through which the inputs must pass in their transformation to outputs.

## Designing the Operations Processes

Before a firm can begin production, it must first determine the appropriate method of transforming resources into the desired product. Often, consumers' specific needs and desires dictate a process. Customer needs, for example, require that all ¾ inch bolts have the same basic thread size, function, and quality; if they did not, engineers and builders could not rely on ¾ inch bolts in their construction projects. A bolt manufacturer, then, will likely use a standardized process so that every ¾ inch bolt produced is like every other one. On the other hand, a bridge often must be customized so that it is appropriate for the site and expected load; furthermore, the bridge must be constructed on site rather than in a factory. It should be noted that various processes are used when manufacturing a product. For example, though most automobiles are made on an assembly line, some of the lines are highly automated while others are highly labor intensive. Planning the operational processes for the organization involves two important areas: capacity planning and facilities planning.

The BFGoodrich Company made a long-term capacity planning decision to expand the aircraft maintenance, repair, and overhaul services of its Tramco subsidiary. This new hangar in Everett, Washington, doubles BFG's capacity for providing aircraft servicing. The 635,000-square-foot hangar accommodates 13 narrow-body or four wide-body planes at one time. The added capacity strengthens BFG's position with international carriers, where there is a growing demand for wide-body aircraft overhaul services.
*Source:* Courtesy of BFGoodrich.

## Planning Capacity

The term **capacity** refers to the maximum load that an organizational unit can carry or operate at a given point in time. The unit of measurement may be a worker or machine, a department, a branch, or even an entire plant. Maximum capacity can be stated in terms of the inputs or outputs provided. For example, an electric plant might state plant capacity in terms of the maximum number of kilowatt hours that can be produced without causing a power outage, while a restaurant might state capacity in terms of the maximum number of customers that can be effectively—comfortably and courteously—served at any one particular time.

Capacity-planning decisions can be both long term and short term. Long-term decisions tend to focus on overall capacity levels, such as with building a new plant. Short-term capacity decisions relate more to the effects that variations in demand have on capacity, as with the fluctuating demand of a seasonal product (such as snow sleds). Usually, long-term capacity decisions are based on demand that has been forecasted over some time horizon. This forecasted demand is converted into capacity needs or requirements. Short-term capacity decisions are based more on deviations from the norm or average demand. Such deviations are critical to the operations system as they may result in ideal capacity at some points in time while resulting in the inability to meet demand at others. U.S. automakers, for example, are struggling to add capacity because demand for trucks has far outstripped supply. GM is running its truck factories round-the-clock, while Ford is switching some plants from making cars to trucks. However, none of the automakers wants to invest in new plants for fear that the truck boom won't last.[1]

Efficiently planning the organization's capacity needs, whether for the long or short run, is an important process for the operations manager. Capacity levels that fall short can result in unmet demand, and consequently, lost customers. On the other hand, when there is more capacity available than needed, operating costs are driven up needlessly due to unused and often expensive resources. To avoid such situations, organizations must accurately forecast demand and then plan capacity based on these forecasts. Another reason for the importance of efficient capacity planning has to do with long-term commitment of resources. Often, once a capacity decision—such as factory size—has been implemented, it is very difficult to change it without incurring substantial costs.

**capacity**
The maximum load that an organizational unit can carry or operate at a given point in time.

**Critical Thinking Challenge:** What determines capacity in area organizations? Have students contact an area manufacturer or service organization and gather information on what determines capacity in the organization as well as how the business plans for capacity needs in the short term and in the future. Have students report their findings to the class.

## Planning Facilities

Once a company knows what process it will use to create its product(s), it then can design and build an appropriate facility in which to make it. Many products are manufactured in factories, but others are produced in stores, at home, or where they ultimately will be used. Manufacturers must decide where to locate their operations facilities, what layout is best for producing their particular product, and even what technology to apply to the transformation process.

**Facility Location.**    Where to locate an organization's facilities is a significant question because, once the decision has been made and implemented, the firm must live with it due to the high costs involved. When a company decides to relocate or open a new facility at a new location, it must pay careful attention to the alternatives for such a move. U.S. executives, for example, are searching for sites in Europe in order to attract greater sales in the 345-million-consumer European Community market. Choosing the right site takes time, patience, and agreement among top managers, and veterans of site searches have learned that the process requires a lot of homework and solid objectives.[2] Though the critical location factors vary by firm, the following are among the most common concerns:  proximity to market, availability of raw materials, availability of transportation, availability of power, climatic influences, availability of labor, community characteristics (quality of life), and taxes and inducements.

The facility-location decision is complex because it involves the evaluation of many factors, some of which cannot be measured with precision. Because of the long-term impact of the decision, however, it is one that cannot be taken lightly.

**Facility Layout.**    Arranging the physical layout of an organization is a complex, highly technical task. Some industrial architects specialize in the design and layout of certain types of businesses. There are three basic layouts:  fixed-position, process, and product.

A company using a **fixed-position layout** has a central location for the product and brings all resources required to create the product to that location. The product—perhaps an office building, a microwave relay station, a house, a hydroelectric plant, or a bridge—does not move. Companies relying on fixed-position layouts are typically involved in large, complex tasks such as construction or exploration. They generally make a unique product, rely on highly skilled labor, produce very few units, and have high production costs per unit.

Firms that use a **process layout** organize the transformation process into departments that group related processes. A metal fabrication plant, for example, may have a cutting department, a drilling department, and a polishing department. A hospital may have an X-ray unit, an obstetrics unit, and so on. Organizations using a process layout deal with smaller-scale products than those requiring a fixed-position layout. Their products are not necessarily unique but significantly different. Doctors, custom-made cabinet makers, commercial printers, and advertising agencies are examples. Such firms tend to create products to customers' specifications and produce relatively few units of each product. Because of the low level of output, the cost per unit of product is generally high.

The **product layout** design requires that production be broken down into relatively simple tasks assigned to workers positioned along the line. Workers remain in one location, and the product moves from one worker to another. Each person in turn performs his or her required tasks or activities. An assembly line is the clas-

**fixed-position layout**
Facility layout in which the organization has a central location for the product and brings all resources required to create the product to that location.

**process layout**
Facility layout in which firms organize the transformation process into departments that group related procedures.

**product layout**
Facility layout in which production is broken down into relatively simple tasks assigned to workers positioned along the line, and the product moves from worker to worker.

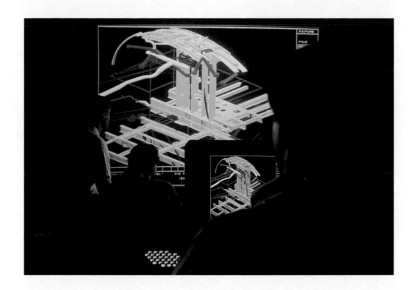

In developing new commercial and military aircraft, the Boeing Company uses computers for design and preassembly. Computer-assisted design allows Boeing engineers to verify how parts will fit together before they are manufactured. The use of computers in product design and preassembly is helping Boeing reduce design errors, rework, and the need to build expensive engineering prototypes.

*Source:* Courtesy of the Boeing Co.

sic example of a product layout. Examples of products produced on assembly lines are automobiles, television sets, vacuum cleaners, toothpaste, and meals from a cafeteria. Organizations using a product layout are characterized by their standardized product, the large number of units produced, and the relatively low unit cost of production.

Many companies actually use a combination of layout designs. For example, an automobile manufacturer may rely on an assembly line (product layout) but may also use a process layout to manufacture parts. A commercial sign manufacturer may rely on the process layout but also use an assembly line to assemble the components of a sign. No matter which facility layout is used, the cost and efficiency of operations depend on the degree to which the layout works effectively.

**Technology.**   Technology is the application of knowledge (tools, processes, procedures) to solve problems. Every industry has a basic, underlying technology that dictates the nature of its transformation process. The steel industry continually tries to improve steelmaking techniques; the health care industry performs research into medical technologies and pharmaceuticals to improve the quality of health care service. Two developments that have strongly influenced the operations of many businesses are computer applications and robotics.

**Computer Applications.**   Computers have been used for decades and on a relatively large scale since IBM introduced its 650 series in the late 1950s. Most of the early applications were of a recordkeeping nature—for example, processing payrolls and maintaining inventory records. Modern businesses are highly dependent on computers for many functions; many of these uses will be discussed in Chapter 21.

The operations function uses computers in the product-design phase as well as in the actual manufacturing of products. These applications are generally referred to as **computer-assisted design (CAD)** and **computer-assisted manufacturing (CAM)**, which are computerized approaches that link the design and manufacturing areas, making information readily available. At Ford Motor Company, for instance, a CAD/CAM system facilitates new product development across its many operating sites, including 15 European countries. Ford's CAD/CAM system plays a critical role in achieving its goals of reducing the time

**computer-assisted design (CAD)**
A computerized approach in the operations function that links the design and manufacturing areas, making information readily available.

**computer-assisted manufacturing (CAM)**
A computerized approach in the operations function that links the manufacturing and design areas, making information readily available.

to get a new vehicle from concept to showroom, communicating with customers, providing more product value for money, and using all resources to reduce the cost of design and manufacturing.[3]

Companies may also use computers to monitor the transformation process, gathering information about the equipment used to produce the product, as well as about the product itself, as it goes from one stage of the transformation process to the next. The computer provides information to an operator who may, if necessary, take corrective action. In the monitoring mode, the computer itself does not take the corrective action, although in some highly automated systems, computers can actually control the production process. A computer compares data generated by the transformation process concerning the operation of the equipment and certain product characteristics with predetermined standards. If these comparisons are favorable, the process continues; if they are unfavorable, the computer is programmed to take corrective action. No direct intervention by human beings is needed.

In **flexible manufacturing**, computers can direct machinery to adapt to different versions of similar operations. For example, with instructions from a computer, one machine can be programmed to carry out its function for several different versions of an engine without shutting down the production line to refit the machines. Also, an athletic shoe manufacturer might invest in a flexible manufacturing system that allows it to make ten different styles and sizes of shoes on the same machinery.

Computers will continue to make strong inroads into production and operations on two fronts—one dealing with the technology involved in manufacturing and one dealing with the administrative functions and processes used by operations managers. The operations manager must be willing to work with computers and must develop a high degree of computer literacy.

**Robotics.**    The industrial robot is less glamorous and considerably less sophisticated than fictional robots such as R2D2 and C3PO in the *Star Wars* movies. An **industrial robot** is a machine designed to move material, parts, tools, or specialized devices through variable programmed motions, for the performance of a variety of tasks.[4] These "steel-collar" workers have become particularly important in industries such as nuclear power, hazardous-waste disposal, ocean research, and space construction and maintenance, in which human lives would otherwise be at risk. The Bechtel Corporation, for example, employed three robots to clean up a contaminated nuclear reactor at Three Mile Island, the site of a much-publicized nuclear accident in 1979. The robots handled the cleanup operation much faster and more efficiently than human beings could have because of the risk of exposure to harmful radiation.[5]

Robots are used in numerous other production and operations environments by companies all around the world. They are especially prevalent in the automobile industry, where they are used to move materials as well as in assembly operations such as spot welding and painting. As a matter of fact, many assembly operations—not just of cars, but of television sets, telephones, stereo equipment, and many other products—depend on industrial robots. Researchers continue to make more sophisticated robots, and some speculate that, in the future, robots will not be limited to space programs and production and operations, but will also be able to engage in farming, laboratory research, and even household activities.

---

**Example:** Computers and statistical process control were used successfully at Granite Rock Company, a 1992 Malcolm Baldrige National Quality Award winner. In the aggregate division, mixtures of different kinds of rock are subjected to statistical process control to ensure that each batch is nearly identical to every other batch.

**flexible manufacturing**
A manufacturing process in which computers can direct machinery to adapt to different versions of similar operations.

**industrial robot**
A machine designed to move material, parts, tools, or specialized devices through variable programmed motions, for the performance of a variety of tasks.

---

## BUSINESS   DILEMMA

*You're the Manager ...What Would You Do?*

THE COMPANY:   **McWendy King**

YOUR POSITION:   **Head of Franchise Operations**

THE PLACE:   **Wichita, Kansas**

McWendy King is one of the largest fast-food restaurant companies in the United States, with over 5,000 units. The restaurant chain has a traditional fast-food menu with hamburgers, chicken, and roast beef sandwiches as well as other specialty sandwiches, salads, french fries, shakes, and so forth. McWendy King owns and directly operates roughly 50 percent of its restaurants, with the rest run by franchisees. Unlike in some other franchise systems, McWendy King franchisees are small-business operators who own just one or two outlets. This gives the franchised restaurants the advantage of being run by local businesspersons who are involved in the daily operations of their outlets. Such owner/operator involvement and control are not as evident in McWendy King's major competitors.

One store manager of a company-owned unit in Peoria, Illinois, wished to experiment with the development and sale of pizzas at his restaurant. After talking with his district manager, the store manager drafted a proposal and presented his ideas to the company's headquarters in Wichita. Company representatives were impressed with the insights, competitive analysis, profitability projections, and operational considerations presented. The executives believed the idea had merit, and they decided to test it in the Midwest region, working closely with the store in Peoria.

Headquarters worked for months developing the perfect fast-food pizza that could be produced as quickly as possible and would require a minimum of equipment investment for the company and franchise restaurants. The company then tested the product in company-owned restaurants in the Midwest region. The final conclusion was that the pizza product would achieve success, but not in the 12-inch size originally offered. Instead, research suggested that if only one size was offered, it should be 16 inches to accommodate small families and those who like to reheat the product for later meals.

McWendy King presented the concept, with all the financial information, to the franchisees. The company's presentation indicated that each store would need to invest approximately $41,000 in equipment and employee training. In addition, because the 16-inch pizza box was too large to fit through the current store drive-through windows, all the stores would have to make structural modifications. The cost to redo each drive-through window was roughly $15,000.

The franchisees were aware that the company was testing the pizza concept, but were not informed along the way of the operational considerations and costs. Unlike the company units that had flat or declining sales, the franchise units, because of the tighter owner control, operated with significantly higher sales. With emotional responses, the franchisees rejected the idea of making such sweeping changes in order to add pizza to the menu. They suggested that the company look into other less costly alternatives for expanding the McWendy King menu.

### Questions

1. As the head of franchise operations, what should you have taken into consideration in evaluating operational changes for the system?
2. Identify and evaluate compromise alternatives to resolve the situation; consider both quality and productivity for each alternative.
3. What is the role of communications between the corporate and franchise organizations?

---

# MANAGING INVENTORY

After a facility is running, operations managers oversee the transformation process and control the inputs and outputs. **Inventory** refers to all the materials a firm holds in storage for future use. There are three basic types of inventory. **Finished-goods inventory** includes those products that are ready for sale, such as a fully assembled automobile ready to ship to a dealer. **Work-in-process inventory** includes those products that are partially completed or are in transit. At McDonald's, for example, a hamburger being cooked represents work-in-process inventory because it must go through several more stages before it can be sold to

**inventory**
All the materials a firm holds in storage for future use.

**finished-goods inventory**
Those products that are ready for sale, such as a fully assembled automobile ready to ship to a dealer.

**work-in-process inventory**
Those products that are partially completed or are in transit.

**raw materials inventory**
Those materials that have been purchased to be used as inputs for making other products.

a customer. **Raw materials inventory** includes those materials that have been purchased to be used as inputs for making other products. Nuts and bolts are raw materials for an automobile manufacturer, while hamburger patties, vegetables, and buns are raw materials for the fast-food restaurant.

Managing operations must be closely coordinated with inventory management. The production of televisions, for example, cannot be planned without some knowledge of the availability of all the necessary materials—the chassis, picture tubes, color guns, and so forth. Also, each item held in inventory—any type of inventory—carries with it a cost. For example, storing fully assembled televisions in a warehouse to sell to a dealer at a future date requires not only the use of space, but also the purchase of insurance to cover any losses that might occur due to fire or other unforeseen events. For this reason, managers must keep a careful eye on the inventory of materials and components when they develop a production plan.

To illustrate inventory management, consider a hypothetical small business—we'll call it Fleet Athletic Shoes, Inc.—that manufactures athletic shoes, which it sells primarily to sporting goods and department stores.

**Example:** Steve Braccini, founder and CEO of Pro Fasteners Inc., an industrial-parts distributor based in San Jose, California, found opportunities not only for supplying parts for manufacturers, but for managing inventory and providing parts on a just-in-time basis. In some cases the company actually maintains depots at the customer's facilities.

## Purchasing

**purchasing**
The buying of all the materials needed by the organization; also known as procurement.

**Purchasing**, also known as procurement, is the buying of all the materials needed by the organization. Fleet Athletic Shoes, for example, must purchase not only leather and other raw materials, but also machines and equipment, manufacturing supplies (oil, electricity, and so on), and office supplies to make its shoes. People in the purchasing department locate and evaluate suppliers for these items. They must also be on the lookout for new materials or parts that will do a better job or cost less than those currently being used. The purchasing department's objective is to obtain items of the desired quality in the right quantities at the lowest possible cost. Moreover, there is a public relations dimension to purchasing: The individuals who work in this area must maintain good relations with suppliers.

The purchasing function is sometimes very complex. The average automobile, for example, has more than 16,000 different parts, each of which is associated with at least one supplier. The importance of the task of purchasing is further revealed by the amount of money spent by various organizations. Further, the nature of the purchasing task is changing and becoming highly competitive. General Motors, for example, has a new strategy for parts purchasing, which it calls Purchase Input Optimization with Suppliers. This strategy enables GM to force suppliers to slash costs in order to compete and keep GM's business. The strategy has two basic phases. In the first phase, GM sends components supplied by a particular vendor back out for requote from that supplier and its competitors in order to establish a lower target price for those components. In the second phase, a team from GM's supplier development department undertakes an intensive five-day review of every aspect of the supplier's production system to streamline suppliers' operations so as to control costs. The new strategy has reduced GM's North American parts budget by more than $1 billion a year.[6]

**Example:** Purchasing is a key to a company's success, according to Michael Schoonover, executive vice president for operations at high-end storage system maker EMC Corporation. A key change in EMC's purchasing processes is a monthly business-review meeting that includes an overview of sales leads, order backlogs, and market intelligence. Suppliers are seen as an extension of the plant-management team and are expected to provide information to EMC.

Not all organizations elect to purchase all the materials needed to create their products. Often, they can make some materials more economically and efficiently than can an outside supplier. Coors, for example, manufactures its own cans at a subsidiary plant. On the other hand, firms sometimes find that it is uneconomical to make or purchase an item, and instead arrange to lease it from another organization. Some airlines, for example, lease airplanes rather than buy them.

Whether to purchase, make, or lease a needed item generally depends on cost, as well as on product availability and supplier reliability.

## Inventory Control

Once the purchasing department has procured the items needed to create a product, some provision has to be made for storing the items until they are needed. Every raw material, part, and piece of equipment has to be accounted for, or controlled. **Inventory control** is determining how many supplies and goods are needed and keeping track of quantities on hand, where each item is, and who is responsible for it.

Inventory managers spend a great deal of time trying to determine the proper inventory level for each item. The answer to the question of how many units to hold in inventory depends on variables such as the usage rate of the item, the cost of maintaining the item in inventory, the cost of paperwork and other procedures associated with ordering or making the item, as well as the cost of the item itself. Several approaches may be used to determine how many units of a given item should be procured at one time and when that procurement should take place.

**inventory control**
The process of determining how many supplies and goods are needed and keeping track of quantities on hand, where each item is, and who is responsible for it.

**Economic Order Quantity (EOQ).** To control the number of items maintained in inventory, managers need to determine how much of any given item they should order. One popular approach is the **economic order quantity (EOQ) model**, which generally identifies the optimal number of items to order while minimizing certain annual costs that vary according to order size. We should note here that the purchase price per item is not generally included because it does not change or vary with order size unless a quantity discount is a factor. The optimal order quantity $(Q_o)$ can be obtained by using the following formula:

**economic order quantity (EOQ) model**
A popular approach to inventory control that identifies the optimal number of items to order while minimizing certain annual costs that vary according to order size.

$$Q_o = \sqrt{\frac{2DS}{H}}$$

where $D$ equals the annual demand in units; $S$ equals the ordering cost (in dollars); and $H$ is the carrying cost (in dollars per unit/year). Carrying and ordering costs typically are estimated values. Thus, the EOQ should be viewed as an approximation rather than an exact quantity.

For example, let's say Fleet Athletic shoes expects to sell 5,000 units (pairs) of its RXII model next year. The company buys shoelaces from a supplier at 10¢/unit (pair) of laces. The carrying costs are 5 percent of the purchase price and ordering costs are $10. How many units of laces should the shoe manufacturer order from its supplier per order?

$$Q_o = \sqrt{\frac{2DS}{H}} = \sqrt{\frac{(2)(5,000)(10)}{(.05)(.10)}}$$

$$= \sqrt{\frac{100,000}{.005}} = \sqrt{20,000,000}$$

$$= 4,472.1 \text{ units of laces}$$

Thus, the optimal order quantity is 4,472 pairs of laces per order. Notice that if Fleet Athletic Shoes orders only 4,472 units next year, there will be an eventual shortfall of 528 units. This provides an excellent illustration of how EOQ provides only an approximation of the number of units to order, rather than the exact number.

By adopting a just-in-time manufacturing approach, Lifeline Systems, Inc., improved product quality, productivity, and customer satisfaction. The 225-employee firm makes a home personal-response system that alerts emergency personnel when its owner needs help. For Lifeline, quality means perfection, for when a customer pushes the help button, the product *must* work. John Gugliotta, Lifeline's vice president of operations (shown here with assemblers), says JIT manufacturing has decreased waste and rework, reduced the time it takes to turn raw materials inventory into finished-goods inventory from 30 days to less than 5 days, and boosted unit production per square foot of factory space by 400 percent since 1987.

*Source:* © 1994 Rick Friedman/Black Star.

**just-in-time (JIT) inventory management**
A concept that minimizes the number of units in inventory by providing an almost continuous flow of items from suppliers to the production facility.

**Teaching Note:** Remind students that the EOQ formula is outdated in the JIT concept where units are made just in time for the customer. Rather, customer orders drive the amount of inventory. Inventories are minimized and the result is decreased holding and carrying costs for inventory as well as minimized insurance costs. Quality is improved as fewer units wait in queues.

**material-requirements planning (MRP)**
A planning system that schedules the precise quantity of materials needed to make the product.

### Just-in-Time Inventory Management.

The **just-in-time (JIT) inventory management** concept minimizes the number of units in inventory by providing an almost continuous flow of items from suppliers to the production facility. It eliminates waste by using smaller inventories, which require less storage space and less investment. To illustrate, let's say that Fleet Athletic Shoes buys 500 units of shoelaces from a supplier per day. Traditionally, its inventory manager might order enough for one month at a time: 11,000 units per order (500 units per day times 22 workdays per month). The expense of such a large inventory could be considerable because of the cost of insurance coverage, recordkeeping, rented storage space, and so on. The just-in-time approach would reduce these costs because shoelaces would be purchased in smaller quantities, perhaps in lot sizes of 500, which the supplier would deliver once a day. For such an approach to be effective, the supplier must be extremely reliable and relatively close to the production facility.

The JIT concept was developed in Japan and, with varying degrees of success, has been adapted to several American companies. Indeed, General Motors, in deciding where to locate its Saturn assembly plant, specifically used proximity to suppliers as a location criterion because the Saturn plant uses the JIT approach and, to allow for frequent deliveries, has to be close to its sources of supply.

### Material-Requirements Planning (MRP).

Another technique firms use is **material-requirements planning (MRP)**, a planning system that schedules the precise quantity of materials needed to make the product. The basic components of MRP are a master production schedule, bill of materials, and an inventory status file. At Fleet Athletic Shoes, for example, the inventory-control manager will look at the production schedule to determine how many shoes the company plans to make. She will then prepare a bill of materials—a list of all the materials needed to make that quantity of shoes. Next, she will determine the quantity of these items that Fleet already holds in inventory (to avoid ordering excess materials) and then develop a schedule for ordering and delivery of the right quantity of materials to satisfy the firm's needs. Because of the large number of parts and materials that go into a typical production process, material-requirements planning must be done on a computer. MRP can be and often is used in conjunction with just-in-time inventory control. Some potential benefits, if these systems are correctly implemented, are reduced inventory, reduced delivery lead times, realistic commitments, and increased efficiency.

**Manufacturing-Resource Planning (MRPII).**    **Manufacturing-resource planning (MRPII)** is another computerized system that helps a company control all of its resources, not just inventory needed for production. It includes data from all divisions within the organization to help executives plan all elements of the firm's operations. Thus, it is sometimes called the "closed loop" MRP because it incorporates all aspects of the company (accounting, marketing, etc.) rather than just the manufacturing component. Here, Fleet Athletic Shoes might, based on marketing research information, utilize MRPII to allocate resources including personnel and materials to various regional areas in order to meet projected swings in demand for the company's products. This is accomplished, by MRPII, through adopting a focal production plan and using a "unified" database to plan, update, or change *all* organizational activities.

**manufacturing-resource planning (MRPII)**
A computerized system that helps a company control all of its resources, not just inventory needed for production.

## Routing and Scheduling

**Routing.**    After all materials have been obtained and their use determined, operations managers must then determine the maximum or optimum level of production. As part of this process, management must consider the **routing**, or sequence of operations through which the product must pass. For example, before employees at Fleet Athletic Shoes can begin sewing together the leather in the shape of a shoe, it must be cut and stretched into the appropriate sizes. Likewise, the material used in the soles of the shoes must be cut to size before it can be attached to the leather uppers. Routing, therefore, establishes the order of operations through which each shoe at Fleet Athletic must pass on its journey, from being sheets and stacks of leather, rubber, and other raw materials to a finished and ready-to-wear shoe.

**routing**
The sequence of operations through which a product must pass.

**Scheduling.**    Once management knows through which departments or work stations the product must pass and in what sequence, it can then schedule the work. **Scheduling** means assigning the work to be done to departments or to specific machines or persons. At Fleet Athletic, cutting leather for the company's high-top basketball shoes might be scheduled to be done by the "cutting and finishing" department on machines designed especially for that purpose.

Many approaches to scheduling have been developed, ranging from simple trial and error to highly sophisticated mathematical procedures. One popular scheduling technique is the **Program Evaluation and Review Technique (PERT).** Managers using this technique first identify all the major activities required to complete a project. To produce a McDonald's Big Mac, for example, involves removing meat, cheese, sauce, and vegetables from the refrigerator, grilling the hamburger patties, assembling the ingredients, placing the completed Big Mac in its package, and serving it to the customer (see Figure 20.2).

Each complete activity is called an *event.* A scheduler arranges each event in a sequence, ensuring that an event that must occur before another event in the process does so. For example, at McDonald's, the cheese, pickles, lettuce, onions,

**scheduling**
The assigning of work to be done to departments or to specific machines or persons.

**Program Evaluation and Review Technique (PERT)**
A scheduling technique in which managers identify all the major activities (events) required to complete a project, arrange the events in a sequence or path, determine the project's critical path, and estimate the time required for each event.

**FIGURE 20.2**

## A Hypothetical PERT Diagram for a McDonald's Big Mac

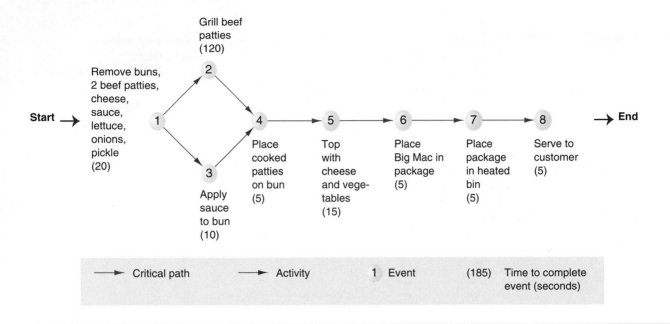

Grill beef patties (120)

Remove buns, 2 beef patties, cheese, sauce, lettuce, onions, pickle (20)

Start → 1

2

3 — Apply sauce to bun (10)

4 — Place cooked patties on bun (5)

5 — Top with cheese and vege-tables (15)

6 — Place Big Mac in package (5)

7 — Place package in heated bin (5)

8 — Serve to customer (5)

→ End

→ Critical path    → Activity    1 Event    (185) Time to complete event (seconds)

**Teaching Note:** Have students pre-pare a PERT diagram for a selected industry or activity of their choice. Have them exchange diagrams with a classmate. Ask students to make sure the sequence is correct and discuss the critical path in each activity.

and sauce cannot be put on a Big Mac before the hamburger patty is completely grilled and placed on the bun. The scheduler depicts the sequence of a project graphically as a path, with arrows to connect events that must occur in sequence, as in Figure 20.2. Finally, the time required for each activity is estimated and noted near the corresponding arrow. The scheduler then totals the time to complete each path. The path that requires the longest time from start to finish is called the *critical path* because it determines the minimum amount of time in which the process can be completed. For example, if any of the activities on the critical path for pro-duction of the Big Mac fall behind schedule, the sandwich will not be completed on time, causing customers to wait longer than they usually would. Thus, PERT allows managers to identify critical activities that can be performed concurrently so as to minimize completion time.

**Gantt chart**
A bar chart that shows the relationship of vari-ous scheduling activities over time.

Still another popular technique used for scheduling purposes is the **Gantt chart**, a bar chart that shows the relationship of various scheduling activities over time. Usually, the scheduling activities are listed vertically and the time frames are listed horizontally. One of the main strengths of the Gantt chart is its simplicity.[7] Consider, for example, a student who is preparing for midterm exams in Accounting 201, Finance 112, and Economics 202. Figure 20.3 illustrates how a Gantt chart could be used in this situation. The student would list courses down the page and the activity time frames across the page. We can see from the chart that the student has studied for Accounting 201 for one and a half weeks, Finance 112 two and a half weeks, and has completed studying for Economics 202. The "v" shows where the project is currently.

**Teaching Note:** For the previous-ly prepared PERT diagram, have students now prepare a Gantt chart and estimate time for completion of the activity or project.

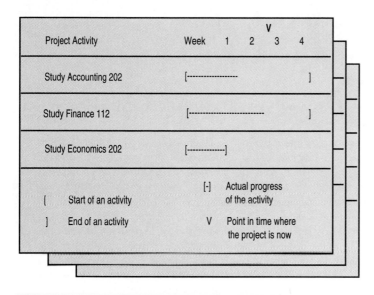

**FIGURE 20.3**

**A Hypothetical Gantt Chart for Studying for Midterm Exams**

## MANAGING QUALITY

Quality, like cost, is a critical element of operations management, for defective products can quickly ruin a firm. A defective shoe, for example, could result in an athlete's injury and expose Fleet Athletic Shoes to lawsuits and declining sales. While we discussed many aspects of managing quality in the context of a total quality management program in Chapter 7, quality is so important that we need to reexamine it in the context of operations. **Quality control** refers to the activities an organization undertakes to ensure that its products meet its established quality standards.[8]

Companies employing TQM programs know that quality control activities should be incorporated throughout the production process, from the initial plans to develop a specific product through the product and production-facility design processes to the actual manufacture of the product. In other words, they view quality control as an element of the product itself and of continuous improvement, rather than as simply a function of the operations process. Regardless of whether a company has a TQM program, to control quality, it must first establish what standard of quality it desires and then determine whether its products meet that standard. The "Quest for Quality" box describes some Korean firms' quality efforts.

### Establishing Standards

Quality control involves comparing the quality of products against established quality standards. Product specifications and quality standards must be established so the company can create a product that will compete in the marketplace.

**quality control**
The activities an organization undertakes to ensure that its products meet its established quality standards.

**Example:** Ritz-Carlton has a total quality push and managers give employees the power to deliver quality at every turn. For example, if a housekeeper feels the hotel needs a new washing machine, she orders it. If a front desk clerk sees a problem with a bill, she takes the charge off and no one has to check with a supervisor first.

# Quest *for* Quality

## KOREAN AUTOMAKERS STRIVE FOR QUALITY

In the past, Korean companies had a reputation for manufacturing cheap products. Today, however, Korea's giant conglomerates, or *chaebol,* realize that to be competitive, they must make quality a top priority. This challenge is particularly important to Korean auto manufacturers. Korea's Big Three—Hyundai, Kia, and Daewoo—plan to triple production by the turn of the century (to approximately 6 million cars per year). They will need to export most of this output to the United States and Europe. To be competitive in these markets, Korean automobiles will need to be produced with consistently higher quality.

According to Yoon Yong-Nam, president of Daewoo Management Development Center, the key to improving quality lies in being able to encourage employees to "join the quality effort voluntarily and with enthusiasm." Daewoo is taking a relatively straightforward approach to improving quality. For example, the company now demands cash refunds from suppliers who produce poor components, and it sent 2,000 auto workers to the Japanese plants of Isuzu and Suzuki (companies with which Daewoo has business ties) to observe Japanese quality methods. In addition, the personal involvement of chairman Kim plays a critical role in Daewoo's drive for higher quality. He frequently visits the factory both day and night.

Daewoo Motor has also installed a "three-level" quality control program. First, each unit of about a dozen assembly workers has its own quality monitor who wears a bright green vest for easy identification. At the end of the line, another group, called the "Q-point," checks for product defects (which have dropped by 65 percent over the past two years). Finally, approximately 2 percent of the cars are examined by a "customer satisfaction" inspector who spends 3½ hours checking 188 different aspects of the car from the paint to the fit of the doors.

Hyundai Motor, the largest Korean automobile manufacturer, also takes the direct approach to increasing quality. The company began by attempting to reeducate everyone involved in making and distributing Hyundai cars. In addition, it sent both union leaders and suppliers to the United States to observe firsthand the intense competition. Now, every Hyundai car is inspected and test-driven at least three times before reaching the consumer—first at the Korean factory, then at the U.S. port of entry, and finally by American dealers. Needed repairs are made at all inspector points, even if it's simply touching up scratched paint.

*Source:* Louis Kraar, "Korea Goes for Quality," *Fortune,* April 18, 1994, 153–160.

---

Fleet Athletic Shoes, for example, may specify that each of its shoes has soles of a specified uniform thickness, that the toe and heel of each shoe be reinforced to a specified level to ensure adequate support, and that each shoe be able to last through a specified number of miles of use. Production facilities must be designed that can produce products with the desired specifications.

Quality standards can be incorporated into service businesses as well. For example, SpaResort Hawaiians, a resort near Tokyo, Japan, specifies down to the milliliter the amount of soy sauce to be served with sushi, and reformulated its restaurants' recipes to eliminate leftovers. It even specifies how much water and fertilizer to use on the resort's palm trees, the water temperature for its swimming and bathing pools, and the time required to check in visitors. Establishing such precise standards and ensuring that those standards were met helped the company boost customer satisfaction and made it the first service company awarded Japan's prestigious Deming Award for quality.[9] Once the desired quality characteristics, specifications, and standards have been stated in measurable terms, the next step is inspection.

To ensure the quality of its milk and specialty dairy products, Dean Foods Company conducts extensive quality control tests. Tests are performed on raw product samples of milk Dean Foods receives from local and regional dairies in 14 states and the Virgin Islands. The company also tests finished product samples of cottage cheese, yogurt, sour cream, whipping cream, and other specialty dairy products.

*Source:* Courtesy of Dean Foods Company.

## Inspection

Inspection reveals whether a product meets quality standards. Some product characteristics may be discerned by fairly simple inspection techniques—for example, weighing the contents of cereal boxes or measuring the time it takes for a customer to receive his or her hamburger. Other inspection techniques are more elaborate. Automobile manufacturers use automated machines to open and close car doors to test the durability of latches and hinges. The food-processing and pharmaceutical industries use various chemical tests to determine the quality of their output. Fleet Athletic Shoes might use a special computer that can accurately simulate long-term usage of a shoe to determine how many miles a runner can expect the shoe to last.

Inspection tests may be classified as performance tests or destructive tests. The repeated opening and closing of car doors to determine the life expectancy of hinges and latches is a destructive test because the test lasts until the product fails. Performance testing, on the other hand, does not destroy or damage the product. Many software companies, for example, use performance tests to find and eliminate bugs in their programs, even asking customers worldwide to help with the tests. IBM asked several thousand customers to test "beta" (not ready for full release) versions of its OS/2 2.1 operating system before releasing the complex program worldwide.

Organizations normally inspect purchased items, work-in-process, and finished items. The inspection of purchased items and finished items takes place after the fact; the inspection of work-in-process is preventive. In other words, the purpose of inspection of purchased items and finished items is to determine what the quality level is. For items that are being worked on—an automobile moving down the assembly line, a booster rocket at an intermediate stage of completion, or an athletic shoe being assembled—the purpose of the inspection is to find defects before the product is completed so that the corrections can be made.

**Example:** Beverly Enterprises, the nation's largest nursing home chain, spends $18 million each year on its quality-assurance program, which monitors facilities in 38 states and the District of Columbia. Facilities are graded each quarter in such areas as housekeeping, laundry, environmental control, nursing care, and food service.

## Sampling

An important question relating to inspection is how many items it should include. If Fleet Athletic Shoes produces more than 500 shoes a day, should they all be inspected or just some of them? At Alaska Airlines, the chef samples food quality by boarding planes about once a month to ask passengers how they like the airline's food. The airline also conducts focus groups and surveys groups of fliers to determine how well it is satisfying its customers.[10] Whether to inspect 100 percent of the output or only part of it is related to the cost of the inspection process, the destructiveness of the inspection process, and the importance of the item to the safety of consumers or others.

Some inspection procedures are quite expensive, use elaborate testing equipment, destroy products, and/or require a significant number of hours to complete. In such cases, it is usually desirable to take a sample of the output and test that. If the sample passes inspection, the inspector may assume that all the items in the lot from which the sample was drawn would also pass inspection. By using principles of statistical inference, management can employ sampling techniques that assure a relatively high probability of reaching the right conclusion—that is, rejecting a lot that does not meet standards and accepting a lot that does. Nevertheless, there will always be a risk of making an incorrect conclusion—accepting a population that *does not* meet standards (because the sample was satisfactory) or rejecting a population that *does* meet standards (because the sample contained too many defective items).

Human life and safety depend on the proper functioning of certain items, such as the navigational systems installed in commercial airliners. For such items, even though the inspection process is costly, the potential cost of flawed systems in human lives and safety is too great not to inspect 100 percent of the output.

**Example:** The principles of total quality management (TQM) were developed 80 years ago by Henry Ford, Sr., and described in his book *My Life and Work*, published in 1926. U.S. executives rediscovered the book in a trip to Japan where they discovered Japanese executives had adopted Ford's book as their industrial bible. Ford did not call his management process TQM but thought of it as common sense.

## MANAGING PRODUCTIVITY

The importance of productivity has increased dramatically in recent years and continues to escalate as a critical concern. For example, when GM's directors appointed John L. Smith, Jr., as CEO, they gave him one mandate: to improve productivity and efficiency. Fulfilling that mandate will not be easy because GM's North American operations are highly leveraged and hugely unprofitable, and the company faces a hostile United Auto Workers union as it tries to reduce its operations in the name of improved productivity. In fact, GM may need as long as five years to catch up with Ford and Chrysler![11]

One of the primary objectives of the operations function is to increase productivity by using resources efficiently. Before we continue, let's establish what productivity is and how it is measured.

### Measuring Productivity

**productivity**
The measurement of the relationship between the outputs produced and the inputs used to produce them.

**Productivity** measures the relationship between the outputs produced and the inputs used to produce them. It is usually expressed as a formula:

$$\text{productivity} = \frac{\text{output}}{\text{input}}$$

In general, productivity measurements can be classified in two ways: partial productivity or total productivity. **Partial productivity** reflects output relative to a single input or some combination of inputs. For instance, labor productivity is a very common concern. Examples of labor productivity include labor hours, machine hours, and number of workers necessary to produce at a given level of output:

**partial productivity**
Output relative to a single input or some combination of inputs.

$$\frac{\text{output}}{\text{labor hours}} = \text{output per hour}$$

$$\frac{\text{output}}{\text{machine hours}} = \text{output per machine per hour}$$

$$\frac{\text{output}}{\text{number of workers}} = \text{output per worker}$$

**Total productivity** reflects all the inputs used to obtain an output(s). For example, if we know that all inputs consist of labor, machines, and materials, we can use the following formula to express the total productivity measurement:

$$\frac{\text{output}}{\text{labor costs} + \text{machine costs} + \text{material costs}} = \text{output per total inputs}$$

Please note that this ratio requires that the inputs and outputs be measured using a common unit such as cost or value. In the above example, the output(s) would need to be converted to a dollar value.

**total productivity**
Outputs relative to all the inputs used.

## The Importance of Productivity

Productivity is important on three levels. Organizations do not have unlimited resources, so they must determine how to allocate their limited resources to different departments or divisions within the firm. Consequently, each department or division must use its allotted resources as efficiently and effectively as possible. Moreover, the most productive departments are those most likely to be given larger allocations of the firm's resources.

From the perspective of an entire organization, productivity is a critical factor in competitiveness. For instance, if a company can achieve the same level of output as its competitors using fewer resources, then it has a competitive advantage. It can charge the same price for its products and generate higher profit margins than its less productive competitors, or it can charge a lower price and thereby increase its sales at the expense of its less productive competitors. Because of poor productivity, GM lost a substantial share of the auto market to competitors such as Ford and Chrysler. In an effort to improve productivity, GM will close six assembly plants and 15 other factories by 1995, reducing its capacity by one-fifth so that it can operate more profitably with its 35 percent market share.[12]

Productivity is also important from a national perspective because there is a close relationship between a country's productivity and its standard of living. High productivity levels are largely responsible for the high standards of living enjoyed by the citizens of the industrialized nations. Moreover, if productivity levels are not in alignment with wage and price levels, the nation's economy may be adversely affected. High wages and prices combined with low productivity, for example, may result in inflationary pressure. Today, there is a serious concern on the part of the U.S. government and business leaders that American productivity increases in many industries have lagged behind those of other nations such as Japan and Korea.

In 1960 the United States accounted for 51 percent of the free world's total output, but its share had fallen to 22 percent by 1980. In contrast, Japan accounted for only 19 percent of the free world's total output in 1960, but its share climbed to 24 percent by 1980.[13] Moreover, over the last several years, the United States has lost its dominance of industries such as TVs, VCRs, cameras, and minor appliances to foreign competitors, particularly Japan. More recently,

**Example:** Threatened with losing a large portion of business from Xerox Corporation, Mid-South Industries, a contract manufacturer, needed to meet efficiency standards that Xerox had set for suppliers to help it trim costs. Jerry Weaver, the CEO, spent two years cutting costs and improving productivity and invested $400,000 to upgrade his assembly line with robotics and other computer automation. Another $1 million went to training workers.

however, productivity in the United States is on the rise. A study of international productivity levels released by the McKinsey Global Institute in 1992 found that manufacturing productivity in the United States is 20 percent ahead of that in Japan and Germany.[14]

## Improving Productivity

Many factors affect productivity, including methods, capital, quality, technology, and management. For example, a student studying for a comprehensive final exam may take a speed-reading course (method) and try to better organize the material (management) with the aid of a computer (capital and technology). The incentive of getting good grades and the personal pride of doing a good job are also important. The point is that all of these factors are potential sources of productivity improvements.

Some key steps toward improving productivity are listed below.

**1.** *Develop adequate productivity measurements.* For example, if Fleet Athletic Shoes measures only the number of shoes made, it may be ignoring other indicators of productivity, such as wasted materials or product quality, that provide a better picture of true productivity.

**2.** *Consider the "entire" or "whole" system when deciding on which operations to concentrate.* For most products, the production process is a closely integrated sequence of events that must take place in exact order to achieve the desired results. If just one of these steps, regardless of its apparent importance, is not performed satisfactorily, the whole production process may be thrown off course. Only by considering the entire system as a whole is it possible to detect relatively minor difficulties that may be causing major problems.

**3.** *Develop productivity improvement methods (such as work teams) and reward contributions.* For example, when USL, a medium-sized pharmaceutical company, established Core Teams to operate its high-volume tablet packaging line, within 12 weeks its line changeover time dropped from four hours to less than two hours, the number of bottles packaged increased by 82 percent, and the number of dollars in back orders fell to zero.[15]

**4.** *Establish reasonable improvement goals.* If goals are set too high, workers may be frustrated when they cannot achieve them. However, if goals are set too low, the company is not likely to reach its potential in terms of productivity because it is not challenging its workers enough.

**5.** *Make productivity improvements a management, particularly top management, priority.* Commitment from management is critical to the achievement of any goal, particularly those concerning productivity improvements. Xerox Corporation, for example, attributes the tremendous benefits realized from its productivity improvements (boosted sales and improved employee morale) to the high commitment from top management. Xerox began by not only rewarding employees for productivity improvements but also recognizing and rewarding managers.[16]

**6.** *Publicize productivity improvements.* Publicizing improvement not only tends to instill a sense of pride in those workers most responsible for the improvements, but also creates somewhat of a challenge to other workers to see if they too can do something that will help the company's overall productivity.

**7.** *Use decision-support systems.* Chapter 21 will discuss those specialized computer systems which allow managers and other workers to consider the effects

c a r e e r s

## Opportunities in Production and Operations

Experts predict that 24 million more jobs will be generated in the United States by 2005 than were generated in 1990. It is expected that, between 1990 and 2005, employment will increase from 123 million to 147 million. Experts predict that executive, administrative, and managerial workers will constitute the fastest growing job segment, and it is likely that many of these jobs will be operations oriented.

Individuals with a production and operations focus can provide needed knowledge to all levels in the organization. Some typical production and operations positions are first-line supervisor, foreman, computer analyst, project analyst, inventory and material planning and control manager, production planning manager, and quality control manager (some of these are discussed in more detail below). Frequently, the top managers of an organization possess production and control skills. One key advantage to an operations focus is that these types of skills are often transferable across both service and manufacturing sectors as well as within each sector. Thus, operations skills not only are critical skills for the organization but also can facilitate an individual's career growth.

Working as a purchasing agent or manager (sometimes referred to as a procurement officer) can be interesting, challenging, and rewarding. According to John Hill, a top industry leader, purchasing is taking on a whole new critical meaning to the organization for four reasons: (1) Purchasing is a profit-making activity, (2) top management is becoming more involved with the purchasing function, (3) purchasing actually begins long before any specifications or requisitions are written, and

(4) it requires highly trained, competent people who are on par with all other departments. Purchasing can offer great growth opportunities, broad organizational exposure, and business training. One electronics company states that its procurement manager candidates must have a bachelor's degree, preferably with a major in engineering or business administration.

Another new hot career area in operations (particularly for inventory and distribution) is the information systems (IS) specialist. In the inventory and distribution area, businesses are looking for individuals who are familiar with telecommunications technologies. Additionally, these people should be well acquainted with image processing for collecting and distributing information, as well as electronic data interchange for the transfer of information. Understanding the needs of customers and being able to translate how those needs can be fulfilled is also a key skill. Finally, because there is such an emphasis currently on economical inventory management, IS candidates should acquire knowledge of just-in-time inventory methods. These individuals might consider a major in information systems with a minor in both operations management and communications.

*Sources:* Jay M. Berman and Theresa A. Cosca, "The Job Outlook in Brief: 1990–2005," *Occupational Outlook Quarterly* 36 (Spring 1992): 6–41; Paul V. Farrell, "Old Pro Pitches Purchasing," *Purchasing World* 34 (December 1990): 36–37; Emily Leinfuss, "Keeping an Eye on Inventory Pays," *Computerworld*, May 4, 1992, 91.

---

of a wide range of possible factors on organizational productivity. As a result, outcomes of decisions can be predicted more accurately than they otherwise could.

**8.** *Link incentives with productivity increases.* For example, rather than merely giving automatic annual year-end bonuses to employees, Fleet Athletic Shoes could base its bonuses on work teams or individual employees successfully meeting preset productivity goals.

**9.** *Provide adequate training.* Dana Corporation, for example, is finding out what a difference proper training can make in its Minneapolis facilities. Its strategy is to train trainers, who come from the company's plants. These new trainers go back to their plants and spread information about human relations, manufacturing techniques, and philosophies. This new strategy has resulted in a 32 percent productivity improvement, a 47 percent reduction in quality costs, and a 77 percent reduction in customer lead time.[17]

**Comment on Box:** Ask a local purchasing agent to address your class on careers in purchasing as well as to discuss what his or her job entails. Contact the National Association of Purchasing Managers to assist you in making contacts in your area.

Employees' attitudes have an important influence on productivity. For instance, it is believed that workers who are committed and have a positive attitude about their jobs and company will have a high overall productivity level, all other things being equal. Some of the ways to increase productivity through employees' attitudes include providing sufficient job training, increasing job autonomy, providing financial incentives, and eliciting and integrating employees' input on productivity issues. For example, since the end of 1990, representatives of companies such as Ford, 3M, and Honeywell have investigated the GE Business Information Center (GEBIC), the company front door for business customers looking for personalized information on GE technical, industrial, and commercial products. What makes GEBIC of such interest to so many companies is not only its evidence of higher customer satisfaction, increased productivity, and reduced costs, but also the fact that GEBIC's own employees planned and implemented the changes that made these results possible. Since the self-directed work force took over GEBIC, customer satisfaction has gone from 94 to 99 percent, productivity has doubled, and the cost savings have been in the millions of dollars.[18]

Unfortunately, when faced with the challenge of improving productivity, managers frequently focus on updating equipment rather than developing employees. Tom Peters and Robert Waterman revealed in their book *In Search of Excellence* that the best-run organizations view their employees "as the root source of quality and productivity gain." These firms achieve high productivity through high employee performance by respecting employees as individuals, trusting them, and "treating them as adults."[19] It is evident, then, that a key way to improve productivity is through employees.

## SUMMARY AND REVIEW

- **Define operations management and identify the activities associated with it.** Operations management is the development and administration of the activities involved in transforming resources into goods and services. Operations managers oversee the transformation process, the planning and designing of operations systems, and the managing of inventory, quality, and productivity.

- **Determine the elements involved in planning and designing an operations system.** Operations planning is necessary before actual production can occur. Product design depends on what customers want and on the organization's technical abilities. Facility layout is the arrangement of the physical layout of an organization. Layouts may be fixed-position layouts, process layouts, or product layouts. The decision where to locate operations facilities is a crucial one that depends on proximity to the market, availability of raw materials, availability of transportation, availability of power, climatic influences, availability of labor, and community characteristics. Technology is also vital to operations, particularly computer-assisted design, computer-assisted manufacturing, flexible manufacturing, and robotics.

- **Specify some of the techniques that managers may use to manage inventory.** Inventory refers to all the materials a firm holds in storage for future use, and includes finished-goods inventory, work-in-process inventory, and raw materials inventory. Inventory control is determining how many supplies and goods are needed and keeping track of how many of each item are on hand, where each item is, and who has responsibility for each item. The economic order quantity (EOQ) model generally identifies the optimal number of items to order while minimizing certain annual costs that vary according to order size. The just-in-time (JIT) inventory concept minimizes the number of units maintained in inventory by providing an almost continuous flow of items from the suppliers to the production facility. Material-requirements planning (MRP) is a planning system that schedules the precise quantity of materials that are needed to make the product. Manufacturing-resource planning (MRPII) is another computerized system that helps a company control all of its resources, not just inventory needed for production.

- **Assess the importance of quality in the operations management process.** Quality is a critical element of operations management because low-quality products can harm a firm. Quality control refers to the activities undertaken to ensure that products meet established quality standards. To control quality, a company must first establish what standard of quality it desires and then determine whether its products meet that standard through inspection.

- **Define productivity, explain why it is important, and propose ways to improve it.** Productivity measures the relationship between the outputs produced and the inputs used to produce them. Partial productivity reflects output relative to a single input or some combination of inputs; total productivity reflects all the inputs used to obtain an output(s). Productivity is

important because it relates to a firm's (or nation's) efficiency in using resources and competitiveness. There are many ways to improve productivity, including developing adequate productivity measurements, developing productivity improvement methods, establishing reasonable improvement goals, publicizing productivity improvements, linking incentives to productivity increases, providing adequate training, and motivating employees to be more productive.

- **Evaluate operations issues in a franchise operation.** Evaluate the scenario described in the "Business Dilemma" box and come up with a compromise solution to the problem. Your solution should enable all outlets to maintain quality and productivity standards.

## Key Terms and Concepts

operations management (OM) 588
inputs 588
outputs 588
manufacturing 590
production 590
operations 590
capacity 593
fixed-position layout 594
process layout 594
product layout 594
computer-assisted design (CAD) 595
computer-assisted manufacturing (CAM) 595

flexible manufacturing 596
industrial robot 596
inventory 597
finished-goods inventory 597
work-in-process inventory 597
raw materials inventory 598
purchasing 598
inventory control 599
economic order quantity (EOQ) model 599
just-in-time (JIT) inventory management 600
material-requirements planning (MRP) 600

manufacturing-resource planning (MRPII) 601
routing 601
scheduling 601
Program Evaluation and Review Technique (PERT) 601
Gantt chart 602
quality control 603
productivity 606
partial productivity 606
total productivity 607

## Ready Recall

1. What is the purpose of operations management?
2. Distinguish between the terms *operations, production,* and *manufacturing.*
3. Compare and contrast a manufacturer versus a service provider in terms of operations management.
4. In what industry would the fixed-position layout be most efficient? The process layout? The product layout? Use real examples.
5. What criteria do businesses use when deciding where to locate a plant?

6. What is flexible manufacturing? How can it help firms improve quality?
7. Explain why organizations using the just-in-time inventory concept must have zero defects in their inventory.
8. Describe the methods a firm may use to manage inventory.
9. When might a firm decide to inspect a sample of its products rather than test every product for quality?
10. Explain why productivity is important to the organization or a nation. Include some steps that can be taken to improve productivity.

## Expand Your Experience

1. Compare and contrast operations management at McDonald's with that of Honda of America. Compare and contrast operations management at McDonald's with that of Citibank, a banking firm.

2. Find an existing company that uses JIT, either in your local community or in a business journal. Why did the company decide to use JIT? What have been the advantages and disadvantages of using JIT for that particular company?

What has been the overall effect on the quality of the company's products or services? What has been the overall effect on the company's bottom line?

3. Interview some local operations managers and ask them what induced their companies to locate in your area.

Compare and contrast the different criteria and report the results to your class.

# The New Marriage between Manufacturers and Suppliers

Today's dynamic business environment has organizations rushing to find new ways to be more cost efficient, provide higher quality, and be more flexible. Some manufacturing firms are responding to these challenges by forming new kinds of relationships with their suppliers. These new relationships are partnerships between manufacturers and suppliers that represent a strong commitment between two entire organizations, rather than the traditional relationship between a purchasing agent and a salesperson. In other words, the manufacturer and the supplier work very closely together as a team.

An example of this new kind of marriage is the relationship between the Donnelly Corporation and Honda. In 1986 Honda selected Donnelly Corporation, based in Holland, Michigan, to make all of the exterior mirrors for Honda cars manufactured in the United States. Honda executives made this decision even though Donnelly had never made exterior mirrors and, in fact, had no factory for making them. A major factor in Honda's choice was its satisfaction with Donnelly as a supplier of interior mirrors. A second factor, of equal importance, was that Donnelly's values and culture aligned perfectly with those of Honda. For instance, both Honda and Donnelly believe that companies should involve and empower their employees.

Donnelly thus built a brand new plant to manufacture exterior mirrors for Honda. To ensure that the partnership got off on the right foot, Honda developed a consulting program to help strengthen Donnelly's operations. This program involved bringing in engineers from Honda to pore over and analyze all aspects of Donnelly's operations—looking for "kinks" in the system. Honda expects that the payoff from this new partnership will be large—with the partnership expected to grow to $60 million by 1997 from $5 million in sales in the first year.

Motorola is another firm looking to enter into partnerships with its suppliers. As with Honda, a critical factor for Motorola is the alignment of company cultures. However, Motorola goes even further than Honda to ensure that the operations skills of the supplier measure up. For example, Motorola teaches a new supplier-partner its own total quality management (TQM) techniques, requiring the supplier-partner to take courses in cycle time reduction and customer satisfaction from its own education program, at Motorola University.

Every two years, teams from Motorola tour suppliers' plants, analyzing their operations on issues such as quality and timeliness. These tours also spark a bit of friendly competition among supplier-partners in that grades are assigned to each supplier-partner based on how well they stack up against each other. In addition, the commodity manager at Motorola rates suppliers using a monthly index that combines both cost and quality, again comparing supplier-partners with one another. Motorola rewards the better performers with more business. Currently, Motorola is encouraging suppliers to analyze, for themselves, how much quality defects can add to their own costs. According to Tom Slaninka, Motorola's procurement chief, suppliers often find 12 to 20 percent cost-reduction opportunities.

Motorola's philosophy is to get suppliers involved from the very start in the design and manufacture of a product. The company has found that the supplier often better understands how to design specialized high-tech parts so that material and manufacturing costs are minimized. Also, suppliers often know how better to avoid design flaws. In fact, Motorola has come to value its suppliers' opinions so much that it has established a 15-member council of suppliers to rate its own operations practices and offer suggestions for improvements. Slaninka says that this arrangement has worked out beautifully in reducing costs because most any kind of error requires the people at both ends to correct it.

A final example of the new trend of manufacturer-supplier partnerships is Betz Laboratories and Allied-Signal. Betz, a Pennsylvania-based producer of industrial water-treatment chemicals, supplies Allied-Signal's plants with water chemicals to keep pipes and equipment working properly and prevent corrosion. Betz also provides its own people, who preside over all the water as it flows throughout the Allied-Signal plant to ensure that the water is as safe as possible and meets all government standards, as well as maintain cost effectiveness. Basically, this is accomplished by high-level teams that consist of both Betz and Allied-Signal engineers and managers. The teams are empowered to test water in any part of the plant and make necessary adjustments. For example, in less than one year, one of the teams found $2.5 million in potential annual cost reductions at one Allied-Signal plant. The savings resulted from using filtered river water instead of buying city water and by recycling water instead of dumping it into the sewer (which had resulted in a sewer charge). By using recycled water in the plant's cooling tower, for example, the Allied-Signal plant saved 300 gallons of water a minute.

Marriages such as the ones Honda, Motorola, and Allied-Signal have entered into represent a relatively new trend for companies today. Some experts suggest that this is a good indi-

cation that U.S. businesses are "smartening up," and that they are learning to cooperate with one another so that they can focus on the real competition—foreign companies.

*Source:* Myron Magnet, "The New Golden Rule of Business," *Fortune,* February 21, 1994, 60–64.

## Questions

1. How do these new kinds of supplier relationships (or partnerships) change the operations function for the manufacturer? For the supplier?
2. What new "roles" will become necessary for the operations managers as a result of these supplier partnerships? What new skills will the operations manager need?

3. Discuss the potential benefits and drawbacks of these kinds of arrangements for the supplier and the manufacturer.

## STRENGTHEN YOUR SKILLS
### *Humor*

According to Malcolm Kushner in *The Light Touch: How to Use Humor for Business Success:*

> *Humor is a powerful management tool. It can gain attention, create rapport, and make a message more memorable. It can also relieve tension, enhance relationships, and motivate people.... In today's competitive business environment, success requires developing your full potential. Every skill counts. And humor can provide the winning edge.*[20]

In this chapter where you have studied about increasing productivity, it is appropriate for you to work on strengthening your humor skills. In a recent executive survey conducted by Accountemps, 96 percent of the surveyed executives believe that people with a sense of humor do better at their jobs than those who have little or no sense of humor. Studies also have shown that people who enjoy their work are more productive, more creative, and have greater job satisfaction.[21]

C. W. Metcalf, consultant and author on the role of humor in managing oneself and others, says you need to develop three humor skills:

- the ability to see the absurdity in difficult situations
- the ability to take yourself lightly while taking your work seriously
- a disciplined sense of joy in being alive[22]

This exercise will help you strengthen the first humor skill by using "Follow-Ups to Murphy's Law." You may be familiar with the original Murphy's Law: "Whatever can go wrong, will."

These laws can help you view your problems from a more humorous perspective, help lessen your stress and frustration, and increase your productivity.

### Instructions

- Break into groups of 3 to 5 students.
- Each group member is to select one law from the list provided below that he or she can relate to the rest of the group from personal experience. For example, a worker at a medical clinic might relate the experiences of a particularly hectic day with the "Follow-Up to Murphy's Law": "The last patient of the day is always the sickest, especially if you're about to go on vacation."
- You are not restricted to the list provided. You may already have a law you use to help you deal with difficult situations, or you may want to create a new one to fit a common problem you face.
- When it is your turn to relate your personal experience, you should include a description of a work-related situation. (If your work experience is limited, you may choose a home- or school-related situation.) Conclude with either how you already use a "Follow-Up to Murphy's Law" to help you deal with the situation or how you will cope with the situation next time it happens by applying the law.

### Follow-Ups to Murphy's Law

1. Nothing is ever as simple as it first seems.

2. Every activity takes more time than you have.

3. It is easier to make a commitment or to get involved in something than to get out of it.

4. Whatever you set out to do, something else must be done first.

5. Every clarification breeds new questions.

6. The greater the importance of decisions to be made, the larger must be the committee assigned to make them.

7. Things get worse under pressure.

8. Opportunity always knocks at the least opportune time.

9. The number of people watching you is directly proportional to the stupidity of your action.

10. It is a mistake to allow any mechanical object to realize you are in a hurry.

11. People who snore tend to fall asleep first.

12. The estimate to repair anything will always be more than it's worth and less than the cost of a new one.

13. Measure twice because you can only cut once.

14. The one time in the day that you lean back and relax is the one time the boss walks through the office.

15. By working faithfully eight hours a day, you may eventually get to be a boss and work twelve hours a day.

16. Every solution breeds new problems.

17. The person at the back of the elevator is always the one who needs to get off at the next stop.

# Managing Information Systems

## Outline

## After reading this chapter, you will be able to:

- Explain why managers need information and the characteristics of useful information.
- Describe a management information system and explain its role in management.
- Specify the basic factors that determine an organization's information management needs.
- Determine how computers can be used in management information systems.
- Distinguish among the basic types of management information systems.
- Summarize the impact of information technology on people, organizations, and information.
- Critique a business's implementation of a management information system.

# Research Technology Brings Customers Closer

Marketing managers often find it quite difficult to keep up with the constantly emerging new technology in the field of marketing research—research that provides information about the wants, needs, and buying behavior of the customers to whom they market their products. Advances in this area are most evident in the retailing sector, where the amount of information obtained on shoppers and their buying habits and preferences has increased astronomically over the last several years, enabling retailers and the companies whose products fill their shelves to dramatically increase the efficiency and effectiveness of their marketing efforts.

Several marketing research firms catering to the specific needs of both retail merchants and product marketers now specialize in high-tech, in-store surveillance services and equipment. Among other things, information gathering and tracking services such as these allow retailers to collect data on traffic patterns in their stores, which affect store and shelf layout. For example, using consumer traffic information, Bashas' Markets Inc. in Chandler, Arizona, found that just 18 percent of grocery store customers pass through the aisle displaying greeting cards, which are high-profit items in customarily low-margin supermarkets. Based on this finding, the Bashas' store-layout manager moved the greeting cards, placing them between the floral department and an aisle with peanut butter, jelly, and health foods that regularly drew over 60 percent of the store's traffic. Shortly thereafter, sales of greeting cards jumped 40 percent.

Although retailers currently benefit most from state-of-the-art, in-store, customer-tracking technology, consumer product firms have also used it to their advantage. Procter & Gamble (P&G) found that placing its products in other than their normal locations greatly increased sales for certain items. For example, during a three-week test period in new locations in Kmart stores, P&G toothpaste sales rose 119 percent, while the company's coffee sales soared more than 500 percent. PepsiCo has also used in-store tracking data to reposition its Frito-Lay snack items and soft drinks in hopes of realizing increased sales as a result of higher traffic by its products, which are customarily located in low-traffic areas.

Procter & Gamble has also used such information technology to boost its ordering efficiency. Under its new continuous product replenishment (CPR) system, whenever a product, say a box of Tide, is "scanned" at the checkout, the information is sent directly to P&G's computer system, which automatically determines where and when to restock the product. Not only does the system reduce mistakes in inventory and improve cash flow, it also ensures that the products customers want are on the shelves when they are ready to buy them.

However, retailers themselves continue to get the most out of in-store tracking technology. In fact, knowledge about shopping behavior and traffic patterns is now becoming so advanced that retailers may soon be able to assign values to certain store locations and charge product marketers for preferential placement, much as real estate agents charge a premium for prime parcels of property.

*Sources:* Bradley Johnson, "Retailers Check Out In-Store," *Advertising Age,* December 16, 1991, 23; "Just-in-Tide Marketing," *Fortune,* March 7, 1994, 75–82; and Michael J. McCarthy, "James Bond Hits the Supermarket: Stores Snoop on Shoppers' Habits to Boost Sales," *The Wall Street Journal,* August 25, 1993, B1.

anagers spend a great deal of time making decisions—planning for future operations, implementing current plans, and evaluating past performance. Managers constantly need information to aid their decision making, information about not only the current situation but also the past and the future. Indeed, in recent years, it has become evident that information must be considered a basic resource much like capital, human resources, raw materials, and plants and equipment. In today's dynamic and increasingly global business world, having timely and accurate information is more important than ever before. At the same time, computers and other information processing technologies are making this information increasingly accessible to organizations of all sizes and functions that know how to capture and use it. In short, the technological revolution has greatly influenced the ways that business is conducted, as well as the activities and responsibilities of managers. Nowhere is this impact more evident and important than in the area of information management.

In this chapter we provide an overview of the nature of organizational information needs as well as the technology available for management of this information. The first half of the chapter discusses the importance of information for business decision making and explains what a management information system is and how it works. The second half examines how information technology is used in managing information.

## INFORMATION AND MANAGEMENT

**Example:** Patrice-Ann Rutledge, executive editor of *Global Business Technology Report*, a Concord, California, newsletter tracking the use of technology in international business, agrees the technology of the 1990s will make international business more feasible and affordable for small companies, particularly due to the latest computer, telecommunications, and facsimile technology.

All managers need information to make decisions so that they may achieve their firms' objectives. Kellogg Company managers, for example, need information about how many boxes of cereal the firm has sold and whether sales measure up to expectations. They need to know whether promotional efforts have been effective in increasing sales and enhancing the firm's image, and if they have set the best price for the firm's products. But they also need information about the quality of Kellogg's products, as well as human resource information about the number, location, and productivity of the firm's employees. The managers need to know how the company's investments are performing and whether its financial resources are contributing to the firm's objectives.

Obtaining and understanding information about these and many other subjects is critical in strategic and tactical planning as well as in implementing business plans. Moreover, such information indicates the success or failure of a firm's past efforts, helping managers to make more informed decisions about future activities. Obtaining, analyzing, and understanding information about the business environment are therefore important activities in any business.

### The Role of Information in Management

**data**

Unorganized facts, statistics, opinions, and predictions gathered from various sources inside and outside the company.

**information**

Data that are relevant for a specific purpose.

Managers need information, not just data. **Data** are unorganized facts, statistics, opinions, and predictions gathered from various sources inside and outside the company. But, confronted with a pile of raw data, a manager would have a hard time making a decision. Data must be sorted and logically organized to produce relevant information. **Information** is data that are relevant for a specific purpose. A sales manager, for example, might want to rank total annual sales by territory over the past five years. Presented with lists of each salesperson's monthly sales reports for those five years, the manager could spend days trying to make sense out of all the names and numbers.

## Characteristics of Useful Information

Although each manager's information needs vary according to his or her function and in terms of factors such as the nature of the company's business, the state of the environment, and even cyclical or seasonal business trends, all managers require accurate, timely, complete, and relevant information. Additionally, it is important to recognize that information is often shared with other departments within the same organization.

*Accurate* information provides a true, reliable picture of the situation. Inaccurate information is of little or no use for decision-making purposes. Consider, for example, a sales manager who has received overstated sales figures and exaggerated sales forecasts from a regional sales representative trying to impress the boss. If the manager uses that information to prepare company-wide sales projections for the next planning period, the result may be misallocation of marketing resources, with the region whose sales representative supplied the inaccurate information gaining a disproportionate percentage of the expenditures. Under this scenario, the firm's other sales regions would not receive optimal marketing support, and the sales and profits of the whole organization might suffer.

*Timely* information is available for use when needed. Timely does not necessarily mean quick or immediate availability; rather, it means information that is accessible precisely when it is needed in the decision-making process. Timeliness depends on each manager's unique situation and needs.

*Complete* information includes all the facts and details required for a particular situation. If a manager receives incomplete information, the decision-making process then takes on an added level of uncertainty and risk. For example, suppose a human resource manager turns in estimates of projected quarterly hirings for only three of the company's four operating regions. To meet approaching deadlines, his superior hastily projects the missing figure based on last year's forecast, failing to consider the likely effect of a slowing economy. Misallocation of resources is the likely result.

*Relevant* information meets the requirements of the manager's particular needs and circumstances. The information needs of a marketing manager, for example, will probably differ considerably from those of a human resources manager. While information regarding the results of a recent direct-mail promotional campaign targeted at purchasing managers of heavy industry clients in Singapore and Malaysia may be highly relevant to the marketing manager, the same information is likely to hold little interest for the human resources manager.

**Example:** Bob Antin, CEO of Veterinary Centers of America, a 20-unit chain of animal hospitals based in Santa Monica, California, has invested in information technology to keep his business growing. Antin invested $100,000 in a state-of-the-art phone system to automatically route calls to his nearest hospital. Previously, each hospital handled its own calls. Antin hopes the phone system will help boost business by 45%.

## MANAGEMENT INFORMATION SYSTEMS

To gain access to accurate, timely, complete, and relevant information, many organizations have turned to management information systems to manage a sometimes overwhelming amount of information. A **management information system (MIS)** organizes past, present, and projected data from both internal and external sources and processes them into usable information, which it then makes

**management information system (MIS)** A system that organizes past, present, and projected data from both internal and external sources and processes them into usable information.

**FIGURE 21.1**

**How an MIS Simplifies the Flow of Information**

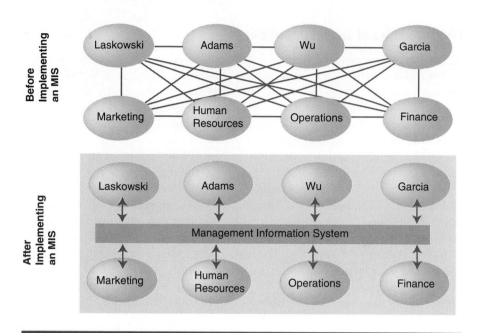

Example:   North Star Steel Company Inc. of Minneapolis, Minnesota, has begun upgrading its MIS department so that all of its customers will be able to take advantage of an electronic data interchange system. This would allow a real-time exchange of order and inventory data for the company's mill products.

available to managers at all organizational levels. Because managers—and other users of MISs—have different needs, information systems must be able to organize data into usable and accessible formats. Frito-Lay managers, for example, were able to pinpoint the problem behind a sales decline of Tostitos chips in San Antonio and Houston supermarkets because the company's MIS made data usable and accessible. Analysis of the data for south Texas showed that a competitor's white-corn tortilla chip was selling well at Tostitos' expense. Based on this information, Frito-Lay introduced a white-corn version of Tostitos, which quickly regained market share for Frito-Lay in those areas. Frito-Lay's MIS obtains daily sales data from retailers, analyzes them for trends, and even alerts managers about problems and opportunities in each of Frito-Lay's markets. By sorting and analyzing data, the system helps managers glean important information quickly without having to sort through "forklift trucks" of data.[1]

## How an MIS Works

The major task of a management information system is to gather, store and update, analyze, and report data. Companies with large management information systems generally employ an MIS manager to coordinate the workings of the system and manage the technicians and specialists who actually process the data.

Users enter data into a **database**, a collection of related data—past, present, and projected—organized for convenient access. Data are stored, typically in a computer, where they are accessible to all authorized users of the system. Although computers are not essential to the storing of data and updating of databases, they greatly facilitate the task, as we shall see later.

**database**
A collection of related data—past, present, and projected—organized for convenient access.

**FIGURE 21.2**

**Determining Information Needs**

Data must be analyzed, or processed, to be in a form useful to MIS users. An MIS can process stacks of sales data and provide a sales manager with a ranking by sales territory, by year, by sales dollar, by sales representative within each territory, or by some other factor. Many companies use their databases to identify and target established customers with special sales promotions because that approach may cost less than trying to bring in new customers. A Sacramento, California, Toyota dealer, for example, used the company's database to target area residents who had bought Toyotas three years before with a mass mailing just before a sale.[2] Figure 21.1 illustrates how an MIS simplifies the flow of information.

## Determining Information System Needs

Every organization has its own unique set of information needs that must be clearly understood before it can design and implement a system to satisfy those needs. To understand them, the designer of the information system must consider both organizational and managerial factors (Figure 21.2).[3]

**Organizational Factors.**    As it does with many other elements, an organization's environment affects its information needs. On a basic level, the more uncertain and complex a company's competitive and technological environment, the greater will be its requirements for accurate, timely, complete, and relevant information. The timeliness of information is at a particular premium in these instances. For example, in the dynamic and unpredictable computer industry, where products become obsolete at ever increasing rates and competition is intense, companies require "real-time" information—that is, information that is developing as it is reported—more so than do companies operating in more stable environments. Companies such as Dell and Microsoft require highly sophisticated information systems not only to monitor rapidly changing environmental conditions, but also to assist in a wide range of business activities designed to keep them ahead of the competition.

An organization's size also affects its information system needs. The larger the firm, the greater will be its need for information in terms of sheer volume. For instance, a large oil company such as Exxon with roughly twice the number of employees and four times the sales of Amoco will require a more elaborate information system than its smaller industry competitor.

Additionally, as the level of organizational diversity—the number of industries in which a firm is involved, its number of divisional units—increases, the nature of the information it requires changes. A highly diversified company such as Time Warner, for example, with a host of broad interests in industries as diverse as publishing, broadcasting, and entertainment services, will require a more complex information system capable of integrating a vast array of interorganizational information into an accurate, timely, complete, and relevant whole. A more narrowly focused organization such as the one that publishes *Reader's Digest* requires a less complex information system. While both organizations need information characterized by these essential factors, the challenge to capture and integrate it is greater in the highly diversified firm.

**Managerial Factors.**    Factors related to the characteristics of individual managers within an organization also affect information system needs. Just as different functional units within an organization have different responsibilities, they also have different information systems needs. For example, managers in a firm's legal department need information regarding legal precedents and ongoing judicial actions that might have current or future implications for the firm. Operations managers need information about new manufacturing technology and the price and quality of resources, while marketing managers need information about the company's sales, prices, and advertising effectiveness.

Although managers of each functional area of a company have unique information needs, these needs cannot be considered in isolation. It is important to consider the degree of interaction between the individual units as well. When managers in different areas need to work closely together, the information system must be coordinated so that each may readily access the information needed. For example, consider a product marketing manager for a large national banking firm who is developing a promotional campaign to introduce a new product targeted at individuals over 55 years of age. In developing the campaign, she must work closely with the manager of the legal department to ensure that advertising claims and product features do not violate any regulations or otherwise expose the organization to legal liability. In such a case, the product marketing manager should be able easily to access usable information about the project to guide her actions and to reduce the possibility of having to redo or rethink either promotional or product strategy.

Another factor that must be considered when assessing information systems needs is the manager's level within the organization. In general, the higher the level of the manager, the less specific and more long-term oriented the information will need to be. At the supervisory level, decisions are generally routine and well-defined; the informational needs of first-line managers can be met by normal information processing activities such as the preparation of financial statements

**Example:** Determining information needs in his organization is the job of Larry Grandia, vice president of information systems at Intermountain Health Care (Salt Lake City, Utah). Grandia joined corporate senior management in setting priorities for affiliates to achieve systemwide objectives. He believes someone in the organization must link information system capabilities with the strategic direction of the organization.

and routine recordkeeping. Middle managers require a broader range of internal information and rapid processing and retrieval of data so that they can develop operating plans for their areas. Managers at the highest levels require broad-based, summarized information to allow them to monitor corporate activities and conduct long-range strategic planning.

Returning to the previous example of the development of a new product at the national banking firm, the executive vice president of marketing may be chiefly concerned with knowing aggregate projected demand and cost figures for the product as a whole over a six-year period. The product marketing manager will need information on first-year projected demand and costs within each of the bank's numerous marketing areas. The manager of an individual bank branch will be concerned with receiving information that will facilitate getting the product up and running on the day of introduction inasmuch as he or she must ensure that bank employees and customers understand procedures, specifications, and features related to the new product.

## Characteristics of Effective MIS Development, Implementation, and Usage

It is useful at this time to consider some characteristics of effective MIS development, implementation, and usage. Generally, an MIS investment should enable the firm to create new business processes; a successful MIS may depend on external systems experts; and the system must be "user/worker-friendly."[4]

**Creation of New Business Processes.**   Rather than merely pouring money and processing power into the automation of antiquated ways of doing business, expenditures in management information systems should be viewed as investments in the creation of entirely new operational processes. For example, heavy-equipment manufacturer Caterpillar was able to return to profitability only after successfully implementing a $1.85 billion information and production systems technology program which totally reengineered the way in which the company tracks and accesses inventory at 17 of its plants.[5] In short, computers themselves are not the key to improved organizational performance:  It is how they are used that determines their true value.

**Use of Third-Party Systems Experts.**   Because any one organization seldom possesses all the knowledge with which to most effectively design, implement, and use an MIS best suited to its needs, successful MISs are often the result of collaboration with third parties who are experts in system matters. However, the company must work closely with these external experts to ensure that its particular needs are adequately addressed. Caterpillar, for example, worked closely with experts from GM's Electronic Data Systems (EDS) division to redesign many of the processes in its new inventory automation system.[6]

**The System Must Be "User/Worker-Friendly."**   To ensure effective usage, MISs should be designed and implemented with the objective of minimizing system user resistance and frustration. Although this complex task is often easier said than done, Table 21.1 discusses several of the more crucial activities to which managers must attend.

**Example:** McKinsey & Co., a management-consulting firm, made capital investments in the fastest-growing area of consulting—information technology—by acquiring Information Consulting Group. McKinsey launched an elaborate international network for making better use of the knowledge its consultants gather on assignments around the world.

**TABLE 21.1**

**Creating User-Friendly Management Information Systems**

| Activities | Explanation |
| --- | --- |
| 1. Carefully test new systems and introduce them in stages. | Employees are likely to resist complicated systems forced on them all at once, or which frequently malfunction during initial periods of use. |
| 2. Involve those who will actually use the system in all stages of MIS development. | No one understands the job to be done better than employees. Also, system users are more likely to accept and be patient with a system they feel they helped develop. |
| 3. Clearly communicate business objectives and how MIS usage helps meet these objectives to system users. | Employees will not likely adopt a new MIS if they do not understand its connection to both overall corporate objectives and their own welfare. Change will not occur without a clear reason to do so. |
| 4. Teach employees system usage by helping them improve their performance. | It is far more important to learn how to do the job better than merely to learn how to use the new system. Once employees realize they can improve their performance, proper system usage will follow. |
| 5. Don't ignore the generation gap. | Many higher-level managers lack advanced computer skills. However, there is no better way to get lower-level system acceptance than through observation of executive-level commitment to, and actual—visible—use of, the system. |

*Source:* Adapted from David Kirkpatrick, "Making It All Worker-Friendly," *Fortune* 128 (Autumn 1993; Special Information Technology Edition): 44–53; and Stratford Sherman, "How to Bolster the Bottom Line," *Fortune* 128 (Autumn 1993; Special Information Technology Edition): 14–28.

## USING COMPUTERS IN MANAGEMENT INFORMATION SYSTEMS

Computers have made giant strides in information processing because of their speed and accuracy in calculating, classifying, storing, sorting, and summarizing data. Consequently, computers have become an important component in many management information systems. Large businesses, for example, typically invest around 8 percent of their total revenues in telecommunications, computers, and other technologies. Such expenditures account for a growing share of corporate spending in the United States, representing nearly 15 percent of all capital investment in 1992, up from just 8 percent in 1980.[7] Worldwide, spending in computer technology totaled some $350 billion in 1992, while training employees to use this equipment cost organizations in the United States alone between $2 billion and $5 billion.[8] At the same time, the occupational segment of "computer professionals and technicians" is considered the fastest growing sector of the U.S. work force, with demand for systems analysts and computer scientists expected to increase nearly 80 percent, and demand for computer programmers projected to climb over 55 percent, by the year 2005.[9]

Although a management information system does not require a computer, its concepts and practices are closely related to those of computers. An MIS processes data into information relevant to users of the system. The large growth in the number of computer installations in both profit and nonprofit organizations reflects significant increases in the amount of available data. Many companies, regardless of size, rely on computer-based information systems to organize, manipulate, and distribute information. Computers are a prime example of the impact of new technology on business practices and capabilities. In the last two decades,

GE Medical Systems replaced 200 pounds of manuals with a computer-based information system to help its field service engineers repair medical imaging machines such as CAT scanners. Before switching to laptops, the engineers estimated they spent 15 percent of their time during a service call traveling to their cars to check procedures and get information from manuals stored in car trunks. Now the company's 2,500 field engineers use laptop computers with CD-ROM readers that allow them to carry all their reference information to job sites. The switch to laptop computers has helped GE Medical raise productivity 9 percent.

*Source:* © Ann States/SABA.

computers have become accessible to just about everyone from kindergarten students to people involved in the most complex business tasks.

## Hardware versus Software

The two main ingredients of any computer system, as described below, are computer hardware and software.

**Hardware.**    Regardless of size, all computers have the same basic physical components, called **hardware.** Computer hardware is generally classified into three categories on the basis of size and computing ability, although technological advances are increasingly blurring the differences between them. Mainframe computers, the largest and fastest computers available, are usually multi-user, general-purpose computers. Because of their large size—they may occupy entire rooms or floors of buildings—and high costs—often in excess of $1 million—they are usually used by large corporations, banks, and government organizations. The very largest mainframes are supercomputers, which have vastly expanded memories and perform more operations faster than standard mainframes. Minicomputers are usually desk-sized computers used in applications too large or too specialized for a microcomputer and too small for a mainframe. Microcomputers—better known as personal computers (PCs)—are the smallest, least powerful, and least expensive of all basic computer types. In wide personal use in the home, microcomputers are also popular in small and large businesses that do not require computers with large memory capabilities. PCs may also be linked together or to minicomputers or to a mainframe as part of a computer network.

Regardless of size, all computer systems consist of (1) a *central processing unit (CPU)*, used for storing data and programs, processing instructions, and performing computations, and (2) *peripheral devices*—keyboard, printer, mouse, monitor, disk drives, modem, CD-ROM—which are used to either enter (input) raw data into the system or transmit processed data (output) between system components. For example, a manager may input data by typing them on his or her computer's keyboard; the processed data may then be printed out on a laser printer or sent to the home office via a modem (a device that allows a computer to communicate over telephone lines).

**hardware**
The basic physical components of a computer.

Frank St. Onge, manager of marketing analysis for lamp-light manufacturer Osram/Sylvania, uses a customized version of Tactician software to show sales reps and wholesalers where competitors are, where customers are, and what areas of the country have the greatest sales potential. The software is part of a geographic information system (GIS) that includes geographic and demographic information from the corporate database. The system enables St. Onge to illustrate and analyze data on digitized maps rather than presenting the information on spreadsheets.

*Source:* © John Madere.

**software**

A computer program or set of commands that instructs a computer to perform various operations, such as reading, analyzing, or storing data in a specified location.

**Software.**    **Software** is a computer program, a set of commands that instruct a computer to perform various operations, such as reading, analyzing, or storing data in a specified location. *WordPerfect,* for example, is a word-processing program used in many companies to create, manipulate, store, and process text such as letters and reports. Some companies employ programmers to create and revise specialized software or they hire outside programmers to do so, but because developing software is both expensive and time-consuming, many businesses now buy ready-made software. The availability of such software has increased markedly in recent years. So many firms now produce software that costs have decreased, making software affordable to most businesses.

Additionally, companies may create or buy software that is specific for their industry. In the insurance industry, new software can help insurers detect suspicious patterns of billing and treatment to identify fraud. Travelers Corporation, for example, uses software that looks for signs of overcharging by doctors and laboratories. A program developed by Aetna Life & Casualty, which finds 500 indicators of fraud a month out of millions of claims, was responsible for 15 percent of the $38 million Aetna recovered in bad health insurance payments in 1992.[10] Companies as diverse as Black & Decker, Hasbro, and Lotus Development are adopting specialized "help desk" software to collect information and troubleshooting guidelines on their products and store them in databases; customer-support personnel can then easily access the data to answer queries about products. Such customer support operations are becoming increasingly important as more customers buy complex products—particularly highly technical ones such as computers or power tools—from discount retailers sometimes unable to supply adequate technical information.[11]

## Computer Networks

**computer networks**
Systems that permit different computers to communicate with each other.

**local-area network (LAN)**
A network in which computers are linked together directly within one building or one plant.

**wide-area network (WAN)**
A network in which computers are linked by telephone lines or long-range communications devices.

Many businesses—particularly those with branch offices—have benefited from **computer networks**, systems that permit different computers to communicate with each other. A network can be a **local-area network (LAN)**, in which computers are linked together directly within one building or one plant, or a **wide-area network (WAN)**, in which computers are linked by telephone lines or long-range communications devices (Figure 21.3). For example, a Westinghouse man-

### FIGURE 21.3

**WANs and LANs**

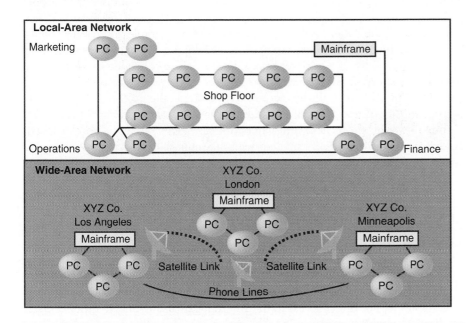

ufacturing plant might have a LAN that allows different computers within the plant to communicate with each other, and to access the plant's mainframe database. All of Westinghouse's manufacturing plants may be linked in a WAN to allow managers in different plants to communicate and transfer information as well as to send data to and receive instructions from the company's headquarters.

A network can connect mainframes, minicomputers, and personal computers. Many networks are centered on a mainframe or a minicomputer (called a *server*) that stores databases and other information vital to all parts of the network and is thus the heart of a firm's management information system. Each user of the network has access to a computer (called a *client*), often a PC, that stores enough software and information for his or her immediate needs and communicates with the rest of the network. Store managers for Mrs. Field's Cookies, for example, have personal computers that help them run their stores. Networking with the home office's minicomputer allows the store manager to transmit data or to obtain information about inventory levels and sales projections. An individual workstation computer may also have specialized software to handle an employee's specific needs and may be hooked up to specialized peripherals, such as printers, plotters (which print sophisticated graphics), scanners (which transfer printed material to computer language), modems, and other devices.

While a manager is most likely to use his or her company's internal computer network, it is also possible to access huge, multiorganization networks. One such network that has dramatically increased in importance in recent years is the Internet, a network of corporate, university, government, and other computer networks around the world. Though it is expensive, more and more companies are linking their own networks to the Net, as it is often called, to allow their employees to communicate with companies, consultants, customers, and other interested

**Example:** The Japanese are abandoning their resistance to computer networking and are now using Internet. In the past year usage has doubled; two million Japanese E-mail addresses and 1,524 networks are now linked to the global network. While they are behind the United States, they are on par with France, Germany, and Great Britain. Jun Murai, the "Internet Samurai," runs a company called Internet Initiative Japan and feels that when the Japanese see something new and convenient, it gets popular pretty fast.

**electronic mail**

The exchange of "letters" or messages from computer to computer; also called E-mail.

**Example:** Developers can access Microsoft Canada Inc. through an E-mail network service to get immediate information on Microsoft development tools and technology. This service is accessed on the Internet and is the first service of its kind by Microsoft anywhere in the world. It will allow software developers to stay current on products and seminars.

**Example:** Daytime TV will get wired in the fall of 1994 when "Days of Our Lives" becomes the first interactive soap opera. Viewers will be able to voice their opinion on the fate of their favorite star by using a handheld wireless control unit developed by Interactive Network. The electronic interactive network will be available in San Francisco, Chicago, Sacramento, and South Bend, Indiana.

people in locations around the globe. Companies with Net access can allow their workers to exchange messages with virtually anyone in the world who has a computer and a modem, to upload or download files from other computer systems or allow users to download files from their own systems, to join discussion groups (called Usenet news groups) on any conceivable subject, and to access other computer networks in order to use their databanks. For example, a software company manager in Brussels whose company is developing a new spreadsheet to run under Windows NT (a computer operating system) may be able to obtain information and source code directly from Microsoft (the marketer of NT) through Internet. The Net currently links some 15 million people in 50 countries, including Japan, Russia, and Mexico, and adds more users in more countries every day. Companies can also access other network services such as General Electric Information Service (GEIS); smaller firms may choose instead to join less expensive commercial online services such as Delphi or NetCom.

## Communicating with Computers

**Electronic mail**—also called E-mail—is the exchange of "letters" or messages from computer to computer. Using the organization's network, individuals can send E-mail to managers, employees, and workers in other facilities across the country and even overseas. Companies that have access to online providers such as CompuServe or direct access to the Internet can also E-mail to others outside the firm. Although E-mail was once the exclusive realm of computer software and hardware marketers, millions of employees now have the capability. Table 21.2 shows some symbols and acronyms E-mailers and news group participants often use to enhance their messages.

One benefit of electronic mail is that businesspeople no longer have to play "phone tag," that is, return another person's phone call only to learn that the person is not in; the process of leaving messages and missing return calls can mean that several days pass before actual contact is made. With electronic mail, you simply leave an electronic message, to which the receiver responds when convenient.

*Electronic bulletin boards* are another method of communicating via computers. Whereas E-mail involves one person sending a message to or more specified receivers, an electronic bulletin board allows the sender to post a message for any participant to read and discuss, just as if he or she had posted a handwritten notice to an actual bulletin board in the hallway for all to see. Many corporate computer networks include an electronic bulletin board where employees can post questions, discuss work (and even nonwork) issues, and air complaints.

More companies are beginning to provide electronic bulletin board services (BBSs) for customer use. A customer having difficulty with a new piece of computer hardware, for example, may be able to "log onto" the manufacturer's BBS and pose questions to online experts as to how to resolve the problem. Some companies are even marketing their products over BBSs. Consumers looking for virus detection and elimination software, for example, may log onto a BBS run by McAfee Associates and download the company's latest virus scanner, mailing payment to the company if they like the program. McAfee, based in Santa Clara, California, gets 90 percent of its $8.4 million revenues from its BBS. Customers of Cleveland-based Book Stacks Unlimited can order books and movies from that company's BBS.[12]

Computer networks also allow managers to hold conferences. In *computer conferencing*, each participant sits at his or her own terminal and types in reac-

**TABLE 21.2**

## Some Symbols and Acronyms Used in Electronic Mail

Because it is not possible in an electronic medium to detect subtle meanings normally conveyed through facial expressions, E-mailers often use symbols to indicate their feelings, to tell the reader what they normally might express with a smile or wink. (Hint: to read the symbols, look at them sideways.) Acronyms serve as a common shorthand.

| | |
|---|---|
| :-) | smile |
| :-> | another smile |
| ;-) | wink (writer is kidding or being sarcastic) |
| :-\| | frown |
| :-( | sad |
| <g> | grin |
| <vbg> | very big grin |
| BTW | by the way |
| FWIW | for what it's worth |
| FYI | for your information |
| RSN | real soon now |
| OTOH | on the other hand |
| IMO | in my opinion |
| IMHO | in my humble opinion |
| LOL | laughing out loud |
| ROFL | rolling on the floor laughing |

tions, questions, ideas, or instructions to others who are also online. Conferencing is particularly useful when the participants are in different locations. For example, the managers of all of Chevrolet's manufacturing plants scattered across North America could hold a computer conference to discuss labor issues or new robotics technology.

## Integrating Information Technologies

Companies today typically strive to integrate their information technology tools to gain maximum benefits. For example, San Francisco-based pharmaceutical distributor McKesson greatly improved its retail distribution system—reducing costly order errors by 70 percent and realizing substantial productivity gains—by using a 12-ounce computer/scanner/two-way radio device that is worn like a cast on the hand and forearm of order fillers in the company's 22,000-item warehouse.[13] Catalina Marketing of Anaheim, California, relies on a personal computer/scanner link-up to issue "on-the-spot" coupons at supermarket checkout counters. The system, which also supplies a wealth of information to both sponsoring companies and retailers, issues the coupons—complementary, competitive, or same product—based on what the shopper purchases and serves a network of 5,000 stores with some 70 million customers.[14]

**Telecommuting**, using telecommunications technology to work from home or other places outside the traditional workplace, is becoming an increasingly popular integration of information systems technologies, boosting organizational performance and helping save the environment at the same time. For example, in Phoenix, AT&T has creatively linked the use of its telecommunications

**telecommuting**
Using telecommunications technology to work from home or other places outside the traditional workplace.

American Express Travel Services' Project Hearth telecommuting program allows travel counselor Faye Compton to work at home. Linked electronically with American Express's phone and data lines, she looks up fares and books reservations on her personal computer. Telecommuting is boosting employee productivity. The typical agent handles 26 percent more calls at home, resulting in a 46 percent average increase in revenue from travel bookings, or about $30,000 annually for each at-home employee. Compton attributes her increased productivity not to working harder but to better concentration because her home office lacks the many distractions of a corporate office environment.

*Source:* © Louis Psihoyos/MATRIX.

technology to the solution of nagging environmental problems caused by high per-capita automobile usage. In response to an order by the state legislature to reduce commuter driving, AT&T set up a pilot telecommuting program with Arizona's largest employer, the state itself. Through use of telecommunications technology—fax, modem, and computer—the 134 participants in the initial program were allowed the opportunity to work from their homes by accessing remote AT&T MISs one day each week. In just six months, participants in the program drove nearly 100,000 fewer miles than they normally would have, preventing some 1.9 million tons of air pollution, while at the same time saving nearly 4,000 hours of active work time that otherwise would have been spent unproductively in transit. Now, several years after completion of the pilot project, AT&T has nearly 450 "telecommuters" in the Phoenix area.[15] Similarly, American Express has also recently successfully linked information systems technologies through telecommuting to dramatically improve the performance of its travel services operations, while at the same time finding that telecommuting employees, especially working mothers, enjoy the opportunity to spend more time at home.[16]

## TYPES OF INFORMATION SYSTEMS

Several basic types of information systems exist, including transaction support systems, decision support systems, executive information systems, and expert systems. Organizations, particularly large ones, often find that they need more than one type of system to satisfy their information management needs.

### Transaction Support Systems

**transaction support system (TSS)**
An information system that handles routine, repetitive business transactions.

Often the first computerized form of information system adopted by an organization, a **transaction support system (TSS)** handles routine, repetitive business transactions. TSSs are best suited for managing high volumes of similar transactions where large amounts of raw data must be summarized. Examples of information that a TSS might be designed to handle include order entry, charges and payments to accounts, and the preparation and transmission of monthly billing statements.

TSSs arc common cnough today that you probably intcract with a widc variety of them on a daily basis. Every time you make a credit card purchase, use an automated teller machine (ATM), or purchase goods that are run through a scanner at a store's checkout counter, you are interacting with a TSS. Although rather common and unsophisticated relative to other types of information systems, TSSs are an integral and irreplaceable part of the overall MIS of many organizations. For example, information gathered from point-of-sale scanners is used by consumer product manufacturers such as Procter & Gamble and RJR Nabisco to track and forecast sales, as well as by retailers such as Wal-Mart and J.C. Penney, to determine shelf-space allocation and to monitor and control levels of inventory.

**Example:** Scanning or bar coding was used by Wrangler, a subsidiary of BF Corporation. The company has set a higher standard for replenishment by taking full advantage of apparel bar coding and electronic data interchange. This new, higher standard has helped in the company's men's jeans division and in the company's ability to move the product quickly, at more than 10 turnovers per year.

## Decision Support Systems

A **decision support system (DSS)** aids managers in decision making by helping them anticipate the possible outcomes of alternative actions. A DSS, for example, can determine how sales and profits might be affected by higher or lower interest rates or how sales forecasts, advertising expenditures, production levels, and the like might affect overall profits. For this reason, a decision support system is often a major component of a business's management information system, as is the casc with the prcviously citcd cxamplc of Frito-Lay.

A **group decision support system (GDSS)**, a special set of computer systems designed to aid group decision making, focuses on expediting the exchange of ideas about the solving of a particular problem within a group setting. Such systems are commonly used in *computerized or electronic brainstorming,* in which all group members can participate at their own pace without fear of interrupting or possibly offending other, more senior members of the group—as can occur with the more traditional face-to-face brainstorming format. Also, due to the higher level of anonymity afforded by computers, GDSSs increase the likelihood of drawing out the thoughts and feelings of more reserved group members as well as getting more honest opinions from the group as a whole. Still another advantage of using GDSSs, over the traditional method of brainstorming, is having a more reliable means of capturing and organizing all ideas generated; anything and everything that comes to mind is quickly and easily input into the system, which collects and stores the information for further analysis and use at later stages of the decision-making process.

**decision support system (DSS)**
An information system that aids managers in decision making by helping them anticipate the possible outcomes of alternative actions.

**group decision support system (GDSS)**
A special set of computer systems designed to aid group decision making.

## Executive Information Systems

One of the more recent developments in decision support systems is the **executive information system (EIS)**, an easy-to-use DSS designed for executives who have limited experience using computers but need access to the firm's database. A properly designed EIS will place summarized key information at the executive's fingertips, ready for rapid retrieval and review. The intent is to allow the executive to monitor and evaluate corporate performance easily, rather than focusing on the details of a specific decision.

San Francisco-based oil giant Chevron Corporation made use of EIS technology during an attempted hostile takeover bid by Pennzoil in the late 1980s. The company's chief financial officer, along with 45 other senior executives, maintained access to stock market operations and to each other by means of electronic mail to closely monitor Chevron stock transactions in real time (as they happened). By being able to monitor the transactions in this manner and to communicate readily

**executive information system (EIS)**
An easy-to-use DSS designed for executives who have limited experience using computers but need access to the firm's database.

Dean Barr, investment fund manager at LBS Capital Management, uses a hybrid expert system—neural network program in making buy-and-sell stock investment decisions. Barr calls the network "the ultimate decision maker." He believes it does a better job more consistently than most analysts do because it is not emotionally involved in the decisions. He says the neural network makes timely suggestions to sell stocks weeks before their prices begin to fall. Stock trading neural network software programs such as Stock Prophet and BrainMaker use many data variables to predict a stock's price trend, including a stock's price and trading volume, futures contracts, and patterns in a company's debt level, cash flow, and earnings estimates.

*Source:* © 1994 Red Morgan.

with one another, they were able to fend off the takeover bid.[17] Other corporations that have effectively used EISs include Mack Truck, Centel, Fisher-Price, and General Dynamics.[18]

## Expert Systems and Neural Networks

**artificial intelligence**

Programs that seek to make computers able to work—to "think"—as much like the human mind as possible.

**expert system**

Decision support programs that mimic human decision-making processes by using a collection of thousands of "if-then" rules to solve complex problems.

**Example:** An expert system called the Safety Expert System was developed by the U.S. Army Medical Research Institute of Infectious Diseases. The system permits retrieval of specific biological and chemical safety information within minutes and can be tailored to meet the needs of an organization.

Decision support programs may incorporate **artificial intelligence**, which seeks to make computers able to work—to "think"—as much like the human mind as possible. The study of artificial intelligence led to the development of **expert systems**, which mimic human decision-making processes by using a collection of thousands of "if-then" rules to solve complex problems. They are often used to capture and computerize rare decision-making expertise, such as that possessed by an individual who has performed a highly complex and specialized task for a number of years. The rare expertise can be preserved either to replace the expert, perhaps on his or her retirement, or to transport the unique knowledge to locations in other parts of the world when it would be impractical, in terms of both risk and cost, to transport the expert.

Expert systems may also be applied to relatively tedious, recurring tasks. For example, an expert system might be programmed to make routine decisions about maintenance on a dam. If the system detects a pressure loss in one inflow channel, it can consider several preprogrammed options and perhaps "choose" to increase water flow from another channel to ensure that sufficient pressure exists to generate electricity.

Expert systems can enhance decision making because they are capable of considering a far larger range of options than can one individual. However, the decisions they make cannot take into account emotional and other human factors, and their use in some applications may therefore be limited. For example, although expert systems are now being used to help marketing managers formulate advertising objectives, advertising researchers caution that such usage requires the employment of at least three human-based validation criteria: (1) the validation of the actual content of the knowledge base, (2) comparison with actual human expert judgment, and (3) a determination of whether use of the expert system actually leads to improved decisions.[19] Thus, while the availability of information

## BUSINESS DILEMMA

*You're the Manager ...What Would You Do?*

THE COMPANY:    Elliott, Layman, and Pierce Advertising

YOUR POSITION:    Account Supervisor, Horizon Automotive

THE PLACE:    Apopka, FL

Elliott, Layman, and Pierce Advertising (ELP) has been a well-respected regional advertising agency in the Orlando area for over 20 years. The agency has won numerous awards for its highly creative print and radio advertising. It specializes in retail service, handling some fast-food accounts, small retail clothing stores, a regional hardware chain, and a dry cleaning franchise. ELP has just pitched and won the largest account it has ever managed, Horizon Automotive, the fifth largest automobile manufacturer in the United States. This account represents approximately $100 million in agency billings over the next year. In light of this major growth, ELP will hire new employees, move into larger facilities, and open a new office in Overton, Missouri, Horizon's home office and main production facility.

Although ELP has the creative talent to handle the account, it lacks the technology that many of its competitors possess. One of the stipulations of winning the Horizon account was that ELP invest in a sophisticated computer system that will, among other things, link ELP to Horizon's central offices and regional dealerships across the country. This stipulation requires not only new computers for ELP's offices, but a fiber optic hookup that will cost approximately $1 million.

ELP will benefit from the computer system in increased employee productivity, faster project turnaround, increased profitability, and reduced overhead in the long term. The system provides electronic mail capability and enables the transfer of sales data and order information on an hourly, daily, weekly, or monthly basis. Additionally, the system will help ELP employees create ads by manipulating images on the screen, changing colors, rotating images, or changing any aspect of ad design, even transmitting a copy to the client for approval. Speed is the main advantage of using a system such as this.

ELP now faces the task of developing a system to handle the information that it will be receiving and sending through the computer network. It has never had a client that provided so much online information to its employees. ELP can now develop an ad campaign or promotion and monitor sales on an hourly or daily basis to evaluate its success. Horizon not only expects this kind of monitoring and evaluation of promotional success, it also expects ELP to conduct research on main ad campaigns to determine the effect of this advertising.

ELP also has been able to set up the computer system to provide advanced human resources management capabilities. The agency's employees can log on to check their benefits, review their profit sharing status, check health insurance information, etc. They can also send questions to the appropriate individual with reference to particular aspects of their personnel file.

ELP has grown from a medium-sized regional advertising agency to one that now handles a major national account. Its information system requirements have given it a unique opportunity to grow and advance. As ELP's account supervisor for the new Horizon Automotive account, you must help integrate and manage the account, using the new information system.

### Questions

1. How should you proceed to educate employees about using the new system?
2. What role should Horizon Automotive play in organizing the system and how should you determine the amount of communication necessary?
3. Discuss how such an information system could be used to benefit other accounts. What are the internal benefits?

---

system technologies such as expert systems represents definite opportunities, they are not likely to completely replace human judgment anytime in the foreseeable future. Such technologies should therefore be used with caution, and only for those distinct tasks for which they are best suited.

Another form of artificial intelligence gaining increasing acceptance among organizations is *neural networks,* which involve actually training the computer to think like the human mind by presenting it with repeated examples of information for use in forming patterns of logic with which to make future decisions.[20] Mellon Bank, for example, implemented a neural network system in 1993 that has greatly

**Comment on Box:** Have students share their answers to the three questions in the "Business Dilemma" box with the class. Discuss the importance of organizing and planning for a new system in advance. How can the input of all user groups be included in the decision? How can they anticipate and plan for future system needs?

improved the detection of credit card fraud. The company estimated that the system, although costing nearly $1 million, paid for itself in roughly six months. Neural networks, which often outperform both expert systems and human judgment, have also recently been applied in judicial, stock trading, real estate appraisal, and airline passenger scheduling settings, as well as for the prediction of bank and thrift failures.[21]

# THE IMPACT OF INFORMATION TECHNOLOGY

Modern organizations have been and will continue to be greatly affected by advances in information technology. To manage information effectively, however, it is important that managers understand the effects and limitations of such technology as they try to establish and implement management information systems.

## The Effects of Information Technology

The effects of information technology on an organization fall into two general categories: organizational effects and performance effects.

**Organizational Effects.**    To keep pace with the rapid rate of technological and environmental change and maintain competitiveness in an increasingly complex and global business marketplace, many organizations are turning to strategic alliances and partnerships of varying permanence with other firms that would have been unthinkable just a few years ago. For example, Apple Computer, lacking the manufacturing capacity to produce its entire line of PowerBook notebook computers, turned to Sony—known for its expertise in miniaturization—to manufacture the least-expensive model in the PowerBook product line. A year later, after sales of more than 100,000 Sony-made models, the joint effort was ended.[22]

**Example:** RJR Nabisco recently implemented better use of information technology to reshape its consumer-products business.

A more advanced and complicated if somewhat controversial form of information-based alliance is currently in the developmental stage. Called "the virtual corporation," it involves a temporary alliance of several independent companies—suppliers, customers, and even traditional business rivals—linked by information technology for purposes of exploiting an opportunity. Each company contributes only its specific expertise to the alliance to form an "ideal organization" for the task at hand. Once the venture has been completed, more likely than not, the group effort will be discontinued.[23] Companies such as Apple, Sony, Intel, Sharp, and Xerox are at the forefront of applying technology to create such alliances, which promise to create both new opportunities as well as new challenges for managers.

Information technology commonly affects internal organizational structure in several other important ways. First, most organizations create a "systems" department, often headed by a chief information officer (CIO), to maintain, upgrade, and find new uses for the MIS, as well as to train users to operate it in an efficient manner. Second, adoption of information technology often leads to staff reductions because of increased individual performance and supervision capabilities. Such reductions can help a firm trim costs and give it a competitive edge. Third, not only are more and more companies replacing workers with technology, but an increasing number are also opting to hire consultants who specialize in information technology management to develop, install, implement, and upgrade their MISs.[24] Finally, at the same time as the above trends are occurring, companies are increasingly also hiring more temporary workers to handle programming, data entry, and other MIS tasks.[25]

**Performance Effects.**   Obviously, one of the primary objectives of a management information system is to improve organizational performance. If managers didn't think that the adoption of information system technology would increase performance, companies would not adopt such technology. Although it is difficult to measure accurately the value of investments made in information technology, and it may take years to do so, there is a growing consensus that such investments pay for themselves in terms of organizational performance gains and returns on investment.

MISs help companies improve performance in several ways. Particularly when computerized, they help companies "crunch numbers" and retrieve information faster and more conveniently, which should serve to improve decision making. MISs can also help companies react better and faster to changes in the environment. Recall the Frito-Lay example cited previously, in which the company's MIS enabled managers to identify a problem and resolve it. MISs can also help improve organizational coordination. Operational managers, marketing managers, and personnel managers often need to work closely together. For example, if the marketing manager projects that demand will increase, the operations manager must work with the human resources manager to ensure that the company hires or reassigns sufficient production workers to handle the increase. An MIS can help coordinate such essential managerial interactions.

**Example:** AT&T will soon begin offering video and data communications to companies that operate toll-free "800" numbers. In time, customers will be able to phone a catalog company like L. L. Bean with their computers and get photos and price lists for outdoor clothing and supplies as they talk to sales representatives on the telephone. Company officials plan to offer the enhanced 800-number services in early 1995.

## Information System Limitations

While computers and information systems provide enormous benefits such as improved productivity and information management, organizations should bear in mind the limitations of the use of information technology. We can classify these drawbacks as performance limitations, behavioral limitations, and health risks. Moreover, the "Ethics Encounter" box describes some ethical issues related to the use of information systems.

**Performance Limitations.**   Although management information systems have the potential to increase overall performance, adopting MIS technology may also have potential negative effects on a firm's bottom line. For example, the organizational effects described in the previous section carry with them possibly not-so-beneficial ramifications. Specifically, managers and scholars involved in the Total Quality Management movement have suggested that selectively replacing long-time organizational employees with information system technology, consultants, or temporary workers not only inhibits the company from learning how to operate most effectively as a cohesive unit, but also results in the loss of expert knowledge these individuals typically hold.[26] In short, some contend that the key to retaining customers is to retain employees. Replacing full-time employees with either information system technology or temporary workers may create a situation that compromises the company's long-term performance at the expense of short-term gains.

Additionally, computerized information systems are expensive and difficult to develop, and organizations may find that an MIS that seems ideally suited to their needs costs even more than anticipated. Additionally, once the system has been purchased, coordinating it—possibly with existing equipment—may be more

# Ethics ncounter

## ETHICAL ISSUES IN INFORMATION TECHNOLOGY

As you read this, a project so colossal is under way that your future—and the future of the United States, even the world—hangs in the balance. Such giants of U.S. communications as GTE, Bell Atlantic, Time Warner, and NYNEX are currently working to build and control a vast, intricate web of electronic networks as part of what many are calling "the rewiring of America." "America's information system" will be a network of networks—nationwide "information highways" built of glass fiber—controlled by a group of companies that will deliver an abundance of services to both homes and businesses. Phone calls, video images, and useful information in practically every imaginable shape and form will one day travel over fiber-optic lines. For the companies involved, the risks are as great as the opportunities. It is difficult to gauge the cost of the project at such an early stage, but just for a company to be actively involved typically requires an investment of at least a billion dollars. For the nation as a whole, the risk is that these companies will not be able to work together fast enough (optimistic estimates project a completion date of 2037) and that, with Japan, Germany, and France currently involved in similar "rewiring" projects, our ability as a nation to compete in an increasingly global economy may suffer as a result.

The risks inherent in technological innovation rest not only on those companies and nations most directly involved. Advances in technology carry with them very real ethical issues affecting the daily lives of people worldwide. Many critics of some of the major companies most directly involved in "the rewiring of America" feel strongly that these companies, by virtue of their gaining access inside millions of homes across the nation,

will take advantage of the situation, both exploiting and invading the privacy of the American public.

Technology-driven ethical issues such as these concern not only massive global projects, but the daily use of computer and surveillance technology by both individuals and companies. Ethical issues concerning business information systems are evident in a wide variety of abuses. For example, a Malaysian bank executive allegedly broke through his employer's elaborate security system in 1990 and looted customer accounts of some $1.5 million. Former employees of Continental Can Co. won a large financial settlement against the company after it was found that they had been victims of a plan to use a human resource management information system to avoid paying pensions. A senior vice president at American Express's North American data center operation allegedly used his privileged access to corporate information to create business for his own private company and to pressure American Express systems suppliers to purchase products from several of his personal ventures.

It is virtually impossible to discuss technology-driven ethical issues without addressing computer crime, once the exclusive realm of bright, boastful, well-educated teenagers (so-called "hackers") who honed their computing skills by breaking into computer systems as stunts to brag about.

Computer crime today involves not only the "playful" misuse of computer technology, but also the malicious deployment of telecommunications technology to steal valuable information, software, phone services, credit card numbers, and cash. According to USA Research, attacks on U.S. workplace computers increased from 339,000 in 1989 to 684,000 in 1991. With an estimated 60 percent of all personal computers linked to one or more computer networks by 1993, that number is certain to escalate.

With increasingly rapid advances in computers and other areas of high technology, new and often confusing ethical issues and risks for both business and individual technology users are sure to continue to arise. Projects like "the rewiring of America," while offering vast opportunities and benefits, carry with them great potential for misuse from which virtually no one is entirely immune. Big Brother may, indeed, be watching.

*Sources:* William G. Flanagan and Brigid McMenamin, "The Playground Bullies Are Learning to Type," *Forbes,* December 21, 1992, 184–189; Andrew Kupfer, "The Race to Rewire America," *Fortune,* April 19, 1993, 42–61; John P. McPartlin, "Ethics," *Information Week,* July 13, 1992, 30–40; Jim Nash, "Technology Raises Many New Ethics Questions," *Computerworld,* October 14, 1991, 89; and Glenn Rifkin, "The Ethics Gap," *Computerworld,* October 14, 1991, 83–85.

difficult than expected. Consequently, a company may cut corners or install the system carelessly, to the detriment of the system's performance and utility.

Like other sophisticated electronic equipment, information systems do not always work all the time. Such costly downtime may be due to a variety of causes. For example, pranksters (called "crackers" or "hackers") or disgruntled employees may sabotage systems that have weak security by damaging programs or entering false data. **Computer viruses**, computer programs concealed inside legitimate programs that change or destroy data kept on a computer, can damage or even cripple a system. Far more common is downtime due to power failures, poor telephone connections, equipment breakdowns, and similar problems, which can result in the phrase many consumers have come to dread: "We're sorry, but the computer is down."

Additionally, the information generated by an information system may not be as accurate, timely, complete, or relevant as needed. The quality of a computer system's output is determined by what is input into the system by programmers and users. Computer people use the acronym GIGO, which means "garbage in, garbage out," to indicate this basic computer premise. If a user makes a mistake entering a formula in a spreadsheet program, the results will be inaccurate and, if the error is not discovered and corrected quickly, it is likely to multiply, spread, and wreak havoc, possibly across the entire organization. For example, a software **bug**, an error in the program, resulted in a **crash**, or service failure, of AT&T's long-distance service in 1991, which ultimately hurt many businesses and individuals unable to complete their long-distance calls.[27]

The use of computers is also limited in situations where highly personal or sensitive information is involved. Wide access to computer files and the sharing of databases can mean loss of individual privacy. Credit records, for example, are sometimes made available to many organizations, and many people object to the widespread dispersal of such information. One reason for their objections is that if a credit record is incorrect, an individual might have trouble obtaining loans or other credit, sometimes without knowing why. Judicious use of computers in such situations is called for.

Information technology is simply not suited for all tasks or problems. Computers may be overused. Managers should remember that business associates, clients, and customers appreciate human contact. For example, a computer might shut off all shipments to a long-time customer who is overdue in paying a bill, whereas a phone call from the credit manager might identify a short-term cash-flow problem and result in a new payment schedule. Additionally, many people simply do not like computers and may even fear them. Without the human element, such customers might be lost forever. Employees, too, may fear that the automation of tasks customarily performed by people might "dehumanize" the workplace, making it a less rewarding environment in which to work.

Computers and information systems are a tool for decision making, not a crutch. Managers must still think for themselves. Even when computers are used in decision support systems, they should support the decision, not make it. A computer can assess quantitative data, but only a human being can contribute gut reactions and intuition.

**Behavioral Limitations.**   While information technology allows managers to access more information than ever before, too much information can overwhelm employees, cause stress, and even slow decision making. Thus, it is important to manage the quality and amount of available information to avoid "information overload."

---

**computer viruses**
Computer programs concealed inside legitimate programs that change or destroy data kept on a computer; can damage or even cripple a system.

**bug**
An error in a software program.

**crash**
A system service failure.

## orner

### Opportunities Increase for Systems Personnel

Positions in information systems technology await qualified college and technical-school graduates in abundance. Computer professionals and technicians—computer programmers, systems analysts, computer scientists, data-processing equipment repair personnel, etc.—have for some time constituted one of the fastest growing segments of the U.S. job market and will likely continue to do so into the twenty-first century. Experts say jobs for computer systems analysts and scientists will increase by nearly 80 percent by the year 2005. Moreover, as applications of emerging technologies, such as 3-D computing and virtual reality, become more commonplace in management information systems, as-yet-unheard-of opportunities for employment in systems technology are sure to develop. For example, over the next ten years, some 1.2 million positions are expected to open up for drafters skilled in application of computer-assisted systems.

Despite the continual flow of new technologies and the jobs created to operate and maintain them, computer programmers are certain to remain in high demand. In fact, by the year 2005, the number of such positions is expected to rise by well over 50 percent, to over 880,000 in the United States alone. Computer programmers write and "debug" software, the detailed instructions a computer must follow to process words, manipulate numbers, and handle other tasks. Because of the rapid advancement of computer technology, programmers must periodically take training courses to keep abreast of the latest developments in terms of both hardware and software application in their specific fields. Most computer programmers are employed by manufacturing firms, banks, insurance companies, data processing service organizations, utilities, and government agencies. For example, 25 percent of the nearly 15,000 employees at San Antonio-based home and auto insurer USAA work in the area of information services.

Regardless of exact job title or industry, the hallmark of information systems positions of the future will be vastly increased responsibility. Advances in technology have created opportunities for individuals who can not only operate or repair systems, but also integrate them to give the organization an innovative edge over competitors. Specifically, versatile systems specialists who can create harmony out of the often intimidating maze of available technology are increasingly assuming front-line strategic responsibility for organizational effectiveness.

There is also a need for systems personnel who can clearly and effectively communicate system capabilities and usage procedures to those individuals—such as middle- and executive-level managers—who must use them to make key strategic decisions. This so-called "soft-side" approach to technology integration is necessary because system users, particularly senior management, often possess limited computer capabilities; without clear explanation, they are likely to be intimidated by the system and not use it to its full capacity. Many companies find it harder to hire college graduates with soft-side system integration skills than those with only technical expertise.

In the quickly evolving frontier of information technology, technical competence is not enough. Tomorrow's computer professionals must also be able to foresee the direction of their company, clearly communicate that vision across the organization, and then assist in actual strategic planning and implementation. As a result, systems positions such as computer programmers once calling only for technical skills are now increasingly demanding knowledge in a broad range of organizational management disciplines such as finance, production management, marketing, and overall leadership capabilities in order to facilitate both career and organizational growth.

*Sources:* Gene Bylinsky, "The Payoff from 3-D Computing," *Fortune,* 128 (Autumn 1993—Special Information Technology Issue), 32–40; "How to Make Cybercash," *Worth,* September 1993, 60–68; Robert Levering and Milton Moskowitz, *The 100 Best Companies to Work For in America,* rev. ed. (New York: Plume, 1994); Louis S. Richman, "Jobs That Are Growing and Slowing," *Fortune,* July 12, 1993, 52–53; *VGM's Handbook of Business & Management Careers,* 2nd ed., Annette Selden, ed. (Chicago: NTC Publishing Group, 1993).

**Comment on Box:** Ask someone who works in the computer industry to speak to your class on technology and information needs for the future. A programmer at your university would be a good choice. How is the employee trained to deal with the changing nature of technology and growing information needs?

Social scientists are concerned that people who frequently use information technology may come to overidentify with information systems, adopting the computer's yes/no pattern of logic to the point that they can no longer tolerate ambiguity. People who suffer from such "technostress" may have difficulty moving between the computerized information system and social relationships.[28] Moreover, when an entire organization becomes overdependent on its information system, any minute interruption or glitch in the system may all but shut the entire operation down.

Managers, especially those relatively unfamiliar with systems operations, may expect an MIS to solve all the problems they encounter. They may expect the system to be so "user-friendly" that they need not waste valuable time reading manuals or attending training sessions. In such cases, dissatisfaction, frustration, and poor system utilization are the likely outcomes.

**Health Risks.**   Finally, there are potentially serious health-related issues that have been raised in recent years about the use of computers and other information technology. For example, there is concern about exposure to low-level radiation emitted by cathode-ray tubes (CRTs) housed in computer monitors. Some studies have suggested that people who work on computers for long periods of time may experience more headaches and miscarriages due to radiation exposure. Also, in early 1993, several national news stories suggested a link between prolonged use of cellular phones and brain cancer. Yet another problem associated with computers, this one well-documented, is carpal tunnel syndrome (CTS), a painful disorder in the hands and wrists caused by repetitive movements on a typewriter or computer keyboard.

**Putting the Limitations into Perspective.**   Novice and intermediate systems users are sometimes heard to say, when describing their level of computer competency, that they "know just enough to be dangerous." This is sometimes true, not only of individual users, but of entire organizations. In general, however, computers and information technology offer many benefits to business as well as to society as a whole. But misuse or overuse can cause misunderstanding, mistakes, and disaster, as well as mental and physical disorders. The rush to adopt "cutting-edge" information management technology and to reap the potentially substantial cost and time savings offered can lead organizations to do so without first considering possibly harmful consequences. The wise information systems user will keep both the advantages and the disadvantages in mind.

# SUMMARY AND REVIEW

- **Explain why managers need information and the characteristics of useful information.** Managers need information to make decisions so that they may achieve their firms' objectives. They need information—data that are relevant for a specific purpose—rather than just unorganized facts, statistics, opinions, and predictions gathered from various sources inside and outside the company. They need information that is accurate, timely, complete, and relevant.

- **Describe a management information system and explain its role in management.** A management information system organizes past, present, and projected information from internal and external sources and makes it available to managers at all levels of an organization. Users enter data into a database, where

the MIS can process it into relevant information that is readily accessible to all users.

- **Specify the basic factors that determine an organization's information management needs.** The basic factors that determine an organization's information management needs are organizational (particularly environment and size) and managerial (especially level and area).

- **Determine how computers can be used in management information systems.** Most management information systems are computerized. Computers can be classified into three categories: mainframes, minicomputers, and microcomputers. Hardware is the physical components of a computer; software is a set of commands that instruct a computer to perform various operations, such as reading data, analyzing data, or storing it in a specified location. Computer networks are systems that permit different computers to communicate with each other; they may be local (LAN) or wide area (WAN) networks. Internal and external networks (such as the Internet) offer electronic mail, bulletin boards, teleconferencing, and access to information systems and databases.

- **Distinguish among the basic types of management information systems.** A transaction support system (TSS) handles routine, repetitious business transactions. Decision support systems (DSSs) are more complex and aid managers in decision making by helping them anticipate the possible outcomes of alternative actions. A group decision support system (GDSS) is a special kind of DSS designed to aid group decision making. Another type of DSS is the executive information system (EIS), designed for executives who have limited experience using computers but need access to the firm's database. Expert systems, which make use of artificial intelligence, mimic human decision-making

processes by using a collection of thousands of "if–then" rules to solve complex problems.

- **Summarize the impact of information technology on people, organizations, and information.** Information technology has many effects, including improving performance and affecting organizational structure. However, it also has many drawbacks including performance limitations (expense, downtime, etc.), behavioral limitations, and health risks. Systems designers need to be aware of both the benefits and drawbacks and try to balance them to create a system that is useful, efficient, and effective in managing the firm's information resources.

- **Critique a business's implementation of a management information system.** Based on your reading of this chapter, determine how to implement a management information system for ELP (hypothetical company presented in the "Business Dilemma" box), considering how to make the system most efficient and effective without intimidating the firm's employees.

## Key Terms and Concepts

data *618*
information *618*
management information system
  (MIS) *619*
database *620*
hardware *625*
software *626*
computer networks *626*

local-area network (LAN) *626*
wide-area network (WAN) *626*
electronic mail *628*
telecommuting *629*
transaction support system (TSS) *630*
decision support system (DSS) *631*
group decision support system
  (GDSS) *631*

executive information system (EIS) *631*
artificial intelligence *632*
expert systems *632*
computer viruses *637*
bug *637*
crash *637*

## Ready Recall

1. What kinds of information do managers need? Distinguish between the terms *data* and *information*.
2. What is a management information system? What is its role in business?
3. How do information needs differ among the three levels of management?
4. How can computers be used in a management information system?
5. What is hardware? What is software? How do they differ?

6. How can managers make use of computer networks in managing information?
7. List the types of management information systems.
8. How can an MIS improve an organization's performance?
9. Why do managers sometimes form unrealistic expectations about the capabilities of an MIS?
10. What are some of the health risks associated with using information technology?

## Expand Your Experience

1. Find some examples of information-sharing alliances such as "virtual corporations." What are some possible problems associated with them? What challenges do such alliances create for managers? Opportunities?

2. Cite examples of how an organization might become overdependent on information technology. How might this overuse of technology affect customers? Employees?

3. Find out what networks your university or college (or even workplace) has available to employees and students. How does it use them to help manage the huge amounts of data required to operate?

# Merck's Strategic Use of Information Systems Technology in an Uncertain Environment

In 1992, two of the ten most profitable industrial corporations in the world were U.S. pharmaceutical companies—Merck and Bristol-Myers Squibb—each with annual profits of nearly $2 billion. Regardless of their past accomplishments and current positions in the industry, they face a highly uncertain future as they anticipate sweeping changes in the nation's health care system as promised by the administration of President Bill Clinton.

It is largely due to the fact that pharmaceutical companies have been so profitable that they have become the "whipping boys" of ongoing health care reform rhetoric. Critics refer to big drug companies as "greedy," and "unconscionable profiteers," and say they illustrate why the nation's health care system is in such a cataclysmal predicament. The pharmaceutical companies certainly expect that they will be affected—probably adversely—by the coming changes, but two years after Clinton's election they still did not know exactly how. Among the possibilities are government regulation of the industry, possibly in the form of price controls. In the event of price controls, which many consider a very real possibility, the practice of many firms of making huge investments in research and development (R&D) to develop new, cutting-edge drugs would become far less attractive. Analysts estimate the average price of developing and introducing a new drug to the market to be around $231 million. Industry proponents maintain that price controls would turn drug companies away from high R&D investments because they would not be allowed to recoup their investments by charging relatively high prices during the early stages of product life—while a new drug is under patent protection. Under price controls, pharmaceutical manufacturers would have little say in the price of their products, regardless of the magnitude of the costs incurred in their development.

Concern over the possibility of impending price controls, as well as other uncertainties, has led pharmaceutical firms to consider and implement a variety of organizational strategies never before seen in the industry—as alternatives to the costly practice of developing new drugs and then marketing them on the basis of product differences. Miles Laboratories, for

example, launched a major new hypertension drug marketed principally on the basis of its being priced 25 percent less than the market leader, an approach previously unheard of among major drug companies. Bristol-Myers Squibb announced that it was entering into a multibillion-dollar strategic alliance with the nation's largest association of not-for-profit hospitals, thus making it the preferred provider of drugs and other health care products for over 1,000 hospitals across the country. Merck, however, announced the most costly and innovative strategic approach of all: For a reported $6 billion, it purchased Medco Containment Services, a large mail-order drug company distributing cut-rate drugs in large quantities to pharmacists and health plans nationwide.

Merck & Company, Inc. was founded in 1887 when chemist Theodore Weicker came to the United States from Germany to establish an American branch of E. Merck AG of Germany. Often named among the most admired firms in the world, and well known as a highly innovative research and development leader in the pharmaceutical industry, Merck—based in Whitehouse Station, New Jersey—posted 1992 profits of $1.98 billion on sales of $9.8 billion, ranking it among the top six corporations worldwide in terms of both profits and sales. Despite its brilliant past successes, the $6 billion it paid for Medco stretched even the deep-pocketed Merck, and industry insiders questioned the soundness of the acquisition. They could not understand why Merck was willing to pay such an astronomical price for what many considered a mere arm of product distribution, one that might hurt the company's reputation as the innovative leader in the pharmaceutical industry.

Merck countered that its critics fail to realize exactly what it has bought and what it plans to do with what it has gained as a result of the merger. Medco, Merck said, is much more than a mail-order distributor of drugs; it is an elaborate, extensive system of industry-specific information and technology. Through the acquisition, Merck has gained access to 90 percent of all U.S. pharmacies—some 1,000 individual pharmacists—and, most importantly, a state-of-the-art database tracking the prescription drug use of some 33 million individuals. Merck plans to use this information and technology to increase sales by getting closer to its customers. Specifically, with the addition of the database, Merck/Medco's information systems can access the prescription drug histories of these 33 million individuals and see which drugs they were taking, then automatically diagnose the individual's probable illness. The system can then tell Merck/Medco which people could be switched over to a drug or drugs made by the company. With this information in hand, the newly formed strategic alliance can then employ the pharmacists gained in the acquisition to persuade doctors to prescribe Merck's products instead of those currently being used.

The Merck/Medco information system can also tell which patients are supposed to be taking certain drugs but have not refilled their prescriptions. The system can track refills and contact physicians or patients directly. It can even set up a program to send refills to the patient or doctor automatically, bypassing the chance of a lapse in needed medication while at the same time increasing sales of Merck products. Indeed, Merck and other drug companies annually lose hundreds of millions of dollars in sales because so many individuals fail, for whatever reasons, to renew their prescriptions. Half of all patients on certain Merck drugs, for example, discontinue usage after a year, regardless of the continuing need for the medication.

Before the merger, Medco had also managed pharmaceutical benefits for some 1,500 health plans across the United States. In the process of so doing, the company was responsible for formulating lists of drugs from which physicians participating in the plan were required to select when prescribing drugs for patients. Merck/Medco will be able to use databases containing information on these health plans to its advantage in much the same manner as it can the databases on individuals. In this case, however, Merck/Medco will be able to locate employers whose workers are covered through the health plans. It can then approach the participating companies and offer its products as alternatives to certain more costly medical procedures. The employers might then attempt to persuade physicians to carry the Merck drugs and use them in appropriate cases in place of surgery or other procedures.

Some in the pharmaceutical industry argue that Merck could have obtained information of the type it gained through Medco for much less than $6 billion. However, others point out that having access to such information at all times, and being able to get it when needed, gives Merck a decided advantage over competitors. The free flow of information between Medco and Merck gives the new information- and technology-based alliance the ability to locate and act on market opportunities almost instantaneously.

*Sources:* "Fortune's Global 500," *Fortune,* July 26, 1993, 188; *Hoover's Handbook of American Business 1993,* Gary Hoover, Alta Campbell, and Patrick J. Spain, eds. (Austin, TX: The Reference Press, Inc., 1993), 772; James Kim, "Selling Point of New Drug: Low Price," *USA Today,* August 9, 1993, B1; David Kreutzer, "Merck, a Lesson in Industrial Policy," *The Wall Street Journal,* August 4, 1993, A10; Shelly Neumeier, "Health Stocks That Should Escape Hillary's Scalpel," *Fortune,* August 9, 1993, 27; Elyse Tanouye, "Bristol-Myers, Hospital Group Set Supply Pact," *The Wall Street Journal,* August 13, 1993; A3; Elyse Tanouye, "Merck Will Exploit Medco's Database," *The Wall Street Journal,* August 4, 1993, B1; Joseph Weber, "Is This Rx Too Costly for Merck?" *Business Week,* August 9, 1993, 28; and Joseph Weber, "Merck Is Showing Its Age," *Business Week,* August 23, 1993, 72.

## Questions

1. What type of information system is Merck/Medco employing?
2. Discuss the various information systems objectives that you feel may be best pursued by Merck/Medco.
3. What sort of organizational and performance effects might Merck's acquisition of Medco have on the company? Do you feel these effects might eventually justify the high price Merck paid for Medco?

---

### STRENGTHEN YOUR SKILLS
## *Solving Puzzling Problems*

Managing information effectively requires you to have the ability to sort and logically organize your data so as to produce relevant information. Computer programmers who design management information systems sometimes use the analogy of solving a very complex puzzle to describe how they develop the components of a computer program. Every "piece of the puzzle" must fit perfectly together with every other piece that it touches until the "picture" is complete.

**Triangle Puzzle**

Illustrated below is a puzzle where 47 triangles fit together to form a complete picture. Think of it as a completed MIS software program.

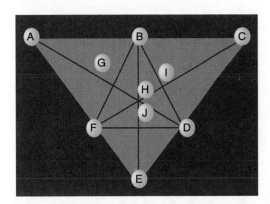

*Source:* Adapted from Edward E. Scannell and John W. Newstrom, *Still More Games Trainers Play* (New York. McGraw-Hill, Inc., 1991), 249–251.

To get beneath the surface to see what went into getting all the pieces to fit together so perfectly, here is your assignment:

- Break into groups of 3 to 4 people each (three is the preferred number for a triangles exercise).
- Your group is to work together to identify as many as possible of the 47 triangles that fit together to complete this picture. Three answers are provided to get you started.
- Consider these two "Hints" and "MIS Applications" as you and your group work together to solve this triangle puzzle.

| Hints | MIS Applications |
|---|---|
| Remember one of the benefits of working in teams to solve problems is that each individual sees things from a different perspective; take advantage of that by having each member view the puzzle from a different side. | To accommodate the many different information needs of the people using the MIS, it is important during its development to get the perspective of everyone who will use the MIS. |
| Consider beginning the problem-solving exercise by taking some kind of systematic approach, such as seeing how many triangles you can identify that originate from a single point (point A, for example) before moving on to a new point. | A systematic approach is often used in developing management information systems because of the necessity of logically sorting and ordering massive amounts of data. |

Your instructor will give you ten minutes to fill in as many of the answers as you can. It will be easier to make sure you are not duplicating if you always write your three letters in alphabetical order. For example, when you find triangle HBG, write it as BGH.

| | | | | |
|---|---|---|---|---|
| 1. ABD | 11. | 21. | 31. | 41. |
| 2. ABE | 12. | 22. | 32. | 42. |
| 3. ABF | 13. | 23. | 33. | 43. |
| 4. | 14. | 24. | 34. | 44. |
| 5. | 15. | 25. | 35. | 45. |
| 6. | 16. | 26. | 36. | 46. |
| 7. | 17. | 27. | 37. | 47. |
| 8. | 18. | 28. | 38. | |
| 9. | 19. | 29. | 39. | |
| 10. | 20. | 30. | 40. | |

# Management
## Control Systems

**Outline**

Introduction
Control in Organizations
The Control Process
Forms of Management Control
Managing the Control Process

**After reading this chapter, you will be able to:**

- Define management control and explain why it is necessary.
- Examine the process through which managers develop and implement control.
- Distinguish among the various forms of control.
- Summarize the elements of effective control.
- Determine why control is sometimes met with resistance and how managers may overcome this resistance.
- Assess an organization's control program.

# The Rise and Fall of Osborne Computer

At the age of 22, Thailand-born Adam Osborne moved to the United States, where he received a doctorate in chemical engineering and went to work for Shell Development Company. Frustrated by corporate bureaucracy, in 1970 he decided to start his own computer consulting company. By the time the personal computer boom began in the mid-1970s, Osborne was considered a computer expert, with nearly a dozen books on the industry under his belt. In 1981 he announced plans to manufacture a new personal computer priced well below those currently on the market. His revolutionary machine—the first portable computer sophisticated enough for business use—hit the market in July 1981. Within a year, Osborne's company had sales of $100 million, surpassing even his most optimistic expectations. Osborne Computer gave computer users what they wanted but were unable to get elsewhere, and it manufactured its products at a fraction of standard industry costs. At the peak of the company's success, it held an estimated 80 to 90 percent share of the rapidly growing market. However, on September 14, 1983, the Osborne Computer Corporation filed for Chapter 11 bankruptcy protection. How could such a seemingly perfect success story turn so sour so quickly?

Adam Osborne was always known for his showmanship. At a West Coast trade fair in 1981, he spent a sizable portion of money that had been set aside to start the company on a dazzling Plexiglas booth that reached nearly to the ceiling, dominating the show. In 1982 he spent $3.5 million on advertising. Plans were laid for further expansion, with more heavy advertising scheduled to lead the way. Osborne Computer knew no limits, no bounds. Who could argue with such success?

Adam Osborne was also slow to give up control of the company as it grew larger and more complex. Even when it became obvious that the demands of phenomenal growth had outstripped his entrepreneurial skills, he continued to run the company almost single-handedly. By the time an experienced team of computer industry executives had been assembled and put into place to assist Osborne with managing his company's expanded operations, it was too late. In April 1983, Adam Osborne was told of staggering company losses: $8 million for the recently concluded fiscal year, a figure updated from $4 million due to the discovery of unrecorded financial liabilities. By the end of the year, the loss had grown to $12 million.

One of the primary reasons for the losses—despite high projected profits that appeared reasonable just months before—was excessive inventories of old, outdated equipment that the company did not even realize it had. Furthermore, the company had no mechanisms in place to indicate how much money it had been spending.

Finally, Adam Osborne had no other choice but to close the company's doors and file for court protection from its creditors, three of whom had brought lawsuits, claiming that the company owed them a total of $4.7 million. No one can really know what might have become of the Osborne Computer Corporation had it been managed more efficiently.

*Source:* Robert F. Hartley, *Marketing Mistakes*, 5th ed. (New York: John Wiley and Sons, 1992): 277–293.

*introduction*

The spectacular rise and fall of the Osborne Computer Company illustrates that organizational growth is not necessarily always good. For growth to be beneficial, it must be closely controlled. The word *control* sometimes conjures up images of a totalitarian state devoid of personal freedom where everything is preordained by a faceless, all-knowing, all-powerful being who often fails to have the best interests of those being controlled in mind. Consequently, individuals, in their roles as organizational employees, often resist being controlled. However, as we will discuss in this chapter, control is vital for efficient and effective organizational operations. The challenge to managers is to understand both the purpose and importance of control, and to use it so that it does not infringe on employees' personal freedoms.

In this chapter, we explore management control systems. As you will see, control is closely associated with many of the other managerial functions discussed throughout this book. We begin by examining the nature of management control, including its purpose, importance, areas, responsibilities, and how it relates to planning. Next, we explore both the control process, as well as the various forms of control most important in organizations. Finally, we look at how to manage the control process and present some common ways in which to ensure its optimal implementation and use.

**management control**
All of the activities an organization undertakes to ensure that its actions lead to achievement of its objectives.

**management control system**
A planned, ordered scheme of management control.

**Example:** Management control systems are implemented by teams for 3M's 23 major businesses. A global plan is crafted by a group executive with global input. The national response to that plan is carried out by each of 3M's international subsidiaries, often in coordination with regional managers. The degree of global, regional, and local authority varies depending on the business. 3M is moving from a top-down control organization to a transnational, global corporation.

## CONTROL IN ORGANIZATIONS

As the Osborne Computer example illustrates, without control, a company has no way of knowing how well it is doing relative to its goals. **Management control** includes all activities an organization undertakes to ensure that its actions lead to achievement of its objectives. A **management control system** is a planned, ordered scheme of management control. It allows managers to readily assess where the firm actually *is* at a point in time relative to where it wants or expects to be. Managers at Osborne Computer should have recognized that the company was not meeting its goals and taken action to deal with the deteriorating situation. But, because the company lacked a system of control mechanisms, they had no way of knowing how bad things actually were.

### The Importance of Control

All the good planning efforts and brilliant ideas in the world do little good if a firm has no system of management control. Control, therefore, is an essential part of effective organizational management. In today's dynamic, unpredictable global business world, control plays a more crucial role than ever before. Specifically, control helps an organization adapt to changing conditions, limits the magnification of errors, assists in dealing with increased complexity, and helps minimize costs.

**Adapting to Changing Conditions.**     Change itself is about the only thing that can be predicted with any degree of certainty in turbulent markets. While change is inevitable, it is the nature of change that defies accurate forecasting. A properly designed management control system can allow managers to effectively anticipate, monitor, and respond to often constantly changing conditions.

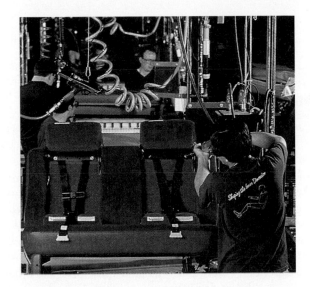

Magna International's internal complexity increased during the 1980s as sales grew thirteen-fold. Plant managers helped fuel the company's explosive growth. They had authority to build factories, take on debt, and sign supply contracts with customers, and their pay was tied to the success of their plants. Burdened with debt, Magna almost went bankrupt in the early 1990s when automobile sales slowed. Top management instituted control measures to reverse the situation. The company sold or shut almost half of its 120 factories and used the proceeds to eliminate its $1 billion of debt. It placed a ban on new debt and shifted its focus from merely supplying parts to designing and building parts, such as the car seat shown that it developed for Chrysler.

*Source:* © Hestoft/SABA.

**Limiting the Magnification of Errors.**   Generally, a small error or mistake does not adversely affect organizational operations. However, a small error or mistake left uncorrected—perhaps one undetected as a result of a lack of control—may be magnified with the passage of time, eventually harming the whole company. For example, a report that underestimates the number of product defects within a manufacturing company may easily lead to perpetuation of a flawed production system, and, with time, tarnish the organization's image. An effective management control system would enable production managers to pinpoint the problem before further damage is done.

**Dealing with Organizational Complexity.**   Today's businesses must contend not only with an increasingly complex external environment, but with increasing internal complexity as well, particularly in highly diversified or rapidly growing organizations. For example, Canadian auto parts manufacturer Magna International grew from a tiny tool and die maker into one of North America's ten largest auto parts makers, manufacturing more than 4,000 components in its nearly 120 plants. However, a lack of centralized executive control over Magna's greatly expanded and complex operations nearly led to disaster. In 1990, its aggressive, undercontrolled strategy in the face of an increasingly complex environment resulted in the accumulation of $1 billion of debt—4.5 times stockholder equity—and to a reported loss of $191 million on sales of $1.6 billion. Only through implementation of tighter organizational control was Magna able to rebound and save itself from bankruptcy. By July 1992, the company was back on track, experiencing higher sales and profits despite having sold off or closed half of its manufacturing plants.[1]

**Minimizing Costs.**   A properly designed system of control can often allow a firm to enjoy considerable cost reductions. In 1989, Seattle-based Boeing, the world's leading aircraft manufacturer, announced that it intended to cut the cost of designing and building a plane by no less than 25 to 30 percent. Boeing proposed to accomplish this objective by designing and implementing a more efficient system of control over the company's $8 billion inventory stock, including adopting the just-in-time inventory management concept. After three years, Boeing's tighter control helped it reduce inventory stocks by $700 million. Industry analysts estimate that if Boeing meets its 1998 goal of reducing the time needed to manufacture a plane from 12 to 6 months, it could cut inventory in half, with potential savings thereafter of $1 billion per year.[2]

## Responsibilities for Control

Traditionally, managers have been responsible for the control process. Most large organizations employ individuals, often called *controllers* (also comptrollers), whose chief responsibility is to coordinate and supervise financial and other control activities. Recent developments in management practices, however, have led to more sharing of responsibility for control activities with lower-level employees. For example, increasing degrees of employee empowerment—allowing operational-level employees more input into organizational policies and procedures—are intended to take advantage of the fact that the people who actually do the work know it better than anyone else does. These workers, especially those with lengthy and specialized experience, can contribute innovative ideas and other useful input about how best to get things done that others not so intimately familiar with the operations processes could not provide.

Ironically, increasing control and control-related responsibilities at lower levels may create the need for still more control. Managers at Corning's Erwin, New York, ceramics plant grouped production workers into teams and gave them new authority to decide, among other things, how production should be scheduled, a form of control in itself. Contrary to their expectations, however, management found that worker performance declined and that a general state of confusion prevailed over the new system. On investigation, they found that the solution lay in more control in the form of additional employee training. Corning management had empowered employees to say how things should be done, but failed to prepare them for that power or for the resulting working environment. After a training program was implemented and workers were allowed to get used to the new system, performance increased, waste declined, and product defects were significantly reduced.[3]

## The Link between Planning and Controlling

For control to be effective, it must be integrated with planning so that managers can readily compare actual results with planned projections. Moreover, the ability to control activities must be considered during the planning process. When developing marketing plans, for example, marketing managers should focus not only on measurable performance criteria such as sales and market share to facilitate effective management control, but also on performance in terms of more subjective and difficult-to-quantify criteria such as company image and employee morale. Although these criteria are less quantifiable than other performance measures, they are controllable and should be closely managed.

The relationship between planning and controlling continues as a long-term cycle. Managers make plans and then use control to evaluate the effectiveness of organizational activities relative to those plans. If the control system indicates that things are proceeding as they should, the current plan should be maintained. However, managers may find the firm is not making adequate progress, in which case, they should revise the current plan. Or, the control system may indicate that the situation—for example, the competitive or economic environment—has changed, warranting the development of a new plan.

**Example:** The link between planning and control is evident at Ames Department Stores, which had a $40 million net profit for 4th quarter 1993 after 5 years of losses. According to president and COO Peter Thornton, this turnaround was caused by inventory control as well as plans for store remodeling and repositioning of the apparel business in 1994 .

**FIGURE 22.1**

**The Control Process**

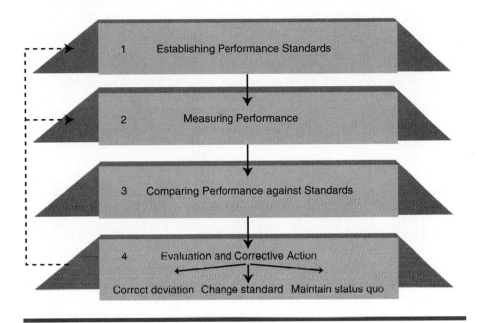

## THE CONTROL PROCESS

The control process consists of four basic steps: establishing performance standards, measuring performance, comparing performance against standards, and evaluation and corrective action (Figure 22.1). The dotted lines in the figure indicate feedback communication.

### Establishing Performance Standards

The first step in the control process is to establish **performance standards**, targets set by management against which actual performance is compared at a future date. Without such standards, managers cannot accurately gauge the effectiveness of the company's efforts. For example, earlier we mentioned that Boeing set goals to reduce the cost of building aircraft by 25 to 30 percent, and the time it takes to manufacture an airplane from 12 to 6 months, by 1998. Based on these goals, Boeing managers might set performance standards of holding no more inventory at any time than is necessary to complete outstanding orders. They would then use these performance standards as benchmarks to track the effectiveness of the company's ongoing efforts.

Ideally, performance standards will be closely related to organizational goals. Like goals and objectives, performance standards should be stated in very clear, easily measurable terms, and they should be realistic given both the internal and competitive environment in which the organization operates.

Performance standards should also reflect organizational strategy and therefore be expected to vary widely among organizations and even internally within a particular organization with respect to different products or markets. A well-

**performance standards**
Targets set by management against which actual performance is compared at a future date.

**Example:** Performance standards may vary by gender. For this reason managers need training in evaluating a woman who may be less assertive, though not necessarily less effective, than a male counterpart according to Robert Monroe, the executive vice president for diversity at Seagram, the beverage maker. His job is to review the company's recruiting, training, and development practices to eliminate gender and racial biases.

established market leader such as Procter & Gamble might set performance standards related to maintaining its market-share leadership position in each of the many product categories in which it competes, while a smaller, less well-known company might set standards related to gaining initial entry and acceptance in a limited number of geographical markets. In international markets where Procter & Gamble is not a market leader to such an extensive degree, its performance standards are likely to reflect different strategic considerations. For instance, the company might set a performance standard for a "new" brand of shampoo introduced in Peru to attain a 4 percent market share in the first six months, even though the same shampoo has long led the domestic market—where the standards reflect the company's objective to maintain its relative competitive position. All other considerations aside, control standards must reflect marketplace realities to facilitate meaningful comparisons with actual performance.

## Measuring Performance

The second step in the control process is measuring actual performance in the context of the specific activities that management wishes to control. In most organizations, this assessment occurs continually. For example, if a company establishes as a performance standard a certain maximum acceptable product defect rate, managers must measure the rate continually to ensure that all products fall below it.

It is sometimes difficult to measure performance accurately. For example, a pharmaceutical company such as Burroughs Wellcome, which concentrates its efforts on relatively "high-risk" drugs in developing fields of medicine, such as AIDS research, that its competitors often avoid, may spend years developing and testing a potential product that may never actually make it to the market. Although it can be difficult to measure performance in such a case, a valid method must be developed to facilitate effective control. The company might measure performance by looking at reviews and testing done on its ongoing projects by other scientists or medical associations, or it could consider performance in terms of successfully combatting individual symptoms of certain diseases in the laboratory, regardless of whether the drug gets to the market.

## Comparing Performance against Standards

The third step in the control process involves comparing measured actual performance against the standards established in step one. Actual performance may match the performance standard exactly, or it may be higher or lower than the target. Management must decide how much deviation from standards will be tolerated before considering corrective action. In some cases, this decision is quite straightforward. If Procter & Gamble sets a standard of being the market-share leader in each product category in which it competes, then it is easy to determine if it has met that standard. In other situations, the decision may not be nearly so simple. If Burroughs Wellcome sets standards for a drug related to combatting specified symptoms of a disease, and the drug fails to meet those standards but receives a number of unexpected positive reviews from experts in the scientific community, Burroughs may decide that it has made acceptable progress anyway. Or, a sales manager might find that while an annual sales increase of 10 percent falls short of the 12.5 percent performance standard, no action is warranted because of unexpected environmental circumstances—such as the surprise introduction of a strong competitive product—during the measurement period.

CEO Sally Frame Kasaks of Ann Taylor, maker and retailer of private-label fashions for professional women, took corrective action to win back customers and turn around the company's poor performance in 1991, when it lost $15.8 million on sales of $438 million. Kasaks installed procedures to monitor store sales nationwide. The control system allows her to mark down merchandise that isn't selling well and to quickly restock hot-selling items. The monitoring system not only enables the company to react quickly and flexibly to customer preferences, it's also reduced prices about 15 percent, making the company more price competitive.

*Source:* © 1994 Red Morgan.

Managers should be constantly aware that unforeseen conditions that may influence control decisions can occur at any time.

## Evaluating Performance and Taking Corrective Action

In the final step of the control process, managers evaluate actual performance relative to standards and then take appropriate action. Performance evaluation calls not only for quantitative and diagnostic skills, but, as already mentioned in the previous step, also for subjective yet crucial decision making. Before deciding how to respond to deviations between performance standards and actual performance, managers in charge of control must determine the reason(s) for the deviation. Specifically, they must determine whether the plan previously laid out was properly implemented and failed to work, or if it was not implemented properly. As illustrated in Figure 22.1, once managers have evaluated the firm's performance, they must decide which of three basic options is the appropriate response: correct the observed deviation, change the performance standards, or simply maintain the status quo.

**Example:** Kraft General Foods, located just outside Chicago, took corrective action by bringing workers from the inner cities to the suburbs. Kraft gives vans to various employees, who are responsible for driving many of the employees that live in the city to and from work. Sears Roebuck links up with private bus and van companies to get some of its city-dweller workers to suburban Chicago.

**Correct the Deviation.**   When actual performance deviates significantly from the performance standard, managers will ordinarily take steps to correct the discrepancy. For example, faced with a higher than acceptable number of customer complaints, managers at a service firm such as McDonald's or NationsBank may decide, after careful investigation, that certain employees or groups of employees need additional customer service training. Corrective action may be called for when performance standards have been exceeded as well. For example, a popular restaurant that easily surpassed its profit or number-of-customer-related performance standards may decide to expand physical facilities, increase hours of operation, or even raise menu prices in an attempt to bring actual performance more in line with standards.

**Change Standards.**   A second option when there is a discrepancy between actual performance and the performance standard is to change the initial performance standards. This option is the likely choice when observation of actual performance leads managers to conclude that the original standards were unrealistic given environmental conditions. Standards may have been set too low or too high, requiring modification for future control activities to be effective.

Gillette's introduction of its Sensor for Women razor illustrates a situation in which standards were initially set too low. Seeing a gap in the market, Gillette managers set out to design and bring to market a new women's razor. The product that served as their solution to this unmet need was so revolutionary in nature that sales skyrocketed well beyond expectations. Only six months after its summer 1992 introduction, Sensor for Women had captured an incredible 60 percent of the market, becoming by far the market leader.[4] Such an unexpected success requires that managers increase future performance standards to more realistic and challenging levels for effective control; otherwise, the passive standards may encourage suboptimal performance when objectives are achieved far too easily. On the other hand, had the Sensor for Women not fared so well, Gillette managers might have had to decrease future performance standards.

**Maintain the Status Quo.**    When performance standards are either met or nearly met, maintaining the status quo—the current course of action—may be the best response. If production managers set an optimistic performance standard of a 50 percent decrease in product defects, and actual performance indicates a 48 percent reduction, the company has obviously made significant progress. Maintaining current production control policies and procedures is generally the proper course of action to take in such a case. Moreover, managers should reward employees for "a job well done," and otherwise encourage them to continue on their current course of action.

## FORMS OF MANAGEMENT CONTROL

In this section, we will look at three levels of control—organizational, operations, and strategic—and then discuss financial control techniques.

### Organizational Control

**organizational control**
A broad-based form of control that guides all organizational activities and oversees the overall functioning of the whole firm.

**Organizational control** oversees the overall functioning of the whole firm. It is a broad-based form of control that guides all organizational activities. The two dominant forms of organizational control are bureaucratic and clan control. While some companies adopt one form to the complete exclusion of the other, most exhibit characteristics of both forms with one exerting noticeably more influence than the other. Figure 22.2 illustrates the characteristics of and differences between the two forms of organizational control.

**bureaucratic control**
An attempt to control the firm's overall functioning through formal, mechanistic structural arrangements.

**Bureaucratic Control.**    **Bureaucratic control** attempts to control the firm's overall functioning through formal, mechanistic structural arrangements. It seeks to gain employee conformance through strict administration of rigid, straightforward policies and procedures, and its reward system focuses on individual employee compliance with either an implied or formal, written code of behavioral standards. As such, bureaucratic control allows limited employee input into organizational activities.

Although its corporate culture has become somewhat less bureaucratic in recent years, IBM was long known for exhibiting strong bureaucratic control ten-

## FIGURE 22.2

### Forms of Organizational Control

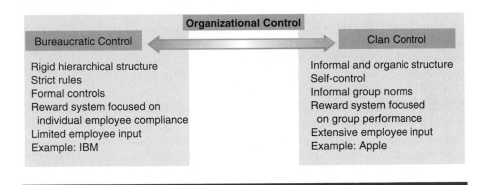

dencies. As stated by one former IBM sales representative, the longstanding traditional dress for male managers at IBM was "...a dark blue pinstriped suit with a freshly starched white shirt; a conservative, striped tie—with the stripes pointing to the heart; and heavy '16-pound Florsheim,' polished, black wing-tip shoes."[5] Using its formal control system, IBM was able to develop such a distinctive, respected, and effective way of conducting business that countless organizations copied it, with varying degrees of success, down nearly to the very last detail.

**Clan Control.**   **Clan control** seeks to regulate overall organizational functioning through reliance on informal, organic structural arrangements. It tries to foster strong employee commitment by vigorously encouraging employee input and group participation. Rather than setting strict behavioral standards as in bureaucratic control systems, clan control relies on self-control and informal group norms to effectively create a relaxed yet sharply focused working environment.

Apple Computer, founded by two young entrepreneurs in a garage in California, has long been recognized for its informal, easy-going, clan-controlled atmosphere. In terms of corporate culture, IBM and Apple were once at opposite ends of a continuum of organizational control. Apple has limited behavioral codes of conduct, focusing instead on allowing employees freedom to design a working environment in which they feel most comfortable and best able to function productively. Apple's rapid rise to the top of the dynamic and unpredictable computer software industry—and its long-term stay there—can be attributed in no small part to its effective use of clan control.

**Bureaucratic or Clan Control?**   Although one form of organizational control is not necessarily "better" than the other, managers should keep several issues in mind when deciding on what form to apply. First, companies seldom use one form of organizational control to the complete exclusion of the other. For example, the formerly highly bureaucratic IBM permits employee participation, and Apple, the classic example of a company exhibiting clan control, does have formal rules that employees must closely follow. Second, control that is too bureaucratic may result in employee alienation as well as failure to recognize and use potentially good ideas often better generated in a more informal setting. IBM's board of

**clan control**
The regulation of overall organizational functioning through reliance on informal, organic structural arrangements.

**Example:**  IBM PC Co. uses both bureaucratic and clan control. The unit operates with a high degree of autonomy free of corporate interference. CFO Edward F. Rogers and CEO Robert J. Corrigan control all costs, expenses, assets, and resources yet they use a group of branch managers empowered to make their own pricing and distribution decisions.

directors apparently felt that the company was missing marketplace opportunities due to an overly bureaucratic orientation when it purposefully hired an industry outsider less inclined toward bureaucratic forms of management as its new corporate chief executive officer in 1993.[6] Third, control that is too clan-oriented might result in an organization with no idea where it is going or one heading in so many different directions that it fails to accomplish anything. Finally, consistency of control orientation is vital. Not only will employees resist drastic change—especially to extreme bureaucratic control—but, after working under one form of organizational control, they may have a hard time adjusting to a change in control. If Apple were to decide suddenly to move to a more radically bureaucratic form of control, managers and subordinates used to the more informal atmosphere would likely have great difficulty adapting to the change. This in fact has been the case in a recent Apple/IBM joint venture. The companies' different philosophies have clashed, with those on the Apple side resisting the influx of the more bureaucratic style of control, although not to an unmanageable degree.[7]

## Operations Control

**operations control**
The regulation of one or more individual operating systems within an organization.

**Operations control** regulates one or more individual operating systems within an organization. Most companies practice three basic forms of operations control—preliminary, screening, and feedback—with the forms differentiated primarily by the focus of the control itself.

**preliminary (or feedforward or steering) control**
A form of operations control that monitors deviations in the quality and quantity of the firm's resources to try to prevent deviations before they enter the system.

**Preliminary Control.**    **Preliminary control** (sometimes also referred to as **feedforward or steering control**) monitors deviations in the quality and quantity of the firm's resources to try to prevent deviations before they enter the system; its focus is on inputs to the product or service production process. In the area of human resources, for example, preliminary control techniques include employee selection, placement, and, where it occurs before formal employment, training of newly hired personnel. Such activities help management eliminate job candidates who are unsuitable for the company's needs. Other preliminary control techniques include inspection of incoming materials used in the production process, as well as capital and financial budgeting—financial control techniques that will be dealt with in more detail later.

Nowhere is the importance of preliminary control more important than in the total quality management (TQM) movement. Although TQM focuses on achieving superior levels of quality and customer value at all levels of the operations process, high-quality inputs are essential for overall organizational quality because they reduce the need for costly inspections (i.e., feedback control) and allow managers to pay more attention to quality problems occurring within internal firm operations.[8] This helps explain why so many organizations have consistently been reducing the number of suppliers of parts and materials to the production process, while at the same time building deeper and more permanent relationships with those vendors they retain.[9] The "Quest for Quality" box discusses how Tyson Foods uses control to produce quality poultry products.

**screening (or yes/no or concurrent) control**
A form of control that regulates operations to ensure that they are consistent with objectives; also called yes/no or concurrent control.

**Screening Control.**    **Screening control** (also called **yes/no or concurrent control**) regulates operations to ensure that they are consistent with objectives; the focus is on the transformation process that converts inputs into outputs. Managers supervising the work of their subordinates, for example, are exerting screening control to ensure that employees' activities will result in achievement of objectives.

During the Great Depression, Arkansas businessman John Tyson developed a method for transporting live poultry over longer distances than was previously possible by installing a food-and-water trough on the transport trailer floor. In 1936, when Tyson bought and transported 500 Arkansas chickens (springers) to Chicago and realized a profit of $235 on their sale, Tyson Foods, Inc., was born. Today, the company, based in Springdale, Arkansas, is the world's largest producer, processor, and marketer of poultry-based food products. With 1992 sales of nearly $4.2 billion, and profits of just over $160 million, Tyson ranks as the 31st largest food-products company in the world, as well as the 23rd most profitable.

Tyson's overriding corporate strategy and the source of much of its success is value enhancement facilitated by tight management control. The company has taken a basic commodity item such as chicken and added value to it. For example, when preparation time and nutritional value became important attributes in the food-selection process in the 1980s, Tyson enhanced its chicken-based products through, among other things, deboning, marinating, individual packaging, and creating pre-cooked entrees and complete meals. Rather than hire outside agencies to perform these value-added activities, the company chooses to handle them internally, thus maintaining a higher degree of control.

The value-enhancement strategy that has allowed Tyson to become a single-source "total food company" doing business on a global scale could not have been successful if it were not for the company's extensive, tight systems of management control. The company maintains control over its poultry operation through total vertical integration of all raw materials,

# Quest for Quality

## TYSON FOODS: VALUE ENHANCEMENT THROUGH TIGHT CONTROL

processing, and manufacturing activities. By managing all steps in the process of bringing poultry products to market—genetic research, breeding, hatching, rearing, feed milling, veterinary and technical services, transportation, and delivery—Tyson can build quality into its many poultry products. While Tyson does not currently maintain such a high degree of control over its other types of products, it nevertheless applies exacting standards. In the company's pork and beef product operations, for example, selection of only the highest grade meats along with the use of state-of-the-art processing technologies ensure customer satisfaction through the production of a broad range of excellent-quality food products. The result of these carefully administered forms of control is a consistent level of superior product quality on which Tyson's growing customer base has come to depend.

As part of its management control efforts, Tyson Foods has created a variety of programs to enhance employees' lives, both in and away from the workplace. For example, more than 200 cross-functional workplace safety teams work to create hazard-free environments at all Tyson Foods production facilities. These teams have helped to make Tyson the leader in worker safety in the food-products industry, with a lost work-day rate that is approximately three times better than competitors' in the

poultry industry, and one-and-one-half times better than all national manufacturers'. Tyson also offers workers an opportunity to enhance their lives outside the workplace through the provision of educational programs that help work team members improve their skills in reading, mathematics, and problem solving.

Tyson Foods continues to expand its operations into new international markets from Great Britain to Angola and Colombia. Anticipating increased business in Mexico as a result of the North American Free Trade Agreement (NAFTA), Tyson announced a $400 million expansion plan scheduled to increase the company's total poultry production by 8.5 million birds per week, as well as to create 8,500 new jobs.

*Sources:* Charles Conner, "Tyson Plans $400 Million Expansion," *The (Memphis) Commercial Appeal,* January 5, 1994; Christy Fisher, "Feeling Big and Healthy," *Advertising Age,* February 17, 1992, 59; Stephanie Anderson Forest, "Tyson Is Winging Its Way To The Top," *Business Week,* February 25, 1991, 57; "Guide To the Global 500," *Fortune,* July 26, 1993, 187; *Hoover's Handbook of American Business 1993,* Gary Hoover, Alta Campbell, and Patrick J. Spain, eds. (Austin, TX: The Reference Press, Inc., 1993), 548; Tyson Foods, Inc., "Tyson Then—Tyson Today," internal video documentary, October 1992; and Tyson Foods, Inc., 1992 Annual Report.

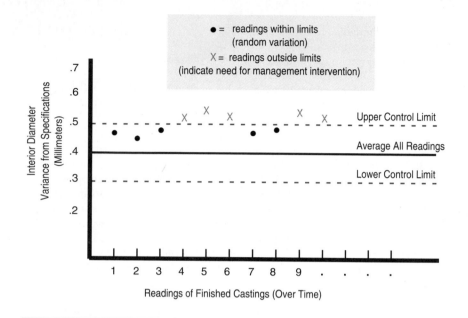

**FIGURE 22.3**

**Hypothetical Statistical Process Control Chart of the Manufacturing Process of Steel Castings**

Delegation of authority provides managers with the power to use both financial—pay raises and promotions or demotions—and nonfinancial—praise or verbal reprimand—incentives to carry out screening control.

In addition to supervisory direction, screening control includes quality and production control measures such as ongoing training programs designed to update continually the skills and knowledge of both managers and nonmanagers. These programs serve as control in that well-trained employees consistently require less formal supervision and control by other means as compared to their less-trained counterparts. The rapid pace of change, caused by technological advances and an increasingly global business environment, has made training-based control programs more popular. Motorola, for example, runs worldwide training programs from Motorola University, a collection of computer-equipped classrooms and laboratories centered at corporate headquarters in Schaumburg, Illinois. In 1992 alone, Motorola University, which also includes regional campuses in Austin, Texas, and Phoenix delivered a total of 102,000 days of training. Motorola calculates that every dollar it puts into training delivers $30 in productivity gains within three years.[10]

Another form of screening control is **statistical process control (SPC)**, which employs "control charts" such as the one depicted in Figure 22.3 to continuously track performance variation over time. The charts provide employees with readily accessible information with which to monitor their work and predict when they are about to exceed control limits and possibly waste organizational resources. Developed by Walter Shewart at Bell Labs in the 1930s and later refined by W. Edwards Deming, SPC is a key TQM tool with which to explain the variation that inevitably occurs in every production process.[11] In short, SPC serves

**statistical process control (SPC)**
An alternate form of screening control that employs "control charts" to continuously track performance variation over time.

to determine whether work processes can effectively be brought under control or if they should be left alone, as well as when manager intervention is necessary.

According to Shewart, management intervention is called for only when the limits of random variation—that occurring strictly by chance—have been exceeded. Otherwise, the level of variance does not significantly affect the performance of the production process and should be left alone, at least for the time being and contingent upon ongoing SPC efforts.[12] Faced with the production process depicted in the SPC control chart in Figure 22.3, managers in charge of screening control should at least be concerned with the specific causes of the intermittent, nonrandom variation, and may want to take immediate action to bring the system back into control. As with all other forms of management control, SPC works best when those individuals being controlled understand the nature and purpose of the control process.

### Feedback Control.

**Feedback control** (also known as **postaction control**) monitors the firm's outputs, the results of the transformation process. Feedback control techniques include (1) the analysis of financial statements to evaluate the actual costs relative to expected (standard) costs through use of standard cost accounting systems, (2) quality control efforts to determine whether the manufacturing process is producing output of an acceptable quality level, and (3) employee performance evaluations to determine whether or not actual performance, in terms of productivity or number of errors, is acceptable. The results of these analyses are fed back into the operating system, where they then affect future output. If, for example, after completing a production run, a company's analysis of cost accounting data indicates that its manufacturing output has cost more than anticipated, management will be alerted to the situation and can take corrective action to prevent the costly deviation from recurring on future production runs.

**feedback (or postaction) control**
A form of control that monitors the firm's outputs, the results of the transformation process; also known as postaction control.

### Multiple Control Systems.

In practice, most companies do not employ the three forms of operational control in isolation. Instead, most use a multiple control system, often using all three forms simultaneously to effectively achieve control of operating systems. For example, computer firms employ multiple control systems in assembling personal computers: Integrated circuits must conform to prescribed quality standards before being installed (preliminary control); various circuit configurations are tested during assembly (screening control); and the completed units are stringently tested before being packed for shipment, pinpointing or correcting operational errors in the system if necessary (feedback control).

In general, operations control methods employed earlier in the production process are less costly than those performed at later stages. For example, while concerned with minimizing deviations from quality standards at all stages in the production process, TQM focuses primarily on controlling the quality of various inputs to the system—i.e., on "doing things right the first time."[13] As we have said, companies have found that the costs associated with correcting mistakes already made far outweigh the costs of controlling initial product quality.[14] Errors first detected by feedback control not only cost the company in terms of product repair or replacement, but they also often result in high long-term costs associated with losing customers who experience poor product quality. When errors are detected early on in the production process by preliminary control, both the short-term and long-term costs associated with poor product or service quality can be avoided.

## Strategic Control

**strategic control**
A form of control whose purpose is to ensure that the organization effectively understands and responds to the realities of its environment.

The purpose of **strategic control** is to ensure that the organization effectively understands and responds to the realities of its environment. Effective strategy leads to the attainment of organizational objectives; effective strategic control should tell managers if their strategies are appropriate given the actual circumstances faced. Without strategic control, managers have no way of knowing—other than eventual goal attainment or failure—if their company is headed in the right direction. Conducting business in such "blind" fashion is sure to lead to less than optimal use of valuable organizational resources as well as missed competitive opportunities.

Effective strategic control is especially important for companies operating in highly complex and dynamic environments; they require more detailed, continuous control than those operating in more stable environmental conditions. For instance, high-technology companies such as Motorola and GE are likely to place great emphasis on control techniques designed to stay abreast of industry developments that might affect organizational strategy or attainment of their strategic goals.

## Financial Control

**Example:** Financial control became easier for LifeUSA, Springfield Remanufacturing Corp., and Chesapeake Packaging Company after they began experimenting in the hopes of changing the thinking of employees and managers. Now individuals at all three firms make more decisions, and key tools—such as the financial records, income statements, and balance sheets—are available to all in the companys' new, open-book management style.

Pure financial control does not exist in the same sense as does operations, organizational, or strategic control, but control of financial resources is so closely related to the use of other resources that financial control is exercised, in part, through proper control in these other areas. For example, if a lack of control in purchasing results in the inefficient use of physical resources—perhaps by not having the right raw materials on hand when needed—the organization's financial resources will not have been used efficiently. Thus, it is important to understand techniques that companies commonly employ to control financial resources. Organizations typically use a number of financial control techniques, many of which are beyond the scope of this book. Here, we focus on the most commonly used and basic methods: budgetary control, analysis of financial statements, and financial audits.

**budgeting**
The process of establishing formal, written plans to control the availability and cost of financial resources.

**budgets**
The formal, written plans for future operations in financial terms.

**operating budgeting**
Budgeting that deals with relatively short-term financial control concerns, such as having sufficient cash on hand to cover daily financial obligations, including routine purchases and payroll.

**capital budgeting**
Budgeting concerned with the intermediate and long-term control of capital acquisitions such as plant and equipment.

**top-down budgeting**
Control budgeting in which top managers establish financial plans and hand them down to middle- and lower-level managers for review and implementation.

**Budgetary Control.**   The principal means of controlling the availability and cost of financial resources is through **budgeting**, the process of establishing formal, written plans—called **budgets**—for future operations in financial terms. Budgeting allows companies to anticipate and control financial resource needs. In a manufacturing company, for example, a cash-flow budget tracks and controls financial resource needs as the firm purchases materials, produces and inventories finished goods, sells goods, and receives cash for them.

There are two main forms of budgeting. **Operating budgeting** deals with relatively short-term financial control concerns, including having sufficient cash on hand to cover daily financial obligations such as routine purchases and payroll. Cash-flow budgeting, as described above, is a form of operating budgeting. In contrast, **capital budgeting** is concerned with the intermediate and long-term control of capital acquisitions such as plant and equipment.

Companies have traditionally developed control budgets in one of three ways. With **top-down budgeting**, top managers establish budgets and hand them down to middle- and lower-level managers for review and implementation. Although top-down budgeting has the advantage of being able to take a broad, corporate perspective and is relatively quick and inexpensive because it involves relatively few people, it fails to consider the input of those employees closest to and

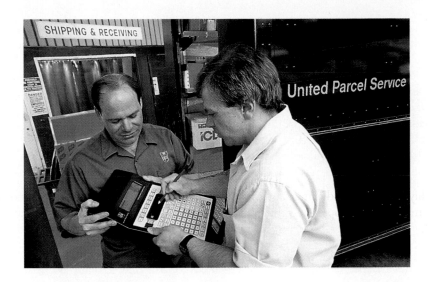

UPS used capital budgeting when management decided to switch from its manual package handling system to a computer-based system for identifying, routing, and tracking packages. The company's capital budget for plant and equipment included $50 million for a global data network, $100 million for a data center, and $150 million for a cellular data network and for creating a machine-readable label that holds more data than bar codes. UPS budgeted $350 million for the development of the Delivery Information Acquisition Device, a custom handheld computer for drivers shown here. The device electronically captures customers' signatures, helping UPS track packages.

*Source:* © John Abbott.

most knowledgeable of actual work responsibilities. **Bottom-up budgeting**, on the other hand, flows up from lower levels of an organization for review by top management. Bottom-up budgeting involves those more directly engaged in the actual tasks covered by the budget; however, its disadvantage is the possibility that those same people may have a somewhat narrow view of their specific tasks, leading them to ignore the effects of their proposed actions on the overall organization. In practice, a form of negotiated budgeting is usually called for. As its name implies, **negotiated budgeting** involves a degree of give and take between upper and lower levels of management to develop the most appropriate form of budgetary control for a given situation.

Regardless of the type or process of budgeting in use, budgeting in general has both advantages and disadvantages as a form of financial control. Its advantages include the fact that it can lead to better coordination of organizational activities because the budgeting process often involves employees from various organizational areas, allowing conflicts to be discovered and discussed before they become actual problems. When done properly, budgetary control also serves as a means of bringing together diverse organizational members to determine overall objectives as well as a means of communicating these plans to the organization as a whole. Finally, in theory, budgeting, especially operating budgeting, implies a need for the organization to adapt continually in the face of constant environmental change.

Disadvantages of traditional budgeting as a means of control include the unavoidable fact that it is difficult to do. Managers must successfully allocate scarce organizational financial resources among many departments and subunits, all with projects that they feel are worthy of full organizational backing. Furthermore, in actual practice, budgeting often involves the extensive use of *incremental budgeting*, the process of merely adjusting the previous period's budget to arrive at the new plan of control. Overreliance on incremental budgeting greatly increases the probability that managers will fail to consider current—and likely changed—environmental conditions. Budgeting also suffers when it is used as a method of legitimizing current power structures, when upper-level managers slash or redistribute financial resources in order to reinforce their power—possibly "paying back" or "rewarding" a subordinate manager—rather than basing their decisions on matters more directly related to overall operational performance.

**bottom-up budgeting**
Financial planning by those employees more directly engaged in the actual tasks being covered and in which information flows up from the lower levels of an organization for review by top management.

**negotiated budgeting**
The give and take between both upper and lower levels of management in developing the most appropriate form of budgetary control for a given situation.

**Example:** Budgetary control was used by Steelcase Company, the multinational manufacturer of office furniture. Its plan for production has a waste-reduction goal of zero loads to the landfill. Research efforts support cost control by focusing on documenting costs of machine and process improvements as well as packaging-source reduction and recycling programs.

**zero-based budgeting (ZBB)**

A method of budgeting in which managers thoroughly reevaluate organizational activities to determine their true level of importance.

To overcome these disadvantages, many firms have turned to **zero-based budgeting (ZBB)**, a method of budgeting in which managers thoroughly reevaluate organizational activities to determine their true level of importance. The key elements of ZBB include identifying objectives, evaluating alternative means of accomplishing each activity, evaluating alternative funding levels (maintain current level or raise or lower levels), evaluating work load and performance levels, and establishing priorities.[15] As a form of financial control, ZBB forces managers to view budgeting as a true management process rather than a simple matter of recycling and adjusting the budget for the previous planning period. As a means of budgetary control, ZBB requires managers to reevaluate all activities to determine their true level of importance and resulting funding level as compared to alternative uses of limited financial resources. This thorough reevaluation of activities and alternative uses of financial resources gives ZBB its name: Everything is considered as if it is a completely new—zero-based—matter. Such an approach is especially appropriate for today's increasingly dynamic marketplace.

Regardless of how effective budgetary control may actually be, it should never be the sole means of a company's financial control. Overreliance on this one—or any other one—method of control may lead managers to ignore other pertinent information that can be uncovered only through the use of other financial control methods. By relying on several forms of financial control, a firm can discover trends through complementary and supportive information that pinpoints potential problems requiring management attention.

**Analysis of Financial Statements.**    Financial statements allow a firm to classify the effects of the many varied transactions that occur in the course of conducting business. The two principal financial statements used in management control are balance sheets and income statements. The **balance sheet**, a snapshot of the organization's financial position at a given moment, indicates what the firm owns and what proportion of its assets are financed with its own or borrowed money. The **income statement**, which shows the profitability of an organization over a period of time—a month, a quarter, or a year—helps managers focus on the organization's overall revenues (from sales and investments) and the costs incurred in generating those revenues. A detailed analysis of such statements helps management determine the adequacy of the organization's earning power and its ability to meet current and long-term obligations.

**balance sheet**

A snapshot of the organization's financial position at a given moment, indicating what the firm owns and what proportion of its assets are financed with its own or borrowed money.

**income statement**

A statement of an organization's profitability over a period of time—a month, a quarter, or a year.

**ratio analysis**

A method used by managers to take information from balance sheets and income statements in order to measure a company's efficiency, profitability, and sources of finances relative to those of other organizations.

Analyzing balance sheets and income statements as a form of financial control answers two basic questions: (1) How much money did the organization make or lose? and (2) What is a measure of the organization's worth based on historical values found on the balance sheet? Using **ratio analysis**, managers take information from the two financial statements so that they can measure the company's efficiency, profitability, and sources of finances relative to those of other organizations. Ratio analysis allows an organization to determine its levels of liquidity and solvency. *Liquidity ratios* indicate an organization's ability to meet short-term (less than one year) debt obligations as they come due. Establishing minimum and maximum performance standards will serve to alert the organization that it has either too little or too much invested in liquid assets—those that can be converted into cash quickly. *Solvency ratios* allow a company to assess its ability to meet long-term obligations. The two ratios reflect the claims of creditors and owners on the organization's assets.

As previously mentioned, analysis of financial statements may occur as a form of feedback control, where managers use information provided in such state-

---

## BUSINESS DILEMMA

*You're the Manager ...What Would You Do?*

THE COMPANY:   Aerodyne Corporation

YOUR POSITION:   Vice President of Ethics

THE PLACE:   Bethesda, MD

Aerodyne Corporation is the fourth largest aircraft manufacturer in the United States. Nearly 50 percent of Aerodyne's sales come from government contracts and the remainder from commercial airlines. Over the past ten years, airlines have experienced intense scrutiny as a result of labor problems, bankruptcies, consolidation, and plane crashes. Aerodyne has been the subject of two investigations that examined the use of defective parts and lack of quality control in certain aspects of the production process. In addition, Aerodyne has come under scrutiny because of expense padding on government contracts. These incidents probably occurred as a result of the company ignoring the potential impact of ethics training and control systems.

Tracy Reynolds was hired two years ago to head an ethics department, with the goal of establishing training systems for the entire company. Tracy's first step was to develop a comprehensive code of ethics, a formal statement of what the company expects in terms of ethical behavior from its employees. Following the development of the code of ethics, employees were provided training on the code's requirements. Additionally, employees were encouraged to report violations without any fear of retribution. A special 24-hour, 800-number, ethics hotline was installed to allow employees to ask anonymous questions about any issue or policy.

Tracy also helped establish systems to monitor compliance with federal procurement laws and installed procedures for the voluntary disclosure of violations to the appropriate authorities. Once these systems were in place, training was done on a region-by-region basis, with Tracy and her four assistants conducting three-hour seminars. Part of each seminar involved discussing ethical issues in the industry, situations that have plagued the company in the past, and procedures for avoiding unethical decisions. Many who reviewed the content of the ethics training seminars felt the frank group discussions of issues and dilemmas were perhaps the strongest part of the training. They helped employees recognize ethical issues and gave them outlets through which to obtain additional information to assist them in making ethical decisions.

### Questions

1. How does the ethical program provide control for Aerodyne?
2. Defend the investment in training and development required by an ethics program.
3. What are the potential benefits of this program?

---

ments to evaluate the organizational output—actual past performance—and to determine the need for changes in future resource acquisitions or operational activities. For example, after analyzing its income statement, Boeing might decide to employ an alternative supplier of a certain component part if it determines that the current supplier's products have generated less-than-optimal results; for another firm, higher-than-anticipated levels of defects in a current supplier's product, for example, may have reduced the profitability of a production process.

**Financial Audits.**   A **financial audit** is a periodic and comprehensive examination of a firm's financial records. As a control technique, audits can tell managers whether the information on which they have been basing decisions has been accurate, a sort of "double-checking" technique of financial control. Audits may be either internal, performed by the organization's own accounting staff, or external, done by qualified independent agencies. External auditing carries the advantage of objectivity; an outsider is unlikely to be so accustomed to the way that things are routinely done within an organization as to overlook common errors. Also, an external agency may be in better touch with new or innovative accounting methods and thus be

**Comment on Box:** Have students relate ethics to control. Many have not considered how an ethics statement and code of conduct helps control an organization and its employees. Why is the code important? What forms of ethics training are necessary? Why? Have students contact local organizations and determine whether they have a formal ethics code.

**financial audit**
A periodic and comprehensive examination of a firm's financial records.

better able to suggest alternative means of enacting more effective financial control. Additionally, an outside auditor is less likely to encounter a conflict of interest.

## MANAGING THE CONTROL PROCESS

As with other processes occurring within a company, control must be carefully managed to be successful. To facilitate effective control, managers must understand how to develop the process as well as to overcome resistance to it. To ensure that control systems continue to operate in smooth fashion, managers must be able to identify signs of inadequate control.

### Developing the Control Process

Because of differing circumstances faced by individual organizations, what makes the ideal control system for one is not necessarily appropriate for another. However, effective control systems are typically well-integrated with planning and are flexible, accurate, timely, and objective.

**Integration with Planning.**    As we said earlier, if control is to be effective, it must be closely linked with the planning process. Specifically, managers must set objectives that may readily be converted into performance standards that will reflect how well plans are being carried out. For example, Boeing managers might set a performance standard of never holding more inventory than is necessary to complete outstanding orders in an effort to evaluate the effectiveness of the company's ongoing operations. Such standards represent an attempt not merely to save a certain amount of money, but also to meet the company's goal of reducing the cost of building planes by 25 to 30 percent. Such a close link with planning ensures that efforts at increased control may be easily and accurately evaluated in terms of meeting organizational objectives.

**Example:** Flexibility of control is a key form of strategy used at Chrysler. Management flexibility, absence of institutional barriers, strong leadership, and urgency of mission helped Chrysler achieve success in the minivan market. Listening to customers also helped Chrysler avoid design errors.

**Flexibility.**    Flexibility is an important factor in the development of an effective management control system to allow the company to respond to changes in the business environment. The more turbulent or complex the environment, the more flexible the control system should be. For example, consider a manufacturing organization such as Xerox (copiers and other office automation equipment) that employs a complicated, multiple-step production system incorporating hundreds or even thousands of raw materials or component parts. Because each step in the production process must follow the successful completion of the previous step, the production control system must be able to monitor and manage each successive step in the process. Likewise, inventory control must account for current and expected levels for each of a multitude of parts and materials. If changes occur in either the production process or the required quantity of materials needed—perhaps due to new technology or changing consumer demand—control must be flexible enough to readily accommodate modifications while remaining effective.

**Accuracy.**    Control systems are useful only to the extent that the information on which they rely (and therefore produce) is accurate. Just as with management information systems, system output can be only as good as system input. If a quality control system somehow permits workers an opportunity to hide product defects,

Motorola's control system includes teaching its suppliers total quality management techniques such as cycle-time reduction and customer satisfaction. Motorola provides suppliers with objective information about their actual performance. Every two years, it sends a team to suppliers' plants to grade them against their competitors on quality and timeliness. Motorola managers also rate suppliers each month on an index that combines costs and quality, comparing them with other suppliers, listed anonymously, and indicating how much Motorola business each gets. Motorola also established a supplier council charged with rating Motorola's quality practices, such as the accuracy of production schedules and design layouts.

*Source:* © Michael L. Abramson.

for example, the potential exists for errors that may render the control system useless because it cannot accurately measure or report on what it is supposed to.

**Timeliness.**    An effective management control system provides performance information when it is needed. In general, the more uncertain and unstable the situation, the more often information will be needed. Marketing managers, for example, will require control-related information pertaining to the sales performance of a new product much more often than they will need such information on a mature, stable product that has been on the market for several years. During the six-month period of the initial launch of Gillette's Sensor for Women product, for example, marketing managers would have required more information at shorter intervals than they would have for more established products such as Gillette Foamy or the company's Trac II razors.

**Objectivity.**    To be effective, the control system must provide unbiased information. The manager who plays favorites with certain subordinates and "lets them off the hook" by submitting information that does not reflect actual performance deficiencies does no one, including the organization as a whole, any favors. If production workers allow defective products to slip through the system, bypassing control, not only might the company's image suffer as consumer complaints surface, but the production unit deemed responsible for the errors may be unfairly reprimanded. Moreover, objective, control-related information calls for managers to assess qualitatively the information they receive. Rather than simply report unusually high sales figures for a region or individual salesperson, a sales manager should look beyond the numbers into how the sales were made. It could be that drastic and unauthorized price concessions or unrealistic guarantees were provided buyers in hopes of gaining sales. Information pertaining to such deviations must be uncovered and reported in detail to facilitate effective management control.

## Understanding Resistance to Control

Implementation of new control systems often implies modified management philosophies as well as new responsibilities for organizational workers. As with other forms of change, such alterations of control systems are likely to be met with resistance. Additionally, common perceptions of control as a force restraining individual or group action adds to the likelihood of employee resistance. In short, managers charged with developing a control system should recognize that employees may resist control. While some employees may be less likely to resist change than others because of personal factors such as what might be called a "zone of indifference," or differing levels of acceptance of authority, common reasons for resistance to control include overcontrol, inappropriately focused control, control that rewards inefficiency, and the creation of enhanced accountability.

**Overcontrol.**    The issue of the appropriate level of control to apply is situational in nature. Levels that might seem overly aggressive or restrictive for management of a team of administrative office workers may very well be essential to the effective control of a sports team or military unit. However, a fine line often exists between the proper level of control and overcontrol, and companies sometimes try to control employees' activities more than they should. For example, an organization that explicitly tells its employees what to wear, when to eat, and what they can and can't do during their free time away from the workplace is likely to experience employee resistance to such overly aggressive practices.

Most employees recognize that control is necessary to the regulation of activities directly related to job performance. In fact, it is the responsibility of management to make sure that this understanding exists.[16] However, when control creeps into the realm of non–job-related behavioral matters, many employees may feel that the organization is overstepping its bounds. Some people, for example, argue that random testing for employee drug or alcohol use is wrong because they feel that companies should not be able to tell them what to do in their free time unless it has a direct, noticeable impact on actual work performance.

Managers must carefully balance the level of control against both situational demands and employee rights. Control for the sake of controlling workers will likely be unproductive from a long-term perspective; it must be firmly founded in terms of actual and relevant job performance in a manner that makes sense to the person being controlled. Overcontrol will likely result not only in low employee morale and commitment, but also in mistrust and even legal hassles with labor-related regulatory agencies, rather than the improved organizational performance desired.

**Inappropriate Focus.**    A production control system that places an extremely high priority on the number of units produced may result in workers who feel they must sacrifice product quality to meet the system's quantity standards. Not only will that company waste resources having to rework defective units, but it may also lose loyal customers who find substandard products. Firms can ill afford to place themselves in such situations, as research has found that it is increasingly more profitable for companies to retain loyal current customers by providing consistently high product quality than to recruit new customers through promotional efforts.[17]

Workers are much more likely to be motivated by a control system that seems to make sense. The principal means by which to achieve this ideal situation is to properly focus management control efforts. For example, at SRC, a Springfield-based manufacturer, operations and financial control efforts are supported by extensive training programs in which each and every employee learns to read financial statements and to understand the impact of his or her work activities on the company's profit structure. Also, employees have almost unlimited access to financial information. Similarly, at the Nashville-based Northern Telecom subsidiary Burgess Oliver, managers have replaced traditional cost accounting figures, often used to set financial-based control objectives, with figures and control terminology that are more meaningful to manufacturing employees, such as the amount of labor hours expended versus the amount projected to accomplish specified production tasks.[18] As these examples illustrate, only when control systems are focused on relevant issues in terms that clearly make sense to those being controlled can they be expected to function optimally.

**Rewards for Inefficiency.**    A former product marketing manager for a major banking company told the authors of his disappointment over the bank's decision to reclaim and redistribute resources that had been earmarked for use in his department in the upcoming final quarter of the year. The manager felt that executive management had merely transferred the resources to another, less-efficient department that had already used up its allotted funds because it "needed" the money more than his department did. In effect, the department receiving the additional resources was rewarded for inefficient performance. The manager responded by structuring his department's budget for the following year so that all resources would be expended before the scheduled fourth-quarter executive budgetary review. While the manager's response may be understandable, it was a misguided strategy devised to counter an ineffective control system, resulting in inefficient use of scarce departmental resources. Regardless of the specific response in this case, a system of budgetary control that rewards inefficiency is likely to be met with resistance because it appears to be unfair, arbitrary, and, most importantly, nonsensical.

**Accountability.**    Even properly designed control may be resisted because it creates additional levels of accountability. Effective control allows managers to pinpoint departmental or individual employee deficiencies. A worker who has been performing inefficiently is likely to resist a control system that shows that he or she is not performing up to standards. However, technological advances—such as the ability to videotape workers or record their phone calls anonymously—that may enhance a company's ability to monitor employees' activities and increase accountability have led to both employee abuse and worker concern and distrust. Managers must carefully consider the possible ethical implications of attempting to secure additional levels of accountability through increased control.

## Overcoming Resistance to Control

Although employees may resist control because of, among other factors, management misuse, control remains a necessary managerial function. Without it, the organization is unlikely to achieve its objectives. The challenge to managers is to exercise control so that employees understand the need for control but are not unduly inconvenienced by it. In general, there are four things managers can do to overcome resistance to control: create effective control, encourage employee participation, and use both management by objectives and a system of checks and balances.

**Create Effective Control.**    Probably the best way to avoid resistance to control is to establish effective control in the first place. This requires both careful planning before implementation, as well as continual monitoring of the effectiveness of the control system, rather than simply doing what has always been done before or what

**Example:** Resistance to control was minimized at Boeing headquarters in Seattle. The company abandoned its secretive management style and moved to open communication, sharing information with employees about goals and even layoffs.

works best for some other organization. Only with thorough planning and maintenance can a control system be properly integrated with overall organizational planning and be as flexible, accurate, timely, and objectively meaningful to those most directly controlled as it should be.

**Example:** Employee participation in teams can help identify and solve small problems and can even help struggling companies begin their quality improvement efforts. But, according to a study by Ernst & Young, teams ultimately lose their value and can distract from broader strategic issues once corporate performance improves.

### Encourage Employee Participation.

More and more companies are realizing the benefits of allowing nonmanagerial employees increased say in the establishment of organizational policies and procedures. Such empowerment can be applied effectively to planning for and implementing a system of control, as employees are less likely to resist a system that they themselves helped create.

Earlier, we mentioned the use of employee empowerment and increased control through additional levels of training at Corning's Erwin ceramics plant. In this instance, Corning managers worked closely with the plant's unionized assembly workers to jointly and radically change the way work was done. To control the level of product quality, they decided to eliminate 21 separate job classifications and replace them with one highly trained product specialist. Managers grouped most of the workers into teams and gave them authority to decide where machines should be placed, who should work on them, and how production should be scheduled. Corning's effort at increasing employee participation in the control process resulted in an increase in productivity and a 38 percent decrease in product defects.[19]

Employee empowerment is a form of control in itself in that empowered employees who know their jobs better, have more responsibility, and exhibit higher levels of commitment simply need to be monitored—controlled—less. Although control in this manner is ordinarily considered in a positive light, some organizational management researchers question the motivation behind increased employee empowerment, arguing that modern quality control efforts in particular are little more than covert attempts on the part of management to extract as much labor as possible from employees with a minimum amount of supervision—that is, management effort. While perceptions such as these may be warranted in some cases, they can be avoided in other instances by carefully educating controlled employees about how the process works and how their work activities affect overall organizational performance.

### Use MBO.

Another way to overcome resistance to control may be through the use of management by objectives (MBO), a management philosophy based on converting organizational objectives into individual objectives. Working closely in concert with management, workers set their own goals, which in turn serve as standards against which to evaluate their actual performance. MBO assumes that allowing employees to set personal objectives will gain their commitment to those objectives, leading to increased performance. Also, employees know before starting work that they will be rewarded on the basis of how well they satisfy and maintain these personal goals and standards. Moreover, MBO links planning and control closely, thus lessening the likelihood that resistance to control will occur.

### Use Checks and Balances.

When properly employed, a system of checks and balances should provide documentation for managerial control decisions. For example, if a production worker is reprimanded for poor-quality work, a properly designed quality control system should provide information pertaining to the exact cause of the inadequate work. Resistance to control decreases because an effective system of checks and balances serves to protect employees as well as management. A reprimanded production worker, for example, should be able to refer to information provided by the control system to see if the cause of the poor-quality work is truly something under his control; the worker can use the system of checks and balances to "prove" his case and hopefully help correct the deviation should he not be directly at fault.

## Signs of Inadequate Control Systems

In addition to understanding ways to overcome resistance to control, managers also need to be aware of the basic signs of a control system that is not operating effectively. Following are some indicators of possible control-related difficulty.

**1.** *A high incidence of employee resistance to control.* A control system that employees continually resist may simply not be right for the specific situation. This is likely to be the case after repeated attempts at either improving the control system or trying to explain or justify it to employees. It may be that employees consider the system excessive, or that the control is inappropriately focused. In this situation, managers must work closely with employees to determine the cause of the resistance and take appropriate action to remedy the situation.

**2.** *A unit meets control standards but fails to achieve its overall objectives.* In this case, it is likely that the link between planning and control is poor. If Boeing, for example, meets its performance standard of reducing the cost of manufacturing aircraft by 25 to 30 percent but finds that it has not met its overall objective of making it more economical for customers to buy new planes instead of maintaining old ones, it is probable that the control standards established did not realistically reflect what it would take to meet the objective. Additionally, the control may be unable to measure what it is supposed to measure or perhaps is not being enforced stringently enough.

**3.** *Increased control does not lead to increased or adequate performance.* The extra control may simply not be needed or it may not be appropriate for the situation. Adding control where it is not needed runs the risk of alienating those controlled and should be avoided.

**4.** *The existence of control standards that have been in place for an extended period of time.* When an organization becomes stagnant in this day and age, it cannot remain competitive. As the environment inevitably changes, so should the organization and its system of management control. Potential dramatic changes in the U.S. health care industry under the administration of President Bill Clinton in the early 1990s, for example, demanded that the many organizations affected continually monitor and revise their control systems to best reflect and deal with changing circumstances.

**5.** *Organizational losses in terms of sales, profits, or market share.* Declining performance is a clear indicator of trouble. Anytime an organization appears to be losing ground from a competitive or financial standpoint, it is wise to examine its control system. Effective control should allow the company to pinpoint the cause of the problem before major losses occur. Inadequate control itself may be, as we saw in the example of the ill-fated Osborne Computer Company at the beginning of this chapter, the root of the problem.

Although an essential managerial function, controlling the complex activities of organizational members is seldom a simple undertaking. The challenge to man-

## Paths to Positions in Management Control

Rapid organizational growth demands tight organizational control. Out of the 100 fastest growing U.S. firms in 1992, the top ten posted an average annual sales growth rate of nearly 150 percent over the previous three to five years. With growth rates so high, demand for a variety of control-related positions will be strong. Moreover, the unpredictable and turbulent nature of the environments faced by most organizations ensures that managers well versed in control methodology will remain in high demand for many years to come.

Pressures to cut costs in the late 1980s and early 1990s resulted in the elimination of 6 million jobs from companies with more than 500 employees. Employees able to integrate and control the growth of day-to-day operations and information networks experienced rapid growth. Additionally, most traditional executive-level positions associated with organizational control remain in demand in a wide variety of firms. Controllers are needed to design increasingly flexible accounting systems, prepare budgets and financial forecasts, and create and maintain auditing mechanisms that track the hectic flow of organizational resources during times of rapid expansion and change. Similarly, there is an increased need for competent personnel to fill the position of treasurer in a wide variety of organizations. Treasurers are responsible for the actual receipt, custody, and properly organized disbursement of company funds to suppliers, employees, insurance agencies, and other relevant parties.

While a college background in finance, economics, accounting, and mathematics is customarily required, the career paths to the positions of treasurer and controller vary with the size, culture, and specific structure of the individual organization. Cost-analysis, budgeting, tax auditing, financial analysis, credit collections, and data processing are entry-level positions leading to possible advancement to executive-level control assignments. However, the majority of individuals reaching such positions have a masters degree in business or a CPA (certified public accountant) certificate.

Additionally, those initially involved in actually providing services, such as nursing personnel, are increasingly learning to manage operations through financial means and other forms of control, particularly in smaller firms experiencing rapid growth.

Total quality control, especially in production and operations, provides many opportunities for employment. Developing benchmarks and efforts to ensure continuous quality improvement must be implemented by employees in all areas of management. Jobs in this area require managers to possess a wide range of knowledge about the organization, suppliers, and customers. Total quality managers, ethics officers, and work-team managers, as well as statistical control inspectors, are all involved in activities to ensure continuous quality improvement.

From a careers perspective, the implications of the high demand for control personnel are twofold. First, environmental uncertainties resulting from competitive pressures and dynamic industry change have created a need for those once trained only in technical fields to at least understand the basic principles and methods of management control. Second, traditionally financial-minded managers well-versed in the application of various forms of control must increasingly understand the peculiarities and information technology of management fields, particularly if they find themselves looking for career change or advancement. In short, there are great opportunities and great challenges for those wishing to apply the principles of management control in business.

*Sources: Hoover's Handbook of Emerging Companies,* Patrick J. Spain, Alta Campbell, and Alan Chai, eds. (Austin, TX: The Reference Press, 1993), 368; Louis S. Richman, "Jobs That Are Growing and Slowing," *Fortune,* July 12, 1993, 52–53; Andrew E. Serwer, "America's 100 Fastest Growing Companies," *Fortune,* August 9, 1993, 40–56; *VGM's Handbook of Business & Management Careers,* 2nd ed., Annette Selden, ed. (Chicago: NTC Publishing Group, 1993).

**Comment on Box:** Invite an area treasurer or controller to your class to discuss the need for control and how control-related positions are changing in organizations. What type of training is needed for careers in organizational control? Is the need for control expected to increase in the future? Why?

agers is to understand the purpose and importance of control, and to use it so that it does not infringe on employees' personal freedoms, but it does maximize organizational performance. As part of this process, it is the responsibility of management to convey the need for control to employees in a manner that facilitates active and voluntary participation in the control process. For this ideal situation to occur, managers must structure and communicate the objectives of the process throughout the organization so that conforming to clearly defined control guidelines makes sense to those being controlled. Responsibility for control does not end after system implementation, nor does it involve the simple inspection of the output of the production process. Through control, managers must constantly look for sometimes hidden signs of inadequate performance at all stages and levels of organizational activity, and they must enact corrective action when warranted.

## SUMMARY AND REVIEW

- **Define management control and explain why it is necessary.** Management control includes all activities an organization undertakes to ensure that its actions lead to achievement of its objectives; a management control system is a planned, ordered scheme of management control. Management control allows managers to readily assess where the firm actually is relative to where it wants or expects to be. It also serves to help an organization adapt to changing conditions, limit the compounding of errors, deal with increased complexity, and minimize costs.

- **Examine the process through which managers develop and implement control.** The control process consists of four steps: establishing performance standards (targets set by management against which to compare actual performance at a future date), measuring performance, comparing performance against standards, and evaluating and taking corrective action. Should discrepancies occur between desired and actual performance, a firm can decide to correct the deviations, change the performance standards, or maintain the status quo.

- **Distinguish among the various forms of control.** Four forms of control are organizational, operations, strategic, and financial. Organizational control regulates the overall functioning of the organization. It includes bureaucratic control (control through formal, mechanistic structural arrangements) and clan control (control through more informal, organic structural arrangements), which can be viewed as opposite levels of organizational control, though most firms make use of both to varying degrees. Operations control regulates one or more individual operating systems within an organization, and can be subdivided into preliminary, screening, and feedback control. Preliminary control monitors deviations in the quality and quantity of the organization's inputs with the objective of preventing deviations before they enter the system. Screening control regulates the transformation process to ensure that

it is consistent with objectives. Feedback control monitors the firm's outputs. Strategic control ensures that the organization effectively understands and responds to the realities of its environment. Financial control includes budgeting (the process of establishing formal, written budgets for future organizational operations), analysis of financial statements (balance sheet and income statement), ratio analysis (measures of the company's efficiency, profitability, and sources of finances relative to those of other organizations using information provided by financial statements), and financial audits (periodic and comprehensive examinations of a firm's financial records).

- **Summarize the elements of effective control.** Effective control systems are well-integrated with planning and are flexible, accurate, timely, and objective. Most importantly, control systems should make sense to those individuals being controlled.

- **Determine why control is sometimes met with resistance and how managers may overcome this resistance.** Common reasons for resistance to control include overcontrol, inappropriately focused control, control that rewards inefficiency, or control that results in enhanced accountability. To overcome resistance to control, managers may create effective control from the outset, encourage employee participation, and employ both management by objectives and a system of checks and balances. Often, workers must be educated about the purpose and function of control, as well as about how their activities relate to control objectives.

- **Assess an organization's control program.** Based on the material presented in the "Business Dilemma" box and throughout this chapter, evaluate the vice president's efforts to control Aerodyne's ethical decision making. You should be able to describe the forms of control being used and address how these efforts will help improve the organization's performance.

## Key Terms and Concepts

## Ready Recall

1. Why is control important? What do you think would happen without it?
2. Why must control be closely integrated with organizational planning?
3. List the four steps in the control process.
4. List and define the four types of control. How do organizational, operations, and strategic types of control differ from one another? How do they relate?
5. Differentiate between bureaucratic and clan organizational control. Which is the better form of control?
6. How does operating budgeting differ from capital budgeting?
7. How is a financial audit used for purposes of control?
8. What are some common reasons for resistance to control?
9. How can managers combat resistance to control? What is the most important factor in this process?
10. How can managers recognize inadequate control systems?

## Expand Your Experience

1. Take a look at your own place of employment (if you are not employed, apply the question to your college or university). Who is responsible for the control function? Cite specific examples of the four forms of control used in your workplace.
2. How effective are control systems that are based on meeting objectives stated in the same terms for both the finance and production departments? Why might control of this nature prove less than optimal? How would you alter the system to be more meaningful for the individual functional departments?
3. Analyze the control system of a local small business (you may have to interview some managers and employees to get enough information). Identify examples of each of the forms of control as practiced within the company. Is the control system adequate? Why or why not? If you judge the control to be inadequate, make some recommendations for improving it.

**CASE**

# Cin-Made: The Effective Transformation of Operations Control

Cincinnati-based Cin-Made, a manufacturer of sturdy paper mailing tubes and other mailing materials, was founded in 1902. During the 1960s and 1970s, Cin-Made was run exclusively by one woman who lived and breathed the company for a total of 25 years. Under her management, the company's system of management control might best be described as benevolent and maternal; she ran it like a family. Many of the company's employees had worked at Cin-Made all their working lives and had never known anything other than the casual, family-oriented atmosphere that prevailed.

As competitive pressures mounted in the early 1980s, both the nature of the work environment and the manner in which operations were—or were not—controlled at Cin-Made led to difficulties. When the hard times hit, the company's owner learned that her employees were not as loyal to her as she had been to them. After being told frankly about the company's rapidly deteriorating financial condition in 1982, union officials flatly denied the owner's proposal to roll back customary annual pay raises to stem the tide of red ink. When she took her case to her employees—her "family"—only two or three people took her side.

In 1984, Cin-Made was sold to two investors who set out to turn the stagnant, troubled company around. Their early efforts at change, especially in the area of increased levels of control, were met with great resistance. The company's only maintenance technician, for example, resigned over what seemed a trivial dispute over wages. When the new owners brought in new, automated equipment to replace the slow, antiquated machinery that employees had worked on for over twenty years, the employees hated it. The owners, however, believed that their authority and intervention were needed to bring the company's erratic operations under control. Overall, Cin-Made's new owners did not make themselves popular with their early efforts at increasing control of the company's operations. In fact, long-time Cin-Made employees considered them brash, young "know-it-alls" trying unsuccessfully to make drastic changes that failed to make sense. Just a few months after the change of ownership, Cin-Made was losing $30,000 per month.

The situation did not begin to improve at Cin-Made until after the settlement of a bitter strike. During the strike, the company's owners operated the machines on the factory floor themselves and soon realized that the jobs were not nearly as simple as they had thought. Consequently, when the strike was finally settled, the humbled owners, reasoning that employees knew the system best, set out to involve shopfloor workers more directly in the operation of the company. To the surprise of the owners, however, these efforts at employee empowerment likewise failed miserably. Workers, accustomed to being told what to do, even if it was the same thing over and over again, did not welcome the change. They still didn't trust the new owners, let alone understand what they were trying to do.

After much consideration, the owners decided that the employees, as a result of decades of following orders, simply did not feel that Cin-Made was "their company." To remedy this, albeit with much early resistance on the part of both union officials and the workers themselves, they froze wages and implemented a profit-sharing plan. The idea was to increase the workers' stake in the everyday operations of the company, with a resultant increased interest in how to improve and better control the production process.

Once the potentially generous profit-sharing system was in place—after extensive education of workers—new forms of operations control were implemented. Gradually, the owners shared increasingly complex information about the operations of the company with front-line employees to facilitate the implementation process. Workers gradually began to accept more

responsibility and to work as a team. In short, they began to control themselves.

Once Cin-Made began to stabilize, the owners set out to implement a total quality management (TQM) program, including statistical process control (SPC). Again, extensive education of all involved parties was required. For example, the company's newly appointed plant manager and eight hourly workers enrolled in a 10-week night school course at a local university. In turn, these employees educated other Cin-Made employees on the "hows" and "whys" of the specific SPC techniques employed. Within a year of SPC implementation, under the direction of the new plant manager, each and every company employee was entering SPC data into the company's computer databank and tracking his or her own scrap material and efficiency. What makes this all the more remarkable is the fact that many Cin-Made workers had only limited mathematical knowledge and, as a result, initially found the concept of SPC very intimidating.

Overall, the effects of the transformation of operations control at Cin-Made have been phenomenal. Once oppositional union committees now handle the tasks of allocating overtime, scheduling layoffs, and deciding when to hire and let go of temporary workers. Employee committees schedule and control production operations for an expanding line of Cin-Made products. Full-time employees routinely monitor the sometimes inconsistent and potentially disruptive activities of temporary workers to control waste and improve overall efficiency. Absenteeism has all but ceased, while productivity has soared some 30 percent. And, most important of all, the effects of the newly implemented control efforts have made themselves readily apparent, as the profit-sharing system designed by Cin-Made's once-hated owners is now generating more money for everyone at the company than they have ever before made. As one long-time—and once highly skeptical—employee put it: "So in the end, I like my job more than I ever used to. I do better work. I make more money. Yes, I suppose Bob Frey [one of the owners] is getting rich on these same profits.... And that's fine."

*Sources:* Robert E. Cole, "Learning From Learning Theory: Implications for Quality Improvement of Turnover, Use of Contingent Workers, and Job Rotation Policies," *Quality Management Journal* 1 (October 1993): 9–25; Robert Frey, "Empowerment or Else," *Harvard Business Review* (September-October 1993): 80–94; Arthur R. Tenner and Irving J. DeToro, *Total Quality Management: Three Steps to Continuous Improvement* (Reading, MA: Addison-Wesley, 1992).

## Questions

1. Why did employees initially resist the new control efforts?
2. Discuss the use of strategic process control at Cin-Made. How has it helped improve the company's performance?
3. How have management control efforts at Cin-Made facilitated the company's growth? How might these efforts help the company expand its operations?

## STRENGTHEN YOUR SKILLS
# *Controlling*

Before beginning this exercise, you will need to review Figure 22.1 (The Control Process) on page 649 and the accompanying text discussion under the heading "The Control Process."

### Procedure

- Break the class into groups of 4 to 6 people. Have each group designate one person to role play the "manager" (this person must be willing for the others to discuss/evaluate his or her performance after completing the exercise). The remaining students in each group will role play the "employees."
- The "manager" will follow the steps of the control process in order to accomplish the objective of having his or her work group correctly complete a work assignment.
- Before each group begins, the "employees" need to sit quietly for two minutes while each "manager" formulates how best to proceed with communicating the work assignment to the employees in his or her work group. *Only* the "managers" may look now at the work assignment on this page (have everyone else cover it with a piece of paper).
- After the managers have their two minutes of planning time, the instructor will announce that the "managers" may proceed as they see fit with their respective employee groups.
- When your work group completes the work assignment, raise your hand and write down the time, as provided by your instructor, that it took your group to complete the work. When all the groups are finished, your instructor will give you the correct answers to the questions. The class will then discuss how various managers used the steps of the control process as identified in Figure 22.1 to help the work groups to function together effectively and efficiently.

Manager _____

Employees _____

Work Assignment[20]

The following questions are to be answered using *only capital letters* from the alphabet. Your group is to get the questions answered correctly as directed by your "manager."

1. What is the only letter open on all sides? _____
2. What are the two curved letters that are the same upside down? _____
3. What are the five letters containing only one single horizontal line? _____
4. What are the three letters with only two parallel horizontal lines? _____
5. What is the only letter with two diagonal straight lines? _____
6. What letter of the alphabet is a bird? _____
7. What letter of the alphabet is part of your head? _____
8. What letter of the alphabet is an insect? _____
9. What letter of the alphabet is a drink? _____
10. What letter of the alphabet is a building extension? _____
11. What letter of the alphabet is a hint? _____
12. What letter of the alphabet is a vegetable? _____
13. What letter of the alphabet is a body of water? _____
14. What letter of the alphabet is a farm animal? _____

Time to complete work assignment _____

Number of correct answers _____

# Notes

## Chapter 1

1. Vida G. Scarpello and Robert J. Vandenberg, "The Satisfaction with My Supervisor Scale: Its Utility for Research and Practical Applications," *Journal of Management* 13(3) (Fall 1987): 447–466.
2. Raymond A. Katzell and Richard A. Guzzo, "Psychological Approaches to Productivity Improvement," *American Psychologist* 38 (April 1983): 468–472.
3. David Kirkpatrick, "CEO Scully on Apple's Future," *Fortune*, February 8, 1993, 11.
4. Henry Mintzberg, *The Nature of Managerial Work* (Englewood Cliffs, NJ: Prentice-Hall, Inc., 1973).
5. Peter Coy, "Two Cheers for Corporate Collaboration," *Business Week*, May 3, 1993, 34.
6. Chuck Hawkins, "After a U-Turn, UPS Really Delivers," *Business Week*, May 31, 1993, 92–93.
7. Laura Zinn and Mary Beth Regan, "The Right Moves Baby," *Business Week*, July 5, 1993, 30–31.
8. Charles Burck, "The Real World of the Entrepreneur," *Fortune*, April 5, 1993, 62–81.
9. Amy Barrett, "Still Dealing After All These Years," *Business Week*, March 29, 1993, 80.
10. Robert A. Katz, "The Skills of an Effective Administrator," *Harvard Business Review* 52 (September–October 1974): 90–102.
11. Alan Deutschman, "Odd Man Out," *Fortune*, July 26, 1993, 42–56.
12. Brian O'Reilly, "How Execs Learn," *Fortune*, April 5, 1993, 52–58.

## Chapter 2

1. Daniel A. Wren, *The Evolution of Management Thought*, 3rd ed. (New York: John Wiley and Sons, 1987), 17.
2. Wren, *Evolution of Management Thought*, 6–7.
3. Wren, 20; and Claude S. George, Jr., *The History of Management Thought* (Englewood Cliffs, NJ: Prentice-Hall, Inc., 1968), 27.
4. Wren, 22–25.
5. Max Weber, *The Protestant Ethic and the Spirit of Capitalism* (New York: Charles Scribner's Sons, 1958; originally published in 1905).
6. Adam Smith, *An Inquiry into the Nature and Causes of the Wealth of Nations* (New York: Modern Library, 1937; originally published in 1776).
7. Smith, *The Wealth of Nations*.
8. Smith, 340.
9. Wren.
10. George, 49.
11. Wren.
12. Frederick W. Taylor, *Scientific Management* (New York: Harper & Row, 1947; originally published in 1911).
13. Wren, 87.
14. Taylor, *Scientific Management*, 21.
15. Taylor.
16. See, for example, Charles D. Wrege and Amedeo G. Perroni, "Taylor's Pig-Tale: A Historical Analysis of Frederick W. Taylor's Pig Iron Experiment," *Academy of Management Journal* 17 (March 1974): 6–27; and Charles D. Wrege and Anne Marie Stotka, "Cooke Creates a Classic: The Story Behind F.W. Taylor's Principles of Scientific Management," *Academy of Management Review* 3 (October 1978): 736–749.
17. The definitions in this section are based on material presented in William A. Ruch, Harold E. Fearon, and David C. Wieters, *Fundamentals of Production/Operations Management*, 5th ed. (St. Paul: West Publishing, 1992).
18. Daniel A. Wren, "In Memoriam: Lillian Moller Gilbreth (1878–1972)," *Academy of Management Journal* 15 (March 1972): 7–8.
19. W. R. Spriegel and C. F. Meyers, eds., *The Writings of the Gilbreths* (Homewood, IL: Irwin, 1953), 284.
20. Spriegel and Meyers, *The Writings of the Gilbreths*, 152–153.
21. The material on Henry Gantt is from unpublished notes prepared by Dr. Richard Lutz, Management Department, College of Business, University of Akron; and "Famous Firsts: Charting a Way to 'Democracy'," *Business Week*, January 11, 1964, 44–46.
22. The material on Morris Cooke is from unpublished notes prepared by Richard Lutz; and "Famous Firsts: Extending the Scientific Gospel," *Business Week*, April 18, 1964, 132–136.
23. Henri Fayol, *General and Industrial Management* (London: Sir Isaac Pitman & Sons Ltd., 1949).
24. The material on Henri Fayol is from the preface and body of Henri Fayol, *General and Industrial Management*, with a foreword by L. Urwick (London: Sir Isaac Pitman & Sons Ltd., 1949).
25. Based on Wren; and Richard Weiss, "Weber on Bureaucracy: Management Consultant or Political Theorist?" *Academy of Management Review* 8 (April 1983): 242–248.
26. Quoted in Reinhard Bendix, *Max Weber: An Intellectual Portrait* (Garden City, NY: Doubleday Co., 1960), 464.
27. Lee D. Parker, "Control in Organizational Life: The Contribution of Mary Parker Follett," *Academy of Management Review* 9 (October 1984): 736–745.

28. "Famous Firsts: Sibyl of a Modern Science," *Business Week,* November 21, 1964, 196ff.

29. Parker, "Control in Organizational Life."

30. Mary Parker Follett, *Creative Experience* (New York: Peter Smith, 1924).

31. Richard H. Franke, "The Hawthorne Experiments: Empirical Findings and Implications for Management," Paper presented at the *Academy of Management* meeting, August 1987, New Orleans.

32. Franke.

33. Wren, 238.

34. This material is based on information in unpublished notes and materials pertaining to the Hawthorne experiments prepared by Dr. Richard Lutz, University of Akron.

35. John G. Adair, "The Hawthorne Effect: A Reconsideration of the Methodological Artifact," *Journal of Applied Psychology,* 1984, 334–345; Alex Carey, "The Hawthorne Studies: A Radical Criticism," *American Sociological Review,* June 1967, 403–416.

36. Franke.

37. Fremont E. Kast and James E. Rosenzweig, "General Systems Theory: Applications for Organization and Management," *Academy of Management Journal* 15 (December 1972): 447–465.

38. Kast and Rosenzweig.

39. Wren, 265.

40. Chester I. Barnard, *The Functions of the Executive* (Cambridge, MA: Harvard University Press, 1938), viii, 6.

41. This material on Chester Barnard is based on unpublished notes prepared by Richard Lutz, University of Akron.

42. Wren, 269.

43. Jeremy Main, "The Curmudgeon Who Talks Tough on Quality," *Fortune,* June 25, 1984, 118–122.

44. Lloyd Dobyns and Clare Crawford-Mason, *Quality or Else* (Boston: Houghton-Mifflin Company, 1991); John Loring, "Dr. Deming's Traveling Quality Show," *Canadian Business,* September 1990, 38–42.

45. Wren, 358–359.

46. Thomas J. Peters and Robert H. Waterman, Jr., *In Search of Excellence* (New York: Harper & Row, 1982).

47. William G. Ouchi and Alfred M. Jaeger, "Theory Z Organizations: Stability in the Midst of Mobility," *Academy of Management Review* 3 (April 1978): 305–314.

## Chapter 3

1. "Drugstores Take the Lead in Incontinence Product Sales," *Drug Topics,* March 21, 1988, 70.

2. Claudia Puig, "Latino Radio Surge: A Coming of Age," *The Los Angeles Times,* January 7, 1993, F1.

3. Judith Crown, "Sales Are Thinning for Fat-free Foods; Just Another Fad? Interest Slim in Many Products," *Crain's Chicago Business,* June 1, 1992, 1.

4. Allan Meltzer, "Times Board of Economists: Massive Aid Program for Russia, as Proposed by Nixon, Isn't the Answer," *The Los Angeles Times,* March 29, 1992, D2.

5. "Maybe, No, No Way," *Automotive News,* June 7, 1993, 2.

6. Carol Loomis, "Dinosaurs?" *Fortune,* May 3, 1993, 36.

7. Paul Thayer, "Survey of International Telecommunications," *Financial Times,* October 15, 1992, 1.

8. Ken Terry, "Talkin' About A Revolution; How Compact Disc Changed the Music Industry Forever and (Mostly) for the Better," *Billboard,* September 26, 1992, CD4.

9. Michael Porter, *Competitive Strategy* (New York: The Free Press, 1980), 97–98.

10. Michael Verespej, "CEOs Under the Magnifying Glass," *Industry Week,* April 19, 1993, 60.

11. John Huey and Andrew Erdman, "Managing in the Midst of Chaos," *Fortune,* April 5, 1993, 38.

12. Thomas McCarroll, "Board Games; In a Fundamental Power Shift in Corporate America, Boards of Directors, Once Tame and Docile, are Turning on Their Masters," *Time,* February 8, 1993, 54.

13. R. Edward Freeman, *Strategic Management: A Stakeholder Approach* (Boston: Pittman, 1984).

14. Freeman, *Strategic Management: A Stakeholder Approach,* 60–61.

15. "Toyota-GM Venture Backed," *The New York Times,* June 29, 1993, C17.

16. Jacqueline Mitchell, "Auto Makers Post Flat Sales in Mid-March: Lackluster Pace Continues from Previous 30 Days," *The New York Times,* June 24, 1993, C3.

17. "McDonald's Net Income Rose 14% in Fourth Quarter," *The Wall Street Journal,* January 28, 1993, C15.

18. Loomis, "Dinosaurs?"

19. S. J. Diamond, "Clever, But Who Thought of It?" *The Los Angeles Times,* December 6, 1991, D1.

## Chapter 4

1. Ed Brennan, "An Open Letter to Sears Customers," advertisement appearing in *The Wall Street Journal,* June 25, 1992.

2. Wendy Zellner, "Not Everybody Loves Wal-Mart's Low Prices," *Business Week,* October 12, 1992, 36–38.

3. Vernon R. Loucks, Jr., "A CEO Looks at Ethics," *Business Horizons* 30 (March–April 1987): 4.

4. "It's a Racket," *Business Ethics* 8 (March/April 1994): 10.

5. "Arthur Andersen Agrees to Settlement Involving Connecticut Real Estate Firm," *The Wall Street Journal,* May 5, 1993, B4.

6. Jim Impoco, "Working for Mr. Clean Jeans," *US News & World Report,* August 2, 1993, 50.

7. Phillip Sulak, "Atochem May Face $10 Million Fine," *The (Bryan/College Station, TX) Eagle,* January 15, 1992, A1, A6.

8. Kenneth Labich, "The New Crisis in Business Ethics," *Fortune,* April 20, 1992, 167.

9. Chris Welles, "What Led Beechnut Down the Road to Disgrace," *Business Week,* February 22, 1988, 124–128.

10. Brett Pulley, "Culture of Racial Bias at Shoney's Underlies Chairman's Departure," *The Wall Street Journal,* December 21, 1992, A1, A4.

11. Thomas M. Jones, "Ethical Decision Making by Individuals in Organizations: An Issue-Contingent Model," *Academy of Management Review* 2 (April 1991): 371–373.

12. Sir Adrian Cadbury, "Ethical Managers Make Their Own Rules," *Harvard Business Review* 65 (September–October 1987): 72.

13. Jo McIntyre, "They Just Did It: Nike's Crusade for Diversity," *Business Ethics* 8 (March/April 1994): 14.

14. O. C. Ferrell and Larry Gresham, "A Contingency Framework for Ethical Decision Making in Marketing," *Journal of Marketing* 49 (Summer 1985): 87–96.

15. Julia Flyn, with Christina Del Valle and Russell Mitchell, "Did Sears Take Other Customers for a Ride?" *Business Week,* August 3, 1992, 24–25.

16. Gene R. Laczniak and Patrick E. Murphy, *Ethical Marketing Decisions: The Higher Road* (Boston: Allyn & Bacon, 1993), 14.

17. Margaret Cunningham, "Walking the Thin White Line: A Role Conflict Model of Ethical Decision Making Behavior in the Marketing Research Process," Ph.D. Dissertation, Texas A&M University, 1991.

18. Ferrell and Gresham, "A Contingency Framework."

19. "Whistle Blower Award," *USA Today,* December 7, 1992, B10.

20. Labich, "The New Crisis in Business Ethics," 168.

21. "More Big Businesses Set up Ethics Offices," *The Wall Street Journal,* May 10, 1993, B1.

22. Archie B. Carroll, "The Pyramid of Corporate Social Responsibility: Toward the Moral Management of Organizational Stakeholders," *Business Horizons* 34 (July/August 1991): 42.

23. Larry Reynolds, "Vice President of the Environment," *Business Ethics* 5 (March/April 1991): 22–24.

24. Emily T. Smith and Vicki Cahan, with Naomi Freundlich, James E. Ellis, and Joseph Weber, "The Greening of Corporate America," *Business Week,* April 23, 1990, 96–103.

25. Smith and Cahan, "The Greening of Corporate America."

26. Joan O'C. Hamilton, "Bugs, Weeds, and Fine Wine," *Business Week,* August 10, 1992, 30.

27. David Woodruff and Thane Peterson, with Karen Lowry Miller, "The Greening of Detroit," *Business Week,* April 8, 1991, 54–60.

28. U.S. Bureau of the Census, *Statistical Abstract of the United States: 1993,* 113th ed. (Washington DC: U.S. Government Printing Office, 1993), 387, 554.

29. Julia Lawlor, "Homeless Can Reserve Room, Job at Days Inns," *USA Today,* July 20, 1990, 2B.

14. U.S. Department of Commerce, "North American Free Trade Agreement: Opportunities for U.S. Industries," NAFTA Industry Sector Reports, October 1993.

15. U.S. Department of Commerce, 1993.

16. Gary A. Knight, "NAFTA Holds Promise for Stronger, Prosperous North America," *Marketing News,* October 25, 1993, 14–15.

17. Owen Ullmann and Judith H. Dobrzynski, "NAFTA: Pro: A Trade Bonanza," *Business Week,* September 13, 1993, 26–28.

18. Douglas Harbrecht, "NAFTA: Con: A Jobs Nightmare," *Business Week,* September 13, 1993, 26–28; and Asra Q. Nomani and Michael K. Frisby, "Clinton Opens Free-Trade Drive, But Side Accords Could Fall Short," *The Wall Street Journal,* September 15, 1993, A16.

19. Harbrecht, "NAFTA: Con: A Jobs Nightmare."

20. John Hillkirk, "It Could Be Trade Boom or Bust," *USA Today,* January 12, 1989, 4B.

21. Nicholas Colchester, "1992 = 1990 + 2 or Thereabouts," in *The World in 1990* (London: Economist Publications, 1990), 49–50; Stephen Young, James Hamill, Colin Wheeler, and J. Richard Davies, *International Market Entry and Development* (London: Harvester Wheatsheaf, 1989), 280–282.

22. "Japan Plan," *USA Today,* February 18, 1994, B1.

23. Mark Memmott, "Transitions Are Like Night and Day," *USA Today,* February 24, 1994, B2.

24. Rose Brady and Peter Galuszka, with Patricia Kranz and Richard A. Melcher, "The Soviet Lurch Toward Capitalism," *Business Week,* October 21, 1991, 50–51.

25. Memmott, "Transitions Are Like Night and Day."

## Chapter 5

1. David A. Ricks, "How to Avoid Business Blunders Abroad," in *International Marketing,* ed. Subhash C. Jain and Lewis R. Tucker, Jr. (Boston: Kent Publishing Co., 1986), 109–111.

2. "Where's the Beef?" *Fortune,* January 24, 1994, 16.

3. Bob Hagerty, "Trainers Help Expatriate Employees Build Bridges to Different Cultures," *The Wall Street Journal,* June 14, 1993, B1, B6.

4. Hagerty, "Trainers Help Expatriate Employees."

5. Patricia Sellers, "Where Killers and Kidnappers Roam," *Fortune,* September 23, 1991, 8.

6. Paul Hofheinz, "Rising in Russia," *Fortune,* January 24, 1994, 92–97.

7. "GATT Costs," *USA Today,* February 24, 1994, B1.

8. Douglas Harbrecht, Owen Ullmann, Bill Javetski, and Geri Smith, "Finally, GATT May Fly," *Business Week,* December 20, 1993, 36–37.

9. Peter Conradi, "PepsiCo, Soviet Union Sign Barter Deal," *The Commercial Appeal,* April 10, 1990, B1, B8.

10. Paul B. Brown, "Over There," *INC.* 13 (April 1990): 105–106.

11. Thomas Gross and John Neuman, "Strategic Alliances Vital in Global Marketing," *Marketing News,* June 1989, 1–2.

12. Thomas V. Greer, "The Maquiladora Program: Nature and Current Status," *Developments in Marketing Science,* Vol XII, Academy of Marketing Science Proceedings, 1989, 108–111; Benito E. Flores, "Mexico's Maquiladora Industries: An Overview and Perspectives," *Texas A&M Business Forum,* Fall 1987, 27–32.

13. O. C. Ferrell and John Fraedrich, *Business Ethics: Ethical Decision Making and Cases* (Boston: Houghton Mifflin, 1994), 195.

## Chapter 6

1. Michele Galen, with Ann Therese, "White, Male, and Worried," *Business Week,* January 31, 1994, 51.

2. Audrey Edwards, Suzanne B. Laporte, and Abby Livingston, "Cultural Diversity in Today's Corporation," *Working Woman* 16 (January 1991): 45–61.

3. Martha Farnsworth Riche, "We're All Minorities Now," *American Demographics,* October 1991, 28.

4. Sue Shellenbarger, "The Aging of America Is Making Elder Care A Big Workplace Issue," *The Wall Street Journal,* November 16, 1993, 1.

5. Shellenbarger, "The Aging of America Is Making Elder Care A Big Workplace Issue."

6. Margaret Usdansky, "Minorities Are Headed Toward the Majority," *USA Today,* December 4, 1992, A1; Margaret L. Usdansky, "Census: The USA's Changing Face," *USA Today,* December 4, 1992, 8A.

7. Usdansky, "Census: The USA's Changing Face."

8. Marilyn Loden and Judy B. Rosener, *Workforce America! Managing Employee Diversity as a Vital Resource* (Homewood, IL: Business One Irwin, 1991).

9. U.S. Bureau of the Census, *Statistical Abstract of the United States: 1993,* 113th ed. (Washington DC: U.S. Government Printing Office, 1993), 395.

10. Kathy Bodovitz, "Black America," in *American Demographics,* Desk Reference Series, 1 (July 1991): 8–10.

11. Margaret L. Usdansky, "College Doesn't Close Blacks' Pay Gap," *USA Today,* September 16, 1993, 3A.

12. Usdansky, "College Doesn't Close Blacks' Pay Gap."

13. "The Corporate Elite: Chief Executives of the *Business Week* Top 1000," *Business Week,* October 19, 1990, 274.

14. Editorial, *USA Today,* December 1, 1992, 10A.

15. USA Snapshots, "National Indian Gaming Association," *USA Today,* December 4, 1992, 1A.

16. Beth Belton, "No Degree? Welcome to the Wage Gap," *USA Today,* February 15, 1994, 1B–2B.

17. Joan E. Rigdon, "Three Decades After the Equal Pay Act, Women's Wages Remain Far From Parity," *The Wall Street Journal,* June 9, 1993, B1, B3; "Women Still Earn Less, But They've Come a Long Way," *Business Week,* December 24, 1990, 14.

18. Rigdon, "Three Decades After the Equal Pay Act."

19. Sue Shellenbarger, "Executive Women Make Major Gains in Pay and Status," *The Wall Street Journal,* June 30, 1993, A3.

20. Ronaleen R. Roha, *Kiplinger's Personal Finance Magazine,* March 1994, 124.

21. Carol Kleiman, "Glass Ceiling Hasn't Risen, Report Shows," *The (Bryan/College Station, TX) Eagle,* October 13, 1991, 1D, 4D.

22. Meredith K. Wadman, "Mothers Who Take Extended Time Off Find Their Careers Pay a Heavy Price," *The Wall Street Journal,* July 16, 1992, B1, B2.

23. Felice N. Schwartz, "Women as a Business Imperative," *Harvard Business Review* 70 (March–April 1992): 106–113.

24. Elizabeth Erlich, "The Mommy Track: Juggling Kids and Careers in Corporate America Takes a Controversial Turn," *Business Week,* March 20, 1989, 126–127; Alex Taylor, "Why Women Managers Are Bailing Out," *Fortune,* August 18, 1989, 18.

25. Bureau of the Census, *Statistical Abstract of the United States: 1993,* 380.

26. Larry Reynolds, "Handicapped Workers Won't Disable Your Company," *Business Ethics* 4 (November/December 1990): 14–15.

27. Taylor H. Cox, Jr. and Stacy Blake, "Managing Cultural Diversity: Implications for Organizational Competitiveness," *Academy of Management Executive* 5 (August 1991): 45–56.

28. Adapted from Taylor H. Cox, Jr., "The Multicultural Organization," *Academy of Management Executive* 5 (May 1991): 34–47; Loden and Rosener, *Workforce America!*

29. Ann M. Morrison, *The New Leaders: Guidelines on Leadership Diversity in America* (San Francisco: Jossey-Bass Publishers, 1992), 23.

30. Cox and Blake, "Managing Cultural Diversity."

31. Shellenbarger, "Executive Women Make Major Gains."

32. Brett Pulley, "Culture of Racial Bias at Shoney's Underlies Chairman's Departure," *The Wall Street Journal,* December 21, 1992, A1, A4.

33. "Shoney's Founder Divests His Stake," *Business Week,* March 22, 1993, 42.

34. Loden and Rosener.

35. Howard Gleckman, Tim Smart, Paula Dwyer, Troy Segal, and Joseph Weber, "Race in the Workplace: Is Affirmative Action Working?" *Business Week,* July 8, 1991, 50–62.

36. Gleckman, et al., "Race in the Workplace."

37. Paula Dwyer and Alice Z. Cuneo, "The `Other Minorities' Demand Their Due," *Business Week,* July 8, 1991, 62.

38. Loden and Rosener.

39. Material in this section is adapted from Loden and Rosener.

40. Loden and Rosener.

41. Alice Cuneo, "Diverse by Design," *Business Week/Reinventing America 1992,* Special Bonus Issue, 72.

42. Kathy Seal, "Know Thy Neighbor," *American Way,* August 15, 1991, 34.

43. Ronita Johnson and Julie O'Mara, "Shedding New Light on Diversity Training," *Training and Development,* May 1992, 25–26.

44. Loden and Rosener.

45. Loden and Rosener, 214.

# Chapter 7

1. Richard J. Schonberger, "Total Quality Management Cuts a Broad Swath—Through Manufacturing and Beyond," *Organizational Dynamics* 20 (Spring 1992): 16–28.

2. Marshall Sashkin and Ken Kiser, "What Is TQM?" *Executive Excellence* 5 (May 1992): 11.

3. Genichi Taguchi and Don Clausing, "Robust Quality," *Harvard Business Review* 68 (January–February 1990): 65.

4. Henry R. Neave, *The Deming Dimension* (Knoxville, TN: SPC Press, 1990), 24.

5. Deming's 14 Points (January 1990 revision) reprinted from *Out of the Crisis* by W. Edwards Deming by permission of MIT and W. Edwards Deming. Published by MIT, Center for Advanced Engineering Study, Cambridge, MA 02139. Copyright 1986 by W. Edwards Deming.

6. Tim Minahan, "Torrington Brass and Steel Takes the Road Less Traveled," *Purchasing,* January 16, 1992, 118–119.

7. Joseph M. Juran, *Juran on Leadership for Quality: An Executive Handbook* (New York: The Free Press, 1989).

8. Artemis March, "A Note on Quality: The Views of Deming, Juran, and Crosby," Harvard Business School Reprint 9-687-011, 1986, 4.

9. March, "A Note on Quality," 5.

10. Lloyd Dobyns and Clare Crawford-Mason, *Quality or Else* (Boston: Houghton Mifflin Co., 1991), 70.

11. Philip B. Crosby, *Quality Is Free: The Art of Making Quality Certain* (New York: McGraw-Hill, 1979).

12. Dobyns and Crawford-Mason, *Quality or Else,* 66.

13. March, 7.

14. March, 13.

15. Armand V. Feigenbaum, "America on the Threshold of Quality," *Quality* 29 (January 1990): 16–18.

16. Hirotaka Takeuchi and John A. Quelch, "Quality Is More Than Making a Good Product," *Harvard Business Review* 61 (July–August 1983): 140.

17. Takeuchi and Quelch, "Quality Is More Than Making a Good Product," 141.

18. Robert W. Schrandt, "Quality Service," *Executive Excellence* 9 (May 1992): 13.

19. Bro Uttal, "Companies That Serve You Best," *Fortune,* December 7, 1987, 98.

20. Joan Brager, "The Customer-Focused Quality Leader," *Quality Progress* 25 (May 1992): 51.

21. Y.K. Shetty, "Product Quality and Competitive Strategy," *Business Horizons* 30 (May–June 1987): 51–52.

22. David A. Garvin, "Competing on the Eight Dimensions of Quality," *Harvard Business Review* 65 (November–December 1987): 101–109.

23. Garvin, "Competing on the Eight Dimensions of Quality," 108.

24. John A. Parnell and Peter Wright, "Generic Strategy and Performance: An Empirical Test of the Miles and Snow Typology," *British Journal of Management* 4 (March 1993): 29–36.

25. Jay B. Barney, "Firm Resources and Sustained Competitive Advantage," *Journal of Management* 17 (March 1991): 99–120.

26. John T. Burr, "The Tools of Quality Part I: Going With the Flowchart," *Quality Progress* 23 (June 1990): 67.

27. Stephen J. Sarazen, "The Tools of Quality Part II: Cause and Effect Diagrams," *Quality Progress* 23 (July 1990): 59.

Notes **677**

28. Sarazen, "The Tools of Quality," 62.

29. Sarazen, 75.

30. John T. Burr, "The Tools of Quality Part VI: Pareto Charts," *Quality Progress* 23 (November 1990): 59.

31. Daniel V. Hunt, *Quality in America: How to Implement a Competitive Quality Program* (Homewood, IL: Irwin, 1992), 67–72.

32. Kenneth R. Thompson, "A Conversation with Robert W. Galvin," *Organizational Dynamics* 20 (Spring 1992): 56–69.

33. David E. Bowen and Edward E. Lawler III, "Total Quality-Oriented Human Resources Management," *Organizational Dynamics* 20 (Spring 1992): 31.

34. Hamid Noori, "The Taguchi Methods: Achieving Design and Output Quality," *The Academy of Management Executive* 3 (November 1989): 322.

35. Noori, "The Taguchi Methods," 323.

36. Noori, 323.

37. John R. Hauser and Don Clausing, "The House of Quality," *Harvard Business Review* 66 (May–June 1988): 63.

38. Michael Piczak, "Quality Circles Come Home," *Quality Progress* 21 (December 1988): 37.

39. Piczak, "Quality Circles Come Home," 38.

40. David A. Garvin, "Quality on the Line," *Harvard Business Review* 61 (September–October 1983): 72.

41. David Bush and Kevin Dooley, "The Deming Prize and Baldrige Award: How They Compare," *Quality Progress* 22 (January 1989): 29.

42. *1994 Award Criteria: Malcolm Baldrige National Quality Award* (Gaithersburg, MD: U.S. Department of Commerce), 13.

43. Bush and Dooley, "The Deming Prize and Baldrige Award," 28.

44. Bush and Dooley, 28.

45. Regina Eisman, "Why Companies Are Turning to Total Quality," *Incentive* 166 (May 1992): 26.

46. Eisman, "Why Companies Are Turning to Total Quality," 24.

47. Gilbert Fuchsberg, "'Visioning' Missions Become Its Own Mission," *The Wall Street Journal*, January 7, 1994, B1, B2.

48. Dana Milbank, "Made in America Becomes a Boast in Europe," *The Wall Street Journal*, January 19, 1994, B1, B6.

49. Robert L. Simpson, "Huge Market Potential in China Lures Auto Makers," *The Wall Street Journal*, January 11, 1994, B4.

50. Bob Davis and Kenneth H. Bacon, "Japan Is Pushed to Promise 20% Rise in Purchase of U.S.–Made Auto Parts," *The Wall Street Journal*, January 18, 1994, A2, A9.

# Chapter 8

1. John A. Byrne, "Enterprise; How Entrepreneurs Are Reshaping the Economy—and What Big Companies Can Learn," *Business Week/Enterprise 1993*, Special Issue, 11–18.

2. Byrne, "Enterprise," 12.

3. "250 Companies on the Move," *Business Week/Enterprise 1993*, Special Issue, 269.

4. Byrne.

5. Darryl Hartley-Leonard, "The Entrepreneurial Spirit," Special Advertising Section, *Inc.* 15 (December 1993).

6. Hartley-Leonard, "The Entrepreneurial Spirit."

7. Michael Gleckman, "Meet the Giant Killers," *Business Week/ Enterprise 1993*, Special Issue, 69.

8. Jay Nathan, "Empowerment as a Workplace Strategy in Small Business," *Review of Business* 15 (Winter 1993/1994): 28–29.

9. Byrne.

10. Joan O'C. Hamilton, "Roger Salquist," *Business Week/ Reinventing America 1992*, Special Issue, 186.

11. Timothy Noah, "Asian-Americans Take Lead in Starting U.S. Businesses," *The Wall Street Journal*, August 2, 1991, B2.

12. Roger Thompson, "Small Business Report," *Nation's Business*, February 1988, 10.

13. "Entrepreneurs: Russell Simmons," *Business Week/ Enterprise 1993*, Special Issue, 119.

14. Noah, "Asian-Americans Take Lead."

15. Wendy Zellner, with Resa W. King, Veronica N. Byrd, Gail DeGeorge, and Jane Birnbaum, "Women Entrepreneurs," *Business Week*, April 18, 1994, 104–110.

16. "Entrepreneurs: Sheri Poe," *Business Week/Enterprise 1993*, Special Issue, 126.

17. Zellner, et al., "Women Entrepreneurs."

18. Gleckman, "Meet the Giant Killers."

19. Linda Romine, "Roadside Seller Hopes to Produce with a New Store," *The Memphis Business Journal*, September 16–20, 1991, 35.

20. "Business 200," Special Advertising Section, *Inc.* 15 (December 1993).

21. A. David Silver, *Entrepreneurial Megabucks* (New York: Wiley, 1985), 146–149.

22. U.S. Department of Commerce, "Malcolm Baldrige National Quality Award, 1991 Award Winner"; and Micheline Maynard, with Mark Land, John Schneidawind, and Chris Wloszczyna, "No Price Tag on Being the Best, Winners Show," *USA Today*, October 10, 1991, B1, B2.

23. Peter Coy, "Start with Some High-Tech Magic," *Business Week/Enterprise 1993*, Special Issue, 24–25.

24. Michael Oneal, "Just What Is an Entrepreneur?" *Business Week/Enterprise 1993*, Special Issue, 108.

25. Sue Shellenbarger, "Some Thrive, But Many Wilt Working at Home," *The Wall Street Journal*, December 14, 1993, B1; and Sue Shellenbarger, "I'm Still Here, Home Workers Worry They Are Invisible," *The Wall Street Journal*, December 16, 1993, B1.

26. Tom Ehrverfeld, "B School Bohemians," *Inc.* 15 (September 1993): 59.

27. Brent Bowers, "This Store Is a Hit but Somehow Cash Flow Is Missing," *The Wall Street Journal*, April 13, 1993, B2.

28. Bowers, "This Store Is a Hit."

29. Robert C. Hill and Sara M. Freedman, "Managing the Quality Process: Lessons from a Baldrige Award Winner; A Conversation with John W. Wallace, Chief Executive Officer of the Wallace Company," *Academy of Management Executive* 6 (February 1992): 76–87; and Mark Ivey, with John Carey, "The Ecstasy and the Agony," *Business Week*, October 21, 1991, 40.

30. Carmella M. Padilla, "Picuris Indians Acquire a Subsidized Stake in Hotel," *The Wall Street Journal*, September 13, 1991, B2.

31. U.S. Bureau of the Census, *Statistical Abstract of the U.S., 1993*, 113th ed. (Washington DC: Government Printing Office, 1993), 541.

32. *Statistical Abstract of the U.S., 1993*, 780.

33. Bruce J. Walker, "Retail Franchising in the 1990s," *Retail Issues Letter*, published by Arthur Andersen & Co. with Texas A&M University, January 1991, 2.

34. Carol Steinberg, "Multi-unit Owners: They're Hooked on Franchising," *USA Today*, September 9, 1993, 9B.

35. Gifford Pinchot III, *Intrapreneuring* (New York: Harper & Row, 1985), 34.

36. Russell Mitchell, "Masters of Innovation: How 3M Keeps Its New Products Coming," *Business Week*, April 10, 1989, 58–63.

37. Larry Armstrong, "Nurturing an Employee's Brainchild," *Business Week/Enterprise 1993*, Special Issue, 196.

38. Hartley-Leonard.

39. Adapted from Carol Kinsey Goman, *Creativity in Business: A Practical Guide for Creative Thinking* (Los Altos, CA: Crisp Publications, Inc., 1989), 5–6 Copyright Crisp Publications, Inc.,

1200 Hamilton Court, Menlo Park, California 94025; 800–442–7477.

40. Emily T. Smith, "Are You Creative?" *Business Week,* September 30, 1985, p. 81.

## Chapter 9

1. Alex Taylor III, "Why GM Leads the Pack in Europe," *Fortune,* May 17, 1993, 83–88.
2. Richard Teitelbaum, "Designs Inc.," *Fortune,* February 8, 1993, 127.
3. Charles Hofer and Daniel Schendel, *Strategy Formulation: Analytical Concepts* (St. Paul: West Publishing, 1978).
4. Peter Burrows, "Compaq Flexes Its PECS," *Business Week,* August 2, 1993.
5. Peter F. Drucker, *The Practice of Management* (New York: Harper & Brothers, 1954).
6. Peter Burrows, "TI Is Moving Up in the World," *Business Week,* August 2, 1993, 46–47.
7. Amy Barrett, "A Retailing Pacesetter Pulls Up Lame," *Business Week,* July 12, 1993, 122.
8. Nancy J. Perry, "Hit 'Em Where They Used to Be," *Fortune,* October 19, 1992, 112.
9. Pete Engardio and Neil Gross, "Acer: Up From Clones—and Then Some," *Business Week,* June 28, 1993, 54.
10. Sunita Wadekar Bhargava, "What's Next, Grunge Bathrobes?" *Business Week,* June 21, 1993, 64.
11. Peter F. Drucker, *The Practice of Management* (New York: Harper & Brothers, 1954).
12. Lori Bongiorno, "Corporate America, Dr. Feelgood Will See You Now," *Business Week,* December 6, 1993, 52.

## Chapter 10

1. For a summary of recent works see James Quinn, Henry Mintzberg, and Robert James, *The Strategy Process* (Englewood Cliffs, NJ: Prentice-Hall, 1988); Cynthia Montgomery and Michael Porter, eds., *Strategy* (Boston: Harvard Business School, 1991); and Henry Mintzberg, *The Rise and Fall of Strategic Planning* (New York: Free Press, 1994).
2. Henry Mintzberg, "The Fall and Rise of Strategic Planning," *Harvard Business Review* 72 (January/February 1994): 107–114.
3. Michael Porter, "Towards a Dynamic Theory of Strategy," *Strategic Management Journal* 12 (Winter 1991): 95–117.
4. Maria Shao, "Everybody's Falling into the Gap," *Business Week,* September 23, 1991, 36.
5. Faye Rice, "Profiting by Perseverance," *Fortune,* January 27, 1992, 84.
6. Alan Farnham, "America's Most Admired Company," *Fortune,* February 7, 1994, 50–54.
7. Sherman Stratford, "The New Computer Revolution," *Fortune,* June 14, 1993, 56–81.
8. David Lieverman, "Keeping Up with the Murdochs," *Business Week,* March 20, 1987, 32–34.
9. Robert Hof and Richard Brandt, "Sun's Next Target," *Business Week,* December 20, 1993, 40.
10. Lien Fahey, *The Strategic Planning Management Reader* (Englewood Cliffs, NJ: Prentice-Hall, 1989).
11. Lien Fahey and V. K. Narayanan, *Macro-environmental Analysis for Strategic Management* (St. Paul: West, 1986).
12. David Woodruff, "Detroit Begins Tailgating Japan's Small Sedans," *Business Week,* December 27, 1993, 38.

13. Zina Mourkheiber, "Opportunity Knocks," *Forbes,* April 12, 1993, 62.
14. Robert Simmons, "How New Top Managers Use Control Systems as Levers of Strategic Renewal," *Strategic Management Journal* 15 (March 1994): 169–189.
15. Catherine Arnst and Peter Burrows, "Showdown in Silicon Alley," *Business Week,* November 1, 1993, 146.
16. Laura Zinn, "Does Pepsi Have Too Many Products?" *Business Week,* February 14, 1994, 64–66.
17. Kelvin Kelly, Aaron Bernstein, and Seth Payne, "Rumble on the Runway," *Business Week,* November 29, 1993, 36–37.
18. Richard P. Rumelt, *Strategy, Structure, and Economic Performance* (Boston: Harvard University Press, 1974); Cynthia Montgomery, "The Measurement of Firm Diversification: Some Empirical Evidence," *Academy of Management Journal* 25 (June 1982): 299–307.
19. Bill Saporito, "The High Cost of Second Best," *Fortune,* July 26, 1993, 99–102.
20. Seth Lubove, "Vindicated," *Forbes,* December 9, 1991, 198, 202.
21. "Renault-Volvo: A Marriage of Necessity," *Fortune,* November 15, 1993, 129–130.
22. Keith Hammonds, "An IBM Division Goes to Loral," *Business Week,* December 27, 1993, 49.
23. Laura Zinn, "Retailing Will Never Be the Same," *Business Week,* July 26, 1993, 54–68.
24. Barry Hedley, "Strategy and the Business Portfolio," *Long Range Planning* 10 (February 1977): 9–15.
25. Michael Porter, *Competitive Strategy: Techniques for Analyzing Industries and Competitors* (New York: Free Press, 1980).
26. Alan I. Murray, "A Contingency View of Porter's 'Generic Strategies'," *Academy of Management Review* 13 (July 1988): 390–400.
27. Ron Stodghill, "Joe Montgomery's Wild Ride," *Business Week,* April 19, 1993, 50.
28. Sandra Atchinson and Andrea Rothman, "Morris Air Is Starting to See Things on Its Radar," *Business Week,* January 25, 1993, 62.
29. Peter Wright, Charles D. Pringle, and Mark J. Kroll, *Strategic Management: Texts and Cases* (Boston: Allyn & Bacon, 1994).
30. Arthur Thompson Jr., "General Motors Corporation," case appearing in *Strategic Management: Concepts and Cases* (Homewood, IL: Irwin, 1992), 629.
31. Tom Peters and Robert Waterman Jr., *In Search of Excellence* (New York: Harper and Row, 1982).
32. Zachary Schiller, "Procter & Gamble Hits Back," *Business Week,* July 19, 1993, 20.
33. Wendy Zellner, "Frito-Lay Is Munching on the Competition," *Business Week,* August 24, 1992, 52–53.

## Chapter 11

1. Helga Drummond, "Another Fine Mess: Time for Quality in Decision Making," *Journal of General Management* 18 (Autumn 1992): 1–14.
2. Herbert A. Simon, *The New Science of Management Decision* (New York: Harper & Row, 1960), 5–6.
3. Otis Port, "Lev Landa's Worker Miracles," *Business Week,* September 21, 1992, 72.
4. Simon, *The New Science of Management Decision,* 5–6.
5. Wendy Zellner, "Frito-Lay Is Munching on the Competition," *Business Week,* August 24, 1992, 52–53.
6. K. J. Radford, *Managerial Decision Making* (Reston, VA: Reston Publishing Company, Inc., 1975), 58–61.

7. Charles Burck, "Blindsided by the Rules," *Fortune*, April 5, 1993, 68–69.

8. Arthur Sondak, "How to Answer the Question, 'What Should I Do?'" *Supervisory Management* 37 (December 1992): 4–5.

9. E. Frank Harrison, *The Managerial Decision-Making Process*, 2nd ed. (Boston: Houghton Mifflin Company, 1981), 53–59; and Radford, *Managerial Decision Making*, 77, 216–218.

10. Herbert A. Simon, *Administrative Behavior* (New York: Free Press, 1947); and James G. March and Herbert A. Simon, *Organizations* (New York: John Wiley & Sons, 1958).

11. Janet Bernard, "Successful CEOs Talk About Decision Making," *Business Horizons* 35 (September–October 1992): 72.

12. Charles R. Holloman, "Using Both Head and Heart in Managerial Decision Making," *Industrial Management* 34 (November–December 1992): 9.

13. Weston H. Agor, *The Logic of Intuitive Decision Making* (New York: Quorum Books, 1986), 5.

14. Carol J. Loomis, "Dinosaurs?" *Fortune*, May 3, 1993, 37.

15. Amitai Etzioni, "Humble Decision Making," *Harvard Business Review* 67 (July–August 1989): 123.

16. Glen Whyte, "Decision Failures: Why They Occur and How to Prevent Them," *The Executive* 5 (August 1991): 25.

17. Joel Brockner, "The Escalation of Commitment to a Failing Course of Action: Toward Theoretical Progress," *The Academy of Management Review* 17 (January 1992): 39.

18. Brockner, "The Escalation of Commitment," 39–61; Barry M. Staw, "The Escalation of Commitment to a Course of Action," *The Academy of Management Review* 6 (October 1981): 577–587; and Max H. Bazerman, *Judgment in Managerial Decision Making* (New York: John Wiley & Sons, 1986), 67–80.

19. Bazerman, *Judgment in Managerial Decision Making*, 75.

20. Tricia Welsh, "The Man Who Blew $10 Billion," *Fortune*, May 17, 1993, 92–95.

21. George P. Huber, *Managerial Decision-Making* (Glenview, IL: Scott, Foresman and Company, 1980), 193–195.

22. Stephen P. Robbins, *Essentials of Organizational Behavior*, 2nd ed. (Englewood Cliffs, NJ: Prentice Hall, 1988), 114–115.

23. Robbins, *Essentials of Organizational Behavior*, 115.

24. Radford, 202.

25. Gayle W. Hill, "Group Versus Individual Performance: Are N + 1 Heads Better Than One?" *Psychological Bulletin* 91 (May 1982): 517–539.

26. Brian S. Moskal, "GM's New Found Religion," *Industry Week*, May 18, 1992, 46–53.

27. Irving L. Janis, *Groupthink*, 2nd ed. (Boston: Houghton Mifflin, 1982), 9.

28. Gregory Moorhead, Richard Ference, and Chris P. Neck, "Group Decision Fiascoes Continue: Space Shuttle Challenger and a Revised Groupthink Framework," *Human Relations* 44 (June 1991): 539–550.

## Chapter 12

1. Steve Weinstein, "Teams Without Managers," *Progressive Grocer* 71 (September 1992): 101–106.

2. Adam Smith, *An Inquiry into the Nature and Causes of the Wealth of Nations* (Hartford, CT: O.D. Cooke, 1811), 7–8.

3. Steve Horton, "Team Effort: A Shift to Self-Directed Work Teams," *American Printer* 209 (June 1992): 30–32.

4. Anat Bird, "Teamwork Pays Off at MasterCard," *American Banker*, June 10, 1992, 11–12.

5. *Organizational Charts*, ed. Judith M. Nixon (Detroit: Gale Research Inc., 1992).

6. Mark Lander, "Mad Avenue Is Becoming Boutique Boulevard," *Business Week*, September 20, 1993, 102–106.

7. Thomas Hoffman, "NCR Eyes Software Growth With New Unit," *Computerworld*, September 27, 1993, 79–105.

8. Jenny C. McCune, "More Power to Them," *Small Business Reports* (November 1992): 51–59.

9. Henri Fayol, *General and Industrial Management* (London: Sir Isaac Pitman & Sons Ltd., 1949).

10. "Purolator Courier, Ltd.," *Business Quarterly* (Spring 1993): 105.

11. Mark Mehler, "Publix Enemy No. 1," *Computerworld*, March 1, 1993, 61–62.

12. Alice LaPlante, "Bankers Trust Trusts Users to Control Bottom Line," *Computerworld*, June 17, 1991, 58.

## Chapter 13

1. John Child, *Organization*, 2nd ed. (New York: Harper and Row, 1984).

2. "EuroDisney Could Face 'La Guillotine'," *The Dallas Morning News*, December 29, 1993.

3. Richard Rumelt, *Strategy, Structure, and Economic Performance*, Harvard Business School Classics (Boston: Harvard Business School Press, 1986).

4. Gareth R. Jones and Charles W.L. Hill, "Transaction Cost Analysis of Strategy-Structure Choice," *Strategic Management Journal* 9 (March–April 1988): 159–172.

5. S.M. Davis and P.R. Lawrence, *Matrix* (Reading, MA: Addison-Wesley, 1977); J.R. Galbraith, *Designing Complex Organizations* (Reading, MA: Addison-Wesley, 1973).

6. Tom Peters, *Thriving on Chaos: Handbook for a Management Revolution* (New York: Alfred A. Knopf, 1988).

7. Robert E. Miles and Charles C. Snow, "Organizations: New Concepts for New Forms," *California Management Review* 28 (Spring 1986): 62–73.

8. Joseph L. Bower, Christopher A. Bartlett, C. Roland Christensen, Andrall E. Pearson, and Kenneth R. Andrews, "Phil Knight: CEO at Nike," in *Business Policy: Text and Cases*, 7th ed. (Homewood, IL: Irwin, 1991), 50–73.

9. Raymond E. Miles and Charles C. Snow, "Causes of Failure in Network Organizations," *California Management Review* 34 (Summer 1992): 53–72.

10. For more on new organizational forms, see Homa Bahrami, "The Emerging Flexible Organization: Perspectives from Silicon Valley," *California Management Review* 34 (Summer 1992): 33–52; Richard A. Bettis, Stephen P. Bradley, and Gary Hamel, "Outsourcing and Industrial Decline," *Academy of Management Executive* 6 (February 1992): 7–22; C. K. Prahalad and Gary Hamel, "The Core Competence of the Corporation," *Harvard Business Review* 68 (May–June 1990): 79–91.

11. Stephen P. Robbins, *Organization Theory: Structure, Design, and Applications*, 2nd ed. (Englewood Cliffs, NJ: Prentice-Hall, 1987); Dan R. Dalton, William D. Todor, Michael J. Spendolini, Gordon J. Fielding, and Lyman W. Porter, "Organization Structure and Performance: A Critical Review," *Academy of Management Review* 5 (January 1980): 49–64; Danny Miller and Cynthia Droge, "Psychological and Traditional Determinants of Structure," *Administrative Science Quarterly* 31 (December 1986): 539–560.

12. Robbins, *Organization Theory: Structure, Design, and Applications*; Dalton et al., "Organization Structure and

Performance"; Miller and Droge, "Psychological and Traditional Determinants of Structure."

13. T. Burns and G.M. Stalker, *The Management of Innovation* (London: Tavistock, 1961).

14. Lee G. Bolman and Terrence E. Deal, *Reframing Organizations: Artistry, Choice, and Leadership* (San Francisco: Jossey-Bass, 1991).

15. Child, *Organization*. The point is also implied in John Child, "Organizational Structure, Environment and Performance: The Role of Strategic Choice," *Sociology* 6 (January 1972): 2–22.

16. Alfred D. Chandler, *Strategy and Structure: Chapters in the History of the American Industrial Enterprise* (Cambridge, MA: MIT Press, 1962).

17. Danny Miller and Peter H. Friesen, "A Longitudinal Study of the Corporate Life Cycle," *Management Science* 30 (October 1984): 1161–1183. See also Robert E. Quinn and Kim Cameron, "Organizational Life Cycles and Shifting Criteria of Effectiveness: Some Preliminary Evidence," *Management Science* 29 (January 1983): 33–51.

18. Chet Borucki and Carole K. Barnett, "Restructuring for Self-Renewal: Navistar International Corporation," *The Academy of Management Executive* 4 (February 1990): 36–49.

19. William McWhirter, "Back on the Fast Track," *Time*, December 13, 1993, 62–71.

20. Gregory G. Dess and Donald W. Beard, "Dimensions of Organizational Task Environments," *Administrative Science Quarterly* 29 (March 1984): 52–73; Douglas R. Wholey and Jack Brittain, "Characterizing Environmental Variation," *Academy of Management Journal* 32 (December 1989): 867–882.

21. L.J. Bourgeois, "Strategic Goals, Perceived Uncertainty, and Economic Performance in Volatile Environments," *Academy of Management Journal* 28 (September 1985): 548–573; Kim S. Cameron, M.U. Kim, and David A. Whetten, "Organizational Effects of Decline and Turbulence," *Administrative Science Quarterly* 32 (June 1987): 222–240; Dess and Beard, "Dimensions of Organizational Task Environments."

22. Janice Castro, "Is Bill Gates Getting Too Powerful?" *Time*, April 4, 1994, 43.

23. Joan Woodward, *Industrial Organizations: Theory and Practice* (London: Oxford University Press, 1965).

24. Henry Mintzberg, *The Structuring of Organizations* (Englewood Cliffs, NJ: Prentice-Hall, 1979).

25. Mintzberg, *The Structuring of Organizations*; and H. Mintzberg, *Structure in Fives: Designing Effective Organizations*, 2nd ed. (Englewood Cliffs, NJ: Prentice-Hall, 1993).

26. "Golf Ball Finder," *Chemical and Engineering News*, March 22, 1993, 88.

# Chapter 14

1. William C. DeLone, "Telephone Job Posting Cuts Costs," *Personnel Journal* 72 (April 1993): 115–118.

2. Dawn Gunsch, "Comprehensive College Strategy Strengthens NCR's Recruitment," *Personnel Journal* 72 (September 1993): 58–62.

3. "Best Practices: Hiring," *Inc.* 16 (March 1994): 10.

4. Mark Thomas and Harry Bull, "Tests Improve Hiring Decisions at Franciscan," *Personnel Journal* 72 (November 1993): 89–92.

5. Scott L. Martin and Loren P. Lehnen, "Select the Right Employees Through Testing," *Personnel Journal* 71 (June 1992): 46–51.

6. *True v. Ladner*, 513A, 2d 257 (1986).

7. Michelle Neely Martinez, "Disney Training Works Magic," *HR Magazine* 37 (May 1992): 53–57.

8. "HR Propels the Launch of A New Production Site," *Personnel Journal* 72 (January 1993): 54.

9. Kelly Allan, "Computer Courses Ensure Uniform Training," *Personnel Journal* 72 (June 1993): 65–71.

10. Sandra O'Neal and Madonna Palladino, "Revamp Ineffective Performance Management," *Personnel Journal* 11 (February 1992): 93–102.

11. Ron Sorenson and Geralyn McClure Franklin, "Teamwork Developed a Successful Appraisal System," *HR Focus* 69 (August 1992): 3–4.

12. Michael Woika, "Pay Plan Based on Performance Motivates Employees," *HR Magazine* 38 (December 1993): 75–77.

13. Richard L. Bunning, "Models for Skill-Based Pay Plans," *HR Magazine* 37 (February 1992): 62–64.

14. Jerry Lullo, "Preparing for Relocations," *HR Magazine* 37 (October 1992): 59–63.

15. G. James Francis, John Mohr, and Kelly Anderson, "HR Balancing: Alternative Downsizing," *Personnel Journal* 71 (January 1992): 71–78.

16. *Wilson v. Monarch Paper Co.*, 939F. 2d 1138 (5th Circuit), 1991, No. 89–2293.

17. *EEOC v. Francis W. Parker School*, USOC NILL., No. 91, C4674, 3/23/93.

18. Anthony P. Carnevale, *America and the New Economy: How New Competitive Standards Are Radically Changing American Workplaces* (San Francisco: Jossey-Bass, 1991), 166–167.

19. Carnevale, *America and the New Economy: How New Competitive Standards Are Radically Changing American Workplaces*.

20. Scott J. Simmerman, *The Book of Square Wheels: A Tool Kit for Facilitators and Team Leaders,* 3rd ed. (Taylors, SC: Performance Management Company, 1994), 1–2.

# Chapter 15

1. Brian Dumaine, "Who Needs a Boss?" *Fortune*, May 7, 1990, 52–60; Joann S. Lublin, "Trying to Increase Worker Productivity, More Employers Alter Management Style," *The Wall Street Journal*, February 13, 1992, B1, B3.

2. Dumaine, "Who Needs a Boss?"

3. Jon R. Katzenbach and Douglas K. Smith, "The Discipline of Teams," *Harvard Business Review* 71 (March/April 1993): 111–120.

4. Katzenbach and Smith, "The Discipline of Teams."

5. Lublin, "Trying to Increase Worker Productivity."

6. Lublin.

7. Richard S. Wellins, William C. Byham, and Jeanne M. Wilson, *Empowered Teams: Creating Self-Directed Work Groups That Improve Quality, Productivity, and Participation* (San Francisco: Jossey-Bass Publishers, 1991).

8. Andrall E. Pearson, "Corporate Redemption and the Seven Deadly Sins," *Harvard Business Review* 70 (May/June 1992): 65–75.

9. Dumaine.

10. Wellins, Byham, and Wilson, *Empowered Teams*.

11. Wellins, Byham, and Wilson.

12. Norman F. Maier, "Assets and Liabilities in Group Problem Solving: The Need for an Integrative Function," *Psychological Review* 74 (July 1967): 239–249.

13. Eric Sundstrom, Kenneth P. DeMeuse, and David Futrell, "Work Teams: Applications and Effectiveness," *American Psychologist* 45 (February 1990): 120–133.

14. Sundstrom, DeMeuse, and Futrell, "Work Teams."

15. Katzenbach and Smith.

16. Bradford McKee, "Turn Your Workers into a Team," *Nations Business* 80 (July 1992): 36–38.

17. McKee, "Turn Your Workers into a Team."

18. Wellins, Byham, and Wilson, 5.

19. Wellins, Byham, and Wilson, 5.

20. David T. Kearns, "Leadership Through Quality," *Academy of Management Executive* 4 (May 1990): 86–89.

21. Wellins, Byham, and Wilson.

22. Nancy K. Austin, "The Death of Hierarchy," *Working Woman* 15 (July 1990): 22–23.

23. Tom Peters, *Liberation Management: Necessary Disorganization for the Nanosecond Nineties* (New York: Alfred A. Knopf, 1992).

24. Robert Albanese and David D. Van Fleet, "Rational Behavior in Groups: The Free-Rider Tendency," *Academy of Management Review* 10 (April 1985): 244–255.

25. Peters, *Liberation Management.*

26. Brian Dumaine, "The Bureaucracy Busters," *Fortune,* June 17, 1991, 36–50.

27. Bruce W. Tuckman and Mary Ann C. Jenson, "Stages of Small Group Development Revisited," *Group and Organizational Studies* 2 (December 1977): 419–427.

28. Connie J. G. Gersick, "Time and Transition in Work Teams: Toward a New Model of Group Development," *Academy of Management Journal* 31 (March 1988): 9–41.

29. Gersick, "Time and Transition in Work Teams."

30. Daniel C. Feldman, "The Development and Enforcement of Group Norms," *Academy of Management Review* 9 (January 1984): 47–53.

31. Richard F. Allen and Saul Pilnick, "Confronting the Shadow Organization: How to Detect and Defeat Negative Norms," *Organizational Dynamics* 2 (Spring 1973): 13–17.

32. Edgar H. Schein, "Organizational Socialization and the Profession of Management," The Third Douglas Murray McGregor Lecture of the Alfred P. Sloan School of Management, Massachusetts Institute of Technology, reprinted in David A. Kolb, Irwin M. Rubin, and James M. McIntyre, *Organizational Psychology: Readings in Human Behavior in Organizations,* 4th ed. (Englewood Cliffs, NJ: Prentice-Hall, Inc., 1984).

33. Feldman, "The Development and Enforcement of Group Norms."

34. Schein, "Organizational Socialization and the Profession of Management."

35. Adapted from Thomas A. Kayser, *Mining Group Gold* (El Segundo, CA: Serif Publishing, 1990).

36. Charles R. Evans and Kenneth L. Dion, "Group Cohesion and Performance: A Meta-Analysis," *Small Group Research* 22 (May 1991): 175–186.

37. Marvin Shaw, *Group Dynamics: The Psychology of Small Group Behavior* (New York: McGraw-Hill, Inc., 1971).

38. Kenneth Thomas, "Overview of Conflict and Conflict Management: Reflections and Update," *Journal of Organizational Behavior* (May 1992): 263–274.

39. Stephen R. Covey, *Principle Centered Leadership* (New York: Summit Books, 1991).

40. Peters.

41. Derived from: Covey; Marsha Sinetar, "Building Trust Into Corporate Relationships," *Organizational Dynamics* 16 (Winter 1988): 73–79; Fernando Bartolome, "Nobody Trusts the Boss Completely—Now What?" *Harvard Business Review* 67 (March/April 1989): 137–139; and Dale E. Zand, "Trust and Managerial Problem Solving," *The Administrative Science Quarterly* 17 (June 1972): 229–239.

42. Peters.

43. Kayser, *Mining Group Gold,* 17.

44. Charles H. House and Raymond L. Price, "The Return Map: Tracking Product Teams," *Harvard Business Review* 69 (January–February 1991): 92–100.

45. Gregory O. Shea and Richard A. Guzzo, "Group Effectiveness: What Really Matters?" *Sloan Management Review* 28 (Spring 1987): 25–31.

46. Peters.

47. Suzyn Ornstein, "The Hidden Influences of Office Design," *The Academy of Management Executive* 3 (May 1989): 144–147.

48. S. E. Asch, "Effects of Group Pressure upon the Modification and Distortion of Judgments," in *Groups, Leadership, and Men,* H. Guetzkow, ed. (Pittsburgh: Carnegie Press, 1951), 177–190.

49. Irving Janis, "Groupthink," *Psychology Today* 5 (November 1971): 43–46, 74–76.

50. Janis, "Groupthink."

51. Janis.

52. Jerry B. Harvey, "The Abilene Paradox: The Management of Agreement," *Organizational Dynamics* 3 (Summer 1974): 63–80.

53. Victor Murray and Jeffrey Gandz, "Games Executives Play: Politics at Work," *Business Horizons* 23 (December 1980): 11–23.

54. This list and the subsequent one on techniques to reduce politics were compiled from Dan Farrell and James C. Petersen, "Patterns of Political Behavior in Organizations," *Academy of Management Review* 7 (July 1982): 403–412; Murray and Gandz, "Games Executives Play"; Don R. Beeman and Thomas W. Sharkey, "The Use and Abuse of Corporate Politics," *Business Horizons* 30 (March–April 1987): 76–130; Blake E. Ashforth and Raymond T. Lee, "Defensive Behavior in Organizations: A Preliminary Model," *Human Relations* 43 (July 1990): 621–648; and Jerry B. Harvey, "Some Thoughts About Organizational Backstabbing: or, 'How Come Every Time I Get Stabbed in the Back, My Fingerprints Are on the Knife?'" *The Academy of Management Executive* 3 (November 1989): 271–277.

# Chapter 16

1. Carolyn Wiley, "Create an Environment for Employee Motivation," *HR Focus* 69 (June 1992): 14–15.

2. Michael Hartline, "The Socialization of Customer-Contact Employees in Service Organizations: Effects on Employee Behaviors and Service Quality Outcomes," unpublished dissertation, University of Memphis, 1993.

3. Y. K. Shetty and Paul F. Buller, "Regaining Competitiveness Requires HR Solutions," *Personnel* 67 (July 1990): 8–12.

4. Judy Quinn, "Employee Motivation Repair Job," *Incentive* 166 (October 1992): 40–46.

5. Abraham Maslow, *Motivation and Personality* (New York: Harper & Row, 1954).

6. "Cost Control: Getting Employees to Care," *INC.* 9 (July 1987): 76.

7. Robert J. House and Lawrence A. Wigdor, "Herzberg's Dual-Factor Theory of Job Satisfaction and Motivation: A Review of the Evidence and a Criticism," *Personnel Psychology* 34 (Winter 1967): 369–389; Victor H. Vroom, *Work and Motivation* (New York: Wiley, 1964).

8. Frederick Herzberg, *Work and the Nature of Man* (Cleveland: World Publishing, 1966); Marvin D. Dunnette, John P. Campbell, and Milton D. Hakel, "Factors Contributing to Job Satisfaction in Six Occupational Groups," *Organizational Behavior and Human Performance* 43 (May 1967): 143–174; C. L. Hulin and P.A. Smith, "An Empirical Investigation of Two Implications of the Two-Factor Theory of Job Satisfaction," *Journal of Applied Psychology* 61 (October 1967): 396–402; Vroom, *Work and Motivation.*

9. House and Wigdor, "Herzberg's Dual-Factor Theory of Job Satisfaction and Motivation."

10. Margaret Lund, "ESOPs Gaining Popularity as Business Tool," *National Underwriter,* March 23, 1992, 20, 32.

11. David McClelland, "The Urge to Achieve," in Louis E. Boone and Donald D. Bowen, *The Great Writings in Management and Organizational Behavior* (New York: McGraw-Hill, 1987): 386.

12. J. Stacy Adams, "Toward an Understanding of Inequity," *Journal of Abnormal and Social Psychology* 67 (November 1963): 422–436; J. Stacy Adams, "Injustice in Social Exchange," in *Advances in Experimental Social Psychology,* 2nd ed., L. Berkowitz, editor (New York: Academic Press, 1965).

13. Vroom, *Work and Motivation.*

14. Lyman W. Porter and Edward E. Lawler III, *Managerial Attitudes and Performance* (Homewood, IL: Dorsey Press, 1968).

15. Daniel C. Boyle, "Employee Motivation That Works," *HR Magazine* 37 (October 1992): 83–89.

16. "Motivation: Turning Mistakes into Lessons," *INC.* 9 (June 1987): 136.

17. Edwin A. Locke, K.M. Shaw, and Gary P. Latham, "Goal Setting and Task Performance: 1969–1980," *Psychological Bulletin* 90 (1981): 125–152.

18. J.R. Hollenbeck, J.R. Williams, and H.R. Klein, "An Empirical Examination of the Antecedents of Commitment to Difficult Goals," *Journal of Applied Psychology* 74 (1989): 18–23.

19. J. Richard Hackman and Greg R. Oldham, *Work Redesign* (Reading, MA: Addison-Wesley, 1980).

20. Carol Hymowitz, "As Aetna Adds Flextime, Bosses Learn to Cope," *The Wall Street Journal,* June 18, 1990, B1.

21. Jaclyn Fierman, "Are Companies Less Family Friendly?" *Fortune* March 21, 1994, 67.

22. Sue Shellenbarger, "Some Thrive, but Many Wilt Working at Home," *The Wall Street Journal,* December 14, 1993, B1.

23. Janet Ruhl, "Part-Time Jobs Are Catching On," *Computerworld,* May 21, 1990, 111.

24. Cathy Trost and Carol Hymowitz, "Careers Start Giving in to Family Needs," *The Wall Street Journal,* June 18, 1990, B1, B5.

25. Kathleen Pease, "Selling with Employee Benefits Communication," *Life and Health Insurance Sales* 135 (February 1992): 12–13.

26. George T. Milkovich and Jerry M. Newman, *Compensation,* 2nd ed. (Plano, TX: Business Publications, 1988); and Edward E. Lawler III, *Organizational Effectiveness* (New York: McGraw-Hill, 1971).

27. Ira Sager, Gary McWilliams, and Robert D. Hoff, "IBM Leans on Its Sales Force," *Business Week,* February 7, 1994, 110.

28. James P. Guthrie and Edward P. Cunningham, "Pay for Performance for Hourly Workers: The Quaker Oats Alternative," *Compensation & Benefits Review* 24 (March/April 1992): 18–23.

29. Laurence Hooper, "IBM Grants Gerstner Pay Package Valued at Up to $3.5 Million," *The Wall Street Journal,* March 31, 1993, A1.

30. Susan Sonnesyn Brooks, "Noncash Ways to Compensate Employees," *HRM Magazine* 38 (April 1994): 38–41.

# Chapter 17

1. Max DePree, *Leadership Is an Art* (New York: Dell Publishing, 1989), 3.

2. James M. Kouzes and Barry Z. Posner, *The Leadership Challenge: How to Get Extraordinary Things Done in Organizations* (San Francisco: Jossey-Bass Publishers, 1987).

3. See Gary Yukl, *Leadership in Organizations,* 2nd ed. (Englewood Cliffs, NJ: Prentice Hall, 1989) for a thorough discussion of the subtleties surrounding the definitions and approaches to the study of power.

4. Adapted from Gary Yukl, *Leadership in Organizations;* and Robert C. Benfari, Harry E. Wilkinson, and Charles D. Orth, "The Effective Use of Power," *Business Horizons* 29 (May–June 1986): 12–16.

5. Brian Dumaine, "America's Toughest Bosses," *Fortune,* October 18, 1993, 38–50.

6. Thomas A. Stewart, "New Ways to Exercise Power," *Fortune,* November 6, 1989, 52–64; and Benfari, Wilkinson, and Orth, "The Effective Use of Power."

7. Ralph M. Stogdill, *Handbook of Leadership: A Survey of the Literature* (New York: Free Press, 1974).

8. Bernard Bass, *Handbook of Leadership: A Survey of Theory and Research* (New York: Free Press, 1981) as summarized in Yukl's *Leadership in Organizations.*

9. Shelley A. Kirkpatrick and Edwin A. Locke, "Leadership: Do Traits Matter?" *The Academy of Management Executive* 5 (May 1991): 48–60.

10. Chester A. Schriesheim and Barbara J. Bird, "Contributions of the Ohio State Studies to the Field of Leadership," *Journal of Management* 5 (Fall 1979): 135–145; Carroll L. Shartle, "Early Years of the Ohio State University Leadership Studies," *Journal of Management* 5 (Fall 1979): 126–134.

11. Steven Kerr, Chester A. Schriesheim, Charles J. Murphy, and Ralph M. Stogdill, "Toward a Contingency Theory of Leadership Based Upon the Consideration and Initiating Structure Literature," *Organizational Behavior and Human Performance* 12 (August 1974): 62–82; L. L. Larson, J. G. Hunt, and R. N. Osburn, "The Great Hi-Hi Leader Behavior Myth: A Lesson From Occam's Razor," *Academy of Management Journal* 19 (December 1976): 628–641.

12. Paul C. Nystrom, "Managers and the Hi-Hi Leader Myth," *Academy of Management Journal* 21 (June 1978): 325–331.

13. Bass, *Handbook of Leadership.*

14. Rensis Likert, "From Production—and Employee—Centeredness to Systems 1–4," *Journal of Management* 5 (Fall 1979): 147–156; and Rensis Likert, *The Human Organization* (New York: McGraw-Hill Book Company, 1967).

15. Robert R. Blake and Anne Adams McCanse, *Leadership Dilemmas-Grid Solutions* (Houston: Gulf Publishing Co., 1991).

16. Paul Hersey and Kenneth Blanchard, "Life Cycle Theory of Leadership," *Training and Development Journal* 2 (May 1969): 4–6.

17. Kenneth Blanchard, Patricia Zigarmi, and Drea Zigarmi, *Leadership and the One Minute Manager* (New York: William Morrow & Company, 1985).

18. Richard Rapaport, "To Build a Winning Team: An Interview with Head Coach Bill Walsh," *Harvard Business Review* 71 (January–February 1993): 110–120.

19. Fred E. Fiedler, "Engineer the Job to Fit the Man," *Harvard Business Review* 53 (September–October 1965): 115–122.

20. Yukl, *Leadership in Organizations.*

21. Ramadhar Singh, "Leadership Style and Reward Allocation: Does Least Preferred Co-Worker Scale Measure Task and Relation Orientation?" *Organizational Behavior and Human Performance* 33 (October 1983): 178–197; and Chester A. Schriesheim and Steven Kerr, "Theories and Measures of Leadership: A Critical Appraisal of Current and Future Directions," in *Leadership: The Cutting Edge,* eds. J.G. Hunt and L.L. Larson (Carbondale, IL: Southern Illinois University Press, 1977).

22. Yukl.

23. Robert J. House and Terence R. Mitchell, "Path-Goal Theory of Leadership," *Journal of Contemporary Business* 3 (Autumn 1974): 81–97.

24. Victor H. Vroom and Phillip Yetton, *Leadership and Decision Making* (Pittsburgh: University of Pittsburgh Press, 1973); and Victor H. Vroom and Arthur G. Jago, *The New Leadership: Managing Participation in Organizations* (Englewood Cliffs, NJ: Prentice-Hall, 1988).

25. "A Master Class in Radical Change," *Fortune,* December 13, 1993, 82–90.

26. Vroom and Jago, *The New Leadership: Managing Participation in Organizations.*

27. Steven Kerr and John M. Jermier, "Substitutes for Leadership: Their Meaning and Measurement," *Organizational Behavior and Human Performance* 22 (December 1978): 375–403.

28. Jon F. Howell, David E. Bowen, Peter W. Dorfman, Steven Kerr, and Phillip M. Podsokoff, "Substitutes for Leadership: Effective Alternatives to Ineffective Leadership," *Organizational Dynamics* 19 (Summer 1990): 21–38.

29. Alan Farnham, "America's Most Admired Company," *Fortune,* February 7, 1994, 50–54.

30. Fred Dansereau, Jr., George Graen, and William J. Haga, "A Vertical Dyad Linkage Approach to Leadership Within Formal Organizations: A Longitudinal Investigation of the Role Making Process," *Organizational Behavior and Human Performance* 13 (February 1975): 46–78.

31. Gary Yukl, "Managerial Leadership: A Review of Theory and Research," *Journal of Management* 15 (June 1989): 251–289.

32. Nancy G. Boyd and Robert R. Taylor, "The Influence of Leader-Subordinate Friendship on the Evaluation of Subordinate Performance," *1992 Southern Management Association Proceedings,* 164–166.

33. Jay A. Conger and Rabindra N. Kanungo, "Toward a Behavioral Theory of Charismatic Leadership in Organizational Settings," *Academy of Management Review* 12 (October 1987): 637–647.

34. M. Potts and P. Behr, *The Leading Edge* (New York: McGraw-Hill, 1987).

35. Conger and Kanungo, "Toward a Behavioral Theory of Charismatic Leadership."

36. Conger and Kanungo.

37. Jane M. Howell and Peter J. Frost, "A Laboratory Study of Charismatic Leadership," *Organizational Behavior and Human Decision Processes* 43 (April 1989): 243–269.

38. James M. Burns, *Leadership* (New York: Harper and Row, 1978).

39. Bernard M. Bass, "From Transactional to Transformational Leadership: Learning to Share the Vision," *Organizational Dynamics* 18 (Winter 1990): 19–31.

40. Bernard M. Bass, "Leadership: Good, Better, Best," *Organizational Dynamics* 13 (Winter 1985): 26–40.

41. Yukl, 210.

42. Bass, "From Transactional to Transformational Leadership."

43. Bass, "From Transactional to Transformational Leadership."

44. Kouzes and Posner, *The Leadership Challenge.*

45. William Taylor, "Message and Muscle: An Interview with Swatch Titan Nicholas Hayek," *Harvard Business Review* 71 (March–April 1993): 98.

46. "Cooper Tire and Rubber: Now Hear This, Jack Welch," *Fortune,* April 6, 1992, 94–95.

# Chapter 18

1. Henry Mintzberg, *The Nature of Managerial Work* (New York: Harper & Row, 1973).

2. David R. Kolzow, "Communication and Leadership: The Critical Foundation for an Effective Economic Development Program," *Economic Development Review* 8 (Summer 1990): 19–23.

3. Frank Burge, "Getting It and Communications Myopia," *Electronic Business* 19 (February 1993): 98.

4. Mary L. Good, "Communication of R&D to Management: A Two-Way Street," *Research-Technology Management* 34 (September/October 1993): 42–45.

5. Robert Snyder and James H. Morris, "Organizational Communication and Performance," *Journal of Applied Psychology* 69 (August 1984): 461–465.

6. Larry E. Penley, Elmore R. Alexander, I. Jernigan, and Catherine I. Henwood, "Communication Abilities of Managers: The Relationship to Performance," *Journal of Management* 17 (June 1991): 57–76.

7. John H. Telford, Jr., "What Does It Take to Get a Plum HR Job?" *Human Resources Professional* 5 (Winter 1993): 36–38.

8. Ken G. Smith and Curtis M. Grimm, "A Communication-Information Model of Competitive Response Timing," *Journal of Management* 17 (March 1991): 5–24.

9. Diana Stork and Alice Sapienza, "Task and Human Messages Over the Project Life Cycle: Matching Media to Messages," *Project Management Journal* 23 (December 1992): 44–49.

10. Mintzberg, *The Nature of Managerial Work.*

11. Michael B. McCaskey, "The Hidden Messages Managers Send," *Harvard Business Review* 57 (November–December 1979): 135–148.

12. Penley, Alexander, Jernigan, and Henwood, "Communication Abilities of Managers."

13. Stork and Sapienza, "Task and Human Messages."

14. Jack R. Gibb, "Defensive Communication," *Journal of Communication* 11 (September 1961): 141–148.

15. Tony Alessandra and Rick Barrera, "Motivating to Excellence," *Security Management* 36 (November 1992): 20, 22; and John M. Wellborn, "Productivity and Pay," *LIMBRA's Market Facts* 10 (November/December 1991): 3–4.

16. Walter Kiechell III, "Breaking Bad News to the Boss," *Fortune,* April 9, 1990, 111–112.

17. Jean B. Keffeler, "Managing Changing Organizations: Don't Stop Communicating," *Vital Speeches of the Day,* 1991, 58:92–96.

18. Keith Davis, "Management Communication and the Grapevine," *Harvard Business Review* 31 (September–October 1953): 43–49.

19. "Spread the Word: Gossip Is Good," *The Wall Street Journal,* October 4, 1988, B1.

20. "A National Study of Middle Managers' Assessment of Organizational Communication Quality," *Journal of Business Communication* 28 (Fall 1991): 348–365.

21. "Spread the Word: Gossip Is Good."

22. Thomas J. Peters and Robert H. Waterman, Jr., *In Search of Excellence: Lessons from America's Best Run Companies* (New York: Harper & Row, 1982); Tom Peters and Nancy Austin, *A Passion for Excellence* (New York: Random House, 1985).

23. Jerry Wofford, Edwin Gerloff, and Robert Cummins, *Organizational Communication* (New York: McGraw-Hill, 1977).

24. Wofford, Gerloff, and Cummins, *Organizational Communication.*

25. Virginia M. Cerullo and Michael J. Cerullo, "Operations Audits of Computer Information Systems: A General Framework," *Internal Auditing* 8 (Winter 1993): 44–52.

26. Howard Banks, "Out-Faxed," *Forbes,* May 10, 1993, 40–41.

27. Sandra G. Hirsh and Jean M. Kimmerow, *Introduction to Type in Organizational Settings* (Palo Alto, CA: Consulting Psychologists Press, 1987).

28. John Huey, "Managing in the Midst of Chaos," *Fortune,* April 5, 1993, 38–48.

29. Michael Liebowitz, "Merrill Merges MBS and ABS Under U.S. Debt Organization," *Investment Dealers Digest,* May 3, 1993, 8.

30. Bruce Bond, "'Listening' as a Sales Function," *Telephone Engineer and Management,* May 15, 1993, 70.

31. Albert J. Narnois, "The Psychology of Auditing," *Internal Auditing* 8 (Winter 1993): 16–23.

32. David Lindo, "Say It with Feeling," *Office Systems* 9 (November 1992): 14, 16.

33. George Manning and Kent Curtis, *Communication: The Miracle of Dialogue* (Cincinnati, OH: South-Western Publishing Co., 1988).

34. Linda M. Dulye, "Toward Better 2-Way: Why Communications Process Improvement Represents the Right Response During Uncertain Times," *IEEE Transactions on Professional Communication* 36 (March 1993): 24–29.

35. Gibb, "Defensive Communication."

36. Gibb.

# Chapter 19

1. William C. Symonds, Jonathan B. Levine, Neil Gross, and Peter Coy, "High Tech Star: Northern Telecom Is Challenging Even AT&T," *Business Week,* July 27, 1992, 54–58; Bart Ziegler, "What Really Happened at Northern Telecom," *Business Week,* August 9, 1993, 27–28.

2. Jean B. Keffeler, "Managing Changing Organizations: Don't Stop Communicating," *Vital Speeches,* November 15, 1991, 92–96.

3. William Taylor, "Message and Muscle: An Interview with Swatch Titan, Nicholas Hayek," *Harvard Business Review* 71 (March–April 1993): 98–110.

4. Laura Zinn, Gail De George, Rochelle Shoretz, Dori Jones Yang, and Stephanie Anderson Forest, "Retailing Will Never Be the Same," *Business Week,* July 26, 1993, 54–60.

5. Rosabeth Moss Kanter, "Championing Change: An Interview With Bell Atlantic's CEO Raymond Smith," *Harvard Business Review* 69 (January–February 1991): 118–130.

6. Tim Smart, "What Do Dogs, Guitars and Choppers Have in Common?" *Business Week,* July 26, 1993, 64–65.

7. Brian Dumaine, "Times Are Good? Create a Crisis," *Fortune,* June 28, 1993, 123–127.

8. Dumaine, "Times Are Good," 127.

9. Dumaine.

10. Bruce Rayner, "Trial-by-Fire Transformation: An Interview with Globe Metallurgical's Arden C. Sims," *Harvard Business Review* 70 (May–June 1992): 117–129.

11. Rayner, "Trial by Fire."

12. Dumaine.

13. Michael Beer, Russell A. Eisenstat, and Bert Spector, "Why Change Programs Don't Produce Change," *Harvard Business Review* 68 (November–December 1990): 158–166.

14. Thomas G. Cummings and Christopher G. Worley, *Organization Development and Change,* 5th ed. (St. Paul: West Publishing Company, 1993), 63.

15. Teresa Joyce Covin and Ralph H. Kilmann, "Implementation of Large-Scale Planned Change: Some Areas of Agreement and Disagreement," *Psychological Reports* 66 (June 1990): 1235–1241.

16. Peter Senge, *The Fifth Discipline: The Art and Practice of the Learning Organization* (New York: Doubleday, 1990).

17. Ann M. Morrison and Nancy J. Perry, "Apple Bites Back," *Fortune,* February 20, 1984, 86–93.

18. Gary McWilliams, "A Radical Shift in Focus for Polaroid," *Business Week,* July 26, 1993, 66–67.

19. Peter Burrows, "Compaq: Turning the Tables on Dell?" *Business Week,* March 22, 1993, 87.

20. Dumaine.

21. Keffeler, "Managing Changing Organizations."

22. Alex Taylor III and Sally Solo, "How Toyota Copes with Hard Times," *Fortune,* January 25, 1993, 78–82; Kathleen Kerwin, "GM's Aurora," *Business Week,* March 21, 1994, 88–94; Andrew Baxter, "Androids on the March—After Years on the Breadline, Modern Robots are Finding Gainful Employment in Europe," *Financial Times,* May 7, 1992, 18.

23. Robert Howard, "The CEO as Organizational Architect: An Interview with Xerox's Paul Allaire," *Harvard Business Review* 70 (September–October 1992): 107–121.

24. Beer, Eisenstat, and Spector, "Why Change Programs Don't Produce Change."

25. Kanter, "Championing Change: An Interview with Raymond Smith."

26. Cummings and Worley, *Organization Development and Change,* 53.

27. Adapted from Cummings and Worley.

28. Kanter.

29. Cummings and Worley, 145.

30. Dumaine.

31. Jacqueline M. Graves, "Leaders of Corporate Change," *Fortune,* December 14, 1992, 104–114.

32. Cummings and Worley, 147.

33. Alan L. Wilgus, "Forging Change in Spite of Adversity," *Personnel Journal* 70 (September 1991): 60–67.

34. Keffeler, 96.

35. Howard, "The CEO as Organizational Architect."

36. Elliott, "The Challenge of Managing Change."

37. Wilgus, "Forging Change in Spite of Adversity."

38. Bart Ziegler, Catherine Arnst, Elizabeth Lesley, Kathy Robello, and Robert D. Hof, "AT&T's Bold Bet," *Business Week,* August 30, 1993, 26.

39. Covin and Kilmann, "Implementation of Large-Scale Planned Change."

40. Cummings and Worley, 151.

41. David A. Nadler, "Managing Organizational Change: An Integrative Perspective," *The Journal of Applied Behavioral Science* 17 (April–June 1981): 191–211.

42. Dumaine.

43. Catherine Cleary and Thomas Packard, "The Use of Metaphors in Organizational Assessment and Change," *Group and Organization Management* 17 (September 1992): 229–241.

44. Cummings and Worley, 156–157.
45. Nadler, "Managing Organizational Change."
46. Cummings and Worley, 157.
47. Graves, "Leaders of Corporate Change."
48. Graves.
49. Cummings and Worley, 2.
50. David A. Nadler, *Feedback and Organization Development: Using Data-Based Methods* (Reading, MA: Addison-Wesley Publishing Company, 1977).
51. Edgar H. Schein, *Process Consultation Volume II: Lessons for Managers and Consultants* (Reading, MA: Addison-Wesley Publishing Company, 1987).
52. Richard E. Walton, *Managing Conflict: Interpersonal Dialogue and Third-Party Roles,* 2nd ed. (Reading, MA: Addison-Wesley Publishing Company, 1987).

## Chapter 20

1. James B. Treece and Kathleen Kerwin, "Detroit: Highballing It into Trucks," *Business Week,* March 7, 1994, 46.
2. Paul B. Finney, "A Hunt for Space," *International Business* 6 (June 1993): 38–44.
3. William Dixon, "Ford's Strategic Multinational Network," *Telecommunications* 25 (December 1991): 39–42.
4. Joseph P. Ziskowsky, "Robotics—the First Step to CIM and the Factory of the Future," *Robotics and Factories of the Future,* ed. Suren N. Dwivedi (Berlin: Springer-Verlag, 1984): 154–160.
5. Gregory L. Miles, with Neil Gross and Mark Maremont, "It's a Dirty Job, But Something's Gotta Do It," *Business Week,* August 20, 1990, 92–97.
6. Joe Cyr, "Waste Removal—Now," *CMA Magazine* 67 (June 1993): 22–25.
7. Everett E. Adam, Jr., and Ronald J. Ebert, *Production and Operations Management* (Englewood Cliffs, NJ: Prentice-Hall, 1992).
8. Ross Johnson and William O. Winchell, "Business and Quality," pamphlet (Milwaukee: American Society for Quality Control, 1989).
9. Robert Neff, "No. 1—and Trying Harder," *Business Week,* October 25, 1991, 20–24.
10. Dori Jones Yang, "Northern Hospitality," *Business Week,* October 25, 1991, 118.
11. Alex Taylor, III, "What's Ahead for GM's New Team," *Fortune,* November 30, 1992, 58–61.
12. Alex Taylor, III, "Can GM Remodel Itself?" *Fortune,* January 13, 1992, 26–34.
13. Adam and Ebert, *Production and Operations Management.*
14. "Watch Out! Industrial Productivity Gains Momentum," *Modern Material Handling* 48 (February 1993): 68.
15. Timothy H. Olson, "Orchestrating Improvement—A Case Study," *Supervision* 53 (June 1992): 11–12.
16. Bill Kelley, "The Power of Incentive," *Incentive* 166 (May 1992): 6–9.
17. Gary S. Vasilash, "Dana's Gresen Plant: Measurably a Winner," *Production* 104 (December 1992): 48–51.
18. John F. Wilfore, "Employees Draw Their Own Road Map for Cultural Change," *Industrial Engineering* 25 (June 1993): 49.
19. Thomas J. Peters and Robert H. Waterman, Jr., *In Search of Excellence: Lessons from America's Best-Run Companies* (New York: Warner Books, 1982): 14–15, 260–277.

20. Malcolm Kushner, *The Light Touch: How to Use Humor for Business Success,* New York: Simon and Schuster, 1990, 18.
21. Karen Matthes, "Lighten Up! Humor Has Its Place at Work," *HR Focus* (New York: American Management Association, February 1993), 3.
22. C. W. Metcalf and Roma Felible, *Lighten Up: Survival Skills for People Under Pressure* (New York: Addison-Wesley, 1992), 17.

## Chapter 21

1. Jeffrey Rothfeder and Jim Bartimo, with Lois Therrien and Richard Brandt, "How Software Is Making Food Sales a Piece of Cake," *Business Week,* July 2, 1990, 54–55.
2. William M. Bulkeley, "Marketers Mine Their Corporate Databases," *The Wall Street Journal,* June 14, 1993, B6.
3. Jesse B. Tutor, Jr., "Management and Future Technological Trends," *Texas A&M Business Forum,* Fall 1988, 2–5.
4. David Kirkpatrick, "Making It All Worker-Friendly," *Fortune* 128 (Autumn 1993; Special Information Technology Edition): 44–53; and Stratford Sherman, "How to Bolster the Bottom Line," *Fortune* 128 (Autumn 1993; Special Information Technology Edition): 14–28.
5. Sherman, "How to Bolster the Bottom Line."
6. Sherman.
7. Sherman.
8. Sherman; and Kirkpatrick, "Making It All Worker-Friendly."
9. Louis S. Richman, "Jobs That Are Growing and Slowing," *Fortune,* July 12, 1993, 52–53.
10. Chris Roush, "Call It Bogus 1–2–3," *Business Week,* December 13, 1993, 97.
11. William M. Bulkeley, "Your Pet Iguana Swallowed a Staple? Computerized Help Desk Will Try to Help," *The Wall Street Journal,* November 1, 1993, B1, B6.
12. Kyle Pope, "To Whom It May Concern," *The Wall Street Journal,* November 15, 1993, R22.
13. Myron Magnet, "Who's Winning the Information Revolution," *Fortune,* November 30, 1992, 110.
14. Magnet, "Who's Winning the Information Revolution."
15. Faye Rice, "Who Scores Best on the Environment," *Fortune,* July 26, 1993, 114; American Telephone and Telegraph Company, "A Safe and Green Tomorrow," internal corporate video documentary, 1992.
16. Sherman.
17. Karen A. Frenkel, "The War for the Executive Desktop," *Personal Computing,* April 27, 1990, 55.
18. David L. Olsen and James F. Courtney, Jr., *Decision Support Models and Expert Systems* (New York: The Macmillan Publishing Company, 1992), 214–215, 219–222.
19. Raymond R. Burke, Arvind Rangaswamy, Jerry Wind, and Jehoshua Eliashberg, "A Knowledge-Based System for Advertising Design," *Marketing Science* 9 (Summer 1990): 212–229.
20. Gene Bylinsky, "Computers That Learn by Doing," *Fortune,* September 6, 1993, 96–102; Linda M. Salchenberger, E. Mine Cinar, and Nicholas A. Lash, "Neural Networks: A New Tool for Predicting Thrift Failures," *Decision Sciences* 23 (1992): 899–916; G.E. Hinton, "Connectionist Learning Procedures," *Artificial Intelligence* 40 (1989): 185–234.
21. Bylinsky, "Computers That Learn by Doing,"; Kar Yan Tam and Melody Y. Kiang, "Managerial Applications of Neural Networks: The Case of Bank Failure Predictions," *Management Science* 38

(July 1992): 926–947; Salchenberger, Cinar, and Lash, "Neural Networks: A New Tool for Predicting Thrift Failures."

22. John A. Byrne, "The Virtual Corporation," *Business Week,* February 8, 1993, 98.

23. Byrne, "The Virtual Corporation."

24. Jaclyn Fierman, "What Happened to the Jobs?" *Fortune,* July 12, 1993, 40–41.

25. Robert E. Cole, "Learning from Learning Theory: Implications for Quality Improvement of Turnover, Use of Contingent Workers, and Job Rotation Policies," *Quality Management Journal* 1 (October 1993): 9–25.

26. James L. Heskett, Thomas O. Jones, Gary W. Loveman, W. Earl Sasser, Jr., and Leonard A. Schlesinger, "Putting The Service-Profit Chain to Work," *Harvard Business Review* 72 (March/April 1994): 164–174; Robert E. Cole, "Learning from Learning Theory"; Frederick F. Reichheld, "Loyalty-Based Management," *Harvard Business Review* 71 (March/April 1993): 64–73.

27. Bruce Sterling, *The Hacker Crackdown* (New York: Bantam Books, 1992).

28. Mary S. Glucksman, "The Dark Side of the Boom," *Omni* 13 (April 1991): 36.

## Chapter 22

1. Brian O'Reilly, "The Perils of Too Much Freedom," *Fortune,* January 11, 1993, 79.

2. Shawn Tully, "Can Boeing Reinvent Itself?" *Fortune,* March 8, 1993, 66–73.

3. Ronald Henkoff, "Companies That Train Best," *Fortune,* March 22, 1993, 62–75.

4. Mark Maremont, "A New Equal Right: The Close Shave," *Business Week,* March 29, 1993, 58–59.

5. Author's personal interview with a former IBM typewriter salesperson, April 6, 1994, Memphis, Tennessee.

6. Catherine Arnst, with Judith H. Dobrzynski and Bart Ziegler, "Faith in a Stranger," *Business Week,* April 5, 1993, 18–21.

7. John Huey, "Managing in the Midst of Chaos," *Fortune,* April 5, 1993, 38–48.

8. Jeanette A. Davy, Richard E. White, Nancy J. Merritt, and Karen Gritzmacher, "A Derivation of the Underlying Constructs of Just-In-Time Management Systems," *Academy of Management Journal* 35 (August 1992): 653–670.

9. Myron Magnet, "The New Golden Rule of Business," *Fortune,* February 21, 1994, 60–64; Davy, White, Merritt, and Gritzmacher, "A Derivation of the Underlying Constructs of Just-In-Time Management Systems"; Joseph L. Cavinato, "A Total Cost/Value Model for Supply Chain Competitiveness," *Journal of Business Logistics* 13, #2 (1992): 285–301; Arthur R. Tenner and Irving J. DeToro, *Total Quality Management: Three Steps to Continuous Improvement* (Reading, MA: Addison-Wesley, 1992).

10. Ronald Henkoff, "Companies That Train Best."

11. Tenner and DeToro, *Total Quality Management: Three Steps to Continuous Improvement*; Artemis March and David A. Garvin, "A Note on Quality: The Views of Deming, Juran, and Crosby," Harvard Business School Reprint 9–687–011, 1986, 1–13.

12. Tenner and DeToro.

13. Tenner and DeToro; Chapman Wood, "The Prophets of Quality," *Quarterly Review,* American Society for Quality Control, Fall 1988; Philip Crosby, *Quality Is Free: The Art of Making Quality Certain* (New York: Mentor Books, New American Library, 1979).

14. Joseph M. Juran, "Made in U.S.A.: A Renaissance in Quality," *Harvard Business Review* 71 (July–August 1993): 42–50; Frederick F. Reichheld, "Loyalty-Based Management," *Harvard Business Review* 71 (March–April 1993): 64–73; Benson P. Shapiro, V. Kasturi Rangan, and John J. Sviokla, "Staple Yourself to an Order," *Harvard Business Review* 70 (July–August 1992): 113–122; Tenner and DeToro.

15. H.W. Allen Sweeny and Robert Rachlin, *Handbook of Budgeting* (New York: John Wiley and Sons, 1987), 649.

16. Willard I. Zangwill, "Focusing All Eyes on the Bottom Line," *The Wall Street Journal,* March 21, 1994, A12.

17. James L. Heskett, Thomas O. Jones, Gary W. Loveman, W. Earl Sasser, Jr., and Leonard A. Schlesinger, "Putting the Service-Profit Chain to Work," *Harvard Business Review* 72 (March–April 1994): 164–174; Reichheld, "Loyalty-Based Management."

18. Zangwill, "Focusing All Eyes on the Bottom Line."

19. Henkoff.

20. Adapted from Edward E. Scannell and John W. Newstrom, *Still More Games Trainers Play* (New York: McGraw-Hill, Inc., 1991), 237–239.

# Glossary

**Abilene Paradox** A situation occuring when members of a group publicly agree on a course of action even though there is an underlying consensus agreement that an alternative course is preferred. **page 450**

**ability tests** Paper-and-pencil quizzes, usually multiple choice, that measure an applicant's knowledge of specific work content or cognitive ability. **page 402**

**acceptance theory of authority** The theory that, in formal organizations, authority flows up, because the decision as to whether an order, or communication, has authority lies with the person who receives the communication. **page 48**

**accommodating style** A style exhibiting low assertiveness and high cooperation. **page 444**

**action research** An approach to change that involves an ongoing process of joint (with clients) problem discovery, diagnosis, action planning, action implementation, and evaluation. **page 574**

**adhocracy** A centralized, informal, but complex organization which tries to maintain flexibility in the face of rapid environmental changes by using a matrix or network formal structure. **page 384**

**adjourning stage** The stage when in which task forces, project teams, or committees complete their task and disband. **page 436**

**administrative management** The universality of management as a function that can be applied to all organizations. **page 40**

**administrative model of decision making** A descriptive approach, recognizing that people do not always make decisions with logic and rationality, that outlines how managers actually do make decisions; also known as the organizational, neoclassical, or behavioral model. **page 309**

**affiliative power** Power that is derived by virtue of a person's association with someone else who has some source of power. **page 496**

**affirmative action programs** Policies designed to increase job opportunities for minority groups through analysis of the present pool of workers, identification of areas where women and minorities are underrepresented, and establishment of specific hiring and promotion goals along with target dates for meeting those goals. **page 166**

**antigroup roles** Behaviors that disrupt the group, draw attention to individual rather than group functioning, and detract from positive interactions. **page 440**

**artificial intelligence** Programs that seek to make computers able to work—to "think"—as much like the human mind as possible. **page 632**

**assessment center tests** Programs that typically simulate managerial tasks. **page 402**

**assimilation** Organizational practices that force minority groups to accept the norms and values of a majority group. **page 165**

**authority** The right to give work orders to others in the organization; associated with a position within an organization, not with the individual occupying that position. **page 334**

**avoidance** The act of strengthening a desired behavior by allowing individuals to avoid negative consequences by performing the behavior. **page 474**

**avoiding style** A style displaying low assertiveness and low cooperation. **page 443**

**balance sheet** A snapshot of the organization's financial position at a given moment, indicating what the firm owns and what proportion of its assets are financed with its own or borrowed money. **page 660**

**behavior modification** An application of reinforcement theory, which involves changing behavior and encouraging appropriate actions by relating the consequences of behavior to the behavior itself. **page 474**

**behavior-based appraisal** A subjective evaluation of the way an employee performs job tasks. **page 408**

**behavioral approach** A view of management that emphasizes understanding the importance of human behavior, needs, and attitudes within formal organizations. **page 43**

**behavioral approach to job design** The design of jobs based on the view that workers are independent parts of the production process whose individual characteristics should be taken into account in forming jobs. **page 340**

**birth** The initial stage when the product is introduced. **page 290**

**body language** The broad range of body motions and behaviors, from facial expressions to the distance one person stands from another, that send messages to a receiver. **page 530**

**bottom-up budgeting** Financial planning by those employees more directly engaged in the actual tasks being covered and in which information flows up from the lower levels of an organization for review by top management. **page 659**

**boundary-spanning roles** Group behaviors involving interaction with members in other units of the organization or outside the organization. **page 441**

**bounded rationality** The idea that people have limits, or boundaries, to their rationality. **page 310**

**brainstorming** A technique in which group members spontaneously suggest ideas to solve a problem. **page 318**

**budget** A plan to allocate resources and expenses for a certain period of time. **page 261**

**budgeting** The process of establishing formal, written plans to control the availability and cost of financial resources. **page 658**

**budgets** The formal, written plans for future operations in financial terms. **page 658**

**bug** An error in a software program. **page 637**

**bureaucracy** A theory of management by office or position, rather than by person, based on rational authority. **page 42**

**bureaucratic control** An attempt to control the firm's overall functioning through formal, mechanistic structural arrangements. **page 652**

**business ethics** Moral principles and standards that define acceptable behavior in business. **page 92**

**business plan** A meticulous statement of rationale for the business and a step-by-step explanation of how it will achieve its goals. **page 223**

**business-level strategy** The area of responsibility usually assigned to the divisional-level managers. **page 282**

**capacity** The maximum load that an organizational unit can carry or operate at a given point in time. **page 593**

**capital budgeting** Budgeting concerned with the intermediate and long-term control of capital acquisitions such as plant and equipment. **page 658**

**capitalism** An economic system wherein the natural laws of supply and demand and free competition within the marketplace will efficiently regulate the flow of resources within a society. **page 33**

**cartel** A group of firms or nations that agree to act as a monopoly and not compete with each other. **page 128**

**cash cows** Those businesses that tend to generate excess cash over what is needed for their continued growth due to their high market share in a slow-growing market. **page 286**

**cause-and-effect diagram** A method for analyzing process dispersion that relates causes and effects; also known as fishbone analysis. **page 193**

**centralization** The pattern of concentrating authority in a relatively few, high-level positions. **page 351**

**certainty** The condition that exists when decision makers are fully informed about a problem, its alternative solutions, and their respective outcomes. **page 304**

**chain of command** An organizing concept that ensures that all positions are directly

linked in some way to top management. **page 349**

**channel** The medium or method used to transmit the intended information and meaning, such as by phone or in person. **page 528**

**channel richness** A channel's ability to transmit information, including the ability to handle multiple cues simultaneously, encourage feedback, and focus personally on the receiver. **page 531**

**charisma** The ability to inspire admiration, respect, loyalty, and a desire to emulate, based on some intangible set of personality traits; a personal source of power. **page 495**

**checksheets** Data-recording forms that have been designed to allow managers to enter data on the form and simultaneously analyze trends in the data. **page 194**

**clan control** The regulation of overall organizational functioning through reliance on informal, organic structural arrangements. **page 653**

**classical approach** An approach to management that stresses the manager's role in a formal hierarchy of authority and focuses on the task, machines, and systems needed to accomplish the task effectively. **page 36**

**classical approach to job design** The design of jobs based on the principles of division of labor and job specialization. **page 338**

**classical model of decision making** A prescriptive approach, asserting that managers are logical, rational individuals who make decisions that are in the best interests of the organization, that outlines how managers should make decisions; also known as the rational model. **page 309**

**closed system** An organization that interacts little with its external environment and therefore receives little feedback from or information about its surroundings. **page 47**

**cluster chain** An exchange in which one person or a selected few share information with only a few others. **page 536**

**codes of ethics** Formalized rules and standards that describe and delineate what the organization expects of its employees. **page 102**

**coercive power** An organizationally based source of power derived from a leader's control over punishments or the capacity to deny rewards. **page 494**

**cohesiveness** The tendency of group members to unite in their pursuit of group goals and to be attracted to the group and each other. **page 441**

**collaborating style** A style displaying both high assertiveness and high competition. **page 444**

**committee** A permanent formal group that does some specific task; may be either a functional or cross-functional group. **page 430**

**communication** The process through which information and meaning are transferred from one person to another. **page 526**

**compensation system** The basis on which an organization gives money, goods, or services to its employees in exchange for their work. **page 410**

**competing style** A management style involving a stance of high assertiveness with low cooperation. **page 443**

**competitors** Other organizations that produce similar, or in some cases identical, goods or services. **page 68**

**complexity** The level of differentiation among structural units, including the specialization of jobs, geographical dispersion, and height of the firm. **page 370**

**comprehensive model of planned change** A step-by-step plan for implementing major change. **page 564**

**compressed work week** A four-day (or shorter) period in which an employee works 40 hours. **page 479**

**compromising style** A style that reflects a moderate concern for both your goals and the other person's goals. **page 444**

**computer networks** Systems that permit different computers to communicate with each other. **page 626**

**computer viruses** Computer programs concealed inside legitimate programs that change or destroy data kept on a computer; can damage or even cripple a system. **page 637**

**computer-assisted design (CAD)** A computerized approach in the operations function that links the design and manufacturing areas, making information readily available. **page 595**

**computer-assisted manufacturing (CAM)** A computerized approach in the operations function that links the manufacturing and design areas, making information readily available. **page 595**

**conceptual skills** The intellectual abilities to process information and make accurate decisions about the work group and the job task. **page 14**

**confidence** A person's faith that his or her decisions are reliable and good. **page 315**

**conformity** Adherence to the group's norms, values, and goals. **page 449**

**conglomerates** Firms that pusue unrelated diversification strategies. **page 284**

**congruence model of change** An approach that emphasizes the interrelationships between the various parts of an organization and how change in one part will cause reactive change in other parts. **page 563**

**consideration behaviors** Patterns of being friendly and supportive by listening to employees' problems, supporting their actions, "going to bat" for them, and getting their input on a variety of issues. **page 498**

**consumerism** The activities undertaken by independent individuals, groups, and organizations to protect their rights as consumers. **page 108**

**content theories** A group of theories that assume that workers are motivated by the desire to satisfy needs and that seek to identify what their needs are. **page 465**

**contingency approach** An approach to management theories that emphasizes identifying the key variables in each management situation, understanding the relationship among these variables, and recognizing the complex system of cause and effects that exists in each and every managerial situation. **page 49**

**contingency plans** Alternate courses of action to be undertaken if certain organizational or environmental conditions change. **page 263**

**contingency theory** The suggestion that successful leadership requires matching leaders with primarily stable leadership styles to the demands of the situation. **page 503**

**continuous technology** A method of production in which raw materials flow continuously through a system that transforms them into finished products. **page 379**

**contract manufacturing** Occurs when a company hires a foreign company to produce a specified volume of its product to specification. **page 137**

**contracting for leadership style** A process whereby employees may not initially agree with a manager's assessment of their developmental level, thus requiring a leader's skill in arriving at an assessment consensus and an agreed-upon leadership style. **page 503**

**control charts** Diagrams that display data over time as well as computed variations in those data. **page 194**

**controlling** Those activities that an organization undertakes to ensure that its activities lead to achievement of its objectives. **page 8**

**coordination** The linking of jobs, departments, and divisions so that all parts of the organization work together to achieve goals. **page 381**

**corporate strategy** The scope and resource deployment components of strategy for the enterprise as a whole. **page 280**

**corporation** A separate legal entity, or body, created by the state, having assets and liabilities which are distinct from those of the owners of the corporation. **page 226**

**cost leadership** A business-level strategy aimed at achieving the overall lowest cost structure in an industry. **page 288**

**cost-of-quality (COQ) accounting system** A system that permits managers to calculate precisely the costs and savings associated with their quality efforts. **page 187**

**countertrade agreements** The bartering of a product for other products instead of for currency. **page 134**

**crash** A system service failure. **page 637**

**cross-functional groups** Groups that cut across the firm's hierarchy and are composed of people from different functional areas and possibly different levels. **page 430**

**cultural conflict** The tension or friction between culture groups that stems from a lack of understanding by one group of the values, attitudes, and behaviors of the other. **page 165**

**cultural diversity** Differences in age, gender, race, ethnicity, nationality, and ability. **page 153**

**customer departmentalization** The grouping of jobs so that the job holders interact with a specific customer group or clientele. **page 344**

**customer division structure** The organization of divisions by customer. **page 363**

**customers** Those who purchase an organization's goods and/or services. **page 66**

**data** Unorganized facts, statistics, opinions, and predictions gathered from various sources inside and outside the company. **page 618**

**database** A collection of related data—past, present, and projected—organized for convenient access. **page 620**

**decentralization** The pattern of dispersing authority to several positions at various levels in the organization. **page 351**

**decision** A choice made from alternative courses of action in order to deal with a problem. **page 302**

**decision making** The process of choosing among alternative courses of action to resolve a problem. **page 302**

**decision support system (DSS)** An information system that aids managers in decision making by helping them anticipate the possible outcomes of alternative actions. **page 631**

**decisional roles** Activities that deal primarily with the allocation of resources in order to reach organizational objectives. **page 12**

**decline** The stage marked by decreases in the product's market share. **page 290**

**decoding** The process of interpreting and attaching personal meaning to the message. **page 528**

**delegation** The assignment of work activities and authority to a subordinate. **page 349**

**Delphi group technique** A technique employing a written survey to gather expert opinions without holding a group meeting. **page 319**

**departmentalization** The grouping of related jobs to form an administrative unit. **page 341**

**diagonal communication** The flow of information, often in matrix structures, between individuals from different units and organizational levels. **page 535**

**differentiation** A business strategy in which the SBU offers a unique good or service to a customer at a premium price. **page 288**

**direct investment** The purchase of overseas production and marketing facilities. **page 138**

**discrimination** Negative behaviors toward people from other cultural groups. **page 163**

**distinctive competence** What a firm does well relative to its competitors. **page 276**

**distortion** A deviation between the sent message and the received message. **page 533**

**diversification** A strategy of acquiring other businesses. **page 283**

**divestment** A strategy of selling off businesses that the company no longer wishes to maintain, either because they are failing or because the company has changed its corporate strategy and does not wish to be in those businesses any longer. **page 284**

**division of labor** The idea of breaking down an entire job into its component parts and assigning each specific task to an individual member; also called specialization. **page 33**

**divisionalized form** A multidivisional structure or hybrid; typically a very large corporation that has organized its departments into divisions. **page 384**

**dogs** Businesses that have only minimal profits or even losses due to their low market share in slow growing markets. **page 286**

**downward communication** The traditional flow of information from upper organizational levels to lower levels, such as job directions, assignment of tasks, performance feedback, and information concerning the organization's goals. **page 534**

**dumping** The sale of products, by a country or business firm, at less than what it costs to produce them. **page 130**

**economic dimension** The overall condition of the complex economies throughout the world. **page 65**

**economic forces** The relationship of people to resources. **page 32**

**economic order quantity (EOQ) model** A popular approach to inventory control that identifies the optimal number of items to order while minimizing certain annual costs that very according to order size. **page 599**

**effectively** Having the intended result. **page 4**

**efficiently** Accomplishing objectives with a minimum of resources. **page 4**

**electronic mail** The exchange of "letters" or messages from computer to computer; also called E-mail. **page 628**

**embargo** The suspension of trade in a particular product by the government. **page 130**

**employee-centered leaders** The most effective managers, who engage in both dimensions of leadership behaviors by getting employees involved in the operation of their departments or divisions in a positive and constructive manner, setting general goals, providing fairly loose supervision, and recognizing employees' contributions. **page 499**

**empowerment** The extent of a group's authority and ability to make and implement work decisions. **page 430**

**encoding** The process of transforming information into understandable symbols, typically spoken or written words or gestures. **page 528**

**entrepreneur** A person who creates a business or product, manages his or her resources, and takes risks to gain a profit. **page 210**

**entrepreneurship** The process of creating and managing a business to achieve desired objectives. **page 210**

**entropy** The tendency of systems to deteriorate or break down over time. **page 47**

**environment** All of those factors that affect the operation of the organization. **page 60**

**equity theory** A theory stating that the extent to which people are willing to contribute to an organization depends on their assessment of the fairness of the rewards they will receive in exchange. **page 469**

**error-free production** A manufacturing process consisting of maintaining machinery and equipment, quality inspection checks, and well-trained employees. **page 183**

**escalation of commitment** The tendency to persist with a failing course of action. **page 314**

**ethical formalism** A philosophy that focuses on human rights and values and on the intentions associated with a particular behavior. **page 99**

**ethical issue** An identifiable problem, situation, or opportunity that requires a person or organization to choose among several actions that may be evaluated as ethical or unethical. **page 94**

**exchange controls** Restrictions on the amount of a particular currency that may be bought or sold. **page 129**

**exchange rate** The ratio at which one nation's currency can be exchanged for another nation's currency or for gold. **page 131**

**executive information system (EIS)** An easy-to-use DSS designed for executives who have limited experience using computers but need access to the firm's database. **page 631**

**expectancy theory** A theory stating that motivation depends not only on how much a person wants something but also on the person's perception of how likely he or she is to get it. **page 470**

**expectancy** A person's expectation that effort will lead to high performance. **page 471**

**expert power** Power or influence derived from a person's special knowledge or expertise in a particular area. **page 494**

**expert system** Decision support programs that mimic human decision-making processes by using a collection of thousands of "if-then" rules to solve complex problems. **page 632**

**exporting** The sale of goods and services to foreign markets enabling organizations of all sizes to participate in global business. **page 134**

**external environment** All of the factors outside the organization that may affect its managers' actions. **page 60**

**extinction** Weakening an undesired behavior by not providing positive consequences. **page 474**

**facilitators** Leaders who help the group overcome internal obstacles or difficulties so that it may achieve desired outcomes. **page 445**

**feedback** The receiver's response to the sender's communication. **page 528**

**feedback (or postaction) control** A form of control that monitors the firm's outputs, the results of the transformation process; also known as postaction control. **page 657**

**finance managers** Managers concerned with the value of the organization's assets and various investment strategies that would increase net worth. **page 18**

**financial audit** A periodic and comprehensive examination of a firm's financial records. **page 661**

**finished-goods inventory** Those products that are ready for sale, such as a fully assembled automobile ready to ship to a dealer. **page 597**

**fixed-interval schedule** A pattern of reinforcement at specified periods of time, regardless of behavior. **page 475**

**fixed-position layout** Facility layout in which the organization has a central location for the product and brings all resources required to create the product to that location. **page 594**

**fixed-ratio schedule** A pattern offering reinforcement after a specified number of desired performance behaviors, regardless of the time elapsed between them. **page 475**

**flexible manufacturing** A manufacturing process in which computers can direct machinery to adapt to different versions of similar operations. **page 596**

**flextime** A work schedule that allows employees to choose their starting and ending times as long as they are at work during a specified time period. **page 479**

**flowchart** A tool that diagrams a process from start to finish, identifying those aspects of the process that need improvement. **page 193**

**focus** A business strategy in which the business concentrates on one part or segment of the market and tries to meet the demands of that segment. **page 289**

**for-profit companies** Companies owned either privately by one or more individuals or publicly by stockholders. **page 20**

**Foreign Corrupt Practices Act** Legislation outlawing direct payoffs to and bribes of foreign governments or business officials by American companies. **page 128**

**formal groups** Groups created by the organization that generally have their own formal structure. **page 430**

**formal organization** The arrangement of positions, as shown on an organizational chart, that dictates where work activities are completed, where decisions should be made, and the flow of information. **page 334**

**formalization** The degree to which the organization's procedures, rules, and personnel requirements are written down and enforced. **page 370**

**forming stage** The stage when group members meet for the first time or two, become acquainted, and familiarize themselves with the group's task. **page 435**

**framing** The tendency to view positively presented information favorably and negatively presented information unfavorably. **page 313**

**franchise** A license to sell another's products or to use another's name in a business, or both. **page 229**

**franchisee** The purchaser of a franchise. **page 229**

**franchiser** The company that sells a franchise. **page 229**

**franchising** A form of licensing in which a company (the franchiser) agrees to provide a franchisee elements associated with the franchiser's business, in return for a financial commitment and the agreement to conduct business in accordance with the franchiser's standard of operations. **page 137**

**free-riding** The tendency of some individuals to perform at less than their optimum in groups, relying instead on others to carry their share of the workload. **page 433**

**functional departmentalization** The grouping of jobs that perform similar functional activities, such as finance, manufacturing, and human resources. **page 343**

**functional groups** Groups that perform specific organizational functions, with members from several vertical levels of the hierarchy. **page 430**

**functional structure** The grouping of jobs according to similar economic activities, such as finance, production and operations, and marketing. **page 360**

**Gantt chart** A bar chart that shows the relationship of various scheduling activities over time. **page 602**

**General Agreement on Tariffs and Trade (GATT)** Legislation, first signed by 23 nations in 1947, providing a forum for tariff negotiations and a place where international trade problems can be discussed and resolved. **page 131**

**general environment** The broad, complex factors that affect all organizations. **page 60**

**general partnership** A complete sharing in the management of a business, with each partner having unlimited liability for the business's debts. **page 226**

**geographic departmentalization** The grouping of jobs according to physical geography. **page 346**

**geographic division structure** The organization of divisions by geographic region. **page 362**

**global business (globalization)** A strategy in which organizations treat the entire world or major regions of it as the domain for conducting business. **page 124**

**global dimension** Pertaining to the general environment, those factors in other countries that affect the organization. **page 65**

**goal-setting theory** A theory which recognizes the importance of goals in improving employee performance. **page 476**

**goal** The final result that a firm wishes to achieve. **page 250**

**gossip chain** The spreading of information by one person to many others. **page 536**

**grapevine** Informal communication channels, found in virtually all organizations. **page 536**

**grid OD** A six-phase organization intervention that comprehensively and systematically attempts to enhance personal management style, team functioning, intergroup organizational functioning, and the organization's ability to improve its method for solving problems, resolving conflicts, and making decisions. **page 577**

**group decision support system (GDSS)** A special set of computer systems designed to aid group decision making. **page 631**

**group-maintenance roles** Behaviors that help the group engage in constructive interpersonal relationships, and help members fulfill personal needs and derive satisfaction from group participation. **page 440**

**group** Two or more individuals who communicate with one another, share a collective identity, and have a common goal. **page 426**

**groupthink** A phenomenon occurring when cohesive "in-groups" let the desire for unanimity, or consensus, override sound judgment in generating and evaluating alternative courses of action. **page 322**

**growth** The stage characterized by dramatic increases in the product's market share. **page 290**

**hardware** The basic physical components of a computer. **page 625**

**Hawthorne studies** A group of studies that provided the stimulus for the human relations movement within management theory and practice. **page 44**

**histogram** A graphic summary of data that enables a user to interpret patterns that are difficult to see in a simple table of numbers. **page 193**

**holding company** An organization composed of several very different kinds of businesses, each of which is permitted to operate largely autonomously. **page 364**

**horizontal communication** The exchange of information among individuals on the same organizational level, either across or within departments. **page 534**

**horizontal coordination** The linking of subunits on the same level. **page 381**

**horizontal specialization** The division of labor at the same level of the organization into simple, repetitive tasks. **page 338**

**human resource management (HRM)** All activities that forecast the number and type of employees an organization will need and then find and develop employees with necessary skills. **page 394**

**human resource managers** Managers concerned with developing and carrying out programs used to make decisions about employees, such as selection, training, and compensation. **page 18**

**human resource planning** The forecasting of an organization's future demand for employees and the future supply of employees within the organization, and the designing of programs to correct the discrepancy between the two. **page 395**

**human-relations movement** A practice whereby employees came to be viewed as informal groups of their own, with their own leadership and codes of behavior, instead of as unrelated individual workers assigned to perform individual tasks. **page 45**

**hybrid structure** A combination of several different structures, the most common form of organizational structure. **page 364**

**import tariff** A tax levied by a nation on goods bought outside its borders and imported into the country. **page 128**

**importing** The purchase of goods and services from a foreign source. **page 134**

**income statement** A statement of an organization's profitability over a period of time—a month, a quarter, or a year. **page 660**

**incremental change** A relatively small change in processes and behaviors within just one or a few systems or levels of the organization. **page 558**

**industrial robot** A machine designed to move material, parts, tools, or specialized devices through variable programmed motions, for the performance of a variety of tasks. **page 596**

**informal groups** Groups that arise naturally from social interaction and relationships and are usually very loosely organized. **page 430**

**informal organization** The relationships among positions that are not connected by the organizational chart. **page 335**

**information** Data that are relevant for a specific purpose. **page 618**

**information overload** The condition of having too much information to process. **page 543**

**information power** Power that is a result of having access to important information that is not common knowledge, or of having the ability to control the flow of information to and from others.   **page 495**

**informational roles**   Activities, such as reports or briefings, that focus on obtaining data important for the decisions the manager needs to make.   **page 11**

**infrastructure**   The physical facilities that support a country's economic activities, such as highways, utilities, schools, hospitals, communication systems, and commercial distribution systems.   **page 131**

**initiating-structure behaviors**   Defining and structuring leader-employee roles through activities such as scheduling, defining work tasks, setting deadlines, criticizing poor work, getting employees to accept work standards, and resolving problems.   **page 498**

**inputs**   Resources such as labor, money, materials, information, and energy that are converted to outputs in the transformation process.   **page 588**

**instrumentality**   A person's expectation that performing a task will lead to a desired outcome.   **page 471**

**integrity tests**   Tests that measure an applicant's attitudes and opinions about dysfunctional behaviors such as theft, sabotage, physical abuse, and substance abuse.   **page 402**

**intergroup team building**   An exercise designed to facilitate functioning between two or more groups by helping the groups understand and deal with areas of conflict.   **page 577**

**internal environment**   All factors that make up the organization, such as the owners, management, employees, and board of directors.   **page 61**

**international business**   The buying, selling, and trading of goods and services across national boundaries.   **page 124**

**International Monetary Fund (IMF)**   Organization established to promote trade among member nations by eliminating trade barriers and fostering financial cooperation.   **page 133**

**interpersonal roles**   Activities that involve interacting with others who may be external or internal to the organization and, at the same time, at a higher or lower level than the manager.   **page 10**

**interpersonal skills**   Those management skills, such as communication, conflict resolution, and leading, that are necessary to work with others.   **page 13**

**intrapreneurs**   Individuals who, like entrepreneurs, take responsibility for, or "championing," developing innovations of any kind within the larger organization.   **page 234**

**intuition**   The immediate comprehension that something is the case, seemingly without the use of any reasoning process or conscious analysis.   **page 311**

**inventory**   All the materials a firm holds in storage for future use.   **page 597**

**inventory control**   The process of determining how many supplies and goods are needed and keeping track of quantities on hand, where each item is, and who is responsible for it.   **page 599**

**job analysis**   The systematic process of gathering information about important work-related aspects of a job.   **page 395**

**job design**   The process of grouping tasks into jobs.   **page 338**

**job enlargement**   A behavioral approach to job design aimed at increasing the number of tasks that comprise a job.   **page 340**

**job enrichment**   A behavioral approach in which jobs are designed to increase the number of similar tasks involved, especially tasks that require information processing and decision making.   **page 341**

**job evaluation methods**   Techniques that determine the value of an organization's jobs and arrange these jobs in order of pay according to their value.   **page 411**

**job rotation**   A behavioral approach to job design involving a deliberate plan to move workers to various jobs on a consistent, scheduled basis.   **page 341**

**job sharing**   A working arrangement whereby two employees do one job.   **page 479**

**job specialization**   The division of work into smaller, distinct tasks.   **page 338**

**job-centered leaders**   Less-effective managers, who are mostly directive in their approaches and more concerned with closely supervising employees, explaining work procedures, and monitoring progress in task accomplishment.   **page 500**

**joint venture**   An agreement by which a company that wants to do business in another country may find a local partner (occasionally, the host nation itself) to share the costs and operation of the business.   **page 137**

**just-in-time (JIT) inventory management**   A concept that minimizes the number of units in inventory by providing an almost continuous flow of items from suppliers to the production facility.   **page 600**

**leader-member exchange (LMX) theory**   A description of how leaders develop "unique" working relationships with each of their employees, based on the nature of their social exchanges.   **page 511**

**leadership**   The process of influencing the activities of an individual or a group toward the achievement of a goal.   **page 492**

**leadership enhancers**   Aspects of the task, subordinates, or organization that amplify a leader's impact on employees.   **page 510**

**leadership neutralizers**   Aspects of the task, subordinates, or organization that have the effect of paralyzing, destroying, or counteracting the effect of a leadership behavior.   **page 510**

**leadership substitutes**   Aspects of the task, subordinates, or organization that act in place of leader behavior and thus render it unnecessary.   **page 510**

**leading**   The act of influencing others' activities to achieve set goals.   **page 7**

**least preferred coworker (LPC) scale**   A measurement of a leader's style consisting of a series of adjective continuums.   **page 503**

**legitimate power**   The influence that comes from a person's formal position in an organization and the authority that accompanies that position.   **page 493**

**licensing**   A trade agreement in which one company (the licensor) allows another country (the licensee) to use its company name, products, brands, trademarks, raw materials, and/or production processes in exchange for a fee, or royalty.   **page 136**

**life and career planning**   The use of structured counseling and group discussions to assist employees in planning career paths and integrating life and career goals.   **page 577**

**limited partnership**   An association of at least one general partner, who assumes unlimited liability, and at least one limited partner, whose liability is limited to his or her investment in the business.   **page 226**

**liquidation strategy**   A strategy in which the firm dismantles an operation and/or sells off parts that may be more valuable as separate entities than as part of the business as a whole.   **page 285**

**local-area network (LAN)**   A network in which computers are linked together directly within one building or one plant.   **page 626**

**lower (first-line) managers**   Those concerned with the direct production of items or delivery of service.   **page 17**

**machine bureaucracy**   A highly structured, formal organization that emphasizes procedures and rules, has a functional formal structure, and contains an informal structure emphasizing complexity, formalization, and centralization. **page 383**

**maintenance factors** Those aspects of a job that relate to the work setting, including, adequate wages, comfortable working conditions, fair company policies, and job security. **page 467**

**management** A set of activities designed to achieve an organization's objectives by using its resources effectively and efficiently. **page 4**

**management by objectives (MBO)** A management philosophy and systematic process through which managers of all levels communicate with subordinates in terms of goals and how specific activities of the subordinates can contribute to reaching these goals. **page 263**

**management control** All of the activities an organization undertakes to ensure that its actions lead to achievement of its objectives. **page 646**

**management control system** A planned, ordered scheme of management control. **page 646**

**management information system (MIS)** A system that organizes past, present, and projected data from both internal and external sources and processes them into usable information. **page 619**

**management science** The field of management that includes the study and use of mathematical models and statistical methods to improve the effectiveness of managerial decision making. **page 38**

**management theory** A systematic statement, based on observations, of how the management process might best occur, given stated underlying principles. **page 35**

**managers** Individuals who make decisions about the use of the organization's resources and are concerned with planning, organizing, leading, and controlling the organization's activities in order to reach its objectives. **page 4**

**manufacturing** The activities and processes used in making tangible products; interchangeable with production. **page 590**

**manufacturing-resource planning (MRPII)** A computerized system that helps a company control all of its resources, not just inventory needed for production. **page 601**

**marketing managers** Managers who develop programs that provide information about the company's goods or services and encourage potential customers to purchase these. **page 18**

**Maslow's hierarchy of needs** The order in which people strive to satisfy the five basic needs as theorized by Maslow—physiological, security, social, esteem, and self-actualization. **page 465**

**mass technology** The production of large numbers of the same product. **page 379**

**material-requirements planning (MRP)** A planning system that schedules the precise quantity of materials needed to make the product. **page 600**

**matrix structure** A structure in which members of different functional departments are chosen to work together temporarily on a specific contract or project. **page 366**

**maturity** The stage when the product's market share either slows or has no growth. **page 290**

**mechanistic organizations** Structures that are highly formal, complex, and centralized. **page 371**

**middle managers** Those who receive broad statements of strategy and policy from upper-level managers and develop specific objectives and plans. **page 17**

**mission** A definition of an organization's fundamental purpose and its basic philosophy. **page 247**

**mission statement** A formal written declaration of the organization's mission; often includes the firm's philosophy, its primary products and markets, the intended geographic scope, and the nature of the relationships between the firm, its stakeholders, and society. **page 247**

**morale** The sum total of employees' attitudes toward their jobs, employer, and colleagues. **page 460**

**moral philosophy** A set of principles that describe what a person believes is the right way to behave. **page 99**

**motivation** An inner drive that directs behavior toward goals. **page 460**

**motivational factors** Those aspects of a job that relate to the content of the work, including achievement, recognition, the work itself, involvement, responsibility, and advancement. **page 468**

**moving** The transition period (state B) during which the behaviors of the organization or department are shifted to a new level (desired state C). **page 561**

**multicultural organizations** Companies that value their culturally diverse employees as assets, and that develop and implement policies designed to promote cultural diversity and equality. **page 168**

**multidivisional structure** The organization of departments together into larger groups called divisions. **page 361**

**multinational corporation (MNC)** A corporation, such as IBM or Exxon, that operates on a worldwide scale, without significant ties to any one nation or region. **page 139**

**munificent environment** An environment in which the organization has a large market for its product and has funds needed to continue operations readily available, and other stakeholder groups are satisfied or pleased with the organization's performance. **page 376**

**negotiated budgeting** The give and take between both upper and lower levels of management in developing the most appropriate form of budgetary control for a given situation. **page 659**

**network organization** A structure, primarily a command unit, that does not make a good or provide a service but instead coordinates agreements and contracts with other organizations to produce, distribute, and sell products. **page 367**

**noise** Anything acting as an information filter, such as knowledge, attitudes, and other factors, that interferes with the message being communicated effectively. **page 528**

**nominal group technique** A process that involves the use of a highly structured meeting agenda and restricts discussion or interpersonal communication during the decision-making process. **page 319**

**nonprofit organizations** Institutions such as governments, churches, and universities that cannot retain earnings over expenses, do not have equity interests, and cannot be bought or sold. **page 20**

**nonprogrammed decisions** Decisions made in response to situations that are unique, relatively unstructured, undefined, and/or of major consequence to the organization. **page 303**

**nonverbal communication** Information conveyed by actions and behaviors rather than by spoken or written words. **page 530**

**norming stage** The stage when conflicts are largely resolved and harmony ensues. **page 435**

**norms** Prescriptions for appropriate behavior of group members that help reduce the disruption and chaos that would ensue if groups members didn't know how to act. **page 436**

**on-the-job training** A technique in which the employee learns the job tasks while actually performing the job. **page 405**

**open system**    An organization that interacts continually with its environment and therefore is well informed about changes within its surroundings and its position relative to these changes.    **page 47**

**operating budgeting**    Budgeting that deals with relatively short-term financial control concerns, such as having sufficient cash on hand to cover daily financial obligations, including routine purchases and payroll.    **page 658**

**operational goals**    Those short-term goals that address activities that must be performed before tactical goals can be fulfilled.    **page 253**

**operational plans**    Plans that are intended to achieve operational goals.    **page 258**

**operations**    Those processes used in the making of both tangible and intangible products.    **page 590**

**operations control**    The regulation of one or more individual operating systems within an organization.    **page 654**

**operations management (OM)**    The development and administration of the activities involved in transforming resources into goods and services.    **page 588**

**organic organizations**    Structures that are less formal, fairly simple, and decentralized.    **page 371**

**organizational change**    Any modification in the behaviors or ideas of an organization or its units.    **pages 334, 554**

**organizational chart**    A pictorial display of the official lines of authority and communication within the organization.    **page 334**

**organizational control**    A broad-based form of control that guides all organizational activities and oversees the overall functioning of the whole firm.    **page 652**

**organizational culture**    The value, beliefs, traditions, philosophies, rules, and heroes that are shared by members of the organization.    **page 19**

**organizational development (OD)**    A systemwide application of behavioral science knowledge to the planned development and reinforcement of organizational strategies, structures, and processes for improving an organization's effectiveness.    **page 573**

**organizational power**    A person's ability to satisfy or deny satisfaction of anothers' need, based on a formal contractual relationship between an organization and the individual.    **page 493**

**organizational structure**    The way managers group jobs into departments and departments into divisions.    **page 360**

**organizations**    Groups of individuals who work together to achieve desired objectives.    **page 4**

**organizing**    The activities involved in designing jobs for employees, grouping these jobs together into departments, and developing working relationships among organizational units and employees to carry out the plans.    **page 7**

**orientation**    The process of familiarizing newly hired employees with fellow workers, company procedures, and the physical properties of the organization.    **page 404**

**outputs**    Goods, services, and ideas that are converted from inputs in the transformation process.    **page 588**

**outsourcing**    A form of direct investment that involves transferring manufacturing or other functions to countries where labor and supplies are less expensive.    **page 138**

**Pareto chart**    A diagram that graphically illustrates the frequencies of key factors that contribute to poor quality.    **page 194**

**partial productivity**    Output relative to a single input or some combination of inputs.    **page 606**

**partnership**    An association of two or more persons who carry on as co-owners of a business for profit.    **page 226**

**path-goal theory**    A model concerned with how a leader affects employees' perceptions of their personal and work goals and the paths to goal attainment.    **page 504**

**perception**    The process through which we receive, filter, organize, interpret, and attach meaning to information taken in from the environment.    **page 533**

**perceptual organization**    The natural and essential process of organizing, interpreting, and attaching value to the selected stimuli.    **page 533**

**perceptual selection**    The choosing of stimuli from the environment for further processing; also known as filtering or screening.    **page 533**

**performance appraisal**    A formal measurement of the quantity and quality of an employee's work within a specific period of time.    **page 407**

**performance gap**    The difference between an organization's desired and actual performance levels.    **page 556**

**performance or work-sample tests**    Examinations that verify an applicant's ability to perform actual job behaviors identified from a job analysis.    **page 402**

**performance standards**    Targets set by management against which actual performance is compared at a future date.    **page 649**

**performing stage**    The stage in which members have reached a level of maturity that facilitates total task involvement.    **page 435**

**peripheral norms**    Norms that are accepted by some, but are not important for organizational success.    **page 437**

**personal power**    A person's ability to satisfy or deny satisfaction of anothers' need, based on an interpersonal relationship between individuals or on his or her personal characteristics.    **page 493**

**personality inventories**    Programs that measure the thoughts, feelings, and behaviors that define an individual and determine that person's pattern of interaction with the environment.    **page 402**

**physical examinations**    Tests that qualify an individual's placement in manually and physically demanding jobs.    **page 403**

**pivotal norms**    Standards that are critical for group success.    **page 437**

**plan**    A set of activities intended to achieve goals, whether for an entire organization, department, or an individual.    **page 244**

**planned change**    The deliberate structuring of operations and behaviors, often in anticipation of environmental forces.    **page 557**

**planning**    The process of determining what the organization will specifically accomplish and deciding how to accomplish these goals.    **page 6**

**policy**    A broadly stated standing plan that provides general principles or guidelines for making decisions in many situations.    **page 261**

**political forces**    The relationship of individuals, their rights, and their property to the state.    **page 32**

**political-legal dimension**    Within the general environment, the nature of the relationship between various areas of government and the organization.    **page 62**

**politics**    The maneuvering by an individual to try to gain an advantage in the distribution of organizational rewards or resources.    **page 452**

**Porter-Lawler expectancy model**    An extension of the expectancy theory stating that satisfaction is the result rather than the cause of performance and that different levels of performance lead to different rewards, which, in turn, produce different levels of job satisfaction.    **page 472**

**portfolio analysis**  A technique allowing for managers to visualize their businesses as a set or portfolio using certain common criteria, such as profitability or growth potential. **page 285**

**positive reinforcement**  The act of strengthening a desired behavior by rewarding it or providing other positive outcomes. **page 474**

**potential new competitors**  Companies not currently operating in a business's industry but which have a high potential for entering the industry. **page 68**

**power**  A person's capacity to influence the behavior and attitudes of others. **page 493**

**prejudice**  Negative attitudes and feelings toward others because of their membership in a different cultural group. **page 163**

**preliminary (or feedforward or steering) control**  A form of operations control that monitors deviations in the quality and quantity of the firm's resources to try to prevent deviations before they enter the system. **page 654**

**primary characteristics of diversity**  Inborn characteristics, such as age, gender, race, ethnicity, abilities, and sexual orientation, that cannot be changed. **page 153**

**primary stakeholders**  Those who have a formal and/or contractual relationship with the firm, such as customers, suppliers, and employees. **page 72**

**problem**  The difference between a desired situation and the actual situation. **page 302**

**procedures**  Step-by-step descriptions that detail the action that firms or individuals undertake to carry out standing plans. **page 262**

**process consultation**  A technique in which a consultant focuses on the dynamic task-related processes and assists the client organization in diagnosing how to enhance these kinds of processes. **page 576**

**process layout**  Facility layout in which firms organize the transformation process into departments that group related procedures. **page 594**

**process theories**  A set of theories that try to determine "how" and "why" employees are motivated to perform. **page 469**

**product departmentalization**  The grouping of jobs or activities around a firm's principal goods and services. **page 344**

**product division structure**  The organization of divisions by product. **page 361**

**product layout**  Facility layout in which production is broken down into relatively simple tasks assigned to workers positioned along the line, and the product moves from worker to worker. **page 594**

**product life cycle**  The cycle of birth, growth, and decline of a product. **page 289**

**product-development teams**  A special type of project team formed to devise, design, and implement a new product. **page 431**

**production**  The activities and processes used in making tangible products; interchangeable with manufacturing. **page 590**

**production and operations managers**  Managers who schedule and monitor the work process that turns out the firm's goods and services. **page 18**

**productivity**  The measurement of the relationship between the outputs produced and the inputs used to produce them. **page 606**

**professional bureaucracy**  An organization that has a functional structure, is medium sized, and works best in stable environments, but has primarily professional employees and a decentralized informal structure. **page 383**

**program**  An intermediate plan that encompasses a wide set of activities with a common focus. **page 261**

**Program Evaluation and Review Technique (PERT)**  A scheduling technique in which managers identify all the major activities (events) required to complete a project, arrange the events in a sequence or path, estimate the time required for each event and note it near the corresponding arrow, and total the time for the completion of each path. **page 601**

**programmed decisions**  Decisions made in response to situations that are routine, somewhat structured, and fairly repetitive. **page 302**

**project**  A subdivision of a program. **page 261**

**project teams**  Groups similar to task forces, but usually responsible for running an operation and in control of a specific work project. **page 431**

**promotion**  The advancement of a current employee to a higher-level job within the organization. **page 413**

**Protestant ethic**  An interpretation of the purpose of life, stating that, instead of merely waiting on earth for release into the next world, people should pursue an occupation and engage in high levels of worldly activity so that they will fulfill their calling. **page 33**

**punishment**  The act of weakening or eliminating an undesired behavior by providing negative consequences. **page 474**

**purchasing**  The buying of all the materials needed by the organization; also known as procurement. **page 598**

**quality**  The degree to which a good or service meets the demands and requirements of the marketplace. **page 182**

**quality assurance teams**  Generally small groups formed to recommend changes that will positively affect the quality of the organization's products. **page 431**

**quality circles**  Groups of managers and employees, representing production tasks, who meet periodically to discuss proposals to seek continuous improvements in the production system. **page 199**

**quality control**  The activities an organization undertakes to ensure that its products meet its established quality standards. **page 603**

**quality function deployment (QFD)**  A set of planning and communication routines that focus and coordinate skills within an organization, first through design, then through the manufacturing and marketing of products. **page 199**

**quality loss function (QLF)**  The idea that a product that fails to meet consumer expectations results in a measurable loss to society. **page 199**

**quantitative approach**  A viewpoint of management that emphasizes the application of mathematical models, statistics, and structured information systems to support rational management decision making. **page 38**

**quantum change**  A large-scale planned change in how the firm operates. **page 558**

**question marks**  Those businesses, that are viewed positively in the sense that they are located in attractive, fast-growing markets, but for which there is a question as to their ability to compete, given their low market share. **page 286**

**quota**  The maximum number of units of a particular product that may be imported into a country. **page 130**

**ratio analysis**  A method used by managers to take information from balance sheets and income statements in order to measure a company's efficiency, profitability, and sources of finances relative to those of other organizations. **page 660**

**raw materials inventory**  Those materials that have been purchased to be used as inputs for making other products. **page 598**

**reactive change**  A situation in which organizational members react spontaneously to external and internal forces but do little to modify these forces or their behaviors. **page 557**

**receiver** The person to whom the information and meaning are sent. **page 528**

**recruiting** The process of attracting potential new employees to the organization. **page 398**

**referent power** Personal power that results when one person identifies with and admires another. **page 495**

**refreezing** The phase in which the organization is stabilized at a new state of behavioral equilibrium (state C). **page 562**

**reinforcement theory** A process theory which assumes that behavior may be reinforced by relating it to its consequences. **page 474**

**related diversification** A firm's acquisition of a business that has some connection with the company's existing businesses. **page 284**

**relationship-oriented behaviors** Behaviors such as being considerate, supportive, and helpful to employees by showing trust and confidence, listening to employees' problems and suggestions, showing appreciation for contributions, and supporting employees' concerns. **page 499**

**relevant norms** Norms that are important, but not as critical as the pivotal norms. **page 437**

**resources** The people, equipment, finances, and data an organization uses in order to reach its objectives. **page 5**

**responsibility** The individual's burden of accountability for attainment of the organization's goals. **page 347**

**reverse discrimination** The result of a company's policies that force it to consider only minorities or women instead of hiring the person who is best qualified. **page 167**

**reward power** Organizational power that stems from a person's ability to bestow rewards. **page 494**

**risk** The condition that exists when decision makers must rely on incomplete, yet reliable information. **page 304**

**risk propensity** A person's willingness to take risks when making decisions. **page 315**

**role** A description of the behaviors expected of a specific group member. **page 439**

**role negotiation** The structuring of interactions between interdependent persons or groups to clarify and negotiate role behaviors and expectations. **page 577**

**routing** The sequence of operations through which a product must pass. **page 601**

**rule** A specific plan that either condones or prohibits certain kinds of behavior. **page 262**

**satisficing** The decision maker's decision to choose the first alternative that appears to resolve the problem satisfactorily. **page 310**

**scaler chain** The principle of organizing whereby authority should flow through the organization from the top down, one level at a time. **page 349**

**scarce environment** An environment wherein money is tight, the market is stagnant or declining, or stakeholder groups are making conflicting or difficult demands. **page 376**

**scatter diagrams** Illustrations allowing management to evaluate the relationship between two variables, using one variable to make a prediction about another variable or characteristic. **page 194**

**scheduling** The assigning of work to be done to departments or to specific machines or persons. **page 601**

**scientific management** A theory within the classical approach that focuses on improvement of operational efficiencies through the systematic and scientific study of work methods, tools, and performance standards. **page 36**

**screening (or yes/no or concurrent) control** A form of control that regulates operations to ensure that they are consistent with objectives; also called yes/no or concurrent control. **page 654**

**secondary characteristics of diversity** Characteristics, such as work background, marital status, and education, that can be changed. **page 154**

**secondary stakeholders** Groups which have a less formal connection to the organization, such as environmentalists, community activists, and the media. **page 72**

**selection** The process of collecting systematic information about applicants and using that information to decide which applicants to hire. **page 400**

**self-directed work team (SDWT)** An intact group of employees who are responsible for a *whole* work process or segment that delivers a product or service to an internal or external customer. **page 431**

**semantics** The different uses and meanings of words, often influencing the effectiveness of a message. **page 541**

**sender** The person who wishes to relay or share particular information and meaning, and initiates the communication process. **page 527**

**simple structure** A structure with few departments, arranged by function, headed by an entrepreneur/owner, and with few technical support staff. **page 383**

**single-use plans** Plans that are used once and then discarded. **page 261**

**situational leadership theory** A leadership model whose premise is that a leader's style should be contingent on subordinates' competence and commitment. **page 501**

**small business** Any business that is not dominant in its competitive area and does not employ more than 500 people. **page 211**

**Small Business Administration (SBA)** An independent agency of the federal government that offers managerial and financial assistance to small businesses. **page 211**

**small-batch technology** The production of small numbers of goods in response to a specific customer request. **page 379**

**social audit** A systematic examination of the objectives, strategies, organization, and performance of the social responsibility function. **page 112**

**social forces** The relationship of people to each other within a particular culture. **page 32**

**social responsibility** The obligation a business assumes to maximize its positive impact and minimize its negative impact on society. **page 105**

**socialization** The process by which an individual learns the norms, values, goals, and expectations of the organization. **page 438**

**sociocultural dimension** The aspect of the general environment that includes the demographics and the values of the society within which an organization operates. **page 62**

**software** A computer program or set of commands that instructs a computer to perform various operations, such as reading, analyzing, or storing data in a specified location. **page 626**

**soldiering** The systematic slowdown in work by laborers, with the deliberate purpose of keeping their employers ignorant of how fast the work can be done. **page 37**

**sole proprietorships** Businesses owned and managed by one individual; the most popular form of business organization. **page 225**

**span of control** The actual number of subordinates over which a position has authority. **page 348**

**stable environment** An environment in which stakeholder demands, and specifically customer desires, are well understood and relatively stable over time. **page 377**

**stakeholder** A person or group which can affect, or is affected by, an organization's goals or the means to achieve those goals. **page 72**

**stakeholder map** A representation of the organization's stakeholders and their stakes. **page 73**

**standing plans** Those plans that deal with recurring, as opposed to unique, situations. **page 261**

**stars** Those businesses that have high market shares and operate in industries experiencing major growth. **page 286**

**statistical process control (SPC)** An alternate form of screening control that employs "control charts" to continuously track performance variation over time. **page 656**

**stereotyping** A type of perceptual organization in which we categorize people into groups based on certain characteristics such as race, sex, or education level, and then make generalizations about them according to their group. **page 533**

**stock** Shares of a corporation that can be bought, sold, given as gifts, or inherited. **page 226**

**storming stage** The stage when conflict usually occurs and in which group members begin to assert their roles, jockey for leadership positions, and make known their feelings about a task. **page 435**

**strategic alliance** A relatively new form of international joint venture formed to create competitive advantage on a worldwide basis. **page 137**

**strategic business unit (SBU)** A separate division within a company that has its own mission, goals, strategy, and competitors. **page 285**

**strategic control** A form of control whose purpose is to ensure that the organization effectively understands and responds to the realities of its environment. **page 658**

**strategic goals** Goals set by higher managers that deal with such general topics as the firm's growth, new markets, or new goods and services. **page 251**

**strategic management** All the processes an organization undertakes to develop and implement its strategic plan. **page 274**

**strategic plans** Plans that are intended to achieve strategic goals. **page 258**

**strategy** A course of action for implementing strategic plans and achieving strategic goals; a general statement of actions an organization intends to take or is taking that is based on the fit of the organization with its external environment. **page 274**

**substitutes** Goods or services that may be used in place of those furnished by a given business. **page 67**

**subsystem** Any system that is part of a larger one. **page 47**

**suppliers** Organizations and individuals who provide resources to other organizations. **page 66**

**survey feedback** The gathering of data through questionnaires and/or personal interviews and the return of that data to employees in a structured form to facilitate discussion and problem solving. **page 575**

**SWOT analysis** The evaluation of the organization's internal strengths and weaknesses and the opportunities and threats associated with the business's external environment. **page 277**

**synergy** The ability of the whole system to equal more than the sum of its parts. **page 47**

**system** An arrangement of related or connected parts that form a whole unit. **page 46**

**systems approach** An approach to management theory that views organizations and the environments within which they operate as sets of interrelated parts to be managed as a whole in order to achieve a common goal. **page 46**

**tactical goals** The intermediate goals of the firm, which are designed to stimulate actions necessary for achieving the strategic goals. **page 251**

**tactical plans** Plans that are designed to achieve tactical goals. **page 258**

**task environment** Those factors that have a direct effect on a specific organization and its managers, including customers, suppliers, competitors, substitutes, and potential new entrants to the industry. **page 61**

**task force** A temporary group of employees responsible for bringing about a particular change. **page 430**

**task-oriented behaviors** Behaviors—such as planning and scheduling work, coordinating employee activities, and providing necessary supplies, equipment, and technical assistance—designed primarily and specifically to get tasks completed. **page 499**

**task-specialist roles** Behaviors oriented toward generating information and resolving problems. **page 440**

**team** A small number of people with complementary skills who are committed to a common purpose, set of performance goals, and approach for which they hold themselves mutually accountable. **page 426**

**team building** The use of structured group experiences to help ongoing work teams function more effectively through better decision making, goal setting, and intragroup communications. **page 576**

**technical skills** The knowledge and ability to accomplish the specialized activities of the work group. **page 14**

**techno-structural redesign** A large-scale intervention that involves redesigning the organizational structure to better address environmental contingencies and better utilize information and process technologies. **page 577**

**technological dimension** Within the general environment, the knowledge and process of changing inputs (resources, labor, and money) to outputs (goods and services). **page 64**

**telecommuting** Using telecommunications technology to work from home or other places outside the traditional workplace. **page 629**

**termination** The separation of an employee from the organization. **page 413**

**Theory X** The assumption that people are naturally lazy, must be threatened and forced to work, have little ambition or initiative, and do not try to fulfill any need higher than security needs at work. **page 45**

**Theory Y** The assumption that people naturally want to work, are capable of self-control, seek responsibility, are creative, and try to fulfill higher-order needs at work. **page 46**

**Theory Z** A management theory involving increased concern for quality of work-life, job security, group decision making, cooperation between groups, informal central mechanisms, and concern for work-family issues. **page 51**

**third-party peacemaking** A process in which a consultant facilitates a conflict resolution between two individuals. **page 577**

**top-down budgeting** Control budgeting in which top managers establish financial plans and hand them down to middle- and lower-level managers for review and implementation. **page 658**

**total productivity** Outputs relative to all the inputs used. **page 607**

**total quality management (TQM)** A management view that strives to create a customer-centered culture which defines quality for the organization and lays the foundation for activities aimed at attaining quality-related goals. **page 182**

**trading company** An organization that acquires goods in one country and sells them to buyers in another country. **page 136**

**training** The process of instructing employees in their job tasks and socializing them into the organization's values, attitudes, and other aspects of its culture. **page 404**

**training and experience form** An application device that presents a small number of the important tasks of a job and asks the applicants whether they have ever performed or been trained in each of the activities. **page 401**

**trait appraisal** A subjective evaluation of an employee's personal characteristics such as attitude, motivation, cooperation, and dependability. **page 408**

**transaction support system (TSS)** An information system that handles routine, repetitious business transactions. **page 630**

**transactional leadership** A more traditional approach in which managers engage in both task- and consideration-oriented behaviors in an exchange manner. **page 513**

**transfer** The reassignment of a current employee to another job at the same level as the original job. **page 413**

**transformational leadership** A style that goes beyond mere exchange relationships by inspiring employees to look beyond their own self-interests and by generating awareness and acceptance of the group's purposes and mission. **page 513**

**transition state** The period during which the organization learns the behaviors needed to reach the desired future state. **page 570**

**turbulent environment** An environment wherein customer or other stakeholder demands are continuously changing or the primary technology of the firm is constantly being improved and updated. **page 377**

**turnaround strategy** A strategy in which the firm attempts, through such measures as cost-cutting, quality enhancement, or the elimination of management positions, to restore economic strength to a declining business. **page 285**

**uncertainty** The condition that exists when little or no factual information is available about a problem, its alternative solutions, and their respective outcomes. **page 304**

**undercapitalization** The lack of funds to operate a business normally. **page 221**

**unfreezing** The disruption of forces maintaining the existing state (state A) or level of behavior. **page 561**

**unity of command** The principle that a subordinate should report to only one immediate superior. **page 349**

**unrelated diversification** The action of diversifying into any business that is potentially profitable for the organization. **page 284**

**upper managers** Those who make decisions about the overall performance and direction of the organization. **page 17**

**upward communication** Communication flowing from lower to higher levels of the organization, such as progress reports, suggestions, inquiries, and grievances. **page 534**

**utilitarian philosophy** A philosophy where believers seek the greatest satisfaction for the largest number of individuals. **page 99**

**valence** The importance of each potential outcome to the individual. **page 471**

**variable-interval schedule** A pattern whereby the period of reinforcement varies between one reinforcement and the next. **page 475**

**variable-ratio schedule** A pattern whereby the number of behaviors required for reinforcement is varied. **page 475**

**venture capitalists** Persons or organizations that agree to provide some funds for a new business in exchange for an ownership interest, or stock. **page 228**

**verbal or oral communication** Words spoken through various channels to convey information and meaning. **page 529**

**vertical coordination** The integration of succeeding levels of the organization. **page 381**

**vertical specialization** The division of labor at different levels of management into different tasks of planning, organizing, leading, and controlling. **page 338**

**Vroom-Yetton-Jago (VYJ) participation model** A model that provides a set of rules for employee participation in decision making. **page 507**

**wage and salary survey** A study that tells the company how much compensation is paid by comparable firms for specific jobs the firms have in common. **page 411**

**Webb-Pomerene Export Trade Act** Legislation allowing selected American firms desiring international trade to form monopolies in order to compete with foreign cartels. **page 128**

**whistle blowing** The act of an employee's exposing an employer's wrongdoing; typically such reporting is to outsiders, the media, or government regulatory agencies. **page 103**

**wide-area network (WAN)** A network in which computers are linked by telephone lines or long-range communications devices. **page 626**

**work-in-process inventory** Those products that are partially completed or are in transit. **page 597**

**World Bank** Financial organization established and supported by the industrialized nations to loan money to underdeveloped and developing countries; formerly known as the International Bank for Reconstruction and Development. **page 133**

**written communication** Information and meaning transferred as recorded words, such as memos, reports, and electronic mail. **page 530**

**zero defects** A program that emphasizes "doing it right the first time," with 100 percent acceptable output. **page 187**

**zero-based budgeting (ZBB)** A method of budgeting in which managers thoroughly reevaluate organizational activities to determine their true level of importance. **page 660**

# Name Index

# Company Index

# Subject Index